THE
NEW BOOK
OF
KNOWLEDGE

THE NEW BOOK OF KNOWLEDGE

Grolier Incorporated, Danbury, Connecticut

VOLUME 1

A

Library of Congress Cataloging-in-Publication Data

The New book of knowledge.—1995 ed.
   p.   cm.
  "Volume 1, A."
  Includes bibliographical references.
  ISBN 0-7172-0526-6
  1. Children's encyclopedias and dictionaries. I. Grolier Incorporated.
AG5.N273 1995   94–42538
031—dc20   CIP
                   AC

ISBN 0–7172–0526–6 (set)

COPYRIGHT © 1995 BY GROLIER INCORPORATED

The publishers wish to thank the following for permission to use copyrighted material:
Harcourt, Brace & World, Inc., and Alfred J. Bedard for "The Emperor's New Clothes" from *It's Perfectly True and Other Stories* by Hans Christian Andersen, translated by Paul Leyssac, copyright 1938 by Paul Leyssac.
Little, Brown and Company for excerpt from *Little Women* by Louisa May Alcott.
David McKay Company, Inc., for excerpts from *Arabian Nights*, edited by Andrew Lang, new edition 1946, copyright 1898, 1946, Longmans Green and Company, Inc., now David McKay Company, Inc.
Harcourt Brace Jovanovich, Inc., for excerpt on measuring star distances from *Space in Your Future* by Leo Schneider, copyright 1961 by Leo Schneider.

Trademark
THE BOOK OF KNOWLEDGE
registered in U.S. Patent Office

PREFACE

THE NEW BOOK OF KNOWLEDGE is uniquely related to the needs of modern young people, both in school and at home. The children and teenagers of today are standing on the threshold of a new world and they must learn to cope with it successfully. Knowledge in every field is bursting its bounds. Old "truths" are becoming invalid; new "truths" are opening vistas never before imagined. Our youth need an encyclopedia that will help them understand the constantly changing realities of the world around them. For that purpose, more than one thousand advisers and contributors, together with a staff of editors, artists, and other specialists, have worked together to create and sustain THE NEW BOOK OF KNOWLEDGE—an encyclopedia designed for the young people of today.

SCOPE

THE NEW BOOK OF KNOWLEDGE is designed for the library and the classroom as well as for practical and educational use at home. It will be useful to a wide range of readers, from very young children to students ready for an adult encyclopedia. The content of the encyclopedia was selected by educators who analyzed the curriculum requirements of school systems across the nation, by librarians familiar with the research needs of children and young adults, and by cultural specialists who considered the interests and needs of the set's users beyond school and library settings. Students will find a wealth of information and clarifications of concepts that will be important and useful in their schoolwork. In addition, the articles have been enriched by many informative projects, experiments, and illustrations.

For children, and the young child in all of us, there are carefully selected illustrations, games, and activities, as well as selections from well-known and much-loved stories, myths, fables, and other classic works of literature. Parents will find much material to use with and read aloud to their children, both for enjoyment and as answers to their questions. These materials will provide important additions to every child's growing-up experiences. They will also help children learn the value of books as sources of information, imagination, and pleasure.

AUTHORITY

The articles in THE NEW BOOK OF KNOWLEDGE are written or reviewed by experts eminent in their fields who understand how to address and write about their subjects in a way that is both informative and interesting to our readership. Almost all of the articles are signed, and the contributor's or reviewer's position appears with each signature so that readers can see the person's authority. Many articles are signed not only by an author but also by a reviewer. The few unsigned articles are written by staff editors who are familiar with the needs and ability levels of young readers and are subject-matter specialists. A complete list of contributors, consultants, and reviewers appears in Volume 20.

ACCURACY

To ensure utmost accuracy, every article, map, drawing, photograph, diagram, chart, and fact box is checked by skilled researchers so that the information provided is correct and current. Where authorities disagree or information is unknown, the reader is so informed. Editorial policy is to present fact, not opinion.

READABILITY

Reading consultants to the encyclopedia have helped the staff design a set that is comprehensible, informative, and interesting. Articles whose subjects appeal to younger children are at lower levels of comprehension, whereas other articles, especially those with a technical vocabulary, are at higher levels. In addition, the editors strive to provide the background information necessary to ensure a complete understanding of every article.

They realize that for information to become knowledge, it must be understood so well that its seekers can both use it correctly and communicate it to others. The editors also make every effort to present information in a style that will capture the reader's interest and imagination. To further assure pleasurable reading, the type in which the set is printed was chosen after careful research in typeface legibility.

ARRANGEMENT and AVAILABILITY of INFORMATION

THE NEW BOOK OF KNOWLEDGE is organized alphabetically in unit letter volumes. Each volume contains an Index that is cross-referenced to the entire contents of the set. Blue paper is used for the Index pages so that they can be easily identified. Printed in front of the Index are hundreds of short informational items that will be found particularly useful for quick reference. They are listed under the heading Dictionary Entries. Articles and Dictionary and Index entries are arranged in alphabetical order, letter by letter to the comma, ignoring hierarchical orders. In addition there is extensive use of *See also* references following articles.

The encyclopedia also includes standing cross-references. These are printed in the same type as article headings and refer the reader to the article or articles where the subject is covered. Other devices that assist the search for information include placing word guides at the bottom of each page close to the page number; placing a page number on every page, or, where this is not possible, on one out of every double spread of pages; organizing long articles into shorter units through the use of bold-face headings; and presenting information in concise forms such as fact summaries, chronologies, charts, graphs, and lists. Finally, the Wonder Questions, which have been a part of the set since the original 1911 edition of THE BOOK OF KNOWLEDGE, appeal to one's curiosity and provide concise information throughout the set about a wide range of topics.

MAPS

THE NEW BOOK OF KNOWLEDGE presents a map program planned especially to meet the needs of its readers. Maps are prepared by skilled cartographers in collaboration with geographers and subject editors. The maps are clear, accurate, informative, attractive, and easy to understand. Information of various kinds is presented on different but related maps, not crowded onto one map. Pictorial symbols, decorative insets, and rich color make the maps appealing to the eye and also provide additional information. There are almost one thousand maps of all kinds in the encyclopedia and most are in color.

ILLUSTRATIONS

THE NEW BOOK OF KNOWLEDGE is printed on a full-color press so that color can be available throughout. There are more than thirteen thousand color illustrations in the set. All of the photographs, illustrations, and maps were selected to complement, extend, and add information to the text and were as carefully checked for accuracy as the text itself. The illustrations appear near the information they illustrate and they are large enough to show details clearly. Most of the artwork was commissioned especially for this publication.

BIBLIOGRAPHY

A comprehensive bibliography in the Home and School Reading and Study Guides points the way to further reading on more than a thousand topics. The recommended readings are grouped by general levels—primary, intermediate, and advanced. These references emphasize that THE NEW BOOK OF KNOWLEDGE is a springboard to learning that will stimulate the curiosity of its readers and lead them to further study.

The Editors

FIRST EDITION STAFF

Martha Glauber Shapp, M.A.
Editor in Chief

Cathleen FitzGerald, B.A., H. Dip. Ed.
Managing Editor

Ben Feder
Designer and Graphic Arts Consultant

Lowell A. Martin, Ph.D.
Vice President and Editorial Director, Grolier, Inc.

EDITORIAL

SOCIAL STUDIES

Chief Editor: Dorothy W. Furman, B.S.

Senior Editors: Sue Brandt, B.A.; F. Richard Hsu, M.A.; Mary B. Irving, B.A.; Jerome Z. Neibrief, B.S.; John Ratti, M.A.; Eugenio C. Villicaña, M.A.

Associate Editors: Jay Bennett; Joyce Berry, B.A.; Claudia H. Cohl, B.A.; Mary-Stuart Garden, B.A.; Carol Z. Rothkopf, M.A.

Assistant Editors: Lorraine Abelson Abraham, B.A.; Marcus Anton Cohen, B.A.; Ellen Gendell, B.A.; Bryna Mandel, B.A.; Paul Schmel, B.A.; Amy Small, B.A.; Annette Stiefbold, M.A.

Editorial Assistants: Cecilia H. Bustos; Judith Glickman, B.A.; Mada Levine, B.A.; Barbara Mathes, B.A.

LANGUAGE AND LITERATURE

Senior Editor: James E. Jarnagin, M.A.

Associate Editors: Marcia B. Marks, B.A.; Janet Stone, B.A.

Assistant Editors: Carol Smith Bundy, B.A.; Lis Shabecoff, B.A.

TECHNOLOGY

Senior Editor: Peter R. Limburg, B.S.F.S., M.A.

Associate Editor: Sara L. Hannum, B.A.

Assistant Editors: Marion Bowman; Arthur G. Hudgins, M.A., Winifred B. Luhrmann, B.A.; Anthony M. Quintavalla, B.A.

EDITORIAL COORDINATOR

Lois C. Schwartz, B.A.

SCIENCE AND MATHEMATICS

Chief Editor: Patricia G. Lauber, B.A.

Senior Editor: Herbert Kondo, M.A.

Administrative Assistant: Anita Sedler

Associate Editors: John S. Bowman, B.A.; Barbara Land, M.S.; Rebecca Marcus, B.A.; Elizabeth Shepherd, B.A.

Assistant Editors: Chica Minnerly, B.A.; Steven Moll, B.A.; Harvey M. Weiss, M.A.

Editorial Assistants: Larry Baker, B.A.; Larry Blaser, M.A.; Stephen Kreitzman, B.A.; Ruth Plager, B.A.

MUSIC AND ART

Senior Music Editor: David L. Buckley, B.A.

Senior Art Editor: David Jacobs, B.F.A.

Associate Editor: Gwendolyn E. Reed, B.A. (Art)

Assistant Editors: Sara Friedman, B.A. (Art); Barbara Kaye, B.A. (Art); Joseph H. Markham, B.A. (Music); Robert Porter, B.F.A. (Art)

SPORTS AND LEISURE; HEALTH, HOME, AND COMMUNITY

Senior Editor: Helen Hull Jacobs

Associate Editors: Eleanor Felder, M.S.; Virginia Gurnee; Sylvia Rosenthal, B.A.

Assistant Editor: Noemie Emery, M.A.

STAFF EDITORS

Elisabeth Freidel Earley, M.A.; Susan Elliott, B.A.; Rosalyn Heith, B.A.; Fay Leviero; Sarah Lee McSweeney, B.A.

COPY EDITORS

Chief Copy Editor: Patricia Ellsworth, B.A.

Senior Copy Editors: Paule H. Jones, M.A.; Sandra L. Russell, B.A.; Damsey Wilson

Staff Members: Philip G. Anthony; Marcy Benstock, B.A.; Jeane Pavelle Garment, B.A.; Philip C. Johnson, B.A.; Naomi Kassabian, M.A.; Marian Klein, B.A.; Martin S. Mitchell, B.A.; Thomas W. Wyckoff

RESEARCHERS

Chief Researcher: Marshall Tulloch, B.A.

Senior Researcher: Thomas Cuddihy, B.A.

Staff Members: Margaret Anderson, B.A.; Lydia Cohen, B.A.; Helen McVey Colvin, B.A.; Margaret Covode, B.A.; Susan Day, B.A.; David Diao, B.A.; Edward Diaz, B.A.; Stephen Elliott, B.A.; Imre Horvath, M.A.; Rita Horvath, B.A.; Leland Lowther, M.A.; Susan Nergaard, B.F.A.; Peter Scarlet, B.A.; Ralph Slayton, B.S.; Camilla Turnbull, B.A.; Sally Valentine, B.A.

PROOFREADERS

Chief Proofreader: Martha L. Moffett, B.S.

Staff Members: Elizabeth M. Elkind, B.A.; Patricia M. Godfrey, B.A.; Susan F. Heimann, M.A.; Louise Oblan-Shor, B.A.

INDEXERS

Chief Indexer: Ruth Hines, M.L.S.

Consulting Indexer: Sarita Robinson, M.A.

Dictionary Index Editor: Sybil Rhoads, B.S.

Staff Members: Diane Gilroy, M.A.; Janet Hadley; Zohreh Kerendian, B.S.; Brenda Kurz, B.A.; Martin S. Mitchell, B.A.; Barbara Paskell, B.A.; Margaret Reed; Carole Schindeler, M.A.; Toni Strauss, B.S.; Barbra Wood, B.A.

MAPS

Map Designer: George Buctel, B.A.

Editor: Linda Keim, B.A.

Assistant Editors: Emily Wood Corbin, A.A.; Margo Dryden, A.A.; Cyril Edoho, M.A.; Arlene Zuckerman, B.A.

OFFICE MANAGER

Joanne Burns

STAFF ASSISTANTS

Kiki Barroso; Rose Ann Bonetti; Sheridan Cogan; Willie May Elcock; Louisa Folta; Anne Hegarty; Ruth Heim; Aline Moyler; Mitzi L. Sanchez; Dorothy Schatten; Minna Sedler; Stephanie Shaffer

ART AND PRODUCTION

Art and Production Director: Verne Bowman, B.F.A.

Production Manager: Charles Behre, B.A.

Assistant Art Director: Chester Prosinski, B.F.A.

Art Coordinator: Rita Maduro, B.S.

Typography Manager: Barbara Effron, B.S.

Typography Coordinators
Tema Harris, B.F.A.; Geraldine Felder Smith

Layout Designers
Susan Colton, B.A.; Ronald Cooper, A.A.S.; Sue Crooks; Nancy Ferguson, B.A.; Mary Ann Joulwan; Sidney Miller; Miriam Troner, B.A.

Staff Artist
Irmgard Lochner

PHOTO EDITORS

Chief Editor: Isabelle Rubin, M.A.

Administrative Assistant: Susan Lewis West, B.A.

Staff Members: Anne Alpert, B.A.; Carol Baker, B.A.; Beverly Bayne, B.A., B.S.; Laura Bustard; Lois Davis, M.A.; Wesley Day, B.A.; Monika Dillon, B.A.; Iris Eaton; Ada Fridman, M.D.; Richard Green, B.A.; Elizabeth Heskett, M.A.; Gloria Hoffman, B.A.; Dorothy Kalins, B.A.; Jane Latta; Diana Lee, B.A.; Alice Lundoff, M.S.; Ivy Minely, B.A.; Barbara Nagelsmith, B.S.; Marjorie Goreff Neuwirth, B.A.; Joan Scafarello, B.A.; Lisl Steiner, B.A.; Patricia Walsh, M.A.

STAFF ASSISTANTS

Linda Bokor; Nancy Hammalian, B.A.; Michael Harvest; Lynn Jacobs, B.S.; Laura Johnson, B.A.; Franklin Schmidt; Marcy Waxman, B.A.; Marjorie Williams

MANUFACTURING

Director: Ed McKenna

Staff: Raymond Labott; Walter Stork

ADVISERS AND CONSULTANTS

Russell L. Adams, Ph.D.
Chairman, Afro-American Studies Department
College of Arts and Sciences
Howard University

Alfred B. Bortz, Ph.D.
Assistant Director,
Magnetics Technology Center,
Carnegie-Mellon University

Hugh C. Brooks, Ph.D.
Director, Center for African Studies,
St. John's University (New York)

Jeanne S. Chall, Ph.D.
Professor of Education and Director of
the Reading Laboratory,
Graduate School of Education,
Harvard University

Suzanne H. Chapin, Ed.D., Ed.M.
Assistant Professor of Mathematics
School of Education
Boston University

Peter Conn, Ph.D.
Professor of English,
University of Pennsylvania
Author, *Literature in America:
An Illustrated History*

Kenneth S. Cooper, Ph.D.
Professor of History,
George Peabody College for Teachers,
Vanderbilt University

Robert I. Crane, Ph.D.
Ford-Maxwell Professor of South Asian History,
Syracuse University

Kathryn Cullen-DuPont
Author, *Encyclopedia of
Women's History*

Lawrence S. Finkel, Ed.D.
Superintendent, Chester Township (New Jersey)
Public Schools

Arthur W. Foshay, Ed.D.
Professor Emeritus,
Research and Field Services,
Teachers College, Columbia University

M. L. Frankel, Ph.D.
Member, National Task Force on Economic
Education

Christine B. Gilbert, B.L.S., M.A.
Coeditor, *Best Books for Children;*
Former Librarian and Adjunct Associate
Professor of Library Science,
Long Island University, C. W. Post Center

John T. Gillespie, M.L.S.
Professor, Palmer Graduate Library School,
Long Island University, C. W. Post Center

Colonel C. V. Glines, M.B.A.
Former Assistant Secretary
of Defense (Public Affairs),
U.S. Department of Defense

William A. Gutsch, Jr.
Chairman, The American Museum—
Hayden Planetarium

Theodore C. Hines, M.L.S., Ph.D.
Professor of Library Science,
School of Education,
University of North Carolina at Greensboro

Daniel Jacobson, Ph.D.
Professor of Geography and Education
and Adjunct Professor of Anthropology,
Michigan State University

A, the first letter of the English alphabet, was also the first letter of the Phoenician, Hebrew, and Greek alphabets. The Hebrews called it *aleph* and the Greeks changed it slightly, calling it *alpha*. The word "alphabet" itself comes from joining the Greek names for the first two letters—*alpha* (A) and *beta* (B). Thus the first two letters have come to stand for all the rest, just as "learning your ABC's" really means learning your DEFGHIJ's as well.

The shape of the letter A has changed slightly from time to time. The legs have been shorter or longer, the crossbar more crooked. But even the earliest traces of the letter look familiar to us. The Phoenician picture symbol for A was probably an ox's head with two long horns. It looked like this: ∠. The later Greek forms stand up straight. By the time the Romans had adapted the Greek alphabet, the A looked very much as it does today.

A is a vowel. It stands for different sounds. Pronounce these words: *fate, bare, am, farm, grass*. You will notice that each A has a different sound. The most common sounds are the long A, as in *fate*; the short A, as in *am*; and the broad A, as in *farm*.

A is a word in itself. It is found before the name of a thing to show that this thing is one of a particular class or kind: a tree, a bird, a worm.

In Phoenician, Hebrew, and Greek, the letter A also meant the number 1. In English too, A has come to mean the first or best. Some schools give A as the highest grade. Grade-A milk and grade-A eggs mean top quality.

In music A is a note; in chemistry A sometimes stands for the element argon. Two of our most common abbreviations employ the A—A.D., for the Latin *anno Domini*, is used with dates and means "in the year of our Lord"; A.M., for *ante meridiem*, is used with times and means "before noon."

Reviewed by MARIO PEI
Author, *The Story of Language*

See also ALPHABET.

AARON, HENRY (Hank). See ALABAMA (Famous People); BASEBALL (Great Players).

SOME WAYS TO REPRESENT A:

Aa *Aa*

The **manuscript** or printed forms of the letter (left) are highly readable. The **cursive** letters (right) are formed from slanted flowing strokes joining one letter to the next.

The **Manual Alphabet** (left) enables a deaf person to communicate by forming letters with the fingers of one hand. **Braille** (right) is a system by which a blind person can use fingertips to "read" raised dots that stand for letters.

The **International Code of Signals** is a special group of flags used to send and receive messages at sea. Each letter is represented by a different flag.

International Morse Code is used to send messages by radio signals. Each letter is expressed as a combination of dots (•) and dashes (––).

Many Asian children learn to operate an abacus in primary school. The best known of the many forms of this instrument is the Chinese *suan p'an* which has a dividing bar across the frame. Beads above the bar count 5 and those below it count 1.

ABACUS

The abacus is a simple calculating machine that is used for doing arithmetic. A modern abacus is made of beads, rods, and a frame. The rods are fastened in the frame, and each stands for a place in the decimal system. One rod stands for units, one for 10's, one for 100's, and so on. The beads are counters. Numbers are added or subtracted by moving the beads on the rods.

The abacus was invented thousands of years ago. It provided a way of doing arithmetic without using written numerals. The numerals of ancient times were very awkward for doing arithmetic. The trouble was that they did not express zero or place value.

For example, compare our numerals with the Roman ones. Our numeral 5 can stand for 5, 50, or 500, depending on the place it is given. In the number 555, each 5 has a different value. The Romans used letters as numerals and expressed place by using a different letter. The numbers 5, 50, and 500 were written as V, L, and D. Without the idea of zero and place, there was no way to make the same numeral stand for more than one number. That is, V could not be made to stand for any number except 5.

This system of numerals made written arithmetic very difficult. So the Romans, like other ancient peoples, used the abacus. The idea of place was built into the abacus. One counter could be made to express 1, 10, or 100, according to its place on the abacus.

The abacus offered an easy way of adding and subtracting and could also be used for multiplication and division.

The abacus was first made by placing pebbles in grooves drawn in soft dirt or sand. Later, the Romans and Arabs learned to make a portable abacus. It was usually a flat piece of wood or metal with grooves or slots for the counters.

The abacus is still widely used today in China, Japan, India, and other countries. Some people can add on an abacus as fast as a person using an electronic calculator. Shortly after World War II a Japanese bank clerk using an abacus was matched against an American soldier using a desk calculator. The two men were given identical sets of business figures that needed addition, subtraction, multiplication, and division. The Japanese clerk, with the abacus, won every time.

Multiplication can be done by adding equal groups. For example, to multiply 12 x 4, you would set up the number 12 on the abacus (one bead in the 10's row and two beads in the 1's row). Then add 12 three more times. Your abacus should show the answer: 48. Division can be done on the abacus by subtracting equal groups.

Reviewed by FORREST M. MIMS, III
Author, *Number Machines*

The drawings on the opposite page show you how to do simple addition and subtraction, as well as addition and subtraction that require exchanging 5 counters for 1.

See also NUMBERS AND NUMBER SYSTEMS.

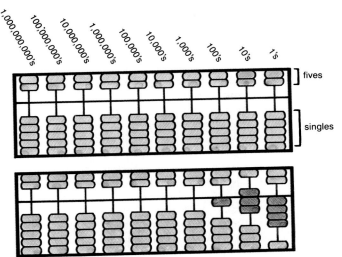

1,000,000,000's
100,000,000's
10,000,000's
1,000,000's
100,000's
10,000's
1,000's
100's
10's
1's

fives

singles

THE CHINESE ABACUS

In a Chinese abacus, each of the five counters below the horizontal divider bar stands for a single decimal unit. A single counter below the bar on the 1's wire represents 1. A single counter below the bar on the 10's wire represents 10, on the 100's wire 100, and so on.

Each counter above the divider bar equals five single decimal units. Therefore a counter above the bar on the 1's wire stands for 5. A counter above the bar on the 10's wire stands for 50, on the 100's wire 500, and so on.

To operate the abacus, counters are moved toward the divider bar. The number 174 is set out at left. Think of the number as 100-70-4. The four counters up against the bar on the 1's wire represent the 4. The 70 is represented by one counter from the top of the 10's wire, which stands for 50, plus two counters from underneath the bar on the 10's wire, which represent 10 apiece. The 50 and the two 10's make a total of 70. The 100 is represented by a single counter from below the bar on the 100's wire.

Simple Addition: 823 + 126

First set out 823
3 on the 1's wire
2 on the 10's wire
8 on the 100's wire

Then move in 126
6 on the 1's wire
2 on the 10's wire
1 on the 100's wire

Read the number shown on the abacus for the answer: 949

Addition with Carrying: 76 + 98

First set out 76
6 on the 1's wire
7 on the 10's wire

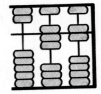

Then move in 98
8 on the 1's wire
(This now makes 14 1's, which must be expressed as one 10 and four 1's — so move the two 5's off the top of the 1's wire and move one 10 up on the 10's wire.)

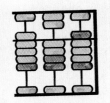

9 on the 10's wire (Adding nine 10's to the 10's that are already shown on the 10's wire would make 17 10's — there are not enough counters to do that. To express 90, move one 100 counter up on the 100's wire, and remove one 10 counter from the bottom of the 10's wire.)

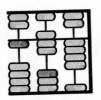

Read the number shown on the abacus for the answer: 174

Simple Subtraction: 137 – 26

Set up 137
7 on the 1's wire
3 on the 10's wire
1 on the 100's wire

Move away 26
Move away 6 from the 1's wire
Move away 2 from the 10's wire

Read the number shown on the abacus for the answer: 111

Subtraction with Borrowing: 44 – 28

Set up 44
4 on the 1's wire
4 on the 10's wire

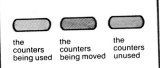

the counters being used

the counters being moved

the counters unused

What the Colors Mean

Move away 28
Move 8 away from the 1's wire
(Take away one counter from the 10's wire and *add* 2 counters to the 1's wire for a net loss of 8.)

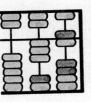

Move 2 away from the 10's wire

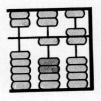

Read the number shown on the abacus for the answer: 16

ABBREVIATIONS

Abbreviations are shortened forms of words and phrases. In the past, when all writing was done by hand, abbreviations saved time and space. Today, although most of what we read is printed, so much information is available that we need abbreviations for much the same reasons.

There are various ways of abbreviating words. A part of the whole word followed by a period may be used. It is often the first syllable or letters, as in Mon. for Monday, Jan. for January, co. for company or county. Some words are shortened to the first and last letters: pr. for pair, yr. for year, Mr. for Mister. In other cases key letters are selected: TV for *television*, pkg. for package. Modern abbreviations often use initials, and many omit periods (CB, mpg, UFO).

Initials for many Latin phrases are used as abbreviations. Here the period is retained. For example, the letters i.e. stand for the Latin *id est*, which means "that is." No., meaning number, goes back to *numero*, the Latin word meaning "by number."

People often make up their own abbreviations, and some of these, like VIP (very important person), come into general usage. Your notebook may contain abbreviations that you have made up yourself.

An **acronym** is a word formed from the initial letters in a phrase or title. It is pronounced as a single word, not as a series of letters. OPEC and NATO, two such forms, stand for the names of organizations—*O*rganization of *P*etroleum *E*xporting *C*ountries and *N*orth *At*lantic *T*reaty *O*rganization. These acronyms, like many others, omit periods.

Some common abbreviations and acronyms are listed below. Others may be found in the dictionary, generally in the regular alphabetical order of words. Some dictionaries list abbreviations in a special appendix.

ISABELLE FORST
Former Assistant Superintendent of Schools
New York City

See also CHEMISTRY for abbreviations of chemical elements; POSTAL SERVICE and individual state articles for abbreviations of state names; UNITED NATIONS for abbreviations of United Nations agencies; articles on letters of the alphabet for abbreviations beginning with those letters.

AAA—American Automobile Association
A.A.U.—Amateur Athletic Union
ABC—American Broadcasting Company
AC—alternating current
ACLU—American Civil Liberties Union
A.D., A.D.—*anno Domini* (Latin, "in the year of our Lord")
ad, advt.—advertisement
adj.—adjective
aka—also known as
ALA—American Library Association
alt.—altitude
A.M., a.m.—*ante meridiem* (Latin, "before noon")
AMA—American Medical Association
anon.—anonymous (giving no name)
AP—Associated Press
assn., assoc.—association
asst.—assistant
att., atty.—attorney
attn.—attention
ATV—all-terrain vehicle
Ave., Av.—Avenue
AWOL—absent without leave
b.—born
B.A., A.B.—Bachelor of Arts
BBC—British Broadcasting Corporation
B.C., B.C.—before Christ
B.C.E.—before (the) common era

biog.—biography
bldg.—building
Blvd.—Boulevard
B.S., B.Sc.—Bachelor of Science
C—Celsius
c., ca.—*circa* (Latin, "about")
cap.—capital
Capt.—Captain
CB—citizens band (radio frequency)
CBC—Canadian Broadcasting Corporation
CBS—Columbia Broadcasting System
CD—certificate of deposit; compact disc
cf.—*confer* (Latin, "compare")
chap.—chapter
CO—Commanding Officer
co.—company; county
c/o—care of
Col.—Colonel
col.—college; column
cop., ©—copyright
CORE—Congress of Racial Equality
corp.—corporation; corporal
C.P.A.—certified public accountant
CPR—cardiopulmonary resuscitation
CPU—central processing unit
CST—central standard time
d.—died; day
D.A.—District Attorney
D.A.R.—Daughters of the American Revolution

DC—direct current
D.D.—Doctor of Divinity
D.D.S.—Doctor of Dental Surgery
dec.—deceased
Dem.—Democrat
dept.—department
dia., diam.—diameter
DNA—deoxyribonucleic acid (chemical carrying genetic information)
Dr.—Doctor
DST—daylight saving time
ed.—edited; edition; editor
e.g.—*exempli gratia* (Latin, "for example")
EKG—electrocardiogram
elev.—elevation
EPA—Environmental Protection Agency
ERA—Equal Rights Amendment
Esq.—Esquire
est.—established; estimated
EST—eastern standard time
ETA—estimated time of arrival
et al.—*et alii* (Latin, "and other"); *et alibi* (Latin, "and elsewhere")
etc.—*et cetera* (Latin, "and the rest")
F—Fahrenheit
FBI—Federal Bureau of Investigation
FCC—Federal Communications Commission
FDIC—Federal Deposit Insurance Corporation
fed.—federal

ff.—following (pages)
FHA—Federal Housing Administration
Fig.—Figure
Gen.—General
GI—government issue
GNP—gross national product
G.O.P.—Grand Old Party, nickname for present Republican Party in the United States
Gov.—Governor
H.M.S.—His (or Her) Majesty's Service; His (or Her) Majesty's Ship
Hon.—Honorable
hosp.—hospital
H.P., HP, h.p.—horsepower
hr.—hour(s)
H.R.H.—His (or Her) Royal Highness
ht.—height
ibid.—*ibidem* (Latin, "in the same place")
ICBM—intercontinental ballistic missile
i.e.—*id est* (Latin, "that is")
ill., illus.—illustrated; illustration
inc.—incorporated; including
I.N.R.I.—*Iesus Nazarenus Rex Iudaeorum* (Latin, "Jesus of Nazareth, King of the Jews")
intro.—introduction
IOU—I owe you
IQ—intelligence quotient
IRA—individual retirement account
I.R.A.—Irish Republican Army
IRS—Internal Revenue Service
J.P.—justice of the peace
Jr.—Junior
KO—knockout
kwhr., kwh.—kilowatt-hour(s)
l.; ll.—line, lines
lab—laboratory
Lat.—Latin
lat.—latitude
Lieut., Lt.—Lieutenant
lit.—literary
lon., long.—longitude
L.P.N.—licensed practical nurse
Ltd.—limited
m.—married, meter
M.A., A.M.—Master of Arts
Maj.—Major
max.—maximum
M.B.A.—Master of Business Administration
M.D.—Doctor of Medicine
med.—medical; medicine
mfg., manuf.—manufacturing
mgr.—manager
MIA—missing in action
min.—minimum; minute(s)
misc.—miscellaneous
mo.—month(s)
M.O.—*modus operandi* (Latin, "method of operation"); mail order

MP—military police
M.P.—member of Parliament
mpg—miles per gallon
mph—miles per hour
Mr.—Mister
Mrs.—Mistress (the original term for a married or unmarried woman)
M.S.—Master of Science
Ms.—Miss or Mrs.
MS, ms; MSS, mss—manuscript; manuscripts
MST—mountain standard time
Mt., mt.—mount; mountain
n.—noun
NAACP—National Association for the Advancement of Colored People
NASA—National Aeronautics and Space Administration
natl.—national
NATO—North Atlantic Treaty Organization
N.B.—*nota bene* (Latin, "note well")
NBC—National Broadcasting Company
NFL—National Football League
NOW—National Organization for Women
OAS—Organization of American States
op. cit.—*opere citato* (Latin, "in the work cited")
OPEC—Organization of Petroleum Exporting Countries
p., pp.—page; pages
P.A.—physician's assistant
par.—paragraph; parallel
PBS—Public Broadcasting Service
PC—personal computer
pd.—paid
Pfc.—Private, First Class
Ph.D.—Doctor of Philosophy
pkg.—package
pl.—plural
P.M.—Prime Minister
P.M., p.m.—*post meridiem* (Latin, "after noon")
P.O.—Post Office
pop.—population
POW—prisoner of war
pr.—pair
pres.—president
prof.—professor
pron.—pronoun
pro tem.—*pro tempore* (Latin, "for the time being"; "temporarily")
P.S.—postscript; Public School
pseud.—pseudonym
PST—Pacific standard time
PTA—Parent-Teacher Association
pub.—public; publisher; published
Q.E.D.—*quod erat demonstrandum* (Latin, "which was to be shown or proved")
q.v.—*quod vide* (Latin, "which see")

RAF—Royal Air Force
rd.—road
RDA—recommended dietary allowance
recd.—received
Rep.—Republican; Representative
Rev.—Reverend
rev.—revenue; revised
R.N.—Registered Nurse
RNA—ribonucleic acid (in cells, chemical used to build protein)
R.O.T.C.—Reserve Officers' Training Corps
rpm—revolutions per minute
R.R.—railroad; rural route
R.S.V.P.—*Répondez, s'il vous plaît* (French, "please reply")
RV—recreational vehicle
SEC—Securities and Exchange Commission
sec.—second
sec., secy.—secretary
Sen.—Senator
sing.—singular
soc.—society
SPCA—Society for the Prevention of Cruelty to Animals
SPCC—Society for the Prevention of Cruelty to Children
sq.—square
Sr.—Senior
SST—supersonic transport
St.—Saint; Street
Ste.—Sainte (French, feminine of Saint)
subj.—subject
supt.—superintendent
syn.—synonym
tbs., T—tablespoon(s)
temp.—temperature
tr.—translation; transpose
treas.—treasury; treasurer
tsp., t—teaspoon(s)
U., univ.—university
UFO—unidentified flying object
UHF—ultrahigh frequency
U.N.—United Nations
UPI—United Press International
USPS—United States Postal Service
U.S.S.—United States Ship
v.—verb; verse
VA—Veterans Administration
VAT—value-added tax
VCR—videocassette recorder
VFW—Veterans of Foreign Wars
VHF—very high frequency
vid.—*vide* (Latin, "see"; used to direct attention, as *vide p. 40*)
VISTA—Volunteers in Service to America
viz.—*videlicet* (Latin, "namely")
v.p.—vice president
vs.—*versus* (Latin, "against")
wk.—week
wt.—weight
yr.—year

ABOLITION MOVEMENT

The abolition movement in United States history was a two-hundred-year campaign to free American blacks from the practice of slavery, or forced labor. The movement, which began in the late 1600's, evolved through several increasingly militant stages before the Civil War (1861–65) brought the issue to a climax. After four years of bloodshed, the victory of the Union forces made possible the ratification of the 13th Amendment (1865), which finally declared slavery illegal in the United States.

Early Activities and Accomplishments

The first recorded abolition meeting took place in 1688 in Germantown, Pennsylvania, among a group of Quakers and Mennonites, whose religious beliefs equated slavery with sin. "What thing in the world," they inquired of other colonists, "can be done worse toward us, than if men should rob or steal us away and sell us for slaves to strange countries?" For the next one hundred years, individuals continued to speak out against forced servitude, but no formal antislavery organization was founded until Benjamin Franklin helped organize the Pennsylvania Society for Promoting the Abolition of Slavery in Philadelphia in 1775. Dozens of similar protest organizations soon sprang up in other Northern states, gaining members beyond religious circles.

The three primary goals of these pioneer antislavery societies were to improve the living conditions of the black population, both slave and free; to challenge suspected false claims of slave ownership; and to petition legislative bodies to emancipate, or free, slaves within their jurisdictions. These initial movements were highly successful, and by 1804 slavery had been abolished in Rhode Island, Vermont, Pennsylvania, Massachusetts, New Hampshire,

At Boston's Tremont Temple in 1860, police and a hostile mob broke up an abolitionist meeting held in memory of the first anniversary of John Brown's execution.

Connecticut, and New Jersey. In addition, the importation of slaves from Africa ended in 1808, according to the terms of the U.S. Constitution (Article I, Section 9).

Militant Abolitionism

A more militant stage of the antislavery movement began in 1829 with the publication of *An Appeal to the Colored People of the World*. Written by David Walker, a freeborn black, the *Appeal* called for a slave revolt in the United States similar to the violent uprisings that had freed Haitian slaves from French colonial rule in the late 1700's. Legislators in Georgia and North Carolina enacted laws to censor what they termed incendiary, or explosive, publications, and African Americans in the South were arrested for distributing copies of Walker's pamphlet.

On January 1, 1831, a young and outspoken white abolitionist from Massachusetts named William Lloyd Garrison published the first issue of his antislavery newspaper, *The Liberator*. The following year he helped organize the New England Anti-Slavery Society in Boston.

In 1833 representatives from eleven states met in Philadelphia to form a national organization, the American

This moving emblem of a man in chains became the unofficial symbol of the abolition movement. It was used to illustrate a wide variety of antislavery publications.

Frederick Douglass

John Brown

John Brown (1800–59), born in Torrington, Conn., was the most radical of the militant white abolitionists and a hero to the slaves. A biography of John Brown appears in Volume B.

Frederick Douglass (Frederick Augustus Washington Bailey) (1817–95), born a slave in Tuckahoe, Md., escaped to the North in 1838. An orator and editor of the antislavery newspaper the *North Star*, he was the most influential of the black abolitionists. A biography of Frederick Douglass appears in Volume D.

James Forten (1766–1842), a free black, born in Philadelphia, Pa., was a major financial contributor to the abolition movement. As a teenager, he served on an American ship during the Revolutionary War and was taken prisoner by the British. After the war, he returned to Philadelphia and became an apprentice to a sailmaker. By 1798 he owned the business and had become quite wealthy. Forten was opposed to the movement to colonize American blacks in Africa. He assisted blacks escaping from the South and became a major financial backer of William Lloyd Garrison's newspaper, *The Liberator*.

Henry Highland Garnet (1815–82), born a slave in Kent County, Md., escaped to New York in 1824 and later became a Presbyterian minister and professional speaker with the American Anti-Slavery Society. At an 1843 National Convention of Free Colored People, he called upon slaves to rise up and "strike for your lives and liberties!" Garnet was the first African American to address the U.S. House of Representatives (1865).

William Lloyd Garrison (1805–79), born in Newburyport, Mass., was perhaps the most outspoken white champion of the abolitionist cause. In the first edition

(1831) of his newspaper, *The Liberator*, Garrison declared slavery an abomination in God's sight. He demanded immediate emancipation, vowing never to be silenced. "I am in earnest—I will not equivocate—I will not excuse—I will not retreat a single inch; and I will be heard!" He co-founded the American Anti-Slavery Society in 1833. For additional information, see the article MASSACHUSETTS (Famous People) in Volume M.

Elijah Parish Lovejoy (1802–37), born in Albion, Me., was a white Presbyterian minister and abolitionist. Opposition to his views in St. Louis, Mo., forced Lovejoy to abandon his position there as editor of a religious newspaper. In 1837 he relocated to Alton, Ill., where he began publishing the *Alton Observer* and tried to establish a chapter of the American Anti-Slavery Society. Within the year, Lovejoy was killed by a mob that came to seize his printing press. He became a martyr to the abolitionist cause.

Robert Purvis (1810–98), a freeborn South Carolinian of a well-to-do family, moved to Philadelphia and became an antislavery activist. He was one of three African Americans who helped organize the American Anti-Slavery Society (1833). Purvis also headed (1838–44) the Philadelphia Vigilance Committee, which assisted hundreds of fugitive slaves on the Underground Railroad. "Slavery," he said, "will be abolished in this land, and with it, that twin relic of barbarism—prejudice against color."

John Brown Russwurm (1799–1851), born in Port Antonio, Jamaica, was a co-founder of *Freedom's Journal*, the first newspaper owned and operated by African Americans. The first issue was published in New York on March 16, 1827. Seeking freedom for slaves, Russwurm favored the back-to-Africa movement of the

day, for which he was burned in effigy by activists opposed to colonization. In 1829 he moved to Liberia, in West Africa.

Profiles

Harriet Beecher Stowe (1811–96), born in Litchfield, Ct., gained international renown for her novel *Uncle Tom's Cabin*. Published in 1852 in reaction to the Fugitive Slave Law, the book increased popular support for ending slavery. A biography of Harriet Beecher Stowe appears in Volume S.

Sojourner Truth (Isabella Van Wagener) (1797?–1883), born a slave in Ulster County, N.Y., became the most famous antislavery spokeswoman. In 1843 she said that God called upon her to "travel up and down the land" and preach his word. She changed her name to Sojourner (meaning traveler) Truth and set out on a lecture tour to speak out about religion, slavery, and women's issues. Although she could neither read nor write, she was a captivating orator. Truth touched her audiences with such declarations as, "I have borne 13 children and seen them most all sold off into slavery, and when I cried out with a mother's grief, none but Jesus heard!"

David Walker (1785–1830), a free black, born in Wilmington, N.C. , settled in Boston in 1827. He became a charter member of the Massachusetts Colored General Association and contributed to *Freedom's Journal*. In 1829, Walker published a 76-page pamphlet, *An Appeal to the Colored People of the World*, urging slaves to rise up against their oppressors, convinced that violence was the only sure way to gain freedom. Walker's *Appeal* outraged slaveholders. He died mysteriously in 1830. Most abolitionists believed he had been poisoned.

William Lloyd Garrison

Harriet Beecher Stowe

William Lloyd Garrison's *The Liberator* was the most militant antislavery publication. Founded in 1831, it was published until emancipation was achieved in 1865.

Anti-Slavery Society. Three African Americans took part in the proceedings, making it the nation's first interracial public advocacy group. Most of its members believed that persistent "moral persuasion" would eventually convince slaveholders of the immorality of slavery, and that the practice would gradually disappear. Others, however, insisted on taking political action and called for the creation of an abolitionist political party.

Political Abolitionism

In 1840 the Liberty Party was organized in Albany, New York. The new party nominated a reformed ex-slaveholder, James G. Birney, for president. Despite the tens of thousands of Americans who called themselves abolitionists, only 7,000 cast their vote for Birney. Even fewer voted for him in 1844.

In 1846, as Congress was preparing to administer the transfer of territory from Mexico, David Wilmot, a U.S. representative from Pennsylvania, offered a provision that would prohibit slavery in land added to the Union.

WONDER QUESTION

What were the Gag Rules?

By 1836, the U.S. Congress had been overwhelmed by the number of petitions from citizens requesting that slavery not be extended into new U.S. territories. Because the reading of these petitions took up so much time, that year the House of Representatives passed a series of resolutions, known as the Gag Rules, to prevent further discussion of the issue. Opponents, led by House member and former president John Quincy Adams, argued that the Gag Rules violated the citizens' First Amendment right to petition the federal government for "redress of grievances." The measures were repealed in 1844.

This Wilmot Proviso became the basis of the new Free Soil Party, which attracted former Liberty Party members as well as antislavery Democrats, known as the Barnburners.

In 1848 the Free Soil Party endorsed former president Martin Van Buren under the slogan "Free Soil, Free Speech, Free Labor, and Free Men." However, when Van Buren drew only slightly more than 10 percent of the vote, support for the Free Soil Party dwindled. By 1856 most of its members had joined the Republican Party, which was organized in 1854 in opposition to the Kansas-Nebraska Act.

The Kansas-Nebraska Act (1854), which overturned the Missouri Compromise of 1820, allowed settlers to vote for or against slavery in their own territories. Nebraskans voted no, but Kansans voted yes. The growing number of "free staters" were enraged, notably John Brown, whose subsequent attacks on Kansas slaveholders gave rise to the name Bleeding Kansas.

Abolitionists already were embittered by the passage of the Fugitive Slave Act (1850) that had made it illegal for any American to assist fugitive slaves. Outrage over this law actually increased support for the Underground Railroad, a secret network of people dedicated to helping slaves escape to the North. Abolitionists were further outraged when the U.S. Supreme Court ruled in 1857, in the Dred Scott Decision, that the Constitution protected slave property throughout the United States. Each of these actions propelled the North and South toward a civil war, which began in April 1861.

On September 22, 1862, as a military measure, U.S. president Abraham Lincoln issued his Emancipation Proclamation, declaring that as of January 1, 1863, any slave residing in a Confederate state would be "forever free." Enforcement of this policy, however, depended upon which side won the war.

On April 9, 1865, the Confederates surrendered to the Union forces and the Civil War came to an end. Eight months later, on December 18, 1865, abolition was assured with the ratification of the 13th Amendment to the Constitution.

RUSSELL L. ADAMS
Chair, Department of Afro-American Studies
Howard University

See also EMANCIPATION PROCLAMATION; UNDERGROUND RAILROAD.

ABORIGINES, AUSTRALIAN

The Australian aborigines are the earliest-known inhabitants of Australia and today are regarded as the native people of that continent. The term aborigine, which comes from the Latin words *ab origine*, means "from the beginning" and can be applied to the native peoples of any region.

▶ TRADITIONAL WAY OF LIFE

It is believed that Australia's aborigines migrated from Southeast Asia more than 30,000 years ago. They probably traveled across the Indian Ocean by raft or dugout canoe.

The aborigines lived in nomadic tribes, and over the centuries they spread out across the continent. Each tribe claimed its own territory and moved from place to place within that territory to hunt, fish, and gather food.

Each tribe was actually an extended family made up of several clans. Clan members lived in family groups of thirty to forty people. Each clan had an emblem called a totem—perhaps an animal or a plant. The totem was honored as a member of the clan and served as a reminder of the clan's common ancestry. The aborigines believed that all things—people, animals, plants, and even rocks—were important parts of nature and of the spirit world.

The aborigines survived for thousands of years by adapting to Australia's often harsh conditions. They were one of the few early peoples to make use of the principle of the lever, using it in the design of a spear-thrower called the woomera. They also used several types of boomerangs, a flat, curved throwing stick made of hard wood. One type, the returning boomerang, was invented by the aborigines and used for sport. When thrown properly, this kind spins through the air and returns to the thrower in a perfect arc. The aborigines also used non-returning boomerang-type weapons for hunting, fighting, and other purposes, but they were not the only early culture to use such a tool. The aborigines also left a rich heritage of artwork in the form of rock carvings and bark and cave paintings.

In 1788, when the first European settlers came to Australia, there were perhaps more than half a million aborigines living there. As the Europeans spread out, many natives were driven from their lands into remote areas. Many others died from foreign diseases.

In Australia's aboriginal societies, adult males are the principal guardians of sacred rites and culture. Ritual dances and body painting are two forms of expression that create a spiritual connection to ancestral origins.

▶ ABORIGINES IN MODERN AUSTRALIA

Today there are less than half as many aborigines in Australia as there were when Europeans first arrived. Less than half of them are considered full-blooded. Most are now of mixed aboriginal-European ancestry. All together, aborigines make up only about 1 percent of today's population. Most live in cities and towns, although a few are trying to preserve some form of the old, nomadic way of life. Unfortunately, the standard of living for most aborigines lags far behind that of other Australian citizens, and in the past few decades, the government has sponsored a number of programs to help the aborigines compete for jobs and housing opportunities.

In recent years, efforts also have been made on the part of the aborigines to regain title to their ancestral lands. They have been successful in regaining ownership of some parts of the Northern Territory and of South Australia. Since 1980, these lands have been administered by the Aboriginal Development Commission. In 1992 the Australian High Court ruled that the aborigines owned Australia before European settlement began in 1788. This ruling should assist them in any future land disputes.

CAROL PERKINS
Author, *The Sound of Boomerangs*

See also AUSTRALIA.

Abraham receiving God's promise of a son, as depicted by a Christian artist of the 1200's.

ABRAHAM

Abraham is called the father of the Jews and is considered to be the founder of their religion. He was the first to believe in one all-powerful God instead of many gods.

Abraham's story is found in the book of Genesis, the first book of the Bible. When Abraham was 75 years old, God commanded him to leave Haran in search of a new home. God promised that a great nation would arise in the new land. Abraham set out with his wife, Sarah, his nephew Lot, and some followers. They traveled into the land of Canaan. God told Abraham that this was the land he would give to Abraham's descendants. Abraham journeyed on toward the south, building altars to God wherever he went. When a famine came, he went into Egypt. He grew rich in cattle, silver, and gold.

When Abraham and his followers left Egypt, both Abraham and Lot grew very prosperous. They acquired so many sheep that their shepherds quarreled over grazing land. Abraham and Lot agreed to separate and live in different places.

Abraham settled in Hebron. Lot and his family settled in Sodom. When Sodom was attacked by the armies of four great kings, Lot was taken captive. Abraham went to his rescue with 318 men and brought Lot and all his goods back to Sodom.

The people of Sodom and neighboring Gomorrah grew very wicked. God told Abraham that he would destroy both cities because no righteous people could be found in them.

But God warned Lot to escape with his wife and two daughters, forbidding them to look behind as they fled. Lot's wife looked back, and she became a pillar of salt.

When Abraham and Sarah had grown very old and were still childless, God promised them a son. God also said that Abraham would have as many descendants as there were stars in the sky and that one day they would dwell in the Promised Land. In time, a son was born to Abraham and Sarah and was named Isaac. The name means "he laughs." God told Abraham that he would keep his promise with Isaac and his descendants.

While Isaac was still a boy, God tested Abraham again. He told Abraham to take Isaac to the top of a mountain and sacrifice him. Abraham loved his son, but he could not disobey God's command. At the place of sacrifice, Isaac asked, "Where is the lamb for a burnt offering?" Abraham answered that God would provide it. Then he built an altar, laid wood on it, bound up Isaac, and laid him on top of the wood. Just as he was about to put the knife to his son, God stopped him. God said, "Lay not thine hand upon the lad, neither do thou any thing unto him: for now I know that thou fearest God, seeing thou hast not withheld thy son, thine only son, from me." Abraham looked up and saw a ram caught in a thicket. He offered the ram in sacrifice. God blessed Abraham for his obedience.

When Sarah and Abraham died, they were buried in the cave of Machpelah in Hebron. After Abraham's death God blessed Isaac.

Christians and Muslims also honor Abraham and trace their belief in one God back to him. The Arabs claim descent from Ishmael, who was Abraham's son by Hagar, Sarah's handmaiden. When Sarah thought she would have no children, she gave Hagar to Abraham.

Abraham's life is regarded as an example of the proving of faith through trial. Because Abraham listened to God, he is called the Friend of God. His unquestioning obedience to God's commands is taken as proof of genuine righteousness.

Reviewed by MORTIMER J. COHEN
Author, *Pathways Through the Bible*

ACCIDENTS. See FIRST AID; SAFETY.

ACCOUNTING. See BOOKKEEPING AND ACCOUNTING.

ACHAEMENIDS. See PERSIA, ANCIENT.

ACID RAIN

Fifty years ago, few people had heard of acid rain. Today, many people all over the world know about this environmental problem that can pollute lakes, rivers, and streams; damage metals and other construction materials; and even pose a health risk to people.

Acid rain is a general term for rain or other precipitation that has been polluted by chemicals called acids. It forms when certain pollutants, such as sulfur oxides and nitrogen oxides, mix with tiny droplets of water vapor in the atmosphere. Smoke from factories and power stations, exhaust fumes from automobiles and trucks, and even gases given off by chemical fertilizers put the pollutants into the air. The pollutants change the clean, fresh water to droplets of acid. These acids fall to earth as rain, snow, or sleet. Even fog can contain acids.

Rain normally contains some acids. This is because carbon dioxide in the air and even smoke from volcanoes mix with rain and make it mildly acidic. This is normal and is not considered a problem. However, sulfuric and nitric acids in rain are a problem. When acid rain falls to earth, it soaks the ground and can make soil, lakes, and rivers abnormally acidic. In badly affected regions, plants and many types of aquatic animals are harmed. Entire lakes and some forest trees can be affected. Even buildings and statues can be damaged by acid rain.

In the eastern United States and southeastern Canada, acids in the air have made the rain ten times more acidic than normal. Acid mists from clouds surrounding trees at high elevations can be 100 times more acidic than normal rainwater.

POLLUTION THAT CAUSES ACID RAIN

When fossil fuels—oil, coal, and gas—are burned, in industrial plants or automobile engines, for example, sulfur oxides and nitrogen oxides are released into the air. One industrial smokestack without pollution controls may produce as much as 500 tons of sulfur oxides each day.

Nitrogen oxides and carbon particles produced by motor vehicles are so plentiful in some large cities that the air is colored by them. Nitrogen oxides also enter the air from the breakdown of agricultural fertilizers. Other

The forest on Camels Hump in Vermont shows the effects of acid rain. Scientists have closely studied this area to collect information on the acid rain problem.

acid-forming chemicals also occur but in smaller amounts. Hydrochloric acid often comes directly from smokestacks. Carbon monoxide and carbon dioxide are produced by motor vehicles.

TRANSPORTING POLLUTION

Because pollutants can travel over hundreds and even thousands of miles, acid rain often affects areas that are far from power plants, which are the main source of pollutants causing acid rain, and heavy automobile exhaust. Many power plants have smokestacks well over 300 feet (100 meters) high. Pollutants in smoke enter the air high above the ground and are carried by winds for great distances. Pollutants from the midwestern United States are regularly carried to New York, New England, and southeastern Canada. Similarly, pollution from Canada is carried by winds into the United States. Norway and Sweden have received acid rain created by pollutants traveling north from England, Germany, Italy, France, and Austria.

▶THE EFFECTS OF ACID RAIN

Millions of tons of acids fall in rain on the United States and Canada each year. The concentration of these acids are too weak to cause burns, but they do produce other less severe effects.

When acid rain falls on metal objects, the objects can begin to change in undesirable ways. Shiny objects become dull and, if the process continues for many years, the metal objects can corrode and lose strength or crumble. Acid rain also affects the surfaces of stone statues and stone or brick buildings.

The way in which acid rain reacts with aluminum causes another serious problem. Aluminum is normally present in soil. If acid rain causes soil acidification, the aluminum in the soil may dissolve in water and be absorbed by plants, where it can damage root cells. Animal cells are also very sensitive to aluminum. In lakes and streams, it can kill the eggs of many kinds of fish and the embryos of salamanders and other amphibians. Aluminum affects ma-

Lime is an alkaline substance that neutralizes acids. In this picture, lime is being pumped into a lake to neutralize the water's increasing acidity.

ture fish by causing the gills to clog with mucus, preventing breathing. Aluminum also disrupts eggshell formation in birds.

Human beings may also be at risk from the effects of acid rain. In moist air, high levels of pollutants from acidic aerosols have been found to affect lung function in experimental studies. People who suffer from asthma, emphysema, and chronic bronchitis are more sensitive to acid environments. Additional studies are necessary to determine whether people are affected at current levels of aerosol acidity.

▶STOPPING ACID RAIN

In 1990, the United States passed the Clean Air Act Amendments, which is a law that will require significant reductions in air pollution by the year 2000. One measure to fight acid rain is to remove from the air those sulfur and nitrogen compounds that become acids. Some of these compounds can be taken out of fuel before the fuel is burned. Or the pollutants can be removed from smoke before the smoke enters the air. Each individual also can play a role in reducing pollution by conserving energy through such activities as cutting back on the use of electricity and car-pooling or using public transportation.

Reviewed by PATRICIA M. IRVING
Director
National Acid Precipitation Assessment Program

ACIDS. See CHEMISTRY.

ACNE. See DISEASES (Descriptions of Some Diseases).

ACOUSTICS. See SOUND AND ULTRASONICS.

The statue on the right shows the damaging effects of air pollution and acid rain. Stone and brick buildings have been similarly damaged.

ADAMS, CHARLES FRANCIS (1807–1886)

Charles Francis Adams was an American historian and diplomat. The son of President John Quincy Adams and the grandson of President John Adams, he was born in Boston, Massachusetts, on August 18, 1807. He graduated from Harvard in 1825, became a lawyer, and later entered politics, serving in the Massachusetts state legislature (1840–45) as a Whig. Adams, who opposed slavery, switched over to the Free Soil Party and ran unsuccessfully as its vice-presidential candidate in 1848. Later he served in the U.S. House of Representatives as a Republican (1859–61).

Adams performed his most important work during the U.S. Civil War. In 1861 he was appointed ambassador to Great Britain by President Abraham Lincoln. The British government had declared itself neutral in the American conflict, yet many prominent Britons openly supported the Confederate states, and several Confederate navy ships were built in England. Adams persuaded the British government not to intervene diplomatically on the Confederate side and to officially ban further shipbuilding for the Confederates (although several ships continued to slip through on the black market).

In 1872 Adams represented the United States on an international committee that settled the so-called *Alabama* claims for damages caused by British-built Confederate ships during the Civil War. The committee assessed Great Britain $15.5 million for damages for building the *Alabama* and other ships, which had violated international neutrality laws.

Adams edited many letters, papers, and diaries of his famous parents and grandparents. Among the most notable is his 12-volume *Memoirs of John Quincy Adams* (1864–67). He died in Boston on November 21, 1886.

MICHAEL WINSHIP
Cornell University

ADAMS, HENRY (1838–1918)

Henry Brooks Adams—historian, novelist, and philosopher—was born on February 16, 1838, in Boston, Massachusetts. Adams came from a distinguished family. His grandfather, John Quincy Adams, and his great grandfather, John Adams, both were former presidents of the United States; his father, Charles Francis Adams, was a historian, diplomat, and politician. Not surprisingly, Henry Adams grew up assuming that he, too, would be an important person one day.

When Adams graduated from Harvard in 1858, he entered a world in which he felt he did not belong. He tried a number of careers, first as his father's private secretary (1861–68). He later became a journalist, and then for seven years he taught history at Harvard.

Finally in 1877, Adams settled down in Washington, D.C. There he suffered a great personal tragedy in 1885 when his beloved wife Marian committed suicide. Adams devoted himself to writing books. In his *Mont-Saint-Michel and Chartres: A Story of 13th Century Unity* (1913), he described the Middle Ages as a time of beauty and spiritual unity, very much unlike the chaotic times in which he felt he lived. It seemed to him that

In 1919, a year after Henry Adams' death, *The Education of Henry Adams* was awarded a Pulitzer prize. It is still considered a classic among autobiographies.

America was a harsh place where only the most brutal and energetic people could succeed, not the most intelligent and idealistic. In *The Education of Henry Adams* (1918), he explored this observation, trying to understand how the world had changed and why he could not adapt to the new society.

Among Adams' other works were two novels, *Democracy, an American Novel* (1880), a political satire; and *Esther* (1884), the story of a woman's search for religious truth. His most important historical work was the multi-volume *History of the United States during the Administrations of Jefferson and Madison* (1884–1891). Adams died in Washington, D.C., on March 27, 1918.

MICHAEL WINSHIP
Cornell University

JOHN ADAMS (1735-1826)
2nd President of the United States

FACTS ABOUT JOHN ADAMS

Birthplace: Braintree (now Quincy), Massachusetts (below)
Religion: Unitarian
College Attended: Harvard College, Cambridge, Massachusetts
Occupation: Lawyer
Married: Abigail Smith
Children: Abigail, John Quincy, Susanna, Charles, Thomas
Political Party: Federalist
Office Held Before Becoming President: Vice President
President Who Preceded Him: George Washington
Age on Becoming President: 61
Years in the Presidency: 1797–1801
Vice President: Thomas Jefferson
President Who Succeeded Him: Thomas Jefferson
Age at Death: 90
Burial Place: First Unitarian Church, Quincy, Massachusetts

John Adams

DURING JOHN ADAMS' PRESIDENCY

The first cast-iron plow was patented by Charles Newbold (1797). *Below:* Disputes between the United States and France led to an undeclared naval war between the two nations and the creation of the Navy Department (1798). *Left:* The U.S. Marine Corps was established as a permanent service by Congress (1798). The Mississippi Territory, including what is now Mississippi and Alabama, was created (1798). The Indiana Territory, including all or parts of present-day Indiana, Wisconsin, Illinois, Michigan, and Minnesota, was created (1800). The capital was moved from Philadelphia to Washington, D.C. (1800).

ADAMS, JOHN. Of all the early presidents of the United States, John Adams has been the least understood and appreciated. His reputation, both during his lifetime and after, has suffered from this lack of understanding. Yet he was a remarkable man who contributed greatly to the creation of the United States during the American Revolution and in its formative years.

▶ EARLY YEARS

Adams was born on October 30, 1735, in Braintree (now Quincy), Massachusetts. His great-grandfather Henry Adams had emigrated from England. But both his grandfather Joseph Adams and his father, John Adams, had been born in Braintree. His mother, Susanna Boylston Adams, came from the nearby city of Boston.

Adams grew up on his father's farm, doing the usual country chores, including feeding the horses, milking the cows, and chopping wood. In 1751, at the age of 16, he entered Harvard, then a small college, and graduated four years later. He then taught school during the day and studied law at night. In 1758 he became a lawyer. Perhaps his most famous case, which showed Adams' characteristic courage, was his successful defense of the British soldiers who were arrested after the Boston Massacre in 1770.

In 1764, Adams married Abigail Smith. She was an intelligent and sprightly woman whose letters are still a source of interesting information. The marriage was happy and successful. It lasted 54 years, until Abigail Adams' death in 1818. Their eldest son, John Quincy, later became the sixth president.

▶ POLITICAL BEGINNINGS

Altogether, Adams spent about 25 years in public life. He became interested in politics quite early in his career as a lawyer. In 1765 a crisis arose when the British Government passed the Stamp Act. This was an unpopular tax on public documents, newspapers, licenses, insurance policies, and even playing cards. Adams wrote powerful articles against the tax in the Boston *Gazette*. These articles

Abigail Adams was the wife of one president, John Adams, and the mother of a second, John Quincy Adams. She was the first First Lady to occupy the White House.

helped to establish his reputation as a political thinker, as an opponent of Britain's colonial policies in America, and as a champion of individual liberties.

The Continental Congress. Adams served as a delegate from Massachusetts to the First Continental Congress in Philadelphia in 1774 and to the Second Continental Congress, which met in 1775. With brilliance and persistence, he argued for American independence from Britain. When the fighting broke out in 1775 that marked the beginning of the Revolutionary War, Adams proposed George Washington as the commander of American military forces.

Adams was a member of the committee that drafted the Declaration of Independence. Although the Declaration was written chiefly by Thomas Jefferson, Adams bore the burden of defending it on the floor of the Continental Congress. It was adopted on July 4, 1776.

Diplomatic Service. Adams' diplomatic career began in 1778 when he was sent to France to help negotiate a treaty of alliance. In 1780 he returned to Europe as minister to arrange for loans and trade agreements in France and the Netherlands. Two years later Adams, together with Benjamin Franklin and John Jay,

signed the preliminary peace treaty with Britain. The treaty, known as the Treaty of Paris, was finally concluded in 1783. It ended the Revolutionary War and crowned Adams' long struggle for American independence.

In 1785, Adams was appointed the first U.S. minister to Britain. He tried to win British friendship and economic co-operation, but without success. One reason was that he was too outspoken in defense of American interests. He was happy to return home in 1788, after having spent some ten years abroad.

Vice President. In the first presidential election in the United States, in 1788, George Washington won all the electoral votes cast for president. Adams became vice president. Both men were re-elected in 1792.

In spite of his general agreement with Washington's policies, Adams was impatient with his position as vice president. Adams was eager to lead and to act. Instead, he had to confine himself to the largely ceremonial job of presiding over the U.S. Senate.

▶ PRESIDENT

Adams' frustration was ended by his victory in the presidential election of 1796. Running as the Federalist candidate, he edged out Thomas Jefferson, leader of the Democratic-Republicans (also called the Republicans). According to the laws of the time, Jefferson thus became vice president. As a result, the new president and vice president belonged to opposing political parties.

John Adams was the first president to occupy the White House. He and Abigail moved in near the end of his term, in the fall of 1800. The President's Palace, as it was then known, was still unfinished and littered with debris.

Adams' one term as president was marked by troubles, both international and domestic. The foreign affairs crisis involved American neutrality at a time when Britain and France were at war. French attacks on American ships stirred up a warlike atmosphere in the United States, even inside Adams' own Cabinet. The situation was aggravated by the so-called XYZ Affair.

The XYZ Affair. Adams had sent a diplomatic mission to France to arrange a treaty. There the diplomats were visited by three agents of the French foreign minister Talleyrand. These agents, known as X, Y, and Z, asked for a bribe of $240,000. When news of this XYZ Affair reached America, it caused an uproar and led to an undeclared war between the United States and France. But despite immense pressure, including that of members of his own Federalist Party, President Adams knew that the United States was not strong enough to fight the French Empire. He persisted in his efforts for peace, which was finally achieved by the Convention of 1800. Adams considered it his great accomplishment. He said, "I desire no other inscription over my gravestone than: 'Here lies John Adams, who took upon himself the responsibility of the peace with France in the year 1800.' "

Adams' courageous but unpopular peace policy and his stubborn independence in other political matters cost him the support of his own party. The leading Federalists, including the powerful Alexander Hamilton, turned bitterly against him. This led to a hopeless split in their party.

The Alien and Sedition Acts. President Adams' unpopularity was aggravated by the Alien and Sedition Acts. These acts were a direct result of the excitement over the trouble with France. The country was divided into pro-French and pro-British groups. Adams' Federalist Party was strongly anti-French. The opposition Democratic-Republican Party, led by Jefferson, was just as strongly anti-British.

The Federalists were convinced that opposition against them was aroused by the French and Irish living in America. They were sure that the country swarmed with French spies.

The Federalists controlled Congress. In 1798 they decided to crush the opposition through legislation that came to be known as the Alien and Sedition Acts.

The Alien Act contained three provisions. One required that the period of naturalization for foreigners be changed from 5 to 14 years. The second authorized the president to deport all aliens considered dangerous to the peace and security of the country. The third gave the president the power to imprison or banish citizens of an enemy country in time of war.

More serious was the Sedition Act, which was aimed at American opponents of the government. This act made it a crime to oppose the administration directly or indirectly. Even those who voiced criticism in print were made subject to harsh penalties.

The Sedition Act resulted in the prosecution of 25 persons and the conviction of 10 of them. All were prominent Democratic-Republicans.

These acts were violently unpopular. They were considered an attack on the basic liberties of the American people. President Adams was not personally responsible for them, but they were passed by his party and he signed them. Therefore the blame fell upon him. In the election of 1800, Adams and his party suffered disastrous defeat. The Federalist Party never recovered.

On March 4, 1801, after the inauguration of President Jefferson, Adams retired from public life. He returned to Braintree and devoted the remaining 25 years of his life to

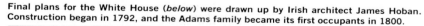

Final plans for the White House (*below*) were drawn up by Irish architect James Hoban. Construction began in 1792, and the Adams family became its first occupants in 1800.

John Adams (*standing, in rust-colored suit*) and the four other members of the drafting committee present the Declaration of Independence to the Second Continental Congress.

intellectual pursuits, mainly reading (philosophy, religion, political thought, science) and letter writing. He resumed his friendship and correspondence with Thomas Jefferson in 1812. The two men had been separated for 12 years because of political differences. On July 4, 1826—the 50th anniversary of the Declaration of Independence—John Adams died at Quincy. That same day Jefferson died at Monticello, Virginia.

▶ **HIS POLITICAL PHILOSOPHY**

Adams expressed his ideas in a number of essays and books, as well as in his letters. There are three main elements in his philosophy. One is Adams' view of human nature. Another is his conception of inequality. The third is his idea of government.

Adams did not agree with democrats like Jefferson that human beings were naturally good and decent. On the contrary, he believed that people were basically selfish and only good because of necessity.

Adams also denied the democratic idea of equality. He pointed out that among all nations the people were "naturally divided into two sorts, the gentlemen and the simple men." The gentlemen, being superior in abilities, education, and other advantages, were therefore qualified to rule.

These views underlay Adams' philosophy of government. Since human beings were greedy and selfish, it was necessary for society to keep them in check. The average person, he felt, could not be entrusted with power.

Adams believed in liberty and was opposed to tyranny. Though he was sometimes accused of being a monarchist, he actually preferred a republic. But instead of a Jefferson-type democracy, Adams favored a republican government run by an aristocracy of talented men.

Such views, expressed with his typical bluntness, gained Adams unpopularity and even hostility among the American people. But he was not one to seek popular favor. He died as he had lived, an independent, tough-minded, somewhat opinionated and irritable Yankee—but always a courageous patriot and scholar.

SAUL K. PADOVER
Editor, The World of the Founding Fathers

IMPORTANT DATES IN THE LIFE OF JOHN ADAMS	
1735	Born at Braintree (now Quincy), Massachusetts, October 30.
1755	Graduated from Harvard College.
1758	Began practicing law.
1764	Married Abigail Smith.
1765	Attacked the Stamp Act in articles in the Boston *Gazette*.
1774–1777	Served in the Continental Congress.
1780	Minister to the Netherlands.
1782	Went to Paris (with John Jay and Benjamin Franklin) to arrange peace treaty with Great Britain ending the Revolutionary War. Treaty of Paris concluded 1783.
1785–1788	Minister to Great Britain.
1789–1797	Vice-president of the United States.
1797–1801	2nd president of the United States.
1826	Died at Quincy, Massachusetts, July 4.

JOHN QUINCY ADAMS (1767-1848)
6th President of the United States

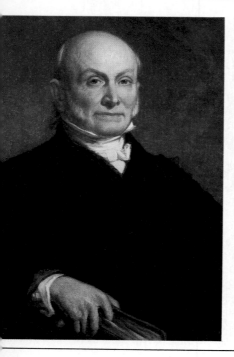

FACTS ABOUT JOHN QUINCY ADAMS

Birthplace: Braintree (now Quincy),
  Massachusetts *(center)*
Religion: Unitarian
College Attended:
  Harvard College,
  Cambridge,
  Massachusetts
Occupation: Lawyer
Married: Louisa
  Catherine Johnson
Children: George, John, Charles Francis,
  Louisa Catherine
Political Party: Federalist, Democratic-
  Republican (National Republican), Whig
Nickname: "Old Man Eloquent"
Office Held Before Becoming President:
  Secretary of State
President Who Preceded Him: James
  Monroe
Age on Becoming President: 57
Years in the Presidency: 1825-1829
Vice President: John C. Calhoun
President Who Succeeded Him: Andrew
  Jackson
Age at Death: 80
Burial Place: Quincy, Massachusetts

DURING JOHN QUINCY ADAMS' PRESIDENCY

Right: The cornerstone of the
Bunker Hill Monument was
laid (1825), commemorating
the famous Revolutionary War
battle. *Below:* The Erie Canal
was opened (1825),
linking New York
with Lake Erie and
the other Great
Lakes and increasing
trade with and settlement of the growing
Midwest. The first iron vessel, built of
sheet iron, in the United States, the
steamboat *Codorus,* was tested (1825) on
the Susquehanna River. Construction of
the Baltimore and Ohio Railroad, the first
commercial passenger and freight railroad
in the United States, was begun (1828).

ADAMS, JOHN QUINCY. Many Americans have
sought the office of president of the United
States and have deliberately shaped their lives
to that end. John Quincy Adams' parents prepared him for the presidency from boyhood.
But although Adams achieved his goal of becoming president, his term in the White House
was overshadowed by his two other political
careers—as America's greatest diplomat and
as its greatest defender of human freedom in
the U.S. House of Representatives.

▶AN UNUSUAL CHILDHOOD

John Quincy Adams was born on July 11,
1767, in Braintree (now Quincy), Massachusetts. His father was John Adams, who would
later become the second president of the
United States. His mother, Abigail Smith
Adams, was the most accomplished American
woman of her time. Young Adams grew up as
a child of the American Revolution, which
began when he was 7 years old.

John Quincy's education began in the village school and continued under his mother's
guidance. His education was inspired by letters from his father, who had been serving in
the Continental Congress in Philadelphia since
1774.

During the Revolutionary War, John
Quincy accompanied his father on two diplomatic missions to Europe. In 1781, at the age
of 14, he acted as French interpreter to his
father on a mission to Russia. In 1783, John
Quincy served as his father's secretary when
the elder Adams was minister to France.
Young Adams was present at the signing of
the Treaty of Paris in 1783, which ended the
Revolutionary War.

In Paris, John Quincy Adams began his famous diary. He was to continue it for over 60
years. On the title page of the first volume was
the proverb that ruled his life: "Sweet is in-
dolence [laziness] and cruel its conse-
quences." Adams never had a lazy day.

Young Adams returned to Massachusetts in
1785 to complete his education at Harvard
College. He graduated in 1787 and then studied law.

He had barely developed a law practice when the French Revolution broke out. Articles Adams wrote for a Boston newspaper attracted the attention of President George Washington. In 1794 Washington appointed the 28-year-old John Quincy Adams minister to the Netherlands. Adams' official dispatches and his letters from the Dutch capital at The Hague convinced the President that this young man would one day stand at the head of the American diplomatic corps.

In 1797, while on a mission from the Netherlands to England, Adams married Louisa Catherine Johnson, daughter of the American consul in London.

From The Hague Adams (whose father was now president) was assigned to the Court of Prussia. There he negotiated a treaty of friendship and commerce. He continued his letters and dispatches about the war of the French Revolution. Because of political reasons, John Adams recalled him after Thomas Jefferson was elected president in 1800.

Adams' experiences had convinced him that the United States must never be caught in the "vortex" of European rivalries and wars. This lesson guided him through his later diplomatic career and influenced United States policy for a century afterwards.

▶ A SHORT TERM IN THE SENATE

When he returned to Boston, Adams found the practice of law frustrating. He had a strong desire to enter politics. In 1803 the Massachusetts legislature elected him to the United States Senate. Though elected as a Federalist, Adams felt that party politics stopped at the ocean's edge. To the disgust of Massachusetts Federalists, he voted for President Jefferson's Embargo of 1807. The embargo was aimed at protecting United States neutrality in the wars between England and France. It stopped all American trade with the two countries. Adams' vote in favor of the embargo cost him his Senate seat. The legislature held a special election ahead of time to replace him with a more faithful Federalist.

▶ DIPLOMAT AGAIN

In 1809 President James Madison appointed Adams the first American minister to Russia. Adams was in Russia when the War of 1812 broke out between the United States and Great Britain. He served on the delegation that brought about the Peace of Ghent in 1814. The following year he became minister to Great Britain, where he served until 1817.

By now Adams was in his 50th year. He was without question the most experienced man in the United States diplomatic service. Because of his European experience, Adams had become a confirmed isolationist. He felt that the future of the United States lay in expansion across the North American continent rather than in European alliances.

▶ SECRETARY OF STATE

In 1817 President James Monroe called Adams home to become secretary of state. The most important achievements of Secretary Adams were the treaties he negotiated, which brought much of the Far West under American control. The famous Transcontinental Treaty of 1819 (ratified 1821) with Spain gave the United States access to the Pacific Ocean. This was the greatest diplomatic triumph ever achieved by one man in the history of the United States. Adams was also responsible for treaties with the newly independent countries of Latin America.

The Monroe Doctrine

John Quincy Adams had a major role in forming the Monroe Doctrine. Adams' words in that famous document made it clear that the United States would not tolerate any new European colonization in the Americas. The doctrine properly bears President Monroe's name. For it was Monroe who in 1823 first declared its principles to the world as American foreign policy.

The Election of 1824

Adams was never a dynamic politician. But his accomplishments brought him before the people in the national election of 1824. There was no real party contest. The old political parties had disappeared during the so-called Era of Good Feeling of Monroe's administration. It was a contest of leaders.

General Andrew Jackson, the hero of the battle of New Orleans during the War of 1812, received a majority of the popular vote. But no candidate received the necessary ma-

The 79-year-old Adams sat for this photograph in 1847, a year before he died.

This portrait of Louisa Catherine Adams, the President's wife, dates from the 1820's. The harp and book symbolize her love of music and literature.

jority in the electoral college. Jackson had 99 electoral votes; Adams, 84; William H. Crawford of Georgia, 41; and Henry Clay of Kentucky, 37. Under the Constitution the election had to be decided by the House of Representatives. The voting there was by states and was limited to the first three candidates. On February 9, 1825, Adams was elected president by a bare majority of states.

John Adams, then 90 years old, was delighted at his son's victory. But Abigail Adams did not live to see the presidency come to rest on her son's shoulders. She had died in 1818.

▶ HIS TERM AS PRESIDENT

President John Quincy Adams appointed Henry Clay secretary of state. Clay had thrown the votes of his supporters in the House of Representatives to Adams rather than Jackson. At once Jackson and his followers raised the cry of "corrupt bargain." That there was a political deal seems fairly certain. But there is nothing to show that it was dishonest.

The charge of corrupt bargain was the beginning of a quarrel with Jackson that marred Adams' administration. Jackson had strong support among the voters of the newly admitted states. Adams, after all, had not received a majority of the popular vote. The Jacksonians were out to get rid of Adams and seize office themselves.

The 4 years of Adams' presidency were prosperous and generally happy years for the United States. Adams' ambition was to govern "as a man of the whole nation," not as the leader of a political party. He believed in liberty with power. He favored more power for the federal government in the disposal of public lands and in building new roads and canals to keep up with the westward movement. He supported federal control and protection of the Indian groups against invasion of their lands by the states.

This program hit at the narrow interpretation of the Constitution under the old Jeffersonian concept of states' rights. It thus aroused Adams' opponents. In the election of 1828, Andrew Jackson was elected president by an overwhelming majority.

With his term as president over, Adams' career seemed finished. He returned sadly to

Quincy, Massachusetts. However, he was still willing to serve his country in any office, large or small. In 1830 he was elected to the House of Representatives. Nothing could have been more pleasing to Adams, for the ghost of the presidency still haunted him. He hoped for the nomination again. But these hopes soon faded.

▶ "OLD MAN ELOQUENT"

During Adams' years in the House of Representatives, the stormy issue of slavery faced the United States. At heart Adams was an abolitionist: he wished to do away completely with slavery. But he was politically prudent, and did not say so publicly. He became a leader of the antislavery forces in Congress but limited his efforts to constitutional means. He sought to abolish slavery in the District of Columbia. He opposed its expansion into the territories of the United States. And he championed the right of petition to Congress for abolition of slavery.

As secretary of state and as president, Adams had tried to obtain Texas from Mexico. But in Congress he resisted to the last the movement for annexation of Texas. By that time the entry of Texas into the Union would have meant the creation of one or more new slave states. On the other hand, he championed the annexation of Oregon, where slavery did not exist. "I want the country for our Western pioneers," he said.

Adams was a patron and supporter in Congress of scientific activities, especially in the fields of weights and measures, and astronomy. He led the movement for establishment

Adams' long career of public service ended in the U.S. House of Representatives. He was elected to Congress in 1830 and died there on February 23, 1848.

of the Smithsonian Institution, in Washington, D.C., one of the nation's foremost centers of learning.

"Old Man Eloquent," as Adams was called, opposed the war with Mexico that followed the annexation of Texas in 1845. He considered it an unjust war. On February 21, 1848, while protesting the award of swords of honor to the American generals who had won the war, Adams collapsed on the floor of the House of Representatives. He died two days later in the Capitol.

During most of his early career as a diplomat, Adams was little known throughout the country. His term as president was unpopular. Always a reserved man, he seemed cold and aloof to the people. His career in the House of Representatives made him a violently controversial figure. It was not until the final years of his life that Adams won esteem and almost affection, especially in the hearts and minds of the millions who hated slavery. Representatives of both political parties journeyed to Quincy, Massachusetts, for his funeral. In death, John Quincy Adams seemed at last to belong to the whole nation.

SAMUEL FLAGG BEMIS
Yale University
Author, *John Quincy Adams and the Union*

See also MONROE DOCTRINE.

IMPORTANT DATES IN THE LIFE OF JOHN QUINCY ADAMS

1767 Born at Braintree (later Quincy), Massachusetts, July 11.
1787 Graduated from Harvard College.
1794 Appointed minister to the Netherlands.
1797 Married Louisa Catherine Johnson.
1797–1801 Minister to Prussia.
1803–1808 Served in the United States Senate.
1809–1814 Minister to Russia.
1814 Headed American delegation that negotiated the Peace of Ghent, ending the War of 1812.
1815–1817 Minister to Great Britain.
1817–1825 Secretary of state.
1825–1829 6th president of the United States.
1831–1848 Served in the U.S. House of Representatives.
1848 Died at Washington, D.C., February 23.

ADAMS, SAMUEL (1722–1803)

Samuel Adams was an American patriot whose skills as an orator and organizer did much to arouse the American colonists against British rule and helped bring about the revolution that created the United States.

Early Years. Adams was born in Boston, Massachusetts, on September 27, 1722. He was a cousin of John Adams, who was to become the second president of the United States. He attended the Boston Grammar School and graduated from Harvard College in 1740. He later returned to Harvard to earn his master's degree. His father was a well-to-do businessman who wanted him to follow a similar career, but Samuel had no talent for business. He studied law but gave it up to devote his time to politics.

Orator and Organizer. In 1765, Adams was elected to the Massachusetts legislature, where he soon became a leader of the radical (anti-British) party. He spoke out against and wrote many angry articles protesting unpopular British laws such as the Stamp Act, which required the purchase of a tax stamp for use on business and legal documents and newspapers. Adams' argument was that the people could not be taxed without their consent. When the British Parliament was forced to repeal the Stamp Act but introduced new taxes under the Townshend Acts in 1767, he delivered fiery speeches against them.

In 1772, Adams organized a committee of correspondence to spread the news of events in Boston and to coordinate the activities of other patriots. By 1773 dozens of such committees had been formed. Eventually extending from Massachusetts to Georgia, they played a vital role in the revolutionary cause.

Boston Tea Party. The British tried to quiet the unrest by repealing most of the unpopular taxes, but they retained a tax on tea. The fact that a British company was given a monopoly on the tea trade, at the expense of American merchants, made the situation even worse.

Matters came to a crisis on the night of December 16, 1773. Adams had demanded the departure from Boston of three British ships carrying tea. When the royal governor of Massachusetts refused, a group of Bostonians, on Adams' prearranged signal and disguised as Indians, boarded the ships and dumped their cargoes into the harbor. The action was celebrated as the Boston Tea Party. But it provoked the British Parliament into passage, in 1774, of what were known as the Intolerable Acts, which closed the port of Boston and restricted colonial liberties.

Independence and After. Events moved rapidly. Adams approved the Suffolk Resolves, calling for a boycott on trade with Britain, and was elected to the First Continental Congress. Named to the Second Continental Congress in 1775, he narrowly escaped arrest by British troops, who fired the shots at Lexington that touched off the Revolutionary War. In 1776, he proudly signed his name to the Declaration of Independence.

Adams' work as an organizer of the revolution was now complete. He played a minor role as a member of the Continental Congress during the war. When peace came in 1783, many people thought he was too much of a firebrand for the new nation and too gruff and critical of opposition. But Adams did serve as lieutenant governor and as governor of Massachusetts before retiring in 1797. He died in Boston on October 2, 1803.

Reviewed by RICHARD B. MORRIS
Columbia University
Editor, *Encyclopedia of American History*

ADDAMS, JANE (1860–1935)

Jane Addams founded Hull House, one of the first settlement houses (centers for social welfare) in the United States. All of her life she crusaded for social reforms, equal rights for women, and world peace.

Born in Cedarville, Illinois, on September 6, 1860, Addams came from a large and moderately wealthy family. At an early age, she decided to do something important with her life. She attended Rockford College in Illinois and later was forced to drop out of medical school due to poor health.

While traveling in London, Addams became impressed with Toynbee Hall, a settlement house founded in 1884, and she decided to attempt a similar project in Chicago. In 1889, with the help of Ellen Gates Starr, a former college classmate, Addams founded Hull House in a run-down mansion to help the immigrants crowded into the poor sections of the city.

By 1907, Hull House had expanded to 13 buildings and was providing important social services, such as child care and adult education. Meanwhile, Addams led successful

Recognizing that private charitable donations could not adequately address the problems of the poor, Jane Addams founded Hull House in Chicago to help the needy.

campaigns against child labor and fought for better housing and an eight-hour working law for women. She also campaigned vigorously to obtain for women the right to vote. Addams lectured all over the country on behalf of social reform and published many books and articles, among them *Twenty Years at Hull House* (1920).

After World War I broke out in 1914, Addams, an ardent pacifist, served as president (1915–29) of the Women's International League for Peace and Freedom. In 1931 she was awarded a Nobel Peace Prize. When Addams died on May 21, 1935, she was mourned by thousands.

ALLEN F. DAVIS
Author, *American Heroine: The Life and Legend of Jane Addams*

ADDITION. See ARITHMETIC.

ADDRESS, FORMS OF

If you were to meet a governor, a rabbi, or the president of the United States, how would you address that person? If you wanted to write a letter to one of them, how would you start your letter?

Forms of address are ways of addressing people in speech or in writing. Some are used in everyday life. For example, Mr., Mrs., Miss, and Ms. are used as courtesy titles for men and women. The term Mr. applies to all men, Mrs. to all married women, and Miss to unmarried women and girls. Some women prefer to be addressed as Ms., whether they are married or not. A physician is addressed as Dr., as are people in the academic world who hold doctorate degrees.

Other forms of address are needed for speaking or writing to persons who hold special positions or offices. For example, Excellency serves as a title for certain high dignitaries of state (as a governor or ambassador) and church (as a Roman Catholic arch-

bishop or bishop). The courtesy title Honorable, given to many government officials, is used in written address and in formal introductions but never in conversation.

Esquire was long used as a form of address for gentlemen. Placed after a name—Ernest Johnson, Esq.—it takes the place of Mr. It is sometimes used today as a form of address for lawyers.

Military personnel are addressed in writing by their title and full name: General George Thompson; Sergeant Marjorie Hall; Commander Virgil Beasley.

Courtesy demands that we use the proper forms of address in speech and writing. The chart on the following page shows how to address various government officials and religious dignitaries.

ISABELLE FORST
Former Assistant Superintendent of Schools
New York City

See also ETIQUETTE; LETTER WRITING.

PERSON	ADDRESS IN WRITING	SALUTATION OF LETTER	SPEAKING TO
The President of the United States	The President The White House	Dear Mr. (or Madam) President:	Mr. (or Madam) President or Sir (or Madam)
The Vice President of the United States	The Vice President The United States Senate	Dear Mr. (or Madam) Vice President:	Mr. (or Madam) Vice President or Sir (or Madam)
The Chief Justice of the United States	The Chief Justice The Supreme Court	Dear Chief Justice:	Chief Justice or Sir (or Madam)
Associate Justice of the Supreme Court	Justice Holmes The Supreme Court	Dear Justice Holmes:	Justice Holmes or Sir (or Madam)
United States Senator (or State Senator)	The Honorable Stephen A. Douglas United States Senate	Dear Senator Douglas:	Senator or Senator Douglas
United States Representative (or State Representative)	The Honorable Charles A. Halleck United States House of Representatives	Dear Mr. (or Mrs.) Halleck:	Mr. (or Mrs.) Halleck
Governor	The Honorable Ella Grasso Governor of Connecticut	Dear Governor Grasso:	Governor Grasso
Mayor	The Honorable Fiorello La Guardia Mayor of New York	Dear Mayor La Guardia:	Mayor La Guardia or Mr. (or Madam) Mayor
Federal Judge	The Honorable Learned Hand Judge of the 2nd U.S. Circuit Court of Appeals	Dear Judge Hand:	Judge Hand or Mr. (or Madam) Justice
Ambassador of the United States	The Honorable Dwight Whitney Morrow The Ambassador of the United States	Dear Mr. (or Madam) Ambassador	Mr. (or Madam) Ambassador or Sir (or Madam)
Foreign Ambassador to the United States	His Excellency, Rubens Ricupero The Ambassador of Brazil	Dear Mr. (or Madam) Ambassador:	Mr. (or Madam) Ambassador or Sir (or Madam) or Excellency
The Prime Minister of Canada	The Right Honourable Lester Pearson, P.C., M.P.[1] Prime Minister of Canada	Dear Mr. (or Madam) Prime Minister or Dear Sir (or Madam):	Mr. (or Madam) Prime Minister or Sir (or Madam)
Premier of a Canadian Province	The Honourable William A. C. Bennett, M.L.A.[2] Premier of the Province of British Columbia	Dear Mr. (or Mrs.) Bennett or Dear Sir (or Madam):	Mr. (or Madam) Premier or Mr. (or Mrs.) Bennett
Rabbi without (or with) a Doctor of Divinity Degree	Rabbi Stephen Samuel Wise (D.D. and/or LL.D., if held) The Free Synagogue of New York	Dear Rabbi (or Dr.) Wise or Dear Sir:	Rabbi (or Dr.) Wise
Episcopal Bishop	The Right Reverend Samuel Seabury, D.D., LL.D.	Dear Bishop Seabury or Right Reverend Sir:	Bishop Seabury
Protestant Minister without (or with) a Doctor's Degree	The Reverend Henry Ward Beecher (D.D. and/or LL.D., if held) Plymouth Church of the Pilgrims	Dear Mr. (or Mrs.) (or Dr.) Beecher or Dear Sir (or Madam):	Mr. (or Mrs.) (or Dr.) Beecher
The Pope	His Holiness Pope John Paul II or His Holiness the Pope	Your Holiness or Most Holy Father:	Your Holiness or Most Holy Father
Cardinal	His Eminence, Cardinal Francis Joseph Spellman Archbishop of New York	Dear Cardinal Spellman or Your Eminence:	Your Eminence or Cardinal Spellman
Roman Catholic Bishop (or Archbishop)	The Most Reverend Fulton John Sheen Bishop (or Archbishop) of Rochester	Dear Bishop (or Archbishop) Sheen or Your Excellency:	Your Excellency or Bishop (or Archbishop) Sheen:
Roman Catholic Priest	The Reverend Joseph Damien de Veuster, SS.CC.[3]	Dear Father Damien or Reverend Father:	Father Damien or Father

[1] P.C.—Privy Council, M.P.—Member of Parliament. [2] M.L.A.—Member of the Legislative Assembly. [3] Letters addressed to members of religious orders include the initials or abbreviation of the order.

ADEN. See YEMEN.

ADENA INDIANS. See INDIANS, AMERICAN (Empires and Other Extended Groups).

ADHESIVES. See GLUE AND OTHER ADHESIVES.

ADJECTIVE. See PARTS OF SPEECH.

ADOLESCENCE

The time of growing up from childhood to adulthood is known as adolescence. It is a period of physical growth. But it is more than that. It is a time for the maturing of mind and behavior as well. The length of time for this period of development varies. Adolescence can start at 9 and end at 18. It can start at 14 and end at 25.

Young people may grow quickly in some ways and more slowly in others. This is why children who may be only 9, 10, or 11 years old may be adolescents in some ways already, while teenagers of 13 or 14 may just be reaching adolescence.

For example, 11-year-old Sue is already 5 feet 4 inches (163 centimeters) tall. Her body is fully developed, and people often think she is 15 or 16. But sometimes she acts very babyish. She has not yet learned to concentrate, so her schoolwork is far below that of others in her class.

On the other hand, Ricky, at 14, is quite thin and short. He looks much younger than he is. But he is the brightest boy in his class. He is editor of his school newspaper, and his teachers and friends know that he is reliable and capable.

Sue is adolescent because of her physical growth, and Ricky because of his maturity of mind and behavior. When they "catch up with themselves," they will be well on the way to adulthood.

During adolescence young people begin to find out about themselves and what they want to do, what kind of people they want to be. It can be a time for self-expression, curiosity, and exploration, a time of discovery and adventure. Slowly but surely boys and girls accept more and more responsibility for their own behavior.

▶ **THE BODY BEGINS TO CHANGE**

Only a short time ago, the adolescent boy or girl had the body of a child. Now many physical changes begin to take place. Girls become aware that their breasts are developing. They begin to have more of a waistline, and there are signs of pubic hair as well as hair under their arms. Boys may notice that their voices are becoming deeper and that there are signs of hair on their faces as well as on their bodies. This period of dramatic physical development is called puberty.

Before, during, or after some of these changes, girls will begin to menstruate and boys will begin to mature sexually. These are normal glandular changes. They show that the organs of reproduction are being prepared for the part they will someday play.

Both boys and girls may feel that their arms and legs are growing too fast for the rest of their bodies. They may feel clumsy and awkward. Glandular changes sometimes cause acne, a skin disturbance. The skin may become oily, and pimples may appear. It is natural for young people to feel strange and uncomfortable about these physical changes. They often seem to occur before the boy or girl feels ready for them. But part of growing during adolescence is getting acquainted with the new self that is appearing and gradually accepting the changes that are taking place.

▶ **FEELINGS ARE CHANGING, TOO**

These body changes affect feelings as well as appearance. The glands and hormones that are bringing about external physical changes are also working toward a new internal balance. This is hard work for the body. There are times when adolescents feel very tired and seem to need a lot of sleep. At times they may feel happy and lively, at other times gloomy and depressed. Ups and downs are natural during adolescence. As the physical changes within become more stable, boys and girls begin to have more control over their feelings.

Adolescents still feel unsure of themselves, so they are annoyed at anything that makes them feel exceptional or different, whether it is wearing glasses or braces or having too many freckles. As young people gain self-confidence through all the experiences of growing and learning, they are able to accept themselves as they are. Then being different becomes a pleasure instead of a disaster.

▶ **ADOLESCENTS CAN HELP THEMSELVES**

An adolescent boy or girl is not merely a spectator who just stands by and watches as all these changes in body and feelings take place.

The adolescent is directly involved. The changes are happening to him or her. Boys and girls can help themselves a great deal during this time. If they have periods of fatigue, they can plan their homework and social activities so that they get extra sleep and relaxation. If they feel full of energy, they can participate in sports at school or go bowling or dancing. They can eat sensibly and take proper care of their bodies.

They can also help themselves by seeking information and advice about the things that are troubling them. At this time a number of questions and worries come up in the minds of adolescents. They want to be free and independent, but they still need the strength and support their parents give them. They are concerned about their future roles as mature men and women. Soon they will be ready to choose careers and adult relationships. Adolescents are often troubled by their suddenly awakened feelings about sex. It is quite normal for people at this age to begin to feel strong physical desires.

Both boys and girls need reassurance and information. They can get information from reading. Or they can talk to their parents. Sometimes it is hard for young people to talk freely and openly with their parents, because the relationship is so close. Then an understanding adult who is not part of the family may be able to help. It may be easier to confide in a favorite teacher or camp counselor. The person whose advice an adolescent seeks should be someone whom she or he trusts and who has enough background and experience to be of help.

If boys and girls feel guilty and unhappy about some of their thoughts, if they keep all their fear and confusions to themselves, they will make this an unnecessarily difficult period.

▶ GROWING UP WITH OTHERS

This is a time that will influence a boy's or girl's choice of adult companions, of a vocation, and even of a marriage partner.

Friends

Making friends and learning how to be a friend take on special importance during adolescence. It is the time that the center of their social world changes from their home environment to their peer-group environment. At first the most important thing is popularity. Boys and girls want to be well liked. They want to do what their friends want to do, and be what their friends want to be. This is all part of feeling unsure.

Later on, young people become more selective about their friends. They begin to choose those who have the same ideas and interests or those who are interesting because they have different backgrounds. As boys and girls develop their own standards, popularity becomes less important to them than the genuine affection of individuals they admire.

Young people often need to make friends among those of their own sex before they feel ready for relationships with the opposite sex. It is natural to feel more at ease with those who are having the same experiences and feelings. Then, as girl-boy friendships begin and become more intense and personal, a girl or a boy has to face some important issues and make some important decisions.

Dating is one problem. Should girls and boys date only one person because it makes them feel safe and popular or because everyone else in the crowd is dating only one person? Or should they go out with many different kinds of people in order to learn more about themselves, to find out what relationships give them the most satisfaction?

The intimacy that develops between a girl and a boy who go out only with each other often brings another problem. How far should an adolescent girl and boy permit this intimacy to lead them? The sexual drive in young people can be very strong. It is a powerful and often disturbing feeling. Girls and boys are also very curious about sex. It is a great unknown. They have certain worries and fears about it, too. Both girls and boys hope that they will be attractive and appealing to members of the opposite sex, but they also feel confused and uncertain about just how this can be accomplished.

As boys and girls mature, they try to understand their feelings about sex. They try to find answers to their questions so that they can set standards for their own behavior. The more responsible and mature they become, the more they think about long-range goals. They are willing to give up immediate satisfactions for something that is more important to them in the future. The more they care about their own feelings and needs, the more sensitive they are to other people. They understand the need for making choices seriously, rather than on a sudden impulse, to avoid hurting themselves and others.

Family

All adolescents have mixed feelings about their families. There are times when boys and girls feel that they could manage very well if only their parents would leave them alone. At other times young people feel uncertain and inexperienced and confused. They wish their parents would take over and tell them what to do.

Many conflicts with parents come up over social relationships. Teenagers are often so eager to belong to a group that they do not always use good judgment in making dates. Then their parents have to step in and help them by keeping some control over their activities. This is especially true when matters of health and safety are concerned. But when boys and girls show signs of greater maturity and sounder judgment, parents usually have more confidence in them and allow them to make more decisions and choices.

Family chores and responsibilities are other common causes of conflict. Teenagers are very much involved with their own interests, and they are apt to forget that as members of the family group they have certain obligations. At times they feel they are being nagged at about everything. Their rooms are untidy, their clothes are not neat, they sleep too late, they talk on the phone too much, they go to bed too late, they are careless with money, they do not allow enough time for homework. At times teenagers feel overwhelmed with criticism. But at other times they may sense that all their parents' comments are really signs of loving and caring.

Sometimes younger brothers and sisters seem to be a nuisance. Teenagers resent babysitting. It interferes with their privacy and cuts into their free time. Older sisters and brothers may tease teenagers, and this makes them feel young and foolish. But all this is only one side of the picture. Adolescents still need their families and the special kind of love a family gives, and their families still need them.

Some rebellion against adult authority is healthy—within limits. An adolescent wants to become a strong and independent person, and that is right. But this is not accomplished by fighting against adults. Learning to be an understanding, cooperating member of the family is, in the long run, the biggest sign of growing up.

But adolescents cannot grow up alone. They need the help and understanding of the adults who are closest to them. Parents can help their teenagers as they mature. One of the best ways is simply by acting as parents. This means being strong and firm when the occasion calls for it. Children may call their parents old-fashioned. They may say, "You do not understand me." But wise parents overlook such expressions. They know that many times teenagers ask for permission to do something they are not ready for. They ask because the whole crowd is asking, and they do not want to be different. But secretly the teenagers want their parents to say "No," to set limits for them. They need to feel that their parents have authority and will use this authority wisely. Teenagers also need to know that their parents will not take a firm stand one day and then give in the next day. They want their parents to be consistent.

Being firm, of course, does not mean being too strict, and being consistent does not mean being stubborn. Understanding parents give their teenagers love and encouragement and let them feel that they are free to grow but have not been set adrift.

▶LOOKING AHEAD

A young child finds it hard to imagine being grown up. Adulthood seems so far away and strange. To a child, what happens each day matters most. The child is not really interested in what will happen next month, next year, or in the next ten years.

During adolescence all that changes. The subjects boys and girls study in school and the marks they get have a great deal to do with their plans for a vocation. Their friendships with other boys and girls and their dating have a clear relationship to adult love and the choice of a marriage partner.

One of the most exciting things about adolescence is that it suddenly brings the future so much closer. Growing up makes adolescence a very special time.

EDA J. LESHAN
Author, *You and Your Feelings*

See also FAMILY.

ADOPTION

Adoption is a way for children who cannot be cared for by their birth parents to become members of another family. Certain laws and procedures create the same legal relation between adoptive parents and a child as the biological one that exists between birth parents and a child. Adoption ends the child's ties to his former parents. After adoption the child has a new and permanent home.

▶ WHY CHILDREN NEED ADOPTION

In most countries children are brought up in families that are made up of a father, a mother, and the children born to them. Some birth parents, however, cannot give the love and care that every child needs. They are often very young and unmarried. They did not think ahead of time about the responsibilities of being parents. These parents may decide, after much sorrow, to give up their child for adoption. They want the child to have a chance to grow up in a family that can provide love and the potential to fulfill the child's needs for security and permanence.

Other children may lose their parents by death, accident, illness, war, or some other disaster. Sometimes parents with serious personal problems neglect or abandon a child. Children may be left for a long time in temporary foster homes or institutions. Then it may become clear that their parents will never be able to take them home. In all these cases someone other than the parents has to decide that adoption will be best for the child.

Families have to be found for children who no longer have parents to care for them. There are many childless people who wish to adopt. They have a great desire to love and bring up a child and to have a child who loves them. Also, some parents who already have children want to share their love and family life with another child who needs parents.

▶ WHO IS ADOPTED

The children who are adopted in the United States are mostly white babies. They go into their new homes shortly after birth. It has usually been difficult to find families for older, handicapped, or nonwhite children. Recently, however, a greater number of these children —especially African American, American Indian, and Asian children—are being adopted.

The total number of children adopted each year in the United States is about 120,000. About half are adopted by a stepparent, by grandparents, or by other relatives. The others are adopted by unrelated people.

▶ HOW ADOPTION TAKES PLACE

Children needing families and people seeking children may be brought together in several ways. The majority of the adoptions by nonrelatives now take place through recognized social agencies.

Physicians, lawyers, clergymen, and other well-meaning individuals have frequently arranged adoptions. Sometimes a dishonest person tries to make money by finding a child for someone willing to pay a high price. Such transactions are illegal.

Arrangements by individuals have in some cases been harmful to a child, to birth parents, or to adoptive parents. An individual cannot usually give the time, help, or protections needed in adoption. Many difficulties are prevented when social agencies are responsible for planning adoption and selecting adoptive parents.

Social agencies are established and supported by concerned people in a community or by state governments. Some agencies have been given the duty by law to protect children and to provide adoption and other social services. Such agencies are known as child-welfare agencies, children's aid societies, or family and children's services.

▶ ADOPTION SERVICES

The purpose of an adoption service is to help children and, also, birth parents and adoptive parents. Social workers, who have special training, skills, and experience, provide the service. They know how to study children and find out what may be best for each child. They work with physicians, psychologists, and lawyers. They use the advice of other experts in selecting suitable parents for a particular child. Then they help adoptive parents take the necessary steps to complete a legal adoption. Agencies usually charge a fee for this service, based on ability to pay.

Parents and older children especially may need continuing help as they become a family. Most problems that occur are the usual ones that all parents and children have. Some of the problems have to do with adoption. For example, adoptive parents are encouraged to help a child understand, as soon as the child is able, what it means to be adopted. It is not easy to explain about adoption. Many adoptive parents would like to keep it a secret. Sooner or later, however, adopted children discover that they have not been born to their parents. Many become upset about it. They wonder why their birth parents gave them up. They may imagine that they would have been happier with those other parents. They are curious about their heredity.

It takes time for children to feel comfortable about being adopted. They have to learn that real parents are the ones who help a child grow up and feel loved. They have to know why parents give up a child. Usually it is because the parents care about the child and want him or her to have a better family life than they could ever provide.

▶LEGAL PROCESS

An adoption must take place according to law. In each state and in most countries, laws have been passed that say how the relationship of parent and child can be ended and a new one created. The laws require certain procedures to be followed. These are designed to protect the various people, and especially the child, involved in an adoption.

The parent-child relation is very important in our society. The law requires that a judge must decide whether it should be broken. A judge must also grant an adoption decree to make the adoption legal and final.

After the adoption has been arranged either by agreement between the natural and adoptive parents or through an agency, the adoptive parents must go to court and ask that lasting family ties between the child and them be established. They must first wait until the child has lived with them for a set period of time. Then the judge has to make sure that the adoption is likely to benefit the child.

The judge considers all the facts obtained in a study of the case and talks with a child if he or she is old enough to understand. In most states, after the decree is granted all court records are sealed. No one can see these without a court order. Then a new birth certificate for the child is issued with the names of the adoptive parents. Lawyers are used in an adoption to see that all legal procedures are properly carried out.

▶TRENDS IN ADOPTION

Adoption is mentioned in ancient legends, myths, and stories. The Bible, for example, describes the adoption of Moses by Pharaoh's daughter. The Roman general Julius Caesar adopted his grand-nephew Octavius.

Formerly the purpose of adoption was to enhance the family unit by providing a childless family with an heir to inherit property or to continue a family name. It was not until 1851, in Massachusetts, that the first adoption law to protect children was passed. Since then people have become more concerned about the child's welfare in adoption.

Gradually ideas about adoption have changed. Adoption is now considered a way to find families for children. Communities and social agencies are trying to give more children the benefits of adoption. One reason is the belief that every child has a right to a caring and supportive family.

Social agencies are using new methods to find families to care for an older child, a sibling group, or a child with handicaps. Legislation has been passed to help families who choose to adopt children with special needs. The adoptive parents of such children are given allowances to help meet the costs of including the child in their family.

People who are members of minority groups are being encouraged to adopt children, and in some states the law allows single persons to adopt children.

Various organizations are engaged in research to find out how to make adoption as satisfactory as possible for children and their biological and adoptive families.

Recently, there has been a trend toward the re-establishment of a relationship, later in life, between adoptees and their birth parents. A few states have passed "open records" legislation that allows the examination of certain adoption records that makes it easier for adult adoptees and their birth parents to secure the information needed to conduct a search for each other. Some states have adoption registries that take information from, and provide information to, any person engaged in such a search.

ZITHA R. TURITZ
Former Director, Standards Development
Child Welfare League of America, Inc.
Reviewed by BEVERLY STUBBEE
Child Welfare Specialist

Crayola® Our toys run on imagination.

Magazine advertisements, such as this one for crayons, must be eye-catching in order to attract the attention of the parents and children who will buy the product.

ADVERTISING

Advertising is part of our daily lives. To realize this fact, you have only to count the television and radio commercials you see and hear in one day, or leaf through the pages of a magazine or newspaper. Most people receive hundreds of advertising messages every day.

▶ WHAT IS ADVERTISING?

Advertising is the difficult business of bringing information to great numbers of people. The purpose of an advertisement is to make people respond—to make them react to an idea, such as helping to prevent forest fires, or to affect their attitudes toward a certain product or service.

At the beginning of the 1900's, advertising was described as salesmanship in print. If this definition were expanded to include television and radio, it would still stand today. The most effective way to sell something is through person-to-person contact. But the cost of person-to-person selling is high. Because it takes a great deal of time, it increases the cost of the product or service. Advertising distributes the selling message to many people at one time.

▶ THE MEDIA

To bring their messages to the public, advertisers must use carriers, such as television, radio, magazines and newspapers, and direct mail. The carrier of a message is called a **medium** of communication, or simply a medium. The five media (plural of medium) just mentioned are the ones most commonly used. Other media include billboards, posters, printed bulletins, and, especially in Europe, films. Unusual methods that have been used to attract attention include skywriting and messages painted on the sails of boats or trailed from high-flying kites.

When advertisers select a medium or a group of media to carry a message, they must think of the kind of product they are selling and the kind of people who are most likely to buy it. They must figure out how to reach the largest possible number of these people at the lowest possible cost. The cost of reaching a thousand people—the cost per thousand—is different in each medium. In print media such as newspapers and magazines, advertisers buy **space** (pages or parts of pages) in which to display their messages. In the broadcast media —radio and television—they buy **time** in which to present them.

28 · ADVERTISING

Most magazines, newspapers, and radio and television stations in the United States depend on advertising for their support. Without advertising, newspapers and magazines would have to charge much higher rates to their readers. In some cases the price would be so high that the average reader would not want to pay it, and the magazine or newspaper would go out of business. Without advertising, radio and television would have to charge their listeners and viewers directly or be supported by the government. There are, in fact, some television services that do not carry advertising and therefore require a viewer to pay a monthly fee to receive their broadcasts. Although pay TV has grown in popularity, advertiser-supported television is still the most popular type of video medium.

Magazines

Magazines cover a wide range of audiences. There are general magazines that reach several million people with varied interests. And there are hundreds of magazines for readers with special interests. They offer the advertiser a good way to reach a particular group of likely customers. An advertiser who is trying to sell washing machines, for example, would select a magazine for homemakers rather than one for hunters or boat owners. And an advertisement for fishing rods would be placed in a fishing magazine rather than in a general magazine or a newsmagazine.

Newspapers

Newspapers carry news, and good advertising is a kind of news. Most newspapers reach an audience that is concentrated in one geographical area—a town, a city, or a county. Most are published daily or weekly. For these reasons, newspapers have several advantages for advertisers. Ads placed in newspapers often bring quick results. And advertising can be placed in newspapers on very short notice. Usually ads can be placed for a specific day— to announce a sale, for example. If the ad had to be published a week or a month in advance, many people would forget about the sale before it took place. An advertiser can also choose to place an ad in a special section of the newspaper, such as the sports section or the food section, or in the classified pages, where ads of similar kinds are grouped together.

Local businesses depend on newspapers to reach customers in their neighborhoods or metropolitan areas. Newspapers also carry a great deal of advertising for nationally sold products. These ads will often list the names and addresses of all of the local dealers carrying the product.

In recent years, transmission of editorial material by satellites has brought us to an age where newspapers can be distributed across the entire country. This has helped to make the newspaper medium increasingly important for national advertisers.

An advertising campaign will often use a famous person to promote a product. Here comedian Bill Cosby and his young friends are enjoying some pudding in a television ad.

Above: Billboards are advertisements made to be read from a distance. They feature large illustrations and short messages. *Below:* Advertisements that promote ideas for the common good are called public service ads.

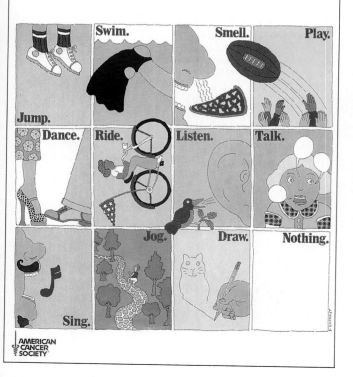

Radio and Television

Nothing has had more effect on advertising than the development of the broadcast media—radio and television. Radio took words off the printed page and gave them a voice and a sound of urgency. Radio lacks the advantage of a visual image, but it reaches places that other media do not because it is portable. Radios can be found in automobiles or can be carried with you wherever you go. Television is the most dramatic of the media. Because it combines sight, sound, and motion, it gives advertisers many ways of catching customers' attention.

Radio and television use every dramatic device possible to get advertisers' messages across. Commercials may be presented as short plays that tell how a new detergent can make doing the laundry pleasant or how a headache remedy can transform someone who is grouchy and ill-tempered into a cheerful, lovable person. Jingles help plant the name of the advertiser's product in the listener's mind. In radio, tones of voice and sound effects—like breaking glass or slamming doors—attract the listener's attention. In addition to the devices used by radio, television uses elaborate sets, picturesque costumes, and cartoons or other types of animation to help put the message across. Filming commercials has become a business in itself.

To attract listeners on a nationwide or regional basis, an advertiser or a group of advertisers sometimes **sponsors** a program—that is, pays for the time and the costs of producing the program. An advertiser may purchase **spot announcements** between or during programs. Today a minute's time on television may cost advertisers several hundred thousand, or even as much as a million, dollars.

Radio and television advertisements can be bought in a number of ways. Commercials can be shown across the entire nation, in certain regions of the country only, or even in just one city.

Outdoor Advertising

Outdoor advertising is one of the oldest media. It is usually colorful and strong on illustration, and it has short selling messages. Billboards are placed in locations where surveys have shown that they will be seen by large numbers of people. They range from lithographed paper sheets pasted together to the

Since the beginning of time, children have thought "CLEAN YOUR ROOM!" means "HIDE THE MESS"

INTRODUCING A BREAKTHROUGH IN PARENT-KID COMMUNICATION

Take this book FREE! with no obligation to buy a thing, ever! See inside

The Survival Series for Kids
WHAT TO DO WHEN YOUR MOM OR DAD SAYS ... CLEAN YOUR ROOM!
Written by Joy Wilt Berry
Pictures by Bartholomew

In direct mail advertising, a business mails an advertisement or catalog to the consumer who is then able to order the product directly from the advertiser.

more permanent and more expensive **painted bulletin** (painted on the billboard or on the side of a building) and the very costly **spectacular**, which uses flashing lights to attract attention. By flashing the lights in proper sequence, the spectacular can create the effect of motion, such as a coffee cup being filled. Spectaculars are sometimes controlled by computers.

Posters are often placed in train stations and in buses and railroad trains. This is called **transit advertising**.

Electronic Media

Rapidly advancing technology is helping to create new ways and new places to advertise. Space satellites have helped to create new TV networks, and the number of programs one can choose to watch has grown dramatically.

We can now use the television set in many different ways. It can be used as part of a personal computer or to play video games. Television sets are appearing in places like shopping malls and hotels to provide information on an interactive, or two-way, basis. For example, suppose you are visiting a strange city and want to find a Chinese restaurant near your hotel that has prices in a particular range. You may, if your hotel subscribes to an interactive database service, get the information by "asking" the television set. The television set is connected to a computer that is programmed to answer certain types of questions.

The use of video cassette recorders has advertisers concerned because TV viewers who have the machines are able to watch the programs at their convenience, thus shifting the time of day when they view commercials. They may also completely eliminate commercials when they watch a recorded program.

Direct Marketing

Direct response is defined as any form of advertising that elicits a measurable response. That is, it encourages people to contact the advertiser directly. It uses all forms of media —direct mail (including catalogs), magazines, newspapers, radio, television, the telephone (toll-free numbers), and the new electronic media.

Direct marketing, particularly direct mail, allows advertisers to target their advertising to very specific audiences, those who would most likely be interested in buying a particular product or service. It is a very personal method of selling.

The computer is an important advertising tool in direct marketing. It is used to build databases that record the purchasing habits of various groups of people.

▶ NATIONAL AND RETAIL ADVERTISING

From the marketing, or selling, point of view, advertising has two main divisions.

National advertising is used to promote products or services that are sold all over the country or over large areas. Examples are products such as automobiles, soft drinks, household appliances, and such services as insurance and air travel. Such products and services are advertised in magazines with nationwide circulation and on nationwide radio and television programs.

Retail advertising is used by local businesses. Unlike most national advertising, retail advertisements give specific prices and dealers' addresses. Department stores, drugstores, automobile dealers, and banks are typical retail advertisers. Most retail advertisements are carried by newspapers, direct mail, and local broadcasting stations. They are usually prepared by the business that is doing the advertising or by a local agency. Some large businesses have special departments to handle retail advertising.

In the United States, about 45 percent of advertising money is spent on retail advertising and 55 percent on national advertising. Of the two types, national advertising has a more direct influence on the products and services the consumer buys. The rest of this article will deal with national advertising. For simplicity's sake, services will be considered products.

▶ THE AGENCY

In most cases, manufacturers and other national advertisers do not produce their own advertising. Instead, they rely on specialists—the advertising agencies. These agencies bring together a number of people with specialized talents in various fields.

The advertising agency is a service company. It is appointed by a client to perform certain functions—planning, creating, researching, producing, and placing printed advertisements and broadcast commercials for that client.

Large agencies employ a variety of specialists, including writers, artists, photographers, film production specialists, musicians, actors, producers, and directors. Experts in economics, law, accounting, marketing, media, management, and research are also involved in the advertising business.

Each client of the agency is served by an account team representing most of these specialties. The team's job is to create the client's advertising. Everything the team does must be approved by the client—the kind of advertising chosen, the media used, and the amount of money spent. The person in charge of the team, called the account manager or account executive, meets often with the client to discuss these matters and to determine how well the advertising has been working.

Creating Advertising

The first step in preparing an advertising campaign is to conduct research on the possibilities of the product. The members of the agency team must come to understand consumers' attitudes toward the product and its competitors, and what qualities of the product, practical or emotional, are most likely to appeal to the buying public. The team finds out the age, sex, occupation, income, personality and special interests of the product's best or prospective customers—the "target group" for the sales message. They learn where the product can be bought and how it is sold and what its usage patterns are. Even such factors as climate, season of the year, and holidays have a bearing on sales. For instance, cold remedies sell best in cold weather, soft drinks in warm weather.

The client and the agency try to make sure that the right selling message reaches the right people in the right place at the right time.

After studying this information, the team's writers and artists, working with the creative director, explore different advertising approaches. They arrive at a good, interesting, and persuasive idea about the product—one that will make it stand out from competing products.

The idea alone is not yet advertising. What is needed now is a way of expressing or dramatizing the idea that will produce in the consumer the thoughts and feelings about the product the advertiser wants to convey. This is not always easy to do because a reader, or a viewer, may get a different message from the one that was intended. A number of different messages may be explored to determine which one communicates most effectively. Layouts are made for printed media such as newspapers, magazines, and posters. Scripts are prepared for radio commercials. A storyboard —a series of pictures with captions for spoken dialogue or written messages—is prepared for each television commercial. Writers and artists work together in developing this material. Today computer-generated graphics are sometimes used in the preparation of storyboards and layouts.

When the rough draft is ready, it is presented to the client for approval. Usually the team designs one ad or commercial as the recommendation. The preliminary draft of a print ad is called a **comp**, or **comprehensive**.

When the client has approved the advertisement, it is put into final form. The agency commissions specialists to prepare finished art or photography, and type is set for printed advertisements. Then the material goes on to an engraver or a printer. Filmed and taped commercials for the broadcast media are also produced outside the agency, by specialists who are hired to do this work.

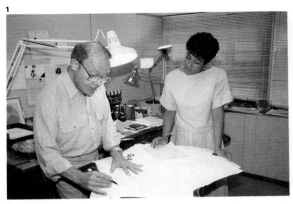

To create the advertisement below, an agency creative team developed the idea (1). The concepts were sketched in color (2). Preliminary drafts, called comps, were reviewed (3), then presented to the client (4). An artist specializing in automotive illustration prepared final art (5). The completed proofs were reviewed (6) and sent to the printer.

33

Meanwhile, media planners at the agency decide on the most efficient way to reach the target group. They also determine the size, color, and dates for printed advertisements; the time periods for broadcast commercials; and the costs in each case. These media recommendations must also be approved by the client. The materials for the completed advertisement are then shipped to the media with authorization for their use on specific dates or for specific periods of time at agreed-upon rates or prices.

The agency checks to make sure that each advertisement or commercial actually appears. If everything is satisfactory, the agency then bills the client. The total cost includes the agency commission; when the agency pays the media, the agency's commission for its service is deducted. Some agencies work for flat fees rather than commissions, and the client pays the agency a sum of money in addition to the cost of producing the advertising.

What Makes Customers Buy?

Advertisers and their agencies have spent great amounts of time, money, and effort trying to determine what makes potential customers want a product. There is no single answer. To find the special quality of a product that will cause people to buy, advertisers often turn to research.

Several kinds of research are employed in advertising. **Marketing research** explores sales patterns, sales problems, and sales possibilities for a product. **Product research** is designed to discover how the public feels about a product. **Copy research** discovers how well an advertisement gets its message across. **Motivational research** unearths the reasons people behave as they do.

A consumer may buy a certain brand of face soap because it is used by a glamorous movie star or sports figure. When selecting a new refrigerator, that same consumer may be attracted to a sleek or colorful style. Or perhaps that consumer is most concerned with how much food the refrigerator will hold and how efficiently a particular model uses energy.

Some advertisements appeal to logic through straightforward presentation of facts about a product. Others appeal more to the emotions. Most advertisements combine logical and emotional approaches. Advertisements offer consumers an opportunity to make their purchasing decisions from among a wide range of choices. One of the important roles of advertising is to provide the consumer with a free and abundant choice.

▶ADVERTISING AS A CAREER

Advertising is a big business—and a fascinating business. It combines writing, art, show business, and science.

The average advertising agency has a need for people with many different kinds of experience and talent. But opportunities are limited. Some estimates suggest that there are probably not more than a few thousand places for newcomers in advertising each year.

Most advertising jobs require the ability to use language with skill. Other important qualities are curiosity and the ability to use imagination in analyzing situations. Retail selling experience is excellent preparation for a career in advertising. The American Association of Advertising Agencies, in New York City, offers information about careers in advertising.

▶HISTORY

Advertising is very old. It can be traced back as far as the public criers of ancient Greece—who, for a fee, shouted out messages about their clients' wares. It first became important in the late 1400's, when the merchants of the rapidly growing cities and towns needed a way to tell people where their goods could be bought.

The first printed advertisement in the English language appeared in 1478. This early ad was the work of William Caxton, England's first printer, who used it to advertise religious books from his own workshop. Caxton posted small printed notices along London's main streets. Besides advertising his product, he identified his shop with a red-striped shield so that customers could find it easily.

This same sort of simple, informational advertising is still used. Examples are the roadside signs that tell travelers that they can buy eggs or take flying lessons just down the road.

The Industrial Revolution, in the 1700's and 1800's, brought a new kind of advertising. Large factories took the place of small workshops, and goods were produced in large quantities. Manufacturers used the newly built railroads to distribute their products over wide areas. They had to find many thousands of customers in order to stay in business. They

Paul Revere & Son,

At their BELL and CANNON FOUNDERY, at the North Part of BOSTON,

CAST BELLS, of all fizes; every kind of Brafs ORDNANCE, and every kind of Compofition Work, for SHIPS, &c. at the fhorteft notice; Manufacture COPPER into SHEETS, BOLTS. SPIKES, NAILS, RIVETS, DOVETAILS, &c. from Malleable Copper.

They always keep, by them, every kind of Copper rafining for Ships. They have now on hand, a number of Church and Ship Bells, of different fizes; a large quantity of Sheathing Copper, from 16 up to 30 ounce; Bolts, Spikes, Nails, &c of all fizes, which they warrant equal to Englifh manufacture.

Cafh and the higheft price given for old Copper and Brafs.   march 10

This early advertisement is a simple listing of the products and services available from Paul Revere's foundry. Compare it to today's advertisements.

could not simply tell people where shoes or cloth or tea could be bought—they had to learn how to make people want to buy a specific product. Thus modern advertising was born. Advertising created new markets and helped to raise standards of living as people came to feel that they had a right to new and better products.

Advertising agencies began to develop in the United States just after the Civil War. At first these agencies merely sold space in the various media, mainly newspapers and magazines. But they soon added the service of writing and producing advertisements. From these beginnings, advertising has developed into a highly specialized profession.

▶ **PROS AND CONS OF ADVERTISING**

Advertising has received a great deal of criticism from various sources. Its critics say that it appeals to unworthy motives like vanity, snobbery, and the fear of being "left out." And they say that high-pressure advertising makes people buy some things that they do not really need and cannot afford. Another common criticism is that some advertising is deceitful.

Most people who work in advertising feel that it can certainly help shape attitudes toward products. But they know from experience that it is not possible to sell a poor product more than once. People may try a product because they are attracted by the advertising, but if they do not like it they simply will not buy it again. Consumers make the choices, and because of advertising they may have many more products from which to choose and are more informed about their choices.

Advertising agencies and the media work against deceptive practices by setting standards within the industry. In the United States there is also some government regulation. Consumers are protected by such agencies as the Federal Trade Commission, the Federal Communications Commission, and the U.S. Postal Service. State and local agencies, as well as private organizations, work to prevent false or misleading advertising.

Advertising is used for public service messages as well as for commercial ones. Smokey the Bear, who for many years warned the public against the dangers of forest fires, was a creation of the advertising industry. Advertising agencies produce the campaigns for organizations such as the Red Cross, helping them to gather money. And advertising is an efficient way of telling large numbers of people about new ideas, useful inventions, and scientific discoveries. Defenders of advertising say that it stimulates the economy by helping to keep production and employment high.

Advertising is an important part of life in a complex society. Often a word or phrase from an advertisement will enter the language, at least for a time. Songs written for use in advertising may become popular apart from their original use. A character seen or heard in advertising may become a favorite with the public. These are some of the ways advertising becomes part of popular culture.

Advertising has been described as the news of the marketplace. Partly because of the influence of advertising, people have learned to want ever better products and services, to take better care of their health, and to improve their way of living. Advertising is an important economic and social force.

DON JOHNSTON
Chairman and Chief Executive Officer
J. Walter Thompson Company
See also MAIL ORDER; SALES AND MARKETING.

AENEID

The most famous work in Latin literature is the *Aeneid*, an epic poem about the hero Aeneas. (An epic is a long narrative poem, written in a noble, complex style, that tells a story of heroic deeds.) Publius Vergilius Maro, whom we call Vergil, began the *Aeneid* about 29 B.C. at the request of the emperor Augustus. Vergil worked on it for over ten years. He meant to spend three more years revising the poem, but he died in 19 B.C. before he could complete it. On his deathbed he asked for his manuscript, intending to burn it because he felt it was imperfect, but his friends refused to give it to him. It was published as Vergil left it.

The twelve parts (called books) of the *Aeneid* tell the story of Aeneas, a legendary ancestor of Augustus. At the end of the Trojan War, when his native city, Troy, was destroyed by the Greeks, Aeneas escaped with his father, Anchises; his son, Ascanius; and a band of followers. He intended to build a new Troy, and searched long for a site. After founding several settlements (which failed) and having many adventures, he and his party were shipwrecked in North Africa and were given shelter in the city of Carthage.

Carthage was ruled by the beautiful Queen Dido, who fell in love with Aeneas and wanted him to marry her. But the gods had chosen him to go on to Italy, where his descendants would found the Roman nation. The messenger of the gods, Mercury, came to Aeneas and reminded him of his destiny. So Aeneas left Dido, who then killed herself in despair.

Aeneas and his men sailed across the Mediterranean and landed at Cumae, in Italy. There he met the sibyl, a prophetess who guided him to the underworld so that he could consult the spirit of his father. Anchises told his son that he was to establish a city in central Italy and that his descendants were to be the founders and citizens of Rome. Then he showed him the souls of the great Romans of the future, waiting for their time to be born; among them was Vergil's own friend and patron, the emperor Augustus.

The last six books of the *Aeneid* tell of the settlement in Italy and the warfare between the Trojans and some of the Italians, who rise against the invaders. The poem ends with a fierce duel between Aeneas and his chief enemy, Turnus. Turnus is killed, and Aeneas' triumph is assured.

Tales of Aeneas and Rome had been told by the older Roman poets Naevius and Ennius. Vergil owes something to them. He also owes a debt to Homer, from whose *Iliad* and *Odyssey* he borrowed freely, intending to create a Roman epic that would rival Homer's work. The wanderings of Aeneas in the first six books are like the wanderings of Odysseus in the *Odyssey*; the fighting in the last six books of the *Aeneid* is like the savage battles of the *Iliad*.

Vergil also follows Homer in using gods as characters in the story. The gods struggle against one another to help or hinder Aeneas. This means that he was not merely a wanderer, but a man with a great mission. Even with a spiteful goddess opposing him, he succeeded, and worked out the will of fate.

The *Aeneid* is a proudly national epic, showing Rome as the chief carrier of civilization. Its poetry is magnificent. It has many fine phrases, such as the opening line, "Arms and the man I sing," the warning, "I fear the Greeks even when they bring gifts," and the advice to Rome, "Spare the conquered and crush the proud." Its scenes and symbols stir our imagination: the golden bough that opens the path to the underworld, the shield of Aeneas decorated with the battles and the champions of future Rome, the description of the fall of Troy, and the mystical vision of heaven filled with noble and happy souls.

The *Aeneid* was the greatest achievement in the golden age of Latin literature, and it has continued to influence poets through the centuries. Dante Alighieri, the greatest Italian poet of the Middle Ages, called Vergil his master and his model. English poetry also has been shaped by Vergil. Shakespeare read him at school, and quotes him several times in his works. Chaucer, Spenser, Milton, and Tennyson all imitated him, each in his own way. Poets in French, German, Spanish, and other European languages also felt his power and tried to equal his artistry. Despite the fact that he himself had imitated Homer, Vergil was one of the great creators of Western literature.

GILBERT HIGHET
Author, *The Speeches in Vergil's Aeneid*

See also VERGIL.

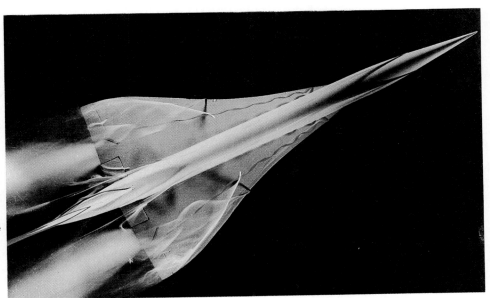

Some aspects of the aerodynamics of flight can be studied by observing models of airplanes in wind and water tunnels. This model of the supersonic airplane Concorde was photographed in a water tunnel. Colored dyes ejected from the top surfaces of its wings into a slow-moving water current show the path of air flowing over the plane at low speeds and how the vortex, or corkscrew of air, gives the wings their lift.

AERODYNAMICS

Aerodynamics is the science that examines what happens when air, or any other gas, is in motion. Its name comes from two Greek words meaning "air" and "power." Aerodynamics sometimes deals with air moving against an object—like wind filling the sails of a boat. Sometimes it deals with an object moving through air—like an airplane flying through the sky. The same laws apply in both cases.

▶PUTTING AIR TO WORK

Long before anything was known about aerodynamics, people noticed that moving air pushed things. The wind scattered leaves and bent tree branches. Strong winds could uproot trees and knock down houses. Hunters could run faster and throw spears farther when the wind was behind them.

In time people learned how to put the wind to work. They built sailboats and windmills. Today we still use the wind in these ways. But an understanding of aerodynamics has opened up many other ways of using the power of moving air. For example, it is an understanding of aerodynamics that has made possible all heavier-than-air craft. This includes spacecraft, airplanes, helicopters, hovercraft—in fact, all aircraft except balloons, which are lighter than air and float in it.

The Dream of Human Flight

People have always envied the ability of birds to fly through the air, and the first flying machines made it possible for people to make their dream of flight come true. Since ancient times there have been myths and legends about people who could fly like birds. Perhaps the best-known story tells of Daedalus, the Greek craftsman who was imprisoned with his son Icarus. Using wax and birds' feathers, Daedalus made two pairs of wings. When he and Icarus put the wings on, they were able to fly away from the prison. But Icarus flew so close to the sun that the wax in his wings melted. The feathers dropped out, and Icarus fell into the sea and drowned.

The flight of Daedalus and Icarus was only a story, but the idea of flying like a bird seemed possible to people for hundreds of years. It was a long time before anyone realized that the human body is simply not built in a way to allow birdlike flight.

Powered flight in a heavier-than-air craft had to await several things. One was an understanding of aerodynamics, which began in the 1700's with a discovery made by a Swiss mathematician who was studying not flight but the flow of water in pipes.

▶BERNOULLI'S PRINCIPLE

The Swiss was Daniel Bernoulli, who came from a family of famous mathematicians and scientists. In the 1730's, Bernoulli began to investigate what happened to water flowing through pipes that were partially blocked. He experimented by putting obstacles of different sizes in pipes and keeping track of differences in the speed and pressure with which the water flowed.

The first thing Bernoulli discovered was that the water flowed faster as it went past an obstacle. Then he discovered that wherever the water flowed faster, it lost some of its normal pressure. On the far side of the obstacle, the flow of water slowed down again and pressure returned to normal.

The explanation is that steadily flowing water has a constant amount of energy. This energy depends on both the speed and the pressure of the water. If more of the energy goes into speed, then there is less for pressure; if less goes into speed, then there is more for pressure. To put it another way, where the speed is great, the pressure is small. This idea is known as Bernoulli's principle.

Other scientists became interested in what Bernoulli had discovered. They began to experiment with what happened inside pipes of different shapes. One of the first to do this was an Italian scientist named Giovanni Venturi. Later, a pipe invented for such experiments was named the venturi tube in his honor.

▶ THE VENTURI TUBE

The venturi tube consists of a short narrow section of pipe called the throat that gradually tapers outward, or grows wider, at each end. Experiments with it revealed an important fact: Air passing through the tube behaves the same as water. When air passes through the tube's narrow throat, it moves faster. When the air moves faster, its pressure decreases. When the air moves beyond the throat into a wider section of the tube, it moves more slowly again and its pressure increases.

A venturi tube can be used to measure the flow rate of a liquid. As a liquid is poured into one end of a venturi tube, recording devices called manometers attached to the throat and to the two wide sections at each end can measure the drop in air pressure at the throat and then calculate the liquid's overall flow rate through the entire tube.

The venturi tube can also be used in many practical ways. A paint sprayer and an automobile carburetor are two devices that depend on it. In each, a liquid is driven forward by an airstream affected by a difference in air pressures. In an automobile carburetor, for example, gasoline is made into a fine spray by being drawn through a small jet attached to the throat of a venturi tube. It is then pulled through the throat and into the tube where it mixes with the air that is being drawn through the tube and into the automobile's engine. The gasoline is sucked through the jet and into the tube because the air pressure outside the venturi tube is greater than the air pressure inside its throat.

▶ WHAT KEEPS A PLANE UP IN THE AIR?

The principle of the venturi tube also applies to an airplane in flight.

The bottom of an airplane wing is flat. This means that the top surface is longer than the bottom. As the plane wing rushes through the air, the particles of air are separated. They move over or under the wing and meet again behind the wing. The air that passes over the wing has a longer way to go, so it must move faster to join the air that passes under the wing. As we saw, more speed means less pressure. So the pressure above the wing is lower than the pressure beneath the wing. The wing, and the plane it is attached to, are forced upward by the higher pressure under the wing. The upward force is called **lift**, and it offsets the downward force of **gravity**. As a plane's speed increases, so does the lift of the plane's wings.

A wing develops lift in a second way. The wing is set into the plane at a slight angle. Air that hits the bottom of the wing is deflected

Because air has a longer distance to travel when it flows over the curved surface of an airplane wing than when it flows under its flat bottom, the air above the wing must move faster. This causes air pressure above the wing to be lower than it is below it, resulting in a force called lift. The angle of the wing also helps develop lift. Air hitting the bottom of an angled wing is deflected downward. The effect of this is to push the wing upward.

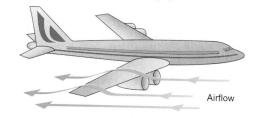

Airflow

downward, pushing the wing upward. The major part of a wing's lift comes from its curved top, and the rest of the lift comes from the bottom.

Other Forces That Act on a Plane

Besides working against gravity, an airplane must work against the resistance of air. Air resists the movement of any object through it. This resistance is called **drag**. The faster an airplane flies through the air, the more drag there is.

An airplane opposes drag with **thrust**. A jet or rocket engine forces a powerful blast of hot air out of the back of the engine to move the plane forward against the air's resistance.

In propeller-driven planes, thrust is provided in another way. The engine turns a propeller rapidly. The propeller pulls its way through air somewhat as a wood screw pulls itself through wood.

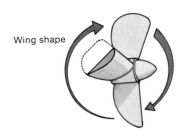

Wing shape

A propeller blade is shaped like an airplane wing—flat on the back side and curved on the front side. As a blade revolves, air passes over the two sides. The air speed is greater when it passes over the curved side so the pressure is less. This means that there is less pressure in front of the propeller than behind it. The propeller moves forward, pulling the rest of the plane with it.

Stalling Speed and Turbulence

There is a certain minimum speed that an airplane must have if the amount of lift is to be greater than the force of gravity. This minimum speed is called the airplane's stalling speed. A plane must be moving faster than its stalling speed to take off, and it cannot stay up in the air if it flies slower than its stalling speed.

An airplane also loses lift if the smooth flow of air over its wings is disturbed. This disturbance is called turbulence. Turbulent air swirls in eddies above the wings.

▶STREAMLINING

Drag is a special problem for designers of high-speed planes because drag increases much faster than speed does. If a plane is to fly at 125 miles (200 kilometers) an hour, the thrust of its engines must overcome a certain amount of drag. But at twice that speed the drag is four times as great, and at three times that speed the drag is nine times as great.

To reduce drag as much as possible, all parts of an airplane exposed to the air are streamlined. Streamlining helps to make the air flow over an airplane as smoothly as possible. A scientist thinks of streamlines as imaginary lines along which particles of air flow smoothly. Streamlines can be made visible in a wind tunnel by letting small tubes blow thin lines of smoke into the airstream. If the

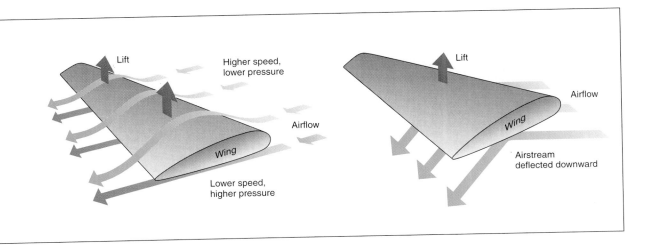

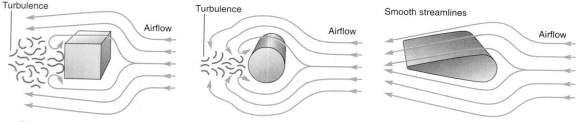

Square shape: high turbulence and drag   **Round shape:** some turbulence and drag   **Teardrop shape:** laminar airflow

The shape of an object determines how smoothly air is able to flow around it. A square shape causes a great deal of drag. As the streamlines break up around it, they cause turbulence. A round shape allows air to flow around it more smoothly. The ideal streamlined shape, however, is the teardrop shape on which the airplane wing is based.

streamlines are smooth, gentle curves, the airflow is called **laminar**. Laminar airflow causes the least amount of drag. If the streamlines break up and become irregular, then turbulence results.

The perfect streamlined shape is neither round like a ball nor pointed like an arrowhead. The shape that causes the least amount of drag is that of a teardrop. However, a perfect, horizontal teardrop shape does not make a good wing. This is because there is no difference in pressure between air flowing above and underneath it. As a result there is no lift. Most airplane wings are shaped like half teardrops. This shape provides the most lift with the least drag.

▶ THE SOUND BARRIER

The designers of modern high-speed planes must also take into account what happens when a plane passes the speed of sound. At sea level the speed of sound is about 760 miles (1,225 kilometers) an hour. At higher altitudes the particles of air are farther apart and the speed of sound is less. As it reaches the speed of sound, an airplane is said to meet the sound barrier.

Air flows smoothly past the wing of a plane flying at less than the speed of sound. But at the speed of sound, the wing produces a thin wave of compressed air, called a **shock wave**. This shock wave increases drag, destroys lift, and, when it moves relative to the wing, shakes the plane violently. A plane must be specially designed to go through the sound barrier safely. Even so, pilots try to go through it as quickly as possible into the smooth flight of **supersonic** (faster than sound) speeds.

Shock waves occur at supersonic speeds as well as at the speed of sound. But the effect of the shock waves on a plane is most severe at or near the speed of sound. The effect is reduced at supersonic speeds.

A shock wave spreads out like the wave formed by the bow of a ship. Just as the ship's waves strike the shore, the plane's shock wave may sweep along the ground below the plane. It causes a thunderlike noise called a **sonic boom**. If a plane is flying low enough, the boom may shake houses and break windows.

Speeds of fast-moving planes are measured in units called **Mach numbers**. The numbers are named after Ernst Mach (1838–1916), an Austrian scientist. A plane traveling at the

A moving airplane causes waves in the air that move ahead of the plane at the speed of sound. When the plane reaches the speed of sound, the waves begin to pile up, forming a sort of wall called a shock wave. When the airplane moves at supersonic speed, the wall bends ahead of the airplane, leaving shock waves behind and causing a sonic boom on the ground.

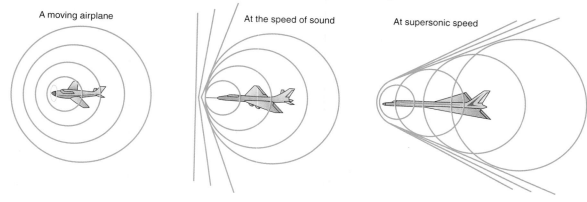

A moving airplane   At the speed of sound   At supersonic speed

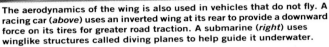

The aerodynamics of the wing is also used in vehicles that do not fly. A racing car (*above*) uses an inverted wing at its rear to provide a downward force on its tires for greater road traction. A submarine (*right*) uses winglike structures called diving planes to help guide it underwater.

speed of sound is said to fly at Mach 1. For a plane flying at twice that speed, the Mach number is 2. A spacecraft re-entering the Earth's atmosphere may travel at Mach 20 or higher.

▶ **OTHER CRAFT**

The principles of aerodynamics apply to several kinds of craft.

Lighter-Than-Air Craft. The lighter-than-air craft such as dirigibles and balloons do not require forward motion to produce lift. They rise because they are filled with a gas that is lighter than air. However, their design must take drag into account, and for controlled, forward motion, thrust must be provided.

Gliders. Gliders have no engines and so have no thrust. For launching they must be pulled forward or shot into the air to overcome gravity. But once in the air, glider pilots use the changing currents to gain lift. By controlling the relationship between lift and drag, glider pilots can keep their craft aloft for many hours. Gliders are sometimes compared to birds. But in many ways birds are more like airplanes, since they create thrust. Only when birds soar can their motion be compared to that of a glider.

Helicopters. Helicopters also use the basic aerodynamic forces. Helicopters have no recognizable wings. But the rotating blades—called rotors—are a combination of wings and propeller. As they revolve, the rotors act like wings by creating lift. By using the controls to tip the rotors slightly, the pilot can make the helicopter travel forward and backward, as well as go up and down and hover, or stand still, in the air.

VTOL Aircraft. VTOL (*v*ertical *t*ake*o*ff and *l*anding) aircraft have the advantages of both standard airplanes and helicopters. They can fly through the air like propeller or jet airplanes at speeds greater than those of a helicopter. These experimental aircraft can also take off and land like helicopters. Engine thrust is used for a straight-up takeoff and for forward movement.

Hovercraft. A hovercraft is meant not to fly high but to hover just above the surface of water or land. The propeller is on the bottom of the craft. When the propeller turns, it pushes air down, against the surface. A "skirt" around the edge of the craft helps to confine the air, allowing the hovercraft to ride a short distance above the surface. A second source of thrust moves the craft forward. Instead of using the lift of a wing, the hovercraft rides on a cushion of air.

IRA M. FREEMAN
Rutgers, The State University of New Jersey

Reviewed by Chuen-Yen Chow
Coauthor, *Foundations of Aerodynamics*

See also AVIATION; BALLOONS AND BALLOONING; BERNOULLI FAMILY; GLIDERS; HELICOPTERS; SUPERSONIC FLIGHT.

AERONAUTICS. See AVIATION.
AESOP. See FABLES; SLAVERY (Profiles).

AFGHANISTAN

Afghanistan is a nation in south central Asia. For much of its history, this mountainous land has been at the center of struggles for wealth and power in Asia. Its strategic location made it a crossroads of both trade and conquest. The greatest conquerors of the past —among them Alexander the Great, Genghis Khan, and Tamerlane—saw Afghanistan as a prize to be won. In the 1800's it was a buffer between competing British and Russian empires. The last foreign power to try to win control of Afghanistan, the former Soviet Union, failed in its attempt in the 1980's.

▶THE PEOPLE

Afghanistan means "land of the Afghans." But the Afghans include a number of different peoples. The most numerous are the Pushtuns (or Pathans), who live in the south. They speak Pushtu. The Tajiks, an Iranian people who live mainly in the northeast, speak Dari, or the Afghan form of Persian. The Hazaras are believed to be of Mongol origin but have adopted a Persian dialect. The Uzbeks and Turkomans, who live on the northern plains, speak languages related to Turkish. The various peoples are united by religion. Afghanistan is a Muslim country, and religion plays an important role in everyday life.

A rugged land, Afghanistan has produced a proud, independent people used to hardship. Centuries of warfare have developed an Afghan fighting tradition that continues to the present day.

Way of Life

In the past many Afghans were nomads. They were constantly on the move, searching the dry plains and plateaus for water and fresh pasture for their sheep, goats, cattle, and camels. Some Afghans still live a nomadic life as animal herders, but most now are settled farmers. The farms are small, and only the simplest hand tools are used. It is quite usual to see farmers plowing their fields with wooden plows or cutting their wheat crops by hand with sickles. Threshing machines are unknown. Farmers often thresh the wheat by hand, or they may walk cattle back and forth across large piles of wheat to separate the grain from the stalks.

Afghans pray before a mosque in Kabul, the capital. The Islamic religion unites the country's varied peoples and plays an important role in their everyday lives.

Life in the villages has changed little over the years. A typical house is built of mud or mud brick and has three or four rooms, furnished with rugs and pillows. Round flat bread and rice are staple foods, together with mutton (sheep), goat meat, chicken, yogurt, and fruit. Traditional clothing for men consists of a turban wound around the head over a skullcap, and a long shirt worn outside baggy trousers. A vest and quilted coat are worn in cold weather. Village women wear a long dress over trousers and a cloth over their hair.

In the cities, European-style clothing or a combination of traditional and modern dress are common. Men often wear a turban and a suit jacket over Afghan trousers. Men of higher social status may wear a suit and tie and the distinctive Afghan karakul (lambskin) hat. Traditionally, women appearing in public were required to wear the *chaderi*, a long garment that covered the body from head to ankle. Many city women, particularly in Kabul, the capital, had given up the *chaderi* for modern dress. Many women in the cities also held jobs outside the home. What effect the new conservative Islamic government will have on the role of women remains to be seen.

Movement of people to the cities increased in recent years, largely because of fighting in the countryside. The largest city is

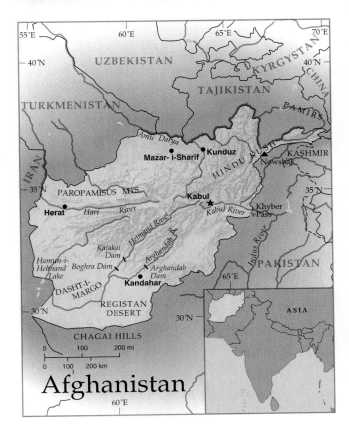

Afghanistan

FACTS and figures

ISLAMIC STATE OF AFGHANISTAN is the official name of the country.

LOCATION: South central Asia.

AREA: 251,772 sq mi (652,090 km²).

POPULATION: 17,000,000 (estimate).

CAPITAL AND LARGEST CITY: Kabul.

MAJOR LANGUAGE(S) (official): Pushtu, Dari.

MAJOR RELIGIOUS GROUP(S): Muslim.

GOVERNMENT: Republic. **Head of state**—president. **Head of government**—prime minister. **Legislature**—Meli Shura (National Assembly). *The government was overthrown in 1992 and an interim government was established.*

CHIEF PRODUCTS: Agricultural—wheat, rice, and other grains; cotton; fruits; nuts; karakul pelts; wool; mutton. **Manufactured**—textiles, processed foods and other agricultural products. **Mineral**—natural gas, petroleum, coal, iron ore, copper, chromium.

MONETARY UNIT: Afghani (1 afghani = 100 puls).

Kabul, which has a population of more than 1 million, including the surrounding area. Other important cities are Kandahar, Herat, and Mazar-i-Sharif.

Only a small percentage of Afghans can read and write. To remedy this, more schools have been built so that all children can have at least six years of elementary education.

Afghanistan's national sport is *buz-kashi*. It is a form of polo, in which players ride horseback. But instead of hitting a ball as in polo, *buz-kashi* players use the carcass of a goat or calf. It is a hard-fought game, and the horses that take part are swift and well trained.

The national dance is called the *attan*. It is intense and warlike. Both the music and the dance itself remind Afghans of their long and hard fight for freedom and independence.

▶**THE LAND**

Afghanistan is wedged between Pakistan, Iran, and the former Soviet Union. It is slightly larger in area than France but much more thinly populated. About two thirds of the land is mountainous. The towering, snow-capped Hindu Kush range and the Pamir mountains rise in the northeast, reaching

Above: The twisting Khyber Pass links Afghanistan with Pakistan. Since ancient times the pass has been a route for both trade and invasion. *Below:* Afghan farmers use the simplest of tools. Wheat is often threshed by hand to separate the grain from the stalks.

heights of over 20,000 feet (6,000 meters). Dry, dusty plains lie north of the mountains. The west and south are desert areas. In the southeast the twisting Khyber Pass links Afghanistan with Pakistan. The most fertile areas are in the east.

Afghanistan has several rivers. But only the Amu Darya (known as the Oxus in ancient times) can be used by ships. Since much of the land is arid (dry), farmers depend on the rivers to provide irrigation for growing crops. Afghanistan at one time had great areas of forest, but these have long since been cut down, causing erosion of the soil. The climate is generally marked by extremes—very cold, snowy winters and hot, dry summers. But temperatures vary from one part of the country to another. Rainfall is slight.

▶ THE ECONOMY

Afghanistan is basically an agricultural country. Most of its people earn their livelihood as farmers or shepherds. The chief crops are wheat, rice, and other grains; cotton; fruits; and nuts. Sheep are raised for food and for their wool and skins. The skins of karakul sheep and lambs provide a valuable fur (one variety is known as Persian lamb) and are a leading export.

Afghanistan is known to have important mineral resources. But their full extent remains to be discovered, and most of the known resources have not been developed. Minerals already found include natural gas, coal, iron ore, copper, chromium, petroleum, and small amounts of gold and silver. Coal is now being mined, but commercial production of petroleum had not yet begun when war broke out.

In the past, most of Afghanistan's industry was based on its agricultural raw materials. Textiles and the processing of fruits and nuts for export were the chief industries. But modern technology offers Afghanistan an opportunity to expand its industry. With the end of the civil war, Afghanistan will be able to make better use of its natural resources. Hydroelectric power, for example, will be available to light Afghan homes and to run factories throughout the country.

Before this can be achieved, however, an economy damaged by years of war must be restored. Agriculture, especially, suffered from the dislocation of people from the land.

▶ HISTORY AND GOVERNMENT

As a crossroads of south central Asia, Afghanistan has known many conquerors and many rulers. With each invasion came new peoples, some of whom settled permanently in the region. Great cities were built, and a prosperous agricultural economy based on irrigation was developed. These achievements were destroyed during the terrible invasions by the Mongols in the 1200's and 1300's. The last foreign rulers of Afghanistan were Baber, the founder of India's great Mogul Empire, in the 1500's and Nadar Shah of Persia (now Iran) in the 1700's.

Independence and Buffer State. In 1747 the Pushtun tribes made Afghanistan an independent kingdom for the first time. But in the following century, the Afghans found themselves caught between the British Empire in India and the expanding Russian Empire in Central Asia. The Afghans struggled hard to keep their independence. They fought two wars against the British before Great Britain was able to take control of Afghanistan's foreign affairs in the late 1800's. For nearly 40 years, Afghanistan served as a "buffer state" between Russia and British-ruled India. In 1919, Afghanistan successfully asserted its full independence again.

After World War II, Afghanistan and Pakistan disagreed over their border. As a result, Pakistan sometimes refused to allow imported goods to reach Afghanistan. This forced Afghanistan to become friendly with the Soviet Union, which offered to send imports through its country.

A Communist Government. Afghanistan remained a kingdom until 1973, when a military coup toppled the monarchy. The leader of the coup, General Mohammed Daoud Khan, was named president and prime minister. Daoud was killed during another coup in 1978, and the government was taken over by a leftist group, which signed a treaty of peace and friendship with the Soviet Union. But most Afghans opposed the new government, and a revolt, led in part by Muslim religious leaders, erupted. Although the Soviet Union sent arms and military advisors to help the government, by the middle of 1979 opposition forces controlled the countryside. In December 1979, thousands of Soviet troops were airlifted into Afghanistan in an attempt to stop the spreading rebellion.

Afghan *mujahidin*, or holy warriors, fought a successful guerrilla war against Soviet occupying forces and the Afghan Communist government.

The Struggle for Afghanistan. More than 100,000 Soviet troops were engaged in Afghanistan. Aided by some Afghan regular troops, they battled Afghan resistance forces called *mujahidin* ("holy warriors"), who waged a relentless guerrilla war against them.

The years of war took a terrible toll. The economy was devastated, with large areas of farmland destroyed by Soviet bombing. At least 5 million Afghans fled the country, most settling in refugee camps in neighboring Pakistan and Iran. The Soviets themselves had suffered some 25,000 troops killed by 1988, when the Soviet government began the withdrawal of its forces. After the last Soviet troops departed in 1989, a struggle began for control of Afghanistan between the *mujahidin* and the Communist government in Kabul, led by President Najibullah. In 1992, Najibullah fled and Kabul was occupied by *mujahidin* forces. An interim government was established, but a struggle for power soon broke out among factions of the *mujahidin*. Although a pact to share power was signed in 1993, the country's political future remains uncertain.

ALOYS A. MICHEL
University of Rhode Island
Reviewed and updated by RICHARD S. NEWELL
Co-author, *The Struggle for Afghanistan*

AFRICA

Africa is the world's second largest continent in area, after Asia. It ranks third in population, after Asia and Europe. Africa is separated from Europe on the north by the Mediterranean Sea. On the northeast, the Suez Canal serves as its traditional dividing line with Asia. The Atlantic Ocean borders Africa on the west, while the Red Sea and the Indian Ocean wash its eastern shores.

Africa lies astride the equator, which divides it almost evenly in half, and is the most tropical of the continents. It is, nevertheless, a continent of great diversity, of broad plateaus and snowcapped mountain peaks, barren deserts and lush rain forests, and enormous rivers and lakes. Africa has the world's longest river, the Nile, and its largest desert, the awesome Sahara.

Africa has been called the probable cradle of humanity because of the many fossils of human ancestors found there. It was the site of one of the world's earliest civilizations, that of ancient Egypt, which flourished in the valley of the Nile thousands of years ago. Numerous African kingdoms, some of great wealth and culture, existed there before the arrival of Europeans, who came first as explorers and then as missionaries and colonists. For much of its modern history, Africa was under the political and economic domination of European powers. It was only in relatively recent

A panorama of Africa. *Opposite page:* The sands of the Sahara, the world's largest desert; a fossil skull of one of the earliest human ancestors; zebras at a waterhole; Mount Kilimanjaro, highest point on the continent; and the awesome Victoria Falls. *Above and right:* Night scene of Cairo, Africa's most populous city; a West African dignitary; and the great pyramids at Giza.

times that the present-day African nations gained their independence and were recognized as an important force in world affairs.

See articles on African art and architecture, literature, and music following this article.

▶ THE LAND

A map of Africa shows the familiar western bulge, the hornlike projection of land in the east (the Horn of Africa), and the land tapering toward the south. Topographically, most of the continent consists of a vast plateau, or tableland, which drops sharply to a narrow coastal belt. The plateau varies in elevation from about 500 to 2,000 feet (150 to 500 meters) in the north and west to more than 3,000 feet (900 meters) in the east and south. In the north, the Sahara separates the Mediterranean coastal plain from the savanna (grasslands) and rain forests to the south. Two smaller but equally forbidding deserts, the Kalahari and Namib, lie at the continent's southern end.

Africa's coastline is more regular than that of most other continents, with fewer bays and other inlets, and as a result, it has relatively fewer good harbors. A number of offshore islands are considered part of the continent. The largest of these, the island nation of Madagascar, lies off the southeastern coast.

Divisions of the Landscape

Mountains and Rivers. The African landscape is broken by modest-size mountain ranges. Among the larger ranges are the Atlas in the northwest, the Ruwenzori in east central Africa, the Cameroon in the west, and the Drakensberg in the southeast. Mount Kilimanjaro, in Tanzania, in eastern Africa, is the highest point on the continent.

In the northeast, in the midst of the barren desert, the Nile has carved out a fertile valley that is one of the most densely populated regions on earth. The continent's second great river, the Congo, drains a vast area in the heart of central Africa. Separate articles on the Congo and Nile rivers can be found in volumes C and N.

Other major waterways include the Niger, which irrigates much of western Africa before emptying into the Atlantic Ocean; and the Zambezi and Orange rivers of southern Africa. The Zambezi flows into the Indian Ocean, and the Orange, which rises in the Drakensberg range, empties into the Atlantic. Africa's rivers generally form rapids and waterfalls as they near the coast, which makes navigation difficult and which long hampered European penetration of the interior. The most spectacular waterfall, Victoria Falls, is located on the Zambezi, at the border of Zambia and Zimbabwe, and drops some 400 feet (120 meters).

Great Rift Valley and Chief Lakes. The Great Rift Valley is one of the continent's most distinctive landforms. Created by ancient volcanic activity and the sinking of the earth's crust, it consists of an enormous trench running along the eastern part of Africa and into south-

western Asia. Within or along the two branches of the valley lie many of Africa's greatest lakes—Victoria (the world's third largest lake), Tanganyika, Malawi (also called Nyasa), Turkana (or Rudolf), Albert, Kivu, and Edward. Lake Chad, which lies at the southern edge of the Sahara, is the continent's largest lake with interior drainage.

For more information on Africa's lakes, see the article LAKES (Africa) in Volume L. An article on the SAHARA appears in Volume S.

The Atlas Mountains of northwestern Africa (*above*) separate the Mediterranean coastal plain from the desert to the south. The waters of the Nile (*left*), the world's longest river, have carved out a fertile valley that is one of Africa's most densely populated regions.

Climate

The climate is largely tropical, except at the northern and southern edges of the continent and in the eastern highlands, which are more temperate. Away from the elevated areas, temperatures remain high throughout the year. The world's highest temperature, 138°F (58°C), was recorded at Azizia, in Libya.

Rainfall varies widely. More than half the continent receives less than 20 inches (500 millimeters) a year, with desert areas receiving much less. It is heaviest in the central equatorial region and along parts of the Atlantic coast, where 100 inches (2,500 millimeters) or more may fall in a year. For much of Africa, the year is marked by alternating dry and wet seasons.

Natural Resources

Minerals. Africa is rich in a variety of mineral resources, including diamonds, gold, cobalt, petroleum, bauxite (aluminum ore), copper, iron ore, chromite (chromium ore), manganese, uranium, and phosphate rock. Much of its mineral wealth, however, still remains to be developed.

Africa is the most tropical of the world's continents. Its central equatorial region consists of thick rain forests, with alternating wet and dry seasons.

FACTS and figures

LOCATION AND SIZE: Mainland Africa extends from: **Latitude**—37°21' N to 34°50' S. **Longitude** —51°24' E to 17°32' W. **Area**—approximately 11,708,000 sq mi (30,324,000 km²). **Highest point**—Mt. Kilimanjaro (Kibo Peak), Tanzania, 19,565 ft (5,963 m). **Lowest point**—Qattara Depression, Egypt, 440 ft (134 m) below sea level.

POPULATION: 700,000,000 (estimate).

CHIEF LAKES: Victoria, Tanganyika, Malawi (Nyasa), Chad, Turkana (Rudolf), Albert, Kivu, Edward.

CHIEF RIVERS: Nile, Congo (Zaïre), Niger, Zambezi, Orange.

CHIEF MOUNTAIN RANGES AND PEAKS: Kilimanjaro (Kibo Peak, Mawenzi); Kenya; Meru; Elgon; Cameroon; **Ruwenzori**—Margherita, Alexandra; **Simen**—Ras Dashan; **Virunga**—Karisimbi, Mikeno; **Atlas**—Djebel Toubkal, Bou Naceur; **Drakensberg** —Thabana Ntlenyana; **Tibesti Massif**—Emi Koussi; **Ahaggar**—Tahat.

CHIEF DESERTS: Sahara (including the Eastern and Libyan deserts), Kalahari, Nubian, Namib.

The discovery of petroleum deposits in the Sahara in the mid-1950's turned Algeria and Libya into major oil-producing countries. Nigeria, Angola, and Gabon are also among the continent's chief oil producers. Much of the world's diamond supply comes from such African countries as Botswana, Zaïre, South Africa, and Namibia. South Africa, which has the continent's most extensive mineral deposits, leads the world in gold production. It is an important exporter of chromite, copper, iron and manganese ore, and uranium, and has most of Africa's limited coal deposits as well.

Zambia and Zaïre have extensive deposits of copper, and Zaïre is the world's major producer of cobalt (used to harden steel). Ghana, once known as the Gold Coast, still mines substantial amounts of gold. Guinea ranks among the world's leading producers of bauxite, while Morocco is one of the leading producers of phosphate rock (used in making fertilizer).

Scattered across the barren desert areas of northern Africa are fertile oases, watered by underground streams. This oasis is in Morocco.

INDEX TO AFRICA PHYSICAL MAP

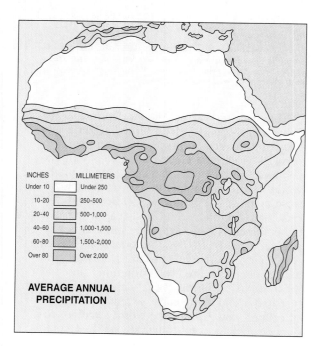

INCHES	MILLIMETERS
Under 10	Under 250
10-20	250-500
20-40	500-1,000
40-60	1,000-1,500
60-80	1,500-2,000
Over 80	Over 2,000

AVERAGE ANNUAL PRECIPITATION

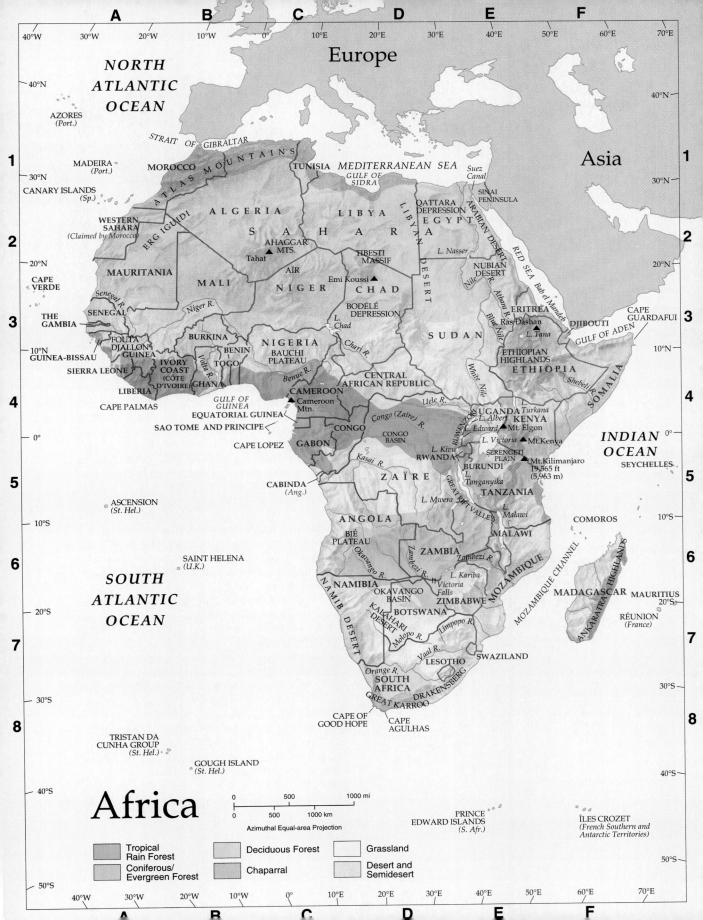

Africa

Legend:
- Tropical Rain Forest
- Coniferous/Evergreen Forest
- Deciduous Forest
- Chaparral
- Grassland
- Desert and Semidesert

Azimuthal Equal-area Projection

Scale: 0 — 500 — 1000 mi / 0 — 500 — 1000 km

COUNTRIES OF AFRICA

COUNTRY	CAPITAL
Algeria	Algiers
Angola	Luanda
Benin	Porto-Novo
Botswana	Gaborone
Burkina	Ouagadougou
Burundi	Bujumbúra
Cameroon	Yaoundé
Cape Verde	Praia
Central African Republic	Bangui
Chad	N'Djamena
Comoros	Moroni
Congo	Brazzaville
Djibouti	Djibouti
Egypt	Cairo
Equatorial Guinea	Malabo
Eritrea	Asmara
Ethiopia	Addis Ababa
Gabon	Libreville
Gambia, The	Banjul
Ghana	Accra
Guinea	Conakry
Guinea-Bissau	Bissau
Ivory Coast	Yamoussoukro
Kenya	Nairobi
Lesotho	Maseru
Liberia	Monrovia
Libya	Tripoli
Madagascar	Antananarivo
Malawi	Lilongwe
Mali	Bamako
Mauritania	Nouakchott
Mauritius	Port Louis
Morocco	Rabat
Mozambique	Maputo
Namibia	Windhoek
Niger	Niamey
Nigeria	Abuja
Rwanda	Kigali
Sao Tome and Principe	São Tomé
Senegal	Dakar
Seychelles	Victoria
Sierra Leone	Freetown
Somalia	Mogadishu
South Africa	Pretoria (administrative)
	Cape Town (legislative)
	Bloemfontein (judicial)
Sudan	Khartoum
Swaziland	Mbabane
Tanzania	Dar es Salaam
Togo	Lomé
Tunisia	Tunis
Uganda	Kampala
Zaïre	Kinshasa
Zambia	Lusaka
Zimbabwe	Harare

Vegetation and Soils. Vegetation zones vary with the climate. Central Africa, with its heavy rainfall, is a region of dense tropical forests. As the climate grows drier north and south of the equator, there is a gradual change from rain forest to a broad belt of savanna, or grassy plains dotted with trees. With decreasing rainfall, the savanna gives way to a drier, steppe region of shorter grasses and thorn bushes with only occasional trees. In the north, the steppe merges into a semidesert region known as the Sahel, which borders the Sahara. The Mediterranean-type vegetation of the northern coast includes such trees as pine, cork, oak, and olive.

In spite of their lush growth, the rain forests have soil that is of limited value for agriculture, while the drier savannas are suitable chiefly for grazing livestock. The most fertile areas are found in the valleys of the great rivers, which have rich alluvial soils. A variety of crops can be cultivated in the Mediterranean coastal zone and parts of eastern and southern Africa. But in general, Africa has nothing comparable to the large grain-growing regions of North America, Europe, and Asia.

Animal Life. Africa's wealth of wild animal life is one of its most important natural resources. The rain forests are home to monkeys, chimpanzees, gorillas, and okapis (shorter-necked relatives of the giraffe), snakes such as the large rock python and the

A broad belt of savanna, or plains dotted with trees (*opposite page*), covers much of the African landscape. It is home to such wildlife as the sable antelope (*left*) and the African lion (*bottom*). The mountain gorilla, by contrast, lives in upland areas.

poisonous African cobra and black mamba, and numerous kinds of birds. Crocodiles inhabit many African rivers. Herds of zebra and antelope graze on the savannas, serving as prey for lions, cheetahs, leopards, and scavenging hyenas. Among the larger African mammals are elephants, two species of rhinoceroses (white and black), and giraffes. Gazelles, foxes, and hares are some of the animals that have adapted to the harsh environment of the deserts. Lemurs (monkeylike primates) are found mainly on the island of Madagascar.

Some of Africa's animals are endangered and others close to extinction, due to population growth, the destruction of their natural habitat, and illegal or excessive hunting. The most threatened species are the black rhinoceros and the mountain gorilla. Elephants, hunted for their ivory, have also greatly diminished in numbers. Several African countries have passed strict laws to protect their wildlife, and game reserves have been established in various parts of the continent. Among the largest are Serengeti National Park in Tanzania, Kruger National Park in South Africa, and Tsavo Park in Kenya.

An article on endangered species appears in Volume E.

▶THE PEOPLE

Of all the world's continents, Africa has the most rapidly-growing population. If it continues its present rate of growth, it is expected to soon exceed Europe as the second most populous continent. Its people are very unevenly distributed across the land, however.

Since much of Africa consists of desert or semidesert land, mountains, and dense rain forests, large areas of the continent are only sparsely inhabited. Other areas, by contrast, are thickly crowded with people. Millions of people live in the valley and delta area of the Nile, where the soil is fertile, and water is available. Parts of the northern, or Mediterranean, coast are also well populated. This region has a generally pleasant climate and, historically, is well situated for trade and other contacts with Europe.

Some of the earliest large African kingdoms originated in western Africa south of the Sahara, and the well-watered parts of this region, particularly along the Gulf of Guinea, are still home to considerable numbers of people. The eastern highlands and the southeastern coast of the continent, with their temperate climates, can also support sizable populations.

Although Africa has a number of large cities, the great majority of its people live in rural areas, as they have traditionally for centuries. Only about one-third of Africans live in urban areas, or cities—less than any of the other inhabited continents. But the rate of urban growth is very high, as increasing indus-

trialization, cultural changes, the hope for a better life in the cities, and other factors attract growing numbers of people from the countryside. Often this strains the abilities of the cities to provide jobs, housing, and services for all who need them.

Racial and Ethnic Groups

Africa is home to a variety of peoples, languages, and cultures. Africans are usually divided into two major racial groups—the Negroid, or black, and the Caucasoid, or white. Black Africans are by far the more numerous, inhabiting a region from just south of the Sahara to the southern part of the continent. Generally considered as related groups are the Nilotic peoples of eastern Africa and the pygmies of central Africa, distinguished by their small stature. The San (Bushmen) and Khoikhoi (Hottentots) may be the most ancient people of the continent. Few in numbers, most live in the southern deserts.

The major Caucasoid groups are the Arabs and Berbers of northern Africa. There are also relatively small numbers of Africans of European origin. The largest of these are the whites of South Africa, descendants of early, mainly Dutch, settlers. The others are remnants of the European colonial period. In addition to the Europeans, Asians, mostly from India, have settled in eastern Africa and parts of South Africa. The intermingling of many of the various peoples over the course of history has created the Africans of today.

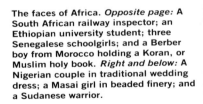

The faces of Africa. *Opposite page:* **A South African railway inspector; an Ethiopian university student; three Senegalese schoolgirls; and a Berber boy from Morocco holding a Koran, or Muslim holy book.** *Right and below:* **A Nigerian couple in traditional wedding dress; a Masai girl in beaded finery; and a Sudanese warrior.**

Africa's varied people speak a multitude of languages. Arabic is the language of these fishermen from northern Africa; the boys on camelback, from Niger, speak Fulani, a major language of western Africa.

Languages

Africa has a multitude of languages, estimated at 1,000 or more, spread across the continent. Some are spoken by large numbers of people; others by relatively few. Languages are often a more accurate way of defining the continent's ethnic groups. They are generally classified into several broad categories.

Afro-Asian and Nilo-Saharan. Afro-Asian languages are spoken mainly in northern and northeastern Africa. They include Arabic, the dominant language of northern Africa; Berber, spoken by the people who inhabited the region before the arrival of the Arabs; and the various languages of Ethiopia, Eritrea, and Somalia. The group also includes ancient Egyptian and its more modern relative, Coptic, as well as Hausa, spoken in northern Nigeria and adjacent areas.

The Nilo-Saharan language family is found in the central Sahara and just south of it, the basin of the Nile, and parts of eastern Africa. It is spoken by people in an area stretching from Mali in the west, through southern Sudan, to parts of Uganda, Kenya, and Tanzania in the east. Its major languages include Dendi, Kanuri, Dinka, Nuer, and Masai.

Niger-Kordofanian and Khoisan. The large Niger-Kordofanian family makes up a majority of the continent's languages and is spoken in most of Africa below the Sahara. In western Africa, its major language branches include Mande, Fulani, and Kwa. The hundreds of languages of the Bantu subfamily are found in central and southern and large areas of eastern Africa. One of the most widespread of the Bantu-based languages, Swahili, which was influenced by Arabic-speaking traders, became a common language of communication for much of the east African coastal region.

The San and Khoikhoi of southern Africa speak languages belonging to the small Khoisan family. They are sometimes referred to as click languages, because of the distinctive sound made in speaking them.

European Languages and Others. European languages were introduced by settlers and colonizers. French is still often used in former French territories in northern, western, and central Africa, as well as in Zaïre, once a Belgian colony. English continues to be spoken by educated people in former British colonies in western, eastern, and southern Africa, while Portuguese remains the official language of Angola and Mozambique. The descendants of the original white settlers of South Africa speak Afrikaans, based on a mixture of Dutch and Bantu languages.

Another distinctive language of the continent, Malagasy, spoken on Madagascar, is of Malayo-Polynesian origin.

Religions

Africa has three main religious faiths—Islam, Christianity, and traditional religions.

Islam, the Muslim religion, arrived in northern Africa with conquering Arab armies. It became the predominant faith of the region, displacing Christianity, and quickly spread into areas immediately south of the Sahara. Christianity survived in Ethiopia and parts of Egypt and, centuries later, was reintroduced to other regions of Africa by European and American missionaries.

A great variety of traditional religions has existed in Africa since earliest times. As a particular society developed, it evolved its own beliefs, which were handed down from

A Catholic priest blesses a Ugandan boy; Muslims in Nigeria pray before a mosque; and a practitioner of traditional religion surveys his artifacts. Islam, Christianity, and traditional religions are Africa's main faiths.

In a rapidly changing Africa, the old and the new frequently meet. Here, in Niger, a skyscraper looms over traditional beehive-shaped thatched homes.

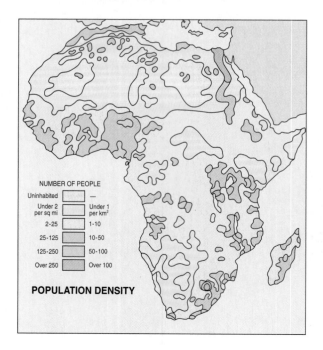

NUMBER OF PEOPLE

Uninhabited	—
Under 2 per sq mi	Under 1 per km²
2-25	1-10
25-125	10-50
125-250	50-100
Over 250	Over 100

POPULATION DENSITY

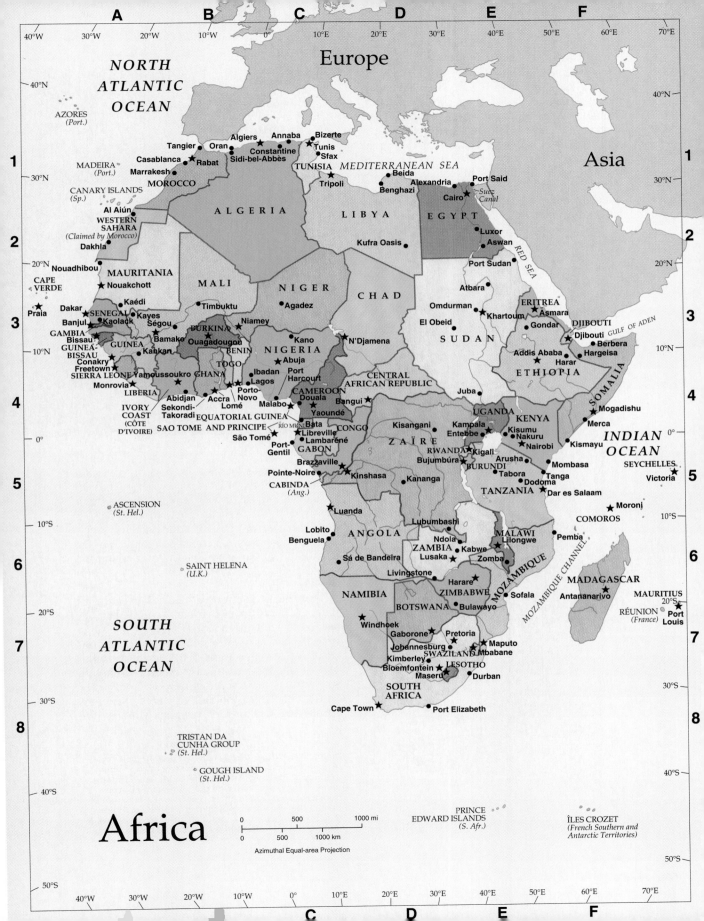

generation to generation, reflecting its cultural as well as its spiritual ideas. Most have as a basic element a belief in spirits, which are thought to exist in such things as trees and mountains, and a reverence for or worship of one's ancestors. Magic is also an important ingredient of many traditional religions and is often used in healing. Although most traditional religions do not deny the existence of many minor gods, most recognize the existence of a supreme creator.

Africa also has small numbers of Hindus and Jews. Hinduism is practiced by the Indian communities living mainly in South Africa and in parts of eastern Africa. Most Jews live in the north and in South Africa.

Education

Along with improvements in health care and economic conditions, the expansion of education has been one of the chief aims of African countries since independence. This has been a major undertaking. The adult literacy rate (the

percentage able to read and write), although it varies widely, still averages only about 25 percent for most of Africa. In addition, with nearly half the African population under 15 years of age, the cost of educating its young people represents an enormous strain on the economies of the continent's poorer countries.

Society

Traditional Society: The Tribe. For centuries much of traditional African society has revolved around the tribe. People of the same tribe usually speak the same language and observe the same customs. They share a similar way of life and a distinctive culture. Although some tribes are small, more commonly they consist of large populations, in some cases numbering millions of people. Most of the

Traditional African society revolved around the tribe, whose members shared a common language, culture, and way of life (*left*). But traditional life is undergoing rapid change, due in part to the movement of people from rural areas to the cities. Tribal conflicts have also caused the large-scale dislocation of peoples. These Rwandan refugees (*top*) fled their homeland because of fighting between the country's two main ethnic groups.

large African tribes, in fact, would be considered nations or nationalities if they lived in Europe.

Tribal society, traditionally, was the center of an individual's life. It offered social and economic security and regulated conduct through tribal laws and customs. It took care of its members in time of need and protected them from hostile outsiders. In return, members gave their services to the tribe. A tribe was usually ruled by a chieftain or a tribal council or, sometimes, by both. In some areas, tribes with similar cultural backgrounds banded together under a paramount chief.

One of the values basic to virtually all traditional African life was the strong attachment to the land. Probably this was because most Africans have always lived off the land. It was considered to belong to all, and not only to the living but to one's ancestors and to future generations as well.

National and Tribal Conflicts. But tribal boundaries do not always correspond to the political realities of modern African countries. The border between Togo and Ghana, for example, cuts through the traditional homeland of the Ewe people. This and similar situations came about because most of Africa's present-day borders were drawn by colonial powers, who divided vast territories among themselves without regard for traditional boundary lines. In a number of instances this has been the cause of conflict and outright civil war. Eventually, it is hoped that as the ties of traditional society lessen, Africans will feel a greater loyalty to their national governments than to their tribes.

Social Change. The traditional ways of life are rapidly changing. Some 200 years of European influence have profoundly affected the thinking and life of many Africans. Improved transportation and communications have brought the outside world even closer to the rural villages. Although many Africans have been reluctant to leave their traditional homelands and the security they represent, each year increasing numbers move to the cities in search of greater opportunities. In spite of improvements in health and standards of living in general, governments often cannot cope with the rapid urban growth or satisfy the people's demands. Economic and social dislocation are frequently the result, often aggravated by civil strife.

WONDER QUESTION

What and where are the Mountains of the Moon?

One of the mysteries of Africa that had perplexed historians and explorers from earliest times was the source, or origin, of the Nile—the mighty river whose life-giving waters enabled the ancient Egyptians to create a great civilization in an otherwise barren land. The Greek geographer Ptolemy (A.D. 90–168) conjectured that the river originated in the heart of Africa, in a vague region that he called the Mountains of the Moon. It was not until the 1870's that the true source of the White Nile, its main tributary, was discovered, chiefly in lakes Victoria, Edward, and Albert. As for the Mountains of the Moon, they are generally, although not always, identified today with the Ruwenzori range, on the border between Uganda and Zaïre. Ptolemy may not have been entirely wrong, however, for the melting snows of the Ruwenzori do contribute to the waters that ultimately feed into the Nile.

Cape Town (*left*), the legislative capital of South Africa, lies on the southernmost tip of the continent. Nairobi (*above*) is Kenya's capital and largest city and one of the chief cities of eastern Africa.

▶CITIES

In spite of a largely rural population, Africa also has a considerable culture based on urban life. Cairo, the capital of Egypt, is the continent's largest city and continues to attract increasing numbers of people from the countryside. Alexandria, Egypt's chief port, is an ancient center of learning and commerce, named for Alexander the Great. Other important cities of the north are Casablanca, Morocco's principal city and port; and Algiers and Tunis, the capitals, respectively, of Algeria and Tunisia.

Southern Africa's major cities include Cape Town, located at the southernmost tip of the continent, and Johannesburg, both in South Africa. Lagos, Nigeria's largest city and chief port, and Abidjan, capital of Ivory Coast, are western Africa's largest urban centers. Dakar, Senegal's capital, is a leading port situated on Africa's most westerly point of land.

Eastern Africa has several major cities. Dar es Salaam, Tanzania's capital and largest city, is one of the region's leading ports. Nairobi is Kenya's chief city and capital, and Addis Ababa is the largest city, commercial center, and capital of Ethiopia. Central Africa's largest city, Kinshasa, the capital of Zaïre, lies on the Congo River.

▶THE ECONOMY

Although rich in terms of its natural resources, most of Africa is in the developing stage, economically. The continent has emerged in only relatively recent times from the colonial period, when it served mainly as a source of raw materials for Europe's industry and as a market for its manufactured goods. Aside from South Africa, the most highly industrialized of the African countries, the continent in general has only begun to develop a modern industrial economy. Agriculture and the mining of its mineral wealth are still the main sources of Africa's income.

Agriculture

Most Africans earn their livelihood from the soil. The great majority practice subsistence farming, growing basic food crops for their own use, generally on small plots of land. Commercial crops, intended for export, are often grown on large plantations. Ordinarily, a variety of crops can be grown in some regions of the continent. In others, the thinness of the soil, the arid climate, and frequent drought make farming difficult.

Northern and Western Regions. Wheat, barley, and grapes flourish on the Mediterranean coast. Date palms, fig trees, and wheat, cotton, and vegetables can be grown in the scattered oases, or watered areas, of the desert regions. In the rainy, tropical areas of western Africa, the main food crops are yams, cassava (a starchy root), and rice. Commercial crops grown here include cacao (from which chocolate is made), coffee, rubber, and palm oil. Ivory Coast is the world's leading producer of cacao, while Nigeria is a major producer of coffee and natural rubber. In the drier savanna, important crops include such grains as millet, sorghum, and corn, peanuts, and cotton.

Eastern and Southern Regions. Corn and wheat, along with millet, cassava, and vegetables, are the major food crops of eastern Africa. Commercial crops include sisal (a fiber from which cord and twine are made), cotton, coffee, tea, and pyrethrum (used in making insecticides). Winter wheat, wine grapes, and other fruits are grown in South Africa's southern Cape province, which has a Mediterranean-type climate. Sugarcane is an important crop in the coastal region of Mozambique and along the eastern coast of South Africa.

Livestock Raising. Livestock raising is an important element of African agriculture, particularly in the savanna and steppe regions. Goats are grazed in the arid Sahel, while farther north, in the Sahara itself, semi-nomadic peoples regularly migrate, seeking pasture for their herds of camels and sheep. Eastern Africa has a distinctive cattle culture, especially among the Masai of Kenya and Tanzania, where ownership of cattle is a sign of wealth and prestige. Smaller domestic livestock, such as pigs and chickens, are kept as part of the traditional subsistance farming. Large-scale commercial cattle- and sheep-raising is carried out in South Africa.

Livestock raising (*left*) is an important part of African agriculture, particularly in regions of limited rainfall. In more fertile areas, such as the Nile Valley (*below*), a variety of crops can be grown.

Mining and Manufacturing

Mining accounts for about half of Africa's total exports and is the major source of income for a number of African countries. For detailed information on Africa's mineral resources and where they are found, see the section Mineral Resources.

While South Africa has a variety of heavy industry, including the production of iron and steel, most African industry consists of light manufacturing. The bulk of the labor force is employed in the processing of foods and other agricultural products and the production of textiles, clothing, and chemicals. Manufacturing is usually concentrated in the larger cities, but many of the newer industries are located near rivers to take advantage of the continent's considerable hydroelectric power potential.

Forestry and Fishing

Forests cover about one-quarter of the continent. But the commercially valuable trees, such as mahogany and other hardwoods, are often widely scattered and transportation is frequently inadequate. Usable areas of forest lie mainly in west central Africa.

Africa is rich in mineral resources. Libya is one of the world's major oil producers (*above*) and Zambia ranks among the leading producers of copper (*below*).

Freshwater fish obtained from Africa's rivers and lakes partially make up for the lack of meat in the diet of most Africans. The major commercial fishing grounds are found off the southwestern coast, where the cold Benguela Current attracts large schools of fish; in the Mediterranean; and in the Gulf of Guinea. Much of the catch is processed for export as fish meal and fish oil.

Transportation

Africa's often difficult terrain and severe climate have combined to hinder transportation over much of the continent. Most of its system of roads and railroads was built during the colonial period to connect the interior with the coastal ports, and its further development has been slow and painstaking. South Africa and the Mediterranean area have the most extensive road and rail networks.

Historically, Africa's rivers and lakes have served as a natural transportation system, although limited by the numerous rapids and falls. Air transportation is now of major importance in areas difficult to reach by other means and in connecting major cities, as well as by linking Africa with the rest of the world.

Africa is believed to have been the home of the earliest humans. Scientists have discovered the remains of humanlike ancestors in eastern Africa who are estimated to have lived more than 3 million years ago. Africa, which has been incorrectly called the continent without a history, may well have the longest human history of all the continents. For more information on this subject, see the articles FOSSILS in Volume F and PREHISTORIC PEOPLE in Volume P.

Northern Africa

Early peoples in the valley of the Nile developed a form of agriculture based on the cultivation of cereal grains, irrigated by the yearly flooding of the great river. In about 3200 B.C., the northern and southern states of the region were united, marking the beginning of Egyptian civilization. A later kingdom, that of Kush (or Nubia), arose just to the south, while in the Horn of Africa, in what is now Ethiopia, the kingdom of Aksum eventually grew out of contacts with southwestern Asia.

The Phoenicians, a people from the eastern Mediterranean, and their successors, the Carthaginians, established themselves on the coast of northern Africa. Their most famous settlement, the city-state of Carthage, was founded in the 800's B.C. The Carthaginians were displaced by the Romans, who by the A.D. 100's had gained control of the entire northern coast of Africa from Morocco to Egypt.

Between the A.D. 600's and 1000's, Arab armies from southwestern Asia swept across northern Africa, bringing with them the Islamic religion and Arabic language that still prevails over most of the region. Islam gradually spread southward, and Arabs later traded and settled along the coast of eastern Africa.

West African Kingdoms

Several ancient African kingdoms flourished in the valley of the Niger River in western Africa. They engaged in trade with the Arabs of the north and became wealthy centers of learning and culture.

The earliest of the great kingdoms of the region, Ghana, originated in the A.D. 300's and reached its height in the A.D. 1000's. It

A European map of 1375 depicts the king of Mali, Mansa Musa, on his throne. Mali was one of the early empires and kingdoms that flourished in western Africa.

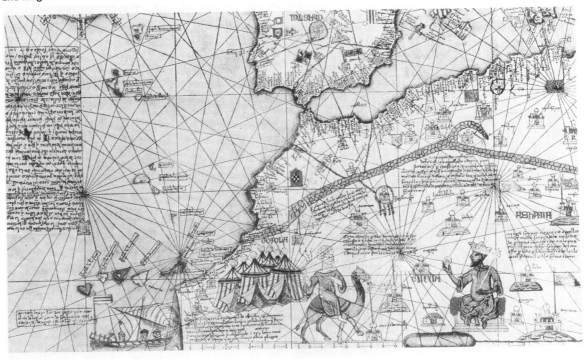

Other European powers began to compete with the Portuguese. They also established forts and trading posts along the coast. But the dense rain forests, disease, the hazards of waterfalls and rapids, and hostility by Africans to foreign encroachment long kept Europeans from penetrating to the inland areas.

European exploration of the interior of Africa first began in the second half of the 1700's, with the discoveries of two Scots—James Bruce, who explored the region of the Blue Nile, one of the two main branches of the Nile River; and Mungo Park, who traveled down the Niger River. One of the most famous African explorers, the Scottish missionary and doctor David Livingstone, made extensive discoveries in central Africa and the lake region of southeastern Africa in the mid-1800's. He was joined by Henry Morton Stanley, who later explored the vast Congo region.

See the article EXPLORATION AND DISCOVERY (Exploring Africa) in Volume E. An article on Stanley and Livingstone appears in Volume S.

was succeeded by the empire of Mali, one of whose chief cities was the fabled Timbuktu. Mali held sway until it was replaced, in turn, as the most powerful western state by Songhai, which at its height during the early 1500's stretched from the Atlantic coast to northern Nigeria. Two modern African nations, Ghana and Mali, have taken their names from these old kingdoms.

European Exploration

European exploration along the coast of Africa began with the Portuguese, who were looking for a convenient water route to India. Bartholomeu Dias rounded the Cape of Good Hope at the southern tip of Africa in 1488. Another Portuguese explorer, Vasco da Gama, visited the eastern coast and reached India in 1498. Soon afterward, the Portuguese established coastal settlements and began trading in gold, spices, ivory, and slaves.

The Slave Trade

The slave trade was a by-product of the opening of Africa. Arabs had long been established in the trade in slaves in eastern Africa. By the 1600's and 1700's, the Portuguese, British, Dutch, and French had joined them. Millions of black Africans were to become its victims before the trade was banned by most European countries in the 1800's. For more information on the slave trade, see the article SLAVERY (the African Slave Trade and other sections) in Volume S.

Top: The British explorer Richard Burton (1821–90) spent years searching for the source of the Nile. His discoveries included Lake Tanganyika. *Right:* The slave trade was one of the tragic episodes of African history, lasting from the 1600's until it was abolished by most European countries in the 1800's.

IMPORTANT DATES

About 3200 B.C. Egypt united under King Menes.

About 2000 B.C. Rise of kingdom of Kush (Nubia).

814 B.C. Phoenicians settle the colony of Carthage in northern Africa.

About 600 B.C. Greeks replace Phoenicians in trade and exploration of Africa.

264–146 B.C. Punic Wars involve Rome and Carthage in a struggle for control of the Mediterranean. Victorious Roman armies destroy Carthage.

168 B.C. Romans conquer Egypt.

A.D. 300's–1000's Kingdom of Ghana flourishes in western Africa.

300's Kingdom of Aksum (in northern Ethiopia) converted to Christianity.

429–439 Vandals conquer northern Africa, which had been part of the Roman Empire.

About 500 Decline of Vandals; northern Africa becomes part of the Byzantine Empire.

640–710 Period of the Arab conquest of northern Africa; introduction of Islam and the Arabic language.

1000's Mali empire conquers Ghana.

1415 Prince Henry the Navigator sends Portuguese expeditions down the western coast of Africa.

1487–1488 Bartholomeu Dias of Portugal discovers Cape of Good Hope.

1497–1498 Portugal's Vasco da Gama sails around the Cape of Good Hope to India.

1500's Songhai kingdom overthrows Mali.

1517 Ottoman Turks conquer Egypt.

1520–1526 Francisco Alvarez of Portugal explores Ethiopia.

1535 Spain conquers Tunis.

1595 First Dutch settlement established on the Guinea coast.

1626 French settle in Senegal.

1652 Cape Town founded by the Dutch.

1660 Rise of the Bambara kingdoms on the upper Niger.

1697 France completes conquest of Senegal.

1768–1773 James Bruce explores the Blue Nile.

1787 Home for freed African slaves set up in Sierra Leone.

1792 Denmark becomes the first country to abolish slave trade.

1795, 1805 Mungo Park explores the Niger River.

1807, 1811 Britain abolishes slave trade.

1814 Cape Colony becomes a British possession.

1815 France, Spain, and Portugal abolish slave trade.

1821 Freed American slaves arrive in Liberia.

1830–1847 France conquers Algeria.

1834 Britain frees all slaves in its colonies.

1836–1840 Great Trek of Boers (descendants of Dutch settlers) to interior of what is now South Africa.

1841 David Livingstone begins exploration of Africa.

1847 Liberia becomes the first independent black republic.

1849 The French establish a home for freed slaves at Libreville in Gabon.

1850's Richard Burton and John Hanning Speke explore source of the Nile.

1866 Diamonds are found in South Africa.

1869 Suez Canal opens.

1871 Henry M. Stanley's search for Livingstone ends successfully in Tanganyika.

1871 Cecil Rhodes starts building his fortune and empire in southern Africa.

1884 Germany annexes South-West Africa, gains control of Togoland and the Cameroons.

1885 King Leopold II of Belgium establishes the Congo Free State as his personal property. Germany acquires Tanganyika. Berlin Conference on African Affairs held.

1886 Gold discovered in South Africa—gold rush begins.

1898 Fashoda Crisis, involving confrontation of Britain and France on the upper Nile, brings the two powers to the brink of war.

1899–1902 Boer War: Britain's defeat of Boers gives it control of South Africa.

1908 Congo Free State is turned over to the Belgian government and renamed the Belgian Congo.

1910 The British colonies in South Africa are united to form the Union of South Africa.

1922 Egypt gains independence from Britain, but British influence remains.

1935 Italy invades Ethiopia.

1941–1943 North African campaign of World War II fought.

1948 South Africa formally adopts policy of apartheid, or racial separation.

1951 Libya gains independence.

1954–1962 Period of Algerian war of independence.

1956 Tunisia, Morocco, Sudan gain independence. Egypt nationalizes the Suez Canal, touching off a Middle East war.

1957 Ghana gains independence.

1958 Guinea gains independence.

1960 Belgian Congo (now Zäire), Cameroon, Central African Republic, Chad, Congo, Dahomey (now Benin), Gabon, Ivory Coast, Malagasy Republic (now Madagascar), Mali, Mauritania, Niger, Nigeria, Senegal, Somalia, Togo, and Upper Volta (now Burkina) gain independence.

1961 Sierra Leone and Tanganyika gain independence. South Africa becomes a republic.

1962 Algeria, Burundi, Rwanda, and Uganda gain independence.

1963 African leaders meet in Addis Ababa to form the Organization of African Unity (OAU). Zanzibar and Kenya gain independence.

1964 Zanzibar and Tanganyika united as Tanzania. Malawi and Zambia gain independence.

1965 The Gambia gains independence. Rhodesia unilaterally declares independence.

1966 Botswana and Lesotho gain independence.

1967–1970 Civil war rages in Nigeria.

1968 Equatorial Guinea, Mauritius, and Swaziland gain independence.

1971 Egypt's Aswan Dam formally opened.

1974 Guinea-Bissau gains independence.

1975 Comoros, Mozambique, São Tomé and Príncipe, Angola, and Cape Verde gain independence.

1976 Seychelles gains independence.

1977 Djibouti gains independence.

1980 Zimbabwe (former Rhodesia) gains independence under black majority rule.

1990 Namibia gains independence.

1993 Eritrea wins independence from Ethiopia.

1994 Inauguration of Nelson Mandela, a black, as president of South Africa marks a turning point in the country's political history.

The Colonial Era

The "scramble for Africa," as the rivalry for African possessions was called, began in the mid-1800's. During the next 50 years, the continent came almost completely under European domination. France and Britain were the main colonial powers, but Portugal, Germany, Spain, Italy, and Belgium also carved out large African empires that were often many times larger than the European countries themselves. By the beginning of the 1900's, the only African states that were still independent were Ethiopia and Liberia. Ethiopia had successfully resisted colonization, while Liberia had been founded, in the early 1800's, as a refuge for freed American slaves.

The March Toward Independence

The end of World War II in 1945 saw the rise of African nationalism as a mass movement. The great march toward independence began in the late 1950's and proceeded swiftly. In 1960 alone, 17 nations won independence. By 1970 most of the continent had freed itself from colonial rule. Independence was generally gained peacefully, although in a few cases it was preceded by years of guerrilla war.

The transfer of authority was usually orderly. In several instances, however, independence was followed by civil war, either immediately or some years later. In some countries, separatists sought to break away

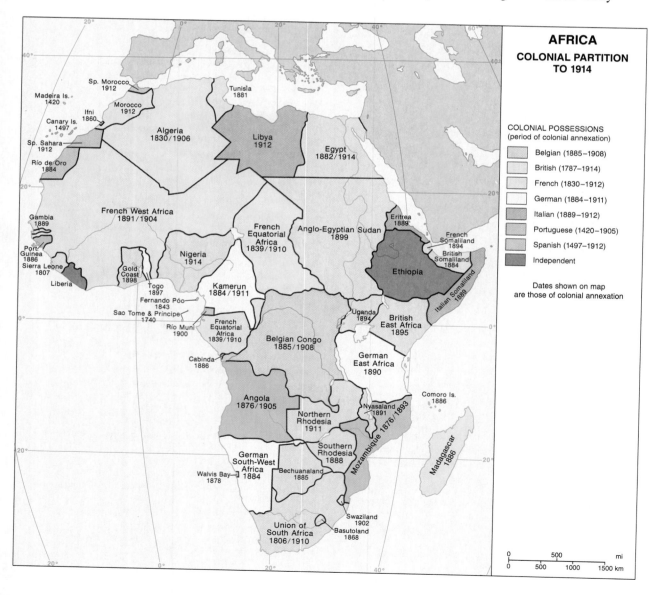

AFRICA

COLONIAL PARTITION TO 1914

COLONIAL POSSESSIONS
(period of colonial annexation)

Belgian (1885–1908)
British (1787–1914)
French (1830–1912)
German (1884–1911)
Italian (1889–1912)
Portuguese (1420–1905)
Spanish (1497–1912)
Independent

Dates shown on map
are those of colonial annexation

The inauguration of Nelson Mandela as South Africa's first black president in 1994 was an event of historic importance.

and form their own nations. This occurred in the Belgian Congo (Zaïre) in 1960 and in Nigeria in 1967. When Angola and Mozambique won independence from Portugal in the 1970's, civil war erupted as opposing political factions fought for power.

Nevertheless, progress toward complete independence continued. Zimbabwe finally gained independence under black-majority rule in 1980. The last of the great African colonies, Namibia (a former German territory administered by South Africa) gained its independence in 1990. Africa's newest nation, Eritrea, won independence from Ethiopia in 1993, after years of fighting. In South Africa the inauguration, in 1994, of Nelson Mandela as its first black president marked a historic turning point in a country where a white minority had long been dominant.

The Future

Much remains to be done, however. Average incomes for most Africans are very low. There are still not enough schools or teachers and relatively few hospitals and doctors compared to Africa's vast size and numbers of people. Traditional ways of life have been disrupted by the migration of people from the countryside to the cities. Tribal and ethnic loyalties that sometimes cross the old European-drawn boundaries have also led to violent conflict in several regions.

The great majority of African nations are dependent on one or two primary exports, chiefly agricultural or mineral products, for much of their income. Their economies are thus subject to changes in world prices for these products. Falling prices, together with increases in the cost of vital imports, have forced many countries to reduce needed social and economic programs. Drought has caused the widespread failure of crops. Famine and civil strife in such countries as Ethiopia, Sudan, Liberia, Angola, and Rwanda have dislocated entire populations, caused the death of large numbers of people, and created a serious refugee problem.

Africans now make up more than one-quarter of the member nations of the United Nations and have an increasingly important voice in world affairs. They are asking for the cooperation of the international community, especially the more developed and prosperous nations, to help solve economic problems that affect not only Africa but much of the rest of the developing world as well.

DONALD J. BALLAS
Indiana University of Pennsylvania
Reviewed by HUGH C. BROOKS
Director, Center for African Studies
St. John's University (New York)
and L. GRAY COWAN
Director, Institute of African Studies
Columbia University

See also articles on individual African countries.

AFRICA, ART AND ARCHITECTURE OF

African art has developed from ancient traditions. Generations before the United States and the nations of Europe became great powers, Africa had known the rise and fall of many great kingdoms. The organization, discipline, laws, and religions of these ancient kingdoms show that Africa has been civilized for thousands of years.

The continent of Africa is often divided into two parts. To the north of the Sahara desert

Prehistoric rock paintings by the San people of southern Africa are the earliest existing examples of African art south of the Sahara desert.

are the peoples known as Arabs, living in such countries as Morocco, Algeria, and Egypt. The articles EGYPTIAN ART AND ARCHITECTURE and ISLAMIC ART AND ARCHITECTURE contain information on the arts of these peoples. This article discusses the arts of the peoples living south of the Sahara.

The land varies greatly across sub-Saharan Africa. Victoria Falls, in Zimbabwe, and snowcapped mountains such as Kilimanjaro are in sharp contrast to dry plains and tropical rain forests. The differences in physical environment produced many different kinds of cultures, each with a distinct artistic tradition.

▶THE FUNCTIONS OF AFRICAN ART

Much of the world's art was made for religious reasons, and African art is no exception.

Ancestor worship, spirits, magic, and other aspects of the religion of African peoples are reflected in their art. Art was also created for marriage ceremonies, for funerals, for honoring leaders, and for festive celebrations.

Nearly all African art has a function. Statues are carved to honor ancestors, kings, and gods. Masks are used in rituals surrounding boys' and girls' coming-of-age ceremonies, at funerals, and for entertainment. Jewelry, clothing, hairstyles, and body painting are sometimes used to signify wealth, power, and social status.

Carved figures are used to guard containers filled with sacred relics of ancestors. Combs, spoons, bowls, stools, and other useful items are elaborately carved and decorated. Objects are made with taste and skill, regardless of their function.

African art is not anonymous, but very few African artists are known by name. Most worked alone or in a workshop composed of a master and one or more apprentices. Because their work often consisted of replacing existing objects that had deteriorated, artists were obliged to conform to the ancient artistic laws. Yet despite these restrictions, African artists managed to express individual imagination and to employ new materials and techniques. If these innovations proved to make the art more effective, they became part of an ever-growing tradition.

▶BEGINNINGS

In prehistoric times, the nomadic San people (also called Bushmen) of southern Africa left many paintings and engravings in caves and on rock faces. These works portray human figures and animals as well as mythological symbols. They show men and women hunting, gathering food, dancing, and performing ritual activities.

Other early works of art are those of the Nok culture, which flourished in northern Nigeria from about 500 B.C. to A.D. 200. The modeled human and animal figures made of terra cotta (fired clay) that have been found in the region are the earliest known sculptures of sub-Saharan Africa. The heads of the figures are several times larger than the heads of real human beings. This is a stylistic convention that, with slight variations, can be observed in the art of most African peoples. Although we do not know why this convention was used in the Nok culture 2,000 years ago, in most African sculpture the head is emphasized because it is the most vital part of the body.

▶ SCULPTURE

Sculpture is Africa's greatest art. Wood is used far more than any other material. This means that much African art did not last, because wood is more easily destroyed than stone or metal. Because of this, there are some gaps in our knowledge of African art history.

An Early Tradition: Ifé and Benin

In the midwestern part of what is now Nigeria, two ancient kingdoms existed, Ifé and Benin. Artists in Ifé were casting metal sculpture by the A.D. 1000's. Archaeological evidence suggests that artists in Benin were casting metal

This cast-metal plaque is characteristic of the art of the kingdom of Benin. There, too, artists followed a tradition of naturalism, often depicting events at the royal court.

as early as the 1300's; their earliest metal sculptures date from the 1400's.

The cast-metal sculpture of Ifé and Benin was naturalistic; that is, the work of art resembled the actual object it was meant to represent. For subject matter the artists used animals, birds, people, and events at the royal court. Benin artists depicted Portuguese soldiers, merchants, and other foreigners who visited the kingdom. Artists also worked in ivory, especially at Benin, where elephant tusks were carved to honor deceased kings.

Ifé and Benin sculpture represents a very different tradition from that of most other African art. In its naturalism, it is closer than any other type of art in Africa to classical Western art.

Regional Styles

Most African sculpture originated in western and central Africa, a vast area containing three main cultural regions: the Western Sudan, the Guinea Coast, and Central Africa. Figure carving is rare in eastern and southern Africa, except among a few peoples in Kenya, Tanzania, and Madagascar.

Many different styles of sculpture exist in western and central Africa, and even within each cultural region. Some stylistic characteristics, however, are common to all the regions. In addition to the "head-heavy" proportions described above, these characteristics are simplified forms, balanced and symmetrical design, and unemotional facial expression. Although the form of a face or figure may be minimal, details are both precise and abundant. For example, figures may have intricately designed hairstyles and body adornments such as necklaces and bracelets.

Western Sudan. This region extends from Senegal through Chad, ranging from semi-desert to grassland to wooded savanna. Sculpted figures tend to be angular and elongated, and the facial features are only suggested. Many of these figures are used in religious rituals; they usually have dull or encrusted surfaces

including that of the Akan people—the Baule of Ivory Coast and the Asante of Ghana—and the Yoruba people of southwestern Nigeria, was made to honor leaders. Here gold and ivory as well as wood were used to make objects of value.

The royal arts of the small kingdoms in the grasslands area of central Cameroon are bold and expressive. Colorful beadwork is used to embellish carved wood thrones and figures. The face, hands, and feet of some sculpted figures are covered with molded sheet brass.

Central Africa consists of an enormous area that extends down the Atlantic coast from Equatorial Guinea to northern Angola and eastward through Zaïre.

In the Ogowe River basin region of Gabon, sculpted guardian figures are placed atop containers holding the sacred relics of deceased ancestors. Among the Kota people, guardian figures are flat metal-sheathed heads with minimal facial features set on lozenge-shaped bases. In contrast, those of the Fang people are single heads or complete figures that are more naturalistic in appearance.

The Kongo people predominate in the Lower Zaïre River basin. Their art displays a greater degree of naturalism than most African sculpture. Gesture and emotion are subtly indicated. Many figures depict a mother with a child on her lap. Because the Kongo were once part of a powerful kingdom, much of their art consists of items made for royalty.

from ceremonial offerings of millet gruel or other liquid substances that have been poured over them.

Guinea Coast. This region extends along the Atlantic Ocean from Guinea-Bissau through central Nigeria and Cameroon. It includes coastal rain forests and inland wooded grasslands. Sculpted figures from this cultural region tend to be shorter and more rounded than those from the Western Sudan region. Figures often have smooth, luminous surfaces. Much art from the central part of the region,

Most African sculpture has simplified forms and a balanced design. *Top:* A terra cotta figure of a horse and rider from Mali has an elongated shape typical of sculpture from the Western Sudan region. *Far left:* A wood sculpture of a mother and child was made by the Yoruba people of Nigeria. *Left:* Much African art serves a practical purpose: In this Luba wood sculpture from Zaïre, "twin" female figures form the support for a headrest.

The Kuba and the Hemba are only two peoples among hundreds in Zaïre who have important sculptural traditions. Kuba figure sculpture portrays ancestral kings seated cross-legged. Standing Hemba figures are rounded naturalistic forms that serve to commemorate ancestors.

Eastern and Southern Africa. This cultural region extends south along the southern Atlantic coast and around South Africa to Ethiopia. Here, in Botswana and Namibia, are found the ancient rock paintings attributed to the San people of the Kalahari Desert. Figure carving is rare in this region. Instead, the arts of personal adornment, including body painting, and of decorating useful objects, such as headrests, spoons, and stools, are very highly developed. In Ethiopia, the art of the highlands reflects the influence of Christianity, which was introduced there in the A.D. 300's. Non-Christian Ethiopians created figurative carvings for use in their own religious worship.

▶ MASKS

Masks are supports for spirits, which according to traditional beliefs are found in nature and in humans and animals. Some spirits are gods. Masks perform a variety of functions: They may be used in rites marking the transition from childhood to adulthood, to enforce the laws of society, to cause rain to fall during periods of drought, and to celebrate gods and ancestors.

Masks are usually worn as disguises, along with a full costume of leaves or cloth, but they are sometimes used for display. They are used in masquerades, which may be performed publicly or secretly. Generally music and dance are part of the event. Although masks may represent male or female spirits, they are almost always worn by men. During the performance, a masked dancer is no longer himself, but the spirit the mask represents.

Face masks are only one type of mask. There are also helmet, or "bucket," masks,

Masks serve a variety of important functions in African society, and distinctive styles of mask making have arisen in different regions. *Left:* A two-faced mask of painted wood was made by the Fang people of Gabon. *Above:* A painted-wood and fiber mask made by the Kuba people of Zaïre is decorated with paint, beads, and shells. *Right:* A wooden mask made by the Songe people of Zaïre is covered with a pattern of finely cut lines.

A wood, iron, and fiber headdress made by the Bamana people of Mali is worn on top of the head.

covering all or half of the head, and crest masks, worn on top of the head. Masks are made from a variety of materials. They may be carved of wood and painted with pigments made from plants or minerals. They may be decorated with animal skins, feathers, or beads. Artists also make masks out of paint fibers, tree bark, metal, or other materials.

▶DECORATIVE ARTS

Goldwork

For centuries, African goldsmiths have used different techniques to create gold objects. They can cast solid forms, hammer gold into shapes, or press thin pieces of gold (gold leaf) onto ready-made objects.

Goldwork prevailed in areas of Africa where gold was mined and used for trade. Gold mines were located in the modern nations of Senegal, Mali, Ivory Coast, and Ghana. Ghana was so famous for its gold that it was once called the Gold Coast. A rare and expensive material, gold was used as currency and worn by kings and important religious and political officials. It was also used to make jewelry and other body ornaments, as well as to decorate weapons.

The Akan people of Ivory Coast and Ghana used metal counterweights to weigh gold dust, which was the local currency from the 1400's to the mid-1800's. Called goldweights, the counterweights were actually miniature sculptures made of cast bronze or brass. They depict animals, plants, human beings, objects, and scenes from everyday life.

Jewelry

Men, women, and children wear jewelry to decorate their bodies or as a badge of distinction. Jewelry includes a variety of objects: hair ornaments, necklaces, earrings, bracelets, rings, and anklets. Artists make jewelry from many different materials. These include gold, silver, brass, iron, and copper, carved ivory, and beads made of glass, amber, stone, or shells.

Textiles

Textiles are woven on looms by both men and women. Locally grown cotton, raffia palm, and a woody fiber called bast are the most commonly used fibers, but silk and wool are also woven.

Among the Kuba of Zaïre, men and women work together to make cloth. First, men weave raffia into square or rectangular pieces. Next, the women embroider designs on the cloth with raffia thread. They can also create a cut-pile effect that resembles velvet. Although Africans commonly wear Western-style clothing, traditional apparel made from locally woven cloth is the proud national dress. Thus weaving remains a vital occupation in many parts of Africa.

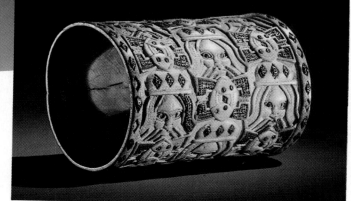

Above: In gold-mining areas of western Africa, small weights such as this were used to weigh gold dust. *Right:* A carved ivory bracelet from the court of Benin.

The skill of African artisans can be seen in the beauty of everyday objects. *Far left:* A woven cotton rug from Sierra Leone has a geometric design. Textiles are woven by both men and women. *Left:* A terra cotta vessel from central Africa. Most African pottery is made by women.

Textile artists create patterns on textiles using various techniques, including weaving, dyeing, stamping, painting, embroidery, and appliqué. Patterns may be plain or extremely intricate, consisting of geometric forms or figures such as animals and birds. Materials such as metallic or glossy threads may be incorporated to enhance the design. Natural or imported dyes are used to color the cloth.

Pottery

Pottery is usually crafted by women, who have made vessels in different sizes and shapes for cooking, storing, and serving food and drink since time beyond memory. The smooth, symmetrical vessels are hand-formed; the mechanical potter's wheel has been introduced only recently.

Potters create designs on the surface of the vessel by burnishing it with a smooth pebble, by cutting lines in with a blade, or by making impressions with combs and other objects. The surface may also be decorated with slip, a thin wash of clay, in a different color than the clay of the vessel. The vessels are fired in the open and may be dipped in a vegetable solution to seal them. Because they are fired at low temperatures, African vessels made by traditional methods do not shatter when used over an open fire.

Some vessels are used for religious rituals or for display as works of art. Such vessels are decorated with modeled figures and are usually made by especially skilled potters.

Basketry

Like pottery and weaving, basketry is a very old craft that is practiced by both men and women. Baskets are essential household objects, used for storage, for preparing or serving food, and for carrying objects.

The techniques and materials used to make baskets are determined by how the basket will be used. There are three basic techniques: coiling, twining, and plaiting (braiding). Vegetable fibers, such as grasses and raffia, are the main materials used. Leather, wood, or other materials may be added for both decoration and strengthening.

▶ PAINTING

Although easel painting was introduced only at the beginning of the 1900's, Africans have always painted. The most ancient evidence is in the prehistoric San rock paintings in southern Africa. In Christian Ethiopia, artists illustrated Bible stories in books, on scrolls, and later on canvas.

African artists have always used paint to decorate surfaces. People painted their bodies when they participated in religious or social rituals and ceremonies, or simply to make themselves more attractive. They have traditionally painted the internal and external walls of their houses and places of worship. Sculpted figures and masks were also painted.

Until European paints were introduced, artists obtained their colors from natural sources, including clay, plant leaves and roots, stones, and minerals.

ARCHITECTURE

A wide range of architectural forms can be found in Africa. The simplest houses are the beehive-shaped houses of the Pygmies of central Africa. The frames of such houses are constructed with flexible branches that are covered with large, fresh leaves. This type of temporary housing suits the Pygmies' nomadic way of life. Agricultural people, in contrast, require sturdy, permanent houses.

Houses may be built with thick mud walls or with sturdy bamboo frames. Roofs may be thatched or covered with corrugated metal. The spacious Islamic mosques in Mali are perhaps the most dramatic example of mud architecture. The royal palaces of the Cameroon grassfields, some of which reach heights of more than 25 feet, are outstanding examples of bamboo-frame structures.

The most noteworthy stone architecture is the complex of buildings constructed during the 1100's to the 1400's at the ancient city of Great Zimbabwe in southern Africa. It is

CONTEMPORARY TRENDS

The traditional art of Africa has had a great impact on modern art. In the early 1900's, European artists came into increased contact with the art of Africa. Artists such as Pablo Picasso and Henri Matisse incorporated elements of African art into their works.

Contemporary Africans create art in a variety of styles. In some societies, traditional religion and social practices have prevailed (usually with modern modifications), and there is a need for sculptors to create masks for initiations and sculptures for shrines, much as their predecessors did. However, they may use modern innovations such as imported paints. Sign painters, graphic artists, photographers, and textile and fashion designers also are part of the contemporary visual art scene.

Some artists are like their counterparts in Europe and America. They are self-taught or trained at universities and art schools. They display their art at exhibitions in art galleries and museums at home and abroad, and have

A wide variety of architecture can be found in Africa. The Ndebele people of southern Africa have traditionally painted the clay walls of their houses with striking geometric designs. Inside walls may also be decorated with painted designs.

remarkable because of its great size and because the stone walls were assembled without mortar.

Important buildings are ornamented with carved and painted doors, door frames, and posts to support the veranda roofs. Kings and other sponsors of elaborate architecture often brought specially skilled sculptors from great distances to work for them.

local and foreign patrons. The content of their art may be African or not; it may be realistic or non-representational—the choice is theirs. The African art that caused a revolution in Western art early in the 1900's continues to inspire artists all over the world, including those born in Africa.

ROSLYN WALKER
Curator, National Museum of African Art

Storytellers play a key role in traditional African society. The stories they perform dramatize important truths, teach moral lessons, and transmit the history of the community. For many years, these stories were not written down but were passed on from one generation to the next by word of mouth. This oral tradition is a vital part of African literature.

AFRICA, LITERATURE OF

This article concerns both the oral traditions and the written literature of the peoples of Africa. While literature is generally considered to be a written body of work, it can also be defined more broadly. This fact is of special significance when discussing the nonwritten oral tradition by which Africans transmit history, culture, and duty from one generation to the next.

▶THE ORAL TRADITION (ORATURE)

In many parts of Africa, the spoken word is considered to be much more powerful than the written word. For centuries, a great deal of the traditional literature of Africa was not written down. It was performed, and passed on by word of mouth. That is why an African philosopher once said, "Whenever an old man dies, it is as though a library had been burned to the ground."

(It should be noted, however, that not all of Africa's literature was of the oral tradition alone. Throughout the many dynasties and civilizations along the Nile River, written literature flourished for centuries and continues to be written in Ethiopia today.)

In recent years, a major debate has taken place among scholars of African literature as to whether the term "literature" should be used to define the oral tradition. The term **orature** emerged from the debate, giving the spoken tradition its own name. African orature serves an important social, religious, and educational purpose. The truths by which the people have always lived are dramatized, providing valuable lessons for social behavior.

The performer or storyteller relies on common experience and shared tradition. As he tells the story to his audience, he also acts out the narrative by means of gestures, facial expressions, body movement, mime, voice modulation, song, and dance. The members of the audience understand according to their ages and social circumstances. A story may mean one thing to the teller, another to the adults, and still another to the children. Everyone learns something from the performance. The good storyteller makes certain that learning takes place by punctuating his performance with proverbs that underscore the social value of the story.

In Africa the spoken word is an art and a celebration of life, to be shared by all who live in the community. Like life, this art constantly changes. When a story is repeated, it will be different because it will have been adapted to the changes in society. The ancestral wisdom, however, is not lost in the changed version. It, too, will have been adapted to the circumstances of the changed times. The actively participating audience, joining in singing and clapping, will be different, too. Each listener will be older and wiser than the last time. In this way, the past and the present remain harmoniously linked in a balanced expression of culture and duty.

Although most people in African society are capable of storytelling, not everyone becomes an expert performer in public. Those who do must be specially trained in the art of eloquence and must learn to sing and play one or more musical instruments because of the importance of music to the oral tradition.

▶FORMS OF THE ORAL TRADITION

Although there are many different forms of orature in Africa, they all share certain themes. Universal traits of human behavior—honesty and dishonesty, charity and greed, bravery and cowardice, wisdom and foolishness—are exposed and examined. The main forms of orature are proverbs, riddles, folktales, poetry, and epics.

Proverbs and Riddles. Proverbs are extremely popular and are used in almost every kind of situation. They are short and witty and are treasured by Africans for the traditional wisdom and universal truths contained in them.

Riddles are commonly used to set the mood for performances and are especially popular with children, who are encouraged to use them to sharpen their wits. Like proverbs, riddles are usually short. Their language is poetic and indirect, relying on metaphor (a way of suggesting a likeness between two objects or ideas) as well as on subtleties of sound, rhythm, and tone. Some examples of African proverbs and riddles are given below.

Proverbs

Sierra Leone: If you climb up a tree, you must climb down the same tree.

Ghana: Only when you have crossed the river can you say the crocodile has a lump on his snout.

Ashanti: The ruin of a nation begins in the homes of its people.

Ethiopia: A fool and water go the way they are diverted.

Riddles

What talks a lot when going, but is silent when coming back? Answer: water gourds. Empty gourds rattle together—"talk"—on the way to be filled. Full gourds do not rattle.

What darts about all day and rests behind a gate of straw at night? Answer: the eye. The straw refers to the eyelashes.

Folktales. Short oral narratives commonly referred to as folktales are told in nearly all societies in Africa. They are used to teach moral lessons, expose trickery, promote heroic behavior, and tell about how or why things came to be. Or they may present a dilemma, challenging the listener to make a choice between two or more equally deserving arguments. Folktales can be purely fictional, or they can be based on real events of the past.

The main characters in fictional folktales are usually **tricksters**—small and normally weak characters endowed with cleverness, cunning, and resourcefulness, which they use to outwit their adversaries. Because they are always motivated by greed and selfishness, tricksters sometimes become the victims of their own excesses.

Trickster characters are usually animals but are sometimes human or part human. Gods may also be used as trickster characters. For example, among the Yoruba people of Nigeria, the god Elegba is the trickster. In Sudan, the clever hare is the subject of these stories. Anansi the spider is the greedy trickster from Ghana, Liberia, and Sierra Leone. In Nigeria and Cameroon, the tortoise is the mischievous hero. The Ethiopian tricksters are Totta the monkey and Koora the crow.

Some of the trickster characters were brought to the Americas by Africans. Anansi stories are still popular in Jamaica, Belize, and Suriname, and the clever hare has become Brer Rabbit in the United States.

Poetry. Poetry is one of the oldest, most highly developed, and most widespread of African oral traditions. It has many forms and is used for a variety of purposes—for religious and sacred practices as well as for such secular (nonreligious) events as birth and marriage celebrations. There is also lyric poetry, political poetry, satirical poetry, and drum poetry.

The practice of poetry requires formal training in the language, history, culture, and music of the society. Performers of poetry are usually identified with a specific social group. In Mali, these performers are called *djeli*; in eastern Zaïre, they are called *karisi*. The Zulu of South Africa call them *imbongi*. The bards, or heroic singers, of Cameroon and Gabon bear the same name as the instrument they play and the type of tale they recite: *mvet*. In Ethiopia, performers called *amina* tell stories in the form of couplets.

Epics. The epic, a major part of Africa's oral tradition, is found mainly in western and central Africa and, to a lesser extent, in eastern and southern Africa. An epic is a long poem that tells about the fantastic deeds of a legendary hero. Often it weaves the ideals and traditions of a people into the story. It is usually narrated to a musical accompaniment.

Sundiata is the national epic of the Malinke people of Mali. It honors the founder of the Mali empire. *Lianja* tells the fabulous story of the epic hero of the Mongo people of Zaïre. Liyongo, the spear lord, gives his name to an epic sung in the languages of eastern and central Africa. These are only three of the many epics of Africa.

▶**AFRICAN LITERATURE IN EUROPEAN LANGUAGES**

During the colonial period, beginning in the 1700's, Europeans introduced their own written languages as tools of power, education, and government. Different peoples with different languages and cultures were grouped together in the various colonial territories. When these territories became independent, choosing one official African language proved difficult. Thus most of the new African states retained the language of their former colonizers as their official language.

The written translation of orature into these foreign languages was natural and inevitable. And as it gains recognition and popularity, orature is being written and translated into more of the major languages of the world. This rapid shift from the oral to the written tradition carries with it the danger that young Africans may choose not to become performers of orature. The risk of losing the tradition, under these circumstances, is quite real.

Learning to write the European languages also produced a new literature: short stories, poems, and novels that were never meant to be recited and plays that were meant to be performed on a stage rather than in a traditional African setting.

Some of these literary forms have been explored by African writers in their own languages. But those who write in English, French, or Portuguese can expect to have more readers. For this reason most recent African literature has been written in these languages. Ethiopia is an exception; written literature in the Ge'ez script has been practiced there for

The famous storyteller (*djeli*, or griot) of Mali, *Djeli* Mamoudou Kouyate, describes his position and role in society just before recounting the great *Sundiata* epic:

I am a griot. It is I, *Djeli* Mamoudou Kouyate, son of Bintu Kouyate and *Djeli* Kedian Kouyate, master in the art of eloquence. Since time immemorial the Kouyates have been in the service of the Keita princes of Mali; we are vessels of speech, we are the repositories which harbour secrets many centuries old. The art of eloquence has no secrets for us; without us the names of kings would vanish into oblivion, we are the memory of mankind. I teach kings the history of their ancestors so that the lives of the ancients might serve them as an example, for the world is old, but the future springs from the past. My word is pure and free of all untruth; it is the word of my father; it is the word of my father's father. . . .

centuries, together with an oral tradition. An example is the epic story of Solomon and Mequeda, Queen of Sheba, which has also been translated into European languages.

African writing in French developed primarily in the regions of western and central Africa once occupied by the French. African literature in English comes from countries in eastern, western, and southern Africa where, for a time, English-speaking people ruled. Portuguese is used in Mozambique and Angola, former colonies of Portugal.

The Negritude Movement. Beginning in the 1930's, some African writers writing in French launched a literary movement known as negritude. Aimé Césaire, a West Indian from the island of Martinique, was the first to use the word. Césaire had been influenced by the African American literary movement of the 1920's known as the Harlem Renaissance. In his greatest poem, *Return to My Native Land* (1939), he defined negritude as a celebration of blackness.

Césaire's friend Léopold Sédar Senghor became the president of Senegal and one of the major writers of his generation. Senghor defined negritude as the cultural heritage, values, and spirit of black African civilization.

The negritude movement also expressed anger. It attacked the white world for racism, for concern with wealth and material things, and for pretending one thing but being another. This anger may be seen in the novels of Ferdinand Oyono from Cameroon, especially in *Houseboy*, the story of an African servant in a white household.

Other writers of the negritude movement include poet Tchicaya U Tam'si of the Congo and novelist Camara Laye of Guinea.

Other Views. Wole Soyinka, a Nobel Prize-winning Nigerian playwright, expressed a different view. Soyinka wrote *A Dance of the Forests* for the celebration of Nigerian independence in 1960. This play is a fantasy in which traditional gods and spirits call up a group of ancestors to accuse them of participating in the European slave trade. "Do not romanticize old Africa," the play is saying.

This no-nonsense attitude is shared by Ezekiel Mphahlele, a South African writer, and by most Africans writing in English. To them, Senghor's idea of traditional African life is unrealistic.

The Nigerian novelist Chinua Achebe has recorded the strife within the traditional African community. He says it is useless to deny social change; the problem is how to meet it. His novels *Things Fall Apart* (1958) and *Arrow of God* (1964) ask whether modern Nigerian leaders can develop the strength of character of certain old chiefs and priests who resisted European ways.

The terrible experience under colonialism and the struggle for independence provided substantial material for African novelists and poets of the new literature. In South Africa, in particular, the new literature played an extremely important role in expressing the Africans' feelings in their struggle against apartheid. But censorship and persecution forced many black writers, such as the poet Dennis Brutus, to flee the country. White South African writers, too, voiced their objections to apartheid. Among the best known of these writers are Alan Paton, Athol Fugard, and Nadine Gordimer.

Women in African Literature. Traditionally, the position of women in orature was secondary to that of men. The early stages of the new African literature also tended to be male-dominated. Recently, however, many women novelists and poets, as well as feminist scholars and literary critics, have emerged. Notable women writers include Ama Ata Aidoo of Ghana, Buchi Emecheta of Nigeria, Martha Mvungi of Tanzania, Grace Ogot of Kenya, Bessie Head of South Africa, and Kebedech Tekleab of Ethiopia.

▶**FILM**

Filmmaking came to Africa after independence in the 1960's. Film, more than written literature, was ideally suited to accommodate the performance aspects of orature. As filmmaking in Africa gained momentum, so did the search for stories suitable for film. Both filmmakers and writers soon turned to the rich oral tradition for their material. As a result, many of the leading African films are patterned after the traditional epics and other forms of orature.

For these reasons, and because they are seen by a great number of people, African films play an important role in keeping the oral tradition alive in modern times.

Some examples of major African films include *Heritage Africa* by Qua Ansa of Ghana, *Yeelen* by Souleymane Cisse of Mali, and *Sarraounia* by Med Hondo of Mauritania. In addition, important writers such as Kenya's Ngugi wa Thiongo and Nigeria's Wole Soyinka have tried their hands at filmmaking.

The number of African filmmakers is growing steadily, along with that of novelists, poets, and playwrights. The work of all these artists constitutes a major contribution to the richness of world literature. African orature and modern literature tell about a world many people of the West have never visited, or even imagined correctly. It is a world that is well worth getting to know.

ABIYI R. FORD
School of Communications
Howard University

The traditional music of Africa is celebrated for its richness and diversity. *Clockwise from upper left:* Percussion instruments such as drums and xylophones are the most common African instruments. However, traditional instruments also include wind instruments such as this wooden horn as well as a variety of stringed instruments.

AFRICA, MUSIC OF

Africans perform and listen to all types of music—popular, classical, and traditional. Traditional music has its roots in the soil of Africa and is extremely diverse: There are more than 700 different languages and ethnic groups in Africa, and each is associated with a particular kind of music.

At one time, scholars assumed that all African music was the same and that it rarely changed. We now know that traditional African music has been changing for centuries. Many changes occurred even before Europeans and other outsiders visited Africa. When people come in contact with each other, through trade, war, or other circumstances, musical ideas are often exchanged. For example, the Asante people of Ghana in western Africa adopted the *donno*, a type of talking drum, from people who lived north of them.

The physical environment, occupation, and social structure of the people also affect their music making. For example, the Khoisan people (also known as Bushmen) of southern Africa used to be nomadic—constantly moving from place to place to hunt and gather foods. Clans of twenty to fifty people lived together as equals, with no political leaders. The Khoisan used few musical instruments; singing was their main form of music making. While the women and girls sang and clapped their hands, the men danced and played drums.

The music of the Baganda people of Uganda, on the other hand, developed in a very different way. In earlier times, their kingdom was one of the largest in eastern Africa. The king's court included several musicians, who played a variety of instruments—drums, trumpets, flutes, harps, lyres, drum-chimes, and xylophones—for the king's private enjoyment and for official activities. Other musicians performed at community events and ceremonies.

▶ MUSIC IN AFRICAN LIFE

Africans perform music when they come together for leisure and recreation. They also use music at religious ceremonies, festivals, and work. Music plays an important role at birth, initiation, wedding, and funeral ceremonies. Songs performed at some events help people remember their history and customs.

In many parts of Africa, adults take their children to special camps for initiation ceremonies. There the elders teach the girls and boys what they need to know about adulthood. The girls learn lullabies as part of child-care training. The boys learn historical songs to teach them the customs of their society. Through music, children may also learn about numbers and language, as well as singing and dancing techniques.

Some musicians in Africa are specialists who receive formal training from a family member or a professional musician. But music is a vital part of everyday life for all Africans. Everyone participates in a performance by dancing, singing, handclapping, or playing a musical instrument. Mothers train their children when they are infants by rocking them to music and singing songs. Among the Fon people in western Africa, children who lose their first tooth have to sing a special song to commemorate the event. Children also learn music by playing games and telling stories.

In many African communities, musicians are admired and respected for the service they perform for the community. But some people believe musicians are lazy because they spend all their time making music. Also, through their music, musicians sometimes warn and criticize people about unacceptable behavior, and this can make them unpopular. However, most people believe that musicians play an important role in society.

▶ **INSTRUMENTS**

Africans perform music on a wide variety of percussion, stringed, and wind instruments.

Percussion Instruments are the most common instruments in Africa. Societies that do not use drums may perform on rattles, bells, sticks, clappers, and stamping tubes.

Percussion instruments are mainly used for rhythm, but some also play melodies. For example, the xylophone has wooden keys of various sizes, which produce different tones when struck with a stick. The Chopi people of eastern Africa include as many as 13 xylophones in ensembles that also include drums, rattles, and whistles. While some of the xylophone musicians play the main melody, others play a supporting repetitive part.

Drums come in a variety of sizes and shapes. Some are small and held in the hand; others are large and are placed on the ground when played. To produce a sound, musicians strike the drum head with sticks, hands, or both. Sometimes the musician scrapes or rubs the drum head with a stick to produce a sound. The Akan-speaking people of Ghana play a drum called *etwie* in honor of their king. The drum is made of wood and covered with the skin of a leopard. When the drum head is rubbed with a stick, the sound that is produced imitates the sound of the leopard. By reproducing the sound of a feared and powerful animal, *etwie* music symbolizes and praises the might and majesty of the king.

Stringed Instruments include musical bows, harps, zithers, lyres, and lutes. The musical bow is the most common stringed instrument in Africa. It has only one string, which is plucked or struck. Harps and zithers are common in eastern and central Africa; eastern Africa is also the primary location for lyres. The lute is found in societies influenced by Arab culture. Lutes can be bowed like a fiddle or plucked like a banjo. The *kora*, a 21-string harp lute, is prominent among the Mandinka people. The *kora* looks like a lute but is played like a harp.

The Talking Drum

Some of the most interesting African drums are known as talking drums because they imitate the tones of African languages. One type of talking drum is the hourglass pressure drum, such as the *dùndún* played by the Yoruba people of Nigeria. It consists of two drum heads connected by cords on an hourglass-shaped frame. The drum is held at the performer's side under the arm. When the cords are pressed by the arm, the drum heads are stretched and the pitch of the drum is raised. Changing the pressure on the cords changes the pitch of the sound produced when the drum head is struck.

Wind Instruments include flutes, reed pipes, horns, and trumpets. The flute is the most widespread. Flutes can be made of wood, bamboo, clay, or other materials and can have as many as seven finger holes. They are played vertically or horizontally. The reed pipe, like the lute, is located in areas influenced by Arab culture. Horns and trumpets are made of animal horns and tusks, wood, gourd, or bamboo and can be either end-blown or side-blown.

▶ CHARACTERISTICS

Singing is the most characteristic way of performing African music. Although people sing solos, singing in a group is more common. Often, one person leads a song and a group of singers responds by repeating the same theme or a variation. This arrangement is sometimes called call and response.

Language or speech serves as the basis for most African melodies and rhythms. Many African languages are **tone languages**, meaning that the pitch on which a word or a syllable is spoken determines its meaning. The high and low sounds of the rhythms played on African talking drums correspond closely to speech. In earlier times, such "talking" instruments informed African people about current events.

In an African performance, music, dance, song, and drama are all important. Although musicians include a variety of musical sounds in their ensembles, percussion is essential. The Ewe people of Ghana include singing, handclapping, rattles, bells, and four or five drums in their ensembles. The bell players perform a repetitive rhythm that serves as the base for all other parts. Some of the drummers and other musicians perform a different repetitive pattern. The leader of the group, playing the largest drum or drums, does not play a repetitive rhythm but **improvises**—spontaneously creates different but related music. When everyone performs the various rhythms and melodies together, this is called **polyphony**. African music is interesting not because of the individual parts that each person plays. Rather, Africans enjoy hearing how the parts interrelate and communicate with each other.

▶ INFLUENCES

Much of today's popular music contains African elements. This is because African Americans have greatly influenced music

The Mbira

One of the most distinctive African instruments is a small percussion instrument called the *mbira* (also known as the *kalimba*, *sanza*, or thumb piano). Rarely found in other parts of the world, it consists of a wooden board or box over which several tongues of metal or bamboo are fastened. When the tongues are plucked (usually with the thumbs), soft sounds are produced. The sound can be modified by wrapping wire around the tongues to produce a buzzing effect, or by attaching a hollow gourd to make the sound resonate (vibrate and grow louder). Many African musicians play the *mbira* as a solo instrument or to accompany singing. Several *mbira* can also be played together in an ensemble, with singing and rattle accompaniment.

throughout the world. When Europeans took Africans as slaves to the Americas, Africans remembered much about the music they performed in Africa. Those in the West Indies and various parts of Central and South America continued to worship African gods and play African instruments.

In the United States, most slaves could not openly practice their African traditions. Slave-owners outlawed drums and other loud instruments when they discovered that slaves could use them to communicate. Instead of playing drums, slaves patted different parts of the body or used handclapping or foot-stomping to make music. When they sang songs, they performed them differently from European Americans. They used a different vocal quality and added bends and slurs to the melody. Also, they created their own songs and styles of music. Spirituals, blues, jazz, gospel, and other forms of popular music come from the integration of African and European elements.

Music from the United States, Europe, and Asia has influenced musicians in modern Africa. Highlife, juju, and soukous are a few of the new forms of popular music that one can hear in dance halls and nightclubs in Africa. Musicians now create new hymns for the church. Also, Africans have begun to compose their own style of classical music. Along with traditional music, each of these types of music plays an important role among the people who live in various cities, towns, and villages throughout Africa.

JACQUELINE COGDELL DJEDJE
University of California, Los Angeles

From left to right: Kathy E. Morris Wilkerson, New Orleans' first female firefighter. NBA All-Star Kevin Johnson takes time out to play with a group of young friends. Dr. James W. Mitchell, Director of Analytical Chemistry at AT&T Bell Laboratories. Farmworkers pick peppers near Atchafalaya, Louisiana.

AFRICAN AMERICANS

African Americans are citizens of the United States who trace at least part of their ancestry to the continent of Africa. Although some are recent immigrants, most are descended from Africans who were brought in slavery to the American colonies and states between the years 1619 and 1808. Today African Americans number approximately 30 million, or 12 percent of the total United States population. The largest communities reside in the states in the Deep South, followed by those in the Northeast, Midwest, and West.

Over the centuries, African Americans have been known by a succession of names. Many of these name changes reflected the African Americans' desire to establish a distinctive identity and to express their pride in their racial heritage. Until the early 1800's, the preferred name was simply African. Later the terms black, colored, and Negro (the Spanish word for "black") came into use. After the 1960's, the terms Negro and colored were largely abandoned in favor of black and Afro-American. Since the late 1980's, the term African American has been preferred.

The African heritage in North America, which dates as far back as any other except Native American, has greatly influenced the American culture through the centuries. African roots are evident in the distinctive African American styles of clothing and adornment, in cooking, and in modern dance. They also are found in African American literature and in orature, or oral history, passed down through the generations, that tell of stories of the African American experience.

Perhaps the strongest influence, however, is found in music, an art form that has always been central to the daily lives of most Africans. African roots can be found in nearly every American music form, from the early spirituals and the gospel singing of religious celebration to rhythm and blues, soul, rock and roll, rap, and the most uniquely American music form of all—jazz.

Today, in music as well as all other forms of mass popular culture, African Americans are more influential than ever. The better part of black creative expression has been directed toward widening the nation's perceptions and understanding of African Americans and their values.

▶OVERVIEW

For three hundred years, European colonists brought Africans to the New World as slaves

A strong antislavery movement helped set the stage for the United States Civil War (1861–65) between the free states in the North and the slave states in the South. Emancipation, or freedom, for the slaves was assured in 1865 by the 13th Amendment to the U.S. Constitution after the North defeated the South.

to clear vast tracts of land for the cultivation of sugar, rice, cotton, and tobacco. The black community in what is now the United States began in 1619 at Jamestown, Virginia, where 20 Africans were traded for water and supplies by Dutch seamen on their way from New York to Suriname, South America. Historians are divided on the issue of whether or not these particular immigrants were slaves or indentured servants (people who were contracted to work for a specific period of time in exchange for voyage costs, food, and lodging). One thing is certain: At least 1 million Africans became unwilling travelers to North America before the United States outlawed the importation of slaves in 1808.

Much of African American history is based on the blacks' struggle to achieve the equality and unalienable rights promised by the founders of a democratic government. In 1776, Thomas Jefferson wrote in the Declaration of Independence, "We hold these truths to be self-evident, that all men are created equal, that they are endowed by their Creator with certain unalienable Rights, that among these are Life, Liberty, and the pursuit of Happiness." Frederick Douglass, an ex-slave and the most prominent black abolitionist of the mid-1800's, challenged this notion of democracy when he declared to the white community, "The rich inheritance of justice, liberty, prosperity, and independence, bequeathed by your fathers, is shared by you, not by me."

But it was not until the ratification of the 14th Amendment (1868) that African Americans were declared citizens in the land of their birth. The 15th Amendment (1870) assured African American men their right to vote.

Slavery had encouraged a false assumption that blacks were inferior to whites. Despite emancipation, discrimination against blacks continued to deprive African Americans of their legal rights well into the 1900's. Fundamental democratic privileges, such as the right to vote, were routinely denied them, and they were set apart from mainstream society by laws designed to keep the races socially separate and politically unequal. Their frustrations finally erupted in a civil rights movement in the 1950's and 1960's, when African Americans began demanding their proper and equal place in society.

The modern-day historian John Hope Franklin has noted, "With an optimism born in hope when only despair was in view," African Americans struggled for equal status "in the land that [African American author] James Weldon Johnson reminded them was theirs by right of birth and by right of toil."

1624 William Tucker, born in Jamestown, Virginia, is believed to have been the first African American born in what is now the United States.

1770 Crispus Attucks, an American patriot, was killed by British troops in the Boston Massacre. He was the first-known African American to die in the American revolutionary movement.

1821 Thomas L. Jennings, a New York tailor, was the first black to receive a U.S. patent, for inventing a dry-cleaning process.

1827 *Freedom's Journal*, the first African American newspaper, was published by co-editors John B. Russwurm and Charles B. Ray, in New York City.

1853 *Clotel: A Tale of the Southern States*, written by William Wells Brown, was the first-known novel written by an African American.

1865 John S. Rock became the first African American lawyer allowed to practice law in the U.S. Supreme Court.

1868 John Willis Menard, the first African American elected to the U.S. Congress, was not permitted to take his seat in the U.S. House of Representatives.

1870 Hiram Rhoades Revels became the first African American to serve in the U.S. Senate; Joseph Hayne Rainey was the first to win election and be seated in the U.S. House of Representatives.

1872 Pinckney Benton Stewart Pinchback, the lieutenant governor of Louisiana, became the first African American elevated to the position of governor.

1893 Dr. Daniel Hale Williams performed the world's first successful heart operation.

1903 Maggie Walker founded the St. Luke Penny Thrift Savings Bank in Richmond, Virginia, becoming the first African American woman to head a bank.

1940 Benjamin O. Davis, Sr., became the first black brigadier general in the U.S. Army.

1940 Hattie McDaniel became the first African American to win an Academy Award for her supporting role in *Gone With the Wind*.

1949 Jackie Robinson of the Brooklyn Dodgers was the first African American to be named Most Valuable Player.

1950 Gwendolyn Brooks became the first African American to win a Pulitzer Prize, for her volume of poetry *Annie Allen*.

1950 Ralph Bunche became the first African American to win the Nobel Peace Prize.

1955 Marian Anderson became the first African American soloist to perform with the Metropolitan Opera in New York City.

1957 Althea Gibson became the first African American tennis player to win a singles championship at Wimbledon, in England.

1962 Mal Goode became the first African American television news correspondent.

1966 Constance Baker Motley became the first African American woman to serve as a federal judge.

1966 Robert C. Weaver became the first African American appointed to a cabinet position, as secretary of the Department of Housing and Urban Development.

1966 Edward W. Brooke, a Republican from Massachusetts, became the first African American elected to the U.S. Senate since the Reconstruction period.

1967 Thurgood Marshall became the first African American appointed to the U.S. Supreme Court.

1967 Carl Stokes, a Democrat, was elected mayor of Cleveland, the first African American to govern a major city.

1968 Shirley Chisholm, a Democrat from New York, became the first African American woman elected to the U.S. House of Representatives.

1975 Daniel "Chappie" James became the first African American four-star general (in the U.S. Air Force).

1975 Virginia Hamilton became the first African American to win a Newbery Medal, for her novel *M.C. Higgins, the Great* (1974).

1977 Patricia R. Harris became the first African American woman appointed to a president's cabinet, as secretary of Housing and Urban Development.

1983 Guion S. Bluford, Jr., became the first African American astronaut to make a spaceflight.

1989 The Reverend Barbara L. Harris, an African American Episcopalian priest, became the first female bishop consecrated by the worldwide Anglican community.

1989 General Colin L. Powell was the first African American named chairman of the Joint Chiefs of Staff, the nation's highest military office.

1990 Walter E. Massey became the first African American executive director of the National Science Foundation.

1990 L. Douglas Wilder, a Democrat, became the first African American elected governor of a state (Virginia).

1992 Mae C. Jemison, M.D., became the first African American woman to make a spaceflight.

1992 Carole Moseley Braun, a Democrat from Illinois, became the first African American woman elected to the U.S. Senate.

1993 Toni Morrison became the first African American to win the Nobel Prize for literature.

Taurian Osborne attending the New Fellowship Missionary Baptist Church in Miami, Florida.

THE ROLE OF THE CHURCH

When Africans were first brought to America, they were forced to abandon their native religions and were taught Christianity. Many embraced the new faith, finding spiritual comfort and hope. In the late 1700's, black churches started to form, and many became centers of African American community life. Their music—spirituals and rousing gospel songs—has since become part of the American musical tradition.

Many black churches led the fight against discrimination, and throughout their history, African Americans have often chosen their leaders from the ranks of the church.

In the 1960's the Nation of Islam challenged the black churches, claiming that Islam is the true religion of African peoples. But most worshipers have remained with the Christian churches, which continue to play an important role in many African American communities.

THE AFRICAN PAST

From the ancient civilization of Egypt of 3000 B.C. to the fall of Timbuktu in the A.D. 1600's, the African continent was the site of a succession of great inland societies, whose names still carry hints of mystery and grandeur—Meroe, Napata, Axum, and Kush. In western Africa along the Niger River, three massive societies rose and fell: ancient Ghana (A.D. 800–1200); Melle (or Mali) (1000–1400); and Songhai (1200–1600). Through trade, commerce, and warfare, these societies grew from small village kingdoms into complex empires, ruled by great kings and covering thousands of square miles. No coastal African society ever matched these inland empires in terms of size, governmental organization, and military power.

Long before Europeans appeared on Africa's Atlantic coast, traditional African societies had traded people for goods. African communities recognized ownership claims to people not belonging to their family or clan. In traditional African exchange systems, claims to the rights of individual slaves were bought and sold along with tangible goods, such as gold and ivory.

The hardships endured by slaves in Africa were softened somewhat by the cultural traditions they shared with their African slaveholders, such as religion and respect for ancestors. By contrast, the European treatment of enslaved Africans from the late 1400's on was influenced by myths of black inferiority and the promise of wealth that could be gained by using slave labor. Few Europeans had any interest in or knowledge of Africa's true history or greatness.

In the 1500's, gold and slaves were traded out of Timbuktu, the legendary city of Africa's Songhai Empire.

PLANTATION BONDAGE ERA (1619–1865)

Over a period of about 350 years, from the early 1500's to the mid-1800's, approximately 12 million Africans were forcibly transported across the Atlantic Ocean to the Americas. Of this number, about 8 percent, or approximately 1 million, were brought to North America (after 1619), with the rest going to the islands of the Caribbean and the shores of Central and South America. Collected by European slave traders working out of western Africa, millions of Africans were taken in exchange for guns, iron, beads, silks, brocades, and other cloths, knives, basins, mirrors, and the like. They were then sold as slaves to colonial plantation owners in the Americas.

The Slave Trade

The business of trading goods for people, and then selling those people as slaves for a financial profit, was initiated and funded by European royalty and merchants. They fi-

This article traces the history of the African American people, from their African roots to the present day. For additional information on specific subjects, refer to the following articles in the appropriate volumes in *The New Book of Knowledge*: ABOLITION MOVEMENT; AFRICA; AFRICA, ART AND ARCHITECTURE OF; AFRICA, LITERATURE OF; AFRICA, MUSIC OF; AMERICAN LITERATURE; CIVIL RIGHTS; CIVIL RIGHTS MOVEMENT; CIVIL WAR, UNITED STATES; COMPROMISE OF 1850; DRED SCOTT DECISION; EMANCIPATION PROCLAMATION; HYMNS (Spiritual and Other Folk Hymns); JAZZ; KANSAS-NEBRASKA ACT; LINCOLN-DOUGLAS DEBATES; MISSOURI COMPROMISE; RACISM; RECONSTRUCTION PERIOD; SEGREGATION; SLAVERY; SPINGARN MEDAL; UNDERGROUND RAILROAD; UNITED STATES, HISTORY OF THE; the history sections of individual state articles; and biographies and profiles of notable individuals.

1526–39 The first Africans arrived in the Americas in the company of Spanish and Portuguese explorers.

1539 Estevanico (Little Stephen), a Moroccan slave who had escaped his Spanish captors, led the first expedition of explorers into the Southwest as far as present-day New Mexico and Arizona.

1565 Africans helped establish North America's oldest European settlement, St. Augustine, Florida.

1619 North America's first slaves were brought to Jamestown, Virginia.

1688 The first formal protest against slavery was made in Germantown, Pennsylvania.

1775–81 At least 5,000 blacks fought in the Revolutionary War, notably at the battles of Bunker Hill, Lexington, Brandywine, White Plains, Concord, and Saratoga. Two of them, Prince Whipple and Oliver Cromwell, crossed the Delaware River with George Washington on Christmas Day, 1776.

From 1619 to 1808, about 1 million black Africans were sold into slavery and shipped across the Atlantic Ocean to what is now the United States.

nanced the trading companies that outfitted ships and their crews and maintained agents on both sides of the Atlantic Ocean.

Over the years, thousands of European ships crisscrossed the Atlantic on this triangular, or three-legged, business route between Europe, Africa, and the Americas. On the journey's second leg, known as the Middle Passage, each ship carried between 200 and 300 Africans to America. During a journey lasting four to six months, the slaves traveled most of the way lying down because there was no room for standing or sitting. They were branded with hot irons, separated by gender, and fed a diet of beans, yams, and corn mush. Some were under 10 years of age. The tightly packed conditions promoted contagious diseases that killed an estimated 20 percent of the blacks as well as many of the white crew members. From the diaries of Africa-based trading company agents, scholars calculate

that an additional 2 to 4 percent of the slaves died before they ever reached the ships. These losses increased the value of the slaves who survived the rigorous crossing.

On arrival in the colonies, slaves were evaluated for their strength and potential work capabilities and put up for sale on the auction block. Most slaves in North America were bought by well-to-do plantation owners living in the Southern colonies, with open areas suitable for commercial agriculture. About 10,000 planters made up the Southern ruling class, each owning 50 or more slaves. Virginia planters George Washington and Thomas Jefferson each held at least 250 slaves, even as they debated the morality of slavery.

Slave Life

Slaves engaged in three basic categories of work—domestic, mechanical, and agricultural. Domestic slaves worked around the slaveholders' homes, cooking, cleaning, and raising the white children. Other slaves were skilled artisans, trained as carpenters, millwrights, masons, tailors, and shoemakers. Most slaves, however, were engaged in some form of farming. Those who were skilled in crop production were more valuable than unskilled farm laborers, or "field hands." As such, they were treated differently, often having better food, clothing, and shelter.

The typical day for a slave began in a lineup for task or group assignments. Except for a short break for a midday meal, work continued until nightfall. Generally the slaves were not required to work on Saturday afternoons or on Sundays, except during certain stages of rice and sugarcane cultivation, when they were required to work 16 to 18 hours a day, seven days a week. If the taskmaster felt it necessary, slaves could be worked to the very limit of their strength.

Weekly food rations were a peck (eight dry quarts) of corn, three or four pounds of bacon

In 1816 the Reverend Richard Allen of Philadelphia was consecrated the first bishop of the African Methodist Episcopal (A.M.E.) Church, the first independent black religious denomination.

1777 Vermont became the first state to abolish slavery.

1787 The Free African Society was founded by Richard Allen and Absalom Jones in Philadelphia.

1817 James Forten presided over the first interstate convention of African Americans. More than 3,000 attended to protest a proposal by the American Colonization Society to deport free blacks to Africa.

1822 Denmark Vesey organized 6,000 slaves in South Carolina in a failed effort to overthrow slavery.

1826 The Massachusetts Colored General Association, established in Boston, became the nation's first African American political group.

1830 A national meeting of African American leaders in Philadelphia was the first time black leaders met to review the problems and status of black Americans.

or salt pork, and perhaps some yams and molasses. This was supplemented with vegetables and salad greens raised by the slaves themselves on patches of ground allowed them near their one-room cabins. Leisure time was enjoyed after the fall harvest season and during major holidays.

Although many slaves were not intentionally mistreated, most slaves lived in constant fear. At the word of any person in authority, a slave could be punished, physically abused, or even sold away from his or her family. Although some considerate buyers made an effort to keep family members together, often children were sold apart from their mothers, and husbands and wives were taken to separate plantations. This disregard for the slaves' emotional needs weakened the foundations of many black families. In spite of such inhumane treatment, there were relatively few slave uprisings in North America, perhaps because there were at least four times as many whites as blacks, and blacks generally did not have access to weapons.

Forced to be submissive and obedient by day, slaves created a different style of life for themselves at night. Between sundown and sunup, they tried to maintain normal family traditions and relationships. Many found comfort in religion, and community gatherings often were centered on religious celebration. They sang hymns and other religious songs called spirituals to lift their burdens and to express their suffering. Songs such as "Nobody Knows the Trouble I've Seen" and "Swing Low, Sweet Chariot" were among the first created in America.

Free Blacks

Not all of the blacks in antebellum (pre–Civil War) America were slaves. "Free blacks" lived and worked in major cities throughout the nation. The rights of free blacks, however, were strictly limited, especially in the South, where so-called Black Codes dictated their behavior. Free blacks were not allowed to express any kind of social or political viewpoint, nor were they allowed to socialize with whites or to carry weapons. Therefore, not surprisingly, black leadership became centered in the North, where blacks enjoyed a greater measure of freedom.

Although Northerners made up only 15 percent of the nation's free-black population, they set the standard for the black community's social and religious values. Free blacks financed neighborhood elementary schools in New York and many other Northern cities. Even in the slaveholding South, where "compulsory ignorance" laws prohibited black education, many blacks taught their children how to read and write during the time permitted for religious instruction. They treasured literacy, even though they were forced to hide it.

The Abolitionist Movement

In the 30 years prior to the outbreak of the Civil War in 1861, free blacks in the North played a major role in the struggle to abolish slavery in the United States. They founded organizations, such as the American Society of Free People of Color, to protest racial prejudice in the North as well as slavery in the South. Free-black churches raised money to support antislavery lecturers and news-

Frederick Douglass was the most famous black abolitionist of his day. In 1845 an antislavery song was published describing his escape from slavery.

1831 Nat Turner led an unsuccessful slave revolt in Southampton County, Virginia. He and many others were hanged for the deaths of more than 50 whites. The uprising led to the nation's first public debate over the morality of slavery.

1840–61 Harriet Tubman, working through the Underground Railroad, rescued more than 300 slaves from the South. She later became a spy and a nurse for the Union Army.

1850 Enactment of the Fugitive Slave Law caused many African Americans and others to flee to Canada to join the abolitionist movement against slavery in the United States.

1857 In the Dred Scott Decision, the U.S. Supreme Court held that slaves, and also free blacks, were not citizens of the United States and therefore had no rights protected by the Constitution.

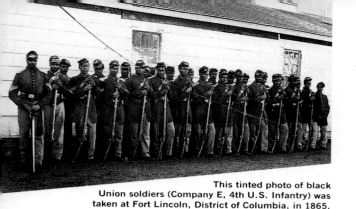

This tinted photo of black Union soldiers (Company E, 4th U.S. Infantry) was taken at Fort Lincoln, District of Columbia, in 1865.

The Civil War and Emancipation

During the course of the Civil War (1861–65), nearly 200,000 African Americans, both slave and free, volunteered to fight for the Union against the slaveholding Confederate states in the South. Black servicemen took part in nearly every major military engagement, although until 1864 they were paid less than white soldiers. They also built fortifications, handled provisions, and served as lookouts. Some also served as spies.

The promise of emancipation was fulfilled when the Union forces won the war in 1865. By the end of that year, the 13th Amendment was ratified, abolishing slavery in the United States. In 1868 the 14th Amendment extended full legal citizenship to African Americans, and in 1870 the 15th Amendment guaranteed voting rights to black men. A profound national social revolution was set in motion.

▶RURAL EMANCIPATION ERA (1865–1915)

Between 1865 and 1915, many Americans left their farms and moved to a town or city, where new jobs were opening up. About 90 percent of the African Americans remained within the eleven ex-Confederate Southern states where they had been raised and where their families had lived for generations.

The Evolution of Black Education

The "social reconstruction" of former slaves began with basic education, the success of which was by far the most dramatic evidence of their new legal freedom. Tens of thousands of ex-slaves, so long forbidden to learn to read and write, now displayed a passion for knowledge so powerful that, in the words of one observer, "it was as if an entire race was trying to go to school."

The nation's first real "teacher corps" consisted of several thousand Northern-born white women who went South to instruct black students, braving the taunts and threats of white

papers, such as the *North Star*, published by Frederick Douglass. The free-black communities of the North supported these publications to the limit of their resources and were the main sponsors of *The Liberator*, edited by the militant white abolitionist William Lloyd Garrison. Blacks also were instrumental in the efforts of the Underground Railroad, a secret society of people who helped thousands of slaves escape from bondage in the South.

As the abolitionist movement rapidly gained followers in the 1840's and 1850's, bitter arguments over states' rights and the existence of slavery pushed the nation ever closer to war. When the Civil War began in 1861, abolitionists prayed for a Northern victory of pro-Union forces that would bring emancipation, or freedom, to the slaves.

In 1863, immigrants in New York City rioted when the U.S. government tried to draft them into the Union Army. Unwilling to fight to free the slaves, they expressed their outrage by lynching blacks in the city streets.

1861–65 Of the 200,000 blacks who served in the Union forces during the Civil War, 72% were from the slave and border states and 28% were from the Northern free states. Nearly 30,000 lost their lives; 21 received the Medal of Honor.

1863 President Abraham Lincoln's Emancipation Proclamation declared the freedom of any slave residing in a state in rebellion against the Union.

▼ The announcement of a military draft prompted Irish American attacks on blacks in New York City, leaving 74 people dead.

1865 The urgent need for food and first aid and other services prompted the federal government to establish the Bureau of Freedmen, Refugees, and Abandoned Lands (later called the Freedmen's Bureau) to assist the 4 million African Americans making the transition from slavery to freedom.

Southerners who feared that blacks would be "overeducated for their places." Within a decade, these teachers were replaced in the classrooms by many of their older black pupils. The faculties of the earliest black colleges and universities remained more white than black for a much longer period, due to the shortage of college-trained blacks.

In 1890 the Morrill Land Grant Act established 17 institutions of higher learning. These tax-supported A & I (Agricultural and Industrial) and A & M (Agricultural and Mechanical) colleges reflected the doctrine of industrial education of the sort promoted by the educator Booker T. Washington at his Tuskegee Institute in Alabama. Washington's theories directly conflicted with those of another prominent black scholar of the era, W. E. B. Du Bois, who believed that blacks should study the liberal arts. This historic debate was but one example of the emerging conflict within the black community over the proper focus of black education.

The post-emancipation educational experience produced a small but highly educated group of African Americans who supported at least a dozen black-issue-oriented newspapers. In 1911, Du Bois, at his own expense, launched *The Crisis*, black America's first race-relations journal, which is still published today. These publications, financed by their readers, boldly explored race relations.

Political Advances

Prior to 1868, John M. Langston had been the only black to hold elective office anywhere in the United States. He had been a city councilman in Brownhelm, Ohio, in 1856. Then between 1868 and 1898, 22 African Americans were elected to the U.S. Congress, including two to the U.S. Senate. At the state and local levels, nearly a thousand gained public office. Many had gained political experience working in the antislavery campaigns.

In 1905, W. E. B. Du Bois, a scholar and early civil rights leader, founded the Niagara Movement, a forerunner of the NAACP, to fight discrimination.

Discrimination and Violence

After the war, during the period known as Reconstruction, blacks in the South were protected by federal troops who occupied the former Confederate states. But when those troops were withdrawn in 1877, blacks found themselves at the mercy of the Ku Klux Klan and similar white-supremacist groups. Violence against blacks became so commonplace that approximately 100,000 fled from the Carolinas, Tennessee, Alabama, and Mississippi to the safer havens of Kansas, Missouri, and Illinois. By 1892, lynchings, or unlawful executions, of African Americans by terrorist groups in the South averaged one every two days.

Two U.S. Supreme Court decisions further undermined the new freedom of African Americans. In 1883, the Court declared that the 1875 Civil Rights Act, which forbade discrimination against blacks in public facilities, was unconstitutional and that local authorities could discriminate for a variety of reasons, including that of race. Most of the former

1865 The 13th Amendment to the Constitution abolished slavery in the United States. African American and white abolitionists celebrated the victory with church programs, speeches, and parades.

1865–70 Howard University, Bowie State University, Morehouse College, Talladega College, Morgan State University, and Fisk University were among the institutions of higher learning founded to educate African Americans.

1868 The 14th Amendment to the Constitution granted citizenship to "All persons born or naturalized in the United States," overturning the Dred Scott Decision (see 1857).

1870 The 15th Amendment to the Constitution affirmed that no citizen may be denied the right to vote due to their race or color.

1875 The U.S. Congress passed the Civil Rights Act of 1875, prohibiting discrimination of blacks in public facilities.

Beginning in the late 1800's, many poor black Southern sharecroppers (*left*) moved to the cities, hoping to find economic prosperity. The oppressive conditions they found in urban centers, however, prompted early civil rights marches, such as one in Harlem in 1912 (*below*).

Confederate states quickly passed "Jim Crow" laws (named for a minstrel show character) that segregated (separated) the races in all public facilities, including schools. The trend climaxed in 1896 with the infamous Supreme Court case *Plessy* v. *Ferguson*, which declared that segregation was constitutional as long as white and black facilities were equal. Seven Southern state legislatures used additional tactics to keep blacks from voting. They began charging blacks money to vote (a poll tax), which few could afford to pay. They also instituted "grandfather clause" voting rules, meaning that voters had to demonstrate their understanding of the federal and state constitutions unless they could prove that one of their grandfathers had voted before January 1, 1867. Since African Americans were not declared citizens until July 23, 1868, few could claim kinship to such an unusual relative. These discouragement tactics successfully eliminated most blacks from the voting process.

Migration to the Cities

After the Civil War, many blacks supported themselves by working as sharecroppers, cultivating sections of other people's land in exchange for a share of the crop as payment. But after a series of economic depressions, in 1872, 1884, and 1893, many found it difficult to feed their families. After each depression cycle, thousands of blacks, as well as whites, abandoned farming and moved to the nearest industrial town or city to look for jobs in manufacturing industries. Many of the blacks who remained in the farming communities joined protest organizations, such as the Colored Farmers' Alliance, which by the 1890's had gained a membership of more than 1 million in nine states. White resistance to this union climaxed in North Carolina, the state with the highest concentration of alliance members. In 1898, after the Southern Democrats who were hostile to black issues won control of the state legislature, a riot broke out in Wilmington, North Carolina. More than 40 people were killed over a period of several days.

1883 Jan Ernest Matzeliger revolutionized the shoe industry with his invention of the shoe lasting machine, which was capable of attaching soles of shoes to their upper parts.

1896 In the ruling *Plessy* v. *Ferguson*, the U.S. Supreme Court upheld the right of a state to

establish separate but equal facilities for blacks and whites, encouraging racial segregation and discrimination.

1903 W. E. B. Du Bois became a national figure with the publication of *The Souls of Black Folk*.

1905 Du Bois and other early civil rights activists launched the Niagara

Movement, calling for an immediate halt to segregation and racism.

1909 The National Association for the Advancement of Colored People (NAACP) was founded by a group of whites and blacks to favorably influence public opinion and to defend the legal rights of African Americans.

Soldiers of the all-black 369th Infantry distinguished themselves at the Battle of the Argonne Forest in World War I. The entire regiment was awarded the Croix de Guerre, France's highest medal for bravery.

►URBANIZATION (1915–1945)

Following the terror of the Wilmington Riot, many Southern blacks headed north to settle in Boston, Newark, Philadelphia, Pittsburgh, Cleveland, Cincinnati, Detroit, Chicago, St. Louis, and Harlem, a section of New York City. Over the next two decades, hundreds of thousands of blacks moved into these urban centers. But on arrival, most discovered overcrowded facilities, inadequate housing, and dead-end jobs. As a result, concerned individuals of both races formed the National Association for the Advancement of Colored People (NAACP) in 1909 and the National Urban League (NUL) in 1911. The NAACP was devoted to the pursuit of civic justice and the NUL to economic fairness.

World War I

When the United States entered World War I in 1917, W. E. B. Du Bois, among others, urged blacks to support the war effort "shoulder to shoulder with our white fellow citizens." Of the 2.2 million African Americans who registered for the draft following the passage of the Selective Service Act in May 1917, a total of 367,000 were actually drafted and 42,000 went overseas to fight in France. More than 600 African Americans received commissions as officers of the U.S. Army to take command of segregated black military units.

During the war, tens of thousands of black men and women found employment as coal miners and in industrial centers where war supplies, such as ammunition, ships, and motor vehicles, were manufactured. These job opportunities brought economic prosperity to many black communities for the first time. Racism, however, continued to undermine the African American community, and competition between blacks and poor whites for limited job opportunities led to a violent cycle of race riots.

Meanwhile, the Ku Klux Klan was rapidly expanding northward and its membership grew to 4 million. Northern lampposts, as well as Southern oak trees, now served as lynching gallows. In 1919 at least 70 blacks were lynched, including 10 African American war veterans wearing full uniform.

The 1920's

This wave of racial hatred divided the African American community itself. The majority of middle-class blacks believed racism could end with full integration of the races, but many working-class blacks, who felt completely removed from white society, supported a new Back-to-Africa movement led by Marcus Garvey. For nearly a million individuals, Garvey was a prophet of black pride, independence, and separatism.

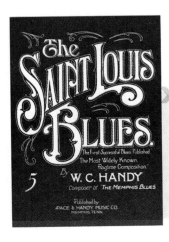

1911 The National Urban League (NUL) was founded to help African Americans find employment.

1914 W. C. Handy, known as the "father of the blues," popularized the blues style of music with the release of his classic "St. Louis Blues."

1918 Approximately 370,000 African Americans distinguished themselves in combat during World War I.

▼ Nearly 100 people lost their lives in hundreds of race riots that erupted in major U.S. cities, partly as a result of competition for jobs among returning soldiers.

About this time, the black middle class began producing a stunning collection of now-classic literary and artistic works. Because so many were created in Harlem, this period of the 1920's became known as the Harlem Renaissance. The works of Langston Hughes, Claude McKay, Countee Cullen, Jessie Fauset, and James Weldon Johnson were widely circulated. Also popular were "race movies," produced for black audiences by Oscar Micheaux.

Marcus Garvey attracted millions of followers with his Back-to-Africa movement in the 1920's.

The Depression Years

Creative expression diminished during the Great Depression of the 1930's, as jobs became increasingly scarce and racial tensions once again exploded. A riot in Harlem in 1935 was directly connected to housing shortages and to a local unemployment rate that exceeded 50 percent. Blacks also were highly frustrated because they felt generally unprotected by the law. In cases involving blacks and whites, the law courts almost always ruled in favor of the whites.

On the positive side, however, the administration of President Franklin D. Roosevelt included blacks in its economic relief efforts. In 1936 the esteemed black educator Mary McLeod Bethune, an associate of the president's wife, Eleanor Roosevelt, formed what was known as the Black Cabinet to deal with governmental problems and policies affecting African Americans. The formation of the Committee for Industrial Organization (CIO) in 1935 extended union membership to blacks who found employment in the automobile, railroad, textile, and tobacco industries and in the building trades. Before this time, they had generally been limited to service jobs, such as janitors and cooks.

World War II

America's entry into World War II in 1941 renewed an old debate concerning the role African Americans should play in defense of the nation. Black service personnel were excluded by law from the United States Marines and by custom from the Air Force. Blacks in the Navy could only aspire to be cooks and kitchen helpers. Despite these barriers, more than 1 million patriotic African Americans joined the armed forces. Pressure from the NAACP and other African American leadership groups persuaded the Marine Corps to drop its policy of discrimination and the Air Force to set up pilot training operations for blacks in Tuskegee, Alabama. By mid-1942 approximately 200 African American officers had received commissions for duty, and by 1945 nearly 500,000 African Americans were serving overseas. It did not escape their notice, however, that while they were fighting for democracy overseas, many were still living in segregation in the United States.

World War II significantly affected the lives of African Americans. Employers in the military industries were ordered by the federal

Mary McLeod Bethune

1925 The first major African American labor union, the Brotherhood of Sleeping Car Porters, was organized by A. Philip Randolph. His work paved the way for the acceptance of blacks in the labor movement of the 1930's and 1940's.

1936 Mary McLeod Bethune helped organize the National Council of Black Federal Officials, known as the Black Cabinet, during the administration of President Franklin Roosevelt.

1939 Concert singer Marian Anderson performed before 75,000 people at the Lincoln Memorial, after the Daughters of the American Revolution (DAR) refused to allow her to appear at Constitution Hall.

BREAKING THE COLOR BARRIER

By the 1940's, blacks had made inroads into mainstream popular culture. Among those who rose to the top were (*clockwise from left*) singer Sarah Vaughan, known as "the Divine One"; Richard Wright, author of the acclaimed novel *Native Son*; jazz great Count Basie and his orchestra; Jackie Robinson, the first black major league player of the 1900's; and the esteemed artist W. H. Johnson.

1940 Richard Wright published *Native Son*, describing the hostile social and economic conditions that can lead blacks into crime.

1941 President Franklin Roosevelt issued Executive Order 8802, prohibiting discrimination in government and in defense industries.

1942 The Congress of Racial Equality (CORE), led by James Farmer, was founded in Chicago to seek nonviolent, direct action to combat discrimination.

1946 The U.S. Supreme Court ruled in *Morgan* v. *Virginia* that segregation in interstate bus travel was unconstitutional.

1948 President Harry S. Truman issued Executive Order 9981, abolishing segregation in the armed forces.

1953 Ralph Ellison won a National Book Award for *Invisible Man* (1952), a story of a black man's efforts to overcome society's stereotypes and assert his individuality.

Left: During World War II, African American artist Horace Pippin, a disabled World War I veteran, painted *Mr. Prejudice* (1943) to show that racial discrimination was weakening the war effort.

Right: "Colored Only" marks the front of a segregated store in Belle Glade, Florida, 1945.

Opposite page, left: Rosa Parks, who refused to yield her bus seat to a white man in 1955, is known as the mother of the modern civil rights movement.

government not to discriminate against blacks when hiring, stimulating another wave of migration to the major cities in the South, Northeast, and West. As their income and wages increased, more African Americans were able to afford to buy automobiles, radios, record players, ready-made clothing, and other luxury items.

▶ MODERNIZATION (1945–   )

Under the administration of President Roosevelt, the executive branch had determined that blacks must be included in federal assistance programs. In addition, the Supreme Court had indicated that it was unconstitutional to exclude African Americans from due process of law. As a matter of record, between the years 1938 and 1948, the NAACP, with Thurgood Marshall as its chief counsel, successfully challenged racial discrimination in housing, interstate travel, graduate-level education, and voting requirements. Within the decade the number of blacks registered to vote rose from 100,000 to more than 1 million, setting the stage for political changes of an unforeseen magnitude.

The Civil Rights Movement

In 1954 the U.S. Supreme Court ruled in the case of *Brown* v. *Board of Education of Topeka* (Kansas) that racial segregation in public schools was unconstitutional, or unlawful. This victory unleashed a new era of civil rights activities, particularly in the South. For example, in 1955, Rosa Parks of Montgomery, Alabama, touched off a boycott of the city's transportation system after she was arrested for refusing to yield her bus seat to a white man. The boycott was led by a young minister named Martin Luther King, Jr., who came to symbolize the civil rights movement.

During the administration (1953–61) of President Dwight D. Eisenhower, the Civil Rights Commission and the Civil Rights Division were created in the Justice Department. This signaled to the nation that civil rights issues were a concern of the executive and legislative branches of the federal govern-

1954 In the ruling of *Brown* v. *Board of Education of Topeka* (Kansas), the U.S. Supreme Court overturned *Plessy* v. *Ferguson* (see 1896) and declared the segregation of public schools unconstitutional.

1955 Dr. Martin Luther King, Jr., led a yearlong boycott of the Montgomery, Alabama, bus system after Rosa Parks, a black seamstress, was arrested for not giving up her seat to a white person.

1956 As a result of the nonviolent Montgomery boycott, the U.S. Supreme Court ruled that segregation on public transportation was unconstitutional.

1957 President Eisenhower signed a civil rights bill and created a commission to investigate civil- and voting-rights violations.

▼ Federal troops were ordered to Little Rock, Arkansas, to ensure the safety of nine black students attempting to enroll in the all-white Central High School.

Right: Most African American civil rights activists were dedicated to nonviolent protest and bore hostility and injustice with dignity and perseverance.

ment. This commitment was put to the test in Arkansas in 1957, when President Eisenhower was compelled to send federal troops to Little Rock to enforce a federal court order to integrate Central High School.

In February 1960, in Greensboro, North Carolina, four young black college students were arrested for refusing to leave a drugstore lunch counter after they had been denied service. Such peaceful methods of protest, which became popular among college students, resulted in the founding of the Student Non-Violent Coordinating Committee (SNCC) in April 1960. Through freedom rides and sit-ins, boycotts and demonstrations, activists tried to evaluate the extent of continued segregation and communicate their findings to the media. Each group encountered violent resistance throughout the Deep South. Some of the most bitter confrontations took place in Alabama, Mississippi, and Georgia.

At the height of the movement, civil rights leaders planned a March on Washington. On August 28, 1963, huge crowds gathered at the Lincoln Memorial in Washington, D.C., to show their support for civil rights and to persuade Congress to pass a comprehensive civil rights bill. Before an audience of more than 200,000 people, Dr. King delivered his stirring speech, "I Have A Dream," in which he envisioned a day when discrimination and social injustice would no longer exist.

In 1964, after extensive debate and with the support of President Lyndon Johnson, Congress passed the Civil Rights Act, prohibiting all racial discrimination in public life. Building on this momentum, Johnson succeeded in getting Congress to pass the Voting Rights Act of 1965, which expanded the scope of the 15th Amendment. Many people then started to believe that because civil rights were now protected by law, further protest would seem excessive. But people continued to protest, venting their anger over the fact that racism and economic inequality remained characteristic of American society.

1960 In Greensboro, North Carolina, four black college students began sit-in demonstrations at an all-white lunch counter. This nonviolent protest method soon spread throughout the South.

1961 Bus loads of black and white youths from the North called freedom riders were organized by

CORE to journey through the South to test the enforcement of desegregation laws on interstate transportation.

1962 Federal troops were ordered to Oxford, Mississippi, to protect James H. Meredith, the first African American to register at the University of Mississippi.

▼ President John F. Kennedy signed an executive order banning discrimination in federally funded housing.

1963 Civil rights demonstrations in Birmingham, Alabama, resulted in police brutality. Late in the year, four young black girls were killed in a church bombing.

Separatism, Militancy, and Black Power

During the civil rights era, a religious group called the Nation of Islam, or Black Muslims, began to grow in strength. The group, founded by Wali D. Farad (Fard) in the 1930's, required its followers to separate themselves from whites. In the 1960's, the two most visible Black Muslim leaders were Elijah Muhammad and Malcolm X. In 1964, however, Malcolm X moved away from the separatist doctrine and founded his own movement, the Organization of Afro-American Unity (OAAU). He was assassinated at a meeting in Harlem the following year.

Also prominent during this time was a group known as the Black Panther Party for Unity and Self-Defense, organized in California by Huey P. Newton and Bobby G. Seale. The Panthers brought attention to such problems as unfair rent evictions and police brutality. Soon they were teaching black history classes and informing people of their rights. "Black Power" became a popular slogan. It was meant to encourage blacks to gain economic and political power and, more importantly, to gain self-pride and dignity. Eventually, however, the Black Panthers grew increasingly militant. They started rejecting nonviolent protest methods and urged blacks to prepare for an armed struggle against the whites. Many people began to fear them.

The civil rights movement headed North and began addressing matters of economic inequality. In response to some police encounters, rioting broke out in black neighborhoods in Harlem, Newark, and the Watts section of Los Angeles. As black ghettos went up in flames, televised newscasts showed African

Top: The dynamic Black Muslim leader Malcolm X was in the process of re-examining his theories of black separatism when he was killed by an assassin in 1965.

Left: In March 1965, blacks and whites marched together from Selma to Montgomery, Alabama, to protest racial discrimination in voting procedures.

1963 On August 20, more than 200,000 blacks and whites participated in a March on Washington, D.C., to protest the lack of federal civil rights legislation. Dr. Martin Luther King, Jr., delivered an electrifying speech, "I Have a Dream."

1964 Malcolm X left the Black Muslim organization Nation of Islam and formed the Organization of Afro-American Unity (OAAU), stressing black nationalism and social action. He was assassinated the following year.

▼ The U.S. Congress passed the Civil Rights Act of 1964, prohibiting racial discrimination in public places and in employment and education.

▼ Dr. Martin Luther King, Jr., won the Nobel Peace Prize.

1965 White resistance to a black voter registration drive led to a Freedom March, from Selma to Montgomery, Alabama, to protest discrimination at the polls.

▼ Congress passed the Voting Rights Act.

Americans chanting threatening slogans like "Burn, Baby, Burn." Then on April 4, 1968, the African American community was dealt a crushing blow when Dr. King, the principal advocate of nonviolence and social justice, was assassinated by a white man in Memphis, Tennessee. The civil rights movement had lost its most respected leader.

Beyond Civil Rights

During the election campaigns of 1968, it became apparent that a conservative, anti–civil rights backlash had begun to take hold of the nation. George Wallace, the defiant, pro-segregationist governor of Alabama, became a popular third-party candidate for president of the United States.

Race relations worsened in the 1970's as national support for issues concerning African Americans diminished. Racial violence returned in the 1980's and 1990's in such communities as Forsyth, Georgia; Howard Beach and Crown Heights, New York; and Los Angeles, California.

Meanwhile, black separatists also attracted new followers. By 1978, Minister Louis Farrakhan, the most influential Black Muslim leader since Malcolm X, began addressing audiences of 8,000 to 10,000 African Americans, who were seeking solutions to social problems that included poverty, drug abuse, crime, and gang violence. By 1990, Farrakhan had become a controversial figure. Many applauded his preaching the virtues of decent and law-abiding behavior. However, many others, especially within the rising and prosperous black middle class, rejected Farrakhan's notion of black superiority and racist tendencies.

The Reverend Jesse Jackson founded the Rainbow Coalition in 1984 to carry on the fight for civil justice and to promote racial tolerance and understanding.

A more positive force within the African American community was the Reverend Jesse Jackson. In 1984, Jackson founded the Rainbow Coalition, a political organization dedicated to social, economic, judicial, and environmental reforms to enrich the lives of African Americans and other minorities. The popular support for Jackson's candidacy for president of the United States in 1984 and 1988 brought African American issues back into the national spotlight.

While two-thirds of the African American community thrived, at least one-third was living in poverty in areas with disproportionately high rates of crime, unemployment, and welfare dependency. Routine concerns of inner-city residents were quality of housing, personal safety, and inadequacy of services.

Despite persistent problems, by the end of the 20th century, the African Americans had also achieved many goals. The community was characterized by its diversity of income levels, occupations, religious affiliations, levels of education, and lifestyles. Increasingly they were represented in the various professions and at all levels of government.

In recent years, many inner-city school systems with large enrollments of African Americans have suffered from a lack of resources and adequate funding. Efforts have been made to raise the esteem and performance levels of

The New York Times

NEW YORK, FRIDAY, APRIL 5, 1968

RTIN LUTHER KING IS SLAIN IN MEMP WHITE IS SUSPECTED; JOHNSON URGES

1968 The U.S. Senate passed a civil rights bill prohibiting racial discrimination in the sale or rental of most housing.

▼ Dr. Martin Luther King, Jr., was assassinated by a white man, touching off a new wave of violence in more than one hundred cities nationwide.

1971 African American members of the House of Representatives founded the Congressional Black Caucus to focus on legislative issues affecting blacks and other under-represented groups.

1986 For the first time, the birthday of Dr. Martin Luther King, Jr., was celebrated as a national holiday (on the third Monday of every January).

1988 In the U.S. presidential primary elections, nearly 7 million people cast votes for Jesse Jackson.

The civil rights movement freed African Americans to pursue professional opportunities and win recognition for their achievements. Among the top achievers are (*top, left to right*) General Colin L. Powell (Ret.), chairman (1989–93) of the Joint Chiefs of Staff, the nation's highest military post; Whitney Houston, one of popular music's biggest stars; Michael Jordan, considered one of basketball's greatest players; Spike Lee, a director who has brought African Americans into the mainstream of film culture; and (*bottom left*) Toni Morrison, winner of the 1993 Nobel Prize for literature.

African American students by exposing them to more information relevant to the accomplishments of black people throughout the world. This approach, called afrocentrism, attempts to reclaim black culture. Toward this goal, Americans have observed Black History Month every February since 1976 to spotlight some of the achievements of African Americans that have long been overlooked in mainstream education—for example, that beautiful poetry once was written by a colonial slave named Phillis Wheatley; that a black engineer named Norbert Rillieux invented a sugar-refining process that is still used today; that black cowboys and the so-called "buffalo soldiers," as well as whites, helped settle the West; that black musicians invented the blues and developed jazz; that an African American explorer, Matthew Henson, reached the North Pole with Robert Peary; that an African American surgeon, Daniel Hale Williams, performed the first successful heart operation; and that African American officers led black soldiers into battle. Thousands of accomplishments such as these, great and small, have profoundly influenced the nation and contributed immeasurably to American culture.

RUSSELL L. ADAMS
Chair, Department of Afro-American Studies,
Howard University

WONDER QUESTION

What is Kwanzaa?

Kwanzaa, meaning "first fruits" in Swahili, is an annual seven-day festival observed by some African Americans during the week of December 26 to January 1. Inspired by an African harvest festival, Kwanzaa was created in 1966 by an American activist named Maulana Karenga to increase awareness of African heritage and to encourage unity.

Kwanzaa teaches seven lessons, or *Nguzo Saba*, one for each day of the week. They are unity (*umoja*); self-determination (*kujichagulia*); cooperation (*ujima*); sharing (*ujamma*); creativity (*kuumba*); purpose (*nia*); and faith (*imani*). The observance includes lighting candles in a holder called a *kinara*, one for each lesson learned. Festivities also may include exchanging gifts and eating an African-style meal known as *karamu*.

AGASSIZ, JEAN LOUIS RODOLPHE (1807–1873)

Long ago the glaciers of the earth began to grow. Great sheets of ice ground their way south from the Arctic. Huge rivers of ice crept down from lofty mountains into the valleys. As thousands of years passed, the ice reached out and covered lands we know today as green and fair.

The man who first drew this picture of a strange and vanished past was a young Swiss scientist named Louis Agassiz. It was Agassiz who realized that there had been an ice age.

Agassiz was born on May 28, 1807, in Môtier-en-Vully, Switzerland. As a boy he showed a strong interest in animals and plants. His mother encouraged him, letting him collect specimens and carry out experiments. His father was a minister, and although far from rich, was determined that his bright son receive a good education. At 10 Louis was sent away to school. Later he studied at several universities.

While at the University of Munich, he began work on the classification of fishes, both living and fossil. His research soon drew the attention of scientists all over Europe. It also helped Agassiz make a decision. He would not practice medicine, as his father wished. He would work in the natural sciences.

By 1832 he was teaching at Neuchâtel, in Switzerland. The 14 years he spent there set the pattern for his life: His home became his workshop. Life was not easy for his wife, Cécile; funds were always low, yet the house was always full of co-workers who lived and ate with the Agassiz family.

In the summer of 1836, Agassiz and two friends climbed one of the great Alpine glaciers. What Agassiz observed caught his curiosity and his imagination. Studies of other glaciers soon convinced him that ice had played a major role in sculpturing the earth. Within a year he announced that a large part of the earth had once been covered with ice.

The geologists of his day were furious. Who was Agassiz to talk about geology? Why did he not stick to his fishes? Agassiz, however, was sure he was right. Year after year he went back up the Alps, gathering the evidence that proved his case.

In 1845 Agassiz was invited to lecture in America. He accepted, and as things turned out, spent the rest of his life in the United States. In his new home Agassiz became famous as a lecturer and teacher.

Agassiz, a leading scientist of the 1800's, was famous for his enthusiastic approach to teaching. He trained an entire generation of naturalists.

In 1848 he became a professor at Harvard University. His wife, whom he had had to leave in Switzerland, was now dead. So Agassiz sent for his children and soon remarried. His second wife was Elizabeth Cabot Cary, a remarkable woman, who later became a founder of Radcliffe College. Mrs. Agassiz encouraged her husband in his work and added to their income by setting up a girls' school on the top floor of the house.

Agassiz was an extraordinary teacher. He treated his students as co-workers. He believed that they should learn to gather facts, rather than learn facts already gathered. The first summer school for studying animals in their natural environment was set up by Agassiz on an island in Buzzards Bay, Massachusetts. He also founded the first natural history museum in America. It is the Museum of Comparative Zoology at Harvard (often known as the Agassiz museum).

Agassiz's enthusiasm for natural history overflowed. His desire to learn as well as to teach endeared him to his students. One wrote, after his death on December 14, 1873, that Agassiz "had been a student all his life long, and when he died he was younger than any of them."

PATRICIA G. LAUBER
Science Author and Editor

See also GLACIERS; ICE AGES.

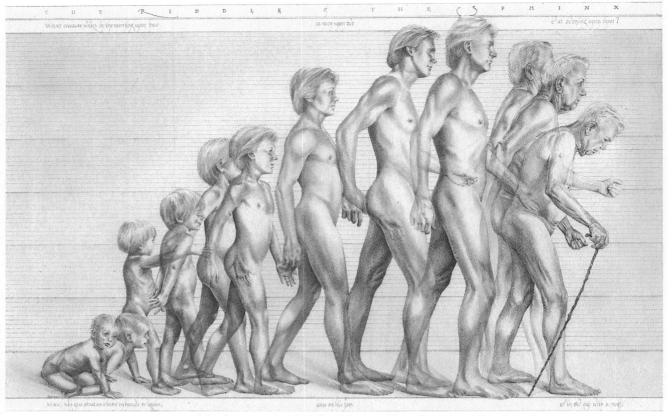

THE RIDDLE of THE SPHINX

WHAT creature walks in the morning upon four, at noon upon two & at evening upon three?

MAN, who goes about as a baby on hands & knees, later on his feet & in old age with a staff.

Aging is a normal part of life. It begins with a phase of growth and development which is followed by a gradual decrease in the body's size and ability to function efficiently.

AGING

Everybody knows that old people are more likely to die than young people. We know it from experience. We also can find the facts and figures in life insurance tables. For example, in an advanced country with a well-fed population only about one in every 1,000 children dies during his or her 12th year. But one in every 20 men aged 70 will die before his 71st birthday.

The risk we run of dying at any particular age is called the **force of mortality** for that age. The force of mortality has been carefully worked out for all ages of people—this is what life insurance rates are based on. Naturally, it grows steadily greater with age. If we kept all through life the same force of mortality that we had at 12—never becoming any more likely to die than we were then—we could all hope to live several hundred years, unless we were very unlucky or careless. The fact that people do not live several hundred years (and only rarely reach 100) is due to a process called **aging.**

We can recognize aging by the gray hair, weakened muscles, wrinkled skin, loss of hearing, and other signs that it produces. It also has a more important effect on us. It reduces our power of staying well and of getting better if we fall ill. A common cold may not be serious in a young person, but its complications may lead to death in an old person.

This loss of the power to stay healthy (and the increase in the likelihood of dying) happens at about the same rate in everybody. As we age, we tend to be like an old automobile—more and more things go wrong with us.

But old cars and radios do not repair themselves. When we are young, our bodies do. What seems to decline with age is the power of self-repair. There comes a time beyond which it is very difficult to stay alive at all. The least thing may be enough to finish us. This is the end of our **life span.**

▶LIFE SPANS IN HUMANS

People and other animals that age have fixed life spans, or characteristic ages of death. Some individuals may die sooner, while strong or lucky ones live longer. But most individuals of a species have about the same length of life. In countries with good food and medical services, the most common length of life in people is between 70 and 80 years. Where there is hunger or little medical care, many people die young. Often death among babies, called **infant mortality,** is very high. For those who survive, the expectation of life is low—perhaps 40 to 45 years.

Women, for reasons not clearly understood, live a little longer on the average than men. This could be because their genetic makeup (two X chromosomes instead of one) gives them a better chance of avoiding defective genes. Also, differences in hormone levels between men and women also appear to affect life span.

Some people, especially if they have come from long-lived families, live longer than others. Some are able to live as much as 20 years beyond the usual limit of life. For example, in England, Canada, and the United States, three out of every 100 babies born will live to be 90 years old. About one out of every 1,000 will live to be 100.

A few people live longer still, up to 107 or 108 years. There is a great deal of argument about the highest age ever reached by a person. Probably it is just short of 120 years. For instance, a man who said he was 117 and the last survivor of the Confederate Army died in Texas in 1959. People who have claimed to be older than 120 have never been able to prove it. Some old people are jokers who tell tremendous tales about their age. Other people are willing to believe these tales because they like the idea of living a long time.

▶ LIFE SPANS IN ANIMALS

We are used to the idea that we will age. We are so used to this that it comes as a surprise to find that there may be some animals that do not age. Sea anemones are an example. Some have been kept for nearly a century without showing any signs of losing vigor. Some kinds of marine worm can even "grow backwards." If starved and kept in the dark, they get steadily smaller. They finally end as a ball of cells, looking rather like the egg from which they came. Under favorable conditions the ball will turn back to a worm and start growing again. They could probably keep growing and "un-growing" indefinitely.

An animal that does not age is not immortal. That is, it is not deathless. Some individuals will die by accident or from disease every year. But such animals do not get *more likely* to die with age. The force of mortality stays the same in them.

It is sometimes said that small wild animals and birds do not age. What really happens is that they do not have a chance to age. Nearly all die by accident before they have a chance to get really old. Few small birds in the wild survive more than a couple of years. But in a cage, protected from hunger and enemies, they can live as long as 20 years and then die of old age.

Most animals are like us in having fixed life spans. But the life spans of different kinds of animals vary greatly. Birds live longer than mammals of the same size. Fish and reptiles, which are cold blooded, live longer still.

Tortoises (land turtles) and sturgeon are probably the two longest-lived vertebrates (animals with backbones). Human beings are the longest-lived mammals. The elephant is the only other mammal that approaches our life span. In spite of what you read in some books, whales and elephants do not live for hundreds of years.

▶ INVESTIGATIONS ON AGING

The study of aging is called **gerontology.** This name comes from the Greek word *gerōn*, which means "old man." The general aim of gerontology is to find out exactly how aging occurs and how, if possible, it can be altered. The ultimate object is to discover if the rate of aging in humans can be slowed down and, if so, by how much. If successful, gerontology could help people stay young and healthy longer.

What Happens During Aging?

We do not yet know why people and animals lose vigor with age. There seem to be three main possibilities.

First, aging might be due to the dying off of cells we cannot replace. The animals that do not age are mostly kinds that can replace all their cells. In people and other vertebrates, cells of the skin, blood, and liver are renewed. But this renewal slows down with age. Other cells, like those of the brain, cannot divide and are never renewed. We keep the same brain cells all our lives, but they get fewer as we get

Gray hair and wrinkled skin are two of the most common signs of aging. Changes such as these may be caused by the body's inability to replace old cells with healthy new ones.

older. Aging may be due simply to a loss of cells or structures that we cannot renew.

A second possibility has to do with cell formation. Aging may be due to a change in the cells that are newly produced throughout life. Perhaps the new cells formed by an old man are different from, and not so good as, new cells in a baby.

The third possibility is that aging is more complicated than this. It may be the result of development. Chemical changes in the body make us grow up. Perhaps these same chemical changes eventually damage the body in some way and make it grow old.

Those are only three of the theories that have been suggested to explain aging. Nobody yet knows for certain which, if any, of them is right.

DNA Repair and the Rate of Aging

Two important facts have been discovered, however, that help us better understand the aging process. The first concerns not the repair of cells but the repair of material inside the cells that makes it possible for them to grow and reproduce.

This material is made up of DNA (short for deoxyribonucleic acid). DNA forms long strands that carry instructions for everything the cell makes or does. (You can read more about DNA in the articles on BODY CHEMISTRY and GENETICS.) Breaks and alterations can form in these strands, but the cell has ways of snipping out errors and mending breaks.

Scientists have found that long-lived animals have cells that are better at making such repairs than cells in short-lived animals, such as mice. It could be that DNA repair is an important factor in remaining vigorous and healthy for a long time.

The second important discovery is that aging can be slowed down. This can be done by slowing growth and development. A great many animals (cockroaches, for example) have shorter lives if they are fed heavily and made to grow as fast as possible. They live longer if they eat less and grow more slowly. Dr. Clive M. McCay, at Cornell University, found that this was also true of rats.

In McCay's experiment, litters of young rats are divided at random into two groups.

One group is fed a normal rat diet; the other gets everything it needs except enough energy-giving food (calories) to grow. The fully fed rats grow up, become adult, live their lives, and die of old age. During the same period of time, the underfed rats stay apparently young. And they can be made to grow long after their fully fed brothers and sisters are dead of old age. This means that aging, then, is not simply a matter of passing weeks and months, but also of the rate of living. McCay's experiment does not mean, of course, that starving people will live longer than the well fed. Starvation in people is a shortage of everything. The rats were short only of enough energy foods for growth.

Aging and the Brain

Much research on slowing down aging is now concerned with the brain. Certain parts of the brain are known to act as the "clocks" that control growing up and becoming adult. There is much evidence that while many aging processes are going on in different parts of the body, it is the brain—in a region called the hypothalamus—that controls and organizes life span.

"Clocks" in the brain are able to determine which cells divide, what substances they make, and how they react to invading bacteria and other foreign substances. They may even control DNA repair. The difficulty for researchers is that because the body acts as a whole, changes in one part of the body affect many other parts. This makes it difficult to determine what exactly the "clocks" are controlling. There may even be many "clocks" in different parts of the body.

Aging and the Immune System

The body's immune system is responsible for repelling invaders, that is, disease-producing viruses and bacteria. Researchers know that old people do not resist infection very well. Studies have shown that this is partly due to changes in the white cells of the blood, an important part of the immune system.

These changes can be reversed, however. A great deal of research is directed at finding ways to do this and at understanding why the changes occur in the first place. Another research effort is aimed at discovering why the immune system sometimes damages the body by mistaking its own cells for enemies. Once

Disabilities or disease may limit the capabilities of some elderly people. However, most can still enjoy simple activities such as a trip through a garden with a friend (*above*) or benefit from the thoughtful attention of a caregiver (*below*).

A scientist studies cells in hopes of uncovering clues about the causes of aging and the factors that determine an organism's life span. Research such as this may one day help us to slow down or completely control the aging process.

we understand the immune system, we may be a lot closer to actually controlling the aging process.

▶RESEARCH ON LIFE SPANS

Another type of research on aging involves the collection of facts about ages and growth rates in animals. It is very hard to study the force of mortality in animals by keeping them for life and recording when they die. The reason is that many live half as long as we do ourselves.

What we need to find out is the force of mortality at different ages in a mixed population of animals. This means we must know the age of each one—but wild creatures do not have birth certificates. For the most part we must rely on research records, though the records are far from complete. In a few cases, however, we can tell the ages of animals by some structure on the animal's body that grows regularly. The shells, bones, or teeth of certain animals lay down a fixed number of marks or rings every year. We can tell the ages of these animals just as we can tell the age of a tree by counting its rings.

Life Spans of Organs and Cells

In addition to studying how long an entire animal or person lives, researchers are explor-ing the life spans of individual organs and cells.

Would our skin or liver age if it were not joined to the rest of us? We know that when a healthy young heart is transplanted into an old person, it does not prevent the older person from aging. But would an older person's heart last longer if it were in the body of a young person?

Scientists have tried to find answers to such questions by putting tissue from an old animal (a mouse, for example) in the body of a young animal. Unfortunately, the experiments have produced unclear results, so scientists have simplified their experiments and turned to studying individual cells.

When human cells are grown outside the body (under special laboratory conditions), they can only divide a limited number of times —the cell culture becomes old and dies out. It is now possible to combine a cell from a young culture with a cell from an old culture. When this is done, however, the only cells that are able to divide continuously and never die out seem to be cancer cells.

Clearly there are still many puzzles to be solved before we have a clear picture of what controls the life span of cells, organs, or entire animals. Some experiments seem to add more questions instead of providing some answers.

Other experiments seem to provide valuable new information, but it cannot be safely used until we have a clearer understanding of the aging process.

▶ THE DREAM OF A LONGER LIFE

Research on aging has raised many interesting questions about how the body works and how it changes over time. But one of the most important questions is whether the ultimate goal of gerontology—to make people live longer—is really a good idea.

People have never liked to think that they would get old or that their lives would end around a fixed age. So there have always been stories about miraculously long lives and about people who regained their youth. A Greek myth tells us of Eos (Aurora), goddess of the dawn, who prayed that her husband, Tithonus, be made immortal. The prayer was granted, but unfortunately she had forgotten to ask that he stay eternally young. So he grew older and older and more and more decrepit until he prayed to be allowed to die.

Poets in the Middle Ages wrote of a Fountain of Youth in which one could bathe and become young. The fountain was a fiction invented by the poets. But there was, at the same time, another group of people called alchemists. They were the inventors of chemistry, though they mixed a great deal of magic in with it. The alchemists took over the dream of eternal youth. They made it one of their three great projects: to change lead into gold, to travel to the moon, and to discover the elixir of life, which would make old people young.

The alchemists failed to achieve these goals. Time passed and scientific knowledge grew. In the light of the new knowledge, the three old dreams seemed less and less likely ever to be realized. Scientists left them to lunatics and frauds. But then more time passed, and the modern age of science arrived. In it the old dreams have started to come true.

Today we can change one metal into another. Astronauts have visited the moon and returned safely. The third of the alchemists' projects, the slowing down of aging, remains the hardest. It has not been achieved, but it no longer seems impossible. Many scientists, backed by a number of governments and by various universities, are now carrying out serious research on aging.

The legendary Fountain of Youth, sought by Ponce de León, was a magic spring that would restore youth to the aged. It is one of the many myths about eternal youth.

Certainly if we only made people live longer, like Tithonus—instead of preventing them from aging as well—it would not be a good thing. On the other hand, there are some people of 80 who are ill or crippled because of age, while others are hale and active. If it were possible that we could all be hale and useful at 80—even if we lived no longer in the end—it would be a great improvement both for individuals and for society. Now we spend nearly a third of our lives learning our jobs. If we lived longer, we could do more work in a lifetime and carry out more of our plans.

The possibility of lengthening life raises some difficult questions. At the moment we do not know for certain whether we can ever hope to change the rate of aging. Yet everyone should think about the problems because scientists are making a serious attempt to find the means of slowing aging. It seems reasonable to think they will succeed eventually—but when and by how much nobody can yet say.

ALEX COMFORT
Author, *A Good Age*

See also OLD AGE.

AGNEW, SPIRO T. See VICE PRESIDENCY OF THE UNITED STATES.

A combine gathers grain in one of the highly productive wheat fields of North America. Large machines capable of working vast farmlands are the basis of modern agriculture.

AGRICULTURE

When you think about agriculture, do you picture a farmer driving a large tractor across a huge field? If you do, you will be partly correct, for a farmer on a tractor certainly represents agriculture. But agriculture is also much more. It is the tank truck driver who carries loads of milk from farms to dairy-processing plants. It is the merchant who sells livestock feed to cattle ranchers. It is the worker who taps rubber trees or plants cotton, tobacco, or potatoes. It is the scientist researching better ways to grow grain, the operator of a grain elevator, the migrant worker picking apples, the worker in a modern ·chicken factory, and even the farm lobbyist trying to get a bill enacted into law. And agriculture is still more. Agriculture includes the raising of every kind of plant and animal that is useful to human beings—and all the people and services that help bring agricultural products to the world's markets.

▶ **MODERN AND TRADITIONAL AGRICULTURE**

Big farm machines and large fields are common in the great agricultural regions of the United States and Canada. Most of the food consumed in these two countries comes from these large modern farms. These farms often produce only one or two products but in very large amounts. The farms are usually named for their chief product, for example, cattle ranches, wheat farms, and dairy farms.

There are other forms of agriculture, which use fewer and smaller machines. Almost half the people of the world are farmers. Most of them are part of "traditional" agriculture,

The article AGRICULTURE discusses the agricultural industry, types of agriculture, important agricultural products, agriculture around the world, general and specialized farming, land management, and agricultural education and history. If you want to read about the business of farming, farming methods, and farm machinery, see the article FARMS AND FARMING.

using animals and their own muscles for power and using the same tools and practices that have been used for centuries.

Traditional farmers grow much of their own food and the fiber for their clothing. They do not spend much for machinery, fertilizer, or other modern materials. Even in the "modern" United States, some people farm in the traditional way. Amish farmers, for example, use no machines, even in such jobs as scooping grain, pitching hay to cattle, milking cows, and hauling the cow manure to the fields to serve as fertilizer.

Many countries have a "dual agriculture," that is, traditional farms in some areas, modern farms in others. But traditional agriculture is losing out. Millions of traditional farmers are moving to crowded cities in search of an easier life. These people must be fed by the modern agriculture that replaces them. Other millions of small farmers have stayed on the farms but have adopted modern practices including the use of fertilizers and high-producing seeds and the efficient use of small machines. Some of these small modern farmers also have jobs off the farm, so they are called "part-time" farmers. Most U.S. farms are part-time farms—even some of the larger ones—because part of the farm family's income is earned off the farm.

Modern agriculture is changing. On future farms, there may be fewer big tractors, as scientists find ways to farm with less energy as well as less human labor. Agriculture is becoming more successful in producing food for all the world's people.

▶ IMPORTANT AGRICULTURAL PRODUCTS

The most important sources of human food are the grains or "cereals"—wheat, rice, corn, and others. Wheat is the most important grain in the United States, Canada, and many other western countries. But much of the world's wheat is grown and eaten in the large Asian nations of China and India. Wheat will grow well in most farming areas, even those with little rainfall, and those where the weather is cold most of the year, as in Siberia in the Russian Federation. Wheat is used to make bread, pasta (such as spaghetti and macaroni), cereals, and numerous other products. Wheat products are growing in popularity, and fortunately, farms are producing enough wheat to keep up with the demand.

An Amish farmer in Pennsylvania cultivates a field with a team of horses. Traditional agricultural methods are still practiced by many peoples the world over.

Rice is grown in areas where the weather is warm throughout the year and rainfall is plentiful. Most rice is grown in wetlands or paddies that are flooded with water during the growing season. Rice is the main food of Asia, but it is a part of the diet in other lands as well. Rice requires more labor than wheat, but it yields more grain per acre.

Corn is the highest producer per acre. It is grown in temperate zones where rainfall is plentiful and summer days are long, such as in the midwestern United States. Corn was first raised by American Indian peoples, and corn *tortillas* ("little cakes") are a basic food in Central and South America.

Other important grains include rye, oats, barley, sorghum, and millet. Sorghum and millet are important foods in some parts of Africa and Asia.

Grains are seeds that usually grow at the top of the plant. But there are also many common

foods that grow underground as roots and tubers of plants. These include potatoes, the basic food of early Europe, and sweet potatoes, an important food in China and the Pacific. Many Africans rely on cassava, another root crop.

Most people eat several kinds of foods to make their diets more interesting and also because a single food is unlikely to provide all the nutrients a human body needs. Meat is a useful supplement to foods made from grains. And because meat comes from animals, it can be moved and stored "on the hoof." Canadian and U.S. agriculture produces meat mainly from cows (beef), pigs (pork), chicken, and turkeys. In other lands some other animals are used. For example, mutton (from sheep) is popular in many countries.

For many people in the world, meat is very expensive. So it may be eaten only on special occasions, and then only as a small part of the meal. As people become wealthier, they eat more meat. For this reason, the use of meat is increasing in the developing countries of Asia.

Eggs and dairy products such as milk and cheese are popular and nutritious foods. To assure that they are fresh and safe to eat, they must be carefully refrigerated, and dairy products must also be processed, that is, specially treated and prepared.

Legumes, such as beans, are another important food. A good source of protein, legumes can even take the place of meat and dairy products in the diet. Soybeans, in particular, are becoming a major source of protein in human diets.

Soybeans are also the source of soy oil, which is used as an ingredient in many prepared foods. Edible oils also come from sunflower seeds, olives, corn, cottonseed, and many other plants.

Because people everywhere enjoy sweets, there is a large world demand for sugar. Sugarcane is the principal export of many tropical lands, such as Cuba. In northern countries, sugar beets are the main source of sugar.

Among the fruits of the world, the banana is the most commonly eaten, and it is becom-

Some countries are especially known for particular agricultural products. Top: On a plantation in the Dominican Republic, a worker cuts sugarcane, the country's leading commercial crop. Left: A good grape harvest assures another fine year for France's world-famous wines.

A Dominican farmer inspects tobacco leaves that have been hung to dry. Though not a food, tobacco is a commercially important agricultural product.

ing even more popular. The second most popular fruit is the orange. Grapes, too, are widely grown because the juice of the grape, as wine, is a popular beverage.

Different countries have different choices of fresh vegetables. Peppers are a favorite among Spanish-speaking peoples. Cabbage is an important vegetable in areas with cold winters, such as Poland, because cabbage can withstand frost. Therefore it can be eaten fresh, after the season for other vegetables is past. The most popular vegetable in the world is the tomato, which is used in more than 100 countries. Another especially popular vegetable is the onion.

There is another group of products in great worldwide demand. These are the so-called "stimulants": tobacco, tea, coffee, and cocoa.

Agriculture produces not only food but also fibers. Cotton, flax (linen), and wool for clothing are among the important fibers produced. Rubber for industry is another important product from agriculture. Some medicines, too, are made from agricultural products.

▶ AGRICULTURE AROUND THE WORLD

Many countries do not have to buy much food from others. They meet their food needs largely from their own agriculture. Even the world's most populous countries, China and India, can meet most of their food needs. Even so, there is a large and lively international trade in agricultural products.

Farmers in the United States supply the nation with hundreds of foods, including the basic foods such as wheat for bread, potatoes, milk, and meat. But bananas, coffee, and tea are grown more easily in the tropics, so these products are imported to the United States, mainly from Central and South America. Africa and Asia provide tropical products for Europe.

Many countries produce more farm products than they need. This surplus (overproduction) is traded for other goods. The United States sends grain and meat to Japan, which sends back radios, cars, and other manufactured goods. Some countries are famous for their farm exports, such as Brazil for its coffee, New Zealand for wool and lamb, and Canada and Australia for wheat.

Taxes on farm exports provide income for governments of developing countries. Governments may also control farm prices, hoping to assure inexpensive food for their own people. But if a government taxes farm products too much, or holds prices too low, farmers may protest.

Farmers have formed farm organizations. These organizations demand that government push farm prices higher, not lower. Farmers demand help in expanding their markets, both at home and outside the country. They also demand better roads, better storage facilities, water for irrigation, and useful agricultural research, all of which help make farmers more efficient and more competitive.

Responding to farmers' demands, some governments have contributed much to agricultural growth. With government help, agriculture in Canada, the United States, and Europe has grown so much that farmers can often produce far more than can be sold at a fair price. Food surpluses drive prices down. So too much growth may lead to hard times on the farms, in farm towns, and in industries that serve farmers. In the United States in the 1980's, for example, many efficient farmers went broke, and so did some banks and equipment companies that served them. Farming is a risky business, especially when it is rapidly changing.

There are countries where agriculture is not rapidly improving. One such country is Russia, a vast land that must import grain to meet its food needs. One reason for the slow agricultural growth is that much of Russian farmland is in cold places where crops often fail. To help provide more food, the Russians have planned engineering projects for capturing water from their rivers to be used for irrigating farmland.

On the continent of Africa, there is a shortage of food, and here, too, the natural environment is part of the problem. African geography offers both advantages and disadvantages for farming. The advantages are lots of unused land that could be made into farms and much water in rivers that could be captured for irrigation to help yield additional crops. The disadvantages are the lack of rainfall in some years and, in tropical Africa, no cold winter to kill off pests and diseases. Farm plants may be attacked by swarms of birds or locusts, by weeds, fungi, insects, and viruses. After the crops are harvested, rats may move in to eat them in the storage places. Diseases attack animals and human beings. Many African farmers suffer from malaria, dysentery, and parasites such as worms.

Agriculture faces many other problems in the developing countries of Africa and of

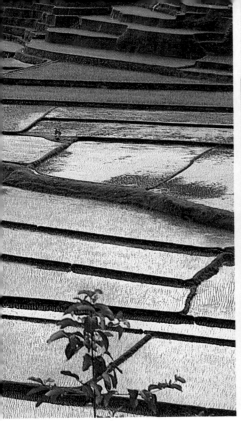

Latin America as well. Some countries are losing forests and grasslands. People cut down too many trees for timber, causing forests to disappear. Animals eat grassy lands bare. When forests and grass are gone, rainwater washes away the topsoil. Beautiful lands turn into wastelands.

Agriculture in Asia sets a good example for the developing world. In most Asian countries, there is now more food per person than ever before, even though the number of people has grown larger than ever. Gains in food production have come about partly as a result of government policies and programs. Countries such as India and China are also overcoming the problems of unpredictable weather and tropical pests.

▶GENERAL AND SPECIALIZED FARMING

A farm where a variety of things are raised is called a general farm. On such a farm there may be a herd of dairy cows whose milk the farmer sells. There may also be hogs, sheep, or poultry to provide extra income and supply some of the family's needs. The farmer may raise some of the hay and grain for feeding the animals. There may be some "cash crop"

Around the world, agriculture takes many forms. Far left: Merino sheep in New Zealand are herded prior to shearing for their excellent wool. Center: In Indonesia, rice is grown in flooded paddies on terraced hillsides. Above: On a *kibbutz*, a collective farm in Israel, workers cultivate a peanut field. Below: A hand-powered machine separates coffee beans from their shells in Colombia.

Specialized farming of beef cattle is a huge enterprise in western regions of the United States and Canada. The structures at the rear of the feedlot are for grain storage.

such as tobacco, soybeans, or vegetables. Cash crops, as the name indicates, are raised to be sold rather than for use on the farm.

General farms usually require constant labor and often cannot use new technologies. As a result, general farms are becoming few in number. In most countries with modern agriculture systems, specialized farming is predominant.

Specialized farms concentrate on one or two products. In North America, some specialized farms are clustered by region. Wheat farms stretch across the Prairie Provinces of Canada and the High Plains of the United States, from Montana and North Dakota through Colorado, Kansas, and Oklahoma.

Sometimes two products fit well together. The dry climate most suitable for wheat lands is also suitable for the grasslands that support beef cattle. The cattle can also graze on young wheat plants. So wheat and beef production often go together.

In the U.S. Midwestern region extending from Nebraska to Ohio, which has heavier rainfall than the High Plains, corn is the favored crop. Corn is a high-yielding crop, producing as much as 200 bushels per acre (500 bushels per hectare). Another important Midwestern crop is soybeans, which sell for high prices. Soybean and corn production go to-

gether because the same farm machinery can be used for both crops and because both thrive during the long humid summer days.

Cotton and soybeans often go together on specialized farms in the humid South—in Mississippi, Arkansas, and Tennessee. Cotton and wheat go together in the dry southern plains of Oklahoma, West Texas, and New Mexico. (Cotton can grow well in dry climates if there is enough irrigation.)

The irrigated valleys of California and other Western states provide fresh fruits and vegetables—even for millions of people living across the continent on the East Coast. In the East, Florida produces vegetables and provides orange juice for the whole nation. There are also other centers for fruit and vegetable production—Michigan, for example.

While some specialized farms, such as fruit and vegetable farms, are located far away from consumers, others, such as dairy farms, tend to be located on the edges of cities. Los Angeles County in California, for example, with one of the world's largest cities, is also one of the United States' major agricultural centers. Dairies located near Los Angeles, like other specialized farms, may do just one thing —in this case they just feed and milk the cows. Many other steps are done elsewhere. For example, the dairy cows were probably born and raised on other farms, to be purchased by the dairy farm just before they were ready to be milked.

Farmers are just one of many groups involved in agriculture. Others include feed and fertilizer suppliers, truckers and shippers, food processors and packagers, distributors, and grocers. There are some kinds of specialized agriculture, in fact, that have no farmers at all. For example, in the United States today, chickens and eggs are produced largely in factories. Not long ago almost every farm had some chickens, which provided eggs and meat for the farm family. "Egg money" from the sale of eggs was an addition to the family income. Now, however, most chickens are raised in large buildings. These "chicken factories" may be owned by grocery store chains or by large companies. Specialized farming has greatly changed the process of food production in highly developed countries. The term **agribusiness** is now used to describe the entire industry involved in the production, distribution, and sale of agricultural products.

▶ LAND MANAGEMENT

Plants grow in the earth's thin skin of topsoil. Because such a small portion of the earth's surface can be used to produce crops, it is very important that farmers do a good job of managing the soil, that is, taking care of it so that it does not become exhausted and is not eroded away by rain and wind. All over the world, much good farmland has been lost to erosion. For example, people seeking timber and food may cut down trees and other vegetation that hold the soil, and they may plow steep hillsides that soon become eroded and barren.

There are ways to control erosion even while improving agriculture to meet all food and fiber needs. Some older practices work well, but many farmers do not use these methods because extra time and effort are needed. These ways include changing crops from year to year (rotating crops) so that high-profit crops are followed by soil-building crops. Or, different crops can be planted side by side in narrow bands (strip cropping). Water erosion can be slowed by cultivating across, rather than up and down, the sides of hills and by digging ridges (terraces) along the sides of hills, which keep water from rushing downhill.

A new practice is "minimum till," in which plant residues (remains) are not plowed under after the harvest but instead are left on the surface to protect soil from wind and rain. Minimum till is easier than other methods, so this is a popular form of soil conservation.

There are other losses of farmland, but these losses are small by comparison to erosion. For example, some farmland is being used for roads, factories, and houses. Some

A modern "chicken factory" can accommodate flocks of more than 100,000 chickens at a time. The birds remain indoors and are fed and watered by machines.

To help prevent soil erosion, this farm uses strip cropping (planting different crops side by side in bands) and contour farming (cultivating across the sides of hills).

land is being polluted by salt and other chemicals carried in irrigation water.

Since our food comes from the soil, the loss of soil is a great concern. In the future, people will thank us if we are able to preserve most of our farmland and other natural resources.

▶AGRICULTURAL EDUCATION

Until the 19th century agricultural education was limited to whatever practical information and folklore a father might hand down to his son. England led the way in scientific agricultural education by establishing an experimental station in 1843 and an agricultural college in 1845. Other European countries soon followed suit. Agricultural education had a hard time winning acceptance. Many farmers were unwilling to change the methods they were used to, and many also disliked and distrusted "book learning."

One of the leaders in the movement to establish agricultural education in the United States was Senator Justin S. Morrill (1810–98), the son of a Vermont blacksmith. It was he who introduced the bill, signed by President Lincoln in 1862, that provided for the establishment of agricultural colleges in every state. Money for these colleges was to come from the sale of public lands granted to the states by the federal government. For this reason these agricultural colleges are known as "land-grant" colleges. Some of the leading universities in the United States began as small land-grant colleges.

Research stations that worked closely with the land-grant colleges were established soon after. They proved their value by the contributions they made to agricultural knowledge. They also were important in developing better types of animals and plants.

The county agents played an important part in bringing the knowledge of the agricultural colleges and research stations to the ordinary farmer. Their on-the-spot demonstrations probably did more than anything else to convince farmers that "book learning" was truly practical.

In Canada, agricultural education on the college level began in 1851 at the University of Toronto. The first agricultural college, St.

Anne's Agricultural School (now affiliated with Laval University), was opened at Ste. Anne de la Pocatière, Quebec, in 1859. The Ontario Agricultural College, founded at Guelph in 1874, was the first institution that succeeded in taking agricultural education to the farmer in much the same way that the county agents did in the United States. The success of the Ontario Agricultural College led to the founding of similar schools throughout Canada.

Typical subjects taught in agricultural colleges nowadays include plant and animal biology, genetics, soil conservation, soil chemistry and the use of fertilizers, bacteriology, entomology and pest control, agricultural engineering, and marketing.

▶ **HISTORY OF AGRICULTURE**

Nobody knows exactly when or where agriculture began. But scientists now believe that it began 8,000 years ago or more when people discovered that the wild grass seeds that they ate as part of their diet would grow if they were placed in the ground at the right time of year. Not only did the seeds grow, but each one produced many more seeds to fill the stomachs of the tribe. This may seem like a small thing to modern people, but for primitive people it was a truly revolutionary discovery. Up until then they had depended for their lives on their luck in hunting and fishing and finding wild plants that they could eat. Being able to grow a part of their own food meant that starvation was no longer such a danger.

As early people learned about raising crops, they came to depend more and more on farming and less on hunting to keep themselves alive. In addition to wild grasses, from which our present-day grains are descended, these early people learned to grow many other plants, the ancestors of today's vegetables.

Permanent settlements grew up where the land was good for farming. As time passed and the population increased, some of these settlements grew into large towns and eventually cities. People who were especially skilled at making things, such as pots, cloth, or tools and weapons, began to work full-time at their specialties. This was the beginning of division of labor.

Agriculture was developed independently by different groups of people in widely separated parts of the world. The knowledge probably spread slowly from each little group of farmers to their neighbors. Today, historians look at the crops early people raised as a clue to how much contact they had with other areas and continents.

Two of the very earliest places where we know that agriculture was practiced were the valley of the Nile River, in northeastern Africa, and the region called Mesopotamia, along the Tigris and Euphrates rivers in southwestern Asia. The little farming settlements of the Nile Valley grew into the mighty civilization of Egypt. A whole series of countries, from Ur of the Chaldees to Babylonia, flourished in Mesopotamia.

Primitive farming methods were extremely crude. Seeds were planted in little holes in the ground made with a sharp stick. Grain was harvested with flint knives or flint-edged sickles or was sometimes pulled up by the roots. The invention of the spade and the hoe made it possible to cultivate the ground. This helped the crops by loosening the soil and keeping down weeds. At first the work in the fields seems to have been done by women, while the men watched the herds, hunted occasionally, and defended the village against its enemies.

Domestic animals were probably kept at first for hunting (such as dogs) or food (such as cows, sheep, and pigs). Eventually it was discovered that some of them could be used to carry loads or pull a plow. This was another great step forward. The first plows were little more than forked sticks pulled through the soil to stir it up. They were hard to pull and did not work very well by modern standards. Still, they made it possible to cultivate more land with less work than had ever been possible with only hand tools.

The Egyptians, the Mesopotamians, and the Chinese developed advanced systems of agriculture. They knew the value of fertilization, irrigation, and drainage. They developed

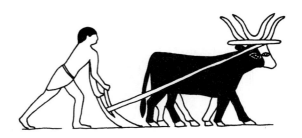

improved varieties of plants and animals by selective breeding. The Chinese, in particular, were skilled at getting the most possible use out of every piece of land. By comparison Europe lagged far behind. The Romans developed fairly advanced methods of farming around the beginning of the Christian Era, but most of their knowledge was lost when the Roman Empire fell apart during the 5th century A.D.

Farming methods in Europe during the Middle Ages were generally crude, wasteful, and inefficient. Very few farmers owned their own land. Most of the land was owned by nobles or the church. It was worked by tenant farmers who were little better off than slaves. On each estate, or **manor,** much of the land was kept as forest, where the nobles hunted for sport. The less fertile land was used as pasture. Hay was gathered from swampy meadows. The cultivated land was divided into three large sections. Crops were grown on two of these sections, while the third lay **fallow;** that is, nothing was grown on it This allowed the land to recover a little of its fertility. Each year a different section lay fallow. In the sections that were cultivated, each peasant was allotted a certain amount of land. The

During the Middle Ages, most farm work was done by hand. Workers are shown harvesting grain with sickles and then tying the stalks into bundles.

fields were usually long, narrow strips rather than squares because this shape made plowing easier. The plow did not need to be turned around so many times at the end of the furrow. The peasant's land strips were usually scattered in different parts of the big field. The average size of the individual allotments was as much as one peasant could plow in one day. Our word "acre" comes from the Latin word *ager,* meaning "field." So does the word "agriculture."

Deep-rooted customs forced all the peasants on a manor to plant the same crops and do their plowing, planting, and harvesting together. Thus there was very little chance for trying out new crops or new farming methods.

Agricultural machinery was unknown, and all farm work except for plowing and harrowing was done by hand. The harrow of those days was an implement like a large rake. It was pulled over the ground after plowing to break up the clods and smooth the surface somewhat. Sometimes a large bundle of brush was used instead. Seeds for grain crops, the main food of the people, were **broadcast** (scattered by hand) over the ground. Since seeds were not covered, many were eaten by birds. Much grain was also lost by inefficient harvesting and storage. Domestic animals were usually small and scrawny from lack of food. The swamp meadows did not yield enough hay to support many animals over the winter; so most of them were slaughtered in the fall. The lack of domestic animals meant that there was never enough manure for the fields. This kept crop yields very low. Under these conditions starvation was never very far around the corner.

The revival of European agriculture really began in the Low Countries (now the Netherlands and Belgium) around the 16th century A.D. The Dutch and Flemish (Belgian) farmers had begun to cultivate two new "wonder crops"—clover and turnips. Clover enriched the soil by adding nitrogen and made very nutritious hay. Turnips made good winter feed for animals. They fitted in well with the primitive scheme of crop rotation. With plenty of feed the farmers could keep herds of animals over the winter. Furthermore, animals could be kept in farmyards during the rest of the year so that the manure could be easily collected. The manure was carefully put on the fields to maintain their fertility.

In America in the early 1800's, much farm work, such as gathering hay, was still done by hand. But agriculture would soon be changed by machines like the reaper.

With more and better food, the animals soon improved in size and quality. Historians call this discovery the Agricultural Revolution.

The new methods spread slowly. But more advances were made in 18th-century England. Pioneer experimenters developed horse-drawn farming machines, improved systems of crop rotation and fertilization, and better breeds of sheep and cattle.

Meanwhile, Europeans were exploring the New World. They returned home with crops previously unknown in Europe—white and sweet potatoes, corn, pumpkins, and tomatoes. Most of these remained little more than curiosities for many years. But one plant, the potato, was found to grow well in cold, damp climates and on poor soils. It soon became an important food item in northern Europe.

Similarly, crops and animals native to Europe and Asia were carried to North America by early explorers and colonists. Later, crops were exchanged between other lands. Coffee, a native of northern Africa, was taken to Brazil and Indonesia. Peanuts, native to South America, were carried to Africa.

As trade between the various countries of the world increased, there was a growing exchange not only of plants and animals but also of agricultural practices and technologies.

Scientific agriculture in the United States had its beginnings in the 1700's. Benjamin Franklin promoted the use of lime to improve acid soils. George Washington and Thomas Jefferson were leading experimenters in scientific farming. Their work was continued by a few wealthy landowners, who corresponded with one another and with like-minded people in Europe.

In the 1800's, the government began to become involved in helping farmers. Agricultural experiment stations were set up. The establishment of land-grant colleges and other institutions brought knowledge of scientific methods and improved techniques within reach of ordinary farmers.

Another advance during the 1800's was the discovery that chemicals could be used as fertilizers. These substances, produced cheaply and in large quantities, increased crop yields even on poor soil. The development of machines like the reaper, binder, and thresher also increased production. Steel plows replaced the less efficient cast-iron plows. The use of power, at first steam and then gasoline, took much of the physical labor out of agriculture.

In the 20th century the major advances have been in three areas—chemistry, breeding, and technology. Modern farming depends heavily on chemical fertilizers and insect-killers. Other chemicals fight plant diseases and kill weeds. Synthetically produced vitamins, hormones, and antibiotics speed the growth of livestock and chickens and control the tenderness of the meat and the amount of fat in it.

Plant and animal breeders, building on the discoveries of geneticists, developed improved breeds of plants and animals. Some plant breeds produce much higher yields per unit of land than earlier breeds. This has been particularly valuable in basic crops such as wheat, rice, and corn. Corn hybrids, for example, enable farmers of today to get three or four times more corn per acre of land than farmers of the early 1900's.

Power-driven machinery and the electrification of farms have also greatly increased pro-

An agricultural scientist records data on sunflower growth. Agricultural scientists work to improve the quality of crops and livestock and to increase food production.

duction. This has led to an increase in the size of farms and a decrease in the number of farm workers. One person operating large, efficient equipment can produce much more than a group of workers without machines.

Farm technology continues to improve. Already, modern agriculture is doing away with the plow, which caused soil erosion and used too much energy from humans, animals, and tractors. Under new "no-till" or "minimum-till" agricultural practices, farmers save time and money.

Agricultural scientists have done much to make agriculture more productive. They have found ways to control terrible plant and animal diseases. For example, one team of agricultural scientists found a vaccine for Marek's disease, from which many chickens were suffering. Other scientists developed a ray gun that can take a plant's temperature, to find out if the plant is sick or thirsty for water.

One of the biggest research findings has been the development of new strains of wheat and rice. Scientists in each rice-growing country have adapted the new strains of rice for the best use by their own farmers.

Scientific breakthroughs may soon be leading to another big change or "revolution" in agriculture. Scientists are learning to change living things by altering their genes. Through "gene-splicing," nature itself can be changed quickly. Food plants may be improved to do a better job of fighting off insects and weeds, with less use of pesticides. Plants may become better able to fertilize themselves and to reproduce themselves each year. Changes in genes can also make grains and other plant foods more nutritious. All these changes would make farming easier and help solve the enormous problems in countries where hunger is a severe problem.

Perhaps the most important effect of the new revolution in genetics is that all people may benefit from it, not just those in highly developed nations. Countries that cannot afford tractors, fertilizers, and other expensive aids to modern agriculture may be able to bypass these things in a simpler, cheaper agricultural system.

There are still many things to be done. For example, some chemicals we have used to grow more food are endangering our health and polluting our soil and water. So we must find ways to produce our food with less use of these chemicals. One way is to find natural biological controls to do the same things chemicals do now. This might seem like looking for miracles. But such "miracles" have happened often, and they have helped agriculture become one of the most progressive, efficient industries in the world.

DON F. HADWIGER
Iowa State University

See also FARMS AND FARMING; CONSERVATION; EROSION; FERTILIZERS; IRRIGATION; NATURAL RESOURCES; PLANT PESTS; SOILS; names of products, as CORN, WHEAT; kinds of farming, as DAIRYING AND DAIRY PRODUCTS; and the agriculture sections of continent, country, and state articles.

AGRICULTURE, UNITED STATES DEPARTMENT OF

The Department of Agriculture (USDA) is one of the 14 executive departments of the United States government. Its purpose is to inspect and grade agricultural products—such as grain, livestock, and dairy products—to ensure the quality and safety of the nation's food supplies; to carry out soil and water conservation programs; to conduct research on crop production, nutrition, pest control, and animal and plant diseases; to grant federal loans to family-size farms and ranches; to aid the hungry and undernourished with supplementary food programs, such as food stamps and school lunches; to provide technical assistance and agricultural training in developing countries; to expand overseas markets for American produce; and to ensure fair prices for farmers as well as consumers.

Departmental Agencies

The Department of Agriculture is headed by the secretary of agriculture. The secretary is a member of the president's cabinet and is the president's principal adviser on agricultural matters. The secretary, who is assisted by a deputy secretary, two undersecretaries, seven assistant secretaries, and various agency administrators, is responsible for the overall planning and operations of the seven agencies listed below.

The undersecretary for **Small Community and Rural Development** manages the Farmers Home Administration; the Federal Crop Insurance Corporation; and the Rural Electrification Administration.

The assistant secretary for **Marketing and Inspection Services** manages the Agricultural Cooperative Service; the Agricultural Marketing Service; the Animal and Plant Health Inspection Service; the Federal Grain Inspection Service; the Food Safety and Inspection Service; the Packers and Stockyards Administration; and the Office of Transportation.

The assistant secretary for **Food and Consumer Services** manages the Food and Nutrition Service, including the Food Stamp Program; the Human Nutrition Information Service; and the Office of the Consumer Adviser.

Secretaries of Agriculture		
Name	**Took Office**	**Under President**
Norman J. Colman	1889	Cleveland
Jeremiah M. Rusk	1889	B. Harrison
Julius S. Morton	1893	Cleveland
James Wilson	1897	McKinley
David F. Houston	1913	Wilson
Edwin T. Meredith	1920	Wilson
Henry C. Wallace	1921	Harding
Howard M. Gore	1924	Coolidge
William M. Jardine	1925	Coolidge
Arthur M. Hyde	1929	Hoover
Henry A. Wallace	1933	F. D. Roosevelt
Claude R. Wickard	1940	F. D. Roosevelt
Clinton P. Anderson	1945	Truman
Charles F. Brannan	1948	Truman
Ezra Taft Benson	1953	Eisenhower
Orville L. Freeman	1961	Kennedy
Clifford M. Hardin	1969	Nixon
Earl L. Butz	1971	Nixon
John A. Knebel	1976	Ford
Robert S. Bergland	1977	Carter
John R. Block	1981	Reagan
Richard E. Lyng	1986	Reagan
Clayton Yeutter	1989	Bush
Edward Madigan	1991	Bush
Mike Espy	1993	Clinton

The undersecretary for **International Affairs and Commodity Programs** manages the Agricultural Stabilization and Conservation Service; the Foreign Agricultural Service; and the Office of International Cooperation and Development.

The assistant secretary for **Science and Education** manages the Agricultural Research Service; the National Agricultural Library; the Extension Service; and the Cooperative State Research Service.

The assistant secretary for **Natural Resources and Environment** manages the Forest Service and the Soil Conservation Service.

The assistant secretary for **Economics** manages the Economic Research Service; the National Agricultural Statistics Service; the Office of Energy; the Economic Analysis Staff; and the Economics Management Staff.

When the Department of Agriculture was established in 1862, its primary functions were to conduct experiments, collect statistics, and distribute seeds and plants. It did not achieve cabinet-level status until 1889. Today the department's headquarters are located at Fourteenth Street and Independence Avenue, S.W., Washington, D.C. 20250.

WILLIAM WHYTE
Public Information Specialist
United States Department of Agriculture

See also FOOD REGULATIONS AND LAWS.

AIDS

In the mid-1970's, a new disease began to emerge—a disease that came to be called AIDS, or *a*cquired *i*mmune *d*eficiency syndrome. Although its cause was unknown, AIDS quickly became recognized as a major health threat. By the end of the 1980's, the number of people known to have AIDS or conditions related to it had grown to more than 1 million. Some 10 million more are thought to be infected without showing symptoms of the disease. Some parts of the world—sub-Saharan Africa, India, Thailand, the United States, and Brazil—have been more severely affected by AIDS than others. But the threat of AIDS is worldwide.

▶ **WHAT AIDS IS**

AIDS is a disease caused by a virus that attacks various cells of the body. Mainly, the virus attacks cells of the body's immune system (such as certain white blood cells) that help fight infection. When the virus attacks these cells, the immune system becomes weak, or deficient. (The name "acquired immune deficiency syndrome" describes the condition that results.) Once the immune system has been weakened by the virus, diseases of all kinds can easily take hold, including some that are rare and do not normally affect healthy people. Eventually, one of these diseases kills the person with AIDS.

AIDS is a progressive disease. At first, people are infected with the virus but show no symptoms. However, they can spread the infection to others. The virus acts slowly, and over time, ten years or more, the immune system becomes weakened. Various symptoms may appear that can last a long time and may or may not be serious. Finally, the disease progresses to true AIDS. This end stage is characterized by certain life-threatening infections, such as pneumonia, and often by nervous disorders and severe weight loss.

▶ **HOW AIDS SPREADS**

The AIDS virus is present in body fluids, and it can be spread only through an exchange of certain of those fluids. This means that it is difficult for most people to get AIDS. In fact, researchers think that AIDS is spread only in four main ways. The virus can be transmitted from one person to another during sexual intercourse. It can be transmitted by an exchange of blood—as when drug abusers share hypodermic needles. A woman who is infected with AIDS can pass the virus to her unborn child through her blood or after birth, through breast milk. And before 1985, when American blood banks began to screen for AIDS, a number of people became infected when they received transfusions of blood or blood products donated by AIDS carriers.

As scientists have learned more about AIDS, they have been able to lay many unreasonable fears to rest. There is no need to avoid someone who has AIDS—you do not catch the disease by touching or being in a room with that person. The virus is not spread by sneezing or through food, drinking glasses, toilet seats, or swimming pools. It is not carried by dogs, cats, or other domestic animals. And there is no evidence that it can be spread by biting insects, such as mosquitoes.

You will not catch AIDS by donating blood because the needles used in this procedure are new. Because blood is now screened, the chances of receiving a transfusion of infected blood are extremely low. And while the virus may be present in an infected person's saliva, scientists know of no case in which AIDS was transmitted by kissing. Also, the risk of becoming infected in a health-care setting is extremely small.

▶ **SEARCHING FOR A CURE**

Great progress has been made in understanding AIDS. The virus that causes the disease was identified in 1983; it is called HIV, or *h*uman *i*mmuno-deficiency *v*irus. Scientists have developed blood tests to find out if people have been infected. These tests look for AIDS antibodies, substances that the body produces in an effort to fight the virus.

But researchers are still a long way from finding a cure for AIDS. Drugs have been found to slow the progress of the disease. But they are not a cure and can cause serious side effects. Nor is there yet a vaccine that will protect people from AIDS. Until one is found, the best defense lies in teaching people to avoid those behaviors that spread the disease.

Reviewed by MERVYN F. SILVERMAN, M.D.
President, American Foundation
for AIDS Research

See also IMMUNE SYSTEM.

AIR. See AERODYNAMICS; ATMOSPHERE.

AIR CONDITIONING

During a hot spell in 1900, people could do very little about the weather except complain about it, unless they could afford to go away to the mountains or the seashore to try to escape the heat. Today air conditioning has made it possible to be comfortable anywhere, even on the hottest, stickiest days of the year. You will almost certainly find air conditioning in the movie theaters you attend, in most of the stores and office buildings where your family shops and works, in the restaurants where you eat, perhaps even in your family's home and car.

▶ WHAT IS AIR CONDITIONING?

Everyone knows that air conditioning makes you feel cool. But an air conditioning system is often used for more than just cooling. It keeps the temperature and humidity, or moisture content, of the air in an enclosed space at just the right level for the comfort of the people inside. It also circulates the air with fans and removes dust from the air with filters. In winter, an air conditioning system can heat the air and, if necessary, add moisture to it. In summer, an air conditioner removes moisture from the air by passing the air over cold pipes that collect water from it, much as drops of water condense on a cold glass of water on a hot, damp day.

This article will focus on how air conditioning cools the air to create an artificial but comfortable climate indoors when there is warm or hot, humid weather outdoors.

▶ HOW AIR CONDITIONING IS USED

Air conditioning has many uses besides keeping us comfortable. Many industries depend on it to keep the air in their plants clean, cool, and at the right moisture level. For example, textile fibers such as wool and cotton will stretch or shrink as the moisture content of the air changes. This causes variations in the quality of the cloth. Too much moisture in the air—or even on a worker's fingertips—will cause delicate metal parts such as rocket components or precision instruments to corrode. The wrong temperature can spoil a batch of antibiotic culture. Proper air conditioning prevents these mishaps.

The deep diamond and gold mines of South Africa use air conditioning to enable miners to work in what would otherwise be suffocating heat, thousands of feet below ground. With air conditioning, atomic submarines can cruise for weeks under water without coming up for air. Air conditioning is involved in every part of the United States space program, from making missiles to tracking them through the atmosphere.

▶ HISTORY

Over the years inventors have devised various air-cooling methods. The ancient Egyptians and Romans were able to get some relief from the heat by hanging woven mats soaked with water across the entrances to their houses so that the incoming air would be cooled by evaporation. In the 1400's, a water-powered fan was built by the artist and inventor Leonardo da Vinci.

As interest in science increased, hundreds of ideas for cooling systems were proposed, but none of them really worked. In fact, many of the methods made people feel worse because they added large amounts of water to the air, making it very humid. Air soaks up water like a sponge, causing people to feel sticky and uncomfortable, especially in hot weather. If the air is dry, the humidity is low and people feel better.

The first machine that kept the humidity low and cooled the air at the same time was developed in 1902 by

A design for an air-cooled suit and hat from the 1800's displays adjustable slats that could be raised to admit cooling breezes to the wearer.

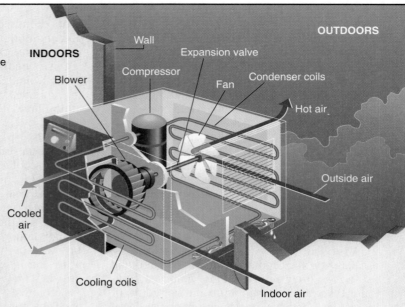

How an Air Conditioner Works

Small air conditioning units are used to cool rooms in houses. Steps 1 through 5 describe how the heat and humidity of the air in a room is removed by an air conditioner, which then blows the cooled air back into the room.

1. The coils and pipes in an air conditioning unit contain refrigerant gas. The refrigerant gas enters the compressor as warm, low-pressure gas and leaves it as hot, high-pressure gas.

2. In the condenser coils, hot, compressed refrigerant gas loses heat to the outdoor air and becomes liquid while it is still warm.

3. The warm, liquid refrigerant passes through the tiny opening of the expansion valve, expands, and partly turns to gas at a low temperature.

4. In the cooling, or evaporator, coils, the refrigerant—now a cold mixture of gas and liquid—takes up heat from the indoor air and leaves the coil as warm, low-pressure gas.

5. The indoor air gives up heat to the refrigerant in the cooling coils and also loses moisture as it is chilled. The moisture condenses on the coils and trickles down to outside drain holes. Cooled air is blown back into the room.

Willis H. Carrier, who is often called "the father of air conditioning." Carrier built this machine for a printing plant in Brooklyn, New York, that had trouble printing in color. Paper stretches when the air is damp and shrinks when the air is dry. Because each color had to be printed separately, printings of different colors on the same sheet of paper did not line up accurately because the paper changed size between printings. Carrier's machine kept the moisture level of the air constant by drawing the air over a row of cold pipes that condensed the excess moisture. This kept the paper at one size and also made the people in the plant feel cool. Carrier's invention marked the beginning of scientific air conditioning.

Air conditioning was soon being used in many factories, such as the plants that made ammunition during World War I. But people generally did not know about this invention until the 1920's, when hundreds of movie theaters, department stores, and restaurants installed air conditioners. People often came into these places just to get relief from the hot, muggy air outdoors.

As air conditioning became more popular during the 1930's, central air conditioning systems were developed. These systems could cool a whole office or apartment building from one centrally located unit, just as one big furnace in a basement could heat an entire building, replacing the need for little stoves in each room. During the same period, small units were developed that could cool a single room. After World War II large numbers of small units began to be used in private homes. A later development, used increasingly in both public buildings and private homes, combined heating and cooling units in one system.

▶ HOW DOES AIR CONDITIONING WORK?

An air conditioning unit does not add coolness to the air; it removes heat. An air conditioner works on the same basic principle as a refrigerator, although it is not designed to produce such low temperatures. Heat is taken from the air by the rapid expansion of a refrigerant, or cooling substance, as it turns from a liquid at high pressure to a gas at low pressure. In small units, which are often used in houses and apartments, the air is cooled directly by the machine. In large, central installations, such as those in office buildings and schools, a machine chills water that is piped to a series of coils. Air from the building is drawn over these coils and circulated through the building by blowers.

For an air conditioning unit to be practical, it must be able to maintain a steady temperature. Otherwise people would have to turn their units off and on continually as the temperature became too cold or too hot. A steady temperature is maintained by a regulating device called a thermostat. The thermostat is set at the desired temperature. It then switches the cooling unit on and off as needed.

Many new types of air conditioning systems are also being developed to eliminate the use of hydrofluorocarbons as a refrigerant. It is thought that hydrofluorocarbons released from many types of popular products such as refrigerators and air conditioning units reach and deplete portions of the ozone layer in the Earth's atmosphere. This activity reduces the effectiveness of the ozone layer, which protects us from harmful radiation from the sun. The designs of these new systems will be based on the latest technological advances, and it is probable that the air conditioning units of the future will be very different from those in use today.

RUSSELL GRAY
President, Carrier Air Conditioning Company
Reviewed by FRANK HARRIS
Product Service Manager, Lennox Industries Inc.

See also HEAT; HEATING SYSTEMS; REFRIGERATION.

AIR FORCE. See UNITED STATES, ARMED FORCES OF THE; CANADIAN ARMED FORCES.

A Central Air Conditioning System

Central air conditioning systems are used to filter and cool all the floors of large buildings at the same time. The arrows show the path of the air as it travels through the filters and supply ducts to each floor. The cool, filtered air comes out of vents on each floor and returns to the air conditioning system.

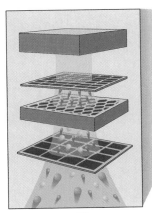

In a Filter

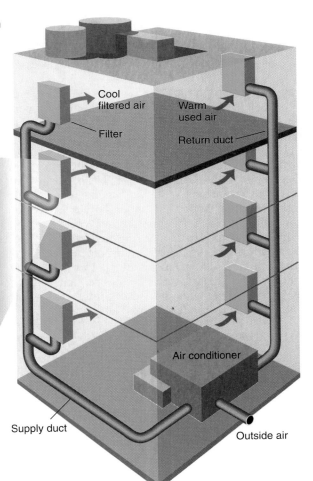

Cool filtered air

Filter

Warm used air

Return duct

Air conditioner

Supply duct

Outside air

A radio-controlled aerobatic (stunt) plane is readied for flight.

AIRPLANE MODELS

No one knows who built the first model airplane. Models of birds, carved from wood and able to fly like gliders, have been found in ancient Egyptian tombs. Early inventors such as Leonardo Da Vinci (1452–1519) built models of their concepts of "flying machines." But the modern hobby of model-airplane building did not really begin until after World War I. The war proved that the airplane was an exciting and practical way to transport people and products. The romance of air travel, together with a natural creative desire, led many people of all ages into the hobby of building miniature models of real airplanes.

▶NON-FLYING MODELS

The easiest-to-build and least expensive model airplanes are constructed from plastic kits. They are made up of pre-molded plastic parts. The parts are very detailed. When they are glued together and painted, the result is a very realistic model of an airplane. They are simple to build, but serious modelers have been known to spend hundreds of hours in research and construction. They try to dupli-cate, as nearly as possible, an actual aircraft—perhaps one flown by a specific pilot in a particular battle. Many modelers go one step further. They build realistic settings, complete with trees and shrubs, buildings, and even miniature people, to create museumlike displays for their airplanes.

In the days before plastic kits, it was common practice to carve models from blocks of wood. That type of construction is mostly limited now to experienced modelers who wish to duplicate an airplane for which no kit is available. It is quite enjoyable to whittle an airplane from a piece of wood. And it is good practice for going on to the next step in model building.

▶FLYING MODELS

This is the part of model-airplane building where the real excitement begins. An airplane is not truly an airplane unless it flies.

There is great variety in the types of models built for flight. They range from the simplest hand-launched glider to very complicated radio-controlled helicopters. Some are scale models of real airplanes. But others are special aircraft designed for contests in which the models are judged for flight duration, precision maneuvers, or speed.

Flying models are classified according to the way they are controlled in flight. The three categories of flying models are free flight, control line, and radio control.

Free Flight

The very early model airplanes were all free-flying. That is, once they were launched, there was no way to control their flight. Free flight remains a very popular activity today. To many modelers there is nothing quite so beautiful as the sight of a model drifting freely on a gentle breeze.

But it is not fun to lose a model if it flies too far. The wise free-flight flier sets the rudder on the airplane to produce a gentle turn. This keeps the model flying in circles overhead.

Free-flight models can be divided into three types—gliders, rubber-powered, and engine-powered. Gliders are relatively simple. They are launched into the air either by being thrown or by being towed on a string (like a kite) and then released for free flight. The towline is attached to a hook on the bottom of the glider. When it reaches altitude, the line is slackened, allowing it to slide off the hook. The glider is then free to soar like a bird.

Rubber-powered models have propellers that are turned by wound-up rubber bands. When the rubber unwinds, it turns the propeller, which causes the airplane to move forward through the air. Some rubber-powered models are very small, with wingspans of no more than 30 centimeters (12 inches). Others have wingspans of close to 2 meters (6 feet). A very special type of rubber-powered model is designed to be flown in large rooms indoors. These super-lightweight models can fly for almost an hour at a time.

Engine-powered models, sometimes called gas models, are powered by engines similar to those used in lawn mowers. But they are small enough to fit in the palm of your hand. These miniature engines produce a great deal of power for their small size. They can fly a model airplane to amazing heights. Once the model rises high enough, the motor is shut off by a timing mechanism, and the airplane is free to glide back to earth.

Free-flight models have one disadvantage. They require large open spaces in which to fly. This was one of the factors that led to the invention of a means of controlling the flight in a small area.

Control Line

Control-line airplanes are flown in circles at the end of two thin steel wires connected to a handle that is held by the pilot. The two wires are usually about 20 meters (65 feet) long. They are attached to a mechanism inside the airplane that controls the up-and-down direction of flight. By moving the handle, pilots can make the airplane do loops, figure eights, and other stunts. They can also control the takeoff and landing.

Control-line airplanes are all powered by miniature engines. There are contests for stunt flying, speed flying, and racing and for scale models.

Radio Control

Remote-control airplanes are the most realistic because they can be controlled in flight without wires or connections of any sort. Every maneuver that a real airplane makes can be duplicated by a radio-controlled model. Sometimes it is difficult to tell whether a model or a real plane is in the sky.

To understand how radio control works, think of your radio or television set. Somewhere outside your house there is a radio or television station transmitting radio waves through the air. You cannot see them or feel them or hear them. But your radio or television is designed to receive these waves and turn them into sound and pictures. Different kinds of radio waves are sent out on different channels, and you can tune your receiver to pick up these waves.

In a radio-control system for model airplanes, there is a transmitter, a receiver, and small electric motors (called servos) to move the airplane's controls. The pilot, using a hand-held transmitter, moves various levers and buttons to transmit different signals on different channels. Inside the airplane, the receiver picks up these signals and activates the servos to move the controls that steer the plane.

On simple radio-controlled models, the only control is the rudder, which steers the airplane right or left. On the most complex models, all the controls of a real airplane are duplicated. These include retractable landing gear, engine throttle, sky-writing smoke in stunt planes, bomb-dropping in war planes, parachute drops, and just about anything else you can think of.

Radio-controlled models come in all types and sizes. There are gliders with wingspans of more than 3 meters (over 10 feet) that can soar for hours when the skillful pilot takes advantage of rising air currents. There are racing planes that fly at almost 200 kilometers (125 miles) per hour. Aerobatic airplanes can loop, roll, spin, and do everything a real air-show plane can do. And there are helicopters that hover and fly backward and sideways just like the real ones. In fact, radio-controlled models can be quite realistic in appearance and flight. Many have been used in motion pictures when it would have been too danger-ous or expensive to use real aircraft.

Remember that flying models are not mere toys. Many of them are fast-moving objects that can fall and cause injury or damage. Care should be taken to fly them only under com-pletely safe conditions.

▶ROCKETS

As the space age has developed, model rock-ets have become an exciting part of the model-ing hobby. But model rockets are not strictly model airplanes. They are not toys, either. They are miniature missiles powered by real solid-fuel rocket motors.

Scale model rocket.

Model rockets are generally constructed of a basic cardboard tube for the body, with a balsa wood or plastic nose cone and balsa tail fins. There are many kits available, and it is best to start with a kit. They are prop-erly designed and built to be completely safe in operation. A homemade rocket can be dan-gerous.

The rocket motor itself is a small cylinder that fits into the rear of the rocket body. Model-rocket motors are dangerous when they are not used properly. In certain places it is necessary to have a license to purchase them. For example, in California, in the United States, you must be at least 14 years of age to get a license. Your local hobby shop can give you full details on how to get a license.

Model-rocket motors are ignited by wires. These are attached at one end to the rocket and at the other end to an electric ignition device placed some distance away for safety. When electricity flows through the wires, the ignition wire in the rocket motor gets hot, just as the wires in a toaster do. This causes the rocket fuel to burn. When the fuel burns, the rocket does not go off like a firecracker. In-stead, a hot, rapidly expanding gas is released. It shoots out through the motor nozzle at a very high speed and pushes the rocket up with a great deal of thrust (power).

A single rocket motor burns for just a few seconds. But it will push the model rocket to altitudes of more than 100 meters (over 325 feet). Multistage rockets use two or more mo-tors, burning one after the other, to get to much greater heights.

Just before the motor burns out, the last little bit of gas pressure actually blows out through the front of the motor. This causes the nose cone of the rocket to pop off and release a parachute. The model rocket then comes down very gently on its parachute, ready for another blast-off.

As with airplanes, model rockets can be scale models of actual rockets and missiles. Or they can be original designs made up by the builder. Contests are often held on military bases, where the models can be tracked by radar to determine how high they fly.

▶YOU CAN DO IT, TOO

When the model-airplane hobby first started, very little equipment was available in

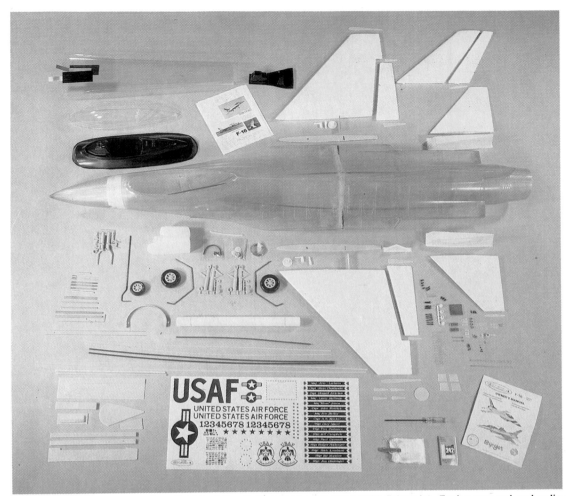

A model kit of the United States Air Force F-16 fighter jet. Engine-powered and radio-controlled, the finished model wil reach speeds of 125 miles (200 kilometers) per hour.

stores. Now, most cities and towns have well-stocked hobby shops, and construction kits are available for all types of airplanes.

The most common construction material is still lightweight balsa wood. But plastics are also popular, especially for complex shapes such as engine cowlings (housing for the engine) and wing tips. Some flying models are all plastic and are almost ready to fly right out of the box.

If you are just becoming interested in model airplanes, the best way to begin is with a well-proved kit of a simple airplane. It is not wise to start off with a big, complex model just because it looks exciting. Start with a model that is within your ability to build. You will soon progress to that big, fancy airplane. If at all possible, try to get advice from an experienced modeler. Read some of the model magazines that are available on newsstands and in hobby shops. If you wish to join a model-airplane club, your local hobby shop will know whether there are any clubs in your area. The Academy of Model Aeronautics in Washington, D.C., can give you information on flying-model contests.

Above all, be patient. Do not rush in building a model. If you follow the directions and work carefully and neatly, all your airplanes will fly like birds.

DON TYPOND
EDITOR, *Model Airplane News*

Airplanes influence many aspects of modern life. Airliners (*above*) carry tourists and business people around the world. Airplanes contribute to increased farm production by aerial spraying of fertilizer and pesticides (*left*). Military fighter planes (*top left*) are an important element in national security. And planes such as the small, slow-flying ultralight (*top right*) are flown just for fun.

AIRPLANES

The airplane has had a greater impact on our lives than any other modern invention. The ability to fly has dramatically increased the speed at which we can travel and decreased the time it takes to receive mail, food, and other goods from far-off places. It has brought us into closer contact with people in other parts of the world, and it has drastically changed the way we wage war.

Yet, until the beginning of the 20th century, the idea of a practical flying machine was only a dream. Balloons and gliders had been flown before 1900, but they were unreliable and could not carry a person over a long distance and land at a chosen destination. It was not until Orville and Wilbur Wright invented and successfully flew the first powered, controllable aircraft that the dream of flight became a reality. On December 17, 1903, the Wrights' plane, the *Flyer,* took off at Kitty Hawk, North Carolina, and flew 120 feet (37 meters).

The airplane has changed greatly since 1903. The wingspan of a modern jumbo jet is longer than the entire distance flown on the Wright brothers' first flight. That flight lasted only 12 seconds; in 1986 a plane named *Voyager* was flown around the world in nine days without stopping or refueling. Airplanes have been flown at more than 4,500 miles (7,300 kilometers) per hour and to altitudes of almost 70 miles (110 kilometers) above the earth. But no matter how fast, high, or far airplanes fly, they are still subject to the same basic principles of flight as the Wright *Flyer*.

HOW AN AIRPLANE FLIES

An airplane is a heavier-than-air craft that can fly only if air flows over its wings fast enough to produce an upward force called **lift.** The force of lift must be strong enough to overcome the force of **gravity,** the force that pulls objects toward the ground. A third force, called **thrust,** is required to move the plane through the air. Thrust is produced by the plane's engine. Thrust must be stronger than another force, called **drag.** Drag is the resistance of the air to anything moving through it. Lift, gravity, thrust, and drag are the four forces that act on every airplane.

The four forces can be experienced while riding a bicycle. The rider pedals, producing thrust by turning the rear wheel against the ground. The sensation of air pushing against the rider can be compared to the force of drag. If the rider holds out one hand with the palm down and slightly tilted to face the oncoming air, the hand will rise. This is similar to the way a wing reacts to one kind of lifting force. Gravity keeps the rider earthbound.

Of the four forces, lift is perhaps the least familiar. It is the result of physical laws that govern the way all liquids and gases behave when they are in motion. Air, a gas, moves faster when it flows past an obstacle. As it flows faster, its pressure is reduced. This law is known as Bernoulli's principle, and it is one of the basic laws of aerodynamics (the study of air, or any other gas, in motion). It is further explained in the article Aerodynamics, in this volume. Bernoulli's principle is used in the design of an airplane's wing to change the air pressure around the wing and produce lift.

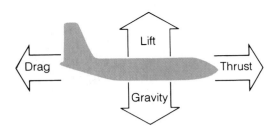

Four forces act on a plane. Thrust is produced by the engine to overcome the drag of air resistance. Air flowing over the wing creates lift, which overcomes gravity.

The airplane's wing is an **airfoil,** a surface that produces lift when air moves over it. A wing has a curved top surface and a relatively flat bottom surface. As the wing moves through the air, the particles of air are separated. They must move either over or under the wing and meet again behind the wing. Air passing over the curved top of the wing has a longer distance to travel and so moves faster than the air passing under the wing. Just as Bernoulli had proved, pressure is reduced in the faster-moving air over the wing. The lower pressure of the air above the wing pulls the wing up. This upward force is lift. As the airplane moves faster, the lift increases, until it is strong enough to overcome the force of gravity and lift the airplane's weight.

More lift is created as the result of another physical law. This is Newton's third law of motion, which states that for every action there is an equal and opposite reaction. In normal flight, the wing is slightly tilted, so the front is slightly higher than the back. When the bicyclist tilted an outstretched hand and felt it rise, that happened because air struck the bottom surface and was deflected, or turned, downward. According to Newton's law, the force of this deflected air exerts an equal force in the opposite direction, in this case, upward against the bottom of the wing or the bicyclist's palm, lifting them upward. This force may provide as much as 25 percent of the lift on a wing.

STRUCTURE

The design of modern airplanes is based on the same aerodynamic principles used by the Wright brothers. But modern airplanes are built with stronger materials and more powerful engines. They fly faster and carry heavy loads or many passengers. They may be single-engine (one-engine) or multi-engine air-

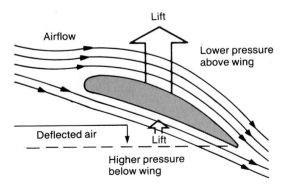

Air travels faster over the curved top of a wing than under its relatively flat bottom. As air moves faster, its pressure becomes lower. This lower pressure produces lift.

planes. Some are owned by large airlines or corporations, while others are owned by individuals. Airplanes are used for business, pleasure, and sports, such as racing or aerobatics. Other airplanes are military fighters, bombers, or transports that carry soldiers, tanks, or other equipment.

All of these aircraft, as different as they may seem, work on the same aerodynamic principles and are made up of the same structural components (parts): the **fuselage**; the **wings**; the **tail assembly,** with **vertical** and **horizontal stabilizers**; and the **landing gear.** All of these components together are called the **airframe.** The other main component of an airplane is the engine, which provides the power.

Fuselage

The purpose of the fuselage, or body of the plane, is to carry the pilot, passengers, and cargo. The oldest fuselage design, the **truss type,** consists of a welded steel framework (truss) covered with tightly stretched fabric, metal, or composites which is painted to provide a smooth surface. The framework absorbs the stresses encountered in flight. The popular Piper Cub, first built in the 1930's and still flown today, has a fuselage of this type, as do many sport, recreational, and utility airplanes still being produced.

A second type of airplane fuselage is **monocoque.** Monocoque is a French word meaning "single shell." No truss is needed because the shell is made of metal or other strong material,

such as composites (compounds) of plastic, fiberglass, and carbon fiber. These are strong enough to absorb the forces of normal flight. Small airplanes are often built with monocoque construction to save weight. But monocoque construction is not strong enough or rigid enough for large cargo planes or airliners. Therefore, most modern commercially built airline aircraft are manufactured using

It takes about four years from the first design of an airliner to reach the full-scale production stage shown here. These planes may be in use for 20 years.

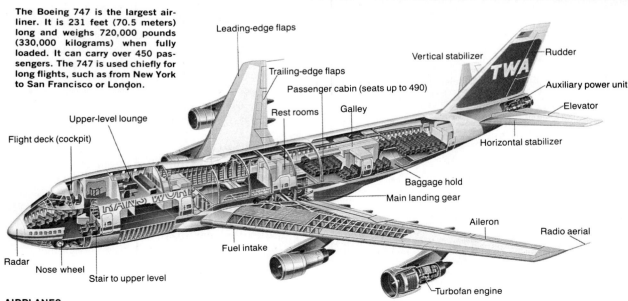

The Boeing 747 is the largest airliner. It is 231 feet (70.5 meters) long and weighs 720,000 pounds (330,000 kilograms) when fully loaded. It can carry over 450 passengers. The 747 is used chiefly for long flights, such as from New York to San Francisco or London.

Leading-edge flaps
Trailing-edge flaps
Passenger cabin (seats up to 490)
Rest rooms
Galley
Vertical stabilizer
Rudder
Auxiliary power unit
Elevator
Horizontal stabilizer
Baggage hold
Main landing gear
Aileron
Radio aerial
Turbofan engine
Fuel intake
Stair to upper level
Nose wheel
Radar
Flight deck (cockpit)
Upper-level lounge

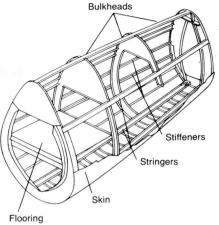

Semi-monocoque construction (*above*) is clearly visible in the fuselage of the airliner being built (*left*). The location of the windows indicates that the floor of the passenger compartment will be near the center of the fuselage. Cables provide temporary support during construction.

the **semi-monocoque** method, in which bracing and stiffeners of metal or other materials are added to the shell.

Modern airliners and military aircraft can fly at extremely high altitudes, where lower air pressure and oxygen content make breathing difficult. Also, the rapid changes in air pressure that occur when changing altitude can cause extreme physical discomfort. Therefore, the passenger cabin and cockpit of modern passenger jets are pressurized. Like the hull of a submarine, the fuselage of a pressurized aircraft is airtight. The air pressure inside the cabin and cockpit is increased by air compressors as the jet gains altitude. In this way, air pressure inside the plane is almost as high as pressure at ground level.

Wings

Airplane wings are designed to be very strong. Beneath the skin, or surface material, of the wing is a framework consisting of one or more **spars,** and **ribs, stringers,** and **formers.** The spars run from the wing root (the part of the wing attached to the fuselage) to the wing tip. Ribs run from the leading edge (front) of the wing to the trailing edge (back) of the wing. This framework provides the wing with its shape and its strength.

The distance from the leading edge to the trailing edge of the wing is called the **chord.** The distance from wing tip to wing tip is the **wingspan.**

Because the wing is an airfoil and thus produces lift, it is relatively flat on the bottom and curved on the top. This curve is called **camber.** Camber is the amount of curvature of the airfoil from the leading edge to the trailing edge of the wing. Thus a wing can have more or less camber, or curve, depending on the purpose for which it is designed.

The design and location of airplane wings vary according to the purpose of the airplane. Many modern airplanes have low wings—that is, wings attached near the bottom of the fuselage. Airplanes that operate out of rough, unpaved airfields often have wings attached near the top of the fuselage. High wings are less likely to hit the ground as the airplane bumps over the rough airfield. High-wing planes include the two-seat Piper Cub and the C-130, a large military plane that carries troops and equipment into grass or dirt air fields.

On most airplanes the wings are attached at a slight angle, so that when viewed from the front they form a shallow V. This angle is called the **dihedral,** and it reduces the plane's tendency to roll from side to side.

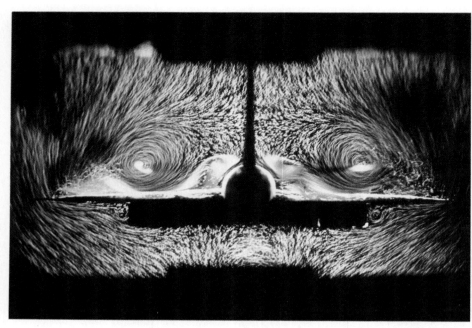

A wind-tunnel test of a model of the supersonic Concorde shows how air flows over its wings when it flies at lower speeds. The pattern changes as airspeed increases. Water containing dyes is injected into the tunnel to make the airflow visible.

► The ribs of the small airplane wing (*right*) show the top curve that gives it an airfoil (lift-producing) shape. Ribs also curve the top of the large airliner wing (*far right*), seen here from a passenger window. The flaps have been lowered to increase the curve. This provides more lift at slow speeds during takeoff and landing.

The shape and thickness of the wing are determined by the speed at which the airplane will be flown. Slower-flying planes have wings that extend straight out from the fuselage, with a very visible curve on the top surface. This provides lift at slow speeds. Faster airplanes have thinner wings. Because the air flows faster over these wings, less curve is needed to create lift. On very high speed jet fighters, the wing appears almost flat on top and is shorter. Such wings are also very thin so they create less drag at high speeds.

Wings on high-speed planes are usually **swept** (angled back). On some planes the two swept wings together form a triangle called a **delta wing.**

Planes with thin, short, swept wings must land at much higher speeds than straight-wing airplanes in order to maintain lift until the plane is on the ground. The F-14 Tomcat, a jet fighter, has variable wings, which can be changed from straight to swept. This allows it to be more easily maneuvered at both low and high speeds.

On each wing of an airplane are hinged movable sections called **control surfaces** with which the pilot controls the movement of the plane. **Ailerons** are control surfaces located on the trailing edge of the wing, near the wing tip. The pilot controls the ailerons by moving the control stick or wheel of the airplane. If the pilot moves the stick or turns the wheel to the right, the right aileron moves up and the left aileron moves down. Air pushing against the upturned right aileron forces the right wing down, while, at the same time, air pushing against the downturned left aileron pushes the left wing up. This causes the airplane to turn and **bank,** (tilt) to the right. A left movement of the stick or wheel causes the ailerons to move in the opposite directions, and the airplane banks to the left.

Many airplanes also have other control surfaces on the wings, called **flaps.** Flaps are usually located on the trailing edge between the aileron and the wing root. Flaps move at the same time in the same direction. When the pilot puts the flaps down, the camber of the wings is increased, thus increasing lift and permitting the airplane to fly at slower speeds. Flaps are put down primarily when landing. Because having the flaps down also creates drag, they are put up for normal flight.

Tail Assembly

The tail assembly, or **empennage,** of an airplane has two purposes: to provide stability and to control direction.

In most situations, a pilot prefers to keep the plane stable, or steady, in straight and

level flight. In most aircraft, this stability is provided by surfaces called stabilizers. A fixed vertical stabilizer prevents the airplane from **yawing** (swinging from side to side). The horizontal stabilizer prevents **pitching** (up and down movement of the nose). On some planes the horizontal stabilizer is located near the nose. Then it is called a **canard.**

Directional control is provided by two control surfaces in the tail. These are the **rudder** and the **elevator.** The rudder is a hinged surface attached to the vertical stabilizer. The pilot moves the rudder by pushing foot pedals. When the pilot pushes the right rudder pedal, the rudder moves to the right. The pressure of the airflow against the rudder pushes the airplane's tail to the left. This, in turn, pushes the nose of the airplane to the right. When making a turn, the pilot uses both the ailerons and the rudder. This is called a co-ordinated turn.

Elevators are the movable control surfaces hinged to the horizontal stabilizer. When the pilot pushes the control stick or wheel forward, the elevators go down. The airflow pushes on the elevators, which makes the tail move up and the nose point down. Pulling the stick or wheel back puts the elevator up so the airflow pushes the tail down and the nose up. These movements are called changing the

A plane rotates around 3 lines, called axes. It rolls around an axis from nose to tail, yaws around an axis from top to bottom, and pitches around an axis from wing tip to wing tip.

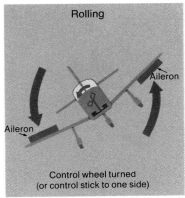

Rolling

Aileron

Aileron

Control wheel turned
(or control stick to one side)

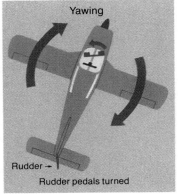

Yawing

Rudder →

Rudder pedals turned

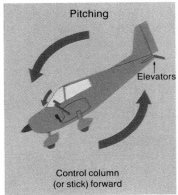

Pitching

Elevators

Control column
(or stick) forward

Planes equipped with special landing gear can land on surfaces other than runways. Planes with pontoons are able to land on water (*below*). Skis can be attached to landing gear (*right*) for winter flying in northern areas. Ski-planes and seaplanes are important means of transportation in remote areas of Canada and Alaska.

pitch of the airplane. On some airplanes, the function of the elevator is served by a horizontal stabilizer that can be moved up or down to control pitch. A horizontal stabilizer designed in this manner is called a **stabilator.**

Most airplanes also have **trim tabs**—small hinged sections of the elevator and rudder. These can be adjusted to stick out into the airflow to exert pressure on the control surface, causing it to move. In situations where a certain amount of pitch or yaw must be maintained for a period of time, the pilot can set the trim tab to hold the control surface in one position, such as a long, steady descent. Thus the pilot is better able to concentrate on other aspects of controlling the plane.

Landing Gear

In the early days of aviation, most airplanes had two wheels in front of the airplane's center of gravity (the point where the plane's weight is evenly balanced). A third, smaller wheel was located in the rear under the tail. Because this arrangement was used successfully for a long time, it is referred to as **conventional landing gear.** Newer aircraft often use **tricycle gear,** which consists of two wheels behind the center of gravity and a third wheel under the nose of the airplane. Aircraft with tricycle gear are easier to control on the ground than those with conventional landing gear. For this reason, tricycle gear aircraft are more popular with most of today's pilots.

All early airplanes were **fixed-gear** aircraft. The wheels remained in place whether the airplane was on the ground or in the air. Today, although many aircraft still have fixed gear, faster airplanes have **retractable gear**—the wheels are pulled up into the fuselage or wings of the airplane. Fixed gear causes a great deal of drag, which slows the airplane down and increases fuel consumption (amount of fuel used). Retracting the wheels into the wings or fuselage reduces drag.

Landing gear may consist of equipment other than wheels. For example, **seaplanes,** special aircraft that take off and land on water, have **pontoons** (floats) instead of wheels.

Flying boats have a boat-shaped hull on which they land. Seaplanes with retractable landing gear for use on land are called **amphibians.** There are also planes that are equipped with skis for landing on snow. Landing on either water or snow requires different piloting techniques from those used to land on pavement.

▶ POWER AND PROPULSION

In order for an airplane to achieve flight, its wings must be pushed or pulled through the air fast enough to create lift. This function of propulsion is performed by the engine. There are three main types of airplane engines: **reciprocating** engines, **jet** engines, and **rocket** engines.

Reciprocating Engines

Reciprocating engines, or piston engines, used in airplanes are very similar to those used in automobiles. In a reciprocating engine, the expanding force of a burning fuel (gasoline) pushes pistons, which in turn rotate a crankshaft. In an airplane, the crankshaft turns the propeller. (You can learn more about how reciprocating engines work by consulting the article INTERNAL-COMBUSTION ENGINES in Volume I.

Reciprocating engines need cooling systems so they will not overheat. The first airplanes had liquid-cooled engines like those of many automobiles. Today, most reciprocating airplane engines are air cooled.

An air-cooled engine is lighter than a liquid-cooled engine because it does not have to carry hoses, radiators, cooling fluid, and circulation pumps. Air-cooled engines must be constructed so that the greatest possible area is exposed to the onrushing air. Air is forced into openings in the **cowling** (engine cover) behind the propeller and then flows over the engine to cool it. Because of their lightness, air-cooled engines replaced liquid-cooled engines for most uses by the 1930's. But liquid-cooled engines continued to be used very successfully for certain types of airplanes because they last longer than air-cooled engines and can produce more power. For example, some of the fastest piston-driven aircraft used during World War II (1939–45), such as the Spitfire and P-51 Mustang, had liquid-cooled engines. The *Voyager,* which in 1986 flew around the world without landing or refueling, used one air-cooled and one liquid-cooled engine.

Opened cowling (engine cover) reveals the four-cylinder engine of a small plane. A cone-shaped spinner reduces drag over the propeller hub.

Propellers. All reciprocating engines turn propellers. Some early airplanes, like the Wright *Flyer,* were pushed into the air by propellers at the rear, while most modern airplanes are pulled into the air by propellers at the front.

The propeller consists of a control **hub** at the center with two or more blades attached. The entire assembly is rotated by the engine, and the blades convert engine power into thrust. The propeller is a **rotating airfoil.** As the blade rotates through the air, lower pressure is created on its curved front surface, pulling the propeller and plane forward.

The angle at which the propeller blade strikes the air determines how much pulling or pushing power it produces. A flatter angle results in high pulling power but low forward speed. Early airplane propellers had fairly flat blade angles that could not be changed. This flatter blade angle was satisfactory as long as airplanes flew slowly, but it was not practical for high-speed aircraft. The problem was solved by **variable-pitch** propellers, invented in 1923. The blades of a variable-pitch propeller can be adjusted so that they have a flat angle for takeoff, when the most power is needed, and steep angles for normal flight, when speed is important. A more recent development is the **constant-speed** propeller, which automatically (without pilot input) adjusts the angle of the propeller blade to maintain a constant forward speed.

Jet Engines

Jet engines have fewer moving parts than reciprocating engines, but they burn a great deal more fuel. A jet engine burns its fuel in an enclosed space called a combustion chamber. The burning of fuel produces hot gases that rush out of the rear opening of the engine at high speed. This powerful jet exhaust pushes the engine (and the plane to which it is attached) forward.

Before leaving the engine, the gases race past a fanlike device called a **turbine,** making it turn. The turbine is mounted on a drive shaft. As the drive shaft turns, it turns another set of fans, called the **compressor,** at the front end of the engine. The spinning compressor packs enormous amounts of air into the combustion chamber, providing the oxygen needed for continuous burning of the fuel. This basic type of jet engine is called the **turbojet.** It powers some of the fastest high-altitude aircraft, such as military fighters and bombers.

The **turboprop** engine is very similar to the turbojet, but it uses the power of the jet exhaust to turn a propeller. Turboprops are used on planes that must use fuel more efficiently, but planes using them do not fly as fast.

Turbofans are jet engines with a second turbine that drives a fan near the front of the engine. This fan, which acts something like a propeller, forces air out through special openings at very high speed. The air passes around the outside of the engine and provides extra thrust without burning extra fuel. The rest of the air enters the engine. Turbofan engines are widely used in modern airliners because they burn less fuel and are usually quieter than turbojet engines used in earlier airliners.

More about how jet engines work can be found in the article JET PROPULSION in Volume J–K.

Rocket Engines

Rocket engines are used very rarely in aircraft today. Rockets require much more fuel than jet engines, so they would require much larger fuel tanks. Also, refueling a rocket is more complicated than putting jet fuel or aviation gas on an airplane. Unlike jet engines, rockets are closed at the forward end. As a solid or liquid fuel burns in the combustion chamber, hot gases rush rearward through a nozzle. Because every physical action results in an opposite reaction, the engine, and the aircraft attached to it, is pushed forward. Rocket engines have been used primarily on experimental types of aircraft such as the Bell X-1, which, in 1947, was the first plane to break the sound barrier. (Rocket engines are described in the article ROCKETS in Volume R.)

New Designs

Today, a great deal of research and development is being devoted to engines and propulsion. Because reciprocating engines are less expensive to operate than jet engines, and because jet engines often make a great deal of noise, many researchers are experimenting with high-performance propeller-driven engines. In the late 1980's, the National Aeronautics and Space Administration (NASA) and several private companies were experimenting

Most jet-powered passenger airplanes have turbofan engines similar to this one with its cowling removed for repairs (*left*). A new turboprop design (*right*) has two propellers, which move in opposite directions. It produces as much power as a turbofan at lower cost.

The *Solar Challenger* flew across the English Channel in 1981, powered only by sunlight. The black areas on the top of its wings are solar cells, which convert sunlight to electricity.

with curved propeller blades, which will be used on airliners of the future. The Beech Starship, which was developed by a private company, uses a rear-mounted **pusher prop,** which is almost as fast as a jet engine and more efficient than a propeller that pulls an airplane through the air.

There have been new developments in power for very light aircraft. Dr. Paul Mac-Cready, an American inventor, built the *Gossamer Condor* in 1977 and the *Gossamer Albatross* in 1979. These were human-powered airplanes in which the pilot pedaled a bicycle-like mechanism that turns the propeller. A later MacCready design known as the *Solar Challenger* flew across the English Channel in 1981 entirely under solar power.

▶**INSTRUMENTS**

Aviation pioneers flew using very simple methods, such as looking for landmarks and other visual references. They also sensed the forces on the airplane through their bodies, so they said they "flew by the seat of their pants." But instruments have become more and more important in aviation. Generally, the larger the airplane, the greater the number of instruments. Even a relatively simple training airplane like a Cessna 152 contains enough instruments to confuse the nonflyer. But a highly complex airplane such as the Concorde, a supersonic airliner, contains many more instruments. As a result, the crew of the Concorde and some other large airliners in-

cludes a special crew member, the flight engineer, whose job is to monitor these instruments and make the necessary adjustments to the engines and other systems. The pilot and co-pilot fly the airplane and also give their attention to flight instruments and navigation instruments.

Engine Instruments

Each airplane, no matter how large or how small, has a number of instruments for each engine. A **tachometer** tells how many revolutions per minute the engine makes. The temperature and the pressure of the air entering the engine, the fuel pressure, the oil pressure, and the engine temperature are usually measured as well. Jet planes use gauges that measure the temperature of the exhaust gases as they exit the tail pipe. Although all aircraft also have fuel gauges, most pilots measure the amount of fuel at the beginning of the flight and mathematically compute their fuel consumption throughout the trip. They use the fuel gauge only as a backup to their own computations.

Flight Instruments

If a pilot is flying low and slow, he or she does not need many flight instruments. However, all pilots need to know four basic types of information. They must know the **heading** (the direction in which the airplane is flying), its altitude, its airspeed, and its **attitude** (pitch and bank in relation to the horizon).

The most basic of all flight instruments is the compass, which indicates the heading of the airplane. The magnetic compass can give a true heading in straight and level flight but has a tendency to be inaccurate when the airplane is turning. For this reason, many larger aircraft use **gyrocompasses,** which are not affected by the turns. (Gyrocompasses are described in the article GYROSCOPES in Volume G.)

Altimeters measure altitude. There are two types of altimeters. One measures the pressure of the outside air, which decreases at a fairly regular rate as the aircraft gains altitude. A pilot, however, must be careful with this type of altimeter because it is affected by changes in temperature and barometric pressure, which in turn are affected by the weather. The **radio altimeter** uses a radio beam to measure the distance to the ground.

The **airspeed indicator** measures the speed with which the airplane moves through the air. The air enters the instrument through a special tube called a **Pitot-static tube,** which is mounted on the outside of the airplane. The faster the plane moves, the more air rushes into the tube, moving a **diaphragm**—a flexible surface inside the instrument—that turns an indicator needle.

An airplane's **airspeed** (speed through the air) is seldom the same as its **ground speed** (speed in relation to the ground). For example, if a plane flies into the wind, this head wind reduces the plane's ground speed but does not affect its airspeed. If the plane is flying at the same airspeed but in the same direction as the wind is blowing, this tail wind increases the speed with which the plane moves over the ground. Ground speed may be calculated by measuring how long it takes to fly a known distance between two points. It also may be measured electronically with DME (Distance Measuring Equipment).

The attitude of the airplane in relation to the ground must be known when flying in clouds or fog. Three instruments can be used to determine the plane's attitude. The **rate-of-climb indicator** tells how many feet per minute the plane is climbing or descending. The **turn-and-bank indicator** shows how many degrees the plane is banked to the left or right. The artificial horizon shows the pitch of the nose above or below the horizon. All commercial aircraft have these instruments.

Navigation Instruments

Navigation is the science of getting to a destination in an airplane without getting lost. The oldest method of navigating an airplane is called **pilotage.** The pilot navigated by watching for landmarks on the ground and comparing them with a map. Pilotage works well at relatively low speeds and altitudes, when landmarks can be seen easily. However, when flying a plane higher, faster, or in clouds or fog, a pilot must be able to navigate without seeing the ground.

If a pilot knows the direction in which the aircraft is headed, its altitude and airspeed, the direction and speed of the wind, and the outside air temperature, he or she can compute, with the aid of a watch, the airplane's position on a flight map without seeing the ground. This is an excellent method of navigation called **dead reckoning.** However, the use of reliable electronic instruments has largely replaced dead reckoning for commercial flights.

The development of radio and electronic navigation has greatly simplified the task of navigating an aircraft. Many aircraft are equipped with automatic **radio compasses** that indicate the direction from which a radio signal is coming. If lost, the pilot simply tunes the radio compass to the frequency of an airport radio range transmitter. An indicator needle shows the way to the station. This is sometimes known as **homing in** on a radio station. The pilot can also pinpoint the airplane's position by tuning in two or three different stations and plotting the signals on a map. The airplane's position will be the point on the map where the directional lines cross. The locations and frequencies of these old-style radio range stations are still given on flight charts used by all pilots.

Radio ranges, however, are being replaced by more effective devices known as VOR's. VOR stands for Very-high-frequency Omnidirectional Range. A VOR radio station sends out 360 course signals spaced one degree apart, radiating like the spokes of a wheel from a radio transmitter. Pilots may select and fly on any of these courses. An indicator in the cockpit tells the pilot the position of the airplane in relationship to the VOR. As previously mentioned, a DME can be used for measuring the exact speed of the airplane. It also measures the exact distance of the airplane from the VOR transmitter.

Military pilots use a radio navigation system known as TACAN (TACtical Airborne Navigation). TACAN works like a combination of VOR and DME and has a longer range.

Several years ago, sailors began using a radio system called loran (*long-range navigation*) aboard ships at sea and in the Great Lakes. Soon, private pilots discovered that loran signals can be transmitted long distances and that the system is extremely accurate. They began experimenting with Marine loran radio receivers. Today, loran plays an important role in aerial navigation across the United States for many types of aircraft.

Inertial Navigation. Today, most commercial aircraft and many military aircraft use inertial navigation. Inertial navigation is accomplished by a computer that uses a very precise program together with a memory, accelerometer (an instrument measuring all directions and rates of movement), and gyroscopes to measure the plane's precise position above the earth's surface in latitude and longitude. The latest developments in precision navigation make use of satellite technology.

Radar. Commercial aircraft and larger general aviation aircraft use radar to find and avoid storm systems. This is an important function because bad weather is the age-old enemy of the pilot. In fact, approximately 40 percent of all general aviation accidents are caused by bad weather. However, the type of radar used in civilian aircraft cannot help pilots detect other airplanes. Another, more complex type of radar is used for this purpose. It is found only in military aircraft, which must locate enemy planes even when they are too far away to see.

Most airplanes have duplicate instruments and flight controls for the captain, who sits on the left, and the co-pilot. The Boeing 747-400 has computer screens displaying flight, navigation, and engine information as well as traditional flight instruments.

Auto Pilot. Automatic pilots are standard equipment on most commercial aircraft, and increasing numbers of military and private aircraft have them as well. The simplest auto pilot is based on two gyroscopes, each of which is connected to the aircraft's controls. When an airplane deviates (strays) from straight and level flight, the gyroscopes detect the change. By means of electrical servomotors (much like those used on radio-controlled model airplanes), they move the controls slightly to return the airplane to straight and level flight. More sophisticated automatic pilots are used by aircraft that have computerized navigation systems. In these aircraft, the auto pilot may be set to fly a particular course at a certain airspeed and altitude. The auto pilot automatically updates its position through the navigation computers while monitoring its speed, altitude, and heading.

Until recently, the dozens, or sometimes hundreds, of instruments in an airplane's cockpit had analog displays; that is, they had clock-type faces with dials and hands. In today's most modern aircraft, these analog instruments have been replaced by digital instruments, which display information in the form of numbers. Also, high technology in the form of computerization and CRT's (Cathode-Ray Tubes) is changing the look of the modern aircraft cockpit. Some corporate aircraft such as the Beech Starship and the Gulfstream IV already have what have been nicknamed "glass cockpits." These areas display on video screens all of the important information needed to fly and navigate an airplane. Many military aircraft and commercial airliners are also beginning to use this highly developed technology.

AIRPLANE DESIGN

An airplane can fly at fast or slow speeds over long or short distances. It can carry hundreds of vacationers around the world or a single person from one side of a major city to the other. The designer of an airplane must keep in mind the task the airplane is to accomplish. Will the airplane fly great distances? If so, the designer will have to provide either very efficient power or the capacity to store a great amount of fuel. Should the airplane's structure be relatively light or heavy? That depends on the cargo it will carry. This might be two persons or a whole company of soldiers and equipment. A large airplane will mean more weight and more drag. As a result, larger engines and wings will be necessary to get it airborne. Crop dusters, aerobatic biplanes, personal transportation aircraft, and airliners all have different design requirements. The airplane designer has many choices to make, and modern technology can help with these decisions.

Recently, airplanes have been designed with the aid of computers. CAD-CAM (Computer-Aided Design and Computer-Aided Manufacturing) is becoming part of the industry. The *Voyager* was designed with the aid of a computer. The design required very light weight, large fuel capacity, relatively high horsepower for propulsion, and efficient engines. After determining these requirements,

The F-15E Eagle and its computer-drawn skeleton are examples of current aircraft design knowledge and technique.

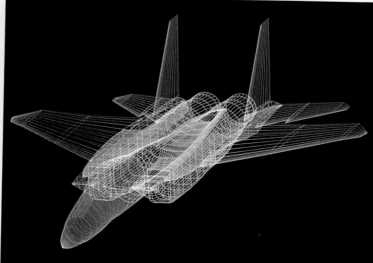

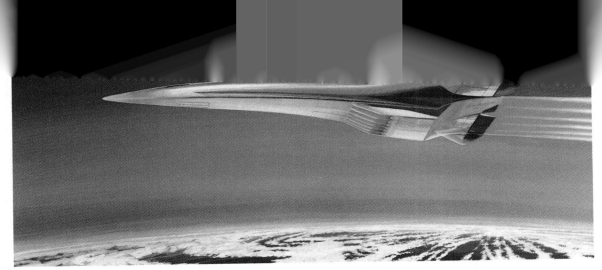

▲ An air-space plane similar to the one in this painting may be built by the year 2000. The orange areas indicate where heat would be created by friction with the air as it flies at about 10,000 miles (16,000 kilometers) per hour.

◄ The Bell XV-15 takes off and lands vertically like a helicopter. Once in flight, the engines rotate to a horizontal position and it flies like an airplane. It is designed to fly to and from the centers of cities.

the designers used computers to solve the complex mathematical problems encountered in designing aircraft.

▶ **THE FUTURE**

Our future in the vast ocean of air above us is limited only by our imaginations. Today, composite materials similar to fiberglass are beginning to replace the metal parts on many airplanes. These materials are stronger and lighter than those they replace. New engine and design technology will permit aircraft to fly higher and farther than ever before. NASA and the Department of Defense are working on a passenger airplane that will fly at the outer edges of the atmosphere. It should cross the Pacific Ocean in only 2 hours instead of the 12 to 14 hours required in the mid-1980's.

Other technological developments are bringing planes closer to home. Planes called VTOL's (Vertical Take Off and Landing) need very little space to take off and land, eliminating the need for long runways. One kind of VTOL, called a tilt rotor, has engines that can tilt to provide either horizontal or vertical thrust. The development of VTOL's allows planes to land at small airports closer to city centers.

At air shows around the world—Paris, France; Oshkosh, Wisconsin; Farnborough, England; Hanover, Germany; and Dayton, Ohio—engineers, designers, and developers all share information that will expand the future of flight.

PAUL H. POBEREZNY
President, Experimental Aircraft Association

See also AVIATION; AERODYNAMICS; GLIDERS; GYROSCOPES; INTERNAL-COMBUSTION ENGINES; JET PROPULSION; NAVIGATION; RADAR, SONAR, LORAN, AND SHORAN; ROCKETS.

Industrial plants pollute the air with smoke and gases that pour from their smokestacks.

AIR POLLUTION

Wherever you go, whatever you do—inside, outside, on top of a mountain, deep in a coal mine—you are always surrounded by a sea of gases. This sea is called the air, or the atmosphere.

The gases of the atmosphere cannot be seen, and we are rarely aware of them. But they are of the greatest importance. Without the atmosphere, people, animals, and plants could not live. Of almost equal importance is the quality of the atmosphere—whether it is pure or **polluted** (meaning impure).

The atmosphere is made up mainly of the gases oxygen and nitrogen, together with water vapor and smaller amounts of carbon dioxide and other gases. But all air contains small amounts of impurities. In rural areas, far removed from factories and heavy traffic, the air may contain pollen from plants, dust from the soil, and even bacteria. These impurities are usually in such small amounts that they are not important.

Air is said to be polluted when it contains enough harmful impurities to affect the health, safety, or comfort of living things. The impurities, or **pollutants**, could be tiny particles of matter or gases not normally found in air.

When people breathe, pollutants in the air may be deposited in the lungs or absorbed into the body. And polluted air can harm animals and plants as well as people. For this reason, our air supply should be closely watched and managed to assure its good quality.

▶ CAUSES OF AIR POLLUTION

There are two main types of air pollution—natural pollution and pollution caused by people. Natural pollutants are windblown dust, pollen, fog, and the like. There have been instances when the ash from volcanic eruptions has been blown across large areas of the earth. And early in the 1950's, forest fires in the southeastern United States blanketed huge areas of the country with smoke so intense that air flights had to be canceled as far away as New York City. Acts of nature such as these are often beyond human control.

The chief concern is the second and perhaps more serious form of air pollution—the pollution caused by people. Most of this pollution is produced by industry and by vehicles such as cars, trucks, and airplanes. It becomes worse as society becomes more industrialized —as more automobiles are produced and driven, new factories are built, and existing factories are expanded. It is most severe in cities, where people and industries are concentrated in large numbers.

The millions of people who live in cities need heat, hot water, and electric power. Most of the energy for these needs comes from burning fossil fuels such as coal and oil. This produces large amounts of gases that enter the atmosphere. Another source of air pollution is the use of fossil fuels in transportation. Public and private vehicles are the source of vast amounts of polluting gases. Sometimes factories produce waste chemicals that escape into the air. Smoke from cigarettes can pollute the air in a closed room. All kinds of surfaces grind against one another, sending tiny particles of dust into the air. Even ordinary wear and tear on brakes and tires produces dust, as do sanding, grinding, and drilling operations.

Warm Air

Cool Air

In a temperature inversion, cool air containing smoke and gases is trapped under warm air, keeping harmful pollutants close to the surface of the earth.

SOME MAJOR POLLUTANTS

Particulate matter is made up of tiny solid or liquid particles. Dust, whether natural or produced by human activity, is particulate. Another example is fly ash, which results from the burning of fuels. Beryllium, used in rockets, and asbestos, used for insulating against heat, are among the materials listed as particulate pollutants.

Oxides of sulfur are gases. They are produced when sulfur-containing fuels, such as coal or oil, are burned. They are also produced in factories where sulfur is used in manufacturing processes. Oxides of sulfur irritate the breathing passages and can damage the lungs.

Carbon monoxide is a poisonous gas produced by the incomplete burning of the carbon in such fuels as gasoline, coal, and oil. Most of the carbon monoxide in the air comes from the exhausts of automobiles and other vehicles that burn gasoline.

Oxides of nitrogen are also produced by automobile engines and other engines. Nitrogen makes up about 78 percent of the air, and oxygen, about 21 percent. Normally these gases do not combine chemically in the air. But in engines that run at very high temperatures, such as those in automobiles, they combine to form gases called oxides of nitrogen.

Photochemical oxidants are formed when oxides of nitrogen combine with other substances present in automobile exhaust. Sunlight promotes the combining process. The photochemical oxidants are the main ingredient of smog, which irritates the eyes and breathing passages.

Laws requiring lower emissions of these pollutants help, but the problems still exist.

Some of these pollutants, such as exhaust gases from cars and trucks, are discharged into the air at street level. Others, such as smoke from power plants and factories, enter the atmosphere at higher levels. When smoke and other pollutants combine with fog, they form **smog**. An article on fog and smog is included in Volume F.

The amount of air pollution is affected by atmospheric conditions such as temperature and air pressure. Because the air near the earth's surface is normally warmer than the air at higher altitudes, air currents usually rise. The rising air currents carry pollutants to the upper atmosphere, where they are dispersed, or scattered. But sometimes the air above the earth's surface is warmer than the air at the surface. When this happens, the warm air stops the flow of rising air currents. This condition is called a **temperature inversion**. The pollutants are trapped close to the surface, where they do the most harm.

High Cost of Air Pollution

The damage caused by air pollution is enormous. In money alone it represents a loss of billions of dollars each year. Many flower and vegetable crops suffer ill effects from car exhaust gases. Trees have been killed by pollution from power plants. Cattle have been poisoned by the fumes from smelters that recover aluminum from ore. Air pollution causes rubber tires on automobiles to crack and become porous. Fine buildings become shabby, their walls blackened with soot that has settled on them. Building surfaces may actually deteriorate because of air pollution.

But the high cost of air pollution is most strikingly illustrated in its damaging effects on the human body. Air pollution causes eye irritations, scratchy throats, and respiratory illnesses. It also contributes to a number of serious diseases. In both the United States and Europe, periods of high levels of air pollution were linked to an increased number of deaths.

Much direct harm is done by air pollution. Scientists are alarmed because the amounts of gases such as carbon dioxide, methane, and nitrous oxide in our atmosphere are increasing. These gases tend to trap the radiation that reaches the earth from the sun. Because the amount of radiation we receive from the sun tends to be constant, if less radiation escapes from our atmosphere, the atmosphere could become warmer. This process would eventually cause the temperature of the earth's surface to rise.

Scientists have been concerned, too, about the widespread use of a substance that may destroy the atmospheric layer that protects us from harmful kinds of solar energy. This substance belongs to a group of chemicals called **chlorofluorocarbons**. It is used as a refrigerant and a cleaner and was once widely used in spray cans.

Another concern is **acid rain**. This is rain or other precipitation that contains oxides of sulfur and nitrogen, along with other chemicals. Acid rain causes damage in lakes and rivers. It poisons the plants and animals that live in the water. Acid rain may also affect crops and other plants, stone buildings and monuments, and drinking water. More information on acid rain may be found in the article ACID RAIN in Volume A.

▶ CONTROL OF AIR POLLUTION

There are three basic approaches to the control of air pollution—**preventive measures**, such as changing the raw materials used in industry or the ingredients of fuel; **dispersal measures**, such as raising the heights of smokestacks; and **collection measures**, such as designing equipment to trap pollutants before they escape into the atmosphere.

Smog has seriously affected more people than any other form of air pollution. It tends to collect over large industrialized cities. Other forms of air pollution are less visible than smog. At right, a government worker uses instruments to check air quality.

Top: Chemical pollutants in the air have eaten away the surface of stone statues of the 1600's that decorate the Palace of Versailles, near Paris. *Bottom:* Exhausts from jet planes create high levels of pollution near airports throughout the world.

Nearly all the highly industrialized countries of the world have some type of legislation to prevent and control air pollution. One difficulty is that pollutants may be carried by the wind from one country to another, often for distances of thousands of miles. The death of lakes in eastern Canada has been caused by acid rain that originated in the United States. Acids produced in Britain and France have caused damage in Sweden.

In the United States, control of air pollution is chiefly the responsibility of the state and local governments. All the states have air quality management programs, which are patterned after federal laws.

The basic federal law dealing with air pollution is the Clean Air Act of 1970. The act was last amended in 1990. Under this law, the federal Environmental Protection Agency set standards for air quality. The agency also placed limits on the amounts of pollutants that could be given off by cars, factories, and other sources of pollutants. The states and industries were expected to develop and carry out plans to meet these standards. Some of the federal deadlines could not be met, and they were extended several times.

Air quality programs have brought improvements in many areas. For example, burning low-sulfur coal and oil in factories and power plants has lowered pollution in many cities. To meet federal standards, automobile engines have been redesigned, and new cars have been equipped with devices such as the catalytic converter which changes pollutants into harmless substances. Because of these new devices, air pollution from car exhaust has also been reduced.

It is not easy to bring about the new developments needed to control air pollution. Many people—physicians, engineers, meteorologists, botanists, and others—are involved in research, seeking new ways. Permanent observatories have been established to measure gradual changes in the atmosphere over long periods of time. The first observatory of this type was established near Mauna Loa, in Hawaii.

Vast sums of money will have to be spent in the future to clean the air and to keep it clean. Often pollution control means higher prices—to cover the cost of control devices in emission systems of new cars, for example. But to most people, the cost is justified. Perhaps the day will come when people everywhere can breathe pure air in cities where the sunlight is no longer blocked by an umbrella of pollution.

FRED H. RENNER, JR.
Office of Regional Programs
U.S. Environmental Protection Agency

See also ACID RAIN; ENVIRONMENT.

In an airport's control tower, sophisticated electronic equipment and a clear view of the airfield below help air traffic controllers direct the takeoffs and landings of planes.

AIRPORTS

An airport is a place where airplanes land and take off. At an airport, passengers and cargo are picked up and dropped off, and airplanes are refueled and serviced.

The first airplanes were small and light and needed only an open, flat area to take off and land. For this reason, and because very few people traveled by air, an early "airport" often consisted of only an unpaved landing field and a **hangar,** a large building in which airplanes are housed and repaired.

Since those early days, flight has become an important means of transportation, and aviation is now a major industry. Today, there are some 36,000 airports of all sizes throughout the world (including nearly 20,000 private airfields). Airports, like airplanes, have become much larger and more complex. In fact, airports in major cities are often so large that they can almost qualify as cities themselves. These large **air carrier** airports handle thousands of flights every day, mainly those of scheduled airlines. They are especially well equipped to accommodate large, jet-engine airplanes.

The vast majority of airports, however, are not as large as the air carrier airports. For example, of the more than 5,500 public airports in the United States, only 10 percent are large enough to handle commercial flights. Most airports are equipped to handle mainly smaller, propeller-driven airplanes owned by businesses or private citizens. Airports that handle this type of airplane and not those of scheduled airlines are known as **general aviation** airports. If a small airport is located near a much larger airport, the small airport is likely to assume a large share of the area's small-airplane traffic and is known as a **reliever** airport.

Although smaller airports are more numerous than large ones, most air travelers—roughly 450,000,000 per year in the United States alone—begin and end their journeys at a large airport.

▶A TRIP THROUGH A LARGE AIRPORT

Your first stop at the airport depends on the means of transportation you have used to get there. You can travel to some airports by train or bus, while others can be reached only by taxi or private car. If you have driven your own car, it must be parked in an airport lot or garage, which may have up to 20,000 parking spaces. From there you may have to board a shuttle bus to take you to your next destination, the terminal.

The Terminal. The terminal building or buildings are the largest at the airport and are the center of many services and activities. All passengers must pass through a terminal when boarding or leaving an airplane. When you arrive at the terminal, you will first go to the airline ticket counter. There, in exchange for your ticket, the airline agent will give you your boarding pass, which gives you permission to sit in a specific seat on the airplane.

The airline agent will attach a cardboard label to your baggage. The label has an identification number that matches one that is stapled to your boarding pass. The label also has a three-letter code, which identifies the airport at which you will land and helps the airline baggage handlers get your bags to the correct airplane. Your baggage will then travel on a conveyor belt into the underground ''belly'' of the airport. On international flights and some domestic flights, the baggage will be checked for weapons. A baggage handler will load all the baggage for your flight onto a cart, drive the cart to the airplane, and load the baggage onto the plane.

While you wait to board your plane, there may be time to visit some of the many shops located in the terminal. These include banks, newsstands and bookstores, restaurants and snack bars, and gift shops. Most international airports also have duty-free shops. If you are visiting a foreign country, you can buy goods at the duty-free shop and bring them home without having to pay duty, or import tax.

Some airports have an observation lounge, where large windows allow you to watch airplanes take off, land, and taxi (move slowly along the ground) to a gate. Gates are the points from which passengers leave the terminal and board the airplane.

Before heading to your gate, you will be screened by an electronic device that detects hidden weapons. Any bags that you are carrying on the plane will be passed through an X-ray machine to be sure they do not contain any weapons. These security checks are necessary to prevent the airplane from being hijacked.

The next stop is your gate, where your airplane is waiting. The distance between the main part of the terminal and the gate may be

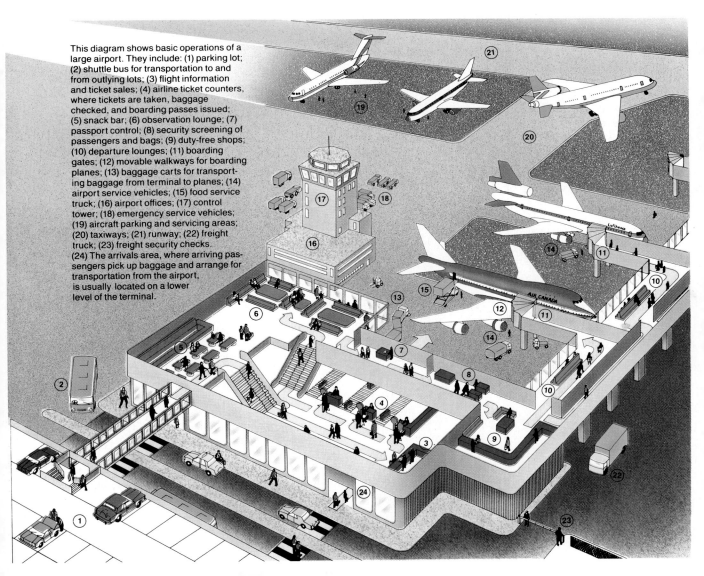

This diagram shows basic operations of a large airport. They include: (1) parking lot; (2) shuttle bus for transportation to and from outlying lots; (3) flight information and ticket sales; (4) airline ticket counters, where tickets are taken, baggage checked, and boarding passes issued; (5) snack bar; (6) observation lounge; (7) passport control; (8) security screening of passengers and bags; (9) duty-free shops; (10) departure lounges; (11) boarding gates; (12) movable walkways for boarding planes; (13) baggage carts for transporting baggage from terminal to planes; (14) airport service vehicles; (15) food service truck; (16) airport offices; (17) control tower; (18) emergency service vehicles; (19) aircraft parking and servicing areas; (20) taxiways; (21) runway; (22) freight truck; (23) freight security checks. (24) The arrivals area, where arriving passengers pick up baggage and arrange for transportation from the airport, is usually located on a lower level of the terminal.

too far to walk. In some airports, you will have to take a quick train ride. In others you will take a shuttle bus to a "mid-field" terminal, which is separate from the main terminal. In still other airports, passengers are transported to their gates on moving sidewalks. When you reach your gate, you will find yourself in a large, open waiting room. From here you will board your plane, most likely via a short, covered walkway.

The Runway. Airplanes take off and land on the runway. Jet planes require very long runways, sometimes as much as 2 miles (3 kilometers) in length. An air carrier airport typically has between two and four runways and may have as many as eight. A runway may look like an ordinary paved road. But, unlike roads built for cars, runways are made of special material able to withstand the impact of 830,000-pound (375,000-kilogram) airplanes. The runways will not crack under extreme cold or heat. Snowplows and salt spreaders keep them clear and ice free in winter. Drainage systems keep them from being flooded during rainy weather. Emergency fire and ambulance crews are always on duty.

The roads that run alongside the runways are called taxiways. They link the runways with the terminal and with other airport buildings, such as storage and service hangars. Lining the runway is a complex system of lights and signs with numbers and letters, which guide pilots in taking off, landing, and taxiing to and from the gates. Pilots are also guided by the ground crew, who steer airplanes into their gate parking positions. (Because airplanes cannot back up, they are often towed out of their gates by trucks.)

Air Traffic Control. Before the pilot can take off, or even start the plane's engines, permission must be given by the airport control tower. The control tower is the nerve center of the airport. From there, all approaches, landings, and takeoffs are directed by radio contact with the pilot. Air traffic controllers, the men and women in the control tower, are skilled at helping as many as 100 planes per hour take off and land without a collision. To do their job, they rely on sophisticated computers and communications systems. In the United States, air traffic controllers are employees of the Federal Aviation Administration (FAA).

Air traffic controllers in charge of ground control tell the pilot when to start the engines

Above: Airport firefighters perform a practice drill. Fire and other emergency teams are on call around the clock in case of accidents. *Below:* An airplane is serviced in an airport hangar. Planes are checked regularly; a major overhaul may take nearly two weeks.

When approaching an airport, the pilot of an airplane is guided by a system of lights that outline the runways and show where the plane should touch down.

THE WORLD'S 10 BUSIEST AIRPORTS

Airport	Passengers per year
1. O'Hare International: Chicago	59,936,137
2. International: Dallas/Ft. Worth	48,515,464
3. Hartsfield Atlanta International: Atlanta	48,024,566
4. International: Los Angeles	45,810,221
5. Heathrow Airport: London	42,964,200
6. Tokyo International (Haneda): Japan	40,233,031
7. International: San Francisco	31,059,820
8. Kennedy International: New York	29,786,657
9. Frankfurt: Germany	28,912,145
10. Stapleton International: Denver	27,432,989

Source: Airports Association Council International

and which taxiways and runway to use. After clearance (permission to take off) is given, the tower gives the pilot instructions to get clear of the airport area and proceed on course. Throughout the flight, the pilot must report at regular intervals to air traffic control centers located along the flight route. The pilot may be directed to change course or altitude to avoid bad weather or other air traffic. As the plane nears the end of its flight, the pilot contacts the control tower at the destination airport (where the plane will land). Air traffic controllers there direct the approach to the airport and the landing of the plane.

Other Facilities. Many operations are carried out at a major airport. Scores of buildings on airport grounds contain airline offices and food kitchens, fire and snow-removal equipment, and medical facilities. Large warehouses store cargo before and after it is shipped. Hangars house planes for servicing and maintenance. (Each airline must have a regular maintenance schedule for its planes, based on number of hours flown.)

All these operations employ staffs of workers. Additional airport workers include police and military personnel and, at international airports, customs and immigration officials. Altogether, up to 35,000 people may be employed at a large airport.

▶ **OWNERSHIP AND CONTROL**

All major civil airports in the United States are owned by the communities or states in which they are located. Airport policy is set by a board, commission, or department of public works. An aviation director is in charge of daily airport operations.

Even though most airports are publicly owned, they usually are not supported by taxpayers' dollars. Large airports are run mainly with money made from fees charged to airlines and other businesses operating in the airport.

More and more, airports are seeking to help their communities by controlling the noise produced by jet airplanes. Originally, most airports were built far from city centers. They have not moved, but the growth of cities has sometimes led to the building of homes near airports. Steps taken to reduce noise for nearby residents include forbidding the use of older, noisier aircraft and closing the airport during times when most people are sleeping.

At the same time, airports must expand to accommodate ever-growing numbers of passengers. One of the major challenges facing today's airport planners is to increase an airport's capacity while also making it acceptable to the community in which it is located.

ANDREW J. SOBEL
Manager, Public Affairs
Airports Association Council International

ALABAMA

The name Alabama comes from an Indian word that scholars believe means "plant gatherers." It referred most likely to the agricultural practices of the Alabama, a tribe of Creek Indians who originally lived in the region.

Alabama's nickname, Heart of Dixie, comes from the state's location in the heart, or center, of the southeastern United States, a region popularly known as Dixie. There are several theories about the origin of the name "Dixie." One claims it came from the French word dix, *meaning "ten." This word was printed on $10 bills used in the state of Louisiana before the Civil War. The bills were called dixies, and eventually the name Dixie, or Dixieland, came to be used for all the cotton-growing states in the South.*

State flag

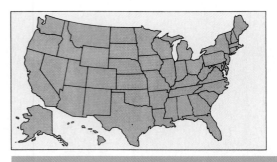

Alabama lies in the southeastern United States, in a region known as the Deep South. Part of its southern border includes the port of Mobile, which connects the state to the seaports of the world. Birmingham is Alabama's most populous city. Montgomery is its capital.

Like its neighbors, Alabama was once a predominantly agricultural state dominated by cotton farming. Although cotton is still grown, forest products and livestock are now more important to the economy. The development of the iron and steel industries in the 1880's, particularly around Birmingham, made Alabama the most industrialized state in the South. Local factories continue to make iron and steel products in addition to tires, textiles, and computer parts. Coal is also mined and processed. However, service-related jobs contribute the most to the state's economy.

Throughout its history, Alabama has experienced its share of conflict and rebellion. The Confederate States of America (CSA) was organized in Alabama in 1861, and Montgomery briefly served as its first capital. Alabama's history also is noteworthy for its long struggle with race relations. The modern civil rights movement began in Montgomery in 1955, when a black woman named Rosa Parks refused to yield her seat to a white person on a city bus. This bold action initiated a year-long boycott of the city bus system, which led to the passage of a federal law banning segregation on public transportation. Furthermore, mass demonstrations in Birmingham in 1963 forced the desegregation of public facilities. Then in 1965, more than 25,000 Americans, black and white, participated in a protest march, from Selma to Montgomery, to end discrimination at the polls and to secure voting rights for all African Americans.

▶ LAND

From north to south, Alabama extends about 330 miles (531 kilometers) from its border with Tennessee to its shoreline on the warm Gulf of Mexico.

Land Regions

Five major land regions cover the state of Alabama. Although the northeastern corner of the state reaches into the Appalachian Mountain system, much of Alabama's interior is made up of flat or gently rolling plains.

The East Gulf Coastal Plain is by far the largest of Alabama's land regions. For many years this mostly flat plain formed the heart of the South's cotton fields.

The part of the plain that today lies within Alabama can be divided roughly into three areas: the **Central Pine Belt** in the northwest, so called because of its abundant pine forests; the **Mobile River Delta** in the southwest; and the **Wiregrass** area in the southeast, named for the coarse grass that used to grow there.

Clockwise from top left: Oakleigh Mansion, near Mobile, is a graceful example of the antebellum (pre-Civil War) plantation homes of the Old South. Beaches along the Gulf of Mexico make excellent playgrounds. Birmingham is Alabama's largest and most industrialized city.

State flower:
Camellia

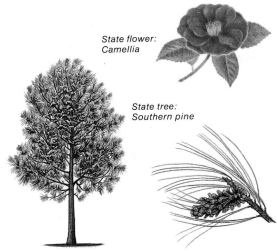

State tree:
Southern pine

FACTS AND FIGURES

Location: Southeastern United States; bordered on the north by Tennessee, on the east by Georgia, on the south by Florida and the Gulf of Mexico, and on the west by Mississippi.
Area: 51,705 sq mi (133,915 km²); rank, 29th.
Population: 4,062,608 (1990 census); rank, 22nd.
Elevation: *Highest* —2,407 ft (734 m) at Cheaha Mountain; *lowest*—sea level, along the Gulf of Mexico.
Capital: Montgomery.

Statehood: December 14, 1819; 22nd state.
State Motto: *Audemus jura nostra defendere* ("We dare defend our rights").
State Song: "Alabama."
Nickname: Heart of Dixie.
Abbreviations: AL; Ala.

State bird:
Yellowhammer

The Black Belt is a long strip of nearly level land less than 50 miles (80 kilometers) wide. Named for its dark-colored soils, it is an especially fertile region and was once known for its large, productive plantations.

The Interior Low Plateau covers a small region of northern Alabama. It is dominated by the broad valley of the Tennessee River, which cuts through the knobby hills of the plateau and makes the soil suitable for farming.

The Appalachian Highlands reach their southernmost extension in northeastern Alabama, where they can be divided into two regions. The **Cumberland Plateau**, which is the southern portion of the Appalachian Plateau, has some good farmland, but it is mainly suited to lumbering and mining. The **Ridge and Valley** Region is made up of narrow valleys between steep mountain ridges. It is known for its mineral riches and picturesque forests of oak and pine.

The Piedmont is a wedge-shaped area to the south of the Ridge and Valley Region. It is made up of foothills, with some rolling land. The state's highest point, Cheaha Mountain, is located here. It rises 2,407 feet (734 meters) above sea level.

Rivers, Lakes, and Coastal Waters

Alabama's geography is marked by an abundance of rivers and lakes. Two main river systems cover the southern three-quarters of the state. The Alabama River and its main tributaries, the Coosa and Tallapoosa rivers, empty the eastern side of the state; the Tombigbee River and its tributary, the Black Warrior River, drain the western side. These two river systems join to form the Mobile River, which empties into Mobile Bay on the Gulf of Mexico. Their junction forms a delta area that covers several hundred square miles of marshes and cypress swamps.

The Tennessee River, flowing east to west, distinguishes the geography of northern Alabama. The Tennessee-Tombigbee Waterway, a canal completed in 1985, ties the Tennessee River system to the Tombigbee River, and thus to the port of Mobile. The Chattahoochee River in the southeast forms part of the border between Alabama and Georgia.

All of Alabama's larger rivers have been dammed, creating many beautiful lakes. The largest is Guntersville Lake, created in the 1930's by damming the Tennessee River.

Alabama's coastline on the Gulf of Mexico makes up a small part of the state's southern border. It stretches only 53 miles (85 kilometers), but because of many bays, inlets, and islands, there are actually 607 miles (977 kilometers) of shoreline. Of the offshore islands, Dauphin Island is the largest.

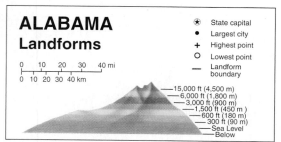

ALABAMA
Landforms

⍟ State capital
● Largest city
+ Highest point
○ Lowest point
— Landform boundary

0 10 20 30 40 mi
0 10 20 30 40 km

15,000 ft (4,500 m)
6,000 ft (1,800 m)
3,000 ft (900 m)
1,500 ft (450 m)
600 ft (180 m)
300 ft (90 m)
Sea Level
Below

Loblolly pine trees surround the swamplands of Gulf Shores State Park, in one of Alabama's southernmost regions. The rare Cahaba lily (*inset*) grows only along some Alabama streams.

Climate

Alabama's climate is quite mild. Winter temperatures rarely drop below freezing and average about 52°F (11°C) in the south and 46°F (8°C) in the north. Summer temperatures tend to be about the same throughout the state, averaging about 80°F (27°C).

Snowfall is unusual, but rainfall is abundant, averaging 65 inches (1,651 millimeters) a year along the coast and about 53 inches (1,346 millimeters) in the northern regions. Hurricanes sometimes blow in from the Gulf of Mexico, occasionally causing damage to shoreline areas.

Plant and Animal Life

Alabama's many flowering trees and shrubs make spring and summer especially beautiful. Azaleas, mountain laurel, rhododendron, orchids, and wild roses dot the landscape. About two-thirds of Alabama is forestland. The pine is the most common tree, followed by oak, hickory, and cedar.

More than 300 species of birds live at least part of the year in the state. These include eagles, buzzards, hawks, ospreys, wild turkeys, ducks, and geese. Rabbits, squirrels, raccoons, foxes, and white-tailed deer are common. Black bears and alligators live in some areas.

Bass, crappie, bluegill, and catfish fill many of the state's freshwater lakes. The commercial products of Alabama's offshore waters include shrimp, snapper, oysters, and crabs.

Natural Resources

One of Alabama's most valuable resources is its waterways. Rivers were once the primary means of transport in the state before roadways were built. Still used for shipping, the rivers provide hydroelectric power from dams on the Coosa, Tallapoosa, Tennessee, Chattahoochee, and Black Warrior rivers.

The fertile soils of the East Gulf Coastal Plain were formed from sediment laid down in the oceans that once covered this region. Most of these soils are sandy loams or clay soils. Unfortunately erosion and many decades of farming have made Alabama's soils less fertile. Some farms are now planted with grasses to improve the soil and provide pasture for cattle, especially in the Piedmont and Black Belt regions.

The state's pine forests are a valuable source of wood pulp, used for making paper products. Tree farms have had the added benefit of controlling erosion and improving the worn-out soils.

Most of Alabama's minerals are found in the northern half of the state. Coal, limestone, marble, sand and gravel, and bauxite (an aluminum ore) are mined. Petroleum is found in the extreme southwestern counties. Iron ore, once an important local resource for steelmaking in the Birmingham area, is no longer heavily mined.

▶ PEOPLE

The majority of Alabamians are descendants of European settlers, mostly of English or Scotch-Irish ancestry. The influence of the Spanish and the French, Alabama's first European settlers, is still evident around Mobile.

About 25 percent of the population is African American. Those of Hispanic or Asian descent together make up only about 1 percent of the population. Less than half of 1 percent are of Native American heritage. Four major groups are native to the state—the Creek, Choctaw, Chickasaw, and Cherokee.

For many decades most of Alabama's population lived in rural areas. Starting in the 1940's, the number of people who worked on farms dropped steadily. By 1960, for the first time, more Alabamians lived in cities than in rural areas. Today 60 percent of Alabamians live in urban centers.

Education

Although public education in Alabama was established in 1854, the state's schools were poorly supported, and there were virtually no schools for black children. Since the early 1900's there have been efforts made to improve education, but Alabama's tax support for schools remains well below the national average. City schools are generally better funded than those in rural areas.

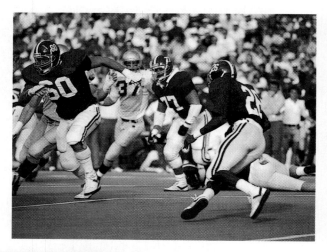

The University of Alabama is the state's oldest public university. Its football team, known as the Crimson Tide (*above*), is consistently ranked among the best in the nation. In the summertime, county fairs (*left*) are held throughout the state. These public festivals give people an opportunity to display and sell homemade foods and crafts.

PEOPLE

Population: 4,062,608 (1990 census).
Density: 78 persons per sq mi (30 per km²).
Distribution: 60% urban; 40% rural.
Largest Cities (1990 census):

Birmingham 265,968	Tuscaloosa 77,759
Mobile 196,278	Dothan 53,589
Montgomery 187,106	Decatur 48,761
Huntsville 159,789	Gadsden 42,523

Persons per sq mi	Persons per km²
over 250	over 100
50-250	20-100
5-50	2-20
0-5	0-2

Huntsville
Decatur
Gadsden
Birmingham
Tuscaloosa
Montgomery
Dothan
Mobile

The state has many colleges and universities, including more than 40 community colleges built during the 1960's.

Athens State College, founded in 1822, is the oldest college in the state. The University of Alabama, founded in 1831, is the oldest state university, with campuses in Tuscaloosa, Birmingham, and Huntsville. Auburn University has the largest student body in the state. There are six other state universities and more than a dozen private colleges, including Tuskegee University, established by Booker T. Washington in 1881.

Libraries, Museums, and the Arts

About 200 public libraries serve the people of Alabama. The largest are located in Birmingham, Montgomery, Huntsville, and Mobile. State history is explored in the Alabama Department of Archives and History in Montgomery and at the Civil Rights Institute, located in Birmingham.

Alabama has more than 50 museums. The Birmingham Museum of Art and the Montgomery Museum of Fine Arts have large collections of paintings and artifacts. The Anniston Museum of Natural History contains an unusual display of 900 specimens of birds. The George Washington Carver Museum at Tuskegee Institute National Historic Site features agricultural exhibits. The U.S. Space and Rocket Center in Huntsville has more than 60 hands-on exhibits about spaceflight. It is Alabama's most popular tourist attraction.

The Alabama Shakespeare Festival, founded in Anniston in 1972, is located in Montgomery. This elaborate performing arts complex offers a variety of plays, from Shakespeare to Tennessee Williams, as well as concerts, lectures, and dance programs.

Alabama is an important center of traditional American music. Spirituals, gospel songs, and string-band music for banjos, fiddles, and guitars are popular.

Although Alabama has no professional sports teams, college football is a major pastime. The University of Alabama team, called the Crimson Tide, is consistently ranked among the best in the nation. The school's traditional rival, Auburn University, was the home of famed football coach John Heisman, in the 1890's. The prestigious Heisman Trophy, named for him, is awarded each year to the nation's best college football player.

Cotton thrives in Alabama's rich river valleys. It was once the state's single most important product, but today it is considerably less important to the economy.

▶ECONOMY

More than one hundred years ago, Alabama's economy was agricultural, based almost entirely on cotton. Manufacturing grew after the Civil War, with iron furnaces and steel mills providing many of the state's jobs. Today the service industries have surpassed agriculture and manufacturing to become the largest and fastest-growing part of Alabama's economy.

Services

More than 70 percent of Alabamians have jobs that provide services to their communities, such as health care, education, government services, police and fire protection, and banking, insurance, and real estate services. Services also include businesses that supply such necessities as food, clothing, transportation, and housing.

Manufacturing

About 23 percent of the state's workforce is employed in manufacturing jobs. Alabama's most important manufacturing industries are those that produce metals, wood products, and textiles. Many of these industries make use of

The manufacture of copper tubing and other fabricated metal products contributes significantly to Alabama's gross state product.

Agriculture

For many years, cotton ranked first among Alabama's crops, but today cotton contributes only minimally to the state's total income from crops. Alabama produces substantial amounts of soybeans, peanuts, vegetables, corn, hay, and oats.

Livestock now brings more than twice as much income to Alabama than cash crops. Broilers (young chickens) are Alabama's single most important agricultural product. Cattle, hogs, dairy products, and seafood from the Gulf of Mexico also are important.

Mining and Construction

About 5 percent of the state's workforce is engaged in mining or construction activities, such as the ongoing building and repair of roads and bridges. Alabama is known for its production of coal and limestone. Other minerals produced in the state include oil, natural gas, clays and shale, marble, mica, sand and gravel, and bauxite.

The state's first producing oil well began operating in Choctaw County, in 1944. Today there are about 2,000 producing oil wells in the state, nearly all of them located in the southwest.

Transportation

Alabama has one of the nation's finest river transportation systems. Completed in 1985, the Tennessee-Tombigbee Waterway provides a water route from much of the eastern United States to the port city of Mobile. Alabama's first railway, between Decatur and Tuscumbia, was completed in 1835. Today the state's railroads are used mostly for freight. Alabama also has an excellent system of more than 140 local airfields. Major airports are located in Birmingham, Huntsville, Montgomery, and Mobile.

the state's own raw materials, such as coal and wood pulp.

About 90 percent of all the steelmaking in the South takes place in Alabama, mostly in and around Birmingham, Anniston, and Gadsden. Factories that make metal products are located throughout the state.

Alabama's forests supply lumber for furniture and other wood products as well as wood pulp for the paper industry. More than 500 paper mills are located in the state.

The textile industry produces yarn, thread, woven fabrics, clothing, and other goods. Chemicals, rubber, and plastics are additional important manufactured products.

PRODUCTS AND INDUSTRIES

Manufacturing: Metals and metal products, paper and wood products, textiles, chemicals, rubber, plastics.

Agriculture: Broilers (young chickens), beef cattle, hogs, dairy products, greenhouse and nursery products, soybeans, cotton, peanuts, corn, hay, seafood.

Minerals: Coal, limestone, oil, natural gas, clays and shale, bauxite, sand and gravel, mica, marble.

Services: Wholesale and retail trade; finance, insurance, and real estate; business, social, and personal services; transportation, communication, and utilities; government.

*Gross state product is the total value of goods and services produced in a year.

Percentage of Gross State Product* by Industry

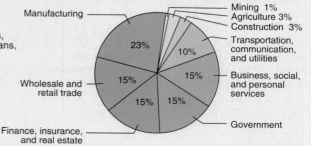

Manufacturing 23%
Mining 1%
Agriculture 3%
Construction 3%
Transportation, communication, and utilities 10%
Business, social, and personal services 15%
Government 15%
Finance, insurance, and real estate 15%
Wholesale and retail trade 15%

Source: U.S. Bureau of Economic Analysis

Communication

About 100 weekly newspapers are published in Alabama; another 24 are published daily. The *Birmingham News* has by far the largest circulation. The *Mobile Register*, founded in 1813, is the state's oldest newspaper still in existence.

Birmingham acquired the state's first licensed radio station, WBRC, in 1925 and its first television stations, WABT and WBRC-TV, both in 1949. Approximately 25 television stations and 240 radio stations operate within the state.

▶CITIES

Alabama's cities are scattered throughout the state. Only four of them have populations exceeding 100,000.

Montgomery, Alabama's capital and third largest city, is often called the Cradle of the Confederacy because in 1861 it became the first capital of the Confederate States of America (CSA). Situated on the Alabama River, Montgomery is a center of agricultural trade. It is the leading cattle market in the southeastern United States, with large ranges and cattle herds in the surrounding area. Industries within the city include textile mills, meatpacking plants, and furniture factories.

Montgomery has several institutions of higher education, including Alabama State University. Auburn and Troy State universities each have a campus there. Faulkner University and Huntingdon College also are located in Montgomery.

Birmingham, Alabama's largest and most industrialized city, is located in central Alabama. It was founded as the small town of Elyton in 1871 and has been called the Magic City because of its rapid growth. Birmingham is the South's major producer of iron and steel. Other area industries manufacture cast-iron pipes, heavy machinery, chemicals, textiles, and wood and paper products. Birmingham is also a cultural and educational center.

Mobile, the state's second largest city and only seaport, was founded by the French and named for the Mobile Indians. Known as Alabama's Gateway to the World, Mobile is a busy industrial and shipping center with chemical plants, shipyards, and seafood industries. It is also a gracious and beautiful resort city, known for its flowers and ancient oak trees draped with Spanish moss.

Huntsville, in the northern part of the state, was one of Alabama's first settlements. For many years it remained a small farming community, but it grew rapidly in the 1950's after the U.S. Army developed a missile research center at the Redstone Arsenal. Today Huntsville is known as Rocket City, U.S.A. The U.S. Space and Rocket Center, the U.S. Space Camp and Space Academy, and the George C. Marshall Space Flight Center, run by the National Aeronautics and Space Administration (NASA), are located there.

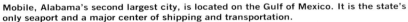

Mobile, Alabama's second largest city, is located on the Gulf of Mexico. It is the state's only seaport and a major center of shipping and transportation.

137

Places of Interest

Bellingrath Gardens and Home, in Theodore, is a beautifully landscaped estate once owned by Walter D. Bellingrath, a local industrialist. The formal gardens are world famous for their springtime displays of azaleas. The home itself is noted for its lovely art objects.

The Birmingham Civil Rights Institute, in Birmingham, is the centerpiece of the city's historic Civil Rights District. On permanent display is a chronological history of the city's role in the civil rights movement.

The Civil Rights Memorial, located outside the Southern Poverty Law Center in Montgomery, stands in tribute to forty people who lost their lives in the struggle for civil rights. It was designed by Maya Lin, the architect who designed the Vietnam War Memorial in Washington, D.C.

Dexter Avenue King Memorial Baptist Church, in Montgomery, was where Martin Luther King, Jr., preached from 1954 until 1960. Now designated a National Historic Landmark in memory of the slain civil rights leader, the church contains a mural depicting events in King's life.

Horseshoe Bend National Military Park, on the Tallapoosa River near Dadeville, marks the site of the last battle of the Creek War of 1813–14. It was there that General Andrew Jackson defeated the heavily outnumbered Creek Indians.

Ivy Green, in Tuscumbia, is the birthplace and childhood home of Helen Keller. Every June a theater company takes part in the Helen Keller Festival to reenact the period in Keller's life during which she learned to overcome her disabilities.

Azaleas in Bellingrath Gardens, in Theodore

First White House of the Confederacy, located in Montgomery, served as the residence of Jefferson Davis, the first president of the Confederacy, during the first months of the Civil War in 1861, when Montgomery was the Confederate capital. The house was originally built in 1835. Civil War items and many period furnishings are on display.

Mound State Monument, a state park and museum in Moundville, near Tuscaloosa, preserves prehistoric temple mounds. Visitors may also explore a reconstructed Indian village.

Russell Cave National Monument, near Bridgeport in northeast Alabama, is the site of Alabama's earliest known human inhabitants. The monument preserves evidence of almost continuous habitation in the cave from at least 7000 B.C. to about A.D. 1650.

Tuskegee Institute National Historic Site, in Tuskegee, includes Tuskegee University, the George Washington Carver Museum, and Booker T. Washington's home, known as the Oaks. The museum includes displays of Carver's agricultural experiments with peanuts and sweet potatoes.

U.S. Space and Rocket Center, in Huntsville, is the world's largest space museum. Visitors can experience the sights and sensations of space travel through dozens of hands-on exhibits. Rockets, space shuttles, training facilities, and research laboratories are also on display.

The center also runs a number of enormously popular space camps, where children and adults can experience many aspects of spaceflight. For more information, see the article SPACE AGENCIES AND CENTERS in Volume S.

State Parks. Alabama has 4 national forests and more than 20 state parks. For more information, contact Alabama State Parks, 64 North Union Street, Montgomery, Alabama 36130.

U.S. Space and Rocket Center, in Huntsville

Sculpture near the Birmingham Civil Rights Institute

▶GOVERNMENT

Alabama's constitution, adopted in 1901, has been amended more than five hundred times. It contains provisions for three branches of government.

The head of the executive branch is the governor, who is elected by the people of the state. Other elected officials in the executive branch include the lieutenant governor, secretary of state, attorney general, treasurer, auditor, and commissioner of agriculture and industry.

The legislative department is made up of a senate and a house of representatives. The members of both of these bodies meet annually and serve 4-year terms.

The highest state court is the supreme court. It consists of a chief justice and eight associate justices elected statewide.

GOVERNMENT

State Government
Governor: 4-year term
State senators: 35; 4-year terms
State representatives: 105;
    4-year terms
Number of counties: 67

Federal Government
U.S. senators: 2
U.S. representatives: 7
Number of electoral votes: 9

For the name of the current governor, see STATE GOVERNMENTS in Volume S. For the names of current U.S. senators and representatives, see UNITED STATES, CONGRESS OF THE in Volume U-V.

The state is divided into 67 counties. Each county is governed by a board of commissioners, known as the county commission.

▶HISTORY

Evidence shows that cave-dwelling Indians lived in Alabama as early as 9,000 years ago. By the time of first European contact in the early 1500's, Alabama was inhabited by the Mississippians, a sophisticated society of Indians frequently referred to as the Mound Builders.

European Exploration and Settlement

The Spanish explored Mobile Bay as early as 1519, but they did not venture into the interior until 1540, when Hernando de Soto led an expedition through northeastern Alabama. He took many Indians captive as he marched from one Mississippian village to the next, searching for gold and other treasure.

One of De Soto's prisoners, the chieftain Tuskalusa, secretly plotted a counterattack at the walled Mississippian town of Mabila, but armor and horses gave the Spanish a big advantage. By the time the Indians surrendered, about 3,000 of them had been killed.

In the late 1600's, English traders from the Carolinas and Georgia traded with the Indians in Alabama. In 1702 the French established Fort Louis on Mobile Bay, which was moved,

Alabama's state government finally settled in Montgomery in 1846. The following year, the capitol building (*above*) was erected in the Greek Revival style.

in 1711, to the present site of the city of Mobile. It became the first permanent white settlement in what is now Alabama.

After the French and Indian War, the Treaty of Paris (1763) ceded most of present-day Alabama to England, which in turn ceded it to the United States in 1783 following the American Revolutionary War. American settlers started moving into Alabama around 1800.

At that time, Alabama's four main tribes—the Creek, Cherokee, Choctaw, and Chickasaw—occupied much of Alabama's good farmland, and they resisted the settlers moving onto their lands. As a result, during the War of 1812 the Indians sided with the British against the Americans. In 1813, in retaliation against an American assault, the Indians at-

This engraving of a plantation in Clarke County in the 1800's shows slaves called field hands engaged in the backbreaking task of picking cotton by hand.

tacked Fort Mims, about 50 miles (80 kilometers) north of Mobile, killing approximately 250 settlers. The Tennessee militia, led by General Andrew Jackson, marched from one Indian village to another, burning and killing. The final conflict came on March 27, 1814, when Jackson defeated the Creek at the Battle of Horseshoe Bend. The Indians signed a treaty that gave most of their territory to the U.S. government. Almost immediately, thousands more settlers poured into Alabama.

Statehood and the Trail of Tears

Settlers organized the Alabama Territory in 1817. Two years later it became a state. Between 1819 and 1846, the state capital was moved three times due to transportation difficulties and Alabama's changing centers of population. State government finally settled in Montgomery in 1846.

In the early years of statehood, settlers pushed for the removal of all Indians from Alabama. In 1830, Andrew Jackson, who was by then the president of the United States, signed the Removal Act, using his power to force the migration of most of Alabama's Indians to Oklahoma. The route the Indians took, on which many thousands died throughout the 1830's, became known as the Trail of Tears.

Cotton, Slavery, and the Civil War

Between 1820 and 1860, due to a booming cotton market, Alabama became one of the wealthiest states in the Union. However, the state's large cotton plantations would not have been as profitable without the use of slave labor. Alabamians, therefore, fiercely resisted a growing movement in the North to abolish slavery, and they objected to the federal government interfering in the affairs of the South-

INDEX TO ALABAMA MAP

• County Seat

Counties in parentheses

★ State Capital

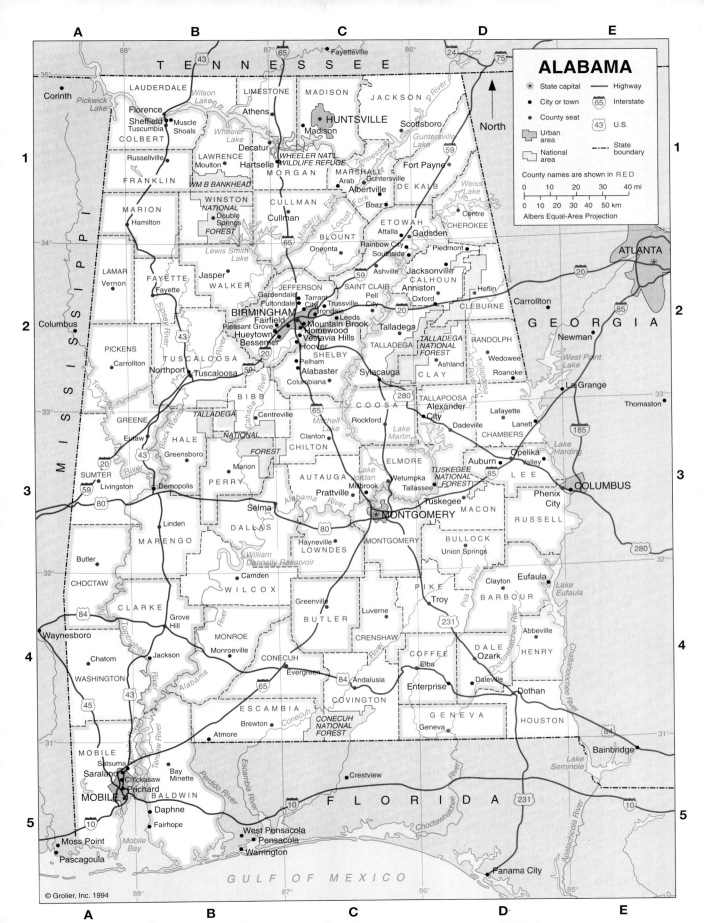

ALABAMA

State capital
City or town
County seat
Urban area
National area

Highway
Interstate 65
U.S. 43
State boundary

County names are shown in RED

0 10 20 30 40 mi
0 10 20 30 40 50 km
Albers Equal-Area Projection

North

© Grolier, Inc. 1994

Famous People

Included among Alabama's most celebrated citizens are three famous educators, George Washington Carver (1864–1943), Helen Keller (1880–1968), and Booker T. Washington (1856–1915); renowned civil rights leader Martin Luther King, Jr., (1929–68); and Olympic track-and-field star Jesse Owens (1913–80). Biographies of these figures can be found in their appropriate volumes.

Helen Keller

Booker T. Washington

Dr. Martin Luther King, Jr.

Henry Louis (Hank) Aaron (1934–   ), born in Mobile, is American baseball's all-time champion home-run hitter. In 1974 he broke Babe Ruth's record of 714 career home runs and went on to hit a career total of 755. For much of his career, Aaron played for the Braves of the National League, first in Milwaukee (1954–65) and then in Atlanta (1966–74). He ended his career with the Milwaukee Brewers (1974–76) of the American League. Along with a lifetime batting average of .305, Aaron holds the all-time record for runs batted in (2,297). In addition to being chosen the National League's most valuable player of 1957, Aaron won the Spingarn Medal in 1975 and was elected to the National Baseball Hall of Fame in 1982.

Ralph David Abernathy (1926–90), born in Linden, was a Baptist minister and civil rights leader. In the 1950's, while a pastor in Montgomery, Abernathy and Dr. Martin Luther King, Jr., planned the 1955 Montgomery bus boycott to protest segregation. Then in 1957, in Atlanta, Georgia, Abernathy helped King establish the Southern Christian Leadership Conference (SCLC) to broaden the civil rights movement through nonviolent means. After King was assassinated in 1968, Abernathy served as SCLC president until 1977. His autobiography, *And the Walls Came Tumbling Down* was published in 1989.

Hugo La Fayette Black (1886–1971), born in Harlan, was an associate justice of the U.S. Supreme Court for 34 years (1937–71). A successful Birmingham lawyer, Black was elected to the U.S. Senate, where he served for ten years (1927–37). A Democrat, Black vigorously supported the New Deal policies of President Franklin Roosevelt, which led to his Court appointment in 1937. Black was a liberal judge who supported government protection of free speech and civil rights.

Paul William (Bear) Bryant (1913–83) is considered by many to be the greatest college football coach of all time. Born in Kingsland, Arkansas, Bryant was head coach at Maryland (1945), Kentucky (1946–53), and Texas A&M (1954–57)

ern states. On January 11, 1861, Alabama seceded (withdrew) from the Union and invited all the other Southern states to join her in withdrawal and in forming a new government. On February 4, 1861, a convention of delegates met in Montgomery and drew up a constitution for the newly formed Confederate States of America. Jefferson Davis was sworn in as president on February 18.

During the Civil War (1861–65), many minor battles took place in Alabama. The most notable action occurred at the naval battle of Mobile Bay in 1864, which the Confederates lost. Union raids late in the war destroyed a great deal of property and left Alabama so impoverished, it took generations to rebuild its economy.

Reconstruction

After the war, several amendments to the Constitution freed the slaves and guaranteed them citizenship and the right to vote. This marked the greatest change in Alabama society since the settlers had displaced the Indians. However, most whites refused to recognize blacks as citizens. They used violence and fraud to strip blacks of their rights and eventually created a system of legal segregation (separation of the races), which allowed whites to treat blacks unfairly. The final blow came in 1901, when Alabama revised its constitution and took away the blacks' right to vote.

Meanwhile, falling cotton prices made farming less profitable. At the instigation of Daniel Pratt, a cotton-gin and textile manufacturer, Alabama began to build railroads and encourage the development of industries. Pratt invested in the iron industry in the new city of Birmingham, which grew rapidly, and in the 1890's, many new cotton mills and sawmills were established.

Alabama in the 1900's

Economic growth accelerated in the 1900's with the expansion of the iron-and-steel, textile, and lumber industries. The development of chemical, rubber, and electronics plants added to the industrial base. An abundance of electricity, generated cheaply by the power of both water and coal, greatly advanced the state's industrial economy.

American involvement in World War I (1917–18) and World War II (1941–45) spurred industrial production and led to the before beginning his 24-year dynasty with the Crimson Tide of the University of Alabama (1958–82). Among his achievements were six national championships; three Coach of the Year awards; 15 victories in a record 29 bowl-game appearances; and a career record of 323-85-17. The Paul W. Bryant Museum in Tuscaloosa commemorates Bryant and University of Alabama football.

William Christopher (W.C.) Handy (1873–1958), born in Florence, is known as the "Father of the Blues." A musician and a composer, Handy popularized the blues style long before the jazz era began. He wrote many popular tunes, including "Memphis Blues" (1912) and "St. Louis Blues" (1914). He also arranged music for films, radio, and theater.

(Nelle) Harper Lee (1926–   ), born in Monroeville, achieved literary distinction with the publication of her only novel, *To Kill a Mockingbird* (1960). The story examines racial prejudice and social injustice in a small Alabama town, as seen through the eyes of an innocent and unbiased young girl. The book won the Pulitzer Prize for fiction in 1961 and was made into a popular film in 1962.

Joe Louis (Joseph Louis Barrow) (1914–81), born near Lafayette, was one of the all-time greatest professional boxers. He was the longest-reigning world heavyweight champion, defending his title 25 times between 1937 and 1949. He won his first heavyweight title in 1937 by knocking out James J. Braddock in 8 rounds. Nicknamed the "Brown Bomber," Louis won 68 victories and lost only 3 fights in his entire professional career.

Rosa Louise McCauley Parks (1913–   ), born in Tuskeegee, sparked the modern civil rights movement when she was arrested in 1955 for refusing to give her seat to a white passenger on a crowded Montgomery city bus, as required by city law. The incident led to a bus boycott, led by Dr. Martin Luther King, Jr., that increased national awareness about racial segregation and dis-

George C. Wallace

crimination practices. In 1979, Parks was awarded the Spingarn Medal for her courageous efforts to further civil rights in the United States. Her memoir, *Rosa Parks,* was published in 1992.

George Corley Wallace (1919–   ), born in Clio, served as governor of Alabama for four terms (1963–67; 1971–79; and 1983–87) and three times was an unsuccessful candidate for president of the United States (1968, 1972, and 1976). A staunch supporter of states' rights and segregation, Wallace came to national attention in 1963 when he defied federal law by attempting to block the enrollment of two black students at the University of Alabama. In later years, however, he softened on civil rights protections and formed a coalition of black and white supporters. While campaigning for the presidency in 1972, Wallace was paralyzed by a bullet in a failed assassination attempt in Laurel, Maryland.

---

establishment of several large military bases in the state. The Great Depression of the 1930's, which brought great suffering to Alabama's farmers, led to the establishment of the Tennessee Valley Authority (TVA) and other federal projects that helped build the state's economy. In the 1950's and 1960's, the nation's space program developed rockets at Huntsville Redstone Arsenal. Rockets built there were used to send up America's first satellite as well as the first astronauts to land on the moon.

Meanwhile, race relations remained strained. As early as the 1940's, African Americans in Alabama challenged racial discrimination in voting. However, their first victory was not achieved until 1956, following a year-long, nonviolent boycott of the Montgomery city bus system, organized by Dr. Martin Luther King, Jr., in response to the 1955 arrest of Rosa Parks. The protest led to the passage of a federal law in 1956 that made discrimination illegal on public transportation and marked the birth of the modern civil rights movement in the United States.

Demonstrations against the continued segregation of public facilities took place in Bir-

mingham in 1963. Abuses by law enforcement officers, such as the use of high-powered water hoses against peaceful demonstrators and the deaths of four black girls, killed by a bomb while attending Sunday school, outraged the nation and prompted the passage of the Civil Rights Act of 1964. Then the following year, Dr. King led a peaceful march from Selma to Montgomery to protest discrimination against blacks at the polls, which directly led to the passage of the Voting Rights Act of 1965.

Meanwhile, many whites deeply resented integration and supported the pro-segregation position of Alabama's Governor George Wallace. By the 1970's, however, most Alabamians, including Governor Wallace, had adjusted to the new order and accepted the rights of all citizens. By 1991, Alabama led the nation in the number of African Americans elected to public office, clearly representing the state's progress toward achieving racial equality.

ROBERT J. NORRELL, PH.D.
Director, Center for Southern History and
Culture, University of Alabama

ALAMO.   See TEXAS.

ALASKA

The Aleuts, one of Alaska's earliest native peoples, called their land alayeksa, *meaning "great land." This gave Alaska its name and also one of its nicknames, the Great Land.*

Alaska is also known as the Last Frontier. For more than two hundred years, newcomers have sought their fortunes from Alaska's wealth of natural resources. Whether pursuing furs, gold, or oil, these hearty pioneers forged their way through an untouched wilderness. Even today, much of Alaska has never been settled or even explored.

Alaska gets more hours of sunlight in the summertime than any other state, giving the state yet another nickname, Land of the Midnight Sun. For nearly three straight months, from May through July, the sun never sets at Barrow, Alaska's northernmost point.

State flag

Alaska is a rugged peninsula located in the northwest corner of North America, approximately 500 miles (800 kilometers) away from the "Lower 48" states. Attu Island, at the westernmost tip of Alaska's Aleutian island chain, lies only 51 miles (82 kilometers) from Russia's Siberian coast.

Covering an area more than twice the size of Texas, Alaska is by far the largest of the fifty states, yet it has fewer residents than any other except Wyoming. Alaska's northern quarter, which lies within the Arctic Circle, is covered by frozen, treeless tundra, yet the southeastern region of the state contains lush rain forests.

Anchorage, Fairbanks, and Juneau, Alaska's capital, are the three largest cities in the state. People there enjoy most of the same conveniences as other American cities. Yet beyond these urban areas, Alaska is rough, wild, and barely populated. Many places can only be reached by airplane. Dog mushing, or sledding, is Alaska's official state sport. Once a major form of transportation throughout this snowbound land, the dog team and sled is still a necessity in some rural areas. Since 1973, the Iditarod Trail Sled Dog Race has been Alaska's most famous sporting event. Dashing from Anchorage to Nome through more than 1,000 miles (1,600 kilometers) of swamps, mountains, and ice, mushers may take as long as three weeks to finish what has been called the Last Great Race on Earth.

The first people to inhabit Alaska came from Siberia, perhaps as long as 40,000 years ago. The descendants of these first settlers—the Eskimos, Aleuts, and various groups of Indians—still thrive in Alaska. Russian explorers discovered Alaska in the mid-1700's, and at once the territory was overrun with fur trappers and merchants. Within a hundred years, they had hunted sea otters and fur seals almost to extinction. When the United States offered to buy Alaska in 1867, many Americans believed Alaska was worthless, and they ridiculed its purchase until gold was discovered there in 1880. Soon tens of thousands of gold rushers swarmed over the Alaskan frontier, hoping to strike it rich.

Alaska's modern history began when the territory achieved statehood on January 3, 1959, and even more important, when oil was discovered in Prudhoe Bay in 1968. Since then, oil has become the mainstay of Alaska's economy as well as the focus of many fierce battles between business people, who wish to develop the land, and environmentalists, who wish to preserve it in its natural state.

▶LAND

Alaska is an enormous peninsula, surrounded on three sides by water. Its 6,640-

Dall sheep and other wildlife thrive in Alaska's vast mountain ranges. Most Alaskans enjoy the challenge of living in such a rugged land and climate. A Russian Orthodox church graces Kodiak Island, where fur traders established their first permanent settlement in 1784.

State flower:
Forget-me-not

State tree:
Sitka spruce

FACTS AND FIGURES

Location: Northwestern North America; bordered on the north by the Arctic Ocean, on the south by the Pacific Ocean and the Gulf of Alaska, on the east by Canada (British Columbia and Yukon Territory), and on the west by the Bering Sea.

Area: 591,004 sq mi (1,530,700 km²); rank, 1st.

Population: 551,947 (1990 census); rank, 49th.

Elevation: *Highest*—20,320 ft (6,194 m), at Mount McKinley; *lowest*—sea level.

Capital: Juneau.

Statehood: January 3, 1959; 49th state.

State Motto: *North to the Future.*

State Song: "Alaska's Flag."

Nickname: (unofficial): The Last Frontier; the Great Land; Land of the Midnight Sun.

Abbreviation: AK

State bird:
Willow ptarmigan

mile (10,686-kilometer) coastline is longer than that of any of the other continental states. The total shoreline, including offshore islands, bays, and inlets, is about 34,000 miles (54,720 kilometers) long.

Alaska encompasses more than 1,000 islands, mostly in the Alexander Archipelago and the Aleutian island chain. The Alexander Archipelago and the thin strip of mainland that borders British Columbia are known as the Panhandle.

Land Regions

Alaska's vast landscape contains four major land regions.

The Pacific Mountain System, in the south, contains the Coast Mountains in the southeast; the St. Elias, Wrangell, Chugach, and Kenai ranges around the Gulf of Alaska; the Aleutian Range, which sweeps southwestward through

ests grow in its eastern and central valleys. Some areas are covered by permafrost, or permanently frozen subsoil. Others are covered with a dense growth of low vegetation.

The Rocky Mountain System reaches its northernmost extension at the Brooks Range. The highest mountains within this range are located in the northeastern part of the state and rise just above 9,000 feet (2,743 meters).

The Arctic Coastal Plain, also known as the Arctic Slope, lies entirely within the Arctic Circle. From the foot of the Brooks Range, this flat and treeless plain slopes northward to the Beaufort Sea and the Arctic Ocean. The soil is largely permafrost.

Rivers and Lakes

The Yukon is the great river of Alaska. It winds across central Alaska more than 1,200 miles (1,900 kilometers) and empties through

Mount McKinley is the highest mountain in all of North America. The Athabascan Indians call it *Denali*, meaning the Great One. Located in Denali National Park in the south central part of the state, it is the crowning point of the Alaska Range.

the Alaska Peninsula and the Aleutian Islands; and the Alaska Range farther inland. The Alaska Range is known for its high peaks and its many glaciers and rivers. Its crowning point is Mount McKinley. Rising 20,320 feet (6,194 meters), it is the highest peak in North America.

The Central Uplands and Lowlands, covering most of central Alaska, is made up of rolling hills, valleys, and low mountain ranges. For-

a huge, swampy delta into Norton Sound. The largest of the Yukon's tributaries in Alaska are the Porcupine, the Koyukuk, and the Tanana rivers. Other major rivers are the Kuskokwim, Susitna, Copper, and Colville rivers.

Alaska has many natural lakes. Iliamna Lake, on the Alaska Peninsula, is the largest, covering about 1,000 square miles (2,600 square kilometers). Becharof Lake, south of Iliamna, is the second largest.

Climate

Alaska's climate varies widely from one region to another. The Panhandle and the coastal plain along the Gulf of Alaska have moderate temperatures and heavy precipitation. High mountains protect these areas from cold northerly winds, and ocean currents warm the shores. Winds off the Pacific Ocean lose their moisture as they collide with the mountains, drenching the area with rain. The average annual precipitation in this region is about 94 inches (2,388 millimeters), although some areas receive twice that amount. The average annual temperature is 41°F (5°C). The Copper River, Cook Inlet, and Bristol Bay areas have colder winters and less rainfall.

Summer and winter temperatures in the interior are more extreme. Average annual precipitation there is about 15 inches (380 millimeters). The growing season in the Tanana Valley near Fairbanks averages only about 100 days, but long hours of summer sunlight help to make up for the short season. The waters of the Arctic Ocean keep Arctic

Lichens cover the ground in the tundra regions of Alaska. This type of vegetation is an important food source for reindeer and caribou.

ALASKA
Landforms

0   100   200   300 mi
0 100 200 300 400 km

⊛ State capital
• Largest city
+ Highest point
○ Lowest point
— Landform boundary

15,000 ft (4,500 m)
6,000 ft (1,800 m)
3,000 ft (900 m)
1,500 ft (450 m)
600 ft (180 m)
300 ft (90 m)
Sea Level
Below

Places of Interest

In the vast expanse of Alaska, there are many places of scenic and historic interest, including remote arctic lands, sites of early Russian settlement, prospectors' trails, the seacoast, spectacular glaciers, and wilderness homes of Alaska's fascinating, varied, and abundant wildlife.

Denali National Park and Preserve, located midway between Anchorage and Fairbanks, contains Mount McKinley, the highest mountain in North America. Originally established in 1917 as Mount McKinley National Park, this popular park preserve contains deep lakes, glaciers, and approximately 300 peaks of the Alaska Range, as well as a wide variety of wildlife.

Gates of the Arctic National Park and Preserve lies completely north of the Arctic Circle. Located in the central Brooks Range, the area is a vast wilderness of mountains, valleys, glacial lakes, and rivers. It was designated a national park in 1980.

Glacier Bay National Park and Preserve, 100 miles (160 kilometers) west of Juneau, can be seen by boat or by air. The park contains more than forty great ice masses between two parallel mountain ranges—the St. Elias to the east and the Fairweather to the west. Whales and seals can be found in Glacier Bay.

Katmai National Park and Preserve, on the eastern shore of the Alaska Peninsula, is the site of the violent volcanic eruption in 1912 that turned green lands

Totem Bight State Historical Park, near Ketchikan

into the Valley of Ten Thousand Smokes. Also remarkable for its wildlife, it is the nation's largest grizzly bear sanctuary.

Kenai Fiords National Park, south and west of Seward on the Kenai Peninsula, includes the Harding Icefield, one of the major ice caps in the United States.

Klondike Gold Rush National Historical Park, at Skagway, preserves historic buildings from the gold rush days, as well as the Chilkoot and White Pass trails, once trekked by prospectors.

Malaspina Glacier is located in the St. Elias Range on Yakutat Bay. The largest glacier in North America, it covers an area about the size of Rhode Island.

Saint Michael's Russian Orthodox Cathedral, a landmark building in Sitka, houses a beautiful collection of icons, or religious paintings.

Sitka National Historical Park, at Sitka, preserves the site where the Tlingit Indians made their last stand against the Russian settlers in 1804. The park also includes a wildlife sanctuary, beautiful spruce and hemlock trees, and a collection of Tlingit totem poles.

Totem Bight State Historical Park, north of Ketchikan, contains a unique collection of Haida and Tlingit totem poles from the 1800's.

Wrangell-St. Elias National Park and Preserve, east of Anchorage, is the largest unit of the National Park System. The Chugach, Wrangell, and St. Elias mountain ranges of the Pacific Mountain System converge here, forming North America's largest collection of peaks higher than 16,000 feet (4,877 meters).

State Parks. For information on state parks and other public lands, such as wildlife refuges, contact the Alaska Public Lands Information Center, 605 W. 4th Avenue, Anchorage, Alaska 99501.

Brown bear catching salmon, Katmai National Park and Preserve

Mendenhall Glacier, near Juneau

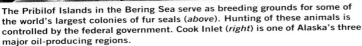
The Pribilof Islands in the Bering Sea serve as breeding grounds for some of the world's largest colonies of fur seals (*above*). Hunting of these animals is controlled by the federal government. Cook Inlet (*right*) is one of Alaska's three major oil-producing regions.

Alaska from being as bitterly cold as the interior. Precipitation in this region averages only about 7 inches (178 millimeters) a year.

Weather in the Aleutian Islands is influenced by the warm Pacific Ocean to the south and the cold Bering Sea to the north. The air is wet and foggy. Average annual temperatures are about the same as those along the Gulf of Alaska, but there is only half as much precipitation. Fierce, gusting winds called williwaws often lash the islands.

Plant and Animal Life

Forests cover about one-third of Alaska. The coastal forests—in the Panhandle and along the Gulf of Alaska —are dense, towering stands of western hemlock, Sitka spruce, and red and yellow cedar. The interior forests contain mostly white spruce, birch, aspen, poplar, and willow. Muskeg bogs, common to much of Alaska, contain spongy masses of plant life—cranberry vines, crowberries, grasses, mosses, and lichens. The dead plants decay slowly because of the low temperatures.

Alaska is home to an astounding variety of wildlife. Black-tailed deer, mountain goats, moose, black bears, and Kodiak brown bears are among the largest animals found in the southeast. Farther north, moose become more plentiful than deer, and grizzly bears and Dall sheep appear. Caribou, a type of reindeer, increase in numbers toward the north, where they travel in herds of thousands. Polar bears live in the far north. Animals that are not native to Alaska but were brought there include reindeer, elk, musk oxen, and bison.

Nearly 400 species of birds make their home in Alaska, including geese, grouse, and ptarmigan and such predatory birds as bald eagles, falcons, hawks, and owls. Wolves and foxes are found throughout most of the state. Animals that are valued for their fur include marten, mink, and beaver. Major game fish include rainbow trout and grayling. The most important commercial fish are salmon, cod, herring, halibut, crab, shrimp, clams, and scallops. Enormous numbers of marine mammals, such as walruses, whales, and seals, thrive in Alaska's bounteous waters.

Natural Resources

Traditionally, Alaska's most prized natural resources were fur, fish, and gold. Today they are petroleum and natural gas. Rich deposits have been found in Prudhoe Bay, the Kenai Peninsula, and Cook Inlet. Gold and silver are known to exist in almost every region of the state. Also, surveys have shown that Alaska holds approximately half of the nation's coal reserves.

Russians (*above*) were the first people to emigrate to Alaska, starting in the late 1700's. Eskimos (*right*) make up the largest segment of Alaska's native population. They include the Inupiat of the northern regions and three Yupik groups—Siberian, Pacific Gulf, and Central Alaskan.

▶PEOPLE

Although Alaska is one of the least populous states in the nation, its population has grown tremendously in recent decades. Three out of every four Alaskans live in five major urban areas. The Anchorage borough is the most densely populated, followed by the Fairbanks, Kenai Peninsula, Matanuska-Susitna, and Juneau boroughs.

Two out of every three Alaskans were born outside of the state and are descended from a variety of nationalities. Many came from other U.S. states to work in Alaska's oil fields or for the government. There are pockets of African, Hispanic, and Asian Americans in urban areas. Approximately 15 percent of the state's population is Native American. The three major groups are the Eskimos, the Aleut, and various Indian communities that include the Haida, Tsimshian, and Tlingit and eleven Athabascan groups. For more information, see ESKIMOS (INUIT) in Volume E and INDIANS, AMERICAN (North American Indians Since 1500: In the Far North and Northwest) in Volume I.

Education

The first schools in Alaska were established by the Russians after the settlement of Kodiak Island in 1784. After the United States purchased Alaska in 1867, educational work among the native peoples was carried on by missionaries. Gradually, as settlers went to Alaska during the 1880's and 1890's, the federal government established public schools. Today each borough or rural district regulates its own public-school system, according to the policies of the State Board of Education. Home schooling and correspondence-course study is common in remote areas.

The state-supported University of Alaska was founded in 1917 in Fairbanks as the Alaska Agricultural College and School of Mines. Today main campuses also are located

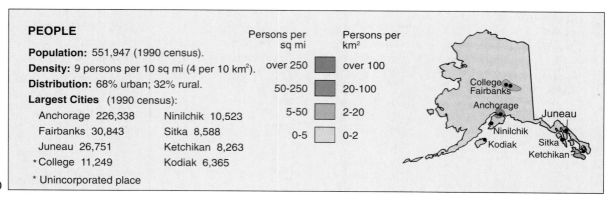

PEOPLE

Population: 551,947 (1990 census).

Density: 9 persons per 10 sq mi (4 per 10 km²).

Distribution: 68% urban; 32% rural.

Largest Cities (1990 census):

Anchorage 226,338	Ninilchik 10,523
Fairbanks 30,843	Sitka 8,588
Juneau 26,751	Ketchikan 8,263
*College 11,249	Kodiak 6,365

* Unincorporated place

Persons per sq mi		Persons per km²
over 250		over 100
50-250		20-100
5-50		2-20
0-5		0-2

in Anchorage and Juneau, with branch campuses in several communities. The state university system offers strong programs in arctic and petroleum engineering, marine sciences, geophysics, and international business and trade. There are three private colleges in the state: Alaska Pacific University, in Anchorage; Alaska Bible College, in Glennallen; and Sheldon Jackson College, the oldest college in the state, in Sitka.

Libraries, Museums, and the Arts

Anchorage's public library system circulates more than a million books a year. Statewide, there are about ninety public libraries and branches. The Alaska State Library in Juneau houses the state's largest collection of state-related books and documents.

The Alaska State Museum in Juneau is the state's leading natural history museum. Displays cover ancient and modern native culture, pioneer and mining history, and Alaskan wildlife. The Anchorage Museum of History and Art highlights centuries of Alaskan art and history. The University of Alaska Museum in Fairbanks features Alaskan history and natural sciences. The Sheldon Jackson Museum in Sitka houses an array of native artifacts. Other museums include the Living Museum of the Arctic, in Kotzebue; and the Trail of '98 Museum, in Skagway.

▶ ECONOMY

Petroleum is Alaska's single most important product. Royalties and taxes on oil alone provide nearly 85 percent of the state's revenues. Fish is Alaska's most valuable export.

Services

Service industries account for more than half of Alaska's annual gross state product (GSP)—the total value of goods and services produced in a year. Government is the largest segment, employing approximately 30 percent of the workforce, including national park workers. Other services, in descending order of importance, are transportation, communication, and utilities; finance, insurance, and real estate services; business, social, and personal services, which include tourism; and wholesale and retail trade.

Manufacturing

Alaska has relatively few manufacturing industries. Its most important manufactured goods are processed seafood products, such as canned salmon and smoked, salted, or frozen fish and shellfish. Wood is processed to produce round logs, lumber, wood pulp, wood chips, and paper.

Agriculture

Due to its harsh climate and rugged terrain, Alaska ranks last among the fifty states in the value of its farm production. Most of Alaska's farming is done in the Matanuska-Susitna Valley north of Anchorage and in the Tanana Valley near Fairbanks. Major farm products are milk, hay, potatoes, lettuce, greenhouse plants, and cattle.

Alaska leads the nation in the value of its seafood catch (*left*). Seaplanes (*below*) bring essential goods to people who live in Alaska's remote regions.

Alaska's fisheries, on the other hand, are extremely productive. They account for half the catch of the entire United States. Groundfish are the most valuable. These include pollack, cod, flatfish, rockfish, and sablefish. Salmon, once Alaska's leading commercial fish, now rivals shellfish for second place. Crab—tanner, king, and Dungeness—are the major shellfish catches. Alaska also supplies much of the world's halibut.

Mining and Construction

Mining contributes more to Alaska's GSP than any other single enterprise. One-fourth of all the petroleum produced in the United States comes from Alaska, making it the leading oil-producing state. More than 1.8 million barrels of crude oil are extracted from Alaska's oil fields every day. About 90 percent of all the state's oil comes from Prudhoe Bay and Ku-

The Trans-Alaska Pipeline carries oil from Prudhoe Bay on the North Slope to the port of Valdez on Prince William Sound, a distance of 800 miles (1,287 kilometers).

paruk on the North Slope. They are the two largest known oil fields in North America. The state also produces about 860 million cubic feet (24.4 million cubic meters) of natural gas a day.

After petroleum, zinc is Alaska's most valuable mineral product. The Red Dog Mine near Kotzebue is the largest zinc mine in the Northern Hemisphere. Valdez Creek Placer Gold Mine is the largest gold producer in the United States, and Greens Creek Mine, near Juneau, is North America's largest silver producer.

All three phases of mining—exploration, development, and production—require construction work, including the building of housing for workers. As new mineral reserves are continually being found, construction continues to be an important support industry in the state.

Transportation

Most people do not realize that Alaska is as close to major European cities as it is to major Asian cities. Air and sea traffic take the polar route across the Arctic region between Europe and Alaska every day. Anchorage and Fairbanks have international airports that provide passenger and cargo service. Modern airports also are located in Juneau, Ketchikan, Kodiak, Sitka, Wrangell, Petersburg, and Nome. Bush planes, flown by bush pilots, handle most of the travel into the rugged interior.

Alaska has one road connection to Canada and the Lower 48, the Alaska Highway. The Alaska Railroad is the principal rail line. Both extend north as far as Fairbanks. Perhaps Alaska's best-known transportation system is the Trans-Alaska Pipeline. This 800-mile (1,287-kilometer) channel transports oil from Alaska's North Slope fields to the port of Valdez for shipping. The port of Valdez is the fourth busiest port in the country. Most of its traffic is domestic, and most of its cargo is oil.

PRODUCTS AND INDUSTRIES

Manufacturing: Processed foods, wood and paper products, electrical and nonelectrical machinery, sand and gravel materials, computer equipment, handcrafted goods.

Agriculture: Seafood, milk, hay, livestock feed, potatoes.

Minerals: Petroleum, natural gas, zinc.

Services: Wholesale and retail trade; finance, insurance, and real estate; business, social, and personal services; transportation, communication, and utilities; government.

*Gross state product is the total value of goods and services produced in a year.

Percentage of Gross State Product* by Industry

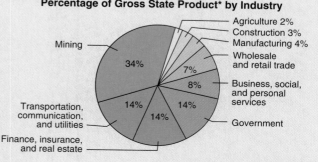

- Mining 34%
- Agriculture 2%
- Construction 3%
- Manufacturing 4%
- Wholesale and retail trade 7%
- Business, social, and personal services 8%
- Government 14%
- Finance, insurance, and real estate 14%
- Transportation, communication, and utilities 14%

Source: U.S. Bureau of Economic Analysis

Communication

Among Alaska's major newspapers are the *Anchorage Daily News*, the *Anchorage Times*, and the Fairbanks *Daily News Miner*. The *Tundra Times*, Alaska's oldest statewide newspaper, reports news of interest to Alaska's Native American population. More than sixty radio stations broadcast in the state, and more than a dozen television stations have satellite transmission.

▶ CITIES

Most of Alaska's large population centers, except for Fairbanks, are in the state's southern coastal region. Small towns and villages dot the interior and the western coast.

Juneau, located in the Panhandle, is Alaska's capital and third largest city. Founded by gold miners in 1880, it was named for Joe Juneau, one of the first prospectors to discover gold in the area.

Juneau, often called the longest city in the world, occupies a long and narrow stretch of land that slopes from the foot of Mount Juneau down to a bustling waterfront on Gastineau Channel. Douglas Island, in the channel, also is part of the city. The mountains cut the city off from the mainland, so visitors must come in by boat or airplane. Attractions include the Alaska State Museum, St. Nicholas Russian Orthodox Church, and a fascinating historic district.

Anchorage, Alaska's most populous city, is home to more than 40 percent of the state's residents. The metropolitan area, known as the Anchorage Bowl, lies between Cook Inlet to the east and the Chugach Mountains to the west. The city was founded in 1915 when the Alaska Railroad was under construction. Today it is the state's commercial and financial center. Revenues from the booming oil

More than 40 percent of Alaska's population lives in the sprawling city of Anchorage (*top*). Juneau (*above*), the state capital, has charming hillside neighborhoods with clusters of brightly painted houses.

industry have financed the construction of the Performing Arts Center, Sullivan Sports Arena, and dozens of office towers and luxury hotels. Earthquake Park, commemorating the 1964 earthquake, offers a scenic view of the city and its surroundings.

Fairbanks, Alaska's second largest city, is the only major population center in the interior. Fairbanks is the northern endpoint of the Alaska Railroad and the state's major highways. Thus it is a transportation hub for travel to the northern and western regions of the state. Fairbanks' international airport also provides travel to and from Asia, Europe, Arctic Alaska, and the Lower 48 states.

The city was founded in 1902 when gold was discovered there. Today it is a main trading center for the Yukon Valley. Its attractions include the main campus of the University of Alaska and a pioneer theme park called Alaskaland. It also serves as the gateway to Denali National Park and Preserve.

Four pillars of Alaskan marble and a statue of a Kodiak brown bear distinguish the entrance to the state capitol building in Juneau.

GOVERNMENT

Alaska remained a territory for 75 years before it became a state. This was the longest territorial period in the nation's history. Anxious for statehood, Alaskans adopted a constitution in 1956, three years before they joined the Union.

Like the United States government, Alaska's state government consists of three branches: executive, legislative, and judicial. The governor is the state's chief executive. Other executive branch officers include the lieutenant governor and the attorney general.

The state's legislative branch consists of a senate and a house of representatives. The legislature convenes in January of odd-numbered years. The normal 120-day lawmaking session can be extended ten days upon a two-thirds vote of the legislators.

The Alaska Supreme Court heads the judicial branch of government. There are also courts of appeals, superior courts, district courts, and local magistrates.

While most other states are divided into counties, Alaska is divided into 13 boroughs organized around population centers. Those

GOVERNMENT

State Government
Governor: 4-year term
State senators: 20; 4-year terms
State representatives: 40; 2-year terms
Number of organized boroughs: 13

Federal Government
U.S. Senators: 2
U.S. Representatives: 1
Number of electoral votes: 3

For the name of the current governor, see STATE GOVERNMENTS in Volume S. For the names of current U.S. senators and representatives, see UNITED STATES, CONGRESS OF THE in Volume U-V.

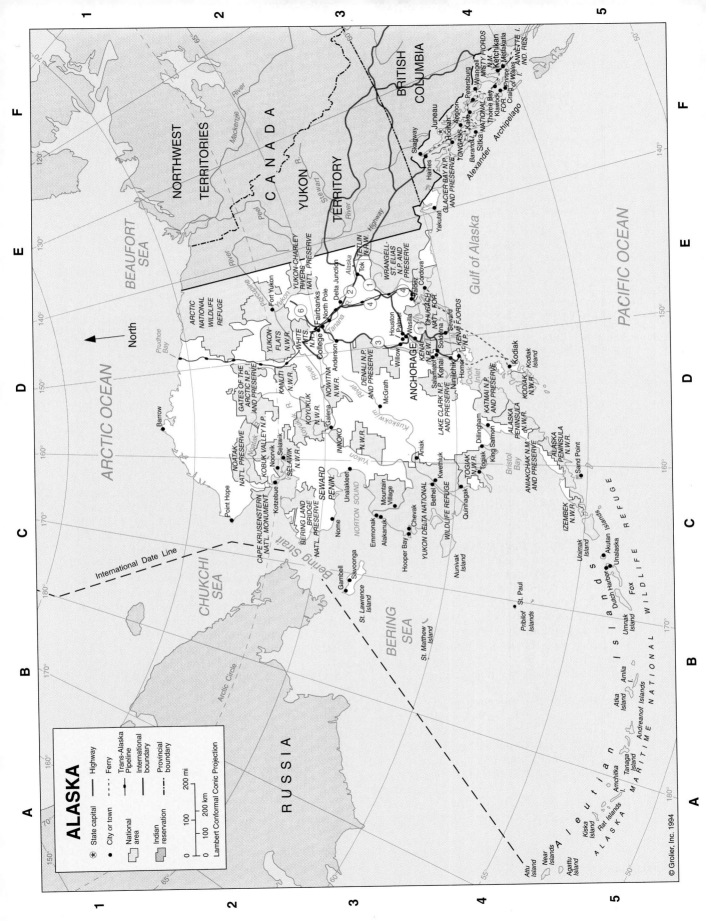

Famous People

Aleksandr Baranov

Vitus Bering

Joseph Juneau

Aleksandr Andreevich Baranov (1746–1819) became the first manager of the Russian-American Company, established in 1799, and served as the first governor (1799–1818) of Russian America. A successful fur trader, he extended Russian settlements in Alaska and sold furs to the United States, Canada, and China. Baranov's settlement at New Archangel (now Sitka) replaced Kodiak as the fur-trading capital. Baranof Island is named for him.

Vitus Bering (1680–1741), a Danish explorer employed by the Russian Navy, was the first European to set foot in Alaska. He also discovered the strait and the sea that now bear his name. A biography of Bering is included in Volume B.

Susan Howlet Butcher (1954–), a world-class sled dog racer, was born in Boston, Massachusetts, and lives in Manley Hot Springs. In 1979 she became the first person to drive a sled dog team to the top of Mount McKinley. In the annual 1,000-mile (1,600-kilometer) Anchorage-to-Nome Iditarod Trail Sled Dog Race, she took first place in 1986, 1987, 1988, and 1990, setting new course records in 1986, 1987, and 1990.

Sheldon Jackson (1834–1909), born in Minaville, New York, was a leading Presbyterian missionary. He went to Alaska in 1884 to minister to the Eskimos and became known as the Bishop of All Beyond. He helped save the Eskimos from starvation by urging the U.S. government to import reindeer from Siberia for domestication. In 1885 he was appointed Alaska's first superintendent of public instruction. Jackson founded many free schools and traveled widely, collecting native artifacts on his way. He was a sponsor of Sitka Industrial School, which was later renamed Sheldon Jackson College.

Joseph Juneau (1836?–99), a French Canadian gold miner born near the city of Quebec, was prospecting with Richard Harris and three Tlingit Indians in 1880 when he discovered gold near present-day Juneau, touching off the Alaska gold rush. The town that sprang up on the site was named Juneau after him.

---

parts of the state that do not belong to a particular borough are governed by the state legislature. Only one Alaskan community is organized under federal law. This is the former Tsimshian Indian reservation of Metlakatla on Annette Island. Otherwise, Alaska's Indian affairs are conducted according to the Alaska Native Claims Settlement Act.

▶ **HISTORY**

It is believed that Alaska's first settlers came to the area possibly as long as 40,000 years ago. These nomadic hunters and gatherers migrated from what is now Siberia, pursuing wild game across the Bering land bridge that once existed between Asia and North America. Three distinct groups of people developed among these early settlers: the Eskimos (Inuit), the Aleut, and various Athabascan and other Indian groups.

Russian Exploration and Settlement

The first Europeans arrived in 1741, when Vitus Bering, a Dane serving in the Russian Navy, landed on Alaska's southern coast. Bering's crew had found not only a new land, but also a new article of trade—the luxurious fur of the sea otter. Soon, Russian hunters and traders were rushing to colonize Alaska. The newcomers took many native Aleuts as slaves, while some settled down and married native women. In 1784, Russian traders established their first permanent settlement at Three Saints Bay on Kodiak Island. This new colony became known as Russian America.

By 1799 the Russian-American Company had been chartered, with Aleksandr Baranov as its manager. Baranov expanded trade eastward into the Alexander Archipelago and built a fort near the present-day city of Sitka on Baranof Island. The native Tlingit Indians, who could not tolerate this invasion of their centuries-old homeland, attacked the fort in 1802 and won back their ground. But Baranov returned in 1804 with fully armed Russian troops and forced the Tlingit to retreat for good. Baranov rebuilt the settlement, New Archangel, which became the capital of Russian America. Later renamed Sitka, it remained the capital of Alaska until 1900.

Near right: When U.S. Secretary of State William H. Seward bought Alaska from Russia in 1867, many people thought the purchase was extravagant and called it Seward's Folly. This cartoon shows Seward (left) and President Andrew Johnson (right) preparing to "cool down" angry congressmen with a chunk of Alaskan ice. *Far right:* In 1897, one year after gold was discovered in the Klondike region of Canada's Yukon Territory, prospectors built the town of Skagway near Chilcoot Pass, which was then the shortest route—over the mountains—to the Yukon.

Susan Butcher

William Louis Paul, Sr. (1885–1977), a politician and lawyer born in Port Simpson, British Columbia, was the first native ever to serve (1925–29) in the Alaska territorial legislature. He fought the Literacy Act in 1925 to protect the natives' voting rights. His advocacy of Tlingit and Haida rights in 1968 paved the way for the Alaska Native Claims Settlement Act of 1971.

William Henry Seward (1801–72), a statesman and outspoken opponent of slavery, was born in Florida, New York. Having served as a New York state senator (1831–34) , as governor of New York (1839–42), and as a U.S. senator (1849–61), he was appointed U.S. secretary of state by President Abraham Lincoln in 1861. During the Civil War (1861–65), he succeeded in preventing European nations from recognizing the Confederate States of America as a legitimate nation. In 1865, Seward was injured in the same assassination plot that killed Lincoln. After his recovery he continued in his post until 1869, under President Andrew Johnson. It was during this time that Seward, a territorial expansionist, purchased Alaska for the United States (1867).

Grigori Shelekhov (1747–95), a Russian fur trader, founded the first Russian colony in Alaska at Three Saints Bay on Kodiak Island in 1784. After his death, his business, the Shelekhov-Golikov Company, formed the basis of the Russian-American Company.

The Alaska Purchase

By the mid-1800's, Russia's interest in Alaska had declined. The colony was expensive to maintain, and the fur trade had ceased to be profitable. In 1867, U.S. Secretary of State William H. Seward arranged to purchase Alaska from Russia for $7.2 million. Many Americans believed it was a foolish idea. Newspaper articles and cartoons ridiculed Alaska, calling it Seward's Folly, Seward's Icebox, Icebergia, and Walrussia. But Seward believed Alaska was a land of great potential.

The Gold Rush

Seward's Folly soon turned to fortune. In 1880, near present-day Juneau, Tlingit guides led prospectors to rich deposits of gold. Year after year, new gold strikes brought additional waves of gold rushers. In 1896, fabulous deposits were found in the Klondike region of Canada's Yukon Territory, and tens of thousands of fortune hunters swarmed through Alaska's Panhandle to get there. After gold was discovered in Nome in 1899, a tent city sprang up overnight. Within a couple of years,

PREPARING FOR THE HEATED TERM.
King Andy and his man Billy lay in a great stock of Russian ice in order to cool down the Congressional majority.

almost 18,000 prospectors had arrived. To help keep order among the gold hunters, Alaska adopted a system of courts and laws in 1900. In 1912, Congress officially declared Alaska a U.S. territory.

The Long Road to Statehood

Alaskans first appealed to Congress for statehood in 1916, but the bill failed to pass. In 1941, when America declared war on Japan and entered World War II, Alaska's strategic importance became clear. More than 150,000 American troops and civilian workers were rushed to Alaska. In only eight months, a 1,523-mile (2,451-kilometer) road was built through Canada to Fairbanks as a military supply route. Now called the Alaska Highway, it is still the only road connecting Alaska with the Lower 48 states.

In 1942, Japan bombed the American naval base at Dutch Harbor in the Aleutian Islands and invaded the islands of Attu and Kiska. Fierce American resistance, with heavy casualties on both sides, managed to free the islands again. This was the only North American territory to be invaded during the entire course of the war.

After the war ended in 1945, the United States entered into the Cold War era with the Soviet Union, reinforcing Alaska's strategic importance. In 1958, Congress approved the Alaska Statehood Act, and on January 3, 1959, President Dwight D. Eisenhower proclaimed Alaska the 49th state.

Hardship and Prosperity

On March 27, 1964, a devastating earthquake, registering about 8.5 on the Richter scale, ravaged Anchorage and much of the Gulf coast and killed 131 people. This was the strongest earthquake ever recorded in North America. Another disaster struck in 1967, when flood waters rushed through Fairbanks, killing five people. Despite these two disasters, which caused damages amounting to nearly $500 million, Alaska prospered. In 1968 the state's economy boomed when massive oil and natural gas reserves were discovered at Prudhoe Bay. Due to profits from oil, the gross state product doubled between 1973 and 1975. Construction of the Trans-Alaska Pipeline began in 1974 to transport the oil to the port of Valdez, and Alaska's population and labor force soared. After the pipeline was completed in 1977 and the oil began to flow, lavish revenues began flowing into the state treasury, allowing Alaskans to abolish the state income tax.

Alaska Native Claims Settlement Act

In 1971, President Richard Nixon signed the Alaska Native Claims Settlement Act, awarding Alaska's Native Americans approximately 44 million acres (18 million hectares) of land and more than $962 million in compensation for past infringements on their land and resources. Eventually 13 regional corporations were organized to manage the money and the economic development of the natives' lands, such as mineral exploration and development. However, some communities resisted economic interests, choosing instead to preserve their territory.

Environmental Concerns

The dark side of the oil boom was its effect on the environment. For example, deep-water blasting destroyed fishing grounds. Exploration on the North Slope endangered the populations of caribou, polar bears, whales, and other animals vital to the Inupiat Eskimos' survival. And leaks in the Trans-Alaska Pipeline threatened wildlife in the lands through which it passed.

In 1978, 56 million acres (23 million hectares) of Alaskan land were designated to be set aside as national parks, monuments, and wildlife refuges. While this protected Alaska's natural areas, it also closed off a vast amount of territory to mineral exploration. The state of Alaska sued to retain access to these lands, but lost. Two years later the Alaska National Interest Lands Conservation Act passed into law.

In 1989 came the worst environmental disaster in Alaska's history. The oil tanker *Exxon Valdez* ran aground in Prince William Sound, spilling millions of gallons of crude oil. Hundreds of miles of shoreline—as well as thousands of birds, fish, and other animals —were coated with thick, black oil. Federal, state, and local governments, oil companies, and environmentalists mobilized to clean up the environment and sort out the damages. The disaster only heightened the debate between land developers and environmentalists.

ANN HEINRICHS
Author, *Alaska*

ALBANIA

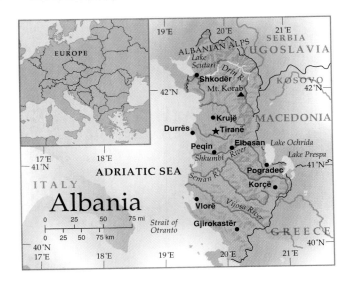

Albanians call themselves Shqiptarë, which means "sons of the eagle." It is an appropriate name because many Albanians live in the high mountains just as eagles do. A fiercely independent people, the Albanians long suffered under foreign domination. For nearly 500 years Albania was a part of the Turkish Ottoman Empire, before winning its independence in 1912. In the early 1990's, Albanians freed themselves from a Communist system of government that had long ruled the country.

▶ THE PEOPLE

Most of the people are Albanians. Greeks are the country's largest ethnic minority. The Albanians were formerly divided into two major groups—the Gegs, in the north, and the Tosks, in the south. The Shkumbi River was the dividing line between the two. The differences in speech and customs between the two groups were largely eliminated during the period of Communist rule. The population is concentrated mainly in and around the major cities of Tiranë (also spelled Tirana), Durrës, Vlorë, Elbasan, and Shkodër. Tiranë is the capital and largest city.

Many people of Albanian ancestry live outside their homeland. Most live in what was Yugoslavia. But there are also large Albanian communities in Greece, Italy, Western Europe, and the United States.

Way of life. In spite of many centuries of foreign occupation, the traditional Albanian way of life was preserved in the high mountain region. In the more isolated areas, the clan

Albania is a small, rugged country. Many of its people, like these schoolgirls, traditionally have lived in the high mountains that make up most of the land.

Albanian Muslims pray at a mosque near Tiranë, the capital. Albania is the only European country in which Muslims make up the majority of the population—a reminder of the centuries-long rule of the region by the Ottoman Turks. Other Albanians belong to the Eastern Orthodox and Roman Catholic churches.

system, based on family relationship, survived until the 1900's. After the Communists took over Albania, they broke up the clan system and seized the land owned by the landlords. The land was divided into small farms, which were then combined into collectives, run by a group of farmers in common, or large state farms, run by the government. This system is now being changed with the restoration of private ownership of farmland.

Striking contrasts between old and new are seen in all of Albania's cities. The huge new apartment houses, modern in appearance, are very different from the narrow, cobblestone streets and oriental-looking bazaars in older parts of the cities.

FACTS and figures

REPUBLIC OF ALBANIA is the official name of the country.

LOCATION: Southeastern Europe.

AREA: 11,100 sq mi (28,748 km²).

POPULATION: 3,400,000 (estimate).

CAPITAL AND LARGEST CITY: Tiranë.

MAJOR LANGUAGE: Albanian.

MAJOR RELIGIOUS GROUPS: Muslim, Eastern Orthodox, Roman Catholic.

GOVERNMENT: Republic. **Head of state**—president. **Head of government**—prime minister. **Legislature**—Parliament.

CHIEF PRODUCTS: Agricultural—wheat, corn, potatoes, cotton, tobacco, rice, sugar beets, fruits, nuts, livestock. **Manufactured**—refined petroleum products, processed foods, textiles, machinery, building materials, fertilizers. **Mineral**—chromite (chromium ore), petroleum, coal, copper, nickel, asphalt.

MONETARY UNIT: Lek (1 lek = 100 quindars).

Language and Religion. Albanian is one of the Indo-European group of languages, but it is unlike any other language spoken in Europe. The Albanian language is used throughout the country. Some Greek is also spoken in the southern part of Albania.

Although the government forbade religious observance, about 70 percent of the people are said to be Muslims; about 20 percent members of the Eastern Orthodox Church; and some 10 percent Roman Catholics. Albania is the only predominantly Muslim nation in Europe.

▶THE LAND

Albania lies on the west coast of the Balkan Peninsula, in southeastern Europe. Small in area, it extends about 200 miles (320 kilometers) from north to south and about 60 miles (100 kilometers) from east to west. On the west are the Adriatic Sea and the Strait of Otranto. Across the Strait of Otranto is the heel of Italy's boot. Yugoslavia borders Albania on the north and east. Greece is on the south. Albania has three natural regions: the coastal lowland in the west, a central hilly belt, and the mountains in the east, north, and south.

The Coastal Lowland. Along the coast is a narrow, formerly marshy lowland. Fast-running streams flow from the mountains to this plain and often flood the land. Until recently mosquitoes thrived in the stagnant water, and few people lived here because of the dangers of malaria. The marshes have since been drained and the land reclaimed.

The Hilly Belt. A narrow strip of hilly land stretches across central Albania, where the mountains and the coastal lowlands meet. At this point the mountains are quite low, and their lower slopes are terraced and planted with tree crops. Here, too, the narrow mountain valleys widen into broad basins. The soils of these basins are fertile and are carefully cultivated. Tiranë, Shkodër, Elbasan, and Berat are important cities in this region.

The Mountains. Nearly three fourths of Albania is mountainous. The highest mountain is Mount Korab, which rises to 9,066 feet (2,763 meters) in northeastern Albania. In the north the mountains are deeply fissured. In the southern parts of the country, they are more rounded and often open up into broad, fertile basins.

Lakes, Rivers, Natural Resources. Albania has three large lakes. They are Scutari, in the north, and Ochrida and Prespa, in the southeast. The country's rivers are short and swift and are not navigable, or usable by ships, except for short stretches. These rivers are, however, an important source of hydroelectric power, which supplies much of Albania's electricity.

About one quarter of the land is wooded. Oak or scrub forests are found in the south, while pine, poplar, and chestnut trees grow along the rivers and at various elevations.

Albania has a number of valuable mineral resources. It is one of the world's leading producers of chromite (chromium ore). Other mineral deposits include petroleum, coal, copper, nickel, and asphalt.

Climate. The coastal lowland and the hilly belt have a Mediterranean climate, typically marked by mild winters and hot, sunny summers. A cold wind called the bora sometimes blows from the mountains to the lowlands. The mountains have a continental climate. Summers here are cool and winters cold and snowy. Although there is considerable rainfall, it is sometimes erratic.

▶THE ECONOMY

Historically, Albania has been one of Europe's least-developed countries. At one time most of its people were farmers, even though the largely mountainous terrain severely limits the amount of land suitable for agriculture. Under Communist rule, Albania had a centrally planned economy controlled by the state, which stressed industrial development.

Agriculture. About half the working population is still engaged in agriculture. The chief food crops include wheat, corn, and potatoes.

The major commercial crops are cotton, tobacco, rice, sugar beets, and fruits and nuts. Sheep traditionally were the most important form of livestock. But chickens, goats, pigs, and cattle are also raised.

Industry and Trade. Manufacturing and mining currently employ about one third of the work force. The chief industrial products are minerals, refined petroleum products, processed foods, textiles, machinery, building materials, and fertilizers.

Albania's chief exports include chromite and other mineral ores, processed foods, and tobacco products. It imports chemicals, metals, and paper and rubber products. A lack of rainfall in the early 1990's forced the importation of grains and other foodstuffs.

Transportation and Communications. The country's most important railroad connects the port of Durrës with Tiranë and Elbasan. Airline service links Tiranë with capitals of neighboring countries. There are some asphalt roads, but many parts of the country have only dirt or gravel roads. In the rugged interior, people may still travel by horseback or in the traditional ox carts.

Radio, television, and other forms of communication were owned by the state.

▶HISTORY AND GOVERNMENT

Early History. The earliest known people of what is now Albania were the Illyrians. The Romans conquered the region in 167 B.C., but they were never able to subdue the mountain-

A nearly deserted factory reflects the economic failures that played an important part in the overthrow of Albania's Communist government.

Below: George Kastrioti, known as Skanderbeg, is Albania's national hero. He briefly united the country against the Ottoman Turks in the 1400's, before it again fell to the Turks after his death. *Right:* Modern Albanians in 1992 celebrated their victory over the Communist regime that had ruled the nation for more than 45 years and had made it the most isolated country in Europe.

ous areas completely. In the centuries that followed, the region fell to numerous rulers. The Ottoman Turks first invaded Albania in 1385. Opposition to the Turks was led by the national hero George Kastrioti, called Skanderbeg, who in 1443 united Albanians against them. After his death in 1468, however, Albania again fell under Turkish rule.

Independence to World War II. Albania declared its independence from a declining Ottoman Empire on November 28, 1912. The years between World War I and World War II were stormy ones for Albania. Ahmet Zogu was named president in 1925. Three years later he gave himself the title of King Zog I. Zog fled when Italy invaded Albania in 1939, just months before the outbreak of World War II. In 1943, a German army occupied Albania.

When the Germans evacuated Albania in 1944, the Communists took control of the country. Albania officially became a "people's republic" under a new constitution in 1946.

Communist Rule. Although Albania had an elected legislature, the People's Assembly,

only the Albanian Labor Party, a Communist party, had been allowed to take part in elections. Real political power had always been in the hands of the party's top leadership.

Albania was led by Enver Hoxha from 1944 until his death in 1985. During these years, Albania followed its own rigid, solitary Communist road. It broke relations with the Soviet Union in 1961 after political disagreements. For a time it had friendly relations with the People's Republic of China, but these also cooled. After Hoxha's death, Ramiz Alia assumed power.

Alia agreed to modest political reforms. Several thousand Albanians were allowed to emigrate in 1990, and in 1991 the first elections were held in which non-Communist political parties were allowed to compete. The result, a victory for the Communists, led to widespread protests, forcing the new Communist government to resign.

It was replaced by a coalition, or alliance, of Socialists (as the former Communists were now called) and representatives of the major opposition parties. In late 1991, President Alia appointed a government made up mainly of Socialists to serve until new elections could be held.

The elections, held in 1992, resulted in an overwhelming victory for the opposition Democratic Party, which won most of the seats in the Parliament, or legislature. Alia resigned and Parliament elected Sali Berisha as the country's new president.

GEORGE W. HOFFMAN
University of Texas at Austin
Revised and updated by NICHOLAS C. PANO
Western Illinois University
Author, *The People's Republic of Albania*

ALBANY. See NEW YORK (Cities).

ALBERT

Albert was the name of one prince consort of Great Britain and two kings of Belgium.

Albert, Prince Consort of Great Britain (1819–61) was the husband of Victoria, queen of England, Scotland, and Ireland. Born Albert Francis Charles Augustus Emmanuel near Coburg, Germany, on August 26, 1819, he was the youngest son of Duke Ernest I of Saxe-Coburg-Gotha.

Albert married Queen Victoria, his first cousin, in London in 1840. He soon became her most trusted adviser. Victoria's ministers feared that Albert, a foreigner, would interfere in British politics, but he used his influence tactfully and wisely and in time became known as Albert the Good.

Prince Albert was known to be strict but kindhearted. He encouraged music and the arts and was extremely interested in science and education. He was instrumental in organizing the Great Exhibition of 1851 and in the founding of Imperial College, London. His other achievements ranged from the abolition of dueling to the introduction of the Christmas tree to England.

Prince Albert and Queen Victoria enjoyed an unusually happy marriage. Unfortunately, he died at 42 from typhoid fever at Windsor Castle on December 14, 1861. Victoria, who had idolized her husband, was so distraught by his early death that she withdrew completely from public life for the next 15 years.

The popular King Albert I led the Belgian resistance against the Germans during World War I. He was one of the few European monarchs not to be overthrown in the political upheavals that followed the war.

Albert, Prince Consort of Great Britain, was husband and first cousin to Queen Victoria. A German prince by birth, Albert worked hard to prove his devotion to his adopted homeland. Although he was considered shy and cold, Albert was actually kindhearted, and it was largely due to his influence that slavery was abolished in the British colonies. Albert's high moral standards also shaped the rigid social conditions now associated with the Victorian era.

Albert I, King of the Belgians (1875–1934) (r. 1909–34), born in Brussels, was the son of Philip, Count of Flanders, and the nephew of King Leopold II. The shy Albert was considered unsuited to his role as king when he succeeded his uncle in 1909. But his tolerant and progressive views, and the popularity of his German-born wife, Queen Elisabeth, won him the affection of his people.

In 1914, at the outbreak of World War I, Germany, disregarding Belgium's neutrality, invaded the country. Albert won the world's admiration for his courage in resisting the invasion. By ordering open the floodgates along the Yser River, flooding the Yser Valley, he prevented the Germans from achieving their critical goal of advancing to the English Channel coast. For the remaining four years of the war, Albert and his army resolutely held on to a few square miles of Belgian territory, becoming a symbol of Belgian resistance.

After the war, Albert continued to support social reform and to work toward improving relations between the opposing Flemish- and French-speaking sections of his population. An enthusiastic mountaineer, he was killed in a climbing accident in the Ardennes on February 17, 1934. He was succeeded by his eldest son, King Leopold III.

Albert II, King of the Belgians (1934–   ), born in Brussels, was the second son of Leopold III. He came to the throne in 1993, succeeding his brother, Baudouin I.

LANCE SALWAY
Author, *Queen Victoria's Grandchildren*

ALBERTA

Alberta's flag (above) and coat of arms (opposite page) both feature a view of the province's wheatfields, plains, foothills, and mountains. The cross of St. George, patron saint of England, recalls Alberta's ties with Great Britain. The provincial bird is the great horned owl (right); the provincial flower is the wild rose (opposite page).

Alberta is one of Canada's three Prairie Provinces. It stretches from British Columbia and the towering, snow-clad Rocky Mountains in the west to the province of Saskatchewan in the east; and from the thinly settled Northwest Territories in the north to the state of Montana in the south. Within the boundaries of Alberta, fields of grain extend father than the eye can see, and cattle ranches dot the foothills of the Rockies.

▶ THE LAND

Alberta has a varied landscape that falls into three landform regions: the Canadian Shield, the Interior Plains, and the Mountains and Foothills.

The Canadian Shield. The northeast corner of Alberta lies in the Canadian Shield. This region occupies 3 percent of the land area of the province. Elevations in the Shield range from 650 to 1,300 feet (200 to 400 meters). Bare rock outcrops are found throughout the area. Only in a few places do patches of soil cover the rocks. The soils are thin and rocky and of little use for agriculture. Many marshes and lakes have formed in depressions created during the Great Ice Age.

The Interior Plains. The Interior Plains occupy almost 90 percent of the land. The plains lie between the Shield in the northeast and the Mountains and Foothills in the southwest. Elevations range from about 650 to 4,000 feet (200 to 1,200 meters).

Contrary to popular opinion about the flatness of the plains, they have a highly varied local relief. The land is flat only in places once covered by ancient glacial lakes. Elsewhere, the plains region is typically rolling. Deep river valleys and a number of hilly areas, especially in northern Alberta, contrast sharply with the surrounding plains. Some of the valleys are now dry (coulees), but at one time they carried away the meltwaters from the retreating ice sheets. The hills are flat-topped remnants of land that was eroded (worn away) by the rivers. The Cypress Hills in the southeast, the Swan Hills south of Lesser Slave Lake, and the Caribou Mountains in the north all rise at least 1,200 feet (370 meters) above the countryside. In a few areas the streams have cut deeply into softer rocks. Small sections of deeply eroded land called badlands have resulted, especially in the lower Red Deer Valley, where dinosaur fossils are often exposed by erosion.

The Mountains and Foothills. This region is located along the southwestern margin of the province. The mountains form the boundary between Alberta and British Columbia. They are also a continental drainage divide between waters flowing into the Pacific Ocean on the one hand, and the Arctic Ocean, Hudson Bay, and the Gulf of Mexico on the other.

Between the plains and the eastern wall of the Rockies lie the rolling foothills, which range in elevation from less than 4,000 to more than 6,000 feet (1,200 to 1,800 meters). West of the foothills tower the ranges of the Rocky Mountains. Here the landscape is composed of jagged, snow-clad peaks and broad, U-shaped valleys. Many small lakes and swift streams are found high in the rocky basins of

the mountains. Thirty of these peaks are at least 11,000 feet (3,300 meters) high. Many of them have glaciers similar to those that once covered the neighboring plains. The mountains offer the tourist some of the most spectacular scenery in the world.

Rivers and Lakes

All the important rivers of the province begin in the snow and ice fields of the Rocky Mountains. Many of the important rivers in central and southern Alberta flow eastward to Lake Winnipeg and then northward to form part of the Hudson Bay drainage system. The Milk River flows about 100 miles (160 kilometers) in Alberta near the southern border. It is a tributary of the Missouri and is part of the Gulf of Mexico drainage. The large rivers of northern Alberta flow northward and form part of the Arctic Ocean drainage.

There are thousands of lakes in Alberta. The largest is Lake Athabasca, although only one third lies in Alberta. The remaining two thirds is in Saskatchewan. Because of its beauty and the large number of tourists who visit it, Lake Louise in Banff National Park is perhaps the best-known lake in Alberta.

Climate

Alberta has a continental climate with long, cold winters and short, warm summers. In winter, the cold is sometimes broken by warm dry winds from the mountains. The Indians call these winds ''chinooks,'' or ''snow-eaters.'' The chinook can cause temperatures to rise sharply in less than an hour.

Except in the Rocky Mountains, annual precipitation ranges from about 16 inches (400 millimeters) in the plains to about 24 inches (600 millimeters) in hill areas. Westerly winds from the Pacific Ocean lose most of their moisture crossing the mountains. The Rockies thus have a higher annual precipitation—from 16 inches (400 millimeters) in the drier valleys to more than 55 inches (1,400 millimeters) in the higher areas. Precipitation there falls mostly as winter snow.

In the plains, most of the precipitation falls as rain in the summer, when it is needed for crops. Autumn is fairly dry, which is good for harvesting grain. The growing (frost-free) season varies from more than 120 days in the southern plains to less than 60 days in the far north and mountain valleys.

Natural Resources

Soils. Alberta's rich soil is one of its major resources. The black soils of the parkland are among the most fertile in the world. The brown soils of the prairies are also fertile, but they are located in the drier parts of the province. Ranching, dryland agriculture, and irrigation agriculture are important in this soil zone. The gray forest soils, which occupy the northern half of the province, have developed under the cover of trees and thus are less suited for agriculture.

Vegetation. The foothills, the eastern slopes of the Rocky Mountains, and large portions of northern Alberta are forested. The forestlands are one of the province's important natural resources.

Left: Erosion of soil and rock has produced the barren terrain of the badlands, in southeastern Alberta. *Above:* The more fertile soil of Alberta's prairies is well suited for growing wheat and other grain crops.

Right: Towering mountain peaks, majestic pine forests, and crystal-clear lakes are among the attractions of Banff National Park, in the Canadian Rockies.

Between the forests and the prairie lies the parkland. Parkland is a region of mixed trees and grassland. To the south and east of the parkland lie the prairies. Almost all the agriculture is located in the prairie and parkland regions.

Minerals. The most important of Alberta's widespread mineral deposits are the mineral fuels: The province contains vast deposits of both crude oil and natural gas. In addition, sulfur is an important nonfuel by-product of Alberta's natural-gas production.

The Athabasca tar sands (sands filled with thick, tarry oils), located along the Athabasca River, contain the richest reserves in the province. But recovery of the oil is costly. Two plants are now in production, and other pilot projects are under way.

Alberta has more than half of Canada's minable coal reserves. Most of the coal is bituminous (soft) coal. It underlies much of the plains area and also occurs in the foothills and along the eastern slopes of the Rockies.

Good-quality sand and gravel occur throughout most of the province; limestone is abundant in the Rockies, and clay and shale are found in the Medicine Hat area. Large deposits of low-grade iron are available in the Peace River district. Alberta also has deposits of gypsum, phosphate, salt, sodium sulfate, and silica sand.

▶THE PEOPLE

Alberta is one of the fastest-growing provinces in Canada. Its population, like those of the other Prairie Provinces, is made up of people from different backgrounds. The greatest number are British in origin. In addition there are large groups of German, Ukrainian, Scandinavian, French, Dutch, or Polish background. Smaller ethnic groups include Russians, Hungarians, Italians, Rumanians, Yugoslavs, Finns, Chinese, and Japanese. About 44,000 native Indians, 27,000 Métis (persons of mixed Indian and European heritage), and 500 Inuit (Eskimos) make their homes in Alberta.

At the beginning of the 20th century more than 70 percent of the people lived on farms or in rural villages. Today more than 60 percent of the population lives in metropolitan Edmonton and Calgary, while 13 percent lives in smaller urban centers.

Agriculture was once the leading occupation in Alberta. Today less than 8 percent of the labor force is employed in agriculture. Increased use of farm machinery requires fewer people to operate the farms. Higher wages offered in other industries also account for the movement away from the farm.

More than half of the people now employed in Alberta work in service industries—education, health, welfare, entertainment, recrea-

Elk Island National Park, near Edmonton, is a preserve for buffalo and other plains animals.

Jasper National Park is also in the Rockies. An article on this park appears in Volume J.

Waterton Lakes National Park, bordering on Montana, is a recreational area. It shares the International Peace Park with Montana.

Wood Buffalo National Park, in northeast Alberta and the Northwest Territories, is famous for its herds of buffalo and other wild animals.

Alberta also has a number of provincial parks that offer a wide variety of recreational opportunities. Best known are **Peter Lougheed Park,** near the site of the 1988 Winter Olympic ski events; **Dinosaur Park,** which contains the fossil remains of prehistoric dinosaurs; and **Writing-on-Stone,** which features monumental stones with inscriptions by prehistoric people.

▶**INDUSTRIES AND PRODUCTS**

Mining. Alberta ranks first among the provinces in mineral production. It produces some 85 percent of Canada's oil and natural gas, making the nation approximately self-sufficient in these mineral fuels.

The most important oil fields are at Pembina, Leduc-Woodbend, Redwater, Swan Hills, and Rainbow Lake. Development of the vast Athabasca tar-sands deposits began in 1964. The first oil was produced in 1967. A second and larger development started operating in 1978. Production from conventional oil wells has peaked and will now slowly decline. Deposits in the tar sands will be increasingly important. Reserves of natural gas are larger than those of conventional oil, and both production and proven reserves are still in the process of expanding.

Much of Alberta's other mineral production is made up of industrial minerals such as clay, sand, gravel, limestone, gypsum, salt, and phosphate. Sulfur, a by-product of natural gas production, is becoming more important. Alberta accounts for most of Canada's sulfur production. Although Alberta has vast coal deposits, coal makes up less than 2 percent of the province's mineral production. But growth in exports to Japan and in the production of thermal power is increasing the demand for coal.

Manufacturing. The food and beverage industry, which includes slaughtering and meat-packing, flour milling, and various other types

tion, transportation, communication, finance, and personal services. Many people are employed in wholesale and retail trades. Manufacturing, construction, mining, forestry, fishing, and trapping are other occupations.

▶**EDUCATION**

Schooling is free for all children in the province and is compulsory for those between the ages of 7 and 15.

Alberta has four universities—the University of Alberta in Edmonton, Athabasca University, the University of Calgary, and the University of Lethbridge. There are 13 community colleges and technical schools. The Banff School of Fine Arts in Banff offers programs in music and the arts in a wilderness setting.

Alberta has more than 100 public libraries. Museums include the Provincial Museum in Edmonton, Glenbow Museum in Calgary, and the Tyrrell Museum of Paleontology near Drumheller. Art galleries and other cultural institutions are widely distributed.

▶**PLACES OF INTEREST**

Banff National Park, in the Canadian Rockies, is noted for its majestic scenery and its wildlife preserve. An article on Banff National Park appears in Volume B.

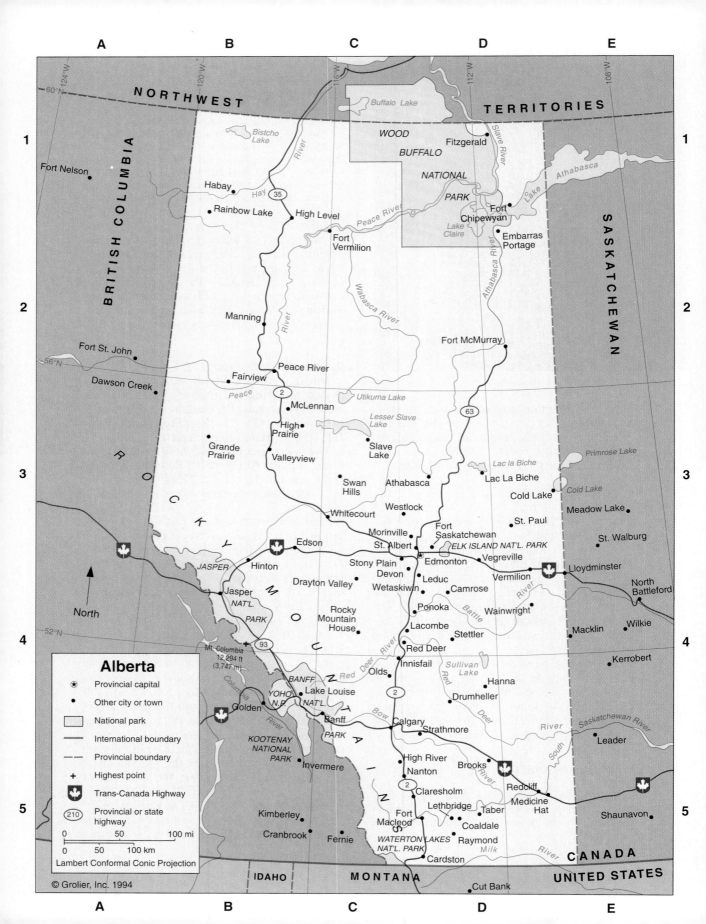

Alberta

- ⊛ Provincial capital
- • Other city or town
- ☐ National park
- ── International boundary
- ─── Provincial boundary
- + Highest point
- 🍁 Trans-Canada Highway
- ⬭ Provincial or state highway

Lambert Conformal Conic Projection

© Grolier, Inc. 1994

NORTHWEST   TERRITORIES

BRITISH COLUMBIA

SASKATCHEWAN

Fort Nelson

Bistcho Lake

WOOD

BUFFALO

NATIONAL

PARK

Buffalo Lake

Fitzgerald

Slave River

Lake Athabasca

Habay

Rainbow Lake

High Level

Hay River

35

Fort Vermilion

Peace River

Fort Chipewyan

Lake Claire

Athabasca River

Embarras Portage

Manning

River

Wabasca River

Fort St. John

Peace River

Fairview

Dawson Creek

Peace

2

McLennan

High Prairie

Fort McMurray

63

Utikuma Lake

Lesser Slave Lake

Grande Prairie

Valleyview

Slave Lake

Lac la Biche

Primrose Lake

ROCKY

Swan Hills

Athabasca

Lac La Biche

Cold Lake

Cold Lake

Meadow Lake

Whitecourt

Westlock

St. Paul

St. Walburg

Edson

Morinville

Fort Saskatchewan

ELK ISLAND NAT'L. PARK

Vegreville

Lloydminster

JASPER

Hinton

Stony Plain

St. Albert

Edmonton

Vermilion

River

North Battleford

Jasper NAT'L. PARK

Drayton Valley

Devon

Wetaskiwin

Leduc

Camrose

Battle

Wainwright

Macklin

Wilkie

North

Mt. Columbia 12,294 ft (3,747 m)

93

Rocky Mountain House

Ponoka

Lacombe

Stettler

Kerrobert

Red Deer

Deer River

Innisfail

Sullivan Lake

Hanna

BANFF

Olds

Red

Red

YOHO N.P.

Lake Louise

NAT'L.

Drumheller

Golden

Banff

2

Columbia River

PARK

Bow

Calgary

Strathmore

Saskatchewan River

KOOTENAY NATIONAL PARK

Invermere

High River

Nanton

Brooks

South

Redcliff

Leader

Kimberley

2

Claresholm

Lethbridge

Taber

Medicine Hat

Shaunavon

Cranbrook

Fernie

Fort Macleod

Coaldale

WATERTON LAKES NAT'L. PARK

Raymond

Milk

River

CANADA

Cardston

Cut Bank

IDAHO

MONTANA

UNITED STATES

0   50   100 mi

0   50   100 km

INDEX TO ALBERTA MAP

An oil sands recovery plant at Fort McMurray. Production of synthetic crude oil from Alberta's vast tar-sands deposits is an important part of the oil industry.

of food processing, depends largely on farm production. It was the leading manufacturing industry in Alberta until the early 1980's, when the refined-petroleum and coal-products industries took the lead. The chemical and chemical-products industries have also expanded rapidly. Other products manufactured in Alberta include metals and fabricated metal products, machinery, cement and concrete, and wood products.

Agriculture. Grain is still the most important agricultural product, but there has been a steady trend toward mixed crop and livestock farming in recent years. Cattle ranching is important. Sugar beets, potatoes, and feed crops are grown in irrigated areas. Where there is enough rainfall, wheat is the most important grain crop. In the parkland region, barley, oats, rye, rapeseed, and flax are grown and livestock is raised.

Electric Power. Most of Alberta's electric power plants use coal and natural gas for fuel. Hydroelectric power plants are located along the Bow and North Saskatchewan rivers and their tributaries. These typically account for less than 5 percent of the electric power produced, because they are used mainly during peak-demand periods. Power generated from huge supplies of coal and gas, together with waterpower, makes Alberta one of the most energy-rich provinces.

Forestry. Forest products account for only a small part of the economy. But forests are so extensive that production could be greatly increased. Alberta's forest products include lumber, plywood, and pulp, as well as railway ties and Christmas trees. Pulp mills are located near Hinton and Grande Prairie.

Fishing and Trapping. Fishing and trapping are of minor importance today. Commercial fishing is confined largely to the northern lakes. Whitefish is the most valuable variety. There are several hundred fur farms in Alberta. Trapping is conducted primarily in the northern forest and, like fishing, is chiefly a part-time occupation.

▶CITIES

Most of Alberta's major cities are located in the southern and central part of the province. Many were first established near rivers that served as waterways. Today an extensive network of railways, highways, and airlines serves all the urban centers of the province.

Left: Cowboys can test their riding skills at the Calgary Exhibition and Stampede, an annual agricultural fair and rodeo. *Right:* Edmonton, Alberta's capital, is a transportation hub of western Canada and a center of industry, culture, and provincial government.

Edmonton, the capital, is located in central Alberta. It serves as a collecting and distributing center for industries connected with agriculture and petroleum and as a transportation hub for the mining regions in the Northwest Territories and the Yukon. Meat-packing and other food processing, oil refining, metal production, and the production of petrochemicals are some of the city's important industries. Edmonton is the home of the Oilers, a National Hockey League team, and of the Eskimos, a Canadian Football League team. The city's metropolitan population is about 760,000. (An article on Edmonton appears in Volume E.)

Calgary, the administrative center of Alberta's oil industry, also has grown rapidly. Food and beverage processing, meat-packing, flour and feed milling, and the production of dairy products are important industries. The annual Calgary Exhibition and Stampede (rodeo) attracts thousands of visitors. The 1988 Winter Olympics were held in Calgary and in mountain areas to the west of the city. Calgary's metropolitan population is about 670,000.

Lethbridge, with a population of almost 60,000, is a major center for food processing. Lethbridge lies in the center of the chinook belt and thus enjoys relatively mild winters.

Early settlers included many Mormons, Hutterites, and Mennonites.

Red Deer, a city of 54,000, is a rapidly growing service center midway between Edmonton and Calgary.

Medicine Hat, a city of almost 50,000, is noted for clay products and pottery. Its ample supply of natural gas provides fuel for factories and for heating Medicine Hat's thriving greenhouse industry.

Other important cities are Fort McMurray, Grande Prairie, Camrose, Wetaskiwin, Lloydminster, Brooks, and Drumheller.

▶**TRANSPORTATION AND COMMUNICATION**

Because most of the people live in the southern part of Alberta, transportation is more highly developed there. However, new roads are being built in remoter areas to aid in economic development and to attract tourists. Transportation by truck is important, and Alberta has a higher percentage of cars in proportion to population than other provinces.

Railways. Alberta is served by two transcontinental lines that provide year-round access to world markets for Alberta's products. Feeder lines serve most communities. One of the latest additions—the Great Slave Railway —will have far-reaching effects on the northern areas through which it passes.

Aviation. Aircraft are used to transport people, machinery, and supplies to the north, where there are few roads and railways. All of the major cities have regular passenger and air freight services, and various airlines link Alberta with the rest of Canada and the world.

Water Transport. Freighting by river was once the only means of shipping heavy goods in Alberta. It is of minor importance today. Water routes still in use today are the Athabasca River from Waterways to lake Athabasca, and the Slave River between Athabasca and Great Slave Lake in the Northwest Territories. In summer, power barges haul heavy freight bound for northern settlements.

Pipelines. Pipelines are the most economical means of transporting the oil and gas produced in Alberta. Oil is transported by pipelines from Edmonton to Superior, Wisconsin; to Sarnia and Port Credit in Ontario; and to the Pacific coast.

Communication. Alberta has nine daily newspapers. Of these, the Edmonton *Journal* has the largest circulation. Numerous weeklies are also published. The province has 14 television stations and 36 AM and nine FM radio stations. Cable television is available in most centers. In addition to the major Canadian networks, the major U.S. networks are picked up through Spokane, Washington.

▶ **GOVERNMENT**

Alberta is a self-governing province. Like the other provinces, it is headed by a premier who represents the controlling party in the provincial assembly. A lieutenant governor, appointed by the Governor-General in Council, is the titular head of the province. He represents the Crown. Alberta is represented in the federal parliament by six senators appointed by the Governor-General and by 25 elected members of the House of Commons. The voting age for provincial elections is 18.

▶ **HISTORY**

The first European to set foot in Alberta was probably Anthony Henday. In 1754 he set out from Hudson Bay to trade for furs with the Indians. Henday explored a large portion of southern Alberta.

After the surrender of New France to the English in 1763, fur traders from eastern Canada and the United States began to tap the rich fur resources of the Canadian west.

Peter Pond, an American from Connecticut, was the first of these men to reach Alberta. He established a trading post on the Athabasca River in 1778. In 1789, Alexander Mackenzie began his famous explorations to the Arctic Ocean; and, in 1793, to the Pacific Ocean.

The Hudson's Bay Company and the North West Company competed for the fur trade of the Canadian west. Soon much of the country between Hudson Bay and the Rocky Mountains was dotted with rival trading posts. Competition was so fierce that there was sometimes bloodshed. But the rivalry ended when the companies united in 1821 under the name of the Hudson's Bay Company.

In 1870 the Dominion of Canada acquired title to the company's lands, and five years later the area known today as Alberta became part of the newly organized Northwest Territories.

Before the transfer of land to Canada, most of the settlers in Alberta were traders, Indians,

---

IMPORTANT DATES

1691	Henry Kelsey of the Hudson's Bay Company reached the eastern border of Alberta.
1754–1755	Anthony Henday of the Hudson's Bay Company was the first white person to enter Alberta.
1778	Peter Pond established the first trading post in Alberta.
1789	Alexander Mackenzie went down the Mackenzie River from Chipewyan to the Arctic Ocean.
1793	Alexander Mackenzie crossed Alberta via the Peace River.
1794	Fort Augustus founded on the site of Edmonton.
1861	St. Albert Mission founded by Father Lacombe.
1870	Canada acquired Alberta from the Hudson's Bay Company.
1874	North West Mounted Police posts established.
1882	The District of Alberta was created.
1883	The Canadian Pacific Railway main line was built across Alberta.
1905	Alberta admitted to Canadian Confederation.
1923	Alberta Wheat Pool organized.
1924	Turner Valley began producing oil.
1947	Oil discovered at Leduc.
1949	Mackenzie Highway to Hay River in the Northwest Territories completed.
1950–1953	Interprovincial Pipeline built between Edmonton and Sarnia, Ontario.
1951	Completion of the St. Mary Dam near Spring Coulee provided irrigation for southeastern Alberta.
1956	Trans-Canada Pipe Line began to carry natural gas from Alberta to eastern Canada.
1964	Development of oil sands at Athabasca began.
1969	Alberta Resources Railway completed.
1976	The Alberta Heritage Fund established to invest oil and gas revenues and thus provide for Alberta's future welfare.
1979	Charles Joseph (Joe) Clark of Alberta became prime minister of Canada.
1988	Winter Olympic Games held in Calgary.

Métis, and missionaries. The best-known mission was St. Albert Mission, founded by Father Lacombe in 1861. It was the province's first successful agricultural settlement.

In 1873 the Canadian Government organized the North West Mounted Police. Mounted Police posts were established in Alberta at Fort Macleod, Fort Saskatchewan, and Fort Calgary. The "Mounties" brought law and order to the region. One of their first acts was to stamp out an illegal whiskey trade in southern Alberta.

The Canadian Pacific Railway reached Calgary in 1883. This was the turning point in the growth of settlement. The first settlers to take advantage of the rail line were ranchers who settled on the rich grazing land in the south.

Toward the end of the 1800's, Canada encouraged immigration by offering land to homesteaders. This, together with more railway construction in western Canada, attracted many settlers. They came from eastern Canada, the United States, and Britain and other European countries. The population of Alberta rose rapidly from about 73,000 in 1901 to more than 375,000 in 1911.

In 1905, Alberta became a separate province. Following World War I, the Depression and drought of the 1930's slowed economic growth. However, population doubled in the years between World War I and World War II. The discovery of oil at Leduc in 1947, followed by even larger oil discoveries elsewhere, touched off the greatest period of economic growth in Alberta's history. Population continued to increase. But by the early 1980's, economic growth had slowed, due in part to a decline in oil prices. Because of this economic recession, migration increased, leading to a decline in population. A partial recovery of oil and gas prices stimulated some economic activity, as did the 1988 Winter Olympics in Calgary and the prospect of a freer trade with the United States.

D. WAYNE MOODIE
University of Manitoba
Reviewed by A. H. LAYCOCK
University of Alberta

ALBUQUERQUE. See NEW MEXICO (Cities).
ALCHEMY. See CHEMISTRY, HISTORY OF.

ALCOHOL

Alcoholic beverages have been known for many centuries, but it was not until the late Middle Ages that the substance alcohol was discovered. Someone—possibly an alchemist in southern Italy—collected a colorless, flammable liquid from heated wine. This liquid, first called *aqua ardens*, or "burning water," was named alcohol in the 1500's.

Today thousands of different alcohols are known. Some are clear, colorless fluids that evaporate readily and mix freely with water. Others are thick, oily liquids that hardly dissolve in water. Some are even solid at room temperature.

Alcohols are made up of atoms of carbon, hydrogen, and oxygen. The carbon atoms form a kind of framework around which the hydrogen and oxygen atoms are arranged. The particular type of alcohol is typically determined by the number and arrangement of these three elements.

Most alcohols are very poisonous. Ethyl alcohol, which is found in alcoholic beverages, is poisonous when taken in large quantities. Methyl alcohol, also called wood alcohol, is so poisonous that a small amount may cause blindness or death. Denatured alcohol, an important industrial solvent, is ethyl alcohol to which poisonous chemicals or unpleasant-tasting substances have been added to make it unfit to drink.

Alcohols are used in enormous quantities in the manufacture of plastics, medicines, synthetic fibers, paints, and other common products. Because other substances mix easily with them, alcohols are used to extract, or remove, flavoring oils, perfumes, and drugs from plant and animal products.

In the home, ethyl alcohol is an ingredient in antiseptics, flavorings, perfumes, liquors, and many medicines. Because of its low freezing point (about $-179°F$, or $-117°C$), red-tinted ethyl alcohol is usually used in outdoor thermometers. Isopropyl alcohol, or rubbing alcohol, is commonly used in both homes and hospitals.

Reviewed by LOUIS I. KUSLAN
Southern Connecticut State University

ALCOHOLISM

Alcoholism is a disease in which the drinking of alcoholic beverages interferes with some aspect of life. A person who drinks alcohol in spite of the fact that it results in loss of health, job, or good relationships with family, friends, and colleagues is said to be suffering from alcoholism.

There is a great difference between casual, or social, drinkers and alcoholics, or compulsive drinkers. The social drinkers drink because they choose to. The compulsive drinkers drink because they must, in spite of knowing that drinking is affecting their lives in a harmful way.

Alcohol is one of a large group of sedative drugs, which includes barbiturates, bromides, and chloroform. A sedative drug is one that causes sleep when used in large enough quantities. Alcohol was one of the earliest sedative drugs used.

Doctors are not sure why people become alcoholics. There does not seem to be a particular type of personality likely to become an alcoholic. Alcoholism may affect people of all races and religions. It may affect both men and women, the old and the young, the rich and the poor.

Health authorities are disturbed by the great increase in the use of alcohol among young people in recent years. Alcohol is by far the most common substance causing drug dependency among the teenage population.

The idea that the alcoholic is a person of bad character and poor morals is no longer widely held. Through the efforts of the National Council on Alcoholism, the American Medical Association, and other organizations, alcoholism is now generally recognized as a disease. The alcoholic is an ill person who needs help and treatment.

Effects of Alcohol

People drink alcohol only for the effect it has on the way they feel. The social drinkers may get a feeling of relaxation and freedom from tension. The alcoholics often show a great change in personality. They may become angry and argumentative, or quiet and depressed. Often a small amount of alcohol causes persons with alcoholism to feel even more anxious, sad, tense, and confused. They then seek relief by drinking more. This is how the alcoholic gets caught up in a web of ever-increasing need for and dependency on alcohol.

Many medical problems affect alcoholics. Serious damage to the liver, heart, stomach, and other organs can result from the overuse of alcohol. Many alcoholics do not eat properly, and some of their ills are caused by poor nutrition as well as by the direct effects of alcohol on the body. The most tragic effect of alcohol, however, is the damage it causes to the brain. Patients find it difficult to concentrate, their memories are affected, and a few suffer even more serious brain damage.

Alcoholism has become a leading cause of death in the young adult population of the United States. This grim statistic is based on accidental deaths resulting from drunken driving; from fires started by carelessly dropped cigarettes; and from overdosage with other sedatives while under the influence of alcohol.

Treatment for Alcoholism

Even though the exact cause of alcoholism is not known, the problems associated with this illness can be treated. For the alcoholic, the use of alcohol in any form must be forever avoided.

To achieve this aim, organizations like Alcoholics Anonymous give patients guidance, support, and hope. Doctors, psychologists, and trained counselors can help motivate the patient to enter into a plan for recovery. Private rehabilitation centers have been established to help the alcoholic recover. Many large businesses have also set up programs to help their employees who are alcoholics.

Several programs were established to help the families of alcoholics better understand their problems. Al-Anon is for the family and friends of alcoholics. Alateen, a division of Al-Anon, is for young people 12 to 20 years of age who live in an alcoholic family situation. Adult Children of Alcoholics (ACOA) helps adults who have problems because they grew up with an alcoholic parent. Research into methods of treatment and even prevention also will help to deal with this major health problem.

STANLEY E. GITLOW, M.D.
Chairman, Committee on Alcoholism
Medical Society of the State of New York

See also DRUG ABUSE.

Louisa May Alcott was one of the first authors to write novels for young people. Her best-loved work, *Little Women*, is based on her own girlhood experiences.

ALCOTT, LOUISA MAY (1832–1888)

Louisa May Alcott, best known as the author of *Little Women*, was among the first authors to write novels for young readers. She was born in Germantown, Pennsylvania, on November 29, 1832. Her father, Bronson Alcott, was a noted educator and lecturer. When Louisa was 2 years old, the family moved to Boston, Massachusetts, where her father opened a school. Six years later, the Alcotts moved to Concord.

There were five children in the Alcott family—Anna, Louisa, Elizabeth, May, and a boy who died in infancy. For the Alcott girls, childhood was not all play. Bronson Alcott's projects failed, one after another, and money became scarce. Louisa realized that she must find a way to help her family.

When she was 16, she began writing stories and sketches and sending them out for publication. She also worked as a teacher. In 1854, Louisa's first book, *Flower Fables*, was published. It was a collection of fairy stories she had made up to tell one of her pupils.

During the U.S. Civil War, Louisa May Alcott served as a nurse in a Union Army hospital in Washington, D.C. She wrote about her experiences in the book *Hospital Sketches*, published in 1863. Her first novel for adults, *Moods*, appeared the following year.

Louisa May Alcott wrote more than 200 books and stories, but her publisher had to urge her to write what became her most famous novel, *Little Women*. She wrote it while she was editor of *Merry's Museum*, a magazine for girls. She based the story on the Alcotts' family life in Concord. The book was published in two parts, in 1868 and 1869. It sold so well that at last she was able to take care of her family. She continued the story in *Little Men* (1871) and *Jo's Boys* (1886).

Many famous people of Concord were friends of the Alcotts. Henry David Thoreau, Ralph Waldo Emerson, and Oliver Wendell Holmes were among those from whom Louisa gathered ideas about the need for social reform. She worked for the abolition of slavery and later for women's right to vote.

Louisa May Alcott died in Boston on March 6, 1888, two days after her father's death.

LOUISE HALL THARP
Author, *The Peabody Sisters of Salem*

An excerpt from *Little Women* follows.

▶LITTLE WOMEN
"What in the world are you going to do now, Jo?" asked Meg, one snowy afternoon, as her sister came tramping through the hall, in rubber boots, old sack and hood, with a broom in one hand and a shovel in the other.

"Going out for exercise," answered Jo, with a mischievous twinkle in her eyes.

"I should think two long walks this morning would have been enough! It's cold and dull out; and I advise you to stay, warm and dry, by the fire, as I do," said Meg with a shiver.

"Never take advice! Can't keep still all day, and, not being a pussy-cat I don't like to doze by the fire. I like adventures, and I'm going to find some."

Meg went back to toast her feet and read "Ivanhoe"; and Jo began to dig paths with great energy. The snow was light, and with her broom she soon swept a path all around the garden, for Beth to walk in when the sun came out; and the invalid dolls needed air. Now, the garden separated the Marches' house from that of Mr. Laurence. Both stood in a suburb of the city, which was still country-like, with groves and lawns, large gardens, and quiet streets. A low hedge parted the two estates. On one side was an old, brown house, looking rather bare and shabby, robbed of the vines that in summer covered its walls, and the flowers which then surrounded it. On the other side was a stately stone mansion, plainly betokening every sort of comfort and luxury, from the big coach-house and well-kept grounds to the conservatory and the glimpses of lovely things one caught between the rich curtains. Yet it seemed a lonely, lifeless sort of house; for no children frolicked on the lawn, no motherly face ever smiled at the windows, and few people went in and out, except the old gentleman and his grandson.

To Jo's lively fancy, this fine house seemed a kind of enchanted palace, full of splendors and delights, which no one enjoyed. She had long wanted to behold these hidden glories, and to know the "Laurence boy," who looked as if he would like to be known, if he only knew how to begin. Since the party, she had been more eager than ever, and had planned many ways of making friends with him; but he had not been seen lately, and Jo began to think he had gone away, when she one day spied a brown face at the upper window, looking wistfully down into their garden, where Beth and Amy were snowballing one another.

"That boy is suffering for society and fun," she said to herself. "His grandpa does not know what's good for him, and keeps him shut up all alone. He needs a party of jolly boys to play with, or somebody young and lively. I've a great mind to go over and tell the old gentleman so!"

The idea amused Jo, who liked to do daring things, and was always scandalizing Meg by her queer performances. The plan of "going over" was not forgotten; and when the snowy afternoon came, Jo resolved to try what could be done. She saw Mr. Laurence drive off, and then sallied out to dig her way down to the hedge, where she paused, and took a survey. All quiet, —curtains down at the lower windows; servants out of sight and nothing human visible but a curly black head leaning on a thin hand at the upper window.

"There he is," thought Jo, "poor boy! all alone and sick this dismal day. It's a shame! I'll toss up a snowball and make him look out, and then say a kind word to him."

Up went a handful of soft snow, and the head turned at once, showing a face which lost its listless look in a minute, as the big eyes

Little Women tells of the daily lives of the four March girls—pictured here with their beloved mother—as they grow from schoolgirls to independent young women.

brightened and the mouth began to smile. Jo nodded and laughed, and flourished her broom as she called out, "How do you do? Are you sick?"

Laurie opened the window and croaked out as hoarsely as a raven, "Better, thank you. I've had a bad cold, and been shut up a week."

"I'm sorry. What do you amuse yourself with?"

"Nothing; it's as dull as tombs up here."

"Don't you read?"

"Not much; they won't let me."

"Can't somebody read to you?"

"Grandpa does, sometimes; but my books don't interest him. . . ."

"Isn't there some nice girl who'd read and amuse you? Girls are quiet and like to play nurse."

"Don't know any."

"You know us," began Jo, then laughed, and stopped.

"So I do! Will you come, please?" cried Laurie.

Left: The Russian emperor Alexander I (reigned 1801–25) helped defeat Napoleon, but failed to fulfill his early promise as a reformer. *Above:* A terrorist's bomb ended the life and reign (1855–81) of Alexander II, who had freed the Russian serfs. *Right:* Alexander III, a son of the assassinated Alexander II, disapproved of reform. His reign (1881–94) was marked by repression and intolerance.

ALEXANDER

Alexander was the name of three emperors and czars of Russia. They set the course of Russian political history between 1801 and 1894 by resisting all efforts to limit their absolute power.

Alexander I (1777–1825) reigned as emperor from 1801 to 1825. As a boy he was raised at the court of his grandmother, the Empress Catherine II (the Great). He was taught, in the spirit of the Enlightenment of the 1700's, to seek justice and to right the social ills of his subjects. He came to the throne, at the age of 23, following a palace revolution that overthrew his father, the Emperor Paul I (ruled 1796–1801), who was murdered.

Alexander's greatest challenge came in 1812, when a French army under Napoleon invaded Russia and captured and burned Moscow. However, the French forces were virtually destroyed in their long retreat through Russia. With Napoleon's final defeat in 1814, Alexander emerged as the most powerful monarch in Europe. He was one of the dominant figures at the Congress of Vienna (1814–15), which restored the old balance of power in Europe after the fall of Napoleon. He was also a founder of the Holy Alliance (1815), which was largely a statement of religious faith and was adopted by most of the European rulers.

Under Alexander, Russia's boundaries were expanded to include central Poland, Finland, Bessarabia, and territories in Transcaucasia. The tragedy of his rule arose from his unwillingness to apply the liberal lessons of his youth to the problems of his country and his subjects. Russian government and institutions, including serfdom, remained much the same at the end of his reign as he had found them in 1801.

Toward the end of his life, Alexander grew moody and melancholy. A legend grew up that he did not die in 1825, but gave up his throne to become a wandering holy man, eventually dying in Siberia in 1864.

Alexander II (1818–81), the nephew of Alexander I, was emperor of Russia from 1855 to 1881. He earned the name of Czar Liberator for his freeing of the Russian serfs.

Alexander was conservative by instinct and sympathetic to the authoritarian style of rule of his father, Emperor Nicholas I (ruled 1825–55). When he succeeded to the throne, Russia was in the midst of the Crimean War (1854–56) against Britain, France, and the Turkish Ottoman Empire. Russia's poor performance in the war prompted Alexander to examine its many neglected problems.

Among these was the institution of serfdom, under which millions of Russian peasants were bound by law to the land of their lords. Beginning with the emancipation of the serfs in 1861, Alexander introduced further reforms in the system of local government, the law, finances, higher education, and the method by which soldiers were recruited.

Alexander expected universal approval of these reforms. Instead, he received demands for even greater reform, including a constitution to limit his absolute authority. After escaping an attempted assassination in 1866, he became disillusioned with his role as reformer and turned his attention to foreign affairs. He extended Russian influence and territory in Central Asia and led Russia into the Russo-Turkish War of 1877–78.

Alexander was killed by a bomb thrown by a member of a revolutionary terrorist group. The assassination occurred only hours after Alexander had signed an order granting some political concessions.

Alexander III (1848–94) was Russian emperor from 1881 to 1894. He succeeded his murdered father, Alexander II, on the throne. One of his first acts was to cancel the modest political concessions made by his father.

Alexander was a gruff, robust figure. Even before coming to the throne, he had been conservative and disapproving of reform. As emperor, he placed restrictions on education and imposed severe censorship of the press. He was intolerant of the many languages, cultures, and religions found among the numerous peoples of the Russian Empire. The Poles, Finns, and Jews became special targets of his repressive policy of "Russification." This was an attempt to force the Russian Orthodox religion and the Russian language on the subject peoples and thus reduce the religious and cultural differences within the empire.

In foreign affairs, Alexander avoided major military conflicts while pursuing a goal of expansion in the Ottoman territories in Europe and Asia. He also abandoned Russia's traditional alliance with Germany and replaced it with a French alliance.

PETER CZAP, JR.
Amherst College

See also CRIMEAN WAR.

ALEXANDER THE GREAT (356–323 B.C.)

Alexander III of Macedon, known as Alexander the Great, was one of the most extraordinary persons of all time. He was a military commander at the age of 18; king at 20; ruler of Greece, western Asia, and Egypt at 24; and conqueror of the Persian Empire at 28. He died at the age of 32, leaving a legend unmatched in history.

Early Years. Alexander was born in 356 B.C. in Pella, Macedon (or Macedonia), in what is now part of northern Greece but was then a separate kingdom. His father, Philip II, had made Macedon into a major power and had conquered the cities of Greece. King Philip hired the Greek philosopher Aristotle as a teacher for the young prince. Thus, Alexander acquired training in war and politics from his father and admiration for the culture of Greece from his teacher.

King of Macedon. When Philip was assassinated in 336 B.C., Alexander became king of Macedon and inherited his father's plans for an invasion of Asia. In 334 B.C. he led a well-

Alexander III of Macedon (Macedonia), known as Alexander the Great, was the foremost general of ancient times. During his brief lifetime of 32 years, he conquered most of the known world of the 4th century B.C. His conquests opened Egypt and western Asia to Greek culture and thought.

trained army of Macedonians and Greek allies across the Hellespont (the Dardanelles)—a strait separating Europe from Asia—and declared war on the vast Persian Empire.

Conquest of an Empire. The young king proved himself to be one of the greatest generals in history. A natural leader of soldiers and a master of military planning, he defeated

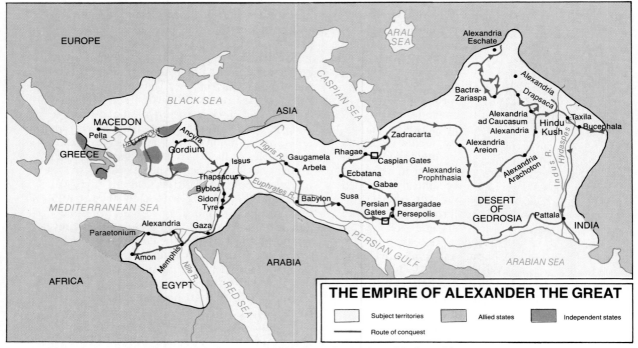

THE EMPIRE OF ALEXANDER THE GREAT

Subject territories   Allied states   Independent states

Route of conquest

Alexander's empire stretched from Greece and Macedon to the borders of India and included Egypt and the Persian Empire. The arrows show his route of conquest.

a variety of armies, including the much larger forces of the Persian Empire. At the core of Alexander's army were the superb Macedonian infantry and cavalry, the best troops of the age.

Egypt, which had been a satrapy (province) of the Persian Empire, fell to Alexander in 331 B.C. Near the mouth of the Nile River he founded Alexandria, the most famous of the many cities he named after himself. In 331, at the Battle of Gaugamela (in present-day Iraq), he defeated the army of the Persian king, Darius III. When Darius was murdered by his own nobles after this defeat, Alexander succeeded him as the new Lord of Asia.

From 329 to 326 B.C., Alexander led his victorious army through the deserts and mountains of central Asia, to the borders of India. He might have crossed into India itself, except for a mutiny, or revolt, among his officers. What had begun as a military campaign to seize the riches and lands of the Persians had become an expedition of exploration. After years of war in lands strange to them, his weary soldiers wanted to return home.

Return Journey: The Death of Alexander. Yielding to his troops, Alexander led the army down the Indus River (in what is now Pakistan) to its mouth in the Arabian Sea. Splitting his forces, Alexander built a fleet to explore the coast between India and the Persian Gulf, while he and the army followed this route by land. The soldiers became lost in the hostile desert of Gedrosia and many of them died.

Eventually, Alexander and the army reached Babylon (in what is now Iraq), his capital in Asia, where he made plans for further explorations and military campaigns. But, after several weeks of illness, caused by malaria, exhaustion, and, perhaps, too many wounds suffered in battle, the 32-year-old Alexander died on June 10, 323 B.C.

His Achievement and Legend. Alexander opened western Asia to Greek thought and culture. His remarkable conquests (he never lost a battle) and his captivating personality established him as a legend. His brief, whirlwind career gave rise to the story that, at one point, he "wept because there were no more worlds to conquer."

EUGENE N. BORZA
The Pennsylvania State University
Author, *Philip II, Alexander the Great, and the Macedonian Heritage*

ALFRED THE GREAT (849—899)

Only one king in the history of the English people has been called "the Great." This was Alfred, who ruled the land of the West Saxons. The youngest son of King Aethelwulf of Wessex, Alfred was born in 849 in Wantage, a town in south central England.

Alfred's father was a very religious man and a friend of Pope Leo IV. Twice before his 10th birthday, Alfred traveled to Rome. Those visits made a lasting impression on the young boy. Alfred came to respect both religion and education, and in later years he learned to speak and read Latin. During Alfred's youth Danish sea rovers, whom we now call Vikings, raided England. The Danish invaders made settlements on the English coast and used these bases for raids farther inland.

Alfred Becomes King.   Alfred's father died in 858. Soon afterward two of Alfred's older brothers were killed in battle. Aethelred, Alfred's last surviving brother, was king when a new invasion of Danes menaced the West Saxon kingdom in 870. The next year has been called "Alfred's year of battles" because he fought against the Danes in nine different places. The most important battle took place at Ashdown. The Saxons defeated the Danes, but Aethelred was wounded and died in the spring. Alfred then became ruler of the war-torn kingdom. He was 22 years old.

The only English king to be honored with the title "the Great," Alfred saved his country from foreign conquest and paved the way for the unification of England.

The next seven years saw times of peace and times of war. In the winter of 878, a Danish force attacked the castle where Alfred was celebrating Christmas. Alfred and a small band of loyal soldiers escaped and hid in the forest until Easter.

Many legends have grown up about Alfred's adventures during those trying times. The most famous is the story of Alfred and the cakes. According to that legend, Alfred, disguised as a farmer, took refuge in a hut in the forest. An old woman who lived there asked him to watch the cakes baking in her oven while she went about her work. Alfred was so busy worrying about his kingdom and planning new battles that he let the cakes burn. When the woman returned, she gave Alfred a severe scolding. But he did not embarrass her by telling her that he was the king.

In 876, Alfred defeated the Danes at Edington. All the nobles of England now turned to Alfred as their leader. Alfred and Guthrum, the pagan Danish chief, signed a peace treaty at Wedmore. Guthrum and many of his followers settled in England and were converted to Christianity. This was an important step toward uniting England. In 886 other Danish invaders attacked England, but Alfred defeated them, too.

Alfred's Reforms.   Alfred turned his attention to strengthening England. English laws were rewritten and clarified. New forts and walls were built to protect towns. But Alfred's most important work was in restoring the learning and education that had existed in England before the Danish invaders swept through the country.

With the help of scholars, Alfred translated several books from Latin to English. These were among the first books ever written in the language of the country and were the foundation of English literature.

When Alfred died in 899, an unknown chronicler wrote, "There passed away Alfred the king . . . the famous, the warlike, the victorious, the careful provider for the widow, the helpless, the orphan and the poor; the most skilled of Saxon poets, most dear to his own nation, courteous to all, most liberal . . . most watchful and devout in the service of God."

Reviewed by KENNETH S. COOPER
George Peabody College
Vanderbilt University

ALGAE

Algae are a diverse group of simple, primitive organisms that have not changed much in form or life processes in millions of years. Most kinds of algae live in water. They get their name from the Latin word for seaweed, *alga* (the plural is algae). Though they are similar to plants in some ways, algae lack many of the familiar plant parts, such as fruits and seeds. Most scientists classify algae in an entirely separate kingdom, called Protista.

Where Algae Are Found

Algae are found in great numbers all over the world. Algae live in freshwater lakes, rivers, ponds, and streams as well as in the salty ocean. They are found at the water's edge, both on sandy beaches and rocky cliffs. Some species are adapted to extreme temperatures, such as those found in hot springs or in polar ice and snow.

Relatives of the freshwater algae also live on land. These are usually greenish algae that cling to soil, trees, or rocks. They obtain their water from the damp ground and moist air. If the soil dries up, these algae stop growing but may remain alive for years.

Certain algae form a cooperative partnership with fungi, living so closely together that they form a single organism called a lichen. Other algae live on the bodies of animals such as turtles or the three-toed sloth.

Most people think of algae as green scum in a pond, but this group of plantlike organisms comes in a great variety of shapes and sizes. Giant kelp (*below*) growing in the Pacific Ocean is just one example.

Reproduction and Growth

Algae reproduce in several ways. Some algae produce specialized cells for reproduction. When two of these cells join, a new cell is formed and grows into the new alga. Other algae have seedlike cells called spores. Once set free, the spores grow into new plants wherever they settle. Other algae reproduce by dividing into two or more parts. Each part then grows into a new plant.

Like green plants, algae are able to make their own food. They can do this because they contain chlorophyll. This is the green-colored substance that, in the presence of sunlight, carbon dioxide, and water, enables a plant to carry out photosynthesis. An article on this process can be found in Volume P.

Despite the presence of chlorophyll, most algae do not appear green. Other coloring matter blocks out the green. The algae in the ocean are chiefly brown, red, yellow-brown, or blue-green. Green algae are usually found in fresh water or on land. One unusual variety is a bright red alga that helps cause a condition in polar regions called red snow.

Types of Algae

Algae differ greatly in size and shape as well as in color. Some are so small that they can only be seen under a microscope; these include the single-celled algae. Many algae are simply rows of cells; they appear as threadlike forms called filaments. Some algae grow with spiky branches; at the bottom of a pond they look like dwarf trees. Some algae grow to a large size. One of the longest plants on earth, a brown seaweed called kelp, may be 100 feet (about 30 meters) long.

The best-known algae are the seaweeds. Seaweeds grow in many different shapes. Some look like land plants, such as moss, asparagus, or mushrooms. There is a light-green sea lettuce that looks like regular leaf lettuce. One seaweed, the sea palm, looks like a little palm tree. And the gulfweed looks as if it has berries; actually, the "berries" are little bladders that keep the plant afloat.

Most of the algae mentioned so far are harmless or helpful to people, but some others can be dangerous. There are algae that spoil water supplies by producing a bad-tasting oil. When certain algae decay in water, they may give off poisons that will kill fish and animals that drink the water. Other algae are poisonous

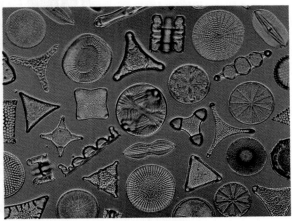

Diatoms are tiny algae usually less than 1/50 inch (0.5 millimeter) across. The glasslike cell walls give each diatom a jewel-like appearance.

to both fish and people. The mysterious, fish-killing "red tides" are made up of tiny organisms that may be algae.

But most algae benefit us, directly or indirectly. Algae and lichens that grow on the land help to keep the soil from washing away. And when these algae decay, they fertilize the plants that people and animals eat.

Algae are especially important to life in the sea. Diatoms, a type of alga, make up a large part of plankton, the floating mass of tiny plants and other micro-organisms on which fish and other sea creatures feed. Algae also supply oxygen to the animal life in the water.

In some parts of the world, especially in Asia, people eat certain seaweeds. Elsewhere livestock are fed seaweeds. From kelp come substances used in making such things as ice cream and rubber tires. And from certain red algae comes the gelatin-like agar-agar. This is the material in which bacteria are cultivated in research laboratories.

In the future algae may become far more important as a food. Scientists have succeeded in growing a single-celled alga, Chlorella, in tanks of water exposed to sunlight. The Chlorella cells grow very fast, using human wastes as their only source of needed materials. Chlorella cells contain a great deal of nutrients. As the world's population grows, Chlorella and other algae may provide a means of overcoming food shortages.

Reviewed by THOMAS GORDON LAWRENCE
Erasmus Hall High School, New York

See also FERNS; MICROBIOLOGY; MOSSES.

ALGEBRA

Algebra is a branch of the science of mathematics that uses numbers, letters, and other symbols, and the basic operations of arithmetic (addition, subtraction, multiplication, and division) to solve problems involving unknown quantities.

Algebra is used constantly by engineers, scientists, and economists and by people who work with computers in banking and in many other industries. Algebra has many practical applications, too. For example, whenever we use a formula to figure out the amount of interest we will earn from a savings account, we are using algebra.

▶USING VARIABLES FOR PROBLEM SOLVING

Arithmetic uses numbers to find answers to problems. You probably know addition problems such as $7 + 5 = 12$. Algebra uses numbers, too, but it also uses other symbols to represent unknown numbers or quantities. Most often these are letters written in italics, such as a, b, c, or x, y, z.

In algebra the letter x is most commonly used to represent an unknown quantity. However, x looks very similar to the multiplication sign $\times$. To avoid confusion, you can write $x \cdot y$ or xy or $(x) \cdot (y)$ to express x times y.

The mathematical statement $3 - 3 = 0$ is also a numerical equation. An equation is a mathematical statement in which the arrangement of numerals and letters and their operating signs on one side of an equals sign ($=$) is equal to an arrangement and its operating signs on the other side of the equals sign. (An arrangement of numerals, letters, and operating signs is often called an **expression**.) For example, this statement means that when 3 is subtracted from 3, the difference is 0. The statement $a - a = 0$ is an algebraic equation. It means that *any* number subtracted from itself has a difference of 0.

In algebra, a letter that can stand for any number is called a **variable**. If *any* number is substituted for a in the example above, the statement will be true. Therefore a is the variable. A number whose value never changes is called a **constant**. In the example above, 0, or zero, is a constant because no matter what a is, whenever it is subtracted from itself, the difference is always 0.

▶ALGEBRAIC EQUATIONS

The use of variables in algebra makes it easier to solve complex problems. For example, consider this situation: A boy and a girl collected $29 for the school fair. The girl collected $3 more than the boy. How much money did each collect?

In algebra the problem would be expressed in this way: Let x represent the unknown number of dollars collected by the boy; then let $x + 3$ represent the unknown number of dollars collected by the girl. This results in the equation $x + (x + 3) = 29$.

When working with equations, it helps to **simplify**, or write a shorter form of, a problem. The first step in simplifying is combining like units, or units that have the same value. When simplifying, the equation must be kept in balance at all times—whatever you do to one side of the equals sign, you must do to the other. There are four ways to simplify:

1. Make both sides larger by adding the same number to both sides.

2. Make both sides smaller by subtracting the same number from both sides.

3. Multiply both sides by the same number, except for the number 0.

4. Divide both sides by the same number, except for the number 0.

These four rules can help us solve the equation $x + (x + 3) = 29$. First, combine the like units by changing $x + (x + 3)$ to $(x + x) + 3$, or $2x + 3 = 29$.

Then, make both sides smaller by subtracting 3 from each side and you will get $2x = 26$.

Now, divide both sides of the equation by the same number, the number 2, and you will get $x = 13$.

Since $x = 13$, we now know that the boy collected $13 and the girl collected $16. This same problem could have been solved using arithmetic, but it is more easily solved using the language of algebra.

Signed Numbers

Signed numbers are often used to solve equations. Signed numbers are **positive numbers** (numbers greater than zero) and **negative numbers** (numbers less than zero). They are sometimes written in parentheses, such as $(+4)$ or (-7), to separate them from the sign that tells you what operation to use.

Signed numbers are often pictured on a number line, with positive numbers to the right of zero and negative numbers to the left of zero.

Adding Signed Numbers. Movement to the right ($\rightarrow$) along a number line indicates addition. For example, let us say that at 6 A.M. the temperature was 5 degrees below zero ($-5°$). By noon the temperature had risen 10 degrees ($+10°$). What was the temperature at noon? In the equation $(-5) + (+10) = x$, the x represents the unknown rise in temperature. To solve the equation, start at (-5) on the number line and move 10 spaces to the right.

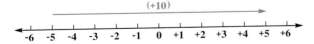

You can see that the temperature at noon was 5 degrees above zero ($+5°$), so $x = (+5)$.

Other Operations with Signed Numbers. The number line can also be used to do subtraction with signed numbers. Movement to the left ($\leftarrow$) on a number line indicates subtraction.

All signed numbers can also be multiplied or divided.

Exponents

In algebra, just as in arithmetic, a short way of writing down particular numbers or expressions is frequently used. Using an **exponent** is a short way of writing a particular number or expression, and it is frequently used in algebraic equations.

In arithmetic, multiplication is a short way of adding equal groups. For example, $3 + 3 + 3 + 3 + 3 = 15$ can also be expressed as $5 \times 3 = 15$. Algebra uses a like procedure.

For example, $2 + 2 = 4$ can be expressed as 2^2, which is read as two squared, or 2 to the second power. Also, $2 \cdot 2 \cdot 2 = 8$ can be expressed as 2^3, which is read as two cubed, or 2 to the third power. The smaller-sized upper numeral in each expression is the **exponent**. The larger-sized lower numeral in each expression is the **base**. The exponent tells us that there is to be a multiplication, and it also tells how many times the base has to be repeated, or multiplied.

In the equation $2^2 \cdot 2^3 = 2^5$, the 2^2 means $(2) \cdot (2)$ and the 2^3 means $(2) \cdot (2) \cdot (2)$. So, $2^2 \cdot 2^3 = (2) \cdot (2) \cdot (2) \cdot (2) \cdot (2)$. The rule is, when multiplying two numbers with the same base, copy the base and add the two exponents. So $(2^2) \cdot (2^3) = 2^5$, or 32.

When you divide numbers containing exponents, you subtract the exponents. For example, $(2^5) \div (2^3) = 2^2$.

▶USING FORMULAS

Many algebraic equations are rules that apply to day-to-day situations. These equations are called **formulas**.

A common formula is used to find the area of a rectangle. It is expressed as $A = lw$, in which A stands for the area, l stands for the length of the rectangle, and w stands for the width of the rectangle. The formula tells us that to find the area of the rectangle, the length must be multiplied by the width. The answer will be expressed in square units.

Using this formula to find how much carpeting is needed for a room that measures 15 feet by 10 feet gives you 150 square feet.

▶COORDINATE GEOMETRY

Algebra is an even more powerful tool when it is combined with geometry to form a graph.

Any equation in algebra can be pictured as a graph. Problems involving more than one equation can be solved by finding where the graphs meet.

Many equations have more than one variable. Usually if one variable is x, the second variable is y, as in $2x + 3y = 12$. The graph of an equation such as $2x + 3y = 12$ is formed by plotting points on a plane, or flat surface, by using **coordinates**—pairs of numbers that give the location of a point. Each point is located by measuring how far it is from each of two lines. The horizontal line is called the x axis. The vertical line is called the y axis. For example, here is a point that is 3 units from the y axis and 2 units from the x axis.

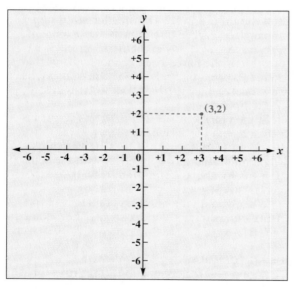

We think of this as 3 units in the $+x$ direction and 2 units in the $+y$ direction and write the location of the point as (3,2). When put into an equation, the point (3,2) is a point for which 3 can replace x and 2 can replace y. If the equation is true, when the variables are replaced by the location of the point on the graph in this way, the point is part of the graph. Because $2(3) + 3(2) = 12$ is true, $(6 + 6 = 12)$, the point (3,2) is on the graph of $2x + 3y = 12$.

Other points on the graph of $2x + 3y = 12$ are (0,4) on the y axis, and (6,0) on the x axis.

$$2(0) + 3(4) = 12$$
$$2(6) + 3(0) = 12$$

When all the points on the graph of $2x + 3y = 12$ are shown, the result is a graph that is a line. Making a graph of an equation often helps us understand the equation better and makes it easier to solve.

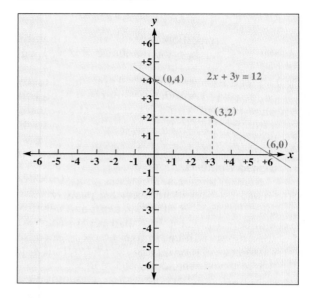

► **THE HISTORY OF ALGEBRA**

The ability to solve algebraic equations goes back almost 4,000 years to the civilizations of Egypt and Babylonia. The algebra of these ancient peoples, however, used words instead of letters to solve equations. It was not until about A.D. 250 that Diophantus, a Greek, used some abbreviations and letter symbols to write out solutions to problems.

The word "algebra" comes from the Arabic word *al-jabr*, which was used about A.D. 825 in the title of a popular book written by the mathematician al-Khwarizmi, which set down the basic rules for solving equations.

Significant contributions to the field of algebra in modern times include the invention of coordinate geometry by René Descartes (1596–1650); the discovery of the *fundamental theorem of algebra* by Karl Friedrich Gauss (1777–1855); the creation of an algebra of logic by George Boole (1815–64); and important discoveries in modern abstract algebra by Emmy Noether (1882–1935).

BRYAN BUNCH
Pace University

See also ARITHMETIC; NUMBERS AND NUMBER SYSTEMS.

ALGER, HORATIO. See MASSACHUSETTS (Famous People).

ALGERIA

Algeria is the second largest country in Africa, after Sudan. It is situated in the northwestern part of the African continent, on the coast of the Mediterranean Sea. Algeria is a nation of great contrasts, where old customs and traditions exist side by side with modern ways. In Algiers, the capital, steel and glass skyscrapers stand alongside the winding, narrow streets of the Casbah, the old section of the city. City dwellers in European-style clothes mingle with desert nomads. The land itself is marked by contrast. Behind a narrow, fertile area along the Mediterranean Sea lies the Sahara—the world's largest desert.

In the 19th century, Algeria came under the control of France, which ruled it for more than 100 years. Algeria won its independence in 1962, after years of violent struggle.

The Casbah is the old section of Algiers, the capital of Algeria. Its narrow, winding streets are lined with closely spaced houses and small shops and markets.

▶THE PEOPLE

Ethnic Groups, Language, and Religion. The first known inhabitants of Algeria were the Berbers, a nomadic people of North Africa. Over the centuries many conquering peoples invaded the land. The Arabs, who came in the 7th century A.D., brought the Muslim religion and the Arabic language to the region. After Algeria came under French rule, large numbers of French settlers, called *colons*, established themselves there.

Today Algeria's population is made up mostly of Arabs and Berbers or people of mixed Arab and Berber stock. Most of the *colons* departed after Algeria became independent. Algeria had a sizable Jewish community, but most of its members have left. Almost all Algerians are Muslims. Arabic is the official language, but French is still widely used.

Way of Life. More than three fourths of the people live in cities and towns along the Mediterranean coast. The others live inland in small villages; on patches of fertile ground in the desert, called oases; or in the desert itself. The traditional Algerian house is built around an open courtyard with a garden. The house has thick walls and is built to keep the sun out and the interior cool. In an oasis village, houses are built of mud brick and enclosed by high mud-brick walls. Nomads in the desert live in dark-colored tents.

▶THE LAND

The ranges of the Atlas Mountains divide Algeria into three physical regions—the Tell, the High Plateau, and the Sahara.

The Tell. The Tell (Arabic for "hill") lies along the Mediterranean. Lowlands on the coast make up a fertile region of farms and orchards. Forests grow on the lower slopes of the hills, and sheep and goats graze higher up. Most of Algeria's major cities are located in the Tell.

The High Plateau. South of the Tell and north of the Sahara lies the High Plateau. Here and there on the plateau are shotts—shallow salt lakes that are dry part of the year. Coarse, prickly drinn and tall esparto grasses grow on the High Plateau.

The Sahara. *Sahara* is the Arabic word for "desert." The Sahara forms the largest part of Algeria. It is mainly a rocky plateau, or hammada, flanked by areas of giant sand dunes called ergs. During the brief rainy season, streams flow through valleys called wadis. When the rains stop, the wadis dry up. Oases are scattered throughout the monotonous desert. These areas of greenery are watered by springs and wells.

Climate. The Tell has mild, rainy winters and dry, hot summers. On the High Plateau summers are also hot and dry, but winters are colder and rainfall is much less. The Sahara is hot by day, but temperatures drop sharply at night. Rainfall is very scanty. In the spring the sirocco—a hot, dry wind from the south—blows across the desert, causing fierce sandstorms.

Natural Resources. Algeria has extensive mineral resources, including petroleum and natural gas (mined in the Sahara), iron ore, phosphates, coal, lead, and zinc.

Pine, cedar, cork oak, olive trees, and evergreens grow in the north. Animal life includes deer, otters, weasels, gazelles, jackals, and wild pigs. Monkeys, hyenas, and panthers live in the remote highlands.

▶**THE ECONOMY**

Agriculture and Fishing. Agriculture employs about one third of the population, but only about 10 percent of Algeria's land is suitable for farming. Grain, wine grapes, tobacco, citrus fruits, olives, and figs are grown on the Tell. On the High Plateau, farmers grow wheat and barley and raise livestock. Nomads raise sheep, goats, and camels on the sparse grazing lands of the Sahara. Dates and other fruits, grains, and cotton are grown in Saharan

oases. However, Algeria must import grain and other foods to meet its needs.

Fishing is carried out in the waters of the Mediterranean, which supplies catches of sardines, tuna, anchovies, and shellfish.

Mining and Manufacturing. Petroleum and natural gas are Algeria's most valuable min-

erals, accounting for most of its income from exports. Although Algeria has relatively small reserves of petroleum compared with some other countries, its natural gas deposits are the fourth largest in the world.

The manufacturing sector of the economy has grown rapidly in recent years. Chief manufactured products include refined petroleum products, iron and steel, textiles, processed foods, fertilizers, assembled motor vehicles, cement, bricks, cork, and paper.

▶CITIES

Most of Algeria's large cities are on the Mediterranean coast.

Algiers. The capital, Algiers, with a population of more than 2,000,000, is Algeria's largest city. It is a major seaport and an important center of transportation, industry, and culture. The winding, hilly streets of the city rise from the half-moon–shaped bay, where there is a bustling, modern harbor. The 19th-century French architecture gives the city a feeling of Marseilles or Paris. But new buildings and roads are also being constructed. Even some of the narrow Casbah streets have been transformed into broad boulevards.

Oran. An important port and industrial city, Oran is the chief outlet for the products of western Algeria. It was founded by Muslims from Spain early in the 10th century.

Constantine. The largest inland city, Constantine was named after the first Christian emperor of ancient Rome. Constantine's port, Skikda, lies on the Mediterranean.

▶HISTORY AND GOVERNMENT

Early History. The Berbers had long inhabited the region when the Phoenicians, a people of the eastern Mediterranean, began to establish colonies along the North African coast in the 12th century B.C. Some of these colonies were in Algeria, but the biggest, Carthage, was in what is now Tunisia. After the Romans conquered Carthage in 146 B.C., they took over Algeria (then called Numidia) as well.

The Vandals, a Germanic people, replaced the Romans in the 5th century A.D. During the

Left: Most of Algeria is desert, broken only by scattered oases. Dates, grains, cotton, and other crops are grown on these small, watered areas.

Right: The port of Algiers is situated on the coast of the Mediterranean Sea. Algeria's largest cities are located in the fertile coastal area.

The ruins of Hippo Regius, near present-day Annaba, are a reminder of past civilizations that ruled in Algeria. Originally settled by the Phoenicians, it later flourished under the Romans and was a center of early Christianity.

6th century, the region fell to the Byzantine, or Eastern Roman, Empire. The Arabs began their conquest of the area during the 7th century. From 1518 to 1830, Algeria was part of the Turkish Ottoman Empire.

French Rule. In 1830 the French invaded Algeria and occupied it after many years of armed resistance by the Algerians.

Early in World War II, France surrendered to Germany. Through the Vichy French puppet government, Germany controlled Algeria. In 1942 the Allied armies recaptured Algeria, and General Charles de Gaulle, leader of the Free French Forces (and later president of France), set up his headquarters in Algiers.

Struggle for Independence. On May 8, 1945, the day the war ended in Europe, thousands of Algerians demonstrated for independence. A confrontation with French *colons* led to violence by both sides. The independence struggle began in earnest in 1954, when the Algerian National Liberation Front (FLN) launched a guerrilla campaign against the French. After more than seven years of bloody civil war, an agreement was reached in 1962 between the FLN and the French Government under President De Gaulle, providing for Algerian independence. A brief revolt led by French military officers opposed to independence was put down, and on July 3, 1962, Algeria officially became independent.

Algeria Since Independence. Ahmed Ben Bella, a leader in the struggle for independence, became president in 1963. He was overthrown in 1965 in a military coup led by Colonel Houari Boumedienne. Boumedienne served as head of a military government and as president of Algeria until his death in 1978.

He was succeeded by Chadli Bendjedid, who became president in 1979 and was re-elected in 1984 and 1988.

The government of Algeria is based on a constitution adopted in 1976 and amended most recently in 1989. The head of state and government is the president, who is elected for a term of five years. The president appoints a prime minister, who handles the day-to-day activities of the government. The legislature is the National People's Assembly, which also is elected for five years.

Until 1989 the FLN was the only legal political party in Algeria. The FLN nominated the president as well as the candidates for the National People's Assembly. Under constitutional amendments approved in 1989, other political parties were permitted to organize. In local elections held in 1990, the first open elections since independence, the Islamic Front for National Salvation (FIS) won control of 32 of the country's 48 provinces as well as a majority of municipal councils. A Muslim fundamentalist party, the FIS seeks to transform Algeria into an Islamic state.

In the first round of legislative elections, held in December 1991, FIS candidates won by a wide margin over the FLN. But in January 1992, the military suspended further elections. President Bendjedid was forced to resign and the military-backed High Council of State was formed to run the country.

ROBERT S. CHAUVIN
Stetson University
Revised and updated by ALF ANDREW HEGGOY
The University of Georgia
Co-author, *Historical Dictionary of Algeria*

ALGONKIAN INDIANS. See INDIANS, AMERICAN.

ALIENS

People who are not citizens of the country in which they live are called aliens. Aliens are required to obtain government permission in order to stay in a foreign country for any lengthy period of time.

Illegal Aliens. An illegal alien is a person who enters a country without the permission of that country's government or who stays beyond the term of his or her visa (permit). Illegal aliens can cause complex problems because they place a burden on public services, such as medical facilities, without paying the taxes that support these services.

Legal Aliens. In the United States the Immigration and Naturalization Service handles alien affairs. This office admits aliens in three categories.

Temporary visitors must obtain visas from the Department of State to enter the country. Visas allow them to travel, attend school, or conduct business for a limited time.

There are several million **permanent resident aliens** living in the United States. They enjoy most of the rights and privileges of American citizens, such as the right to hold a job or to own property. They also share many of the same duties, such as paying taxes. However, they cannot vote or hold most public offices. In addition, every January they must provide the U.S. attorney general with their correct address. Resident aliens over the age of 18 must carry an identification card, more commonly known as a "green card."

The third category is made up of **refugees,** people who have been forced to leave their homelands because of war or persecution. Most refugees are admitted into the United States under a special procedure called parole. They may eventually achieve resident-alien status.

Any alien in the United States who does not follow U.S. Government laws and regulations can be deported (required to leave the country), according to the Alien Act of 1798. In addition, the activities of aliens from enemy countries may be restricted during times of war.

ROBERT RIENOW
Author, *The Great Unwanteds: Illegal Aliens and the American Challenge*

See also CITIZENSHIP; IMMIGRATION; NATURALIZATION; PASSPORTS AND VISAS.

ALLEN, ETHAN (1738–1789)

Ethan Allen was a hero of the American Revolutionary War and a leader in the fight for Vermont's statehood. He was born in Litchfield, Connecticut, probably on January 10, 1738. As a young man he fought in the French and Indian War (1754–63).

In 1769, Allen settled in Vermont, which was then known as the "New Hampshire grants." A heated dispute arose between the colonial governors of New York and New Hampshire because each claimed that land for his own colony. Allen felt that the original settlers from New Hampshire had the strongest claim. Unfortunately for them, Britain decided otherwise and granted the land to New York.

This action prompted Allen and his friend Seth Warner to organize a militia called the Green Mountain Boys. In 1770 the group took up arms against the intruding New Yorkers to prevent them from taking over their land. The governor of New York declared Allen an outlaw and offered a reward for his arrest.

In April, 1775, the Revolutionary War began. On May 10, Allen, with his Green Mountain Boys and some Connecticut militia, succeeded in capturing the British fort at Ticonderoga, New York, on Lake Champlain. Four months later, Allen and his men failed in an attempt to capture Montreal, and Allen was taken prisoner.

On his release in 1778, Allen returned to continue the fight for Vermont's independence. However, the Continental Congress refused to recognize Vermont's claim to statehood. Allen considered having Vermont annexed to Canada, but the plan fell through.

Ethan Allen died on February 12, 1789, in Burlington, Vermont. Two years later, in 1791, Vermont became the 14th state of the Union.

Reviewed by RICHARD B. MORRIS
Editor, *Encyclopedia of American History*

ALLERGY. See DISEASES.

ALLIGATORS. See CROCODILES AND ALLIGATORS.

ALLOYS

An alloy is a substance formed by combining a metal with other metals or non-metals. Brass is an alloy made with the metals copper and zinc. Steel is an alloy made with a metal—iron—and a non-metal—carbon. Alloys are usually made by melting the ingredients and mixing them together.

The special characteristics of a metal, such as its flexibility, hardness, strength, and resistance to corrosion, are called **properties.** Alloying makes it possible to create materials with just the right combination of properties for a particular use.

Almost every metallic substance used today is an alloy of some kind. But the idea of making alloys is not new. It was known by people in ancient times.

Thousands of years ago, people discovered that they could use copper instead of stone to make their tools. Copper was easier to work with than stone and was fairly easy to obtain. Perhaps the only trouble with copper was that it was not hard enough for some uses. About 3500 B.C. it was found that if tin, another fairly soft metal, was combined with copper, a very hard material was produced. This material was the alloy called bronze.

The discovery of how bronze is made was probably accidental, but it turned out to be an important event. Bronze was a better material for many purposes than either of the two metals that composed it. The alloy was so widely used that this period of history became known as the Bronze Age.

Bronze is only one example of an alloy that is used because it does a certain job better than many pure metals. Airplanes must be built of material that is both light and strong. Aluminum is light enough, but it is not strong enough for this purpose. Steel is strong enough, but it is too heavy. But combining aluminum with copper, magnesium, and other metals yields an alloy that is light, yet strong enough to stand up to the stresses of flight. Similarly, adding nickel, vanadium, chromium, and other metals to steel produces a stronger metal. This saves weight by making it possible to reduce the thickness of parts.

Steel is an extremely versatile and useful metallic material. In the United States alone, about 100,000,000 metric tons of steel are produced each year for use in everything from skyscrapers to saucepans.

Alloying steel with other metals produces materials called **alloy steels,** which are suitable for a wide variety of purposes. Manganese alloy steels are used to make machines such as rock crushers and power shovels, which must withstand extremely hard use. Stainless steel, which contains chromium and sometimes nickel and manganese, is a hard, strong substance that resists heat and corrosion. Stainless steels are used for such things as jet engines, automobile trim, knives, forks, and spoons, and kitchen equipment.

▶**CLASSES OF ALLOYS**

Alloys are divided into two main classes: ferrous and non-ferrous. The term **ferrous** (from the Latin word *ferrum,* meaning "iron") applies to alloys, such as steel, whose base metal is iron. Alloys that contain little or no iron, such as aluminum and copper alloys, are called **non-ferrous.**

There is an important difference between alloys and impure metals. Both are mixtures, but alloys are mixtures that have been deliberately combined in definite proportions. Impure metals are accidental mixtures that vary greatly in their make-up.

▶**ALLOY STRUCTURES**

Why does an alloy have different properties from the metals that compose it? To understand the answer to this question, something must be known about how atoms line up to form the inner structure of metals.

When a metal is melted, the atoms of the metal move about freely. When the metal cools and becomes solid, the atoms form clusters of a certain shape, called **crystals.** There are three main types of crystal structure. Two of these crystal structures are shaped like cubes, with the atoms at various places on the cubes. The third type is a more complicated structure that has a six-sided, or hexagonal, shape.

These clusters of atoms, or crystals, also form larger groups called **grains.** These grains can be seen with the aid of a microscope. In a pure metal, such as copper, all the grains look alike.

Certain metals can mix together so closely when they are melted that the grains all look

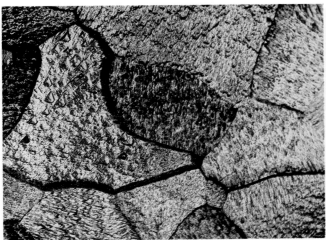

Clusters of metallic crystals form geometric shapes, called grains, in a sample of pure gold. The grain structure here is magnified 160 times.

When copper is added to gold to form an alloy, the atoms of each metal interact, and the grain structure changes. Magnification is the same as the photo at left.

alike when the alloy becomes solid, just as they do in a pure metal. When two metals are so completely mixed, they are said to be in **solid solution.** One such solid solution is the alloy of copper and nickel called cupronickel. In this alloy copper is the base metal; that is, more copper than nickel is used in making the alloy. Cupronickel is stronger and harder than copper but less able to conduct heat or electricity. The addition of nickel to the copper has created new properties that neither copper nor nickel alone has.

These new properties are created by the difference in the sizes of the atoms of copper and the atoms of nickel. When the nickel atoms enter the crystal structure of the copper, they replace some copper atoms. Because the nickel atoms are of a different size, the crystals of copper are distorted, or warped out of their normal shape. Although the grains of the alloy appear to have the same shape as the grains of the base metal (copper), the smaller units, the crystals, have been changed. This change in the shape of the copper crystals is the reason the alloy has different properties from the copper and nickel of which it is made. Every metal has atoms of different size from those of all other metals. Thus, whenever a solid-solution alloy is formed, a distortion of the crystal structure of the base metal will always take place, and new properties will be created.

Some metals do not mix completely with each other. These metals are said to be **partially soluble** in each other. They form two or more different kinds of grains when the alloy solidifies. The different kinds of grains are called **phases.** They are actually solid solutions containing different proportions of the two metals. Some kinds of brass, an alloy composed of copper and zinc, have this kind of structure.

There is a third type of constituent in some alloys. The metals combine to form an **intermetallic compound,** which has a crystal-and-grain structure quite different from either of the pure metals. In an aluminum-copper alloy, for instance, a small amount of copper goes into solid solution with the aluminum. The rest of the copper combines with aluminum atoms to form an intermetallic compound composed of two atoms of aluminum and one atom of copper. Thus, the aluminum-copper alloy is made up of three components: a large amount of aluminum, a small quantity of copper in solid solution, and tiny particles of the intermetallic compound.

Although intermetallic compounds are usually hard and brittle, their presence in an alloy in small amounts is very valuable. Such alloys combine the toughness of solid solutions with the hardness of intermetallic compounds.

We owe jet airplanes, television, and many other technical marvels to alloys. These metal mixtures made it possible to turn engineers' and scientists' ideas into reality.

JOHN A. RING
Union Carbide Corporation

See also BRONZE AND BRASS; IRON AND STEEL; METALS AND METALLURGY.

ALMANACS. See REFERENCE BOOKS.

ALPHABET

An alphabet is a group of signs that is used to write a language. The signs—called letters—express all the individual sounds that people use when they speak.

We think of the letters of our alphabet as having a fixed order—beginning with A and ending with Z—but that is only because we learned it that way. The letters originally were made up as they were needed, rather than in any logical pattern. We could easily change the order of the letters in our alphabet and it would not affect the way we write or speak.

The ancestor of the alphabet we use for writing English was created more than 3,000 years ago. Our alphabet is called the Latin or Roman alphabet because it is taken directly from the alphabet used by the ancient Romans. The Romans adapted this alphabet from the one used by the Etruscans, another people who lived in Italy, who in turn had borrowed it from the Greeks. The Greeks had taken the alphabet from the Phoenicians, a Semitic people who lived along the eastern end of the Mediterranean Sea. Which Semitic people actually originated the concept of the alphabet remains a mystery. But by about 1000 B.C., several groups of peoples speaking related languages—including the Arameans, the Phoenicians, and the Hebrews—were all using this same basic system for writing their languages.

▶ FORERUNNERS OF THE ALPHABET

An alphabet is a writing system that expresses the sounds of language. We call such a writing system phonetic (''by sounds''). An alphabet has signs for the smallest individual speech sounds. We call these individual sounds **phonemes** (''sound units''). Another type of phonetic writing system that is not considered an alphabet uses signs to stand for **syllables.** Syllables are speech units that are made up of phonemes. A syllable can be a complete word or part of a word, but it must contain a vowel sound.

A third type of writing system has signs that stand for complete words regardless of how many syllables the word has. Even though we have an alphabet, we sometimes use signs for complete words in order to save time and space. For example, all of our numerals are word signs. It is much easier to write 1945 than to use our alphabet to spell out ''one thousand nine hundred forty-five.'' Other common word signs that we use include & for ''and,'' + for ''plus,'' and $ for ''dollar.''

Word Writing Systems. The earliest writing systems, which came into use about 3000 B.C., used almost all word signs. These were the hieroglyphic writing of ancient Egypt and the cuneiform writing of the ancient Sumerians. The main disadvantage to a writing system that uses only word signs is that it needs a large number of signs because there are many words in a language. Look at the size of the dictionary. Imagine having to learn a different sign for every word in the dictionary in order to be able to read and write.

Actually, in a word writing system the same sign often stands for several related words. The reader must decide which of the words the writer meant with the sign he used. But such a system still needs about 1,000 signs. Chinese is one of the only modern languages to use a word writing system.

Word-Syllabic Writing Systems. Because of the drawbacks of using only word signs, the Sumerians and Egyptians quickly developed signs for syllables, which they used in combination with word signs. This was a tremendous improvement over using word signs by themselves because the exact word the writer intended to use could be expressed more accurately.

The Sumerians indicated vowel sounds in their syllabic signs. This meant that they needed a sign for each consonant plus each vowel. (In English, for example, different signs would be needed to express the syllables ba, be, bi, bo, bu, da, de, di, do, du, and so on.) The Egyptian signs were simpler. They stood for the consonant plus any vowel. In this system the reader had to supply the correct

The Etruscan alphabet, which reads from right to left, is one of the ancestors of our alphabet. This carving, made about 700 B.C., was probably used for teaching.

vowel, which caused some confusion. It would be like writing "ht" in English and leaving it to the reader to decide whether the letters meant hot, hat, hit, or hut. The advantage of the system was that the number of syllabic signs needed was reduced to the number of consonants in the language.

Syllabic Writing Systems. The Semitic peoples of Syria and Palestine developed purely syllabic writing systems. Their systems were very simple because they eliminated word signs completely and, like the Egyptians, their signs expressed consonants plus any vowel. This simplification was an important step in the development of the alphabet.

Because vowels were not expressed by the writing, these syllabic systems—called **syllabaries**—were not true alphabets. Alphabets have a sign for each phoneme in the language. But the Semitic syllabaries developed into the alphabets used today. The most important of the Semitic syllabaries were the Phoenician, from which the Greeks developed their alphabet, and the Aramaic.

The Phoenician Writing System. The earliest example of Phoenician writing that we have is from the city of Byblos and dates from about 1000 B.C., but the writing system was surely in use before this. Byblos was a major center of commerce. It was so important in the trade in papyrus, a paperlike material used for writing, that its name gave the Greeks their word for "book" (biblos) and the English language its "Bible." Some scholars think that Byblos may have been the place where the Semitic writing system was first created, but there is no direct evidence for this.

The Phoenician writing system had 22 signs. Each sign had a name, the first sound of which was the sound that the sign represented. In many cases the signs can be recognized as pictures of the object that forms the name of the sign. The first sign was called *aleph*, which was the Phoenician word for "bull," and the sign looked like a bull's head.

The second sign, called *beth*, represented the sound "b." It was the Phoenician word

for "house," and the letter looked something like the plan of a simple house. You can go all the way through the Phoenician script in this manner, finding meanings for almost all of the names of the signs and relating the signs to the names. The last sign was *taw*, which meant "sign" or "mark." It was in the shape of a simple cross.

This, then, was the writing system that the Greeks adapted to write their own language.

▶**THE DEVELOPMENT OF THE ROMAN ALPHABET**

Greeks. When the Greeks adapted the Phoenician writing system to their own language, some time before the 8th century B.C., they made a very significant change. They created signs for vowels and used them each time a vowel occurred. Simple as this sounds, it was the last important step in the development of writing systems that had been going on for more than 2,000 years. The Greek writing system was truly an alphabet, because each sound in the language now had its own sign. Every word could be written accurately with a system that used a very small number of signs.

The Greeks did not invent new signs for the vowels but simply converted some of the Phoenician signs that they did not need for their own language into vowel symbols. They also added some letters and later dropped others to create the 24-letter Greek alphabet. When the Greeks borrowed signs from the Phoenicians, they kept the names for the signs, although they had no meaning in Greek. Thus *aleph* became *alpha,* and *beth* became *beta.* It is from the names of these two letters that our word "alphabet" comes.

Etruscans. The next step in the alphabet's journey was to the Etruscans. They were a people of northern Italy who were influential during the 11th to 6th century B.C. The Etruscans wrote their language using an early Greek alphabet, with some modifications. The most important offshoot of the Etruscan alphabet was the Roman alphabet.

EVOLUTION OF THE ROMAN ALPHABET

Phoenician		Early Greek		Early Etruscan	Early Roman	Classical Roman	Modern Roman
𐤊	'ALEPH	Δ	ALPHA	A	A	A	A
𐤁	BETH	8	BETA	B	8	B	B
𐤂	GIMEL	𐤂	GAMMA	𐤂	>C	C	C
𐤃	DALETH	Δ	DELTA	D	D	D	D
𐤄	HE	ξ	E(PSILON)	ξ	ξ	E	E
𐤅	WAW	ϝ	DIGAMMA	ϝ	ϝ	F	F
						G	G
I	ZAYIN	I	ZETA	I			
𐤇	ḤETH	⊟H	(H)ETA	⊟	⊟H	H	H
⊗	ṬETH	⊕	THETA	⊗			
𐤉	YOD	ζ	IOTA	I	I	I	I
							J
𐤊	KAPH	K	KAPPA	K	K	K	K
𐤋	LAMED	𐤋	LAMBDA	𐤋	𐤋	L	L
𐤌	MEM	𐤌	MU	𐤌	NM	M	M
𐤍	NUN	𐤍	NU	𐤍	N	N	N
𐤎	SAMEKH	Ξ	XI (CHI)	⊞			
O	'AYIN	O	O(MICRON)	O	O	O	O
𐤐	PE	𐤐	PI	𐤐	𐤐q	P	P
𐤑	ṢADE	M	SAN	M			
φ	QOPH	φ	KOPPA	Q	Q	Q	Q
𐤓	RESH	𐤓	RHO	𐤓	qq	R	R
W	SIN	ζ	SIGMA	ζ	ζ	S	S
X	TAW	T	TAU	T	T	T	T
							U
		YV	U(PSILON)	Y	V	V	V
							W
		φ	PHI	φ			
		X	CHI (XI)	X	X	X	X
		↑↓	PSI	Y			
							Y
							Z

The Roman alphabet, which is used to write English and many other modern languages, developed over thousands of years. From left: The Phoenician syllabary was an important early writing system. From it the Greeks developed their alphabet, which spread to the Etruscans. The Romans adapted the Etruscan alphabet. By the 3rd century B.C., 21 of the capital letters that we use today had been perfected by the Romans.

Romans. The Romans adapted the Etruscan alphabet, probably beginning in the 6th century B.C. Of the 26 letters of the original Etruscan alphabet, the Romans accepted 20.

By the 3rd century B.C. the Roman alphabet consisted of 21 letters: A, B, C, D, E, F, G, H, I, K, L, M, N, O, P, Q, R, S, T, V, and X. Only J, U, W, Y, and Z remained to be added to the alphabet. When the Romans conquered Greece in the 1st century B.C., a large number of Greek words were taken into the Latin language. The Romans found it necessary to borrow some Greek letters in order to write these new words. The Greek letter *upsilon* had developed into a sound between *u* and *e,* and the Romans gave it the name *wye.* The letter *zeta* had been rejected five centuries earlier and its place in the order taken by G, but it was now

OTHER MAJOR ALPHABETS

The Roman alphabet is just one of the writing systems used by the world's people today. Other important alphabets are listed below.

Arabic	ا ب ت ث ج ح خ د ذ ر ز س ش ص ض ط ظ ع غ ف ق ك ل م ن ل ا و ي
Cyrillic	АБВГДЕЁЖЗИЙКЛМНОПРСТУФХЦЧШЩЪЫЬЭЮЯ
Gaelic	ᴀ ʙᴄ ᴅ ᴇ ꜰ ɢ ʜ ɪ ʟ ᴍ ɴ ᴏ ᴘ ʀ ᴄ ᴜ
Greek	ΑΒΓΔΕΖΗΘΙΚΛΜΝΞΟΠΡΣΤΥΦΧΨΩ
Hebrew	א ב ב ג ד ה ה ו ו ז ח ט י כ כ ל מ נ ס ע ף פ פ צ ק ר ש ש ת
Hindi	अ आ इ ई उ ऊ ऋ ए ऐ ओ औ क ख ग घ ङ च छ ज झ ञ ट ठ ड ढ ण त थ द ध न प फ ब भ म य र ल व श ष स ह

accepted and along with Y placed at the end of the alphabet after X. This brought the total number of letters to 23. This was the alphabet used during the time of the Roman Empire. J, U, and W were added much later and were more a matter of developments in handwriting than of a real need for separate letters.

Capital and Small Letters. In ancient times, all writing was done in what we call capital (or uppercase) letters. Small (or lowercase) letters developed later.

The Roman letters were perfected by the 1st and 2nd centuries A.D. The form known as square capitals was written with great precision, especially on stone, and the letters were very symmetrical and well proportioned. These forms are what we still use for our capital letters today.

The small letters of our modern alphabet developed more gradually. While square capitals were fine for stone inscriptions, everyday writing, done with a pen or brush on papyrus or parchment, required more flexibility and speed. The everyday script, which used much rounder forms of the letters (still capitals), was called cursive. Writing materials were expensive, so the scribes who copied books tried to fit as much lettering as possible on a page and in the process created a number of "book hands." These two factors—the need to write quickly and the need to save space—led to the development of our small letters.

▶ **TODAY'S ALPHABETS**

Many different alphabets are used in the world today, but with the possible exception of the Korean alphabet all of them developed in one way or another from the Semitic writing system.

The Cyrillic Alphabet. We have already seen how the Greek alphabet developed from the Phoenician and how the Roman alphabet developed from the Greek. Two other alphabets also developed from the Greek but at a much later date. In the 9th century A.D., the Glagolitic and the Cyrillic alphabets were devised to write the Slavic languages. Both were based on the Greek alphabet then in use. Glagolitic was more popular at first but eventually was replaced by Cyrillic, which is not as complicated. Cyrillic in various forms is used today in Bulgaria, Russia, Ukraine, Belarus, and present-day Yugoslavia.

Other Alphabets. Except for those areas that use the Greek and Cyrillic alphabets, some form of the Roman alphabet is used throughout Europe. Almost all of the rest of the world's alphabets developed from the Semitic syllabary known as Aramaic. The alphabets derived from the Aramaic include those used to write the modern Semitic languages—Arabic, Hebrew, and Syriac. Alphabets used in India and Southeast Asia and the Mongol script are also derived from the Aramaic.

In the 3,000 years since its invention, the alphabet has proved to be a very durable and flexible tool for expressing language. It has been adapted successfully to many languages. Apparently it is here to stay.

ROBERT M. WHITING
The Oriental Institute
The University of Chicago

See also WRITING; articles on the individual letters of the alphabet.

The snowcapped Alps extend across much of south central Europe. The highest Alpine peak, Mont Blanc (to left of center), lies on the border between France and Italy.

ALPS

The Alps are a great mountain system of south central Europe, famed for the spectacular beauty of their snowcapped peaks.

Extent and Divisions. From the coast of the Mediterranean Sea, the Alps stretch for a distance of about 680 miles (1,100 kilometers). They form the boundary between France and Italy and extend across Switzerland, northern Italy, southern Germany, Austria, and the Balkan peninsula. They are usually divided into three main sections: Western, Central, and Eastern Alps. Some of the principal Alpine mountain ranges are the Maritime, Ligurian, Rhaetian, Pennine, and Bernese Alps in the Western and Central Alps; and the Noric and Carnic Alps, the Hohe Tauern and Dolomites, and the Julian and Dinaric Alps in the Eastern Alps.

Peaks, Glaciers, Rivers. Mont Blanc, on the border between France and Italy, is the highest peak in the Alps, rising 15,781 feet (4,810 meters). The Matterhorn, on the Swiss-Italian border, although lower in elevation, is noted for its steep, knifelike ridges, which have long challenged mountain climbers. There are more than 1,200 Alpine glaciers, or slow-moving bodies of ice. The largest, the Aletsch Glacier, covers an area of about 66 square miles (171 square kilometers). Several important rivers, including the Rhine, the Rhône, and tributaries of the Po, rise in the Alps.

Plant and Animal Life. A variety of plant and wild animal life thrives at elevations below the highest summits. Grapes are cultivated in the southern valleys. Oak, beech, and other trees grow on the lower slopes, while evergreens are found at higher elevations. Above the tree line are meadows, often used for grazing livestock. The edelweiss is the most famous of Alpine flowers. The chamois (a kind of antelope), ibex (a wild goat), and golden eagle all live above the tree line.

Passes and Tunnels. There are about 50 Alpine passes, or natural gaps in the mountains. Some of these were used in older historical times by invading armies crossing into Italy. The best-known passes include the Brenner, between Austria and Italy; the Great St. Bernard and the Simplon, between Switzerland and Italy; the Montgenèvre, the Little St. Bernard, and the Mont Cenis, between France and Italy; the St. Gotthard in Switzerland; and the Arlberg in Austria.

Numerous railroad and highway tunnels have made travel across the Alps much easier. The Simplon Tunnel, extending for 12.3 miles (19.8 kilometers) between Switzerland and Italy, is one of the world's longest railroad tunnels. The St. Gotthard Road Tunnel in Switzerland, completed in 1980, is the world's longest highway tunnel, with a length of 10.1 miles (16.3 kilometers).

Reviewed by Daniel Jacobson
Michigan State University

ALUMINUM

In the 1800's, people already knew that aluminum was the most abundant metal in the earth's crust. They had even been able to extract the blush-white metal from its ores. But the cost of refining it was still so high that Emperor Napoleon III of France still had his finest dinner spoons made of it in the 1860's. Metallurgists were in the position of having discovered a great treasure house of extremely useful metal without having found the key that would unlock it. When a way was found to refine the metal cheaply in 1886, aluminum became an important part of nearly every industry in the world.

Aluminum makes up between 7 and 8 percent of the earth's crust. Although it is so abundant, its existence was not suspected for a long time. This is because it is never found in nature as a pure metal but is combined with other chemical elements in compounds that are very hard to break down.

Aluminum compounds are found in many minerals, and all clay contains aluminum. Many of the most beautiful precious stones are basically nothing but colored aluminum compounds. Rubies and sapphires, for example, are aluminum oxide with traces of other elements. Emeralds contain aluminum along with beryllium, chromium and silicon.

The most important ore of aluminum is bauxite, a type of clay. It generally contains from 40 to 60 percent aluminum oxide.

The existence of aluminum was predicted in 1808 by the English scientist Sir Humphry Davy. However, he was unable to solve the problem of extracting the metal from its ore. In 1825 the Danish scientist H. C. Oersted produced the first aluminum metal the world had ever seen—but in an amount too small even to conduct experiments. The German scientist Friedrich Wöhler succeeded in extracting aluminum in powder form in 1845 and made the first discoveries about aluminum's properties.

Aluminum's career as a luxury item ended in 1886 with the simultaneous discoveries of Charles M. Hall in the United States and Paul Héroult in France. The two men had independently hit upon the same solution to the problem of converting aluminum ore into the metal aluminum cheaply enough for everyday use.

The Hall-Héroult process is basically the same one used in today's two-step process of aluminum refining. Bauxite ore is refined to produce aluminum oxide, a white powder, which is also called alumina. Alumina in turn must be further processed to produce aluminum. It was this second step that held back aluminum production for so many years.

Hall and Héroult found that alumina could be dissolved in molten cryolite, an icy-looking mineral found in Greenland, and then broken down by passing an electric current through the molten mixture. The current separates the alumina into aluminum and oxygen. The aluminum settles at the bottom of the cell and is drawn off periodically. More alumina is added to keep the process going. About 2 pounds (0.9 kilogram) of alumina are needed to make 1 pound (0.45 kilogram) of aluminum metal.

Aluminum's many characteristics combine to make it suitable for many products. An important characteristic is its light weight. Aluminum weighs two thirds less than such common metals as iron, copper, nickel, or zinc. Its lightness makes aluminum useful in the manufacture of building materials, bus and truck bodies, and automotive and airplane parts. About 90 percent of the total weight of a typical four-engine aircraft is aluminum.

Aluminum also conducts electricity well. For this reason it has replaced copper for high-voltage electric transmission lines. Since it is lighter than copper, electric lines of aluminum need fewer supporting towers.

Because it is a good conductor of heat, aluminum makes good cooking utensils. If just one edge of an aluminum pan is heated,

---

FACTS ABOUT ALUMINUM

CHEMICAL SYMBOL: Al

ATOMIC WEIGHT: 26.98

SPECIFIC GRAVITY: 2.7 (a little more than 2½ times as heavy as water).

COLOR: silvery white with a bluish tinge.

PROPERTIES: soft and easily shaped; resists corrosion; nonmagnetic; good conductor of heat and electricity; forms compounds that are hard to break down.

OCCURRENCE: third most abundant element in the earth's crust (after oxygen and silicon); most abundant metal in the earth's crust.

CHIEF ORE: bauxite.

CHIEF SOURCES: Australia, Guinea, Jamaica, Brazil, Russia.

In England and certain other countries, aluminum is called aluminium.

the heat will spread evenly through the pan. With many other metals, "hot spots" that cause food to stick and burn may form.

Besides being a good conductor of heat, aluminum is also a good insulator. This is not as confusing as it seems. The metal's shiny surface reflects heat rays away.

Why doesn't aluminum rust? It would seem that aluminum's quickness to react with the oxygen in the air would make it subject to corrosion. But actually it is this very quickness to react with oxygen that protects aluminum against corrosion. When aluminum is exposed to the air, it immediately combines with some of the oxygen to form a thin, tough, colorless film that protects the metal against further chemical action and thus prevents rusting.

Aluminum also stands up well against most acids, but it is attacked by strong solutions of alkalies, such as lye and ammonia, and of salts, including common table salt. Salt solutions cause pitting and form a dull film on the metal. Aluminum boats that are used in salt water need a protective coating, usually of clear plastic. Aluminum cooking vessels do not usually show this pitting and dulling

because in most homes they are shined with abrasive pads after use.

Although aluminum is naturally light and flexible, it is not especially strong for a metal. There are two ways to increase its strength. One is by cold-working (hammering or rolling the metal at room temperature). This compresses the metal and makes it harder. When very high strength is needed, the other method—alloying—must be used.

The metals most frequently alloyed with aluminum are copper, manganese, nickel, magnesium, zinc, iron, and silicon. Because of its higher strength, most of the aluminum used for machine parts and for structural parts in airplanes, automobiles, and buildings is in the form of alloys.

To help ensure a sufficient supply of aluminum in the coming years, efforts are being made to recycle, or re-use, aluminum products such as soft-drink cans. In addition to conserving ore supplies, recycling uses much less energy than does refining.

ROBERT E. ABBOTT
Senior Associate Editor
Product Engineering Magazine

ALVAREZ, LUIS WALTER (1911–1988)

Luis Walter Alvarez is known for his research on subatomic particles—the tiny particles of matter that make up the atom. Alvarez's research improved our understanding of the forces that hold together the **nucleus**, or center, of the atom. These forces are considered to be among the strongest in the universe.

Alvarez was born on June 13, 1911, in San Francisco, California. He studied physics at the University of Chicago, from which he received his Ph.D. in 1936. He then went on to become a professor of physics at the University of California at Berkeley.

In 1941, the United States entered World War II. Many scientists wanted to help the war effort, and Alvarez, who was then working on microwave radar research, developed a type of radar system that was used to locate bomb-

ing targets, and a ground-controlled approach radar system that was used to land aircraft in bad weather. In 1943, Alvarez was asked to join the team of scientists at Los Alamos Scientific Laboratory in New Mexico that was developing the atomic bomb.

After the war, Alvarez returned to his study of the atom. With associates at the University of California, he developed the hydrogen **bubble chamber**, which he used to identify many subatomic particles. In 1968, he won the Nobel prize in physics for this research.

In 1980, he helped to publicize the theories of his son, the geologist Walter Alvarez, that a large asteroid collision with the Earth may have led to the extinction of the dinosaurs.

Alvarez died on September 1, 1988, in Berkeley, California.

RACHEL KRANZ
Editor, Biographies
The Young Adult Reader's Adviser
See also ATOMS.

ALZHEIMER'S DISEASE. See DISEASES (Descriptions of Some Diseases).

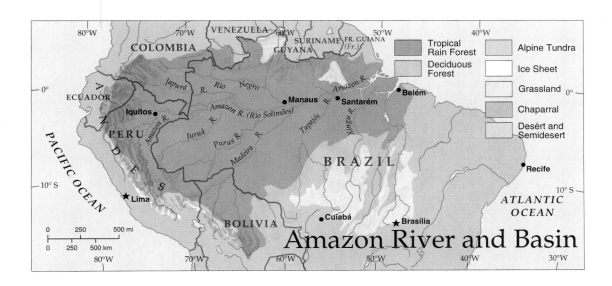

Amazon River and Basin

Tropical Rain Forest	Alpine Tundra
Deciduous Forest	Ice Sheet
	Grassland
	Chaparral
	Desert and Semidesert

AMAZON RIVER

The Amazon is South America's most important river and the second longest river in the world. Only the Nile, in Africa, is longer. The Amazon carries more water than the Mississippi, the Yangtze (the longest river in China), and the Nile together. In a single second the Amazon pours more than 55,000,000 gallons (200,000 cubic meters) of water into the Atlantic Ocean. This tremendous flow is caused by heavy tropical rains and melting snow in the Andes mountains. The Amazon's huge drainage basin—the world's largest—covers more than one third of the South American continent.

The River's Course. The Amazon is about 3,900 miles (6,276 kilometers) long. It begins high in the snow-fed Andean lakes of Peru, tumbles rapidly down the mountains, and then flows eastward across the low plains of Brazil before emptying into the Atlantic Ocean. On its journey the Amazon gathers additional water from hundreds of rivers. Some of its major branches are more than 1,240 miles (2,000 kilometers) in length. These include the Rio Negro and the Japurá, Juruá, Purus, Madeira, Tapajós, and Xingu rivers. In some places the river is so wide that one cannot see the opposite shore. During the rainy season the river frequently overflows its banks and floods the surrounding lowland areas.

The Amazon basin is only sparsely populated. Most of its inhabitants live along the course of the great river, which is their chief means of transportation.

Above: Timber is one of the Amazon basin's most valuable resources. The region also has deposits of gold, bauxite (aluminum ore), copper, tin, and other minerals.

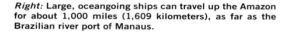

Right: Large, oceangoing ships can travel up the Amazon for about 1,000 miles (1,609 kilometers), as far as the Brazilian river port of Manaus.

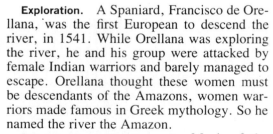

Exploration. A Spaniard, Francisco de Orellana, was the first European to descend the river, in 1541. While Orellana was exploring the river, he and his group were attacked by female Indian warriors and barely managed to escape. Orellana thought these women must be descendants of the Amazons, women warriors made famous in Greek mythology. So he named the river the Amazon.

Resources and Development. Much of the Amazon basin is sparsely populated. The region is covered with some of the world's densest rain forests, which are a source of valuable timber. There are rich deposits of gold, bauxite (aluminum ore), copper, tin, manganese, and iron ore. Several highways have been built, but the river remains a major form of transportation. Oceangoing ships can travel upstream about 1,000 miles (1,609 kilometers) to Manaus, in Brazil. Smaller vessels travel as far as the port of Iquitos, in Peru.

The Amazon basin has been called one of the earth's last frontiers. The eight countries of the Amazon basin—Bolivia, Brazil, Colombia, Ecuador, Guyana, Peru, Suriname, and Venezuela—signed the Treaty of Amazon Co-operation (called the Amazon Pact) in 1978. Under the terms of the treaty, these nations have agreed to jointly develop and share the great wealth of the region. However, because the Amazon basin is home to varieties of plants and animals found nowhere else on earth, many scientists have opposed large-scale development of the area.

Reviewed by DANIEL JACOBSON
Michigan State University

AMERICAN COLONIES. See THIRTEEN AMERICAN COLONIES.

AMERICAN LITERATURE

From the beginning, the literature of America has been created by the many voices of its diverse people. Before the Europeans came to settle in the 1500's and 1600's, the many tribes of Native Americans created a rich oral heritage of songs, chants, and tales. With the arrival of white settlers, America's formal literature began: first in travel books, then in religious writing, finally in the poems, novels, and plays that would eventually record and reflect America's national development.

Over the past four centuries, as the country expanded politically and economically, literature has expressed the aspirations and achievements of all the races and creeds that make up the nation. What began as a small and elite literary culture on the eastern seaboard has grown to encompass a sprawling modern society. In spite of their differences, almost all Americans have shared a commitment to their country's democratic possibilities and a fascination with the meaning of American identity; these two themes have been recurrent topics in American literature.

▶ THE COLONIAL EXPERIENCE

Because the Indians did not practice writing, their ancient traditional material has not survived in its original form. (See feature, Indian Art and Culture, on this page.) It was left to the white explorers and colonists, who brought books and writing with them from England, France, and Spain, to begin the written record that has become American literature.

Promotional Literature

European settlers came to the New World for many reasons. Some were seeking adventure or commercial profit, while others were fleeing religious persecution. All these men and women were urged on by a literature of exploration and promotion—the earliest American advertising—which pictured the New World as a fruitful garden, a land overflowing with abundance and opportunity. Captain John Smith's attractive account of Virginia (1608) was the first book written in English in America, and his *Description of New England* followed several years later.

Other writers, such as Francis Higginson, also produced books, pamphlets, and poems celebrating the golden promise of America.

Throughout the first one hundred years of English settlement, beginning with Jamestown in 1607, most of the literary achievement of the colonies was the work of New England's Puritans. The Puritans were the best educated of the English colonists and the most firmly committed to literary activity. It was the Puritan settlers of Massachusetts who founded the colonies' first institute of higher learning. Harvard College (now Harvard University) was founded in 1636, just a few years after the colony itself was established. The first printing press was set up at Harvard in 1639, and the first book was published there the following year.

Indian Art and Culture

Indians lived on the American continent for hundreds of years before European settlers began to arrive in the 1500's and 1600's. They created a rich oral literature: songs, chants, fables, and stories. Because of language differences, it is hard for English-speaking readers to appreciate Indian literature. However, the two songs printed here in translation suggest the subtle power of the originals:

Love Song
A loon I thought it was
But it was
My love's
Splashing oar.
(Chippewa)

Song of Failure
A wolf
I considered myself,
But the owls are hooting
And the night
I fear.
(Teton Sioux)

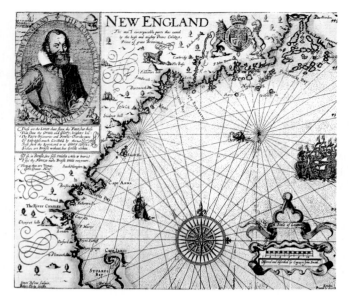

A portrait of English explorer John Smith and a map of the Massachusetts coastline appeared in his *Description of New England*, published in 1616.

Puritan Prose Writing

In their own opinion, the most valuable possession that Puritan men and women brought with them from England was their religion. Above all, they placed their faith in the Bible, which they believed contained the revealed word of God. At the center of their worship, they wanted to hear the Bible read and interpreted. The preacher was thus a leading figure in the community, and the sermons that were preached in Puritan meetinghouses became the first real literary texts produced in the English-speaking New World. The sermons followed a standard format, in which a phrase from the Bible was read and then explained at great length—some sermons went on for more than two hours. The most famous of all the Puritan preachers was Jonathan Edwards, who served as minister of Northampton, Massachusetts, for 24 years. He wrote important philosophical books, including *The Freedom of the Will* (1754), but he is best remembered for a sermon he preached in 1741, "Sinners in the Hands of an Angry God."

Religion was also the major theme of other Puritan writing, including the thousands of diaries produced by men and women alike. Their deep concern with sin and salvation led the Puritans into a habit of daily spiritual examination, which they recorded in their diaries. Part of the Puritan influence on later American literature was this preoccupation with the self. Thomas Shepard, Michael Wigglesworth, and many other Puritan diarists filled daily journals with the details of each day's religious striving. Over and over, they return to a few simple but profound themes: God's sovereign power and the complete dependence of each person on God's mysterious choices.

Puritan minister Jonathan Edwards wrote on religious and philosophical subjects. He is most famous for his sermon "Sinners in the Hands of an Angry God," which he preached to his congregation in 1741. It expressed the Puritan belief that eternal torment awaited sinners after death.

Many of the Puritan diaries are grim and relentless, shrill warnings against any sort of human pleasure. At least one, however, written by Samuel Sewall, reveals a more modern point of view. While still respectful of Puritan values, the diary also introduces newer ideas of happiness and self-fulfillment. Sewall was a prosperous Massachusetts merchant whose long life spanned the end of the 1600's and the early decades of the 1700's. He presided over the Salem witchcraft trials (and later apologized for sentencing convicted "witches" to hang), and he wrote the first antislavery pamphlet in America, *The Selling of Joseph* (1700). Sewall's diary is one of the major works of early American literature. The daily entries provide a vivid self-portrait as well as a valuable record of daily life in colonial New England.

Along with their sermons and diaries, the Puritans also produced a large number of histories. These, too, are important literary texts. Like all the other writing of the Puritans, their histories were anchored in religious belief. *Of Plymouth Plantation* (1630–50), by William Bradford, *The Wonder-Working Providence of Sion's Savior in New England* (1653), by Edward Johnson, and *Magnalia Christi Americana* ("Christ's Great Deeds in America"; 1702), by Cotton Mather, all shared a God-centered view of history. The Puritan historians believed that human events acted out a divine plan—and they believed that they and their fellow Christians were at the heart of that plan.

Puritan Poetry

The men and women of colonial New England also wrote a great deal of poetry, though most of it was conventional and dull. Only a few Puritan poets rose above mediocrity, and only two, Anne Bradstreet and Edward Taylor, achieved real distinction.

Anne Bradstreet immigrated to New England with her husband in 1630 and lived the rest of her life in Massachusetts. She bore eight children and supervised a large, relatively prosperous household. Because she was a woman, she faced opposition as a writer, but her book, *The Tenth Muse, Lately Sprung Up in America* (1650), was the first volume of poems published by a resident of the New World. She wrote a number of long, formal epics. Her best poems, however, are briefer

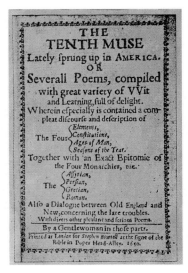

The Tenth Muse, a collection of poems by New England writer Anne Bradstreet, won praise in the American colonies and in England when it was published in 1650.

and more personal verses on her family and her daily domestic obligations. She wrote love poems to her husband, as well as other poems that celebrated the births and mourned the deaths of her children and grandchildren.

For 58 years, from 1671 until the end of his life, Edward Taylor served as minister of the frontier town of Westfield, Massachusetts. Nearly all his poems are closely connected to his preaching and devotions; more than two hundred, called *Meditations*, were written in response to the same biblical texts on which he was preaching. Taken as a group, they are among the most remarkable verse sequences in American literature. They draw on familiar religious traditions, combining the images of the Bible with the language of everyday colonial life. They tell of the encounter between God and the individual soul, often achieving great emotional power through the use of elaborate metaphors and dramatic action.

Southern Writing

Very little significant literature appeared in the South during the 1600's and 1700's. Ebenezer Cooke wrote a funny poem, "The Sot-Weed Factor" (1708), a savage attack on America's rude wilderness conditions. A more important text is the diary of William Byrd II, a wealthy Virginia planter who owned the largest library in the colonies and thought of himself as simply a transplanted Englishman. His diary, unlike those written by the Puritans, contains little reference to God or salvation. Rather, Byrd's diary records his everyday routine: what time he got up, what he ate and read, the journeys he took. Byrd's daily entries provide glimpses into middle-class life in Virginia, from farming practices to relations between masters and slaves.

Benjamin Franklin

By the late 1700's, America's several colonies had existed as dependencies of England for almost two hundred years. America was growing rapidly in population and economic importance, but its literary culture lagged behind. The first American whose work and writing received international recognition was Benjamin Franklin. A scientist, diplomat, businessman, and writer, he rose to success from humble beginnings and seemed to embody the American dream of opportunity.

Franklin's writing, from the humorous "Dogood Papers" (1722) he published as a teenager, through the hugely popular *Poor Richard's Almanac* (1733–38), is always marked by shrewd common sense and independent thought. His *Autobiography,* written between 1771 and 1788, is one of the landmarks of American literature. Franklin's self-portrait, written in a strong, straightforward style, captures the accents of real speech. That style is his chief legacy to the nation's literary tradition.

Political Writing

As America moved toward independence, literature reflected the changing political situation. Some of the most important writing of this period was produced in support of revo-

American Literature 1700–1900

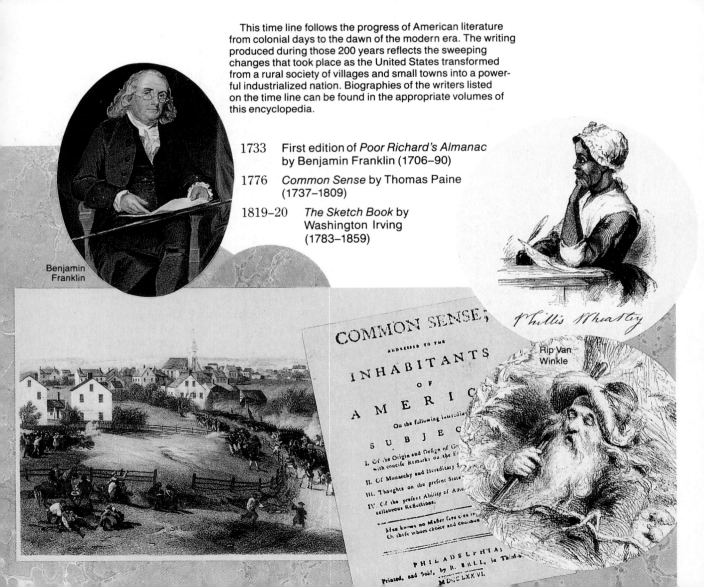

This time line follows the progress of American literature from colonial days to the dawn of the modern era. The writing produced during those 200 years reflects the sweeping changes that took place as the United States transformed from a rural society of villages and small towns into a powerful industrialized nation. Biographies of the writers listed on the time line can be found in the appropriate volumes of this encyclopedia.

1733   First edition of *Poor Richard's Almanac* by Benjamin Franklin (1706–90)

1776   *Common Sense* by Thomas Paine (1737–1809)

1819–20   *The Sketch Book* by Washington Irving (1783–1859)

Benjamin Franklin

Phillis Wheatley

Rip Van Winkle

COMMON SENSE;
ADDRESSED TO THE
INHABITANTS
OF
AMERIC
On the following interesting
SUBJEC

I. Of the Origin and Design of Go
with concise Remarks on the E

II. Of Monarchy and Hereditary S

III. Thoughts on the present State

IV. Of the present Ability of Ame
cellaneous Reflections.

Man knows no Master fave crea
Or those whom choice and common

PHILADELPHIA;
Printed, and Sold, by R. BELL, in Third
MDCCLXXVI.

lution. Thomas Paine's *Common Sense,* published on the eve of the Revolutionary War in early 1776, sold more than 100,000 copies in two months and helped to lead the nation toward its demands for independence. The letters of men and women like John and Abigail Adams, Thomas Jefferson, and James Madison eloquently recorded a dangerous and pivotal period in history.

Out of the continuous discussion and debate emerged the Declaration of Independence and the Constitution, two documents of unequaled importance in political history, which have also earned a high place in American literature. The Declaration, which was officially submitted by a committee, was in fact mostly the work of one man, Thomas Jefferson. Although he was a southern aristocrat and slaveholder, Jefferson established himself as one of the nation's most articulate domestic voices. His library of about six thousand volumes served as the foundation of the Library of Congress, and his writings and building designs strongly influenced America's taste in architecture. His *Notes on the State of Virginia* (1784) made important contributions to American natural science.

Early Black Writing

The Constitution demonstrated the limits as well as the strengths of American democracy. Women were denied the vote, and black

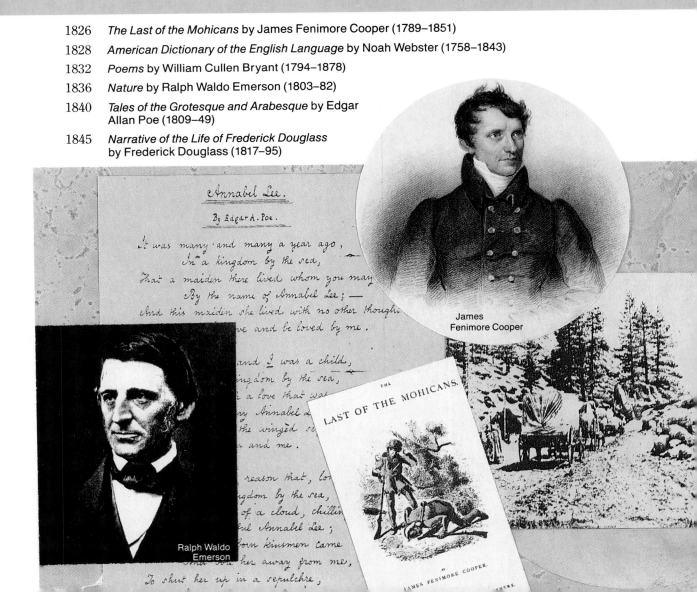

1826   *The Last of the Mohicans* by James Fenimore Cooper (1789–1851)

1828   *American Dictionary of the English Language* by Noah Webster (1758–1843)

1832   *Poems* by William Cullen Bryant (1794–1878)

1836   *Nature* by Ralph Waldo Emerson (1803–82)

1840   *Tales of the Grotesque and Arabesque* by Edgar Allan Poe (1809–49)

1845   *Narrative of the Life of Frederick Douglass* by Frederick Douglass (1817–95)

James Fenimore Cooper

Ralph Waldo Emerson

LAST OF THE MOHICANS

JAMES FENIMORE COOPER.

Americans were defined as property rather than human beings. Slavery had flourished from the earliest colonial settlements: the first slave ship arrived in Virginia in 1619, the year before the *Mayflower* brought the Pilgrims to Plymouth. Slavery was supported by the Constitution, but the debate over the place of black people would occupy an increasingly central role in the debate over the nation's identity throughout the 1800's and 1900's.

Much of African-American culture mingled the African tribal heritage with artistic forms adapted from white European traditions. Phillis Wheatley, the only black writer who gained national recognition in the colonial years, accepted a cooperative relationship to white so-ciety and religion. Her volume, *Poems on Various Occasions,* published in 1773, contains verse that is conventional in style and safely patriotic and Christian in sentiment.

An altogether different tone can be found in the work of Olaudah Equiano, known as Gustavus Vassa. Taken from Africa and enslaved as a child, Equiano eventually earned his freedom and became a leading figure in the abolition movement. His life story, *The Interesting Narrative of the Life of Olaudah Equiano, or Gustavus Vassa, the African* (1789), is an early and important black autobiography. The book contains unforgettable scenes that reveal the cruelty of slavery and the distance that still separated America's democratic ideals from

Oliver Wendell Holmes

Herman Melville

UNCLE TOM'S CABIN;
LIFE AMONG THE LOWLY.

Walt Whitman

reality. (See feature, Slave Narratives, on the following page.)

Literary Nationalists

In the years before and after the Revolution, writers and intellectuals tried to define America's cultural identity. In *Letters from an American Farmer* (1782), St. John de Crevecoeur asked, "What is an American?," and answered his own question by appealing to "a new race of men." One of the busiest groups of literary nationalists in the late 1700's was a band of New England poets and essayists known as the Connecticut (or Hartford) Wits. These men, including such figures as Timothy Dwight, Lemuel Hopkins, and painter John Trumbull, produced satires, epics, and hymns to the New World landscape.

Joel Barlow, one of the youngest members of this group, was more radical in politics and more talented as a writer. He believed that his most important work was *The Columbiad* (1807), a long and tedious narrative in couplets that celebrates American history from the time of Columbus. In fact, modern readers find the best of Barlow's many poems to be *The Hasty Pudding* (1793), a mock-epic in praise of the cornmeal mush eaten in farmhouses all across the nation. In a series of humorous scenes, Barlow contrasts America's plain but wholesome food with the tasteless delicacies favored in Europe.

1866   *Snow-Bound* by John Greenleaf Whittier (1807–92)

1868–69   *Little Women* by Louisa May Alcott (1832–88)

1884   *Adventures of Huckleberry Finn* by Mark Twain (1835–1910)

1890   *Poems* by Emily Dickinson (1830–86)

1895   *The Red Badge of Courage* by Stephen Crane (1871–1900)

1903   *The Ambassadors* by Henry James (1843–1916)

Huckleberry Finn

John Greenleaf Whittier

Emily Dickinson

Slave Narratives

Autobiographies written by ex-slaves made a major contribution both to the politics and the literature of the 1800's. No books told more about the reality of the slave system than the personal narratives of such men and women as Moses Roper and Harriet Jacobs. The most famous of these autobiographies was written by Frederick Douglass (pictured), who was also the leading figure in the black abolitionist movement before the Civil War. Douglass' *Narrative* (1845) is the eloquent story of his own successful quest for freedom. It inspired thousands of Americans, white as well as black, to join together to demand the end of slavery.

Such comparisons were common in the early years of the Republic. They form the entire theme of *The Contrast,* a play that Royall Tyler wrote and staged in 1784. It was the first significant play written in America and the first to be professionally produced.

Early Fiction

The Power of Sympathy (1789), by William Hill Brown, is usually identified as the first American novel. It was written in imitation of English sentimental fiction of the time. So, too, were the works of other writers in the early Republic. *Charlotte Temple* (1791), by Susanna Haswell Rowson, one of the first American best-sellers, and *The Coquette*

(1797), by Hannah Foster, are both melodramatic tales involving seduction, desertion, and death. Charles Brockden Brown brought the mystery and violence of the European "gothic novel" to American settings in such novels as *Wieland* (1798) and *Arthur Huntley* (1801). *Modern Chivalry* (1815), by Hugh Henry Brackenridge, is a huge book that follows its characters across the American backwoods.

Among the most notable southern fiction was the work of William Gilmore Simms, whose *Yemassee* (1835) includes passages of realistic description and lively dialogue. A more sinister southern literary form was the "plantation novel," which defended slavery as a benevolent institution. John Pendleton Kennedy published the first such novel, *Swallow Barn,* in 1832.

Irving and Cooper

Two New Yorkers created some of the most memorable characters and stories in early American fiction. Washington Irving published his *Sketch Book* in 1820, which introduced the unforgettable Ichabod Crane and Rip Van Winkle, both of whom have become enduring parts of America's folklore. Irving's work was a triumph in Europe as well as the United States. The English novelist William Thackeray called him the first "ambassador" from "the New World of Letters to the Old."

The first novel by James Fenimore Cooper also appeared in 1820. Son of a wealthy landholder, Cooper was skeptical of democracy, but he invented several of the themes that would occupy the attention of later American novelists. *The Spy* (1821) is a melodrama about the Revolution, while *The Pilot* (1823) is a sea story based on the career of John Paul Jones. The most important of Cooper's novels are the five volumes in the Leatherstocking series, beginning with *The Pioneers* (1823) and including *The Last of the Mohicans* (1826) and *The Deerslayer* (1841). In these novels, Cooper dealt with the rapid westward march of white settlement and the destruction of the frontier. He also presented an idealized portrait of the woodsman. Natty Bumppo, badly dressed and poorly educated but brave and honest, is a figure of American myth.

Romanticism

Romanticism was a movement in art, music, and literature that began in the late

1700's and continued into the first half of the 1800's. It was a reaction against the Age of Reason of the 1700's, a period when reason was stressed as the best way to discover truth. In contrast, romanticism emphasized emotion and individual feelings over reason and logic. Followers of romanticism were drawn to the beauty of unspoiled nature. William Cullen Bryant was the first American poet to respond to the new movement. His poems "Thanatopsis" (1821) and "A Forest Hymn" (1825) spoke of nature with affection and reverence.

A more extreme kind of romanticism can be found in the work of Edgar Allan Poe. Poe earned very little success in his brief life, but he has had a great influence on European as well as American literature in the years since his death. His poetic theories were ahead of their time, insisting on beauty and the emotional nature of poetry. He pioneered in the mystery story, and the detective he invented, C. Auguste Dupin, looks forward to a later fictional detective, Sherlock Holmes. Poe's tales of the grotesque, such as "The Black Cat," "The Pit and the Pendulum," and "The Fall of the House of Usher," have fascinated generations of readers. No later writer has created images of fear and pain that are more vivid than Poe's.

▶ THE EARLY 1800's

New England Poets

In the years before the Civil War, Boston, which traced its intellectual leadership back to the Puritans, remained the literary capital of the United States. In particular, the poets Henry Wadsworth Longfellow, Oliver Wendell Holmes, and John Greenleaf Whittier enjoyed national admiration.

Longfellow was professor of modern languages at Harvard for twenty years. His textbooks, as well as his volumes of poetry, were highly regarded in Europe as well as America. His long narrative *Song of Hiawatha* (1855), modeled on a Finnish epic, was once among the country's most popular poems. Longfellow's verse was always skillful, but his subjects tended to be familiar and his techniques were usually quite conventional.

Oliver Wendell Holmes, who was for many years professor of anatomy at Harvard, was a respected essayist and poet. He had a great talent for conversation, which he demon-

strated in his most familiar book, *The Autocrat of the Breakfast Table* (1858).

John Greenleaf Whittier, the son of poor Massachusetts farmers, had no college education. He supported himself as a laborer and journalist and wrote a large number of popular poems celebrating the landscape and simple people of rural New England. For many years, he was also active in the cause of abolition, and he wrote many essays and poems demanding the end of slavery. In this cause, he was joined by other prominent New England writers, especially William Lloyd Garrison and James Russell Lowell.

Emerson, Fuller, and Thoreau

The 1830's and 1840's were the years of what was called "the American newness," and it was Ralph Waldo Emerson who gave that phrase its meaning. A graduate of Harvard and a minister, Emerson abandoned Christianity in his twenties and spent the rest of his long life proclaiming a new American philosophy. Above all, Emerson believed in the essential goodness of nature and the freedom of the individual. (See feature, Transcendentalism, on the following page.)

In 1836, Emerson published *Nature,* a small book but one of the most influential in American literature. In *Nature,* Emerson demanded that his fellow citizens reject the authority of the past and of Europe to create their own genuine culture. He repeated this argument the following year, in a lecture at Harvard on "The American Scholar." This speech has come to be regarded as America's declaration of literary independence. Emerson declared that every age must write its own books, and that each new generation must see the world for itself.

A remarkable group of men and women gathered around Emerson, including Margaret Fuller and Henry David Thoreau. Fuller was the first editor of the transcendentalist magazine *The Dial* and the author of a landmark book in the history of feminism, *Woman in the Nineteenth Century* (1845). She shared Emerson's anger at American materialism, but she went much further than Emerson in criticizing the inequalities of American society.

Thoreau also shared many of Emerson's ideas, including his belief in the spiritual power of nature and the need for individual self-reliance. On the Fourth of July, 1845, he

Transcendentalism

Transcendentalism is best known as a movement of New England writers and philosophers, led by Ralph Waldo Emerson and Henry David Thoreau (pictured), that occurred in the 1800's. Transcendentalism covered a wide range of ideas, but its central concepts remain influential: Transcendentalists' belief in the divinity of the human soul and the value of individual thought led to reforms in religion and education. Their philosophy of living in harmony with nature has become an accepted part of American thinking. Thoreau's concept of civil disobedience — the right to protest unjust laws by disobeying them — was adopted by such later reformers as Martin Luther King, Jr.

moved into a cabin he had built on the shores of Walden Pond in Massachusetts. He spent the next two years living alone—reading and writing, eating the vegetables he grew in his own garden and the fish he caught in the pond. Years later, he told the story of that experience in his most famous work, *Walden* (1854). The book is also a lesson in values, in which Thoreau argues for simple living and rejects the dependence of modern civilization on technology and machines. *Walden* continues to influence American attitudes toward nature and the environment.

Histories

In the 1800's, history was regarded as a form of literature. The country was still relatively young, but the search for a distinctive national identity included the rediscovery of the American past. Some historians wrote

about the lives of individual heroes, such as Christopher Columbus, Thomas Jefferson, and especially George Washington. Other writers tried to include the whole nation; they wrote large narratives, often in several volumes, that treated American history as an epic tale. The most important of these books were *The History of the Conquest of Mexico* (1843), by William Hickling Prescott, *The Oregon Trail* (1849), by Francis Parkman, and the monumental *History of the United States* (1834–76), which George Bancroft worked on for half of his long life. These books express quite different attitudes toward the United States and its democratic politics, but all of them accept the assumption that America had a special destiny.

Nathaniel Hawthorne

The American past also provided Nathaniel Hawthorne with his main subject. His own ancestors had been among the Puritans who settled in early Massachusetts, and he was both fascinated and horrified by these grim, self-righteous religious crusaders. He had lived for a while in the utopian (model) community of Brook Farm, but that experiment was a failure and only convinced him that human nature was essentially flawed. He wrote one novel satirizing Brook Farm, called *The Blithedale Romance* (1852), but all his work is colored by his pessimism. He wrote only four novels, but one of them, *The Scarlet Letter* (1850), is among the major works in American literature. This sad account of human weakness and intolerance is set in Salem of the 1600's, a shadowy, mysterious landscape that is at the same time quite real.

Herman Melville

Herman Melville was one of Hawthorne's chief admirers, but his own work is much more concerned with the American present than its past. The years before the Civil War were a period of unprecedented expansion and exploration. The American frontier moved westward, and American ships sailed all the oceans of the world. That seafaring inspired a great many novels and travel books, including *Two Years Before the Mast* (1840) by Richard Henry Dana, Jr., a memoir of Dana's personal experiences as a common sailor.

Melville also worked as a seaman. He shipped on the whaler *Acushnet* in 1841 for an

18-month voyage to the South Pacific. This journey gave him the material for his first books, *Typee* (1846) and *Omoo* (1847), which were popular travel books. But Melville's voyaging also prepared him for his greatest novel, *Moby-Dick* (1851), in which the hunt for the white whale becomes a vast symbolic quest. The *Pequod*'s Captain Ahab, one of the most memorable characters in American literature, leads his men to their doom through the sheer strength of his will.

Moby-Dick was a commercial failure, as were the rest of Melville's writings. His novels, stories, and poems would only begin to receive recognition in the 1900's. He spent the last several decades of his life working as a customs inspector in the port of New York. During those years, he wrote little. However, one of his late works, *Billy Budd* (discovered and published after his death), which tells of an essentially decent man overtaken by tragedy, is among his masterpieces.

Whitman and Dickinson

America's two greatest poets were Walt Whitman and Emily Dickinson. Although they lived at the same time, their lives and their poetry were different in almost every respect.

Whitman lived most of his life in New York City, Long Island, and Camden, New Jersey. As a young man, he worked in dozens of different jobs, from carpenter to schoolteacher to journalist; in the Civil War, he served as a nurse for wounded soldiers. Out of his wide experience, he invented a radically new kind of poetry, using very little rhyme or conventional meter, which influenced all later generations of American writers. He said that the United States were themselves the greatest poem. Whitman wrote about himself as a way of writing about America and the nation's democratic beliefs. In the opening lines of his most famous poem, called "Song of Myself" (1855), he declared:

I celebrate myself and sing myself,
And what I assume you shall assume,
For every atom belonging to me as good belongs to you.

Emily Dickinson lived her entire life in Amherst, Massachusetts. Much of her poetry is based on the ordinary events that filled her daily life: housekeeping, gardening, reading, conversation. She had a sharp sense of humor, but she was also fascinated with death: nearly 600 of her 1,775 poems have to do with dying and death and funerals. Dickinson's poems are typically short, many of them only 8 to 16 lines. However, she compressed a great range of emotional experience into her verse.

Stowe, Lincoln, and the Civil War

In the 1840's and 1850's, the debate over slavery became the most serious crisis facing the United States. Politicians such as Senators Daniel Webster of Massachusetts and Henry Clay of Kentucky tried to find grounds for compromise, but the divisions between North and South grew increasingly bitter. Northern opposition to slavery was significantly hardened by the publication of *Uncle Tom's Cabin* (1852), which proved to be the most popular and the most influential novel published in America during the 1800's. The book's author, Harriet Beecher Stowe, was the daughter and wife of ministers. She had seen the evils of slavery firsthand, and she was committed to abolition. Abraham Lincoln said that *Uncle Tom's Cabin* started the Civil War; that was not literally true, but the novel did serve to crystallize the North's opposition to slavery.

The Civil War itself produced one great writer: President Abraham Lincoln. He had little formal schooling, but he read widely to educate himself. Like his personal style, his writing was plainspoken, earthy, and humorous. At the same time, he maintained a quiet dignity that helped the nation to endure the most serious crisis in its history. His speeches, including "The Gettysburg Address" and the Second Inaugural, are documents of supreme importance to American literature and politics.

▶THE LATER 1800's

The years following the Civil War were a period of unprecedented economic growth. The South had been devastated, but in the North, industry and prosperity increased greatly. Cities grew tremendously in size. For example, in the four decades from 1860 to 1900, New York City grew from 750,000 people to 3.5 million. The nation's population, including millions of immigrants, rapidly expanded westward. The new railroad system linked the most distant parts of the country in an efficient transportation network. New fortunes were created; men such as Cornelius

Vanderbilt, John D. Rockefeller, and J. P. Morgan became familiar figures in the daily press. Because of the country's fascination with wealth and material values, these years were sometimes called the "Gilded Age."

James and Twain

Many writers and artists found the culture of America to be unfriendly, anti-intellectual, and even uncivilized. As a result, several of them actually left the United States for longer or shorter periods to live and work in Europe. The most famous of these early expatriates was Henry James, one of the major novelists of the late 1800's and early 1900's. James used the contrast between Europe and America, which he called the "international theme," as a central subject in many of his stories and novels. He was especially interested in the psychology of his characters, and he employed a subtle prose style in order to reveal the inner life of his heroes and heroines. He also developed theories of fiction that would influence later generations of writers.

Unlike James, Mark Twain had begun as a poor boy and had worked in dozens of different jobs before finding his career as a writer. Although he believed in the promise of democracy, he was a stern critic of American society. His masterpiece, *The Adventures of*

Henry James lived in England for many years. His novels often contrast the values of the young United States with the age-old traditions of Europe.

Huckleberry Finn (1884), is a brilliant comedy, but it also contains a strong attack on the slave system and the corruption of national ideals. Like all of Twain's best novels, including *The Adventures of Tom Sawyer* (1876), *Huckleberry Finn* employs a strong and believable colloquial (conversational) English. Twain said that "the soul of the people, the life of the people" was in their everyday speech, and his own greatest achievement was in his literary use of the ordinary language of America's people.

Frontier Humor

Twain's style grew out of the tall tales and frontier humor of the Old Southwest (a region stretching from Georgia to Missouri). The isolation and lawlessness of the frontier gave rise to an oral tradition of jokes and stories that eventually made its way into print. Some of the major humorists were Augustus Baldwin Longstreet, George Washington Harris, and Bret Harte. Harte's stories, such as "The Luck of Roaring Camp" (1868) and "The Outcasts of Poker Flat" (1869), were vivid portrayals of life in the mining camps of the California gold rush.

Realism

The emergence of the frontier humorists, who came from the West and South, demonstrated that American literature was becoming a more national achievement. Another important writer from the Midwest was William Dean Howells, who was born in Ohio and who eventually became one of the most influential novelists and editors of the late 1800's. In his fiction as well as his essays, Howells spoke as the champion of a new realism, which took ordinary, middle-class life as its subject. His many books include *The Rise of Silas Lapham* (1885) and *A Hazard of New Fortunes* (1890).

The years after the Civil War produced many important realist writers, including Rebecca Harding Davis, Edward Eggleston, and Hamlin Garland. Davis' "Life in the Iron Mills," which was published in the *Atlantic Monthly* magazine in 1861, was an angry work that revealed the oppression of workers. Eggleston's *Hoosier Schoolmaster* (1871) was set among the common people of Indiana, while Garland's *Main-Travelled Roads* (1891) exposed the hard and bitter lives of farmers and villagers in the Midwest.

New England Women Writers

New England continued to produce important writers in the later 1800's, including a group of remarkable women: Rose Terry Cooke, Mary E. Wilkins Freeman, and Sarah Orne Jewett. Each of these women, in different ways, explored the narrow, rural lives of men and women who had been left behind in the great changes that followed the Civil War.

Cooke's stories emphasized the loneliness and poverty of New England life. Freeman was especially interested in the sufferings of women. Her stories, collected in such volumes as *A Humble Romance* (1887) and *A New England Nun* (1891), portrayed the effects of isolation and outworn traditions on individual lives. Jewett emphasized the relationships among women that help them to cope and survive. In her masterpiece, *The Country of the Pointed Firs* (1896), men are mostly absent. The story centers on the daily lives of women, whose quiet activities—gardening, knitting, quilting, visiting, talking, praying—have replaced the more familiar adventures of male fictional heroes.

Southern Writing

Much of the literature produced by white writers in the South after the Civil War looked back affectionately at plantation life before the war. There were significant exceptions, including the work of George Washington Cable, Lafcadio Hearn, and Kate Chopin. Cable, who served in the Confederate army, later became a spokesman for black rights. His major novel, *The Grandissimes* (1880), was an attack on the racism and moral hypocrisy of the South.

Hearn was born in Greece and lived for a while in New Orleans before settling permanently in Japan. One of his early books, *Gombo Zhebes* (1885), was a collection of Creole proverbs. It was one of the earliest attempts to preserve American folk tales and treat them seriously.

Kate Chopin was born in St. Louis and also lived for a while in New Orleans. The mother of six children, she was widowed at the age of 30 and supported herself with her writing. Her most successful work, collected in *Bayou Folk* (1894) and *A Night in Acadia* (1897), was a series of sketches based on the Creole people and customs, which she had observed while she lived in New Orleans. Her tales provide vivid glimpses of the passion that lies beneath the surface of respectability. Her masterwork, *The Awakening* (1899), sympathetically explores the emotions and desires of its heroine.

Naturalism

The tremendous economic and political changes of the late 1800's were accompanied by a philosophy of competition and rugged individualism. Sometimes called "social Darwinism," this philosophy argued that human relations involved an endless struggle, in which only the "fittest" survived. Traditional concepts of justice and morality were threatened by a harsher view of human life in which individual choice mattered less than heredity and environment.

One literary outcome of this new point of view was the movement known as naturalism. Influenced by such European writers as Emile Zola and Gustave Flaubert, naturalism depicted men and women as controlled by instincts or passion, helpless in the face of economic and social circumstances.

Two of the major American naturalist writers were Stephen Crane and Frank Norris. Crane's poems and fiction continually assert the cruelty and indifference of the universe. *Maggie: A Girl of the Streets* (1893), which is set in the slums of New York's Lower East Side, tells the pitiable story of a young girl whose poverty drives her into prostitution, despair, and death. Crane's most famous novel, *The Red Badge of Courage* (1895), strips away the patriotic feeling surrounding the Civil War to reveal the horror of war's reality. The novel's young hero, Henry Fleming, experiences battle as confused, terrifying, and ultimately meaningless. Crane called the novel "a psychological portrait of fear." As such, it is a brilliant success.

Like Crane, Frank Norris believed that force ruled human lives. His major work was a projected three-volume "epic of wheat," which would take in the whole nation and its economic life. Only the first two volumes were completed before Norris' death, but the first of them, *The Octopus* (1901), is his chief work. Loosely based on California history, the novel is mainly a study in the power of destiny. In Norris' view, nature is a vast machine, and human beings are insignificant atoms in a large, mysterious design. It was a view widely shared as the 1800's ended.

Shortly after the turn of the century, Henry Adams said that, in the year 1900, "history broke in halves." He made the statement in his autobiography, which he called his *Education* (1907), a book that examines the sense of complete separation that divided the 1800's from the 1900's. What Adams had in mind was the transformation of the United States from a politically insignificant and agricultural society of villages and small towns into the world's leading industrial and military power. Technology, immigration, and the growth of large cities permanently changed the nature of American life. By 1900, the world of Henry Adams' childhood had disappeared.

Wharton and Dreiser

The city itself became a major subject of fiction and poetry. Novelists as different as Edith Wharton and Theodore Dreiser shared a deep interest in America's new urban life.

Wharton was the child of a socially prominent family in New York City, and many of her books reflect that background. Her finest book was *The House of Mirth* (1905). This novel, one of Wharton's earliest, traces the career of a poor but ambitious young woman whose failure in a money-driven society leads her to despair and death. Throughout the rest of her long career, Wharton wrote dozens of novels and stories in which her characters are defeated by the power of social convention.

Theodore Dreiser, who came from Indiana, grew up in poverty. His parents were German immigrants, and his books reveal his lifelong interest in the fate of poor and outcast people. His first novel, *Sister Carrie* (1900), was a landmark in American literature. Set in Chicago and New York, the novel provides the fullest and most realistic portrait of city life that any writer had yet created—from glamorous restaurants and theaters to sweat shops and tenements. The book's heroine is a poor girl who yearns for money and comfort. A creature of her desires, she is typical of all Dreiser's characters.

The Mass Media and the Muckrakers

At the turn of the century, new printing technologies made it possible to publish magazines and newspapers much faster and more cheaply than in the past. This was the period when the modern "mass media" developed, including hundreds of weekly and monthly magazines, and daily newspapers that sold as many as a million copies. Publishers competed ruthlessly with one another for readers by cutting prices and by introducing special features.

Some of the most important journalists were called "muckrakers." These were a group of men and women who investigated corruption and conspiracy in every aspect of American politics and business. They wrote articles on subjects ranging from oil companies and child labor to the life insurance industry and city government. Their exposés led to the passage of strong reform laws.

The most famous muckraking work was a novel, *The Jungle,* by Upton Sinclair. Published in 1906, this book shocked readers all over the country with its revelations about the Chicago meat-packing industry. The novel showed that the meat Americans were eating was unhealthy and that the workers in the packinghouses were severely exploited.

Willa Cather

Willa Cather began her career as an editor of *McClure's,* one of the principal muckraking magazines. Born in Virginia and raised in frontier Nebraska, Cather often used the Midwest and Southwest in her fiction. Her best novels, including *O Pioneers!* (1913) and *My Antonia* (1918), commemorate the efforts of prairie people, especially women, to maintain their dignity and find fulfillment despite the endless labor and harsh conditions of their lives. Much of her work looks back to an earlier America, in which values were supposedly simpler and more heroic.

Black Writing

For blacks, the early 1900's were a period of increased discrimination and oppression. In 1896, the Supreme Court had declared that segregation was legal. "Jim Crow" laws, which denied blacks equal access to education, employment, health care, and transportation, were passed throughout the South. The Ku Klux Klan, founded just after the Civil War, renewed its persecution of blacks; lynchings were a terrible feature of black life.

Black responses to this worsening racial situation were varied. Booker T. Washington, the most influential leader of his generation, argued for a gradual approach and for cooperation with whites. Washington's autobiogra-

Two writers of the early 1900's were Willa Cather and W. E. B. DuBois. Cather's novels chronicled the heroism of American pioneers, especially women. DuBois sought to combat racial prejudice and obtain equal opportunity for blacks through such writings as *The Souls of Black Folk* (1903).

phy, *Up From Slavery* (1901), tells the story of his progress from poverty and illiteracy to the presidency of Tuskegee University, a position that gave him international prestige.

W. E. B. DuBois felt that Washington was self-serving and compromised too often with white demands. DuBois, who was born in Massachusetts and earned his doctorate at Harvard, argued for a more militant position. He wrote many essays and books in the course of his long life, all of them devoted to combating white racism and demanding equal opportunity for blacks in all areas of American life. One of DuBois' most famous books was *The Souls of Black Folk* (1903). It was here that he gave his famous description of the "double consciousness" of American blacks: "an American, a Negro; two souls, two thoughts . . . two warring ideals in one dark body."

Some of the other important black writers of the early 1900's included poet Paul Laurence Dunbar and Charles Waddell Chesnutt, a novelist and short-story writer. Chesnutt offered realistic portraits of slavery and of the years that followed the Civil War. His novels *The House Behind the Cedars* (1901) and *The Marrow of Tradition* (1901) suggested that life for blacks in the United States was getting worse rather than better.

Modernism

In the early years of the 1900's, many different groups were demanding reform and renewal: black writers, labor organizers, supporters of women's rights, and muckraking journalists. The same spirit of protest also touched literature and the other arts. On both sides of the Atlantic, a dizzying variety of new artistic movements flourished. **Modernism**, as much of this new work and theory came to be called, was based on the belief that all the existing structures that governed life and art—social, religious, and political—had broken down. Order was replaced by fragments, and the typical modernist work often seems difficult to understand.

Three American writers who made major contributions to the modernist movement were Gertrude Stein, Ezra Pound, and T. S. Eliot.

Gertrude Stein studied philosophy and psychology with William James at Harvard. She went on to complete two years of medical school at the Johns Hopkins University before moving permanently to Paris early in the century. Her home became a famous meeting place for artists and writers. It was also a gallery for the dozens of paintings Stein collected—works by Picasso, Matisse, and many other modern masters. Her own writing, in such books as *Three Lives* (1909) and *Tender Buttons* (1914), was eccentric and often difficult to understand. However, her advice and her example made her a key figure in the new artistic developments.

Ezra Pound and T. S. Eliot joined forces briefly, in England before World War I (1914–18), to attempt to revitalize the art of poetry. They identified Victorian conventions and cliches as the enemy, and they insisted that all writers must work on new assumptions. Just before the war, Pound edited an anthology of "imagist" poetry that had an immense influence on later writers. Imagism, according to Pound, demanded that poetry be based on concrete images, and that it use the flexible rhythm of ordinary speech.

The first undeniable masterpiece of American modernism was Eliot's long poem "The Love Song of J. Alfred Prufrock" (1915). Opening with a passage from Dante's *Inferno*, "Prufrock" is the extended self-portrait of a timid middle-aged man.

Robinson and Frost

Despite modernism's influence, important work was done in the early 1900's of a more familiar sort. In particular, Edwin Arlington Robinson and Robert Frost used the scenes and voices of New England to create memorable poetry. Robinson's poems are often set in a fictional New England town called "Tillbury." His typical characters are joyless men and women who spend their days contemplating their own failure. "Eros Turannos" (1916), one of his finest poems, portrays a woman's desperate and self-destructive love for a man she knows will betray her.

Robert Frost was probably the best-known American poet of the 1900's. His first volumes, *A Boy's Will* (1913) and *North of Boston* (1914), gained him a popularity that he kept through half a century. Unlike the modernists, whose verse was difficult and obscure, Frost wrote poetry that was based on ordinary speech and was accessible to a large audience. He was born in California, but he lived most of his long life in New England. His poetry is filled with the landscapes, seasons, and people of that region.

The Chicago Renaissance

In the years before World War I, Chicago was the scene of important American experiments in poetry and fiction. The magazine *Poetry,* brilliantly edited by Harriet Monroe, published some of the most significant new verse, including the work of Carl Sandburg. Sandburg was the son of Swedish immigrants, and his poetry is always sympathetic to the concerns and experiences of ordinary men and women. He established his reputation with *Chicago Poems,* published in 1916.

The most important prose writer associated with the Chicago Renaissance was Sherwood Anderson. His third book, and his one masterpiece, was *Winesburg, Ohio* (1919), a collection of two dozen tales set in the small town of the volume's title.

The poet Carl Sandburg wrote about the life of ordinary people, most famously in *Chicago Poems*. He also collected folk songs and wrote tales for children.

▶ BETWEEN WORLD WARS

The 1920's were known as the "Jazz Age": bootleg liquor was sold in spite of Prohibition, jazz bands played in illegal nightclubs, gangsters battled in city streets. The end of World War I brought a decade of prosperity to America, but it was also a period of moral disillusionment. Many people came to believe that the war had betrayed the ideals of freedom and democracy for which so many had fought and died. The most famous poem of the 1920's, T. S. Eliot's *The Waste Land* (1922), presented an image of the modern world as morally sterile. For Eliot and other writers, the postwar years were a time of anxiety and doubt. These themes were shared by many of the novelists, poets, and playwrights of the period.

Novelists

Sinclair Lewis wrote a series of important novels satirizing the materialism and prejudices of the American middle class. *Main Street* (1920) exposes the conformity and dullness of Gopher Prairie, a midwestern town based on Sauk Centre, Minnesota, where Lewis grew up. *Babbitt* (1922) was perhaps Lewis' most important book. The title character, a smooth-talking real estate salesman, embodies every vice that Lewis associated with America's culture of commerce: ambition, greed, and dishonesty.

Ernest Hemingway was one of several writers who had served in World War I. Born in the suburbs of Chicago, Hemingway found work as a reporter after graduating from high school. He went to Italy in the last months of the war as an ambulance driver and was seriously wounded. His novels, especially early ones such as *The Sun Also Rises* (1926) and *A Farewell to Arms* (1929), tell of the injuries that war inflicts on ordinary men and women. He developed a prose style of rigorous simplicity that influenced American writing throughout the rest of the 1900's.

F. Scott Fitzgerald gave the Jazz Age its name. He created memorable fictional portraits of the immoral but glamorous people who drank and danced through the decade. *The Great Gatsby* (1925) is his masterpiece, a book that T. S. Eliot called "the first step the American novel has taken since Henry James." Jay Gatsby is not merely a gangster and hustler. He is also a tragic figure, whose rise and fall comment sadly on the collapse of the American Dream in the 1900's.

Poets

The 1920's were a period of exceptional achievement in American poetry. The work of William Carlos Williams, Marianne Moore, and Wallace Stevens gave distinction to the decade; so too did the work of several important black poets. (See feature, The Harlem Renaissance, on this page.)

Williams was a physician who insisted that poetry must be faithful to everyday experience. He favored things over ideas, writing about daily life in a language of street-corner speech. Marianne Moore wrote in a more specialized vocabulary but also took the familiar scenes of the world as her subject. She wrote about everything, from animals in the zoo, to science, to baseball. Wallace Stevens was especially interested in the unique role of the creative imagination. He wrote in a richer, more elaborate style than Williams or Moore. Many of his poems explore the ways in which individuals might resist the growing power of the state.

The Harlem Renaissance

The 1920's witnessed an outpouring of prose and poetry by black writers. The movement came to be called the Harlem Renaissance, because it was centered in Harlem, a community in New York City. Langston Hughes (pictured, bottom left, with other writers) was an important contributor to the movement. So, too, were Countee Cullen, Claude McKay, and Jean Toomer. The work of these writers had little in common, but all explored black American life from a black point of view. They often based their writings on black oral traditions and folklore; some of the poets used the rhythms of jazz in their verse. In 1925, Alain Locke published the landmark anthology *The New Negro*, which celebrated the diversity, skill, and self-confidence of the new black writers. The movement ended with the Great Depression of the 1930's, but its influence lived on in later black writers.

Eugene O'Neill

Beginning before World War I and continuing through the 1920's and 1930's, the work of Eugene O'Neill revolutionized American theater. O'Neill was an Irish Catholic and the son of a theatrical father, and his life is often revealed in his plays. He experimented constantly, using masks and other devices to dramatize the hidden psychological truths of his characters. His major plays include *The Emperor Jones* (1920), *The Great God Brown* (1926), *The Iceman Cometh* (1946), and *Long Day's Journey Into Night* (1954).

The Crash and the Great Depression

The Jazz Age ended when the stock market crash of October 1929 ushered in the longest and deepest economic depression in American history. Thousands of banks and factories closed, and millions of workers lost their jobs. The suffering was made worse by a sustained drought in the Midwest, the worst in a century. President Franklin D. Roosevelt used the programs of the "New Deal" to create jobs, but hardship continued throughout the 1930's.

Protest Literature

Some of the most popular writing of the 1930's—for example, Margaret Mitchell's *Gone With the Wind* (1936)—offered escape from the problems of the Depression. However, many writers were politically committed; most of them held left-wing (radical) beliefs. A group who sided with the workers in their struggles were known as "proletarian writers." Some of the most significant protest texts were left-wing plays, especially the work of Clifford Odets. Odets' *Waiting for Lefty* (1935) dramatizes a New York taxi strike and the efforts of oppressed workers to organize.

James T. Farrell wrote about the lower-middle-class Irish neighborhood in South Chicago where he had grown up. Although he published more than forty volumes of fiction, essays, and poetry, his most important books were his earliest, the three novels that make up the *Studs Lonigan* trilogy (1932–35). The three books follow Studs from his adolescence to his early death, a victim of his background and of his own greed and violence.

The two most influential protest writers of the 1930's were John Dos Passos and John Steinbeck. Dos Passos was a veteran of World War I; his work consistently took the side of the common man and woman against the forces of big government. His best books, the three volumes of the *U.S.A.* trilogy (1930–37), are a brilliant chronicle of American life in the early 1900's.

All of Steinbeck's work expresses his deep sympathy with the nation's poor and disadvantaged. *The Grapes of Wrath* (1939), which won the Pulitzer prize and was made into a motion picture, was one of the most controversial and important novels of the decade. The Joad family's journey to California in search of a new life is a true American epic.

Southern Writing

A significant group of southern writers appeared in the years between the two world wars. The earliest was Ellen Glasgow, who treated the southern past in a realistic and often ironic way. Many of her best novels, including *Virginia* (1913) and *Barren Ground* (1925), deal with the status of women in the changing South.

Two other important prose writers were Thomas Wolfe and Katherine Anne Porter. Wolfe's huge novels, especially *Look Homeward, Angel* (1929) and *Of Time and the River* (1935), are based on his own memories of his southern boyhood in North Carolina. Katherine Anne Porter's best works were her short stories and novellas, such as *Flowering Judas* (1935) and *Pale Horse, Pale Rider* (1939). Her work is distinguished for its superb craftsmanship and psychological subtlety.

A group of southern poets, known as "The Fugitives," gathered at Vanderbilt University in Tennessee. They were conservative in their opinions, supporters of earlier rural southern values against the pressure of northern industrialism. The group included John Crowe Ransom, Allen Tate, and Robert Penn Warren.

William Faulkner

The most highly regarded southern novelist of the 1900's was William Faulkner. Almost all of his books are set in the small Mississippi town in which he grew up. Turned into fiction as Yoknapatawpha County, this region became the scene of more than a dozen intricate and eloquent novels. Beginning with *The Sound and the Fury* (1929), and continuing through such books as *Absalom, Absalom!* (1936) and *Go Down, Moses* (1942), Faulkner created dozens of memorable characters and episodes. His principal theme was southern history. He was fascinated by the evil of slavery, and his novels often retell the collapse of the old southern slave empire in the catastrophe of the Civil War.

Black Writing

The range and diversity of black writing in the 1930's is demonstrated by the contrasting work of Zora Neale Hurston and Richard Wright. Hurston was trained as an anthropologist, and she was especially interested in the folk customs and tales of the South and the Caribbean. Her nonfiction writing, including the essays in *Mules and Men* (1935), made a distinguished contribution to African-American culture. Her finest novel, *Their Eyes Were Watching God* (1937), is set in the black communities of the South and also makes use of black oral traditions.

Richard Wright also insisted on the central importance of folklore to black life and literature. He grew up in poverty in rural Mississippi, moved to Chicago, and was active in radical politics in the Depression decade. His essays, stories, and novels all record his personal experience with American racism and oppression. His novel *Native Son* (1940) was a turning point in American literature. The violent story of a young black man named Bigger Thomas, this novel permanently expanded the range of black writing.

▶ LITERATURE SINCE WORLD WAR II

World War II (1939–45) provided the subject for several important novels, in particular *The Naked and the Dead* (1948), by Norman Mailer, and *From Here to Eternity* (1951), by James Jones. The years since the war have been a period in which American dominance as an international power has been accompanied by doubts about America's proper global role. The international hostility of the Cold War defined relations between the United States and the other nations of the world for forty years.

In the shadow of that long conflict, America went through important transformations: the civil rights movement, along with the struggle of women and other groups toward equality; the upheavals of the 1960's, which called many traditional values into question; the Vietnam War, which deeply divided the nation for more than a decade. The poetry, drama, and fiction of these years have recorded the turmoil that has reshaped American society.

Postwar Poetry

Throughout the years since World War II, much excellent poetry has been written in traditional forms, using conventional subjects. The formal poets who did this work, including Elizabeth Bishop and Richard Wilbur, believed in the value of intelligence, contemplation, and civilization. Their verse tends to be restrained, ironic, and often complex.

Experimental Poets. The postwar years have also produced poetry of political protest and experimental verse of all sorts. (See feature,

The Beats

Beginning in the mid-1950's, a group of young writers known as the "beats" began publishing unconventional poems and novels that challenged middle-class American values. The members of the group celebrated freedom of the individual, and many of them were associated with the protest movements of the following decades. The most important beat works are probably *On the Road* (1957), an autobiographical novel by Jack Kerouac (pictured), and *Howl* (1956), a long poem by Allen Ginsberg. Other beat writers were the poets Lawrence Ferlinghetti and Gregory Corso and the novelist John Clellon Holmes.

The Beats, on preceding page.) A group of writers who became known as "confessional poets" published some of the most important recent verse. The confessional writers used their own lives, including their most intimate problems, as the subject matter of their poetry. The group included Robert Lowell, John Berryman, and Sylvia Plath.

Lowell's *Life Studies* (1959), which combined shocking personal revelations with superb craftsmanship, influenced a generation of writers. Berryman's *Dream Songs* (1964–68) was a kind of versified diary in which alcoholism, failure, and death are frequent topics. Plath, who committed suicide at age 30, wrote poems in which anger and despair merge in thoughts of dying; her best work was published, after her death, in *Ariel* (1965).

Black Poets. Gwendolyn Brooks won the first Pulitzer prize awarded to a black writer for her second volume of poetry, *Annie Allen* (1949). Her poetry became increasingly militant after 1967, when she and other writers in the Black Arts Movement dedicated their work to the task of social change.

Robert Hayden makes extensive use of black history and folklore in his poetry; his books include *Figures of Time* (1955) and *A Ballad of Remembrance* (1962). Hayden's "Runagate, Runagate" pays tribute to Harriet Tubman, who escaped from slavery and then helped hundreds of others to freedom.

Postwar Drama

In the years following the war, the leading playwrights were Arthur Miller, Tennessee Williams, and Edward Albee. Miller's *Death of a Salesman* (1949) has been perhaps the most important play of the past four decades; the tragedy of the central character, Willy Loman, went beyond personal failure to encompass the collapse of the American dream.

Tennessee Williams wrote more than two dozen full-length plays. Several of them, including *The Glass Menagerie* (1944), *A Streetcar Named Desire* (1947), and *Cat on a Hot Tin Roof* (1955), are among the classics of recent American theater. Edward Albee wrote more experimental plays than Miller or Williams, often short works influenced by the European "theater of the absurd." In a typical Albee play, a small group of characters engage in verbal and even physical abuse, sometimes for no apparent reason.

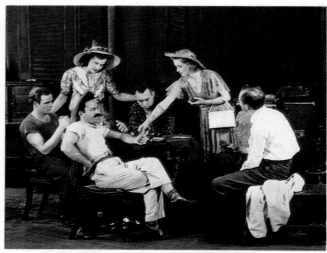

A scene from *A Streetcar Named Desire*, by Tennessee Williams. Williams wrote more than two dozen plays. Many have become classics of American theater.

More recent playwrights whose work has commanded attention include Sam Shepard and David Mamet. Many of the best contemporary dramatists have been women, including Wendy Wasserstein; Beth Henley, who won the Pulitzer prize for *Crimes of the Heart* (1981); and Marsha Norman, who won the Pulitzer for *'Night Mother* (1983).

Postwar Fiction

The early postwar mood of alienation and discontent was best captured in the 1951 novel *Catcher in the Rye,* by J. D. Salinger, in which young Holden Caulfield dreams of protecting all the world's children from danger. Other writers of the period whose work focused on the anxieties of the middle class were John Cheever and John Updike.

Southern Fiction. Although the American economy had become increasingly national, the South remained a separate literary region after World War II. Some of the main writers of that region have included Robert Penn Warren, Eudora Welty, Flannery O'Connor, William Styron, and Walker Percy.

Warren won distinction both as a novelist and a poet. His best novels were his earliest ones, in particular *All the King's Men* (1949), a fictional account of the Louisiana politician Huey Long. Eudora Welty has written some of the finest short stories of the century, memorably evoking the people and landscapes of the rural South. Her first collection, *A Curtain of Green and Other Stories* (1941), remains her masterpiece.

Flannery O'Connor's stories combine the grotesque and the supernatural; her work is filled with outcasts and marginal people. William Styron has chosen subjects that range from the Nazi death camps, in *Sophie's Choice* (1979), to an 1800's slave revolt, in *The Confessions of Nat Turner* (1967). Walker Percy, a physician and a Catholic, continually explored the decay of faith in the modern South. His novels include *The Moviegoer* (1961) and *The Last Gentleman* (1966).

Jewish Fiction. Among the most significant recent writers were several Jewish novelists who examined the debate over older values that followed World War II. This group included Saul Bellow, Bernard Malamud, and Philip Roth. Bellow, who won the Nobel prize in 1976, has created memorable characters and urban scenes. He writes in defense of the individual and of traditional culture; his finest novels are perhaps *Henderson the Rain King* (1959) and *Herzog* (1964).

Bernard Malamud was the son of Russian immigrants. His stories and novels often resemble folk tales and allegories. In much of his work, including his best book, *The Assistant* (1957), Malamud created characters who are defeated by circumstance but maintain their faith. Philip Roth has shown a lifelong interest in the problem of moral authority. His most famous book to date has been *Portnoy's Complaint* (1969).

Black Writers. The past few decades have been a triumphant period for black writers. In 1952, Ralph Ellison published *Invisible Man,* one of the most important novels of the post-war era. The book combines realism, folklore, and fantasy to tell the story of its narrator's life and his discovery of American racism.

James Baldwin was the son of a storefront preacher, an eloquent and bitter man. Baldwin's first and best novel, *Go Tell It on the Mountain* (1953), is based on his own childhood experiences. In addition to fiction, he produced some of the most brilliant essays of his time. Collected in such volumes as *Notes of a Native Son* (1955) and *Nobody Knows My Name* (1961), these essays make up a passionate denunciation of racial injustice.

Postwar black writing has encompassed the remarkable accomplishment of gifted women, including Toni Morrison and Alice Walker. Morrison's fiction celebrates the language and the heritage of tales that define the American black experience. Her principal novels, such as *Song of Solomon* (1977) and *Beloved* (1987), for which she received the Pulitzer prize, combine a detailed knowledge of history with myth and fantasy. Alice Walker's major novel, *The Color Purple* (1982), is written as a series of letters that reveal the oppression and liberation of a woman named Celie.

Other talented black women writers have included Margaret Walker, Paule Marshall, and Toni Cade Bambara.

Experimental Fiction. Over the past several decades, a number of writers have undertaken a wide range of technical experiments in fiction. Vladimir Nabokov, a Russian émigré, used parody, multilingual jokes, and intricate plots to focus attention on the nature of fiction itself. Donald Barthelme worked in fragments, word games, and fairy tales. His stories have been collected in such volumes as *Come Back, Dr. Caligari* (1964). John Barth has created narratives in which storytelling itself becomes the main subject.

Contemporary Diversity

The most evident hallmark of contemporary American literature is its great range and diversity. From the "minimalist" realism of Raymond Carver to the enormous and complex novels of Thomas Pynchon; from the brilliant reportage of Joan Didion to the finely crafted fables of Cynthia Ozick—recent American writing has represented the widest variety of styles and subjects.

The nation's ethnic minorities have produced distinguished work. Maxine Hong Kingston, in such books as *Woman Warrior* (1976), has dramatized the tensions between past and present in Asian-American culture. The main character of *Bless Me, Ultima* (1972), by Rudolfo Anaya, learns to base his life in the modern world on the foundation of tradition. The novels of the Native American writer Leslie Marmon Silko, including *Ceremony* (1978), combine realistic narrative with the songs and legends of the Indian past.

PETER CONN
University of Pennsylvania
Author, *Literature in America:
An Illustrated History*

AMERICAN REVOLUTION. See REVOLUTIONARY WAR.

AMMUNITION. See GUNS AND AMMUNITION.

AMOEBA. See MICROBIOLOGY; PROTOZOANS.

AMPHIBIANS

They can be found under the damp logs on forest floors; propelling themselves through the waters of streams, lakes, and ponds; burrowing into the ground; bounding through woodlands with great leaps; or waddling across dry, sandy desert. These smooth-skinned **vertebrates** (animals with backbones) called amphibians inhabit all parts of the world except Greenland and Antarctica.

There are three main groups of amphibians: frogs and toads, salamanders and newts, and caecilians. As they go through their early growing stages, the three groups look similar; but as adults, they look very different. Frogs and toads have four legs and no tails. Their hind legs are long and strong. They use their well-developed back legs for jumping and swimming. Salamanders and newts have tails their entire lives. They also have four legs as frogs and toads do. However, their short, weak legs are suited to walking rather than jumping. Caecilians, which have no legs, are burrowing animals that look a lot like giant earthworms.

Scientists have identified more than 4,000 kinds, or **species**, of amphibians. More species are still being discovered, particularly in the rain forests of Africa, South America, and Southeast Asia.

▶ **CHARACTERISTICS OF AMPHIBIANS**

Amphibians are ectothermic—that is, they depend on external heat sources, such as the sun, to raise their body temperature. Most amphibians spend the early part of their lives in water and the adult part on land. During the early, aquatic period, amphibians use gills for respiration. Later on land, most breathe through lungs. Amphibians can also absorb oxygen through their skin, which is generally smooth, moist, and scaleless. In some species of salamanders, the lungs do not function; all respiration is through the skin and the mucous membranes of the mouth.

Senses. Amphibian senses are well developed. Frogs and toads have excellent sight and depend on their eyes to find food. Salaman-

ders have good eyes and also a keen sense of smell. When they hunt for food, they use both sight and smell. For the burrowing life of caecilians, good eyesight is not a necessity. They either have very small eyes or no eyes at all. Caecilians hunt mainly by smell. They have two tentacles, or feelers, near the mouth. As they move through the ground, the tentacles pick up food scents.

A toad has a short, stout body with warty skin.

Eating Habits. In their aquatic larval stage, young amphibians vary in their diets. Some eat mainly plant material. Others eat only insects and other animals. Still others eat a mixture of plant and animal food. Adult amphibians, however, are almost entirely meat eaters and make insects the bulk of their diet.

Producing Sounds. Most amphibians are able to produce some kind of sound. Frogs and toads use their voices to communicate warnings, defend themselves, and send mating calls. However, except for frogs and toads, amphibians do not have well-developed voices. Caecilians and most salamanders and newts are limited to sounds such as coughs and grunts. The sounds they produce are not used as a form of communication.

Defenses. Many different kinds of mammals, snakes, and birds hunt the amphibian. When threatened, amphibians that closely match the colors in their environment may hide from their enemies by simply staying very still. Some salamanders have tails that break off. The salamander quickly escapes as

The American bullfrog (*left*) is the largest North American frog.

its attacker chases the twitching tail. Many amphibians have poison-secreting skin glands. The poison irritates the mouth of the attacker, and it does not take much time before the attacker willingly lets go of its prey.

▶LIFE CYCLES

In most species of amphibians, the young animals, or **larvae**, that hatch from the eggs resemble fish in certain ways. They must live in water. They have tails that they use to propel themselves. They take in oxygen through gills. Gradually, the larvae undergo changes that turn them into land-dwelling adults. Such a change of form is called a **metamorphosis**.

As full-grown adults, most amphibians are small creatures. They usually are no longer than 6 inches (15 centimeters) and weigh less than 2 ounces (57 grams). The largest amphibian is the Japanese giant salamander, which grows to 5¼ feet (1.6 meters) in length. One species of caecilian also reaches lengths of more than 4 feet (1.2 meters).

Frogs and Toads. Frogs and toads are the most widespread of all the amphibians. They usually live in wet or moist places such as ponds, marshes, or rain forests, but there are some toads that are able to live in dry areas, including deserts. In frogs and toads, fertilization of the eggs is almost always external. The male fertilizes the eggs as they are being released into the water by the female.

The larva that hatches from an egg is called a **tadpole** or **polliwog**. It has a tail and gills. The larva grows and develops over a period of time that lasts from two weeks to two years; then, metamorphosis to the land stage begins. The gills are absorbed and the animal develops lungs. Legs develop and the tail disappears. Finally the animal has the characteristics of an adult frog. It climbs out of the water and onto land. It continues to grow until it reaches its full size. When it is mature, it returns to the water to mate and breed.

There are exceptions to this typical pattern. In one species, for example, the male frog carries strings of eggs wrapped around his hind legs until they hatch. In other species, there is no aquatic larval stage; the froglets that hatch from the eggs look like miniature adults.

Salamanders and Newts. Salamanders and newts generally live in lakes and streams and

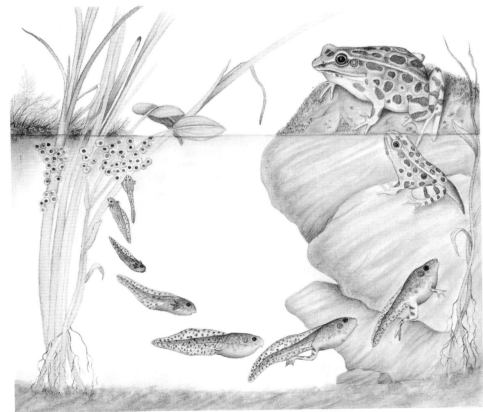

An Amphibian Life Cycle

Most amphibians, such as this leopard frog, develop from eggs laid in water. When a frog egg hatches, a tadpole emerges. The young tadpole is very much like a fish—it has gills, lidless eyes, and a finlike tail. Slowly, the tadpole changes into an animal, with well-developed legs and lungs, that can live on land.

Arching its tail in warning is part of the defensive behavior of the salamander called ensatina (*opposite page*). In addition to the warning posture, the salamander secretes a poisonous slime that irritates and repels attackers.

During its land stage of development, which lasts two to three years, the red-spotted newt feeds on snails, small insects, and worms.

A salamander (*right*) can be identified by grooves that run down its sides.

under damp logs on forest floors. In most tailed amphibians, fertilization occurs internally within the female's body. After courtship, the male deposits a packet of sperm, called a **spermatophore**, on the bottom of the pond. In species that breed on land, the male places the spermatophore on moist ground. The female picks up the spermatophore and stores it in her **cloaca**, a chamber at the base of the tail that opens to the outside of the body. When the female lays her eggs, they pass through the cloaca, where the sperm fertilize them.

The larvae of salamanders and newts are similar in appearance to the adults. The main difference is that the young animal has feathery gills on the outside of its neck. After two to four months, the larva changes into an adult. It loses the gills and forms air-breathing lungs.

Caecilians. The caecilians are found only in the tropics and subtropics. Most live in underground burrows; however, there are caecilians that spend all their life in water.

Fertilization is internal in caecilians. Most species deposit their eggs in water. Some caecilians lay eggs on land. After depositing her eggs, the female caecilian may coil herself around them to keep the eggs safe from predators until they hatch. The caecilian larvae have tails and live in water. Like frogs and toads,

The limbless caecilian lives in underground burrows.

they gradually lose their tails and turn into adults.

▶ **AMPHIBIANS AND THEIR ENVIRONMENT**

Amphibians have an important role in the environment. They help maintain the balance of nature in many areas: sometimes because they are food for other animals, including humans; other times because they eat large amounts of insect pests and larvae.

In many parts of the world, amphibians are disappearing from areas where they once were common. People's activities appear to be the main cause of this decline. Habitats are destroyed as marshes and other wetlands are drained; forests are cut down; and homes, roads, and other structures are built. Automobiles also kill thousands of amphibians each year. In many places, amphibians are run over as they cross the roads built between their homes and their spawning grounds. Chemical substances from acid rain and pesticides also harm amphibians when they are absorbed through their moist skin. Amphibians also absorb dangerous chemicals when they eat insects that contain pesticides.

As the important contributions of amphibians have become recognized, efforts have been made to protect them. Measures enacted by some countries that protect the environment from the harmful effects of acid rain and the misuse of pesticides also help protect amphibians. Countries, such as India, have banned the export of frog legs (considered a delicacy in some parts of the world) to protect their amphibian population. In many parts of Europe, toad tunnels have been built to help toads safely cross the roads that block their travel to spawning grounds.

JENNY TESAR
Author, *Introduction to Animals*
Reviewed by JOHN L. BEHLER
Curator, Department of Herpetology
The Bronx Zoo

See also FROGS AND TOADS.

AMUNDSEN, ROALD. See NORTHWEST PASSAGE.
ANATOMY. See BODY, HUMAN.

This stone tablet is believed to represent a king of Lagash and his sons. One of the world's oldest cities, Lagash flourished about 4,500 years ago. It was located between the Tigris and Euphrates rivers in what is now Iraq. The region, once known as Mesopotamia, is often called the cradle of civilization.

ANCIENT CIVILIZATIONS

In a museum in Paris there is a small carved stone tablet. It was found on the broad plain between the Tigris and Euphrates rivers in the country of Iraq. The tablet shows the king of Lagash and his sons. If you look at a map of modern Iraq, you will not find Lagash. It was a city that disappeared long ago, for this tablet is at least 4,500 years old.

Words carved on the tablet in a strange script say that the king of Lagash brought timber from the mountains to build temples for the gods. But this is not all the tablet tells us. It also tells us that the people of this land lived in cities, had governments, built temples, and —most important of all—knew how to write. In brief, the tablet tells us that people living on the plains of the Tigris and Euphrates rivers had a civilization 4,500 years ago, before 2500 B.C.

Visitors to Egypt usually go to see the huge stone pyramids that are about as old as the tablet from Lagash. The pyramids, too, tell a story. They tell us that the Egyptians had architects who understood enough mathematics to plan these enormous structures with amazing accuracy. The pyramids tell of the many skilled stonecutters and masons and the thousands of people who lifted, tugged, and pushed these stones into place. The Egyptians had to have rulers to command and direct the labor of so many people. Such a government would have required scribes to keep records, and we know from other carved stones that the Egyptians did have writing. The pyramids, temples, and tombs tell us that the Egyptians, too, had a civilization 4,500 years ago.

A library of clay tablets, discovered in 1975 in Syria, gives us information about the ancient city of Ebla, which existed more than 4,000 years ago. It was thought to be a lost city until the clay tablets were discovered.

On the island of Crete, there are traces of another civilization just as old. Carved stone seals and the remains of palace walls have been found there. Piles of bricks on the plains of the Indus River in Pakistan tell of cities that stood there, too.

It is possible that people living in North China on the Hwang Ho (Yellow River) had a civilization equally old. But no carved stones or ruins have been found that tell of it.

People today speak of these civilizations as ancient civilizations because we think of the centuries before A.D. 500 as ancient times. But ancient times do include most of the human history. Civilization grew old even within what we now call ancient times. For example, a king who reigned in 540 B.C. took much interest in digging up ruins of temples built hundreds of years earlier, in what he regarded as ancient times. The time span between the building of the pyramids and the birth of Christ is greater than the time from the birth of Christ to the present.

THE CIVILIZATION OF THE SUMERIANS AND BABYLONIANS

Civilization was not new 4,500 years ago in the lands along the Tigris and Euphrates rivers. Much earlier, the Sumerian people had settled there and had begun to build cities. The Sumerians first entered the plain before 3000 B.C. Semites, people from the dry grasslands south and west of the Euphrates, also settled along the rivers. The Semites adopted many Sumerian ways of living.

Each city had its own ruler, who governed the city within the walls, as well as the areas nearby. As the number of cities and people increased, each city tried to get more land. Sometimes, cities quarreled about land and water for irrigation. At times the quarrels led to war, and the more powerful cities gained more lands. Babylon, one of the Semite cities, conquered and ruled the whole plain known as Babylonia—the land of Babylon. A separate article on Babylonia appears in volume B.

Temple Cities and Priests

The Sumerians built their cities around temples, called **ziggurats.** These were large towers that looked like pyramids. At the top of the ziggurat was a shrine that held an image of the city's god. At different seasons of the year,

priests made offerings to the god. The Sumerians believed that their crops, their health, and the safety of their city depended on the favors of the god. The priests said that they acted for the god. They collected such things as grain, wool, and silver from the people to offer the god. These payments to the god were a form of tax.

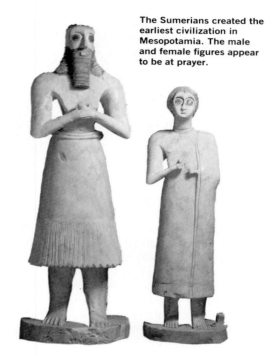

The Sumerians created the earliest civilization in Mesopotamia. The male and female figures appear to be at prayer.

Sites of some of the world's ancient civilizations. The earliest developed in the regions of such great rivers as the Tigris and Euphrates, the Nile, and the Indus.

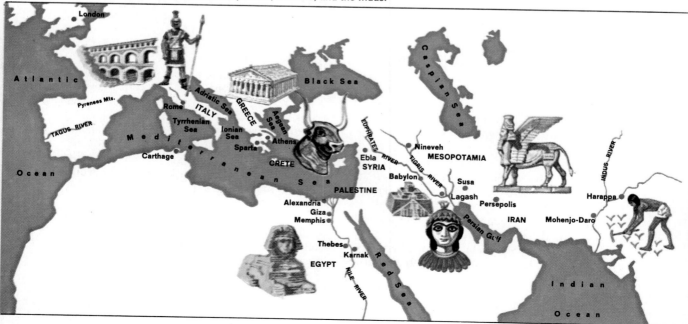

Building Cities with Clay

There was little timber or stone on the river-bottom land where the Sumerians built their cities. But clay was plentiful. They packed moist clay into molds and dried the clay in the sun. In this way they formed flat bricks that could be stacked upon each other to build the walls of houses, shops, palaces, and the ziggurat. The main disadvantage of the sun-dried bricks was that they crumbled after a time, even in a dry climate. But the builders discovered that if they baked the moist bricks, the heat hardened the clay. The bricks then remained firm even in wet weather. A wall built of fire-baked bricks set together with asphalt would stand for a very long time. The Sumerians and Babylonians used fire-baked bricks for their more important buildings.

Writing on Clay Tablets

The Sumerians wrote on clay. They pressed the end of a stick into the soft clay, making little three-cornered marks. They combined these three-cornered marks to form signs that stood for words. Since the marks looked like wedges, this form of writing is called cuneiform, which means "wedge-shaped." The Babylonians, as well as other peoples, borrowed cuneiform writing from the Sumerians. For more than 2,000 years people in this part of the world wrote with these little wedge-shaped marks.

Clay tablets were heavy and awkward to handle, but they lasted for centuries. A paper book buried in the ground for 3,000 years would have rotted away completely. But a clay tablet, carefully dug up, remains in good condition. Scholars in modern times have found thousands of the Sumerian and Babylonian tablets. These tablets tell many things about this ancient civilization. They tell of business and trade, for there are letters from merchants to their agents. There is a "farmer's almanac," which gives instructions about each season's work in the fields. A Sumerian physician wrote down some favorite medical remedies. One of the most interesting tablets describes what children did in school 4,000 years ago. They hurried to school because their teacher would beat them with a cane if they were late. The teacher also used the cane to punish children for talking, leaving the school

King Hammurabi receives the insignia of royal office from a god. Beneath the sculpture is the Code of Hammurabi, one of the world's oldest sets of laws. The detail below shows the cuneiform writing on the stone, the earliest fully developed system of writing that is known.

without permission, and not doing lessons properly.

The Oldest Written Laws in the World

People living together in cities must have laws. The Sumerians and Babylonians wrote their laws on tablets of clay and stone. These are some of the oldest known written laws. One law provided that people would have to pay a certain amount of silver if they entered an orchard that was not their own and were caught there for stealing. The most famous collection of early laws was issued by Hammurabi, king of Babylon, around 1750 B.C. His code declared that Hammurabi was like a real father to his people. He gave them laws "to cause justice to prevail in the land, to destroy the wicked and evil, that the strong might not oppress the weak." Most of our knowledge of the code comes from a tablet found in Susa, Iran, in 1901.

All people were not equal in Babylon. Some people were aristocrats, some were commoners, and some were slaves. People were not treated in the same way by the laws. If a free man knocked out the eye of another free man, he could lose his own eye as punishment. Slaves were still less fortunate. The laws treated them like property. The Sumerians and Babylonians were not the only slave owners in ancient times. Almost all ancient civilizations allowed slavery. Frequently prisoners of war were kept as slaves rather than killed.

More Trade and Better Products

People living in a city did not have to make everything they used. Instead, they could spend their time making one kind of product that they traded for things they needed. A weaver would make cloth and trade it to the potter for dishes, to the merchant for grain, and to the metalsmith for tools. Since weavers spent their time doing only one kind of job, they learned to do it well. They made much finer cloth than part-time weavers could. The same was true of potters, smiths, barbers, and people with other skills.

In the Sumerian and Babylonian cities, artisans devoted themselves to their special jobs. The fine metalwork, jewelry, and stone carving that they produced show the skill of these specialized workers.

▶ **EGYPTIAN CIVILIZATION**

Civilization in Egypt is older than the oldest pyramid. About 3200 B.C. a king named Menes (also called Narmer) brought the land along the Nile River under his rule. For more than 3,000 years, Egypt remained one of the richest and most civilized lands in the world.

The Egyptians had a system of writing. Instead of using clay tablets, they wrote on sheets of papyrus. These were made from strips of the papyrus reed, which grew along the Nile. Papyrus does not last as well as clay tablets. But since the Egyptian climate is dry, many ancient writings have survived. There is a letter from a boy-king to one of his captains, asking that the captain bring back a dancing dwarf from central Africa. There are collections of wise sayings, including one that advised a young man to "think much, but keep thy mouth closed." One essay by a soldier tells how difficult it is to serve in a cold, foreign land. Such writings tell the thoughts of people who lived thousands of years ago.

The God-Kings and Their Officials

The Egyptians thought of their kings, whom they called pharaohs, as gods who had power over the Nile River. The Nile flooded each year and brought water to the fields. Since the prosperity of the people depended on the king, they had to give the king a part of what they produced.

The king supposedly ruled the entire land. But no one person could actually manage so large a kingdom alone. Egypt was in fact ruled in the king's name by an army of officials. The king's chief assistant, called a vizier, appointed the most important officials. They in turn appointed other officials, who appointed still lesser ones. Every district had its official, who was the government representative best known to the common people. The district official served as chief of police, judge, overseer of the irrigation canals, and tax collector.

Religion

The Egyptians worshiped many gods and goddesses. The most important was Re, the sun god. Egyptian kings were thought to be descended from Re, and "son of Re" was part of a king's official title. Re was associated with other gods, including Osiris, king of the underworld, and Isis, wife of Osiris.

In addition, every community had its local deity. Some of these gods became identified with Re and thus gained a higher status. For example, Amon, a god worshiped by the people of Thebes, later became Amon-Re, an important deity throughout Egypt.

Many Egyptian gods were pictured as having the bodies of humans and the heads of animals. For example, Horus, the son of Osiris and Isis, was often depicted with a human body and a hawk's head. Anubis, a god of the dead, had the head of a jackal.

An important aspect of the religion of ancient Egypt was the belief in life after death. This belief led to the practice of mummifying, or preserving, the bodies of the dead and to the construction of elaborate tombs to house the bodies of kings and other important people. Many beautiful sculptures and paintings were created for the tombs. (You can read more about these arts in EGYPTIAN ART AND ARCHITECTURE in Volume E.)

Tombs and Temples

Stone was plentiful in the Nile Valley. And Egyptian builders had a good supply of material to build tombs and temples for the god-kings and their officials. The pyramids were tombs designed to protect the bodies of the kings. The bodies were placed in the burial chambers within these huge heaps of stone. The first pyramid was designed by the architect Imhotep for King Zoser. The largest was built by King Khufu (called Cheops by the Greeks). It took more than 2,000,000 blocks of stone, each with an average weight of more than 2 metric tons, to build Cheops' Great Pyramid. This pyramid stood close to the Nile River, so that during the high-water season barges could float across to it. The pyramid was about 145 meters (480 feet) high. It was the tallest structure in the world for more than 4,000 years. People spoke of it as one of the seven wonders of the world.

Later, kings built other kinds of tombs. Some were cut from solid rock cliffs. Rooms inside the tombs were furnished like rooms in a palace, so that the dead would not want for anything in the next life. Beds, benches, clothing, food, tools, and even games were placed in the tombs. Painters covered the walls with pictures that showed familiar scenes of people working in shops or in the fields or boating on the river. Some of the tombs were

This gold death mask of King Tutankhamen was found in his tomb. The king died at 18 or 19, in about 1325 B.C.

never opened until recent years. Thus people today can still see the furnishings and paintings made so long ago.

The Egyptians also built temples such as the temple for the god Amon-Re at Karnak. This temple is famous for its huge stone columns with elaborate carvings.

Science of the Egyptians

Science grows partly out of the need to know. The Egyptians, for example, needed to know how to mark time so that they would know when to expect the Nile's yearly flood. The river rose in early summer and left behind a rich deposit of soil in which farmers planted crops. The Egyptians discovered that they could keep a record of time by observing the position of the stars and the sun. They invented a calendar that was divided into 12 months of 30 days each. They used the remaining 5 days of the year for religious rites.

Egyptian physicians learned some things about the human body, and they tried to cure diseases. They knew that the pulse was caused by the beating of the heart and that the brain controlled the arms and legs. Egyptians, like most ancient peoples, believed that evil spirits caused sickness. They tried to drive the evil spirits out by magical spells and words. Physicians also made medicines of olive oil, honey, and many kinds of herbs and other ingredients. It is hard to say whether any of these medicines worked. If patients believed that a medicine or magic would help them, it may actually have done so. The Egyptians did set broken bones successfully. They used splints and casts made of linen, glue, and plaster.

Statues Large and Small

Egyptian sculptors were among the best of ancient times. They carved both wood and stone. They made small busts and huge statues of kings as high as seven-story buildings. The Great Sphinx of Giza has the head of a king on the body of a lion. At its tallest point, the figure is 20 meters (66 feet) high.

The portrait statues were remarkably lifelike. Some years ago workers who found a wooden statue of an official called it "sheikh of the village" because they thought it looked like their village mayor. Queen Nefertiti died more than 3,300 years ago. But people can still admire her beauty because of the skillful artists who carved her portrait. Her husband was Amenhotep IV.

A Woman Ruler, a Conqueror, and a Religious Reformer

Nefertiti is not the only famous Egyptian woman. Queen Hatshepsut ruled the country for over 20 years. She put up monuments throughout the land on which she referred to herself as pharaoh, or ruler. One monument tells of an expedition that she sent to Somaliland, on the Red Sea. The expedition returned with rare spices, sweet-smelling woods, gold, ivory, ebony, and apes.

Hatshepsut's nephew, Thutmose III, ruled after her death. He tried to wipe out all memory of the woman who had ruled as pharaoh. Thutmose had his aunt's statues smashed and her monuments covered over with stone walls. But after a time, the walls fell down, revealing Hatshepsut's words.

Thutmose was a soldier who was not content to rule only Egypt. He conquered the cities and kingdoms of Palestine and Syria and made a large empire for himself in the 1400's B.C. Thutmose was one of the most famous military leaders of ancient times.

Amenhotep IV, who ruled in the 1300's B.C., was not a soldier, but he is as famous as Thutmose the conqueror. Amenhotep, unlike most Egyptians, did not worship many gods. Instead he believed only in Aten (or Aton), the sun god. Amenhotep changed his name to Akhenaten (or Akhnaton). He wrote hymns in praise of the sun god. He also tried to stop the worship of the old gods, but he did not succeed. After his death the old worship was restored. Later records written by priests who served the old gods always referred to Akhnaton as "that criminal."

▶ EBLAITE CIVILIZATION

Ebla was one of the ancient world's important trading cities from about 2400 to 2000

This carving is of Nefertiti, one of the most famous of Egyptian queens, who lived in about 1360 B.C.

This painting was found in a tomb at Thebes, the capital of ancient Egypt.

One of the most important trading cities of ancient times, Ebla was located in what is now Syria. The figure at the right of this sculptured ritual basin, which dates from about 1800 B.C., may be one of the many gods worshiped by the people of Ebla.

B.C. Today Ebla is only a large mound in northern Syria, about 34 miles (55 kilometers) southwest of Aleppo. We would know little about Eblaite civilization if there had not been a fire in the palace library 4,000 years ago. It may seem strange that a fire preserved a library. Fire destroys paper books and records. But this was a library of clay tablets. The fire that destroyed the palace baked the tablets so that they became as hard as bricks. Nearly 15,000 of the hardened tablets lay buried until 1975, when an Italian archeologist discovered them.

What the Tablets Tell about a Trading City

About 30,000 people lived within the walls of the ancient city of Ebla. Most of the city dwellers were probably officials and their families. Tablets list the amounts of wheat, barley, and wine collected to support the large number of officials. The fact that there were many officials suggests that Ebla was the center of a large kingdom. Kings ruled the land with the help of a council of high officials. The tablets give the names of some kings. It is thought that each king was elected for a term of 7 years.

The tablets prove that Ebla was a great trading center for timber, fine cloth, rare gems, and metalwork. Eblaite traders carried goods to distant places—to Egypt, the Sumerian cities, the island of Cyprus, and even to Iran.

Scribes kept business records with cuneiform marks on clay tablets. Ebla had a school where scribes learned this Sumerian way of writing. Some students' tablets have been found with the names of the students who wrote on them and of the teachers who corrected the mistakes. Scribes wrote the Sumerian language as well as Eblaite. When the tablets were first found in 1975, no one could read Eblaite. Fortunately, the discovery of word lists with both Sumerian and Eblaite words provided a key. These word lists made it possible for scholars to learn that Eblaite is the oldest known language of the Semitic group. Hebrew and Arabic also belong to this group.

The Eblaites appear to have had many gods. They worshiped more than 500, many of them borrowed from other peoples.

The tablets tell that Eblaite kings conquered other cities. And remains in the mound show that Ebla itself was conquered several times. The burning of the palace library took place when a rival king captured the city about 2250 B.C. The conquest did not destroy Eblaite civilization, for the Eblaites rebuilt their city. But it may have weakened the city. Even through a later war with the Amorites, about 2000 B.C., Ebla remained a trading city. It was conquest by the Hittites, about 1650 B.C., that finally destroyed Ebla. After that date, Ebla was almost forgotten.

▶ INDUS CIVILIZATION

A hundred years ago historians could not have written about the ancient civilization on the plains of the Indus River. The story of that civilization still lay buried in mounds. The first hint of buried cities came in the 19th century. Workers digging for a railroad bed found some unusual carved stone seals. No one paid much attention to the seals at that time.

The ruins of Mohenjo-Daro, one of the chief cities of the great Indus civilization, were discovered in what is now Pakistan. The city flourished between 2500 and 1800 B.C.

After 1920, scholars unearthed the ruins of buried cities on the Indus Plain. Then they realized that the strange seals were but a few of the things left behind by people who lived about 4,000 years ago.

Cities with Sewers

The Indus cities were fairly large. It is thought that Mohenjo-Daro and Harappa, two of the main cities, each had as many as 20,000 inhabitants. The cities were laid out in regular blocks with streets and alleys. The remains of brick walls and platforms mark where the buildings once stood. Houses were generally built around an unroofed court. The rooms of the house opened onto the court. Some houses had bathrooms with drains connected to sewers that ran beneath the paved streets. A thick-walled fort served as a place of safety for the people in time of danger. Mohenjo-Daro had a large pool that may have been used for religious ceremonies.

The World's First Cotton Farmers

The Indus people were the world's first cotton farmers. They also grew wheat, barley, and melons and kept livestock—sheep, cattle, water buffalo, camels, horses, and donkeys, among other animals.

The Indus farmers paid their taxes in grain. One of the most important buildings in the city was a large granary (a storehouse for grain). It was built of timber on a brick platform. This made it high enough to keep the grain safe from the river's floodwaters. The granary served as the ruler's ''bank,'' where the wealth, in the form of grain collected from the people, was kept.

Weapons, Tools, and Toys

Most of the people were farmers, but there were artisans in the Indus cities. They must have spent most of their time working at a single craft. Metalsmiths made fine bronze weapons such as swords, knives, daggers, and spearheads. They also made things for every day use such as razors, hairpins, fishhooks, axes, hammers, and saws.

The cities had toymakers who made play things for children. They made rattles, marbles, little clay carts, and animals on wheels that could be pulled by a string. Perhaps the

Small stone seals carved with animal figures were probably used by Indus merchants to mark their goods. The writing on the seals has not been deciphered.

Indus children had the world's first toy with moving parts—a little clay bull with a head that moved when someone pulled a string.

Trade with Faraway Lands

Beads were found in the Indus ruins. This tells us that the people liked ornaments and that they traded with faraway lands. Some of the beads are like those worn by the Sumerians and Babylonians. Silver, gold, asphalt, and precious stones show that there was trade with Afghanistan, Iran, and southern India.

Writing That No One Can Read

A great many carved stone seals have been found since the first ones were dug up more than a century ago. The Indus people probably used the stones to mark lumps of clay, which were used to seal goods. Each person may have had an individual mark. The seals usually have animals carved on them and some strange writing. No one today can read this writing.

What Happened to the Cities?

How could cities with thousands of people disappear and be completely forgotten? Scholars know only that about 1500 B.C. some disaster struck the Indus cities. Perhaps invaders conquered them. People died in the streets of one of the cities, and no one was left to bury the bodies. After a time, walls fell down and covered the bones. The winds of many centuries blew dust over the mound of ruins. People of later times seeing the mounds never guessed that a city once stood there. It was only when people began to dig that the secret came out.

▶ **ASSYRIAN AND PERSIAN CIVILIZATIONS**

A thousand years after the time of Hammurabi, Babylon was no longer a great power. Other peoples had grown strong. Among them were the Assyrians, who lived in the hilly country north of the Babylonian plain. In 710 B.C. the Assyrians conquered Babylon and then went on to conquer other lands. The Assyrian king Ashurbanipal, who ruled from 669 to 626 B.C., had an empire that included Egypt as well as Babylonia.

Fierce Warriors and Iron Weapons

Assyrian kings boasted of their fierceness and the terrors they inflicted upon those who opposed them. One king grimly declared that he dyed the mountain red with the blood of his foes.

The Assyrian army was both fierce and well armed. Soldiers no longer fought with bronze weapons. They used iron swords, lances, and axes, and they wore iron helmets and armor. Iron dulled the best bronze blade. Assyrian horsemen drove swift battle chariots. It is no wonder that the Assyrian kings conquered an empire.

The King's Library

King Ashurbanipal boasted of his victories, but he was at least as proud of his learning and his library. He probably declared that he had mastered the noble art of writing. It is said that he could even read the beautiful writings of the Sumerians. The Assyrians used

This detail of a carving made in ancient Persia shows Darius I with a servant holding a parasol over him.

the cuneiform writing of the Babylonians. Ashurbanipal's library consisted of thousands of clay tablets. He instructed his officials to search for any old writings in the cities of the empire. It is said that one official wrote from Babylon that he had found an original tablet that Hammurabi the king prepared. Much of what we know about Sumerian and Babylonian writings comes from the tablets found in the ruins of Ashurbanipal's palace.

The Assyrian scribes produced histories of the reigns and wars of their kings. From these writings, we have learned a great deal about the terrors of their conquests. Other armies were probably as brutal, but they left few records of their horrors.

The Assyrian Empire came to a sudden end. Their fearful methods did not keep the conquered peoples quiet. A few years after Ashurbanipal's death, Babylonia revolted. With others, the Babylonians captured and destroyed Nineveh, the Assyrian capital, in 612 B.C.

The Coming of the Persians

Babylon did not long remain free. In 539 B.C. it was conquered by the army of Cyrus the Great, king of the Persians. The Persians were an Iranian people who gave their name to the high land east of Babylonia. The Persians went on to conquer still more lands. Darius I, who ruled from 522 to 486 B.C., controlled an empire that reached from the Indus River to the Aegean Sea. It included Egypt as well as Babylonia. Assyria had never ruled so large an empire.

Zoroaster and the Rule of an Empire

Darius followed the teachings of a Persian prophet called Zoroaster (or Zarathustra). Zoroaster taught that life was a constant struggle between a god of good, Ahura Mazda, and a spirit of evil. Wise people, said Zoroaster, should put themselves on the side of good and justice. For rulers this meant that they should keep peace and order throughout their realm. Darius tried to follow Zoroaster's teachings in at least this one respect. He allowed the people he conquered considerable freedom as long as they remained peaceful. He allowed them to manage most of their own affairs. Although they had their own kings, Darius was recognized as the "king of kings." To make sure that taxes were paid, he placed a governor and a general in every district of his empire. To keep watch on these officials, he sent special agents to travel about their districts.

The Persians built roads between the main cities of the empire. About every 23 kilometers (14 miles) there were rest stations with inns and stables. Royal messengers changed horses at each station so that they could cover long distances rapidly. They could carry a message from Sardis to Susa, a distance of 2,400 kilometers (1,500 miles) in less than two weeks.

The Persian Empire was the largest empire the world had yet seen. In addition to Iran, it included what are now the countries of Turkey, Egypt, Israel, Jordan, Lebanon, Syria, Iraq, Afghanistan, and part of Pakistan.

For more information, see PERSIA, ANCIENT in Volume P.

Persepolis was the royal capital of the ancient Persian Empire. Its buildings were burned by Alexander the Great in 331 B.C. after his conquest of the Persians.

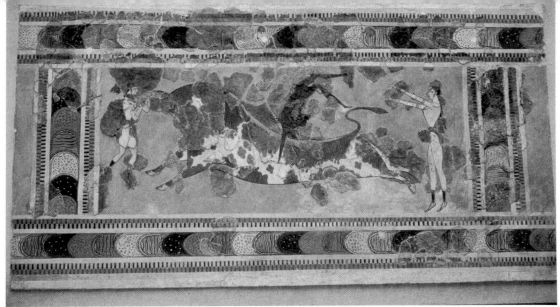

A wall painting in the palace of Minos at Knossos depicts the acrobatic bull-fighters of ancient Crete. The painting dates from the Middle Bronze Age.

▶CRETAN CIVILIZATION

Four thousand years ago the people of Crete depended on the sea for both their wealth and safety. Crete is an island in the Mediterranean Sea, well situated for trade. The Cretans traded wheat, wine, linen, olive oil, and cypress timber for goods from Egypt, Syria, Italy, and lands still farther away. They also depended on the sea for defense. They built no walls around cities because they counted on their navy to keep enemies from their shores.

A statue of a young man, dating from the 6th century B.C., in a temple of the god Apollo in Boeotia, Greece.

Knossos and the King's Palace

Knossos was the greatest of the Cretan cities. Thousands of people lived there. The king's palace was a rambling structure covering 2 hectares (5 acres). It contained an open court, a throne room, chapels, and apartments for the king and his attendants. There were rooms where wheat and olive oil were stored in jars nearly as tall as a human adult. Paintings showing scenes from daily life decorated the walls. Bits of the paintings that remain show us how these people looked.

The people of Knossos watched performances in outdoor theatres. They liked active sports such as boxing. They had an unusual exhibition in which acrobats turned somersaults in midair, coming down on the backs of charging bulls. "Bull leaping" would have made most rodeo contests of today look tame.

Throughout Knossos there were signs of the city's wealth. Women wore gold jewelry and elaborately ruffled skirts. The palaces and houses contained fine pottery and carved stone figures. The king and the nobles had chariots complete with spare wheels, which were necessary because of the rough cobblestone streets.

Trade was important in Crete, but most people were not traders. They worked on the land, growing wheat, olives, figs, and grapes. They tended goats and sheep and drove ox teams. The people gave the oxen such names as Dapple and Darkie, Blondie and Bawler.

Disaster Strikes: A Civilization Forgotten

The prosperity of Knossos came to an end about 1400 B.C. Disaster struck the city, but just what happened is not clear. Perhaps the sea no longer kept invaders away. People continued to live at Knossos, but the great days were past. After 1100 B.C. the old civilization disappeared and was almost entirely forgotten within a few hundred years. The world has learned of the ancient cities only since 1900, when scholars digging among the ruins found the walls of palaces and houses. Among other things, diggers found a number of clay tablets with writing on them. It was clear that there were two different kinds of writing, but both were in an unknown script. It was 1952 before anyone could read these tablets. Then scholars discovered that these ancient writers used an early form of Greek on one group of tablets. But the other writing still remains a complex mystery.

▶ GREEK CIVILIZATION

Athens in the year 447 B.C. was not the largest city in the ancient world. But it was surely one of the liveliest and most interesting. In that year builders began working on the Parthenon, the beautiful temple built in honor of the goddess Athena. The Parthenon stands on the high rocky hill called the Acropolis. Some of the most brilliant people of the ancient world were in Athens in those days, writing books and plays and teaching. There was interesting talk in the homes, on the streets, or wherever people gathered.

Athens was a leader of the Greek cities. This does not mean that Athens ruled Greece, for in those days each city ruled itself. The city-states sometimes united against a common enemy, as when the Persians invaded Greece in 490 and 480 B.C. But they also fought among themselves. The Peloponnesian Wars (431–404 B.C.) brought two groups of

This wall carving of the Greek goddess Athena dates from the 5th century B.C.

Greek vase from the 6th century B.C. depicts the legendary heroes Achilles and Ajax playing dice.

During the time of Pericles, the great temple known as the Parthenon was built in Athens, Greece. These sculptures were part of the temple's magnificent decorations.

cities into conflict. One group was led by Athens and the other by Sparta.

The Democracy of Athens

Athens had an early form of democracy, with government by the citizens. But only men could hold citizenship. Five hundred men made up the council, which had direct charge of city affairs. This council met about three times a month. The men discussed and voted on laws and such important matters as going to war or making peace. Every year a new group of 500 was chosen by drawing names. In this way all men had a chance to serve on the council. The Athenians drew names for all officials except the generals. These were elected each year and could be re-elected any number of times. Pericles was elected general every year except one from 461 to 429 B.C. He was so important as a leader that these years are called "the age of Pericles."

Sparta—A City of Soldiers

Sparta differed from Athens in many ways. In both cities, all men served in the army in wartime, but in Sparta military service was the main duty of all males. A boy began his military training at age 7 and continued it until he was an old man. The laws of Sparta closely regulated what a citizen did. Because a citizen was always a soldier, he could not carry on trade in a foreign land or travel without permission.

The Spartans paid great attention to military training because they were afraid. They had conquered their neighbors and enslaved them, and they feared a slave revolt.

Art and Literature

The Greeks did not build the largest structures of ancient times. No Greek building could compare in size with the pyramids. But the Greeks did erect some of the most beautiful buildings of any time. An example is the Parthenon, at Athens. Only the ruins of the Parthenon stand today. It was blown up during a battle in A.D. 1687. Yet even in ruins the Parthenon remains one of the world's most famous and lovely buildings.

The Greeks produced many things of beauty —pottery, metalwork, and sculpture. It was said that the sculptor Phidias "made marble breathe."

Most Greek children studied Homer's *Iliad* and *Odyssey*, long epic poems that tell of the gods and heroes. The Greeks admired different kinds of poetry, including the verses of a woman named Sappho.

Greek playwrights wrote about subjects well known to their audiences. A play was judged by the beauty of its language rather than the originality of its plot. In the 5th century B.C., Aeschylus, Euripides, and Sophocles moved people deeply with their tragic plays. Aristophanes made them laugh with his uproarious comedies.

Sports and the Olympic Games

The Greeks held games in honor of the gods. Athletes from all the Greek cities took part in the Olympic Games, held in August every four years. They wrestled, boxed, threw the discus and javelin, and ran races. The prize for a victor was only a wreath of leaves. But the honor of winning the wreath was so great that the athletes trained for years to compete for it.

The Desire To Know

The Greeks were eager to learn about the heavens, the world, and themselves. Some searched to discover the elements from which all matter is made. Others studied the sky and carefully observed the sun, moon, and planets. The Greeks knew that the earth was round, and they were not far wrong in their estimations of its size.

The Greeks learned about different peoples and their history. In the 5th century, Herodotus traveled among the Persians, Babylonians, and Egyptians and wrote a history of the world he knew. At about the same time, the Greek physician Hippocrates studied diseases. He described cases he had observed and suggested remedies. He drew up rules of ethics (morals) for those who practiced medicine, which doctors still respect.

Wisdom is more than knowledge alone. Those Greek thinkers who searched for deep understanding called themselves philosophers —"lovers of wisdom." Socrates, his student Plato, and Plato's student Aristotle were among the greatest Greek philosophers. Their ideas still influence modern thinkers.

Greek Civilization Outside Greece

The Greeks were a restless people. They established colonies around the shores of the Mediterranean and Black seas. In 334 B.C., Alexander the Great, the Greek-speaking ruler of Macedonia, waged war against the Persian Empire. Within ten years he conquered the Persians and ruled an empire that extended from Greece east to the Indus River. Alexander established cities throughout his empire that became centers of Greek civilization.

After Alexander's death a Greek ruler of Egypt established the Museum, a kind of university, at Alexandria. There many famous Greek thinkers studied and wrote. The fact that people still study their works tells something important about Greek civilization. The ideas of the Greeks have lasted longer than many of their monuments. For more information on Greek civilization see GREECE, ANCIENT in Volume G.

▶ROMAN CIVILIZATION

When Alexander was conquering his empire in the east, Rome was fighting wars to control Italy in the west. In the years from 265 B.C. to A.D. 14, the Romans won control of the lands around the Mediterranean. For hundreds of years Rome ruled a great empire, which included Egypt and Greece.

Roman conquest did not mean that Roman ways replaced those of the conquered peoples. It was often the other way. Romans adopted many Greek ideas and ways of thinking. The Romans had no real philosophy. If they wished to study this subject, they had to have Greek teachers. They found the

The greatest general of ancient times, Alexander the Great conquered much of the then known world. He introduced Greek civilization to Asia and sought to unite the peoples of East and West.

View of the Roman Colosseum and, in front of it, the Arch of Constantine.

literature of the Greeks more interesting than their own. In fact, the poet Vergil, who lived from 70 to 19 B.C., modeled his great epic poem, the *Aeneid,* on the epics of Homer. The Romans produced important histories and writings about politics, such as those by Cicero.

The Romans as Engineers and Builders

The Romans were excellent engineers. They built a network of good roads. Official messengers and troops moved rapidly over swamps, rivers, and mountains because of good bridges, paved causeways, and tunnels. A Roman bridge still spans the Tagus River in Spain.

Good engineers provided Rome with a better water supply than almost any other ancient city. Stone aqueducts brought pure water from springs sometimes more than 64 kilometers (40 miles) away. Rome had a huge arena, the Colosseum, where over 45,000 people could watch athletic contests, combat between gladiators, chariot races, and other spectacular events. The huge dome on one of ancient Rome's most famous buildings, the Pantheon, still stands.

An aqueduct in Segovia, Spain—one of more than 200 built by the Romans.

Roman coins from the reign of the emperors Nero (*right*), A.D. 54–68, and Constantius II (*left*), A.D. 337–361.

The Romans adopted much of the culture of Greece. The painting above depicts the Greek myth of Narcissus, who fell in love with his own reflection. The mosaic below represents the Academy of the Greek philosopher Plato.

Peace and Justice

The Roman Empire included many different peoples, each with its own language, religion, and customs. The Romans did not force people to give up their own ways so long as they did not interfere with the welfare of the empire. They allowed people to worship their own gods, and they let them manage many of their local affairs. But the Romans could not, of course, use everybody's language. Latin, the Roman tongue, served as the language of government wherever Rome ruled. In some areas Latin came to replace other languages. Portuguese, Spanish, French, Romanian, and Italian all developed from Latin.

The Romans also developed a system of law for the empire. They learned that a law was more likely to be obeyed when it was fair. Roman laws grew increasingly reasonable and fair in the course of time. The Romans saw that the purpose of law is justice. What is justice? The Romans said that it was giving people what was due them. The fact that Roman law lasted so long shows how well they did this. A number of modern countries base their law on that of the Romans.

The Romans did not give the ancient world its greatest art or philosophy, but their contribution was not small. The Roman Empire gave the peoples of that time a peaceful world that allowed them to prosper.

KENNETH S. COOPER
George Peabody College

See also ALEXANDER THE GREAT; ANCIENT WORLD, ART OF THE; BYZANTINE EMPIRE; CITIES; EGYPTIAN ART AND ARCHITECTURE; GREECE, ART AND ARCHITECTURE OF; GREEK MYTHOLOGY; POMPEII; ROMAN ART AND ARCHITECTURE; ROMAN EMPIRE; TROJAN WAR; WONDERS OF THE WORLD; ZOROASTRIANISM.

ANCIENT WORLD, ART OF THE

On the shores of the eastern Mediterranean Sea, where Europe meets Asia and Asia meets Africa, are the remains of ancient cities. These cities lay buried for centuries. When the ruins were dug up, the works of art that were found revealed that this region was one of the first in which civilization was known.

Some of the earliest sculpture of civilized people was created in Mesopotamia, the land between the Tigris and Euphrates rivers. Much of this sculpture was carved on stone slabs, and the slabs served as backgrounds. This kind of sculpture is known as relief. Sculpture-in-the-round—three-dimensional sculpture, free from background—was also created, but it has not survived so well.

Ancient Mesopotamia was the home of many different nations. Certain characteristics of art lasted for thousands of years and were present in the art of every nation. These characteristics were established by the Sumerians, the first civilized people of Mesopotamia. They developed one of the first known empires in history, and their art influenced the Egyptians as well as all later Mesopotamian civilizations.

▶ SUMER (3200–2000 B.C.)

Most of the art that survives from the first 500 years of Sumerian civilization has been found in the ruins of temples. Several bronze statuettes of animals prove that these ancient people knew and used metal. White stone statues of human figures were decorated with

These panels of many-colored stones and shells once decorated a temple in the ancient Sumerian city of Ur. British Museum, London.

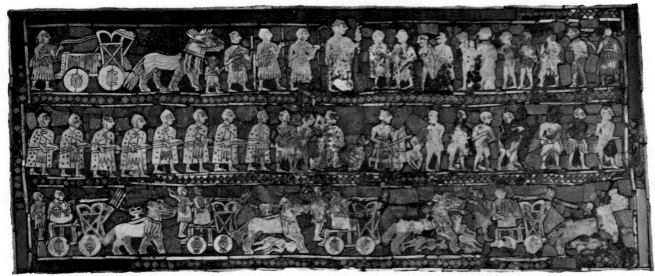

Small statues of worshipers were placed in Sumerian temples. Those at right have stylized features including huge, bulging eyes. The temple statue of the ruler Gudea (*left*) is a later example. Its sculptor may have tried to carve a likeness of Gudea's features.

colored stones. Bowls, vases, bottles, and other containers (called vessels) were made of stone for religious use. The outsides of the vessels were decorated with relief carvings of animals and plants.

Around 3000 B.C. the Sumerians entered their first truly great age, called the Early Dynastic period. Sculpture during this period was created to stand in the temple of the god of the city. Sculptured worshipers stood with their hands clasped in front of their bodies—a gesture of respect before the god. Sometimes the figure held a cup that may have contained an offering to the god. Clothing was solid and stiff; there was no suggestion that a body was beneath it. Most of the artist's skill was concentrated on the head. Eyes were enormous and bulging. The long beards of men had heavy, crosswise ridges. If the figure had hair, it was long and braided, but often heads were shown shaved.

Sumerian sculpture was carved from stone, which had to be imported. There was very little stone in Mesopotamia. The most popular stone was gypsum, which is soft, satiny, and white, and looks like mother-of-pearl.

During this period sculpture gradually became more delicate and lifelike. The rocklike clothing was replaced by more natural-looking skirts, and beards were formed with hundreds of tiny curls. The mouths of these statues are slightly upturned and give life to the face.

Sumerian art reached a peak during the time of the famous ruler Gudea. The sculptures made of Gudea and his family were among the greatest achievements of Sumerian art. Sometimes the statues were seated and sometimes they were standing. Gudea's body was a heavy mass of stonelike drapery as in early Sumerian sculpture. An attempt may have been made to carve a likeness of Gudea's features on the statues.

Sumerian Architecture

Mesopotamia was a land without stone or forests. The usual materials for buildings were mud and reeds. Homes were built of reeds from the marshlands. Sometimes the reeds were tied in great bundles and set in two rows. The tops were bent together and tied. Other

Sumerian temples stood atop towering structures called ziggurats. An artist's reconstruction shows the ziggurat at Ur as it probably looked in ancient times.

Sumerian sculptors worked with metal and colored stones. This offering stand of wood, gold, and lapis lazuli depicts a ram rearing up against a flowering tree.

homes were rectangular and constructed of woven reed. Often the reed building was entirely covered with mud and painted.

The only other buildings that we know about are temples. The temple of the local god was both the spiritual and physical center of a Sumerian city. Built of bricks made of mud and dried in the sun, it stood on a raised platform or tower made of the same material. This temple tower is called a **ziggurat.** The ziggurat was an artificial mountain built in successively smaller stages, like a pyramid. At the top of the "mountain" was the temple of the city-god. Great staircases led from the ground to the summit. The brick walls of the ziggurat often were decorated with colored stones, mother-of-pearl inlays, large paintings, and rows of copper animals.

The ziggurat developed by Sumerian architects became the main form of ancient Mesopotamian architecture. As far as we know, the ziggurat at Warka was the first. The ziggurat built for the moon-god in the city of Ur during the Neo-Sumerian period has remained in better condition than earlier ones. This is because its architects had learned that bricks baked in an oven were much stronger than bricks simply dried in the sun. However, nothing survives of the shrine.

▶ BABYLONIA (2000–1100 B.C.)

Three centuries of war followed the end of the Sumerian Empire. City-states within Mesopotamia fought with each other, and barbarian tribes invaded the Tigris-Euphrates region. Finally in the 18th century B.C., Hammurabi, ruler of the city of Babylon, became the ruler of Sumer and Akkad and united the warring city-states.

Sculpture during the time of Hammurabi was more naturalistic (lifelike) than ever before in Mesopotamia. Although it is not certain, the stone heads that have been found were probably meant to represent Hammurabi. The king was shown as a bearded man with very large eyelids and wearing a cap. Portraiture was unusual in Mesopotamia, but in Egypt—the great nation to the west—royal

In Babylonia, sculpture became increasingly naturalistic, or lifelike. This stone head was intended to represent a particular person—probably King Hammurabi.

portraits were being created. It is likely that Egypt influenced Babylonian art.

Hammurabi recorded his famous laws on a large stone called a **stela.** The laws were written on the lower three quarters of the stone; the top quarter was carved in bold relief, with a figure of a seated god before whom Hammurabi stood. The scene was intended to give religious authority to the laws.

Like the Sumerians, the Babylonians used bronze as well as stone for their sculpture. One bronze statue from the First Dynasty was of a kneeling man. His face was covered with gold. On the base of the statue a carved inscription requested long life for the king, perhaps Hammurabi. Other surviving bronze statues include one of a spirited group of wild goats standing on their hind legs and another of a ram bearing an inscription to a god.

The Kassites, mountaineers from the east, slowly pushed their way into Babylon after the death of Hammurabi. The First Dynasty fell around 1600 B.C., and the Kassite barbarians made themselves masters of Babylonia. Although they adopted Babylonian culture, the Kassites produced very little art.

Babylonian Architecture

Only a few ruins remain of the architecture of the First and Kassite dynasties. Many Sumerian buildings were rebuilt, and the architecture of new buildings was copied from Sumerian styles. The Kassite royal palace was larger than most earlier buildings. Around 1450 B.C. a new temple was built at Warka for the worship of the mother-goddess. It was not on a ziggurat, but was small and rectangular. Reliefs in brick depicting huge gods formed a continuous band of decoration on the outside walls of the temple.

The Kassite Dynasty fell to the Assyrians in about 1100 B.C. Until the 6th century B.C., the Babylonians were attacked, overrun, crushed, and conquered many times. But they survived to rise again and to make Babylon one of the great cities of the ancient world.

▶ MINOAN CIVILIZATION (2000–1200 B.C.)

More than 5,000 years ago the Mediterranean island of Crete was inhabited by people known as the Minoans. The Minoans developed a civilization around the same time that the Sumerians began theirs. Nothing was known about this civilization until the 20th

Frescoes—paintings done on wet plaster—decorated the walls of the Minoan palace at Knossos. One of the most important figures was the king-priest (*left*). Painted pottery statues known as snake-goddesses (*right*) were created by the Minoans about 1600 B.C.

century, and little is certain about its history and earliest art.

The sculpture of the Minoans—at least what has survived—is small and very different from the sculpture of Mesopotamia. Figures of animals and people were made of bronze, stone, ivory, or terra-cotta (red clay). The Minoans sometimes baked clay statuettes and painted them. In contrast to Mesopotamian sculpture, Minoan figures were shown in motion: representations of worshipers had upraised arms; animals were shown running; an acrobat was depicted jumping over a bull. Slender young men and women were portrayed with impossibly small waists and narrow hips. Figures of men had arms crossed on their chests. Women wore narrow corsets beneath their breasts, flaring skirts, and high headdresses.

Around 1600 B.C. the Minoans created statuettes known as snake-goddesses. However, these sculptures probably represented priestesses rather than goddesses. Made of painted pottery, these figures are similar to earlier Minoan work—they are dressed in the same manner—but their outstretched arms have snakes coiled around them.

Ivory figurines were originally enriched with gold details now lost. Common subjects were young athletes leaping over bulls, a child at play, or a child attended by nurses. Bronze sculpture almost always represented a Minoan at prayer.

Relief sculpture on a large scale was probably unknown to the Minoans. Most carving in relief was done on stone vessels. Subjects included farmers marching and singing, and people boxing, wrestling, bull leaping, or just standing. The Minoans also created a great many delicate, tiny seals carved on gems. Some scholars believe that all adult Minoans had their own seal designs.

Minoan Architecture

The Minoans did not build temples. Religious ceremonies were conducted outdoors or in the palaces. The palace was the center of the Minoan community. It was, of course, the residence of the royal family and the seat of government, but it was also used as a storehouse for merchandise and contained workshops where goods were manufactured.

The palace was usually built on a hillside and was made up of many low, rectangular units. Roofs were flat, and foundations were made of stone. Two or three stories was the usual height; the first story was stone and the ones above were probably of mud bricks.

A great court paved with stones was built in the center of the palace. Religious ceremonies were conducted in this court. It is thought that this central court was planned first, and as new parts were needed they were built around it. Corridor walls were decorated with large frescoes—paintings done on wet plaster. Because the building was constructed in separate parts, many staircases and corridors were needed. Walls and sometimes even floors may have been covered with alabaster. Ceilings were held up by painted wooden columns, which were circular or oval. They were unusual because they were smaller at the base than at the top. No one is certain why the columns were made in this way.

Comfort was important to the Minoans. Their palaces and country houses sprawled over large areas, and there were many passageways and windows. Sunlight poured into every part of the buildings, and there was a great feeling of spaciousness. Elaborate bathrooms—undoubtedly the first in Europe—contained terra-cotta tubs, drains, and toilets.

In the course of many centuries, the great Minoan palaces were destroyed several times. Scholars cannot be absolutely certain of the causes, but earthquakes, tidal waves, or fires were among the natural causes. There may also have been uprisings and invasions. But each time, the Minoans rebuilt their palaces. Then, around the year 1200 B.C.,

the Minoan civilization came to a sudden end. The Dorian tribes from the north took over Crete along with much of the Greek mainland. The Minoan buildings, along with all Minoan art, were lost for the next 30 centuries.

▶THE HITTITES (1400–1200 B.C.)

Anatolia, a land in Asia Minor, was the home of the ancient peoples known as the Hittites. Around 1400 B.C. the Hittites extended their empire eastward as far as Mesopotamia.

Except for their statuettes in bronze, the Hittites made no sculpture-in-the-round that we know of. Hittite sculpture, in fact, was so completely a part of Hittite architecture that the two arts must be discussed together.

The Hittites built on an enormous scale. Unlike Mesopotamia, Anatolia was rich in stone and wood. The foundations of their military, civil, and religious buildings were of stone. In early Hittite buildings, stones 3 meters (10 feet) high were used in rough blocks. Later, stone that had been trimmed was used. Above the stone first level, the buildings were constructed with bricks and wood. Parts of the structure that received the most use—such as window sills and thresholds—were reinforced with stone.

Hattusas, the capital city of the Hittite Empire, was enclosed in a great wall. One of the gates was guarded by two stone lions, one on each side. The lions had been carved in very high relief from huge stones, and the remaining part of the boulders rose as high as 3 meters above the lions. Other gates were protected by sphinxes (lions with human heads) that were carved in the same way. The lions and sphinxes appeared to have grown out of the stone.

Marching figures carved in relief from stone slabs were placed along the walls of Hittite buildings on the ground level. The slabs were of either limestone or dolerite, a coarse-grained stone that had to be coated with plaster or gesso (chalk mixed with glue) to create a smooth surface. The marching figures represented a religious procession. Most of these reliefs were at Yasilikaya, which was probably a holy shrine or religious center. Gods were shown wearing flowing robes and often standing on sacred animals.

Great stone lions over 3,000 years old still stand at the ruins of Bogazkoy, a meeting place of the ancient Hittites.

Some of these reliefs were carved on the sides of cliffs at Yasilikaya, and elaborate buildings with open courts and great staircases led to the cliffs. Egyptian and Minoan designs were often included in the reliefs, a sign of trade and communication between empires. Yasilikaya may have been the coronation place of the Hittite kings.

Hittite art did not have a chance to develop fully. In the 13th century B.C., the empire was overwhelmed by invasions of barbarians from the north and by an army of mysterious peoples called the Peoples of the Sea, whose origins are unknown.

▶ ASSYRIA (900–600 B.C.)

In the centuries that followed the decline of the Hittites, the Assyrians gradually built a great empire. The Assyrians were similar to the Babylonians in language, law, and religion, but they were much more brutal. Their civilization was based on the army, and their art reflected their love of war and violence. Only a few sculptures-in-the-round have been found. One is of an early emperor, Ashurnasirpal II. In style it resembled sculpture from the Early Dynastic period of Sumer.

In the long, rectangular rooms of Assyrian buildings, there were large gypsum slabs carved in relief. The carvings often showed fierce battles or hunting scenes. Complicated and horrible scenes of torture and bloodshed and of vicious animals may have been highlighted with black, red, and yellow paint.

Assyrian reliefs give us a picture of cities, fortresses, costumes, and daily life of a people forever lost to us. From these reliefs we know the kind of furniture the Assyrians used, although only bits and pieces of real furniture have been found.

The Assyrians also carved reliefs of gigantic human-headed bulls, each with five legs. These huge creatures always appear in pairs as guardians of a palace. Placed near an entrance, they were sometimes combined with figures of men of superhuman size.

Reliefs of ivory were used by the Assyrians to decorate chests, thrones, chairs, and other furniture. Often the reliefs were gilded (coated with gold) and inlaid with colored glass and stones. Common subjects of the sculpture were plants, real and imaginary beasts, musicians, and a woman standing at a window.

Assyrian Architecture

The chief cities of Assyria were Nimrud, Khorsabad, and Nineveh, the capital. Following an ancient custom, cities were enclosed within great walls to keep enemies out. The buildings in the cities of Assyria were made of mud bricks and looked much like the buildings of Sumer. The buildings were not very high, but were spread over a large area and contained a great many rooms.

Only the ziggurat towered high over the city walls. At Khorsabad the Assyrians erected a spectacular ziggurat reaching as high as a twelve-story building of today. It was probably built in seven levels, and each one was painted a different color.

Inside and outside of every important Assyrian structure, color played an important part. Colorful glazed bricks in various patterns decorated the walls. Sometimes the outside walls were whitewashed and the inside decorated with frescoes. Ceilings were held up by wooden columns resting on stone bases. The combination of wooden columns, glazed brick, stone reliefs, and frescoes of flowers and animals created rich and impressive effects that never grew monotonous.

The stone carvings of the warlike Assyrians frequently illustrated hunting and battle scenes. This 7th century B.C. relief from Nineveh depicts King Ashurbanipal hunting.

Five-legged winged bulls with human heads (*left*) protected the gates of Assyrian palaces. A carved amber statue of the Assyrian king Ashurnasirpal II (*right*) dates from the 9th century B.C. It is one of the few surviving Assyrian sculptures-in-the-round.

In 640 B.C. the Assyrian Empire controlled more of the Middle East than it ever had before. Yet, less than 30 years later the empire no longer existed. In 612 B.C. it was invaded and crushed by a combined army of Chaldeans and Medes.

▶ THE CHALDEANS (615–539 B.C.)

When the Chaldeans and Medes divided the Assyrian Empire in two, southern Mesopotamia and the lands west of the Euphrates River became the Chaldean, or Neo-Babylonian, Empire. The Chaldeans were the descendants of the Babylonians, who had ruled the ancient world before the rise of the Hittites and Assyrians.

Babylon was restored as the capital of a great empire. Temples from the old First and Kassite dynasties were rebuilt. The best-known Chaldean king, Nebuchadnezzar, built the Hanging Gardens of Babylon. His palace was built in levels, and each level had a terrace planted with flowers and shrubs. The pillars that supported each level were hollow and were used as wells.

Little remains of the art of the Chaldeans. Their famous ziggurat is hardly more than rubble today. It is likely that this ziggurat was the Tower of Babel mentioned in the Bible, for it was Nebuchadnezzar who conquered and destroyed Jerusalem, enslaved the Hebrews, and carried them to Babylonia. The ziggurat and palace were made of baked bricks. The exteriors were decorated with

The stairway leading to the royal audience hall at Persepolis is decorated with relief sculptures of animals and processions of the king's guards.

reliefs in glazed brick. Bright yellow bulls and sparkling white dragons were set against backgrounds of rich blue or green. Babylon during this period became a glowing expression of its luxury-loving people.

▶THE PERSIAN EMPIRE (550–332 B.C.)

In the middle of the 6th century B.C., the Persians conquered all of Mesopotamia. The Persian Empire eventually spread to Egypt and Europe in the west and into India in the east. The Persians permitted religious freedom —they returned the Hebrews to Palestine— developed an alphabet, and introduced simple systems of arithmetic.

Persia's religion (Zoroastrianism) did not require temples. Services were conducted at an altar in the open. The chief royal palaces were at Susa and Persepolis. The Persians continued the ancient Mesopotamian custom of building their palaces on platforms or terraces of mud brick. Persepolis, which was started about 520 B.C., was built on a series of these

platforms. The throne hall and the audience hall were separate buildings of immense height and were built with forests of tall columns— many more than were needed. Elaborately carved and painted, the columns were topped by enormous capitals (tops of columns) carved with bulls or dragons. The architects continued the earlier Mesopotamian use of huge stone statues of bulls and human-headed bulls as guardians of gates. At Susa reliefs of molded and glazed bricks representing lions and dragons were used as wall decorations in the palace. They date from early in the 4th century B.C.

Sculpture-in-the-round was almost unknown in Persia. A few heads of men, all of them small, were created, and some sculptures found in Egypt may be of Persian origin. But relief sculpture was made for the exteriors of buildings and to line the walls of staircases. The majority of the reliefs were made of limestone often almost black in color. But even this handsome stone was enriched with paint

in a wide range of colors, and details were gilded.

Egyptians and other foreign craftsmen were brought to Persepolis to sculpt the reliefs. Foreign influences can be detected, but the work must have been closely supervised by the Persians. These very decorative reliefs represent the king receiving foreign envoys bearing tribute. Sometimes the king is shown in combat with a demon. Persian art was very decorative, but was not especially original.

In 331 B.C. the Greek conqueror Alexander the Great overran the Persian Empire and destroyed the palace of Persepolis. The defeat of the Persians marks the end of the great cultures of the ancient Middle East. The rise of the Greeks marks the beginning of modern civilization.

JOHN D. COONEY
Author, *Late Egyptian and Coptic Art*

See also ANCIENT CIVILIZATIONS; ARCHITECTURE; EGYPTIAN ART AND ARCHITECTURE; SCULPTURE; WONDERS OF THE WORLD.

ANCIENT WORLD, MUSIC OF THE

In primitive times, music was a means to an end. People used it as a bridge to power. They used it to call in the gods of healing. They used music to bring rain to ensure a good harvest. Hunters expected added strength and accuracy after chanting the correct magic words and melody.

Dramatic changes took place in music about 6,000 years ago. The advanced civilizations of the Sumerians and the Egyptians appeared on the historic scene at this time and set music on a new path. Music received a new personality. No longer was it primarily a tool for religion and magic or for the daily functions of life. Music became an end in itself, an art to be appreciated for its own sake. The change was not abrupt, for primitive people sometimes danced, sang, and played instruments for the sheer joy of making music. But music truly became an art when it was taken over by professional musicians.

Kings, princes, and nobles demanded entertainment in their leisure time. They supported a great many professional singers, dancers, and instrumentalists. These musicians were trained from childhood, and they became highly skilled. They raised music to the level of a special trade or profession. Female musicians were particularly popular and they were often attached in large numbers to the royal courts.

Professional musicians were also heard in the temples, since religion still made use of music. The priests, who could read and write, were often also scholars. They were trained in mathematics, science, and philosophy. (Such subjects were not developed among primitive peoples because they had no written language.) The well-educated priests applied their knowledge to music and made other dramtic changes in this art. For the first time music could be written down, since the priests developed a special music notation. They also looked for the mathematical and scientific bases of music. This led to the first organized music theory, which contained information

An Egyptian wall painting shows female musicians playing the double oboe, long-necked lute, and harp.

A mosaic dating from about 2800 B.C. shows a musician of ancient Sumeria playing a lyre.

A double-reed instrument is shown in an ancient Etruscan wall painting.

on the types of scales, melodies, and rhythms the professional musician had to learn and guided him in tuning his instruments.

The Sumerians

In the ancient cities of Mesopotamia, near the Tigris and Euphrates rivers, Sumerian and later Babylonian court musicians sang and played their harps and long-necked lutes. Temple musicians participated in ceremonies honoring Shamash, the sun god; Ningirsu, the god of war; and other gods. The sacred prayers were sung by large choirs trained at the temple schools. The priests wrote their theories of religion, science, and music on clay tablets in wedge-shaped symbols. They also wrote down many prayers and hymns, often with the accompanying music written alongside the text. Unlike modern Western notation, each special sign for writing the music represented groups of notes rather than single notes. The written prayers, religious myths, and sacred music were probably kept secret and hidden from the eyes of those outside the clergy.

In addition to the harp and long-necked lute, the Sumerians favored another string instrument, the lyre. Instead of a neck the lyre has two separate arms connected by a crossbar. The flute and oboe also appeared, although wind instruments were generally not as popular as strings. Two oboes were usually bound together in a V shape and played at the same time. One of the pair probably played the melody, and the other droned a single continuous note. This melody-and-drone style of music has persisted to modern times in the Middle East and in India, where the double-wind instrument is still found.

Many of the Sumerian instruments were played at the religious ceremonies. For example, the god of wisdom, Ea, was worshiped in a sacrificial bull ritual featuring a large, goblet-shaped metal drum. Special hymns at this ceremony were accompanied by the double oboe.

The Egyptians

The civilization of ancient Egypt first appeared along the Nile River about 4000 B.C., perhaps a few hundred years later than that of Sumer. Like the Sumerian and Babylo-nian kings, the Egyptian pharaohs had many professional musicians. These are often shown on tomb paintings and sculptures playing, singing, and dancing in groups rather than as soloists. A typical musical group of about 2500 B.C. might have had several of the Egyptians' favorite instrument, the large curved harp, standing upright. There might also have been some flutes and a double clarinet consisting of two clarinets glued together. However, the most important part of the group was the singers, who were also conductors. These conductors accomplished more than conductors of modern times, for their special finger, hand, and arm motions were a special sign language. By holding the palm upward or making a circle of the thumb and forefinger, for example, they could indicate to the accompanists what melodies and rhythms to play. A similar sign language is still used today in Egypt and India.

Many musicians were exchanged as gifts between the kings of ancient times. Pharaoh Pepi II, who ruled Egypt for more than 90 years in the 26th and 25th centuries B.C., even received presents of skilled Pygmy dancers from the Congo. Much later, when Egypt became a conquering nation, many such gifts began to pour in. The pharaohs received hundreds of music girls and their instruments from Mesopotamia and other parts of southwest Asia after conquering this region in about 1500 B.C. Among the new instruments were the lyre, long-necked lute, double oboe, and tambourine. The girls seem to have brought with them a more exciting style of music, which the Egyptians soon adopted.

Little is known of the melodies and rhythms of the ancient Egyptians. However, their harps were tuned to one of the most popular scales of ancient times (and of modern Japan). This is one of the pentatonic, or five-note, scales, which can be illustrated on the piano by the tones A F E C B. No doubt other scales were also used by the Egyptians. Like the Sumerians, the Egyptians enjoyed a touch of harmony in their music, such as the drone. The drone is a steady, continuous note with a hypnotic effect. However, it was always merely a backdrop to the more important part of the music, the melody.

The sistrum, a rattle with jingling cross-bars, was played at the festivals of the

Egyptian cow-headed goddess Hathor. Although the goddess is no longer worshiped, an instrument similar to the sistrum is still played in Ethiopian Coptic churches.

The Hebrews

Although the ancient Sumerian and Egyptian civilizations faded away in history, ancient Hebrew traditions continue to the present day. Some modern Hebrews, such as those in Yemen and Iraq, have lived alone and have not been influenced by surrounding people. Their religious music, therefore, is probably very much like the music of King Solomon's temple from the 10th to 6th centuries B.C.

In this temple professional male choirs sang at daily and special ceremonies. They sang the psalms of David and other religious texts, often in the form of two choruses answering each other. There was also a soloist who chanted the different parts of the Old Testament and at certain points was answered by the congregation. Most of the melodies

Ancient Greek singers sometimes accompanied themselves on the kithara.

sung at the temple were made up of tiny melodic patterns of a few notes each. Like little formulas, these patterns could not be changed in themselves. They could, however, be strung together in different ways to form a large variety of melodies. This idea is connected with the old Sumerian music notation described above and with some later Hebrew and Christian music notation. In such types of notation, a single written sign stands for a group of musical tones that make up a tiny melodic pattern. In fact, some of the melodies of the early Christian Church are exactly like some Hebrew religious melodies sung today in Yemen, Iraq, and Iran.

The ancient Hebrews played many instruments. In the temple large professional orchestras of harps, lyres, and cymbals accompanied the choirs. Horns and metal trumpets were played by the priests. The sound of the 120 trumpets played by the priests at the opening of Solomon's temple, an event described in the second chapter of Chronicles, must really have been shattering. Outside the temple shepherds and other people played the lyre, which was King David's favorite instrument, the flute, and the oboe. Women played the tambourine, often dancing and singing as they played.

The Greeks

In the 9th century B.C., when Homer wrote his great poems the *Iliad* and the *Odyssey,* Greece was on the way to becoming a great civilization. Like Sumeria, Egypt, Persia, and nearby nations, Greece shared in the general Oriental culture of the Middle East. Through royal gifts, conquests, and migrations, musicians and instruments were interchanged throughout this entire area. As a result the music of these ancient civilizations had many things in common. One of these was the melody patterns. Another was the lack of any real harmony, a feature that developed much later in Europe, after the Middle Ages. Melody and rhythm were strongly emphasized in the ancient world, as they still are in the Middle East and India.

The Greeks were so interested in melody and rhythm that of all the ancient nations they developed the most elaborate theories on these subjects. Since all melodies are based on scales, the Greek scientists soon set to work in this direction. The great mathematician Euclid was one of the first to organize all the important Greek scales in one system, in the 4th century B.C. These scales, or modes as they are often called, had seven notes each. Earlier the Greeks had favored five-note scales, the most important resembling the ancient Egyptian harp scale A F E C B. In fact, two famous hymns of the 2nd century B.C., sung to Apollo at his shrine in Delphi, still had sections in this very old scale. The popular Greek aulos, a shrill double oboe often heard at the exciting spring rites of the god Dionysus, was also frequently played in this five-note scale, even as late as the 2nd century A.D.

When the seven-note modes were organized, they received the names of various people and places in Greece, such as Dorian, Phrygian, and Lydian. All of these modes can to some extent be played on the white keys of the piano. The C major scale is a good example of the Lydian mode, and all the white keys between any two E's on the piano give the Dorian. In the Middle Ages the Christian Church used the same Greek names for its own musical scales.

The Greeks were very fond of psychology. They felt that mental and physical health could be directly influenced by different scales and rhythms. The philosopher Aristotle, for example, said the Phrygian mode should be used to inspire enthusiasm, and the Dorian to produce calm in a person. Many of these ideas were applied to musical education, which in Arcadia, Sparta, and other places was required for most people from childhood on.

The lyre was the national instrument of Greece. Amateurs usually played a light type of lyre made of a tortoise shell. Professionals played the famous kithara, a heavier lyre said to be Apollo's favorite instrument. Composers often wrote their lyre melodies in a special notation in which each note was represented by a letter of the alphabet.

As in other ancient nations, singing was very popular in Greece. Professional soloists, especially poets who sang their own poetry, were in great demand by the nobility. Even more important were the choruses, some of which contained hundreds of singers. Choruses sang hymns to the gods and sang at athletic competitions, where they won prizes. Resembling opera, Greek drama usually included choruses that also danced and acted. A chorus leader would beat out the rhythm with a special sandal having a loose, flapping sole. His conducting was very helpful to the musicians, since Greek poetry and music had complicated rhythmic patterns made up of long and short beats.

Ancient music left many traces in early Europe, particularly in its instruments and in the Gregorian chant of the Christian Church. Eventually Europe broke away from its heritage from other parts of the world and developed its own musical ideas.

ROSE BRANDEL
City University of New York, Hunter College

ANDERSEN, HANS CHRISTIAN (1805–1875)

When I was a very young boy, just discovering the world of books and stories, Hans Christian Andersen was a magic name to me. I used to laugh and cry over his tales—especially *The Ugly Duckling*. You see, I was a gawky, lonely child, too, and now that I have found my place in the world, I think of the story as *my* story.

When I was chosen to play Hans Andersen in the movie and went to Denmark to learn as much about him as I could, I found out from townspeople whose grandparents had been Andersen's neighbors that *The Ugly Duckling* was really Hans's story. This made me feel a great kinship for him and gave his story special meaning.

In many ways his life was like a fairy tale. Out of the poverty of his boyhood, out of years of hardship, loneliness, and ridicule he came to be one of the honored men of his time. He was a friend of all the great people of his day and a welcome guest in the palaces of princes and kings. Yet the purity of his heart, his simplicity, his faith in God and man, never changed. Throughout his life he saw the world with the clear and innocent eyes of childhood. He understood children, and they loved to sit at his feet while he wove a spell of enchantment and wonder.

On a sunny September day in 1819, when Hans was only 14, he left his hometown of Odense to seek his fortune in the great capital city of Copenhagen. He was very tall, gawky, and awkward, with yellow hair. He had a big head and a big nose. He wore a long coat, wooden shoes, and a peaked cap. In his pockets was enough money to last him a day or two, until he became—as he was sure he would—an actor in the Royal Theatre.

With high hopes he said good-bye to his mother and grandmother—the two people in the world who loved him dearly and whom he dearly loved. As the coach that took him to the boat rumbled away, he may have been thinking not only of the unknown experiences ahead but of the life he was leaving behind.

In the one-room cottage where he had lived with his parents was his father's cobbler's bench, but no one was beside it now. His father had died several years before. In the new house where Hans had lived after his mother had remarried was the toy theater his father had made. The little figures wore costumes that Hans himself had cut out of bits of cloth while the shoemaker, working at his trade, told his son stories from *The Arabian Nights* and old Danish legends.

Left behind too was the church where he had been confirmed only a few weeks before. On that day, Hans had worn new shoes outside his trousers so that people could see them. He had been very proud when his shoes creaked as he walked down the aisle. But later he was ashamed that all through the confirmation service, he had thought only of his new shoes. Many years later he wrote *The Red Shoes,* about a selfish girl who behaved in much the same way. Hans put many pieces of his own life into his fairy tales. He never forgot that his mother as a young girl had been forced to go begging. This led him to write *The Little Match Girl,* so full of compassion for the unfortunate ones of this earth. His own story, *The Ugly Duckling,* points out that sometimes the qualities that make you feel lonely, different, and out of place are the very qualities that, when properly used, can make you shine.

The people of Odense had never known what to make of Hans. They thought he might be a little daffy. When he recited long pas-sages from plays or did a clumsy dance or insisted on singing, they could hardly help laughing. Everyone advised him to learn a trade, but this he would not do. He was forever saying that he was going to be famous, that he knew he would have to suffer, but in the end, God would make his dreams come true.

When Hans got off the little boat at Copenhagen, he prayed to God to give him help. He then went to the home of a great lady of the theater to seek her help. To the lady's astonishment, he tried to dance the role from the ballet *Cinderella.* Instead of helping him to become a famous actor, she had him hastily shown out.

Many people of the theater and wealthy families of the city tried to help him, without much success. His dancing master gave up, and so did his singing teacher. Directors of the Royal Theatre sympathized with his efforts to write plays but finally concluded that Hans needed an education. One of the directors of the theater raised money to send him away to school. These next few years were the unhappiest of his life. At 17, Hans was much older than the other students, and the schoolmaster found endless ways to make fun of him. Finally when word of Hans' plight reached his benefactors in Copenhagen, he was removed from the school and put into the hands of a private tutor.

After his schooling, Hans spent many years in travel and in writing poems, books, and plays, which met with some success. It was not until he was 30 that he wrote any fairy tales. The first small book of fairy tales became popular almost immediately, and from then on his fame grew rapidly, spreading from country to country. Hans had found himself at last. The rest of his life was a happy and a busy one.

In 1867 he returned to Odense to be honored by the great of his country. Standing on the balcony of the hall where the ceremonies had been held, he saw below him the city square, full of people who cheered him, and bright with thousands of candles burning in the windows of all the buildings. The whole of Odense had been illuminated just for him.

DANNY KAYE

On the following pages is one of Hans Christian Andersen's best-loved fairy tales.

▶ THE EMPEROR'S NEW CLOTHES

Many years ago there lived an Emperor who was so exceedingly fond of fine new clothes that he spent all his money on being elaborately dressed. He took no interest in his soldiers, no interest in the theater, nor did he care to drive about in his state coach, unless it were to show off his new clothes. He had different robes for every hour of the day, and just as one says of a King that he is in his Council Chamber, people always said of him, "The Emperor is in his wardrobe!"

The great city in which he lived was full of gaiety. Strangers were always coming and going. One day two swindlers arrived; they made themselves out to be weavers, and said they knew how to weave the most magnificent fabric that one could imagine. Not only were the colors and patterns unusually beautiful, but the clothes that were made of this material had the extraordinary quality of becoming invisible to everyone who was either unfit for his post, or inexcusably stupid.

"What useful clothes to have!" thought the Emperor. "If I had some like that, I might find out which of the people in my Empire are unfit for their posts. I should also be able to distinguish the wise from the fools. Yes, that material must be woven for me immediately!" Then he gave the swindlers large sums of money so that they could start work at once.

Quickly they set up two looms and pretended to weave, but there was not a trace of anything on the frames. They made no bones about demanding the finest silk and the purest gold thread. They stuffed everything into their bags, and continued to work at the empty looms until late into the night.

"I'm rather anxious to know how much of the material is finished," thought the Emperor, but to tell the truth, he felt a bit uneasy, remembering that anyone who was either a fool or unfit for his post would never be able to see it. He rather imagined that he need not have any fear for himself, yet he thought it wise to send someone else first to see how things were going. Everyone in the town knew about the exceptional powers of the material, and all were eager to know how incompetent or how stupid the neighbors might be.

"I will send my honest old Chamberlain to the weavers," thought the Emperor. "He will be able to judge the fabric better than anyone else, for he has brains, and nobody fills his post better than he does."

So the nice old Chamberlain went into the hall where the two swindlers were sitting working at the empty looms.

"And so the Emperor set off in the procession under the beautiful canopy, and everybody . . . said 'Oh! how superb the Emperor's new clothes are!' "

"Upon my life!" he thought, opening his eyes very wide, "I can't see anything at all!" But he didn't say so.

Both the swindlers begged him to be good enough to come nearer, and asked how he liked the unusual design and the splendid colors. They pointed to the empty looms, and the poor old Chamberlain opened his eyes wider and wider, but he could see nothing, for there was nothing. "Heavens above!" he thought, "could it possibly be that I am stupid? I have never thought that of myself, and not a soul must know it. Could it be that I am not fit for my post? It will never do for me to admit that I can't see the material!"

"Well, you don't say what you think of it," said one of the weavers.

"Oh, it's delightful—most exquisite!" said the old Chamberlain, looking through his spectacles. "What a wonderful design and what beautiful colors! I shall certainly tell the Emperor that I am enchanted with it."

"We're very pleased to hear that," said the two weavers, and they started describing the colors and the curious pattern. The old Chamberlain listened carefully in order to repeat, when he came home to the Emperor, exactly what he had heard, and he did so.

The swindlers now demanded more money, as well as more silk and gold thread, saying that they needed it for weaving. They put everything into their pockets and not a thread appeared upon the looms, but they kept on working at the empty frames as before.

Soon after this, the Emperor sent another nice official to see how the weaving was getting on, and to enquire whether the stuff would soon be ready. Exactly the same thing happened to him as to the Chamberlain. He looked and looked, but as there was nothing to be seen except the empty looms, he could see nothing.

"Isn't it a beautiful piece of material?" said the swindlers, showing and describing the pattern that did not exist at all.

"Stupid I certainly am not," thought the official; "then I must be unfit for my excellent post, I suppose. That seems rather funny—but I'll take great care that nobody gets wind of it." Then he praised the material he could not see, and assured them of his enthusiasm for the gorgeous colors and the beautiful pattern. "It's simply enchanting!" he said to the Emperor.

The whole town was talking about the splendid material.

And now the Emperor was curious to see it for himself while it was still upon the looms.

Accompanied by a great number of selected people, among whom were the two nice old officials who had already been there, the Emperor went forth to visit the two wily swindlers. They were now weaving madly, yet without a single thread upon the looms.

"Isn't it magnificent?" said the two nice officials. "Will Your Imperial Majesty deign to look at this splendid pattern and these glorious colors?" Then they pointed to the empty looms, for each thought that the others could probably see the material.

"What on earth can this mean?" thought the Emperor. "I don't see anything! This is terrible. Am I stupid? Am I unfit to be Emperor? That would be the most disastrous thing that could possibly befall me.—Oh, it's perfectly wonderful!" he said. "It quite meets with my Imperial approval." And he nodded appreciatively and stared at the empty looms—he would not admit that he saw nothing. His whole suite looked and looked, but with as little result as the others; nevertheless, they all said, like the Emperor, "It's perfectly wonderful!" They advised him to have some new clothes made from this splendid stuff and to wear them for the first time in the next great procession.

"Magnificent!" "Excellent!" "Prodigious!" went from mouth to mouth, and everyone was exceedingly pleased. The Emperor gave each of the swindlers a decoration to wear in his buttonhole, and the title of "Knight of the Loom."

Before the procession they worked all night, burning more than sixteen candles. People could see how busy they were finishing the Emperor's new clothes. They pretended to take the material from the looms, they slashed the air with great scissors, they sewed with needles without any thread, and finally they said, "The Emperor's clothes are ready!"

Then the Emperor himself arrived with his most distinguished courtiers, and each swindler raised an arm as if he were holding something, and said, "These are Your Imperial Majesty's knee-breeches. This is Your Imperial Majesty's robe. This is Your Imperial Majesty's mantle," and so forth. "It is all as light as a spider's web, one might fancy one had nothing on, but that is just the beauty of it!"

"Yes, indeed," said all the courtiers, but they could see nothing, for there was nothing to be seen.

"If Your Imperial Majesty would graciously consent to take off your clothes," said the swindlers, "we could fit on the new ones in front of the long glass."

So the Emperor laid aside his clothes, and the swindlers pretended to hand him, piece by piece, the new ones they were supposed to have made, and they fitted him round the waist, and acted as if they were fastening something on— it was the train; and the Emperor turned round and round in front of the long glass.

"How well the new robes suit Your Imperial Majesty! How well they fit!" they all said. "What a splendid design! What gorgeous colors! It's all magnificently regal!"

"The canopy which is to be held over Your Imperial Majesty in the procession is waiting outside," announced the Lord High Chamberlain.

"Well, I suppose I'm ready," said the Emperor. "Don't you think they are a nice fit?" And he looked at himself again in the glass, first on one side and then the other, as if he really were carefully examining his handsome attire.

The courtiers who were to carry the train groped about on the floor with fumbling fingers, and pretended to lift it; they walked on, holding their hands up in the air; nothing would have induced them to admit that they could not see anything.

And so the Emperor set off in the procession under the beautiful canopy, and everybody in the streets and at the windows said, "Oh! how superb the Emperor's new clothes are! What a gorgeous train! What a perfect fit!" No one would acknowledge that he didn't see anything, so proving that he was not fit for his post, or that he was very stupid.

None of the Emperor's clothes had ever met with such a success.

"But he hasn't got any clothes on!" gasped out a little child.

"Good heavens! Hark at the little innocent!" said the father, and people whispered to one another what the child had said. "But he hasn't got any clothes on! There's a little child saying he hasn't got any clothes on!"

"But he hasn't got any clothes on!" shouted the whole town at last. The Emperor had a creepy feeling down his spine, because it began to dawn upon him that the people were right. "All the same," he thought to himself, "I've got to go through with it as long as the procession lasts."

So he drew himself up and held his head higher than before, and the courtiers held on to the train that wasn't there at all.

ANDERSON, MARIAN (1897–1993)

Visitors to a small church in Philadelphia, Pennsylvania, were amazed by the beautiful voice of a 6-year-old girl singing in the choir. She was Marian Anderson, born in Philadelphia on February 27, 1897. As a child she loved to sing all kinds of songs, but her favorites were the hymns she sang in church. This little girl eventually became known as one of the greatest singers of her time.

It was not easy for Marian Anderson to acquire a musical education. She was black in a racially prejudiced society, and her family was poor. But when she was in her twenties, she won a scholarship. It enabled her to travel and study in Europe. She made her European concert debut in Berlin, and her fame spread quickly. Her singing delighted huge audiences in every major European city. The great composer Jean Sibelius dedicated a song to her when she visited him in Finland.

News of her success in Europe reached America. At her homecoming concert in New York City in 1935, she received thunderous applause. But in 1939 she was prevented from giving a concert at Constitution Hall in Washington, D.C. Many people felt that her race was the reason. Undaunted, on Easter Sunday of the same year, she gave a free concert for an audience of 75,000 from the steps of the Lincoln Memorial.

As her fame increased, Marian Anderson toured all parts of the world. In 1955 she became the first black singer to appear with the Metropolitan Opera. The U.S. State Department sent her on a goodwill tour of Asia in 1957, and the following year, she served as a U.S. delegate to the United Nations. She was awarded the Presidential Medal of Freedom in

Marian Anderson, a contralto with a rich, mellow voice, overcame racial prejudice to become one of the greatest singers of modern times.

1963. The Marian Anderson Award, which she established in 1942, helped young students pay for their musical education.

On April 18, 1965, Marian Anderson gave a farewell concert at Carnegie Hall, in New York City. But she continued to be honored with awards and tributes. She died in Portland, Oregon, on April 8, 1993. Her autobiography is *My Lord, What a Morning* (1956).

Reviewed by FLORENCE JACKSON
Author, Blacks in America series

ANDERSON, MAXWELL. See NORTH DAKOTA (Famous People).

Tropical
Rain Forest

Coniferous/
Evergreen Forest

Deciduous
Forest

Grassland

Chaparral

Desert/
Semidesert

Alpine Tundra

Ice Cap

Andes

Cotopaxi, located in the Andes south of Quito, Ecuador, is the world's highest active volcano.

ANDES

The Andes form the longest and one of the highest mountain systems in the world. Only the Himalayas in south central Asia are taller and more rugged. The ranges of the Andes stretch about 7,200 kilometers (4,500 miles) along the west coast of South America, from the Caribbean Sea in the north to Tierra del Fuego, an island group at the southern tip of the continent.

Within the Andes there are many different kinds of lands and ways of life. There are great modern cities and small Indian villages where people live much as their ancestors did centuries ago. There are dense forests and barren plains, fertile farmlands, and stony soil where little grows. The capitals of four South American countries lie high in the Andes—Caracas, Venezuela; Bogotá, Colombia; Quito, Ecuador; and La Paz, Bolivia.

Many peaks in the Andes are over 6,100 meters (20,000 feet) high—taller than any peaks in North America. Aconcagua, in Argentina, is the highest mountain in the Western Hemisphere. It rises to 6,960 meters (22,835 feet). Many Andean peaks are volcanic. Some are inactive, but others still erupt at times. Cotopaxi, in Ecuador, is the highest active volcano in the world. It rises to 5,896 meters (19,344 feet).

There are few passes through the Andes, and the mountains form a great barrier to transportation and communication in South America. The northern Andes lie in Colombia, Venezuela, and Ecuador. The central Andes are in Bolivia, Peru, northern Chile, and northern Argentina. The mountains in some parts of the central Andes are extremely high and wide. The southern Andes, at the tip of the continent in Argentina and Chile, are the lowest part of the system.

Two of South America's major river systems—the Amazon and the Orinoco—begin in the Andes. High in the mountains between Bolivia and Peru is Lake Titicaca. It is the largest lake in South America and the highest navigable lake in the world.

The climate in the Andes changes with the elevation above sea level. At the lowest elevation, below 900 meters (about 3,000 feet), the climate is tropical. This is called the *tierra caliente* ("hot land"). It is a region of dense green jungles and rivers filled with crocodiles. Crops such as fruits and vegetables, cotton, and tobacco grow well at these elevations.

At slightly higher elevations, the climate is cooler. In the northern Andes, this region is the source of much of South America's fine coffee. At 2,100 meters (7,000 feet) the *tierra fría* ("cold land") begins. Evergreen trees and wheat grow well here.

Between 3,000 and 4,000 meters (10,000 and 13,000 feet) is the treeless, windswept region known as the puna. Only a few hardy crops like potatoes and barley can be grown on these high mountainsides. High above, between the puna and the snowfields, is the *páramo* ("wasteland"), where nothing but mosses and lichens can survive.

The Andes provide the world with many important minerals such as copper, tin, and petroleum. There are smaller quantities of gold and silver. Coal deposits are limited.

Many interesting animals live in the Andes. There are llamas, guanacos, alpacas, and vicuñas—all members of the camel family. Chinchillas are highly prized for their valuable fur. There are cougars, or mountain lions, and small deer called guemal. Tiny hummingbirds, brilliantly colored, dart about in the Andean forests. Soaring above the towering, snowcapped Andes are the huge condors, the largest of the vultures and one of the world's largest flying birds.

About a third of all the people in South America live in the Andes, most of them in crowded cities and towns. In the Andes of Bolivia, Peru, and Ecuador, there are many descendants of the ancient Incas and other Indians who lived in the area before the Spanish conquest in the 1500's. Many of these peoples still speak only Indian tongues. The southern Andes are sparsely populated.

Deep gorges, steep slopes, and towering heights make it difficult and costly to build roads and railroads through the Andes. The Central Railroad of Peru, for example, is one of the world's highest railroads. It climbs to an elevation of 4,836 meters (15,865 feet). But in recent times the airplane and some modern highways have opened up areas that were once almost completely cut off from the outside world.

Reviewed by DANIEL JACOBSON
Michigan State University

A girl of the Peruvian Andes sits by the roadside above terraced fields. Below: Llamas parade before Sacsahuamán, a fortress built by the Incas outside Cuzco.

ANDORRA

Andorra is a tiny country located high in the Pyrenees mountains of southwestern Europe, between France and Spain. Although few people know much about it, Andorra is an ancient land, whose people have lived in the region since Roman times and whose form of government dated from the Middle Ages.

▶ THE PEOPLE AND THEIR LAND

In addition to the native Andorrans, the population includes many Spaniards and a small French minority. The official language is Catalan, which is spoken in the Spanish province of Catalonia. Spanish and French are also widely used. The people are Roman Catholics.

Andorra is a rugged land. Surrounded by the high peaks of the Pyrenees, the country is broken by deep gorges and narrow valleys. It is drained by the Valira River and its tributaries. Andorra's beautiful mountain scenery and cool, dry summer climate make it popular with tourists. In winter there are heavy snowfalls, which have led to the development of several fine ski resorts. Andorra has neither railroads nor a major airport and can be reached only by automobile or bus.

▶ THE ECONOMY

Because of its location and isolated mountainous terrain, Andorra served for centuries as a corridor through which goods were smuggled between France and Spain. So profitable was the smuggling business that it was often called Andorra's national industry. Today, however, tourism dominates the economy, accounting for most of Andorra's income.

Since little of Andorra's land is suitable for farming, agriculture is not a main source of wealth, and Andorra must import much of its food. The leading crops are oats, barley, and fruit. Tobacco is grown for export. Many mountain pastures are dotted with flocks of sheep. Mining, stone quarrying, and lumbering are carried out on a limited basis. Andorra also has a number of hydroelectric plants that supply electric power to Spain. Until 1983,

Andorra had no income tax. Until recently, it had no customs duties (taxes), and many items are imported into the country for sale to tourists at bargain prices. Andorra also receives income from the sale of its beautiful postage stamps to collectors around the world.

▶ HISTORY AND GOVERNMENT

According to tradition, Andorra was established late in the 700's when the emperor Charlemagne granted the people a charter of independence for their help in fighting the Muslim Moors, who had invaded the region from Spain. Nevertheless, for many years, Andorra was fought over by the French counts of Foix and the Spanish bishops of Urgel. Finally, in 1278, a treaty was signed at Les Escaldes, a small town near Andorra la Vella, the capital. By the terms of this treaty, the count of Foix and the bishop of Urgel were made co-princes of Andorra. Later the rights of the count of Foix were inherited by the kings of France, and when France became a republic, by the president of France.

Following a centuries-old custom, Andorra sent each of its two co-rulers a token tribute each year. The French president received the sum of 960 francs, while the bishop of Urgel received 460 pesetas, together with a supply

---

FACTS and figures

PRINCIPALITY OF ANDORRA (Principat d'Andorra) is the official name of the country.

LOCATION: Southwestern Europe.

AREA: 175 sq mi (453 km²).

POPULATION: 58,000 (estimate).

CAPITAL AND LARGEST CITY: Andorra la Vella.

MAJOR LANGUAGES: Catalan (official), Spanish, French.

MAJOR RELIGION: Roman Catholic.

GOVERNMENT: Co-principality. **Heads of state—** president of France, bishop of Urgel (co-princes). **Head of government—**chief executive (president) of the Executive Council.

CHIEF PRODUCTS: Agricultural—tobacco, oats, barley, fruit, livestock. **Manufactured—**tobacco products, lumber. **Mineral—**iron ore, building stone.

MONETARY UNIT: French franc (1 franc = 100 centimes), Spanish peseta (1 peseta = 100 céntimos).

of chickens, cheeses, and hams from each of the districts of Andorra. Each of the "princes," as the co-rulers are still referred to, sent a representative to Andorra. These representatives served as joint chiefs of the small Andorran police force and as judges in the criminal courts.

Because of the dual relationship with France and Spain, there are two school systems, one supported by France, the other by Spain. There is both a French- and a Spanish-owned radio station, each broadcasting in its own language. Andorra uses both French francs and Spanish pesetas as its legal money.

The Andorran legislative body is the General Council of the Valleys, which is made up of 28 elected members, four from each of the seven districts. The council chooses the chief executive, or president, who selects and heads the Executive Council, or cabinet of ministers.

A break with Andorra's past came in 1993, when Andorrans, in a referendum, approved the country's first constitution, which provides for a parliamentary form of government. It retains the Spanish and French co-princes as heads of state, but with much reduced powers.

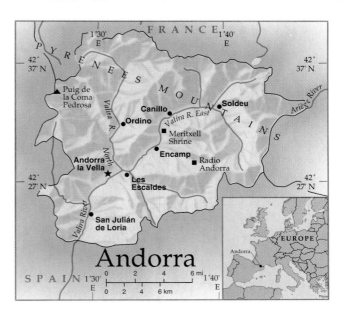

Andorra's traditional diplomatic isolation is also likely to undergo some changes with its admission to the United Nations, also in 1993.

PAUL C. HELMREICH
Wheaton College (Massachusetts)

ANDRÉ, MAJOR JOHN. See ARNOLD, BENEDICT; SPIES (Profiles).

ANEMIA. See DISEASES.

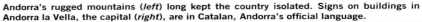

Andorra's rugged mountains (*left*) long kept the country isolated. Signs on buildings in Andorra la Vella, the capital (*right*), are in Catalan, Andorra's official language.

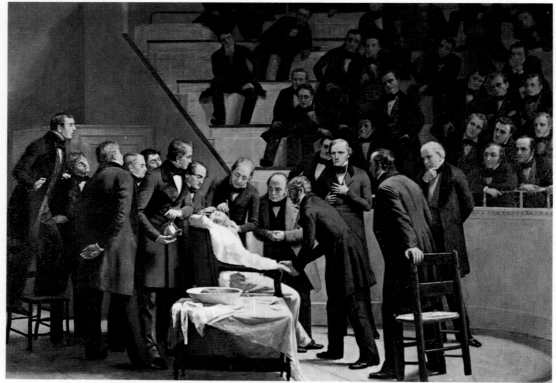

Ether as a safe and effective anesthetic during surgery was first demonstrated in public in 1846 by William T. G. Morton (the man holding the flask in the painting above).

ANESTHESIA

When you have to have an operation, you are given an **anesthetic.** This is a substance that keeps you from feeling pain. Some anesthetics prevent the nerves from sending messages of pain to the brain; others affect the brain itself. In either case you feel nothing when you are operated on. This condition is called anesthesia.

▶PAIN RELIEVERS OF OLD

From the earliest times people have looked for ways to relieve pain. They discovered that drugs made from certain plants could be used to kill pain. Doctors then tried using the same drugs during operations. Among these drugs were opium, mandrake, and hashish. But none of them was really very good. Small amounts had little effect. Large amounts often killed the patient.

Alcoholic drinks were tried as a means of inducing anesthesia (making the patient unconscious). But the patient often regained consciousness as soon as the first cut was made.

Even as late as the 1840's there seemed to be no safe and satisfactory way of putting a patient out of pain during an operation. So in most cases the patient was simply held or tied down, and the doctor worked as quickly as possible. Operations were limited to those that could be done in a few minutes. Even so, many patients did not survive the pain and shock.

▶THE START OF MODERN ANESTHETICS

The story of modern anesthetics begins with scientific studies of gases and ways they could be used. As early as 1799 the English chemist Humphry Davy had described nitrous oxide as a gas that was "capable of destroying physical pain." But many years passed before anyone used it as an anesthetic.

In the meantime people had discovered that breathing small amounts of nitrous oxide produced a pleasant sensation. In fact, nitrous oxide was known as laughing gas. By the 1840's people had also discovered the pleasures of breathing in ether. (Ether is a liquid that quickly turns into a gas when exposed to air.) They held parties called "ether frolics." Such parties were silly, but one good came from them. Many medical students and doctors were introduced to these gases at the parties.

One doctor who learned about ether at a frolic was Crawford W. Long of Jefferson, Georgia. In 1842 he painlessly removed tumors from the neck of a patient who had breathed in ether. This was probably the first truly effective anesthetic ever used in an operation on a human being. But Dr. Long did not publish his discoveries, and other doctors did not learn of his success.

By this time many doctors were experimenting with anesthetic gases. Horace Wells, a dentist in Hartford, Connecticut, was working with nitrous oxide. Unfortunately, when he tried to demonstrate it in public, something went wrong. The patient screamed with pain as his tooth was pulled. Dr. Wells fled to the sound of boos.

Success came to Wells's former partner, William T. G. Morton. At the Harvard Medical School, Dr. Morton met Charles T. Jackson, who suggested trying ether. Morton did. First he tried it on animals, including his own dog. Then he tried it on himself. It proved to be a safe and effective anesthetic.

By 1846, Morton was ready to demonstrate how ether could be used in surgery. He persuaded John C. Warren of the Massachusetts General Hospital to try operating on a patient who had been given ether. The day set was October 16. A group of doctors and students had been invited to observe. Many of them were sure that the ether would not work and had come only to laugh at Morton.

The patient was strapped to a chair in the usual way. Morton placed a tube in his mouth. The tube was connected to a glass globe filled with ether. Breathing the fumes into his lungs, the patient fell asleep.

Dr. Warren began to operate. Expecting the usual outcry, he made the first cut. There was silence. The doctor finished the operation. When the patient became conscious, he announced that he had felt no pain.

News of this success spread quickly. The way to modern, painless surgery was open. Oliver Wendell Holmes, an American doctor and poet, applied the term "anesthesia" to the condition produced by ether. The word is from the Greek and means "loss of feeling."

The search for more and better anesthetics was stepped up. James Simpson, an English doctor, was dissatisfied with ether because it irritated the lungs. Seeking a substitute, he found that chloroform had an anesthetic effect. In 1847 he gave it to a woman during childbirth, and she suffered no pain. Chloroform became very popular after 1853, when Queen Victoria took it during delivery of her seventh child.

Since then many anesthetics have been developed, each with its own special properties. Today, doctors can choose from many anesthetics the one best suited to the patient and the operation.

▶GENERAL AND LOCAL ANESTHETICS

There are two main types of anesthetics: general and local.

A general anesthetic makes the patient lose consciousness. A local anesthetic affects only part of the body. For example, if you have your tonsils out, you are given a general anesthetic so that you sleep through the operation. But if you need only a few stitches in your arm, you are given a local anesthetic that kills pain only in that area.

General Anesthetics

A general anesthetic works by first entering the bloodstream. The blood carries the drug to the central nervous system. Once there, the anesthetic acts on the nerve cells of the brain. These cells lose their ability to send and receive messages. No sensations are felt, and the patient loses consciousness.

General anesthetics are usually given either as a gas to be breathed in or as a liquid to be injected into a vein. The anesthetic may be given by an **anesthesiologist,** a physician who specializes in this work. Sometimes it is given by an **anesthetist,** a specially trained nurse or technician. Monitoring, or watching, the patient's vital signs is a very important part of giving an anesthetic. This means that the anesthetist must closely observe the pulse, blood pressure, color of the skin, and appearance of the eyes to check the depth of anesthesia.

The Local Anesthetic

A local anesthetic blocks the nerves at the area of the operation. The chemical may be applied to the surface of the body, to act on the nerve endings in the skin. Or it may be injected with a needle, to block nerve impulses to the brain and thus prevent the feeling of pain. Tooth extractions are often done in this way, with the anesthetic injected into the gum.

A method called spinal or regional anesthesia may be used for some abdominal operations or for the delivery of a baby. Nerves to the lower part of the body branch from the spinal cord. A single injection into the fluid surrounding the spinal cord blocks large numbers of nerves. The patient remains conscious and relaxed and feels no pain.

▶ WHY A RANGE OF ANESTHETICS IS NEEDED

Every anesthetic has both advantages and disadvantages. There is no single all-purpose anesthetic. Doctors choose what seems best for the patient and the kind of operation. They may choose one particular anesthetic. Or they may use several together.

Any good anesthetic must free the patient from pain, be safe and dependable, and prevent struggling movements. In most cases the muscles must be relaxed in order for an operation to be performed successfully.

Ideally, an anesthetic should also be pleasant to take, put the patient to sleep rapidly, have the smallest possible effect on the heart and lungs, and wear off quickly, leaving no unpleasant aftereffects.

A preanesthetic (before the anesthetic) drug is given to help prepare the patient for the anesthetic. It makes sure that the anesthetic will work smoothly and reduces anxiety, especially in children. The drugs most frequently used as preanesthetics are Demerol or Seconal, which make the patient drowsy, and Valium, which relaxes the patient. These drugs also help to reduce the aftereffects of anesthesia, such as nausea.

▶ OTHER KINDS OF ANESTHESIA

Anesthetics are drugs that act chemically on the nerves of the body. But there are other ways to produce anesthesia.

One way is to lower the temperature of a part of the body—an arm, for example—by packing it in crushed ice. As the temperature goes down, sensation in that part is dulled. The same effect can be produced by spraying the area with a fast-evaporating chemical, such as ethyl chloride. The chemical evaporates quickly, causing the skin to cool sharply so that all sensation is lost. A quick operation can then be performed.

For operations on internal organs, the body is cooled by a technique called **hypothermia.** The body is cooled well below its normal temperature of 37°C (98.6°F), and a general anesthetic is given. With this technique the body's need for oxygen is lowered, and the heartbeat is reduced or even stopped. This allows surgeons to perform difficult brain and

---

SOME WELL-KNOWN ANESTHETICS

These are all chemical anesthetics, identified by names in common usage. All are made in a laboratory.

GENERAL ANESTHETICS

CHLOROFORM: Clear liquid with a sweet odor. Quickly changes into gas. Stronger than ether, but not as safe in large amounts. Unlikely to burn or explode. Can damage liver. An early anesthetic, now rarely used.

CYCLOPROPANE: Colorless, sweet-smelling gas. Produces quick and deep anesthesia. Useful especially in diseases of the heart and respiratory system, when a high level of oxygen must be provided to the tissues. But its use is limited because it can explode.

ETHER: The chemical ethyl ether or diethyl ether. A colorless liquid that quickly changes into gas. Produces deep but safe anesthesia for long operations. Strong odor. Irritates breathing passages and lungs. Leaves patient feeling sick after operation. Burns and explodes easily. An early anesthetic, now replaced by newer ones.

FLUOTHANE: Trade name for the chemical halothane. A liquid that quickly changes into gas. Stronger than ether. May cause liver damage in a few patients. No unpleasant aftereffects. Unlikely to burn or explode. Now the most widely used anesthetic.

NITROUS OXIDE: Colorless, sweet-smelling gas. Produces unconsciousness quickly. No unpleasant aftereffects. Unlikely to burn or explode. Produces light anesthesia and must be used with stronger drugs. Used often in dental work or short operations. One of the first anesthetics. Also known as laughing gas.

PENTOTHAL: Trade name for thiopental sodium. A chemical solid that is dissolved in liquid before being injected into veins. Puts patients to sleep and makes them forget operation. Not a true anesthetic, so must be used in combination with other anesthetics for long operations. Few unpleasant aftereffects, but not safe for people with heart or lung trouble.

LOCAL ANESTHETIC

NOVOCAIN: Trade name for the drug procaine hydrochloride. Injected into area of pain. Commonly used in dental work and minor operations. Related anesthetics include those known by trade names Carbocaine, Metycaine, Nupercaine, Pontocaine, and Xylocaine.

---

heart operations, because the body part under surgery is nearly bloodless.

Hypnosis is a very old way of producing a state of anesthesia. Before the development of chemical anesthetics, it was often the most effective way to control pain. The hypnotist-doctor suggests to the patient that no pain will be felt. The sensation of pain is then absent until the patient is awakened. But not everyone can be successfully hypnotized. And hypnosis cannot be used in major operations.

Acupuncture is a method of anesthesia that was developed in China, where it is routinely used in place of or in addition to conventional anesthesia. In acupuncture, fine needles are inserted under the skin and twirled rapidly. Hundreds of specific acupuncture points on the body are known. In acupuncture anesthesia the patient remains conscious and relaxed and does not suffer the nausea or other unpleasant aftereffects of chemical anesthesia.

Today anesthesia makes possible long and difficult lifesaving operations that were never before dreamed of. The search for new and better anesthetics still goes on. So do the efforts of scientists to learn more about the way in which anesthesia works.

SARAH R. RIEDMAN
Author, science books for children

See also DRUGS; MEDICINE, HISTORY OF.

ANGELICO, FRA (1400?–1455)

One of the most beloved artists in history was the Italian painter Fra Angelico. He was so saintly that legends grew up around him. One story relates that when he fell asleep while working on a painting, angels came down from heaven to finish it for him.

Fra Angelico was born near Florence. His real name was Guido di Pietro. He took the name Fra Giovanni da Fiesole at about the age of 20, when he entered a monastery in Fiesole. There he became famous for his paintings and illuminated manuscripts.

In 1436, Fra Angelico was transferred to the San Marco monastery in Florence. It is said that when the pope saw San Marco after Fra Angelico redecorated it, he offered to make the artist archbishop of Florence. But Fra Angelico refused, explaining that he could better serve the church by painting. About 1445 the pope called him to Rome to paint frescoes (wall paintings done on wet plaster) at the Vatican. Fra Angelico's frescoes use soft, yet clear colors and graceful lines to tell stories from the Bible.

Fra Angelico died in Rome on February 18, 1455. The names Fra Angelico ("angelic brother") and Il Beato ("the blessed one") were given to him after his death because he was devout—in his life and in his art.

Reviewed by S. J. FREEDBERG
National Gallery of Art (Washington, D.C.)

ANGELOU, MAYA. See ARKANSAS (Famous People).
ANGLO-SAXONS. See ENGLAND, HISTORY OF; ENGLISH LANGUAGE.

A detail from Fra Angelico's 1437 altarpiece at Perugia, Italy. The scene is from the life of St. Nicholas.

ANGOLA

The nation of Angola is located on the southwestern coast of Africa bordering the Atlantic Ocean. One of the largest countries on the African continent, it is greater in area than France, Germany, and the United Kingdom combined, although its population is relatively small for its size. Angola was for centuries a colony of Portugal. It finally gained its independence in 1975, but in the years since, the country has been torn by a bitter and destructive civil war.

The People. The people of Angola are related to the Bantu of central and southern Africa. Of the many Bantu groups, the largest in Angola are the Ovimbundu, the Kimbundu, and the Bakongo, who together make up about 75 percent of the population. The Ovimbundu, the largest group, live in the central highlands and are known for their skill as traders and ironworkers. The Kimbundu live near the cities of Luanda, the capital, and Malange, and have been most influenced by European ways. The Bakongo live in the northwest.

Angolans of mixed European and African ancestry are called mestiços. Although they form a small percentage of the population, they play an important part in the country's economic and political life. About 400,000 Portuguese once lived in Angola, but most left after its independence. Portuguese remains the official language, but various Bantu languages are widely spoken. Some Angolans are Christians, while others follow traditional African religions.

The Land. Most of Angola consists of a vast plateau, which rises to its greatest height at Bié in the country's central region. A narrow strip of lowland runs along the Atlantic Ocean coastline, and the northern region is covered with tropical rain forests. In the south, Angola borders the northern edge of the great Kalahari Desert. Angola's land also includes a small area in the far north called Cabinda, which is separated from the rest of the country by the territory of neighboring Zaïre. Most of the major rivers rise in the central plateau and empty into the Atlantic.

Angola's climate varies with location and elevation. The coastal area and south are generally hot and dry. The plateau region is cooler and receives more rainfall.

The Economy. Agriculture and mining are the basis of the country's economy. Most Angolans are subsistence farmers, who grow food for their own use. Their chief food crops are corn, cassava (a starchy root), sweet potatoes, and bananas. The most important commercial crops are coffee and sugarcane, followed by cotton and sisal (used in making cord and twine). Angola is rich in minerals, especially petroleum, which provides the bulk

Luanda is Angola's capital and largest city, a major port, and the country's economic center. Founded by the Portuguese in 1575 and situated on Angola's long Atlantic Ocean coastline, it is considered one of western Africa's most attractive cities. It has suffered damage during the long civil war that began after Angolan independence in 1975.

REPUBLIC OF ANGOLA is the official name of the country.

LOCATION: Southwestern coast of Africa.

AREA: 481,351 sq mi (1,246,700 km²).

POPULATION: 10,500,000 (estimate).

CAPITAL: Luanda.

MAJOR LANGUAGE: Portuguese (official), various Bantu languages.

MAJOR RELIGIOUS GROUPS: Christian, traditional African religions.

GOVERNMENT: Republic. **Head of state and government**—president. **Legislature**—National Assembly.

CHIEF PRODUCTS: Agricultural—coffee, sugarcane, cotton, sisal, corn, cassava, sweet potatoes, bananas. **Manufactured**—processed food, fish meal, textiles, beverages. **Mineral**—petroleum, diamonds, iron ore.

MONETARY UNIT: Kwanza (1 kwanza = 100 lwei).

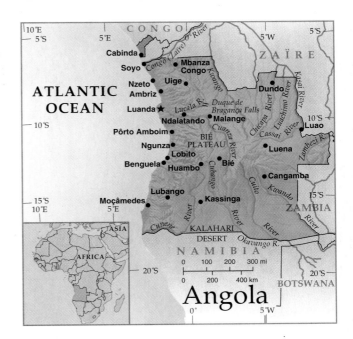

Angola

of its export income. It also has sizable deposits of diamonds, iron ore, and other minerals.

Angola suffered the loss of many skilled European workers, who left after independence. The civil war that followed was particularly destructive, and the country's economy is expected to take years to recover.

History and Government. Bantu peoples first moved into Angola from central Africa in the 1300's. The country was named for Ngola, ruler of an ancient Kimbundu kingdom.

European penetration of the region began with the Portuguese explorer Diogo Cão, who reached the mouth of the Congo River in 1482. The Portuguese founded the capital city, Luanda, in 1575. However, disease, the tropical climate, and resistance by the Africans prevented them from gaining complete control of the territory until 1918.

Independence. Angola underwent a long struggle to win independence. Armed revolts against Portuguese rule broke out in 1961. They were followed by years of guerrilla warfare, until a new government in Portugal granted independence to Angola in 1975. But independence led to a battle for power among rival liberation groups.The Popular Movement for the Liberation of Angola (MPLA) estab-lished a Communist-style government, headed by Agostinho Neto as president.

Civil War. It was opposed by the National Union for the Total Independence of Angola (UNITA), led by Jonas Savimbi. The conflict brought the intervention of outside powers. The MPLA was aided by the former Soviet Union and by Cuba, which sent troops to Angola, while the United States backed UNITA.

Government support for the independence movement in neighboring Namibia involved it in clashes with South Africa, which then administered Namibia. An agreement to withdraw Cuban forces, signed in 1988, was one of the conditions for Namibian independence (achieved in 1990). After the Luanda government accepted a demand for democratic elections, a peace accord was signed by the government and UNITA in 1991.

The elections, held in 1992, resulted in a government victory in the legislature. In the presidential vote, however, José Eduardo dos Santos (who had succeeded Neto in 1979) fell just short of a majority against Savimbi. This would have required a run-off election between them, but Savimbi rejected the results, leading to a resumption of the civil war. Although a new cease-fire was agreed to in 1993, it was short-lived. By early 1994, UNITA controlled about two-thirds of the countryside, including the second largest city, Huambo.

HUGH C. BROOKS
Director, Center for African Studies
St. John's University (New York)

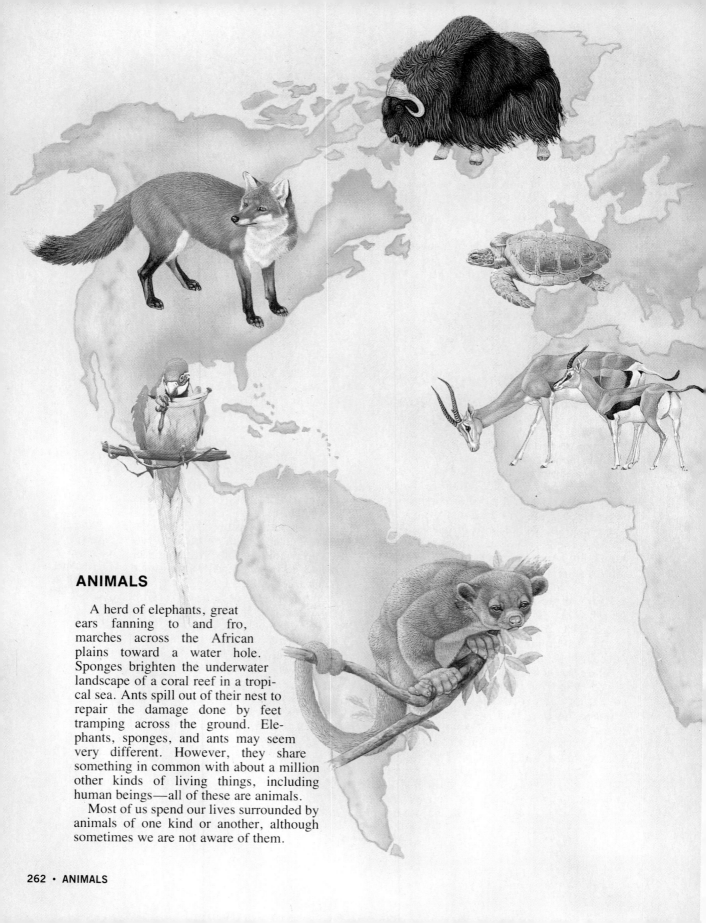

ANIMALS

A herd of elephants, great ears fanning to and fro, marches across the African plains toward a water hole. Sponges brighten the underwater landscape of a coral reef in a tropical sea. Ants spill out of their nest to repair the damage done by feet tramping across the ground. Elephants, sponges, and ants may seem very different. However, they share something in common with about a million other kinds of living things, including human beings—all of these are animals.

Most of us spend our lives surrounded by animals of one kind or another, although sometimes we are not aware of them.

Insects abound, sometimes in places where they are not particularly welcome. Small fish, frogs, and salamanders live in streams, ponds, and lakes and even in the middle of big cities. Some animals, such as raccoons, are out and about only after dark.

Animals live almost everywhere on Earth. They inhabit the deepest, darkest parts of the sea, where plants cannot survive. They are found on the highest mountain peaks and can survive in the coldest parts of Antarctica, where temperatures plunge to −72°F (−22°C). Even hot springs, with water heated to more than 100°F (38°C), are home to some kinds of insects.

The classification of living things started when early humans grouped organisms according to whether they were considered helpful or harmful. Today living things, such as plants (*above left*), fungi (*above*), and bacteria (*left*), are separated into groups based on shared traits.

▶ THE WORLD OF LIVING THINGS

Scientists classify all living things by assigning them to related groups according to similar characteristics, or traits. This orderly arrangement of all living things is called **scientific classification**. The largest groups of living things are called kingdoms.

For a long time, all living things were divided into just two kingdoms: animals and plants. If a living thing had body parts, such as a head, eyes, and limbs, and could move about, it was considered an animal. If a living thing was green, had leaves, and was stationary, it was considered a plant. However, even using such characteristics, scientists found it difficult to place some living things in either kingdom. A few kinds of plants, such as the Venus's-flytrap, move as they open and close their leaves to catch insects and feed on them. Some animals do not have heads or limbs; others, such as sponges, are anchored in place for most of their life and cannot move around.

Another characteristic, the method of getting food, was also used to group living things into kingdoms. Animals cannot make their own food; they must take food from their surroundings. In order to get the nourishment they need, they must eat either plants or animals that feed on plants. Plants, on the other hand, are able to make the food they need to survive by taking carbon dioxide from the air and water and nitrates from the soil, along with energy from sunlight. But even when they used the method of nourishment as a characteristic, scientists found organisms that were difficult to classify as either a plant or an animal. Some did not seem to belong to either group.

Over time, it became clear that all living things could not be assigned to just two groups. As a result, most scientists now divide all living things into five kingdoms. Animals make up one kingdom. Plants make up another. Certain one-celled organisms, some of which have characteristics of both plants and animals, belong to yet another kingdom, called Protista. Bacteria and fungi each have their own kingdoms, too. The living things in the same kingdom share more of the same characteristics than the living things in different kingdoms.

Within a kingdom, organisms are separated into subgroups depending on the characteristics they share. Major groups, called phyla, include animals that share one or more characteristics. Animals within each phylum are also separated into groups called classes according to certain differences between the animals. The classes are further divided into orders; the orders into families; the families into genera; and the genera into species.

With each subdivision, the relationship between the living things becomes stronger and the members of the group share more of the same characteristics of body structure and behavior. With the final separation into species, the members of a species share so many of the same basic characteristics that they look alike. Within a species, the members can mate with others in their group and produce offspring. The young develop in the same manner as the parents and grow to look very much like the parents. Human beings are a species. So are raccoons, American robins, and bullfrogs.

For more detailed information on how scientists classify living things, see the article LIFE in Volume L.

With tiny microscopic creatures, such as this protozoan, it is sometimes impossible to tell which are plants and which are animals. Many scientists prefer to group these forms into a separate kingdom called Protista.

▶ THE ANIMAL KINGDOM

The animal kingdom can be divided into two general main groups: **vertebrates**, made up of animals that have a backbone, and **invertebrates**, made up of animals that do not have a backbone. Throughout the animal kingdom, there are about 40,000 different species of vertebrates and more than 1 million known species of invertebrates.

Vertebrates, which include human beings, have a bony structure, or skeleton, inside the body. The skeleton, which grows as the animal does, is the framework that gives an animal its body shape. The skeleton also supports and protects the soft insides of an animal's body.

Many invertebrates, such as insects, crabs, and lobsters, wear their skeleton outside their body. The tough outer coat, which is like a

shell enclosing the body, is called an **exoskeleton**. The hard but lightweight structure is made up of sections, like the armor of a medieval knight. When invertebrates outgrow their exoskeleton, the shell splits and a new one is formed. Some invertebrates have no skeletons. Instead, they have soft bodies held together by strong, flexible fibers.

There is an endless variety of shapes, sizes, and traits within the animal kingdom, yet groups of animals are similar in certain ways. Some, such as humans (*right*), have two pairs of limbs; others, such as crabs (*below right*), have tough outer coats covering their bodies; still others, such as elephants (*below*), eat only plants.

Although they are very different looking, the flamingos (*above left*), the tree frog (*above*), the cheetah (*far left*), and the tree python (*left*) share certain characteristics as members of the animal group called vertebrates. All vertebrates have a backbone formed from cartilage or bony tissue, or both. In addition, the body of a vertebrate is usually divided into a head and a trunk and has two-sided symmetry —that is, the left and right sides are alike.

Animal Groups

Vertebrates and invertebrates can be further divided into subgroups. Each subgroup has its own unique combination of traits.

Vertebrates. Human beings are **mammals**, as are elephants, dogs, and whales. It may be hard to imagine that such different-looking animals have some of the same characteristics, but they do. Mammals are the only vertebrates that have hair and feed on milk from their mothers when they are babies. Mammals also are the only vertebrates whose young grow within the mother and receive nourishment from her before birth, although a few primitive kinds, such as the platypus, hatch from an egg.

Whether they live in the water like a whale or on land like a person, mammals breathe air through their lungs. They are also **warm-blooded** animals, which means they are able to maintain a constant body temperature no matter what the temperature of their surroundings is.

Similar to mammals, **birds** are warm-blooded and breathe air through lungs. However, birds are feathered instead of hairy. They hatch from eggs and bring food to their young. Unlike most vertebrates, birds do not have teeth. Instead, they have a hard beak, or bill, that is used to get food.

Reptiles are covered with scales instead of hair or feathers. They are **cold-blooded**—that is, their body temperature depends on the temperature of their surroundings. If a reptile, such as snake or crocodile, is too hot, it must move to the shade. If it needs warmth, it must get into the sun. Like birds and mammals, however, reptiles breathe air. Reptiles hatch from eggs, either inside or outside the mother.

Frogs, salamanders, and caecilians are **amphibians**. These cold-blooded animals are free of hair, scales, and feathers. Most live part of their life in water and part on land. Young amphibians use gills to breathe oxygen from the water. As they grow into adults, their body changes and they can live on land, using lungs to breathe air.

Fish, another vertebrate class, mainly use gills to breathe. Like reptiles and amphibians, fish are cold-blooded and cannot regulate their body temperature internally. Fish, which appeared about 500 million years ago, were the first animals to have a backbone.

Invertebrates. As a group, **arthropods** contain the largest number of species in the animal kingdom. The great variety in this group includes insects, spiders, crabs, lobsters, centipedes, and millipedes. All arthropods have jointed legs and an exoskeleton that contains a stiff, horny material called chitin.

Sponges are a group of animals that live at the bottom of oceans and other bodies of water. They spend their adult lives attached to rocks and other underwater objects. Although sponges vary widely in shape, color, and size, they all have a skeleton made up of either minerals or a protein called spongin.

There are about 100,000 known kinds of **mollusks**, which include snails, scallops, slugs, clams, oysters, and octopuses. The soft, boneless body of the mollusk is usually protected by a hard shell. Wherever mollusks live —in water or on land—they must keep their bodies moist to stay alive.

The **coelenterates** include jellyfish, sea anemones, corals, and sea fans. Coelenterates are soft-bodied animals with a body wall formed by at least two layers of cells. Most of the 9,000 species live in the sea.

The invertebrates commonly referred to as "worms" actually consist of four major groups—**flatworms**, **roundworms**, **ribbon worms**, and **segmented worms**. All have soft, slender bodies, but no limbs. Earthworms, tapeworms, and leeches are among the several thousand kinds of worms.

The sea is home to many invertebrates. Under the water's surface, coral animals (*below*) display a riot of colors, while the red crab (*below right*) scrambles along the seashore.

▶THE VARIETY OF ANIMAL LIFE

Groups of animals may share some traits, yet every kind of animal has its own life-style and way of surviving. Sometimes the traits that make the living patterns different are very small; the great blue heron and the little blue heron are an example. They both are long-legged birds that wade into water to stalk small creatures, such as fish and frogs. They both live in marshes or other wetlands. However, the great blue heron is about twice the size of the little blue heron. The difference in size means that they feed in the same place, in a similar manner, but at different depths.

Each kind of animal is suited to living in a particular kind of environment, or **habitat**. An animal fits into a **niche** within its habitat—that is, it has a specific role within its community. Wetlands, such as marshes, are the habitat of herons, while their niche is that of a bird that wades to catch small water animals.

The heron's behavior and body structures enable it to survive within its particular habitat and niche. While wading, a heron will freeze its movements; motionless, it looks for a fish or a frog. When the heron sees its prey, it quickly extends its long neck and with its bill seizes the startled prey.

The climbing perch, an Asian fish, has another type of life-style. It lives in small ponds that sometimes dry up during times of drought. When this happens, the perch behaves in an unusual way for a fish: It creeps over the ground to another pond that still holds water. The climbing perch can do this because it has strong, flexible fins that act almost like legs. It also has a lunglike organ that allows it to breathe air as it travels out of water and over land.

The difference in their sizes allows the great blue heron (*top*) and the little blue heron (*bottom*) to have separate niches within the same shared habitat.

The traveling behavior, fins, and air-breathing organ of the climbing perch are like the heron's long legs and hunting behavior. They are all changes, or **adaptations**, of a living thing geared to a particular way of life. Every animal has its own special adaptations that improve its chances of survival.

Animals do not adapt on purpose; they adapt by chance. The adaptation of the giraffe's ancestors is an example. It may appear that the ancestors of the giraffe grew a long

---

Did you know that . . .

the bird called an oxpecker spends almost its entire life clinging to the back of a hoofed animal such as this impala? The oxpecker performs a valuable pest-removal service by removing bloodsucking ticks and blood-flies from the impala's body. In return, the impala allows the oxpecker to rest and sleep and even court and mate on its back.

There are many patterns of living within the same forest community. Some animals are most active during the day, others are most active during the night.

Animals of the Day
Clockwise from top right: woodpecker, cardinal, chipmunk, rabbit, coyote, lynx, and squirrel.

Animals of the Night
Clockwise from top right: flying squirrel, red fox, badger, woodcock, raccoon, mule deer, barn owl, and bat.

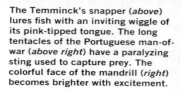

The Temminck's snapper (*above*) lures fish with an inviting wiggle of its pink-tipped tongue. The long tentacles of the Portuguese man-of-war (*above right*) have a paralyzing sting used to capture prey. The colorful face of the mandrill (*right*) becomes brighter with excitement.

neck so they could feed on leaves in trees; however, that is not the way it happened. Millions of years ago, a giraffe ancestor was born with a neck that was longer than the neck of the other animals in its group. It was not much longer than the neck of the others, but long enough so the animal could reach higher for food than the rest of the group. All the offspring of the long-necked ancestor had the same trait. Because more food was available to them, the long-necked animals had a better chance of surviving. As time passed, they survived in greater numbers than their short-necked relatives. Slowly the long-necked animal developed into the giraffe of today.

Amazing Animals

Adaptations create the astounding variety within the animal kingdom. Some animals are brilliantly colored; others are drab. Some animals are huge; others are so tiny that they cannot be seen without a microscope. Some are slightly unusual; others are utterly fantastic. Some animals share the traits of many animals; others seem to have traits that are quite unique.

The Colorful. The mandrill, a large baboon from Africa, is one of the most colorful mammals. Its face is bright red and blue. Many birds are also brilliantly colored, especially the males. The bird of paradise is one of the most colorful, and beautiful, birds. It lives in the jungles of the South Pacific islands. Its feath-

---

Did you know that . . .

the bee hummingbird, which weighs about 1/20 ounce (1.6 grams) and grows to about 2 inches (5 centimeters) in length, is the smallest living bird? Tiny and quick, this flying machine moves its wings at the fantastic rate of 70 times a second, propelling it along at speeds of up to 60 miles (97 kilometers) per hour.

The fierce-looking Komodo dragon is the biggest lizard in the world. It can reach 12 feet (3.6 meters) in length and more than 250 pounds (113 kilograms) in weight.

ers of scarlet, yellow, green, and blue form long trailing plumes or feathery capes. The shimmering colors gleam like metal in bright sunlight. In South America lives a group of frogs, known as poison dart frogs, that are as colorful as any birds. The small animals are bathed in vivid greens, reds, yellows, and black.

The Curious. The tapir is a jungle animal with an unusual appearance. Big as a pony, the tapir looks like a combination of several animals. It has a body shaped like that of a rhinoceros; a large, tapering head similar to that of a pig; and a nose, or snout, that looks like a shortened version of an elephant's trunk.

The Portuguese man-of-war is an interesting-looking water animal. Its body contains a balloonlike float that acts like a sail. Long tentacles dozens of feet long hang from its body and trail through the water as winds blow the man-of-war across the ocean.

Coral animals, which build reefs by secreting (giving off) limestone, have tubelike bodies with colorful tentacles, resembling petals, around the top.

The Big, the Small. When it comes to large size among animals, most people think of the extinct prehistoric reptiles called dinosaurs. Although not all dinosaurs were large animals (some were no bigger than a house cat), there were some plant-eating dinosaurs more than 85 feet (25 meters) long and weighing 80 tons.

As immense as some of the dinosaurs were, no dinosaur was as large as one animal that lives today. The great blue whale is the largest animal ever known. It grows up to 100 feet (30.4 meters) in length and may weigh more than 130 tons—that is more than the com-

bined weight of thirty elephants. The huge bulk of the whale is supported by water. A land animal of the same size would need such a heavy skeleton and large muscles to support all its weight that it probably would not be able to lift its legs.

Some land animals do reach enormous size. The biggest land animal is the African elephant, which can be more than 13 feet (3.9 meters) high at the shoulder and weigh about 9 tons (10 metric tons). The African white rhinoceros is another heavyweight. It weighs up to 6,000 pounds (2,721 kilograms). Even certain birds can be considered giants. The ostrich, the largest living bird, can tower 8 feet (2.4 meters) high and weigh almost 300 pounds (136 kilograms).

At the other end of the size scale, the smallest animals with a backbone include the goby fish of the Philippines and the Cuban pygmy tree frog, neither of which grows to more than half an inch (0.5 centimeter) in length. The insect-eating shrew, which is the smallest mammal on land, weighs about as much as a dime.

Did you know that . . .

the largest structures ever built by living creatures are coral reefs? Some reefs are more than 1,000 miles (1,609 kilometers) in length. The reefs, such as this one surrounding a blue lagoon off the coast of Belize in the Caribbean Sea, consist of living coral polyps and their skeletal remains piled on top of one another. The strange and beautiful formations take millions of years to build.

The polar bear fears only killer whales and walruses as it makes its way along the Arctic shores. A thick coat of fur and a layer of fat keep the polar bear warm on the cold and barren tundra.

▶ANIMALS AND THEIR HABITATS

A polar bear, its black nose twitching, makes its way across the treeless landscape along the shores of the Arctic Ocean, hunting for small mammals, such as ground squirrels, and eating berries. This cold, icy, dry region is called a **tundra**. During the summer, the sea fringing the tundra is free of ice. When one area of the tundra is picked clean of food, the polar bear will swim miles through the sea to reach a new destination.

In winter when the ocean freezes over, the bears wander hundreds of miles across the ice hunting for seals. Finding an opening in the ice, the bear crouches near the hole, waiting patiently to ambush a seal when it comes up from the water below for a breath of air.

Winter lasts six months in the Arctic, and during most of that time the sun never rises. Temperatures drop far below 0°F (−18°C). Polar bears are adapted in many ways to life in the northernmost part of the world. Under its skin lies a thick layer of fat, called blubber, that serves as insulation to protect the bear against the cold. Over the skin is a thick, woolly undercoat of hair, which also helps the bear keep warm. An outer coat of stiff hairs, which sheds water like a raincoat, helps the

bear stay dry. In addition to its layer of fat, keeping dry helps the bear stay warm. Such adaptations enable the bear to live in its cold, harsh environment.

The polar bear would not survive on the hot, open **grasslands** of East Africa. The climate is too warm and dry for the bear. Although the short-legged polar bear is not slow, it is not adapted for rapid pursuit, which is something it would need in order to catch the fast-running antelopes that live in large herds on the African grasslands.

The cheetah, a medium-sized spotted cat, is suited to hunting antelopes. Long-legged and swift as an arrow, the cheetah can catch fast-running antelopes, such as gazelles. The cheetah lacks blubber, and its fur is not as thick as the bear's. Just as a bear would not last long on the grasslands of the African plains, a cheetah would perish in the Arctic.

Because animals are adapted to different environments, the distribution of animal life throughout the world changes from place to place. The animals in one area can be very different from the animals living in another area. Climate and plant life are the main factors that determine the community of animals that live in a particular region. The African plains, for example, do not receive enough rain for forests to grow. But there is enough rain for grasses to thrive on the plains. Large herds of antelopes and zebras feed on the grasses. In turn, cheetahs, lions, and other predators (animals that kill others for food) stalk the herds.

Parts of Africa that are rainy enough for trees have vast forests, often called **rain forests**, or **jungles**. Grass eaters cannot find enough food in the forests. If the grass-eating antelopes and zebras are not in the forest, neither are the lions or cheetahs. But the jungle teems with other types of animals—monkeys, birds, snakes, and frogs are just a few of the kinds of animals that fill the jungle from the damp, shaded floor to the tops of the tall trees that shoot hundreds of feet into the air.

Some African animals, such as the elephant and buffalo, inhabit both grasslands and forest. However, forest elephants and buffalo generally are smaller than their grassland relatives. Smaller size makes it easier for an ani-

The boldly colored poison dart frog (*right*), which is usually less than 2 inches (5 centimeters) long, carries in its skin glands the most powerful animal poison known.

Animals abound amid the thick tangle of plants in the rain forest (*below*). Many of the animals spend their entire lives in the trees and never descend to the ground.

mal to get around among the trunks of the giant jungle trees.

Other types of animals live in **deciduous forests**, which are found in areas with moderate temperatures and rainfall and cold winters. The leaves of many of the trees in a deciduous forest turn from green to vibrant shades of red, yellow, and orange. The colorful display occurs once a year before the trees shed their leaves. Along with the white-tailed deer, which feeds largely on buds, new shoots, and leaves, nut-eating gray squirrels, bobcats, and many types of birds can be found in the deciduous forests of the northeastern United States.

Farther north are cold **coniferous forests**, with cone-bearing evergreens such as pines and spruces. Moose, which are the largest member of the deer family, feed on water plants in the many wet areas that dot the forests. The large hooves of the moose spread out to keep it from sinking into the waterlogged soil as it wanders through the forest. The many seeds of pine and spruce cones are food for the birds, red squirrels, and other small mammals that make their home in the coniferous forest.

The animals that live in **deserts** are very different from the animals that are found in the tundra and forests. Desert animals must be able to stand scorching heat and go without water for a long time. To escape the sun's heat, many desert animals, such as certain lizards, spend the warmest part of the day in underground burrows. Some animals, such as kangaroo rats, have developed so that they do not need to drink water. They get all the moisture they need from the juices of the plants they feed on.

The marten (*left*), a tree-climbing member of the weasel family, leaps gracefully from branch to branch as it hunts squirrels and other prey in the coniferous forest.

Animals of the northern coniferous forest (*below*) are well adapted to the cold winters. Some animals hibernate, while others travel to warmer climates to seek food and shelter.

Desert wildlife (*above*) must adapt to scorching daytime heat, cool night temperatures, and a scarce supply of water. The land iguana (*below*) nibbles on desert plants, such as cactus, for nourishment and water.

Like the polar bear and cheetah, all species are adapted to particular environments. Polar bears and cheetahs are each bound to just one environment. Even so, they move through many different habitats within their environment. The polar bear roams through the tundra from an ice field to the rocky seashore. Cheetahs hunt on grasslands so dry that they are almost desert, as well as on those that are dotted with thorny shrubs.

Some species manage to live in more than one environment and habitat. The wolf travels from the coniferous forest, where it hunts moose, farther north to the tundra, where it hunts musk oxen. Coyotes, which eat plant and animal products, roam deciduous and coniferous forests, grasslands, deserts, mountains, and lowlands. They can live in climate that is hot or cold, moist or dry.

In contrast to the coyote and wolf, there are species that live in only a tiny habitat within an environment. The Devil's Hole pupfish is one. All Devil's Hole pupfish inhabit a single freshwater pool near Death Valley in western Nevada. Within the pool, the pupfish stay over a ledge about the size of a basketball court. No other species of vertebrate lives within such a confined area.

Wherever it lives, each species of animal has its own way of life unlike that of any other. There are as many different life-styles among animals as there are species.

Broad, winglike fins propel the stingray through water (*above*). Victims have a difficult time escaping the fatal clasp of the bald eagle's talons (*right*).

▶ THE BODY OF AN ANIMAL

By looking at the different body structures of an animal, it is possible to get information about how an animal lives. A shape, foot, bill, jaw, and tooth can all be clues to an animal's life-style. For example, it is reasonable to assume—by looking at its long neck—that the plant-eating giraffe eats leaves high in trees.

Shape. Whales and fish are totally different types of creatures. However, the body of a typical fish has the same streamlined and torpedo-shaped body as that of a whale. Their similar shapes are both adaptations to living in the water. With a streamlined shape, an animal can move through water with less effort. The pointed head of a water animal, such as a fish, wedges water aside. The long, slender body glides behind, almost as if it is following through a "hole" in the water made by the head.

Other fish, such as the stingray, have flattened bodies that resemble a pancake. Even though their bodies are not torpedo-shaped, they are streamlined in another way. A stingray's body can grow to about 5 feet (1.5 meters) wide. However, from the top surface of its body to the bottom, it is only a few inches deep.

Another fish, the moray eel, has a long, slender, snakelike body. Its shape allows it to slither into crevices and holes in reefs after the octopuses and crabs that are its prey. Water animals are not the only animals that need flexible, streamlined bodies. The weasel, a land animal, also has a snakelike body. Its

slender, flexible body enables it to snake through underground burrows to catch the rabbits and rodents it feeds on.

Feet and Legs. The feet of some birds have powerful toes tipped with sharp, hooked claws, or **talons**. Talons are characteristic of birds that hunt, such as eagles and hawks. With the talons, the hunter bird seizes its prey. Once it has the victim within its grasp, the talons automatically tighten to hold the victim fast.

The favored diet of birds of prey varies greatly. The red-tailed hawk catches rodents, ground birds (such as pheasants), lizards, and snakes with its strong talons. The bald eagle feeds largely on fish that are caught near the surface of the water.

The curved, sharp claws of cats are used in much the same manner to grab and hold prey. However, the cat has an additional feature important to a land animal: It can withdraw, or retract, its claws into sheaths within the toes. This protects the claws when they are not needed to grasp prey. Withdrawing its claws also allows the cat to step softly when stalking its prey. Cats—from lions to house cats—creep up as close as they can to their prey before they pounce on it with a final rush.

The sidewinder uses a series of flat S-shaped loops to move its long, limbless body over the desert sand.

One cat is an exception—the cheetah. It has blunt claws, similar to a dog's, that it cannot withdraw. It also hunts more like such members of the dog family as wolves and African wild dogs than a cat. The cheetah does not quietly stalk its prey before pouncing and grabbing with its claws; rather, the cheetah runs down its prey, knocking it to the ground, and with its strong jaws grabs the throat of its victim and suffocates it.

The lynx, a cat that lives in the cold coniferous forest, has large, broad feet. As the lynx travels over the snow in search of prey, its feet act like snowshoes, keeping the cat from sinking into the snow. The spider monkey and the gibbon have unusually long fingers and toes, which they hook over branches as they swing through the trees.

Jaws and Teeth. Because animals have different ways of feeding, the body structures used for eating are different—even within the same family of animals. All birds use their beaks, or bills, to obtain food; however, among birds, there are many different kinds of bills. The woodpecker uses its chisel-like bill to chip away the bark and wood from trees and get to the insects hiding underneath. The pine grosbeak uses its short, heavy bill to crush seeds. The heron uses its long, spearlike bill to grab fish and frogs.

The spotted hyena hunts other animals, but it also feeds off the remains of animals killed by other predators, such as lions. With its large, powerful jaw muscles, the hyena is able to carry off and eat the bones and other remains that most animal jaws cannot crack.

A fish with strong jaws and heavy, wide teeth is the parrot fish. Similar to the hyena, the parrot fish uses its jaws for crushing. Found in the warm waters surrounding coral reefs, the parrot fish crushes the rock-hard coral to feed on the small, soft animals that secrete it.

The teeth and jaws of animals that eat plants are different from those of animals that eat other animals. Plant-eating animals, such as horses, generally have broad, flat-edged teeth for chewing leaves and grass; meat-eating animals, such as dogs, have long, sharp teeth for tearing and chewing flesh.

The spider monkey (*far left*) uses its long slender limbs to swing from branch to branch as it quickly makes its way through the tropical rain forest habitat. The anhinga (*left*) is a long-necked diving bird that uses its pointed bill to spear fish. Once it has captured its prey, it tosses it into the air and gulps it down. The distinctive body of the platypus (*below*) is well equipped for swimming. It has webbed feet and a broad flat tail that the water-loving platypus uses to steer itself.

▶HOW ANIMALS MOVE FROM PLACE TO PLACE

Animals move from place to place in different ways. Some animals travel through air or water; others travel across land. Animal movement requires work. The body must be lifted or moved forward or both. A variety of body structures help animals move. Microscopic animals that live in fluid are able to travel by moving hairlike body extensions called **cilia**. Other animals depend on fins, legs, or wings to help them move.

Animal Movement in Water

Some water animals use a form of jet propulsion to move. The squid fills its body with water and then forces it out the end of its body in a violent rush. The backward force of the water pushes the squid ahead.

A streamlined shape and fins enable fish to move through water. Fish propel themselves by pushing the tail fin back and forth against the water. Muscles along the fish's body contract and relax, first on one side, then on the other, causing the tail to sweep forcefully from side to side. The tail fin does the majority of the work while the other fins are used by the fish to keep its balance in the water.

Other water animals, such as whales and dolphins, also have streamlined bodies and tail fins that do the bulk of the swimming work. However, rather than a side-to-side motion, they are propelled through the water by powerful up-and-down movements of their tails.

Animal Movement on Land

Most land animals move around on legs that extend from the sides or undersides of their body. The legs of an animal must be strong enough to support and lift it. The best support is provided when the legs are extended directly under the body, as in most mammals. Animals such as amphibians and reptiles often

have legs that extend outward from the sides of the body and use them to leap or crawl along rather than stand and walk.

An animal with two legs must keep one in contact with the ground to stay upright. An animal with four legs needs to have three of them on the ground, at least when walking. Three legs hold up the body while the fourth moves forward into a new position. When a four-legged animal runs, it has only two legs planted at the same time—each foot is lifted just before setting down the one ahead of it. However, the motion is so quick the animal does not fall down. Some large, fast animals, such as elks, lift all four feet in the middle of a galloping stride.

The Speed of Animals

How fast animals can move from place to place varies greatly among animals. The fastest speed (which is presented here) and the slowest speed of an individual animal also can be quite different.

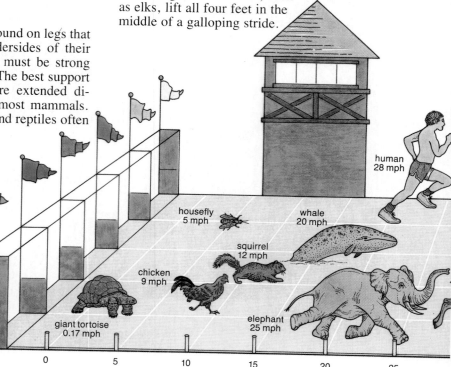

housefly
5 mph

whale
20 mph

squirrel
12 mph

human
28 mph

chicken
9 mph

giant tortoise
0.17 mph

elephant
25 mph

0   5   10   15   20   25

They may look clumsy, but manatees (*left*) are expert swimmers. Clocked at speeds of more than 200 miles per hour, the peregrine falcon (*above*) is the fastest animal in the world. Other cats wait and then pounce, but the cheetah (*right*) races after its prey.

Animal Movement in the Air

Animals travel through the air by gliding and by powered flight. Gliding animals, such as the flying squirrel, have thin flaps of skin extending from the sides of their body. The skin flaps act as parachutes to support them as they leap from a tree into the air. Along with the gliding squirrel, there are gliding frogs, lizards, and fish.

Powered flight requires wings that lift an animal by pushing down against the air. (See the article BIRDS for a detailed description of bird flight.) Most birds and many insects fly. The only mammal that flies is the bat.

▶HOW ANIMALS FEED

Animals spend much of their time seeking the food they need to survive. Animals that feed on meat, such as tigers and wolves, are called **carnivores**. Some meat-eating animals do not hunt for themselves; instead, they clean up the remains of animals killed by other predators. Such animals are called **scavengers** and include hyenas and vultures. Animals that only feed on plants are called **herbivores**. Some animals feed on both meat and plant matter. They are called **omnivores**.

Each species of animal has evolved its own special way of finding the food it needs. Some animals hunt for food in groups, while others hunt alone. Some animals have highly developed senses that help them find food, and others have special body structures that help attract food to them. Some animals gather food, but others lie in wait to trap food.

Animals That Eat Meat. The hunting styles of carnivores are related to the type of prey on which they feed. Wolves and cheetahs hunt

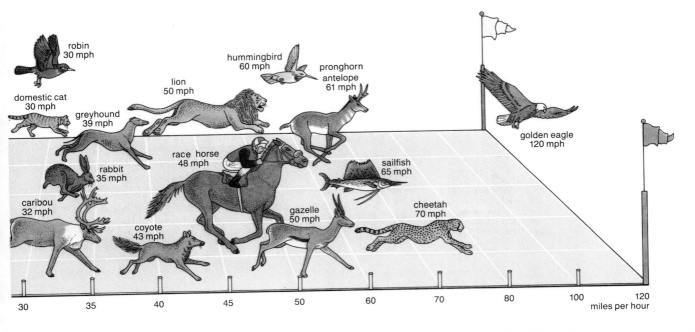

robin
30 mph

domestic cat
30 mph

greyhound
39 mph

lion
50 mph

hummingbird
60 mph

pronghorn antelope
61 mph

golden eagle
120 mph

rabbit
35 mph

race horse
48 mph

sailfish
65 mph

caribou
32 mph

coyote
43 mph

gazelle
50 mph

cheetah
70 mph

30   35   40   45   50   60   70   80   100   120
miles per hour

A pack of wild African dogs (*above*) tears at the flesh of a trapped wildebeest. The deadly emerald tree boa (*right*) wraps around its prey and tightens its coil until its victim suffocates.

fast-running, four-legged herbivores. Both kinds of animals pursue the same prey, but in different ways. The cheetah's pursuit, reaching speeds of over 50 miles per hour (80 kilometers per hour), is rapid but brief. If it does not catch its prey within about 600 feet (183 meters), it gives up and searches for another victim.

Wolves, which are very intelligent, hunt in groups, or packs. The members of a wolf pack take turns chasing their victim. They are able to stay fresh during a chase that sometimes lasts for miles. The prey is left exhausted—an easy target for the hungry pack. Wolves also set up ambushes. It is common for a wolf pack to surround its prey, circling in closer and closer until the victim is trapped. There is little chance that the frantic victim will escape the group attack.

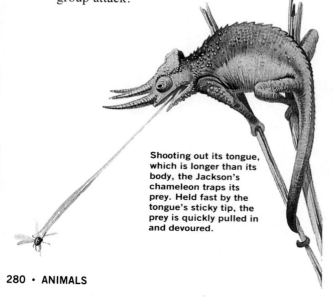

Shooting out its tongue, which is longer than its body, the Jackson's chameleon traps its prey. Held fast by the tongue's sticky tip, the prey is quickly pulled in and devoured.

There are spiders that hunt insects and other small invertebrates in the same manner as some large animals hunt their prey. In fact, some of these spiders are called "wolf" spiders. They are able to pursue their prey with astonishing speed. Most spiders, however, wait for food to come to them. They build webs to trap insects that fly and holes in the ground, with trap doors, to catch insects that crawl.

Rattlesnakes usually hunt at night for small mammals. Special organs in the rattlesnake's head sense the heat given off by the mammal's body. Once it finds its prey, the rattlesnake attacks. Two long fangs inject a poisonous material called venom into the victim. A rattlesnake's venom kills most victims in seconds. Immediately, the injected venom begins to digest the prey—before the snake has even swallowed it.

The jellyfish, a water animal, also uses special organs and venom to catch its prey. The long tentacles of the jellyfish, which can reach up to 50 feet (15 meters) in some species, trail underneath its body as it floats in the water. The tentacles are armed with cells that have stingers. When the cells touch something, the stingers are immediately triggered and shoot out to deliver venom that kills or paralyzes the prey. The helpless prey is then drawn in and eaten.

Although many animals do not have a separate sense organ just to help them hunt, one or more of their senses are highly developed and serve to help them find food. Predatory birds, such as hawks and owls, hunt by sight. Not only are they able to see their small animal prey from great distances, they also have a wide field of vision. Sight, along with a keen sense of smell, helps many animals, such as dogs and wolves, locate their prey.

A water animal that uses a lure to capture its prey is the angler fish. Projecting from its head is a long stalk with a colorful tab of fleshy tissue at the end. When prey swim near, the angler fish wiggles the brightly colored lure. As the victim comes close to examine the wormlike flesh, the angler fish's jaws open wide and the prey is sucked in.

Some animals, such as barnacles, are stationary and must gather food from the surrounding environment. Barnacles spend their adult life attached to rocks or floating objects. Inside its shell, the barnacle is a small, shrimplike animal with long, feathery limbs. As the tide washes over the barnacle, the top of its shell opens and out pop the feathery limbs. The barnacle sweeps its limbs through the water, catching tiny water animals and then kicking the trapped food into its mouth.

Some animals catch food while performing a service for another animal. Cleaner shrimp creep over the bodies of fish, removing pests and parasites as they go along. In the exchange, the shrimp gain a meal and the fish is rid of harmful pests.

Animals That Eat Plants. Plant eaters range from very tiny insects, such as aphids, to huge land animals, such as elephants. In much the same way as meat-eating animals have developed special feeding patterns, each species of plant eaters has evolved its own way of finding and eating food. Some plant eaters feed on grasses; others feed on leaves, seeds, or flowers; still others feed only on plant products, such as nectar. One thing that is common to all animals that only eat plants is that most of their time is spent searching for food and eating it.

Most plant eaters need to take in large amounts of food to get the nourishment they need. The colobus monkey of Africa spends most of its time in trees gathering and eating leaves. Most other monkeys, which have a varied diet, cannot digest leaves. The colobus has a special stomach that allows it to digest the approximately 6 pounds (2.7 kilograms) of leaves that it gathers daily to meet its energy requirements. Even with that amount of food,

the colobus dozes as often as possible to conserve energy.

Water plants are an important source of food for animals such as canvasback ducks, brants (a kind of small goose), manatees, and marine iguanas. The marine iguana, a seagoing lizard that lives on the remote Galápagos Islands, feeds mainly on a type of seaweed called sea lettuce. The spiny invertebrates called sea urchins graze on algae in the water. With its rough, sandpaperlike teeth, the sea urchin scrapes off the algae growing on rocks and other surfaces.

The praying mantis (*right*) grasps its insect prey with the sharp hooks on the ends of its long, strong forelegs. Its usual diet consists of insects; however, the praying mantis may seize and eat small tree frogs.

At a height that can reach up to 18 feet (5.5 meters), giraffes (*below*) are the tallest animals in the world. They are able to browse among the branches of trees and tall shrubs, plucking the succulent vegetation with their long tongues.

When under attack, musk oxen (*right*) form a defensive circle with their horns pointing outward. The young are safe on the inside of the circle. Because the armadillo (*below right*) is protected by a powerful wall of body armor, it does not have to be quick to flee from an enemy.

Hummingbirds are among the animals that feed on plant products. The hummingbird uses its long bill to reach deep into flowers and extract the sweet nectar. Some species of bats also feed on nectar, lapping it up with long, thin tongues.

Animals That Eat Everything. Raccoons and people have something in common. They are both omnivores—that is, they eat all sorts of plant and animal products. Omnivores are among the most successful of all animals because they are not restricted to one food, or even a few foods. If one kind of food runs out, they turn to another. Adaptability to many foods enables an animal to exist in many different habitats. Raccoons are able to live in forests, grasslands, wetlands, and even in big cities. Rodents, sheep, deer, gourds, and insects can all be meals for the coyote.

Some human activities create a greater variety of food for omnivores. Raccoons and other animals, such as bears, relish the food garbage produced by people. Another food source created by people is the remains of animals killed by vehicles on the highway.

▶ **HOW ANIMALS DEFEND THEMSELVES**

A species cannot survive unless it can defend itself against its enemies. The threat of attack from other animals, including human

beings, is ever present. The risk of battle is the same for each animal: There is a winner and a loser. Yet even the winner may be wounded, sometimes seriously, making it more likely that it will be the loser in the next battle.

Animals have general and specialized methods of defense. In most situations, animals prefer to escape danger without fighting. Animals use two general defenses to avoid fighting—freezing and fleeing. When danger appears, an animal will remain motionless in an attempt to make itself undetectable to its predator, sometimes even playing dead. If the danger continues and the predator gets too close, the animal will flee. How close different predators can come before they pose a threat and the animal flees is known as **flight distance**. For example, a herd of Thompson's gazelles will graze without concern even though lions are within sight, as long as they are far enough away. If a lion comes too close, within about 200 yards (183 meters), the gazelles will take flight.

Although it has a preference for small water creatures, the raccoon has a large and varied diet that includes birds' eggs, corn, fruit, nuts, seeds, and small land animals.

Camouflage. Natural camouflage is a way of hiding in the open. When an animal blends into or resembles its surroundings, it can often remain undetected if it stays still. This not only helps an animal avoid enemies, it also helps an animal get close to its prey.

Color and shape can conceal an animal. Insects known as walking sticks have bodies that resemble brown twigs in shape and color. A walking stick will spend long periods of time without moving. Frozen in place on a branch of a tree or shrub, the insect seems to be part of the plant. Many tree-dwelling jungle animals, such as the tree python of Asia, are

without a built-in defense—when the colors or patterns are the same as those of animals that are harmful. An example is the harmless hoverfly that is safe from many attacks because it looks like a stinging wasp.

Chemical Warfare. Some creatures defend themselves with chemical weapons. The chemicals are delivered in a variety of ways, such as the foul-smelling spray of the skunk, the venomous bite of a snake, the fierce stings of a jellyfish, and the stab of a stingray.

Not all chemicals are injected or sprayed. Some animals have skin glands that produce

Camouflaged by long grasses, the tiger can quietly stalk its prey and avoid its enemies. Without its striped markings, the shape of the tiger would stand out from the background of plants and earth in its habitat.

green like the year-round color of their environment. It is difficult—for an enemy and prey—to detect the python when it is coiled in the branches.

Warning Signals. The bright colors and patterns of some animals are a warning signal to enemies that they should stay away. Some boldly colored animals are venomous; others have glands that emit (give off) a harmful or irritating substance; still others sting or taste bad. At times the signal is hidden until danger appears. When threatened, the foul-tasting Oriental fire-bellied toad turns over to reveal its brightly colored belly.

The striking pattern of the black-and-white fur of the skunk, the vivid colors of the poison dart frogs, and the bright bands of the poisonous coral snake all say "stay away!" However, if a predator ignores the signal, one encounter is generally enough for any predator, if it can survive, to learn to avoid such animals.

Bright colors can also be useful to animals

poisonous substances. The chemical oozes out onto the animal's skin. When a predator grabs hold with its jaws, it is poisoned. Other animals, such as the stonefish, have body parts containing poison that is released on contact.

Armor. Scales, shells, and spines provide many animals with protective armor. The pangolin (or scaly anteater) is an ant-eating mammal covered on its back and sides with tough triangular scales that have razor-sharp edges. If threatened, the pangolin can raise its scales to slash its enemy or roll up into a tight ball, protecting its unarmored belly.

The soft flesh of turtles, tortoises, clams, crabs, and many other marine animals is protected by a hard shell. When danger threatens, they simply pull their body back into their snug enclosure and wait for the danger to pass.

The hedgehog, echidna (or spiny anteater), and porcupine are protected by a covering of strong, thick spines. Under attack, the spiny animals will protect exposed underparts and offer the enemy a sea of sharp, powerful spikes.

▶ **HOW ANIMALS COMMUNICATE**

Animals use many signals, including some that are silent, to communicate with one another. Each species shares a language of sound and behaviors that is recognized by all its members.

Animal Calls. Each animal sound has a meaning. Calls are used for many reasons, including to warn or defend, to claim territory, to help find a mate, and to announce that food has been found. If frightened, a young alligator utters a shrill distress call. The call alerts other young alligators to the danger. The call also draws adult females to the young alligators. The nearness of the adult females provides protection for all the young, so the call serves as a warning and a defense.

A distress call can also confuse an enemy. When a frog is frightened, it lets out a loud squeak. The sudden loud sound can startle the enemy just long enough for the frog to jump away.

Animals that live in large groups such as bird flocks often use food calls that let the group know where a source of food can be found. A tern (a type of small gull) that sights a school of small fish swimming through the water utters a screamlike call.

Not all animal sounds are made with the voice. The ruffed grouse is known for its drumming sound. A male ruffed grouse trying to establish its territory or attract a mate will stand on a log and beat the air with its wings, creating a thumping sound. Although the beating is slow at first, it ends with a rapid whirring noise.

Silent Signals. Body characteristics and behaviors provide the silent signals that many animals use to communicate. The shape of a body part, the color of fur, or a pattern of movement can send a message from one animal to another.

Some signals are used so that members of a particular species can identify one another. The horns of each species of antelope have a unique shape—some are straight spikes, others are spiraled, and still others are long and curved. Antelopes are able to recognize one another by the shape of the horns.

Scent is an important communication tool that some animals use to establish ownership. A male wolf urinates on shrubs and bushes to let other males know he is around and in charge of his territory. Scent is also used by members of the same species to identify one another and in mating.

Another silent mating signal is the flashing light that the firefly emits. Fireflies use their flashing signal to attract members of the other sex. Each species of firefly has its own pattern of flashes.

Using postures and facial expressions, animals can transmit a great number of messages that are either friendly or hostile. When a young animal whose mother is disciplining it turns over on its back exposing its soft stomach, it means the offspring knows the mother is in charge. In a meeting of two adult animals, the animal that assumes the same posture is saying "I give up."

▶ **HOW ANIMALS REPRODUCE**

For a species to exist, its members must reproduce their kind. There are two main types of reproduction in the animal kingdom: asexual reproduction, in which a new offspring is produced by one parent, and sexual reproduction, in which a new offspring is produced by two parents.

Asexual Reproduction. Asexual reproduction is carried on by simple animals, such as sponges, jellyfish, flatworms, and those that make coral. When a coral animal reproduces, small projections, called buds, form on its body. The buds grow on the parent and develop their own feeding organs. Soon they split off the parent as a new, separate offspring.

Coyotes, which live throughout the United States, Canada, and Mexico, communicate by howling. The eerie howl of the coyote is usually heard during the evening, night, or early morning.

During sexual reproduction, the sponge (*above*) releases sex cells into the surrounding water. The courting frigate bird (*above right*) inflates its huge red pouch to attract females. Orangutans and their young (*right*) enjoy a close relationship.

Another form of asexual reproduction is called **fragmentation**. During fragmentation, an animal, such as a flatworm, divides into two halves. After dividing, each fragment of the flatworm forms the body parts it is missing and becomes a complete new individual.

Sexual Reproduction. During sexual reproduction, two sex cells, an egg cell from a female and a sperm cell from a male, join to create a new offspring. The sperm of some animals, such as mammals, unites with the egg inside the female's body in a process called fertilization. The fertilized egg grows inside the female until the offspring is fully developed and ready for birth.

The fertilization process does not always take place inside the female during sexual reproduction. Some animals produce young without ever coming together to mate. Many fish and aquatic animals, such as frogs, release eggs and sperm into the water when individuals of both sexes are near one another. Fertilization is then a matter of luck. The chances of it occurring are increased in animals that send out signals to attract the opposite sex to them during the release of the cells. Male frogs, for example, emit mating calls that draw the females to them.

Care of the Young. Typically, animals that release sex cells but do not stay around to care

for the offspring produce vast numbers of eggs. The female ocean sunfish, which can weigh 1,000 pounds (454 kilograms), can produce 28 million eggs in a single season. The unprotected eggs of the sunfish are threatened by wind, waves, and predators. But because so many eggs are produced, some have a chance of surviving and continuing the species.

Animals that have small numbers of young usually provide some sort of care for them. The female Pacific salmon builds a nest of pebbles and gravel for her 800 eggs. Birds and mammals, which may have only a few, or even a single, offspring, protect and feed their young. Some mammals, such as human beings, care for their young over many years.

►CYCLES AND PATTERNS OF ANIMAL LIFE

The lives of animals involve regular cycles and patterns that are related to changes in their surroundings. There are many cycles of varying length that occur in an animal's life. Cycles may correspond with an animal's need to find food, a mate, or a new, less-crowded home.

Migration

Many animals, such as the wildebeest, monarch butterfly, gray whale, and Pacific salmon, are great travelers. The regular movement of animals over a set route is called a **migration**. Although all sorts of animals—mammals, fish, insects, and amphibians—migrate, birds are the best-known animal migrants. In the autumn, many birds travel south to spend the winter in a warmer climate. In the spring, they return north to nest and breed.

The champion travelers are the Arctic terns. Each year, Arctic terns travel between the Arctic and Antarctic, logging up to 25,000 miles (40,225 kilometers) of travel. Other birds migrate very short distances. Ptarmigans, which are ground birds common to the cold regions of the Northern Hemisphere, simply move down the mountainside a few hundred yards to escape severe winter weather.

Hibernation

Some cycles help animals survive sharp seasonal changes in temperature. **Hibernation** is a sleeplike state that protects animals against the cold and decreases their need for food. Many different kinds of animals hibernate, including some species of birds, mammals, insects, reptiles, and amphibians. When cold weather approaches, animals that hibernate burrow into the ground, curl up under leaves, or tuck away in dens. Their heartbeat, breathing, and other bodily functions slow down. They do not move. Because they are inactive, they do not need food. Most hibernating animals eat large quantities of food during the autumn. The food is stored in their body as fat and supplies the energy as they need it during hibernation.

Population Cycles

Some species go through cycles in their population. The ruffed grouse, a chickenlike bird of North America, has a population cycle of six or seven years. At the height of the cycle, the numbers of grouse explode. Then they decrease, year by year. At the lowest point of the cycle, the numbers gradually begin to increase.

Such cycles are partly tied to food supply. When food is abundant, more animals survive and have young. Eventually, however, the number of animals exceeds the food supply. Animals die and the population drops. With fewer animals around, food becomes increasingly more available. As it does, the population of the animals once again begins to increase.

Dense clouds of monarch butterflies (*below*) travel from Canada and the northern United States as far south as Mexico to escape the winter's cold. Huge herds of wildebeests (*right*) migrate over the grassy plains of Africa in search of food and water.

▶ANIMALS AND PEOPLE

Animals provide people with food, transportation, and protection. Animals also spread disease, such as rabies and Lyme disease, and compete with humans for food. In the long run, however, the fate of the animal kingdom is in human hands. People and their activities have so changed the balance of nature that many species will only survive if they have help from humanity.

Early people—and some still today—hunted wild animals as a source of food and clothing. Scientists believe that the need to band together and hunt helped human society become more complex. Actually, we still depend on hunting for an important food source—fish. Harvesting fish from the sea really is just another form of hunting wild animals.

Domestic Animals. Our domestic animals, such as cows, horses, and dogs, were bred from their wild ancestors by people. Dogs were domesticated about 14,000 years ago. Their ancestors probably were wolves that fed on garbage near human camps and then became tame. Dogs help people hunt, serve as guards, and, most of all, bring them happiness as pets.

Cattle and horses were domesticated from wild ancestors more than 5,000 years ago. Ever since, they have served as a means of transportation and, more important, have provided food. People have controlled the breeding of domestic animals to produce types with beneficial characteristics. Wild cattle, for instance, can be fierce. Early cattle breeders eliminated the fierceness by allowing only certain cattle to mate—those that seemed more docile (easy to control) than others. They passed this docile tendency on to their descendants.

Animal Symbols. Animals have always served as symbols for people. This is still true today. Evidence of animals used as symbols can be found throughout the world—in the names given to sports teams, in the art that is produced, and in the religions that consider some animals to be sacred.

Diseases from Animals. Some animals pass diseases to people. Many animals, such as raccoons, can spread rabies. If a rabid animal bites someone, that person will die unless treated. At one time, a person with rabies was doomed, but modern medical treatment has ended this threat.

Giraffes, elands, and rhinoceroses roam an animal preserve in Woburn, England. Preserves are part of an effort to protect and breed endangered animal species.

In recent years, another disease spread by animals has been on the increase. It is called Lyme disease, after the town in Connecticut in which it was first discovered. It is carried by a tick that can live on deer and other animals. Fortunately, not all ticks carry Lyme disease, and, with antibiotics, it is treatable.

▶WILDLIFE CONSERVATION

Humans present far more danger to animals than they to us. All over the world, species of animals are threatened with extinction because of people. Human populations are exploding. People need land, food, and natural resources. This means that habitats on which animals depend are taken up for human wants. Human activities cause pollution that destroys habitats and the animals that rely on them. The same pollution threatens human life.

Animals help keep the balance of nature. Moreover, they should be appreciated for themselves, as well as for what they do for us. While people are a threat to animals, people can also help them. Across the world, conservationists are working to keep animal species healthy, to save them from extinction and make our world better for animals—and for people.

EDWARD R. RICCIUTI
Co-author, *The Audubon Society Book of Wild Animals*

See also AMPHIBIANS; BIOLOGICAL CLOCK; BIRDS; ENDANGERED SPECIES; FISHES; INSECTS; LIFE; MAMMALS; OYSTERS, OCTOPUSES, AND OTHER MOLLUSKS; SPONGES; REPTILES; WORMS.

The Road Runner always gets the better of Wile E. Coyote, his hapless pursuer, in a popular series of animated cartoons. Through the technique of animation, imaginary creatures appear to live and move.

ANIMATION

The word "animate" comes from the Latin word *anima*, or soul, and literally means "to give life to." In filmmaking, animation is a technique that makes inanimate (lifeless) drawings or objects appear to live and move. Animation is most often used to make cartoon movies and television shows. It can also be used in television commercials or in educational films. Animation is sometimes used in combination with live action in movies.

Unlike live-action films, which record the movements of living actors, animated films create an illusion of motion. Bugs Bunny never really dove down his rabbit hole, Mickey Mouse never really kissed Minnie, and Gumby never really waved good-bye. The movements of these imaginary creatures occurred only on film.

Because animation is not limited to recording things that really happened, it can show viewers many things that live action cannot, from the movements of a single atom to a view of an entire galaxy. An animated character can fly without wings, fall off a cliff without getting hurt, or be squashed flat as a pancake and pop back into shape. The only limits to what animation can show are the limits of the artist's imagination.

▶ANIMATION TECHNIQUES

There are two basic types of animation. In one technique, two-dimensional (flat) drawings are animated. The other technique involves the animation of three-dimensional objects such as puppets or clay figures. (A third type of animation, done with computers, is discussed in the box "Computer Animation" on page 290.)

To make an animated film, a series of drawings—or an object placed in a series of positions—is photographed, one picture at a time, by a motion picture camera. In each picture, or **frame**, the subject's position is changed slightly. When the completed film is run, the subject appears to move.

Artists and writers first prepare a **storyboard**, which is an illustrated script. The storyboard looks like a giant comic strip, with sketches showing the action of the story and dialogue (the characters' spoken lines) written under each sketch. Next, the music and the dialogue are recorded. Then the work of animation begins.

Two-Dimensional Animation. The animation of drawings is the technique most often used to create animated films and television shows.

The animators follow a chart listing the length of time and number of frames needed for each word, sound, and action in the entire script. To look smooth and natural, a single action that takes one second of screen time may require as many as 24 drawings. For example, if a script calls for a character to raise his hand, the first picture the animators draw shows the character with his hand at his side. In the next drawing, his hand is raised slightly, and a third drawing shows his hand still higher. Drawing after drawing is made in this way until, in the 24th drawing, the action is completed. More than a million drawings may be used in an animated feature film. Most television cartoons use fewer drawings per second. As a result, the characters' movements may not look as lifelike.

The animators draw every movement of every character that will appear in the film. When the drawings are completed, they are traced onto sheets of clear plastic called **cels**. Colors are then painted on the reverse sides of the cels. Other artists paint the backgrounds in the film. The finished cels are laid over the backgrounds and photographed with a special camera that shoots one frame of film at a time. The camera operator follows a chart that tells the proper sequence of the cels and which background is needed for each frame. The operator takes a picture, removes the cel and replaces it with the next one, then takes another picture. The soundtrack, containing the music, dialogue, and sound effects, is added after the photography is completed.

Some animated films are made without using cels. Instead, the drawings themselves are photographed. Pencil, charcoal, and colored pencil can produce subtle, shaded effects that are very different from the bright colors of the painted cels.

Three-Dimensional Animation. Three-dimensional figures and objects can be animated using a process called **stop-motion photography**. Animators often work with special puppets, which are made of flexible plastic molded around a jointed metal "skeleton." In recent years, figures and objects made of clay have become popular subjects of stop-motion animation.

Using a special motion picture camera, animators film the figure or object. After each frame is photographed, the camera is stopped,

Below: Three favorite animated characters are Elmer Fudd, Bugs Bunny, and Daffy Duck. *Below right:* In the film *Who Framed Roger Rabbit?*, humans appeared to interact with cartoon characters. *Right:* Animated clay figures enliven a television ad for California raisins.

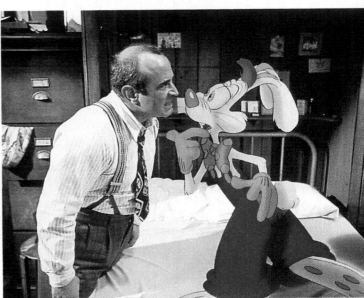

The title character from the computer-animated film *Tin Toy*, which won an Academy Award in 1989.

Computer Animation

Some of the most exciting developments in animation are taking place in the field of computer graphics, in which artists use computers to produce images and animate them. Computer animation is used to create video games and films, as well as graphics and special effects for television and movies.

Computer graphics techniques vary, depending on the kind of equipment and the software (instructions that tell the machine what to do) that are used. But most computer graphics systems have certain features in common.

The inside surface of a computer screen is coated with thousands of tiny dots of light-sensitive chemicals called phosphors. Each dot is called a picture element, or **pixel**. The pixels are arranged in clusters of three, with each pixel responsible for producing one of the three primary colors of light: red, blue, and green. These colors can be combined to produce all the colors an artist might need. Using a computer graphics program, the artist tells the computer which pixels to light up. The glowing pixels create the image on the screen.

The amount of detail in the image depends on the number of pixels on the screen. Most home computer screens have comparatively few pixels, and pictures drawn on them often show little detail. But a powerful computer used by an animator may have millions of pixels on the screen. With these machines it is possible to produce highly detailed images.

Once the artist has produced an image and stored it in the computer, the machine can be instructed to calculate all the slight adjustments in position that are needed to give the appearance of motion. It can also make all the necessary changes in light, shading, and perspective. Each succeeding computer-generated image is photographed and used to make a single frame of film. When the film is run, the effect is one of movement.

Computer animation can be used to create effects that would be difficult or impossible to achieve using drawings. For example, surfaces such as metal, glass, and plastic can be given extremely lifelike textures. For this reason, computer animation is often used to create realistic settings and backgrounds. However, some filmmakers continue to use traditional animation techniques to bring characters to life.

CHARLES SOLOMON

and the animators adjust the figure's position slightly. When the film is developed and projected, the figure appears to move.

Stop-motion photography is used to make short animated films and television commercials. It is also used to animate the imaginary creatures that appear in live-action fantasy and science-fiction movies. The giant ape King Kong, as well as some of the creatures in the *Star Wars* series, were animated using stop-motion techniques.

▶ **HISTORY OF ANIMATION**

The first animated film, *Humorous Phases of Funny Faces*, was made in 1906 by J. Stuart Blackton, an American newspaper illustrator. Blackton filmed a series of faces that had been drawn on a blackboard and also used a variety of other techniques. Another early animated film, *Gertie the Dinosaur*, was created by the American cartoonist Winsor McCay in 1914. In this film, for the first time, a character drawn of lines seemed to live and breathe on the screen.

Audiences liked these animated cartoons. Soon many American film studios were producing animated films, which were shown in movie theaters before the feature films. The Pat Sullivan studio produced one of the most famous characters of the silent-film era, Felix the Cat. The Fleischer studio produced cartoons featuring the character Ko-Ko the Clown and later created Betty Boop, Popeye, and Superman cartoons.

The first successful animated cartoon with sound was *Steamboat Willie* (1928), which introduced the character Mickey Mouse. This film was produced by Walt Disney, who was to become the most famous American producer of animated films. Disney's series of Mickey Mouse cartoons and another series called *Silly Symphonies* were very popular with audiences.

The success of his early cartoons enabled Disney to launch an ambitious training program for his artists. They studied anatomy, drawing, acting, and motion to improve their animation. The results of this training can be seen in Disney's *Snow White and the Seven Dwarfs* (1937), which was the first feature-length animated film made in the United States. Other important Disney films followed, including *Pinocchio* (1940), *Fantasia* (1940), *Dumbo* (1941), and *Bambi* (1942).

Right: Snow White and the Seven Dwarfs, released by the Walt Disney studio in 1937, was the first feature-length animated film made in the United States.

Below: The beloved Disney character Mickey Mouse made his first appearance in 1928 in *Steamboat Willie*, the first successful animated cartoon with sound.

By the end of World War II (1939–45), leadership in the field of animation had passed to two major film studios, Metro-Goldwyn-Mayer (MGM) and Warner Brothers. At MGM, William Hanna and Joseph Barbera made cartoons featuring Tom and Jerry, a cat and a mouse. Warner Brothers cartoons, directed by Tex Avery, Chuck Jones, and Friz Freleng, starred Bugs Bunny, Daffy Duck, and many other characters. These cartoons owed much to the early Disney films, but they were faster-paced, with a slapstick humor. During the 1950's, United Productions of America (UPA) introduced a flat, modernistic drawing style in cartoons featuring Gerald McBoing-Boing and Mr. Magoo.

During the 1960's, television networks began broadcasting children's cartoons on Saturday mornings. Some cartoons were shown in the evenings, during prime time. The most successful television animation studio was Hanna-Barbera, which introduced the Flintstones, the Jetsons, Yogi Bear, and hundreds of other characters.

During the 1980's, feature-length animated films again became popular. *An American Tail* (1986) was the first animated film from the producer Steven Spielberg. The Disney studio released *Oliver and Company* (1988) and *The Little Mermaid* (1989). *Who Framed Roger Rabbit?* (1988), produced jointly by Disney and Spielberg, combined animation with live action. Animation returned to prime-time television with the Fox Network's *The Simpsons*. These developments, along with experiments in computer animation (see box), promised to bring about the most exciting period in animation since its heyday some 50 years earlier.

CHARLES SOLOMON
Author, *Enchanted Drawings:
The History of Animation*

See also DISNEY, WALT.

ANNAPOLIS. See UNITED STATES, ARMED FORCES OF THE; MARYLAND.

ANOREXIA NERVOSA. See DISEASES.

A vast ice sheet (*far right*) covers Antarctica, making the continent inhospitable to life. The only human inhabitants are scientists from many nations, who have established bases (*right*), where they spend part of the year studying the frozen continent. Penguins (*below*) and other animals thrive in the waters off Antarctica.

ANTARCTICA

Antarctica is the coldest, windiest, most desolate continent on earth. Almost all of its area is covered with a vast ice sheet, which reaches a thickness of about 5 kilometers (3 miles) near the South Pole. This ice sheet holds 70 percent of the world's fresh water. Even so, much of Antarctica is considered a desert because many places receive so little precipitation—less than 76 millimeters (3 inches) a year, in the form of snow.

No people are native to Antarctica, but about 40 scientific stations are scattered around the continent. Each summer some 2,000 scientists come to Antarctica to study its environment. About 250 people spend the harsh winters there.

▶THE LAND

Larger than the United States and Mexico combined, Antarctica covers an area of about 14,000,000 square kilometers (5,405,000 square miles). Much of the continent is mountainous, and high peaks protrude through the ice sheet. A great mountain range, the Transantarctic Mountains, divides the continent and ice sheet into East Antarctica and West Antarctica.

At the edges of Antarctica lie enormous ice shelves—some as large as the state of Texas.

Mountain glaciers (slow-moving masses of ice) flowing from the continent's center feed into the ice shelves. Regularly, pieces of ice break off to become icebergs, some of which may be 60 to 100 kilometers (37 to 62 miles) wide.

The ocean around Antarctica is formed by the southern parts of the Pacific, Atlantic, and Indian oceans. Much of this southern ocean is frozen all year long. In winter a thick belt of ice 480 to 1,600 kilometers (300 to 1,000 miles) wide surrounds Antarctica. Although much of the ice melts during the summer, the sea ice still extends between 160 and 800 kilometers (100 and 500 miles) from the continent.

▶THE CLIMATE

Surprisingly, Antarctica receives more sunlight than the equator, but the snow-covered ice sheet and the sea ice surrounding the continent reflect the heat back into space. Although the weather along the coast is considerably milder, inland the average winter temperature is about −70°C (−94°F). In July, 1983 (in the middle of the Antarctic winter), Soviet scientists at their Vostok Station recorded the world's lowest temperature: −89.2°C (−128.6°F).

Fierce winds, called katabatic winds, control Antarctica's weather and make the climate inhospitable to people. Gravity draws cold air

from the interior down the slopes of the ice sheet to the coast. As the air becomes colder, the wind speed increases. Along the coast, winds up to 322 kilometers (200 miles) an hour have been recorded.

▶ANIMAL LIFE

Although plants and animals may have once thrived in Antarctica, today the continent itself is almost empty of life. Only a few hardy insects, primitive plants such as mosses and lichens, and one type of grass survive along the warmer coast of the Antarctic Peninsula near South America. Farther inland, in areas free of ice, lichens and simple organisms called algae have adapted to the cold, dry environment by living in the cracks and cavities of rocks. Some scientists believe that astronauts might find similar organisms on Mars.

The sparseness of life on land contrasts greatly with the variety of life in the southern ocean. About 27 types of seabirds breed in the Antarctic region. Among these are the penguins—the most familiar of which are the small Adélie penguins and the larger emperor penguins. Six types of seals frequent the southern ocean. Of these, Weddell, Ross, crabeater, and leopard seals breed in or near Antarctica. Blue, fin, sei, humpback, and sperm whales also are commonly seen in Antarctic waters. Tiny sea creatures called krill are especially important to Antarctica's marine (sea) ecosystem—the community of living organisms and their environment. Shrimplike animals, krill serve as food for whales, seals, birds, and fishes. In turn, krill feed on plants and smaller animals.

▶ANTARCTICA'S PAST

More than 200,000,000 years ago, Antarctica, South America, Africa, Australia, and India formed one enormous continent that scientists call Gondwana. Gradually, large pieces of the earth's crust separated, and Antarctica was isolated from the other continents. (For more information on how the continents were formed, see the article EARTH and EARTH, HISTORY OF.)

Although the ice hides much of Antarctica's past, scientists have uncovered the fact that millions of years ago the continent had a tropical climate. During the past century, coal, petrified (mineralized) tree trunks, and fossils (the remains or imprints) of leaves and sea creatures have been discovered in Antarctica. In 1969, American geologists discovered the fossil jawbone of a small, four-legged reptile in the Transantarctic Mountains. This reptile was about 1.2 meters (4 feet) long and had lived in Antarctica more than 200,000,000 years ago.

For many years scientists searched for fossils of mammals. In 1982, American geologists discovered fossils of a small, rodentlike

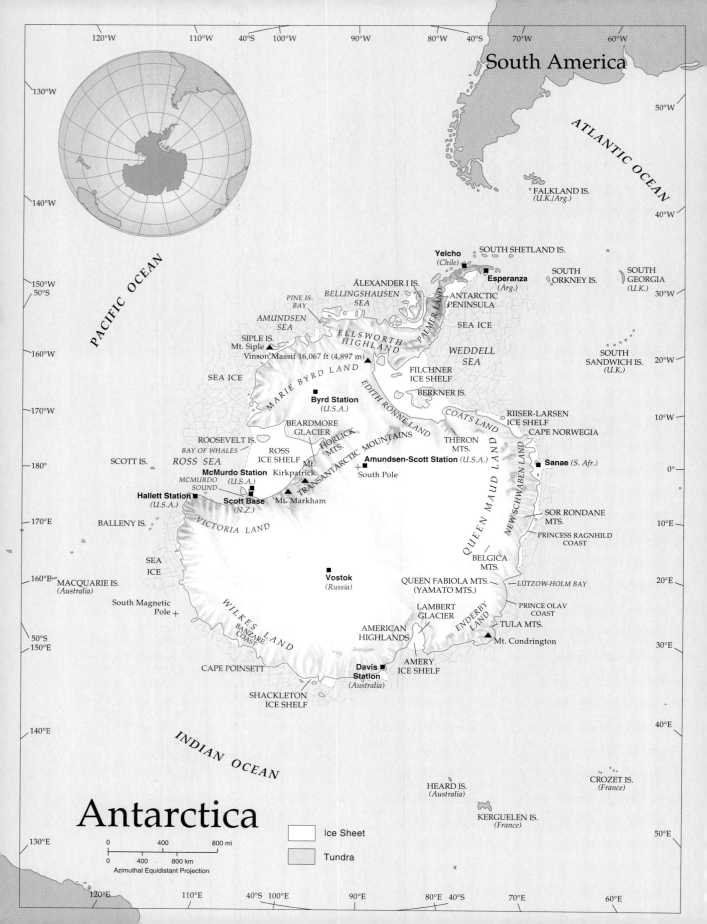

Antarctica

Ice Sheet

Tundra

0   400   800 mi
0   400   800 km
Azimuthal Equidistant Projection

marsupial (a pouched mammal like an opossum) that lived in Antarctica between 55,000,000 and 40,000,000 years ago. Because this marsupial was similar to mammals found in South America and Australia today, the discovery supported the theory that Antarctica was once joined to these two continents. The largest fossil yet found in Antarctica, that of a 30-foot (9-meter)-long whale said to be 40,000,000 years old, was discovered in 1987.

▶ EXPLORATION AND DISCOVERY

For centuries it was believed that an Antarctic continent existed, but its existence remained unproved. Between 1772 and 1775 the British navigator Captain James Cook sailed around Antarctica but did not sight it. In 1820 an American sealing ship under Captain Nathaniel Palmer reached the Antarctic Peninsula. Palmer, a British naval officer named Edward Bransfield, and a Russian admiral named Fabian von Bellingshausen are all generally credited with having "discovered" Antarctica at about the same time.

Between the 1820's and 1900, expeditions from the United States, France, and Britain explored the oceans and coast of Antarctica. In the early 20th century, explorers turned their attention landward. The race to be the first to reach the South Pole, at approximately the center of the continent, was the climax of the heroic age of Antarctic exploration. Although many men tried, the first to reach the South Pole was Roald Amundsen of Norway on December 14, 1911. Close behind him was Robert F. Scott, a British naval officer, who reached the pole on January 17, 1912, but died along with his men on the return trip.

In the years that followed, explorers and scientists from many countries traveled to Antarctica. Among them was Admiral Richard E. Byrd of the United States. Byrd led three expeditions to Antarctica between 1928 and 1941. In 1929 he became the first to pilot an airplane over the South Pole. Byrd and others changed Antarctic exploration by introducing tractors, airplanes, icebreaking ships, and radios and prepared the way for modern scientific investigation of the continent.

The modern age of Antarctic research began with the International Geophysical Year (IGY) of 1957–58. During the IGY, twelve nations established 55 scientific stations in Antarctica.

▶ THE ANTARCTIC TREATY

In December, 1959, in Washington, D.C., Argentina, Australia, Belgium, Chile, France, Japan, New Zealand, Norway, South Africa, the Soviet Union, the United Kingdom, and the United States (all participants in the IGY) signed the Antarctic Treaty. The treaty became official in 1961. Since then, four additional nations have signed it, and 16 others have agreed to observe its provisions.

The Antarctic Treaty provides that Antarctica shall be used only for peaceful purposes. Ordinary military activities, nuclear tests, and the disposal of nuclear wastes are forbidden. The treaty also guarantees the free exchange of scientific ideas and information among the nations. It does not recognize the many territorial claims by countries to Antarctica. In addition, there are several special international agreements designed to preserve Antarctica's environment.

▶ ANTARCTICA: PRESENT AND FUTURE

Scientists study Antarctica not only to learn its secrets but also to solve problems that affect the whole world. Antarctica's climate, the ice sheet, and the southern ocean have an effect on weather and oceans worldwide. The question of the ice sheet's stability is vital to scientists studying how carbon dioxide affects our climate. What will happen to the ice sheet if increased carbon dioxide in the atmosphere makes our climate warmer? Scientists are also concerned about the atmosphere's thinning ozone layer, a problem severe over Antarctica.

Antarctica's future may not be limited to providing scientists with information. Some countries now catch krill to feed people and animals. Antarctica is believed to have valuable mineral resources, including petroleum, coal, and precious metals. However, Antarctica's harsh climate makes finding and developing these resources difficult. In addition, people and governments want to ensure that Antarctica's unique environment will continue to be protected. In 1991, after more than two years of negotiations between members of the Antarctic Treaty, 24 countries signed an agreement that prohibited mining and oil drilling for 50 years.

WINIFRED REUNING
Division of Polar Programs
National Science Foundation

See also ARCTIC.

ANTEATERS

The solitary creature journeys slowly through the dry grass, sniffing the ground with its long tubelike snout. Finding a hidden ant or termite nest, it uses its strong front claws to slash it open. Its wormlike tongue, which can reach 2 feet (.6 meters) in length, darts in and out of the nest, greedily licking up the ants. Each day, this hungry mammal—the giant anteater—eats thousands of insects.

The three species, or kinds, of anteaters can be found roaming rain forests and grassy plains from southern Mexico to northern Argentina. Anteaters belong to a group of mammals, called Edentata (meaning "without teeth"), that also includes sloths and armadillos. Other animals are sometimes called anteaters, such as aardvarks and spiny anteaters; however, they are not part of the same family.

There is a wide range in size among the species of anteaters. The giant anteater measures about 6 feet (1.8 meters) from its head to its bushy tail and can weigh up to 110 pounds (50 kilograms). The tamandua, or collared anteater, measures about 42 inches (106 centimeters) from head to tail and weighs about 9 pounds (4 kilograms). The silky, or pygmy, anteater, which is about the size of a squirrel, measures about 13 inches (34 centimeters) from head to tail and weighs about a pound (.45 kilograms).

Anteaters and Their Young. Anteaters live solitary existences, each one within its own territory. Males and females only come together to mate. About 180 days after mating, the female anteater gives birth to one baby.

Immediately after birth, the baby anteater climbs up onto its mother's back. It leaves its secure spot only to nurse or when the mother feeds. When it is about 3 months old, the young anteater ventures from its mother to find food for itself. The baby anteater stays with its mother until the mother becomes pregnant again.

The Life of an Anteater. The giant anteater lives on the ground—usually in open forests and savannas. Unlike its smaller night-feeding relatives that spend most of their lives in the trees, the giant anteater stays on the ground and seeks its food chiefly by day. When resting, the giant anteater often takes over the empty burrow of another animal or sinks into a shady ditch, covering itself with its broad tail.

Walking about on the knuckles of its front feet to protect its long sharp claws, the giant anteater spends most of the day searching for food. It uses its keen sense of smell to find nests of ants and termites. The giant anteater is a careful diner, quickly taking a small portion of the insect population before it can be bitten by the ants. The food is swallowed whole and broken down in its muscular stomach. The quantities of earth, sand, tiny twigs, and small stones that the giant anteater regularly takes in also help in the digestion of its food.

The Anteater and Its Environment. The enemies of the giant anteater include jaguars and pumas. When defending itself, the giant anteater will stand up and slash out with its strong front limbs and long claws.

Humans are also a threat to anteaters. In the process of clearing land for crops, grazing, and construction, they destroy the anteater's environment. Even though the anteater helps control the populations of insect pests, many people consider the anteater too dangerous to protect.

Reviewed by James G. Doherty
Curator of Mammals
The Bronx Zoo

See also Mammals.

Bounding gracefully across the plains of Africa, impalas (*above*) can jump as high as 8 feet (2.4 meters) in a single leap. Safe within the protective camouflage of tall grasses, a baby Grant's gazelle (*left*) is nuzzled by its mother.

ANTELOPES

Antelopes are usually slender, graceful mammals that have two-hoofed toes on each foot and hollow horns. Although they are sometimes thought to be part of the deer family, antelopes are actually more closely related to cattle. Antelopes, cattle, and other animals such as bison, buffaloes, goats, and sheep all belong to the same family, called Bovidae.

Most antelopes live in Africa. There are also several species, or kinds, of antelopes found in Asia. While there are no true antelopes in North America, a close relative of the antelopes, the mountain goat, makes its home in the Rocky Mountains of North America.

▶CHARACTERISTICS OF ANTELOPES

There is great variety in the size of antelopes. The smallest, the royal antelope of Africa's western coast, is about the size of a rabbit. It measures about 10 inches (25 centimeters) high at the shoulder and weighs about 8 pounds (3.8 kilograms). The largest antelope, the giant eland of West Africa, is about the size of a large cow. It measures 6 feet (1.8 meters) high at the shoulder and can weigh more than 1,200 pounds (544 kilograms).

The appearance of the various species of antelopes seems to vary as much as the size does. Their smooth coat of hair is generally brightly colored with variations of white, gray, or brown. Several species have more distinctive coloring, such as the bongo, which is red with vertical white stripes, and the male sable antelope, which is nearly all black with white markings on its face, belly, and rump.

In some kinds of antelopes, both males and females have horns; in others only males have horns. Antelopes keep the horns all their life, unlike the antlers of deer, which are shed each year. The horns can be many different shapes and sizes—long and curved, short and ringed, spiral, or lyre-shaped.

The strong slender legs of the antelope enable it to leap high and run fast. The impala can jump 8 feet (2.4 meters) high, and the black buck of India can reach speeds of about 60 miles (97 kilometers) per hour.

Plants, such as leaves and grasses, make up the diet of the antelope. The antelope must tear its food from the plant by pressing the front teeth in the lower jaw against a hard pad in the upper jaw. The food is only slightly chewed before it is swallowed. After the food

Although actual fights between antelopes are rare, these greater kudu males have locked horns in a pushing match to resolve a territorial conflict. One of the males will eventually give in and withdraw from the match with head lowered and tail tucked between his legs.

passes to the stomach, it is called cud. At a later time, the cud is forced back into the mouth to be chewed thoroughly with the back molars before it is swallowed again. Antelopes and other animals, such as deer, cattle, sheep, and goats, that eat in this manner are called cud-chewers, or **ruminants**.

▶ ANTELOPES AND THEIR YOUNG

Some male and female antelopes mate throughout the year, while others mate at a certain time of the year. The time between mating and the birth of the offspring varies from about five and a half months to about nine months, depending on the kind of antelope. Usually, only one baby is born at a time.

Most females living in herds leave the herd and find a secluded area in which to give birth. After giving birth, the mother licks the baby antelope, or calf, to rouse it. Within minutes, the calf is able to stand on its own.

In the first few months of life, the mother antelope may hide the calf in tall grass or bush when she feeds. Because calves, as well as sick and old antelopes, are easy catches for predators, many do not reach adulthood.

▶ THE LIFE OF THE ANTELOPE

Antelopes, which live in herds, alone, or in pairs, can be found in a variety of habitats, or environments: grassy plains, dense tropical forests, hot deserts, high mountains, and even swamplands. The antelope spends much of the day, except for the hot afternoon, feeding, drinking, and ruminating (chewing its cud). During the afternoon when the sun is at its hottest, the antelope rests.

Many kinds of antelopes are territorial. This means that males mark an area as their own and guard it against other males. Although males spend much of their time defending their territory from other males, females are allowed to enter the territory so that mating can take place.

Hyenas, wild dogs, and large cats (such as lions and leopards) prey on antelopes. The smaller antelopes are also threatened by eagles, small cats, and pythons. These shy creatures often protect themselves by running away from predators. Some antelopes that live in herds use signals to warn others of danger; the springbok is one antelope that alerts others by leaping high into the air when it senses an enemy is near.

▶ ANTELOPES AND THEIR ENVIRONMENT

For at least 2 million years, humans have hunted antelopes for food. The beauty of some antelopes has made them a target for hunters who desire their skins or horns. Others have hunted them solely for sport.

The long years of hunting have left some antelopes, such as the bontebok and the giant sable, scarce; others, such as the bluebuck, have been completely wiped out. Recent efforts have been made to protect some antelopes in parks and in private reserves. Additional efforts have focused on preserving the wild antelopes by establishing game ranches where antelopes would be raised, much like cattle, for meat. With commercial antelope meat available, it would be less likely that the wild antelopes would be hunted as a food source.

LYNN MARCINKOWSKI WOOLF
Science Writer
Reviewed by JAMES G. DOHERTY
Curator of Mammals
The Bronx Zoo

See also HOOFED MAMMALS.

ANTHONY, SUSAN B. (1820–1906)

For more than fifty years, Susan B. Anthony was a leading force in the women's rights movement and a tireless campaigner for woman suffrage. The 19th Amendment, which finally granted women the right to vote, was not ratified until 1920, 14 years after her death. However, in recognition of her lifelong struggle to gain equality for women, it is often called the Susan B. Anthony Amendment.

Born in Adams, Massachusetts, on February 15, 1820, Susan Brownell Anthony was the second of eight children. Although she grew up at a time when society discouraged women from voicing their political viewpoints, Anthony was raised by her Quaker parents to believe that women are equal to men and deserve equal opportunities.

Due to her parents' influence, Anthony eventually became involved in two important reform movements of the day—antislavery and temperance (to stop people from drinking alcoholic beverages). While working for temperance, Anthony developed extraordinary leadership skills.

In 1850, Anthony met Elizabeth Cady Stanton, an eloquent leader in the developing women's rights movement, and the two women developed a lifelong friendship and working partnership.

Anthony and Cady Stanton realized that no matter how capably led, women would never have the power to bring about changes in society unless they first won control over their own money and won the right to vote. They therefore petitioned the New York state legislature to pass a law giving women the right to keep any money they earned. (At that time, the law stated that a married woman's earnings belonged to her husband.) It took them six years, but in 1860 the state finally voted in favor of women's property rights.

Anthony also became active in the antislavery movement, and during the Civil War she promoted passage of the 13th Amendment. When slavery was finally abolished in 1865, Anthony believed that the antislavery and women's rights reformers should continue working together to win voting rights, both for the newly freed slaves and for women. To her dismay, many of the antislavery reformers chose to focus on black suffrage, and they turned away from the women's cause.

In 1870, the 15th Amendment was ratified, giving the vote to black men, but not to women. To test the law, Anthony went to the polls in Rochester, New York, in 1872 to vote in the presidential election. Her bold attempt got her arrested, and she was tried and fined $100 (which she refused to pay). Although she lost her case, Anthony's trial won additional support for her cause.

Susan B. Anthony's efforts on behalf of women's rights led to woman suffrage in 1920.

In the late 1800's, many new states were being admitted to the Union, and Anthony traveled through each one, urging people to make woman suffrage part of their state's constitution. After covering thousands of miles by train, wagon, and on horseback, she realized she would have to change her tactics. Instead of fighting the same battle state by state, Anthony began to push for an amendment to the United States Constitution. In 1878 a woman suffrage amendment was put before Congress for the first time, but it was defeated.

In 1890 the National Woman Suffrage Association, formed by Anthony and Cady Stanton in 1869, merged with another women's group and became the National American Woman Suffrage Association. Anthony continued to be a guiding force and took over the presidency of the newly merged organization in 1892. When she retired in 1900, the organization's annual convention was crowded with members from all over the country.

Susan B. Anthony died in Rochester, New York, on March 13, 1906, confident that the new generation of reformers would achieve her goal and obtain the vote for women.

In 1979 and 1980 the Susan B. Anthony dollar coin was minted in her honor. She was the first woman ever to be pictured on a U.S. coin in general circulation.

SUSAN MALONEY CLINTON
Author, *The Story of Susan B. Anthony*

See also STANTON, ELIZABETH CADY.

ANTHRAX. See DISEASES (Descriptions of Some Diseases).

A cultural anthropologist may live with a people to learn about their culture. It will take many months of fieldwork to complete a study of this Pygmy group in Zaïre.

ANTHROPOLOGY

Why are people in some parts of the world called by their mother's family name instead of by their father's? Why do people scattered over the face of the earth speak related languages? What did human beings look like when they first began to use stone tools or make pottery?

Such questions are dealt with by the science of anthropology. Scientists who work in this field are called anthropologists. The word "anthropology" comes from two Greek words —*anthropos* ("human being") and *logos* ("study"). Anthropology, then, is the study of human beings and human culture.

Anthropology is a young science, which took shape only in the mid-1800's. Until that time, few individuals had made a serious study of different peoples. European explorers had long been bringing back stories about peoples of Africa, Asia, and the Pacific islands, peoples of different sizes and colors. These people brought up their children and ran their societies in ways unknown to Europeans. Their languages had sounds that Western people had not heard before. To most Westerners then, such customs were strange, uncivilized, or even wrong. They thought that these distant peoples should learn about European ways. The goal was not to understand their ways but to change them.

By the mid-1800's, some Westerners were beginning to hold rather different ideas. Perhaps, they thought, what was best for one group of people might not be best for another. Perhaps it was not desirable to make everyone over in the European image. Perhaps other peoples and their ways should be studied for their own sakes. From such ideas grew the science of anthropology—the study of people, both past and present, near and far away.

Studying all the peoples who have lived on earth is a big job, and anthropologists approach this study in several ways. **Physical anthropologists** are concerned mainly with people as physical, biological creatures. By studying fossil remains of ancient people, physical anthropologists learn about our origins. They also try to understand the physical variations among different human groups today.

In contrast, **cultural anthropologists** study how people live throughout the world. Anthropologists who specialize in archaeology also study social life, by digging up the remains of ancient cultures. In this way, **archaeologists** are able to bring to anthropology an understanding of the human past. **Anthropological linguists** add an important view by concentrating on one aspect of human life— language. They search for the origin of human speech and of the various languages, and they study how languages change.

PHYSICAL ANTHROPOLOGY

Physical anthropologists have been working for more than a century with the bones of very ancient people. They study the shapes of heads, the sizes of brain cases, and the lengths of limbs. All these measurements give hints about how the human race has changed since its beginning. For example, anthropologists have noticed that ancient skulls held smaller brains than those of modern people. This shows that brain size increased as humans evolved.

Physical anthropologists are also interested in modern people's physical traits, such as types of skin, eyes, hair, blood, and diseases. Some of the basic information about these traits comes from the work of biologists and physicians. Physical anthropologists combine all this information and look for new patterns. Are several inherited physical traits related to one another? In what way do these traits differ around the world?

The physical anthropologist tries to find out how people's physical traits relate to their way of life. And if anthropologists can find out how people have changed in the past, they may be able to suggest how people may adapt in the future. For more information on the work of physical anthropologists, see the article PREHISTORIC PEOPLE in Volume P, and the article RACES, HUMAN in Volume R of this encyclopedia.

CULTURAL ANTHROPOLOGY

The word "culture" takes on a special meaning for the anthropologist. A **culture** is the entire way of life that a group of people learns—everything the group has, makes, thinks, believes, and passes on to children. Culture includes knowledge, belief, art, morals, law, custom, and all other habits and abilities that members of the group acquire.

Cultural anthropology has two main goals: (1) to describe the cultures of all human groups and (2) to explain the similarities and differences among them.

The first cultural anthropologists began their studies among peoples living in distant lands. Many of these groups were then considered to be "primitive" because they had not developed writing, did not use metals, or lived in villages rather than cities. Actually these cultures were highly developed in terms of art, religion, family structure, and so on. But they seemed simpler to study than larger industrial societies.

Cultural anthropologists such as Margaret Mead often went alone to some isolated island or faraway village. Often they came from universities that wanted to document and study such people. Some were sent by the government responsible for the people.

The anthropologists had to win the trust of the people they studied. The people sometimes thought the anthropologists were crazy or perhaps evil spirits because they wore funny clothes and wrote in a strange language. If the people accepted them, the anthropologists settled down to live with the people for a while, and perhaps were adopted into a family. Then the anthropologists were ready to study all the different aspects of the culture. Over the years, anthropologists have concentrated on several important aspects of people's lives.

A physical anthropologist at the National Museum in Nairobi, Kenya, compares the skull of a humanlike creature found in Africa with other ancient skulls.

African bushmen hunting food.

Eskimos ice fishing.

Women of India gathering grain.

Exchanging goods in a Thai market.

Shopping for food in America.

An anthropologist might do a comparative study of how different cultures obtain food and how this activity changes through time. In small, traditional cultures, men usually do the hunting and fishing, while women gather plant foods. As villages and towns develop, food may be obtained by specialized groups who are farmers or who raise animals for meat. They bring the food to markets, where it is sold or exchanged for other items.

A People's Livelihood. How do people make a living—by hunting, fishing, farming, or trade? How people feed themselves affects every aspect of their lives. In Siberia, for example, there were once people whose whole way of life depended on herds of horses and sheep. Because the livestock needed fresh pasture, the people could not settle in one place. They moved about with their tents and all their belongings. They had no central government, and they had no major ceremonies because it was too difficult for large groups to get together. Like early American cowboys, the Siberians defended their grazing lands against strangers. Many people thought they were fierce.

The Tewa Indians of New Mexico, on the other hand, depended on the corn, beans, and squash they grew. They lived in large apartment houses called pueblos. Because their fields were near home, the Tewa could live in their pueblos all year round. These Indians had permanent officers who governed the pueblo and planned ceremonies months in advance. The Tewa Indians had little need to fight, and they became known as a peaceful people. Yet if they had lived like the nomadic Siberians, they might have developed very differently.

The Family. All people live in families. But anthropologists have found that family groups may be arranged in many different ways.

Anthropologists try to learn why families differ from culture to culture. Who, they ask, arranges a marriage? How do children find out the rules of their culture? How are old people treated? In some societies the aged are neglected and even left to die. But other groups look up to elders as guides and teachers. The answer usually depends on how the group is living and whether the people have any means of taking care of the weak. Anthropologists have learned that the family cannot be understood unless the total way of life of a people is understood as well.

Government. Some families are gathered into clans, large groups who consider themselves related. Clans sometimes form even larger groups, such as tribes. Tribes can join into nations. Such changes come about slowly and may bring many political and social problems. The anthropologist tries to learn who really holds the power in a new grouping.

War and Games. There has rarely been a group in human history that did not fight. But why do people fight? For land? For slaves? To defend themselves? To avenge an insult? Anthropologists try to discover how a people's beliefs about war are related to livelihood, education, religion, and so on.

There is much to learn from the way people play. For example, games show whether people like to count and calculate. Play reveals character, which may be competitive or peaceful.

Knowledge. The anthropologist tries to learn everything that the group of people knows. What do they understand about the earth, the stars, the animals? Can they write? Can they count? If not, how do they record their knowledge? Some peoples use picture writing; others learn to count using knots or sticks. Many peoples learn by memorizing what they hear instead of what they read.

Religion and Mythology. Religion is a difficult subject for anthropologists to study. Early travelers often thought that tribal peoples had no religion at all. We now know that all human groups have some kind of religion. But most people hesitate to reveal their religious beliefs to strangers.

Connected with religion is mythology, ancient tales about spirits, gods, and other superhuman beings. These tales often tell much about the way a people think life should be lived.

How Cultural Anthropologists Work

Today universities and governments see a need for understanding not only small, traditional societies but also those people with whom we trade and to whom we send aid. Clearly no single investigator could ever find out all that needs to be known about a group of people. So anthropology has had to develop new methods.

More and more, cultural anthropologists work in teams. Among them may be anthropologists who specialize in psychology, music, economics, or ecology; a physical anthropologist; and perhaps a doctor. The research team does not work together every day because members are busy with their own specialties. But the scientists consult frequently and often combine their findings. Many use tape recorders and cameras to record words, music, dances, and everyday life.

The anthropological research team does not simply walk into a village or a camp and settle down to ask questions, as the single investigator did in the early days of anthropology. Generally, modern anthropologists talk to the group's leaders and ask permission to study the group. They explain that their studies will provide a history of the people's culture. Often the people are pleased that someone really wants to understand their ways. Several American Indian tribes have even asked for anthropologists to make such a study.

People in developing nations have come to appreciate that anthropologists can help them adjust to new ways. Traditional styles of life are changing almost everywhere in the world. Cultural anthropologists can often help ease such changes. Their studies can show where new ways could fit in and where they would just not work. For instance, flat, open countryside may appear to be right for tractors. But tractors are of little use if the land is farmed in small patches by isolated families or if people cannot afford gasoline to fuel the tractors.

►ARCHAEOLOGY

Archaeologists contribute to the work of anthropology by digging up and studying things made by people in earlier periods of history. The archaeologist uses a dental pick and a shovel, among other tools. But the goals are the same as those of cultural anthropology: to record the way people live and to explain cultural differences and similarities.

A linguistic anthropologist tapes the speech of a Navaho group. Use of the tape recorder has speeded study of the language, music, and oral literature of many cultures.

Archaeologists help us understand how cultures have changed over centuries. By studying the past, they can discover long-range trends. Archaeologists try to find out how early human societies adapted to the areas where they lived and why some groups began to grow crops and raise animals. They trace patterns of family life and political organization by studying the development of towns and cities. Their studies of ancient conflicts help identify causes of war. Archaeologists are even beginning to understand prehistoric religions and other beliefs—their forms and functions. In this way, archaeology contributes to anthropology's overall goals.

For more information on archaeology, see the article ARCHAEOLOGY in this volume.

▶ LINGUISTICS AND ANTHROPOLOGY

Anthropological linguists are trained in the history and nature of speech. They are especially helpful to cultural anthropologists working among people who speak a little-known language.

Well-trained linguists can write down any sound that human beings can make, even if they have never heard it before. An international system (International Phonetic Alphabet), which has a symbol for each sound, is used. After recording the individual sounds, the linguist then divides the stream of sounds into units that reflect the people's "words" and sentences. Today much work is done with tape recorders. Computers also help in working out many of the details.

When linguists have recorded all of the sounds in a language, they can then analyze the grammar. It was once thought that many little-known languages had no grammar. We now know that most of these languages have precise, complicated grammars. But they often differ markedly from familiar, more widely spoken languages.

In some of these languages, for example, someone who wanted to say "We go . . ." would have to use different forms of the verb that mean "We two go," "We three go," and so on.

The linguist must usually work out these points by experimentation because most people have never tried to explain their language to anyone. When the general shape of the language begins to emerge, the linguist can compare and perhaps relate it to other languages.

Languages can be grouped into several "families," which have the same general sounds and kinds of grammar. Most of the languages of Europe—Greek, Latin, French, German, English, Slavic, and the Scandinavian languages—fit into one family, called Indo-European. There was probably once a main language from which these languages branched. This happened at different times as groups of people moved away and developed other habits. Tracing the history of languages throws light on human history.

The same sort of study can be made of languages throughout the world. At first, to Western anthropologists, there seemed to be countless African languages. Some have never been completely recorded. But after many years of study, these languages have been grouped into eleven families. The same is true of American Indian languages. They were once numbered in the hundreds but now are grouped into six large families.

Linguistics also helps anthropologists learn other things. The customs of different peoples can be seen in the things they talk about. For example, the Arabic language has dozens of special words that describe the behavior of camels. Just from studying the language, an anthropologist can learn that the camel plays an important part in the life of Arabs.

▶PREPARING FOR A CAREER IN ANTHROPOLOGY

Until recently very little anthropology was taught in high schools. But the situation is changing as educators learn how anthropology can help people understand world history and the politics of today. Still, most anthropologists begin their training in college. A young person wishing to study anthropology should look over the catalogs of various colleges to see what courses they offer.

Students who have decided to concentrate on anthropology must choose additional courses related to their specialties. Cultural anthropologists need a good background in history, sociology, and psychology. Physical anthropologists must know a great deal of biology and physiology. Archaeologists must study geology, surveying, and paleontology (the scientific study of past life on earth). Basic computer training is now required for almost all anthropology students.

No matter which areas they plan to concentrate in, all students must begin with an introductory course that traces human history. This course is important because it shows how people evolved, or developed, and how anthropologists study that evolution.

Students also take courses describing the work of anthropologists among different preliterate peoples (those who have not developed writing). Later, should they visit such a people, they will be able to compare its culture with those of similar peoples. They can notice where that group is different and work out the reasons. And the people may appreciate the students' being familiar with their ways.

Some of the reading and course work can be done only in graduate school. Students who show promise may also be allowed to join a team of anthropologists on a project. On occasion, undergraduate and even high school students may take part in anthropological fieldwork, especially archaeological expeditions. Most universities and museums can supply information about such opportunities.

Anthropologists today are employed by universities, colleges, museums, governments, and sometimes by private firms. In the United States many archaeological sites are protected by law. Federal, state, and local agencies hire archaeologists to enforce these laws. Archaeologists are also employed to save information from sites about to be destroyed by development. Physical anthropologists are also involved in many of these programs.

Cultural anthropologists study people in their own countries as well as those in other countries. At home they work in such diverse places as universities, psychiatric institutions, and government. Almost anyone who deals with people can use a background in cultural anthropology. Training in anthropology is useful to those who serve as diplomats or as technical advisers. A knowledge of various cultures prevents people from thinking that their way is the only way. It helps them understand when and how a people might change to their advantage, as well as when change may be harmful, difficult, or unnecessary.

LOUITA D. WILSON
University of Colorado at Boulder
RUTH M. UNDERHILL
Formerly, University of Denver
DAVID HURST THOMAS
Curator, American Museum of Natural History

See also ANCIENT CIVILIZATIONS; ARCHAEOLOGY; PREHISTORIC PEOPLE; RACES, HUMAN; LANGUAGES.

ANTIBIOTICS

At one time or another, almost everyone has used an antibiotic, like penicillin or Terramycin. You may use an antibiotic ointment for bad scrapes or cuts. The doctor may order an antibiotic to help you get over pneumonia, scarlet fever, boils, and other infections.

Antibiotics work so well against so many infections that they are often called "miracle drugs." But a more accurate name would be "microbe drugs," for that is what antibiotics are.

Microbes are tiny living things. Bacteria are microbes. So are molds. There are many, many kinds of microbes in the world. Some of these microbes are used by man to make antibiotics.

Antibiotics are chemicals. When the chemicals are put into your body, they kill or stop the growth of certain kinds of germs. They help your body fight disease. That is why these medicines are called antibiotics. The name was first applied to these medicines in 1942. It comes from two Greek words meaning "against life." Antibiotics work against many of the forms of life that we call germs.

▶ MICROBE AGAINST MICROBE

Like other living things, microbes produce complex chemicals within their bodies. Some of the chemicals made by one kind of microbe may kill other kinds of microbes. In making antibiotics, scientists take advantage of this killing ability. They choose microbes whose chemicals work against the microbes that cause disease. If these chemicals can be made in large enough quantities in laboratories, they may be used as antibiotics.

Microbes are found just about everywhere, in immense numbers. Scoop up a handful of moist, rich soil, and you are also holding millions of bacteria and molds that live in the soil. These microbes are far too small to be seen without a microscope. But when the molds grow in colonies, the colonies are large enough to be seen with the unaided eye. Spots of gray, green, or pink fuzz are sometimes seen growing on bread, cheese, or fruit. The spots are colonies of molds.

One mold may produce millions of microscopic cells called spores. The light, tiny spores may be carried far from the parent mold by currents of air. One spore can produce a new mold if it settles in a place where living conditions are right. In a short time, the mold may grow into a colony.

▶ THE FIRST ANTIBIOTICS

More than 3,000 years ago ancient peoples stumbled on the discovery that some molds could cure. The Egyptians, the Chinese, and Indians of Central America used molds to treat rashes and infected wounds. However, they did not understand either diseases or treatments. Many of them thought in terms of magic. They believed that molds drove away evil spirits that caused disease.

As time passed, men slowly gained some knowledge of disease. But true understanding began only in fairly recent times. In the 1860's the French scientist Louis Pasteur showed that many diseases are caused by bacteria. Later he also said that man might learn to fight germs with other microbes.

Two German doctors were the first men to make an effective medicine from microbes. The doctors, Rudolf Emmerich and Oskar Löw, carried out their experiments in the 1890's. Among other things, they proved that the germ that causes one disease may cure another.

The two men took germs from infected bandages and grew them in test tubes and bottles. They managed to isolate a particularly vicious germ that caused green infections in open wounds. The germ was a bacterium called *Bacillus pyocyaneus*. Then they put some of these germs into test tubes containing other known disease germs. A strange thing happened. The *Bacillus pyocyaneus* wiped out the other disease germs, which were causes of cholera, typhoid, diphtheria, and anthrax.

Emmerich and Löw used *Bacillus pyocyaneus* to make a medicine, which they called pyocyanase. It was the first antibiotic to be used in hospitals, but unfortunately it was ahead of its time. No one yet knew how to control production or how such a chemical worked. Also, the medicine did not have the same effect on all patients. Many people were cured of typhoid, diphtheria, and the plague, but others only became sicker. So pyocyanase was abandoned.

Other scientists went on looking for a safe

and effective antibiotic. They tried hundreds of microbes, but none produced the magic cure-all they hoped to find.

The first real breakthrough was made in the summer of 1928 by a research scientist named Alexander Fleming. It was made because Fleming grasped the meaning of a small mishap in his laboratory.

▶ THE DISCOVERY OF PENICILLIN

At the time, Fleming, a Scottish bacteriologist, was on the staff of a hospital in London, England. He was studying a germ called *Staphylococcus aureus,* which caused many ailments from boils to brain disease. In order to study the germs, Fleming grew colonies of them in small glass plates called petri dishes. Each dish held a gelatin food to nourish the germs.

One day Fleming found a spot of green mold in one dish. It was growing on the gelatin among the germs. He realized that a spore from some mold must have settled on the dish while it was uncovered. But Fleming did not throw out the spoiled dish, because something unusual caught his attention.

There was a clear, germ-free ring of gelatin around the mold. This meant that the mold had killed the staphylococcus germs there. Fleming watched the mold grow for several days. As the green mold spread, it killed more and more germs.

Many earlier workers had made this same observation. But Fleming, studying the mold with great care, suspected he had found a remarkable medicine. But there was much he had to learn before he could be sure. Could he extract the chemical used by this mold to destroy the bacteria? Would the same chemical kill other germs? Would this chemical prove to be "friendly" to the human body? If so, could it be produced in quantity?

Fleming set out to find the answers. For the rest of the summer he gave all his attention to the mysterious mold. It grew and grew. Fleming noticed tiny drops of liquid on the surface of the mold. Perhaps this was the chemical that was destroying the germs.

Fleming drew off the liquid, drop by drop. He found that this liquid could kill germs in a test tube. Since the name of the mold was *Penicillium notatum,* he called the liquid penicillin. Other scientists showed later that penicillin could cure certain infections in mice and rabbits, without harming the animals.

Fleming published his findings in a British medical journal in 1929. Strange as it now seems, the article attracted little attention. Scientists thought it would take too much time and money to produce a useful amount of penicillin. Like pyocyanase, penicillin had been discovered before scientists were ready to develop it.

The Sulfa Drugs

Then, too, a "wonder drug" was discovered shortly afterwards in Germany. It was Prontosil, a substance used as a dye. When taken into the body, Prontosil changes into an active germ-killing drug called sulfanilamide. It was found that this drug could cure pneumonia, scarlet fever, and blood poisoning.

During the early 1930's, laboratories began to make other drugs in the same family. These were known as sulfa drugs and were powerful weapons against disease. But the sulfa drugs had serious drawbacks. Too small a dose could make a disease worse. Too large a dose could upset the body's defense system

The effectiveness of penicillin is visible in this bacteria culture. The area on top was treated with penicillin, and no bacteria have been able to grow there.

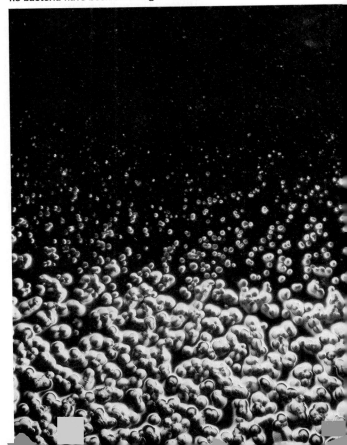

and prevent a cure, because sulfa drugs did not kill germs. They weakened germs and gave the body's defenses a chance to kill the germs. So scientists continued to search for an effective antibiotic. One of them was Dr. René Dubos of the Rockefeller Institute (now Rockefeller University) in New York City.

▶ ANTIBIOTICS FROM SOIL MICROBES

Dubos, a French-born scientist, was seeking a cure for pneumonia. He was seeking it in the soil, which scientists had long viewed as a possible source of germ killers. Dubos was determined to take microbes from the soil and see whether they could be made to work for people.

Experimenting with microbes from a New Jersey cranberry bog, Dubos obtained a substance he called tyrothricin. This chemical killed pneumonia germs in test tubes with amazing speed. Hopefully, he tested it on mice and rabbits. But it proved harmful to the animals as well as to the germs. The search for a pneumonia cure would have to continue. Still, progress had been made. Dubos had shown that antibiotics could be obtained from microbes in the soil.

▶ SUCCESS WITH PENICILLIN

Meanwhile, two scientists in England had taken up Fleming's work with penicillin. By 1939 Dr. Howard Florey and Dr. Ernst Chain were convinced that penicillin could save countless lives—if a way could be found to make it in quantity. They wanted to grow the mold in large tanks. But Fleming himself pointed out: "The mold does not like growing in tanks. You cannot simply put it into a tank and expect good results. It just grows on top and you get a poor yield. It likes plenty of air, so you have to blow in air and keep the fluid moving, and you have to blow in air without microbes. . . ."

It was a difficult problem in chemical engineering. Also, by this time World War II had begun and England was under heavy attack. So, in 1941 Dr. Florey traveled to the United States and asked for help. Government laboratories and private drug manufacturers co-operated to find a way to produce penicillin in large amounts. Within 2 years they had found it. Soon drug companies were producing penicillin in huge tanks. Then

an American researcher found a new kind of penicillium mold on an over-ripe canteloupe. It grew much faster and produced 200 times more penicillin than the mold Fleming had found. By 1945 the United States was making enough penicillin to treat several million patients a year.

▶ THE SEARCH FOR OTHER ANTIBIOTICS

Penicillin had proved its worth against pneumonia, scarlet fever, abscesses, and several other diseases. It was also highly effective against yaws, a disease that affects many people in the tropics. But it had no effect on germs that caused typhoid, poliomyelitis, influenza, and many other diseases. Research scientists continued their hunt for antibiotics.

One of the leaders in the search was an American, Dr. Selman A. Waksman. Turning to microbes of the soil, he looked for a cure for intestinal diseases like dysentery and typhoid. Finally he discovered streptomycin. This drug proved effective against many diseases that penicillin could not cure, such as bubonic plague, a deadly epidemic disease.

Now medical science had penicillin and streptomycin, each effective against particular diseases. But doctors wanted a **broad-spectrum** antibiotic—that is, a single antibiotic that could cure many different diseases.

Research scientists began a worldwide search for more helpful soil microbes. Anybody who traveled was asked to pick up samples of soil. Airline pilots, tourists, missionaries, students, and soldiers all co-operated. Thousands of samples poured in to be tested.

The tests produced results. One laboratory discovered Aureomycin, an antibiotic that does the work of both penicillin and streptomycin. Another laboratory discovered Chloromycetin; it proved effective against many diseases including typhus, typhoid, whooping cough, and certain intestinal ailments.

Then, in 1949, a laboratory that had run off more than 100,000 tests turned to a sample of soil from Indiana. From that test came Terramycin, one of the most effective antibiotics ever found. Terramycin can be used against many bacterial diseases.

Even so, the search goes on. Drug companies continue to seek new antibiotics in nature. And their chemists are learning to make

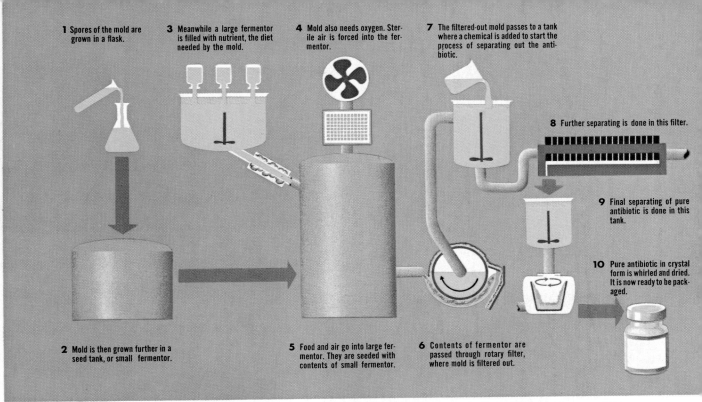

1 Spores of the mold are grown in a flask.

3 Meanwhile a large fermentor is filled with nutrient, the diet needed by the mold.

4 Mold also needs oxygen. Sterile air is forced into the fermentor.

7 The filtered-out mold passes to a tank where a chemical is added to start the process of separating out the antibiotic.

8 Further separating is done in this filter.

9 Final separating of pure antibiotic is done in this tank.

10 Pure antibiotic in crystal form is whirled and dried. It is now ready to be packaged.

2 Mold is then grown further in a seed tank, or small fermentor.

5 Food and air go into large fermentor. They are seeded with contents of small fermentor.

6 Contents of fermentor are passed through rotary filter, where mold is filtered out.

This flow chart shows the main steps taken in the production of Terramycin, one of the most effective antibiotics known. Here biology, chemistry, and engineering are all at work.

or **synthesize** some antibiotics without the help of microbes. These synthetic antibiotics are made from chemicals in the laboratory. Chloromycetin and cycloserine are two antibiotics from microbes that scientists are able to make synthetically. But with many antibiotics, it is difficult for chemists to imitate the work of the microbes. So microbes are used to make half of the antibiotic molecule, and chemists attach the other half. Antibiotics made in this way are called **semi-synthetics**.

Scientists have also learned how to improve antibiotics that are already in use. In hospitals, for example, antibiotics are sometimes combined. Sometimes scientists treat an antibiotic with chemicals to change it into a new one. In the laboratory, scientists are "educating" microbes to make special antibiotics. They do this by changing the microbes' living conditions, such as food, light, or temperature. The change in living conditions may cause a change in the chemicals that the microbes produce.

▶ **WHY MORE ANTIBIOTICS?**

Perhaps it seems odd that scientists keep trying to find new or different antibiotics when

they already know so many. But there are several good reasons for this.

One is that scientists are never content with what they know. They always want to learn more, to explore the unknown.

A second reason has to do with the problems created by antibiotics themselves. A third concerns the discovery of new uses for antibiotics.

Problems with Antibiotics

For a number of years antibiotics seemed to be winning the battle against disease. Then doctors noticed that some germs were not being killed. Some kinds of bacteria were no longer affected by an antibiotic that used to kill them.

For example, doctors had expected streptomycin to conquer tuberculosis, but the antibiotic was not doing the job. It killed some kinds of tuberculosis germs but not others. Some of the bacteria even seemed to make a nourishing meal out of the poison that should have destroyed them. It was as if a new race of super-germs had developed—and they probably had.

When an antibiotic attacks a colony of

Penicillium chrysogenum, a mold that yields penicillin.

Power of a new antibiotic is tested against six different kinds of germs (*left*); of four antibiotics tested against a single germ species (*right*), two were effective.

Streptomyces rimosus, used in making Terramycin.

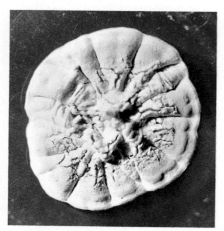

Streptomyces griseus, used in making streptomycin.

Some living molds and microbes, like *Penicillium* and the *Streptomyces*, produce germ-killing substances that are harmless to people. Scientists use these substances in antibiotic medicines to cure hundreds of diseases, some formerly incurable.

germs, it usually destroys all of them. But if some survive, they are the ones best able to resist the antibiotic. The super-germs then multiply, producing more super-germs. Soon a new army of germs exists, and they are germs that the antibiotic cannot destroy.

A second problem has also resulted from the use of antibiotics. Microbes, you remember, compete for food, water, and living space. The winners thrive and spread. The losers become few in number and are not very active. Now suppose something wipes out the winners, which is what antibiotics are doing. The former losers suddenly have room to develop. They become active—and people begin to suffer from new kinds of infections.

The best way to attack such problems is with new or different antibiotics. If one anti-biotic cannot control a germ, perhaps another can.

New Uses for Antibiotics

Farmers have put antibiotics to work in different ways. They add small amounts of antibiotics to the feed of pigs and chickens. The antibiotics speed up growth, so that the animals are ready for market earlier. Exactly why this happens is not fully understood. Today scientists do not agree about the wisdom of using antibiotics to promote growth.

Farmers have also found that antibiotics are of great value in keeping their animals in good health. There was a time when fatal diseases used to sweep through barnyards. Today these epidemics are rare. And the usefulness of antibiotics does not end with the animal's lifetime. Antibiotics are also used as preservatives. In some parts of the world, although not in the United States, antibiotics are used to keep meat and fish from spoiling on the way to market.

On many farms, fruit trees and vegetable plants are sprayed with antibiotics to prevent certain diseases.

Those are a few of the new uses that have been found for antibiotics. Because of these uses, many people have an interest in new antibiotics and what they can do.

▶ FUTURE RESEARCH

The field of antibiotics holds many unanswered questions. For example, no one is sure how or why microbes produce antibiotic chemicals. Do they always produce these chemicals, under all conditions? Or do they produce the chemicals only under laboratory conditions? Many scientists now believe that only "captive" microbes make antibiotics. They think that the laboratory diet may stimulate the microbes to produce these chemicals. But no one is sure.

Do microbes use antibiotic chemicals themselves? Again no one knows. If microbes produce these chemicals under natural conditions, they may also make use of the chemicals. Such chemicals may be a weapon in the war among microbes. Or the chemicals may cause faster growth. Then the faster-growing microbes crowd out the others.

How Antibiotics Work

Other questions have to do with the way that antibiotics work inside our bodies. How do antibiotics cure diseases? What actually happens when an antibiotic overcomes a microbe? Why does a particular chemical kill some kinds of microbes without killing others?

So far, these questions have not been fully answered. In spite of all the antibiotics that have been used successfully, no one knows the full story of how they work.

For instance, disease germs multiply so fast that a few can become a billion in 24 hours. One germ splits into two. Two become four, and the four become eight. This continues until a whole population of germs spreads over an infected wound or into the bloodstream. Given in time, an effective antibiotic stops this growth. How does the antibiotic do this?

Emmerich (*left*) made a crude antibiotic in 1890's. Chain (*right*) helped develop penicillin in 1940's.

Florey (*above left*) shared Nobel prize with Fleming and Chain. Dubos (*above right*) found germ killers in the soil. Below left, Waksman, discoverer of streptomycin, is visited by Fleming, penicillin pioneer.

Scientists have learned some facts about the way that antibiotics do their work against bacteria. In one group of experiments, penicillin was added to a liquid in which bacteria were growing. The bacteria began to bulge. Their cytoplasm, or living material, spilled out, and the bacteria died. Evidently the penicillin affected the cell wall, a stiff outer layer that holds the bacterial cell in shape. Another antibiotic, Terramycin, was used in other experiments. It prevented the bacteria from making substances they must have in order to live. These experiments show how some antibiotics work in the laboratory. Scientists believe they probably work the same way within the body.

Antibiotics for Virus Diseases

Many diseases are caused not by bacteria but by viruses. Among the diseases caused by viruses are polio, influenza, the common cold, measles, and perhaps some kinds of cancer. Research scientists have tested the anti-virus power of antibiotics in experiments with eggs and mice. They were able to slow the growth of the viruses in these cases. Some medical scientists hope that they will be able to develop antibiotics to control virus diseases in people.

BARBARA LAND
Formerly, Columbia University

Reviewed by TIMOTHY H. CRONIN
Central Research, Pfizer Inc.

Growing Penicillium Molds

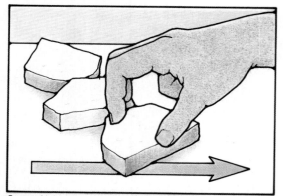

Step 1: Using three pieces of stale bread, wipe each piece lightly across a windowsill or kitchen floor. Even though you cannot see them, there are microbes on the surface of the floor and windowsill that the bread will pick up. The bread or mold that develops should not be eaten or tasted.

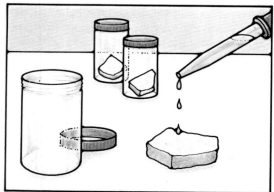

Step 2: Microbes need moisture to grow, so sprinkle each piece of bread with water and put each into a jar. Then place one jar in a warm, dark place (such as a cupboard); place another jar where it will get strong sunlight (such as on a windowsill); place another jar in the refrigerator.

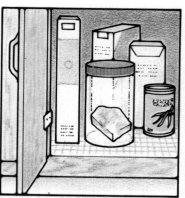

Step 3: In a few days, check each jar. Although most bread contains chemicals to slow the growth of molds, there will probably be several different molds growing. If not, wait a few days and look again. Soon you will see mold colonies growing. If one of these colonies is blue-green, it is probably penicillium mold.

ANTIBODIES AND ANTIGENS

The human body is quick to recognize foreign organisms that enter it. "Foes" must be attacked or otherwise got rid of. The most common of these foes are viruses, bacteria, and other microscopic organisms. The body recognizes these foes by the chemicals within them called **antigens**. To counteract these foreign invaders, the body produces its own chemicals, protein molecules called **antibodies**. Each kind of antigen causes the production of a specific kind of antibody. Antibodies appear in the body fluids such as blood and lymph and in the body's cells.

Doctors learned to make use of the antibody system for defense long before they had any idea that antibodies existed. As early as 1796, Edward Jenner, an English country doctor, discovered that if he gave people a case of the mild disease cowpox, he prevented them from getting the serious disease smallpox. What Jenner did not know is that the diseases are caused by closely related viruses. They are so closely related that the cowpox antibody will counteract the smallpox antigen.

Injecting an antigen to start the production of antibodies is now called **vaccination**. (It is one kind of immunization—making a person immune.) The antigen injected is a **vaccine**. These terms are based on *vacca*, the Latin word for "cow," because Jenner's vaccine was made from the cowpox virus.

Today doctors know of several ways that people become immune to diseases. Some people inherit a natural resistance to certain diseases. Over the years they build up an immunity that keeps them from ever getting certain diseases. But most antibodies are acquired only after the body has been exposed to a known antigen. The antigen may be carried by some organism that enters the body on its own, or the antigen may be artificially injected with a needle.

When a specially prepared antigen is injected into a person, it is called **active immunization**. The person actively produces the antibodies that fight off the foreign matter. The antibody defense system then remains on the alert, ready to deal with any later invasion. This procedure can be used to protect people against tetanus, typhoid, cholera, polio-

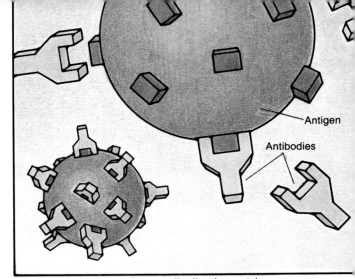

The immune system produces antibodies that match the patterns of specific antigens, much like a lock and key match each other. When antibodies (shown in blue) and an antigen (shown in red) meet, the antigen is put out of action when the antibodies lock onto it.

myelitis, typhus, Rocky Mountain spotted fever, smallpox, yellow fever, diphtheria, whooping cough, and plague.

Antibodies may also be produced in animals by injecting them with antigens. The antibodies are then transferred directly to a person. These antibodies are immediately ready for action. This is called **passive immunization** because the person plays no part in the production of antibodies. Passive immunization disappears within a few weeks. Active immunization gives much more lasting protection.

The substance taken from the immunized animal or person for passive immunization is called **antiserum**. If used early enough, it can prevent such diseases as measles and tetanus. Sometimes an antiserum can be used after the antigen has entered a person's body, as in measles, tetanus, and diphtheria. Antiserums against bee and snake venom have also been developed.

Both antigens and antibodies are large molecules. Scientists believe that the antibody molecule combines with a particular antigen molecule, the two fitting like a key and a lock. In the chemical reaction that takes place, the antigen loses its power to cause the disease.

L. D. HAMILTON
Brookhaven National Laboratory

See also IMMUNE SYSTEM; VACCINATION AND IMMUNIZATION.

ANTIDOTES. See POISONS AND ANTIDOTES.

ANTIGUA AND BARBUDA

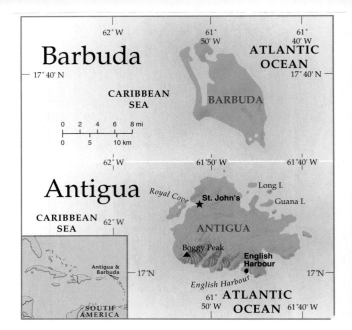

The nation of Antigua and Barbuda forms part of the Leeward Islands chain in the eastern Caribbean Sea. The country is made up of three islands—Antigua, Barbuda, and the tiny, uninhabited island of Redonda. A former British dependency, Antigua and Barbuda gained full independence in 1981.

▶ THE PEOPLE AND THE ECONOMY

Over 90 percent of the people are of black African descent. The rest are of British, other European, Asian, or mixed ancestry. English is the official language. Most of the people live on Antigua, the largest island. St. John's, the capital, located on Antigua, has almost one-third of the total population.

Sugar and cotton were once the most important products of the islands. Tourism is now the main source of the country's income, employing about one-quarter of the labor force. Industries include the manufacture of rum, clothing, and household appliances and the assemblage of automobiles. An oil refinery on the island of Antigua processes imported crude oil for export.

FACTS and figures

ANTIGUA AND BARBUDA is the official name of the country.

LOCATION: Caribbean Sea.

AREA: 171 sq mi (442 km²).

POPULATION: 66,000 (estimate).

CAPITAL AND LARGEST CITY: St. John's.

MAJOR LANGUAGE(S): English (official).

MAJOR RELIGIOUS GROUP(S): Christian.

GOVERNMENT: Constitutional monarchy. **Head of state**—British monarch, represented by a governor-general. **Head of government**—prime minister. **Legislature**—Parliament (consisting of a House of Representatives and a Senate).

CHIEF PRODUCTS: Sugar, cotton, vegetables, rum, clothing, household appliances, assembled automobiles.

MONETARY UNIT: East Caribbean Dollar (1 EC dollar = 100 cents).

▶ THE LAND

The island of Antigua is largely flat but has some rolling hills that are covered with lush vegetation. Barbuda is a wooded island and is noted for its fine beaches of pink and white sand. The climate is generally sunny and warm, with temperatures ranging from 71 to 86°F (22 to 30°C). Rainfall is light. The islands are subject to hurricanes. One of the most destructive, Hurricane Hugo, struck in 1989.

▶ HISTORY AND GOVERNMENT

Christopher Columbus visited Antigua in 1493. The first Spanish and French colonists were succeeded by the British. Antigua officially became a British colony in 1667. Barbuda became part of the colony in 1860.

Tobacco was the first commercial crop. It soon gave way to sugarcane, which was harvested by slaves brought from Africa. The slaves were freed in the 1830's, when slavery was abolished in the British colonies.

After a period of internal self-government, the islands became independent as Antigua and Barbuda on November 1, 1981.

The British monarch, represented by a governor-general, is recognized as the nation's head of state. The head of government is the prime minister. The legislature, or Parliament, consists of an elected House of Representatives and an appointed Senate.

HOWARD A. FERGUS
University of the West Indies (Montserrat)

ANTILLES. See CARIBBEAN SEA AND ISLANDS.

ANTIQUES AND ANTIQUE COLLECTING

Antiques are objects once in everyday use that are prized today for their artistic, decorative, or historical value. Opinions vary on how old an object must be to be considered an antique, but most collectors agree on an age of at least one hundred years.

The most valuable antiques are masterpieces of furniture, glass, pottery, and metal made by skilled artisans in past centuries. Because these items are rare and highly sought after, they are often too expensive for the casual collector. But another category of antiques is available to almost everyone at reasonable prices: Everyday glassware and furniture, old bottles and tools, cracker boxes and tobacco tins are all popular for decorating homes. They have special appeal as reminders of life in the past.

▶ FURNITURE

One of the most important fields of antique collecting is furniture. Most in demand is furniture made before 1830, when mechanized factory production became widespread. Furniture of the 1700's is especially desirable because of its fine design.

In England, beautifully crafted furniture was made during the reign of Queen Anne (1702–14). Queen Anne chairs, tables, highboys, and other pieces are distinguished by a gracefully curving leg, called a **cabriole** leg. The Queen Anne style remained popular for many years. After about 1740, English furniture design was strongly influenced by three outstanding cabinetmakers and furniture designers: Thomas Chippendale, George Hepplewhite, and Thomas Sheraton. Their names were given to the styles they designed.

A distinctly French style of furniture design was established during the reign of Louis XIV (1643–1715) and lasted until the French Revolution (1789–99). Many collectors believe that furniture made during the reign of Louis XV (1715–74) is among the finest ever made. Louis XV furniture is characterized by serpentine (curving) shapes and luxurious carving and inlays.

In colonial America, cabinetmakers copied English designs to produce beautiful furniture in native American woods. Some of the finest American formal furniture of the period was made in New York, Philadelphia, and Boston. Other furniture was produced in smaller towns, such as Newport, Rhode Island, and in rural communities, such as those of the Pennsylvania Dutch and the Shakers, a religious community. Shaker furniture, in particular, is admired for its sturdy construction and the simple beauty of its design.

Left: A highboy made in Massachusetts about 1750 has the curving cabriole leg characteristic of Queen Anne furniture. *Below left:* A French desk from the reign of Louis XV has a graceful form and decorative inlaid patterns. *Below right:* Shaker furniture, made by members of an American religious community, is admired today for its simple beauty.

The condition of antique furniture is an important consideration for collectors. Much antique furniture has remained in good condition because of its sound hand-crafted construction. A piece of furniture in good original condition, retaining the beautiful glow (patina) that age has given to its surface, is highly desirable. However, careful restoration can enhance the value of a damaged piece.

▶GLASS

Antique glass is one of the most popular collectibles. A wide range of glass objects—tumblers and goblets, vases and pitchers, plates and candlesticks—was produced in many countries, and collectors delight in the variety of patterns and colors. One of the earliest kinds of glass was blown glass, which is formed by blowing air through a pipe into a lump of hot, melted glass. Later varieties include pressed glass, in which the hot glass is shaped and given a surface pattern by being pressed into a mold; and cut glass, in which glass is decorated with patterns cut into the surface. (More information about these glass-making processes can be found in GLASS, in Volume G.)

One of the most famous American glass companies was founded in Sandwich, Massachusetts, in 1825. Sandwich pressed glass, which was made in many shapes and colors, is prized by modern collectors.

A lamp with a glass shade in the "dragonfly" design is one of many works created in the late 1800's and early 1900's by American glassmaker Louis Comfort Tiffany.

A pressed-glass candlestick in the shape of a dolphin was made by the Sandwich Glass Company about 1850. Pressed glass is shaped by pressing the hot glass into a mold.

Glass made in the late 1800's by master glassmakers has also become collectible. Some of the most famous makers of this "art glass," which included vases, bowls, and lampshades, were Emile Gallé of France, Thomas Webb of England, and Louis Comfort Tiffany of the United States.

It is difficult to tell old glass from new. Experts look for an irregular shape, signs of wear on the base, or imperfections such as bubbles in the glass itself. One way to identify handmade blown glass—early or modern—is to check the base for a **pontil mark**. A pontil is an iron rod used to handle the hot glass while it is being shaped. When the glass is broken off the pontil, a mark is left on the base. The pontil mark may be either rough or, if polished, smooth.

▶POTTERY

Clay can be shaped and baked into plates, cups, and other useful articles; this is called pottery. Many types of pottery, such as earthenware, are very porous, that is, they are easily penetrated by liquids. Therefore, pottery was often given a thin, glassy coating called a glaze. Glazes could be

A salt-glazed stoneware jug decorated with a bird design in cobalt blue was made in the United States in the first half of the 1800's. Sturdy stoneware vessels were often used to store food.

This teapot is an example of jasperware, a kind of unglazed stoneware made by the potter Josiah Wedgwood in Staffordshire, England. Jasperware usually features white figures silhouetted against a pastel background—often the delicate shade that has come to be called "Wedgwood blue."

decorative as well as protective.

One type of earthenware is called redware because of its red color. Redware was sometimes decorated with a cream-thick slip (fine clay mixed with water and coloring). The slip was placed in a funnel and applied to the piece before its final baking, much the way a baker decorates the top of a cake.

A very strong kind of pottery called stoneware does not require a protective glaze to resist water. This quality made it very useful for food storage. Many sturdy and practical stoneware crocks, jugs, churns, and milk pans were made in colonial times. The pieces most in demand today are those decorated with cobalt blue designs and covered with a transparent salt glaze.

The finest kind of pottery is porcelain (also called china because it was first made in China). It is hard and translucent, that is, light will show through it.

Some of the most collectible pottery was made in Staffordshire, England, during the 1700's and 1800's. A famous Staffordshire potter, Josiah Wedgwood, created jasperware, a kind of unglazed stoneware decorated with classical scenes. Staffordshire ware includes many other types of pottery, including fine china made by Josiah Spode and Thomas Minton and pottery molded in the shapes of dogs and other figures.

Potters have marked their wares with many different signs. The marks scratched, indented, or painted on pottery may tell who made the piece and from what country it came. A well-known mark is the crossed swords that appear on Germany's Meissen china (also called Dresden). However, many old pieces of china are unmarked. For this reason, a collector also judges the value and age of a piece by inspecting its condition, checking for wear on the base, and examining its glaze for small age cracks (called crazing). The shape of a piece and its decoration are also considered.

▶METALWORK

Because metalworking techniques changed greatly after 1830, age is an especially important factor to collectors of metal objects. Silver made in London during the 1700's is of great interest to serious collectors. American and French antique silver is also popular.

Some of the earliest silver items were cups and tankards (drinking mugs). Later silversmiths made tea sets, knives and forks, and other tableware. English silver was stamped

Right: This painted-tin coffeepot was made in the northeastern United States about 1825–50. Tin objects decorated with colorful painted designs are called toleware.

Below: This silver porringer is an example of the work of Paul Revere, a leading American silversmith who became famous as a Revolutionary War patriot.

Biscuit boxes, washstands, copper pots, and old railroad signal lights are just a few of the many collectible items that can be found at an outdoor flea market. Though not always beautiful or rare, objects such as these are valued as reminders of life in the past. They are generally available at reasonable prices, making them especially appealing to beginning collectors.

with marks identifying the maker, the year, and the town in which the piece was made. The thousands of marks are explained in books, which help collectors identify silver pieces.

Pewter, a metal made by combining tin and copper, was also used to make tableware. Like silver, pewter was often marked with symbols, such as an eagle or a rose and crown, that can help identify a piece's origin.

Brass, an alloy of copper and zinc, is an attractive metal that was used to make fireplace andirons, candlesticks, and other useful objects. Many have become highly sought-after antiques. Copper, like brass, is a soft metal that is easy to form and has good color. It is also an efficient conductor of heat, so it was often used to fashion cooking pots. The insides of the pots were coated with tin so that food would not come into contact with the copper. Copper was also made into weathervanes, which today are often used indoors as folk-art decorations. The green color acquired by weathered copper is also admired.

Tin-coated steel was shaped into candlesticks, lanterns, and all kinds of boxes and trays. Tin objects sometimes were decorated

with painted designs; these objects are called **toleware**.

Antique iron is also collected. Cooking forks, pot trivets, and other wrought-iron objects, hand-forged by blacksmiths, were used in American colonial times. Cast-iron objects, which are shaped by casting hot metal in a mold, include everything from old cooking pots to decorative urns.

Samplers were hand-stitched by girls to show their needlework skills. The name and dates on this sampler tell us that it was made by a 10-year-old girl in 1773.

▶OTHER KINDS OF ANTIQUES

Antique clocks are very popular objects to collect. Clocks were mass-produced in Connecticut during the 1800's, and examples are fairly easy to find today. More highly valued are clocks made during the 1600's and 1700's, which show outstanding craftsmanship. Antique guns and powderflasks, swords, lamps, and books each have a following.

In recent years, collectors have shown increased interest in textiles, mainly handmade quilts and **samplers**—examples of hand-stitching created by girls to show their embroi-dery skills. Many other items are considered "collectibles," including early toys, dolls and dollhouse furniture, penny banks, buttons, old signs and posters, and even vintage postcards. These objects are not always beautiful or rare. But they provide a fascinating glimpse of the people and customs of earlier times. Follow your interests and let them lead you into the adventures of collecting.

Reviewed by WAYNE MATTOX
President, Woodbury (Connecticut)
Antiques Dealers Association

See also FOLK ART; FURNITURE DESIGN.

ANTISEPTICS. See DISINFECTANTS AND ANTISEPTICS.
ANTITOXINS. See VACCINATION AND IMMUNIZATION; DISEASES (Prevention of Disease).

ANTONY, MARK (83?–30 B.C.)

Mark Antony (Marcus Antonius) was a Roman general and statesman and one of the rulers of Rome after the death of Julius Caesar. His love for the Egyptian queen Cleopatra was the subject of William Shakespeare's tragedy *Antony and Cleopatra*. He is also a major figure in Shakespeare's *Julius Caesar*.

Antony was born in 83 or 82 B.C. into an aristocratic Roman family. Through his mother, Julia, he was a cousin of Julius Caesar. Antony served with distinction under him during the conquest of Gaul (most of present-day France) in 54–50 B.C. He also backed Caesar in his struggle with the Roman general Pompey. In 48 B.C. he brought precious reinforcements to Caesar and commanded his left wing at the Battle of Pharsalus, in Greece, where Pompey was defeated.

In 44 B.C., Antony shared the consulship, Rome's highest office, with Caesar. When Caesar was assassinated that same year, Antony seized the reins of power for himself. He skillfully negotiated between the opposing groups—the republicans, who had conspired in the assassination, and Caesar's followers—to prevent civil war.

Antony's greatest rival for supreme power in Rome was to be the young Octavian, Caesar's adopted son and heir. Octavian first sided with Cicero, a famed orator and a leader of the republicans, to weaken Antony. But he then joined Antony and Lepidus, a former lieutenant of Caesar's, in a triple alliance, the Triumvirate. Cicero and other republicans were executed.

Mark Antony was one of the rulers of ancient Rome after the assassination of Julius Caesar. His struggle for supreme power with a co-ruler, Octavian, led to his defeat and death. Antony's love for Cleopatra, queen of Egypt, was the subject of William Shakespeare's tragedy *Antony and Cleopatra*.

In 42 B.C., Antony defeated the republican forces led by Brutus and Cassius, Caesar's assassins, at the Battle of Philippi in Greece and won control of Rome's eastern provinces. He later failed to conquer the Parthian Empire and tried to strengthen himself by an alliance with Cleopatra. Relations with Octavian remained strained, in spite of Antony's marriage to his sister, Octavia, in 40 B.C. Their struggle ended in the naval Battle of Actium in 31 B.C. A defeated Antony and Cleopatra fled back to Egypt, where they committed suicide. The triumphant Octavian went on to become (as Augustus) the first emperor of Rome.

ALLEN M. WARD
University of Connecticut
Coauthor, *A History of the Roman People*

See also CAESAR, GAIUS JULIUS; CICERO, MARCUS TULLIUS; CLEOPATRA.

ANTONYMS. See SYNONYMS AND ANTONYMS.

ANTS

Ants emerged on the earth more than 100 million years ago. Since that time, these tiny insects have developed amazingly varied kinds of existences. But no matter how different their lives are, none live alone. Ants are social insects, that is, they live together in organized communities, or **colonies**. The population of an ant colony varies depending on the species of ant. Some ants live in colonies that contain only a few members. Others are part of colonies that contain hundreds, thousands, or even millions of members.

Ants, which along with bees and wasps make up the insect order Hymenoptera, can be found on every continent except Antarctica. **Myrmecologists**, biologists who study ants, have discovered and given scientific names to almost 9,000 species, or kinds, of ants. Each year many new kinds are discovered, and scientists estimate that there may be as many as 20,000 different species in the world.

▶THE CHARACTERISTICS OF ANTS

Ants are small, usually drably colored creatures that range in size from 1/25 inch (0.1 centimeter) to more than 1 inch (2.5 centimeters) in length. The many different species of ants all share similar body structures.

The Body of an Ant

Like all insects, the ant is an invertebrate (animal without a backbone) with a body divided into three main sections: head, thorax, and abdomen. Within these sections are organs that allow ants to sense the world around them, breathe, process food, communicate with others, move, and reproduce. The delicate internal organs are protected by an **exoskeleton**, which is the hard outer covering of the body. Along with protecting the ant's internal organs, the strong exoskeleton gives the ant its body shape and provides places of attachment for the muscles.

Head. The head of an ant has several important structures: antennae, scent glands, eyes, and mouth.

The antennae of an ant are the most noticeable structures of the head. The antennae serve as organs of smell and touch, performing tasks much like those of the human nose and fingertips. The antennae are also used in communication. Ants may tap other ants with their antennae to beg for or offer food or to recruit other ants to go to a food source located outside the nest.

The scent glands are used in another form of communication. Messages are sent through chemicals, called **pheromones**, given off by the scent glands. The smell of these chemicals warns other ants in the nest of danger.

The mouth of an ant is a small hole at the front end of the head. On either side of the mouth is a pair of strong, bladelike jaws called **mandibles**. The shape of the mandibles may be quite different in different kinds of ants and may also vary within a species. Ants use their mandibles for a variety of purposes. They use them to carry their tiny, delicate eggs, cut up food, attack prey, and fight enemies. Mandibles are even used for communication. Some ants bang their mandibles on the floor of their

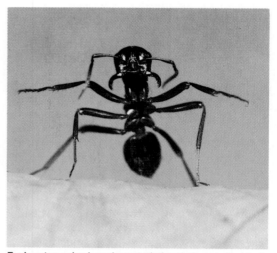

Each ant species has characteristics that are suited to its own way of life. An army ant (*above*) displays the menacing mandibles that it uses to overwhelm prey. The long, muscular hind legs of a jumping ant (*below*) help it to jump several times its body length!

nests or snap them together to produce a danger signal that can be heard by other ants.

While some kinds of ants have very small eyes or no eyes at all, most ants have two different kinds of eyes—compound eyes and simple eyes. The large compound eyes, one on each side of the head, are made up of many lenses placed close together that work to produce a single visual image. The three simple eyes, or **ocelli**, are near the center of the head. The ocelli sense the brightness and the direction of light. Using the ocelli, ants can sense polarized light, a form of light humans cannot see. Using polarized light, ants can find the position of the sun in the sky. Ants use the position of the sun as a compass point to find their way to and from their nest.

Thorax. The thorax is the middle part of an ant's body. There are three pairs of legs attached to it. The front legs, which are used to dig through soil, are thicker and stronger than the middle and hind legs. In most ants the middle and hind legs are very similar in size. But in the jumping ants of South America, the hind legs are longer and more muscular than the middle legs.

In ants that have wings, the two pairs are attached to the upper sides of the thorax. In most species of ants, the males and young queens have wings; workers do not. Winged ants use their wings only during the mating flight. Once they have mated, the males die and the young queens break off their wings because they no longer need them.

Abdomen. An ant's abdomen has three major parts. The first part, which lies close to the thorax, is called the **propodeum**. On its surface, the propodeum often has spines, ridges, or bumps that are unique to each species of ant. The middle part, or **pedicel**, is made up of one or, sometimes, two moveable segments. The pedicel has a slender, waistlike form. Like the propodeum, the pedicel also has surface features unique to each ant species. These surface features are useful in recognizing different species.

The large rounded part of the abdomen is known as the **gaster**. Some species of ants have a sting at the end of the gaster. Because the sting developed from an egg-laying device, only the female can have a sting. The sting is used mainly to capture prey and for defense. **Venom**, or poison, produced in

The Body Structures of an Ant

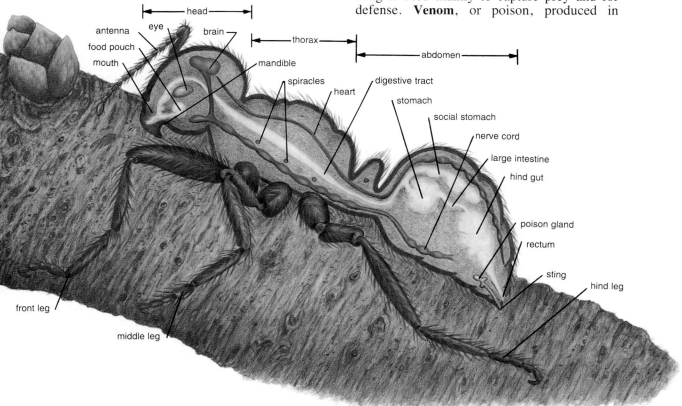

front leg
middle leg
antenna
eye
head
brain
food pouch
mouth
mandible
thorax
spiracles
heart
digestive tract
abdomen
stomach
social stomach
nerve cord
large intestine
hind gut
poison gland
rectum
sting
hind leg

glands at the tip of the gaster is injected into the victim through the sting. But not all ants have useful stings. Some have stings so small or shaped so that they cannot be inserted into prey. Some of these ants produce formic acid or other kinds of venom that are sprayed or dabbed onto prey.

Inside the Body. The nervous system of an ant consists of the brain, nerve cord, and nerves. The brain is very tiny, but compared to the ant's body size, it is one of the largest brains in the insect world. The brain serves as the control center for all the body functions and processes. From the brain, a nerve cord extends along the lower side of the ant's body to the tip of the gaster. Nerves branch out along the nerve cord, carrying messages from the brain to other parts of the body and from other body parts to the brain.

Like other animals, ants take in oxygen during the process of respiration. The oxygen enters the body through small holes called **spiracles** on the sides of the thorax and abdomen. A network of tubes carries the oxygen throughout the ant's body. Carbon dioxide, a waste product formed during energy production, leaves through the spiracles.

The blood system of the ant is responsible for bringing digested food to the organs, muscles, and nervous system. It also takes away waste material. The ant's heart is part of a long tube that runs along the top of the ant's body from the head to the gaster. Blood is sucked up into the heart through tiny openings along the tube. As the heart contracts, blood is forced toward the head of the ant. There, blood pours out through an opening, bathing the brain and then flowing backward through the rest of the body. The cycle repeats continuously, nourishing and cleansing the body.

An ant's digestive system is a long tube that extends from the mouth to the end of the gaster. Within the abdomen, the tube widens to form pouchlike organs. An important organ of the digestive system is the **crop**, or "social" stomach. Liquid food, gathered during feeding expeditions, is stored in the crop. Ants returning to their nest regurgitate (bring up) the food to share with colony members. Food that is not stored in the crop passes to the stomach, where it is digested, then to the hind gut, where most of the food is absorbed into the

blood. Material that is not absorbed travels through the hind gut to the rectum. Waste absorbed from the blood also is deposited in the rectum. After most of the water is reabsorbed from the waste material, it passes out of the body through an opening called the **cloaca**.

▶THE LIFE OF ANTS

Although there is great variety in how ants live, there is one trait they all share—all ants live in colonies. Within the different colonies, ants perform similar tasks: making nests, producing young, and feeding.

Members of the Colony

Ant colonies contain male and female members. However, most of the time the colony is populated only by females. Each ant colony has at least one queen, who is more of an egg-producing factory than a ruler. Some ant species have several queens in a colony, while a few kinds have hundreds. Male ants have short life spans, appearing in great numbers during the mating season. Once their job— flying out and mating with the winged queens from another colony—is accomplished, they die. Most of the colony is composed of workers, small wingless females that do not breed. Some colonies also have larger, big-headed workers called major workers.

Members of an Ant Colony

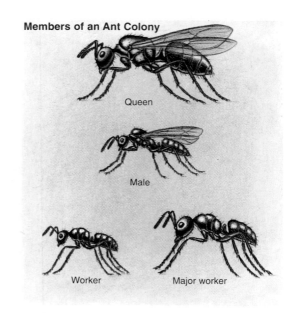

Queen

Male

Worker   Major worker

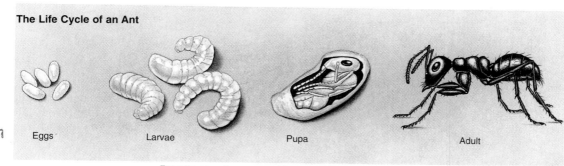

The Life Cycle of an Ant

Eggs　　　Larvae　　　Pupa　　　Adult

From the eggs the queen ant lays, wormlike larvae hatch. The larvae spend their time eating and growing. They enter the pupal stage when their growth as larvae is complete. During the pupal stage, an ant slowly takes on the adult form.

There may be more than one species of ant in a colony. For example, slave-making ants kidnap other ants and bring them back to work in the colony. Young queens of other kinds of ants leave their own colony to take over another species' colony. After killing the colony's queen, the invader queen forces the workers to raise its young. Eventually all the host ants are replaced by the invading ants.

Other kinds of animals, usually other invertebrates, may be "guests" of the colony. The guests are usually scavengers, eating leftover food or waste in the nest. Sometimes these invertebrates feed on the young or adult ants. The invaders may also use special chemicals to repel attacking ants or to fool ants into accepting them into the colony. In tropical rain forests, social wasps, bees, or even birds may live in part of an ant nest, or they may build separate nests nearby.

The Ant's Life Cycle

There are four stages in the development of an ant: egg, larva, pupa, and adult. The mating flights of males and young queens mark the beginning of the cycle. During the flight, a male deposits sperm (male sex cells) inside a queen's body. The queen stores the sperm until she is ready to lay eggs.

With mating accomplished, the male has fulfilled his only function for the colony, and he dies. The queen busily searches for a favorable location to start a new nest. When she finds a suitable place, she settles in, breaking off the wings she will never need again. After the queen prepares a nest, she lays a few eggs each day. As the eggs pass out of her body, they are fertilized by the stored sperm.

Within a few days of being laid, the eggs hatch. From the eggs, the wormlike forms called larvae (plural of larva) emerge. The lar-

vae are fed by the queen. Depending on what they are fed, the larvae will develop into either queens or workers. The larvae, which spend most of their time eating, grow in size over the next few weeks. When their growth is complete, they enter the pupa stage. Some pupae (plural of pupa) spin a protective cocoon of silk; others are covered only by their skin. During the pupal stage, the ant slowly takes on the form of an adult. After about two or three weeks, its development is complete and the adult ant emerges.

The Ant's Home

Most ants make their homes in soil or rotting wood. Nests in soil or wood consist of chambers and narrow tunnels. Ants travel the tunnels to reach the chambers and the outside. In the tropics, many species nest in plants.

Some soil-nesting ants build a mound full of chambers and tunnels. The mounds are built of soil, small pebbles, twigs, grass blades, and leaf fragments. Some kinds of ants build nests without soil. They make nests with a paperlike

Did you know that . . .

ants were used in the first-known instance of biological pest control? More than 2,000 years ago in southern China, farmers gathered the silk nests of the green tree ant. They took the nests from nearby forests and moved them to the orange groves on their farms. Because the ants are aggressive predators, eating any and all insects that cross their path, the ants helped keep the groves free of pests.

Ant mounds can hold interesting collections of objects. The chambers and tunnels of some have yielded fossils, minerals, even tiny nuggets of gold.

material, called **carton**, made of plant fibers stuck together with saliva. The carton nest may be simple sheets of material covering the spaces in bark or rocks in which the ants live. Or the nest may have a ball-like structure.

In addition to soil and carton, parts of plants also are used to make nests. Certain species of tropical tree ants weave a nest of leaves and silk. Groups of workers pull leaves together while others move silk-producing larvae (newly hatched ants) back and forth from the edge of one leaf to the other until the two leaves are firmly attached.

How Ants Obtain Food

Ants feed on a wide range of foods. Some ants eat only plant matter, such as seeds. Others feed on the fungus they carefully grow. But most kinds of ants are predators and scavengers—with a taste for sweets. They catch and eat small invertebrates, especially other insects, and they also eat already dead prey. They even steal prey from other small predators. Ants satisfy their taste for sweets by consuming plant sap, nectar, and fruit. The resourceful ants also get their sugary treats by raiding the hives of honeybees and the homes of human beings.

▶ KINDS OF ANTS

Because ants have developed such elaborate and distinctive methods of feeding, they are often grouped together according to how they obtain food.

Harvester Ants

Seeds are part of the diet of many kinds of ants. However, they make up almost the entire diet of harvester ants, who gather seeds directly from plants or from the ground. These ambitious ants gather many more seeds than can be eaten at one time. The uneaten seeds are stored in special chambers in their nests, so there is always a ready supply of food.

Before the seeds can be eaten by the adults, they must be processed by the larvae. Workers break up the seeds into small pieces and feed them to the larvae. The larvae are able to digest the starchy seeds because they have a starch-digesting enzyme, which is missing in the adults. In the stomach of a larva, the seeds become a soft, pulpy mass. The larvae regurgitate some of this partially digested food for the adult ants. The different digestive abilities of the adults and larvae help ant colonies make use of food resources neither could use without the other.

Fungus-Grower Ants

Fungus-grower ants, found in the warmer portions of North and South America, have a very specialized diet. They have nests with large chambers deep in the soil. In these chambers, fungus growers cultivate special molds. The molds produce swellings that are eaten by the ants.

The fungus must be grown on beds of compost (decayed organic matter). Most fungus-grower ants farm their fungus crop on compost made from the droppings of plant-eating insects, such as caterpillars. Leaf-cutter ants are fungus-grower ants that make compost from pieces of fresh leaves, flowers, and fruits. The ants drink some of the plant juice from these materials but use most of it to raise the fungus that they and their larvae dine on.

Slave-Maker Ants

Slave-maker ants raid the nearby nest of a closely related species and steal its brood. The

slavers carry the stolen brood to their home nest, where the slave ants already present eat most of the brood that is brought in. The brood that is not eaten matures and adds to the slave force of the colony.

To establish a new colony, mated slave-maker queens find a young or weak colony of a related species and invade it. The invaders kill the colony's queen and get the orphaned workers to raise their babies. The population of the colony increases as the slave-maker offspring mature and begin raiding other colonies. The colony remains a mixture of slave-maker ants and kidnapped ants.

Gatherer Ants

Several ant species have certain workers called **repletes** that, like other ants, store liquid food in their crops. Most replete-former ants are known as honey ants. They live in the deserts of North America and Australia. The liquid, usually honeydew or nectar, is gathered during the rainy season when plant growth is rapid and sap-feeding insects are abundant. Storing the liquid food allows these ants to have energy and water available during long dry spells.

Another replete-former lives in the oak woodlands of North America. This unusual ant is active in autumn, on warm winter days, and in early spring. Its main food is the rotting flesh of dead insects and earthworms. The ants collect the liquid from this softened meat during the time of year when many dead invertebrates are available. During summer, these "winter ants" stay underground and raise the year's brood with the liquefied invertebrate flesh stored in the crops of the repletes.

When its abdomen becomes so swollen with liquid food that it can barely walk (*left*), the gatherer ant called a replete must remain in the nest.

Slave-maker ants must depend on their slaves to perform such tasks as grooming the queen (*below left*), raising their brood, and building their nest.

Like miniature gardeners, leaf-cutter ants gather leaves (*below*) and other vegetation to prepare a bed on which to grow their fungus crop.

A herder ant "milks" aphids to get honeydew by stroking the insects with its antennae. It may also eat some of the aphids for meat.

Herder Ants

Herder ants live with sap-feeding insects in a special relationship that resembles the way human beings tend and herd cattle and other livestock. Some herder ants live underground with small insects called root aphids. The aphids feed on the sugary sap of the roots growing through the ant nests. To get rid of the excess sugar and water in their sap diet, the aphids discharge a sweet secretion called honeydew. Ants love to eat this sweet waste product. At times the ants also eat some of the aphids for meat. Ants that live this way often get all of their nutrition from aphids.

The herder ants of the Asian rain forest live with relatives of aphids called scale insects. These ants live in the warm, humid rain forest. The queen ant and her brood hide in the middle of swarms of workers on the soft new growth of forest shrubs. The scale insects suck sap from the plant twigs, and the ants harvest honeydew and scale insect meat for food. When the nest twig grows old and woody, the ants move, transporting their scale insects to a new "pasture"—that is, a new young twig.

Army Ants

When it comes to feeding, many ants are specialists, seeking out and preying on only one kind of food. Army ants are one such example. Many army ants only attack the nests of other ants, stealing and eating their broods. However, they have been accused of eating just about everything—from invertebrates to dogs, even humans!

Army ants have no permanent home. Each night the workers come together, creating a shelter out of their joined bodies. With the morning sun, bands of ants stream out from their temporary quarters, searching for food. When they find their prey, these ferocious ants swarm around it, attacking the victim with their long mandibles.

▶ANTS AND THEIR ENVIRONMENT

Ants serve several valuable functions. They help maintain the balance of nature by consuming large numbers of other insects and serving as a food source for other animals. They enrich the soil as they dig their burrows, loosening and mixing the dirt. Ants benefit human beings when they feed on insect pests, such as those that attack cotton plants and orange trees. But some of the same habits that make them helpful make them harmful. Ants can be household pests, infesting food and sometimes delivering painful stings. Some ants damage homes and other buildings by burrowing into the wood. They are agricultural pests when they feed on crops.

Over the years, myrmecologists have watched the same changes in the health of ant populations as in other species. Ants characteristic of endangered ecosystems—including the eastern tall grass prairie of North America, the rain forests of Asia, the savannas of northern Africa, and the hay meadows of Europe—are headed for extinction along with the other life-forms found in those habitats. In every way, the future of ants is linked to that of other life on our planet. Some species will increase; many others have already decreased and will continue to do so. Some may become victims of extinction.

JAMES C. TRAGER
Editor, *Advances in Myrmecology*

See also ANTEATERS; INSECTS.

APACHE INDIANS. See INDIANS, AMERICAN.

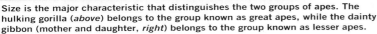
Size is the major characteristic that distinguishes the two groups of apes. The hulking gorilla (*above*) belongs to the group known as great apes, while the dainty gibbon (mother and daughter, *right*) belongs to the group known as lesser apes.

APES

Apes are hairy, long-armed animals without tails. They are intelligent creatures with large and complex brains, belonging to a group of mammals called **primates**. Human beings, monkeys (which are sometimes mistaken for apes), and a number of more primitive animals, such as lemurs, also are primates.

Of all existing animals, apes resemble human beings the most. The similarities between apes and human beings have led most scientists to believe that millions of years ago, apes and human beings shared a common ancestor. Some of the shared characteristics include highly developed nervous systems, excellent eyesight, broad flat chests, and flexible fingers and toes with nails instead of claws.

Although apes and human beings share many characteristics, there are significant differences. People, who are capable of more complicated tasks, have larger, more complex brains. Human beings also take longer to develop, have less body hair, and longer life spans. But probably the most important differences are that people have the ability to communicate with spoken language and to stand upright and walk on two legs.

▶ CHARACTERISTICS OF APES

All apes are divided into two families, or groups, based chiefly on size. There are great apes and lesser apes. The great apes, which

belong to the family Pongidae, include four species, or kinds, of apes: the gorilla, orangutan, chimpanzee, and bonobo, or pygmy chimpanzee. The largest of the great apes, and the largest primate, is the gorilla. A male can weigh about 600 pounds (272 kilograms) and stand more than 5 feet (1.5 meters) tall. The lesser apes, which belong to the family Hylobatidae, include nine species of gibbons. Gibbons are the smallest apes. They usually weigh 10 to 20 pounds (4.5 to 9 kilograms) and stand about 2 feet (0.6 meter) tall.

The various species of apes share many of the same characteristics. Their lively faces are more or less naked with flat noses and jaws that are thrust forward. Because they have mobile facial muscles, apes are able to display a wide range of facial expressions. Their eyes, which are directed forward, are capable of full-color vision. Hairless external ears are positioned on the sides of their heads. The trunk is well muscled with arms longer than legs. The siamang gibbon is the ape with the longest arms. Its arms, which may be more than twice as long as its body, span a distance of about 5 feet (1.5 meters). Apes have long-fingered hands with flat nails and opposable thumbs, that is, thumbs that can be placed against other fingers. Hair, varying in color from black to shades of reddish brown, covers their bodies.

Apes live in a variety of habitats. Gorillas are forest animals, found in tropical Africa. One population, the western lowland gorilla, lives in west central Africa. The eastern lowland gorilla lives about 600 miles (965 kilometers) away, in central Africa. Still another population, the mountain gorilla, inhabits mountains in east central Africa. Orangutans are also forest animals. However, their habitats on the Indonesian islands of Borneo and Sumatra distinguish them from other great apes—they are the only existing great apes of Asia. Chimpanzees are adaptable apes that make their home in Africa. They live in forests and in grasslands near wooded areas. Tropical forests in central Africa are home to the bonobos. Gibbons inhabit the airy heights of forests of Southeast Asia.

The devoted mother orangutan will spend years alone with her young offspring, roaming through the forest.

Apes are both land- and tree-dwellers. On land, apes typically move about on all fours with the knuckles of their front hands on the ground. Exceptions are the orangutan, which closes its hands into fists, and the gibbon, which walks with its long arms held high. Although all apes can climb trees, some are much more comfortable moving about high above the ground—the orangutan and gibbon seldom come down from their lofty habitats, while gorillas rarely climb trees.

Most apes are very social animals. In fact, they need to be around each other. When apes do not have contact with each other, they become depressed and dejected. Their sociability extends to their mode of parenting. Apes are dedicated parents that spend a lot of their time raising their offspring. Rather than have many offspring, apes produce a few young that are cared for by both male and female parents. Their care extends over several years until the young are able to take care of themselves.

▶ THE LIFE OF APES

Except for the solitary orangutan, apes live in groups. Some groups, like those of the gibbons, are small and consist of an adult pair and their young. A gorilla group, which may reach two dozen members, includes a few adult males, some younger males, and females and their offspring. Chimpanzees live in groups of between 15 and 80 individuals. The largest groups, or communities, are formed by the bonobos. A single community can have close to 150 members.

The gibbon is well adapted to a tree-dwelling existence. When it must navigate an open space between trees, the gibbon projects itself through the air for distances up to 32 feet (10 meters).

To get sufficient nourishment, a gorilla (*above*) consumes huge quantities of plant matter. A chimpanzee (*left*) uses a stick tool to search a rotted log for tasty insect morsels.

Although the various groups may be large and noisy, apes are generally peaceful creatures. Apes engage in threatening displays or aggressive behavior when guarding their territories against intruders or when males compete with each other for status, or rank, within a group. Males with the highest status usually mate with the most females. Gibbons are an exception. The male mates with only one female, and it stays with that female for life.

Apes are active during the day hunting and foraging for food. Gorillas are strict vegetarians. Other apes have a varied diet but feed mostly on plant matter. The fruit, roots, and leaves of plants and the bark of trees are consumed. Gibbons often eat birds' eggs, insects, and spiders as well as plants. Chimpanzees and bonobos add small mammals to their plant diet. In their quest for food, apes—especially chimpanzees—will develop and use tools. The episodes of eating are broken up by naps and playtimes with offspring.

When apes are sexually mature, at about 7 years of age, they are able to mate. Although twins are sometimes born, generally only a single offspring is produced by the female. The offspring stays with its mother for three to six years. The young apes are sheltered by their family group as their elders prepare them for the tasks of their adult lives.

At night, apes retire to sleeping nests. Some, like the tree-dwelling orangutan, build their nests high above the ground by bending twigs and branches to form a springy platform in the trees. Other apes, such as the gorilla, gather leaves, grasses, and other plant material to make their ground nests comfortable.

▶ APES AND THEIR ENVIRONMENT

Few animals threaten the lives of apes. Large cats, such as tigers and leopards, do hunt apes for food. But it is people who have seriously reduced the ape population. People have hunted apes for food and captured and traded them to stock zoos and for use in scientific research.

By far the greatest threat to apes is the loss of their habitats. Tropical forests and woodlands throughout the world, including those inhabited by apes, are being eliminated by human activity. Some are cut for lumber. Others are cleared to make room for agriculture or industries such as mining. As people have cleared land for development, apes have been pushed from their homes into lands that are poor habitats. The inferior lands cannot supply the apes with what they require to survive. Consequently, their numbers have dwindled.

Various methods are being used to protect the world's ape population. In many countries, laws have been enacted that make hunting or trading apes illegal. No longer are apes taken from the wild to supply zoos and research centers. Instead, apes are bred in captive-breeding programs. Zoos also have established captive-breeding programs as a way of ensuring that the various species of apes will not become extinct. In addition, many conservation groups are working hard to establish forest sanctuaries where apes can be protected and their habitat preserved.

EDWARD R. RICCIUTI
Coauthor, *The Audubon Society Book of Wild Animals*

See also MAMMALS.

| Bartholomew | Andrew | | Simon Peter | | Jesus | Thomas | Philip of Bethsaida | | Jude |
| James the Younger | | Judas Iscariot | | John | | James the Elder | | Matthew | | Simon the Cananaean |

APOSTLES, THE

The Apostles were 12 men especially appointed by Jesus Christ "that they should be with him, and that he might send them forth to preach, and to have power to heal sicknesses, and to cast out devils." Later Jesus sent them forth two by two. He "gave them power over unclean spirits; and commanded them that they should take nothing for their journey, save a staff only; no scrip, no bread, no money in their purse."

The word "apostle" comes from a Greek word meaning "to send away." Today it is sometimes used for religious missionaries.

Christ's 12 Apostles came from different backgrounds. Four were fishermen. Matthew, a tax collector, was the only wealthy man.

Like people everywhere, the Apostles had different personalities. Peter was a dependable leader with an independent nature. James the Younger was strict and severe, but respected for his justice. Philip liked to ask questions. Christ nicknamed James the Elder and his brother John "Sons of Thunder" because they had quick tempers. Thomas is known as "Doubting Thomas" because at first

he would not believe that Christ had risen from the dead. Some of the Apostles were quiet men, content to listen and to learn. Others were impatient. Because Peter, James the Elder, and John had a deeper understanding of Jesus' teachings, they were chosen to be with Jesus at the most important times.

Following Jesus' lifetime the Apostles traveled near and far. It is believed that Thomas went to India and Andrew reached what is now Russia. The teachings of Christ were spread throughout Asia Minor and most of the Roman Empire. The experiences of some of the Apostles are recorded in the New Testament.

According to a custom of the time, some of the Apostles were given new names when they took up their new responsibilities. The 12 Apostles are usually named in this order:

Simon, renamed Peter; a fisherman. Christ said, "Thou art Peter, and upon this rock I shall build my church."

Andrew, a fisherman; brother of Simon Peter. Saint Andrew's cross is so named because of the traditional belief that Andrew died on a cross made in the form of an X. He is the patron saint of Scotland, Greece, and Russia.

James the Elder (also called James the Greater), a fisherman; son of Zebedee. James was the first to die as a martyr in Jerusalem.

John, a fisherman; brother of James the Elder; author of the Fourth Gospel. He was known as "the disciple whom Jesus loved."

Philip of Bethsaida, who, when he became an Apostle, led his friend Nathanael (renamed Bartholomew) to Christ.

Bartholomew, Philip's friend. He was the son of Talmai (Bar Talmai in Hebrew). It is thought that his new name, Bartholomew, came from Bar Talmai.

Matthew, a tax collector. He preached in Judea, and is the traditional author of the First Gospel. Tradition also says that he brought Christianity to the East.

Thomas (also called Didymus, which means "twin"). He showed great faith by offering to accompany Jesus to Jerusalem, where some sought to stone him.

James the Younger (also called James the Less, or James the Little). Some scholars say that this is the James who welcomed Saint Paul to Jerusalem when many were suspicious of Saint Paul's conversion to Christianity.

Jude, or Judas (also called Thaddaeus), brother of James the Younger (though some scholars think he was the son of James).

Simon the Cananaean, martyred in Persia. "Cananaean" means one who is zealous or eager. Simon was so named for his devotion to Judaism before becoming a Christian.

Judas Iscariot. He betrayed Jesus for 30 silver coins. When Jesus was condemned to death, Judas repented and hanged himself.

Matthias was chosen by the 11 Apostles to replace Judas Iscariot. Tradition says he brought Christianity to ancient Ethiopia and Macedonia.

Paul of Tarsus (originally named Saul) was not one of the chosen 12, but is called an Apostle and is as respected as the others.

Reviewed by JAMES I. MCCORD
President, Princeton Theological Seminary

APPALACHIAN MOUNTAINS. See NORTH AMERICA.
APPENDICITIS. See DISEASES.

APPLE

The apple is the most important tree fruit of the temperate regions of the world. Apples have been grown and used as food since the dawn of history. Charred remains found in Stone Age lake dwellings in central Europe show that prehistoric peoples ate apples. There are carvings of apples on ancient tombs and monuments in the Middle East.

The apple appears often in the myths and folklore of ancient civilizations. In Greek mythology, Hercules traveled to the end of the world to bring back the golden apples of the Hesperides. A golden apple—the apple of discord—caused a quarrel that led to the Trojan War. A Norse myth tells of magic apples that kept people young forever. The Halloween game of bobbing for apples had its beginning among the ancient Celts as a way of foretelling the future.

Apples were brought to America by the earliest European settlers. At first apples were used mainly for cider, which was a popular beverage in England and northern France, where most of the early colonists came from. Cider is another name for apple juice. Hard cider is apple juice that has fermented. It contains a small percentage of alcohol—about as much as beer.

As the frontier moved westward across the continent, apple trees followed. One of the first things a settler did after clearing the land and building a cabin was to plant a few apple trees in the yard.

▶ORIGIN OF THE APPLE

Although there are numerous kinds of wild, or crab, apples native to different parts of the world, the kind from which the familiar cultivated apple developed came from the mountains of southwestern and central Asia, between the regions of the Black and Caspian seas and eastward from there. This ancestor of the modern apple, which still grows wild, is smaller and more sour than our present varieties, but the tree on which it grows resembles our cultivated trees.

People selected the best fruit from the wild trees for eating and used seed from the better fruit for planting. In this way the quality of apples was gradually improved.

▶ VARIETIES

A number of distinct varieties of apple were raised in the lands north of the Mediterranean Sea several centuries before the time of Jesus. Since then thousands of varieties have been named and grown in different parts of the world. Most of these have now disappeared from commercial production, although many different varieties are still grown in various parts of the world.

Fragrant white blossoms in the spring are followed by shiny, colorful fruit in the fall.

In the United States and Canada, about 25 varieties are grown extensively, although there are small plantings of many other kinds. Apple varieties must meet certain requirements before growers are willing to invest time, money, and labor in them. First of all, the trees must be productive. Second, the fruit must be attractive-looking and of good size. Its flavor and texture must appeal to most people. Finally, the fruit must keep well in storage. This is why so few varieties are grown on a large scale.

Nearly all our present important varieties originated as chance seedlings. Since about 1900, scientific breeding work has resulted in the development of some fine new varieties. Most of these are not yet widely grown.

The leading variety of apple in the United States is the Delicious, which originated from a seedling tree found on a farm at Peru, Iowa, about 1881. Most of the Delicious apples are now raised in the northwest Pacific states and British Columbia, though some are grown in nearly all apple-growing regions.

The McIntosh is the leading variety in Canada, New York, and the New England states. McIntosh trees are all descended from one chance seedling found on a pioneer farm in Ontario in 1796. The original tree survived, bearing apples, until 1908, although it was badly damaged by a fire.

Other leading varieties include the Golden Delicious, Rome Beauty, Jonathan, Stayman, York Imperial, and Winesap. The Northern Spy is a favorite in Canada. Some of these varieties are also grown in Europe, Japan, South America, and Australia along with the local kinds.

▶ THE TREE

In good soils unpruned apple trees will reach 30 to 40 feet (9 to 12 meters) in height. But when apples are grown for market, the trees are pruned to prevent them from becoming this tall. The trees in most commercial orchards are kept to a height of less than 20 feet (6 meters).

The apple tree is "rounded"—that is, it is about as broad as it is high. The branches are twisted and spreading. The fruit of most commercial varieties is red, but there are also varieties that bear yellow, green, russet, and striped fruit. Apple wood is dense, hard, and heavy. Because the tree has a short trunk and many branches, it is not used for lumber. Apple wood is sometimes used for carved ornaments, in furniture, and in lasts, or forms, for making shoes.

Apple trees generally do not begin to blossom and bear fruit until they are 5 to 8 years old. They reach maximum production at about 20 years, and commercial orchards are

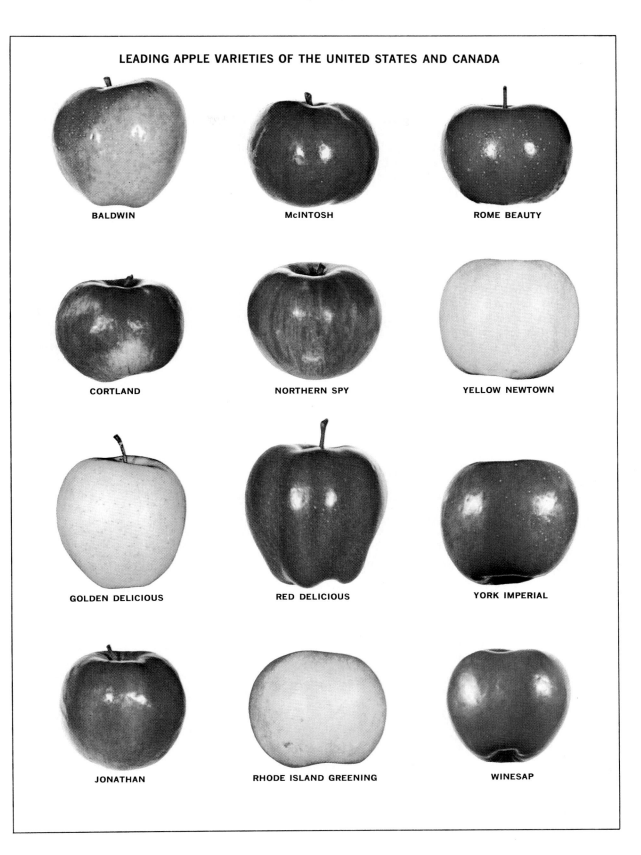

LEADING APPLE VARIETIES OF THE UNITED STATES AND CANADA

BALDWIN

McINTOSH

ROME BEAUTY

CORTLAND

NORTHERN SPY

YELLOW NEWTOWN

GOLDEN DELICIOUS

RED DELICIOUS

YORK IMPERIAL

JONATHAN

RHODE ISLAND GREENING

WINESAP

generally replaced when the trees are 35 to 40 years old. Although the trees would live much longer, the fruit produced on old trees is generally smaller and poorer in appearance.

▶ **MANAGING THE APPLE ORCHARD**

A great deal of intensive work must be performed in the commercial orchard. Each year the trees should be pruned, usually in late winter. This prevents them from becoming too tall or too thick and bushy and results in larger, better-colored fruit. The trees must be fertilized to make them grow and bear properly. Nearly all apple orchards need nitrogen fertilizers. Other elements such as potassium and magnesium may also be needed.

Frost, insect pests, and fungus diseases are among the most serious problems the apple grower faces. Open apple blossoms are killed when the temperataure drops a few degrees below freezing, and crops are often lost because of spring frosts that kill the blossoms. Commercial orchards generally are planted on slopes or high ground to reduce this danger, since cold air tends to sink. Some apple growers protect their orchards with heaters where frost occurs in blossom time.

Many insects attack the apple tree. One of the worst is the codling moth, which lays its eggs on or near the fruit. When the eggs hatch, the larvae bore into the fruit and a "wormy" apple results. Other insect pests include scales, aphids, and mites. Diseases caused by fungi and bacteria, such as apple scab and fire blight, can also infect the flowers, fruit, and leaves of the apple tree.

Repeated spraying is often necessary to keep the fruit free of insects and diseases. Because pests appear at different times of the growing season, some areas may need 12 to 14 sprays per year. New varieties of apples are now being bred that are resistant to certain kinds of insects and fungi. This reduces the need to spray so often.

▶ **PROPAGATION**

Apple trees do not "breed true." That is, new trees grown from seeds do not produce fruit that is exactly like the parent tree's. Trees for orchards are therefore produced by budding or grafting. A bud or a short piece of a twig taken from a parent tree is inserted into a young seedling tree so that it grows and forms the top of the new tree. The new tree

How to Sprout Apple Seeds

1. The first step in sprouting apple seeds is to collect some seeds from an apple. Once you have gathered the seeds, soak them in warm water overnight.

2. There are a number of different kinds of containers you can plant your seeds in — flowerpots, milk cartons, or coffee cans. The container should have one or more drain holes in the bottom and be able to hold about 1 quart (0.9 liter) of moist soil. To prepare the container, place small stones or pebbles in the bottom and fill it to the top with soil. Water the soil and press it down farther into the pot. Make sure there is a dish underneath to catch the water that drains out of the soil. To plant the seeds, place a few seeds on top of the soil about 1 inch (2.5 centimeters) apart. Then push them about a 1/2 inch (1 centimeter) under the surface with your finger. Gently pat the soil down and water it again.

3. The pot should be kept in a warm, sunny place. Be sure to check the soil every day and keep it moist. It may take several weeks for you to see tiny green stalks and leaves pop through the soil. Once the seedlings have grown about 2 inches (5 centimeters), each one can be put in its own container to grow. As they grow, the seedlings will continue to need sunshine and water. You also can fertilize them with houseplant fertilizer. Eventually the apple plants will need to be replanted in larger containers. Check with your local garden center to find out at what intervals they will need to be transplanted.

will then produce fruit exactly like that of the tree from which the bud was taken.

By budding or grafting onto certain kinds of roots, it is possible to produce trees that never become very large. Such trees are called dwarfs. Dwarf trees, besides being easier to spray, prune, and harvest, usually bear fruit earlier. Dwarf trees are popular for home planting and are used commercially on a large scale. Since they can be planted close together, the yield of fruit is generally increased by using dwarf trees.

▶HARVESTING AND STORAGE

Some varieties of apples mature in midsummer, others in late fall. Most kinds are ready for picking in September and October. The fruit must be picked by hand and carefully handled, for it will spoil if it is bruised.

The fruit is firm when picked but softens quite rapidly after picking unless it is put into cold storage. Apples will soften as much in one day at room temperature as they will in ten days in cold storage. Therefore, if the fruit is to be held for winter or early spring markets, it must be put at once in cold storage and cooled rapidly to about 32°F (0°C). It is held there until time for marketing.

Apples will keep even better in controlled atmosphere storage: The fruit is put into airtight rooms, and the oxygen level in the room is reduced from the 20 percent present in normal air to about 3 percent. At the same time the carbon dioxide content, normally present only in trace amounts, is increased to 2 to 5 percent. (The exact figures vary for different kinds of apples.) This slows down the life processes of the fruit cells and helps keep the fruit from softening. The controlled atmosphere, together with low temperatures, can keep some kinds of apples in good eating condition up to a year. But very few apples are stored more than nine months.

▶LEADING APPLE AREAS

Apples can be grown in nearly all the temperate areas of the earth. Most kinds can endure winter temperatures down to −20°F (−29°C), and some kinds can withstand temperatures as low as −40°F (−40°C).

In the United States, Washington, New York, Michigan, Pennsylvania, and California are leading producers of apples. In Canada, British Columbia, Ontario, and Nova Scotia

Apple pickers with long ladders harvest the ripe fruit. Canvas-bottomed pails protect apples from bruising.

lead. Apples are the leading tree-fruit crop in most of Europe. Australia, New Zealand, Japan, Chile, and Argentina also produce many apples. Apples do not thrive in the tropics, for the trees require a period of cold and dormancy to grow and bear fruit properly.

▶USES OF APPLES

Apples have many uses. They are eaten fresh, cooked, dried, and canned. Their juice is used for drinking and for making vinegar. Apples furnish valuable minerals and vitamins and add bulk to the diet. Fresh apples help clean the teeth and reduce tooth decay.

Almost 54 million short tons (49 million metric tons) of apples are produced each year in commercial orchards in the United States alone. About 60 percent of the crop is sold as fresh fruit. The rest is canned commercially as applesauce and as sliced apples for apple pie filling or is crushed and pressed for apple juice or vinegar.

Reviewed by MORRIS INGLE
West Virginia University

See also FRUITGROWING.

APPLIQUÉ. See NEEDLECRAFT.

April

No one really knows how April got its name. Some people think the month was named for Aphrodite, the Greek goddess of love. Others think that it came from the Latin word *aperire,* meaning "to open," referring to the opening of spring buds and flowers.

Place in year: 4th month.
Number of days: 30.
Flowers: Sweet pea and daisy.
Birthstone: Diamond.
Zodiac signs: Aries, the Ram (March 21–April 19), and Taurus, the Bull (April 20–May 20).

1
- **William Harvey** born 1578
- **Otto von Bismarck** born 1815
- *April Fools' Day*

2
- **Charlemagne** born 742
- **Hans Christian Andersen** born 1805
- **Émile Zola** born 1840
- U.S. mint established, 1792
- First American motion picture theater opened, Los Angeles, California, 1902

3
- **Washington Irving** born 1783
- Pony Express began in U.S., 1860

4
- Redesigned American flag adopted, 1818
- North Atlantic Treaty signed, 1949
- Martin Luther King, Jr., assassinated, 1968
- Liberation Day in Hungary
- National holiday in Senegal

5
- **Jean Honoré Fragonard** born 1732
- **Joseph Lister** born 1827
- **Booker T. Washington** born 1856

6
- **Raphael** born 1483
- Church of Jesus Christ of Latter-Day Saints (Mormon) founded, 1830
- Robert Peary and Matthew Henson reached the North Pole, 1909
- U.S. declared war on Germany, entering World War I, 1917

7
- **William Wordsworth** born 1770

8
- Ponce de León claimed Florida for Spain, 1513

9
- **Charles Steinmetz** born 1865
- First tax-supported public library in America founded by people of Peterborough, New Hampshire, 1833
- General Robert E. Lee surrendered the army of Northern Virginia to General Ulysses S. Grant, ending U.S. Civil War, 1865

10
- **Matthew C. Perry** born 1794
- **Joseph Pulitzer** born 1847
- London and Plymouth companies chartered by King James I of England, 1606

11
- **Charles Evans Hughes** born 1862
- Napoleon I abdicated, 1814

12
- **Henry Clay** born 1777
- U.S. Civil War began at Fort Sumter, 1861
- Salk polio vaccine declared effective, 1955
- Soviet Major Yuri Gagarin orbited the earth, 1961
- U.S. space shuttle Columbia launched, 1981

13
- **Thomas Jefferson** born 1743
- Edict of Nantes freed the French Huguenots, 1598
- Metropolitan Museum of Art founded in New York City, 1870

14
- First edition of Noah Webster's dictionary published, 1828
- Abraham Lincoln assassinated, 1865
- *Pan American Day*

15
- **Leonardo da Vinci** born 1452
- **Henry James** born 1843
- The ocean liner *Titanic* sank, 1912

16
- **Wilbur Wright** born 1867
- **Charlie Chaplin** born 1889
- Queen's birthday in Denmark

17
- **Nikita Khrushchev** born 1894
- National holiday in Kampuchea
- Evacuation Day in Syria

18
- **Clarence Darrow** born 1857
- Paul Revere's ride, 1775
- Great earthquake and fire, San Francisco, 1906
- Independence Day in Zimbabwe

19
- The American Revolutionary War began in Lexington, Massachusetts, 1775
- Republic Day in Sierra Leone

20
- **Adolf Hitler** born 1889
- U.S. abandoned the gold standard, 1933

21
- **Charlotte Brontë** born 1816
- **Elizabeth II** born 1926
- Legendary founding of Rome, 753 B.C.
- Spanish-American War began, 1898
- *San Jacinto Day* in Texas

22
- **Immanuel Kant** born 1724
- **Vladimir Lenin** born 1870
- Oklahoma Territory opened to settlers, 1889
- *Arbor Day* in Nebraska

23
- **William Shakespeare** born 1564
- **Joseph M. W. Turner** born 1775
- **James Buchanan** born 1791
- **Stephen A. Douglas** born 1813
- **Sergei Prokofiev** born 1891
- **Lester Pearson** born 1897

24
- U.S. Library of Congress established, 1800

25
- **Oliver Cromwell** born 1599
- **Guglielmo Marconi** born 1874

26
- **John James Audubon** born 1785
- **Eugène Delacroix** born 1798

19
- An explosion and resulting meltdown at the Chernobyl nuclear plant near Kiev, Ukraine, led to the worst crisis in the history of commercial atomic power, 1986
- Union Day in Tanzania

27
- **Samuel F. B. Morse** born 1791
- **Ulysses S. Grant** born 1822
- National holiday in Afghanistan; Togo

28
- **James Monroe** born 1758
- Maryland became the 7th state, 1788
- Mutiny on the British ship *Bounty,* 1789

29
- Emperor's birthday in Japan

30
- George Washington inaugurated as first president of the U.S., 1789
- Louisiana Purchase, 1803
- Louisiana became the 18th state, 1812
- War in Vietnam ended, 1975
- Queen's Day in the Netherlands
- King's birthday in Sweden

Second or Third Sunday in April: *National Library Week* begins. **First Sunday in April:** Daylight Savings Time begins for much of the U.S.
Third Monday in April: *Patriots' Day* in Maine and Massachusetts. **Third Friday in April:** *Arbor Day* in many states. **Holidays or holy days that may occur in either April or March:** *Palm Sunday; Holy Week and Easter; Passover.* **In April or May:** Independence Day in Israel.

The calendar listing identifies people who were born on the indicated day in boldface type, **like this**. You will find a biography of each of these birthday people in *The New Book of Knowledge.* In addition to citing some historical events and historical firsts, the calendar also lists the holidays and some of the festivals celebrated in the United States. These holidays are printed in italic type, *like this.* See the article HOLIDAYS for more information.

Many holidays and festivals of nations around the world are included in the calendar as well. When the term "national holiday" is used, it means that the nation celebrates an important patriotic event on that day—in most cases the winning of independence. Consult *The New Book of Knowledge* article on the individual nation for further information on its national holiday.

AQUACULTURE

Aquaculture is the raising of fish and other animals and plants in controlled water environments. Most often these organisms are raised for food, but they also can be raised for scientific or industrial purposes or for recreational use, such as sport fishing.

Aquaculture is not a new idea. An ancient Egyptian hieroglyphic from 4,000 years ago shows a picture of a fish farm, and in China, carp have been raised for food for more than 3,000 years.

Many kinds of animals and plants are raised successfully through aquaculture. Fish, especially carp, trout, salmon, and catfish, are the most important crops. About 10 percent of the world's supply of fish is produced through aquaculture. Shellfish, such as clams, mussels, oysters, and shrimp, are an important part of the industry. Octopuses, squid, pearl oysters, and seaweed, which is used for food in many Asian cultures, also are raised through aquaculture.

Aquaculture can take place in tanks on land or in artificial or natural bodies of water. Depending on the species, or kind, of organism being raised, salt water, fresh water, or brackish (somewhat salty) water is used. Sometimes flooded lands, such as rice paddies or coastal wetlands, serve as aquaculture pens. Aquaculture is even possible in open water, such as rivers or ocean coastlines, if the plants or animals can be confined with nets or cages.

There are many advantages to raising animals and plants in this manner. Each harvest is predictable, which is an improvement over traditional fishing methods. The quality of the animals and plants can be controlled through diet, breeding programs, and the use of medicines. In addition, crop productivity can be improved because the organisms are more easily protected from predators and contamination by pollutants.

Aquaculture is a rapidly expanding industry. China, which has a long history of aquaculture, is the leading producer of aquatic products. However, many countries contribute to the world's commercial harvests, including the United States, Norway, Japan, Thailand, and Ecuador. As the supplies of fish and shellfish from the world's oceans decrease, the aquaculture industry is destined to become a more and more important way of supplying the world's growing population with food.

BARBARA WIESE
Science Writer
See also FISH FARMING; FISHING INDUSTRY.

AQUARIUMS

Even a beginner can have a successful home aquarium, with crystal-clear water, beautiful plants, and colorful fishes. There are just a few principles involved in keeping an aquarium. If you learn what they are and follow them, you will avoid the mistakes that people often make when they put one together.

▶CHOICE AND LOCATION OF THE TANK

It is best to buy a rectangular tank that is at most about 3 inches (7 or 8 centimeters) higher than it is wide. Globes or tall, narrow tanks are not good because there is too little water surface open to the air. The water in a wider tank can take in more oxygen. This is important for the health of the fish. The water takes in oxygen from the air, and the fish absorb this oxygen through their gills. Fish give off a gas called carbon dioxide, just as people do when they breathe. The carbon dioxide must escape into the air through the surface of the water, or the fish will suffocate.

It is important to keep metal out of a fish tank. The slightest bit of metal in the water can be poisonous to fish. Paints, soaps, detergents, and certain plastics and chemicals must also be kept out of the tank. Insecticides are especially deadly to fish. Limestone products, such as marble chips, seashells, coral, and coral sand, should be avoided. They dissolve and make the water too hard. The best minerals for use in an aquarium are quartz, sandstone, and granite.

For protection, a glass cover should be kept on the tank. Do not worry that the fish will not get enough air. No tank cover fits so tightly that it keeps out the air that is needed. Finding the proper location for the tank is important, too. Sudden changes in temperature, either hotter or colder, are bad for fish.

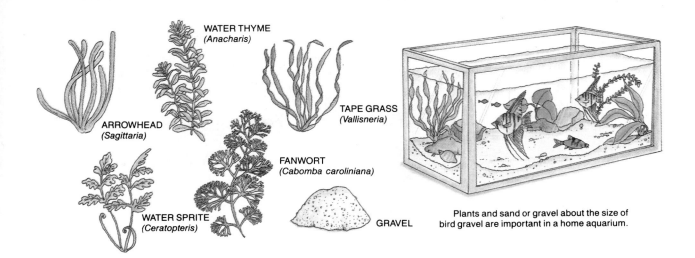

WATER THYME
(Anacharis)

ARROWHEAD
(Sagittaria)

TAPE GRASS
(Vallisneria)

FANWORT
(Cabomba caroliniana)

WATER SPRITE
(Ceratopteris)

GRAVEL

Plants and sand or gravel about the size of
bird gravel are important in a home aquarium.

A tank filled with water is very heavy. A 13-gallon (50-liter) tank weighs more than 110 pounds (50 kilograms) when filled. That is why the aquarium needs a firm resting place and why a filled tank should never be moved. It is impossible to move a full tank without cracking its glass or making it leak.

▶ GRAVEL, WATER, AND PLANTS

The gravel, water, and plants put in the tank are all important to the health of the fish and the beauty of the aquarium.

Gravel or sand is not necessary except when using rooted plants, but it makes a more natural-looking setting for the fish. Material about the size of bird gravel or a little larger is best. Too fine a sand packs tightly and holds back the growth of plants. If gravel is used, it should be carefully washed.

The most important single element of an aquarium is the water, and unless it is kept in good condition, neither fish nor plants will stay healthy. The best water for fish is water in which they have already lived. This is called "conditioned water."

People who keep aquariums speak of two kinds of dirt in a tank: clean dirt and dirty dirt. Clean dirt means the waste products of the fish themselves. This need not be removed. Dirty dirt means such things as uneaten food and the bodies of dead fish. This kind of dirt should be removed.

Beginners will have to start with plain tap water in the tank. Letting it stand until it comes to room temperature will get rid of any chlorine that may have been added to the water to purify it. Chlorine is harmful to fish. The fish may be placed in the water as soon as it has reached room temperature. At first the water may look slightly cloudy or milky. But this is typical of water in a new aquarium. If the fish are fed very little for the first two weeks, the water should clear up and stay crystal clear for an unlimited time.

In spite of everything you may have heard, fish in the usual aquarium do as well without plants as they do with plants. In a process known as photosynthesis, plants use the energy from sunlight to make their own food. In this process, carbon dioxide is taken in and oxygen is given off. However, there is usually enough oxygen in the water in a clean, well-maintained aquarium to take care of the breathing requirements of the fish.

Underwater plants, however, add a great deal to the beauty of an aquarium. Plants that grow in water also provide more natural surroundings for the fish. The fish can hide in the leaves of the plants and lay their eggs on them. In addition, well-planted tanks are less apt to develop green water.

The amount of light the tank receives has much to do with the kinds of plants that will grow well in it. It is best to experiment with several different types to discover which ones will do best. Plants for an aquarium will be found in shops that sell fish and other aquarium supplies. Fanwort (*Cabomba caroliniana*) and waterweed or water thyme (*Anacharis* or *Elodea*) require strong light. Tape grass or eelgrass (*Vallisneria*), arrowhead (*Sagittaria*), and floating fern or water sprite (*Ceratopteris*) need somewhat less. Cryptocorynes, which have broad, heart-shaped leaves, do well with still less light. Tanks that need artificial light will require a light for eight or nine hours a day.

Cardinal tetra.

Rock beauty (Holocanthus tricolor).

Red tuxedo swordtails.

Killifish (Nothobranchius rachovi).

▶ **FEEDING THE FISH**

More pet fish die from overfeeding than from any other cause. Fish should be fed only three times a week. At a single feeding they should be given only as much food as they can eat up completely in ten minutes. You can judge the correct amount by feeding the fish from the flat end of a toothpick and standing by to see that each bit of food is totally eaten up before giving any more.

Snails or catfishes can be added to the tank to act as scavengers. They will eat a certain amount of leftover food and decaying leaves of underwater plants, but no scavenger alive can handle the problem of overfeeding if it goes on day after day.

When feeding fish, use as many different foods as possible. In addition to the dried foods that are already packaged, try finely chopped raw lean meat, liver, raw fish, shrimp, clams, the yolk of hard-boiled eggs, cooked oatmeal, boiled spinach, and fresh lettuce. **Tropical fishes** and many kinds of fishes that live in colder water relish all these foods.

Fish also enjoy some living food once a week. In a pet shop you can find live *Daphnia* (water fleas), enchytraeids (white worms), and *Tubifex* (red worms). Earthworms, chopped up for small fish, are excellent.

▶ **SELECTING THE FISHES**

Before setting out to buy fishes, it is important to understand that some of them can live only in water that is kept at a certain temperature. The water in which many tropical fishes live must be kept at a temperature that ranges from 72 to 80°F (22 to 27°C). For certain tropical fishes, an electric heater with a thermostat is required to control the temperature of the water.

Goldfish usually do not need any temperature control. Minnows, certain darters, sunfishes, catfishes, suckers, sticklebacks, gars, and mud minnows do not need it either. But they must not have sudden changes in temperature. None of these fishes should be kept in a room in which the temperature drops more than 10°F (5°C) at night.

Black scarftail guppy.

Common veiltail goldfishes.

Pyjama Apogon.

When buying fishes for the first time, it is best to get the less expensive kinds. The **guppy**, a small tropical fish that bears living young, is probably the best of all fishes for beginners because of its color, strength, and the number of young fish it bears. Although it is a tropical fish, the guppy does not need specially treated water.

Other strong fishes that are not quite as sturdy as guppies are the brightly colored platyfishes, swordtails, and black mollies. They are in the same family as guppies and also have living young. Tetras, *Corydoras* catfishes, Siamese fighting fish, and angelfish are also good fish for beginners to raise.

Not all fishes get along well together. Many, like the sunfishes, crappies, paradise fish, and Siamese fighting fish, are fighters, especially at breeding time. Guppies, platyfishes, danios, tetras, and *Corydoras* catfishes are the best fish to buy if you plan to keep several kinds in one tank.

Be sure your tank is large enough for the number of fish you plan to buy. Next to overfeeding, overcrowding kills most pet fish. When fish come to the top of the tank gasping, it is a sign of overcrowding. For goldfish a safe rule is to allow 2 gallons of water for each inch (3 liters for each centimeter) of the fish's length, not counting the tail. North American fishes, such as sunfishes or minnows, need at least this much water. For tropical fishes allow one forth of this amount. It is better to start an aquarium with too few fish and add to it gradually and carefully than it is to start with a crowded tank.

When one of the fish acts sick, it should be put into a small aquarium by itself so that the other fish do not become sick, too. The most common disease of tropical fish is white spots, or ichthyophthirius ("ich" for short). It is hard to cure a sick fish, but you can ask about remedies at your pet shop.

If there are both male and female fish in the tank, the female may lay eggs. They often look like seed pearls, and settle on the plants. These eggs should be placed in a separate aquarium, too, before the larger fish eat them up. This is done by taking out the part of the plant on which the eggs have settled and putting it in another tank. When the eggs develop into tiny fish, they may be fed small amounts of hard-boiled egg yolk, crushed fine.

If you follow these suggestions, you should be able to start a successful home aquarium of your own. You can have many moments of pleasure watching your fish swim lazily along or dart quickly about in your tank.

JAMES W. ATZ
Former Curator, New York Zoological Society

AQUINAS, SAINT THOMAS (1225?–1274)

Saint Thomas Aquinas, patron saint of all Catholic universities, colleges, and schools, had a powerful influence on the thinking of his time. Yet as a student in Cologne, his silence in the classroom and his heavy build earned him the nickname of "dumb ox." His fellow students and professors soon discovered, however, that he was not stupid, but a deep and humble thinker.

Thomas was born in the castle of Rocca Secca near Aquino, Italy. His father was Landulf, Count of Aquino, and his mother was Theodora, Countess of Teano. When he was 5, he was taken to the abbey of Monte Cassino for his schooling. He stayed there until he was about 13 and later studied at the University of Naples for five years.

When Thomas was about 19, he joined the Dominican order, despite the objections of his family. He was eventually allowed to complete his studies in Paris and Cologne under Albertus Magnus, the most renowned professor in the Dominican order.

Thomas himself became famous as a teacher, winning admiration for the clarity and power of his thought. He developed a philosophy that combined Christian beliefs with the teachings of the Greek philosopher Aristotle.

About 1266, Thomas began writing his most famous work, the *Summa theologica*, a scientifically arranged study of theological teaching and Christian philosophy. He never finished it. On December 6, 1273, he experienced such a spiritual revelation at Mass that he could write no more. The revelation made all his writings appear as nothing to him.

Thomas died on March 7, 1274. He was made a saint in 1323 and a doctor of the Church in 1567. His writings fill 20 thick volumes and include much on Aristotle.

HARRY J. CARGAS
Editor, *The Queen's Work*

AQUINO, CORAZON C. (1933–   )

From 1986 until 1992, Corazon Aquino, the widow of slain Philippine political leader Benigno Aquino, Jr., served as president of the Philippines. With the support of most Filipinos, in 1986 she led a "People Power" revolution to overthrow President Ferdinand Marcos, who had been in power since 1965. She campaigned to replace his government with one based on "justice, morality, decency, freedom, and democracy."

Corazon (Cory) Aquino was born in Manila on January 25, 1933, the fourth of the six children of Jose Cojuangco and Demetria Sumulong. As a young woman she attended the College of Mount St. Vincent in the United States. In 1953 she married Aquino, a journalist and politician. They had five children.

Benigno Aquino rose quickly in politics. When in 1973 it appeared that he could win the Philippine presidential election, Marcos declared martial law and put his popular rival in jail. In 1980, Aquino was permitted to go to the United States for medical treatment, and Corazon accompanied him.

In 1983, Benigno Aquino was shot and killed when he returned to the Philippines. Many people held Marcos responsible for his death. Corazon, a housewife with no political experience, returned to the Philippines to lead the opposition movement against Marcos in her husband's place. In 1985, more than 1 million Filipinos petitioned her to run for president.

Marcos appeared to be the victor in the election of February 7, 1986, but many charged that he had tried to fix the election. With the support of the military, Aquino led the people in a campaign of nonviolent resistance and forced Marcos to resign.

When Aquino took office, she established a newly elected Congress, called for a new constitution, freed Marcos' political prisoners, and restored the people's civil liberties.

Aquino's new administration faced many serious challenges: Rivals tried to overthrow her government, and Communist rebels threatened the new democracy. Aquino was also faced with reviving the economy, which had suffered after years of corruption under Marcos. In 1992, Aquino was succeeded as president by her former defense minister, Fidel V. Ramos.

ISABELO T. CRISOSTOMO
Author, *Cory: Profile of a President*

ARABIA.   See MIDDLE EAST; SAUDI ARABIA.

ARABIAN NIGHTS

Hundreds of years ago professional story-tellers in India and the Middle East made up the stories now known as *The Arabian Nights*. Later on, groups of these stories were put together. One group was translated from Arabic to French by Antoine Galland in the early 1700's. His *Mille et une nuits*, or *A Thousand and One Nights*, introduced these Oriental tales to the Western world.

All the collections have one thing in common. A heroine, Scheherazade, tells the different stories. She recites the tales for a very good reason: She must save her life.

Scheherazade was married to Sultan Shahriyar, who had killed his first wife when she was unfaithful to him and then all his later wives in revenge against women. Scheherazade did not want to suffer the same fate. On her wedding night she began to tell her husband a story and stopped just before she reached the end. The Sultan allowed her to live another day in order to hear the end of her tale. The next night she finished the story and began another one even more fascinating than the first. Again she stopped before the ending, gaining another day of life.

And so it went, for a thousand and one nights. Finally the Sultan realized that Scheherazade was a good and faithful wife, and the couple lived happily ever after.

The stories supposedly told by Scheherazade are understandably popular. Nowhere does one find treasures more magnificent, beasts more fabulous, or magicians more cunning. Excerpts from two of the best-known stories follow.

In **Aladdin and the Wonderful Lamp** a magician poses as a long-lost uncle to the unsuspecting Aladdin. The two leave the city and arrive at a secret place, where the magician kindles a fire, throws powder on it, and says some magic words. The earth trembles and opens, revealing a flat stone with a brass ring to raise it by. With the help of more magic words, the stone is moved and steps appear.

"Go down," said the magician. "At the foot of those steps you will find an open door leading into three large halls. Tuck up your gown and go through them without touching anything, or you will die instantly. These halls lead into a garden of fine fruit trees. Walk on till you come to a niche in a terrace where stands a lighted lamp. Pour out the oil it contains and bring it to me." He drew a ring from his finger and gave it to Aladdin, bidding him prosper.

Aladdin found everything as the magician had said, gathered some fruit off the trees and, having got the lamp, arrived at the mouth of the cave.

The magician cried out in a great hurry, "Make haste and give me the lamp." This Aladdin refused to do until he was out of the cave. The magician flew into a terrible passion, and throwing some more powder on the fire, he said something, and the stone rolled back into its place.

The magician left Persia forever, which plainly showed that he was no uncle of Aladdin's, but a cunning sorcerer who had read in his magic books of a wonderful lamp which would make him the most powerful man in the world. Though he alone knew where to find it, he could only receive it from the hand of another. He had picked out the foolish Aladdin for this purpose, intending to get the lamp and kill him afterward.

For two days Aladdin remained in the dark, crying and lamenting. At last he clasped his hands in prayer, and in so doing rubbed the ring, which the magician had forgotten to take from him.

Immediately an enormous and frightful genie rose out of the earth, saying, "What wouldst thou with me? I am the slave of the ring and will obey thee in all things."

Aladdin fearlessly replied, "Deliver me from this place," whereupon the earth opened, and he found himself outside. As soon as his eyes could bear the light he went home, but fainted on the threshold. When he came to himself he told his mother what had passed, and showed her the lamp and the fruits he had gathered in the garden, which were in reality precious stones. He then asked for some food.

"Alas, child," she said, "I have nothing in the house, but I have spun a little cotton and will go and sell it."

Aladdin bade her keep her cotton, for he would sell the lamp instead. As it was very dirty she began to rub it, that it might fetch a higher price. Instantly a hideous genie appeared and asked what she would have.

She fainted away, but Aladdin, snatching the lamp, said boldly, "Fetch me something to eat!"

The genie returned with a silver bowl, twelve silver plates containing rich meats, two silver cups, and a bottle of wine.

Another *Arabian Nights* favorite is **The Forty Thieves**. The hero, Ali Baba, is a poor woodcutter. Here is how he finds out what the forty thieves are up to.

One day, when Ali Baba was in the forest, he saw a troop of men on horseback, coming toward him in a cloud of dust. He was afraid they were robbers and climbed into a tree for safety. When they came up to him and dismounted, he counted forty of them. They unbridled their horses and tied them to trees.

The finest man among them, whom Ali Baba took to be their captain, went a little way among some bushes and said, "Open, Sesame!" so plainly that Ali Baba heard him. A door opened in the rocks and, having made the troop go in, he followed them and the door shut again of itself.

They stayed some time inside and Ali Baba, fearing they might come out and catch him, was forced to sit patiently in the tree. At last the door opened again and the forty thieves came out. As the captain went in last he came out first, and made them all pass by him; he then closed the door, saying, "Shut, Sesame!" Every man bridled his horse and mounted, the captain put himself at their head, and they returned as they came.

Then Ali Baba climbed down and went to the door concealed among the bushes and said, "Open, Sesame!" and it flew open. Ali Baba, who expected a dull, dismal place, was greatly surprised to find it large and well lighted, and hollowed by the hand of man in the form of a vault, which received the light from an opening in the ceiling. He saw rich bales of merchandise—silk stuffs, brocades, all piled together, gold and silver in heaps, and money in leather purses. He went in and the door shut behind him. He did not look at the silver but brought out as many bags of gold as he thought his asses, which were browsing outside, could carry, loaded them with the bags, and hid it all with fagots. Using the words, "Shut, Sesame!" he closed the door and went home.

Reviewed by CAROLYN W. FIELD
The Free Library of Philadelphia

Originally nomads of the desert, most Arabs today live in cities such as Cairo (*left*). The capital of Egypt and the most populous city in the Arab world, Cairo was founded in the A.D. 900's by Arab conquerors. Only a relatively few Arabs, like these Bedouins in Qatar (*below*), still follow the nomadic way of life, traveling over age-old routes, seeking pasture and water for their livestock.

ARABS

The name "Arab" refers to the peoples who speak Arabic as their native language. The Arabs originated in the deserts of what is now Saudi Arabia, which occupies most of the vast Arabian Peninsula. However, the impression that Arabs are still people of the desert—that is, Bedouins or nomads—is inaccurate. Most Arabs today are city dwellers. Nomads make up less than 10 percent of the Arab population, which numbers nearly 200 million.

The Arab World. Geographically, the Arab world stretches across North Africa and includes most of the countries of the Middle East, except for Iran, Turkey, Israel, and Cyprus. The nations of the Arab world are Algeria, Bahrain, Egypt, Iraq, Jordan, Kuwait, Lebanon, Libya, Morocco, Oman, Qatar, Saudi Arabia, Sudan, Syria, Tunisia, the United Arab Emirates, and Yemen. Mauritania is also often included.

In addition, about 1.8 million Palestinian Arabs live on the West Bank of the Jordan River and in the Gaza Strip, territories occupied by Israel since the 1967 Arab-Israeli War. Nearly 800,000 Arabs live in Israel itself. Arabs have also emigrated to many parts of the world.

The Arabs are a diverse people, but there are basic elements that link most of them. The most important of these are the Islamic religion and the Arabic language, and the culture and history associated with them.

Religion. The great majority of Arabs are Muslims, or followers of the religion of Islam. There are also significant numbers of Christian Arabs, particularly in Egypt, Lebanon, Syria, and among the Palestinians. In Lebanon, Christians of various denominations make up about 40 percent of the population.

Islam originated in the Arabian Peninsula more than 1,300 years ago. It spread rapidly through much of Asia and Africa, so that today some of the largest Muslim countries and communities are outside the Arab world.

Islam, whether Arab or non-Arab, has two major branches—Sunni Islam and Shi'i Islam. Sunni Islam is the larger branch and most Arabs are Sunnis. However, Shi'ites are a majority in Iraq and make up the single largest religious community in Lebanon. Bahrain's population is about 70 percent Shi'ite, while some other small Persian Gulf states have important Shi'ite minorities.

For more information, see the article ISLAM in Volume I.

An Arab girl and her brother (*left*) study the Koran (Quran), the sacred book of Islam, the religion of the Muslims. Islam originated in the Arabian Peninsula in the 600's and spread to much of Asia and Africa. A miniature painting of the 1200's (*right*) depicts a caravan of Arab pilgrims on the way to Mecca, the holiest city of Islam. If they are able to do so, Muslims are expected to make at least one pilgrimage (*hajj*) to Mecca in a lifetime.

The Arabic Language. Arabic belongs to the Semitic group of languages, which also includes Hebrew. The languages of Arabs and Jews thus are closely related. More broadly, Arabic is a part of the Hamito-Semitic family, which can be traced back to ancient Egyptian and includes some languages of Ethiopia.

The Arabic alphabet has 28 characters, which are written from right to left. Arabic script has two main forms—Kufic and Nashki. Kufic is angular in shape. Nashki is rounded and flowing with the letters joined. A modified Arabic alphabet is also used in the languages of some non-Arab Muslim countries.

Arabic developed among the Bedouins of the Arabian desert. Its growth was greatly encouraged by a tradition of poetry that was highly elaborate in its oral (spoken) form before being written down. With the coming of Islam in the A.D. 600's, the Koran (Quran), the sacred book of Islam, became the model for the future use of the language. It was the one text that all Arab (and later all non-Arab) Muslims learned. Educated Muslims memorized the Koran completely and it became the standard for classical Arabic.

As the Koran accompanied the Arab conquests, its message and style spread across the Islamic world. Eventually, variations in the spoken language developed. Today, certain dialects, especially the Moroccan, are difficult for other Arabs to understand, but all share a common written language. Arabs also can communicate orally by speaking in the classical Arabic used for writing.

Arab History and Civilization. References to Arabs as nomads and camel herders of northern Arabia appear in writings as early as the 800's B.C. The name was later applied to all inhabitants of the Arabian Peninsula.

Arabs were then a tribal society. They were grouped together according to family heritage, tracing their origins back to a common ancestor. But tribal society in the Arabian Peninsula was always fragmented because of the harsh desert conditions. Tribes broke up into smaller clans, who roamed the desert, stopping at oases (fertile areas) and wells for food and water. No great Arab state appeared until the coming of Islam.

Mohammed. Islam originated in the city of Mecca, in what is now western Saudi Arabia. Mecca was the birthplace, in about A.D. 570, of the prophet of Islam, Mohammed (or Muhammad) ibn Abdullah. Mohammed preached a monotheistic religion—a belief in one God—like that of Jews and Christians. When faced with opposition from the people of Mecca, he fled to Medina, to the north. The Muslim calendar begins with this migration, called the Hegira (Hijra), in A.D. 622, because it marked the beginning of a separate Muslim community. Mecca and Medina today are the two holiest cities of Islam.

See the article MOHAMMED in Volume M.

The Spread of Islam. At the time of Mohammed's death in 632, Mecca and most of the tribes of the Arabian Peninsula had accepted Islam. A century later an Islamic empire, under Arab leadership, ranged from Spain across North Africa and most of the present-day Middle East to Central Asia and northern India. Spain, conquered by Arabs from North Africa in 711, was the center of a great Arab-Islamic civilization, with major contributions by Jews, until the end of the 1400's.

Islam was the motivating force behind this conquest, but non-Muslims were not forcibly converted to Islam. Different religions were tolerated. Christians and Jews were permitted to practice their faiths as long as special taxes were paid to Muslim rulers.

The Caliphates. The Muslim rulers who succeeded to the political leadership of Islam first held by the Prophet Mohammed were known as caliphs. There were two great caliphates or dynasties of Arab origin—the Umayyad and the Abbasid. Umayyad rule lasted from 661 to 750 and was centered in Damascus (the present capital of Syria). The Abbasids ruled between 750 and 1258 from their capital of Baghdad (the modern-day capital of Iraq).

Arab Achievements. Islamic civilization, including both Arab and Persian (Iranian) influences, flourished under the Abbasids. Its accomplishments included advances in literature, philosophy, and medicine. Greek philosophy, including the works of Plato and Aristotle, was translated into Arabic as well. The translations passed, by way of Muslim Spain, to European Christian scholars, thus preserving one of the great heritages of Western civilization. Islamic medical texts were used in Europe until the 1600's.

Arab scholars also made important contributions in mathematics. What we call Arabic numerals (the symbols we use for our numbers) actually originated in India and were modified by the Arabs. But Muslim mathematicians invented algebra, which comes from the Arabic *al-Jabr*.

Some words from Arabic literature have also come down to us. Probably the best known is "genie," from the Arabic *jinn*, a spirit that appears in "Aladdin and the Wonderful Lamp" and other tales, part of the collection of stories most commonly known as *The Arabian Nights*. See the article ARABIAN NIGHTS in this volume.

The Arabs also developed a distinctive style of art and architecture. See the article ISLAMIC ART AND ARCHITECTURE in Volume I for information on this subject.

Arab Decline. At the height of its power, the Abbasid Caliphate was immensely

The Arabs are united by their use of the Arabic language, shown here in a page from the Koran (Quran). The many faces of the Arab world include a Syrian man (*right*); a Bedouin chief (*far right*); a woman from Sudan in traditional dress (*below*); and Egyptian schoolchildren (*below right*).

wealthy, dominating trade between Europe and Asia. But the collapse of the dynasty in 1258 meant the end of Arab leadership of the Islamic world. Its later rulers were the Ottoman Turks, whose empire, centered in Constantinople (present-day Istanbul), included most of the Arab lands.

As the Ottoman Empire itself declined in the 1800's, many of the Arab lands were taken over as colonies by European powers. At the start of World War I in 1914, all of North Africa was under European control. Algeria, Tunisia, and Morocco were ruled by France; Libya was an Italian colony; and Egypt was dominated by Britain. By 1918, when the war ended, what was left of the Ottoman Empire had fallen apart.

At the 1919 peace conference, Britain and France were awarded the remaining Arab lands, with the understanding that they would foster the development of the peoples of these regions toward self-government. Syria and Lebanon went to France, and Iraq and Palestine went to Britain.

The Palestine Question. Palestine represented a special case. During World War I, British officials had suggested to Arab leaders that Palestine would be included in areas to be

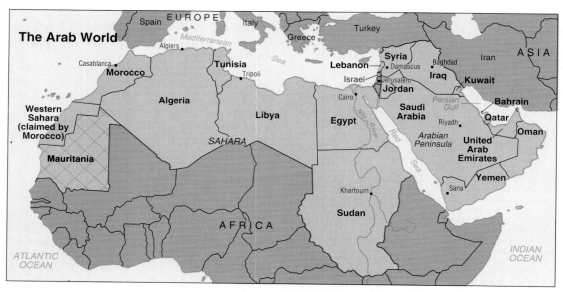

The landscape of the Arab world is as varied as its people. An Iraqi farmer (*below*) plows a fertile area in the upper valley of the Tigris and Euphrates rivers. By contrast, most of the Arabian Peninsula (*right*) is made up of desert.

granted Arab self-determination. The British then promised Palestine to leaders of the Zionist movement, which called for a Jewish state in Palestine. The origin of the Arab-Israeli conflict lies in the history of these conflicting promises as well as Palestinian Arab opposition to Jewish claims in the region.

See the article PALESTINE in Volume P and the one on ZIONISM in Volume W-X-Y-Z.

Recent History. Most of the Arab lands won their independence in stages after World War II ended in 1945. Some did so peacefully, others after a struggle. The creation of the Jewish state of Israel in part of Palestine in 1948 set off hostilities that led to five Arab-Israeli wars —in 1948, 1956, 1967, 1973, and 1982. The conflict continues today, particularly over the claims of the Palestinian Arabs to their own state in the West Bank and Gaza.

In addition to Arab-Israeli hostility, there have been clashes between Arab regimes or within the countries themselves because of territorial ambitions or ideological differences. The civil war that wracked Lebanon from the mid-1970's to late 1990 (and may erupt again) reflected the struggle for political power between different religious communities. The conflict was intensified by the aims of surrounding nations and the Palestine Liberation Organization (PLO), which most Palestinian Arabs look to for leadership.

Iraq's invasion of Kuwait in 1990 was caused by its desire to gain more shoreline on the Persian Gulf as well as control of Kuwait's vast oil reserves. The quick defeat of Iraq in a short war in 1991, by a coalition led by the United States, ended this threat, but the long-term results of the war still remain to be seen.

Workers drill for offshore oil in the Red Sea. Oil is the most valuable resource in the Arab world, with the largest deposits found in Saudi Arabia.

Arab Society Today. In spite of political conflicts and differences among them, the Arab peoples have many things that continue to unite them. In addition to a common written language and values rooted for the most part in Islam, Arabs also have a sense of a shared history. This includes both greatness under past Muslim dynasties and forced submission to foreign rulers in more recent times.

Traditional Arab cultural values have always strongly stressed family ties and unity, which can be important in forming political factions. Such relationships have become less common in the large cities, where the growth of modern professions has created new political and economic alliances. Many educated young people now marry as they choose, whereas once it was assumed that marriages would be arranged by families. Some Arab countries demand stricter allegiance to traditional ways. Saudi Arabia, for example, is an extremely conservative society.

Resources. Arab countries vary greatly in economic development. Except for oil, most have little in the way of natural resources. Saudi Arabia and the small Persian Gulf states, once home only to small numbers of nomadic peoples, now have incredible wealth due to oil. At the same time, countries with rich historical pasts are poor today.

Kuwait, for example, a country the size of New Jersey, has the world's second largest oil reserves (Saudi Arabia has the largest) and a per capita (per person) income of about $15,000 a year. By contrast, Egypt, a center of Arab and Islamic culture with a large population, has a per capita income of only about $710 a year. This disparity has led educated people from the poorer Arab nations to seek work in the wealthy Persian Gulf states. It has also bred resentment among some of the poorer countries.

Agricultural productivity is high in Arab lands, but good farm land is often scarce because of a limited water supply. Population growth, which is much too high in countries such as Egypt, is another important factor in the future of the Arab world.

CHARLES D. SMITH
San Diego State University
Author, *Islam and the Search for Social Order in Modern Egypt*

See also ISRAEL; MIDDLE EAST; and articles on the individual Arab countries.

Each kind of arachnid has special traits. The scorpion (*far left*) gives birth to live young, the spider (*left*) produces silk, and the tick (*above*, before and after feeding) lives on other animals.

ARACHNIDS

Arachnids are very small, typically land-dwelling animals that belong to the class Arachnida. Among the approximately 74,000 species, or kinds, of arachnids, the best known include spiders, scorpions, mites, ticks, and daddy longlegs. Arachnids range in size from the tiniest of mites that are only 1/250 inch (0.1 millimeter) long to the scorpions that can reach 7 inches (18 centimeters) in length. Most, however, are less than 1 inch (2.5 centimeters) long.

In their basic appearance, arachnids resemble insects. Both arachnids and insects have segmented bodies, jointed legs, and a tough, hard outer covering, or **exoskeleton**. Under close examination, however, the two groups are seen to be quite different. While insects have three main body parts, wings, six legs, compound eyes, and antennae, arachnids have two main body regions, eight legs, simple eyes, and two pairs of limbs that are modified for grasping, biting, and touching. Unlike insects, they do not have wings or antennae.

Each kind of arachnid has distinguishing characteristics that set it apart from the others. **Spiders** possess venom glands and inject venom into their prey through fangs on their jaws. They also have abdominal glands that produce silk, which is used for special tasks such as capturing prey, courting a mate, and forming a sac for their eggs. Because spiders consume large amounts of insects, they are economically important biological-control agents.

Scorpions are easily recognized by their tapered bodies and their large size. Clawlike appendages alongside the jaw are used to seize prey. With the prey in its grasp, the scorpion whips its tail, which is tipped with a venomous stinger, forward and over the back to deliver an injection of toxic venom. Among the larger arachnids, scorpions are unusual because rather than laying eggs, they give birth to living young.

Mites and **ticks** are the smallest arachnids. Their bodies are saclike and appear to have only a single region. The feeding habits of mites and ticks vary. Ticks are parasitic; that is, they live on other creatures and are harmful to them in the process. Mites can be parasites as well as plant eaters, predators, and scavengers. Both ticks and mites can be harmful to people. Ticks can carry serious diseases, such as Rocky Mountain spotted fever and Lyme disease. Many mites are significant pests of crop plants, stored products, and domestic animals. Some mites also carry disease.

Daddy longlegs, or **harvestmen**, are named for their extremely long, slender legs. When attacked by a predator, a daddy longlegs can shed a leg to avoid capture. A new leg will regrow at the next molt, when the daddy longlegs sheds its skin. Many species have an additional defense—they have glands that produce secretions disagreeable enough to discourage predators. Most species of daddy longlegs are scavengers, feeding on dead insects and fallen fruit.

MAY R. BERENBAUM
Department of Entomology
University of Illinois

See also SPIDERS; TICKS.

ARBITRATION. See INTERNATIONAL RELATIONS; LABOR-MANAGEMENT RELATIONS.

ARBOR DAY. See HOLIDAYS.

ARCHAEOLOGY

Archaeologists are detectives who investigate the past. They are interested not in crimes and criminals but in discovering how people used to live.

Using all the clues available, archaeologists try to piece together a picture of the people they are investigating. The goal is to learn what sort of environment the people lived in. If the people lived in houses, the archaeologist wants to know how they built and furnished their houses. The archaeologist is also interested in what they ate, how they obtained and prepared food, and what kind of tools they used. The archaeologist tries to discover something about their relations with neighboring people—whether they were friendly and exchanged goods or whether they were enemies and fought each other. And the archaeologist tries to learn something about their customs, about their religious beliefs, and about their political practices.

▶THE STUDY OF PHYSICAL REMAINS

The word **archaeology** comes from two old Greek words—*archaios* (''ancient'') and *logos* (''study'' or ''talk''). From these two words you can see that ''archaeology'' means the study of the past. Archaeologists base their study on physical remains—the objects that people leave behind. They may find an arrowhead, a stone axe, or a clay tablet with writing on it. These objects are called **artifacts,** and archaeologists study them for clues to how people lived in the past. Archaeologists also find animal and plant remains. A charred basket full of seeds, a burned wooden post, or the bones of animals can tell the archaeologist something about the physical environment the people lived in, what they ate, and perhaps how they got their food.

Some archaeologists are concerned only with early peoples who had not discovered how to write. These are the peoples that we know the least about. But some ancient peoples left written records that tell about their times. Archaeologists may excavate places where such people lived.

Together, archaeologists and historians who can read the writings piece together a picture of the people—the archaeologists study the physical remains, and the historians study the writings.

▶KINDS OF ARCHAEOLOGISTS

When you think of an archaeologist, you may think of a person in a sun helmet who digs up gold and mummies. You may think of someone who works with the Indian arrowheads or pueblos of the southwestern United States. These people are both archaeologists, but each has specialized in something that is of personal interest.

Archaeologists usually decide as students what they want to specialize in. Sometimes it is a particular region or people. They may be interested in the Western Hemisphere—perhaps in the Indians of the American Southwest or the ancient Aztecs of Mexico. They may choose a specialty in the Eastern Hemisphere —the biblical peoples of the Middle East, the ancient Egyptians, or the classical Greeks and Romans. Often archaeologists decide to study a particular time period or a particular problem. The interest may be in the time when people were using stone tools or when people first learned how to plant and grow their own food. Or the archaeologist may be interested in the problem of how cities first began or how writing was invented. Most archaeologists read with interest about what goes on in areas that are not their own.

Of course, there are differences in what archaeologists must study to become specialists in their fields. A classical archaeologist interested in ancient Greece or Rome will study much art history, classical literature, ancient Greek and Latin, and history. Students interested in prehistory (that is, before writing was invented) will spend their time studying methods of excavation and analysis, as well as anthropology. (Anthropology is the science that is concerned with how people developed over the years. It studies the different social customs that existed in the past and those that are present today in various parts of the world.)

▶WHY ARCHAEOLOGY EXISTS

There are many reasons for the existence of archaeology. People have always been curious about how other people lived in the past. They have wanted to know how certain skills and practices developed. For example, how and why did people first start writing, and where did the alphabet come from? When did people start using metal instead of stone to make tools? And how did people begin to develop certain forms of organization—such as kinship and governments? People have been fascinated by such questions for a long time.

Archaeologists can study the way people have behaved over thousands of years. Such a long time range allows archaeologists to see the many similarities between ourselves and the people of long ago. For example, thousands of years ago bread was made from flour that was ground from wheat, mixed with water, and then baked near an open fire. Today we may buy our bread in supermarkets, but it is still made chiefly of flour and water. There are many examples like this. In studying them, we come to understand ourselves and our own problems better.

▶HISTORY OF ARCHAEOLOGY

Archaeology as we know it today is a young science. But for several hundred years people have been interested in digging up the past.

Around 1770, Thomas Jefferson excavated an Indian burial mound in Virginia and carefully wrote down what was contained in the mound. Jefferson was probably the first American digger who could be called scientific. He not only wrote down what was coming out of the ground but also noted the order in which the objects were found. Other people could then read his report and understand what he had found and where. This kind of careful reporting is extremely important in archaeology, but more than 100 years passed before it became the generally accepted thing to do.

Another famous man with an interest in archaeology was Napoleon Bonaparte. When he made his conquering expedition to Egypt, he took along skilled artists and scientists as well as his army. He wanted these people to investigate, record, and draw all the artifacts of ancient Egypt that they could find. He established a place for studying artifacts in Cairo. The objects were meant for the Louvre museum in Paris. But because of an English victory over the French in 1801, the artifacts all went to the British Museum in London.

Both Jefferson and Napoleon were ahead of their time in archaeology. Many important finds were made in the 1800's, but most of them were not recorded as carefully as the finds of these two men. Many people working at this time had no formal training in archaeology. Some were European government officials who were working in foreign countries such as Iraq, India, or Egypt. They became interested in archaeology as a hobby. Some were wealthy people who could afford to organize and conduct their own expeditions. Sometimes these excavations were conducted like fancy picnics—especially in England and

Artifacts left by early people help archaeologists learn more about the past. The Egyptian statue at left shows a baker kneading dough —many people today make bread much the same way. Treasures from the tomb of King Tutankhamen, such as the king's solid gold coffin (*opposite page*), show the wealth of Egypt's pharaohs.

France, where there were many Roman ruins dating from the time when Rome ruled Britain and Gaul. Lovely mosaic floors (made of tiny bits of colored stones), Roman burial grounds, and the ruins of villas were all fascinating to the picnic-diggers. But these people viewed their finds only as pretty or curious objects. They gave little thought to the fact that the objects might be clues to understanding the lives of the people who had made them.

Archaeologists must know the order in which things have come out of the ground and which groups of things were found together. Only then can they accurately reconstruct the scene of life in the past. No detective wants the clues removed from the scene of the crime before they can be studied in their relationship to one another. And no archaeologist can use clues that have been removed and mixed up.

▶CHOOSING A PLACE TO DIG

Archaeology today is not at all what it was at the time of Jefferson, Napoleon, or the picnic-diggers. Archaeologists today choose as students what they want to specialize in. They choose a specific problem to work on and a geographic area where they may find the answers. The area may be Europe, with the beautifully painted caves of southern France and Spain or the Roman ruins of Britain. Or it may be Asia, which holds much biblical material—as well as traces of the first farmers, who lived long before biblical times. In Africa some archaeologists search for signs of the first humans, and others study Egyptian pyramids. In the Western Hemisphere, they investigate the many kinds of American Indians who lived in straw huts, mud houses, or tepees —depending on their part of the country and the tribe to which they belonged. In Mexico an archaeologist can work with the ancient Aztec civilization. And in what are now Guatemala and Yucatán, the Mayans once had an extensive civilization, as did the Incas of Peru.

How an Archaeologist Finds a Site

Once archaeologists have defined the questions they want to answer and chosen the place where they think the answers will be found, they must obtain permission from the government of that country. Next, a **site** must be picked. A site can be any place where people in the past have lived, worked, built something, buried someone, or done anything that

has left a trace. It may be in a cave or in the open. The national museum of the country (or, in the United States, the museum of the state) may make suggestions. It may know of a site that might yield artifacts from the period of time in which the archaeologist is interested. Or perhaps another archaeologist who is interested in a different period has found such a site and will give it up. But usually the archaeologist and the staff must go out and search for a site themselves.

The search may begin with a study of aerial photographs of an area in which the archaeologists are interested. They know that people of long ago had to have water and so probably built their villages along or near banks of rivers. These rivers may still exist today, or there may be simply the dried-up beds of what once were rivers. But the old beds, like the rivers, will show up in a detailed aerial photograph. The archaeologist may decide to start the search for a site near the rivers of the old riverbeds. If so, the team sets out, probably in jeeps if the country is rough.

What Remains at a Site

A mound like those found in the Middle East is a good example of a site. People of long ago generally built their houses of wood, reed, stone, unbaked mud, or mud brick. In heavy rain or wind storms, these houses gradually melted down or fell in. But the houses had been built in a certain place for a reason. The place was close to water or good land or was easy to defend. And as other people came along, they also liked the location and built their houses in the same spot. Houses kept falling in, and people kept building new houses in the same place. Gradually a mound of earth and artifacts rose up above the level of the surrounding ground. The mounds do not look like natural hills. In some cases, if the water supply has remained good, there may still be a village on top of a mound. But usually a change in water supply, an attack by neighbors, or some other mishap drove away the people who lived in a village hundreds or thousands of years ago. All that remains to be seen is a mound itself—an unnatural hump on the landscape.

All the people who lived on these mounds did some digging, perhaps to make a foundation for a new house or to bury garbage. In doing this, they dug up pieces of pottery or tools from the layers of houses below. Then when people no longer lived on the

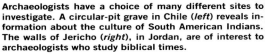
Archaeologists have a choice of many different sites to investigate. A circular-pit grave in Chile (*left*) reveals information about the culture of South American Indians. The walls of Jericho (*right*), in Jordan, are of interest to archaeologists who study biblical times.

mound, nearby farmers came. They plowed the earth for crops, turning it over and mixing it more. Because of all this, a few artifacts from the various layers of the mound worked up to the surface. They lie in the fields and pastures of present-day farmers.

When archaeologists are out looking for a site, they ask farmers whether they have noticed any hills with stray bits of pots and tools. If so, the farmers may take the archaeologists to look at the places where the artifacts were seen. Otherwise, the archaeological team must carefully examine the area in which it is interested, traveling by car, by donkey, and on foot.

Archaeologists seek sites with artifacts that look as though they belonged to the people or the time range that interests them. When some are found, a site is chosen for digging. Part of the archaeologist's training was to come to know the great variety of things that men and women made in the past. Just as you can tell the difference between an automobile made years ago and one made today, so can archae-

ologists recognize broken bits and pieces of artifacts made at different times. For instance, if the people they are interested in had not yet discovered how to harden pottery by baking, the archaeologists will not dig a site that seems to have much baked pottery on the surface. People who made such pottery lived too recently for the period of time being studied.

▶ DIGGING A SITE

After an archaeologist has decided on a site, the excavation is begun. In countries where it is expensive to hire workers, the persons who do the actual digging are usually archaeology students. In other countries, where wages are lower, the archaeologist hires local workers.

The site, whether a cave or a mound, is usually made up of many layers. The people who inhabited the bottom layers were the earliest. The people who lived in the top layers came later. The layers may have been built one right after another, with a new house being constructed as soon as the old one fell down. Or people may have moved

away from the site, leaving it unoccupied until other people settled there some time later. When people lived steadily on a site, one layer is much like the next. Only small changes occur in the shape of pots and tools and in ways of doing things. But in the second case, there may be very great changes from one layer to another. The great changes are caused in part by the longer amount of time between the building of layers, during which people may have discovered different ways of doing things. The changes are also caused by the fact that a different group of people may have moved in, with their own way of doing things. An early group of people may not have known how to bake pottery to make it hard. A later group may have made very good pottery. Thus, small and orderly changes tell an archaeologist that there probably was continual life on the site. But a sharp change in the way things were made or done indicates that there was a gap in living on the site or a strong influence from some outside group. Archaeologists may have to dig through several layers of artifacts before they find any from the period being studied.

Choosing the Most Promising Area To Dig

Once a site is found, archaeologists must decide where to dig. Excavating the whole site would be expensive and unnecessary—the archaeologist can get a good idea of what life at the site was like by carefully choosing places to dig. First, test pits are dug. The test pits may reveal the size of the settlement, interesting buildings, and areas that did not have many houses at all. One deep cut may also be dug into the side of the mound. The side cut shows approximately how many layers are in the site.

How the Digging Is Done

When the test diggings have shown the most promising areas, the archaeologists are finally ready to begin a full excavation. With surveying equipment, they divide the site into smaller units, marked on the ground with stakes and rope. The archaeological team then digs away the soil in the chosen areas. The excavators search the dirt carefully for clues. Sometimes the dirt is sifted through screens to recover small bits of bone and stone. Sometimes it is put in big tanks of water to recover plant material such as small seeds. After all the artifacts and other materials are carefully collected, the dirt goes to a dumping area near the site.

When the soil has been removed from the top of the digging area, the archaeologist begins to see the different layers. Sometimes they are natural layers of mud or clay left by heavy rainstorms. Sometimes they are cultural layers (layers deposited by people)—broken pots left on a floor inside a house, for example. The archaeologist tries to find and uncover each layer.

If archaeologists are excavating a site with many buildings, they may see the outlines of the lower parts of walls. Some walls made of packed mud or mud brick are very much like earth, but they are slightly harder. Careful excavators can feel this extra hardness. Using special small, light picks, they can usually tell by feel what they are hitting—a pot, a skeleton, or the wall of a house. Excavators also have trowels, brushes, and other special tools. They may use very delicate tools, like those of a dentist, to excavate a burial or uncover pieces of burned wood.

If the archaeologist is excavating a settlement with houses, the area inside each room is carefully cleared down to the floor. When this job is done, a whole house may appear or, if the area is large enough, several houses.

When the houses have been cleared, the archaeologist records the layout of the settlement. The staff photographer takes pictures of the houses, perhaps from a high photographic tower. Someone else draws an architect's plan of the houses, which includes careful measurements. Such records must be accurate and complete because once they are made, the walls and floors are cleared away, and this layer is gone forever.

The whole site may be excavated in this way. A representative sample of each layer is carefully dug out and recorded. If time and funds allow, the earliest layer may be reached.

Each of these great archaeological discoveries casts light on an ancient culture. The remains of the city of Machu Picchu, Peru (*opposite page*), hint at the extent of Inca civilization. The ruins of Pompeii (*above right*) reveal details of everyday life in the ancient world. Bakery millstones can be seen in this photograph. The discovery of King Minos' palace at Knossos, Crete (*below right*), provided evidence that Greek legends about Minos were based on fact.

▶THE STAFF AND ITS JOBS

The staff of an archaeological expedition is made up of students and full archaeologists. It must include people with a variety of talents and special knowledge. It needs people to dig and to supervise the digging on the site. It needs people who have specialized in the study of pottery, stone or metal tools, clay figures, and so on. It also needs a photographer and a person skilled in making architectural drawings. There may be a need for someone who can read what was inscribed on ancient tablets, scrolls, or stone, if the site is expected to have such things. There may also be some natural scientists—such as zoologists, geologists, and botanists—whose specialized knowledge is necessary to complete the picture of how people lived in the past. And finally, there is a camp manager, who takes care of bookkeeping, running the household, and supervising the kitchen.

Sorting and Labeling

Every expedition must have special large tents or workrooms where the materials can be cleaned, sorted, labeled, and recorded. Small and delicate objects are taken to this workplace at the end of each day's digging. Other artifacts—like broken pottery, heavy stone objects, or animal bones—may first be cleaned and sorted in a cleared area near the site.

All the material is carefully labeled according to where it was found, and a written description of these finds is made each day. The materials are then carefully put in bags or boxes for further study.

For example, here is what happens to the pieces of broken pottery, called **shards**. The pottery specialist cleans the pieces as well as possible and then studies them to see whether any pieces might fit together to make a whole pot. Next, the unusual pieces are picked out, and the specialist selects enough of the other pieces to make a small sample of the whole pile. These pieces are labeled in waterproof ink to indicate exactly where they were found. They are put aside for further study by the archaeologists at the end of the digging season.

Meanwhile, work on the smaller and more delicate objects goes on in the indoor workroom. The specialists in bone tools, stone or metal tools, clay figures, and the like sort, clean, and label their artifacts. A record is kept of all of these objects, and the particularly interesting ones are drawn and photographed.

▶FINANCING AND FINISHING A SITE

The season of digging goes on until its time runs out. Often this is at the end of summer, when students and teachers must go back to school. In some places, the digging is done in the fall and winter months because the summer is too hot for work. Most archaeologists work for either a museum or a university, and they must do something besides digging and studying what they find. If they are employed by a university, archaeologists are expected to teach some classes and perform other academic duties.

Then, too, there is the problem of money. Archaeologists can dig only so long as funds are available. All the money for an expedition usually does not come from a university or a museum. Part of it may come from wealthy people who are interested in archaeology. Some may come from a foundation. In the

A site is divided into sections, and the excavation team digs away the soil to the desired level (*opposite*). The soil is sifted carefully to recover bits of bone and pottery (*above*). An archaeologist uses a soft brush to expose a find without damaging it (*below*).

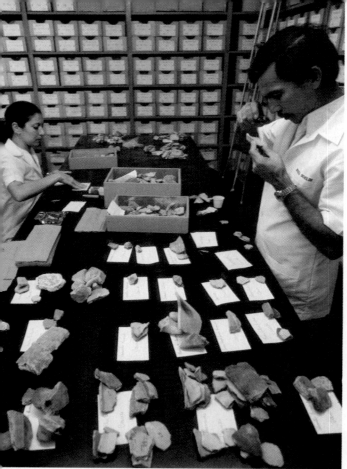

All the objects found at a site—such as these pottery shards—must be cleaned, sorted, and accurately labeled. Then they are stored in boxes for future study.

United States, several large private foundations have special funds for scientific work of various kinds. The United States Government also has such a foundation. Well-trained archaeologists who present carefully prepared and worthwhile research designs, or plans, may get money from one or more foundations. But because an expedition is very expensive, the money is usually spent quickly.

Because archaeologists have other work to do and because it is not always easy to obtain the necessary money, digging seasons are seldom long. An expedition that lasts as long as nine months will probably dig only every three or four years. Many archaeologists dig each year, but for just two or three months. Sometimes archaeologists can finish digging a site in the time allowed. But more often the team must go back again in the next digging season. Some large, complex sites have been dug for many seasons and are still not finished.

When the digging is finished, the team must check all the records, drawings, photographs, and notes to be sure there is a complete set for use in the final study. If the team is working in a foreign country, the director of the country's museum will list all those artifacts that the expedition may keep. Each country has its own laws. Some national museums claim most of the artifacts an expedition finds but allow the archaeologists to borrow some to study at home. Archaeologists never know until the last minute which artifacts they will be allowed to keep—if any at all. For this reason, the records must be thorough if they are to complete their study.

When the archaeologist learns what may be kept, the fragile objects are wrapped in soft tissue or cotton wool, and everything is packed in large crates. If the archaeologist intends to go back to the same area, the house or tent equipment is stored nearby. The expedition is then ready to return home and begin the long study of what has been found.

▶ STUDYING ARCHAEOLOGICAL EVIDENCE

The excavation is only the first part of an archaeologist's work. At the site, the archaeologist mainly gathers information. After the excavation, the archaeologist must analyze and interpret the finds.

During this period of study, the archaeologist really begins to find out what life was like in the time being investigated. Drawings on pieces of pottery may show the kinds of clothing the people wore. If they lived before the time of pottery, a bone needle may show that they sewed skins together for clothing or had some sort of woven fabric of wool or flax. Two kinds of rubbing stones probably mean that they knew how to grind wheat into flour.

Other Scientists Aid the Archaeologist

The natural scientists mentioned before are very important in this final study of artifacts. Some of the artifacts will be pieces of grain or impressions of pieces of grain in floors. It is also likely that there will be many pieces of animal bone, with some made into needles, spoons, and beads.

Botanists who are experienced in this sort of work study the plant remains—often charred seeds or their impressions (if the seeds have disintegrated). They can tell what kinds of plants grew in the area, what kinds of food the people ate, and whether they grew the food themselves. If there are impressions of a fabric, the botanist can sometimes tell whether it was a vegetable fabric (like cotton or linen) and if so, what sort of plant was used.

The zoologist examines the bones to find out what kinds of animals lived in the area. These findings are compared with the findings of the botanist. Together, they can reconstruct a picture of what the natural environment was like at the time being studied. The zoologist can suggest which animals the people ate and whether they kept cows, sheep, and goats. If there are impressions of a fabric that was made of animal hair, the zoologist can tell what animal the hair came from.

The geologist identifies the main kinds of stones that the people used to make tools and ornaments. Some of these stones may come from places far away. The archaeologists then know that the people they are studying either traded or traveled over long distances for this material. The geologist's work is also important in understanding many aspects of the ancient environment.

If archaeologists use the information that the natural scientists supply, they will learn a great deal about the people being studied. Botanists and zoologists, along with geologists, can even tell how many trees and animals there may have been. They can tell what the weather was like from evidence such as tree rings. And there are many other things they can deduce about the countryside in ancient times.

Using all the information, archaeologists finally write reports or books describing the investigations. These reports let other people know what has been learned. The report of one archaeologist can help others with a problem. Suppose, for example, that archaeologists discover an object that cannot be identified. Through reading, they may learn that someone else has found a similar object under circumstances that made it clear how the object was used. In one case, archaeologists had found a certain kind of flint blade. They were unable to determine its use. Finally, some of the blades were found set into handles. Archaeologists realized that the blades formed part of a sickle or scythe. Possibilities like this make it very important for all archaeologists to publish their findings. Only through co-operation can the fullest picture of life long ago be formed.

▶DATING A SITE

How do archaeologists go about finding the dates of the people being studied? There are many ways. But it is important to remember that dates given for times before writing was common are approximations. The approximations may be bolstered by the newest scientific methods, but archaeologists cannot be sure that they are exact.

An archaeologist works on a mammoth skull. The bones of animals can be used to reconstruct extinct creatures. They can also help archaeologists determine what the natural environment was like at the time being studied.

Dating by Comparison

Comparing a site with others is the oldest and most commonly used method for dating. The material that has been discovered may be similar to that found in other sites already dated. This suggests an approximate date for the new find. There are several reasons why the date can only be approximate. For one thing, different styles of decorating pottery or making tools lasted for different amounts of time in different places. So it is not certain that the two sets of artifacts were made at the same time. In ancient days, ideas spread slowly. They were carried from one village to another by merchants. This means, for example, that people did not learn to make the same kind of pottery at the same time. One group learned first. Later, the idea spread to another group.

Archaeologists study how the ways of making and decorating things developed through time. It does not surprise them that a carpenter's saw from Colonial Williamsburg, in Virginia, is a much cruder tool than a saw now sold in hardware stores. You yourself could easily tell which was the older and which the newer of the two saws.

Dating by Scientific Methods

Many different scientific methods are available to archaeologists. At the excavation, they cannot use laboratory equipment for dating. But they can take many samples to send to laboratories for analysis. These samples must be taken carefully if the results of the analysis are to be useful in dating.

Perhaps the most common samples taken by archaeologists are carbon-14 samples. All living things receive a set amount of radioactive carbon (carbon-14, or C-14) from the outer atmosphere. When a plant or animal dies, the carbon-14 begins to leave it at a known rate. Scientists can measure—in a machine called a counter—the amount of radioactive carbon left in any artifact made of material that was once alive (such as wood, grain, and bone). Then, by figuring backward, they can set an approximate date for the artifact. Scientists are working to make the carbon-14 method more exact. But it is useful even now for comparing objects less than 50,000 years old with other objects that have also been dated by the carbon-14 method.

The potassium-argon method is another way of dating with radioactivity. This method can be used only when the site has been covered with volcanic rock soon after people lived on it, because the date represents the time when the volcanic rock cooled. Radioactive changes turn potassium into argon over a very long time. Therefore, archaeologists can use this method only when studying very ancient fossils from sites covered with volcanic rock. The potassium-argon method could not be used,

By comparing similar objects from different countries, archaeologists can see how two cultures advanced. The gold stag from Scythia (*left*) dates from the late 7th century B.C. The jade stag (*right*) was carved in China during the Chou Dynasty (about 1028–256 B.C.).

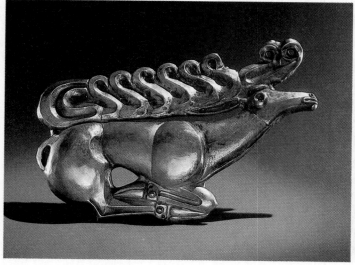

The flint blade below, along with others like it, was excavated at Jarmo, Iraq. It could not be identified, but was saved by archaeologists (see box at right). Later, finds from other sites, such as a fresco from an Egyptian tomb (above), revealed that the blades were used to cut grain.

for example, to date a recent site like Pompeii, which was covered with lava in A.D. 79.

Counting tree rings is another method of dating. If wood was used in building houses and it has not rotted away, its rings may be very useful in estimating the age of the wood, as well as the weather in the area over a period of time. Tree rings grow wide or narrow, depending on each year's weather. Based on the comparison of bands of many trees, a master chart is made. It shows the weather for every year in a particular region. When a piece of wood from an ancient site in the region is found, its pattern of bands can be matched against the master chart. In this way an archaeologist can tell when the wood was cut and first used.

The study of pollen grains provides another way of dating. The kinds of trees and shrubs that grow in a particular area change over long periods of time. Scientists drill into the ground, or into a lake bottom, using long, hollow metal tubes. They bring up cylinders, or cores, of material that contain pollen grains from ancient vegetation. Then they study the pollen grains from the different levels in a core. This gives an overall picture of the kinds of plant life that grew in the area and what changes in climate occurred.

In dating an ancient site, scientists analyze the kinds of pollen grains found there. Comparing these grains with grains in the overall picture of the area, as recorded in a master chart, provides a clue to the age of the site.

Still another method of dating depends on the study of magnetic particles in clay. These particles line up with the earth's magnetic field, like millions of tiny compasses. Scientists know that the earth's magnetic field has shifted many times in the past, and they know when these shifts took place. During such a shift, the magnetic particles in the clay also shift, re-aligning themselves with the new direction of the earth's magnetic field.

But this re-alignment does not occur in clay that has been heated to a very high tem-

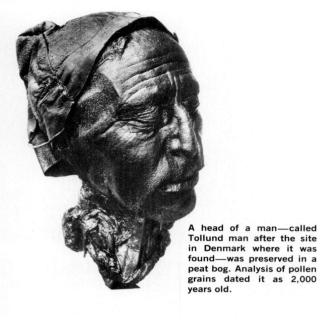

A head of a man—called Tollund man after the site in Denmark where it was found—was preserved in a peat bog. Analysis of pollen grains dated it as 2,000 years old.

perature. The magnetic particles in the floor of an ancient clay oven, for example, are fixed in the pattern that they had when the oven was first fired. By comparing this pattern with the known shifts in the magnetic field, scientists can calculate the age of the oven.

Using these various methods of dating, an archaeologist can get a fairly good idea of when a certain people lived. And scientists are working on still other ways to help the archaeologist date materials.

Archaeology, as a scientific profession, is relatively new. There are many problems in human development and human history yet to be solved. But the methods by which they can be solved are becoming more scientific.

Even so, each problem that is solved often raises new problems, and new ways of solving these need to be found. The radioactive-dating methods were not even dreamed of until the late 1940's. And it is probably that future years will bring other new and important changes for archaeology.

▶THE TRAINING OF AN ARCHAEOLOGIST

As archaeology changed from a hobby and a picnic sport to a scientific profession, more and more importance was laid on the training of archaeologists. In particular, an archaeologist must know how to define an important problem. An archaeologist does not go out and dig just anywhere for the pleasure of discovering artifacts. There must be a purpose—an archaeological problem that needs solving.

It takes many years of hard work to become an archaeologist. The training may begin as early as high school. Young people who are interested in archaeology should realize that both a college and a graduate degree are needed. It may be necessary to read and speak several foreign languages, depending on where the students wish to work. Many important reports are published in French and German. Future archaeologists start one of these modern languages in high school. Latin and Greek are necessary if one is interested in classical archaeology. Students may also learn to type, and they may study mechanical drawing.

It is best to start with a well-planned liberal arts course. Students should learn to express ideas in writing easily and well, so that they can prepare clear and interesting reports. Particularly useful for students of prehistory are courses in geology, geography, botany, and zoology, to help them understand the natural environment. They need at least one year each of chemistry, physics, and biology so that they can understand methods for dating and the information the natural scientists will supply later on. In college, the students continue with foreign languages. They may try to learn the languages of the countries in which they are interested so that they can talk with workers there. They may also study ancient scripts such as Sumerian, Akkadian, or Egyptian, if they are interested in these periods. Finally, the archaeologist should have a good foundation in anthropology, history, and art history.

The Archaeologist Studies Anthropology

A study of anthropology helps the archaeologist to see how other peoples are different from ourselves. What is important to us may not matter at all to someone who lives in a different part of the world or has a different cultural background. Certainly the objects used in daily life in Arctic regions differ from those used near the equator. Archaeologists must realize that people today, like those in the past, do not necessarily all think and behave in exactly the same ways. Through anthropology, students of archaeology can learn how different peoples live and feel and think about things. This is very important because archaeologists depend heavily on their understanding of the present when they reconstruct how people lived in the past.

The Archaeologist Studies Recorded History

In the same way, an archaeology student needs to learn as much history as possible, especially the history of the chosen area. Usually we think of history as coming from the writings of an earlier people themselves. But these people probably did not describe everything they did, or how they lived, or what their countryside looked like. In ancient times—before the invention of paper, pens, and pencils—writing was difficult. Only a few scribes wrote what the priests and kings told them to write. These people may have left us only descriptions of battles, hymns to the gods, and a few business letters. Nevertheless, interesting ideas did slip in, and the archaeology student must learn as much as possible about these writings. From what the people wrote of themselves (and from the knowledge gained through anthropological training), the archaeologist forms a better picture of their lives. These writings may also show what the ancient people took to be good or bad, useful or worthless. All this helps archaeologists understand what they find.

For example, archaeologists study Greek writings about foreign trade carried on by ships. Now suppose that an archaeologist, working as a skin diver, discovers the underwater wreck of a Greek trading ship. The description of the ship can be recorded as well as the type of cargo. The direction in which the ship was headed may also be deduced. Such discoveries add much to Greek history as recorded by the Greeks themselves.

The Archaeologist Studies Art History

Most of the artifacts an archaeologist finds are everyday tools and objects. But occasionally, some art objects may be found—things that must have had special value to the people who owned them. This is why the study of art history is important. Greek vases and Egyptian tomb paintings, for example, often have wonderful pictures of Greeks or Egyptians doing all kinds of things. In the pictures, they are actually using many of the tools, weapons, and objects that the archaeologist finds.

Rounding Out the Training

On their own, archaeology students can learn much by trying to do things as ancient people did. For example, they can try to chip stone into a rough tool and use it to cut a small log. Or they can take wet clay, make a simple pottery bowl, dry it in the sun, and then bake it over an open fire.

During the summers, archaeology students will probably work on one of the digs that most large universities run. This gives them a chance to learn how digging should be done.

After college the archaeology student usually enters a graduate school to work toward a doctoral degree.

Archaeologists may find work with a university or museum after graduate school. After working with older and more experienced archaeologists on their digs, the young archaeologists may eventually have digs of their own and their own students working with them.

ROBERT J. BRAIDWOOD
GRETEL BRAIDWOOD MANASEK
University of Chicago

Reviewed by MAGGIE DITTEMORE
University of Chicago

See also ANTHROPOLOGY; PREHISTORIC PEOPLE; RADIOACTIVE DATING.

A diver lifts an amphora (vase) from the wreck of a Roman ship that sank some 1,900 years ago off the coast of Turkey. Such discoveries add to recorded history.

ARCHERY

People have been shooting bows and arrows for at least 20,000 years. Some famous paintings of archers are at least that old. These paintings, showing people hunting huge deer and bison with bows and arrows, were found on cave walls in France and Spain.

In the earliest days people depended on hunting for food and clothing. American Indian people were still hunting with the bow in the late 1800's. Even today there are people in the jungles of South America and Africa who rely on their skill in archery to obtain some of their food. For many centuries the bow was a weapon of war, and nations rose and fell because of it.

Archery is a sport enjoyed by people everywhere. It may surprise you to learn that many hunters today pursue deer, bear, and other animals with bows and arrows. These archers are called bowhunters. Most archers, though, shoot at targets of various kinds. Many schools, playgrounds, parks, camps, and organizations such as the Boy Scouts and Girl Scouts have archery programs in which young people are taught to shoot the bow and arrow.

In the United States, the National Archery Association sponsors the Junior Olympic Archery Development (JOAD) program, in which thousands of boys and girls are enrolled. American archery winners in recent Olympic Games started their training in the JOAD program.

Whether you shoot in the backyard or anywhere else, remember this: Used properly, bows and arrows are not dangerous. But you must be careful. You should never handle bows and arrows as if they were toys. Handled improperly, bows and arrows can be dangerous instruments.

▶ SHOOTING

If you have never shot a bow and arrow, it is best to get some instruction. This is provided by schools, clubs, and other organizations. Sporting goods and archery stores often will teach you the first steps or provide booklets on the subject.

When you are learning to shoot, stand sideways to the target and about 10 feet (3 meters) from it. If you are right-handed, hold your bow in your left hand. Left-handed archers should hold the bow in the right hand. Grip

Shooting an arrow

1. In nocking the arrow, place the nock of the arrow about ⅛ inch (3 millimeters) above the center of the bowstring.

2. Stand sideways to the target, with your bow arm straight out. The arrow is on the arrow rest. Do not grip the bow too tightly.

3. Draw the bowstring back until it is against your jaw. Look through the bowsight, concentrating on the target.

the bow's handle firmly, but not too tightly. use the same sort of grip you would employ if you were picking up a suitcase.

Place the arrow's slotted plastic **nock** (the string notch at the end of the arrow) about ⅛ inch (3 millimeters) above the center of the bowstring's length. Most archers make a little knot of thread there so they can place the arrow at the same spot for every shot. Now place your three middle fingers on the string, bending them at the first joint of each finger, with the nock between the index and middle fingers. Do not clamp down on the nock with your fingers. Simply hold it firmly.

Place the forward part of the arrow on the shelf above the bow's handle. If you are right-handed, this means on the left side of the bow.

Now you are ready to draw back the string. As you start to do this, push your left arm out in front of you. Draw the string straight back to your face. Do not twist your fingers around the string. Bring your fingers to the corner of your mouth. Look at the target. If the target is close, as it should be when you are learning, make sure your left arm is pointed below the bull's-eye. If you are shooting from about 30 to 40 feet (9 to 12 meters), your left hand should be pointed directly at the bull's-eye. The farther back you go, the higher you will need to hold your left hand.

When you think your hand is properly aimed—and you will need to shoot a few arrows before you are certain—let the arrow go by simply opening your string fingers and pulling them back slightly. Follow through—that is, keep that position until the arrow strikes the target.

▶ EQUIPMENT

Most bows now used by young people are made of layers of fiberglass and wood. Such bows are called **composite,** or **laminated,** bows. Many beginning archers, however, use bows made entirely of fiberglass, which are sturdy and almost impossible to break. Bows of wood are also available, but they do not stand up as well.

Almost every bow is graded according to weight. But the number that you see written on a bow does not give the weight of the bow. It stands for the amount of force needed to pull back the string. Young archers usually shoot bows that are between 15 and 30 pounds (6.8 and 13.6 kilograms). Many adults, but very

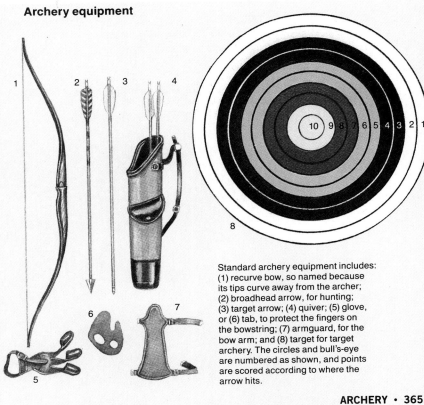

4. Let the arrow go by opening your string fingers, pulling them back slightly. Keep this position until the arrow strikes the target.

Archery equipment

Standard archery equipment includes: (1) recurve bow, so named because its tips curve away from the archer; (2) broadhead arrow, for hunting; (3) target arrow; (4) quiver; (5) glove, or (6) tab, to protect the fingers on the bowstring; (7) armguard, for the bow arm; and (8) target for target archery. The circles and bull's-eye are numbered as shown, and points are scored according to where the arrow hits.

few young people, use the **compound bow.** In a compound bow, the bowstring is passed through a series of pulleys to enable the archer to draw, or pull back, the string more easily.

Most arrows are made of fragrant Port Orford Cedar from Oregon. But many experts prefer arrows made of aluminum tubing or fiberglass. Turkey feathers are generally used for the **fletching** (feathers on an arrow). Most arrows have steel points, but hunters shoot arrows with sharp-bladed tips called **broadheads.** These should only be used for hunting.

All archers should wear a leather or plastic armguard. This is worn on the arm above the hand in which the bow is held. Its purpose is to prevent the string from hitting or slapping the arm. All archers wear a three-fingered glove or a piece of leather called a **tab** on the fingers used to draw back the bowstring. Arrows are carried in a leather **quiver,** worn at the archer's side or on the back.

Many adult archers, and an increasing number of young archers, use a **bow sight** for greater accuracy in shooting. A bow sight is attached above the bow's handle. The position of the bow sight can be adjusted. Looking through the bow sight, the archer lines up the sighting marker (called the ''reticle,'' or ''bead'') with the center of the target.

▶GAMES, ROUNDS, TARGETS

Two basic forms of archery have long been popular—target archery and field archery.

In target archery you shoot most often at a 48-inch (122-centimeter) target. It has five rings—gold, red, blue, black, and white—each divided into two scoring areas. The center area of the gold circle counts 10 points, and the rest of the ring counts 9. The two scoring areas in the red ring count 8 and 7 points, in the blue ring 6 and 5, in the black ring 4 and 3, and in the white ring 2 and 1.

You always shoot six arrows in a series, or **end,** and then score them. An archery match is called a **round.** For young archers, a round consists of 4 to 24 ends (24 to 144 arrows) shot at distances as short as 20 yards (18 meters) and as long as 60 yards (55 meters). The National Archery Association in Colorado Springs, Colorado, sends information about rounds to young people all over the world.

In field archery the targets are smaller and are usually black and white. The bull's-eye and the ring next to it count 5 points. The third and outer rings count 3 points. Targets are set up in the woods at different distances and four arrows are shot at each.

Field archery clubs in the United States, Canada, Australia, and many other countries shoot under the rules of the National Field Archery Association, which has headquarters in Redlands, California. Parks, schools, and camps have other games and rounds that will help you sharpen your skill.

WILLIAM STUMP
Author, *Archery Handbook*

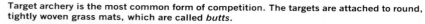

Target archery is the most common form of competition. The targets are attached to round, tightly woven grass mats, which are called *butts*.

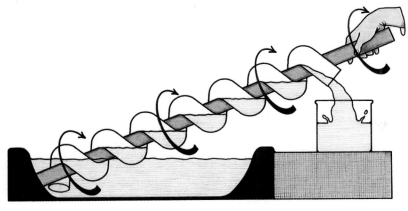

One of Archimedes' many clever inventions is the water screw. As it turns, water is scooped into the lower end and moves upward through the coils. You can make this simple device with a few feet of flexible tubing, a sturdy rod such as a broomstick, and some cloth tape to hold the top and bottom ends of the tubing in place.

ARCHIMEDES (287?–212 B.C.)

"Give me a place to stand, and I can move the world." The man who is supposed to have spoken those words was Archimedes, a Greek mathematician and inventor who lived some 2,200 years ago. It was not an idle boast. Archimedes was one of the first people to develop the science of mechanics. He understood that a person with a mechanical device such as a lever could move many times his or her own weight. Challenged by the king to prove his point, Archimedes did so. He arranged a device that allowed the king to move a large ship all by himself.

Archimedes was born about 287 B.C., in Syracuse, a Greek settlement on the island of Sicily. Little is known about his personal life except that his father was an astronomer and may have been related to the king of Syracuse. Also, at some time in his life, Archimedes studied in Alexandria, Egypt, a center of Greek culture.

Archimedes is best known for his many inventions. Among other things, he invented a compound pulley; a sphere that imitated the motions of the heavenly bodies; and a water screw to raise water. He himself most valued his work in mathematics and scientific theory. But his fame rests on inventions and the legends that grew up around him.

One legend tells how Archimedes made his most important discovery. The king, it seems, had ordered a new crown. It was supposed to be made of solid gold, but the king suspected the jeweler of cheating. He asked Archimedes to tell him if the crown was solid gold.

At first Archimedes could not think how to do this. Then one day the answer came to him as he was getting into his bath. Legend has it that he rushed naked into the streets shouting, "Eureka [I have found it]!"

What had happened was very simple. The bath was full, and it overflowed as Archimedes climbed into it. This started him thinking about the way objects displace water. And he suddenly saw how to solve his problem.

First he took a quantity of gold and a quantity of silver, each equal in weight to the crown. The weights of gold and silver were equal, but their volumes were not. The silver, being less dense, was bulkier than the gold.

Next Archimedes took two vessels filled to the brim with water. He placed the gold in one and the silver in the other. The silver, being bulkier, caused more water to overflow. Archimedes concluded that when a solid sinks in water, it displaces its own volume of water.

Finally he tested the crown against the equal weight of gold. When placed in water, the crown caused more overflow. Therefore, the crown had to contain metal other than gold. This metal made it bulkier and caused the greater overflow.

Further experiments resulted in what is now known as Archimedes' principle: An object in a fluid is buoyed up by a force equal to the weight of the displaced fluid.

When Archimedes was an old man, the Romans attacked Syracuse. He turned his creative mind to defense and invented several weapons that held off the enemy. It is claimed that he built a huge system of mirrors that burned Roman ships by concentrating the sun's rays on them. Syracuse, however, was defeated in 212 B.C., and Archimedes was killed. The story goes that he was drawing mathematical figures in the sand when a Roman soldier struck him down. But Archimedes was so highly respected that the Roman commander buried him with full honors.

JOHN S. BOWMAN
Author, *Prehistory and Early Civilization*

ARCHITECTURE

Architecture is the art of building. Unlike sculpture, painting, or music, it is an art that has a practical basis. Each building serves a definite and special purpose. People living in different ways have developed different styles of architecture to suit their special needs.

Every age demands its own style of architecture, for buildings must suit the way of life of the people who use them. We are living in an exciting period of this art, a time of great experimentation. New engineering techniques and new materials are making possible buildings that never could have been built before.

The American architect Frank Lloyd Wright proposed a building 1 mile (1.6 kilometers) high. R. Buckminster Fuller, an American engineer and designer, suggested the possibility of making a kind of roof, or dome, big enough to cover a whole city or even a region. By using such a dome, he thought, we could control climate and make frozen lands or deserts into livable places. For the most part, these plans are still dreams. But skyscrapers have been built that reach heights of over one quarter of a mile (0.4 kilometer). During your lifetime you will see other kinds of buildings designed for new ways of living.

Every day we move in and out of buildings designed to suit the way we live—our homes, schools, the stores where we shop. We take these buildings for granted, but just like the factories and office buildings necessary to industry, and the courthouses, city halls, and post offices necessary to government, they reflect the life of our times. Airports and railroad stations fulfill the needs of modern systems of transportation. Towering skyscrapers accommodate the vast numbers of people who work and live in our large cities.

Architecture is an art. But as every picture is not a work of art, neither is every building. To create real architecture the architect—the designer of the building—must succeed in

When designing a building, an architect considers its setting and function and the needs of the people who will use it. Top: The upward sweep of the U.S. Air Force Academy chapel recalls traditional church spires and expresses the building's spiritual function. Center: The dream of owning one's own home is fulfilled for many people by functional, affordable houses such as these. Bottom: The thin, sliding walls of a Japanese home are opened in fine weather, allowing indoors and outdoors to become one.

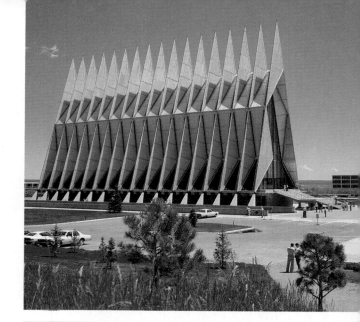

Right: An indoor shopping mall in Toronto, Canada, provides both an attractive setting for shoppers and the convenience of year-round climate control. Below right: The sail-like shells of the Sydney Opera House, Australia, unite the building with its site in the harbor and also hide its high stage and scenery loft. Bottom: Where land is available, a low, sprawling building is the most useful shape for a manufacturing plant. Below left: In crowded cities like Chicago, where land to build on is limited, buildings soar upward to gain space.

The remains of the great hall of the Temple of Amon-Re still stand at Karnak, Egypt. The hall had 134 huge stone columns, the tallest of which were 69 feet (21 meters) high.

certain ways. First, the practical requirements of the building must be met. It must be strong, of sound construction, and suitable to its function. It must also be satisfying to look at. The different parts of a building must be in harmony with each other. Much of the beauty of architecture comes from its proportions—the balance of size and shape of its parts. An architect has to be an artist and a technician.

Construction is a science. The various possible ways to build a structure have been worked out by experiment. Builders of the past had to discover the nature of materials—which ones were strong and which were weak. They had to find out how much weight a material could bear and whether it would resist sun and rain. They had to learn from experience how to hold materials together. The development of architecture has been a long, long process.

▶THE EARLIEST ARCHITECTURE

At first, people lived in caves. Then, experimenting with whatever material they could find—wood, mud, stone, plants—they started to build homes to protect themselves and their families from weather and danger.

Building was much easier after people learned what could be done with mud. Formed into cubes, cylinders, and many other shapes, mud could be dried in the sun or baked in a

fire to make a hard, strong building material. And mud was easy to repair and was durable.

The first builders learned that round or oval buildings were the simplest kind to construct. All they needed to do was lay stones of nearly equal size in a circle or oval on the ground, using enough mud for mortar. Mortar can be made of many materials—sand, straw, or pebbles mixed with mud or clay. Its purpose is to bind together stones or bricks in a strong and lasting way.

Early builders also used wood for roofs and supporting posts. But wood easily catches fire, so important buildings meant to be permanent were often built of stone. The first great stone buildings were probably made in Egypt.

▶EGYPTIAN TOMBS AND TEMPLES

The ancient Egyptians believed that their kings, called pharaohs, were gods. This belief

This article discusses the development of architecture throughout history. The architecture of individual countries is surveyed in numerous articles, such as UNITED STATES, ART AND ARCHITECTURE OF. See also the names of periods and styles of architecture, such as GOTHIC ART AND ARCHITECTURE. Biographies of architects Philip Johnson, Le Corbusier, Ludwig Mies van der Rohe, I. M. Pei, Louis Sullivan, Christopher Wren, and Frank Lloyd Wright can be found in the appropriate volumes of this encyclopedia.

affected their architecture. The pharaohs' palaces were used only during their lifetimes. The palaces did not have to be sturdy. They could be made of mud brick. But a pharaoh's tomb would be used forever. It had to withstand time and weather. For their eternal homes, therefore, the pharaohs built great pyramids of stone. These tombs are still standing after 5,000 years.

The first pyramid was build around 2700 B.C. Built in the form of six great steps, it was about as high as a 20-story building. This step pyramid was the tomb of King Zoser and was built by the architect Imhotep. This is the earliest record we have of both architect and client. Nothing had ever before been built on so large a scale.

The pyramids were surrounded by small rectangular buildings called **mastabas.** These were the tombs of court officials. A sloping passage connected each pyramid with the riverbank, where there were temples in honor of the kings.

Egyptian Temples

The pharaohs built many temples to the gods during the New Kingdom (1580–1100 B.C.). A good example is one at Karnak, where there is a series of temples built and rebuilt over a period of 1,200 years, from 1550 to 323 B.C.

Egyptian temples were surrounded by a high wall. There was one great gate, placed between two towers called **pylons.** The statue of the god was placed at the back of the temple, and approaching it must have been a dramatic and awe-inspiring experience. The few worshipers who were allowed inside went from large, light courtyards through ever smaller and darker rooms until they reached the last one, where the god's face was lighted by only a tiny shaft of light. The massive walls were about 25 feet (8 meters) thick. Many huge stone columns supported the ceilings of the large halls. Walls and columns were often decorated with designs carved into the surface of the stone and brightly painted.

▶MESOPOTAMIAN ARCHITECTURE

While the Egyptians were building pyramids and temples of stone, the people living between the Tigris and Euphrates rivers (the area called Mesopotamia) were building towns and temples of mud brick and reeds. There

was little timber and stone in Mesopotamia. The people often covered the outsides of buildings with glazed tiles. The glazes were made from the same ingredients as glass, melted at a high heat and fused with the bricks to make a hard, shiny surface.

Houses were built in a row on a street and had only one entrance on the street side. The rooms were arranged around an open central courtyard and the windows looked into it. There were usually no windows at all on the outside street walls.

Ziggurats

Because the Mesopotamians lived on a flat plain, high places came to have a religious meaning to them. Therefore they built their temples, called **ziggurats,** to look like miniature mountains. On a huge foundation they added terrace after terrace, each one smaller than the one beneath, until the top of the mountain was reached. These terraces were made of solid brick. On the very top of the ziggurat was a small building for the use of the god. The outside walls of the ziggurat were covered with glazed and molded brick. But the ziggurats have not lasted as well as the stone temples of Egypt. When the glazed exterior bricks were destroyed, the sun-dried bricks crumpled into a great dusty mound.

▶ASSYRIAN PALACES

Temples and towns much like those of the Mesopotamians were in use for several thousand years. Then, about 1200 B.C., a new nation of builders, the Assyrians, came into Mesopotamia. They built royal palaces of brick, decorated with stone carved and painted with scenes of court life. Our knowledge of their architecture is from these carved pictures, for most of the palaces were destroyed by wars.

▶PERSIAN PALACES

In the 6th and 5th centuries B.C., the Persians built great cities. One of the most famous is Persepolis, begun by King Darius I about 500 B.C. and continued by Xerxes I. This city was really one gigantic royal palace. Built on the plain on a huge stone foundation, it could be seen from a great distance. Everything about the palace was planned to impress people with the grandeur of the Persian ruler. A great flight of steps led up to the entrance. Of the many large rooms in the palace, the greatest was the throne room. It was an impressive sight, its flat roof held up by 100 very tall, slender stone columns. The capitals of these columns were carved in the shape of the heads of horses and bulls.

Persepolis is important not only for its size and beauty but also for its influence on the architecture of other countries.

▶MINOAN PALACES

The Minoans, who lived on the island of Crete, in the Mediterranean Sea, were a seafaring people. By 2000 B.C. the Minoan kings had such strong navies that they were able to build unfortified palaces, and to consider comfort and elegance rather than safety.

The great palace of Knossos, which was built over a long period of time, covered about 4 acres (1.6 hectares). It was built around a large courtyard. Each wing of the palace was about 400 feet (120 meters) long and at least two stories high. Each had a special use. The rooms included a shrine for the god-king, his living quarters, and the quarters of the queen.

The Lion Gate, in the ancient city of Mycenae, is an example of post-and-lintel construction, in which two upright posts support a horizontal beam, or lintel.

All parts of the palace were connected by a very complicated system of passageways and stairs.

The pleasure-loving Minoan court lived in luxurious and cheerful surroundings. Large windows let sunlight into the rooms. Floors were covered with gypsum, a mineral that has a satinlike sheen, and walls were painted with brightly colored pictures. The elegant palace at Knossos was destroyed about 1400 B.C., but we do not know whether by fire, earthquake, or enemy invasion. No one ever returned to live there again, and the ruins became a great grass-covered mound. The palace was not discovered until the 20th century, when Sir Arthur Evans, an English archaeologist, dug it out and reconstructed it.

▶GREEK ARCHITECTURE

About the time that Knossos was destroyed, a new civilization with different ideas about architecture was developing on the Greek mainland. Because inland cities needed strong fortifications, the Greeks from very early times built their cities on hills.

The city of Mycenae, built about 1300 B.C., was surrounded by massive stone walls. The gates of the city were set back in the walls so that attackers would be caught in a small space. Only the foundations of the houses remain, but the Mycenae gate is still standing. Built about 1250 B.C., it is a fine example of **post-and-lintel** construction.

In post-and-lintel construction, a pair of upright posts supports a horizontal beam called a lintel. It is one of the basic kinds of construction and is used for doors, windows, or the entire frame of a building. The stone posts of the Mycenae gate support a gigantic stone lintel. One piece of stone is 16 feet (5 meters) long and 8 feet (2.4 meters) wide.

The highest area of a Greek city was called the **acropolis.** In each city the acropolis came to represent two ideas: safety and a sacred area for the gods. If a king needed a big house, it followed that a god needed a bigger one. So temples were the largest buildings and were placed in the center of a city.

Greek architects wanted the proportions and the shapes of their buildings to be clearly visible. Egyptian temples were most often placed so that only the front could be seen and the viewer was not able to tell the building's size or shape. But the Parthenon, the great temple

The Parthenon, the most famous of all Greek temples, was built in the Doric style in the 5th century B.C. It was dedicated to the goddess Athena, patron of the city of Athens.

of the goddess Athena in Athens, is so placed that when Greeks entered the great gate of the acropolis, they saw the corner and two sides of the building. At one glance they knew exactly what its shape and dimensions were.

Although the Greeks built many kinds of buildings, the most important to them, and to later ages, was the temple. Almost always rectangular, the temples were built on a foundation of stone. Three or more steps led up to the temple, and the outside walls were surrounded by columns. Inside the columns was a walk that led all around the **cella,** or inner chamber. The cella was often divided into two parts that did not open into each other, but only to the outside. In one room was a statue of the god, in the other the god's treasures. The most famous of all Greek temples is the Parthenon, built in the middle of the 5th century B.C. by the architects Ictinus and Callicrates. Built of marble, its perfect and graceful shape dominated the Athens acropolis. It was decorated with magnificent sculpture that was brightly painted.

The Architectural Orders and New Techniques

Among the great contributions the Greeks made to architecture were the orders, developed from the post and lintel. The orders are styles for a column and its parts (shaft, capital, and usually a base) and the entablature (architrave, frieze, and cornice) that it supports. There were three Greek orders—**Doric, Ionic, and Corinthian.** Later the Romans and others added more, and the orders have been used in architecture ever since.

Architectural ideas and new methods of construction often spring from the discovery of new materials. Wooden posts and lintels, sun-dried brick, and cut stone all played their parts in the development of architecture. When people began to use metal, a further change occurred.

By using molten metal the Greeks learned how to bind a horizontal line of stones together. They cut T-shaped slots into the top edge of each stone opposite a similar slot in the next stone. This made an H shape into which they poured molten lead. When the lead hardened, the stones were held firmly together. Later iron was added to the lead.

For buildings too wide to roof in stone, the Greeks used cut timber to make a truss for the roof. A truss is really a triangle made by two slanting rafters meeting at the top and held by a tie beam at the bottom side of the triangle. The Greeks covered the truss with clay tiles baked at a high heat.

▶ROMAN ARCHITECTURE

Because the Greeks were fighting disastrous wars among themselves toward the end of the 5th century B.C., they had little time to develop new ideas in architecture. But in Italy the Romans began to build a great city filled with enormous public buildings. An acropolis and an **agora** (marketplace) had been the main open spaces of the Greek cities. In Rome the chief feature was a **forum** (public square). The Romans introduced their architecture into the many countries they conquered. Towns and cities all around the Mediterranean were built according to Roman designs.

Every Roman city had at least one forum, and the great cities, like Rome, often had many. In the forum were the temples, law courts, senate house, and other public buildings. The market area was usually alongside the forum.

The great buildings of Rome were not only complicated feats of engineering and planning but were beautiful as well. The Romans made their buildings suit their functions. They used different plans for temples, markets, theaters, palaces, amphitheaters, and public baths.

The Arch and Vault

The Roman masons, who were very skillful in using brick and stone, developed a roof form called the **arch and vault.** An arch is made by using wedge-shaped stones, later called **voussoirs,** placed with the narrow end on the inside of the arch, the wide end on the outside. An arch may be round, pointed, or a combination of these. It may be used as an entrance, repeated along a wall as decoration, or used to support a heavy roof.

A connected series of arches built one behind the other forms a **barrel** or **tunnel vault.** When two barrel vaults intersect, they form a **groined vault.** Roman engineers mastered the problem of roofing wide areas by using great arched vaults supported on piers (pillars). In the Basilica of Constantine (built about A.D. 300), they were able to roof an open space 75 feet (23 meters) wide.

Roman engineers also succeeded in building **domes.** Domes are really a development of the arch. A dome can take many shapes, but it is basically like a teacup put upside down over an open circle. In one of the largest Roman temples, the Pantheon, the dome spans an opening of 142 feet (43 meters).

▶EARLY CHURCH ARCHITECTURE

The Emperor Constantine made Christianity the official religion of the state in A.D. 326. This meant that many churches were required in a very short time.

Christian worship demanded a style of architecture very different from the religious architecture of Greece and Rome. Temples had served as a house for the god, a storehouse for treasures, and as a background for outdoor ceremonies. Christians worshiped together inside their churches. Therefore the builders of the first churches adopted the design not of temples, but of the Roman public halls called **basilicas.** The basilica plan provided the open space necessary for Christian worshipers to gather and windows to light the interior. Many churches are still built in this style today.

The plan of the basilica is a rectangle divided lengthwise into three parts. The widest part in the center is called the **nave.** On either side of the nave are two aisles, which are usually not as high as the nave. A line of columns divides the nave on either side from the aisles and supports the upper walls of the nave, known as the **clerestory.** The church is lighted by windows cut into the walls of the side aisles and into the clerestory. At one end of the building is a semicircular projection called an **apse.**

The exteriors of the first basilica churches were usually simple and undecorated; it was the inside that was important. To focus attention on the altar, which was the center of the rites, the builders placed it toward the end of the long, low building. The lines of columns seem to march toward the altar, leading the eye of the worshiper to the most important place. As church architecture developed, every part of the church came to have a special function, even the decoration. Sculpture, mosaics, or wall paintings were intended to teach the Bible stories.

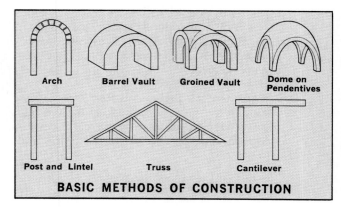

Arch | Barrel Vault | Groined Vault | Dome on Pendentives

Post and Lintel | Truss | Cantilever

BASIC METHODS OF CONSTRUCTION

▶BYZANTINE CHURCHES

Barbarian invasions weakened the Roman Empire. In 410, Rome itself fell to invaders from the North, and Roman traditions died out in the West. But for eleven centuries a civilization based on Greek and Roman ideas was kept alive in what remained of the empire in the East. The capital of the Eastern Empire was the rich city of Constantinople (now Istanbul, Turkey), on the shores of the Bosporus. The city had once been called Byzantium, and Byzantine is the name that we give to the architecture that developed in this area.

Byzantine churches were usually built in the form of a Greek cross, a cross with four equal arms. Domes made of brick and mortar were the most common form of roof, and Byzantine architects became expert in making them. They learned how to raise a round dome over a square space. They did this by means of **pendentives,** triangular forms with curved sides that look as though they were cut out of a ball. Pendentives are built up from the corners of the square space. The base of the dome rests on their uppermost edges.

The interiors of Byzantine churches were richly decorated with colored marble and with bands of lacy stone carving. Walls and domes were often covered with brilliant mosaics—designs and pictures made of pieces of colored glass stuck into plaster.

The greatest church in the Byzantine style is Hagia Sophia, in Istanbul. It was begun by the Emperor Justinian in 532. The dome of this church, which is covered with gold mosaics, is one of the most magnificent ever made. A person standing beneath it feels a sense of great open space. The light falling from windows cut in the bottom of the dome casts a shimmering light throughout the church.

The Byzantine style spread to Greece, Russia, and finally through Venice to western Europe.

▶THE DAWN OF WESTERN ARCHITECTURE

The year 800 is usually considered the beginning of Western architecture. In that year, in Rome, Charlemagne was crowned emperor of the Holy Roman Empire. This empire covered much of Europe. The event was important to architecture because Charlemagne wanted to revive the glory of the old Roman Empire. On his way back and forth between

The domed cathedral Hagia Sophia, built in the 6th century, is a triumph of Byzantine architecture. Numerous windows fill the richly decorated interior with light.

Aachen, his German capital, and Rome, he visited Ravenna, where he saw Byzantine buildings. In Nîmes, in the South of France, he saw a Roman temple and amphitheater. All the lessons that Charlemagne learned from Rome and Byzantium were applied on a simpler scale in his own lands. Although most of these buildings were destroyed, we know about them from excavations and old records. At Aachen he built an eight-sided domed chapel and a large palace. Compared to the buildings of ancient Rome, Charlemagne's chapel was crudely made, for over the centuries techniques of construction had been forgotten.

▶ROMANESQUE ARCHITECTURE

About the year 1000 a revival of building began in Europe. All the buildings built between 1000 and 1200 bear the general name **Romanesque.** They all have certain characteristics in common, such as thick walls, small windows, round arches, short, thick columns, and a heavy and massive appearance. But there is great variety in different countries and even within each country. The greatest amount of building was done in France, and there every section of the country had its own local style of church.

During the Romanesque era the simple basilica plan was made more elaborate. To provide more altars, chapels were built off the side aisles and the apse. A semicircular aisle called an **ambulatory** was placed between the apse and its chapels. **Transepts** were extended on either side of the nave to make the church into the shape of a cross. Architects began to make the main facade of the church into an important architectural feature. The doors were placed inside arches, and these arches were covered with carved decoration. Towers were raised on either side of the entrance. By the end of the 11th century, most churches also had a tower above the crossing of nave and transepts.

The Development of Rib Vaulting

Architects had learned that a long, rectangular building could be roofed with a barrel vault, a groined vault, or a series of domes. But the masons in France were not satisfied with any of these systems, for the buildings were too heavy, low, and dark. By experimenting they learned how to push up the center of the roof to make a pointed vault. To do

this the interior of the church was divided into rectangles of nearly equal size. Next a wooden centering (a temporary wooden support) in the shape of a pointed vault was built to hold the stones in place until the mortar set.

The great achievement of the architects of the Romanesque era was the development of rib vaulting for ceilings.

To make a **rib vault,** architects divided the nave of the church into rectangles. They used a pier at each of the four corners of the rectangle and constructed ribs to a central point. The ribs supported a thin web of ceiling, but the real weight of the roof was carried down the ribs and through the piers into the ground.

At first there were four ribs for each vault. But this arrangement was too heavy, and in France a vault with six, rather than four, ribs made possible a higher, lighter, and more beautiful vault. As architects became more skillful the vaults were divided into more and more parts, and the ribs were decorated with carving. Together with the six-part vault, the French architects used a pointed arch that made the building higher than the old, round arch.

The French church builders also began to use a new type of **buttress.** A buttress is a support to strengthen the walls of the building by receiving the thrust from the vaulting. At first buttresses were built flat against the walls. The new kind was called a **flying buttress,** because it arched away from the outside of the church. The flying buttress pushed in against the walls and balanced the weight of the roof, which pushed out.

▶GOTHIC ARCHITECTURE

By 1150 the masons and architects in northern France had discovered three building techniques that they combined to form a new style called **Gothic:** the rib vault, the pointed arch, and the flying buttress. All these building methods aided the architects in building higher and higher churches and in stressing the vertical line in the design. Steeply slanting roofs, pinnacles crowning the flying buttresses, slender spires, all make the Gothic churches look as though they are reaching into heaven.

Cathedrals

Large churches called cathedrals were built in the cities where bishops had their thrones. In France, Spain, Italy, Germany, and En-

The Cathedral of Notre Dame in Paris was built between 1163 and 1250. Its high walls are supported by flying buttresses, an important element of Gothic architecture.

gland, masons made the roofs of these great churches higher and higher and the walls thinner. This meant that a great deal of engineering and machinery was necessary. It also made possible large windows that, filled with stained glass, flooded the churches with color.

During the Romanesque and Gothic eras, masons and architects traveling from one job to another spread the new ideas and building techniques. This led to a kind of international style of building in Europe. However, there was still a great deal of local variety.

In England the churches were longer and lower than in France. Some of the most important cathedrals there are those at Canterbury, Lincoln, and Salisbury. In Spain and Germany the Gothic style was also important. But in Italy many architects continued to use designs inspired by buildings of the ancient Roman Empire.

Monasteries

At the same time that churches and cathedrals were rising in the towns and cities monasteries were being built in the countryside. Because of the different kinds of buildings needed by the religious orders, the monasteries were almost like towns. There was a church, a dormitory where the monks slept, a kitchen, a guesthouse for visitors, an infirmary for the sick, and a writing room. An important feature of monastic architecture was the **cloister,** a covered passage built around an open court. There the monks could walk sheltered from the sun and rain.

Castles

During the Middle Ages people lived in houses or castles. Castles were built to be safe and strong. Little was done to make them comfortable to live in. Some castles were just outposts to house a garrison of soldiers, but others were the homes of knights and their families.

Castles were so strongly built that they seldom fell to attackers except through treachery or after a long siege. But the owners of the castles were always at war with each other. As towns grew up and local wars decreased, a new style of architecture was developed to fit a new way of living.

▶RENAISSANCE AND POST-RENAISSANCE ARCHITECTURE

The **Renaissance** began about 1400 in Italy, in the city of Florence. Renaissance means rebirth. Throughout Europe there was a rebirth of interest in the art and literature of ancient

Greece and Rome. In architecture there was a rebirth of interest in the ancient Roman ruins so common in Italy. For 500 years beautiful buildings were built in the Renaissance style: palaces for kings, large houses for nobles and rich merchants, town halls, law courts, marketplaces, theaters, and churches. The main characteristics of these buildings are order and balance. The architect Leon Battista Alberti (1404–72) described the Renaissance idea of beauty in a building. Alberti wrote that beauty came from "the harmony and concord of all the parts achieved in such a manner that nothing could be added or taken away or altered except for the worse."

Renaissance architects used few new methods of construction or new materials, but they had many new ideas about what a building should be. Many of them published their theories in books that are still useful. One of the most important ideas was that people should feel their full size in a building.

Italy

During the 15th century an architect named Brunelleschi (1377–1446) designed the first Renaissance buildings in Florence. The very first was the Hospital of the Innocents, for orphans. This building is different from most of those that had been built before. When people looked at a Gothic cathedral, their eyes wandered from one part to another. They saw the parts of the building separately. Brunelleschi's building is meant to be seen as a whole. The facade has a series of delicate columns that support graceful arches. On the second floor, square windows are placed above the arches. Instead of a feeling of great weight, there is a feeling of lightness. People could feel important here, not small and weak as they might feel in a medieval building.

Brunelleschi designed the church of Santo Spirito around squares and according to a mathematical pattern. When people step into the church, they can tell that the nave is twice as high as it is wide and that the ground floor and the clerestory are the same height. The theory of beauty based on arithmetic was carried further by other architects in Italy.

Italian Renaissance Palaces. An important Renaissance contribution to architecture was made in the design of palaces. The palaces built in Florence in the 15th century were constructed of great blocks of stone. The facades

were generally divided into equal sections and were usually three stories high. The proportions were based on the proportions of a human being—a supposedly ideal division into two dimensions: foot to waist and waist to head. These proportions were so popular that they were used in buildings throughout Europe and the Americas.

St. Peter's. In 1506, Pope Julius II asked an architect named Donato Bramante to rebuild the church of St. Peter, in Rome, which was badly in need of repair. The foundation of what was to become an entirely new church was laid in the same year. Many of the great artists of the 16th and 17th centuries contributed to the design of St. Peter's. Raphael, Peruzzi, the Sangallos, and Michelangelo were the most important of these artists. The immense dome that dominates the building was designed by Michelangelo, who modeled it after the dome in Florence that had been designed by Brunelleschi. Higher than a football field is long, the dome of St. Peter's is supported by only four gigantic piers. The church and its magnificent dome is one of the greatest achievements of the Renaissance.

France

The new Renaissance style begun in Italy rapidly spread north over the Alps. One reason why this happened was that masons, architects, and clients traveled. Also, at the end of the 15th and at the beginning of the 16th centuries, several kings of France went to Italy to try to conquer part of that country. Their wars were unsuccessful, but they liked the new style of architecture and persuaded Italian architects to work for them in France.

Châteaux. King Francis I of France (ruled 1515–47) built large palaces called **châteaux** that were influenced by Italian designs. Usually built near the Loire River, these châteaux served as residences for the court, which traveled from one part of the country to another. A major difference between French and Italian Renaissance buildings was that the French continued to use some Gothic forms, such as steep roofs.

During the 16th century not only the king and nobles but also well-to-do members of the middle class built châteaux in France. Many of these people also built large houses in the towns, where they carried on their business in comfortable and handsome surroundings.

The palace of Versailles, in France, was built in the last half of the 17th century. The splendor of its many rooms reflects the wealth and power of the French kings.

The Palace of Versailles. In the last half of the 17th century, Louis XIV, king of France, built a huge palace outside Paris, in the village of Versailles. The palace is so large that 5,000 people were able to live in it. It is over one quarter of a mile (0.4 kilometer) long. It was meant to impress everyone who saw it with the power of France. Other European kings tried to imitate the palace, but none was able to build on such a grand scale.

England

The 16th century was a period of great building activity in England. Some of the most important structures were large country houses. These houses reflected ideas brought back to England by English people who had traveled to the Low Countries (now Holland and Belgium), to France, to Germany, and to northern Italy, especially Venice.

But the Renaissance style came later to England than to other countries. The earliest part of Hampton Court Palace, which was begun about 1520, is still medieval in style. But when a new wing was added, toward the end of the 17th century, it was built in the Renaissance style.

In 1616, Inigo Jones (1573–1652) designed an important house at Greenwich for the queen. It was one of the first times in England that a small private house was built for an important person. A significant feature was that the rooms were arranged so that the queen was able to have more privacy than in her palace. Designed in the form of a bridge, the queen's house is two stories high and has a road running between the two ground-floor wings. On the second floor the wings are joined together by a large room. The house was imitated all over England, and engravings and plans were taken to the English colonies in North America, where they were much copied.

St. Paul's Cathedral. Sir Christopher Wren was one of the greatest English architects. After the Great Fire of London, in 1666, which destroyed much of the city, he set about rebuilding the churches. Wren designed 52 new churches, which are known for their simplicity and the ingenious designs of their different steeples. Architects in the English colonies in America were very much influenced by these churches, and they imitated the style.

The most magnificent of all the buildings designed by Wren is St. Paul's Cathedral, in London. Its dome is a masterpiece of calculation and construction.

The Karlskirche, in Vienna, is an excellent example of Baroque architecture. Its twisted columns and ornate decoration were meant to convey drama and movement.

▶BAROQUE ARCHITECTURE

During the wars and revolutions in 17th-century Europe, many buildings were destroyed. But a surprising number of new ones were built. Many of the buildings designed during this unsettled period are in a new style called **baroque.** The main characteristic of baroque architecture is movement. Architects wanted their buildings to be exciting and to give the impression of activity. They did this by making dramatic contrasts of light and shadow and by using curved shapes. To give the illusion of movement to the exterior of buildings, they made the facades of the buildings curve, as an S does. Light striking these curves makes them appear to move.

Architects tried to outdo each other in using new and dramatic shapes. They designed col-umns, arches, and vaults that were more and more elaborate than the Renaissance forms on which they were based. For example, instead of straight columns they often used twisted ones. The interiors of baroque churches are decorated with fantastic shapes modeled out of stucco and stone and often painted and gilded. Domes and ceilings are painted with clouds and flying figures of angels. If you look up at these ceilings, you get the illusion that there is no roof and that you are looking right up into the sky. The baroque style was most popular in Austria, Germany, Italy, and Spain.

▶THE PALLADIAN STYLE IN ENGLAND AND THE UNITED STATES

The works of some architects have had a great influence, either while they were living or after they died. Such an architect was Andrea Palladio (1508–80), of Vicenza, in Italy. Palladio's buildings tended to be symmetrical and sometimes identical when seen from any of their four sides. If you were to draw a cross through the center of a Palladian plan, you would, generally, end up with four identical quarter plans. Palladio not only built beautiful country houses near Venice but he published his designs and wrote about them. In 1715, more than 100 years after Palladio's death, his designs were published in England. A young Englishman, Richard Boyle, earl of Burlington, saw these designs and was so pleased with them that he went to Italy to look at the houses. With him he took an architect named William Kent to study Palladio's houses on the spot. When they returned to England, Burlington and Kent made the Palladian style very popular. Following Palladio's work they designed spacious, well-arranged houses with simple exteriors.

In the middle of the 18th century the Palladian style was also popular in the English colonies, especially in Virginia and throughout the South. Plantation houses like Westover, built about 1730 on the James River, were Palladian adaptations in brick. When he rebuilt Mount Vernon, George Washington used the Palladian style.

Thomas Jefferson, the third president of the United States, was an architect as well as a statesman. He thought that the new republic should have a suitable style of architecture. While Jefferson was the American minister to

France in the late 18th century, he visited Nîmes. Like Charlemagne, who had been there 1,000 years before, Jefferson admired the Roman temple called the Maison Carrée. The temple was actually built later, but Jefferson probably thought that it had been built during the time of the Roman Republic, whose laws he admired. He had a model of the temple made and sent it back to Virginia, and so the state capitol in Richmond came to look like a Roman temple.

▶ THE 19TH CENTURY

Architects soon began to imitate building styles besides those of ancient Rome. In Europe and America, buildings were designed in the styles of ancient Greece and Egypt and of the Middle Ages. In the early years of the Renaissance, architects had copied earlier styles too, but in a very different way. The difference came from two important changes. In the 1800's, for the first time in centuries, new building materials were available. And new kinds of buildings—such as factories, railroad stations, and high office buildings— were needed. The new materials included cast iron, steel, reinforced concrete, and large sheets of glass. Toward the end of the 1800's, young architects rebelled at using the styles of the past for these new materials and buildings.

The Beginning of a Modern Style

One of the first buildings in a modern style was built in the United States by the architect Louis Sullivan (1865–1924). It was the Guaranty Building, in Buffalo, New York, built in 1894. It had a steel frame. On the upper floors, which house offices, the windows are all alike to show that similar work is done in all of them. The roof projects on all sides so that a person can see exactly where the top of the building is. Sullivan believed that a building should show how it is constructed. "Form follows function," he said. This means that the shape, or form, of a building must contribute to its usefulness, or function. Sullivan did not try to hide the fact that his office buildings were constructed on a steel frame. Other architects were combining the new steel-frame construction with the old styles.

Reviewed by PETER BLAKE, A.I.A.
Former Managing Editor, *Architectural Forum*

The Villa Rotunda (*left*), a country house in Vicenza, Italy, was built by the Renaissance architect Palladio. The Palladian style influenced later architects, including Thomas Jefferson, who designed the Rotunda of the University of Virginia (*right*).

The 20th century is one of the greatest periods in the history of architecture. It brought a revolution in the design of buildings that has seldom, if ever, been matched in earlier times. Twentieth century architecture can be divided into three periods, separated by the two world wars.

Before World War I

Between 1900 and 1914 a few architects broke decisively with traditional architectural styles and ways of planning interior spaces. The Austrian architect Adolph Loos (1870–1933) helped influence the course of contemporary architecture. Loos wrote an essay, *Ornament and Crime* (1908), in which he proclaimed that architectural ornamentation of any kind is immoral in modern society. Ornament had always been a major part of architectural design. After Loos, it was not.

The break with tradition was made possible in part by improvements in building materials. In Germany, Walter Gropius (1883–1969) designed the Fagus Shoe Last Factory (1911), using products of new technology—especially steel, plate glass, and reinforced concrete. Concrete, reinforced with wire mesh or steel rods, is a very strong material. Used as a floor slab, it will support itself even if extended beyond the posts that hold it up. Gropius took advantage of this characteristic. He did away

with the usual corner post and replaced it with panes of glass that were held in place by thin pieces of steel. The result was a building that seemed to weigh very little—even to float.

In the Chicago area, Frank Lloyd Wright (1869–1959) experimented with new possibilities for interior spaces. Wright disliked the boxlike rooms of most houses. He therefore used fewer partitions between rooms. In this way, the whole interior seemed to flow together into one large, continuous space. Most of his designs, such as the Robie House (1909) in Chicago, had long, low silhouettes that were in harmony with the flat Midwestern landscape.

Between World War I and World War II

After World War I, the rebellion against tradition resulted in the development of a new architectural style. This style was marked by simple, geometric lines and the use of concrete, steel, and large areas of glass. The lead-

Below: Falling Water, a house designed by Frank Lloyd Wright, seems to become a part of the surrounding landscape. Right: The Seagram Building, designed by Ludwig Mies van der Rohe and Philip Johnson, rises behind the courtyard of Lever House in New York City. Its simple, boxlike shape is typical of the international style.

The chapel Notre Dame du Haut at Ronchamp, France, designed by Le Corbusier in 1950, pointed the way to new concrete forms. Its unusual curving shape has the expressiveness of sculpture.

ers of its development were Gropius, Le Corbusier, and Mies van der Rohe. In the 1930's, architectural historians gave the name **international style** to the movement.

Gropius founded a design school, called the Bauhaus, located in Weimar, Germany. He wanted to train a new generation of designers who were well informed about many fields of art. He felt that machine technology required a certain kind of rational design that used pure geometric shapes and smooth surfaces. In 1926, Gropius designed a new building to house the school in Dessau. The flat-roofed building was arranged in a pinwheel plan. The design expressed the different activities taking place inside by the different treatments given the five major parts of the building. The workshops, which needed a great deal of light, had glass walls. The office and classroom blocks had smaller windows set in white stucco walls.

The most important architect in France after World War I was Swiss-born Charles Édouard Jeanneret (1887–1965), who took the name Le Corbusier. In 1923 he published a book called *Towards a New Architecture*, which became a basic source of the modern movement. Le Corbusier sought to set standards for modern architectural design based on those developed for cars, airplanes, and ocean liners. He

felt that engineers had a better understanding of how to use modern materials than did architects.

In 1925, Le Corbusier produced a plan for Paris that involved tearing down much of the old city (but leaving certain historical buildings) and erecting great steel and glass towers, widely separated by gardens and highways. This vision of urban renewal was not carried out. But it became the source for most housing projects involving tall buildings.

In the late 1920's, Le Corbusier designed a series of houses, the most famous of which is the Savoye House, at Poissy-sur-Seine, near Paris. This rectangular stucco house is raised up on thin pillars, called **pilotis.** It appears to hover over the field in which it was built. Long, thin windows light the interior.

The third founder of the new style was the German-born American architect Ludwig Mies van der Rohe (1886–1969). He used glass extensively in buildings with precise, angular lines. He expressed his design principles in the saying "Less is more." The architecture of Mies van der Rohe is often considered the most elegant of the 20th century.

In the late 1930's, some architects began to use heavier materials such as stone and brick, often in combination with steel, glass, and concrete. The Kaufmann House (1937–39) at

Bear Run, Pennsylvania—designed by Frank Lloyd Wright—is one of the most impressive of the houses designed in this period. Called Falling Water, the house extends out from a rocky slope and hovers over a waterfall. Its reinforced concrete platforms, or "trays," form a dramatic composition that blends architecture and landscape.

After World War II

After World War II almost the whole world came to embrace the international style. The masters of the style, each moving in a new direction, took the lead in the immediate postwar years. Gradually, architecture began to move away from the boxlike severity of the years between the wars.

Le Corbusier expanded the use of reinforced concrete. In the late 1940's, he designed the Unité d'Habitation, a big apartment building in the French city of Marseilles. He put the building on thick concrete legs instead of thin stilts. He made the entire structure of reinforced concrete, which was left rough to show the marks of the wooden boards that held the wet concrete in place while it dried. On top of the building he placed large concrete ventilators that look like big pieces of sculpture.

But the building that really pointed the way to new concrete forms was Le Corbusier's chapel Notre Dame du Haut at Ronchamp, France, designed in 1950. Its boldly curved

After 1950, concrete continued to be used to create bold, expressive forms. Above: Frank Lloyd Wright used a revolutionary spiral design for the Guggenheim Museum, in New York City. Below: Y-shaped buttresses support the thin concrete vault of the Little Sports Palace in Rome, designed by Pier Luigi Nervi.

roof is made of a thin shell of reinforced concrete held together by concrete struts, like the metal struts inside the wing of an airplane.

In the early 1950's, Mies van der Rohe designed the Lake Shore Drive Apartments in Chicago. These were among the first big rectangular steel and glass towers. They set a standard for the steel and glass commercial buildings that came to dominate the skylines of cities all over the world during the great postwar building boom. A notable example is the 38-story Seagram Building (1956–58) in New York City, designed by Mies and Philip Johnson (1906–   ).The metal parts on the outside are bronze, and the glass is tinted gray. Because Mies was looking for general solutions that would fit almost any problem, he could design apartment and office buildings that are almost identical.

The Finnish architect Alvar Aalto (1898–1976) came to occupy a very important place in world architecture in the postwar years. Aalto moved away from the international style to develop buildings in which people would feel at ease. His buildings featured open, skylit spaces, curving lines, and natural materials such as pale birch wood. The best known of his designs were civic buildings constructed in Europe. Aalto's buildings often have unexpected shapes. These shapes reflect the purposes that the buildings serve. Baker Hall (1948), a dormitory at the Massachusetts Insti-

Above left: Alvar Aalto designed this stadium for the Polytechnial School in Otaniemi, Finland. Above right: Citicorp, in New York City, has energy-efficient double-glass and aluminum walls. Its slanted roof, which faces south, was designed to hold solar collectors.

I. M. Pei used the triangle—considered the most stable structural form—as the basic element in his design for the East Wing of the National Gallery of Art in Washington, D.C.

tute of Technology in Boston, is an example. The dormitory has a curved facade facing the Charles River to give every room a view of the water. The other side, facing the campus, is angular. It reflects the lounges, staircases, and bathrooms inside and is in keeping with the shapes of buildings nearby.

The differences among the types of buildings designed by Corbusier, Mies van der Rohe, and Aalto set the stage for the incredibly varied architecture of the years after 1950. The uses of reinforced concrete continued to expand dramatically. Thin concrete vaults spanned enormous spaces, especially in the stadiums and arenas designed by the Italian architect Pier Luigi Nervi (1891–1979). Concrete was also used to create bold, expressive forms, such as the Trans World Airways terminal at Kennedy International Airport in New York City, designed by Eero Saarinen (1910–61). Other examples are the sail-like vaults of the Sydney Opera House, in Sydney, Australia, designed by the Danish architect Joern Utzon (1918–   ), and Frank Lloyd Wright's spiral design for the Guggenheim Museum in New York City.

Concrete was also used by Louis I. Kahn (1901–74), an important architect working in the 1950's and 1960's. His design for the Salk Institute for Biological Studies in La Jolla,

California, used concrete piers and a concrete truss system. This created large, open laboratory spaces, in which scientists could arrange their equipment in any way they wished. Above each laboratory floor is a floor that does nothing but hold all the mechanical equipment for the laboratories below. Each scientist also has a private study that looks out onto a quiet interior court and has a view of the Pacific Ocean.

Two other important architects of the period were Edward Durell Stone (1902–78) of the United States and Oscar Niemeyer (1907–   ) of Brazil. Stone's best-known buildings include the Museum of Modern Art in New York City and the John F. Kennedy Center for the Performing Arts in Washington, D.C. Niemeyer was the chief architect of Brasília, the new capital city of Brazil constructed during the 1950's.

Beginning in the 1950's, some architects broke completely with the simplicity that was the mark of the international style. This movement is known as **postmodernism.** In 1966, Robert Venturi (1925–   ) published a book called *Complexity and Contradiction in Architecture*. He was dissatisfied with the bland, repetitive look of many modern buildings. Architecture, he argued, should be complex and filled with contradictions, as is life itself.

Recent Trends in Architecture

Architects have developed as many new ways to use steel and glass as they have concrete. R. Buckminster Fuller (1895–1983) designed what he called geodesic domes with very light steel rods, put together in triangles. These can be covered with thin sheets of glass or plastic to keep the rain out. Fuller even designed a geodesic dome that, if built, would cover the whole of Manhattan Island in New York City.

The triangle is considered the most stable structural form. It can also be one of the most beautiful forms, as shown in I.M. Pei's design for the East building of the National Gallery of Art (1978) in Washington, D.C. Pei used the triangle as the basic form of his design and repeated it in skylights, courtyards, and other details.

One of the most spectacular of the recent steel and glass buildings is the Georges Pompidou National Center for Art and Culture in Paris. This building, also known as the Beaubourg, opened in 1977. It was designed ten years earlier by Renzo Piano and Richard Rogers. The front is dominated by an escalator, enclosed in a glass and steel tube, that moves visitors up to all the floors through the thin steel struts that form the structural system.

The Georges Pompidou Center has given new life to an old part of Paris, just as the remodeling of the 19th-century Quincy Markets has done for an old part of Boston. Both projects deal successfully with the important issue of bringing the centers of old cities back to life.

Early in the 1900's architects talked of destroying the architecture of the past. During the 1950's many cities, particularly in the United States, undertook urban renewal programs. Many older buildings were destroyed to make way for blocks of high-rise buildings. Today, architects want to preserve older buildings that are of historic importance and make them useful once again—or to design new buildings so that they fit comfortably with the old. Architects also have shown a renewed interest in adapting styles of the past. For example, many postmodernists have added classically inspired ornamentation to their buildings.

In the 25 years immediately following World War II, most buildings were designed with little thought to energy conservation.

The Humana Building, in Louisville, Kentucky, was designed by Michael Graves. The ornamentation on the building's exterior is characteristic of postmodernism.

Then, in the 1970's, it became more apparent than ever before that fuel resources were limited. People wanted homes, offices, and public buildings that used fuel economically. Architects turned toward designs that include using solar energy and better insulating materials. There was also a renewed emphasis on relating new structures to their environment.

EUGENE J. JOHNSON
Williams College

See also ANCIENT WORLD, ART OF THE; BAROQUE ART AND ARCHITECTURE; BUILDING CONSTRUCTION; BYZANTINE ART AND ARCHITECTURE; CATHEDRALS; GOTHIC ART AND ARCHITECTURE; GREECE, ART AND ARCHITECTURE OF; ISLAMIC ART AND ARCHITECTURE; RENAISSANCE ART AND ARCHITECTURE; ROMANESQUE ART AND ARCHITECTURE.

ARCTIC

Surrounding the geographic North Pole is a deep, ice-covered ocean, the Arctic Ocean, which is bordered by the northern parts of the continents of North America, Europe, and Asia. This is the Arctic region. Here, periods of continuous daylight alternate with periods of continuous darkness for days to months at a time. Cold pervades the region. But unlike the southern polar region of Antarctica, which has no native human inhabitants, people have lived in the Arctic for thousands of years. Because of its location, its geography and climate, and its wealth of natural resources, the Arctic region is politically, scientifically, and economically important.

The boundaries of the Arctic region are measured in different ways. The Arctic is sometimes defined as the area north of the Arctic Circle, an imaginary line around the globe at 66° 30′ (66 degrees, 30 minutes) north latitude. Other ways of determining the region's limits include the tree line, the most northerly point at which trees will grow, and the extent of polar sea ice and of permafrost, or land that is permanently frozen.

▶GEOGRAPHY OF THE ARCTIC

The Arctic is dominated by the Arctic Ocean and a vast treeless plain called the tundra. Unlike Antarctica, which is an ice-covered continent, much of the Arctic consists of ice-covered seas.

The Arctic Ocean. The Arctic Ocean, which covers approximately 5 million square miles (13 million square kilometers), makes up about two thirds of the Arctic region. East of the island of Greenland, the Arctic Ocean connects with the Atlantic Ocean. West of Greenland the Arctic flows through Baffin Bay, Davis Strait, and shallow outlets between the northern islands of Canada. The Arctic Ocean joins the Pacific Ocean through the Bering Strait, which separates Alaska from what is now northeastern Russia (formerly part of the Soviet Union). Although its extent varies from summer to winter, ice covers the Arctic Ocean year-round, making navigation frequently difficult and dangerous. From October to June the ocean is completely ice-locked, and only submarines can cross it completely by passing under the ice. At times, icebergs, which break off the ends of glaciers, float south into the shipping lanes of the Atlantic Ocean and create hazards to navigation.

The Tundra. The tundra begins on the land area of the Arctic about where the tree line ends. When the summer sun melts the ice and snow cover, the Arctic tundra becomes a rich green living carpet of plants. But beneath a thin layer of soil lies ground that is always frozen. This permafrost forms whenever the temperature of the ground stays continuously

The frozen Arctic Ocean (*far left*) dominates the Arctic region. The people of the Arctic have survived in their harsh environment by developing simple but useful equipment, such as the dog sled (*center*). When the summer sun melts its covering of ice, the tundra (*left*) blooms with plants and flowers.

below the freezing point, 32° F (0° C), for two or more years. Most of Greenland, much of Alaska, half of Canada, and parts of Scandinavia, Russia, Mongolia, and Northeast China are affected by permafrost. Its greatest recorded thickness—4,900 feet (1,500 meters) —is in Siberia.

Not all of the land in the Arctic region is covered by the tundra. Rocky, mountainous islands quite different from the flat tundra are scattered around the Arctic Ocean. Greenland is almost completely covered by a large ice sheet, with mountains ringing its coast.

See the article TUNDRA in Volume T.

▶CLIMATE

Although low temperatures are the major characteristic of its climate, the Arctic is not always bitterly cold. During the summer, temperatures over the Arctic Ocean are near 32° F (0° C). Winter temperatures, however, average between −22° and −31° F (−30° to −35°C). It is colder over land areas, especially over the Greenland ice sheet, where a winter temperature of −87° F (−66° C) has been recorded. In the subarctic, a region just south of the Arctic, winters are colder but summers are warmer. The lowest temperature ever recorded here was −90° F (about −68° C) in Siberia.

Like Antarctica, the Arctic receives little precipitation (rain or snow). The generally low temperatures limit the amount of moisture that can be held in the air and consequently the amount of snow that will fall. In March and April, when the greatest amount of snow covers the ground, the average depth in the Arctic is 8 to 20 inches (20 to 50 centimeters). The snow, however, remains for 10 months of the year.

The Arctic year is divided into a long, cold winter and a short, cool summer. Because of its geographical position, the Arctic is marked by long periods of darkness and daylight. At the North Pole the sun remains above the horizon for six months at a time and below the horizon for another six months, giving in effect six months of daylight, followed by six months of darkness.

▶PLANT AND ANIMAL LIFE

Plants and animals are plentiful in the Arctic. More than 90 types of plants grow not far from the North Pole. Closer to the Arctic Circle scientists have identified 450 varieties of plant life. In summer the tundra is covered with flowers and various plants, including lichens, mosses, grasses, and small shrubs. More than a hundred types of birds live in the Arctic. Musk oxen, caribou, reindeer, foxes, wolves, bears (including polar bears), valuable fur-bearing animals such as ermine and sable, snowshoe hares, and lemmings (small, mouselike animals) thrive in the region. The Arctic waters are rich in fish, including salmon, cod, and rockfish, and many kinds of seals, whales, and porpoises.

▶ARCTIC PEOPLES

The Arctic has been populated by small groups of people for thousands of years. They probably followed herds of reindeer, caribou, and musk oxen from Central Asia northward and eventually adapted to the environment. One of the most widespread peoples in the region are the Inuit, commonly called Eskimos. They are found in Alaska and Canada, as well as Greenland and Siberia. Indians also live in some areas of the North American Arctic region, especially in Alaska and Canada. For more information on the Inuit, see the article ESKIMOS (INUIT) in Volume E.

Perhaps the best-known people of the European Arctic region are the Lapps, who live in the northern areas of Finland, Norway, and Sweden and in parts of Russia. Many Lapps still follow their traditional ways of life as hunters and reindeer herders. But as the Arctic is increasingly exploited for its natural resources, they are being trained for more settled occupations, such as farming and mining. For more information on the Lapps, see the article LAPLAND in Volume L.

In Siberia, in the Asian Arctic region of Russia, the native peoples include the Chukchi, Koyaki, and Yakuts, as well as some Inuit and Lapps. Most continue to follow their traditional occupations—herding reindeer, hunting, fishing, and fur trapping. An article on Siberia appears in Volume S.

All of the native Arctic people have developed a unique ability to survive in their harsh environment by skillfully using the few materials available to them. From snow, ice, and animal skins and bones they have fashioned a simple technology that enables them to build shelters, weapons, and such forms of transportation as sleds and kayaks (small, skin-covered boats). Land and sea animals and fish provide their main source of food.

▶NATURAL RESOURCES

The natural resources of the Arctic can be divided into four main groups—furs, whale products, fish, and minerals. In the early days of Arctic exploration, seals attracted fur traders. Because of the region's large whale population, a booming industry soon developed in whale oil, whalebone, and other products from these great creatures. Today, because many marine animals are in danger of being wiped out, their hunting is limited by international agreements.

The Arctic seas provide some of the oldest and most productive fishing areas in the world. The amount that can be caught by any country, however, is controlled by national territorial limits and by other internationally recognized agreements.

The Arctic's mineral resources include coal, copper, diamonds, gold, iron, lead, zinc, nickel, and tin. Large petroleum and natural gas deposits exist in the northern areas of Alaska, Canada, and Russia. Petroleum from Alaska and Canada is transported south by pipelines.

▶EXPLORATION AND DISCOVERY

The first recorded explorers of the Arctic were the Norsemen who sailed from Norway to Iceland, Greenland, and North America. By the mid-1500's, British and Dutch merchants and sailors began exploring the Arctic in search of a northeast passage to China and India. Although these explorers did not find the passage, they did learn more about the Arctic. These searches also opened up sea trade with Russia and led to the development of the whaling and sealing industries.

About the same time, other British explorers were searching for a northwest passage to Asia around the North American continent. In 1576, Martin Frobisher sailed for the first time to Canada's Baffin Island. Within the next 40 years, Davis Strait, Baffin Bay, and Hudson Bay had been explored. An article on Henry Hudson, the explorer of Hudson Bay, is included in Volume H. Between the early 1600's and 1800's the attention of merchants and explorers focused on developing land routes to support the fur trade. As a result of these explorations, two British explorers, Samuel Hearne and Alexander Mackenzie, followed Canadian rivers northwest to the Arctic Ocean. An article on Mackenzie appears in Volume M.

During the 1700's and 1800's explorers continued to search the Arctic for the elusive Northwest Passage. This route was not found until the early 1900's, when Norway's Roald Amundsen became the first person to sail northwest from the Atlantic Ocean through the Arctic to the Pacific Ocean. His voyage lasted from 1903 to 1906. (Amundsen later commanded the first expedition to reach the South Pole of Antarctica.)

Once the Northwest Passage was discovered, explorers turned their attention to the North Pole. During these expeditions much scientific information also was obtained, including data on sea ice and the Arctic Ocean collected by the Norwegian explorer Fridtjof Nansen. In 1909 an American expedition led by Robert E. Peary successfully reached the North Pole for the first time. A separate article on Peary appears in Volume P.

Since the beginning of the 1900's advances in technology have expanded Arctic exploration. The first flight over the North Pole was accomplished by the American Richard E. Byrd in 1926. (An article on

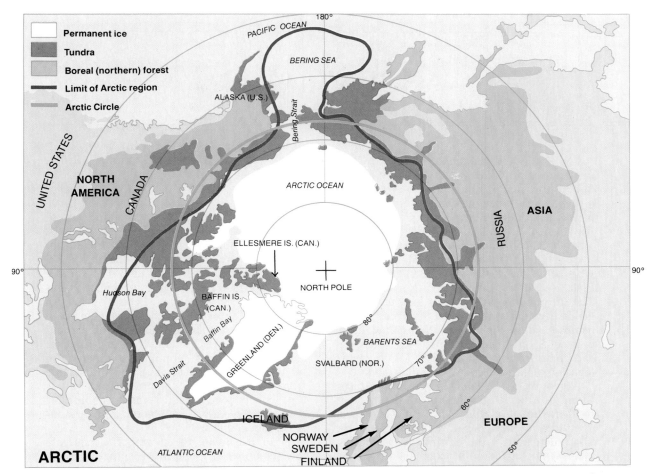

The strategic importance of the Arctic region lies in its central location between the continents of North America, Europe, and Asia.

Byrd appears in Volume B.) In 1958 the U.S. nuclear-powered submarine *Nautilus* became the first ship to reach the North Pole, by traveling under the Arctic ice. In 1977 the nuclear-powered Soviet icebreaker *Arktika* was used to explore the frozen Arctic Ocean. Scientists completed a 7-year exploration project on the ecology of the Bering Sea in 1983.

▶THE ARCTIC TODAY

Political and Strategic Importance. National territorial rights are recognized for all Arctic land areas. But the extent to which nations can control Arctic coastal waters is still unresolved. With the growth of the offshore oil industry in the Arctic, control of its waters will become more important. The Arctic's strategic importance lies in its central position between North America, Europe, and Asia. In 1993, Russia, Norway, Sweden, Finland, Iceland, and Denmark formed the Council of the Euro-Arctic Region, to promote trade and to clean up areas contaminated by radiation and other pollution.

Research and Environmental Protection. Most scientific research in the Arctic concentrates on its climate and its unusual geographical and physical characteristics. In addition, environmental research and protection have become increasingly important as new technology enables us to tap the mineral resources of the region. This is vital because the ecology of the Arctic can be easily disrupted or damaged and recovers very slowly and sometimes not at all. As a result, the United States, Canada, and many European nations have established strict measures to protect this unique, fascinating, and invaluable region of the world.

WINIFRED REUNING
Division of Polar Programs
National Science Foundation

See also ANTARCTICA.

ARGENTINA

More than 450 years ago, Sebastian Cabot explored some of the waterways of southern South America. Friendly Indians went down to greet him when he landed on the riverbanks. Like other European explorers, Cabot was excited when he saw the silver jewelry worn by the Indians. Cabot believed he had discovered a land rich in silver. Thrilled by what he had seen, he gave the name Río de la Plata, "river of silver," to a great estuary. The surrounding country was later named Argentina, which means "land of silver." These names have remained, even though the disappointed Spanish later learned that the silver had come from the mountains of Peru, more than 1,600 kilometers (1,000 miles) away.

Argentina is a land of great contrasts. Tierra del Fuego, the group of islands at its southern tip, is a cold, wet land where penguins thrive. In the hot, humid Chaco, the lowland region of the north, giant anteaters, jaguars, pumas, and other animals of the subtropics abound. In the west are the towering Andes mountains. Seven of the snow-capped peaks rise to more than 6,700 meters (22,000

feet) above sea level. In the east are the flat, prairielike plains of the Pampa.

▶THE PEOPLE

Most of the people in Argentina are of European stock. The remainder are mestizos (persons of mixed European and Indian ancestry) and a few pure-blooded Indians.

Between the years 1858 and 1930, more than 6,000,000 people left their homes in Europe to settle in Argentina. People of Spanish and Italian ancestry are the most numerous. There are also many descendants of French, Swiss, Austrian, German, Russian, English, and Scottish settlers. Immigrants still arrive in large numbers. Recent immigrants often come from Poland and other countries of eastern Europe. Since the mid-1900's, many people have come to Argentina from neighboring Latin-American countries.

When the Spanish first came, the relatively few Indians they found in Argentina were nomadic hunters. Wars broke out when the Spaniards tried to seize the land. Many Indians were killed, and there was little inter-

Iguazú Falls, one of the most striking sights in Argentina, lies on the border with Brazil. The cataracts plunge about 64 meters (210 feet) into the Iguazú River.

ARGENTINE REPUBLIC (República Argentina) is the official name of the country.

LOCATION: Southern part of South America.

AREA: 1,068,297 sq mi (2,766,889 km²).

POPULATION: 33,000,000 (estimate).

CAPITAL AND LARGEST CITY: Buenos Aires.

MAJOR LANGUAGE(S): Spanish (official).

MAJOR RELIGIOUS GROUP(S): Roman Catholic.

GOVERNMENT: Republic. **Head of state and government**—president. **Legislature**—National Congress (consisting of the Senate and Chamber of Deputies).

CHIEF PRODUCTS: Agricultural—wheat, corn, cotton, sugarcane, soybeans, grapes, alfalfa, livestock (especially cattle and sheep). **Manufactured**—processed livestock products (especially beef, leather goods, and dairy products), other processed foods, petroleum products, wine, iron and steel, chemicals, paper, machinery, automobiles and other vehicles. **Mineral**—petroleum, coal, iron ore, smaller deposits of other minerals.

MONETARY UNIT: New peso (1 peso = 100 centavos).

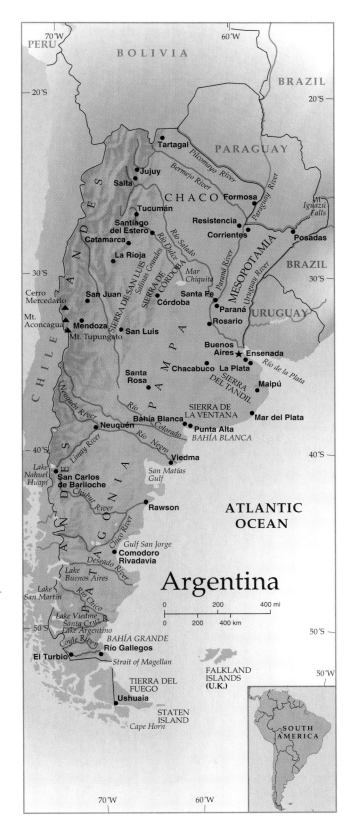

marriage between the Spanish and the Indians. As a result, Argentina has far fewer mestizos than any other Latin-American country. The few remaining Indians generally live in isolated areas.

The eastern plains are by far the most densely settled part of Argentina. The rest of the country tends to be sparsely populated, although cities have also developed in other regions, particularly where the surrounding land can be irrigated by streams running down from the Andes.

Way of Life

Argentina is one of the most highly urbanized countries in the Western Hemisphere. It has been more urban than rural since about 1910, and today more than 85 percent of the people live in cities and towns. Buenos Aires, the capital of Argentina, is one of the world's largest and most international cities.

Wealthy and middle-class Argentines in large cities live in comfortable houses or apartments and dress in European-style clothing. People on the streets of Buenos Aires look very much like Parisians or New Yorkers. Many women still have their own dressmakers, and men often have their suits made to order. But the trend among young people is to buy their clothes ready-made in fashionable shops. Since the 1930's many poor people have moved from the countryside to the cities in search of jobs. The urban poor often live in slums on the edges of the cities and are unable to find full-time employment.

Argentines eat their dinner very late. Although the children may eat early in the evening, adults seldom eat dinner until 8 o'clock. Many families begin their meal as late as 9 or 10 o'clock. Nearly every lunch and dinner starts with homemade soup. The second course is frequently Argentine beef. Macaroni, spaghetti, vermicelli, and other *pastas* made popular by Italian immigrants are often served. Nearly everyone drinks wine with lunch and dinner. The wine is often diluted with seltzer water.

In the countryside the best known residents are the gauchos—the cowboys of Argentina. The word "gaucho" describes a way of life rather than race or ancestry. During Argentina's early days, the gauchos played an important part in the settlement of the country. Many stories were written about the way they lived and their heroic deeds. Today they tend herds of cattle on the great *estancias* (ranches) of the Pampa.

The gauchos' clothes are colorful. Gauchos wear full, billowing trousers called *bombachas*. These are tucked into leather boots adorned with big spurs. Gauchos wear bright neckerchiefs and bright sashes or wide leather belts decorated with coins. On cold days they drape shawls, or ponchos, of sheep or llama wool around their shoulders. The *facon*, a highly decorated knife with many uses, is worn sheathed at the back of the belt. The gauchos often use it at mealtimes to cut strips of raw beef to be broiled over an open campfire. Ranch owners and men in small towns often wear gaucho clothing. Women in rural areas usually wear European-style clothing.

Religion

Most Argentines are members of the Roman Catholic Church. The government helps to support the church, and the constitution re-quires that the president be a Roman Catholic. Argentina has a fairly large Jewish population, and all religious groups are guaranteed religious freedom.

Education and Culture

The Argentines are proud of their school system. The nation has one of the highest literacy rates in all of Latin America. Public education is free and separate from the church. But many parents send their children to private parochial schools.

All boys and girls between the ages of 6 and 14 must attend elementary school. The schoolchildren wear knee-length smocks, called *delantales,* over their everyday clothes. The boys button their smocks down the front. The girls' smocks button down the back. President Domingo F. Sarmiento, who served from 1868 to 1874, made wearing smocks a law so that rich and poor children could feel equal in school.

When they are 14, boys and girls take examinations to enter one of various types of secondary schools. Some secondary schools are for students who plan to go to college. Others train young people to teach primary school or prepare them for careers in business, industry, or trade.

Argentina has several national universities. The largest is the University of Buenos Aires. There are also numerous provincial and private universities located in various parts of the country.

Symphony concerts and opera, the theater, and ballet are all very popular in Argentina. The Teatro Colón, or Columbus Theater, in Buenos Aires is the largest and most elaborate theater. Famous North American and European singers often appear there.

When Argentine dance is discussed, most people think of the tango, but the *chacarera,* the *zamba,* and the *milonga* are also popular. Argentine folk tunes are a combination of Spanish and Indian music. The most popular musical instrument is the guitar. Many people learn to play the guitar when they are children.

Among Argentina's earliest authors was a mestizo named Ruy Díaz de Guzmán. His work, *La Argentina,* is a history of the early days of settlement. Domingo Sarmiento wrote a book called *Facundo,* an attack against dictators. In 1872, José Hernández wrote a long epic poem called *Martín Fierro*. This tale about the life of the early gauchos has become a classic. The works of several more recent writers have been translated into other languages and have become known throughout the world. One of these writers, Ricardo Güiraldes (1886–1927), wrote a famous novel, *Don Segundo Sombra,* that tells of a boy who becomes a man when he lives and rides with gauchos. Probably the most widely known Argentine writer of this century is Jorge Luis Borges (1899–1986). He wrote many books of poetry and prose dealing with the European character of Argentine society.

Argentina is one of the leading book and newspaper publishers in Latin America. Newsstands and bookshops abound in Buenos Aires and other large cities. Because many Argentines speak more than one language, a large number of newspapers are printed in languages other than Spanish.

▶ **THE LAND**

Argentina ranks second to Brazil in area among Latin-American countries. It occupies most of South America's long tip and is somewhat triangular in shape. It extends for 3,700 kilometers (2,300 miles) from north to south and varies in width from 1,450 kilometers (900 miles) in the north to less than 16 kilometers (10 miles) on Tierra del Fuego.

Argentina claims an additional 1,190,000 square kilometers (460,000 square miles) of territory, mostly in Antarctica. It also claims the Falkland Islands (which it calls Islas Malvinas) and the nearby South Georgia, South Sandwich, South Shetland, and South Orkney islands. All of these islands lie in the Atlantic Ocean off the coast of Argentina. But they have been ruled by Britain since 1833, and most of the people there are of British descent.

Natural Regions

There are five natural regions in Argentina. These are the Andean region, the Chaco, Mesopotamia, the Pampa, and Patagonia.

Andean Region. The Andes mountains form most of Argentina's western border with Chile. The highest and most impressive peaks are found midway in the range, not far from the beautiful city of Mendoza. Snow-capped Aconcagua, the highest mountain in the Western Hemisphere, towers to 6,960 meters (22,835

The spectacular Aconcagua is the highest peak in the Western Hemisphere. It sometimes can be seen from as far away as 145 kilometers (90 miles).

feet). Nearby Cerro Mercedario and Tupungato are nearly as high. West of Tucumán, on the border with Chile, is Ojos del Salado, the hemisphere's second highest mountain.

The northern Andes are high and dry. The mountains rise from a high, windswept plateau called the Puna. Some of the rivers of this region empty into salt lakes in the mountains and foothills. Some lakes have dried up and left great salt flats called *salinas.* The largest salt flat is the Salinas Grandes, in a deep depression between the foothills of the Andes and the Sierra de Córdoba.

In the southern Andes, the mountains are lower and rise to about the level of the Puna. The southern Andes remind visitors of the Swiss Alps and are often called the Alps of Argentina. San Carlos de Bariloche is the center of one of Argentina's most popular tourist areas. Thousands of tourists visit nearby Nahuel Huapí National Park in summer.

Skiers and other winter sports enthusiasts visit it in winter.

The Chaco. The most northerly of Argentina's lowland regions, the Chaco is a very wide, wooded plain. Four broad rivers—the Pilcomayo, Bermejo, Salado del Norte, and Dulce—cross the Chaco. These rivers often overflow their shallow banks in the wet season (October through April) and flood large areas of the Chaco.

Mesopotamia. Mesopotamia lies between the Paraná and Uruguay rivers. The name comes from a Greek word meaning "between the rivers." The region includes a portion of the Paraná Plateau in the northeast. Waterfalls are formed as rivers tumble down from this plateau. The Iguazú Falls, on the Iguazú River where it meets the Paraná, are the largest. They are 64 meters (210 feet) high and 4 kilometers (2½ miles) wide.

The Pampa. The Pampa lies south of the Chaco and stretches to the Río Colorado. This is the heart of Argentina's ranch country. The Pampa forms a huge semicircle of lowlands, centering on Buenos Aires. In the east is the humid Pampa. In the west is the dry Pampa. The land rises gradually toward the west. There are few hills or trees, and the land appears perfectly level. The only relief features are the Sierra del Tandil and the Sierra de la Ventana. These hills rise to more than 1,200 meters (4,000 feet) just north of Bahía Blanca.

Patagonia. Patagonia is the name given to the cold, dry, and windy plateaus south of the Río Colorado. The name comes from the Spanish word *patagones,* which means "big feet." The early Spanish explorers noticed the big feet of the local Indians. They called the land Patagonia, or "The Land of People with Big Feet." Tierra del Fuego, the bleak and windswept island at the southern tip of Argentina, is a part of Patagonia. Argentina owns the eastern part of the island, and Chile controls the west.

Climate

The Pampa has a healthful, temperate climate. Mild temperatures and regular rainfall make it one of the best farming regions in Argentina. Summer comes in January because Argentina is in the Southern Hemisphere. In the summer, temperatures average 21°C (70°F). Winter temperatures (July) average 9°C (49°F). Rainfall varies from over 970 millimeters (38 inches) a year in the eastern, humid Pampa to less than 500 millimeters (20 inches) in the western, dry Pampa.

Since northern Argentina lies in the subtropics, both the Chaco and Mesopotamia have hot summers and warm, frost-free winters. Summer temperatures average 27°C (80°F), and winter temperatures average 13°C (55°F). Mesopotamia, the wettest place in Argentina, receives over 1,500 millimeters (60 inches) of rain a year. Less rain falls in the west and south. Tucumán, Córdoba, Mendoza, and other places farther west are too dry for farming without irrigation.

In Patagonia, winters are cold, with temperatures slightly above freezing. Summer temperatures are around 18°C (65°F). Strong winds sweep across Patagonia and make the winter seem colder than it really is. Rainfall is light, especially in the east. Most places receive less than 280 millimeters (11 inches) of rain a year.

Natural Resources

The Pampa is Argentina's most valuable resource. It produces most of the country's agricultural wealth and provides nearly all its exports. The hardwood forests of the Chaco and Mesopotamia are also important. One valuable tree is the red quebracho. Tannin, a substance made from the bark of this tree is used in tanning leather.

Argentina does not have many valuable mineral resources except oil. There is a major oil field near Comodoro Rivadavia, in northern Patagonia, and offshore oil deposits were discovered in 1979. There are coal deposits in Patagonia and near Mendoza. Some silver, tin, copper, iron, manganese, gold, nickel, lead, tungsten, and zinc are also found. Sulfur, salt, and other chemicals are present in the *salinas.*

Argentina has many waterfalls and swift streams. They are beginning to be harnessed for hydroelectric power, but in general they are too far from the population centers of the Pampa. The Iguazú Falls and the snow-fed streams from the Andes are the greatest future sources of power.

▶THE ECONOMY

Traditionally, Argentina has been an agricultural country. The economy is still based

The gaucho is the cowboy of Argentina. The country is a leading exporter of beef, and cattle are vital to the economy.

largely on meat, wool, and cereals. Farm products make up about 90 percent of Argentina's exports. But the majority of the work force is employed in service industries such as government, education, trade, banking, and transportation. Manufacturing also employs more people than agriculture.

Agriculture

Agriculture is big business in Argentina. Cattle raising is one of the oldest and still one of the leading industries. Wheat, grown mainly on the Pampa, is the major crop.

The steel plow, invented in 1837, allowed Argentine farmers to cut through the thick sod of the Pampa to plant wheat and corn in the fertile soils. By the early 1900's, Argentina had become one of the world's major wheat exporters. Other important grain crops are corn, grown near Rosario, and barley, oats, and rye, grown on the drier edges of the Pampa.

Cotton is the most important crop in the subtropical north, where many rivers irrigate the land. Most of the cotton is grown without artificial irrigation in the Chaco.

Yerba maté, a South American holly, is a special crop grown in the northeast. The herb tea brewed from maté stems and leaves is a favorite beverage of the people of Argentina, neighboring Paraguay, and southern Brazil.

Irrigation has turned parts of western Argentina into vast gardens. Hundreds of orchards and vineyards are found in the western regions. Table and wine grapes, olives, apples, pears, and peaches are the leading fruits. Citrus fruits are grown just north of Buenos Aires. Oilseeds, tobacco, and soybeans are other important crops.

Cattle once roamed the Pampa in semi-wild herds. They were valued mostly for their hides and for tallow until the development of refrigeration opened new markets for Argentina's beef in the late 1800's. Other inventions also helped the cattle industry. Well-drilling machinery made it possible to use underground sources of water to raise cattle on the dry parts of the Pampa. And barbed wire enabled ranchers to fence in great *estancias* where they could improve their cattle. Improved strains of beef cattle and scientific methods of cattle raising were introduced. Cattle raising is most important in the Pampa and Mesopotamia, where cattle are raised on huge ranches. Alfalfa is widely grown throughout the Pampa. It is used mainly as feed for cattle.

Sheep are raised in the east and in many other parts of the country. Horses, goats, and poultry are also raised.

Manufacturing and Trade

Manufacturing is concentrated in the east, particularly around the cities of Buenos Aires, Córdoba, and Rosario. Many other cities have industries that serve nearby farms and ranches.

The chief industries are based on livestock —meat processing and packing and the making of such products as leather goods from hides and textiles from wool. Wine making and the processing of sugar, oilseeds, grains, fruit, and other foodstuffs are also important. The plastics, iron and steel, machine tool, engineering, and chemical industries, among others, are expanding rapidly. Many kinds of consumer goods are manufactured, including paper, tobacco products, beverages, automobiles, and clothing.

Other Industries

Argentina has sufficient petroleum and natural gas to satisfy most of its own needs. Small quantities of other minerals are extracted, mostly for local use. Fishing is important in coastal areas.

Tourism is a growing industry. Among the popular tourist spots are the Andean resorts, the lake district around San Carlos de Bariloche, seaside resorts like Mar del Plata along the Atlantic coast, the spectacular Iguazú Falls, and the city of Buenos Aires. Most tourists are from other Latin-American nations.

Transportation and Communication

The country's railroads are government-owned. They link Buenos Aires with almost every part of the country and with Chile, Bolivia, Peru, Paraguay, Uruguay, and Brazil. Buses and trucks are increasingly important as Argentina's roads improve. But most paved roads are still in the eastern part of the country. The Río de la Plata system (the Paraná, Uruguay, and Paraguay rivers) is the only important navigable waterway. Domestic air transport covers most of the country. The city of Buenos Aires is served by many international airlines, including the state-owned Aerolíneas Argentinas.

▶ CITIES

Buenos Aires, on the Río de la Plata, is Argentina's capital and by far its largest city. Greater Buenos Aires is the home of about one third of the nation's people. Most of Argentina's manufacturing, ocean shipping, and commercial businesses are located there. An article on Buenos Aires is included in Volume B.

Rosario, on the Paraná River, is Argentina's second largest city. At Rosario the Paraná River is deep enough to permit the docking of oceangoing ships. This has made the city an important manufacturing, commercial, and export center for the Pampa.

Córdoba is Argentina's third largest city. Its university, one of the oldest in the Western Hemisphere, was founded in 1613. La Plata and Tucumán are important industrial centers, and Mendoza is famous as the center of Argentina's wine-producing region.

▶ GOVERNMENT

According to the constitution adopted in 1853, Argentina has a republican, representative, and federal system of government. Each of the provinces has its own constitution, but the powers of the provincial governments are sharply limited by the federal government.

The Avenida 9 de Julio (Avenue of July 9th) is one of the largest boulevards in the world. The obelisk in the center honors the 400th anniversary of the founding of Buenos Aires.

The government is made up of three branches—the executive, the legislative, and the judicial. The executive branch is headed by a president, elected (with a vice president) for six years by an electoral college chosen by the people. Presidents are not eligible for immediate re-election. The legislative branch is the National Congress, which consists of the Senate and the Chamber of Deputies. Senators are elected by the provincial legislatures for nine years. Deputies are elected directly by the people for four years. The judicial branch includes the Supreme Court and other courts. Judges are appointed by the president with the approval of the Senate.

Argentina is composed of 22 provinces, a federal district, and the national territory of Tierra del Fuego. Each province has its own elected governor and legislature.

▶ HISTORY

Early History and Spanish Rule. Argentina's earliest inhabitants were Indians. Several groups lived in the area long before the Europeans arrived. Most were nomadic hunters and food gatherers, although others practiced farming.

Juan Días de Solís, a Spanish navigator, visited the shores of the Río de la Plata in 1516. Other explorers followed him. A Spanish expedition arrived in the region in 1536, but the first Spanish settlement in what is now Argentina was not established until 1553.

During the 1500's and 1600's, Argentina was a part of the Spanish colony of Peru. A Spanish colonial law required that all trade from Argentina pass westward through Peru and Bolivia. This law made the west the most important part of the country. Trade prospered in the western cities of Santiago del Estero (founded in 1553), Tucumán (1565), Córdoba (1573), Mendoza (1561), San Juan (1562), Salta (1584), La Rioja (1591), Jujuy (1594), and San Luis (1596). These cities, founded by colonists who came over the mountains from Peru, were the centers of Argentina's Spanish colonial life.

In 1776, Spain divided its empire and made Argentina a part of the viceroyalty of the Río de la Plata. Buenos Aires became the capital of the viceroyalty. This new colony included all Argentina, Uruguay, and Paraguay, southern Bolivia, and parts of Chile and Brazil.

But the eastern parts of the country made little progress under Spanish rule. By the end of the 1700's, the *porteños* (as the inhabitants of Buenos Aires were called) had grown very restless. The *porteños* took advantage of Napoleon's invasion of Spain and revolted on May 25, 1810. On July 9, 1816, the western provinces joined Buenos Aires, and independence was formally declared. Under the leadership of General José de San Martín, Argentina's greatest hero, the Argentines drove the Spanish from neighboring Chile and the area around Lima, Peru. (A biography of San Martín appears in Volume S.) The last Spanish forces in Peru were defeated at Ayachucho in 1824 by rebel troops under the leadership of the Venezuelan general Antonio José de Sucre.

Independence. Independence from Spain did not lead to immediate peace and prosperity. For many years there were bitter disputes between the central government in Buenos Aires and the leaders of the interior provinces. These disputes resulted in years of civil war. Juan Manuel de Rosas came to power in 1829 and finally united the country. He ran Argentina as a dictator for more than twenty years, until the people drove him from power in 1852. The following year most of Argentina adopted a constitution similar to that of the United States. But Buenos Aires did not join the confederation until 1862.

During the last half of the 1800's, Argentina developed many new industries and became one of the wealthiest countries in Latin America. Two noted presidents during this time were General Bartolomé Mitre, who was elected in 1862, and his successor, Domingo F. Sarmiento. Both encouraged Europeans to settle in Argentina, and Sarmiento made schooling compulsory (required) for all Argentine children.

The Perón Era. In 1930, when the Argentine economy was in a state of near-collapse due to the worldwide Great Depression, army officers took over the government. Since that time, the military has often played an active role in governing the country.

In 1946, Juan Perón won control of the government. He appealed to the working people, vowing to make Argentina a strong industrial nation. He raised the workers' wages at the expense of the farmers. Farm production fell so low that Argentina was on the brink of bankruptcy. The country was divided into two opposing groups—the Peronistas (Perón's followers) and the anti-Peronistas.

Perón's rise to power had been greatly aided by his second wife, Eva (known as Evita), who was especially popular among the workers in the cities. But continuing economic problems and political conflicts weakened Perón's control of Argentina. In 1955 he was ousted from office by the military and forced into exile. The country then alternated between military and civilian rule. Perón returned from exile and was elected president in 1973. His third wife, Isabel Perón, became vice president. When Perón died in 1974, Isabel Perón became the first woman head of government in the Western Hemisphere. Her administration was marked by soaring inflation and political terrorism. In 1976 she, too, was removed from office by the military.

Recent History. Using severe measures, the military government restored order. But economic failures and Argentina's defeat in a short war with Britain over the Falkland Islands in 1982 discredited the policies of the country's military rulers. In free elections held in 1983, Raúl Alfonsín, the leader of the moderate Radical Civic Union Party, was elected to the presidency.

One of Alfonsín's first acts was to permit civilian review of the actions of Argentina's military officers. Some were accused of responsibility for the disappearance of at least 6,000 people during the war against terrorism in the late 1970's. In foreign affairs, Argentina signed a friendship agreement with neighboring Chile in 1984. Under the agreement, the two countries agreed to peacefully resolve a long-standing dispute over their boundary in the Beagle Channel.

Carlos Saúl Menem, the candidate of the Justice Party (a Peronist party), won election as president in 1989. His party also won a majority in the Chamber of Deputies and the provincial legislatures. Menem's greatest challenge is Argentina's economy, which is burdened by one of the world's highest inflation rates and a huge foreign debt.

ROBERT L. CARMIN
Ball State University

ARISTOTLE (384–322 B.C.)

Aristotle was one of the most important citizens of ancient Greece. He never won a battle or held a political office, but he was a famous teacher and one of the greatest philosophers who ever lived.

Only a few facts are known about Aristotle's childhood. We know he was born in Stagira, a town in northeastern Greece, in 384 B.C. His father was court physician to Amyntas II, King of Macedonia, who was the grandfather of Alexander the Great. It seems likely that Aristotle learned something about science from his father.

▶ **ARISTOTLE THE STUDENT**

When Aristotle was about 17 years old, he went to study in Athens, an important Greek city-state. He became a pupil of the finest teacher of his day, the philosopher Plato.

The young men at Plato's Academy spent several years studying mathematics, astronomy, and government. When they had mastered these studies, they were asked to think about some of the problems at the heart of Greek philosophy: What is happiness? What is the good life? Plato's method of teaching stressed learning how to think clearly.

Aristotle studied under Plato for about 20 years. He was an excellent student. Plato called him "the mind of the school." When Plato died in 347 B.C., Aristotle left the academy and began to develop his own method of teaching.

There was nothing, it seemed, that did not capture Aristotle's interest. How does the mind work? How can we learn what is true and what is false? What is the best form of government? These were only a few of the problems with which Aristotle wrestled.

Aristotle tried to find the answers by observing the world around him. He believed that every event had a logical explanation and that conclusions could be formed from investigation and observation.

▶ **ARISTOTLE THE TEACHER**

Aristotle's fame was great by the time he left Plato's school. When King Philip II of

Macedonia was looking for a teacher for his son Alexander, he chose Aristotle. It is hard to know how much Aristotle influenced Alexander the Great, but we do know that teacher and pupil became lifelong friends.

After Alexander became king of Macedonia, Aristotle returned to Athens. In 335 B.C., with money contributed by Alexander, Aristotle opened a school called the Lyceum. It is from Aristotle's school that the high schools of France and Italy take their names: *lycée* and *liceo*.

Many subjects were taught at the Lyceum, and there were various aids for learning. Aristotle collected the first large library of ancient times. There was a museum of natural science, a garden, and a zoo.

After the morning classes Aristotle lectured to anyone who wanted to listen while he paced up and down the covered walk (called the *peripatos*) outside of his school. For this reason those who accepted his philosophy were called **Peripatetics**.

Aristotle lived and taught in a world that was very different from the one that Plato knew. In Plato's time every citizen understood the part he was to play in the life of Athens and his responsibility to the government of the city-state.

While Aristotle taught at the Lyceum, Athens lost its independence and became only a small part of Alexander's empire. As citizens of an empire, the Athenians had to adjust to a new form of government.

Aristotle urged each man to seek his own place in the world by learning how to live a good and useful life. A happy life could be found by living according to the "golden mean." By the "golden mean" Aristotle meant the middle way between two extremes. For example, he said the middle way "between cowardice and rashness is courage."

Twelve years after Aristotle opened his school, word reached Athens that Alexander the Great had died. At that time the people of Athens were divided into two groups—those who had learned to live under Alexander's rule and those who still hated it. When news of his death came, Alexander's enemies turned on his friends. Aristotle was prosecuted, like Socrates, for offending against religion. Rather than stand trial, he left Athens. He died soon afterward, in 322 B.C.

Copied from a Greek original, this Roman statue of Aristotle is in the Spada Gallery, Rome.

▶ ARISTOTLE'S BOOKS

Of the 400 books that Aristotle is said to have written, only a small number have come down to us. But they are remarkable books. Aristotle's works seem to have been an encyclopedia of Greek learning of the 4th century B.C. There are books on astronomy, physics, poetry, zoology, oratory, biology, logic, politics, government, and ethics.

Aristotle's books were studied after his death. They were used as textbooks in the great centers of learning: Alexandria, Rome, and the universities of medieval Europe. No other man influenced the thinking of so many people for so long.

Even today Aristotle's books are an important influence because we still use his method of investigation and observation. He classified and related all the knowledge of his time about the world. Modern scientists have found that many of the observations he made more than 2,000 years ago are correct. He showed us that every statement should be supported by evidence. Aristotle's key to knowledge was logic and his basis for knowledge was fact.

Reviewed by GILBERT HIGHET
Author, *The Classical Tradition*

ARITHMETIC

When you keep score in a game, when you count your change, when you compare baseball batting averages or try to balance your checkbook, you are doing arithmetic. Arithmetic is a way of working with numbers. It is a branch of the science of mathematics.

▶NUMBERS AND NUMERALS

People begin using arithmetic when they are very young. Their earliest experiences, however, have to do with quantity, not with counting. Just by looking at them, a child too young to count knows that four toy blocks are more than two.

We think that early human beings had the same kind of **number sense**. They could not count, but they could tell by looking that they had as much of something as they needed or wanted.

As time passed, people needed more than just a sense of quantity. They needed to keep an actual count of things, such as how many sheep were in a herd or how many days it took to travel to a good hunting spot. People probably first used pebbles or their fingers to count. Then, at some unknown time thousands of years ago, numbers were discovered and number names were invented. These numbers are called **counting numbers**, which we also call **natural numbers**. Much later, zero was added to the counting numbers. Zero and the counting numbers together make up **whole numbers**.

People in ancient civilizations also developed different numeral systems, or ways of writing numbers. The Babylonians, Egyptians, Greeks, and Romans all had their own systems. These early systems were complicated and difficult to use. Then around 750 A.D., a new numeral system came into use. It was developed by the Hindus in India and was spread to other parts of the world by Arab traders. The Hindu-Arabic system includes only ten symbols. These symbols are 1, 2, 3, 4, 5, 6, 7, 8, 9, 0. The ten symbols of the Hindu-Arabic system can be used to write any number, no matter how great or how small, and they are still used today.

▶OPERATIONS WITH WHOLE NUMBERS

Once people had numbers and written numerals, they were able to work with them in different ways to solve everyday problems. They discovered that numbers can be used to perform four basic processes, or operations. These operations are addition, subtraction, multiplication, and division. Each operation is represented by a sign: $+$ for addition, $-$ for subtraction, $\times$ for multiplication, and $\div$ for division. Another way to show division is with this sign: $\overline{)}$

It is important to know when to use the different operations and how they relate to one another.

Addition

Addition is a way of operating with numbers. It is the process of putting groups of like things together to find their total number or quantity. Counting forward is another way of finding a total number or quantity. Addition is faster than counting forward except when you are counting forward only a few numbers.

In order to add, you must know the basic addition facts. An addition fact is made up of two parts: two numbers from 0 to 9 that are to be added, called the **addends**, and their **sum**, or the answer to the addition.

$$4 + 6 = 10 \qquad 9 + 8 = 17$$

In the first example, 4 and 6 are the addends and 10 is the sum. In the second example, 9 and 8 are the addends and 17 is the sum.

ADDITION TABLE
This table can be used to find the basic addition facts, the sums of any two numbers from 0 to 9. To find the sum of 3 + 4, for example, find the 3 in the far left-hand column. Go along that row until you get to the column with 4 at the top. You will be on the 7, and 3 + 4 = 7.

+	0	1	2	3	4	5	6	7	8	9
0	0	1	2	3	4	5	6	7	8	9
1	1	2	3	4	5	6	7	8	9	10
2	2	3	4	5	6	7	8	9	10	11
3	3	4	5	6	(7)	8	9	10	11	12
4	4	5	6	7	8	9	10	11	12	13
5	5	6	7	8	9	10	11	12	13	14
6	6	7	8	9	10	11	12	13	14	15
7	7	8	9	10	11	12	13	14	15	16
8	8	9	10	11	12	13	14	15	16	17
9	9	10	11	12	13	14	15	16	17	18

This next problem lets us compare addition and counting forward. Suppose you cycled 8 miles on Monday and 5 miles on Tuesday. You could find out how many miles you cycled in all by counting forward or by adding.

Counting forward	or	Addition	
8 9, 10, 11,		8	addend
12, 13		+ 5	addend
		13	sum

When you are adding large numbers, it can be helpful to look at the numbers as if they were written in columns. Each column has a value and each one can be added in a sequence from right to left. The column names are **ones**, **tens**, **hundreds**, and **thousands**. If you were adding 1,268 and 2,159 this way, you would begin in the ones column to the far right and move left to the tens column, then to the hundreds column, and then to the thousands column.

Thousands	Hundreds	Tens	Ones
1	2	6	8
2	1	5	9
3	4	2	7

The greatest number you may write in any column is 9. What do you do when the sum in a column is more than 9?

In this example, the sum in the ones column is 17. You may think of 17 as 1 ten and 7 ones. Write 7 in the ones column and add the 1 ten to the other numbers in the tens column.

Add in the tens column: $1 + 6 + 5 = 12$. Think of the 12 tens as 1 one hundred and 2 tens. Write 2 in the tens column. Add 1 to the hundreds column.

Adding in the hundreds column, you get $1 + 2 + 1 = 4$. Write 4 in the hundreds column.

Adding in the thousands column, you get $1 + 2 = 3$. Write 3 in the thousands column. The sum is 3,427.

Subtraction

Subtraction is the opposite of addition. One kind of subtraction involves finding the number of objects remaining in a group after some of the objects have been removed. Counting back is another way of finding the number remaining. Subtraction is usually quicker than counting back. To use the subtraction method you must know the basic subtraction facts. For every addition fact there is a related subtraction fact. They can each be written down in two ways, which are shown below.

Addition Fact	Related Subtraction Fact
6 + 5 = 11	11 – 5 = 6
6	11
+ 5	– 5
11	6

When you use subtraction, you subtract from a number called the **minuend**. The number you subtract is the **subtrahend**, and the answer you get is the **difference**.

Suppose you had 15 postage stamps and you used 7 of them to mail letters. You could find out how many stamps you had left by counting back or by subtracting.

Counting back	or	Subtracting	
15 14, 13, 12,		15	minuend
11, 10, 9, 8		– 7	subtrahend
		8	difference

When you are subtracting large numbers from one another, the idea of place value can be useful. For example, if you are subtracting 35 from 92, you could think of the numbers in this way:

$$92 = 9 \text{ tens and } 2 \text{ ones}$$
$$-35 = 3 \text{ tens and } 5 \text{ ones}$$

The 9 tens and 2 ones can also be written as 8 tens and 12 ones. All you do is change 1 ten into ten ones. This gives the following:

92	= 8 tens and 12 ones	minuend
– 35	= 3 tens and 5 ones	subtrahend
57	or 5 tens and 7 ones	difference

You can check your results by adding the difference to the subtrahend. You should get the minuend.

Subtraction is also used to compare numbers. Suppose you compare the temperatures of a 19-degree day and a 35-degree day to find out how much warmer the 35-degree day is. You may think, What number added to 19 will make 35? You can do it this way:

19° to 20°	=	1 degree
20° to 30°	=	10 degrees
30° to 35°	=	5 degrees
		16 degrees

On paper, the operation of subtraction will provide a quick answer:

$$35 \text{ degrees}$$
$$-19 \text{ degrees}$$
$$16 \text{ degrees}$$

×	1	2	3	4	5	6	7	8	9
1	1	2	3	4	5	6	7	8	9
2	2	4	6	8	10	12	14	16	18
3	3	6	9	12	15	18	21	24	27
4	4	8	12	16	20	24	28	32	36
5	5	10	15	20	25	30	35	40	45
6	6	12	18	(24)	30	36	42	48	54
7	7	14	21	28	35	42	49	56	63
8	8	16	24	32	40	48	56	64	72
9	9	18	27	36	45	54	63	72	81

MULTIPLICATION TABLE
This table can be used to find the basic multiplication facts, the products of any two numbers from 1 to 9. To find the product of 6 x 4, for example, find the 6 in the far left-hand column. Go along that row until you get to the column with 4 at the top. You will be on the 24, and 6 x 4 = 24.

Multiplication

Multiplication is a quick way of adding equal, or same-size, groups.

To do multiplication, you must know the basic multiplication facts. For example, you know that $3 \times 8 = 24$ is a basic multiplication fact. Read it as "3 eights equal 24." In a multiplication fact, the number being multiplied by another number is the **multiplicand**; the number used to multiply by is the **multiplier**; and the answer is called the **product**.

Suppose a pack of bubble gum contains 5 pieces; how many pieces are there in 3 packs? You can get the answer by adding equal groups or by multiplying.

Adding equal groups or Multiplying

```
       5
       5          5   multiplicand
    +  5        x 3   multiplier
      15         15   product
```

Division

Division is the process of splitting a group into equal parts or groups. It is the opposite of multiplication.

To divide you must know some basic division facts. For example, $6 \div 3 = 2$ is a division fact. In a division fact, the number to be divided by another number is called the **dividend**; the number it is to be divided by is

called the **divisor**; and the answer is called the **quotient**.

Suppose you have 24 soccer cards. If you can put 8 cards on each page in a photo album, how many pages will you fill? To find the number of pages, you can subtract equal groups or you can divide.

Subtracting equal   or   Dividing by 8
  groups of 8

```
     24                              3  quotient
   -  8                  divisor  8 )24  dividend
     16
   -  8
      8
   -  8
```

You can check your division results easily by using multiplication. Multiplying the quotient and the divisor should give you the dividend: $3 \times 8 = 24$.

In division you cannot divide by zero. For example, you may know that 24 cannot be divided into groups of 0.

Operations with Fractions and Decimals

You have been reading about addition, subtraction, multiplication, and division. All of the numbers in the examples you have seen are whole numbers. There are other kinds of numbers as well.

Fractions are numbers that represent parts of a whole, for example, one-half ($\frac{1}{2}$) of an apple, two-thirds ($\frac{2}{3}$) of a mile, or one-fourth ($\frac{1}{4}$) of a dozen.

Another way to express fractions is with decimals. For example, the fraction $\frac{1}{4}$ is 0.25 when written as a decimal.

Working with fractions and decimals is more complicated than working with whole numbers. However, the basic operations of arithmetic—addition, subtraction, multiplication, and division—can be applied to fractions and decimals.

▶USING CALCULATORS AND COMPUTERS

The operations of arithmetic can be performed by different methods. Calculations that may not have to be exact can often be done in your head. Sometimes using a pencil and paper helps you get an accurate answer quickly. When you need to do many operations or work with large numbers, calculators and computers are the most efficient way to work.

USING ESTIMATION STRATEGIES

Estimation is an important step in the process of using arithmetic operations to solve number problems. Estimation involves using clues to make a sensible guess, or estimate. For example, an estimate tells *about* how many of something there may be, or *about* how large or small something may be. You have probably used estimation many times. For example, you may have estimated how long it might take you to get to school, or how much money you might need to buy an outfit for a special occasion, or how much wood you might need to make a bench. Until you actually made the trip or priced the purchases or made specific measurements, you really did not have an accurate amount. But an estimate gave you a good enough picture to begin with. All estimation strategies involve using numbers that are easy to work with mentally.

Here are several strategies:

1. One way to estimate is to **round** each number to the nearest ten, hundred, thousand, and so on, before you add, subtract, multiply, or divide. For example, to estimate the sum of 48 + 11 + 42 + 29, round each number to the nearest ten, then add.

    $$48 \longrightarrow 50$$
    $$11 \longrightarrow 10$$
    $$42 \longrightarrow 40$$
    $$+\,29 \longrightarrow +\,30$$

2. **Clustering** is used when several numbers cluster near a single number. In the example 43 + 59 + 61 + 38, two of the numbers cluster near, or are close to, 40 and two are close to 60. The sum can thus be estimated as 2 × 40 plus 2 × 60, or 200.

3. **Comparison** also involves rounding numbers. In the example 47 + 39, comparison tells you that both numbers are less than 50. Therefore, their sum is less than 100.

4. Estimation can also be done by using front digits. This is called **front-end** estimation. To estimate 7,556 − 1,321, subtract the thousands: 7,000 − 1,000 = 6,000. Then adjust the answer: 556 is more than 321, so the answer must be *more than* 6,000.

5. A way to estimate quotients is to use **compatible numbers**, or numbers that are close to each other. For example, to divide 355 by 12, think of a number close to 355 that can be divided by 12 evenly: 360 ÷ 12 = 30.

6. In situations that require an exact answer, estimation is also helpful. Whether you compute with pencil and paper or with a calculator, it is a good idea to use estimation to check yourself and determine whether a particular answer to a problem is reasonable. If it is not, you should do the computation again.

Using estimation when you work with numbers will help you avoid careless errors.

Imagine, for example, that a recycling center collected 5,937 glass bottles, 7,365 plastic bottles, 3,779 metal cans, and 6,985 paper bags. What method would you use to calculate the total number of containers collected? It might be difficult to get an exact answer by performing this addition mentally. An accurate answer could be found in a reasonable amount of time using a pencil and paper. But a calculator would probably be the best choice to provide the correct answer quickly. Although computers can be used to perform lightning-fast calculations, they are best used for complex tasks, including organizing and displaying mathematical data, setting up graphs, and exploring mathematical patterns.

LYNN FLETCHER
Educational Writer
Reviewed by WILLIAM M. FITZGERALD
Professor of Mathematics
Michigan State University

See also DECIMAL SYSTEM; FRACTIONS; MATHEMATICS; NUMBERS AND NUMBER SYSTEMS; NUMERALS AND NUMERATION SYSTEMS.

ARIZONA

In 1736, a Yaqui Indian prospector discovered chunks of silver lying on the ground near a Spanish mining camp known as Arizonac. Pima Indians, who call themselves the O'odham ("the People"), lived in the region where the silver was found. Some scholars believe that the name Arizonac came from two Pima Indian words, ali and shonak, which mean "small springs." Because many of the first European miners and settlers were Basques from northern Spain, other scholars think that the word derived from the Basque term arritza onac ("valuable rocky places"). Whatever its origin, the name Arizonac eventually became Arizona.

State flag

Because of its dry climate and sparse vegetation, Arizona is a state where the geological bones of the earth—its mountains, canyons, mesas, and valleys—dominate the landscape. In the north, the Grand Canyon of the Colorado River cuts a mile deep through rock formations that are nearly 2 billion years old. In the south, the Sonoran Desert stretches in a series of broad valleys and rugged mountain ranges deep into Mexico.

Arizona has one of the most varied natural environments in North America. North of Tucson, the Mount Lemmon Highway climbs 6,000 feet (1,830 meters) up the Santa Catalina Mountains, passing in the course of a one-hour drive through desert, oak woodland, pinyon pine and juniper woodland, pine forest, and spruce-fir forest.

Arizona's cultural environment is just as varied. Arizona is part of the American Southwest, a region where many different groups encountered one another and fought for control of water and land. The descendants of those peoples continue to live there today. Arizona is a state in which many different ways of life coexist.

It is also a place where the past exists side by side with the present. People have inhabited Arizona for at least 11,000 years; today it is one of the fastest growing states in the nation. Despite its well-deserved reputation for wide-open spaces, Arizona is one of the most urban states as well, with two-thirds of its population residing in Phoenix and Tucson.

Most Arizonans work in those cities at manufacturing jobs or in service industries. Tourism is particularly important to the economy. Arizona's spectacular national forests, parks, and monuments draw millions of visitors to the state each year.

These national treasures underscore the importance of the federal government in Arizona. The U.S. government controls some 70 percent of Arizona's land. It also funded the giant water projects that provide much of the state with water for drinking, irrigation, and hydroelectric power.

▶LAND

Arizona is the sixth largest state in area. The Colorado River forms the western boundary with California. The northeastern corner touches the borders of Utah, New Mexico, and Colorado to form the Four Corners—the only point in the United States where four states meet. Although Arizona is landlocked, its southwestern border with the Mexican state of Sonora is less than 50 miles (80 kilometers) from the Pacific Ocean's Gulf of California.

Land Regions

Three major land regions—the Colorado Plateau, the Central Mountain Zone, and the Basin and Range—cross the state, giving Arizona great biological diversity as well as stunning natural beauty.

Clockwise from left: A desert vista includes ancient rock inscriptions left by Arizona's first inhabitants. Sightseers descend into the Grand Canyon—the state's best-known landmark—on mules. Native American culture is a vital part of modern Arizona life.

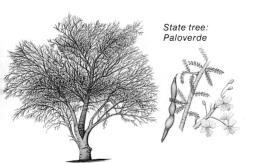

State flower:
Saguaro cactus blossom

State tree:
Paloverde

FACTS AND FIGURES

Location: Southwestern United States; bordered on the north by Utah, on the east by New Mexico, on the south by Mexico, and on the west by Nevada and California.

Area: 114,000 sq mi (295,260 km²); rank, 6th.

Population: 3,677,985 (1990 census); rank, 24th.

Elevation: *Highest*—12,633 ft (3,853 m) at Humphreys Peak; *lowest*—70 ft (21 m) along the Colorado River in Yuma County.

Capital: Phoenix.

Statehood: February 14, 1912; 48th state.

State Motto: *Ditat Deus* ("God enriches").

State Song: "Arizona."

Nickname: Grand Canyon State.

Abbreviations: AZ; Ariz.

State bird:
Cactus wren

The Colorado Plateau is Arizona's largest land region. Stretching into Utah, Colorado, and New Mexico, it extends across Arizona from the northwest to the southeast. The Colorado River and its tributaries have carved steep gorges into the layers of sedimentary rock that form the region. The deepest and best known of these gorges is the Grand Canyon. In between are high **mesas** (flat-topped hills), broken by volcanic craters and peaks.

The southern edge of the Colorado Plateau is the Mogollon Rim, which rises north of Prescott and runs south and east into New Mexico. With elevations of more than 7,000 feet (2,130 meters), it supports the largest stand of ponderosa pines in the world. The rest of the Colorado Plateau is lower and drier, with sparser vegetation. It includes the Painted Desert, famous for its barren rock landscapes, and Monument Valley, where spires of eroded rock tower over the high desert floor.

The Central Mountain Zone, below the Mogollon Rim, is an arc of mountain ranges that separates the Colorado Plateau from the Basin and Range. It is one of the wildest, most rugged regions of Arizona. Ranges such as the Bradshaws, Mazatzals, and Sierra Anchas cross northwestern and central Arizona. To the east are the White Mountains and the Blue Range. Much of Arizona's mineral wealth is concentrated in this region.

The Basin and Range, Arizona's third land region, extends across the western United States and Mexico. Most of Arizona's Basin and Range belongs to the Sonoran Desert, two-thirds of which lies in Mexico.

The Basin and Range is composed of isolated mountain ranges separated by broad, fertile valleys. As the region approaches Tucson, the valleys narrow and the mountains loom higher, reaching elevations of 8,000 to 12,000 feet (2,440 to 3,660 meters). Biologists call these high ranges **mountain islands**. By that they mean that the mountains contain plants and animals not found on the valley floors—the desert "oceans"—that surround them. Mountain islands occur throughout the state, but they are most distinctive in southeastern Arizona.

Above: The Mogollon Rim forms the southern edge of the Colorado Plateau. *Below:* The San Francisco Peaks, north of Flagstaff, are the state's highest mountains.

Rivers and Lakes

Although much of Arizona is desert country, rivers have shaped its landscape and its history. The Colorado River, the greatest river in the West, flows through or along Arizona's borders for nearly half its length. All other major rivers and streams in Arizona empty their waters into the Colorado.

The major tributary of the Colorado in northern Arizona is the Little Colorado River, which arises in the White Mountains. The Gila River and its major tributary, the Salt River, drain central and southern Arizona. They also provide most of the water that irrigates Arizona farms. The Verde River in central Arizona and the Santa Cruz and San Pedro rivers in southern Arizona also flow into the Gila system.

All of Arizona's major rivers have been dammed to provide water for irrigation and hydroelectric power. Those dams have created artificial lakes where Arizonans fish, boat, and

Hoover Dam, on the Colorado River between Arizona and Nevada, generates hydroelectric power and supplies water for agricultural and human use.

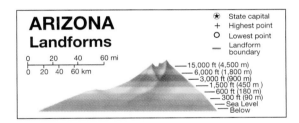

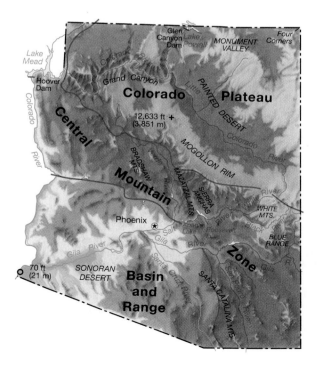

water-ski. Major dams along the Colorado River include Hoover Dam, which formed Lake Mead, and Glen Canyon Dam, which flooded magnificent Glen Canyon to create Lake Powell. Roosevelt Lake, Apache Lake, Canyon Lake, and Saguaro Lake are strung like beads along the Salt River.

Climate

Most of Arizona has a very dry climate. Precipitation (rain and snow) varies throughout the state according to the elevation of the land. Lowland areas like Yuma in the southwest average less than 5 inches (127 millimeters) of rain a year. Rain or snow on the tallest mountain peaks may exceed 30 inches (762 millimeters).

Arizona's moisture arrives during two distinct rainy seasons. During July and August, summer thundershowers provide about two-thirds of the annual rain. Winter storms bring about one-third.

Much of Arizona is as hot as it is dry. Average temperatures for January range from 50°F (10°C) in the lowlands to 30°F (−1°C) in the highlands. July temperatures average 90°F (32°C) in the lowlands and 65–75°F (18–24°C) in the mountains. Temperatures in the

deserts occasionally reach 120°F (49°C) in summer. Many portions of the desert endure more than 100 days of 100°F (38°C) heat a year.

Because Arizona is so hot and dry, farming is impossible without irrigation. The average number of days without a killing frost ranges from 240 around Yuma to 100 days at higher elevations in northern Arizona.

Plant and Animal Life

Arizona's varied environments support many different species of plants and animals. Black bears and elk inhabit the Mogollon Rim and the high mountain country. Herds of pronghorn antelope dart across the grasslands while bighorn sheep clamber over the summits of desert mountain ranges. Coyotes, mountain lions, bobcats, and mule deer range from the deserts to the mountains.

Perhaps the most distinctive plants and animals are those that have adapted to the hot, dry climate of the desert. Cacti such as the giant saguaro and the thorny cholla have broad, shallow root systems that quickly suck up scarce moisture, which is stored in their spongy stems. The tiny kangaroo rat has specialized kidneys that enable it to extract moisture from seeds, so it does not need to drink.

Natural Resources

Arizona is rich in minerals, particularly silver, gold, and copper. Black Mesa in northern Arizona contains enormous deposits of coal. Forests of ponderosa pine and Douglas fir stretch across the Mogollon Rim, while broad valleys in central and southern Arizona have soils suitable for farming. The only limitation on agriculture is water.

Because there are no major rivers south of the Gila, southern Arizona obtains most of its water from aquifers (underground deposits of water). Until 1993, Tucson was the largest city in the United States that pumped all its water from below ground. Now the canals and pipelines of the Central Arizona Project bring water from the Colorado River 335 miles (540 kilometers) across the desert to Phoenix, Tucson, and the farmers of south central Arizona.

▶ PEOPLE

Between 1940 and 1990, Arizona transformed itself from a rural to an overwhelmingly urban state. On the eve of World War II, 499,261 people lived in Arizona. By 1990, Arizona's population had soared to 3,665,228. More than 85 percent of those people live in cities and towns.

Most Arizonans come from other places, particularly California and the Midwest. Arizona society is mobile: For every ten people who settle in Arizona, seven move away.

Native Americans, in contrast, have inhabited Arizona for thousands of years and today make up about 5 percent of Arizona's population. Most belong to the 14 major Native American groups that occupy Arizona—the Navajos or Diné (the largest group), Hopis,

Western Apaches, Yavapais, Hualapais, Havasupais, Quechans, Mojaves, Maricopas, Cocopahs, Akimel O'odham, Tohono O'odham (formerly called Papago), Yaquis, and Southern Paiutes. Some 70 percent of Native Americans live on the state's 22 reservations.

Mexican Americans make up about 20 percent of the state's population. Some are recent immigrants from Mexico, particularly Sonora. Others come from families that have lived in Arizona for nine or ten generations.

Americans of European descent make up about 70 percent of Arizona's population. African Americans compose 3 percent, and about 2 percent of the state's residents are Asian Americans. All these relatively new arrivals join with American Indians and Mexican Americans to make Arizona one of the most multicultural states in the nation.

Education

The Arizona territorial legislature established the first public school system in 1871. There are three state universities. The University of Arizona in Tucson and the Arizona Territorial Normal School (now Arizona State University) in Tempe were founded in 1885. Northern Arizona University in Flagstaff was created in 1899.

Arizona also has numerous public community colleges, including Navajo Community College, which is run by the Navajo Nation. Private institutions include Grand Canyon College and the University of Phoenix, both in Phoenix; Prescott College, in Prescott; and the American Graduate School of International Management, in Glendale.

Libraries, Museums, and the Arts

Arizona has an active public library system, with bookmobiles and computers connecting rural communities with libraries in larger towns. The Arizona Historical Society,

Authentic dances of old Mexico are performed at a festival in Sedona. Arizona shares many cultural traditions with Mexico, its neighbor to the south.

founded in 1884, operates its main museum in Tucson. Museums that focus on Arizona's Native American heritage include the Arizona State Museum of the University of Arizona in Tucson; the Museum of Northern Arizona in Flagstaff; and the Heard Museum and the Pueblo Grande Museum, both in Phoenix.

Museums and botanical gardens devoted to the biological diversity of Arizona and the Sonoran Desert include the Arizona-Sonora Desert Museum west of Tucson, the Boyce Thompson Southwestern Arboretum near Superior, and the Desert Botanical Garden in Phoenix. The Phoenix and Tucson art museums contain important collections of Western, Mexican, and Native American art.

The Arizona Theater Company and other professional theater companies present plays in Tucson and Phoenix. Both Phoenix and Tucson have professional symphonies.

Arizona is internationally renowned for research in astronomy, anthropology, biology, and geology. One of the most important research institutions is the Desert Laboratory on

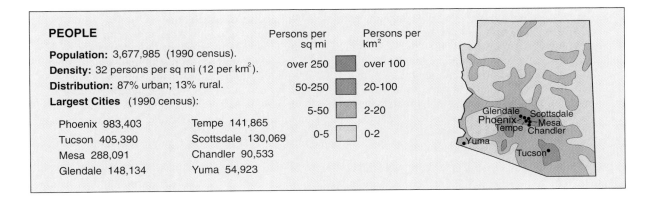

PEOPLE

Population: 3,677,985 (1990 census).

Density: 32 persons per sq mi (12 per km²).

Distribution: 87% urban; 13% rural.

Largest Cities (1990 census):

Phoenix 983,403	Tempe 141,865
Tucson 405,390	Scottsdale 130,069
Mesa 288,091	Chandler 90,533
Glendale 148,134	Yuma 54,923

Persons per sq mi	Persons per km²
over 250	over 100
50-250	20-100
5-50	2-20
0-5	0-2

Above: Kitt Peak National Observatory, west of Tucson, is a world-renowned center of astronomical research. *Right:* Technicians inspect computer chips. Many Arizonans are employed in the electronics industry.

Tumamoc Hill in Tucson, where scientists have been studying the ecology of the Sonoran Desert for nearly a century. Another is the Kitt Peak National Observatory, west of Tucson.

▶ECONOMY

Before World War II, Arizona's economy was dominated by the so-called Three C's: copper, cattle, and cotton. Those industries remain important, but today most Arizonans work in the manufacturing or service sectors of the economy. More job growth was anticipated with the passage in 1994 of the North American Free Trade Agreement (NAFTA), which established a free-trade zone among Mexico, Canada, and the United States.

Services

More than 75 percent of Arizona's workers are engaged in service occupations. Many of these industries arose to serve the large numbers of tourists who visit the state each year. Businesses located along the Arizona-Sonora border rely heavily on customers from Mexico. Among the most important service industries are business, social, and personal services, such as banking, health care, and hotels and restaurants. Wholesale and retail trade are also important service activities.

Many Arizonans work for the local, state, or federal government, running public schools, administering federal and state lands, and managing Indian reservations and military installations. Other service industries are finance, insurance, and real estate and transportation, communicaton, and utilities.

Manufacturing

Manufacturing employs about 15 percent of Arizona's workforce. Leading products are machinery, transportation equipment, and electrical and electronic equipment.

Many manufacturing jobs are in the electronics and aerospace industries and rank high in terms of average annual salary. However,

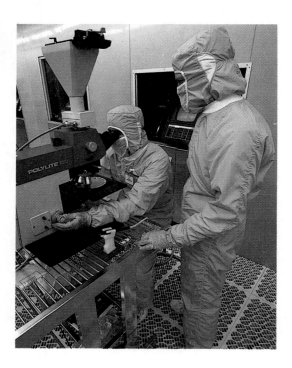

because many of these companies depend on government defense contracts, employment in manufacturing can be uneven. For example, the collapse of the Soviet Union and the end of the U.S.-Soviet arms race in the early 1990's led to layoffs in some Arizona electronics and aerospace companies. Nonetheless, the general trend in manufacturing seems to be expansion.

Mining and Construction

Mining, especially copper mining, was formerly the most important industry in Arizona. Today mining employs less than 1 percent of Arizona's workforce. The copper industry slumped in the 1980's, and although production rose again in the early 1990's, fewer miners were needed because of changes in technology.

A cattle drive on the Fort Apache Indian Reservation. Ranching, once a mainstay of the Arizona economy, remains an important industry in rural areas of the state.

Coal mining is restricted to Black Mesa in northern Arizona. On thousands of acres leased from the Navajo Nation and the Hopi tribe, coal is stripped from the ground with enormous draglines. Some of the coal fuels the Navajo Generating Station at Page. Mixed with water, the rest slides down a 274-mile (441-kilometer)-long pipeline to a power plant on the Colorado River in southern Utah.

Arizona's rapid growth has created employment opportunities in the construction industry. Federal projects such as the digging of irrigation canals also employ construction workers.

Agriculture and Forestry

Agriculture, ranching, and forestry remain important industries in rural Arizona. Arizona is a leading producer of cotton. Thousands of acres of alfalfa, wheat, vegetables, and citrus fruit are also cultivated. Although agriculture uses 80 to 85 percent of Arizona's water, it employs less than 3 percent of the state's workforce.

Ranching is a statewide industry, with most ranchers grazing their cattle and sheep on Arizona's public lands. About 40 percent of Arizona's total dollar value for agricultural production comes from livestock sales. The logging industry employs almost as many Arizonans as copper mining. Nearly all the timber is cut in northern Arizona, where most of the sawmills are located as well.

Transportation and Communication

Arizona is linked to the rest of North America by five interstate highways and two transcontinental railroads, the Santa Fe and Southern Pacific.

Two major international airports in Phoenix and Tucson connect Arizona to the nation and the world. More than 20 million people pass through Sky Harbor Airport in Phoenix each year. Because of its sunny skies, Arizona also has several major air bases, including Luke Air Force Base outside Phoenix and Davis-Monthan in Tucson.

All major Arizona cities have daily newspapers, and many rural communities have weekly newspapers. Radio and television stations, most originating from Phoenix and Tucson, broadcast throughout the state.

PRODUCTS AND INDUSTRIES

Manufacturing: Electrical and electronic equipment, transportation equipment, aerospace equipment, machinery.

Agriculture: Cattle, cotton, dairy products, lettuce, wheat, citrus fruit, sheep.

Minerals: Copper, silver, gold.

Services: Wholesale and retail trade; finance, insurance, and real estate; business, social, and personal services; transportation, communication, and utilities; government.

*Gross state product is the total value of goods and services produced in a year.

Percentage of Gross State Product* by Industry

Business, social, and personal services — 20%
Finance, insurance, and real estate — 17%
Wholesale and retail trade — 16%
Government — 14%
Manufacturing — 12%
Transportation, communication, and utilities — 9%
Construction — 8%
Agriculture 3%
Mining 1%

Source: U.S. Bureau of Economic Analysis

Places of Interest

Mission San Xavier del Bac

Grand Canyon National Park

Petrified Forest National Park

Betatakin Cliff Dwelling, Navajo National Monument

Many of Arizona's spectacular natural attractions are preserved as national forests, parks, and monuments. Some of the most outstanding are included in the descriptions below.

Canyon de Chelly National Monument, on the Navajo Nation in northeastern Arizona, is a sandstone canyon shaped like the talon of a hawk. At Spider Rock, a great sandstone spire, the cliffs rise nearly 1,000 feet (305 meters) above the canyon floor. Canyon de Chelly contains Anasazi Indian ruins built at the base of cliffs and in caves. The two most spectacular ruins are White House and Antelope House. Navajo (Diné) Indians farm small plots and graze their herds of sheep and cattle within the canyon.

Grand Canyon National Park is perhaps the most famous national park in the world. Set aside as a forest reserve in 1893 and a national park in 1919, the Grand Canyon attracts millions of tourists each year. An article on the Grand Canyon can be found in Volume G.

Kitt Peak National Observatory, on the Tohono O'odham Reservation, is a world-renowned center of astronomical observation and research.

London Bridge, in Lake Havasu City, is a historic stone bridge originally built in London, England, that was taken down and reassembled in Arizona. It spans an inlet of the Colorado River.

Mission San Xavier del Bac, south of Tucson, was founded as a Jesuit mission among the O'odham (Pima) Indians by Padre Eusebio Francisco Kino in 1700. The church itself, built by Franciscans in the late 1700's, is a magnificent example of baroque architecture and art. San Xavier continues to be used as a place of worship by the O'odham of the San Xavier Reservation.

Navajo National Monument, in northern Arizona, contains some of the most spectacular Anasazi cliff dwellings in the Southwest. Cliff dwellings such as Keet Seel and Betatakin appear to be timeless extensions of the sandstone cliffs to which they cling; in fact, anthropologists believe they were built, occupied, and abandoned between A.D.1267 and 1300.

Petrified Forest National Park, east of Holbrook, preserves prehistoric trees that turned to rock millions of years ago. The fallen trees and logs are scattered over thousands of acres. The park includes a portion of the **Painted Desert,** a barren area whose rock formations are tinted in shades of red, blue, and purple.

Roosevelt Dam, on the Salt River east of Phoenix, is the foundation of modern Arizona. Completed in 1911 by the National Reclamation Service, the dam controlled flooding along the Salt. It also provided the irrigation water and hydroelectric power to turn the Salt River Valley into one of the largest agricultural oases in the Southwest and Phoenix into the largest metropolitan center between California and Texas.

Saguaro National Monument consists of two units east and west of Tucson. Both protect dense stands of giant saguaro cactus in the Tucson Mountains and the foothills of the Rincon Mountains. Tohono O'odham (Papago Indians) are still allowed to harvest saguaro fruit in the monument in the early summer.

San Pedro Riparian Conservation District, along the San Pedro River in southeastern Arizona, was set aside by the federal Bureau of Land Management to preserve one of the last stretches of natural river habitat in Arizona. It protects great forests of cottonwoods and many species of birds and animals.

Tombstone, in Cochise County, became a mining boomtown after silver was found in the area in the 1870's. It is the site of the O.K. Corral, where Wyatt Earp, Doc Holliday, and other gunfighters took part in a famous shootout.

State Areas. Arizona maintains numerous state parks that preserve its natural beauty and its historical heritage. For more information, contact the Arizona State Parks Office, 800 W. Washington, Suite 415, Phoenix, Arizona 85007.

▶ CITIES

Arizona has two major metropolitan areas. The largest is Phoenix and its satellites of Mesa, Glendale, Tempe, and Scottsdale. The other is the Tucson metropolitan area.

Phoenix is Arizona's capital and largest city. It became the territorial capital in 1889 and the state capital in 1912. Today it is a center of commerce and industry. Sun City, one of the first planned retirement communities in the United States, is part of the Phoenix metropolitan area. An article on Phoenix appears in Volume P.

Tucson, Arizona's second largest city, is located on the Santa Cruz River in the south central part of the state. Its name comes from a Pima Indian phrase meaning "at the foot of black mountain." Tucson was founded by the Spanish in 1775. It was the territorial capital from 1868 to 1877. An article on Tucson appears in Volume T.

Mesa, Arizona's third largest city, was founded by Mormon settlers in 1878. Originally an agricultural center, Mesa now anchors the rapidly urbanizing eastern portion of the Salt River Valley known as the East Valley.

Glendale began as an agricultural community promoted by canal-company developers in the late 1800's. Today it is the key city in the northwestern portion of the Phoenix metropolitan area. The American Graduate School of International Management is located there.

Tempe was known as Hayden's Ferry when it was founded in 1872 at a crossing on the Salt River. Like other cities in the Salt River Valley, its agricultural origins have largely

Above: The state capitol in Phoenix. *Below left:* The capital since 1912, Phoenix is also Arizona's largest city and a center of commerce and industry.

given way to urban and industrial growth. Arizona State University is located there.

Scottsdale, located east of Phoenix, was founded in 1896 by Winfield Scott, a former army chaplain. Today the city, which calls itself "The West's Most Western Town," has many popular resorts and is a center of Western and Native American art markets.

Yuma, on the Colorado River in the southwestern portion of the state, is the center of a thriving agricultural area that includes the Wellton-Mohawk Valley along the lower Gila River. Thousands of tourists winter in the Yuma area each year.

▶ GOVERNMENT

The state constitution was drafted in 1910 and approved by the people in 1911.

The governor heads the executive branch of the state government. The legislative branch is composed of a senate and a house of representatives. The judicial branch includes a supreme court of five justices.

Elected boards of supervisors administer Arizona's 15 counties. Most cities have city managers and city councils as well as mayors.

GOVERNMENT

State Government
Governor: 4-year term
State senators: 30; 2-year terms
State representatives: 60;
2-year terms
Number of counties: 15

Federal Government
U.S. senators: 2
U.S. representatives: 6
Number of electoral votes: 8

For the name of the current governor, see STATE GOVERNMENTS in Volume S. For the names of current U.S. senators and representatives, see UNITED STATES, CONGRESS OF THE in Volume U-V.

▶ HISTORY

People have occupied Arizona for at least 11,000 years. Early peoples survived by gathering wild plant foods and hunting game. Farming began about 1000 B.C. in well-watered areas such as the Tucson Basin.

Beginning about A.D. 200, Arizona's three major pre-European cultures developed. The Anasazi inhabited the Colorado Plateau, where they built cliff dwellings and large pueblos. The Mogollon occupied the highlands of eastern Arizona and western New Mexico. The Hohokam lived in central and southern Arizona. Along the Salt and Gila rivers, the Hohokam created the largest pre-European system of irrigation canals in North America.

Spanish Exploration and Settlement

The first European to enter Arizona was Fray Marcos de Niza, a Franciscan missionary. In 1539, the Spanish government sent him to search for the legendary Seven Cities of Cíbola, which were supposedly made of gold. A year later, a much larger expedition led by Francisco Vásquez de Coronado investigated de Niza's claims that he found the Seven Cities among the Zuni Indians of northwestern New Mexico. Those claims proved false, and Spain lost interest in Arizona until the late 1600's. Between 1687 and his death in 1711, Jesuit missionary Eusebio Francisco Kino established missions in northern Sonora and southern Arizona.

The arrival of the Europeans changed Indian life in Arizona in both good ways and bad. Old World diseases, such as smallpox and measles, killed thousands of Native Americans. But the Europeans also introduced horses, cattle, and sheep as well as crops, such as wheat, that could be grown in the winter.

Some Indians, such as the Pimas, became reluctant allies of the Spaniards. But others, particularly the Apaches, resisted the Spaniards and raided their settlements for horses and cattle. Because of Indian resistance, Spanish Arizona was confined to the valley of the Santa Cruz river. The first major Spanish settlement was Tubac, founded as a **presidio** (military garrison) in 1752. In 1775, the Spaniards transferred the presidio to Tucson.

Mexican Arizona

When Mexico won its independence from Spain in 1821, Arizona became part of the

new republic of Mexico. The Mexican government awarded nine large land grants to Mexican ranchers in southern Arizona. However, by the 1840's the ranchers had been driven from the land by the Apaches.

In 1846, war broke out between Mexico and the United States. The Treaty of Guadalupe Hidalgo in 1848 ended the war and gave to the United States the territory of New Mexico, which included present-day Arizona north of the Gila River. Six years later, in 1854, Mexico sold southern Arizona to the United States under the Gadsden Purchase.

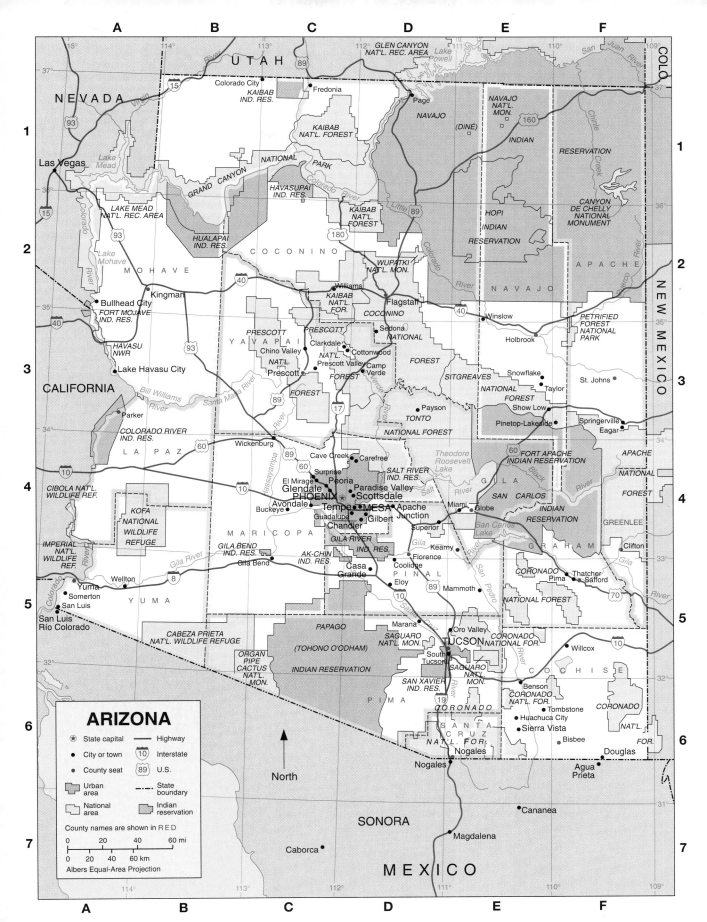

Famous People

Bruce Babbitt (1938–), who grew up in Flagstaff, was elected attorney general of Arizona in 1974. From this position he unexpectedly succeeded to the governorship of the state on the death of the incumbent governor in 1978. Elected to two terms in his own right, Babbitt crusaded against land fraud and forged the Groundwater Management Act, which strictly regulated the pumping of Arizona's groundwater. President Bill Clinton appointed Babbitt U.S. secretary of the interior in 1993.

Cochise (1810?–74) was chief of the Chokonen band of the Chiricahua Apaches. He was one of the greatest Apache war leaders and diplomats of the 1800's. From his homeland in southeastern Arizona, Cochise and his fellow Chiricahuas fought both the U.S. and Mexican governments. He finally made peace with the United States in 1871. Cochise spent the last years of his life trying to negotiate a lasting peace between the Chiricahuas and the United States government.

Barry Goldwater (1909–), born in Phoenix, was one of the architects of the modern conservative movement in the United States. He served as U.S. senator from Arizona from 1953 to 1987. In 1964, he won the Republican nomination for president but lost the national election to Lyndon Johnson. Goldwater served as chairman of the Senate's Armed Services Committee and its Intelligence Committee.

Carl T. Hayden (1877–1972) was born in Tempe. He grew up watching the farmers of the Salt River Valley battle floods and droughts, especially during the disastrous years of the 1890's, and developed a lifelong interest in water control. He pursued this interest when, upon Arizona's admission to the Union in 1912, he became the state's first representative in Congress. Hayden remained in Con-

Barry Goldwater

gress until 1927 and then entered the U.S. Senate, serving from 1927 to 1969. In 1968 he secured approval for the Central Arizona Project, fulfilling his lifelong dream.

George W. P. Hunt (1859–1934), a rancher in the Salt River Valley, was president of Arizona's constitutional convention (1910) and was elected the state's first governor (1912). He went on to win re-election six more times. Hunt was a champion of the Arizona labor movement and an enemy at times of the big copper companies. He also was the president of a bank in Globe.

Helen Hull Jacobs (1908–), born in Globe, was a tennis champion in the 1920's and 1930's. She was the first person to win the U.S. women's singles title four years in a row. She also took the singles title at Wimbledon, England,

Territorial Arizona

During the Civil War (1861–65), most Arizonans favored the South. Confederate troops occupied Tucson in 1862 but were soon driven out by Union forces. Arizona was separated from the territory of New Mexico in 1863. Prescott, the center of a mining district, became the first capital of the Arizona Territory.

After the Civil War, more prospectors, ranchers, and farmers moved to Arizona. The newcomers invaded the traditional lands of several Indian groups, who defended their homelands and tried to drive the miners and ranchers out. By the 1870's, most of these groups had been defeated and settled on reservations. But the Chiricahua Apaches, under such leaders as Cochise and Geronimo, waged brilliant campaigns of guerrilla warfare against both the U.S. and Mexican governments. With the surrender of Geronimo in 1886, Apache armed resistance ended.

Development and Statehood

The arrival of railroads in the early 1880's transformed Arizona's economy, enabling Arizona's major products—cattle, copper, and cotton—to be transported throughout the country.

The number of cattle in the territory increased from about 5,000 in 1870 to 1.5 million in the early 1890's. Arizona ranchers shipped most of their cattle by railroad to California or the Midwest to be slaughtered.

Copper mining did not become feasible until technological changes in the late 1800's enabled mining companies to extract low-grade ores. Huge underground and open-pit copper mines in Bisbee, Superior, Ajo, and other boomtowns made Arizona the largest producer of copper in the United States.

Large-scale agriculture could not take place in Arizona until rivers had been dammed to control floods and provide irrigation water. The Salt River Project, a federally funded irrigation project, constructed the Theodore Roosevelt Dam on the Salt River near Phoenix. The dam, which was completed in 1911, allowed farmers in the Salt River Valley to cultivate several hundred thousand acres of land.

A movement to make Arizona a state arose in the 1890's, but not until 1910 did Congress allow Arizona to draft a constitution and apply for statehood. Arizona became the 48th state on February 14, 1912. Phoenix, which had been made the territorial capital in 1889, became the state capital.

where she was a six-time finalist. Jacobs was elected to the Tennis Hall of Fame in 1962.

Estevan Ochoa (1831–88), with his partner Pinckney Randolph Tully, operated one of the largest long-distance freighting companies in the Arizona Ter-

Estevan Ochoa

Helen Hull Jacobs

ritory. Ochoa also was a territorial legislator and a founder of the Arizona public school system. During the 1870's, he was a leading citizen of Tucson, serving as the first Mexican mayor of the city in 1875.

Sandra Day O'Connor (1930–) grew up on her family's ranch in Duncan. She served in the Arizona state senate and as a judge in the Arizona court system before becoming, in 1981, the first woman appointed to the U.S. Supreme Court. O'Connor is profiled in SUPREME COURT OF THE UNITED STATES in Volume S.

Linda Ronstadt (1946–), born in Tucson, is a well-known pop singer. Having first gained fame in the world of rock and country-rock, she later returned to her Southwest roots, recording albums of Mexican folk songs. Ronstadt springs from a musically prominent Tucson family. Her paternal grandfather, a native of Mexico who moved to Tucson as a young man, founded one of the city's first orchestras. Her aunt, **Luisa (Ronstadt) Espinel** (1892–1963), was a well-known performer of Spanish and Latin-American folk music during the 1920's and 1930's.

Stewart Udall (1920–), born in St. Johns, won fame as both a politician and an environmentalist. He practiced law in Tucson and served in the U.S. House of Representatives from 1955 until 1961, when President John F. Kennedy appointed him U.S. secretary of the interior. He held that post until 1969. His brother, **Morris Udall** (1922–), succeeded him in Congress, serving from 1961 until 1991.

Later Developments

Beginning with World War II (1939–45), Arizona transformed itself from a rural to an urban state. Because of Arizona's good flying weather, the War Department built air bases throughout the state, training thousands of pilots there. The government also opened defense plants in Arizona. In addition, the war increased the demand for Arizona copper and other products.

Growth continued after the war ended. Wartime military and defense activities triggered a boom in electronics and aerospace manufacturing. The state's population grew as soldiers who had been stationed in Arizona returned there to live. Arizona's sunny, dry climate, now tempered by the use of air conditioning, attracted many new residents.

Arizona's Native Americans, who had been denied the right to vote in state elections until 1948, also profited from the economic boom. In the 1960's several tribes opened businesses on their reservations. In 1974 a long-standing land dispute between Hopi and Navajo tribes was settled by Congress. Land in northeastern Arizona that had been used jointly by the two tribes was divided between them. But the new boundary lines forced the relocation of many

Indian families, and the settlement became a source of bitter controversy between Hopis and Navajos.

As the shift from rural to urban land uses continued, Arizona cities competed with farmers for water. The Salt River Project, which had turned the Phoenix area into an agricultural oasis in the early 1900's, now provided the water and power for Phoenix's phenomenal urban growth.

Arizona also tapped the water of the Colorado River. Under the terms of the Colorado River Compact, which Arizona signed in 1945, the state was entitled to 2.8 million acre-feet (3.5 billion cubic feet) of water from the Colorado each year. (An acre-foot equals enough water to cover an acre with a foot of water.) Congress finally approved the Central Arizona Project (CAP) in 1968. The CAP water was originally destined for agricultural use. By the time it finally reached Tucson in 1993, however, people were consuming much of it. As Arizona continues to grow, the struggle for water among various groups will undoubtedly intensify.

THOMAS E. SHERIDAN
Curator of Ethnohistory
Arizona State Museum

ARKANSAS

Early French explorers are credited with naming Arkansas after the Arkansa (or Arkansea) Indians. These Indians called themselves the Quapaw, meaning "downstream people," because they had settled in Arkansas after migrating down the Mississippi River. It was the tribes native to the region who named the newcomers the Arkansa, which in their own language meant "south wind people."

When the United States acquired Arkansas as part of the Louisiana Purchase of 1803, the spelling was changed to Arkansaw *to match its pronunciation, but it was soon changed back again. Ongoing confusion over the spelling and pronunciation finally prompted the state legislature to pass a law in 1881: The name of the state would be spelled* Arkansas, *but it would be pronounced* Arkansaw.

State flag

Arkansas is a southern state, located along the western bank of the Mississippi River. Its eastern and southern regions are covered by open plains that support large plantations on which cotton, soybeans, rice, and other cash crops are grown. To the north and west lie rugged highlands, featuring the beautiful Ozark Plateau and the Ouachita Mountains.

Much of Arkansas's history is linked to its agricultural past. Until 1865, state politics were dominated by slave-holding plantation owners, who supported withdrawal from the Union during the Civil War; in the 1880's dissatisfied small-scale farmers founded a new political party to protect their interests; and during the Great Depression of the 1930's, black and white tenant farmers and sharecroppers joined together to form the nation's first biracial farmers' union.

Despite the steady growth of manufacturing and the service industries in more recent years, the state continues to be associated with its agricultural production. Today Arkansas is the nation's leading producer of rice and poultry.

The largest segment of Arkansas's population lives in the farming regions in the south and east. However, the entire state is becoming increasingly urbanized and large numbers now live in central Arkansas, in or near Little Rock, the state's capital and largest city. The population in the northwest is also expanding due to the growth of tourism, the poultry industry, and retirement communities.

The state's official nickname, the Land of Opportunity, was adopted in 1953 to advertise the state's many assets and to attract new industries. The nickname the Natural State, which appears on Arkansas's state license plates, is the state slogan.

▶ LAND

From east to west, Arkansas rises from the plains of the Mississippi Delta to the Ozarks and the Ouachita Mountains.

Land Regions

The land is divided into two main geographic regions—the lowlands in the southeast and the highlands in the northwest.

The Lowlands include the Mississippi Alluvial Plain, often called the Delta, and the West Gulf Coastal Plain. The Delta, which lies in the east along the Mississippi River, covers nearly one third of the state. The West Gulf Coastal Plain lies in the south-central part of the state and extends into neighboring Louisiana and Texas. The entire lowland area is relatively flat. It was once swampland, but most of it has been drained and put to agricultural use.

Natives of the Ozarks dedicate themselves to preserving regional customs and the unspoiled rural beauty of the Highlands. Ozark heritage celebrations, such as the annual Arkansas Folk Festival in Mountain View, feature traditional folk music, arts, and crafts.

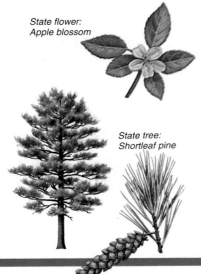

State flower:
Apple blossom

State tree:
Shortleaf pine

FACTS AND FIGURES

Location: South central United States; bordered on the north by Missouri, on the east by Tennessee and Mississippi, on the south by Louisiana, and on the west by Oklahoma and Texas.

Area: 53,187 square miles (137,754 km²); rank, 27th.

Population: 2,362,239 (1990 census); rank, 33rd.

Elevation: *Highest* — 2,753 feet (839 m) at Magazine Mountain; *lowest* — 55 feet (17 m) along the Ouachita River.

Capital: Little Rock.

Statehood: June 15, 1836; 25th state.

State Motto: *Regnat populus* ("The people rule").

State Song: "Arkansas."

Nicknames: Land of Opportunity (official); Natural State; Diamond State.

Abbreviations: AR; Ark.

State bird:
Mockingbird

The Highlands are dominated by the Ozark Plateau and the Ouachita Mountains, with the Arkansas Valley between them. The Ozarks are sometimes referred to as mountains, but they are actually three eroded plateaus of increasing height: the Salem Upland, the Springfield Upland, and the Boston Mountains. The Ouachita Mountains, located in west-central Arkansas, rise more than 2,000 feet (610 meters). They are heavily wooded and known for their natural hot springs. The Arkansas Valley is lower-lying than the two regions it separates, and yet it has several high peaks of its own, including Magazine Mountain, the highest point in the state.

Rivers, Lakes, and Springs

Four great rivers flow through Arkansas: the Mississippi, the Arkansas, the Red, and the White. The Mississippi forms most of the state's eastern border. The Arkansas flows southeastward through the center of the state and empties into the Mississippi. Both rivers play important roles in transportation. Along with the White River and the Red River, they also serve as homes for wildlife and as places for recreation.

Dams have been constructed in a few of the smaller rivers, creating large artificial lakes. These lakes are chiefly in the Highlands and provide flood control, hydroelectric power, and recreation. Lake Chicot in the southeast is the state's largest natural lake.

Thermal springs attract tourists and other people who believe that bathing in them is good for their health. The water temperature at Hot Springs, a well-known resort, reaches about 140°F (60°C) at the surface. Mammoth Spring near the Missouri border is another well-known hot spring.

Climate

Arkansas enjoys a humid subtropical climate. Because of its inland location, Arkansas receives cold air masses from the heart of the North American continent in winter and hot air masses in summer. Far enough south, it also receives warm, moisture-laden winds from the Gulf of Mexico. The result is a relatively mild climate and an eight-month growing season that permits the cultivation of a wide range of crops.

July temperatures average about 80°F (27°C). The Highlands enjoy cooler summer nights than do the Lowlands. Similarly, the Highlands have somewhat colder winters. Average January temperatures in the state range between 36°F (2°C) and 48°F (9°C).

Most of the precipitation falls as rain, with the southern half of the state receiving more than the north. Snow sometimes falls in the northern mountains, but it is rare in the south. Arkansas ranks seventh among all 50 states in the amount of rainfall received. It averages about 49 inches (1,245 millimeters) per year.

Far left: The sandstone cliffs of Petit Jean Mountain overlook the beautiful Arkansas Valley. *Left:* Agriculture thrives in Arkansas's fertile Mississippi Delta region. *Right:* The soothing effects of the natural hot mineral springs in the Ouachita Mountains attract tourists from all over the world.

Plant and Animal Life

One hundred years ago, Arkansas was nearly covered by great forests of deciduous and evergreen trees, but today the majority of wooded land in the Mississippi and Arkansas river valleys has been cleared for farmland. Arkansas also has grasslands on its eastern prairies and in two counties in the northwest.

Many kinds of wildlife abound in Arkansas. Deer, fish, wild turkeys, and migrating ducks and geese, which feed in the rice fields, are abundant. Trout, largemouth bass, and small-mouth bass are among the many popular game fish. Squirrels, opossums, rabbits, weasels, and many other small mammals are found throughout the state. Black bears, which had nearly disappeared from the state, have been brought back and now thrive in the Boston Mountains.

Natural Resources

Arkansas's soils, forests, and minerals provide the raw materials that are so important to the economic life of the state.

The state's most fertile soils are its limestone and alluvial soils, which produce many different crops when properly fertilized and cultivated. The soils in the rice-growing areas have a subsoil that will not let water drain easily, which helps irrigate the rice.

Despite clearing by early settlers, forests still cover approximately one half of the state and are important economically. Softwood forests of shortleaf pine and loblolly pine are found in the south; hardwood forests of oak and hickory are found in the north, in the Mississippi Valley, and along southern streams.

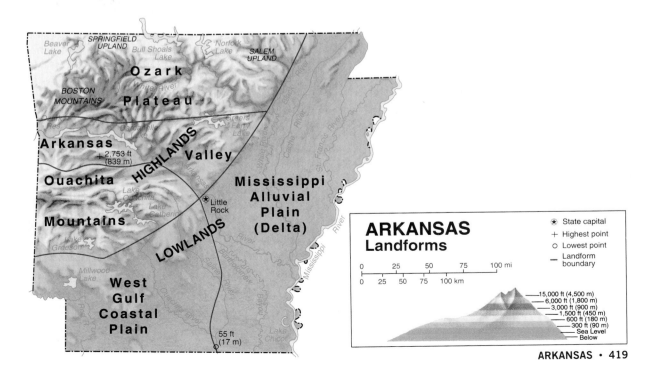

Left: Arkansans who live in rural areas enjoy the benefits of country living, but increasing numbers are moving to urban areas in search of economic opportunities. *Above:* University of Arkansas football fans huddle for warmth at Razorback Stadium in Fayetteville.

Most of the state's minerals are located in the West Gulf Coastal Plain and the Arkansas Valley. They include petroleum, natural gas, natural-gas liquids, clays, coal, and bauxite, from which aluminum is obtained. Stone is quarried in the highlands. Diamonds also are found in abundance, although they are no longer mined commercially.

▶**PEOPLE**

The people of Arkansas are known as Arkansans or Arkansawyers. Approximately 54 percent live in urban areas; the other half live in rural areas—places with fewer than 2,500 residents. The Lowlands are more populous than the Highlands due to the Lowlands' productive agriculture, mineral wealth, and transportation facilities. The Highlands attract retired people because of the beautiful scenery, moderate cost of living, and pleasant climate.

The Caddo, Osage, and Quapaw Indians originally inhabited Arkansas, but few remain there today. In the 1800's, most were forced onto reservations in Oklahoma as a result of the westward expansion of Anglo-Americans.

Most of the Anglo settlers that first came to Arkansas were descendants of colonial southerners, most of whom had originally come from northwestern Europe. They brought with them to Arkansas the traditions and practices of the Old South, notably cotton production and slavery. Later settlers included Germans, Italians, Chinese, and Lebanese, who came to work on Arkansas's farms and railroads and in the lumber mills and mines.

Since the 1970's, Arkansas has shown a consistent gain in overall population. The African-American population, however, has declined and today stands at about 16 percent.

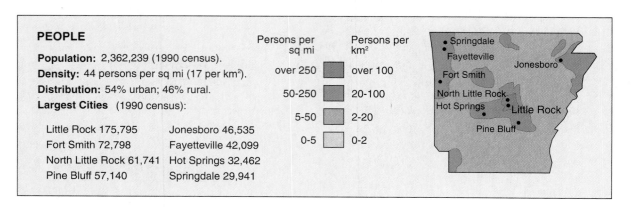

PEOPLE

Population: 2,362,239 (1990 census).
Density: 44 persons per sq mi (17 per km²).
Distribution: 54% urban; 46% rural.
Largest Cities (1990 census):

Little Rock 175,795	Jonesboro 46,535
Fort Smith 72,798	Fayetteville 42,099
North Little Rock 61,741	Hot Springs 32,462
Pine Bluff 57,140	Springdale 29,941

Persons per sq mi	Persons per km²
over 250	over 100
50-250	20-100
5-50	2-20
0-5	0-2

Springdale
Fayetteville
Jonesboro
Fort Smith
North Little Rock
Hot Springs
Little Rock
Pine Bluff

Education

When Congress created the Arkansas Territory in 1819, it set aside a section of land in each county for public schools. In 1843, the state legislature established a system for public education, but until the Civil War, most of the schools in operation were private. Today's public school system is largely based on a plan established by the state constitution in 1868.

Arkansas has 17 accredited four-year colleges and universites. The largest is the University of Arkansas, which has its main campus at Fayetteville; other campuses at Little Rock, Monticello, and Pine Bluff; and a medical sciences campus at Little Rock.

Other state-supported four-year institutions are at Jonesboro, Conway, Russellville, Magnolia, and Arkadelphia. Private four-year colleges include the University of the Ozarks in Clarksville, Hendrix College in Conway, and Harding University in Searcy.

Libraries, Museums, and the Arts

Arkansas's first library system was established in the mid-1800's. However, the growth of public libraries was slow, partly because the people lived in widely scattered rural areas. The Arkansas Library Commission was established in 1935 to address this problem. It maintains a book collection at Little Rock from which volumes are sent by mail to individuals, schools, and organizations. Bookmobiles operate throughout the state, and most of the cities support free public libraries.

The fine arts are represented in Arkansas by various activities. Little Rock has a choral society, an opera company, a repertory theater, and a symphony orchestra. Fort Smith and Pine Bluff also have · symphony orchestras. Poets and writers have settled in Eureka Springs in northwest Arkansas where they have developed a lively and productive literary and artistic community.

The Arkansas Arts Center, in Little Rock, contains the state's most important collection of paintings and other fine arts. Also of note in Little Rock is the Museum of Science and History. The University of Arkansas Museum in Fayetteville contains Arkansas Indian artifacts and many science and natural history exhibits.

Arkansas is rich in folklore and legends. The Ozark Folk Center in Mountain View celebrates Arkansas folk culture. It provides live demonstrations of traditional arts and crafts during the summer. The library at the University in Fayetteville has a large and unusual Arkansas folklore collection that includes tape-recorded histories and stories told by Arkansas residents.

▶ECONOMY

In the past, Arkansas depended almost entirely on its farm products for its income. Products such as cotton, livestock, and poultry remain important income producers. However, in recent years services and manufacturing have become the state's primary economic activities.

Services

Arkansas's various service industries employ 70 percent of the state's entire work force. Wholesale and retail trade (the buying

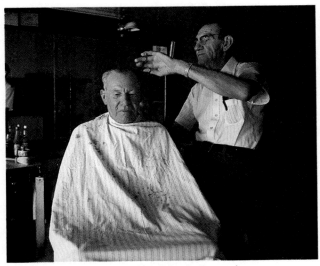

Most people in Arkansas make a living in the service industries. Personal services include such everyday activities as barbering and hairdressing.

and selling of industrial and personal goods) are the most profitable within the services category. They are followed by financial services (banking, insurance, and real estate); professional and personal services (such as medical, tourist, and other social services); and government (which includes the maintenance of state-supported schools, hospitals, and the like). Remaining service industries are in transportation and communication.

Arkansas is the nation's leading producer of rice (*above*) and broiler chickens (*right*). The state's economy once depended on agriculture, but today it is based more on the service industries and on manufacturing, particularly food processing.

Manufacturing

Manufacturing employs about 25 percent of Arkansas's work force. The most important manufacturing industry is food processing, including the canning of fruits and vegetables and the processing of poultry and livestock.

Industries that make electrical equipment also are profitable. Among Arkansas's many products are electric motors, refrigerators and ranges, air conditioners, television sets, and lightbulbs. Arkansas factories also produce clothing, plastic and metal products, and chemicals.

Agriculture

Arkansas's Lowlands belong to a wider region of the South known as the Cotton Belt, and farmers there once grew only this crop. Cotton production has since declined in importance, but it still brings much income to the state. Today Arkansas ranks sixth in the nation in cotton production.

Today rice and soybeans are Arkansas's most profitable cash crops. In fact, Arkansas rice farmers supply an international market, including Japan. Arkansas is also the nation's leading producer of broiler chickens.

Arkansas's forests provide the raw material for many of its manufacturing industries. Pine is used for wood pulp, which is used to make paper; oak and hickory are used to make furniture, barrels, and railroad ties.

PRODUCTS AND INDUSTRIES

Manufacturing: Food processing, electrical machinery and equipment, lumber and wood products, paper products, fabricated metal products, chemicals, nonelectrical machinery, rubber and plastic products.

Agriculture: Broiler chickens, soybeans, rice, wheat, cotton, eggs, milk, beef cattle, turkeys, sorghum grain, cottonseed, hogs, oats, hay, corn, grasses, grapes, snap beans, tomatoes.

Minerals: Petroleum, natural gas and natural gas liquids, bauxite, barite, coal, granite, gypsum, sand and gravel, limestone, marble.

Services: Wholesale and retail trade; finance, insurance, and real estate; business, social, and personal services; transportation, communication, and utilities; government.

*Gross state product is the total value of goods and services produced in a year.

Percentage of Gross State Product* by Industry

Manufacturing 24%
Mining 1%
Construction 5%
Agriculture 5%
Transportation, communication, and utilities 11%
Government 11%
Finance, insurance, and real estate 13.5%
Business, social, and personal services 13.5%
Wholesale and retail trade 16%

Source: U.S. Bureau of Economic Analysis

Mining and Construction

Petroleum and natural gas are important mineral products as are quartz crystals and crushed stone. Arkansas is the nation's leading producer of bauxite, the principal source of aluminum. It is also a leading producer of barite, a mineral used in the manufacture of paper, rubber, and other products. Mining and construction activities employ approximately 4 percent of the work force.

Transportation

The Mississippi River, the greatest river transportation system in the United States, has always been an important trade route to Arkansas. The Arkansas River also is used for limited amounts of freight traffic.

Four major and 24 short-line railways, covering 2,500 miles (4,000 kilometers) of tracks, operate within the state. Three of its rail systems are among the nation's largest: Burlington Northern, Inc.; the Union Pacific Railroad Company; and the Southern Pacific Transportation Company. Bus passenger service and bus and truck freight services also are important to the state's transportation systems. Arkansas has approximately 270 airports and airfields, and about one dozen commercial airlines serve the state. The principal airports are located in Little Rock and Hot Springs.

Communication

Until recently, Little Rock published two major daily newspapers, the *Arkansas Democrat* and the *Arkansas Gazette*. The *Gazette*, first published in 1819, had been the oldest newspaper in continuous publication west of the Mississippi River. The two newspapers combined to form the *Arkansas Democrat-Gazette*. More than 200 radio stations and 17 television stations broadcast throughout the state.

▶CITIES

Four cities in Arkansas have populations exceeding 50,000. Only one, Little Rock, has more than 100,000 people.

Little Rock, the state capital and largest city, was founded in 1820. Its name comes from a rocky outcropping on the Arkansas River that marked the early settlement. Located near the center of the state, Little Rock is a major market for cotton, soybeans, and other agricultural products. It is also the leading transportation and trade center and the home of a large number of industries. Many historic buildings, such as the old Capitol, are located here.

Fort Smith, a historical border city between Arkansas and what was once called Indian Territory, grew up around a fort built in 1817. It is now an important market center on the Arkansas River, serving western Arkansas and eastern Oklahoma. It is also a leading industrial center, producing refrigerators, heating equipment, paper cups, light metal products, and furniture.

North Little Rock is an industrial city across the river from Little Rock. Among its products are clothing, cosmetics, wood products, ma-

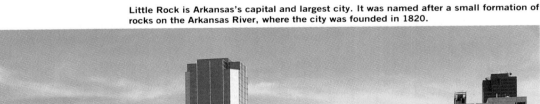

Little Rock is Arkansas's capital and largest city. It was named after a small formation of rocks on the Arkansas River, where the city was founded in 1820.

Places of Interest

Crater of Diamonds State Park, near Murfreesboro

Ozark Folk Center, in Mountain View

Blanchard Spring Caverns, near Mountain View

Buffalo National River, in the Ozarks

Arkansas Post National Memorial, near Gillett at the mouth of the Arkansas River, marks the first permanent European settlement (1686) in the Lower Mississippi River Valley. Founded by Henri de Tonti, it served as Arkansas's first territorial capital (1819–21).

Buffalo National River was the first in the United States to be designated a national river (1972). Canoeists and rafters enjoy its exciting rapids and waterfalls and its scenic canyons, cliffs, and forests. It winds for 132 miles (212 kilometers) through the Ozarks.

Blanchard Spring Caverns, located near Mountain View in the Ozark National Forest, is one of the largest caverns in the United States. It contains many dramatic stalactite and stalagmite formations. The surrounding forest, one of three national forests in the state, is known for its rugged beauty.

Crater of Diamonds State Park, near Murfreesboro, is the only active diamond mine in North America. Discovered by farmer John M. Huddleston in 1906, it is no longer mined commercially. Visitors,

however, may hunt for diamonds and keep whatever they find. More than 60,000 gems have been collected, some with a value of more than $100,000.

Eureka Springs, a resort town in the Ozarks, is known for its picturesque Victorian homes and tourist entertainments.

Hot Springs National Park, in Hot Springs, features a health spa and resort. Its naturally hot mineral waters reach a temperature of about 140°F (60°C). One million gallons flow from the spring each day. Visitors come to bathe in the mineral waters, which are said to be beneficial to one's health. The site was established as a national park in 1921. Thoroughbred racing is featured at nearby Oaklawn Park from February through April.

MacArthur Park, in downtown Little Rock, is home of the Arkansas Arts Center and the Museum of Science and History. The museum occupies the Old Arsenal Building, built in 1838, which was the birthplace of General Douglas MacArthur. The park is named for him.

Ozark Folk Center, in Mountain View, preserves Ozark folk arts. Craftspeople

demonstrate traditional skills, such as blacksmithing, candle making, quilting, and weaving. Musicians also give live folk-music performances.

Pea Ridge National Military Park, located near Rogers, commemorates the largest Civil War battle fought west of the Mississippi River. More than 26,000 troops took part in the battle, which took place March 7–8, 1862. At the battle's end, Union forces had defeated the Confederate troops.

Toltec Mounds, in Scott, is an ancient ceremonial complex made of earthen mounds. The mounds once had buildings on them, probably used for religious purposes. They were built between A.D. 700 and 950 by people of the Plum Bayou Culture. Mistakenly named for Indians from Mexico, they are among the largest and most complex ancient sites in the Lower Mississippi River valley.

State Parks. Arkansas has 44 state parks and 3 state museums. For information, contact Arkansas State Parks, Department of Parks and Tourism, One Capitol Mall, Little Rock, Arkansas 72201.

chinery, and food products. Together with Little Rock it forms a large metropolitan area with a population of more than 390,000.

Pine Bluff, founded in 1819, is a commercial center in a rich agricultural region. It produces paper and other wood products, clothing, and light metal products. It is a major transportation hub for the southeastern part of the state.

▶GOVERNMENT

The government of Arkansas is organized under the constitution adopted in 1874 and its various amendments. The 1874 constitution was the state's fifth. The first was adopted in 1836 when Arkansas became a state. The second was adopted when Arkansas withdrew from the Union in 1861. Others were adopted as a result of the Civil War and its aftermath.

All of the constitutions have provided for three branches of government, with largely separate powers. The legislative branch, called the General Assembly, consists of two bodies: the Senate and the House of Representatives. Senators are elected to 4-year terms, representatives to 2-year terms.

The executive branch consists of a governor and six other state officers—the lieutenant governor, secretary of state, attorney general, treasurer, auditor, and land commissioner. Each is elected by the people to a 4-year term. Other members of the executive branch are appointed by the governor, with approval by the state senate often required.

The judicial branch interprets and applies the law. Four kinds of state courts make up this branch. They are the minor courts, the circuit courts, the chancery courts, and the Supreme Court. The Supreme Court consists of a chief justice and six associate justices, all elected to 8-year terms.

County and city governments have authority in various local matters, including taxation.

Arkansas's state capitol in Little Rock was modeled after the United States Capitol in Washington, D.C. The granite and marble structure was completed in 1915.

Important county officers are the county judge, county and circuit clerks, sheriff, assessor, collector, and treasurer.

▶HISTORY

Three Indian groups lived in the Arkansas region at the time of first contact with European explorers: the Quapaw in the east, the Caddo in the Ouachita and Red river valleys of the southwest, and the Osage in the west.

European Exploration

The first Europeans to visit Arkansas were Spanish explorers, who arrived in 1541 looking for gold. They were led by Hernando de Soto, who died in Arkansas the following year.

The next wave of visitors came 130 years later, when French explorers Father Jacques Marquette and Louis Jolliet traveled by canoe down the Mississippi River and reached the Arkansas River in 1673. In 1682, a French nobleman named Robert Cavelier, Sieur de La Salle, also traveled down the Mississippi to claim the river and its wide valley for the king

---

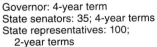

GOVERNMENT

State Government
Governor: 4-year term
State senators: 35; 4-year terms
State representatives: 100;
2-year terms
Number of counties: 75

Federal Government
U.S. senators: 2
U.S. representatives: 4
Number of electoral votes: 6

For the name of the current governor, see STATE GOVERNMENTS in Volume S. For the names of current U.S. senators and representatives, see UNITED STATES, CONGRESS OF THE in Volume U-V.

French explorers Father Jacques Marquette and Louis Jolliet first encountered the Quapaw Indians in 1673 when their expedition reached the Arkansas River.

of France. His faithful lieutenant, Henri de Tonti, returned to Arkansas in 1686, and at the mouth of the Arkansas River he founded a settlement the French called *Aux Arcs* (pronounced Ozarks), Arkansas's first permanent European settlement. Later it was renamed Arkansas Post.

The Louisiana Purchase and Statehood

Arkansas, which was claimed at various times by both France and Spain, was part of an enormous region that was called Louisiana. In 1803, the French emperor Napoleon I sold the territory to the United States. After the Louisiana Purchase, Arkansas was part of the Missouri Territory. Then in 1819 it became its own territory, with its own territorial governor. On June 15, 1836, Arkansas became the 25th state.

Withdrawal from the Union

In the early 1860's, with the threat of civil war surrounding the question of slavery, Arkansas voted against seceding (withdrawing) from the Union, unlike many other Southern states that seceded and formed the Confederate States of America. But after the Civil War began at Fort Sumter, South Carolina, on April 12, 1861, Arkansas joined the Southern states and seceded from the Union on May 6.

The Civil War and Reconstruction

The Civil War brought devastation and bitterness to Arkansas. About 60,000 Arkansans fought for the Confederacy; however, as many as 15,000 joined the Union forces. The largest battle that was fought west of the Mississippi River took place in Arkansas, at Pea Ridge on

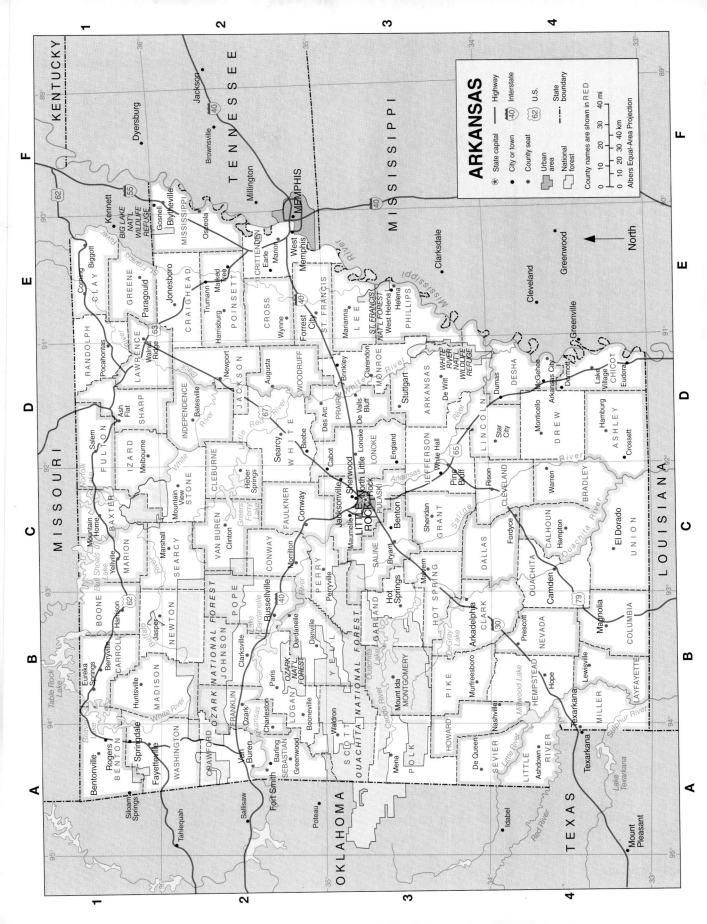

Famous People

Maya Angelou (1928–), born Marguerite Johnson in St. Louis, Missouri, was raised in Stamps. Her autobiography, about growing up during the civil rights movement, is entitled *I Know Why the Caged Bird Sings* (1970). Other works include *All God's Children Need Traveling Shoes* (1986) and *I Shall Not Be Moved* (1990). In 1993 she read a poem at the presidential inauguration of fellow Arkansan Bill Clinton that she wrote especially for the occasion.

Hattie Wyatt Caraway (1876–1950) was born near Bakersville, Tennessee, but later settled in Arkansas. A Democrat, she was the first woman elected to the U.S. Senate. In 1931 she completed her deceased husband's Senate term and was elected in her own right in 1932 and

Maya Angelou

Bill Clinton

1938. She sponsored an early version of the Equal Rights Amendment.

Johnny Cash (1932–), born in Kingsland, is a popular country music singer, guitarist, and composer. One of his first hit songs, "I Walk the Line," was recorded in 1956. He has won numerous Grammy Awards and has appeared in films and on television.

William Jefferson (Bill) Clinton (1946–), born and raised in Hope, was elected 42nd president of the United States in 1992. He had previously served twelve years as governor of Arkansas. A biography of Bill Clinton appears in Volume C.

Jay Hanna (Dizzy) Dean (1911–74), born in Lucas, was one of baseball's greatest pitchers. As a member of the St. Louis Cardinals, he led the National League in strikeouts for four years (1932–36) and in 1934 he won thirty games and the NL Most Valuable Player Award. In 1937 he injured his arm and was traded the following year to the Chicago Cubs. After his retirement in 1941 he became a sports announcer. He was elected to the National Baseball Hall of Fame in 1953.

March 7–8, 1862. Union forces won the battle and secured much of Arkansas and Missouri for the United States. After Union forces captured Little Rock in September 1863, the war was effectively over for Arkansas, although the civilians continued to suffer greatly. Arkansas was readmitted to the Union in 1868 but was occupied by federal troops until 1874.

Politics and Segregation

In the 1880's, many of Arkansas's tenant farmers and sharecroppers suffered due to low farm prices. In part, they blamed the Democrats who ruled the state legislature, and in 1886 they formed their own protest organization, the Agricultural Wheel, and ran "Wheeler" candidates for political office. The Democrats, in order to control dissent and drive a wedge between white "Wheelers" and black "Wheelers," passed laws that made it difficult for blacks to vote. Also, lynchings and other violence toward blacks increased.

Improvements and Reforms

In the early 1900's, during a period known as the Progressive Era, Arkansas's educational system was improved; a board of health was created; and a commission was formed to oversee the state's business interests. But in

spite of this era of optimism, Arkansas soon faced many setbacks.

In the 1920's a major depression in agriculture ruined many farmers. Then a tragic flood in 1927 killed many people and destroyed much of that year's crops. Four years later, as the Great Depression of the 1930's was getting underway, a great drought again ruined crops. The government's New Deal programs brought relief to farm owners but to few farmworkers. As a result, black and white tenant farmers and sharecroppers banded together to form the Southern Tenant Farmer's Union, the first biracial union in the nation's history. The group succeeded in bringing attention to the plight of farm laborers.

In the early 1940's, World War II helped Arkansas's economy, but at the same time, thousands of people left the state, either to serve in the armed forces or to work in defense-related industries. With the work force depleted, farmers began to rely more on machinery to harvest the crops, and eventually agriculture became fully mechanized.

Integration

In 1954, the U.S. Supreme Court declared that segregating black and white students in separate schools was unconstitutional. Arkan-

James William Fulbright (1905–) was born in Sumner, Missouri, but grew up in Fayetteville. A Rhodes scholar and lawyer, he served two terms as a U.S. representative (1942–45) and served five terms as a U.S. senator (1945–74) from Arkansas. In 1946 he sponsored the Fulbright Act, which provides scholarship funds to students studying abroad. As chairman of the Senate Foreign Relations Committee (1959–74), he was one of the chief congressional opponents of American involvement in the Vietnam War. The College of Arts and Sciences and the Institute of International Relations, both at the University of Arkansas, are named for him.

John Harold Johnson (1918–), born in Arkansas City, founded (1942) the Johnson Publishing Company, which publishes *Ebony* and *Jet* magazines. Johnson has also been highly successful in the fields of book publishing, radio broadcasting, and cosmetics. He was awarded the Spingarn Medal in 1966.

Scott Joplin (1868–1917) was probably born in the border town of Texarkana. The son of former slaves, this musical genius became known as the King of Ragtime. Joplin's lively compositions include the still-popular "Maple Leaf Rag" and "The Entertainer." However, he was not recognized as a serious composer until long after his death; he was awarded a Pulitzer prize in 1976.

Douglas MacArthur (1880–1964), born in Little Rock, was one of the United States' most brilliant generals. As commander of the U.S. Army in the Pacific during World War II (1941–45), his bold strategies helped defeat the Japanese. MacArthur also commanded (1950–51) the United Nations forces during the Korean War. A biography of Douglas MacArthur appears in Volume M.

Edward Durell Stone (1902–78), born in Fayetteville, was a noted architect. Often his buildings were designed around a courtyard, with bands of filtered light coming through the roofs and

Douglas MacArthur

ceilings. Among his best-known designs are the Museum of Modern Art (1937) in New York City; the U.S. Embassy (1954–58) in New Delhi, India; and the Kennedy Center for the Performing Arts (1964–69) in Washington, D.C.

In 1957 federal troops were sent to Arkansas to protect the first black students to enroll at the all-white Little Rock Central High School.

sas resisted the courts and continued to segregate the students until 1957, when nine black students attempted to attend the all-white Little Rock Central High School. Governor Orval E. Faubus called out the Arkansas National Guard to prevent them from entering the school. In response, President Dwight D. Eisenhower ordered federal troops to Arkansas to enforce the integration. After a period of crisis and adjustment, the schools integrated without further incident.

Recent Trends

Today the farm economy of Arkansas is struggling, and some of its counties are among the poorest in the nation, especially those in the Delta region. However, the state's economy is growing overall, and population continues to rise. New businesses are coming to the state and some industries are growing rapidly, especially tourism. Arkansas is working harder than ever to live up to its nickname as a land of opportunity for all.

JEANNIE M. WHAYNE
Arkansas Historical Association

ARLINGTON NATIONAL CEMETERY. See NATIONAL CEMETERY SYSTEM.

ARMADA, SPANISH. See ENGLAND, HISTORY OF; SPAIN.

ARMENIA

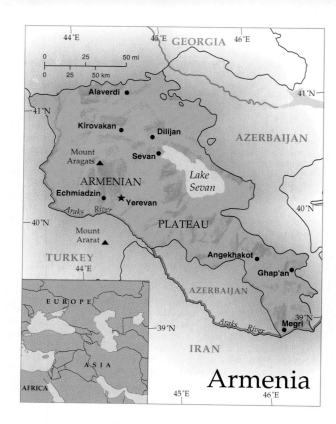

Armenia

The ancient homeland of the Armenians was a large, mountainous plateau in western Asia, which included part of what is now eastern Turkey. Armenians had inhabited the plateau continuously from the 500's B.C. Their kingdoms could be found in the region from earliest times to 1375. From this date until 1918, however, no Armenian state existed.

For most of this period its people were ruled as part of the Ottoman Turkish, Persian, and Russian empires. Between 1918 and 1920 a free Armenian republic struggled to survive, before becoming a part of the Soviet Union. Armenia remained a Soviet union republic until 1991, when it declared its independence. The present-day Republic of Armenia occupies a small area in the northeastern corner of its historic homeland.

▶ THE PEOPLE

A Dispersed People. Armenians have been dispersed, or scattered, to many corners of the world. About half now live outside Armenia. Armenian communities have grown up in the Middle East, Russia, Western Europe, and the United States, among other places.

More than 90 percent of the Armenian republic's people are Armenian. Ethnic minorities include Azerbaijanis and Russians. The capital and largest city is Yerevan (sometimes spelled Erevan), with a population of more than 1 million.

Language and Religion. Armenian is a distinctive language with its own alphabet. Although it belongs to the large Indo-European language family, it is not related to any other living language.

Armenians have been Christians since the early A.D. 300's and claim to be the first to have adopted Christianity as their official state religion. Outside of Armenia, the church is often the center of Armenian social and community life. The head of the Armenian Apostolic Church is the Catholicos, who resides in the holy city of Echmiadzin, near Yerevan.

Custom and Tradition. Although Christmas and Easter are the most important holidays, two others are widely observed by Armenians. Vartanantz celebrates an event in A.D. 451, when Armenians under Vartan Mamikonian fought to the death against the Persians to preserve their religion. And on April 24th, Armenians commemorate the destruction, in 1915, of the Armenian community in Turkey. (See History section.)

Armenian foods are similar to that of other Middle Eastern peoples. A typical Armenian

FACTS and figures

REPUBLIC OF ARMENIA is the official name of the country.

LOCATION: Western Asia.

AREA: 11,500 sq mi (29,800 km²).

POPULATION: 3,300,000 (estimate).

CAPITAL AND LARGEST CITY: Yerevan (Erevan).

MAJOR LANGUAGE(S): Armenian.

MAJOR RELIGIOUS GROUP(S): Christian.

GOVERNMENT: Republic. **Head of state**—president. **Head of government**—prime minister. **Legislature**—parliament.

CHIEF PRODUCTS: Chemicals, electronic equipment, synthetic rubber, textiles, wheat, barley, cotton, fruits and nuts, copper.

meal might include lamb, rice pilaf, eggplant, yogurt, and a sweet dessert like baklava. Armenians pride themselves on their close family ties and the importance of hospitality. Children are taught respect for Armenian culture and traditions.

Notable Armenians. Armenians have gained renown in many fields. Among those prominent in Soviet life were the composer Aram Khachaturian, the astrophysicist Victor Ambartsumian, former world chess champion Tigran Petrosyan, and the onetime president of the Soviet Union, Anastas Mikoyan. Notable Americans of Armenian ancestry include the playwright William Saroyan, composer Alan Hovhaness, former California governor George Deukmejian, Jr., singer and actress Cher (who is also part Cherokee Indian), and businessmen Alex Manoogian and Kirk Kerkorian.

▶THE LAND

The Armenian plateau is a rugged highland averaging about 5,000 feet (1,500 meters) in elevation. It is crossed by numerous valleys and by swift-flowing rivers, broken by rapids and falls. Historic Armenia had its chief population centers in the valley of the Araks River (also called Aras or Araxes) and the region around Lake Van. Lake Van now lies within Turkey. Two other great lakes can be found on the plateau—Sevan in Armenia, and Urmia, now part of Iran.

Most of Armenia consists of a high, rugged plateau ringed by mountains and crossed by numerous valleys and swift-flowing streams. The woman at right wears traditional Armenian dress.

The highest point on the plateau, Mount Ararat (Masis to Armenians), now lies in Turkey. Mount Aragats, the highest peak in the Armenian republic, rises 13,435 feet (4,095 meters) above sea level. The history of the land has been marked by destructive earthquakes. In 1988 two Armenian cities were devastated by a massive earthquake that killed more than 25,000 people.

Armenia has a generally dry climate, often with extremes of temperature. Winters are long and cold; summers are usually short and hot. Despite the harshness of the climate in winter, Armenia was one of the earliest agricultural areas cultivated by humans. The soil can be quite fertile, especially when irrigated. Copper is the chief mineral resource.

▶THE ECONOMY

Until the mid-1900's, most Armenians were peasant farmers. But with the great drive toward industrialization in the Soviet Union during the 1930's, Soviet Armenians began to

move to the towns to work in factories. Today the majority of Armenians live in urban areas (cities and towns) and industry is the most important element of the economy. Major manufactured products include chemicals, electronic equipment, synthetic rubber, and textiles.

The chief crops include wheat, barley, cotton, and fruits and nuts—particularly apricots, peaches, walnuts, and grapes for Armenian cognac, or fine brandy. Livestock, including sheep and goats, are grazed on meadows.

▶HISTORY

Urartu to Tigranes I. The first important state in what became Armenia was the kingdom of Urartu, with its center around Lake Van. In the 600's B.C., new tribes migrated to the region, probably from the west. They mingled with the earlier inhabitants to form a distinct people, first mentioned as "Armenians" in the mid-500's B.C. Ruled for many centuries by the Persians, Armenia became a buffer state between contending Greeks and Romans to the west and Persians and Arabs to the south.

Armenia reached the height of its power and extent under King Tigranes (or Tigran) I, the Great (reigned 95–55 B.C.). Tigranes founded an empire of many different peoples, but it was eventually conquered by the Romans.

Christianity and Conflict. In A.D. 314, the Armenian king Tiridates (or Trdat) III was converted to Christianity. In the early 400's, Saint Mesrop (known as Mashtots) created an alphabet for Armenian, and religious and historical works in that language began to appear. Yet the various noble houses of Armenia frequently fought with one another and with their kings. Although united by language and religion, Armenians were seldom unified under a single monarch.

The invasion of the Seljuk Turks in the 1000's led to the collapse of the independent Armenian kingdoms in Armenia. A new state, known as Lesser Armenia, was formed along the Mediterranean Sea. In 1375, however, this kingdom also fell, overrun by Mamelukes from Egypt. In the 1500's most of historic Armenia was conquered by the Ottoman Turks, who ruled it until the early 1900's. Eastern Armenia was under Persian rule until 1828, when it was absorbed into the Russian Empire.

Ottoman Rule. For centuries, Armenians in Turkey maintained relatively peaceful relations with their Ottoman masters. During the late 1800's, however, they began to suffer increasingly from discrimination, heavy taxation, and violence. In 1894–96, hundreds of thousands of Armenians were massacred with the approval of Sultan Abdul-Hamid II. Armenians were hopeful that when the Young Turk Revolution of 1908 overthrew Abdul-Hamid, a period of peace and co-operation would follow.

But when World War I broke out in 1914 and Turkey went to war with Russia, Armenians found themselves on both sides of the battlefield. In 1915 the Turkish government deported the Turkish Armenians, who were driven into the Syrian desert. In the process, between 600,000 and 1.5 million died of hunger and thirst or were killed outright, in what has been called "the first genocide of the 20th century."

Soviet Republic. Some survivors fled abroad. Others found refuge in Russian Armenia, where in 1918, after the Russian Revolution, an independent Armenian republic was established. It survived only briefly. Threatened by a nationalist movement in Turkey, the government turned the new state over to the Soviet Communists in 1920. Armenia was the smallest of the 15 republics making up the Soviet Union. With the disintegration of the Soviet Union in 1991, the second independent Armenian republic came into being.

Armenia Today. The first president of the new Republic of Armenia, Levon Ter Petrosyan, was elected in 1990. Armenia has a parliament from whose members are chosen the prime minister and other ministers responsible for the operation of the government. Many political parties compete freely.

The new republic faces serious problems. Its economy is weak. Many buildings destroyed in the 1988 earthquake have not yet been rebuilt. Armenians and Azerbaijanis have fought over the territory of Nagorno-Karabakh, which lies in neighboring Azerbaijan but whose people are mostly Armenian. Nevertheless, with control over their own nation and government, Armenians are now able to shape their own future.

RONALD GRIGOR SUNY
University of Michigan
Author, *Armenia in the 20th Century*

The use of armor peaked between the 1300's and the mid-1500's. The soldier's suit was worn in France about 1550. The horse displays Venetian armor dating from 1575.

ARMOR

When primitive people began to use weapons, they were faced with new problems. Their bodies needed more protection. They learned to use shields of wood or tough animal hide to protect themselves from the enemy's clubs or stone axes. This was the earliest armor.

Later the ancient Egyptian and Assyrian soldiers wore heavy cloth jackets or shirts to add to their protection. These were made of many layers of quilted linen.

▶METAL ARMOR

The first metal armor was made of bronze. It was probably used by the Greeks about 2000–1800 B.C. They hammered bronze into helmets to protect their heads. They also covered their wooden shields with thin metal sheets.

The Romans were the first to make wide use of iron for armor. Roman soldiers protected their bodies with leather vests covered with thin strips of bronze or iron. Sometimes they covered their legs with metal shin guards. Helmets shielded the head. Roman helmets had broad, curving metal sidepieces to protect the cheeks. Brims came down to cover the forehead and the back of the neck.

Steel was not used in armor much before the Middle Ages. Armor made of steel was even stronger and more flexible than that made of iron. Whole suits of steel protected the medieval knight from head to toe. Sleeves, shin guards, and even gloves with jointed fingers were carefully shaped from thin metal plates. Hinges, joints, and rivets fastened the suits to make them flexible. Helmets had movable visors, or lids that dropped over the face when fighting began.

Some knights wore flexible armor of chain mail. Such armor was made of hundreds of tiny steel rings linked together to form a kind of steel cloth. Shirts of chain mail slipped over the head and reached to the knees.

Plate armor had to be carefully fitted to the body. The armorer heated the metal and

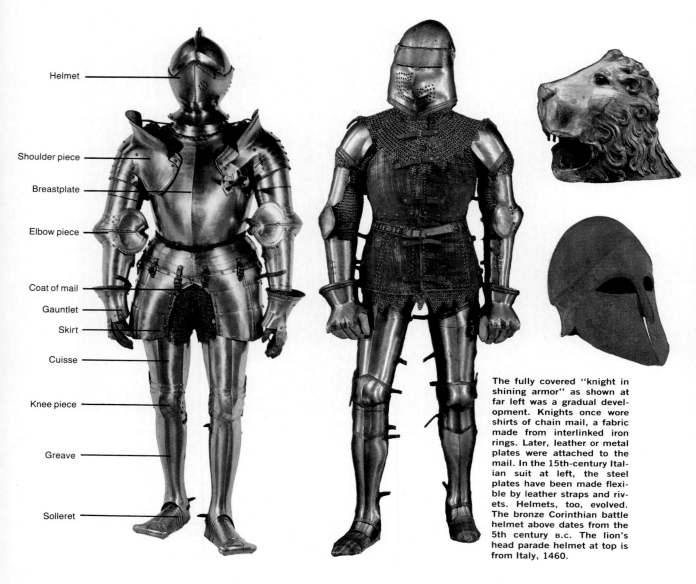

Helmet

Shoulder piece

Breastplate

Elbow piece

Coat of mail

Gauntlet

Skirt

Cuisse

Knee piece

Greave

Solleret

The fully covered "knight in shining armor" as shown at far left was a gradual development. Knights once wore shirts of chain mail, a fabric made from interlinked iron rings. Later, leather or metal plates were attached to the mail. In the 15th-century Italian suit at left, the steel plates have been made flexible by leather straps and rivets. Helmets, too, evolved. The bronze Corinthian battle helmet above dates from the 5th century B.C. The lion's head parade helmet at top is from Italy, 1460.

shaped it with tools. Working like a tailor, the armorer measured, tried on, and shaped again. Sometimes beautiful designs were etched into the steel. The shield was usually decorated with inlaid metal in several colors.

Full armor had many disadvantages. Because it was so expensive to make, only the well-to-do noble or knight could afford a suit of armor. Even worse was its great weight. A special servant or knight-in-training called a squire had to help the knight put on his armor and mount his horse. Drawings from the Middle Ages show knights being hoisted onto their horses by derricks or cranes. If the knight was thrown to the ground by his enemy, he was usually unable to struggle to his feet. His opponent could then easily kill him with his sword or spear.

▶THE DECLINE OF ARMOR

Gunpowder (invented centuries before by the Chinese) reached Europe about the end of the Middle Ages. A foot soldier with a gun could now pierce the heaviest armor that a man was able to carry on his body. Armor began to lose its usefulness. However, early explorers of the American continent continued to use armor against Indian arrows. But by the time of the American Revolution, armor appeared only in fancy-dress uniform.

Far left: A suit of Japanese armor dating from the 16th century is made of steel, silk braid, gilt bronze, deerskin, bear pelt, and gilt wood. Center: A suit of English armor dating from the 16th century is made of brass, leather, and velvet. It was fashioned at the Royal Workshop at Greenwich, the finest armor maker in England. Above: A parade helmet, made of silver and bronze, and shield, made of brass, silver, and gold, were crafted for King Louis XIV of France about 1700.

▶ARMOR IN MODERN FORM

In World Wars I and II, metal helmets were used to protect the head and neck from pieces of flying metal. Lightweight flexible aluminum body armor was tested in the Korean War. Fliers in World War II and in Korea wore thick coveralls padded with fiberglass. These gave protection from cold as well as from shell fragments. Some police officers wear armor in the form of bulletproof vests. Still another type of modern armor is the protective helmet such as those worn by construction workers or motorcyclists.

Today a new type of armor has been designed to help astronauts explore outer space. Space suits are thickly padded and fit snugly from neck to toe. A helmet, covering the entire head, is fitted with earphones, microphones, and a supply of oxygen. With such protection astronauts can face the great strains of rocket launching and space travel. As long as people must protect their bodies against enemy weapons and the forces of nature, they will try to design better armor.

JAMES HOERGER
John F. Kennedy School
(Great Neck, New York)

ARMS CONTROL. See DISARMAMENT.
ARMY. See UNITED STATES, ARMED FORCES OF THE; CANADIAN ARMED FORCES.

ARNOLD, BENEDICT (1741–1801)

No other American is remembered in quite the same way as Benedict Arnold. He was a brave soldier, a patriot—and a traitor.

Arnold was born in Norwich, Connecticut, on January 14, 1741. At the age of 14, he ran away from home to fight in the French and Indian War. Later he became a captain in the Connecticut militia. When the Revolutionary War began in 1775, Arnold was already an experienced soldier. He helped Ethan Allen capture Fort Ticonderoga. Then Arnold proposed a daring plan to capture Quebec, the key to British Canada. The attack on Quebec failed, but Arnold proved himself a heroic soldier.

In 1777, General John Burgoyne marched south from Canada. Arnold played a major role in bringing about Burgoyne's surrender at Saratoga.

In June, 1778, Arnold was placed in command of Philadelphia. There he married Peggy Shippen, the daughter of a wealthy Loyalist (supporter of the British). Life in Philadelphia was pleasant but very costly. Soon Arnold was deeply in debt. In 1779 he was charged with using his position for personal profit and employing soldiers in his command as personal servants. A court martial cleared him of most of the charges but recommended that the commander in chief reprimand him. General Washington issued the reprimand but softened it with the promise of a high position in the future.

Meanwhile, Arnold had begun a traitorous correspondence with British General Sir Henry Clinton. Arnold gave him important military information. He did this in anger because he felt that the Continental Congress had not given him the promotions he deserved. He was also desperate for money. The court martial and reprimand increased his anger.

In 1780, Arnold was given command of the fort at West Point, New York. He immediately entered into a plot to surrender this strategic post to the British. In return Arnold was to be made brigadier general in the British Army. He was also promised money.

British Major John André met with Arnold on September 21, 1780. As André was returning on horseback to New York City, some American soldiers stopped and searched him. They found incriminating papers hidden in his stocking. When Arnold learned that André had been captured, he fled to a British ship that took him down the Hudson River to New York City. André was executed as a spy.

The British gave Arnold about £6,315, though he had asked for considerably more. He was also given the command of a small British force. He fought against Americans in Virginia and Connecticut. In 1781, after the war ended, he left for England with his wife and children. He died there on June 14, 1801, an unhappy man, distrusted by the British as well as the Americans.

Reviewed by RICHARD B. MORRIS
Editor, *Encyclopedia of American History*

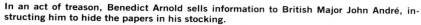

In an act of treason, Benedict Arnold sells information to British Major John André, instructing him to hide the papers in his stocking.

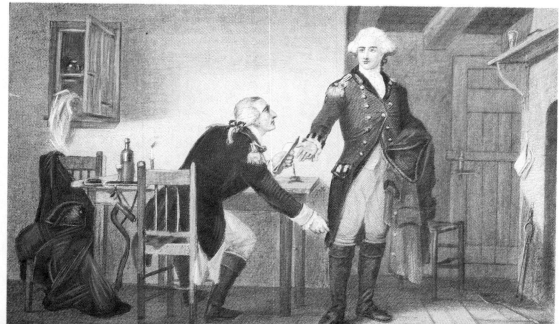

ART

Art is one of humanity's oldest inventions. It existed long before a single farm was planted, before the first villages were built. Art was already thousands of years old when writing appeared; in fact, the letters of the first alphabets were pictures. People were probably shaping objects and scratching out images even as they turned their grunts and cries into the first systematic spoken languages.

People are still making art; they have never stopped. Just about every society, from the oldest to the youngest and from the most primitive to the most advanced, has created works of art. No wonder that the sum of all this creation is called "the world of art." Art is a world in itself, a world as round and full and changeable as the world we live in and, like the earth, a whole of many distinct parts. Removing a wedge from the whole and studying it is like touring a country or visiting an era in the past. One wedge describes the ideals of the ancient Greeks. Another defines the interests of the French in the Middle Ages. Still another demonstrates the ideas that shaped the Renaissance in Italy. Another reflects the traditions that had meaning in Japan in the 1700's, or China in the 900's, or India in the 1600's. But seen as

Every society, in every time and place, has created art. *Clockwise from top:* Artists use a variety of styles and techniques to depict the world around them, from the detailed realism of Albrecht Dürer's *Hare*, to the utter simplicity of *Princesse X*, by Constantin Brancusi. Hans Hofmann's *Rhapsody*, on the other hand, is completely abstract —it does not represent any recognizable object. The Inuit artist who carved a polar bear from whale bone chose a familiar subject and a readily available material.

The Metropolitan Museum of Art, Gift of Renate Hofmann, 1975.

This article discusses theories about the origins and meanings of art. It also suggests ways in which we can learn about a people or culture by studying the art they created. *The New Book of Knowledge* contains many articles that provide specific information on the arts of various cultures. For example, the arts of the peoples of Africa are discussed in AFRICA, ART AND ARCHITECTURE OF. The arts of individual countries are surveyed in numerous articles, including CHINESE ART; FRANCE, ART AND ARCHITECTURE OF; INDIA, ART AND ARCHITECTURE OF; JAPANESE ART AND ARCHITECTURE; LATIN AMERICA, ART AND ARCHITECTURE OF; and UNITED STATES, ART AND ARCHITECTURE OF THE.

Look up the names of periods and styles of art to find such articles as GOTHIC ART AND ARCHITECTURE, IMPRESSIONISM, ISLAMIC ART AND ARCHITECTURE, and MODERN ART.

The basic components of art are discussed in COLOR and DESIGN. There are also articles on art forms, such as COLLAGE, DRAWING, PAINTING, SCULPTURE, and WATERCOLOR. Other articles cover the history and collections of famous art galleries, including HERMITAGE MUSEUM, LOUVRE, METROPOLITAN MUSEUM OF ART, and NATIONAL GALLERY OF CANADA. Consult the Index to find the many biographies of artists contained in this encyclopedia.

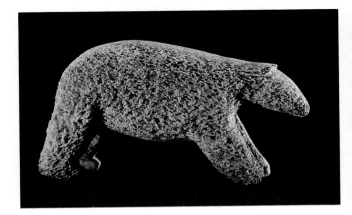

Below: Prehistoric people may have created likenesses of animals, such as this bison carving, as a form of hunting magic. *Left:* Kachina figures made by Pueblo Indians are representations of ancestral spirits.

a whole, the world of art reveals a broad picture of all of humanity; it summarizes the ideals, interests, and ideas of all people in all eras. It tells us what has been on people's minds in generation after generation, from the dawn of humanity to the present day.

Art, then, is a product of the human mind and a mirror of that mind—a record of human progress. And like the mind, and like the societies that progress has created, art is rich, complicated, and sometimes quite mysterious.

▶ THE MEANINGS OF ART

Actually, most people do know what art is. The trouble comes when they try to define it. No one definition satisfies everyone's idea. No one definition seems broad enough to cover every object in an art museum. And some definitions are too broad—they may apply to everything in the museum, but they also apply to many things that clearly are not art.

Despite the difficulty of defining art, we can make certain observations that help us to understand what art is. Art is a product made by people that expresses the uniqueness of the maker, of the society to which the maker belongs, of all humanity, or of all of these. The product appeals to the intellect and to the

senses, especially to the sense of beauty. The product can assume a variety of forms—a musical composition, a ballet, a play, or a novel or poem. This article, however, deals only with the "fine" arts: drawing, painting, sculpture, and architecture.

It is our intellect that makes humans unique. People have created religion, science, and technology to make their struggle for survival easier. They have created art to measure the worth of these and all human enterprises against the quality of life. European medieval art dealt almost exclusively with religion. Italian Renaissance art reflected the growing interest in the sciences. Much Oriental art conveys the idea of a harmonious, well-ordered universe. Art of the modern era is very much a product of the age of technology.

Art—or at least great art—almost always gets at the truth. Great artists are expert observers and their work reflects life as they see it.

▶ ART AS A RECORD

The earliest art that we know about was painted on the walls of caves during the Old Stone Age—roughly 20,000 years ago. Most of the pictures depict animals—bison, reindeer, ibex—the animals that early people hunted and depended on for survival. We cannot be completely sure why these images were painted, but we can guess that hunters created likenesses of their prey in order to capture its spirit. Having taken the spirit, the hunters found it easier to take the body. And since early people were very good hunters, whose mastery of weapons gave them an advantage over much stronger creatures, they must have believed that the magic worked.

About 5,000 years ago, the first great civilization began emerging from humanity's intelligent struggle for survival. And with them came monumental art—art created to proclaim the greatness of a civilization and to last forever. In Egypt and Mesopotamia gigantic pyramids were erected, the tombs within decorated with carvings and paintings showing the great deeds of the rulers buried there. Clearly, these ancient peoples had no intention of ever disappearing. Even their utensils and vessels were meant to last eternally.

Mesopotamian and especially Egyptian art dwelt on the achievements of rulers. This was so mainly because the rulers were thought to be gods, or at least to have intimate contact with gods. And it was fitting, too, because the ruler was regarded as the living embodiment of the nation: Pharaoh and Egypt were one and the same. The individuality of the human being was seldom even recognized, much less celebrated.

Then came the Minoans and Mycenaeans and the Greeks, and people had their day. The early statuary of the Aegean peoples was said to represent gods and goddesses, but the forms were becoming ever more recognizably human. This in itself seems to indicate that people were beginning to appreciate their own importance. Like the ancient Hebrews, they proclaimed themselves made in their gods' image—not perfect, perhaps, but nonetheless godlike. By the Classical Age (400's B.C.) in Greece, even that pretense was dropped. Greek sculptors began portraying spear bearers and charioteers with bodies as perfect as those of the gods Apollo and Dionysus.

Greek art idealized the human form. We do not believe that there were no Greeks with pot bellies or bowlegs; but we can conclude that the Greeks thought enough of themselves to find great satisfaction in showing themselves as ideal beings. And so we admire the Greeks not so much for what they were, but for the ideals they set up for themselves.

The Greeks' high regard for the individual is also reflected in their architecture. Greek architects took great pains to proportion their structures so that people could use them comfortably: The ceilings are never so high, the rooms never so massive that a person feels small or lost within. This is another example of how we use art, which expresses ideals, to learn about a people of the past.

Roman art, like Roman civilization, was based to a large extent on the Greek model. But the Romans carried their concern with the individual a step further. One Roman statue is a representation of an old, big-nosed citizen with a stern expression on his face. No one

Portrait sculptures by Roman artists show their interest in portraying subjects realistically. The deeply lined face and stern expression of this sculpture of an old man reflect his individuality and character.

would call it an idealized portrait. Yet, as one studies it, the face gradually appears handsomer; it seems to reflect great character, wisdom, integrity. With such works the Romans are saying that the individual need not meet prescribed standards to be beautiful.

When invasions by Germanic tribes into western and southern Europe became too troublesome for the Romans to deal with, the emperor Constantine (280?–337) moved his capital eastward to the site of the old city of Byzantium. The new capital was called Constantinople, in his honor. Constantine also was the first Christian emperor, and thus his eastern empire, called the Byzantine Empire, became the first Christian civilization. There the traditions of ancient Greek and Roman art were remolded to fit the needs of Christianity. Under the emperor Justinian (483–565), Constantinople was built up as the first great Christian city.

The soaring heights and rich decoration of Gothic cathedrals, such as Reims Cathedral in France, were meant to inspire churchgoers with the glory of God.

The Roman Empire in western Europe came to an end in the A.D. 400's. The following period, from about 500 to 1500, is called the Middle Ages. The Germanic peoples who established kingdoms in the former empire were greatly influenced by Roman civilization. They learned the Roman tongue and adopted Christianity. They turned their artistic skills to making Christian art, using the intricately carved and decorated style that characterized their art.

The early Middle Ages were years of confusion and disorder in western Europe. Yet during this period the great Frankish king Charlemagne established a large empire that included much of western and central Europe. Elsewhere—in the Byzantine Empire, northern and western Africa, and the Far East—great civilizations flourished.

During the later Middle Ages, a new and monumental style of architecture called Gothic (the name was given to it much later) developed in the West. All over France, Germany, and England, grand cathedrals rose, one after another, each more lavish than the others. Nearly all the art of this period, which lasted into the 1500's in some parts of Europe, was devoted to decoration of the cathedrals. Columns were surrounded with statues; doorways were richly carved; beautiful stained-glass windows colored the sunlight pouring in; carefully cut and polished wood formed the altars; huge, heavy tapestries hung between chapels; mosaic tiles formed mazelike patterns on the floors. It was as if all artistic creativity was focused on the glorification of God and the church.

Gothic architecture tells us a great deal about how society regarded people. The Gothic cathedral is high, heaven-reaching, enormously empty. Inside, one cannot help feeling small and humble. And all the statues —the saints on the columns, the demons over the doors—are watching and warning.

Early in the 1400's, the God-centered outlook of the Middle Ages slowly began to change. First in Italy and then throughout Europe, the individual human being became a main concern of art. This attitude, known as humanism, is what distinguished the Renaissance from earlier periods. It is what made the Renaissance go down in history as a great age for humanity. And again, it was in art that the spirit of humanism was expressed most clearly.

Humanism affected not only the content of art but the very way in which art was created. For if art said that people were individuals, worthy of recognition for their beliefs, were not the people who made art very special individuals, deserving credit for their accomplishments? So, with the Renaissance, the artist took on a new importance. And the recognition that the artist received added a new facet to art.

In Eastern lands, as in the West, art from its earliest days was an ever-growing record of what was most important to people. Art in Japan often reflects an appreciation for the beauty of nature. Early Japanese painting tended to be delicate, airy, and romantic, reflecting the graceful life of the Japanese court. Later, when Japan was ruled by militaristic

The Metropolitan Museum of Art, Bequest of Mrs. H. O. Havemeyer, 1929.

emperors, art became harsher and more realistic. The 1700's and 1800's saw the development of the Japanese woodcut. Woodcuts, which are inexpensive to reproduce, were meant to reach a wider audience—to bring beauty within reach of the hardworking common people.

The arts in India have almost always had a religious content. However, this was often combined with an interest in earthly life. Sculpture, in particular, often portrayed gods and goddesses as vital and lifelike beings. Indian painters developed original and expressive styles of manuscript illustration.

China's artistic tradition is one of the oldest in the world, dating back to 5000 B.C. A respect for tradition and reverence for nature is reflected in Chinese art and architecture. Calligraphy, the art of beautiful writing, was considered one of the most important visual arts.

▶ ART OF THE ARTIST

Art since the Renaissance has remained a record of humanity and a reflection of the ideas that concern people. But since the Renaissance this record has come down to us in a series of very personal statements.

The great Italian artist Michelangelo believed that the truth of any matter existed in nature. The artist's job was to seek that truth and capture it in his art. He once described

sculpture as the act of "liberating the figure from the marble that imprisons it." In other words, the forms that he depicted so dramatically in his work already existed; his job was to find them and free them.

A later Italian painter, Caravaggio, sought the truth in everyday occurrences, such as the pleasures of making music. Even in his paintings of religious events, he clothed the participants in the apparel of his own time, and placed them in commonplace settings, such as taverns. Saints were often pictured as poor people with plain garments and bare feet. Caravaggio seemed to be saying that all people, even the most humble, have value.

The paintings of the Dutch artist Rembrandt may represent the peak of humanism. In a very special way, Rembrandt's subject matter was the soul of man. He painted religious subjects, portraits of prosperous Dutch citizens, and he painted simple portraits of poor people and of himself. But whatever he painted, his figures always appear lit from within, as if they were filled with all the suffering—and the beauty—of humanity. Rembrandt is telling us that with all the pain, corruption, and helplessness that characterize human life, the human spirit is still filled with all the glory and good of God's light.

The 1600's and 1700's were the "age of kings" in Europe. The courts of the European nations dominated much artistic activity. Many artists were dependent on the kings and aristocrats who

Above: In his painting *The Jewish Bride*, Dutch artist Rembrandt van Rijn portrays the tender affection of a newly married couple. Rembrandt's work, in its expression of the dignity of the human spirit, may represent the peak of humanism in art. *Right:* In *The Third of May, 1808*, Spanish artist Francisco Goya protests the invasion of his country by Napoleon's armies—and attacks the nature of war itself.

Near left: A sculpture made by the Kota people of Gabon represents the spirit of the dead. It is constructed of wood covered with sheets of copper and other metals. The shapes and patterns of African art influenced many modern European and American artists, including Pablo Picasso. *Far left:* Picasso, like other modern artists, experimented with new ways of looking at things. *Girl Before a Mirror* uses bright colors and flattened shapes in its portrait of a young woman.

ruled the continent. And yet great artists can never be slaves—except to the search for truth. As the abuses of the monarchs stirred the common people to greater and greater resentment, the artists often joined in the protests. For example, when Napoleon's armies invaded Spain in 1808, the Spanish artist Francisco Goya turned his talents to an assault on the French. His paintings and engravings include works that are savage attacks on the French invaders, and even more savage—and lasting—attacks on war itself.

Another Spaniard, Pablo Picasso, made a similar statement 130 years later. His well-known painting *Guernica* tells the story of the Spanish Civil War as directly as any text. And it is not only about a destroyed Spanish city; it is about war.

The 1800's and 1900's saw a remarkable increase in the speed at which civilization changes. We have come through an Industrial Revolution into an age of technology into a space age. Artists have kept pace with all these changes.

The ways in which artists approach art have been in a state of constant re-evaluation in the last 150 years. The impressionists began a process that led to a breakdown in the importance of subject matter. With these French artists came an interest in the technique used to apply paint to canvas. Concern with forms for their own sake led to cubism and then to abstractionism, in sculpture as well as painting. By the mid-1900's painting and sculpture seemingly came together in a search for new forms.

The 1900's also saw a growing appreciation of the arts of non-Western cultures. Once dismissed as "primitive," the arts of African and Native American peoples were now admired for their vitality and directness of expression. African sculpture, in particular, influenced a number of modern artists, including Picasso. As modern communications have allowed ideas about art to become ever more widely spread, the influence of cultures on one another has continued.

What is the truth of our own age, as expressed in art? That question cannot yet be answered. As we study the art forms of our age, each of us can draw our own conclusions.

DAVID JACOBS
Author, *Master Painters of the Renaissance*

ART DECO. See DECORATIVE ARTS (The Industrial Age).

ARTERIOSCLEROSIS. See DISEASES (Descriptions of Some Diseases).

ARTHRITIS. See DISEASES (Descriptions of Some Diseases).

CHESTER ALAN ARTHUR (1829-1886)

21st President of the United States

FACTS ABOUT ARTHUR

Birthplace: Fairfield, Vermont
Religion: Episcopalian
College Attended:
  Union College,
  Schenectady, New York
Occupation: Lawyer
Married: Ellen Lewis Herndon
Children: William, Chester,
  Ellen
Political Party: Republican
Age on Becoming President: 50
Office Held Before Becoming President:
  Vice President
President Who Preceded Him:
  James A. Garfield
Nickname: "The Gentleman Boss"
Years in the Presidency: 1881–1885
Vice President: None
President Who Succeeded
  Him: Grover Cleveland
Age at Death: 56
Burial Place: Albany,
  New York

DURING ARTHUR'S PRESIDENCY

Below, left: The U.S. Senate ratified (1882) the Geneva (or Red Cross) Convention of 1864. Congress passed the Pendleton Civil Service Act, which established the U.S. Civil Service Commission (1883). *Below:* The Brooklyn Bridge was completed (1883); at the time it was the world's longest bridge. Construction of the first building known as a skyscraper, the 10-story Home Insurance Building, was begun in Chicago (1883). The Linotype, the first practical typesetting machine, was patented (1884) by Ottmar Mergenthaler. *Above:* The Washington Monument in Washington, D.C., was dedicated (1885).

ARTHUR, CHESTER ALAN. On July 2, 1881, President James A. Garfield was shot in the back by an insane man. For two months the President lay between life and death. On September 19, Garfield died, and early the next morning Vice-President Chester Alan Arthur became the new president of the United States.

Arthur was a handsome man. Tall and broad-shouldered, he impressed people with his dignified bearing and elegant manners. He was courteous and friendly.

But many people considered the handsome vice-president unfit to be president. Arthur had long been associated with the spoils system. Under this system government jobs were awarded for service to a political party, whether the candidates were honest and able or not. In fact, the man who killed President Garfield explained that he did so because he had been refused a government job. People were alarmed that Arthur, a product of the spoils system, had become president.

Arthur's administration, however, proved to be quite different than his country expected.

It was marked by honesty and by the replacement of the spoils system with the present Civil Service system based on merit.

▶ EARLY YEARS

Chester Alan Arthur was born October 5, 1829, in Fairfield, Vermont. He was the oldest son in a family of seven children. His father, William Arthur, was a Baptist minister.

The Arthur family moved about a great deal. The Reverend William Arthur was a man of strong beliefs and did not hesitate to speak his mind to his congregations. As a result, he did not stay in one place very long. At the age of 15, Chester entered Union College, in Schenectady, New York. He helped pay for his college expenses by teaching school during vacations. He studied hard and, in 1848, graduated with honors. Arthur then studied law. But he continued to teach to support himself until 1853, when he went to New York City to begin his career as a lawyer.

The future president first gained prominence when he became involved in the slavery question that was soon to lead to civil war. William Arthur had been opposed to slavery, and Chester shared his father's feelings. He sympathized with the plight of blacks and took part in two important cases in their defense. In one his law firm gained freedom for eight blacks accused of being runaway slaves.

The other case dealt with the problem of segregation. It arose when Lizzie Jennings was not allowed to ride on a streetcar in New York City because she was black. Arthur won $500 for her in damages. And the court decision stated that blacks had the same right to ride on New York streetcars as anyone else.

▶ ARTHUR ENTERS POLITICS

Like most lawyers of the time, Arthur also took part in politics. In 1860 he helped organize the New York State Republican Party, and he supported its candidate for governor. As a reward the governor made Arthur engineer in chief and then quartermaster general of New York State. During the Civil War Arthur's position was very important, for all Union Army volunteers were equipped by the state before they were sent on to the Army. Arthur proved skillful and honest in providing thousands of New York soldiers with food, shelter, guns, tents, and other equipment.

▶ COLLECTOR OF NEW YORK

Arthur's work for the Republican Party brought him to the attention of Senator Roscoe Conkling, the political boss of New York State. Arthur became Conkling's lieutenant and worked with him to win the election of Ulysses S. Grant in 1868. For his help President Grant in 1871 appointed Arthur collector of customs for the port of New York.

The collector was in charge of the New York Custom House, which received most of the customs duties of the United States. He also had the power to distribute more than 1,000 jobs. Under the spoils system these jobs went to faithful Republicans. They were expected to work for the party as well as for the Custom House. In the years that Arthur held the position, he simply followed the old system, although he himself remained an honest and able administrator.

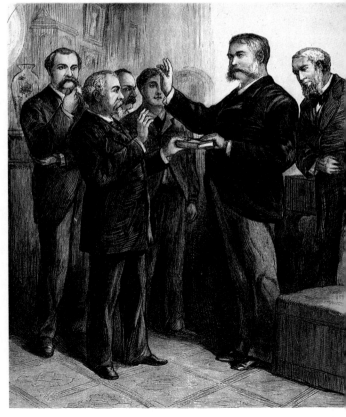

In this newspaper cartoon of the 1880's (*above*), President Arthur turns his back on his old crony, Boss Roscoe Conkling. The woman represents the Republican Party. After President James A. Garfield was assassinated in 1881, Chester Arthur was inaugurated as 21st president at his home in New York City (*below*).

But many people were becoming angry about the inefficiency of the spoils system. They wanted a merit system, under which officeholders would be chosen on the basis of ability. In 1877 Rutherford B. Hayes, a believer in the merit system, became president. Hayes ordered an investigation of the New York Custom House, and in 1878 Arthur was dismissed from his post. The conflict caused a deep split in the Republican Party. The supporters of the old system became known as Stalwarts. The reformers were called Half-Breeds.

▶ VICE–PRESIDENT

In 1880 the Republicans who met to pick a new candidate for president were still bitterly divided. The delegates voted 36 times before they agreed on a candidate whom no one had expected—James A. Garfield, a Half-Breed. However, Senator Conkling was Garfield's political enemy. And to gain the support of the Stalwarts, the Garfield men nominated Arthur for the vice-presidency. The Republicans won in a close election. Ten months later Garfield was dead, and Arthur became the 21st president of the United States.

Ellen Lewis Herndon (*below*) married Chester Alan Arthur in 1859. She died in 1880, before he became president. Their young daughter, Ellen, was raised in the White House by President Arthur's sister.

▶ PRESIDENT ARTHUR SURPRISES MANY PEOPLE

As president, Arthur surprised both his friends and enemies. Arthur wished to make a good record for himself and was eager to be renominated and re-elected. He knew that he would never gain the support of reform and independent voters if he acted simply as a tool of Boss Conkling.

Arthur therefore determined not to let his administration be disgraced by the spoils system. He also tried earnestly to deal with some of the serious political problems the nation faced. But he was not so successful as he wished because he never had the full support of Congress.

For many years the Senate and the House of Representatives had gained power at the expense of weak presidents. Even such a strong personality as Abraham Lincoln had trouble with Congress. And his successors—Johnson, Grant, and Hayes—had let themselves be dominated by powerful Congressional leaders. Arthur was especially defenseless. He had become president by accident, and he did not command the support of any strong group in Congress.

Furthermore, Congress was itself divided. Both the Democratic and Republican parties were split into warring groups like the Stalwarts and the Half-Breeds. Some questions, such as the tariff (the tax on goods imported into the country), also divided the legislators. Other issues, such as the currency, set farmers, laborers, and manufacturers fighting one another.

Most important of all, the country was expanding and growing rich. Many people thought only of what they could get for themselves. Their representatives did not vote according to what was best for the nation as a whole. Instead they voted for laws that would gain the most for their supporters. Under such conditions it was difficult even for an able president to work out a good national policy. Arthur tried his best. But his achievements were limited.

The Pendleton Act and the Merit System

Before Arthur took office, it became known that some postal officials had collected money illegally in arranging mail routes. They were brought to trial in the famous Star Route cases. They were never convicted, but the trial made many more Americans aware of the evils of the spoils system.

With President Arthur's support, Congress now tried to introduce the merit system. In 1883, Arthur signed a law that helped take thousands of government jobs out of politics. This was the Pendleton Civil Service Act. It required candidates for many government jobs to pass tests before they could be accepted. Men who qualified were protected against being dismissed for political reasons. The Pendleton Act was the beginning of the present United States Civil Service.

Too Much Money and Chinese Exclusion

During the 1880's the United States had an unusual problem: there was too much money in the treasury. In one year the government collected $80,000,000 more than it spent. This kept money out of circulation, hurt business, and caused prices to fall. Arthur wanted to solve the problem by lowering the tariff. Congress, however, refused to do so. It preferred to spend the money on a "pork-barrel" bill. This was a law that authorized federal funds to be spent on river and harbor improvements. Such a law won votes for the congressmen and senators of the favored states. Arthur rejected the bill even though he knew that this would make him unpopular. But Congress passed it over his veto, and the tariff problem was not solved during Arthur's term in office.

Congress also passed the Chinese Exclusion Act of 1882 against the president's wishes. Its aim was to prevent Chinese from immigrating to the United States. Arthur op-posed the bill because it violated a treaty between China and the United States. His opposition forced Congress to rewrite the law so that it had fewer harsh restrictions against the Chinese.

▶ NOT ALL WAS POLITICS

In 1859 Arthur had married Ellen Lewis Herndon, the daughter of a Virginia naval officer. Mrs. Arthur died in 1880, before her husband became president. Each day President Arthur honored her by placing fresh flowers in front of her picture.

The President's favorite sport was fishing. He was considered one of the best salmon fishermen in the country. Arthur was also fond of good food and companionship. He enjoyed the dinners to which he was invited and hated to leave. Since none of the guests could politely leave before the President, the dinners sometimes lasted until midnight.

Arthur liked elegant surroundings, and he had the White House completely redecorated. He installed new plumbing, a new bathroom, and the first elevator in the White House. His sister, who acted as hostess, helped him make it Washington's social center.

▶ ARTHUR IS REJECTED BY THE REPUBLICANS

In 1884 the Republicans did not renominate Arthur for president. The Half-Breed reformers were still not satisfied with him, and his old Stalwart friends, of course, were now against him. James G. Blaine was nominated and later lost the election to Democrat Grover Cleveland.

Arthur returned to his old law practice. But his health was failing. On November 18, 1886, at the age of 56, he died at his home in New York.

Chester Arthur was an honest and courageous president. But the political situation of his times did not permit him to deal successfully with the country's great problems. The greatest achievement of his administration was the Pendleton Civil Service Act. However, he will be best remembered as the spoils system politician who became president by accident, and who proved himself a better man than anyone expected.

OSCAR HANDLIN
Harvard University

ARTHUR, KING

In romance and legend, in music and art, King Arthur and his Knights of the Round Table are among the world's best-known heroes. For centuries they have been favorites of storytellers in many different countries.

The tales, as they are most often told today, are set in Arthur's court at Camelot, in a castle with noble towers and a great hall. In the great hall stood the Round Table, where only the best and most valiant knights could sit. Because the table had no head and no foot, all the knights seated around it were of equal rank. Each knight has his own seat with his name carved on it. The knights were bound by oath to help one another in time of danger and never to fight among themselves.

The tales tell of the wise and courteous Sir Gawaine; the brave Sir Percival; Sir Lancelot, who loved King Arthur's wife, Guinevere; the traitor Sir Modred, who seized the throne and tried to wed Queen Guinevere; the noble Sir Bedivere, who received Arthur's last commands before he died; and Sir Tristram, the knight of many skills. One seat at the Round Table had no name on it. It was reserved for the knight who found the Holy Grail, the cup supposedly used by Christ at the Last Supper. The seat was finally won by Sir Galahad, the purest and noblest of all the knights.

Religion and magic run through all the stories about Arthur and his knights. On the side of good was the mighty magician Merlin, who was Arthur's adviser. On the side of evil was the wicked sorceress Morgan le Fay.

THE STORY OF ARTHUR

The story of King Arthur and his knights, as told in *Le Morte Darthur* ("The Death of Arthur") by Sir Thomas Malory, begins with the death of Arthur's father, King Uther Pendragon. Following the king's death, there was strife and civil war among England's nobles. The nobles finally gathered in a church to ask God to show them who their rightful king should be. As they came out of the church they saw a sword in an anvil mounted on a great stone. On the sword it was written that whoever could pull the sword out of the stone would be the next king of England. None of the nobles could withdraw the sword.

Although he was the king's son, Arthur was not with his father when he died. Arthur had been given to the magician Merlin for safekeeping shortly after his birth. Merlin had known that King Uther's death would cause a struggle for power among the nobles and that Arthur's life would be in danger, so Merlin gave the baby to Sir Ector and his wife to raise as their own, not telling them that the baby was King Uther's son.

Some months after the sword appeared in the stone, a great tournament was held and Sir Ector, his son Sir Kay, and the young Arthur all attended. When Sir Kay discovered that he had left his sword at the inn where they were staying, he sent Arthur after it. The inn, however, was closed because everyone had gone to the tournament. But Arthur remembered seeing a sword stuck in a stone in the churchyard nearby. Without knowing what it meant, he removed the sword easily, and, after further proofs, Arthur became king.

His reign was full of victories. Many of these he owed to another sword, an enchanted one called Excalibur. Here is Malory's tale, adapted by Mary MacLeod, of how he got it.

Leaving Sir Pellinore, King Arthur and Merlin went to a hermit, who was a good man, and skilled in the art of healing. He attended so carefully to the King's wounds, that in three days they were quite well, and Arthur was able to go on his way with Merlin. Then as they rode, Arthur said, "I have no sword."

"No matter," said Merlin, "near by is a sword that shall be yours if I can get it."

So they rode till they came to a lake, which was a fair water and broad; and in the midst of the lake, Arthur saw an arm, clothed in white samite, that held in its hand a beautiful sword.

"Lo," said Merlin, "yonder is the sword I spoke of."

With that they saw a damsel rowing across the lake.

"What damsel is that?" said Arthur.

"That is the Lady of the Lake," said Merlin, "and within that lake is a rock, and therein is as fair a place as any on earth, and richly adorned. This damsel will soon come to you; then speak you fair to her, so that she will give you that sword."

Presently the damsel came to Arthur, and saluted him, and he her again.

"Damsel," said Arthur, "what sword is that which yonder the arm holdeth above the water? I would it were mine, for I have no sword."

"Sir Arthur, King," said the damsel, "that sword is mine; the name of it is Excalibur, that is as much as to say *Cut-Steel*. If you will give me a gift when I ask you, ye shall have it."

"By my faith," said Arthur, "I will give you what gift ye shall ask."

"Well," said the damsel, "go you into yonder barge, and row yourself to the sword, and take it and the scabbard with you, and I will ask my gift when I see my time."

So King Arthur and Merlin alighted, and tied their horses to two trees, and went into the barge, and when they came to the sword that the hand held, Arthur lifted it by the handle, and took it with him. And the arm and the hand went under the water; and so they came to the land, and rode away.

Some years later, Arthur married Guinevere, the daughter of a king he had helped in battle. After their marriage, Arthur set up his court at Camelot. There he gathered the most chivalrous princes to be his Knights of the Round Table. The stories of their feats and adventures—tournaments, battles, and quests for the Holy Grail—are all part of the Arthurian legends.

At the end of Arthur's reign, while he was away from Camelot, Sir Modred tried to take over the kingdom and marry the queen. But Arthur returned and defeated Modred in battle, killing him with his own hands. As Modred fell, he lifted up his sword and mortally wounded Arthur. Arthur's body was mysteriously carried away to the island of Avalon. According to legend, King Arthur would return one day.

▶**SOURCES OF THE ARTHURIAN LEGENDS**

The book that is the chief source today for all the legends about Arthur and his knights was written by an Englishman, Sir Thomas Malory. It was printed in 1485 and was one of the first books to come from the press of the first English printer, William Caxton. Although the tales were written in English, the title of the book, *Le Morte Darthur* ("The Death of Arthur"), is French and most of the tales were adapted from various French versions of the legends.

Tales about Arthur were particularly popular in France during the 1100's and 1200's. Originally, however, the Arthurian tales came from Celtic sources—from myths belonging to the Irish and British races and from early accounts of the history of Britain.

The first of these histories to mention Arthur was written in Latin by Nennius, a Welsh priest who lived in the 800's. He tells of a Celtic military commander named Arthur who in the 500's won twelve battles against the Saxon invaders of Britain. This is the original Arthur and it is all we know of him. Legends grew up around him, however, and he became a popular Welsh hero. When some of the Celtic people migrated from Britain to France, they carried the tales about Arthur to their new neighbors, the French and the Normans. Wandering minstrels spread the tales even farther as they visited the courts of Europe and Followed European armies into lands of the eastern Mediterranean.

About this same time, in the 1100's, another Welsh priest, Geoffrey of Monmouth, wrote down some of these tales in a book called *Historia Regum Britanniae* (History of the Kings of Britain). Although he pretended that the book was a translation into Latin of "a very old book in the British language," it was his own creation. He made Arthur into a king and surrounded him with nobles and barons from western Europe. In 1155, a Norman monk named Wace translated Geoffrey's *Historia* into French, adding material from other sources and leaving out parts. His *Roman de Brut* contains the first mention of the Round Table. Wace's poem was used by a priest named Layamon, who was the first to write about Arthur in English.

Between 1170 and 1181, a Frenchman, Chrétien de Troyes, wrote poems based on the Arthurian legends that were highly regarded for their style. His material was probably taken from Celtic origins. He is an important source for the story of the Holy Grail.

The Arthurian legends have attracted many writers in English since Layamon. Stories about Arthur were written in the 1400's by Sir Thomas Malory; in the 1800's by Lord Tennyson, Algernon Swinburne, Matthew Arnold, and William Morris; and in the 1900's by T. H. White.

The Arthurian legends have also been expressed in music and art. In music, the most famous composer to make use of these legends was Richard Wagner. In art, several of John Singer Sargent's mural paintings depict the quest for the Holy Grail.

Reviewed by CAROLYN W. FIELD
The Free Library of Philadelphia

ARTICLES OF CONFEDERATION. See UNITED STATES, GOVERNMENT OF THE; UNITED STATES, HISTORY OF THE.
ARTIFICIAL INTELLIGENCE. See COMPUTERS.
ARTIFICIAL RESPIRATION. See FIRST AID (Rescue Breathing).
ARTILLERY. See GUNS AND AMMUNITION.
ART NOUVEAU. See DECORATIVE ARTS (The Industrial Age).

ASBESTOS

Asbestos is the common name for six fibrous, or threadlike, minerals. The fibers of these minerals are soft and flexible. They can be woven into cloth or mixed with a binding material and molded into any shape.

Asbestos comes in two main forms. Ninety-five percent is *chrysotile*, from the mineral *serpentine*. The other form, *amphibole*, includes five minerals—*crocidolite*, *amosite*, *anthophyllite*, *tremolite*, and *actinolite*.

Both forms of asbestos developed when cracks in the earth's rocks filled with water containing many minerals. Over millions of years, heat and pressure evaporated the water but left the fibers of asbestos.

The biggest deposits of asbestos are found in Canada, the Russian Federation, and South Africa. Smaller deposits are located in the United States. Asbestos is mined like coal—from open pits or through tunnels.

Asbestos is a most valuable substance. It will not burn or melt. It resists acids as well as other strong chemicals, and it is a good insulator against heat or the flow of electricity.

The ancient Greeks and Romans were among the early users of asbestos. They wove the fibers into burial cloths, tablecloths, and long-lasting lamp wicks.

Since the 1700's, dozens of new uses for asbestos have been found. By the 1900's, asbestos was used in such products as automobile brake linings, roofing shingles, furnace linings, floor tiles, and firefighter suits.

In the 1960's, scientists discovered that inhaling asbestos fibers can cause cancer or serious lung disease. This led the U.S. government to ban all mining of asbestos and to order its removal from schools and other buildings. The government set a deadline of 1997 for discontinuing all uses of asbestos.

A 1989 scientific study, however, showed that asbestos did not always cause disease. The danger to health depended on the amount of fibers in the air, the type of asbestos, and the size of the fibers. Still, experts urge people to avoid exposure to asbestos.

GILDA BERGER
Science Writer

ASCORBIC ACID. See VITAMINS AND MINERALS (Vitamin C).
ASHLEY, WILLIAM HENRY. See FUR TRADE IN NORTH AMERICA (Profiles).

ASIA

Asia is the largest and most heavily populated of the world's continents. It occupies nearly one-third of the earth's total land surface and is home to about 60 percent of its people. Asia is bounded on three sides by oceans (and their various seas): the Arctic Ocean on the north, the Pacific Ocean on the east, and the Indian Ocean on the south. On the west its traditional boundaries are the mountains and bodies of water separating it from Europe. The Suez Canal divides Asia from Africa on the southwest; and the narrow Bering Strait, which links the Arctic and Pacific oceans, separates it from North America.

Asia is a continent of enormous extremes. It has the world's highest peak—Mount Everest, on the border between Tibet, a region of China, and Nepal. It also has the lowest point on the earth's surface—the shoreline of the Dead Sea, on the Israel-Jordan border. Asia has some of the most densely populated regions in the world, including the two most populous countries, China and India. At the same time, large areas of Asia are too dry, too cold, or too mountainous to support any but limited numbers of people.

Asia was the birthplace of the world's earliest civilizations and its major religions. It was the site of once-vast empires of great wealth and cultural and scientific achievement. These great empires declined with the rise to power

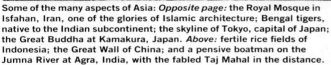

Some of the many aspects of Asia: *Opposite page:* the Royal Mosque in Isfahan, Iran, one of the glories of Islamic architecture; Bengal tigers, native to the Indian subcontinent; the skyline of Tokyo, capital of Japan; the Great Buddha at Kamakura, Japan. *Above:* fertile rice fields of Indonesia; the Great Wall of China; and a pensive boatman on the Jumna River at Agra, India, with the fabled Taj Mahal in the distance.

of European nations, several of which ruled large regions of Asia as colonies until the mid-1900's. The end of colonial rule marked the emergence of the nation-states of present-day Asia.

▶THE LAND

Physically, Asia forms the much larger, eastern portion of an enormous landmass known as Eurasia (Europe and Asia), which stretches from the Atlantic to the Pacific oceans. But although physically linked, Europe and Asia have had such distinct histories that they are usually considered separate continents. The generally accepted dividing line between them runs along the Ural Mountains, the Caspian Sea, the Caucasus Mountains, the

Black Sea, and the Bosporus and Dardanelles straits that connect the Black Sea with the Mediterranean.

Numerous islands, including those making up the nations of Japan, Indonesia, and the Philippines, ring the continent and form part of it. The interior is marked by some of the world's most imposing physical features. In the heart of the continent, standing like an enormous wall, is the great chain of the Himalayas, of which Everest is a part. The Himalayas are themselves part of an even larger mountain system that runs from Turkey in the west to China in the east. Asia has some of the most forbidding deserts on earth, including the Gobi of Mongolia and China, the Syrian, and the Rub' al Khali (Empty Quarter) of

Saudi Arabia. Vast treeless plains, or steppes, cover much of Central Asia. Farther north is the broad belt of forest known as taiga.

Regions of Asia

Asia can be divided into a number of distinct regions, although geographers do not always agree on which countries belong in which regions.

East Asia. East Asia is one of the centers of Asian civilization. It consists of China, Korea, Japan, and Taiwan. Historically and geographically, East Asia is dominated by China, which includes more than 75 percent of the region's territory. Three important rivers flow through parts of China: the Huang He (Yellow River) of North China, the Chang Jiang (Yangtze) of Central China, and the Xijiang (Si Kiang) of South China.

Korea is a long, mountainous peninsula, sit-

gyzstan, Tajikistan, Turkmenistan, and Uzbekistan, which gained independence with the breakup of the Soviet Union in late 1991, are usually considered part of Central Asia, although they are sometimes included in North Asia. Mongolia is often considered a part of the region, too.

Covering a vast area, Central Asia consists mainly of high plateaus, mountains, deserts, and steppe land. Tibet, for example, forms one great plateau rising some 15,000 feet (4,500 meters). Because of its mountainous terrain, limited rainfall, and generally poor soil, however, the region has a relatively small population for its size.

South Asia. South Asia includes India, Pakistan, Bangladesh, Afghanistan, Sri Lanka, Maldives, and the small Himalayan countries of Nepal and Bhutan. For the most part, this region is one of great population density, with

Much of Southwest Asia consists of desert, such as the Rub' al Khali of Saudi Arabia, seen here. Southeast Asia, by contrast, has large areas of tropical rain forest.

uated between China and Japan. Japan itself consists of four large islands and a number of smaller ones lying off the eastern coast of Asia. The island of Taiwan lies off the southeastern coast of the Chinese mainland. Historically a province of China, it is the seat of the Republic of China, which opposes the Communist government of the People's Republic of China on the mainland.

Central, or Inner, Asia. This is a rather imprecisely defined region. Included within it are Tibet and the Xinjiang-Uygur Autonomous Region of western China. Kazakhstan, Kyr-

a variety of climates. It extends from the high Himalayas in the north to the Indian Ocean in the south, forming a huge triangle, dominated by India. The Arabian Sea is situated on one side of this great triangle and the Bay of Bengal is on the other.

Southeast Asia. Southeast Asia includes areas on both the Asian mainland and neighboring islands. Burma (Myanmar), Thailand, Laos, Cambodia, and Vietnam are situated on the mainland. Indonesia, Singapore, and the Philippines are island countries, while Malaysia lies on both the mainland and islands.

Mount Everest, the world's highest peak, rises in the great mountain chain of the Himalayas, which stands like an enormous wall in the heart of Asia.

Tiny, oil-rich Brunei, the smallest of the Southeast Asian nations, is located on the large island of Borneo, which belongs to Malaysia and Indonesia. Indonesia is the largest and most populous of the region's countries.

The climate is tropical, with numerous areas of dense population. Four great rivers flow through mainland Southeast Asia—the Mekong, the Chao Phraya, the Salween, and the Irrawaddy.

FACTS
and figures

LOCATION: Mainland Asia. **Latitude**—1° 16′ N to 77° 41′ N. **Longitude**—26° 04′ E to 169° 40′ W. **Area**—approximately 17,297,000 sq mi (44,780,000 km²). **Highest point**—Mt. Everest, 29,028 ft (8,848 m). **Lowest point**—Dead Sea, about 1,300 ft (400 m) below sea level.

POPULATION: 3,200,000,000 (estimate).

PRINCIPAL LAKES: Aral, Baikal, Balkhash, Tungting, Urmia, Koko Nor.

PRINCIPAL RIVERS: Chang Jiang (Yangtze), Huang He (Yellow River), Amur, Lena, Mekong, Yenisei, Ob, Indus, Irtysh, Brahmaputra, Salween, Euphrates, Amu Darya, Ganges, Olenek, Kolyma, Syr Darya, Irrawaddy, Tarim, Xijiang (Si Kiang), Tigris, Chao Phraya (Menam).

PRINCIPAL MOUNTAIN RANGES: Himalayas—Mt. Everest, Kanchenjunga, Lhotse I, Makalu, Lhotse II, Cho Oyu, Dhaulagiri, Nanga Parbat, Annapurna; **Karakoram**—K2 (Mt. Godwin Austen), Gasherbrum I, Broad Peak; **Kunlun**—Ulugh Muztagh; **Hindu Kush**—Tirich Mir; **Tien Shan**—Pobeda Peak, Khan Tengri; **Elburz**—Mt. Demavend; **Altai**—Tabun Bogdo, Belukha; **Barisan**—Mt. Kerinchi; **Taurus**—Ala Dag; **Sulaiman**—Takht-i-Sulaiman, twin peaks; **Ural Mountains**—Naroda.

PRINCIPAL DESERTS: Gobi, Rub' al Khali, Syrian, Nafud, Taklamakan, Kara Kum, Thar, Kyzyl Kum.

Southwest Asia. Southwest Asia makes up most of the region called the Middle East. It includes the countries of Turkey, Iran, Syria, Lebanon, Israel, Jordan, Iraq, Kuwait, Saudi Arabia, Yemen, Oman, the United Arab Emirates, and the island nation of Cyprus. The Sinai Peninsula, a territory of Egypt lying east of the Suez Canal, is also considered a part of Asia geographically.

Southwest Asia has a generally hot and dry climate, with little rainfall. But an area of rich soil in the shape of a semicircle, called the Fertile Crescent, stretches between the Mediterranean Sea and the Persian Gulf. Here,

Bactrian camels graze on the high steppe that makes up much of Central Asia. Although one of Asia's largest regions, it has a relatively small population.

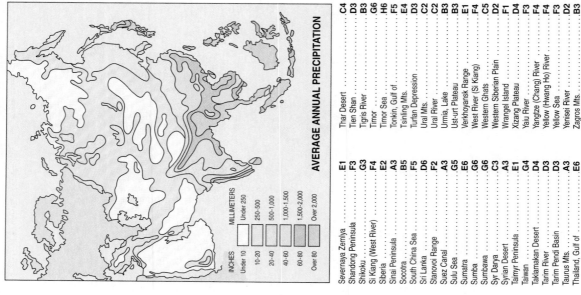

AVERAGE ANNUAL PRECIPITATION

INCHES	MILLIMETERS
Under 10	Under 250
10-20	250-500
20-40	500-1,000
40-60	1,000-1,500
60-80	1,500-2,000
Over 80	Over 2,000

INDEX TO ASIA PHYSICAL MAP

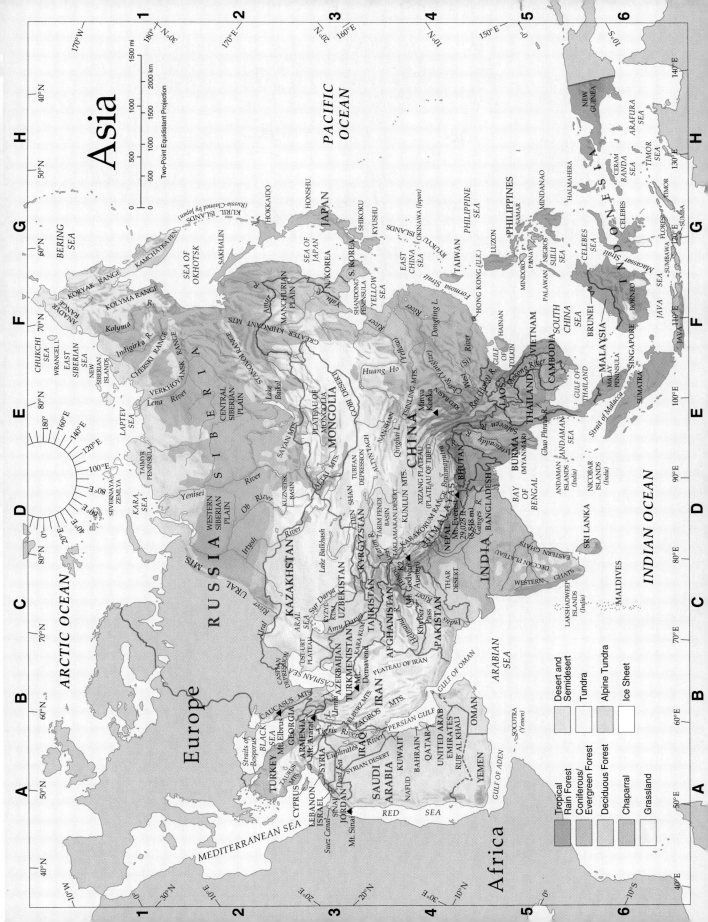

Asia

Two-Point Equidistant Projection

PACIFIC OCEAN

ARCTIC OCEAN

INDIAN OCEAN

MEDITERRANEAN SEA

Europe

Africa

Legend:
- Tropical Rain Forest
- Coniferous/ Evergreen Forest
- Deciduous Forest
- Chaparral
- Grassland
- Desert and Semidesert
- Tundra
- Alpine Tundra
- Ice Sheet

North Asia is another vast but thinly populated region. It is often frozen in winter, when reindeer sleds become a convenient form of transportation. The Chang Jiang, or Yangtze, is East Asia's major river and the longest in China. Nearly half of China's people live in the river's great basin.

where the Tigris and Euphrates rivers provide sufficient water for irrigation, some of Asia's and the world's oldest civilizations arose thousands of years ago.

To the traditional nations of the region can be added three countries—Armenia, Azerbaijan, and Georgia, which also gained independence from the former Soviet Union in 1991. They are sometimes called Transcaucasia or the Transcaucasian republics because of their location on or near the Caucasus mountain range between Europe and Asia.

COUNTRIES OF ASIA*

COUNTRY	CAPITAL
Afghanistan	Kabul
Armenia	Yerevan
Azerbaijan	Baku
Bahrain	Manama
Bangladesh	Dhaka
Bhutan	Thimbu
Brunei	Bandar Seri Begawan
Burma (Myanmar)	Rangoon (Yangon)
Cambodia	Phnom Penh
China, People's Republic of	Beijing
Cyprus	Nicosia
Georgia	Tbilisi
India	New Delhi
Indonesia	Jakarta
Iran	Tehran
Iraq	Baghdad
Israel	Jerusalem
Japan	Tokyo
Jordan	Amman
Kazakhstan	Alma-Ata
Korea	
North Korea	Pyongyang
South Korea	Seoul
Kuwait	Kuwait
Kyrgyzstan	Bishkek
Laos	Vientiane
Lebanon	Beirut
Malaysia	Kuala Lumpur
Maldives	Male
Mongolia	Ulan Bator
Nepal	Katmandu
Oman	Muscat
Pakistan	Islamabad
Philippines	Manila
Qatar	Doha
Saudi Arabia	Riyadh
Singapore	Singapore
Sri Lanka	Colombo
Syria	Damascus
Taiwan (Republic of China)	Taipei
Tajikistan	Dushanbe
Thailand	Bangkok
Turkey	Ankara
Turkmenistan	Ashkhabad
United Arab Emirates	Abu Dhabi
Uzbekistan	Tashkent
Vietnam	Hanoi
Yemen	Sana

*Russia includes territory in both Asia and Europe, but the majority of its people live in Europe. Azerbaijan, Georgia, Kazakhstan, and Turkey also have areas of territory in Europe.

North Asia. This is another vast but thinly populated region, which extends across the northern part of the continent from the Ural Mountains to the Pacific Ocean. Most of North Asia consists of the region known as Siberia and lies within present-day Russia. Bordering the Arctic Ocean on the north, with the coldest winter temperatures on the continent, it is often inhospitable to human settlement, although it is rich in mineral resources.

See the separate articles on the Himalayas, the Middle East, Mount Everest, Palestine, Siberia, and Southeast Asia in the appropriate volumes.

Natural Resources

Minerals. Asia is rich in mineral resources, although a good part of its mineral wealth is still untapped. Deposits of coal, iron ore, and copper are found in East Asia, while South Asia is rich in manganese. Southeast Asia is

Fishing begins at sunrise on the Mekong River, the chief waterway of Southeast Asia. The plains and delta of the river form a fertile rice-growing area, traditionally cultivated with the aid of water buffalo, probably the most useful domesticated animal of the region.

one of the world's chief sources of tin, with Malaysia being the world's largest producer. North Asia's extensive mineral resources include bauxite (aluminum ore), iron, gold, lead, zinc, and silver.

Southwest Asia, particularly the Persian Gulf area, is the world's single largest source of petroleum, with an estimated one-half of the total supply. Other important sources of petroleum are in Azerbaijan, China, and Indonesia. China also has the world's largest deposits of anthracite (hard coal) and tungsten. Turkey has large chromium deposits, and India has enormous deposits of mica.

Soils and Vegetation. Much of Asia has poor soils, particularly in the interior, which is too high, dry, or cold for good soil to have developed. Nor are the soils of the subtropical and tropical regions necessarily very productive. The most fertile places, where crops can most readily be grown, are located along the river valleys and some coastal areas, and it is here that the densest populations are found. In a few cases, such as the island of Java in Indonesia, the soils are fertile because of their volcanic origin.

Vegetation ranges from the mosses and other simple plant life of the frozen tundra along the North Asia coast to the lush tropical rain forests of Southeast Asia. Between the two lie the belt of northern forest (taiga), the grasslands of the semi-arid steppes, and deserts with little or no vegetation at all.

Its forests are among the continent's major natural resources. The taiga belt is the world's largest area of woodlands, and Southeast Asia's tropical rain forests include such valuable hardwoods as teak and mahogany. Logging, however, has suffered from a lack of transportation in some areas, and in others from overcutting.

Animal Life. Asia is home to a variety of wild and domestic animal life. Most wild animals inhabit the less-populated areas.

Polar and brown bears, Arctic foxes and hares, mouse-like lemmings, the rare Siberian tiger, reindeer, elk, and such valuable fur-bearing animals as ermine and sable are found in North Asia. The Bactrian (two-humped) camel is a vital beast of burden in the arid lands of Central Asia, while the Arabian (one-humped) camel performs the same function in the deserts of Southwest Asia. The hardy yak, a shaggy-haired ox, thrives in the high, wind-

Animals unique to Asia include the Komodo dragon, largest of the lizards; the shy orangutan; and the Indian (or Asian) elephant, which has smaller ears than its African cousin.

swept Tibetan plateau, where it is the most important form of livestock.

Birds are found throughout the continent. The most gorgeously plumaged inhabit the tropical areas of South and Southeast Asia, which are also home to monkeys and apes. The orangutan lives only in the dense tropical forests on the islands of Sumatra and Borneo. India has a number of large mammals, including the Bengal tiger, the Indian rhinoceros, and the Indian (or Asian) elephant. The water buffalo is probably the most important domesticated animal of the region, invaluable in plowing its rice fields.

Large reptiles include crocodiles and a wide variety of snakes, among them the deadly Indian cobra and the enormous python. The Komodo dragon, the world's largest lizard, can be found on a few of the Indonesian islands. East Asia's most distinctive mammal is the giant panda, which is native only to the bamboo forests of interior China.

Climate

Asia has almost all the varieties of climates known. In general, it has what is called a continental climate—that is, one marked by wide seasonal and temperature ranges and limited rainfall. Much of the continent is cold and dry in the winter and warm and dry in the summer. Because of its great size, many areas are far from the sea. As a result, the interior of Asia is never touched by the winds that bring moisture from the oceans. Most of Central Asia is alternately cold and warm, but always dry.

Temperature. The high mountain ranges that cross Asia act as a huge wall. They keep the cold winds of the Arctic from blowing to the south and the hot winds of the south from blowing north. Therefore, average tempera-

tures in the areas north of the mountains are lower than they would normally be at the same latitude elsewhere in the world. Siberian winters, for example, are among the coldest on earth. The average January temperature is about $-60°F$ ($-51°C$). In the town of Verkhoyansk, in northeastern Siberia, the winter temperature has dropped to $-90°F$ ($-68°C$).

The hottest parts of Asia are in the southwestern region. The area around the Persian Gulf is one of the hottest in the world, with land temperatures often reaching 120°F (49°C).

Rainfall. Rainfall in Asia is also affected by the size of the continent and its mountain ranges. Some regions receive a great deal of rain, while others receive little. Winds carrying moisture from the ocean bring rain to the near side of the mountains, leaving the far side of the high mountains generally dry.

Examples of this uneven rainfall can be seen throughout Asia. Parts of Southwest Asia receive as little as 4 inches (100 millimeters) of rain a year, while northeastern India is one of the wettest regions on earth. Southeast Asia is often hit by heavy rains, which may cause widespread flooding. Parts of southern China also receive much rainfall. Most of the rest of the continent tends to be dry.

Winds. Many parts of Asia are subjected to very strong winds. One such wind, called the Seistan, blows through Iran, in Southwest Asia, for about six months of the year at extremely high speeds. Many desert areas in Central Asia have similar winds. Winds from the plateau of Tibet have blown thousands of tons of soil (loess) hundreds of miles eastward to China. The heating and cooling of the land in interior Asia causes great masses of air to rush in and out of this area. Because of the height and location of the mountains, the winds usually move in an east–west direction.

The monsoons of the Indian Ocean are seasonal winds. For about six months each year they blow from northeastern India across the peninsula, carrying warm air out to the Indian Ocean. From June to September they reverse their direction and blow from the southwest. They then carry rain to the land, creating the wet monsoon season. If these returning winds do not carry enough rain, then crops fail and famine may result. The farmers of South and Southeast Asia are thus dependent upon the wet monsoon for their livelihood.

▶THE PEOPLE

Asia's population, already very large, is growing rapidly. This is due partly to the high birth rate in some of the Asian nations and partly to the declining death rate. Modern medicines, better health care and diet, and other improvements in living standards have helped to increase the average life span of most Asian people. At the present rate of growth, it is estimated that the population of Asia will double by the early 2000's.

Population Density

Asia's population is not spread out evenly over the continent. Most of the people live in three regions—South, Southeast, and East Asia. Therefore, even though more than one-half of Asia's land lies in North and Central Asia, less than one-tenth of Asians live there.

Population densities vary widely. Southwest Asia has fewer than 60 people per square mile (25 per square kilometer). But in South, Southeast, and East Asia, the highest population densities in the world are found. Often the population is even denser than the figures would indicate, since the bulk of the people are concentrated in the most fertile areas, usually along riverbanks or in coastal regions. In China, for example, the great majority of the people live in the eastern part of the country, along the coast and in the fertile basins drained by the great rivers. The average population density in these areas can be as high as four to six times the overall density of the country.

Racial and Ethnic Groups

Asians are as varied as their landscape. Attempts to classify them differ, but they can be divided into a number of broad categories.

Mongoloid peoples, including Chinese, most Japanese, Koreans, Mongols, and Tibetans, make up by far the largest group. The Han Chinese, who constitute most of China's population but are concentrated in the east, are the largest single ethnic group. Turkic peoples occupy a vast area stretching from northwestern China across Central Asia to Turkey and Azerbaijan. North Asia is also home to some Turkic ethnic groups, as well as to considerable numbers of European Russians.

Malay peoples inhabit Indonesia and the Philippines, while most mainland Southeast

Asians are a Malay-Mongoloid mixture. South Asia includes two main ethnic groups: Indo-Aryans in northern India, Pakistan, Bangladesh, and most of Afghanistan and Sri Lanka; and Dravidians in southern India and part of Sri Lanka. Aside from Turkey, the Transcaucasian countries, and Iran (whose people are mainly Indo-Aryan), the great majority of Southwest Asians are Semites, chiefly Arabs but also including Jews, most of whom live in Israel. The people of Cyprus are of Greek (the majority) and Turkish ancestry.

Other distinctive Asian racial groups include the few remaining Ainu of northern Japan and the Negritos and hill people of South and Southeast Asia. These are believed to be the original inhabitants of the regions.

Languages

The peoples of Asia can also be defined by their languages. The language names are similar to, but not always the same as, the ethnic classifications.

South Asia has two major language divisions—the Indo-Iranian (or Indo-Aryan), part of the large Indo-European family; and the Dravidian. The Indo-Iranian branch is divided into dozens of languages, including Hindi, Urdu, Bengali, Punjabi, and Sinhala. The many languages of the Dravidian family of southern India include Tamil, Telugu, Kanarese, and Malayalam. Persian, spoken in Iran, and the Pushtu and related languages of Afghanistan are also Indo-Iranian.

Chinese, Tibetan, and most of the languages of mainland Southeast Asia belong to the Sino-Tibetan family. Mandarin Chinese is the world's most widely spoken language. Japanese and Korean are separate languages, sometimes classified in the Altaic family. The Malayo-Polynesian family includes languages of Malaysia, Indonesia, the Philippines, and most of the Pacific islands.

The major language of Southwest Asia, Arabic, belongs to the Semitic family, as does Hebrew, spoken in Israel. The Osmanli Turkish of Turkey, the Azeri Turkish of Azerbaijan, and their related languages of Central and North Asia are Altaic. Armenian and the Greek spoken on Cyprus are Indo-European, while Georgian belongs to the small Caucasian language family.

Faces of Asia: *Opposite page:* a young Saudi Arabian with his cellular telephone; elderly Tajiks from Central Asia; a Russian mother and daughter from Siberia, in North Asia; a Sri Lankan girl gathering tea leaves; and a young Israeli woman. *Below and right:* a Chinese in cap and tunic; a girl from the Philippines and a boy from India; and Japanese schoolchildren.

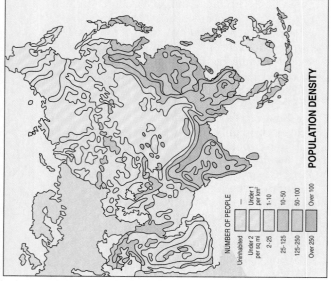

POPULATION DENSITY

NUMBER OF PEOPLE

	Under 1 per sq mi	—	Uninhabited
	Under 2 per km²		
2-25	1-10	
25-125	10-50	
125-250	50-100	
Over 250	Over 100	

Chief Cities in Asia (by population)

Over 7,000,000

Bombay,* India
Beijing† (Peking), China
Calcutta,* India
Seoul, Korea

Shanghai† China
Tianjin (Tientsin),* China
Tokyo, Japan

3,000,000 to 7,000,000

Baghdad, Iraq
Bangkok, Thailand
Guangzhou (Canton), China
Delhi, India
Dhaka, Bangladesh
Ho Chi Minh City (Saigon),* Vietnam
Istanbul,* Turkey

Jakarta, Indonesia
Karachi, Pakistan
Madras, India
Pusan, South Korea
Shenyang, China
Tehran, Iran
Wuhan, China

2,000,000 to 3,000,000

Ahmadabad, India
Bangalore, India
Chengdu (Chengtu), China
Chongqing, (Chungking), China
Hanoi, Vietnam
Harbin, China
Hyderabad, India
Lahore, Pakistan
Nagoya, Japan

Nanjing (Nanking), China
Osaka, Japan
Rangoon, (Yangon), Burma
Xian (Sian), China
Singapore, Singapore
Surabaya, Indonesia
Taipei, Taiwan,
(Republic of China)
Yokohama, Japan

*Metropolitan area
†Municipality, including surrounding counties

INDEX TO ASIA POLITICAL MAP

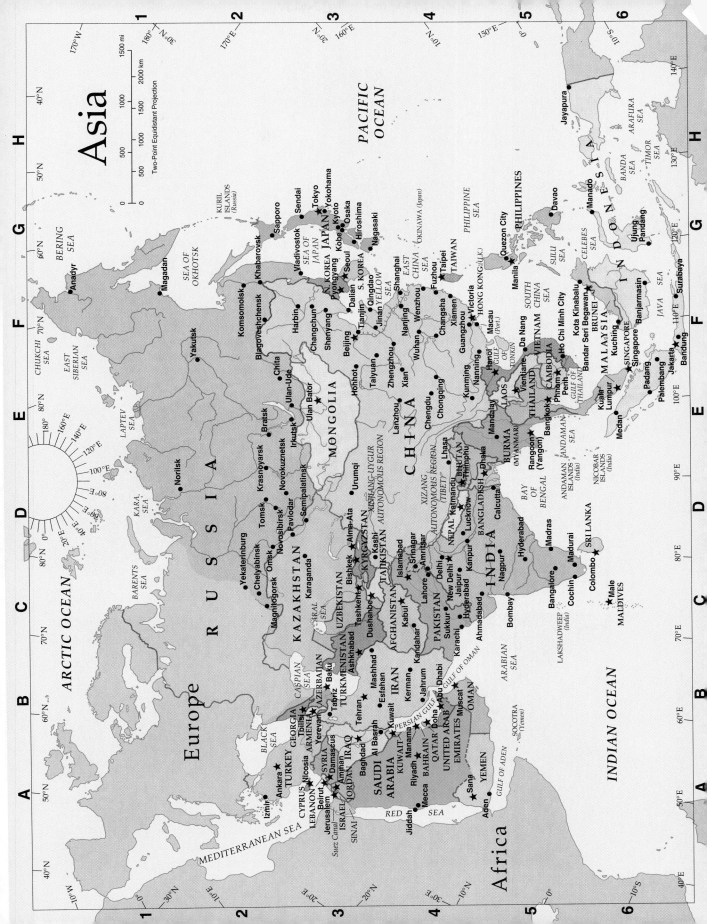

Asia

Religions

Three of the world's great religions, Judaism, Christianity, and Islam, originated in Southwest Asia. Islam, the religion of the Muslims, eventually became the dominant faith of the region and spread to Central Asia and parts of South Asia (chiefly what are now Pakistan, Bangladesh, and Afghanistan) and Southeast Asia (mainly present-day Indonesia and Malaysia). Together with Hinduism and Buddhism, Islam remains one of the major religions of Asia.

Christianity was re-introduced to Asia by missionaries, and Judaism was re-established as the religion of Israel in recent times. Today, Christians predominate in Cyprus, Armenia, Georgia, and the Philippines, and make up about 40 percent of the population of Lebanon. Most of the Russians of North Asia are Christian, and there are significant communities in other parts of Asia.

Hinduism originated in India and is the chief religion of that populous country, which also has an important Muslim minority. India's religious heritage also includes Sikhs, Jains, and Parsees, or Zoroastrians. The origins of Zoroastrianism were in ancient Persia

(Iran), where it was eventually supplanted by Islam. Buddhism also developed in India, based on the teachings of Siddhartha Gautama, called the Buddha. But it has relatively few followers in India today. Most Buddhists are now found in China, Japan, Korea, and mainland Southeast Asia.

Taoism is a native religion of China, which developed from the philosophy of Lao-tzu, while Shinto is the original faith of Japan. China has also been strongly influenced by Confucianism. Named for its founder, Confucianism is not a religion but a system of ethical teachings. Through China, it has influenced the thinking of other countries of East Asia as well as areas of Southeast Asia, partic-

Asia was the birthplace of the world's major religions: an orthodox Jew at the Western Wall in Jerusalem (*top*); Muslims kneeling in prayer (*right*); a Buddhist monk with statues of the Buddha (*below*); Christian dignitaries (*below right*); a Hindu holy man (*opposite page, top*).

ularly Vietnam. In addition, such early religious beliefs as animism and shamanism still survive in some parts of Asia.

Articles on the major religions of Asia can be found in the appropriate volumes. An article on Confucius appears in Volume C. Also consult RELIGIONS OF THE WORLD in Volume Q-R.

The Arts. Many Asian countries have a long tradition of cultural achievement in art, architecture, and literature. For detailed information on this aspect of Asia, see the following articles in the appropriate volumes of this encyclopedia:

ANCIENT WORLD, ART OF THE; CHINESE ART; CHINESE LITERATURE; INDIA, ART AND ARCHITECTURE OF; INDIA, LITERATURE OF; ISLAMIC ART AND ARCHITECTURE; JAPANESE ART AND ARCHITECTURE; JAPANESE LITERATURE; ORIENTAL ART AND ARCHITECTURE.

Education

The scholar has always been a respected member of the community in Asia. In China, the most revered figure, Confucius, was a scholar and teacher. Asia's tradition of learning is also very old, the first Chinese university having been founded in 124 B.C. But until modern times education was a privilege enjoyed only by the well-to-do, and the great mass of Asians could neither read nor write. Not until the latter half of the 1800's did most Asian countries begin to adopt the goal of universal education for all of their people.

The majority of Asian countries today have compulsory school attendance laws, and almost all of them have policies designed to keep children in school longer. Fees that prevented many children from attending school have been gradually abolished or lowered. The literacy rate (the percentage of people able to read or write) has risen dramatically, although it still varies widely from country to country. In higher education, there is at least one college in every major city, and many cities have several colleges and universities. The academic standards of many of them compare favorably with those of the best universities in the world.

▶CITIES

Although the majority of its people live in rural areas, Asia has some of the largest cities to be found anywhere in the world. Population trends are also marked by increasing urbanization, or the movement of people from rural areas to the cities.

The largest urban centers are located in East, South, and Southeast Asia. They include Tokyo, the capital of Japan; China's great municipalities of Shanghai; Beijing, the capital; and Tientsin (Tianjin); South Korea's rapidly growing capital of Seoul; the Indian cities of Bombay, Calcutta, and Delhi; and Jakarta, Indonesia's capital.

Many cities originated close to natural transportation routes. Istanbul, Turkey's largest city, one of the most favorably located, lies on the waters separating Europe and Asia. Formerly called Constantinople, it is a historic city and the only one situated on two conti-

Jakarta is the capital of Indonesia and the largest city of Southeast Asia. Like other rapidly growing Asian cities, it has new sections built in the most modern style.

Istanbul (*left*), Turkey's largest city, is strategically located on the waters separating Europe and Asia. Formerly called Constantinople, it was once the capital of the Roman Empire. Jerusalem (*above*) is an ancient city holy to three religions—Judaism, Christianity, and Islam.

nents. Other Southwest Asian cities, such as Iraq's capital of Baghdad, while smaller, are also of great historical and cultural interest. The importance of Jerusalem, a city holy to three religious faiths, far outweighs its relatively small size.

Articles on the cities mentioned can be found in the appropriate volumes.

▶THE ECONOMY

About two-thirds of Asia's people earn their livelihood from the land. The most fertile areas are in South and Southeast Asia and in the eastern part of East Asia. Here, where the continent's population is most densely concentrated, every bit of usable land is intensely cultivated. Most farms traditionally were small, providing families with a subsistence living. In recent years Asian countries, to keep up with their fast-growing populations, have sought to increase crop production through the use of irrigation, improved seeds, and modern farm machinery.

Industrialization has been the major goal of nearly every economic development program carried out in Asia since the end of World War II in 1945. Japan is the greatest example of an Asian nation that has succeeded dramatically in industrializing itself. Many of Asia's cities,

in addition, have developed into important manufacturing centers, producing a wide variety of goods.

Agriculture

Rice, which needs a warm and wet climate to grow, is the major crop in the southern regions of Asia. Southeast Asia, eastern India, southern China, Korea, and Japan are the important rice-growing areas. Farther north, in the drier regions, cereal grains such as wheat, barley, and millet are grown. China, northern India and Pakistan, and Central Asia are major wheat- and corn-growing areas.

Rubber is an important commercial crop in Malaysia, the world's leading producer of natural rubber, and other countries of Southeast Asia. Most of the world's tea comes from India, China, Sri Lanka, and Japan. Sugarcane is grown mainly in India, Taiwan, and the Philippines. Cotton is a major product in China, India, and countries of Central Asia. Soybeans and silk come largely from China. Jute, used to make burlap and twine, is Bangladesh's chief export. Coconuts and palm oil come from South and Southeast Asia, while peanuts are grown in China and India. Dates and oranges are the specialties of the countries of Southwest Asia.

Nomadic herders in Southwest and Central Asia, where the land is often suitable only for grazing, depend largely on their livestock. Many small farmers throughout Asia raise poultry for food. India and North Asia produce much cheese and butter, and North Asia and China lead in beef, pork, mutton, and lamb. Wool is a major product in Central Asia.

Manufacturing

Japan is not only the most highly industrialized nation in Asia; it ranks among the top two or three world industrial powers. It is the world's chief shipbuilding country and, along with the United States, the largest producer of automobiles and other motor vehicles. It is either first or among world leaders in the manufacture of steel, aluminum, chemicals, television sets and videocassette recorders, and computers and other high-technology products. Japan has achieved this with few mineral resources of its own. It must import the raw materials with which to manufacture these goods for export.

India and China are a distant second to Japan in industrial output. India is an important producer of textiles, cotton clothing, steel, electrical machinery, and electronic equipment. China's industrial heartland has traditionally been in its northeastern region (sometimes called Manchuria), the site of large iron and coal deposits. A main goal of the country's leaders is to make China one of the world's major industrial powers by the early 2000's.

South Korea has been making its mark recently as a rapidly growing industrial nation, and Taiwan has become one of the world's leading trading states. Turkey has long had a significant industrial capacity, while Pakistan, Indonesia, and Malaysia, as well as Singapore and Israel, are also becoming important industrial countries.

Mining and Fishing

Asia has virtually all the minerals needed for industrial growth, although some deposits remain to be developed, particularly in the lightly populated North Asia region. For detailed information on these minerals and where they are found, see the section Natural Resources (Minerals).

Fishing is an especially important industry in Asia. Japan is the world's leading producer of processed fish, and China ranks second. Japan's fishing industry is one of the most modern in the world, equipped with floating canneries that process the fish right after they are caught. Russia and Japan also have large whaling fleets. The waters of the Persian Gulf

About two-thirds of Asians earn their livelihood from the land. Rice, here being planted in China's Sichuan province, is one of the continent's major crops. Automobiles are assembled at a plant in South Korea, which is rapidly becoming one of Asia's leading industrial areas.

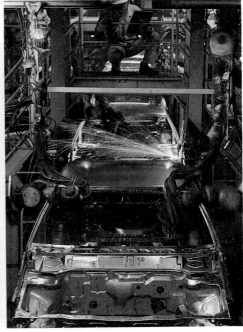

Oil refineries such as this one in Saudi Arabia process much of the world's fuel supply. Southwest Asia has about half of the world's known oil reserves.

are famed for their natural pearls, while Japan produces much of the world's supply of cultured pearls.

Lumbering

Russia is the world's leading producer of sawed wood, and a large part of its lumbering is done in Asia. Japan is also an important world producer of sawed wood. In spite of its rich forest resources, Asia as a whole has a shortage of lumber. Many Asian countries are now carrying out reforestation programs—that is, the planting of trees for future use. These projects, which replace lost timber areas, also help prevent floods and soil erosion.

Transportation

Geography has hindered the development of both transportation and trade in Asia. Transportation has been easiest on or near the coasts and along the great rivers, which have been the main avenues of transportation in much of the continent for centuries. In the North, however, the Arctic climate keeps the coastal areas icebound for the better part of the year. In parts of Asia transportation is still a matter of using old caravan trails. Merchants still cross the deserts of Southwest and Central Asia on camels, although the camels are gradually being replaced by vehicles designed for desert travel.

The first Asian railroads were built after the arrival of the Europeans, mainly during the late 1800's and early 1900's. Some new lines were built after World War II, and others are now under construction. The Trans-Siberian Railroad is the only rail line crossing the whole vast expanse of Asia. It is also the world's longest continuous railroad, linking the Russian capital of Moscow in Europe with the Pacific Ocean port of Vladivostok. The line was expanded in recent years, but the harsh climate and rugged terrain make further work difficult. Today, Japan, India, and China have the most extensive rail systems.

The roads and highways of Asia, with some exceptions, are generally poor. Increasingly, air transport is being used to reach formerly inaccessible areas.

Modern methods of transportation in Asia can be seen in Japan's system of turbo trains. Popularly known as "bullet trains" because of their shape and high speed, they can travel at 160 miles (260 kilometers) an hour. Here the bullet train passes Mount Fuji on the main Japanese island of Honshu.

The sculpture at left was discovered at Mohenjo-Daro, part of the Indus Valley civilization. One of three main sites of early Asian civilization, it flourished 5,000 years ago in what is now Pakistan. Later Greek and Roman influence is reflected in the ruins at Palmyra, in modern-day Syria, a city-state that briefly held power during the A.D. 200's.

▶HISTORY

The history of Asia began in three great river valleys—the Tigris-Euphrates in Southwest Asia, the Indus in South Asia, and the Huang He (Yellow River) in East Asia. In these three areas, civilizations developed that give Asia its special place in the world today.

Early Civilizations

The Tigris-Euphrates Valley was the site of several early civilizations. From 3500 B.C. to 600 B.C., a succession of great states arose in the region. The Sumerians, Babylonians, and Assyrians developed writing, law, and commerce. The code of Hammurabi (about 1800 B.C.) was one of the first written law codes in the world. Around 600 B.C., the Persians, under Cyrus the Great, established an empire that stretched from the shores of the Mediter-

ranean Sea to northern India. The empire was expanded by later Persian kings, among them Darius the Great.

The ruins of Harappa and Mohenjo-Daro are signs of early civilization in the Indus Valley of South Asia. In about 1500 B.C., Indo-Aryan invaders came through the mountains of northwestern India to establish the Hindu civilization. Traces of this early beginning remain to this day, and the tradition of Hinduism is still one of the most important influences in modern India.

For additional information on these periods of Asian history, see the articles ANCIENT CIVILIZATIONS (sections on Sumerian, Babylonian, and Indus Valley civilizations); and PERSIA, ANCIENT.

The earliest civilization in China developed along the northern reaches of the Huang He during the 1500's B.C. China's history was marked by successive dynasties, or ruling families. Some ruled for centuries; others for only a short period. The last dynasty, the Qing (or Manchu), was overthrown and a republic established in 1912.

Period of Development and Expansion

After 500 B.C., several great religions and empires grew up in Asia. In 334 B.C., Alexander the Great began his conquest of western Asia. His invasion brought Asia into direct contact with Greek civilization. Meanwhile the first great Indian empire, the Maurya, was established in the 320's B.C., creating unity in India. Under its greatest ruler, Asoka, Buddhism briefly flourished and the great monumental art of India began.

Farther east, in China, the Han dynasty (202 B.C.–A.D. 220) established an empire and extended its influence into Central and Southeast Asia. Under its great emperor Wu Ti, the Han adopted Confucianism. During this period other great religions took form. Chris-

Confucius, China's great sage and teacher, lived from about 551 to 479 B.C. His system of ethics has influenced Chinese thinking from ancient times to the present.

IMPORTANT DATES

About 3200 B.C.	Beginnings of civilization: Sumerians develop cuneiform writing; early urban culture in the Indus Valley; China emerges from the Stone Age.
About 1750 B.C.	Hammurabi, King of Babylonia, introduces world's first uniform code of laws.
About 1500 B.C.	Shang dynasty flourishes.
About 1300's B.C.	Phoenicians develop the first alphabet.
1200's B.C.	Moses leads the Exodus, receives the Ten Commandments.
1028–256 B.C.	Chou dynasty: beginning of China's Iron Age.
600–300 B.C.	Upanishads written; crystallization of the caste system in India.
563? B.C.	Birth of Buddha.
551? B.C.	Birth of Confucius.
500's B.C.	Cyrus the Great founds the Persian Empire.
274–232 B.C.	Asoka unites two-thirds of India; rules according to Buddhist laws; sends out missionaries.
202 B.C.–A.D. **220**	Han dynasty in China: height of ancient Chinese civilization; paper and porcelain invented.
4 B.C.	Birth of Christ.
A.D. **330**	Constantine I moves the capital of the Roman Empire to Byzantium, renamed Constantinople (now Istanbul).
618–906	Tang dynasty in China: printing invented; administration centralized.
622	Beginning of the Muslim era; Mohammed (570–632) flees from Mecca to Medina and organizes the Commonwealth of Islam.
632–1100	Growth of Arabic civilization under the influence of Islam.
960–1279	Sung dynasty in China: beginning of modernity; diffusion of learning; use of compass; gunpowder developed.
998–1030	Muslims invade Punjab: mixing of Hindu and Muslim cultures.
1096–1290	Era of Crusades: increased contact between East and West.
1206–1227	Genghis Khan (1167?–1227) establishes the Mongol empire, conquers large parts of Asia and Europe.
1260	Kublai Khan becomes emperor of China.
1271–1295	Travels of Marco Polo bring first detailed knowledge of Asia to Europe.
1368–1644	Ming dynasty drives out Mongols, reunifies China.
1369–1405	Tamerlane conquers much of Southwest Asia, invades India.
1453	Constantinople captured by the Ottoman Turks: end of the Eastern Roman (Byzantine) Empire; beginning of the Ottoman Empire.
1498	Vasco da Gama sails to India, opens water route to the East.
1514	Portuguese make first landing in China.
1521	Ferdinand Magellan claims Philippines for Spain.
1526	Mogul Empire in India founded by Baber.
1549–1551	St. Francis Xavier introduces Christianity in Japan.
1600–1868	Tokugawa period in Japan: ban on all foreigners begins a long era of isolation.
1644–1912	Qing (Manchu) dynasty rules China.
1756–1763	Britain becomes dominant power in India after the Seven Years' War.
1839–1842	Opium War between Britain and China.
1853–1854	U.S. Commodore Matthew Perry lands in Japan: end of Japanese isolation.
1857–1858	Sepoy Rebellion (Indian Mutiny) in India.
1868	Meiji Restoration begins in Japan.
1869	Suez Canal opens.
1894–1895	Sino-Japanese War.
1898	Spanish-American War: United States acquires the Philippines.
1900	Boxer Rebellion in China.
1904–1905	Russo-Japanese War: Japan emerges as world power.
1911–1912	Revolution in China led by Sun Yat-sen: China becomes a republic.
1923	Turkey becomes a republic under the leadership of Mustafa Kemal (Atatürk).
1931	Japan invades Manchuria.
1941	Japan attacks Pearl Harbor, bringing United States into World War II.
1945	Atomic bombs dropped on Hiroshima and Nagasaki; Japan surrenders; World War II ends.
1946	Jordan and the Philippines win independence.
1947	India and Pakistan gain independence.
1948	Israel created; Burma and Ceylon (now Sri Lanka) become independent; North and South Korea established.
1949	Communists win control of mainland China: Nationalist government retreats to Taiwan; Indonesia gains independence.
1950–1953	Korean War.
1950	Chinese troops enter Tibet.
1954	North and South Vietnam, Laos, and Cambodia established.
1957	Malaya gains independence.
1959	Tibetans revolt against China; Dalai Lama flees.
1960	Cyprus gains independence.
1961	Kuwait gains independence.
1962	Border clashes between China and India.
1963	Malaysia formed.
1965	Maldives and Singapore gain independence.
1967	Yemen (Aden) gains independence.
1971	Bangladesh gains independence.
1975	Vietnam War ends; civil war in Lebanon; Sikkim incorporated into India.
1976	North and South Vietnam united.
1979	Egypt and Israel sign peace treaty; Shah overthrown in Iran; Soviet forces invade Afghanistan.
1980–1988	War between Iran and Iraq.
1984	Brunei gains independence.
1988–1989	Soviet Union withdraws its troops from Afghanistan.
1990	Yemen (Sana) and Yemen (Aden) are united; Iraq invades and occupies Kuwait: U.S. and allied forces are sent to the region.
1991	Gulf War ends with defeat of Iraq; breakup of the Soviet Union creates eight new Asian nations.
1994	Palestinians assume limited self-rule in Jericho on the West Bank and in the Gaza Strip, after an accord is signed between Israel and the Palestine Liberation Organization (PLO).

Period of Colonialism

With the arrival in India of the Portuguese navigator Vasco da Gama in 1498, Europeans actively entered the life of Asia. Aware of Asia's many riches, the Europeans began to carve out colonial empires. In the 1500's, Portugal established colonies in India, and Spain acquired the Philippines. The English, French, and Dutch joined the rush for colonies in the 1600's. By the end of the 1800's, Britain governed most of what is now India, Pakistan, Bangladesh, Sri Lanka, Malaysia, Singapore, and Cyprus. France ruled modern Vietnam, Laos, and Cambodia; and the Netherlands controlled Indonesia. Among the few remaining independent Asian states were China, Japan, Korea, Siam (now Thailand), Persia (now Iran), and the Ottoman Turkish Empire. The United States won the Philippines from Spain, and Korea was later colonized by Japan, in 1910. Russia and the Soviet Union also ruled a great Asian empire.

Nationalism and Independence

The desire for self-rule and unity—called nationalism—was the most powerful force in Asia during the 1900's. Asian nationalism grew rapidly. It reached its height in the years after World War II, when the following nations were born: Mongolia in 1945; Jordan and the Philippines in 1946; India and Pakistan in 1947; Burma, Ceylon (now Sri Lanka), Israel, and North and South Korea in 1948; and Indonesia in 1949.

tianity appeared in Southwest Asia, and Buddhism began to spread to East Asia.

The A.D. 600's saw the rapid rise of Islam. Its followers conquered most of North Africa, Southwest Asia, and northern India. In East Asia, China flourished under the Tang and Sung dynasties from about A.D. 600 to 1200. In the 1200's, Genghis Khan, the Mongol conqueror, gained control of much of Asia, from China to Russia.

Amid great pomp, Suleiman I (*top*) ascends the Ottoman Turkish throne in 1520. The Ottoman Empire lasted nearly 400 years more, but gradually diminished in power. A British warship (*right*) fires on flimsy Chinese craft in the first Opium War (1839–42), which arose over Chinese efforts to bar imports of the drug. China's defeat forced it to cede Hong Kong to Britain and to open ports to foreign trade.

Mohandas K. Gandhi followed a policy of nonviolence, which eventually proved successful, in his struggle to win India's independence from Britain.

in the introduction of its political ideas and institutions. Some of the newly independent Asian nations adopted Communist forms of government. Others developed parliamentary systems. Most Asian countries, however, assumed a nonaligned, or neutral, position in their dealings with the great powers. This policy had first been announced officially at the Bandung Conference in Indonesia in 1955.

Recent History

The nations of Asia are playing an increasing role in world affairs. Japan's economic strength makes it respected, and sometimes feared, by other nations. China, with more than one-fifth of the world's people, is a major power, especially since the breakup of the Soviet Union. India's size and great population make it dominant in South Asia, and the oil-producing countries of Southwest Asia are vital to the world economy.

The ideal of peace envisioned at the Bandung Conference, however, has been difficult to achieve. In the years since, wars and civil wars have broken out in many parts of Asia.

In South Asia, India and Pakistan have gone to war several times, chiefly over the state of Jammu and Kashmir. Afghanistan has been the site of years of war and civil war. Sri Lanka has been torn by violent ethnic hatreds. Civil conflict also raged in Kampuchea, until a fragile peace was agreed to in 1991.

Cambodia, Laos, and North and South Vietnam became independent in 1954. The Federation of Malaya followed in 1957; Cyprus in 1960; and Kuwait in 1961. Malaysia established itself in 1963. Maldives won independence in 1965, as did Singapore, which seceded from Malaysia. Yemen (Aden) won its independence in 1967, and Bangladesh (formerly East Pakistan) did so in 1971.

In 1976, following the end of the long Vietnam War, North and South Vietnam were united. Brunei gained independence in 1984; and in 1990, Yemen (Aden) and the older nation of Yemen (Sana) were united into a single republic. Armenia, Azerbaijan, Georgia, Kazakhstan, Kyrgyzstan, Tajikistan, Turkmenistan, and Uzbekistan all won independence in 1991.

Perhaps the most far-reaching effect of Western tradition on Asia was

In Southwest Asia, Israel and the surrounding Arab nations have fought numerous wars. Lebanon was devastated by years of conflict. Iran and Iraq were at war from 1980 to 1989. A second Persian Gulf war erupted in 1990, after Iraq's invasion of Kuwait. Iraq's action, condemned by the United Nations, brought a swift response from U.S. and allied forces, which forced an Iraqi retreat in 1991. A hopeful

An awesome cloud marks the atomic bombing of Hiroshima, Japan, by the United States in 1945, which hastened the end of World War II.

Japanese commuters arrive for work. Japan recovered quickly from the destruction of World War II, becoming a world economic power.

sign was an accord signed in 1993 and implemented in 1994 by Israel and the Palestine Liberation Organization (PLO), which gave Palestinians limited self-rule in Jericho on the West Bank and in the Gaza Strip.

The major problems facing Asia today are economic and political ones. The Asian countries wish to develop their natural resources, industries, commerce, and agriculture. To do this, however, they must have stable governments and, above all, they must have peace.

EDWARD W. JOHNSON
Chairman, Political Science Department
Montclair State College

HYMAN KUBLIN
City University of New York
Author, *The Rim of Asia*

See also articles on individual Asian countries.

ASQUITH, HERBERT HENRY (1852–1928)

British statesman Herbert Henry Asquith, 1st Earl of Oxford and Asquith, served as prime minister from 1908 until 1916. He was the last leader of the Liberal Party to serve as prime minister.

Asquith was born on September 12, 1852, in Morely, Yorkshire. He was a brilliant student at Oxford University and later became a successful lawyer in London. In 1886, Asquith won his first election to Parliament. He quickly became a leader within the Liberal Party, serving as home secretary (1892–95) and as chancellor of the exchequer (1905–08) before succeeding to the premiership, following the death of Henry Campbell-Bannerman in April 1908.

Asquith presided over a highly controversial government of the moderate left. Legislation passed during his first years in office included massive social reforms, including the provision of old-age pensions, unemployment insurance, national health insurance, minimum wage standards for miners, and protection of trade unions. However, Asquith was at his best when dealing with constitutional issues, such as limiting the power of the House of Lords, accomplished by the Parliament Act of 1911, and negotiating home rule for Ireland.

In 1914, Britain entered World War I. Unfortunately, Asquith did not prove himself an effective or forceful war leader. Many people

thought his judgment was far too restrained, and in the third year of the war he was pushed out of office in favor of the more dynamic David Lloyd George. Although he continued to lead the Liberal Party until 1926, Asquith never again held office. In 1925 he was created Earl of Oxford and Asquith and entered the House of Lords. He died on February 15, 1928.

ROY JENKINS
Lord Jenkins of Hillhead
Author, *Asquith*

ASSYRIA. See ANCIENT CIVILIZATIONS.

ASTEROIDS. See COMETS, METEORITES, AND ASTEROIDS.

ASTHMA. See DISEASES (Descriptions of Some Diseases).

ASTOR, JOHN JACOB. See FUR TRADE IN NORTH AMERICA (Profiles).

Sally Ride, aboard the *Challenger*, learned how to eat in the weightlessness of space. Notice the special food tray designed for the astronauts.

ASTRONAUTS

Throughout history, a few people have dared to dream that one day human beings might leave the surface of the Earth and explore the heavens. During the last thirty years that dream has come true, and a select group of men and women from several nations have journeyed into space.

The men and women who travel in space for the United States are called **astronauts** (from a Greek word meaning "sailors of the stars"). Those sent into space by the former Soviet Union are called **cosmonauts** (from a Greek word meaning "sailors of the universe"). Astronauts and cosmonauts may be sent into space for different reasons. Their mission may be to gather information about the Earth, the moon, or the rest of our solar system; to perform experiments; to launch, repair, or retrieve space satellites or telescopes; to study how being in space affects people and other living organisms; and to learn what effect space has on nonliving substances.

Selecting Astronauts

The people who become American astronauts are selected by NASA, the National Aeronautics and Space Administration. Today, some astronauts are test pilots, others are scientists or engineers. All astronauts must have graduated from college and have at least a bachelor's degree. They must also have either extensive experience as jet pilots or an advanced degree or professional experience in engineering or in the biological or physical sciences. There is no age limit. The height limit ranges from 64 to 76 inches (163 to 193 centimeters) for pilots, and from 58½ to 76 inches (149 to 193 centimeters) for scientists and engineers. All astronauts must meet rigorous standards of physical health and mental fitness.

Training Astronauts

Today's American astronauts are trained to fly in the space shuttle. They must learn how to control the spacecraft, monitor its many systems, launch satellites, and conduct scientific experiments. Astronauts must also be prepared to handle any emergencies that might happen and to endure the physical and emotional stresses that occur during spaceflight.

Astronauts are trained at NASA's Johnson Space Center near Houston, Texas. They learn the space shuttle's propulsion, navigation, environmental, and computer systems. They learn how to use the shuttle's long robot arm to release satellites into orbit and how to use the tools and equipment carried on board the shuttle. Astronauts also learn how to put on, and work in, the space suits that must be worn if they venture outside the shuttle. In addition, they take classes in subjects such as astronomy, navigation, geology, oceanography, and meteorology.

Astronauts also fly a certain number of hours each month in training jets—the pilots practice flying, the scientists and engineers develop navigation and communication skills and practice working as part of a crew.

Once an astronaut is assigned to a spaceflight, she or he begins training with the other members of the crew. A typical crew is composed of two astronauts with test pilot backgrounds and three or more astronauts with either science or engineering backgrounds. The crew trains together to learn to work as a team and to learn about the experiments or space satellites on their particular flight. An important part of the training takes place in the spaceflight simulator—a device that reproduces many of the shuttle's maneuvers and responses during flight. In the flight simulators, astronauts practice all phases of spaceflight, including launch, orbit, re-entry, and landing. They also learn how to respond when a system malfunctions and how to communicate with mission control.

Living and Working in Space

Being in space is quite different from being on Earth. This is because astronauts and all the objects around them are weightless. Astronauts move around in the shuttle by pushing off from a wall and floating from one place to another. They can perform somersaults and can easily lift satellites that would weigh thousands of pounds on Earth.

Weightlessness also makes eating and sleeping different from what astronauts are used to on Earth. Most of the food is similar to what is eaten on Earth, but some of it is specially prepared. Foods that are sticky, like beef stew or pudding, are the easiest to eat because they stick to utensils instead of floating away before they can be eaten. A drink cannot be poured in space because the liquid would simply float out of the pitcher or glass. To solve this problem, liquids are served in closed containers, and astronauts drink through straws.

When they sleep, some astronauts strap themselves into sleeping bags, which can be attached to the walls with a fabric like Velcro so that they do not float around; others float freely in the middle of the room as they sleep. They can sleep right side up, upside down, or sideways—all positions feel exactly the same in weightlessness.

Compared with earlier spacecraft, today's shuttle is relatively roomy. The air inside is the same as in any living room and the temperature is controlled. Astronauts wear regular clothes during spaceflight. But if they have to go outside, either to conduct experiments or to repair something, they must put on pressurized space suits that provide breathable air and that protect them against the vacuum of space.

During spaceflight, astronauts are very busy conducting experiments, operating equipment, and monitoring different systems. There is some time, though, for just looking at the Earth through the small windows of the shuttle.

Milestones

Yuri Gagarin of the former Soviet Union became the first person in space on April 12, 1961. In February 1962, John Glenn became

WONDER QUESTION

Why are astronauts weightless?

During spaceflight, the space shuttle is held in orbit around the Earth by gravity. This means that astronauts are not "away from gravity," as many people think. Astronauts are weightless because they and the space shuttle are continually falling toward Earth under the force of gravity—just as you would be if you jumped out of an airplane. Imagine jumping out of an airplane carrying a scale to weigh yourself. If you could stand on the scale while you and it were falling, the scale would read zero—you would be weightless. This is exactly the same situation that astronauts find themselves in when they are in orbit. The shuttle and everything inside it, including astronauts, are weightless because they are not resisting gravity, they are all falling together under the force of gravity.

If the space shuttle is falling, why does it not crash into the Earth? The reason is that although the shuttle is falling toward Earth, it is also traveling very fast horizontally. The speed given to the space shuttle by its rockets when it is launched allows it to reach and travel at a certain altitude in space. It is the force of gravity at that altitude that forces the shuttle to fall just enough to stay in a circular orbit that is always at the same distance from the Earth.

the first American to orbit the Earth. The first woman in space was Valentina Tereshkova of the former Soviet Union, who orbited the Earth in June 1963. In March 1965, Soviet cosmonaut Alexei Leonov became the first person to leave a spacecraft on a "spacewalk." On July 20, 1969, the American astronauts Neil Armstrong and Edwin Aldrin became the first human beings to set foot on the moon. John Young and Robert Crippen were the first astronauts to fly in the space shuttle, in April 1981. Sally Ride, who orbited the Earth in the shuttle in June 1983, was the first American woman in space.

The achievements of these and many other brave men and women have made the human dream of space travel come true. These individuals are truly sailors of the skies.

SALLY K. RIDE
Professor of Physics
University of California, San Diego

See also SPACE EXPLORATION AND TRAVEL; SPACE SHUTTLES.

ASTRONOMY

Astronomy is the study of everything in the universe. It is also one of the oldest sciences. For thousands of years, people have gazed at the sky to try to learn about the stars, the planets, and all of the other objects in the universe. Paintings of astronomical events thought to be about 10,000 years old have been found in caves in Europe; and marks that may represent the phases of the moon have been found on artifacts more than 30,000 years old. Aside from such examples, however, the earliest astronomers left no written records of their studies.

▶THE ORIGINS OF ASTRONOMY

Long before the invention of the telescope people noticed many things in the sky. They noticed, for example, that the stars move across the sky from east to west during the course of an evening. They noticed that certain other points of light, which we now know are planets, move through the sky at different speeds. They also observed that the moon goes through phases, or seems to change shape night after night.

Starting about 10,000 years ago, people used their knowledge of the changing positions of the sun and stars to determine when to plant and harvest crops. Between 4,000 and 5,000 years ago, people in England constructed a grouping of large stones to act as a kind of astronomical observatory. Known as Stonehenge, we believe this grouping of stones was used to measure the changing position of the sun as it rises. These positions could in turn be used to determine the changing of the seasons.

The movements of the sun, moon, and planets also became the basis for the study of **astrology**, which held that such movements had an effect on people's lives. Although astrology was unscientific, it led to careful studies of the heavens and to the development of the science of astronomy. The first records of astrologers date back to ancient Babylon about 3,000 years ago. But people also studied the skies in ancient Egypt, China, Mexico, and other parts of the world.

▶ASTRONOMERS OF ANCIENT GREECE

Since the earliest astronomers lived before recorded history, we can only guess at what they knew. Our first real knowledge of ancient astronomy dates from about 2,500 years ago, when ancient Greek astronomers carefully recorded what they had learned.

Among the earliest Greek astronomers was Thales (640–546 B.C.), who was supposed to have predicted an eclipse of the sun around the year 580 B.C. An eclipse of the sun occurs when the moon moves in front of the sun and blocks its light. Supposedly, the sudden darkness caused by this eclipse was so startling that soldiers laid down their arms in the middle of a battle and called a truce. Whether this story is true or not, it is probably true that Thales had the ability to predict eclipses. This tells us that Greek astronomy had reached a fairly advanced stage by Thales' time.

Our knowledge of other Greek scientists is more accurate. The mathematician Pythagoras (582?–500? B.C.) suggested that the Earth was round, which we now know is true. The astronomer Eratosthenes (275?–195? B.C.) calculated, quite accurately, the diameter of the Earth. He did this by comparing the length of shadows cast at noon in two different cities. He knew that the Earth must be round because the shadows were of two different lengths, which told him that the sun was shining at different angles on these two cities. By comparing the length of the shadows, he could calculate the Earth's diameter. In fact, he came very close to the correct diameter. The philosopher Aristarchus (310?–230? B.C.) suggested that the Earth and other planets revolved around the sun, but this idea did not catch on for more than 2,000 years.

Stonehenge may have been an early observatory used to study the movement of the sun across the sky.

Early astronomers, like those in this tapestry, helped change ideas about the order of the universe. By the 1500's, astronomy had become an important science, and careful measurements were being made of the changing positions of the sun, moon, stars, and planets.

The most famous and influential Greek astronomer was Aristotle (384–322 B.C.), a philosopher whose reputation extended into many areas of study. Aristotle's greatest contributions in astronomy dealt with **cosmology**, the study of the nature of the universe. Aristotle believed that the Earth was at the center of the universe and that the stars and other planets were inside crystal spheres surrounding it. According to Aristotle, these spheres rotated around the Earth at different speeds, which was why the stars and planets moved through the night sky at different speeds.

Like Aristotle, the Greek thinker Ptolemy (A.D. 90?–168?) also believed that the Earth was at the center of the universe. His book on astronomy, which became known as the *Almagest* (Arabic for "the greatest"), was one of the most influential books in the history of astronomy. The idea of an Earth-centered universe, known as the Ptolemaic System, was the accepted view for more than 1,000 years.

A number of articles cover topics relating to astronomy and space. For more information about them, see ASTRONAUTS; BLACK HOLES; COMETS, METEORITES, AND ASTEROIDS; CONSTELLATIONS; COSMIC RAYS; ECLIPSES; GRAVITY AND GRAVITATION; MILKY WAY; MOON; NEBULAS; OBSERVATORIES; PLANETARIUMS AND SPACE MUSEUMS; PLANETS; PULSARS; QUASARS; RADIATION; RADIATION BELTS; RADIO AND RADAR ASTRONOMY; ROCKETS; SATELLITES; SOLAR SYSTEM; SPACE AGENCIES AND CENTERS; SPACE EXPLORATION AND TRAVEL; SPACE PROBES; SPACE RESEARCH AND TECHNOLOGY; SPACE SATELLITES; SPACE SHUTTLES; SPACE TELESCOPES; STARS; SUN; TELESCOPES; UNIVERSE; and articles on the individual planets—MERCURY, VENUS, EARTH, MARS, JUPITER, SATURN, URANUS, NEPTUNE, and PLUTO.

▶ **A REBIRTH OF ASTRONOMY**

During the Middle Ages in Europe, little scientific knowledge was accumulated, and the science of astronomy was nearly forgotten. However, the knowledge of the ancient Greeks was preserved by the Arabs, who translated Greek works into Arabic. If not for the Arabs, most Greek knowledge, including astronomy, would have been lost forever.

By the 1200's, Europeans had begun to re-examine Greek knowledge. But it was not until the 1500's that new ideas in astronomy had begun to form. One of the first people to suggest that Aristotle and Ptolemy were wrong was the Polish astronomer Nicolaus Copernicus (1473–1543). Copernicus believed that the sun, not the Earth, was at the center of the universe. He also revived Aristarchus' idea that the Earth revolved around the sun. In fact, Copernicus believed that all the planets revolved around the sun in circular orbits and that the moon revolved around the Earth. As it turned out, parts of his theory were wrong, but Copernicus was closer to the truth than Aristotle or Ptolemy.

One of the most significant points of Copernicus' theory was its explanation for the phenomenon of **retrograde motion**, in which some of the planets sometimes appear to slow down and even move backward in the sky. Copernicus explained that the planets all revolve in their own orbits around the sun. As

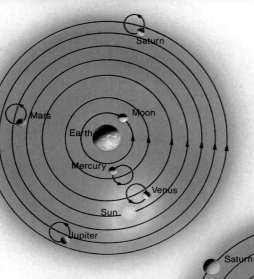

Ptolemy thought that the Earth was the center of the universe and that the sun and planets circled the Earth. Planets also moved in smaller circles, called epicycles.

Copernicus was the first to realize that the Earth, moon, and planets orbit the sun. However, he was wrong in believing that the orbits were perfect circles.

the Earth overtakes another planet and passes it, it appears from Earth that the other planet is slowing down and then moving backward. In fact, the planet's direction is not changing at all. What the observer is experiencing is an effect that is similar to the feeling people have that objects in their field of vision are moving backward as they pass them. For example, a car moving next to your car will seem to go backward as you are going by it.

Copernicus' theories were published in 1543 in a book entitled *De revolutionibus orbium coelestium* ("On the Revolutions of the Heavenly Spheres"). This important book influenced the work of many generations of astronomers.

Later in the 1500's, Danish astronomer Tycho Brahe (1546–1601) built an observatory to study the heavens. Although telescopes had not yet been invented, Brahe designed sophisticated instruments to measure the movements of the stars and planets. Like Copernicus, Brahe believed that the sun was at the center of the universe. Brahe's young assistant, Johannes Kepler (1571–1630), also

believed in the theories of Copernicus. When Brahe died, he left his records to Kepler, who used them to make a remarkable discovery about the planets. He discovered that the planets were moving around the sun in ellipses (ovals), rather than in circles as Copernicus had assumed.

At about this same time, the Italian scientist Galileo Galilei (1564–1642) was making even more remarkable discoveries. Galileo was the first astronomer to use a telescope to study the sky, and he saw things no one else had ever seen. He saw mountains and valleys on the moon, four moons around the planet Jupiter, and strange dark spots on the sun. He even saw something that he called "handles" sticking out of the side of the planet Saturn. They later turned out to be its famous rings. Galileo supported Copernicus' theories and attacked the ideas of the ancient Greeks.

Although Galileo believed, like Copernicus, that the planets orbited the sun, he could not explain why. The person who answered that question was the English scientist Isaac Newton (1642–1727). Newton discovered that all objects produce a force called gravity that attracts other objects. A large object like the sun produces enough gravity to hold the planets in orbit around it. Moons orbit planets for the same reason. Because of Newton's discoveries, scientists came to accept Copernicus' idea that the Earth and other planets revolve around the sun.

▶DISCOVERIES ABOUT THE UNIVERSE

The discoveries of Isaac Newton marked the beginning of modern astronomy. But there was still much to be learned about the solar system and the universe. Since Newton's time, astronomers have learned a great deal.

The Planets and Their Moons

Until the 1700's, astronomers believed that there were only six planets: Mercury, Venus, Earth, Mars, Jupiter, and Saturn. Then, in 1781, the astronomer William Herschel (1738–1822) and his sister Caroline Herschel (1750–1848) discovered a seventh planet. The discovery of this planet, called Uranus, caused

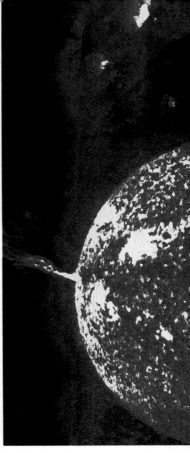

great excitement because it was the first new planet to be discovered since ancient times. Prompted by this discovery, astronomers began looking for other new planets. In 1846, the German astronomer Johann Galle (1812–1910) spotted the planet Neptune, although its presence had been predicted earlier by the English astronomer John Couch Adams (1819–92) and the French astronomer Jean Joseph Leverrier (1811–77). Finally, in 1930, the American astronomer Clyde Tombaugh (1906–) located the planet Pluto, which had been predicted by the American astronomer Percival Lowell (1855–1916).

The existence of the Earth's moon has always been known. But the existence of other moons, or satellites, in the solar system was not known until Galileo discovered moons orbiting Jupiter in 1610. Gradually, other moons were discovered as well. The only planets that have no moons are Mercury and Venus.

Comets and Asteroids

For thousands of years, people had seen strange steaks of light pass through the night sky every few years. The English astronomer Edmund Halley (1656–1742) realized that these streaks of light were actually small objects orbiting the sun. These objects, known as comets, begin their long elliptical orbits far beyond the outermost planets. Attracted by the sun's gravity, they fall inward toward the sun and are then propelled back out to the outer reaches of the solar system.

Comets are made mostly of ice and dust. As a comet nears the sun, evaporation causes gases in its head, or **coma**, to glow. The solar wind (electrically charged particles from the sun) blows back some of these gases to form a brilliant, glowing tail that may be more than 60 million miles (100 million kilometers)

We have learned a great deal about objects in space. Comets like Halley's (*above*) are made of ice and dust. The sun (*right*) is a star made of hot gases that often shoot miles above its surface.

long. Scientists think that comets come from a cloud of ice and dust orbiting the sun at a distance of more than 10 trillion miles (16 trillion kilometers). This cloud, called the Oort Cloud after Dutch astronomer Jan Oort (1900–92) who first predicted its existence, is left over from the earliest days of the solar system.

Another group of objects in the solar system are asteroids, a number of small bodies located between the orbits of Mars and Jupiter. Asteroids may be the remains of a planet that never quite formed. The first asteroid was discovered in 1801 and was named Ceres. Since then, thousands more have been discovered.

The Sun and the Stars

After Galileo observed dark spots on the sun, it was many years before other discoveries about it were made. Beginning in 1826, the German astronomer Heinrich Schwabe (1789–1875) began counting sunspots. Over time, he discovered that these sunspots appear in cycles during which their number varies. In 1851, the Scottish astronomer Johann von Lamont (1805–79) noted that disturbances in the Earth's magnetic field happened during the periods of greatest sunspot activity. These early discoveries opened the way for other discoveries about the sun's effects on the Earth, the sun's temperature, and the process that causes the sun's heat and light.

In time, astronomers realized that the universe is much larger than our solar system and that the sun is actually a star just like others in the night sky. These stars are globes of extremely hot gas heated by nuclear reactions in their interiors. One of the first to try to measure the distance to a star was the Dutch astronomer Christian Huygens (1629–95). Huygens was unsuccessful, but in 1838, the German astronomer Friedrich Wilhelm Bessel (1784–1846) measured the distance to a star named 61 Cygni (the star numbered 61 in the constellation Cygnus) and found that it was 66 trillion miles (106 trillion kilometers) away.

Stars beyond our solar system are so far away that astronomers invented a new unit to measure their distance. That unit, known as the **light-year**, represents the distance a beam of light travels in a year. Although light seems to travel instantly from place to place it does not. It actually moves at an extremely fast speed, about 186,000 miles (300,000 kilometers) per second. A light-year is about 6 trillion miles (9.6 trillion kilometers). The star

we see today left the star 4.33 years ago. This means that we actually see Alpha Centauri as it was 4.33 years in the past. Most stars are millions of light-years away, and the light we see left them millions of years ago.

Binary and Variable Stars. Once astronomers began to study the stars beyond our solar system, they made a number of surprising discoveries. Most stars have other stars orbiting with them, making them part of multiple star systems. Some of these systems consist of only two stars, called **binary stars**. ("Binary" means "made up of two things.") Other systems consist of more than a dozen stars moving around one another in complex orbits.

Astronomers also discovered that stars do not always shine with a consistent brightness. Some grow brighter and dimmer over a period of time. These stars are called **variable stars**.

Classification of Stars. Some of the most important discoveries about stars have been based on their spectra, the plural form of **spectrum**. A spectrum is the range of colors observed in an object that produces light, such as a star. A rainbow is an example of a spectrum. Scientists can study the spectrum of a star by letting the light from the star pass through special instruments. Sometimes certain colors are found to be missing. Because these missing colors appear as dark or bright lines in the spectrum, they are called spectral lines. These lines tell astronomers about the chemical elements that the star is made of.

Omega Centauri, the brightest star cluster in the sky, is 22,000 light-years from Earth. Halley's comet, above it, is about 4 light-minutes from Earth in this picture.

THE TWENTY NEAREST STARS

STAR	DISTANCE IN LIGHT-YEARS	STAR	DISTANCE IN LIGHT-YEARS
Sun	about 8.3 light-mins.	Yale 343.1*	9.0
		Ross 154	9.6
Proxima Centauri*	4.3	Yale 5736	10.3
Alpha Centauri A*	4.3	Epsilon Eridani	10.8
Alpha Centauri B*	4.3	Yale 5475	10.9
Barnard's Star*	6.0	Yale 2730	10.9
Wolf 359	7.7	61 Cygni A*	11.1
+36° 2147	8.3	61 Cygni B*	11.1
Sirius A*	8.7	Epsilon Indi	11.4
Sirius B*	8.7	Procyon A*	11.5

* member of binary or multiple star system

The first astronomer to photograph the spectrum of a star was Henry Draper (1837–82) in 1872. In the

61 Cygni is therefore 11 light-years from Earth.

Soon after Bessel measured the distance to 61 Cygni, the Scottish astronomer Thomas Henderson (1798–1844) measured the distance to Alpha Centauri at 4.33 light-years. A star's distance in light-years indicates how long ago the light we see now left that star. With Alpha Centauri, for example, the light

1880's, American astronomers Edward Pickering (1846–1919) and Annie Jump Cannon (1863–1941) divided stars into classes based on the lines in their spectra and the bright background, or **continuum**, on which the lines are observed. The star classes they created, named O, B, A, F, G, K, and M, are arranged according to temperatures, with the hottest stars in class O and the coolest in class M.

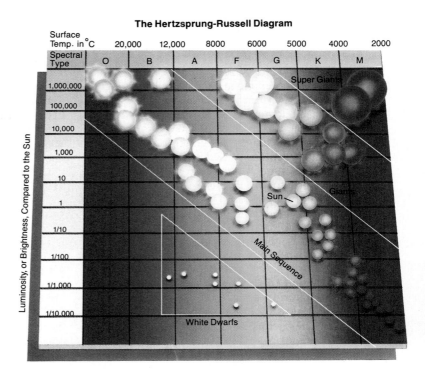

Most stars fall in the area of the H-R diagram known as the main sequence because they obey the rule that hotter stars are brighter and cooler stars are dimmer. However, a few stars are cool and bright or hot and dim and they fall outside the main sequence.

In the early 1900's, the Danish astronomer Ejnar Hertzsprung (1873–1967) and the American astronomer Henry Norris Russell (1877–1957) studied both the spectral classes of stars and their **luminosity**, or brightness. They discovered that temperature and brightness are closely related, with the hotter stars being brighter and the cooler stars being dimmer. These two scientists created a diagram, known as the Hertzsprung-Russell (or H-R) diagram, showing these relationships. This diagram has helped scientists learn how stars are born and how they die.

Detailed analysis of star spectra led British-American astronomer Cecilia Payne (1900–79) to conclude that most stars are made of the same chemical elements. This information also contributed to our understanding of the lifetimes of stars and why stars shine.

The Birth and Death of Stars. A star begins its life as a cloud of mostly hydrogen gas and dust floating in space. If something disturbs this cloud, such as a passing star, it can begin to collapse, and the gravity that is produced attracts other particles of gas and dust. As the cloud shrinks, the speed at which these particles fall toward the center of the cloud causes it to heat up and glow, forming what astronomers call a **protostar**. When the protostar reaches a certain temperature, a process known as hydrogen fusion begins, fueled by the hydrogen gas present. Hydrogen fusion creates such tremendous heat that the protostar tries to explode outward, but the powerful gravity of the gas and dust particles prevents this from happening. Instead, the protostar remains perfectly balanced between exploding and collapsing, and it becomes a star.

Stars have life expectancies ranging from a hundred or so million years to trillions of years, depending on their size. A very massive star uses up, or burns, its nuclear fuel very rapidly and has a relatively short life span. A

star with a very low mass burns its fuel much more slowly and lasts much longer. Medium-sized stars, like our sun, use up their hydrogen in about 10 billion years.

Eventually, a star begins to run out of hydrogen gas and hydrogen fusion ceases. At that point, it begins to collapse again, generating even more heat. The star becomes so hot that other gases, such as helium, begin new processes of fusion. These new fusions generate such tremendous heat that the star expands greatly, becoming what is known as a **red giant**. While the outer layers of red giants are relatively cool, these stars are very bright because of their tremendous size.

As a red giant runs out of fuel, it collapses once more. If the original star was relatively small, the red giant will collapse into a small, dense form called a **white dwarf**. A white dwarf appears very dim because of its small size, but it is very hot. If the original star was massive, the collapsing red giant will generate so much heat that the star explodes. The resulting explosion is called a **supernova** and is millions of times brighter than an ordinary star. The part of the star left behind by the explosion becomes a **neutron star**, a rapidly spinning star that is even smaller and denser than a white dwarf. If the original star was extremely massive before it exploded, the neutron star would also collapse and would never stop collapsing. It would become a **black hole**, which is so dense and has such an enormous gravitational pull that even light cannot escape from it. A black hole has never been seen but would probably appear as a dark hole surrounded by a spiral-shaped halo of hot particles attracted by its gravity. Matter that falls into it can never escape.

Neutron stars often emit bursts of radio waves into space. Because the neutron stars spin rapidly, these radio waves are detected by radio telescopes as a pulsating signal, with a single pulse for every rotation. Because of these pulses, the first neutron stars discovered were known as pulsating stars, or **pulsars**.

Galaxies and Other Objects

For centuries, astronomers have been aware of small glowing clouds of matter in the universe. These clouds are called **nebulas**. Some are clouds of gas and dust left behind by supernova explosions like the Crab Nebula, which formed more than 900 years ago, or by other interstellar events. Others are protostars starting to form.

In the early 1900's, scientists discovered that some nebulas are actually very distant **galaxies**, or great clouds of stars. Our sun is part of the Milky Way galaxy. As astronomers studied these distant galaxies with telescopes that became more and more powerful over time, they saw that there are billions of galax-

ies in the universe. Most are clustered together in groups. The Milky Way galaxy is part of a small cluster known as the Local Group. When astronomers look at galaxies they see bright stars and glowing gases. But they have also learned that much of the matter in galaxies is invisible. This dark matter makes up about 90 percent of all the mass of the universe.

Certain galaxies, called Seyfert galaxies, appear to have violent explosions taking place in their centers, which may result from heat generated by giant black holes at their centers. There is some evidence that such a black hole may exist inside the Milky Way galaxy.

At the very edge of the visible universe, scientists have detected extremely bright objects known as **quasars** (short for "quasistellar objects"). Some of these quasars are billions of light-years away. Because the light from these distant objects takes billions of years to reach us, quasars may be galaxies at early stages of their existence.

The Development of the Universe

By the 1920's, astronomers had noticed that galaxies outside the Local Group were moving away from our galaxy. The American astronomer Edwin Hubble (1889–1953) also noticed that the farther away a galaxy was, the faster it was moving. In fact, clusters of galaxies were moving away from one another, suggesting that the universe was expanding.

Profiles

Friedrich Wilhelm Bessel (1784–1846) is considered to be one of the most skillful and diligent astronomical observers of his time. A self-educated astronomer, Bessel's calculations on the orbit of Halley's comet in 1804 brought him fame and a position at Lilienthal Ob-

Annie Jump Cannon

Sir Arthur Stanley Eddington

servatory in Germany. His contributions included the determination of the positions of more than 75,000 stars and the first accurate calculation of the distance of a star from the earth, which was perhaps his greatest achievement.

Annie Jump Cannon (1863–1941) is recognized as one of the foremost woman astronomers. After studying astronomy at Radcliffe College, Cannon was appointed to the staff of Harvard College Observatory in 1896, where she worked for the rest of her life. She was one of the first women to receive a Harvard faculty appointment. One of her greatest achievements was her preparation of *The Henry Draper Catalogue*, a system still used to classify stars. Cannon proved that stars could be grouped into a few

basic types arranged according to their color, which indicated a star's surface temperature. During her lifetime, Cannon classified well over 350,000 stars. She received numerous honors, including an honorary doctorate from Oxford University, the first awarded to a woman.

Sir Arthur Stanley Eddington (1882–1944) is noted for his work on the internal dynamics of stars. After graduating from Trinity College at Cambridge, England, Eddington served first as chief assistant at the Royal Observatory at Greenwich and then as director of the Cambridge Observatory. His pioneering work on stars proved that a star's energy is transported by radiation from its interior to its surface. He also determined the relationship between a star's mass and its brightness. Eddington became an important supporter of Einstein's theory of relativity. His observation that starlight is deflected (bent) around the sun during solar eclipses provided evidence to confirm Einstein's theory that gravitation causes light to bend. Eddington won many honors for his work.

Astronomers realized that if the universe is expanding, there must have been a time when all the galaxies were closer together. In fact, at some time in the distant past, all the galaxies may have been crushed into an area in space made up of a dense soup of particles smaller than atoms. By studying the speed at which galaxies are moving apart, astronomers theorized that about 15 to 18 billion years ago a tremendous explosion, which they call the Big Bang, may have started the expansion of the universe. At that time, these particles, which make up most of the matter in space, formed into hydrogen and helium atoms, and began to expand and move outward. Over millions of years, stars and galaxies began to form, but scientists are not sure how these particles formed galaxies in the shapes and patterns that exist in the universe today.

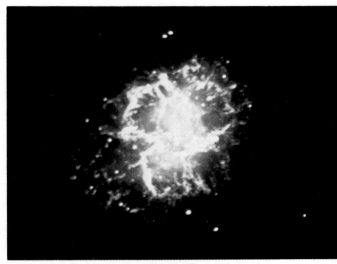

Telescopes help astronomers study the Crab Nebula, the remains of a supernova with a neutron star at its center, about 5,000 light-years from Earth.

▶ THE TOOLS OF ASTRONOMY

Most objects studied in astronomy today are so far away that astronomers must gather information about them from a distance by using special instruments. The first astronomical instrument, of course, was the human eye, and many early astronomers devised instruments to measure the motion of the stars and planets.

One of the most important instruments ever developed by astronomers is the optical telescope. ("Optical" means "making use of light.") The lenses and mirrors of optical telescopes focus the light entering them in such a way that distant objects appear larger and brighter. Optical telescopes also allow astronomers to see many more objects than are visible to the naked eye. The earliest type of optical telescope, developed in the 1600's, was the **refracting telescope**, which is basically a tube with a lens at each end. Another type of optical telescope is the **reflecting telescope**. In a reflecting telescope, one of the lenses is replaced with a mirror. Most of the larger telescopes are reflecting telescopes.

George Ellery Hale (1868–1938) was one of America's foremost astronomers. Hale studied physics at Massachusetts Institute of Technology but devoted much of his spare time to astronomy. One of his first achievements was the invention of the spectroheliograph, an instrument for photographing the sun. His greatest achievements, however, involved telescopes. His first triumph was in overseeing the construction of the 40-inch refracting telescope at Yerkes Observatory in Wisconsin—the largest of its kind in the world. Hale was also involved in the construction of a 100-inch reflecting telescope at the Mount Wilson Observatory in California and the 200-inch reflecting telescope at Mount Palomar Observatory in California.

The **Herschel Family** were distinguished English scientists of German origin who were noted for their work in astronomy. **William Herschel** (1738–1822) was a pioneer in almost every branch of modern astronomy. An avid builder of telescopes, he established his reputation in 1781 with the discovery of the planet Uranus. William is also noted for his classifications of star clusters and nebulas, his discovery of binary (double) star systems, and his theories on the structure of the universe. He was the first to establish the motion of the solar system and to try to determine the direction of its movement. He was also the first to suggest the existence of infrared radiation. **Caroline Lucretia Herschel** (1750–1848), William's sister, began her work in astronomy as her brother's assistant. However, she is also noted for her own research. In 1786 she observed her first comet, and by 1797 she had discovered seven more. She also discovered many new nebulas. **John Frederick William Herschel** (1792–1871), the son of William Herschel, began a career in mathematics and law but devoted himself to astronomy after his father's death in 1822. John Herschel discovered more than 1,000 binary stars and almost 2,000 nebulas and star clusters in the skies of the Southern Hemisphere. He also pioneered the use of photographic techniques in astronomy. A founding member of the Royal Astronomical Society, he received a knighthood for his achievements.

George Ellery Hale

William Herschel

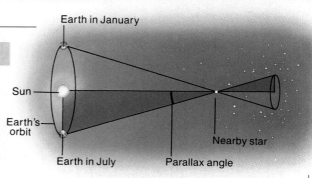

Earth in January

Sun

Earth's orbit

Earth in July

Nearby star

Parallax angle

How do astronomers measure distances in space?

Astronomers have different methods of measuring the distance of objects in space. One way is through something called the **parallax**. When viewed from two different points, a star appears to shift position slightly in the sky. The angle of the parallax is the amount of this shift. Astronomers determine a star's parallax by observing the star at intervals of several months, during which time the Earth has moved between different points of its orbit. Astronomers can calculate the star's parallax from these observations and then use mathematical formulas to determine the star's distance from the Earth.

The parallax method works well for nearby stars but not for measuring the distance of stars and galaxies that are very far away. To do this, astronomers compare the luminosity, or actual brightness, of an object with its brightness as observed through a telescope. This method is based on the fact that the fainter an object appears when viewed from Earth, the greater its distance.

Astronomers often use this method to measure distances to variable stars. The luminosity method can also be used to measure the distance of galaxies.

To measure the most distant objects in space, astronomers use a method involving the objects' spectral lines of light, as measured by special instruments. Astronomers have discovered that if the spectral lines of an object shift toward the red end of the spectrum, it means the object is moving away. The greater the shift, the faster the object is moving. Astronomers also discovered that the farther away an object is, the faster it is receding. Using these facts, astronomers are able to calculate the distance of even the most remote galaxies and quasars.

In the late 1800's and early 1900's, telescopes were combined with cameras to take photographs of objects in the universe. Photographic plates can gather light from objects better than the human eye can, and because of this, very dim objects not visible to the eye can be seen in a photograph. Other instruments, such as **spectrometers** and **photometers**, can also be attached to telescopes to measure the spectrum of an object or the brightness of its light. A telescope receives information carried by visible light. Because it

---

Profiles

Marquis Pierre Simon de Laplace (1749–1827) was a noted French mathematician and astronomer. Laplace's greatest achievements were in the area of celestial mechanics. He explained the properties and motions of the sun, the planets, and the moon, and the gravitational interactions among them. His work was especially significant in that it proved that the solar system was basically a stable system. Laplace is also noted for his nebular hypothesis, which theorized that the solar system evolved from a rotating mass of gas that condensed to form the sun, the planets, and their various satellites.

Henrietta Swan Leavitt (1868–1921) became interested in astronomy at Radcliffe College. In 1902 she was appointed to a permanent position at Harvard College Observatory and soon became head of its department of photographic photometry. Leavitt's job was to determine the photographic magnitudes, or brightness, of the light from distant stars. Her work was the basis for statistical investigations of the Milky Way galaxy until the 1940's. Leavitt is also noted for her study of variable stars—stars whose brightness varies. During her career she discovered roughly 2,400 variable stars—about half of all those known at the time. Of particular importance was her observation that the brighter the star, the longer its period of brightness. This discovery enabled other astronomers to determine the size of the Milky Way galaxy and its distance from other galaxies.

Percival Lowell (1855–1916) studied Mars from his own private observatory near Flagstaff, Arizona. He claimed to see clear signs of vegetation on the planet's surface, a view finally disproved by unmanned probes in the 1960's and 1970's. Lowell predicted a planet lying beyond Neptune, but it was not until after his death that the planet Pluto was discovered. He was the first to realize that the best observations require superior atmospheric conditions. His observatory was one of the first to be built far away from the lights and smog of civilization.

Henrietta Swan Leavitt

Percival Lowell

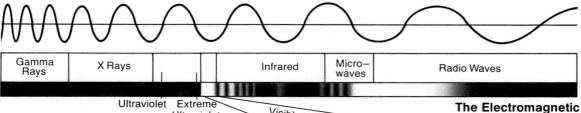

| Gamma Rays | X Rays | | | | Infrared | Micro–waves | Radio Waves |

Ultraviolet   Extreme Ultraviolet   Visible Light

The Electromagnetic Spectrum

Electromagnetic radiation is energy with both electric and magnetic elements. It travels through space in the form of waves. The spectrum extends from short to long wavelengths —from zero to infinity. Visible light can be seen in the rainbow of colors that is reflected by sunlight passing through a glass prism.

Prism

Sunlight

radiates outward from a light-producing object such as a star, visible light is said to be a form of radiation. The visible light that radiates from stars is one of several types of radiation known as **electromagnetic radiation**. Other types of electromagnetic radiation are listed above. Many stars and other astronomical objects produce these other types of radiation, but they are invisible to the human eye. Astronomers have built special telescopes that operate from space satellites. These are used to study forms of radiation that cannot be detected easily on the Earth's surface because our atmosphere blocks them.

The Earth's atmosphere tends to distort visible light from the stars as well. This distortion is what makes stars seem to twinkle, and it interferes with astronomers' studies. In the late 1980's, the United States launched a reflecting telescope, the Hubble Space Telescope, into orbit around the Earth where it could photograph stars and gather information about distant galaxies without many of the distortions caused by the Earth's atmosphere.

Although the Hubble has a flaw in its primary mirror, it has taken many striking and important photographs for astronomers to study.

Some of the newest telescopes use a technique known as "adaptive optics" to compensate for atmospheric distortion. The lenses of these telescopes are computer controlled and can actually change shape to help eliminate distortion. Astronomers often watch what these telescopes are viewing on video screens, and use computers to analyze and create images of the new information.

Charles Messier (1730–1817), a French astronomer, was noted for his discoveries of comets and his catalog of nebulas. While working as clerk for the astronomer Joseph Nicolas Delisle, Messier observed many comets and began compiling lists of nebulas. His list of nebulas, published in a catalog in 1784, remains his most enduring contribution to astronomy. This list includes the Crab Nebula and the Andromeda galaxy. Messier gave each a number prefixed by the first letter of his last name (such as M31 for the Andromeda galaxy), many of which are still used today. Messier also observed eclipses, sunspots, and the new planet Uranus. A skilled observer, he left mathematical calculations to others.

Maria Mitchell (1818–89) was the first woman astronomer in the United States. Mitchell was introduced to astronomy by her father, a noted amateur astronomer. While working as a librarian at the Nantucket Atheneum, Mitchell discovered a faint comet and was awarded a medal from the King of Denmark for her achievement. From 1849 to 1868, Mitchell worked at the U.S. Nautical Almanac Office, where she computed the positions of Venus at regular intervals. When Vassar College opened in 1865, Mitchell was appointed professor of astronomy and director of the college observatory. Mitchell was also an activist in women's causes. In 1848 she became the first woman elected to the American Academy of Arts and Sciences.

Harlow Shapley (1885–1972) began a career as a crime reporter and took up astronomy largely by accident while studying in college. From 1914 to 1921, Shapley worked at the Mount Wilson Observatory in California. While there, he began to study a group of variable stars called Cepheids. His research, coupled with observations by Henrietta Swan Leavitt on star magnitudes, helped him determine the size of the Milky Way galaxy and the location of the solar system within it. From 1921 to 1952, Shapley served as director of the Harvard College Observatory. One of his major discoveries was the identification of two dwarf galaxies. Shapley was also instrumental in developing the Harvard observatory into a major research institution.

Harlow Shapley

Maria Mitchell

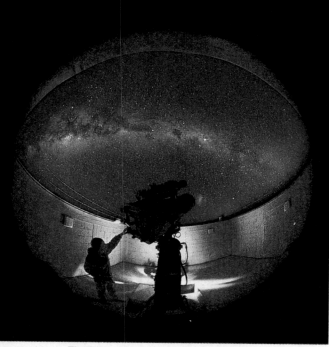

The future of astronomy is as exciting as its past. Today we can only study the stars in the Milky Way galaxy. Some day we may travel to them.

One of the most important astronomical advances of this century has been the development of space probes, which use rockets launched into space to examine the planets and moons of the solar system at a closer distance and to send the information they gather back to Earth. In our solar system, many of the larger moons and all of the planets except Pluto have been studied by space probes. This has led to a new science called comparative planetology, which compares other planets with the Earth and expands our understanding of the geology of the Earth.

►EXTRATERRESTRIAL INTELLIGENCE

People have long wondered whether the Earth is the only place in the universe with intelligent life. So far, there have been no signs of any kind of extraterrestrial life (life "outside the Earth"). In 1976, for instance, a space probe sent to Mars examined the Martian soil for signs of living bacteria, but none were found.

It is possible, however, that life exists elsewhere in the universe. After all, it is a vast place, with billions of galaxies and trillions of stars. Some people think that planets are orbiting at least some of these stars, although nothing has been proven yet. If other planets do exist, some may contain a form of life. Per-

haps there may even be intelligent life elsewhere in the universe. This study of life in outer space is called **exobiology**. So far this science is purely theoretical since no samples of life in outer space have ever been found.

In recent decades, a group of scientists have supported a research effort they call SETI, the *s*earch for *extra*terrestrial *i*ntelligence. These scientists use large radio telescopes to listen for special signals with patterns different from ordinary radio waves that might signal other civilizations. So far, no such signals have been detected.

►CAREERS IN ASTRONOMY

Astronomy really incorporates many different fields of science. Astronomers do far more than study the sky. Some astronomers are theoretical astronomers, who take the data collected by various instruments and devise theories about what they mean. Other astronomers are in charge of space probes, which travel into outer space and send back data from the planets and other objects in the solar system and beyond. Still other astronomers, called archaeoastronomers, study the history of astronomy in the distant past. Others teach at schools and universities, educating the next generation of young astronomers. A few very lucky astronomers fly in the space shuttle, where they can perform astronomical experiments in outer space itself.

Astronomy is one of the most exciting areas of modern science, and over the last few centuries, astronomers have completely changed the way that we view the universe. As an astronomer, you could have the very same opportunity.

CHRISTOPHER LAMPTON
Author, *Astronomy; From Copernicus to the Space Telescope*
Reviewed by KATHERINE HARAMUNDANIS
Co-author, *An Introduction to Astronomy*

See also ASTRONAUTS; BLACK HOLES; COMETS, METEORITES, AND ASTEROIDS; CONSTELLATIONS; COSMIC RAYS; ECLIPSES; GRAVITY AND GRAVITATION; MILKY WAY; MOON; NEBULAS; OBSERVATORIES; PLANETARIUMS AND SPACE MUSEUMS; PLANETS; PULSARS; QUASARS; RADIATION; RADIATION BELTS; RADIO AND RADAR ASTRONOMY; ROCKETS; SATELLITES; SOLAR SYSTEM; SPACE AGENCIES AND CENTERS; SPACE EXPLORATION AND TRAVEL; SPACE PROBES; SPACE RESEARCH AND TECHNOLOGY; SPACE SATELLITES; SPACE SHUTTLES; SPACE TELESCOPES; STARS; SUN; TELESCOPES; UNIVERSE; articles on individual planets.

ATHLETICS. See OLYMPIC GAMES; PHYSICAL EDUCATION; articles on individual sports.

ATLANTA

Atlanta, the capital of Georgia, rose from the ashes of the Civil War to become the center of trade, transportation, and industry in the southeastern United States. Today more than 2.3 million people live in Atlanta's greater metropolitan area, and approximately 395,000 live within the city limits.

Atlanta is located in the northwestern part of Georgia. Transportation has played an important part in its history. The city was founded in 1837 at the end, or terminus, of the Western and Atlantic Railroad. At first it was simply called Terminus. The name was changed to Atlanta in 1845.

During the Civil War, Union General William T. Sherman recognized Atlanta's importance as a Confederate supply center. His troops took the city in 1864, and most of its buildings were burned. But Atlanta was rapidly rebuilt. It became the state capital in 1868. By 1900, the city was prosperous and growing. But it was small in comparison to cities like New York and Chicago. Then, during the 1960's, Atlanta became a major city, its skyline studded with skyscrapers.

Banking, retailing, and tourism are important to Atlanta's economy. Its factories produce textiles, automobiles, steel, paper, furniture, and food products. One of Atlanta's most famous products, the soft drink Coca-Cola, is sold around the world.

Atlanta is still a transportation center. Railroads and highways crisscross and encircle the city. Its airport is one of the busiest in the United States. In 1979 the city opened the first section of a high-speed rail system that will link the downtown area with the suburbs.

The heart of Atlanta is an intersection called Five Points. Office buildings, hotels, banks, shops, and restaurants spread out from this point. Peachtree Street, Atlanta's best-known street, runs to the north. The gold-domed state capitol stands to the south. East of Five Points is the grave of civil-rights leader Martin Luther King, Jr.

Atlanta is a center of education and culture as well. Georgia State University and Georgia Institute of Technology are among its institutions of higher education. Several colleges and universities are clustered at Atlanta University Center, west of Five Points. The city's symphony orchestra and its ballet, opera, and theater companies perform at the Atlanta Memorial Arts Center, which also houses an art school and the High Museum of Art.

There are many things to do and places to go in Atlanta. Atlanta Stadium is home to the city's professional baseball and football teams. The city also supports a professional basketball team. Fernbank Science Center has a planetarium and a forest preserve. Historical displays can be seen at Swan House. Wren's Nest, the home of Joel Chandler Harris, author of the Uncle Remus stories, is open to the public. And Grant Park, one of the largest of the many parks, has a zoo. The Cyclorama, a huge circular painting of the Battle of Atlanta, is also in Grant Park. It is a vivid reminder of Atlanta's past.

JOHN RAYMOND
The Atlanta *Constitution*

Peachtree Center, a modern office and hotel complex, has become a symbol of Atlanta's growth.

ATLANTIC OCEAN

The Atlantic Ocean is the world's second largest body of water. Covering about one fifth of the earth's surface, it is exceeded in size only by the vast Pacific Ocean. As a link between four continents—Europe, Africa, North America, and South America—the Atlantic Ocean has played an important role in modern world history.

The word "Atlantic" is derived from Greek mythology, referring to the Titan Atlas, who gave his name to the Atlas mountain range of North Africa. To the later Romans, the Atlantic was the region beyond the Atlas Mountains. The Atlantic Ocean was also thought to be the site of the legendary land of Atlantis, which was said to have been swallowed up by the sea many centuries ago.

Area and Location. Counting all its adjacent seas, the Atlantic Ocean has an area of more than 41,000,000 square miles (106,000,000 square kilometers). Without them, the ocean still covers an area of some 31,830,000 square miles (82,440,000 square kilometers). The Atlantic Ocean extends from the Arctic region in the north to Antarctica in the south. Some geographers consider the Arctic Ocean to be a separate body of water, while others consider it a part of the Atlantic. The Atlantic is bounded on the east by Europe and Africa, and on the west by North and South America.

At its narrowest, between the bulge of Brazil (in South America) and the city of Dakar in Senegal (in Africa), the Atlantic is about 1,850 miles (2,980 kilometers) across. At its broadest, between Florida and the Strait of Gibraltar, it is more than 4,000 miles (6,400 kilometers) wide. The Atlantic Ocean is divided by the equator into two major parts, the North Atlantic and the South Atlantic.

The Ocean Floor. The Atlantic Ocean has an average depth of about 12,800 feet (3,900 meters). The deepest spot is in the Puerto Rico Trench, in the North Atlantic, which reaches a depth of 27,510 feet (8,385 meters).

The ocean floor is divided into two valleys by the Mid-Atlantic Ridge. This S-shaped ridge runs from north to south and rises about 6,000 feet (1,830 meters). Where it rises above the surface, the ridge forms a number of small islands, including the Azores, Ascension, St. Helena, and Tristan da Cunha.

Shorelines and Coastal Waters. Compared to the fairly straight coast of the South Atlantic, the North Atlantic has a very irregular shoreline. The greatest indentations are on the eastern side of the Atlantic. They are formed by the Baltic, North, Mediterranean, and Black seas. The coastal waters on the western side include Hudson Bay, the Gulf of Saint Lawrence, the Gulf of Mexico, and the Caribbean Sea. Water from most of the great river systems of the world flows into the Atlantic. These rivers give the Atlantic the largest drainage area of any ocean. Such drainage, from about half of the world's land area, includes many dissolved minerals and makes the Atlantic the saltiest of the oceans.

Currents: Warm and Cold. The North and South Atlantic have several strong currents that affect the climate of nearby land areas. The direction of these water currents is similar

to that of the wind currents. In the North Atlantic they flow in a clockwise direction; in the South Atlantic, counterclockwise.

The Gulf Stream of the North Atlantic carries warm water northward from the tropics along the eastern coast of the United States and then turns northeast toward Europe. The Gulf Stream makes western Europe warmer than areas of the same latitude in eastern North America. The cold Labrador Current flows from the Arctic Ocean along the eastern coasts of Greenland and Canada until it meets the Gulf Stream. It is the Labrador Current that gives northern New England and eastern Canada their cold climates. It also carries icebergs and fog southward, where they often endanger shipping. In the South Atlantic the warm Brazil Current travels in a southerly direction from the equator along the eastern coast of Brazil.

The Sargasso Sea, a part of the Atlantic lying between the West Indies and the Azores, is a region of relatively still water and little wind. In the days of sailing ships, vessels were often becalmed there.

Historical Background. To the ancient Greeks and Romans, the Atlantic Ocean marked the boundary of the known world. Few early peoples, except for the seafaring and trading Phoenicians, ventured beyond the Mediterranean Sea. Vikings later colonized Iceland and Greenland, and in about A.D. 1000 founded a short-lived settlement in North America. It was not until Christopher Columbus' epic voyage of 1492, however, that large-scale exploration of the Atlantic began. Trade routes were established, followed by European settlement in the Americas. With improvements in technology, the Atlantic, which had once been a barrier to human expansion, became a vital highway between the Old World of Europe and the New World of America. In the centuries since, the importance of this link has continued.

DANIEL JACOBSON
Michigan State University

ATLANTIC PROVINCES. See NEW BRUNSWICK; NEWFOUNDLAND; NOVA SCOTIA; PRINCE EDWARD ISLAND.

ATLASES. See MAPS AND GLOBES.

ATMOSPHERE

The Earth is surrounded by layers of gases we call air, or our atmosphere. Our atmosphere serves us in many ways. It keeps a portion of the sun's radiation from reaching the Earth's surface, which prevents our planet from becoming boiling hot during the day. At night, it keeps the heat that is generated by the sun's rays during the day from escaping too quickly. This protects the Earth's surface from temperatures of extreme cold. Because the atmosphere moderates temperatures and screens out dangerous radiation from the sun, the Earth is able to support life.

The atmosphere also helps make the Earth a more pleasant place to live. Air carries sound waves, which let us hear voices and music. The molecules, particles, and water droplets in the air can scatter sunlight, giving rise to blue skies, red sunsets, and rainbows.

▶ WHAT OUR ATMOSPHERE IS MADE OF

Air—our atmosphere—is a mixture of colorless gases, water vapor, and dust particles. Nitrogen is the most abundant gas in the atmosphere. Almost four fifths of air is made up of nitrogen. The next most abundant gas is oxygen. Nearly one fifth of air is oxygen, which is an essential element for almost all life. People need oxygen to breathe and to turn food into energy. Another gas in the atmosphere is carbon dioxide. Although it is present in very small amounts, it is vital to life on Earth. Green plants use carbon dioxide in the process of making their food.

Our air contains traces of still other gases. Helium and hydrogen are found in very small amounts, as are argon, krypton, neon, and xenon. Some gases, like methane, nitrous oxide, and dimethyl sulfide, are emitted into the atmosphere from the Earth's surface largely as a result of biological processes in plants and animals. Others, such as carbon monoxide and a class of molecules called *chlorofluorocarbons* (CFC's), enter the atmosphere as a result of human activities, especially in industry. A third class of molecules, like ozone, is formed in the atmosphere usually as a result of chemical reactions caused by sunlight acting on the other molecules there.

Water vapor in the atmosphere is water in a gaseous form. It is found mostly in the lowest few miles of the atmosphere, but it can be found higher up as well. It enters the atmosphere from bodies of water such as oceans, lakes, and rivers, and by evaporation from the Earth's surface. When conditions are right, clouds and fog can form from this vapor. The water in clouds can evaporate back into the atmosphere or fall to Earth as precipitation, such as rain, sleet, or snow.

The lower atmosphere is filled with countless specks of dust—tiny particles of matter from soil, fires, plants, salt spray, volcanoes, or meteors, most too small to be seen.

▶AIR HAS MASS AND EXERTS PRESSURE

Although it may feel as though air does not have mass, it does. A cubic centimeter of dry air has a mass of about 0.00118 grams when it is at sea level and at a temperature of 77°F (25°C). If we could measure the mass of all of the molecules in the atmosphere, the total would be staggering, about 5,700,000,000,000,000,000 (quadrillion) tons.

The air presses down on us and against us from all sides. Something like a ton of air is pressing against you at this moment. You are not aware of this because pressure within your body balances the pressure of the air outside of it.

Air pressure is 14.7 pounds per square inch (1.036 kilograms per square centimeter) at sea level. It is greatest there because that is the bottom of the atmosphere. The higher you go, the thinner the air becomes. For example, at 10 miles (16 kilometers) above sea level, the density of the air is only about one tenth of the density at the Earth's surface.

▶LAYERS OF ATMOSPHERE

Our atmosphere is made up of the troposphere, the stratosphere, the mesosphere, the thermosphere, and the exosphere.

The Troposphere

This lowest layer of the atmosphere is where we live, and it is also the layer that we know the most about. Like the other atmospheric layers it varies in size. The troposphere extends from sea level to an altitude of almost 12 miles (19 kilometers) above the equator, but only about 5 miles (8 kilometers) above the North and South poles.

Most of the Earth's population lives within the area about 1 mile (1.6 kilometers) above sea level. But scientists have learned that peo-

---

OZONE DEPLETION

Scientists have been monitoring concentrations of ozone in the upper stratosphere since evidence for ozone depletion was found over Antarctica in the mid-1970's. Ozone acts as a shield that protects us from much harmful ultraviolet radiation from the sun. Ozone depletion occurs when chlorofluorocarbons exposed to the strong ultraviolet radiation in the stratosphere release chlorine atoms. The chlorine atoms help break down ozone into ordinary oxygen, reducing the amount and effectiveness of ozone in our atmosphere. Chlorofluorocarbons are industrially produced molecules used for air conditioning and refrigeration, as propellants for aerosol sprays, and as blowing agents for foams.

The total amount of ozone over a station in Antarctica where people were living and working was shown to have decreased by about one third between the mid-1970's and the mid-1980's. Measurements from a satellite showed this depletion occurred over all of the continent. By the early 1990's the amounts of ozone over Antarctica were about half those of the 1970's. The TOMS (Total Ozone Mapping Spectrometer) program continues to map daily levels of ozone over Antarctica from satellites in space. In this photograph, the wide bands of lavender and dark purple indicate areas of ozone depletion on this date.

A unique spectrometer maps levels of ozone in the Earth's atmosphere in Dobson units, a measure of the thickness of ozone over a broad area.

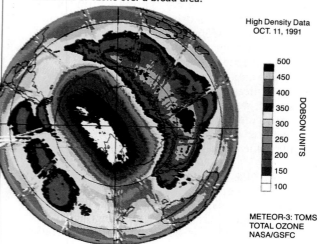

High Density Data
OCT. 11, 1991

DOBSON UNITS

500
450
400
350
300
250
200
150
100

METEOR-3: TOMS
TOTAL OZONE
NASA/GSFC

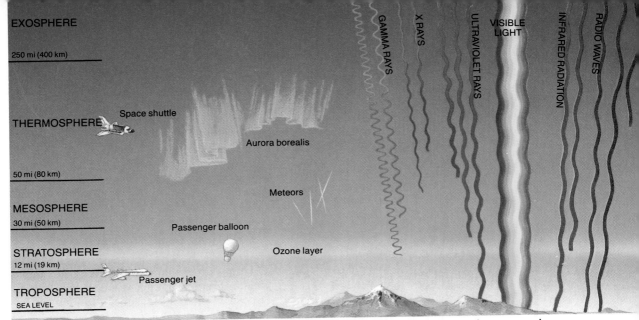

EXOSPHERE

250 mi (400 km)

THERMOSPHERE — Space shuttle

50 mi (80 km)

MESOSPHERE

30 mi (50 km)

STRATOSPHERE

12 mi (19 km)

TROPOSPHERE

SEA LEVEL

Aurora borealis

Meteors

Passenger balloon

Ozone layer

Passenger jet

GAMMA RAYS

X RAYS

ULTRAVIOLET RAYS

VISIBLE LIGHT

INFRARED RADIATION

RADIO WAVES

The many layers of the Earth's atmosphere—the troposphere, stratosphere, mesosphere, thermosphere, and exosphere—protect us from much harmful radiation from space.

ple can go about 3½ miles (5.6 kilometers) above the Earth's surface before they must use pressure suits and oxygen masks.

Most of our weather takes shape in the troposphere. Winds pick up water vapor from which clouds and rain form. Air currents move up and down, while winds blow north, south, east, and west, carrying warm or cold air.

Instruments carried aloft in balloons and on satellites have proven that the temperature in the troposphere drops steadily as one goes higher. There is a drop of about 3.5 to 5.5°F for each 1,000 feet (2 to 3°C for each 300 meters). At the top of the troposphere the temperature usually approaches −70°F (−56°C). Under certain conditions, temperatures as low as −117°F (−82°C) can be reached. This process slows near the top of the troposphere.

The area in which the temperature stops changing as you go higher in altitude is called the tropopause. This marks the boundary between the troposphere and the stratosphere. Winds reach their greatest force at the level of the tropopause. Most of the fast-moving winds called jet streams are found here. They move along at speeds of up to 200 miles (320 kilometers) an hour.

The Stratosphere

The second layer of air is the stratosphere. Temperatures in the stratosphere increase with altitude from the lower boundary (the tropopause) to the upper boundary (the strato-

pause). The stratopause is about 30 miles (50 kilometers) above sea level and the temperature there is typically about 32°F (0°C). The increase in temperature is caused by a layer of ozone. This gas absorbs most of the ultraviolet radiation that comes from the sun and changes it to heat energy, which is transmitted to other gas molecules in the stratosphere.

Ordinarily only between one and ten of every million molecules in the stratosphere are ozone molecules, but these molecules are very important to life on Earth. Ozone absorbs much of the sun's ultraviolet radiation, which can cause skin cancers and cataracts in people, so that only small amounts reach Earth.

The stratosphere is very stable, with little or no upward or downward movement of air. The air in the stratosphere is very dry, with only two to six molecules of water for every million molecules of air.

The Mesosphere

Above the stratosphere, the air becomes even thinner, and the temperature again falls. Beginning at a height of about 30 miles (50 kilometers) and extending up to about 50 miles (80 kilometers) is the mesosphere. At the top of the mesosphere, temperatures may be lower than −103°F (−75°C).

The Thermosphere and the Exosphere

The thermosphere reaches a height of perhaps 250 miles (400 kilometers) above sea level. It is remarkable for its electrical activity and range of temperatures. At the bottom of this layer, temperatures are below freezing. At the top, they exceed 2200°F (1200°C), caused by direct exposure to the sun's radiation.

Atoms and molecules of gas in the very thin air of the thermosphere are bombarded by radiation from the sun. They are broken into smaller, electrically charged particles called **ions** in a region referred to as the **ionosphere**. Here electric currents can flow, as they do in a neon tube or fluorescent light.

The ionosphere reflects some radio waves back to Earth. This allows radio communication between widely separated places on Earth. For example, radio waves beamed from North America bounce off the ionosphere and can be received in Africa. Without the bounce, the waves would simply continue out into space.

The exosphere, the outermost layer of the atmosphere, continues out into space until it eventually merges with the atmosphere of the sun. The atmosphere here is extremely thin. Atoms and molecules travel so rapidly, particularly at the upper levels, that they regularly escape the Earth's gravitation and become part of the gases in space.

▶**CHANGES IN THE ATMOSPHERE**

The atmosphere has remained fairly stable for many millions of years, but its temperature and composition can and do change with time. Natural occurrences can cause changes in the composition of the atmosphere, for example, when ashes and hot gases are thrown into the atmosphere during volcanic eruptions.

People also cause changes in the atmospheric composition. The burning of fossil fuels such as coal and gasoline release carbon dioxide into the atmosphere. Agricultural activities such as cattle raising, rice production, and the burning of tropical rain forests and grasslands release methane, carbon monoxide, and nitrogen oxides. Many industrial processes release oxides of sulfur and nitrogen and traces of metals into the atmosphere. Some processes send chlorofluorocarbons into the stratosphere. Since the start of the Industrial Revolution during the late 1700's, the amount of carbon dioxide in the atmosphere has increased by 30 percent and the amount of methane has doubled.

Increases in the amounts of carbon dioxide in the atmosphere may cause temperatures around the Earth to rise. Chlorofluorocarbons in the stratosphere cause the loss of ozone, which can allow unsafe levels of ultraviolet radiation to reach the Earth. Because of their impact, activities that can cause changes in the Earth's atmosphere need to be better understood and are being studied. Today there are many tools available for conducting these studies, including the research balloons, space shuttles, and space satellites that make observations and collect data and sophisticated computers that help scientists interpret it.

Dr. Jack A. Kaye
Office of Space Science and Applications
Earth Science and Applications Division, NASA

See also AIR POLLUTION; CLIMATE; EARTH; WEATHER; WINDS AND WEATHER.

ATOMIC BOMB. See NUCLEAR ENERGY.
ATOMIC ENERGY. See NUCLEAR ENERGY.

WONDER QUESTION

Is the Earth's atmosphere warming?

Many scientists think that small changes in its composition will cause the atmosphere at the Earth's surface to become warmer. They are alarmed because the amounts of gases such as carbon dioxide, methane, and nitrous oxide in our atmosphere are increasing. These gases tend to trap the radiation that reaches the Earth from the sun. Because the amount of radiation we receive tends to be constant, if less radiation escapes from our atmosphere, the atmosphere could become warmer.

The problem is complex because many factors need to be considered. For example, if the surface atmosphere of the Earth warms, more water may evaporate from the Earth's surface. This would affect the formation of clouds and the amounts and patterns of wind and rainfall. Both of these changes could affect temperatures around the world but precisely how and whether or not the effects would be long-lasting is not fully understood.

Records going back many years show a temperature increase, but the increase has been interrupted by periods of cooling. So far, the evidence does not clearly show whether or not "global warming" is occurring. However, the possible effects of global warming, should it occur, would be so serious that research is continuing on a global scale.

ATOMS

Atoms are the building blocks of our world —tiny units that make up everything around us. In the same way that wheels, bands, screws, and pins fit together to make a clock or a toy, atoms of various kinds fit together to form the substances around us.

At one time or another almost everyone has taken apart a toy or a clock to see what made it work. The result is simply a collection of parts. Some people can figure out how to put the parts together again, to rebuild the toy or clock. And a few people can even work out ways to make entirely new devices out of the toy or clock parts.

Modern scientists have learned to do very much the same kind of thing with matter. **Matter** is anything that takes up space and has weight. Air, water, rock, and even people are composed of matter. (Light and heat do not have weight, and so they are not classed as matter.) All matter can be split into smaller and smaller pieces. There is a limit, however, to how small the pieces can be. A molecule is the smallest piece that keeps the characteristics of the original substance. For instance, a sugar molecule is the smallest piece that is still like sugar.

With special equipment a molecule can be broken down into still smaller parts. These are **atoms**. A sugar molecule breaks down into 12 carbon atoms, 22 hydrogen atoms, and 11 oxygen atoms.

If all these atoms are put back together properly, they will again form a sugar molecule. But by arranging carbon, hydrogen, and oxygen atoms in different groups, still other substances can be made. Alcohol and starch are two of them. To put it another way, molecules of sugar, alcohol, and starch are formed of the same three kinds of atoms. It is the proportions and arrangement that determine which molecule will be made.

This one example shows why atoms are called the building blocks of matter. All the kinds of matter in the world are made from only about 100 kinds of atoms.

Curiously, the idea of the atom is far from new. About 2,500 years ago certain Greeks began to wonder what would happen if they took a piece of wood and kept cutting it into smaller and smaller pieces. Could they go on forever making smaller pieces? They decided that this was impossible. Eventually there would be a piece (too small to be seen) that could not be divided. They reasoned that everything was made out of such tiny particles.

Today we have a more complicated idea of the atom. We know that objects are not made up of simple particles but of molecules that are built up out of atoms. We know that atoms themselves are made of still tinier particles. But traces of the Greek idea remain. We still think of atoms as the building blocks of matter, and the word ''atom'' itself comes from a Greek word meaning something that cannot be cut or divided into smaller parts.

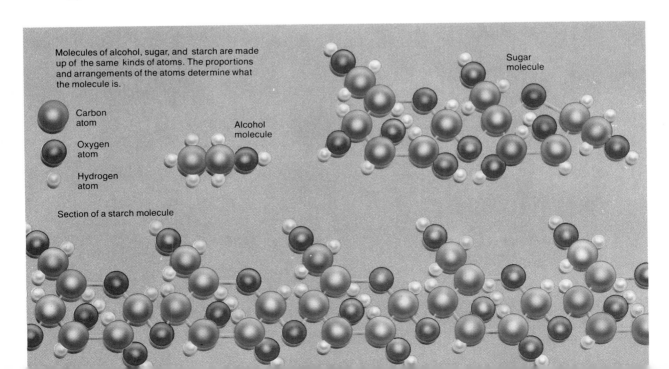

Molecules of alcohol, sugar, and starch are made up of the same kinds of atoms. The proportions and arrangements of the atoms determine what the molecule is.

Carbon atom

Oxygen atom

Hydrogen atom

Alcohol molecule

Sugar molecule

Section of a starch molecule

BASIC FACTS ABOUT THE ATOM

Atoms are so small that they cannot be seen under the most powerful optical microscopes. Yet scientists are able to tell one kind of atom from another. They have learned to measure the size of atoms and the weight of atoms. They have learned about the particles that make up atoms.

The following questions and answers sum up some basic facts about atoms.

How big is an atom?

An atom is smaller than anything you can imagine. Even a speck of dust is gigantic when compared with an atom. It would take about 2,500,000 atoms, placed side by side, to stretch across the head of a pin.

Atoms are also lighter in weight than anything you can imagine. It would take more than 2,000,000,000,000,000,000,000 (sextillion) atoms of uranium to weigh just $\frac{1}{28}$ of an ounce (1 gram).

Atoms are so small that scientists may never be able to see the details of one. The instruments they use can reveal the positions of atoms in solids and show how an atom acts on various materials. But they do not show the structure of the atom itself.

How many kinds of atoms are there?

So far, scientists have discovered 90 kinds of atoms in nature and have made 18 more, for a total of 108. These are known as **elements**. The lightest element found naturally is hydrogen, and the heaviest one is uranium.

All the elements created recently in the laboratory are heavier than uranium. Einsteinium and Californium (for the scientist Albert Einstein and the state of California) are the imaginative names given to two of these artificially made elements. Scientists expect to be able to create still heavier ones. But most of these laboratory-created atoms exist only in small amounts and only for very brief periods of time. They are very unstable (that is, they break down quickly), which explains why they are not found in nature.

How do atoms combine?

Most atoms do not exist singly in nature but are found combined in molecules. When atoms of the same kind combine with one another, they form molecules of the chemical elements. These are the simplest forms of matter.

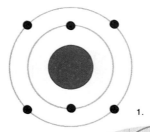

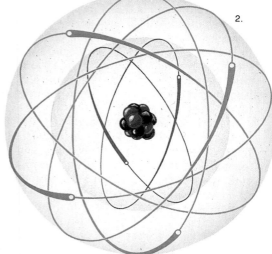

Atoms are too small to be seen, but there are several ways to depict them. A diagram of a carbon atom (1) shows six electrons circling the nucleus. A three-dimensional view (2) shows protons and neutrons in the nucleus.

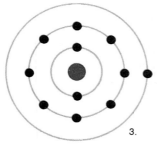

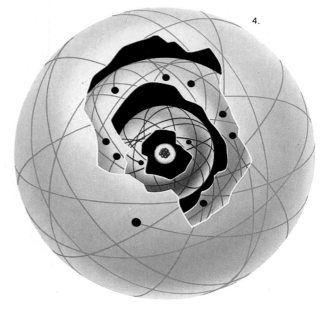

A diagram of a sodium atom (3) shows eleven electrons circling the nucleus. Scientists now think that electrons do not have fixed orbits. Instead, they surround the nucleus in a series of shells, or layers (4). An electron may travel anywhere in its shell.

When atoms of different kinds combine, they form molecules of **chemical compounds**. Compounds are made up of two or more elements, and the elements are always combined in exactly the same ratio. Water, for example, is a compound made up of hydrogen and oxygen. A water molecule contains two hydrogen atoms and one oxygen atom. Oxygen is much heavier than hydrogen, however, so there is always exactly eight times as much oxygen, by weight, as hydrogen.

We rarely see a pure element. Most elements are seen in pure form only in the laboratory. Some exceptions are pure gold and diamonds. (A diamond is made up of pure carbon.) But apart from a few exceptions such as these, most of the materials around us are made up of compounds or mixtures of elements. Even such common objects as copper wire and aluminum pans have small amounts of other elements mixed in.

Although only about 90 elements exist in nature, they combine to make up the almost endless variety of things we see in the world. In fact, most of the world is made up of only about 20 elements. The elements are like the letters of the alphabet. There are only 26 letters. Yet thousands of words are made by combining them in different ways. The compounds of matter are like words, but they are made up of elements instead of letters.

What holds matter together?

The molecules that make up the world of matter are bound to one another by electrical charges. This molecular force of attraction originates with the atoms that make up the molecule. Molecules are bound together most tightly in solids. They move back and forth constantly, with a speed that depends on temperature, but they are held in a rigid structure and do not move far from their fixed positions. In liquids the temperature is higher, and the molecules move faster. They are still held together, but they can slide easily past each other. In gases the molecules move fast enough to overcome the force of attraction, and they can move about freely.

▶THE STRUCTURE OF ATOMS

Although the details of atoms have never been seen, scientists have put together a picture of the atom based on its effects on other matter.

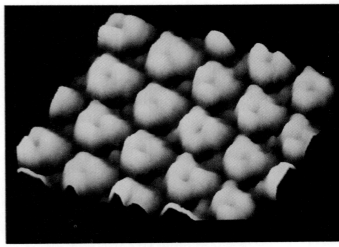

A scanning tunneling microscope can reveal the arrangement of atoms in molecules. Here, each cluster of lumps is a molecule of benzene; each smaller lump is an atom.

In some ways an atom resembles a tiny solar system. At the center of the atom is a **nucleus** (the plural is **nuclei**). Tiny particles of matter called **electrons** travel around the nucleus, somewhat as the planets travel around the sun. (The electrons do not travel in fixed orbits as the planets do, however.)

The nucleus consists of two kinds of particles bound to each other. These particles are called **protons** and **neutrons**. Because they are found together in the nucleus, protons and neutrons are sometimes called **nucleons**. Protons and neutrons can be split into still smaller particles. But protons, neutrons, and electrons are considered to be the three main kinds of particles making up atoms.

An atom is enormous compared with the size of its nucleus. Imagine an atomic nucleus the size of a pea. In such an atom some of the electrons would be moving at a distance of about ¼ mile (400 meters) from the nucleus. Thus, as tiny as it is, an atom consists mainly of empty space.

What are the main kinds of atomic particles like?

A proton is a particle of matter that carries a positive charge of electricity.

A neutron is a particle of matter that weighs just a little more than a proton. But a neutron has no electrical charge.

An electron is a negatively charged particle that is much lighter than a proton or a neutron. An electron weighs about ⅟₁₈₀₀ as much as one of these particles.

The proton and the electron have exactly the same amount of electrical charge. Because an atom normally has the same number of electrons as protons, the positive charges of the protons cancel out the negative charges of the electrons. This balance means that the atoms making up the world of matter are normally electrically neutral.

How does one kind of atom differ from another?

All atoms are made up of the same kinds of particles—electrons, protons, and neutrons. Atoms differ from one another in the number of particles they are made of. For example, oxygen has 8 electrons, 8 protons, and 8 neutrons; aluminum has 13 electrons, 13 protons, and 14 neutrons. These differences are expressed as atomic number and atomic weight.

Atomic Number. The atomic number is simply the number of protons that the atom has. Because the number of electrons that an atom has is equal to the number of protons, the atomic number also tells how many electrons an atom has.

Oxygen has 8 protons and therefore an atomic number of 8. Aluminum has 13 protons and an atomic number of 13. Each element has a unique number of protons and a unique atomic number. The periodic table lists the elements in order of their atomic numbers. (The table is shown in the article ELEMENTS, CHEMICAL in Volume E.)

Isotopes. All atoms of a given element have the same number of protons and electrons. But the atoms of a given element do not always have the same number of neutrons. Atoms that differ in their number of neutrons are called isotopes. Most elements are mixtures of two or more isotopes. An iron pot, for example, is made up of a mixture of four isotopes of the element iron.

All the isotopes of a given element have nearly the same chemical properties. But they differ in their weight. For example, the simplest atom, the common hydrogen atom, has one proton and no neutrons. An isotope of hydrogen called deuterium contains a neutron in addition to the proton. It weighs approximately twice as much as the ordinary hydrogen atom. Deuterium has the same atomic number as hydrogen and therefore also contains one electron. Like ordinary hydrogen, deuterium can combine with oxygen to form water. The water formed by deuterium is called **heavy water**. It is used in some nuclear reactors.

Some isotopes do not occur naturally. Scientists have learned how to produce them in the laboratory. There are more than 1,000 known isotopes. Most of them are artificially made and are generally unstable, existing for only a very brief time. The nucleus of an unstable atom loses particles, so that the atom becomes stable and ordinary.

Atomic Weight. The atomic weight of an element is the average weight of the element's atoms. Because atoms are very tiny, their actual weight is a very small number. However, an atom's weight is concentrated in the nucleus, which is made up of protons and neutrons. All protons weigh the same, no matter what element they are in. So do all neutrons. Thus an atom's weight can be expressed by adding together the number of protons and neutrons.

Scientists have decided to use one commonly found type of atom as a reference for atomic weight and to compare all other atoms with it. This reference is the most abundant isotope of carbon, which is called carbon-12. An atom of this isotope is defined as having exactly 12 units. An atom that weighs twice as much as carbon-12 would have an atomic weight of 24 units.

Because the atomic weight of an element is the average weight of all that element's natural isotopes, it is rarely a whole number. The average atom of iron, for example, is 4.63 times heavier than carbon-12. Thus the atomic weight of iron is 4.63 multiplied by 12, or 55.85 units.

Are there other atomic particles?

Experiments have shown that the model of an atom made up only of protons, neutrons, and electrons is far too simple. Hundreds of new particles have been discovered. Among them are mesons, pions, neutrinos, and positrons. All these particles, along with protons, neutrons, and electrons, are called **subatomic particles**.

Unlike protons, neutrons, and electrons, most subatomic particles exist only for very brief periods. They are formed when atoms are broken apart in laboratories or in nuclear reactors. They also occur naturally in cosmic rays.

Scientists often refer to the hundreds of particles that have been discovered as the "subatomic zoo." However, certain particles have some properties in common, and scientists have been able to group them into three main families. In the current view, called the standard model, all matter is made up of just two kinds of particles, **quarks** and **leptons**. Scientists think that quarks and leptons are truly elementary—that is, so far as is known, they cannot be broken down into smaller parts. The forces between these particles are transmitted by a third category of particles, the **bosons**.

What are quarks?

Protons and neutrons are no longer thought of as being elementary particles but rather as being made up of quarks. The strange name of these particles comes from *Finnegan's Wake,* a novel by James Joyce that contains many made-up words. A bartender in the novel calls out, "Three quarks for Muster Mark." There are thought to be six kinds of quarks, each with a whimsical name: **up**, **down**, **strange**, **charmed**, **top**, and **bottom**. (Some scientists prefer the names **truth** and **beauty** for the last two.) Because there are six types, quarks are often said to come in six flavors.

One of the most extraordinary properties of quarks is that they have fractional charges. Scientists consider the amount of charge carried by an electron to be the basic unit of electrical charge. Until the discovery of quarks, they did not think anything had less charge than an electron. But the up quark, for example, has a positive charge equal to two thirds the charge of an electron. The down quark is negatively charged, with one third the charge of an electron.

A proton is made up of three quarks in two flavors—two ups and a down. Thus its total charge is +1. A neutron is also made up of

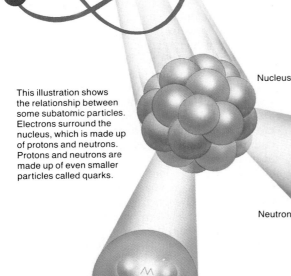

This illustration shows the relationship between some subatomic particles. Electrons surround the nucleus, which is made up of protons and neutrons. Protons and neutrons are made up of even smaller particles called quarks.

Nucleus

Neutron

Electron

Proton

Quark

THE SIX FLAVORS OF QUARKS		
Name	Symbol	Charge*
Up	u	+2/3e
Down	d	−1/3e
Charmed	c	+1/3e
Strange	s	−1/3e
Top	t	+2/3e
Bottom	b	−1/3e
* Charge as a fraction of the charge of an electron.		

three quarks—two downs and an up. Thus its charge is 0. The various flavors of quarks can be combined in similar ways to produce all the other known particles that are not leptons or bosons.

What are leptons?

Electrons belong to a different family of subatomic particles, the leptons. The word "lepton" comes from the Greek word *leptos,* meaning "small." The lepton family consists of six particles that can be grouped in three pairs. The first pair consists of the electron and a particle called a **neutrino** that is associated with it. The second pair consists of a particle called the **muon** and its neutrino. And the third pair is made up of the **tau particle** and its neutrino.

Additionally, experiments have shown that an antiparticle exists for every lepton. Antiparticles have the same weight as their particles, but they have the opposite charge. For example, the antiparticle of the negatively charged electron has a positive charge. It is called a **positron**.

What are bosons?

The bosons are fundamental particles that transmit forces between other particles. For example, in the traditional view an atom's electrons are thought to be bound to the nucleus by the attraction of opposite electrical charges. Scientists now speak of this **electromagnetic force** as being transmitted by the exchange of bosons. You can picture the exchange as a stream of particles passing back and forth.

The boson that transmits the electromagnetic force is called a **photon**. There are three other forces that bind together the elementary particles that make up atoms. Each of these forces has a different boson.

The force that holds the nucleus together is called the **strong force**. It binds quarks together. The boson that transmits this force is called a **gluon**. The familiar force of **gravity** —the force that causes objects to fall to the earth and that keeps the earth in orbit around the sun—is associated with a boson called the **graviton**. The fourth force, called the **weak force**, is responsible for radioactivity (the process by which unstable atoms break down). It is transmitted by the exchange of **Y** and **Z particles**.

How do scientists study atoms?

Scientists study the way molecules fit together in solids by using such tools as X rays and electron microscopes. The most sophisticated tools, such as the scanning tunneling microscope, can show the positions of atoms.

To learn more about the structure of matter, scientists use equipment that can speed up subatomic particles and make them very energetic. These energetic particles can then be shot at atoms of various elements. The bombardment breaks down the nuclei of the target atoms into many different particles. The new particles pass through detectors, and in this way they can be studied. This process is sometimes called **atom smashing**.

The machines that smash atoms are called **particle accelerators** because they force the subatomic particles to travel at very high speeds. Some accelerators, such as the **cyclotron**, whirl the particles faster and faster in a circular path and then let them smash into a target element. A **linear accelerator** speeds up charged particles in a straight line.

Many machines use a device called a **storage ring** to collect a large number of accelerated particles for a given experiment. The particles are gathered and guided by powerful magnets, which keep them circulating in the ring for hours at a time. Then they are extracted in a bunch for the experiment. The more particles in a bunch, the better the chance of hitting a target.

To increase the force in these experiments, particles are sometimes sent toward each other in **colliding beams**. In this case, the target particles as well as the bombarding particles are accelerated in a storage ring. But they travel around the ring in opposite directions. At a command from the operating scientist, the two beams are smashed together. The same principle is at work when two cars collide—the damage is greater when the cars collide head on than when one car is standing still.

When unstable atoms break down through radioactivity, they give off particles and other forms of radiation. These radiations can be detected and measured with various devices. In some, such as the **Geiger counter** and the **dosimeter**, the radiations produce small electric currents that move a needle on a dial or cause clicking sounds. Another instrument, called the **cloud chamber**, has water vapor in a transparent chamber. When radiations pass

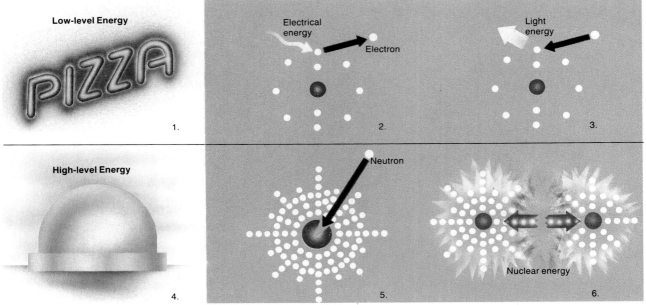

Low-level Energy

1.

Electrical energy

Electron

2.

Light energy

3.

High-level Energy

4.

Neutron

5.

Nuclear energy

6.

The light of a neon sign (1) is produced by low-level energy. Electricity dislodges an electron from an atom of neon gas (2). As the electron falls back into place, light is given off (3). A nuclear reactor (4) releases high-level energy. A neutron splits the nucleus of a uranium atom (5). Two other atoms are formed, and much energy is released (6).

through the water vapor, the vapor condenses into droplets along their tracks. A **scintillation detector** contains a transparent crystal that produces flashes of light, or scintillations, whenever radiation passes through it. The flashes can then be counted and analyzed.

▶**ATOMS AND ENERGY**

When a nucleus breaks down through radioactivity, energy is given off. The source of this energy is some of the atom's mass. (**Mass** is the amount of matter in a substance.)

Scientists have found that mass and energy are equivalent to each other—that is, mass can be changed into energy, and energy can be changed into mass. But the total amount of mass and energy in the universe is always the same. Scientists call this principle the law of conservation of mass and energy.

Radioactivity is one type of nuclear reaction. (A **nuclear reaction** is an event that produces a change in one or more atomic nuclei.) Energy can be released in other nuclear reactions as well—when a heavy nucleus splits (a reaction called **fission**) or when two light nuclei combine to form a heavier nucleus (a reaction called **fusion**). In each case, some mass is changed into energy. A small amount of mass can produce a great amount of energy in these reactions. The energy that is released is called nuclear energy.

What is the difference between nuclear energy and atomic energy?

In everyday speech, the terms "atomic energy" and "nuclear energy" are often used to mean the same thing—energy released from the nucleus of an atom. But scientists prefer to call this energy nuclear energy because atoms and their particles are involved in other kinds of energy, too. For instance, electricity involves a flow of electrons. The energy released by burning coal involves shifts in electrons among atoms.

Strictly speaking, electricity and coal burning could be called atomic energy. But people usually use the terms electric energy and chemical energy to describe these forms of energy. Like certain other forms of energy, electricity and coal burning are considered **low-level energy**. Such forms of energy do not involve the nucleus of the atom.

The nucleus is the source of **high-level energy**. This high-level energy comes only from the nucleus, and it is extremely powerful. Energy released by nuclear fission is used to run power plants that generate electricity. Nuclear fusion occurs in the sun and supplies most of its energy.

Reviewed by ALBERT STWERTKA
Author, *Revolutions in Physics*

See also ELEMENTS, CHEMICAL; NUCLEAR ENERGY; RADIOACTIVE ELEMENTS.

ATTILA (406?–453)

Attila, the legendary king of the Huns, devastated the western half of the Roman Empire between A.D. 451–52. He was so feared by Christians, he became known as a barbarian "Scourge of God," or instrument of God's wrath.

The Huns were originally a nomadic tribe of Mongols, who came out of central Asia in the late 300's and invaded Europe. They were good horsemen, arming themselves with short, powerful bows, which they shot from horseback with devastating effect. About A.D. 400 they settled in the region later known as Hungary.

In 434, Attila succeeded his uncle as leader of the Huns. He won such respect as a warrior that Hunnish communities from the western borders of China to the Danube River accepted his kingship. In 445 Attila launched a campaign against the Roman Empire. In 447 his horsemen overran the Balkan lands, raiding the whole of Greece and threatening Constantinople, the seat of the Roman Empire in the East.

In 451 Attila turned westward and, in his most famous campaign, crossed the Rhine River, penetrating deeply into Gaul (France). Although he successfully besieged the city of Orléans, Attila was defeated later that year in the decisive battle of Châlons by the Roman general Flavius Aetius, who had formed an alliance with Theodoric I, King of the Visigoths.

The defeat did not prevent Attila from embarking on another campaign in 452. That summer his horsemen crossed the Alps to ravage Italy, and Pope Leo I allegedly paid Attila protection money to save Rome from attack.

Attila died suddenly in 453. Although he probably died from heart failure, legend says he was murdered by his bride, a Burgundian princess. His scattered empire disintegrated with his death, but so terrible was his impact on Christian Europe that Attila appears in the epic poems of several countries, most notably as Etzel in the German *Nibelungenlied*.

ALAN PALMER
Author, *Quotations in History*

ATTLEE, CLEMENT (1883–1967)

Clement Richard Attlee, leader of Great Britain's Labour Party from 1935 to 1955, served as prime minister (1945–51) following World War II. As the first prime minister to have a Labour majority in Parliament, Attlee introduced a series of social welfare programs, most notably the National Health Service.

Born in 1883 in a London suburb, Attlee studied at Oxford University, practiced law for four years, then became a social worker. His sympathy for the poor in London's East End slums led him to join the Labour Party.

Elected member of Parliament (MP) in 1922, he held junior cabinet posts in the short-lived Labour governments of 1924 and 1929–31 and became the Labour Party leader in 1935. During World War II, Attlee served as deputy prime minister (1942–45) in Winston Churchill's wartime coalition (multiparty) government. Then, with a landslide victory in 1945, he became prime minister.

At home, Attlee introduced national health care and brought the utilities and railroads into public ownership. In foreign affairs, he backed the creation of the North Atlantic Treaty Organization (NATO) and supported the United Nations' stand against Communist aggression in Korea. Attlee himself regarded the transition of the British Empire to a Commonwealth, marked especially by the government's granting of independence to India and Pakistan (1947), as his greatest achievement.

Although Attlee narrowly won the 1950 election, economic difficulties led to his defeat the following year. After his retirement in 1955 he was given a title of nobility as 1st Earl Attlee. He died on October 8, 1967.

ALAN PALMER
Author, *The Penguin Dictionary of Modern History*

ATTUCKS, CRISPUS. See REVOLUTIONARY WAR (Boston Massacre).

AUDIO SYSTEMS. See HIGH-FIDELITY SYSTEMS; SOUND RECORDING.

AUDUBON, JOHN JAMES (1785–1851)

In the early 1800's John James Audubon was living on the American frontier. He dressed in buckskin and wore his hair long, but he was a different kind of pioneer. His work was the lifelike painting of birds in their natural surroundings.

Audubon was born on his father's plantation in Les Cayes, Santo Domingo (now Haiti), on April 26, 1785. The father, a trader and sea captain, returned to France in 1789, taking his son with him. In the town of Nantes, young Jean Jacques—the French for John James—went to school, but his real interests were the outdoors and painting.

In 1803 John was sent to live at Mill Grove, an estate his father owned near Valley Forge, Pennsylvania. After a short time he went back to France, returning to Pennsylvania in 1806. Audubon later moved to Louisville, Kentucky, where he set up a general store. In 1808 he married Lucy Bakewell, a neighbor from Mill Grove, and took her to Louisville. But the store soon failed, as did all the other business ventures that Audubon tried. Instead of attending to business, he was usually exploring the wilderness.

At first Audubon hunted for food and sport, but he became more and more interested in studying birds. He sketched them in the wild. Then, to get more detail, he began to bring specimens home. He made his paintings in watercolor and chalk. Audubon also made the first known banding experiments on American wild birds. He tied thread around the legs of baby birds and later observed that some had returned to their place of birth to nest.

By 1819, Audubon was bankrupt. He now had only one aim: to complete his collection of bird paintings for publication. In 1821 he traveled down the Ohio and Mississippi rivers, searching for birds and earning a little money by painting portraits. When he arrived in New Orleans, he sent for his wife and two sons. Lucy became a governess and was the main support of the family for the next twelve years.

Audubon began a search for someone to publish his work. Reproduction of his paintings required great skill and expense. In 1826, having failed to find a publisher in America, Audubon went to England and Scotland, where he was well received. He was elected to the Royal Society of Edinburgh in 1827.

A painting of meadowlarks nesting in a field by John James Audubon, who roamed the wilderness identifying, observing, and drawing the birds of North America.

In London that same year, Audubon finally found financial support, as well as an engraver who could reproduce his bird paintings. During the next eleven years, *Birds of America* appeared in four large volumes, one of the rarest and most ambitious works ever published. Between 1831 and 1839, with the help of the Scottish naturalist William Macgillivray, Audubon also wrote five volumes of text to accompany the engravings. This work contained life histories of nearly 500 bird species.

The books brought him money and fame. In 1841, Audubon was able to buy a Hudson River estate. He worked on a book and paintings of the animals of North America, which his sons completed after his death on January 27, 1851.

Audubon's interest in all wildlife is honored by today's National Audubon Society, which is dedicated to the protection of wild creatures and their habitats.

JOHN S. BOWMAN
Author and Science Writer

August

August was the sixth month of the early Roman calendar. It was called *Sextilis,* which means "sixth." The Roman emperor Augustus renamed the month August in honor of himself.

Place in year: 8th month.
Number of days: 31.
Flower: Poppy.
Birthstone: Sardonyx or peridot.
Zodiac signs: Leo, the Lion (July 23–August 22), and Virgo, the Virgin (August 23–September 22).

1
- **Herman Melville** born 1819
- Colorado became the 38th state, 1876
- Confederation Day in Switzerland

2
- First federal census in the U.S. began, 1790

3
- Christopher Columbus began his famous voyage from Spain and eventually reached the New World, 1492

4
- **Percy Bysshe Shelley** born 1792
- John Peter Zenger acquitted of libel, 1735
- U.S. agreed to buy Danish West Indies (now Virgin Islands) from Denmark, 1916

5
- Cyrus Field completed first transatlantic cable, 1858
- First U.S. corporation tax adopted by Congress, 1909
- U.S. atomic submarine *Nautilus* became first vessel to cross the North Pole underwater, 1958

6
- **Daniel O'Connell** born 1775
- **Alfred, Lord Tennyson** born 1809
- **Sir Alexander Fleming** born 1881
- Gertrude Ederle became first woman to swim across the English Channel, 1926
- Hiroshima bombed by the U.S. in first military use of an atomic bomb, 1945
- Independence Day in Bolivia

7
- **Ralph Bunche** born 1904
- Dedication of the International Peace Bridge between the U.S. and Canada, 1927

8
- The Spanish Armada defeated by Britain, 1588

9
- **John Dryden** born 1631
- Richard M. Nixon resigned as president, 1974
- National holiday in Singapore

10
- **Herbert Hoover** born 1874
- Missouri became the 24th state, 1821
- Smithsonian Institution founded, 1846
- Independence Day in Ecuador

11
- Independence Day in Chad

12
- Thomas Edison invented the phonograph, 1877
- The U.S. annexed Hawaii, 1898

13
- **Annie Oakley** born 1860
- **Fidel Castro** born 1926

14
- U.S. Social Security Act approved, 1935
- End of fighting, World War II, 1945
- Strike began at Lenin Shipyard in Gdansk, Poland, leading to gain of workers' rights never achieved before in a Communist regime, 1980

15
- **Napoleon I** born 1769
- **Sir Walter Scott** born 1771
- Panama Canal officially opened, 1914
- National holiday in Congo; South Korea

16
- The American colonists won the Battle of Bennington (Vt.), 1777

17
- **Davy Crockett** born 1786
- Robert Fulton's *Clermont* sailed up Hudson River to become first commercially successful steamboat, 1807
- National holiday in Gabon
- Independence Day in Indonesia

18
- Virginia Dare became first English child born in America, 1587

19
- **Orville Wright** born 1871
- **Manuel Luis Quezon** born 1878
- American ship *Constitution* won naval battle with the British *Guerrière,* 1812

20
- **Bernardo O'Higgins** born 1778
- **Oliver Hazard Perry** born 1785
- **Benjamin Harrison** born 1833

21
- Lincoln-Douglas debates began, 1858
- Hawaii became the 50th state, 1959

22
- **Claude Debussy** born 1862
- The *Savannah,* first American steamship to cross the Atlantic Ocean, launched, 1818

23
- Liberation Day in Romania

24
- Mount Vesuvius erupted in Italy, destroying Pompeii, A.D. 79
- Massacre of St. Bartholomew. Under orders from Charles IX, numerous Huguenots, or Protestants, massacred, 1572

25
- **Althea Gibson** born 1927
- Independence Day in Uruguay

26
- **Antoine Lavoisier** born 1743
- **Geraldine Ferraro** born 1935
- The 19th Amendment to U.S. Constitution gave women the right to vote, 1920

27
- **Lyndon Baines Johnson** born 1908

28
- **Johann Wolfgang von Goethe** born 1749
- **Leo Tolstoi** born 1828
- Martin Luther King, Jr., delivered "I have a dream . . ." speech to 250,000 citizens at the "March on Washington" to demand passage of new civil rights laws, 1963

29
- **John Locke** born 1632
- **Oliver Wendell Holmes** born 1809
- **Charles Franklin Kettering** born 1876

30
- **Lord Ernest Rutherford** born 1871

31
- National holiday in Malaysia; Trinidad and Tobago

The calendar listing identifies people who were born on the indicated day in boldface type, **like this.** You will find a biography of each of these birthday people in *The New Book of Knowledge.* In addition to citing some historical events and historical firsts, the calendar also lists the holidays and some of the festivals celebrated in the United States. These holidays are printed in italic type, *like this.* See the article HOLIDAYS for more information.

Many holidays and festivals of nations around the world are included in the calendar as well. When the term "national holiday" is used, it means that the nation celebrates an important patriotic event on that day—in most cases the winning of independence. Consult *The New Book of Knowledge* article on the individual nation for further information on its national holiday.

AUGUSTINE, SAINT (354–430)

Saint Augustine, one of the most respected Christian thinkers of his time, was born in the year 354. His Latin name was Aurelius Augustinus. His mother, later known as Saint Monica, was a devout Christian. His father, a Roman government official, was not a Christian. The family lived in Tagaste, a small town in North Africa, which was then part of the Roman Empire.

As a young man, Augustine was often in trouble. His parents sent him away to school to keep him busy. He studied Greek, Latin, and philosophy. In 370 he went to Carthage, the center of learning in Africa, where he later opened a school. During his years there, Augustine searched for a way to worship God and to live his life, but no one religion fully satisfied him.

In 383 he traveled in Italy. There he came under the influence of Saint Ambrose, then bishop of Milan. Ambrose instructed him in the Christian faith, and in 387 Augustine was baptized a Christian.

In 388, Augustine returned to Tagaste, where he lived a quiet life of prayer and studied to become a priest. He was ordained in 391 and was made bishop of the nearby city of Hippo in 395. Augustine continued to write and to preach there until his death on August 28, 430.

Today, Saint Augustine is best remembered for his writings. In addition to his sermons and letters, he wrote more than 200 books, the most famous of which are *The City of God* and the *Confessions of Saint Augustine*. In *The City of God,* he defends Christianity and the Catholic Church. In the *Confessions,* Augustine retraces his life and his search for faith. He was the first to use "confessions" as a form of autobiography. His frankness, keen mind, and self-knowledge make this life story one of the most interesting and inspiring ever written.

Saint Augustine's feast day—the day on which the Catholic Church honors him—is August 28.

Reviewed by MSGR. JOHN PAUL HAVERTY
Archdiocese of New York

AUSTEN, JANE (1775–1817)

The English novelist Jane Austen began writing as a child to amuse her sister and brothers. Their father was a parson at Steventon, in Hampshire, where Jane was born on December 16, 1775.

Young Jane's stories made fun of the fashionable novels of the day, in which ladies were very delicate. In *Love and Friendship,* which she wrote when she was 14, her two heroines "fainted alternately on the sofa."

The first of Jane Austen's novels to be published was *Sense and Sensibility,* in 1811. Two years later came *Pride and Prejudice.* The Prince Regent (later King George IV) read *Mansfield Park,* which was published in 1814. He admired it so much that he asked the author to dedicate her next novel to him. *Emma,* with the royal dedication, was published in 1816. But Jane Austen still did not sign her name to her novels. Some of her friends would talk to her about them without knowing she was the author. She had to fit in her writing among her many social and household activities. Much of the time, she said, "Composition seems to me impossible with a head full of joints of mutton and doses of rhubarb." She was often ill during the writing of her last novel, *Persuasion,* and she died in Winchester on July 18, 1817. *Persuasion* and *Northanger Abbey* were published the next year.

Although her books are about courtship, Jane Austen never married. But she led an active social life. In her novels she wrote about the kind of life she knew best—"three or four families in a country village"—instead of inventing colorful people and adventures. The famous historical novelist of her time, Sir Walter Scott, appreciated her special qualities. "The big bow-wow strain I can do myself," he wrote, "but the exquisite touch which renders ordinary commonplace things and characters interesting . . . is denied to me. What a pity such a gifted creature died so early."

JULIET MCMASTER
University of Alberta (Canada)

AUSTRALIA

Australia is both the world's smallest continent and its sixth largest country. Located in the Southern Hemisphere between the Pacific and Indian oceans, it is a land of startling contrasts. Most of its people live in cities or suburban areas. Yet there are lonely areas of the country occupied only by the aborigines, Australia's first inhabitants. Lush, tropical forests —with animals and plants found nowhere else in the world—cover the northeastern coast. Vast grasslands, dotted with flocks of sheep and herds of cattle, stretch across parts of the interior as far as the eye can see. Much of inland Australia is desert—dry, barren, and uninhabited. But in the southeast, snow lies on the high Australian Alps.

The Commonwealth of Australia is made up of six states. Five are on the mainland—New South Wales, Victoria, Queensland, South Australia, and Western Australia. The sixth is the island state of Tasmania. There are also two federal territories on the mainland— the large Northern Territory and the small Australian Capital Territory, which includes Canberra, the federal capital.

Australia also administers a number of small islands in the Pacific and Indian oceans, as well as the Australian Antarctic Territory.

▶THE PEOPLE

The ancestors of the aborigines are thought to have migrated to Australia more than 30,000 years ago, probably from the mainland or islands of Asia. The first European settlers arrived in Australia from Britain in 1788. They founded the colonies that later became the

Canberra is the capital of Australia. The emblem seen through the window is the national coat of arms, which features an emu and a kangaroo, animals found only in Australia.

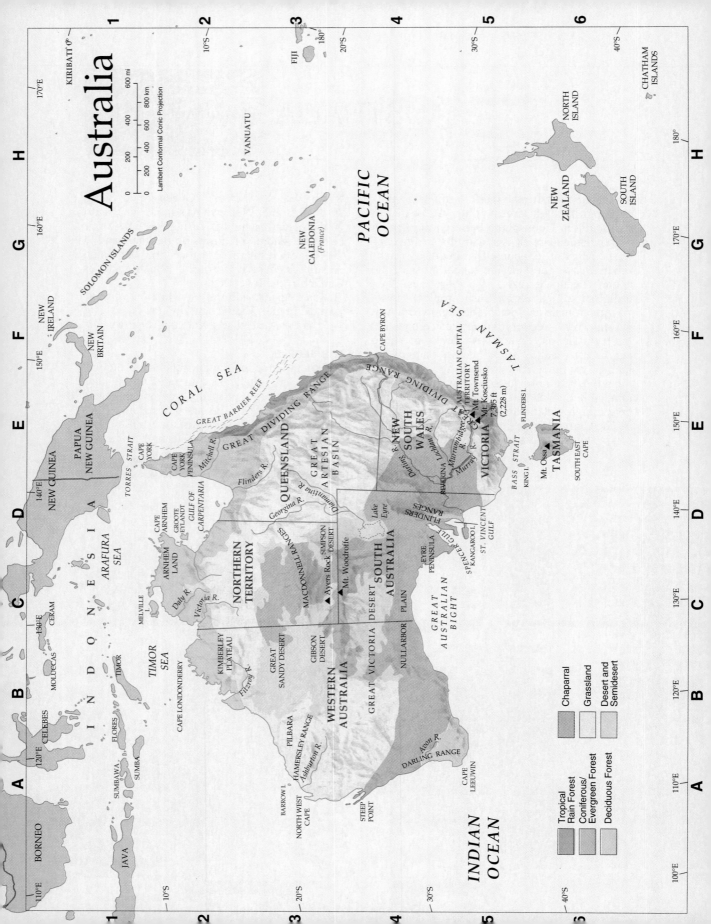

Australia

Lambert Conformal Conic Projection

0 200 400 600 800 km
0 200 400 600 mi

Legend:
- Tropical Rain Forest
- Coniferous/Evergreen Forest
- Deciduous Forest
- Chaparral
- Grassland
- Desert and Semidesert

Australian nation. Since then the development of the new land has been remarkable. Today Australians live in a country with an advanced political and industrial structure and enjoy one of the world's highest standards of living.

How Australians Live

Most Australians live near the coast, mainly in the east, southeast, and southwest, where the climate and soil are best suited to their needs. Life for most of the people is agreeable. History, climate, and natural inclination combine to give Australians an easygoing, informal manner. This dates back to pioneer

INDEX TO AUSTRALIA PHYSICAL MAP

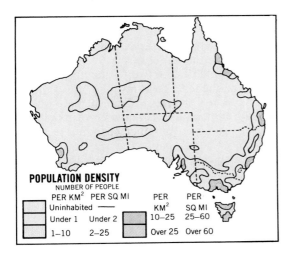

POPULATION DENSITY
NUMBER OF PEOPLE

PER KM²	PER SQ MI		PER KM²	PER SQ MI
Uninhabited	—		10–25	25–60
Under 1	Under 2		Over 25	Over 60
1–10	2–25			

FACTS and figures

COMMONWEALTH OF AUSTRALIA is the official name of the country. The name comes from the Latin *terra australis incognita*, or "the unknown southern land."

LOCATION: Southern Hemisphere, between the Pacific and Indian oceans.

AREA: 2,967,895 sq mi (7,686,848 km²).

POPULATION: 17,000,000 (estimate).

CAPITAL: Canberra.

LARGEST CITY: Sydney.

MAJOR LANGUAGE(S): English.

MAJOR RELIGIOUS GROUP(S): Christian.

CHIEF PHYSICAL FEATURES: Highest point—Mt. Kosciusko, 7,305 ft (2,228 m). **Lowest point**—Lake Eyre, 53 ft (16 m) below sea level. **Chief rivers**—Murray, Darling, Murrumbidgee. **Chief mountain peaks**—Mt. Kosciusko, Mt. Townsend, Mt. Bogong, Mt. Ossa, Mt. Woodroffe.

GOVERNMENT: Independent self-governing federation. **Head of state**—British monarch, represented by a governor-general. **Head of government**—prime minister. **Legislature**—Federation parliament (made up of the Senate and House of Representatives).

ECONOMY: Chief agricultural products—wheat, barley, wool, beef, mutton, fruit, sugarcane. **Chief manufactured products**—iron and steel, motor vehicles, machinery, electronics equipment, electrical appliances, chemicals, aircraft, textiles, food processing, tobacco, wood products. **Chief minerals**—iron, coal, petroleum, bauxite, lead, zinc, copper, nickel, rutile, zircon, uranium, diamonds. **Chief exports**—metals, ores and gems, grains, wool, meat, coal, raw sugar.

MONETARY UNIT: Australian dollar (1 dollar = 100 cents).

days, when individual character and ability—rather than family status or possession of wealth—stood out in the struggle with nature. Their homes and apartments are well built and are usually equipped with modern electrical appliances. The majority of Australians own their own homes. A large proportion of them own automobiles and television sets.

City Life. The main centers of population are the state capitals—Sydney, Melbourne, Brisbane, Adelaide, Perth, and Hobart. These cities have tree-lined streets, lovely parks, large department stores, and supermarkets. Sydney has been compared with San Francisco, while Melbourne has been compared with large cities in Britain.

Everyday life in the cities is much like life in any modern city. Men and women leave home in the mornings to go to offices or factories, while the children go off to school. Most Australians have two free days each week, and there is ample time for outdoor activities.

Like most Australians the city people are involved in sports. Public tennis courts, golf courses, and bowling greens are found in all cities. Swimming, surfing, and yachting are popular throughout the year in cities near the sea. Horse racing is very popular. Spectator sports are well attended. Many people watch amateur and professional Australian Rules football, cricket, and tennis matches.

Symphony concerts, operas, and other musical events are held in the larger cities. Most large cities have art galleries. Australia has produced many world-famous artists, dancers, actors, singers, and musicians.

Country Life. The differences between country and city living are rapidly disappearing as communications bring the city closer to the country and give the country easier access to the city. Sheep raising was Australia's earliest economic activity, and it is still the leading farm activity. Large sheep stations dot the inland plains of the east and southwest. They belong to some of Australia's most distinguished families, who have owned them for several generations. Sheep farmers are called graziers in Australia. With the help of hired workers and wonderfully trained sheep dogs, which look like small collies, they take care of thousands of sheep.

Shearing crews come to clip the sheep once a year. The shearers are highly skilled, and

Two-way radios often provide school instruction in the Australian outback. Australia has pioneered methods of teaching children living in isolated areas.

they travel from station to station in the course of their work. For weeks before their visit, sheep are brought into the station headquarters from the most distant pastures. A good shearer can clip as many as 150 to 200 sheep a day.

After shearing, the wool is baled and stored in the woolshed. It is then taken to market, where it is sold at auction. Picnics, dances, horse races, and other celebrations are held after the auction. These events are especially festive if the wool has brought good prices at the auction.

Some of the larger sheep stations form complete little communities. Most large stations have houses for the owner and the staff, vegetable gardens, a dairy, storage sheds, and a tool-repair shop. Some of the larger stations even have their own one-room schools and power plants to generate electricity.

Smaller farms are found in the irrigated areas and nearer the cities. Most of them belong to farmers of British descent, but some farms belong to or are run by Australians of German or Italian descent. Wheat is the leading crop on the larger farms. Dairy products, fruits, vegetables, chickens, and hogs are produced on the smaller farms.

Life in the Outback. The sparsely settled interior of Australia is known as the outback. Cattle raising is the chief economic activity. Ranches, called stations, vary in size from about 4 square miles (10 square kilometers) to nearly 6,000 square miles (more than 15,000 square kilometers).

The loneliness of life in the outback is rapidly disappearing. Many stations have their own airstrips for use by their own and other planes. Trucks, with trailers often linked together like railroad cars, transport cattle to market much faster than they could be moved by the older method of droving (driving them in herds). At the same time, ranch workers on their horses are giving way to crews operating from trailer trucks.

Outback children are far from any school. Some children go to boarding schools in the cities, but most listen at home to a program called School of the Air. Assignments are given out over the radio, and the children mail in their homework to be graded.

The radio also helps when people become ill. In the early days many sick people died because there were no hospitals or doctors nearby. But today the Royal Flying Doctor Service makes doctors and dentists available throughout the outback. The flying doctor can be called in by radio in an emergency. Some of the doctors fly vast distances every year to care for their scattered patients.

Radio also reduces some of the loneliness of life for people in the outback. It provides most of their entertainment, and people sometimes use it to chat with distant neighbors.

A member of the Royal Flying Doctor Service visits a patient in central Australia. This service provides medical and dental care in remote areas.

The Australian Government has set up special schools for aborigine children. Vocational and other training is also provided for aborigine adults.

The New Australians. Nearly one out of every four Australians has arrived here since 1947. Most of these immigrants came from the United Kingdom, and the population is still largely composed of people of British ancestry. Until the 1970's, most of the remainder of new Australians came from other parts of Europe. Since then, the greatest surge of immigration has been from Asia, with Australians of Asian ancestry now making up about 4 percent of the population. Efforts to help the newcomers become a part of Australian society have been highly successful.

The Aborigines. The Australian aborigines live mainly inland and in the remote northern coastal areas. Most of them no longer live the nomadic tribal life of their ancestors. Another group of aboriginal inhabitants live on small islands in the Torres Strait between Australia and Papua New Guinea. Together the two aboriginal groups total more than 160,000, but fewer than half are considered pure-blooded. The Australian aborigines belong to an ethnological group known as Australoids. Before European influence reached them, they moved continually from place to place, hunting animals and gathering food. The Torres Strait Islanders are largely Melanesian in origin.

The aborigines have the right to enroll and vote in federal elections. Except for those who have chosen to live as tribal nomads, all are entitled to the full range of social benefits available to other Australians. There are special government welfare, housing, and education programs designed to assist aboriginal people, particularly those living in remote areas. A significant number of aborigines continue to live on government reservations, where their traditional way of life is protected.

Language

English is the language spoken in Australia. But it is spoken with a distinctive accent—not English or cockney, as is sometimes mistakenly believed. The Australians have enlivened the language with a rich variety of their own expressions—so much so that their conversation is sometimes hard for an English-speaking foreigner to follow. See the table at left for some distinctive Australian words and phrases.

Education

Education is compulsory in Australia. Children must begin school when they are 6 and stay until they are at least 15. Children in Tasmania must stay in school until they are 16. Most children start in infants' classes at the age of 5. There are government-supported, or state, schools in all populated parts of the country. Australia also has many private schools. As in England, the leading private schools are called public schools. The school year begins in late January or early February and ends in mid-December. Summer in the Southern Hemisphere begins in December.

Elementary school studies include social studies, arithmetic, health education, nature study, reading, and art. Games such as cricket, Australian Rules football, soccer, rugby, and basketball are taught as part of physical education classes. Swimming, tennis, hiking, camping, and singing are some of the popular activities out of school. Children in most state and private schools wear their own uniforms.

Australia has about 20 universities and a number of colleges that offer courses leading to undergraduate and advanced degrees. Since 1974, students wishing to attend universities and colleges have not had to pay tuition. The Australian National University is mainly for graduate students, but undergraduate courses are given there.

The Sydney Opera House, designed by the Danish architect Joern Utzon, has a roof shaped like billowing sails. In the background is the Sydney Harbour Bridge.

Religion

The majority of Australians belong to various Protestant churches. By far the largest of these is the Church of England. There are also many Methodists and Presbyterians and much smaller numbers of Lutherans, Baptists, and Congregationalists. About one-fourth of all Australians are Roman Catholics. There are also smaller numbers of Jews, Muslims, and members of the Orthodox Eastern Church.

The Arts in Australia

Australia's early poets, novelists, and short-story writers were basically Europeans who found both the country and the society unfamiliar. For this reason it was some time before Australia's literature truly reflected the Australian environment and developed national characteristics.

There is now a growing body of clearly Australian literature. Among the more recent poets who have achieved recognition are Kenneth Slessor, Judith Wright, Christopher Brennan, Douglas Stewart, and A. D. Hope. The work of the "bush balladists" is still remembered. These were the poets who wrote about Australia through the eyes of the pioneers who were developing it. Foremost among them were Andrew Barton (Banjo) Paterson and Henry Lawson. Paterson wrote the final form of the ballad "Waltzing Matilda," which has practically become the national song of Australia.

The short story has been a vital form of literary expression since Henry Lawson turned the campfire yarn into a work of art. Among the best-known contemporary short-story writers are Hal Porter, Gavin Casey, Alan Marshall, Geoffrey Dutton, D'Arcy Niland, and Frank Moorehouse.

The novel in Australia has developed its own character since the publication in 1917 of *The Fortunes of Richard Mahony* by Henry Handel Richardson (the pen name of Henrietta Richardson). Among the contemporary Australian novelists whose works have had worldwide distribution are Patrick White, who won the Nobel Prize for literature in 1973, D'Arcy Niland, Jon Cleary, Ruth Park, Morris West, Peter Mathers, Colleen McCullough, David Ireland, and Thomas Keneally.

There are public art galleries in all state capitals and in the larger provincial towns. The Melbourne National Gallery, one of the best endowed, has the nation's finest collection of works by masters of the Italian, Dutch, Flemish, French, Spanish, and English schools. The Australian National Gallery in Canberra houses a fine collection of Australian art.

As with literature, art in Australia began as a reflection of European values of form and light. Most of the early paintings were by European artists with fond memories of their homelands. In the latter half of the 1800's, Swiss painter Louis Buvelot became one of the first to master the Australian landscape. Following him was a group of painters—Arthur Streeton, Tom Roberts, and others—who found the techniques of impressionism an ideal medium for the naturalistic painting of Australian scenes. After the impressionists came another school, including Hans Heysen and Elioth Gruner, who painted the country's scenery more formally.

In recent years, styles have become either starker or more complicated. Notable contemporary artists are Sir Russell Drysdale, Sidney Nolan, Arthur Boyd, John Passmore, and Donald Friend. The best known is probably Sir William Dobell, an exuberant romantic with a fine sense of color and superb technique. Sir William Dargie has been noted for his portraits. There is also a vigorous abstractionist movement in Australia.

An interesting development in Australian painting was the emergence of a school of aboriginal painters. These artists took quickly to watercolor technique when it was introduced to a mission station at Hermannsburg, west of Alice Springs. Their works have been exhibited and have found ready sale in Aus-

tralia and overseas. Albert Namatjira, who died in 1959, was the best known of the aboriginal painters.

In music and drama many Australian artists have become internationally famous. The beautiful voices of opera singers Dame Nellie Melba, Dame Joan Sutherland, Peter Dawson, Marjorie Lawrence, and Harold Blair have delighted music lovers throughout the world. The music of composers Percy Grainger and Arthur Benjamin has also won international recognition. The acting of Cyril Ritchard and Errol Flynn and the piano concerts of Eileen Joyce attracted large audiences. Ray Lawler, whose play *Summer of the Seventeenth Doll* was produced in London and New York, is a leading Australian playwright. Jazz musicians such as Ray Price and Don Burrows, popular singers such as Olivia Newton-John and Helen Reddy, and numerous rock bands have also won popularity with audiences all over the world.

Filmmaking developed early in Australia; one of the first feature films was made there in 1906. Beginning in the 1970's, the Australian film industry gained international prominence through the work of such filmmakers as Bruce Beresford, Peter Weir, Gillian Armstrong, George Miller, and Fred Schepisi. Many of these Australian directors went on to further fame in Hollywood, as did such actors as Mel Gibson—an American who began his acting career in Australia—Judy Davis, and Paul Hogan.

▶ THE LAND

Australia is the world's largest island and its smallest continent, although it is more commonly referred to as a continent than an island. Its total area is about the same as that of the United States, excluding Alaska and Hawaii.

Australia extends from Cape York in the north to South East Cape in the south—a distance of 2,300 miles (3,700 kilometers)—and from Steep Point in the west to Cape Byron in the east—a distance of 2,600 miles (4,000 kilometers). Off its northeastern coast lies the Great Barrier Reef, the world's longest coral reef. Asia is the continent nearest to Australia. The islands of Indonesia form stepping-stones between the two continents. To the west of Australia stretches the vast Indian Ocean. The icy shores of Antarctica lie to the south. New Zealand is to the east.

A woman diver examines some of the coral formations that make up the Great Barrier Reef. The reef is one of Australia's most popular tourist attractions.

The red monoliths of Mount Olga, in the Northern Territory, are part of a national park. The aborigines call Mount Olga *Katajuta* (many heads).

Natural Regions

Australia's major landforms are low plateaus and broad, level plains. Unlike Europe, Asia, or the Americas, Australia has no very high mountains or deep valleys.

Three natural regions extend as broad bands from north to south across the continent. These are the Eastern Highlands, the Central Lowland, and the Western Plateau.

Eastern Highlands. The long range of hills and low plateaus along Australia's eastern coast is known as the Eastern Highlands, or the Great Dividing Range. Australia's highest point, Mount Kosciusko, is in the part of the highlands known as the Australian Alps. The eastern slope of the mountains is too steep for farming and is mainly forested. The western slope is gentler and is divided into large wheat farms and sheep stations. Rivers flowing to the east are short and swift, while rivers flowing westward are longer and sluggish. Much of their flow is lost through evaporation.

Off the east coast of Queensland is the Great Barrier Reef, the world's largest coral formation. It runs along the coast for 1,250 miles (2,000 kilometers). It is separated from the mainland by shallow, sheltered water. A few islands in this stretch of water have become popular resorts. The area is a favorite spot for skin diving.

Central Lowland. The Central Lowland is a broad, flat interior basin that stretches from the Gulf of Carpentaria in the north to Spencer Gulf in the south. It occupies about one-third of the continent.

The northern section around the Gulf of Carpentaria is very narrow. It is covered with scrub and grass vegetation and is used mainly for raising cattle. The rivers flow only during the wet season.

In the southern section is Lake Eyre, a vast depression that is the lowest point in Australia. Lake Eyre has no outlet. Most of the time it is a large expanse of dried, salty mud. But in unusually rainy years it becomes filled with salty water.

Much of the Central Lowland lies over an area known as the Great Artesian Basin. There, warm, slightly salty water is trapped within the rock layers below the ground. When wells are bored deep into the water-bearing rocks of the basin, the water rises to the surface under its own pressure. Graziers have drilled thousands of wells in this region to get water for their sheep and cattle.

In the southern section of the Central Lowland are the Murray River and its three main tributaries—the Darling, Lachlan, and Murrumbidgee. The Murray is Australia's most important river. It flows for 1,600 miles (2,600 kilometers) from its source in the Australian Alps to its mouth in South Australia. The Darling is longer, but it is less important because it often runs dry in drought years. The Darling joins the Murray at Wentworth. Between the Murray and the Lachlan is the Riv-

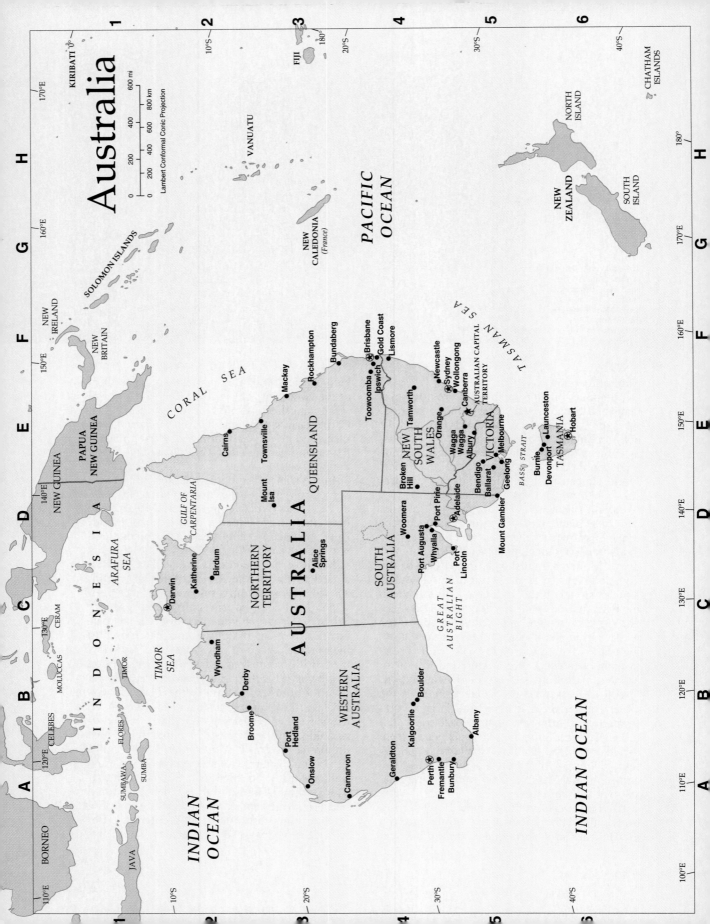

INDEX TO AUSTRALIA POLITICAL MAP

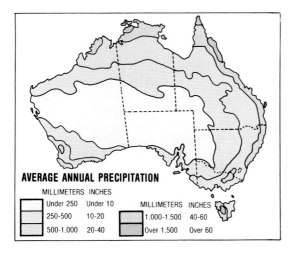

AVERAGE ANNUAL PRECIPITATION

MILLIMETERS	INCHES
Under 250	Under 10
250-500	10-20
500-1,000	20-40

MILLIMETERS	INCHES
1,000-1,500	40-60
Over 1,500	Over 60

erina, one of Australia's leading wheat farming and grazing regions.

Western Plateau. The Western Plateau is a vast upland region that occupies more than half the continent. The interior of the plateau is made up of the Great Sandy Desert, the Gibson Desert, the Great Victoria Desert, and the Nullarbor Plain.

Alice Springs and Kalgoorlie are the only important towns in the interior of the plateau. Alice Springs is a thriving cattle center at the end of a newly rebuilt railroad line from Adelaide. It is the railhead for the surrounding cattle country. Kalgoorlie is the center of Australia's gold-mining industry. All the water for Kalgoorlie and nearby mining towns is piped far across the desert from an artificial lake on the Helena River, a tributary of the Swan River east of Perth.

A few places on the edge of the plateau receive rainfall regularly. One such region is the scrub-and-grassland country of the north around Darwin. Cattle raising is the leading industry in this region. The second non-desert region is in the southwest near Perth. This region receives enough rain in winter so that wheat farming and sheep raising are possible. The Eyre Peninsula, jutting out into the Indian Ocean west of Spencer Gulf, is another non-desert region.

Climate

Because Australia lies in the Southern Hemisphere, winter comes in June and summer in December. People often swim in the ocean during their Christmas holidays.

Temperature. The one-third of Australia that lies north of the Tropic of Capricorn has tropical temperatures. Darwin, on the north coast, has average monthly temperatures of around 80°F (27°C).

The rest of Australia has a moderate climate. Summers are generally hot and winters mild. Winters are often warm enough for Australians to enjoy tennis, lawn bowling, and even surfing. It is warm enough during the winter for cattle and sheep to stay outdoors, so farmers do not have the expense of building barns to shelter their animals.

Rainfall. Most parts of Australia do not receive enough rainfall. In some places droughts occur occasionally. In other places they occur seasonally. Particularly severe droughts affected every state in Australia in

WILDLIFE of AUSTRALIA

GREEN SEA TURTLE · CROCODILE · CORAL · DEVILFISH · CUSCUS · GIANT CLAM · CLOWNFISH · SEA STAR · DINGO · WATER BUFFALO · BUDGERIGAR · PARROT · FRILLED LIZARD · REGENT BOWERBIRD · EMU · RABBIT · FLYING SQUIRREL · COCKATOO · KOALA BEAR · KOOKABURRA · SHARK · KANGAROO · SPINY ANTEATER · LYREBIRD · PLATYPUS · MARLIN · FAIRY PENGUIN · TASMANIAN DEVIL

1978 and again in 1982–83. Lack of rainfall is one of the major reasons for Australia's small population.

Only one-sixth of the continent—a belt of land along the north, east, and southeast coasts —receives more than 40 inches (1,000 millimeters) of rain a year. Wide areas in the interior receive less than 10 inches (250 millimeters) of rainfall each year.

Australia's humid lands extend in a belt along the northern coast and parts of the northeastern and eastern coasts. The southeastern coast and the island state of Tasmania have a marine type of climate. Rain falls throughout the year, and snow is common on the higher mountains.

Southwestern Australia has a Mediterranean climate. Rainfall is distributed throughout the year, but more rain falls during the winter. Summers are warm and sunny.

The northern coast has a monsoon climate. Rain falls only in summer, when the moisture-bearing northwest monsoon blows onto Australia from Asia. Summers are hot and sticky, and grass and trees grow rapidly. Rivers often flood. Winter is almost completely rainless, and the country becomes dry and parched.

Pastures dry up, and cattle must find what grass they can in the few moist places discovered by the cattle drovers.

Farther inland are somewhat drier areas that receive between 10 and 30 inches (250 and 750 millimeters) of rain a year. The rain falls evenly throughout the year in the east. But the northern areas, like the humid monsoon areas along the northern coast, receive most of their rain in summer and are dry during the winter. The semi-arid regions in the south and southwest receive most of their rain in winter and are dry during the summer.

Australian Wildlife

Australia has an extraordinary collection of birds and animals. Many of them are found only there. Early explorers were so surprised by the emu and the kangaroo that they described the continent as the land where birds "ran instead of flying and animals hopped instead of running."

Australia is the home of two of the world's most primitive mammals—the platypus, or duckbill, and the spiny anteater. They belong to the group of mammals known as monotremes, the only mammals that lay eggs. The platypus is a furry creature. It has webbed feet and a long snout shaped somewhat like a duck's bill. The spiny anteater looks more like a porcupine.

Australia is famous as the home of the marsupials, or pouched mammals. A newborn marsupial is extremely tiny and spends the first months of its life in a pouch on the underside of its mother's body. The kangaroo is perhaps the best known of Australia's marsupials. There are more than 40 different kinds of kangaroos in Australia, in many different colors and sizes. The big red kangaroo and the gray kangaroo may be as tall and heavy as a human adult. A smaller kangaroo, known as the wallaby, is about the size of a large dog. The smallest variety is the rat kangaroo. Australia's famous koala is also a marsupial. The koala is a quaint creature that resembles a teddy bear. It spends most of its life in eucalyptus trees and feeds only on the leaves of these trees. Various small opossums, sometimes called flying squirrels, are unusual animals that glide from tree to tree.

Among other animals found in Australia is the dingo, a wild dog that was probably brought to Australia by the aborigines. It is yellowish brown and has a bushy tail.

The kangaroo shares the Australian coat of arms with the emu, Australia's largest bird and also one of the largest in the world. Like the ostrich, the emu cannot fly but is a swift runner. The cassowary is related to the emu and can sprint at high speeds. Another curious bird is the kookaburra, a large kingfisher that is often called the "laughing jackass." The bush country rings with its rowdy laughter. The brolga, an Australian crane, is sometimes called the "native companion" because many people working in the forests and outback used to keep a tame brolga around the camp. Other Australian birds are graceful lyrebirds, brilliantly colored parrots, and the great white cockatoo. Black- and white-backed magpies are rarely absent from the skies of southeastern and southwestern Australia.

Several animals introduced by the Europeans have run wild in Australia. These include the buffalo, brought from India, the European rabbit, brumbies (wild horses), and camels. Buffalo were brought to the north coast as work animals in the early 1800's. They escaped and multiplied and now inhabit the swampy river valleys around Darwin and the Gulf of Carpentaria. Each year, hunters shoot thousands of them for their thick hides.

Rabbits were introduced more than 100 years ago. There are now so many of them in Australia that they are pests. Australian sheep farmers wage constant war against the rabbits because they destroy much valuable grass. Many properties are surrounded by rabbit-proof fences, but fences intended to protect very large regions have failed. For many years the farmers have laid poison bait and plowed up large underground rabbit colonies. They introduced a disease called myxomatosis (or myxo). This disease is deadly to rabbits but harmless to other animals. But many rabbits have now developed resistance to the disease, and Australians are seeking a more effective way to solve the rabbit problem.

Natural Resources

Australia is rich in some natural resources and poor in many others. The most valuable agricultural resource is the vast grassland in east central and southeastern Australia. Thousands of sheep and cattle are grazed on these pastures. They supply most of the meat and wool that Australia sells to the rest of the world. Australia also has abundant mineral resources, many of which have been discovered in recent times. Principal among them are iron ore, coal, bauxite (aluminum ore), petroleum and natural gas, diamonds, and uranium.

Australia's soils are relatively poor. Usually they need to be fertilized for crop production. More serious is a shortage of water over most of the continent. But Australia has taken bold steps to help overcome this problem. The capacity of its water storage facilities has been greatly multiplied. The most remarkable undertaking is the Snowy Mountains Hydro-Electric Scheme. This vast project, which also produces electricity, stretches across the Australian Alps in southeastern New South Wales. It is one of the greatest achievements of its kind in the world. By means of a system of dams and tunnels, it makes possible the storage of huge amounts of water behind nine major dams and greatly increases the quantity of water available for irrigation. Water from coastal rivers is diverted through a series of tunnels so that it flows into the inland river systems of the Murray and Murrumbidgee. The water is used to generate electricity in a number of power stations. Other major projects are being carried out in all the states to increase the supply of water and electricity.

Softwoods are scarce in Australia, but there are large areas of hardwoods in the far southwestern part of Western Australia and the Great Dividing Range. The native eucalyptus tree and the wattle tree are especially common. Large plantations of North American pine and other softwood trees have been established. They should provide enough softwood to meet the needs of the future.

▶ THE ECONOMY

Australia has a diversified economy, combining agriculture, mining, and manufacturing. Although it has only limited fertile land, Australia is a major producer and exporter of agricultural products. Its wealth of mineral resources has made mining vital to the country's economy. Manufacturing, however, has been the most rapidly growing economic sector. Australia's trade, once mainly with Britain and Europe, has increasingly been directed toward Asia and the Pacific.

Manufacturing

Australia's manufacturing industries have grown tremendously in the years since the end of World War II. Today, manufacturing employs about one-quarter of the country's workforce and contributes nearly one-third of its total annual value of production.

Since World War II, the industries that have developed most are those associated with rapid technological changes and rising standards of living. Those that have grown at the fastest rates are the engineering industry and the manufacture of vehicles, construction materials, and chemicals. Products of these industries have been able to replace imports to a great extent. Factories have been turning out—and often exporting—a wide range of goods. These include diesel-electric locomotives, motor vehicles, agricultural and earth-moving equipment, roller bearings, machine tools, cathode-ray picture tubes, synthetic fibers, electronic equipment and appliances, power cables, fiberglass, plastics, fertilizers, pharmaceutical and veterinary products, and petrochemicals.

One of the most important factors in the nation's continuing industrial development is the prosperity of its iron and steel industry. The Broken Hill Proprietary Company Lim-

ited (BHP) and its subsidiaries produce nearly all Australian steel. This company, the largest in Australia, has expanded rapidly. In addition to iron and steel, it has manufactured alloy steels, wire, and other metal products. It is now facing intense foreign competition.

In spite of its small population, Australia has a large domestic market for automobiles. The motor vehicle industry in Australia has long employed more people than any other industry. It has met much of the local demand for motor vehicles, and some vehicles have also been exported. But imported vehicles are a challenge to this industry. Other notable industrial groups include aircraft, textiles, food processing, tobacco, and wood products.

Investment from overseas—most of it coming from the United States, Britain, and Japan —has played a significant part in the development of Australia's manufacturing and mining industries.

Agriculture

Australia has more sheep than any other country in the world and produces nearly one-third of all the world's wool. The merino is the most important breed. It produces more wool than any other breed of sheep. The sheep country is mainly in New South Wales, Western Australia, Victoria, and South Australia.

Australia is also a large producer of meat. More than half of all the meat is beef. Lamb and mutton and smaller amounts of pork and poultry make up the remainder. Much of the beef comes from the large cattle stations in the tropical north country, but many beef cattle are also raised in the sheep areas. Australians eat less than half of the meat produced. The rest is exported in chilled, frozen, or canned form. The United States is an important customer. Japan, the Middle East, and Britain also buy large amounts of Australian meat. Exports of livestock for slaughter in the Middle East are growing.

Dairying is important near the cities along the eastern and southern coasts, where fresh milk is needed daily. The dairy farms are much smaller than the northern cattle stations. Butter, cheese, and other dairy products are produced for home use and for export.

Wheat grows well in eastern and southwestern Australia. The wheat farms are usually very large and mechanized. Many wheat growers also keep sheep as an additional source of income. The sheep are put to graze on the stubble after harvest. Australia exports the greater part of its wheat. Most of the wheat is bought by such countries as China, India, Egypt, Iran, Iraq, Indonesia, and Japan. Barley is another major grain crop.

Fruits are abundant in several places. Pineapples and tropical fruits are grown on the north Queensland coast. Peaches, plums, and citrus fruits flourish near Perth. Apples, plums, and peaches come from Tasmania, and citrus fruits from irrigated areas in the Riverina. The Barossa Valley near Adelaide is known as a wine-making center. Sugarcane is grown along the northeastern coast. Australia is one of the world's leading exporters of sugar.

Mining

Australia has been an important mineral producer since gold was first discovered in the 1850's. For many years, gold was the most important metal, but now it is outranked by coal, iron ore, lead, copper, tin, and zinc. The area around Kalgoorlie in Western Australia is now the center of the nation's gold-mining activity.

Iron ore, chiefly from the Pilbara region of Western Australia, has become one of the nation's most valuable mineral products. Deposits in Western Australia are estimated to total nearly 25,000,000,000 (billion) tons. Australia's exports of iron ore depend more and more on the demand from Japan, which has replaced Britain as Australia's principal trading partner.

Coal is also an important mineral product. Coal is mined in New South Wales and in Queensland. Lignite (brown coal) is mined in Victoria. Coal is used to generate much of Australia's electricity, and large quantities have been exported to Japan and other countries.

Since the end of World War II, the production of oil has become one of Australia's major industries. Most of the oil comes from a vast field off the coast of Victoria, in Bass Strait. Other fields are located west of Brisbane and at Barrow Island, off the northwest coast of Western Australia. Australia now produces enough oil to satisfy most of its domestic needs.

Australia is the world's leading producer of bauxite, used to make aluminum, nearly all of which is exported. Bauxite is mined at Weipa, Queensland; in the Darling Range in Western Australia; and at Gove, Northern Territory. Other important minerals include lead and zinc, at Broken Hill and Mount Isa; copper, from Mount Isa; nickel, near Kalgoorlie in Western Australia; and mineral sand concentrates of rutile and zircon, from the eastern seaboard. There are also vast reserves of uranium near Darwin in the Northern Territory. Diamonds are mined in the Northern Territory and elsewhere. Australia is now the world's largest producer of diamonds.

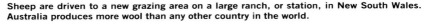

Sheep are driven to a new grazing area on a large ranch, or station, in New South Wales. Australia produces more wool than any other country in the world.

Much of Australia's iron ore comes from mines in Western Australia. Australia is one of the world's major producers of iron ore.

Transportation and Communications

Transportation is well developed. Roads are extensive along the coast. Many of the roads in the outback are unpaved. These red clay roads can be clearly seen from the air. Australia is one of the most highly motorized countries in the world, with one motor vehicle for every two people. Trains are fast and modern. Australia also has one of the largest domestic aviation networks in the world. More than 10,000,000 passengers, as well as considerable amounts of freight, are carried each year on flights within Australia. The outback is particularly dependent on air service as a means of transportation.

Australia is in direct air communication with the major cities of the world. Qantas, Australia's overseas airline, operates services from Sydney to countries around the world. Many other international airlines have regular services to Australia.

The government maintains Australia's internal telegraph and telephone service. The government also operates a network of radio and television stations. Short- and long-wave radio stations are scattered throughout the country. Individually operated voice radios bring distant neighbors closer together in the sparsely settled north. Television is available in most of the populated areas of the country. There are both state and commercial television stations in operation. The larger cities have two or more daily newspapers, and many local papers are published in smaller towns. There is also a wide range of magazines and other periodicals.

▶AUSTRALIA'S STATES AND TERRITORIES

In 1901 the six self-governing colonies of New South Wales, Victoria, Queensland, South Australia, Western Australia, and Tasmania joined together in a federation. The colonies became states, and the federation was called the Commonwealth of Australia.

New South Wales

Almost one third of the people of Australia live in New South Wales, the most populous state. Most people live along the east coast, and more than one half are in Sydney, the capital and largest city. Sydney is also the largest city in Australia. The state of New South Wales is filled with contrasts. People can ski in the mountains in the southern part of the state or visit an almost tropical beach in the north.

New South Wales is Australia's leading industrial state. Most manufacturing is located along the narrow coastal plain. Sydney is the most important center. Other industrial towns include Newcastle and Wollongong. A great variety of products, from ships and motor vehicles to television sets and other appliances, are made in New South Wales. Coal deposits have greatly helped the state's industrial development. Cheap electricity from power plants that use coal and from the Snowy Mountains Hydro-Electric Scheme are expected to attract even more industries.

The farmlands of New South Wales are nearly all west of the Great Dividing Range, at the western foot of the highlands. Beef cattle are important in the drier northwestern sec-

Many aborigines and part-aborigines are learning modern ways. Some work on the large cattle ranches.

tions of the state. Bananas are grown on the north coast. Dams provide irrigation water for the dry lands in the southwest, where rice, citrus fruits, grapes, tomatoes, and other vegetables are grown. Sheep graze extensively in central and western New South Wales, which produces one third of Australia's wool.

Victoria

Victoria is the second smallest state in area and the second largest in population. Most people live in the south. Melbourne is the capital and largest city. Other important towns include Geelong and Ballarat.

Sheep and wheat are the chief products in the southwest and on the plains in the northwest. Cattle raising is the leading activity in the drier foothills of the Eastern Highlands. Many cattle are sent up to pastures in the mountains for the summer. Citrus fruits, grapes, peaches, and apricots are grown on irrigated lands along the Murray River. Truck and dairy farmers supply Melbourne and Geelong with fresh fruits, vegetables, and milk.

Large deposits of lignite from Gippsland, a district east of Melbourne, have helped Victoria's industrial development. Most of the lignite is compressed into briquettes that are used to make electricity. Some is made into gas, which is sent by pipeline to Melbourne. There are also large hydroelectric power stations in the state.

Queensland

The tropical northeastern corner of Australia is in Queensland, Australia's second largest state. Queensland has long stretches of beautiful beaches. These are popular vacation spots for people from the southern states.

In spite of its size, Queensland has a population smaller than that of either New South Wales or Victoria. Most people live along the narrow coastal plain in the east, while the dry interior of the state is thinly populated.

The climate along the east coast is hot and humid. Sugarcane, cotton, and other tropical crops are the leading products. Gold, copper, and coal are mined along the coast. Brisbane, the capital and largest city of the state, is located in the southeast. Few people live along the northern and northeastern coasts, where the rainy summers and dry winters of the monsoon climate make life and farming more difficult.

The vast interior of Queensland is sparsely populated. Some sheep and wheat are produced on the Darling Downs in the southeast, and cattle raising and mining are the leading industries elsewhere. Underground water is the one reliable water source. Artesian wells line all the stock routes between the grazing grounds and the railheads.

Mining communities in the interior are widely scattered. Copper, silver, lead, zinc, coal, and bauxite are mined.

South Australia

In area, South Australia is the third largest state. Most of its people, farms, and industry are in the southeast. Adelaide is the capital and largest city. Woomera is the site of a rocket range and orbital tracking station.

Most of South Australia is too dry for farming. Some wheat is grown east of the Flinders Range and along the eastern margin of Spencer Gulf, but elsewhere all farming depends on irrigation or underground sources of water. From the irrigated lands along the lower course of the Murray River come large quantities of apricots, pears, peaches, nectarines, and grapes. Some of the grapes are used to make wine, and some are dried for raisins, sultanas, and currants. Figs, citrus fruits, and plums are also produced. Beef and dairy cattle are raised on irrigated pastures, and sheep graze on the natural grasslands.

Some of Australia's most unproductive desert lands occupy the remainder of the state. Isolated cattle stations along the railroads to

Perth and Alice Springs and occasional training centers for aborigines are the only signs of civilization.

South Australia has valuable mineral deposits. Iron ore is mined and shipped to the New South Wales steel mills. Coober Pedy is the site of one of the world's largest opal mines.

Western Australia

Nearly 400 years ago, Europeans first touched at the northwest coast of what is now the state of Western Australia. They described it as rugged, dry, and inhospitable. Their description still fits all but the southwestern corner of the state. Barren desert stretches across this largest state of the commonwealth. Only occasionally is the view broken by an isolated mining town or a lonely cattle station.

Nearly all of Western Australia's people and most of the wheat farms, sheep stations, and fruit orchards are in the southwestern corner of the state. This section is connected with the cities in eastern Australia by a railroad across the empty Nullarbor Plain.

Perth, the capital and largest city of Western Australia, is located on the Swan River. Fremantle, the ocean port for Perth, is Australia's largest west coast port and the one nearest to Europe. Albany was an important station for the whaling fleets that once fished in the Antarctic and Indian oceans. Fishing is still important in Western Australia.

Gold was first discovered in Western Australia in 1885, at Hall's Creek, and mining towns sprang up overnight. The richest finds were at Coolgardie in 1892 and Kalgoorlie in 1893. Both of these gold mining towns are in the middle of the desert and depend on a pipeline from near Perth for all their water. The Pilbara region has large iron-ore deposits, and Port Hedland is a major port for both iron ore and salt. Large quantities of bauxite are mined in the Darling Range, and oil is extracted at Barrow Island.

Tasmania

Tasmania, the island state, is sometimes called the apple isle because it once produced most of Australia's apples. It is also famous for its rugged scenery and for the delicious scallops caught along its rocky coasts. At the foot of Mount Wellington is Hobart, the capital and largest city of the island. Other important centers are Launceston and Devonport. A ferryboat connects Devonport with Melbourne on the mainland across Bass Strait.

Tasmania is one of the few places in Australia that has adequate rainfall all year. Tasmania is Australia's leading producer of hops, apples, pears, and berries of different kinds. Potatoes also flourish in this climate and are grown as a specialty in some areas.

The abundance of water has greatly helped the industrial development of the state. Hydroelectric plants are located at many places throughout the island. Many industries that use large amounts of electricity have been attracted to this source of power. There are zinc-refining centers, aluminum smelters, and pulp

Grapes are a major crop in the irrigated areas near Adelaide. Much of the harvest is used for making wine.

and paper mills. Tin, copper, lead, and tungsten are other important mineral products of Tasmania.

Northern Territory

The Northern Territory, which became self-governing in 1978, is the least populated and least developed part of Australia. Crocodiles and wild buffalo still live in some of the marshy coastal swamps. Darwin, the capital, is the only large settlement in the north. Over 90 percent of the city was destroyed by a tropical cyclone in 1974, but rebuilding began at once. Alice Springs, generally called Alice or the Alice, is the only town in the south.

The climate along the coast is hot and wet in summer but too dry for farming in winter. Cattle raising on large stations and mining are the leading industries. Some rice is grown on experimental farms. Copper, gold, uranium, and mica are mined.

▶AUSTRALIA'S CITIES

Most of Australia's people live in the six capital cities of the states and in Canberra, the federal capital. About two out of every five Australians live in Sydney or Melbourne.

Sydney

Sydney, on the east coast, is Australia's largest city and the capital of New South Wales. It was founded on January 26, 1788, and was the first European settlement in the country. Sydney is the home of one fourth of all Australian industry and is the center for Australia's engineering, chemical, and oil-refining industries. Sydney has an excellent harbor and is Australia's leading seaport. Many people enjoy sailing, and the harbor is dotted with boats.

Almost all of the city's older buildings have roofs made of terra cotta tile. The business district is an interesting mixture of old and new. Many buildings, such as the State Parliament House, St. James Church, and the Supreme Court Building, are reminders of the 1800's. But office and apartment buildings made of concrete and glass are rapidly replacing some of the older structures. The Sydney Opera House, opened in 1973, is strikingly modern in design. Another important Sydney landmark is Centrepoint, the tallest building in Australia. The city also has many lovely parks and gardens. A separate article on Sydney appears in Volume S.

Melbourne

Melbourne, which is at the head of Port Phillip Bay, is Australia's second largest city and the capital of Victoria. It is considered the financial center of the nation. From 1901 to 1927 it was the seat of the federal government. Its harbor is the most important on the south coast and the natural outlet for the production of the southeastern part of the country. Old stone buildings and arcades give the city an Old World appearance that often reminds visitors of cities in England.

Melbourne's industrial district lies west and southeast of the city, mainly along the coast. The factories manufacture heavy engineering products, power-station equipment, electrical goods, wool and cotton textiles, clothing, and chemicals. Melbourne is closely tied with Geelong, a nearby industrial city. A separate article on Melbourne appears in Volume M.

Brisbane

Brisbane, on the east coast, is Australia's third largest city and the capital of Queensland. It is the only large Australian city with a subtropical climate. Numerous parks and gardens make Brisbane one of Australia's most beautiful cities. Brisbane is the principal export center for the state's wool, meat, wheat, sugar, and mineral products. Textiles, shoes, and clothing are produced in the city. During World War II, many thousands of Americans passed through Brisbane, which was the headquarters of United States forces in Australia. A monument in the city commemorates the cooperation between the two countries.

Adelaide

Adelaide, the capital of South Australia, is Australia's fourth largest city. The central city is surrounded by a belt of parkland. All the suburbs lie beyond.

Performers from all parts of the world visit Adelaide to take part in the Adelaide Festival of Arts, which is held every two years. The city is also Australia's largest wine-exporting center. Wine from the Barossa Valley is loaded onto oceangoing ships at Port Adelaide on St. Vincent Gulf.

Perth, the capital of Western Australia, is the largest city on the west coast. It is one of the fastest-growing cities in Australia.

Perth

Far to the west of Adelaide is Perth, the capital of Western Australia. It is the major west coast city and Australia's fifth largest city. Perth is said to be Australia's most beautiful city. It reminds many Americans of cities in southern California. Its port, Fremantle, is at the mouth of the Swan River.

The mining boom has brought dramatic changes to Perth. Until 1969 the highest building was 15 stories. Today several skyscrapers are many stories taller. There has been a great deal of investment in such areas as light industry, suburban development, and city buildings. Among the notable recent additions to the city are an entertainment center, a new art gallery, and extensive freeways.

The Perth industrial complex includes the world's largest wheat terminal. This is located at Kwinana, on Cockburn Sound, which is a U.S. Navy port of call.

Hobart

Mount Wellington makes a beautiful background for Hobart, the capital city of Tasmania. Hobart, founded in 1804, is Australia's second oldest city. The city is surrounded by a small but flourishing agricultural area. Fruit, hops, dairy products, wool, and hides are exported through the city. Nearby are large hydroelectric power stations that generate electricity for use in Hobart's flourishing pulp-and-paper industry. Zinc and other metals are smelted near Hobart.

Canberra

Canberra, the national capital, is an important seat of learning and scientific achievement as well as a city of public administration and a center of diplomacy. The site was selected in 1908, and in 1911 an international competition was held to choose a plan for the city. An American architect, Walter Burley Griffin, submitted the prizewinning plan. Construction of the city began in 1923, and four years later the parliament moved from Melbourne to Canberra. Now all branches of the federal government are located in Canberra. An area of 2,432 square kilometers (939 square miles) around the city is designated as the Australian Capital Territory.

Residential suburbs surround a central core where the government buildings, embassies of other nations, and the Australian National University are located. Today the Australian National University is one of the principal centers of nuclear research in the country. It is regularly visited by scholars from other countries. A separate article on Canberra appears in Volume C.

▶GOVERNMENT

Australia is an independent, self-governing nation and a member of the Commonwealth of Nations. The federal government in Canberra conducts national affairs. Each state has its own parliament. Australia was the first country to use the secret ballot. Every Australian citizen over 18 years old is required to vote.

Legislative authority rests with the Federal Parliament, made up of the Senate and the House of Representatives. Each state has ten senators, and each territory has two. The House of Representatives is elected on the basis of population. Its membership is required to be, as nearly as possible, twice that of the Senate. The governor-general is the Queen's representative in Australia, but the actual head of the government is the prime minister. The prime minister is the leader of the governing party or parties in the parliament and is assisted by a cabinet. In 1975, the parliament and the prime minister were unable to resolve a bitter dispute. The governor-general, for the only time in Australia's history, used his authority to remove the prime minister from office.

The High Court of Australia is the judicial branch of the federal government. It interprets the constitution and settles disputes between the states. State governments administer state affairs. City, town, and shire councils manage the affairs of smaller state localities.

▶ HISTORY

Even in medieval times there were stories about a large continent in the Southern Hemisphere. But Europeans had never seen it. They wondered what it was like and whether it was inhabited. They called this land *terra australis incognita*, or "the unknown southern land."

Discovery and Exploration

The Dutch were the first Europeans to visit Australia. They sighted it while making their journeys between the Netherlands and the island of Java, a Dutch colony in what is now Indonesia. Ships sailing from the Netherlands to Java used to go around the southern tip of Africa (the Cape of Good Hope) and then sail across the Indian Ocean with the westerly winds. Many navigators sailed too far east before turning north toward Java and found themselves on the west coast of Australia. They later gave the name New Holland to this western part of the continent.

But the Dutch did not know how far east this southern continent extended, and in 1642, Captain Abel Janszoon Tasman was sent out to discover what lay in the east. Tasman sailed too far south and failed to see the mainland, but he did visit the island now called Tasmania in his honor. He named this island Van Diemen's Land. Tasman then continued eastward to New Zealand. Later he explored Australia's north coast and gave Dutch names to places like Groote Eylandt.

No careful explorations of the continent were made for another century or so. Then in 1770 the English captain James Cook sighted the east coast of Australia and named it New South Wales. He visited Botany Bay, near what is now modern Sydney, and reported back to England that the bay and much of New South Wales looked good for settlement. In London the British Government was concerned about the Revolutionary War in America and did not listen to his suggestions. For many years the British had been sending convicts to the American colonies to relieve overcrowded jails in England. When the colonies won their independence, the British looked around for another place to send their convicts. It was decided to send some to Botany Bay on the coast of New South Wales.

Early Settlement

In May, 1787, the first group of convicts and a few soldiers left Portsmouth, England, for the trip to Australia. Eleven ships and about 1,500 men made the trip. The ships reached Botany Bay in mid-January, 1788. But a few days after their arrival, the governor of the group decided that Port Jackson (now Sydney Harbour), a little farther north, was a better place for a colony. He took the fleet there and established a settlement, which he named Sydney.

More convicts followed, and new penal colonies were established in other parts of the continent. Hobart, on Tasmania (then known as Van Diemen's Land), was established in 1804. Another colony, which later became the city of Brisbane, was begun at Moreton Bay, on the eastern coast, in 1824. Albany, in southwestern Australia, was founded in 1826.

The coastline of Australia was only vaguely known at this time. In fact, not until 1798 did George Bass, a naval surgeon and explorer, sail along the south coast. He proved that Tasmania was an island. The strait separating the island from the continent was named Bass Strait in his honor. And not until 1801 did Matthew Flinders, a captain in the Royal Navy, discover and chart Kangaroo Island

and Spencer and St. Vincent gulfs along the south coast.

Life was very difficult for the early convicts and for the soldiers in charge of the colonies. The colonies depended on ships from England for all their food and supplies. Farming was difficult, and there were few tools. It was at this time that Captain John Macarthur began breeding fine merino sheep for their wool, at Camden, near Sydney. He sent his first batch of wool to England in 1807. The wool industry flourished and later became Australia's most important industry. The merino, originally a native of the dry and dusty plains of Spain, was to prove well suited to life in Australia's interior.

IMPORTANT DATES

1642	Abel Tasman sighted and named Van Diemen's Land (Tasmania).
1770	New South Wales was claimed for Britain.
1788	First British settlement was founded at Port Jackson (Sydney Harbour).
1797	John Macarthur began raising merino sheep.
1798	George Bass sighted the strait (Bass Strait) named in his honor.
1803	Matthew Flinders completed the first circumnavigation of the Australian coast.
1813	An expedition crossed the Blue Mountains.
1825	Van Diemen's Land separated from New South Wales.
1829	Swan River colony (Western Australia) was begun.
1836	Colony of South Australia was first settled.
1851	Victoria separated from New South Wales; gold was discovered in both colonies.
1853	Van Diemen's Land became Tasmania.
1859	Queensland separated from New South Wales.
1862	John McDouall Stuart crossed Australia from south to north.
1891	First federal convention was held.
1892–1893	Gold was discovered in Western Australia.
1898	Second federal convention was held.
1901	Commonwealth of Australia was formed.
1914–1918	Australia fought in World War I.
1925	Parliament moved from Melbourne to Canberra.
1939–1945	Australia fought in World War II; Japanese planes bombed Darwin (1942).
1945	Australia became one of the original members of the United Nations.
1950	Australia contributed forces to the U.N. command in the Korean War; Australia became a member of the Colombo Plan.
1951	ANZUS Security Treaty between Australia, New Zealand, and the United States was signed.
1965–1972	Australian troops fought in the Vietnam War.
1970	Australians celebrated the 200th anniversary of Captain James Cook's landing at Botany Bay.
1974	Darwin was destroyed by a tropical cyclone.
1978	The Northern Territory was granted internal self-government.
1984	Residents of the Cocos Islands voted to become part of Australia.
1988	Australia Day marked the bicentennial (200th anniversary) of British settlement in Australia.

Many convicts earned their freedom and stayed on in Australia, but at first, free English settlers were outnumbered in all of the penal colonies. As more settlers saw the opportunities of the new continent, various free colonies, quite apart from the penal colonies, were founded. The first free colony was the Swan River colony, established in 1829 in southwest Australia. The free colony of South Australia was first settled in 1836. Settlers from Tasmania and New South Wales established the Port Phillip District in New South Wales in 1835–37. This became the colony of Victoria in 1851.

For 25 years the New South Wales colony was restricted to a narrow stretch of lowland along the east coast. Then in 1813 three explorers—Gregory Blaxland, William Lawson, and William Charles Wentworth—found a way across the Blue Mountains behind Port Jackson. They were the first Europeans to see the vast plains beyond the Great Dividing Range. Two years later, Bathurst, the first inland settlement, was established.

Other explorers went farther inland. In 1824, Hamilton Hume came across a river in the interior that he called the Hume River. In 1829, Captain Charles Sturt explored the Darling and, not knowing that he had rediscovered the Hume River, renamed the Hume River the Murray River. In 1836, Major Thomas Mitchell explored the Darling River and the grassy plains of the Riverina.

Close behind the explorers came the sheep drovers, always on the lookout for new grazing lands. Some of Australia's most distinguished families are descended from these pasture seekers. Most of the early graziers were squatters. They had no legal title to the land and just settled, or squatted, wherever they saw land that would provide good grazing for their sheep.

Later explorers made longer journeys into the desert and the north. One of them was Edward John Eyre, who in 1841 came upon the great salt lake in central Australia that now bears his name. Another was Friedrich Wilhelm Ludwig Leichhardt, who in 1844 and 1845 traveled overland from Brisbane to the north coast. John McDouall Stuart in 1861 and 1862 journeyed from Adelaide in the south to near the site of Darwin in the north.

Nationhood

The six early colonies grew and became states of modern Australia. The original colony of New South Wales occupied almost all of the eastern half of the continent when it was founded in 1788. Three other colonies were later separated from New South Wales. One was Tasmania, which became a colony in 1825. Another, Victoria, became a colony in 1851, and a third, Queensland, was separated in 1859. Western Australia grew up around the Swan River colony, founded in 1829. What became the Northern Territory was originally a part of South Australia. The six colonies all became self-governing during the latter half of the 1800's.

The independent colonies soon realized the need to act together on certain matters. And toward the end of the 1800's, they began to seek a basis for federation. A first constitution was drawn up in 1891, and a second in 1898. The constitution was approved by the British Government, and on January 1, 1901, the six separate colonies became states in the new Commonwealth of Australia.

History Since Independence

The new government soon established a system of tariffs, or duties on imports. This protected domestic markets from foreign competition, as well as serving as a form of taxation. The government also set up an immigration policy that encouraged British settlers to come to Australia.

With the outbreak of World War I in 1914, Australia joined forces with Britain and its allies. In World War II, Australia again took part on the side of Britain. Its forces fought first in the Middle East and then in the Pacific, nearer its own shores, when Japan entered the war in 1941. Japanese planes bombed the city of Darwin in 1942.

Australia has become increasingly active in world affairs since World War II. It is a charter member of the United Nations. In 1950 it helped establish the Colombo Plan, an international effort designed to assist developing nations in southeastern Asia. In that same year, Australian troops were sent to Korea as part of the U.N. command. Australia signed the ANZUS defense pact with the United States and New Zealand in 1951 and joined the now-defunct Southeast Asia Treaty Organization (SEATO) in 1954. A significant proportion of Australia's national income each year is allocated to assisting the developing countries, especially those in the South Pacific region. Australia is an active member of the South Pacific Commission, which promotes co-operation among its members in the South Pacific.

Since World War II, the Australian government has devoted much effort to breaking down the isolation of the remote areas of the nation by expanding transportation and communication facilities and establishing programs like the Royal Flying Doctor Service and radio and correspondence schools. The Department of Aboriginal Affairs was created to improve opportunities for the aborigines.

Increased demand and a scarcity of imports during World War II provided a major stimulus to Australian industry. In the economic boom that followed the war, Australia was faced with a shortage of labor. The government assisted immigrants from many countries to come to Australia. Under the program millions of new immigrants have been resettled successfully. When, in the 1970's, a decrease in the rate of population growth brought renewed concern for Australia's economic security, the government, for the first time, encouraged immigration from Asia. The loss of Australia's preferential trading status with Britain, after British entry into the European Community in 1973, also prompted the government to shift its traditional trading patterns from Europe to Asia.

During the 1980's and into the early 1990's, Australia faced a number of economic problems. It was difficult to find markets for Australian coal, and the rising cost of steel hurt the country's industry. Widespread floods, following severe drought, reduced farm yields. Inflation and unemployment became important political issues.

On a more positive note, 1988 marked the bicentennial, or 200th anniversary, of British settlement in Australia. The historic event was celebrated as Australia Day, with several million people joining in the festivities at Sydney Harbour, the site of the landing of the first settlers from Britain.

CHARLES M. DAVIS
University of Michigan

See also ABORIGINES, AUSTRALIAN.

AUSTRIA

The people of Austria call their country Österreich, which can be translated as "eastern realm." The origin of the name dates back to the A.D. 900's, when Austria was an eastern border region of the Holy Roman Empire. From this beginning, Austria itself grew into a great empire. It reached its height in the 1500's, when the Habsburgs, its ruling family, controlled lands that stretched from Austria to Spain and included the vast Spanish colonial possessions in the Americas.

Although the empire declined from this high point, it survived for another 400 years, until its collapse in 1918, at the end of World War I. From its ruins modern Austria emerged, along with other present-day nations of central and eastern Europe.

▶ THE PEOPLE

The Austrians are of various ethnic backgrounds, but most share a common language, religion, and culture.

Language and Religion. German, the official language of Austria, is spoken by almost all of its people. The chief non-German-speaking peoples—Slovenes, Croats, and Hungarians —speak German as their second language. Austrians also take pride in their regional dialects of German, such as the *Wienerisch* spoken in Vienna, the capital.

The great majority of Austrians are Roman Catholics. Many saints' days and church holidays of the Roman Catholic Church are widely celebrated. A small number of people belong to various Protestant churches. Austria had about 84,000 Jews before World War II, but by the end of the war, only a few remained. Many had been killed by German and Austrian Nazis, and thousands had fled their homeland.

Education. School is compulsory for Austrian children between the ages of 6 and 14. All children must attend elementary school, or *Volksschule*, for four years. Students may then go on to several different kinds of secondary schools. A student wishing to prepare for college attends a *Gymnasium*. Trade and technical schools train students for non-academic careers. The University of Vienna, founded in 1365, is the oldest and best known of Austria's universities.

Mountains are Austria's dominant land feature, making up some two thirds of the country's total area. The snow-covered Grossglockner ("great bell"), the highest peak in the Austrian Alps, can be seen in the distance.

Life in Vienna, Austria's capital and largest city, is both colorful and elegant. *Top left:* Folk musicians provide outdoor entertainment. *Above:* Coffeehouses have been popular meeting places since coffee was first introduced here in the 1600's. *Left:* The famed Vienna Choir Boys perform wearing their traditional sailor suits.

Dress. Austrians in the large cities wear modern clothing. But for holidays and special occasions, people sometimes put on traditional local costumes. The women wear a *Dirndl*, which is a colorful dress with aprons and elaborately embroidered headdresses. Men and boys wear short leather pants, called *Lederhosen*, and simple shirts and jackets made of homespun linen or a coarse woolen cloth called *Loden*.

Holidays. Religious holidays and other festivals are joyful occasions in Austria. In some regions there is a boisterous festival for scaring away the winter. The villagers wear ugly masks and make as much noise as they can with bells and drums.

A favorite holiday throughout Austria is December 6, or Nikolo Day. This is the day when Saint Nicholas, or Nikolo (Santa Claus), visits Austrian children. The night before, children leave their shoes where Nikolo will find them. In the morning, children who have been good find presents in their shoes, but those who have been bad find only lumps of coal and potatoes.

Weddings are very special occasions in the villages, where they are celebrated with much singing and dancing. One of the most exciting dances to watch is the *Schuhplattler*, in which the men slap first their thighs, then their knees, and then the soles of their feet while the women twirl around them in their bright dresses. The dancers are accompanied by the music of zithers or violins. The musicians play faster and faster toward the end of the dance until the dancers are out of breath.

In January and February, just before the Roman Catholic period of Lent, Austrians enjoy the carnival season, known as *Fasching*. Elaborate costume balls are often part of the festivities, especially in the cities.

Other Special Events. Three music festivals that are held in Austria each year attract thousands of music lovers from all over the world. The Vienna drama and music festival is held in June. The Salzburg festival, held in August, features the works of Wolfgang Amadeus Mozart (who was born in Salzburg) and other composers. The Bregenz festival, also held in August, specializes in light opera.

REPUBLIC OF AUSTRIA (Republik Österreich) is the official name of the country.

LOCATION: Central Europe.

AREA: 32,374 sq mi (83,849 km²).

POPULATION: 7,700,000 (estimate).

CAPITAL AND LARGEST CITY: Vienna.

MAJOR LANGUAGE: German (official).

MAJOR RELIGION: Christian (mainly Roman Catholic).

GOVERNMENT: Republic. **Head of state**—president. **Head of government**—chancellor. **Legislature**—Federal Assembly (composed of a National Council and a Federal Council).

CHIEF PRODUCTS: Agricultural—wheat, barley, and other grains, potatoes, sugar beets, livestock, dairy products. **Manufactured**—metals and metal products, machinery, textiles, chemicals, lumber, wood products, processed foods. **Mineral**—magnesite, iron ore, graphite, lignite (brown coal), zinc, lead, petroleum, natural gas, bauxite, copper.

MONETARY UNIT: Schilling (1 schilling = 100 groschen).

Another favorite pastime of Austrians is a visit to a café, or coffeehouse. There one can meet friends, chat, read the newspapers, and enjoy delicious coffee and pastries.

Sports. Mountain climbing, swimming, waterskiing, and sailing are favorite summer sports. The cold, snowy winters are perfect for skiing and ice-skating. Skiing is so much a part of the Austrian way of life that school-children take ski courses between February and April as part of their schoolwork.

Soccer is Austria's most popular spectator sport. Large cities have huge stadiums and regularly scheduled soccer games. Soccer players are great heroes to Austrian children. Even the smallest Austrian village has its own amateur soccer team.

▶**THE LAND**

Austria is wedged between eight other countries. Switzerland and tiny Liechtenstein lie to the west and Germany to the northwest. The Czech Republic and Slovakia are situated on the north, Hungary on the east, and Italy and Slovenia on the south. Austria has five natural regions—the eastern Alps, the Alpine Foreland, the Granite Uplands, the Vienna Basin, and the Styrian Basin.

The Alps. The Alps, which cover about two thirds of the country, have three main divisions—the Northern Limestone Alps, the Central Alps, and the Southern Limestone Alps. The highest mountains are in the Central Alps. Austria's highest peak, the Grossglockner ("great bell"), is located there. Deep valleys lie between the main ranges.

Alpine Foreland and Granite Uplands. The Alpine Foreland lies between the Alps and the Danube River in the provinces of Salzburg, Upper Austria, and Lower Austria. It is a region of fertile hills and valleys where cattle graze and vegetable crops are grown. The cities of Salzburg and Linz are both in this region.

Just north of the Danube River are the rolling, forest-covered hills of the Granite Uplands. They occupy the parts of the provinces of Lower Austria and Upper Austria that lie north of the Danube River.

Vienna and Styrian Basins. The Vienna Basin, in eastern Austria, is the country's heartland. It contains all of Austria's best farmland and is also the center of Austrian industry. Vienna lies in the middle of the Vienna Basin.

The Styrian Basin, in the province of Styria, is situated to the south of the Vienna Basin. It is quite fertile, with grain crops and fruit grown in its broad valleys.

Rivers. The Danube is Austria's most important river and one of Europe's major commercial waterways. When the sun is not shining, the Danube looks brown and muddy and very different from the beautiful "Blue Danube" for which Johann Strauss, Jr., named one of his great waltzes.

Other important rivers are the Inn, Salzach, and Enns. All are tributaries (branches) of the Danube. Fed by melting glaciers in the Alps, they flow too swiftly for river traffic. But they are an important source of hydroelectric power, which provides much of Austria's energy needs. Hydroelectric power is also exported to neighboring countries.

Climate. Three of Europe's major climatic regions meet in Austria. Northern Austria has an Atlantic type of climate with mild, rainy winters and cool, moist summers. Southern Austria has a Mediterranean climate with hot, dry summers and mild, rainy winters. Eastern Austria has the hot summers and cold winters typical of the continental climate.

The mountains have their own characteristic climate, marked by heavy snowfall in winter. An unusual feature of the mountain climate is the *Foehn*, a warm, dry wind that blows from the high mountains. The *Foehn* "eats up" the snow from the ground. Farmers are delighted to see the snow disappear, for it means that they can soon drive their livestock up to the mountain pastures for the summer. But they also fear the destructive avalanches that sometimes hurtle down the mountainside when the melting snow becomes dislodged.

▶ **THE ECONOMY**

The Austrian economy is based chiefly on industry. Agriculture, although still important, plays a much smaller role economically than in former times.

Industry. Austria industrialized rapidly in the years after the end of World War II. In 1946 a number of basic industries, such as iron and steel, mining, and utilities, were nationalized, or brought under state control, by the government. Today, industry employs nearly 40 percent of the work force. It provides a similar percentage of the country's gross national product (the total value of goods and services produced in a year).

The leading manufactured goods include metals and metal products, machinery, textiles, and chemicals. Tourism is also important. Millions of visitors come to Austria each year, particularly to Vienna and the Alpine resorts.

Mining. Austria has a number of valuable mineral resources. It is the world's leading producer of magnesite and an important producer of graphite. Most of Austria's iron ore comes from the Erzberg ("Ore Mountain") in Styria. Bauxite (aluminum ore), lignite (low-grade brown coal), copper, lead, and zinc are also mined. Austria has some petroleum and natural gas but it still must import fuel.

Agriculture and Forestry. Because Austria is so mountainous, only about 20 percent of its land can be cultivated. Nevertheless, Austrian farmers supply most of the country's food needs. Most of the suitable farming land is in the Alpine valleys. Wheat, barley, and other grains, potatoes, and sugar beets are the leading crops. Various fruits and vegetables are grown and some wine is produced. Cattle and sheep provide large quantities of meat, milk, butter, and cheese.

Austria's forests provide valuable lumber and the raw materials for a variety of wood products, including paper.

▶ **MAJOR CITIES**

The majority of Austrians are city-dwellers. About one third of the population live in the five largest cities—Vienna, Graz, Linz, Salzburg, and Innsbruck.

Vienna is the capital and largest city. Its location on the Danube River at the edge of the East European plain has made it an important city throughout history. See the separate article on Vienna in Volume U-V.

Graz is Austria's second largest city and the capital of the province of Styria. A manufacturing center, it is also noted for its many parks and gardens. Linz is the capital and cultural heart of Upper Austria. Salzburg, situated on the Salzach River is considered one of the world's most beautiful cities. Its annual music festival attracts many visitors. Innsbruck, the capital of Tyrol, is probably best known for its ski resorts. It was the site of the 1964 and 1976 Winter Olympic Games.

Austria's cultural heritage includes many great figures in music, literature, and art. Among the most important are (*top row, from left*) composers Joseph Haydn, Wolfgang Amadeus Mozart (as a boy), and Franz Schubert; (*bottom row, from left*) authors Arthur Schnitzler and Franz Kafka; and painter Oskar Kokoschka (in a self-portrait).

▶CULTURAL HERITAGE

Austria and lands that were once a part of the Austrian empire have produced many important figures in the world of music, literature, and art. Only a relatively few names can be cited here.

Music. Much of the world's great music was written by Austrians or by composers who made Austria their home.

The greatest period of Austrian music, from about 1730 to 1830, produced Joseph Haydn, Mozart, Ludwig van Beethoven (who lived in Vienna most of his life), and Franz Schubert. The two giants of music in the 1800's were Johannes Brahms (who spent the last twenty years of his life in Vienna), and Anton Bruckner. The Strauss family, especially Johann, Jr., and Johann, Sr., made the Viennese waltz world famous. Gustav Mahler continued the great Viennese tradition into the early 1900's. Arnold Schoenberg and Alban Berg were two of the leading modern composers.

Austria is also the birthplace of one of the most famous Christmas carols—"Silent Night" (*Stille Nacht*), written on Christmas Eve, 1818, by Franz Gruber and Joseph Mohr.

See the article on German (and Austrian) music in Volume G.

Literature and Art. In literature, Austrians have made important contributions to drama, poetry, the short story, and the novel. The dramatist Franz Grillparzer, in the 1800's, combined the German classical tradition with Austrian and modern elements. Hugo von Hofmannsthal wrote plays and poems, as well as librettos for operas by the German composer Richard Strauss, in the late 1800's and early 1900's. At about the same time, Arthur Schnitzler was writing plays and stories on psychological themes.

The poet Rainer Maria Rilke and the short-story writer and novelist Franz Kafka are two of the greatest literary figures from this same period. Kafka (whose short life was spent in Prague, now the capital of Czechoslovakia) wrote symbolic stories about the anxiety of modern life. Other important authors from the first half of the 1900's include novelists Robert Musil, Stefan Zweig, and Franz Werfel.

The beginnings of the modern period of Austrian art are reflected in the paintings of Gustav Klimt. Klimt, who died in 1918, was a leader in the movement that led to expressionism. His work influenced two other important 20th century Austrian artists, Oskar Kokoschka and Egon Schiele.

▶GOVERNMENT

Austria is a federal republic made up of nine provinces: Burgenland, Carintha, Lower Austria, Upper Austria, Salzburg, Styria, Tyrol, Vienna, and Vorarlberg.

The president of Austria, who is elected for six years, is the head of state. The national legislature is the Federal Assembly, composed of the National Council and the Federal Council. The National Council is elected by the people for 4-year terms. The Federal Council, which has only limited powers, is elected by the provincial legislatures. The president appoints the chancellor (prime minister) to head the government. The chancellor and ministers of the government are usually members of the political party with the largest number of seats in the National Council, and they are responsible to that body.

Each of the provinces has its own legislature and governor, with control over its local affairs.

▶HISTORY

Early History. The discovery of ancient burial grounds shows that Austria was inhabited in prehistoric times. About 15 B.C. the region was conquered by the Romans. One of their settlements, Vindobona, eventually became the city of Vienna. With the collapse of the Roman Empire in the West in the A.D. 400's, the region fell to eastern invaders. Not until the time of Charlemagne's empire in the 700's was a stable government re-established.

In 976 the Holy Roman emperor Otto II gave part of Austria to Leopold of Babenberg. The Babenbergs ruled for 300 years. When the line died out, Austria passed to the kingdom of Bohemia (now part of the Czech Republic).

Rise of the Habsburgs. In 1278, Rudolph of Habsburg, who was then Holy Roman emperor, defeated the Bohemian king Ottokar II at the Battle of Marchfeld. Rudolph acquired the Austrian lands, which he and his descendants were to govern continuously until 1918. During that time, Austria became the center of a vast Habsburg empire that often dominated the rest of Europe. The German princes elected a Habsburg to rule the Holy Roman Empire for all but five years between 1438 and 1806, when the empire came to an end.

Austria's real power came from those lands that it owned outright and ruled by heredity. The Habsburgs expanded these possessions, often by military alliances with other countries. They frequently sealed these alliances by offering their sons and daughters in marriage to the children of other rulers.

The greatest matchmaker of all was Emperor Maximilian I. His marriage to Mary of Burgundy in 1477 eventually gave him control of the prosperous Low Countries and parts of northern France. Maximilian then arranged for his son Philip to marry Juana, heiress to the throne of Spain.

Height of Power: Charles V. In 1516, Philip's son, Charles of Ghent, inherited the throne of Spain as King Charles I. When Charles's grandfather Maximilian died in 1519, he became emperor, as Charles V, as well. Charles ruled over more territory than any previous European monarch.

Charles's empire was so vast that he gave Austria to his younger brother Ferdinand in 1522. Through his marriage to Anne of Hungary and Bohemia, Ferdinand was chosen ruler of both these kingdoms in 1526. The House of Austria now governed two empires. Through Charles V, the Spanish branch ruled Spain, the Low Countries (the Netherlands, Belgium, and Luxembourg), much of Italy, and Spain's American colonies. At the same time, the Austrian branch headed by Ferdinand ruled in Austria, Hungary, what is now Germany, the Czech Republic, Croatia, Slovenia, half of Romania, and parts of northern Italy.

A painting from about 1515 depicts three generations of the Habsburg family, which ruled Austria for some 600 years. The emperor Maximilian I is at the left.

Two Centuries of Wars. The Habsburgs' empire soon came under attack from two directions. From the east the Ottoman Turks conquered most of Hungary, which they held until the end of the 1600's. To the west other European rulers attacked Austria and Spain because they feared that the Habsburgs had grown too powerful. Most notable of the conflicts was the Thirty Years' War, which began in 1618 and involved most of Europe before ending in 1648. Although defeated in the Thirty Years' War, Austria was able to win back Hungary from the Turks. See the article on the Thirty Years' War in Volume T.

In 1701 the Habsburgs were at war again. The last Spanish Habsburg, Charles II, had died the previous year, and Louis XIV of France claimed the vacant throne for his grandson Philip of Anjou. England and the Netherlands joined Austria and the Holy Roman Empire against France in the so-called War of the Spanish Succession. The war ended in compromise in 1714. Louis' grandson Philip got Spain and its American colonies. Austria received what was left of the Spanish Netherlands (today's Belgium and Luxembourg) as well as most of Spain's possessions in Italy.

Maria Theresa. Yet another war of succession broke out in 1740, when Emperor Charles VI died without male heirs. Normally, women could not inherit the throne. But before he died, Charles VI had issued a will, called the Pragmatic Sanction, that left his entire empire to his eldest daughter, Maria Theresa. Immediately after Charles's death, several foreign rulers tried to seize Maria Theresa's inheritance, in what became known as the War of the Austrian Succession. After eight years of war she lost the wealthy province of Silesia, but held on to the rest of her empire.

Maria Theresa strengthened the power of Austria's ruler against the country's powerful nobles and church leaders. She also continued the Habsburg policy of making political marriages. She ended nearly three centuries of hostility between France and Austria by marrying her daughter Marie Antoinette to the future King Louis XVI of France. Marie was intelligent but unpopular in France. Her life ended tragically in 1793, when she was executed (along with her husband, Louis) during the French Revolution. An article on Marie Antoinette appears in Volume M.

Joseph II. Maria Theresa's son, Joseph II, helped his mother to rule. After her death in 1780, he became sole ruler. Among his many reforms, Joseph freed the serfs, who had been bound by law to the land they tilled, and drastically reduced the power of the nobles and the church. His Edict of Tolerance granted religious freedom to Protestants and Jews in the Austrian lands.

Napoleon and Metternich. The outbreak of the French Revolution in 1789 had renewed Austria's age-old rivalry with France. The victories by the French general Napoleon brought about many changes, including the destruction, in 1806, of the Holy Roman Empire that Austria had controlled for so long. To save Austria itself, the new emperor, Francis II (who had come to the throne in 1792), gave his daughter, Archduchess Marie Louise, to Napoleon in marriage in 1810.

The clever policies of Francis' chief minister, Clemens von Metternich, contributed to the final defeat of Napoleon and France in 1814. In that year, Metternich invited the other European rulers to meet in Vienna. At this Congress of Vienna, many of the borders that Napoleon had redrawn and the monarchs that he had overthrown were restored.

For more than thirty years, Metternich used repressive measures in an effort to protect Europe's rulers from the growing forces of liberalism and nationalism.

Revolution of 1848: Francis Joseph. But it was impossible to ignore the increasing feelings of nationalism among the Austrian empire's many different peoples. In 1848 a revolution erupted, which was put down only after much bloodshed. Metternich was dismissed, and Emperor Ferdinand, who had come to the throne in 1835, abdicated in favor of his 18-year-old nephew, Francis Joseph.

Francis Joseph was forced to agree to several constitutional reforms. The most lasting was the Great Compromise of 1867, which gave Hungary equal status with Austria in the new dual monarchy of Austria-Hungary.

Tensions remained, however, between the various ethnic groups, especially the Czechs and Germans of Bohemia. In addition, neighboring countries desired those parts of the empire that contained peoples who spoke their language.

Breakup of the Empire. In 1914 a Serb nationalist assassinated the heir to the imperial

The empire of Austria-Hungary reached its peak in 1914, just before the outbreak of World War I. The empire collapsed in 1918, with Austria-Hungary's defeat.

throne, Archduke Francis Ferdinand. The event led to the outbreak of World War I, in which Austria-Hungary and its main ally, Germany, were defeated.

The aged Francis Joseph did not live to see the final breakup of the empire. He had died in 1916, after a reign of 68 years. His successor, Charles I, the last emperor, was compelled to accept the end of the Habsburg empire in October 1918. At the peace conference that followed, Austria and Hungary were divided into two much smaller republics. Most of their former territory went into the creation of two new nations—Czechoslovakia and Yugoslavia, and part of a re-established Poland. In addition, Italy received much of the Austrian Tyrol, while Romania acquired Transylvania from Hungary.

Republic of Austria.   With the loss of its empire the young Austrian republic faced severe economic difficulties. Economic problems led to political strife. Most Austrians favored *Anschluss*, or union, with Germany, although this had been forbidden by the peace treaties. In 1938, Nazi Germany's Austrian-born dictator Adolf Hitler sent troops into Austria, which became the German state of Ostmark. Thus, Austria was part of Germany during World War II. When the war ended in 1945, both Austria and its capital were divided into American, British, French, and Soviet zones of occupation. The occupation forces left Austria in 1955, after it signed a treaty agreeing to a policy of permanent neutrality.

Austria Today.   In the years since, Austria has enjoyed both economic prosperity and political stability. Vienna benefited from Austrian neutrality by serving as a favorite meeting place for many international bodies. In 1972 an Austrian, Kurt Waldheim, was elected secretary-general of the United Nations. A controversy did arise in 1986, after Waldheim was elected president of Austria. Jewish groups and others around the world criticized him for his World War II army service with Nazi forces that committed war crimes in the Balkans. Waldheim denied knowledge of these atrocities and likely did not participate in them. But most Austrians were relieved when he decided to retire from politics at the end of his term in 1991.

The Austrian government has pressed for membership in the European Community (EC). However, many Austrians are reluctant to abandon the country's neutral position or sacrifice their identity in a new economic union with a powerful Germany. The Austrians are eager to maintain an identity separate from that of Germany. Although speaking the same language, Austrians point to their country's distinctive history and culture. Like the Germans, they are an industrious and prosperous people. But they consider themselves warmer and more easygoing than their neighbors to the north.

GEORGE W. HOFFMAN
University of Texas at Austin
Author, *Austria*

CHARLES W. INGRAO
Purdue University
Author, *The Habsburg Monarchy, 1618–1815*

See also HABSBURGS; HOLY ROMAN EMPIRE.

AUTOBIOGRAPHY.   See BIOGRAPHY, AUTOBIOGRAPHY, AND BIOGRAPHICAL NOVEL.

Autographs

Asking your friends to write in an autograph album may start you on a hobby that will last the rest of your life. There are two million autograph collectors, and every year they spend enormous sums to add signatures, letters, and documents to their collections. Your hobby need not be expensive, though. It all depends on what autographs you collect.

The word "autograph" comes from the Greek words *autos*, meaning "self," and *graphos*, "written." Sports stars who write their names for you on a tournament program or piece of paper are giving you their autographs. So are performers who sign your theater programs and authors who sign your copies of their books.

Many collectors prefer to solicit signatures and letters from celebrities in person or by mail. If you write to famous persons for their signatures, be sure to enclose self-addressed, stamped envelopes for the replies. Signatures are very interesting, but letters are more dramatic and usually more valuable. It is often a good idea to ask your correspondent an interesting question. The greatest autograph collection in the United States is in the Morgan Library in New York City. It was started by the financier J. P. Morgan (1837–1913) when he was only 12 years old and began writing to Methodist Episcopal bishops for their signatures.

The ancient Romans collected autographs, and letters of Virgil and Caesar were prized. In Europe during the Renaissance, students collected the autographs of their friends in pocket-size albums called *alba amicorum* (albums of friends). Today autograph collectors gather documents, letters, diaries, manuscripts, and composers' original scores.

The most popular collection in the United States is a set of the presidents' autographs. These can be either simple signatures cut from documents or letters handwritten and dated while the president was in office. In England and other European countries there is a similar interest in kings and queens, emperors, presidents, and dictators. It is not always easy to obtain an authentic presidential signature. Many presidents have used "proxy signers"—persons who have learned to imitate the signatures of other persons to relieve them of some of their work. Nowadays, too, electrical devices that make it possible to sign letters automatically—with one's own pen—have reduced the number of original signatures.

Another popular collection is that of the autographs of the signers of the U.S. Declaration of Independence. The two rarest signatures are those of Button Gwinnett and Thomas Lynch, Jr. Button Gwinnett was killed in a duel with his political rival 9 months after signing, and Lynch died when he was only 30. A letter of Button Gwinnett's was once auctioned off for $51,000. A complete set of signers' autographs was sold in 1978 for $195,000. But documents of many signers—Robert Morris, for instance—are available for less than $100.

Authors' original manuscripts are also particularly prized. Today many writers give their collected works to universities or other institutions so that the works will be kept together and preserved. If this had been done in earlier times, we would not have lost all of Shakespeare's original manuscripts. Even his signature is scarce. Only six authentic ones are known to exist. If another authentic signature were to turn up, it would sell for at least $1,000,000.

Books that are collected for their autographs fall into four types. Signed books have only the author's signature in them. Inscribed books include names of both author and owner of the book. The owner asks the author to write both their names. An inscription might read "To Ben Martin from Rosa Lopez." A presentation book is one the author presents to someone, writing in it to show it is a gift. The fourth type is quite different. It is valued for its association with something or someone that interests the collector. Usually it is a book that has belonged to a famous woman or man and has a signature or inscription inside to prove it.

When autographs are put on the market to be sold, they are classified as follows:

Cut Signature—a signature torn or cut out of the flyleaf of a book or from a letter.

D.S. (Document Signed)—a signature on a document that is more or less intact.

L.S. (Letter Signed)—a letter dictated to a secretary and signed by the author.

A.L.S. (Autograph Letter Signed)—a letter written personally in longhand and signed by the author. This is the most valuable.

Other factors deciding the value of an autograph are rarity, quality, and demand.

Some autographs sold during the 1970's, mainly at auctions, brought these prices:

A handwritten letter signed by Richard Nixon as president—$6,250; a short handwritten speech by John F. Kennedy—$8,000; a Paul Revere expense account, signed by John Hancock—$70,000.

Of course, what the letter is about has a great deal to do with its value. It does not even have to have been written by a famous person. The correspondence and diaries of people of no public importance who lived during unusual times, such as a soldier describing his experiences during the Civil War, may give valuable information or shed new light upon the happenings of those times.

In caring for your collection, it is wise to follow a few simple rules: Never attempt to make major repairs yourself, but be sure to take care of small breaks and tears to prevent further damage. Use thin strips of ordinary tissue paper applied with common white library paste on one side of the tear only and, if possible, not over writing. Never use glue or tape. Fold as little as possible. Remove clips and pins. Avoid direct light, heat, and dampness. Keep letters flat in folders and the folders flat on a shelf so the letters will not slip down and wrinkle.

Whatever type of collection you have, you will find many other enthusiastic collectors who will trade with you. Dealers will help you buy and sell autographs and check whether an autograph is authentic. Their catalogs give important information on available autographs and their prices. Many museums and libraries have excellent autograph collections you will wish to see.

Reviewed by CHARLES HAMILTON
Author, *Collecting Autographs and Manuscripts*

WILLIAM SHAKESPEARE
1564-1616

MARTIN LUTHER KING, JR.
1929-1968

BABE RUTH
1895-1948

WOLFGANG AMADEUS MOZART
1756-1791

LOUIS PASTEUR
1822-1895

SIMON BOLIVAR
1783-1830

FRANCIS DRAKE
1540?-1596

ISAAC NEWTON
1642-1727

CHARLEMAGNE
742-814

JEANNE D'ARC
1412-1431

MARK TWAIN
1835-1910

REMBRANDT
1606-1669

AUTOMATION

For thousands of years people have been devising tools and machines to make their work easier. The development of hand tools made it possible to cut and shape wood, stone, and metal. The next great step was combining mechanisms such as the lever, the wheel, and the inclined plane into machines that could grind flour, press wine and oil, and pump water to irrigate farmland. At first, people or animals provided the power for these crude machines. Then the forces of nature were harnessed to the waterwheel and windmill. Later, the steam engine and the electric motor were used to power more sophisticated machines. The latest stage in this process of **mechanization**, using machines instead of hand labor, is automation.

▶ WHAT IS AUTOMATION?

Automation is the technique of making a machine or a mechanized process self-regulating and self-controlling. Machines can perform many tasks that are impossible to do by hand, and they can do the work faster and more accurately. But machines must be operated by people. With automation the machines either operate themselves or are controlled by other machines, without a human operator. Of course, people must make the machines, set the controls, and keep them running properly. But once the machines have been put in working order, automation allows them to do the jobs they have been "instructed" to do until they are shut off or break down.

Automation may be used to perform a single task, such as sorting cards or filling cement sacks. Several automatic machines performing different tasks may also be linked together to form an automated production line. Some processes, such as oil refining, may be completely automated from start to finish. Others may be partly automated.

Automation is possible whenever a process can be broken down into simple, repetitive operations. But not all things can be done by automation. Machines cannot replace people in tasks involving judgment, imagination, artistic creation, and personal care or service. This includes tasks such as making business decisions or designing and building complex machines or structures; painting a picture, writing a novel, or arguing a court case.

How Automation Works

Automation involves three basic components: a **machine** to perform work, a **control** to detect and measure error, and **feedback** to correct the error. The heating system of a house is an example of a simple automated system. The machine is the furnace, which is

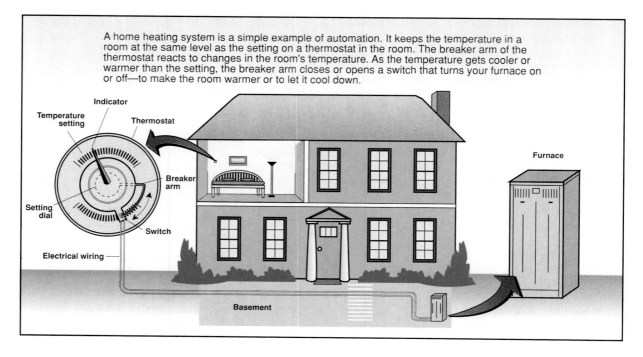

A home heating system is a simple example of automation. It keeps the temperature in a room at the same level as the setting on a thermostat in the room. The breaker arm of the thermostat reacts to changes in the room's temperature. As the temperature gets cooler or warmer than the setting, the breaker arm closes or opens a switch that turns your furnace on or off—to make the room warmer or to let it cool down.

automatically supplied with fuel and lighted by an electric spark or a pilot flame. The control is the thermostat, a combination of a thermometer that measures room air temperature and a switch that turns the furnace on and off. When the temperature in the room falls below the thermostat setting, the switch turns on the furnace. When the room temperature rises to the setting on the thermostat, the switch turns off the furnace. The error is the difference between the thermostat setting and the actual temperature in the room. Feedback takes place when the thermostat reacts to the error and turns the furnace on or off as needed.

What is Feedback?

Feedback means sending information about a process to the control unit so that the control unit will "know" what to do. Although the use of feedback in automation is fairly new, its principles have been known for a long time. In fact, feedback occurs everywhere in nature. If you touch something very hot, feedback flashes the sensation to your brain so that you pull your hand away. Feedback allows you to read this page. After you read one word, feedback signals a control center in your brain that tells the muscles in your eye to move to the next word. This process is very complicated; yet it happens thousands of times a day without your even thinking about it.

▶ HISTORY OF AUTOMATION

Although automation is quite new, some of the ideas behind it are over 200 years old. In 1784 James Watt invented a gadget called a governor to keep the steam engine he invented running at a constant speed. It was one of the first examples of the automatic control of machinery. Watt's governor consisted of two metal balls attached to a vertical shaft driven by the engine. As the shaft turned, the balls tended to fly outward because of centrifugal force. The balls were also linked to a lever that opened and closed the engine's throttle. If the engine ran too fast, the balls flew out and caused the lever to close the throttle and let less steam into the engine. With less steam the engine's speed dropped and the balls moved closer together. When the speed had dropped far enough, the governor caused the throttle to open wider and let in more steam.

In 1801 a French weaver named Joseph-Marie Jacquard invented a loom that could automatically make cloth with complicated woven patterns. This loom was controlled by cards with holes punched in them. As each card moved into place it adjusted the loom to weave part of the pattern. The idea of giving orders to machines by using punch cards was later used in computers.

A big step toward automation was taken near the end of the 1800's. Tallying the results of the United States census had become very difficult because of the growing population and the amount of information collected. The director of the Bureau of the Census devised a system for handling this huge and complicated task by machine. He used punch cards. The holes on each card were arranged in a pattern that stood for the information gathered by the census takers. For instance, a man's age, the city where he lived, and the number and ages of his children might all be shown by holes punched in particular positions on the card. These cards were then fed into machines that tallied the data and gave the Census Bureau correct totals.

People have sought faster ways of doing arithmetic ever since they began to use numbers. The first mechanical calculator, the abacus, was invented over 2,000 years ago, possibly by the Egyptians. It is still used in China and Japan. People using an abacus have been known to calculate faster than someone using an electric calculator.

Over the centuries people have tried to make calculators that would work with gears like a machine instead of with beads sliding on wires like the abacus. But most of these machines failed because parts could not be made accurately enough. Early in the 1900's, mechanical calculating machines were perfected. These early machines were cranked by hand. In 1930 a gear-driven machine powered by an electric motor was invented.

The first electronic calculating machine— the computer—was devised by scientists during World War II. This machine was called the Electronic Numerical Integrator and Calculator (ENIAC). It was designed to solve extremely complicated problems encountered in gunnery. Since ENIAC, computers have come a long way. ENIAC had 18,000 vacuum tubes and filled an entire room. One of today's microprocessors weighs less than a pound, can do work 20 times faster than ENIAC, and can be held in the hand.

▶AUTOMATION AT WORK

Automation may be used for a number of purposes on many different kinds of machines. Automation can be used to aim a battleship's guns and keep them on target, to land a spacecraft on the moon, to keep supersonic airplanes flying on course at the proper speed and level, to manufacture automobile parts, to let a person dial long distance without the help of an operator, or to do most of the work in an office. Even many home appliances have been partly automated. Washing machines, for example, automatically fill with water of the right temperature, wash the clothes, change the water, rinse the clothes, and spin them until they are partially dry.

Although the basic ideas of automation were known years ago, they were not put to great use in manufacturing until World War II. Instruments capable of measuring most kinds of error and methods of feeding the information back to the machines' controls had not yet been developed. It is not difficult to apply automation to simple tasks like regulating the heating system of a house by using an electric switch in a thermostat. But measuring very small amounts accurately and feeding this information back to a cutting machine is something very different. Such delicate work could not be done until the development of electronics.

The increased use of automation came about as a result of knowledge gained from the application of electronics in World War II. After the war, much of this knowledge was applied to the development of computers such as ENIAC. A lot was learned about electronics by studying these early computers at work.

Programming Machines to Work. The new knowledge of electronics led, in turn, to the development of the binary system of numbers later used in computers. The binary system contains only two digits, 1 and 0. The computer indicates numbers through groups of electronic tubes or transistors. Each tube or transistor indicates 1 by conducting an electric current and 0 by not conducting current. This "on-off" or "yes-no" characteristic was adapted for use in automated machine tools as well as in computer circuitry.

To control a machine tool, a **program**, or set of instructions, is recorded on tape in a binary-number code. The numbers may be punched into the tape or recorded magneti-

cally. This program tape is then placed in a tape reader, an electronic device that reads the holes or magnetic waves on the tape and operates small electric or compressed-air motors called **servomotors** built into the machine tool. The servomotors move the tool into the correct position to perform the task programmed on the tape. To do this, the machine's job has to be broken down into a series of simple step-by-step operations. For instance, the program to operate a cutting tool sets the tool's speed, governs the number of passes the cutting tool will make, and controls the depth of the cut.

A spectacular example of industrial automation is the manufacture of automobile parts. One automated production line, for instance, can take in a rough block of metal and deliver it at the other end as a finished automobile engine block. At each stop, or station, along the line, several different tools go into action. By the time the block comes off the line, hundreds of separate operations have been performed. Holes have been drilled in at exactly the right places, finished to perfect smoothness, tested for correct size, and inspected for defects. All of this work has been carried out by machines.

Although many of the operations involved in making engine blocks and other automobile parts were being done by automatic machines, parts had to be moved from machine to machine by workers. After World War II, however, special automatic transfer machines were introduced that could move engine blocks and other parts from station to station. They picked them up from one machine tool and placed them at the next one in exactly the right position. Transfer machines transformed a series of uncoordinated automatic operations into a truly automated process.

The Use of Computers in Automation. As long as a job can be broken down into steps and is repetitive, a computer can take the place of a machine operator. In some cases it can do things that no human operator can do. In a milling machine, for instance, the piece to be worked on is fastened to a table that has three possible motions: back and forth, right and left, and up and down. Each of these motions can be performed in increments of less than 0.001 inch (0.025 millimeter). A computer can direct all motions precisely and quickly, so that in a few minutes the piece can be shaped into forms that an expert machinist

Right: An operator in this plant in Valley Forge, Pennsylvania, can monitor the complex operations that provide electrical power to several neighboring states. *Below:* A plant supervisor at a control panel in this Georgia paper mill can keep the machinery that produces paper working efficiently.

Electronic instruments constantly measure the process and feed back information to the computer. These measurements are compared with the settings on the computer's program. If there is an error (for example, in the flow of oil at a refinery), the computer will correct it by sending a new signal to the machines. Of course, the process must be continually monitored by operators.

Computer programs were originally punched on cards or tape. But the high speed at which many automated plants operate made it necessary to record programs magnetically instead. Information is transferred from a master program to special magnetic tapes. If a change in any part of the program is necessary, it can be made on the master program and a new magnetic tape is made from that—or the outdated sections can be replaced by new sections of magnetic tape.

Other Uses of Automation. Automation is often used in the storage, arrangement, and retrieval of information. Almost any kind of information can be recorded on punch cards or computer tapes and stored in data banks. This information can be retrieved almost instantly with the aid of a computer.

Automation is also used in the circulation systems of some libraries. When a book is withdrawn, a machine records the call number of the book and the borrower's library-card

could not duplicate even after many hours of work.

In some automated plants, computers control the entire production process. In these plants the job involves a continuous, nonstop process as in refining oil, rather than a series of separate operations. Because computers can operate machines under conditions that no person could cope with, they are now used in many industries.

number. This information is stored in a computer and can be used to find out what books are out and who has them. The computer can also print a list of books on any subject that a borrower wants to research. The actual work of taking books from the shelf and returning them is still done by hand. But the computer automatically supplies information on book borrowing in a fraction of the time it would take a person to check a card file.

In offices or banks, computers are used for many tasks. For instance, a check cashed in a bank is entered into a computer, which subtracts the amount from the correct checking account. At the end of the month, the computer prints statements from the information stored in its electronic "memory" and sends them to the bank's customers.

Stores use automation to record the number of items sold and the number still in stock. Each time an item—a cooking pot, a baseball bat, a sweater—is sold, the salesclerk enters a series of code numbers from the price tag into a computerized register. These codes indicate such things as the type of item and its price. A computer also keeps track of when an item was last ordered and how many were ordered

at that time. This sort of information used to be compiled by people. But a computer does it faster with fewer mistakes.

▶THE ROBOTS ARE HERE

In some factories today, robots do many of the jobs that people find dangerous, uncomfortable, or boring. These robots cannot walk and talk as robots do in science fiction movies. They look a bit like huge dental drills or big boxes with long arms. The arm can be fitted with a "hand," or mechanical gripper, that picks up parts and moves them. This hand can be replaced with a spray head to paint cars or other objects traveling down an assembly line. It can also be replaced with an electric arc to weld metal parts.

Japan uses more factory robots than any other country. But the United States leads in robot technology. The automotive industry is the largest user of robots in the United States. These robots are used primarily for welding and spray painting automobile bodies.

Factory robots are run by small computers, which must be programmed by people. Many robots can respond to simple spoken commands, such as "move," "left," and "right."

Automation has moved from the factory and office into our day-to-day lives. *Left:* A microcomputer simplifies record keeping in a dry-cleaning shop. *Right:* Supermarket checkout is fast and accurate as a computer with a scanner "reads" and prints out prices.

Robots at work in an automobile factory near Detroit, Michigan. Only two human workers can be seen in the picture. Can you find them?

In the future, robots will have visual systems that will enable them to "see." They will also be able to identify objects by touch. These robots will be able to select a particular part from among many different parts. And they will be able to assemble different parts to construct a device, a machine, or even a new robot.

▶ HOW AUTOMATION AFFECTS OUR LIVES

By making it possible for machines to replace people, automation has created a revolution in the ways we do things. But like all revolutionary discoveries, automation has both good and bad sides.

On the good side, automation does away with much of the drudgery and some of the hazards of certain types of work. Machines are taking over more and more tasks that are boring, unpleasant, dangerous, and unhealthy. Manufacturers are able to produce the same quantity of goods with fewer workers. And in some cases, automation enables more goods to be produced. This increased production helps lower the cost of items and makes them cheaper for consumers. A lot of products are better made because automated equipment is more accurate than the human hand and eye.

On the bad side, many workers—both highly skilled and unskilled—may be left without work if machines replace them. Some people can be retrained to do work that has not yet been automated. Many programs to retrain workers who have lost their jobs because of automation have been created. But there is as yet no completely satisfactory program to teach people new trades.

Some people point out that every improvement in machines has caused some workers to lose jobs. However, in the long run there has been an increase in the total number of jobs. Other people point out that there is no guarantee that this will always be true. And history shows that when automation creates new jobs, it takes time for these new jobs to develop.

HAROLD I. SHARLIN
U.S. Department of Commerce
Reviewed by JONATHAN SCHLEFER
Technology Review

See also ROBOTS; COMPUTERS; MANUFACTURING; TECHNOLOGY; UNEMPLOYMENT AND UNEMPLOYMENT INSURANCE.

AUTOMOBILE MODELS

How would you like to own a large fleet of motor vehicles—everything from luxury cars and racing cars to trucks and vans, from station wagons and buses to four-wheel drive jeeps? You might even have vehicles representing different periods in automotive history. Owning such a fleet is possible—in miniature—for those who build and collect automobile models.

▶ HOBBY WITH A HISTORY

People began collecting toy cars shortly after the first cast-metal models were made in the early 1900's. The first model-car building kits did not appear until the 1930's, and they were only blocks of wood with wheels. Plastic model kits appeared after World War II. During the 1950's and 1960's, automobile dealers offered assembled plastic models of new full-size cars. These models are rare, and they have become valuable collector's items.

The first model automobiles with internal-combustion engines were available in the 1930's. These models burned fuel to produce power. They were guided by rollers along elevated rails on a wood or concrete track. Some were guided by control lines like those used on model airplanes.

Model cars with electric motors did not become widely available until the 1950's. At first these cars were guided by rails. But by 1960 most were guided by a system using a slot, or narrow opening, in the track. A slotless system, in which cars are guided by a curb or wall, appeared in the early 1970's. Radio control was being used in model cars with fuel-burning engines by 1965. By about 1975 a combination of rechargeable batteries and an electric motor controlled by radio signal was perfected.

▶ TYPES OF MODELS

Automobile models are the most popular type of hobby miniature. There are models of every imaginable type of vehicle. Most models are available ready-made in metal or in plastic or as plastic kits to be put together. There are also powered racing models that duplicate both the action and the appearance of full-size automobiles.

The size of a model as compared to the size of the real vehicle is called its **scale**. The scale is expressed as a proportion (such as 1:43) or as a fraction (such as $\frac{1}{43}$). The larger the proportion or fraction, the larger the model. A $\frac{1}{43}$ scale model automobile is about the size of a credit card; a $\frac{1}{8}$ scale model is about the size of a briefcase. The smallest size, $\frac{1}{87}$ scale, is known as HO scale.

Collector's Cars

Unpowered, ready-made model cars are by far the most popular. These vehicles can range from tiny plastic cars costing a couple of dollars to all-metal desk-size models costing hundreds or thousands of dollars. The most popular collector's cars are metal models with some plastic details, in $\frac{1}{43}$ scale.

Most plastic model kits must be glued together and painted. But kits with simple snap-together construction are also available. Both types of kits include full interior, engine, and chassis details, such as windshield wipers, chrome trim, and hoods and doors that open and close. The most common scale for American model kits is $\frac{1}{25}$, but there are hundreds of kits available in sizes ranging from $\frac{1}{87}$ to $\frac{1}{8}$ scale.

Racing Cars

The two main types of model racing cars are tabletop racers, which run on special tracks, and radio-controlled models, which are usually raced outdoors.

Tabletop Racers. Racing slot and slotless model cars requires almost as much "driving" skill as racing full-size automobiles. Slot cars must stay in a narrow slot to get the electric power needed to move them. The cars must be carefully guided through turns so they do not spin out of their slots.

This $\frac{1}{16}$ scale 1957 Chevrolet has working doors.

Left: A ¹⁄₁₂ scale electric-powered radio-controlled racing car. **Right:** If carefully guided, electric slot racers can zoom around a curved track at terrific speeds.

Slot cars are run by an electric-powered motor, which turns gears that drive the rear axle. Metal strips on each side of the slot carry the electric power. When these strips make contact with the metal pickup strips on the bottom of the car, which are called shoes, electricity is transferred from the track to the car motor. A hand-held control is used to change the car's speed.

Slotless cars are also powered by electricity but it is supplied by batteries carried inside the cars. These cars can be run on the floor or on the ground in straight-line races. When they are used on an oval or wiggly track, however, walls are used to guide the cars. Such tracks are really troughs that force the cars to steer when they push against the walls. Usually, each car has its own trough or lane and the race continues until the batteries run down or the cars are picked up by hand and turned off. There is no remote control with these simple electric racing cars.

Radio-Controlled Racers. In radio-controlled cars, a hand-held transmitter sends radio signals to a receiver in the car. These signals control the car's speed and direction. Most radio-controlled cars are powered by battery-operated electric motors. But some are powered by internal-combustion engines fueled by gasoline.

The most popular size for radio-controlled model cars is ¹⁄₁₂ scale. Some of these models can exceed speeds of about 30 miles (50 kilometers) an hour. The radio-controlled cars respond quickly to any movement of the transmitter levers. With practice, the "driver" can duplicate all the maneuvers of a real racing car.

More expensive radio-controlled cars have powerful transmitters and receivers that use different radio frequencies. This allows several cars to be raced at one time. In the United States, people using these larger transmitters must obtain special permits from the Federal Communications Commission.

Both electric- and gasoline-powered radio-controlled cars can be raced outdoors. Paved parking lots and school yards are ideal places. Some cities even have special tracks. Electric-powered cars can be raced indoors, but they need a very large area. Radio-controlled dune buggies an other off-road vehicles are raced outside in the dirt.

ROBERT SCHLEICHER
Author, *Model Car Racing:
Tabletop & Radio-Control*

Left: The start of the Indianapolis 500. Cars begin the race in eleven rows of three. The starting positions are determined in time trials that take place during the days just before the race.

Below: Formula One cars roar through the curving streets of Monaco during a Grand Prix race.

AUTOMOBILE RACING

When automobile racing began in the 1890's, the speeds were like those of a fast horse and buggy. The first major race, held in 1895, was from Paris to Bordeaux, France, and back. The winner averaged only 15 miles (24 kilometers) an hour. But the speeds of racing automobiles increased every year. By the 1960's, the racing automobile was nearly as fast as some kinds of airplanes.

Automobile racing includes events and classes for almost every kind of four-wheeled vehicle. The racing rules and formulas are established so that the vehicles in each class perform as much like the others as possible.

Racing takes place on many kinds of tracks. There are oval tracks, drag strips, and twisting tracks built around oval tracks. There are also cross-country races on public roads or on dirt and sand. If a car is designed for one type of track, it can sometimes be raced on other tracks if minor changes are made to the car.

The emphasis in automobile racing has shifted away from pure speed. Race car designers now concentrate on improving the cornering speeds, braking, and fuel economy of their machines. Top speeds on a straight course have not increased much since the 1960's. But racing cars are getting around the tracks faster. This is because of improvements in tires, design, brakes, and aerodynamics (the study of the way in which air affects moving objects). It can be said, then, that winners of races are determined by the abilities of the

drivers, the car designers, and the mechanics.

Modern racing cars have been made safer with stout metal frame bars, nonexploding fuel tanks, and built-in fire extinguishers. Race courses are now usually lined with safety barriers to help stop cars that go out of control. Safety helmets and fireproof driving suits provide more protection for the driver. But racing is still a dangerous sport, and the driver must be highly skilled.

▶GRAND PRIX RACING

Grand Prix racing and sports-car racing are the only forms of automobile racing that are popular worldwide. The Grand Prix cars are meant to be the best road-racing machines. The top Grand Prix class is Formula One. It has this name because the cars must be built according to a set formula. The overall winner of Grand Prix Formula One races is really the "world champion" because many countries compete only in this type of racing.

The Grand Prix cars look and perform much like the cars that race in the famous Indianapolis 500. But they have smaller engines, better brakes, and more cornering speed. They have only one seat, are low to the ground, and have no fenders. In the past, Grand Prix races were held on public roads. Today many places, including Monaco; Long Beach, California; and Miami, Florida, use downtown streets for open-wheel race car events. All other races are held on tracks. Whether on public-road courses or on racetracks, Grand Prix races are about 150 to 250 miles (240 to 400 kilometers) long.

▶SPORTS-CAR RACING

No other mass-produced vehicle is as fast as a sports car over winding and twisting roads. Racecourses that imitate such conditions are called road racetracks. These tracks are used for both production and prototype classes of sports-car racing. The production cars are regular sports cars. They are rebuilt for more reliability. But the parts are all regular parts. Only a roll bar and an open exhaust system are allowed as modifications of the cars that the public can buy. The prototype sports cars are built almost exactly like Grand Prix cars. They have a special body and engine not found in sports cars for sale to the public.

There are several sports-car classes, which are based on engine size. Sports-car races range from 30-minute regional races to international endurance events like the 12-hour racing at Sebring, Florida, and the 24-hour race at Daytona, Florida.

▶SPEEDWAY RACING

The most common type of speedway track is oval and measures about 1 mile (1.6 kilometers) around. Many classes of cars—such as Midgets, Sprint cars, Quarter Midgets, and Indianapolis-500-style "Championship" cars —race on these tracks. All but the "Championship" cars often compete in regional or local racing series that use both paved and dirt tracks.

The "Championship" cars have a single-seat cockpit, a powerful engine in the rear, and no fenders. Throughout the year, "Championship" cars compete in races, some as short as 100 miles (160 kilometers) and some as long as 500 miles (800 kilometers). "Championship" racing climaxes at the Indianapolis (Indiana) Motor Speedway each Memorial Day weekend at the end of May. The famous Indianapolis 500 race (so named from its length of 500 miles) is held at that time on the speedway's 2½-mile (4-kilometer) oval track.

▶STOCK-CAR RACING

There is something especially exciting about watching a race when the automobiles

Left: During a "pit stop" at the Indianapolis 500, mechanics make repairs and fill the fuel tank in a matter of seconds. *Right:* Tightly bunched cars in a stock-car race vie for the lead position.

Smoke pours out from the engine as this specially built "dragster" accelerates quickly to begin its run.

look like the family car. In racing, such automobiles are called stock cars. There are many different stock-car classes. A stock car can be a car manufacturer's latest model, or it can be an old model called a jalopy. Some stock cars can reach 180 miles (290 kilometers) an hour on the banked turns of the large paved oval tracks. Jalopies are often the stars of the races held on dirt-track ovals at county fairs. In some countries, stock cars are raced on road racetracks.

The rules for most classes of stock-car racing specify that only the outward appearance of the car and some of the major parts must be truly "stock," or standard. All the other parts —including the wheels, brakes, and moving engine parts—are special racing parts. A tubular steel frame is welded inside the "stock" body to protect the driver and to provide the extra strength needed for faster cornering speeds.

▶ DRAG RACING

Short races in which automobiles accelerate to top speed on straight courses have become very popular. These races are called drag races in the United States and sprint races in many other countries. Drag racers can accelerate from a standing start to more than 280 miles (450 kilometers) an hour on a ¼-mile (0.4-kilometer) track. There are drag-racing classes for just about every type of automobile from compact sedans (enclosed cars) to hot-rod roadsters (open cars) and from stock to "hopped up" cars. Some specially built "dragsters" are about twice as long as normal passenger cars. Often they have no fenders. The fastest drag racers can reach speeds of more than 250 miles (400 kilometers) an hour in less than six seconds.

▶ THE LAND SPEED RECORD

Racing enthusiasts used to have areas closed off on weekends for speed contests. Today only a few of these areas are left. The most famous is Bonneville Salt Flats near Wendover, Utah. Most of the world's land speed records have been set there. Malcolm Campbell went 301.1 miles (484.5 kilometers) an hour in 1935. Craig Breedlove reached 600.6 miles (966.4 kilometers) an hour in 1965, and Gary Gabelich drove 622.4 miles (1,001.4 kilometers) an hour in 1970. In 1979, Stan Barrett went 739.7 miles (1,190.2 kilometers) an hour.

▶ OFF-ROAD RACING

Vehicles with four-wheel drive—such as Jeeps, dune buggies, and special rear-engine racing machines—compete in a variety of automobile races on dirt, off regular roads. The best-known off-road vehicle races are those on the dirt roads and trails of Baja, Mexico. Similar natural courses are sometimes laid out around the outside of paved race courses. Off-road vehicles also compete on many of the dirt-track ovals. Or they use the same types of twisting dirt or sand tracks with jumps that motorcycles race on. There are even some "sand drag" acceleration races for off-road vehicles, where sand dunes or beaches are the race courses.

ROBERT SCHLEICHER
Author, *The Model Car, Truck & Motorcycle Handbook*

See also KARTING.

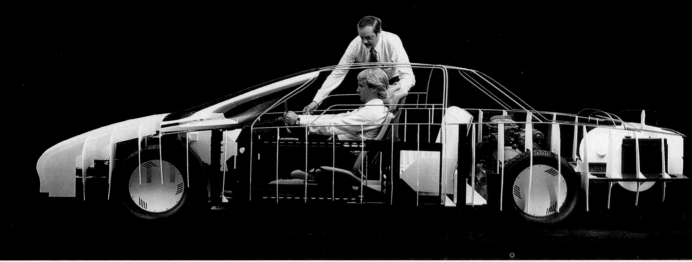

The comfort of the driver is studied in an open model of the design for a new automobile.

AUTOMOBILES

Frightened English farmers rushed to their windows on Christmas Eve, 1801, when they heard loud clanking and hissing on their quiet country road. What they saw was a smoke-belching, steam-powered horseless carriage. It was driven by their neighbor, Richard Trevithick, who had built the odd carriage.

None of them knew it at the time, but it was the first practical use of mechanical power to move a vehicle. Other strange machines had been invented before, and some of them had even moved on their wheels. But Trevithick's was the first to actually do what it was supposed to do—making it the world's first true "automobile."

An automobile is a self-propelled land vehicle that can carry passengers or freight. Unlike a train, an automobile can travel on land without rails. Trucks and buses are automobiles designed for special uses. Race cars are automobiles that run on a race course, and offroad vehicles are automobiles that run on rough ground or sand.

Trevithick's self-propelled carriage could carry passengers over land at a speed of nearly 10 miles (16 kilometers) per hour. Neither his neighbors nor even Trevithick himself appreciated the importance of his achievement. He considered his noisy carriage—with its huge wood and metal wheels and horizontal boiler that puffed out clouds of wood smoke—little more than a toy. He finally took it apart so that he could sell the engine to a mill owner.

The First Experiments

No one person invented the automobile. Many inventors living and working in different countries and at different times contributed to its development. Many of the inventions that went into the creation of the automobile were small in themselves, but together they were important.

The first recorded use of a self-powered vehicle was in 1769. Nicolas Cugnot, a French military engineer, designed and built an awkward but workable three-wheeled vehicle powered by a steam engine. The vehicle was intended as a tractor for hauling heavy cannons. It had a short career. It went out of control during a trial run and crashed.

Only a few years after Trevithick's steam engine, American inventor Oliver Evans built a steam-powered dredge (a machine used to clear sediment from waterways). The machine was equipped with wheels so that it could move on land. To demonstrate to the public that steam could move land vehicles as well as boats, Evans drove his machine around Philadelphia's Center Square for several days. Then he put it to work dredging the waters around the docks in the Schuylkill River. Evans hoped the demonstration would persuade wealthy people to back him in manufacturing steam vehicles. But most people of those days did not think his invention was practical.

Because of the work of Trevithick and Evans, steam-powered vehicles rapidly gained popularity in England. A number of compa-

Built by Nicolas Cugnot in 1769, the earliest self-propelled vehicle was powered by a steam engine. It was almost impossible to steer and crashed on a trial run.

nies were formed to operate steam-powered passenger coaches. But these early steam coaches soon ran into opposition. Stagecoach and railroad operators resented and feared their competition. Farmers disliked the noisy, smelly coaches, and turnpike owners charged them extra high fees. They did this to make up for the damage the steam vehicles supposedly did to the roads. Beginning in 1831 the British Parliament passed a series of very strict laws regulating the use of self-propelled vehicles. The strictest was the Red Flag Act of 1865. It was so named because one of the provisions of the law required a person to walk ahead of all ''road locomotives'' to warn of their approach. The various laws imposed such high taxes and so many limitations that steam coaches could not operate without losing money. This hurt automobile development in England until the Red Flag Act was repealed in 1896.

Forerunners of the Modern Automobile

Meanwhile, experiments in Europe and in the United States were pushing ahead. Building on the work of earlier scientists and engineers, French engineer Jean Joseph Étienne Lenoir completed a workable internal-combustion engine in 1860. This one-cylinder engine ran on coal gas ignited by an electric spark. The Lenoir engine was designed as a stationary power plant for factories. But a small model was used experimentally in 1863 to power a road vehicle.

About 1865 an Austrian inventor, Siegfried Marcus, built and road tested a simple four-wheeled vehicle with an internal combustion engine that used liquid fuel. Ten years later he produced a second liquid-fueled vehicle. It also ran successfully and is now preserved in a museum in Vienna.

Nikolaus A. Otto, a German inventor, built the most direct ancestor of today's automobile engine in 1876. Otto's engine used the four-stroke principle of operation—intake, compression, power, and exhaust. Automobile engines of today operate on this principle. Otto's original engine, like Lenoir's, operated on coal gas, but it was soon adapted for use with other fuels. Otto's invention provided a relatively light and powerful engine that was important to later developments.

Gottlieb Daimler and another German, Karl Benz, are usually credited with being the earliest builders of successful automobiles with internal-combustion engines. Each produced a motor car in 1886. Daimler's greatest contribution was his light, reliable, medium-speed gas engine. The design formed the basis for the modern automobile engine. Daimler's first machine was intended mainly for testing an all-purpose engine that could be used in boats, trains, and airplanes. But Benz concentrated on the idea of a vehicle fitted with a gasoline motor. He worked hard on a design combining the motor, body, chassis (frame and wheels), and other parts into an efficient unit.

In the early 1890's, a French engineer, Emile Levassor, produced a chassis to fit Daimler's engine. The resulting vehicle, called a Panhard-Levassor, is regarded by many automobile historians as the first real forerunner of the modern automobile. It was the first motor vehicle in which the frame was made separately from the body and suspended from the axles by springs. It also was the first to have the engine in front and the now-standard clutch-and-gear transmission.

Between 1880 and 1900, the concept of the automobile emerged. It was still a rarity that only a wealthy person could own. But people were beginning to take it seriously as a method of transportation. Most of these early automobiles were powered by steam or electricity. But the internal-combustion engine was soon to take its place as the standard automobile engine.

The electric car was superior to the steamer or the gasoline car in several ways. It ran quietly and smoothly, without the vibration and

DEVELOPMENT OF THE AUTOMOBILE
In the panel at the right and in panels on the pages that follow, the history of the automobile is shown through photographs. Each car is a notable example of the engineering or design of its time.

smelly fumes of its rivals. It was easy to control. It did not require a complicated set of gears or clutches to transmit the power to the wheels or to run in reverse. There were few moving parts to wear out. But it had a serious defect. It could not carry with it an adequate power source. The batteries ran down, usually after a distance of about 20 to 40 miles (30 to 65 kilometers), and had to be recharged. It was obviously more convenient to add a few gallons of gasoline to a fuel tank than to recharge or replace a heavy battery. Besides, batteries large enough to power an automobile were very costly. Another disadvantage of the electric automobile was its generally low speed—12 miles (19 kilometers) per hour was a good speed for most electric cars in 1900.

Steam-driven cars were even more popular than electrics in the late 1890's and early 1900's. More than 100 different makes of American steamers were placed on the market in those years. Steamers offered more power than electrics, quiet operation, and smooth

1906 Stanley Steamer

1907 Rolls Royce Silver Ghost

Electric cars were briefly popular. They were quiet and easy to operate but slow. Most could travel only about 40 miles before their batteries needed recharging.

Baker
Electrics

Read pages six, seven, eight and nine of the new Baker Electric catalog very carefully. If you have not received a copy write for it now. It contains the most informing statement about electrics ever published.

1909 Model T Ford

1928 Model A Ford

1931 Bugatti Type 41 Royale

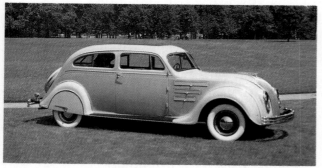

1934 Chrysler Airflow

1935 Dusenberg SSJ

1941 Lincoln Continental   1937 Cord

performance. But their drawbacks were serious. It took a long time to build up steam, and doing so was a complicated procedure. Owners feared, sometimes with good reason, that a boiler explosion or accident might result from the fire under the boiler.

Today, the best remembered of the steam cars are the Stanley Steamers. They were made in Newton, Massachusetts from the late 1890's well into the 1920's by Francis and Freelan Stanley, who were identical twins. In 1906 a Stanley Steamer set a new world's land speed record at Ormond Beach, Florida. It hurtled across the sand at 127.6 miles (205.9 kilometers) per hour. By the time the last steamers were made in the mid-1930's, some very efficient and dependable machines were being produced.

The internal-combustion engine is much more complicated than either the steam engine or the electric motor. It has many more moving parts that can wear out. In its early days, it was tricky and temperamental. It frequently broke down or simply refused to start. But there are good reasons why it eventually became the standard power plant for automobiles. With all its failings, it produced more power in relation to its weight than the other engines. When it broke down, it was relatively easy to repair. Its cruising range was limited by the amount of fuel in its tank and not by the availability of water or the endurance of batteries.

The Early Years

Two brothers, Charles E. and James F. Duryea, were the first Americans to manufacture and market a successful gasoline-powered automobile. James Duryea completed the first Duryea automobile in 1893, in Springfield, Massachusetts, working with his brother's design. Their second car was the winner of the first American automobile race, on Thanksgiving Day, 1895. The course was about 55 miles (88 kilometers) long, from Chicago to Evanston, Illinois, and back. In 1895 the Duryeas established the first American automobile manufacturing company.

Ransom E. Olds opened his first factory in 1899 in Detroit, Michigan. When the factory burned down in 1901, Olds came up with an idea that enabled him to continue production and that was a major breakthrough in automobile manufacturing. Instead of making all the

Henry Ford created the first assembly line to manufacture automobiles. At the stage shown, Model T chassis move along the line while the car bodies are lowered onto them. At the next step, the body will be fastened in place.

parts in his factory, he developed careful specifications and had the parts made with great precision by a number of small manufacturers. The parts were then brought to the factory for assembly into cars.

The idea of standardized parts was further developed by Henry M. Leland who founded the Cadillac Company. His cars were made of completely interchangeable parts. In a test in 1908, three Cadillac cars were completely taken apart by the Royal Automobile Club of Britain, and three cars were reassembled using a mixture of parts from the original cars. The three reassembled cars ran perfectly.

Although Olds and Cadillac developed the idea of standardized and interchangeable parts, it was Henry Ford who developed mass production. In 1908 the Ford Motor Company produced the famous Model T Ford. His idea was to produce a motor car that the average person could afford, operate, and maintain. The first Model T Ford sold for $850.00, but Ford knew that he could bring the price down if he could develop an efficient way of manufacturing the cars. Ford developed the first assembly line in 1914.

The basic idea of the assembly line was to move the car on a moving conveyor belt while workers on each side added parts as the car moved along. Often the parts were brought to the workers on another conveyor belt. Each worker had a specific relatively simple task to perform as compared with assembling an entire engine. The use of standardized interchangeable parts also produced a better product that could be easily repaired at lower cost. Before the assembly line, it had taken more than twelve hours to assemble a Model T. New Model T's now came off the assembly line at the rate of one car every 24 seconds. By 1915 the price of a Model T had dropped to $440.00, and by 1925 a Model T could be bought for $290.00

A major advance in 1912 was the invention of the electric starter, an electric motor that starts the gasoline engine. Before the development of the electric starter, the gasoline engine had to be started by cranking it by hand. This took considerable strength and was also dangerous. If the car were not cranked properly, the crank could kick back and cause a fractured thumb or arm.

World War I proved the value of the gasoline automobile. Trucks and ambulances were used in great numbers during the war, and the war proved to be a testing ground for automotive design. In addition, members of the armed services became familiar with automobiles and what they could do.

In the period 1900 through 1920, a great many changes took place in the automobile. During this time, closed cars that protected the drivers and passengers from sun and rain became more common. However, it was not until 1923 that closed sedans became more common than open cars.

Many technical advances improved the function of the automobile. The braking system of the cars improved as cars became more powerful and traffic increased. Early cars had mechanical brakes only on the rear wheels requiring a great deal of force from the driver to stop the car. In the 1920's, cars first had mechanical brakes on all four wheels. By the 1930's most cars had four-wheel hydraulic brakes. Low-pressure balloon tires took the place of hard-riding high-pressure tires. Safety glass that did not shatter when broken was introduced in the 1920's and helped prevent serious injury from even minor accidents. During the 1930's most cars were also equipped with heaters and radios. At this time cars also began to take on a smoother shape to offer less wind resistance.

During World War II, vast numbers of automobiles and trucks were manufactured for use by the military. Again the war provided a testing ground for new ideas. By the late 1940's, many cars had automatic transmissions, power brakes, and power steering.

During the 1950's, cars became lower, longer, and wider. Many cars were styled with rear fins and great amounts of chrome.

In the 1960's the United States became increasingly concerned with air pollution caused by automobiles, and a number of devices were added to automobile engines to decrease the amount of harmful chemicals released into the air. Later the Federal Clean Air Act of 1970 established standards to control the amount of harmful gases emitted by automobiles.

In the 1970's a gasoline shortage and an increase in gasoline prices created a great interest in smaller cars that used less fuel. The federal government passed laws requiring that new automobiles average 27.5 miles per gallon by 1985. During this time safety regulations were also instituted that required automobiles to better withstand crashes.

In the 1970's and 1980's the trend shifted to smaller cars that were fuel efficient. Other conveniences such as air conditioning and power windows, seats, and door locks became common.

By today's standards the early automobiles were uncomfortable and difficult to operate. But the many inconveniences did not discourage potential buyers. Many people believed that the automobile represented a new frontier for the 20th century. The fact that a person could have independent transportation by mechanical means was considered a miracle of modern technology. It has certainly proved to be so.

1942 Jeep

1947 Volkswagen Beetle

1951 Studebaker

1957 Ford Thunderbird

1959 Cadillac

1964½ Ford Mustang

1984 Plymouth Voyager

1965 Toyota Corona

1985 Chevrolet Corvette

1973 Mercedes Benz 280 SEL

1988 Acura Legend

1973 Honda Civic

1989 Suzuki Samurai

1978 Volvo

1989 Ford Taurus

▶ HOW AN AUTOMOBILE WORKS

Modern automobiles are complex machines made up of thousands of metal, plastic, glass, and rubber parts. They are reliable, comfortable, and safe. Although the sleek, modern automobile has changed greatly from the noisy and smelly cars of the 1890's, it has the same basic systems.

Most cars are powered by an internal-combustion engine. An **electrical system** provides the power to start the engine and, in gasoline engines, provides the sparks that ignite the fuel. Electricity is also required for electric devices such as lights, horns, radios, and heater fans.

Engines have **lubrication systems** to reduce the friction of their moving parts. They have **cooling systems** to carry away the great heat created by combustion. They have a **fuel system** to store and carry fuel to the engine. An **exhaust system** carries away the waste products of combustion.

The engine and all the parts that carry power to the wheels make up the **drive train.** In addition to the engine, the parts of the drive train include the **transmission,** the **drive shaft,** the **differential,** the axles, and the wheels that move the car, called the **drive wheels.** Some cars have the drive wheels in the front, some have drive wheels in the rear, and in other cars, all four wheels are drive wheels.

All cars have a **steering system** to connect the steering wheel to the front wheels. A **brake system** slows and stops the car. A **suspension system** protects the car and passengers from the bumps and dips in the road.

The basic structure to which all these parts are attached is the **chassis.** The **body** of the car consists of the external parts such as the fenders, hood, roof, doors, and trunk lid and the internal fittings of the passenger compartment. These fittings include the seats and the dashboard, which displays instruments that monitor such things as engine temperature, oil pressure, speed, and distance driven.

The Engine

The engine is the first part of the drive train. Most cars today are powered by internal-combustion engines. These engines burn a gaseous mixture of air and either gasoline or diesel fuel inside hollow cylinders. Most modern automobile engines have four, six, or eight cylinders. The cylinders in four-cylinder engines are generally arranged in a line. The cylinders in six-cylinder engines are arranged either in a

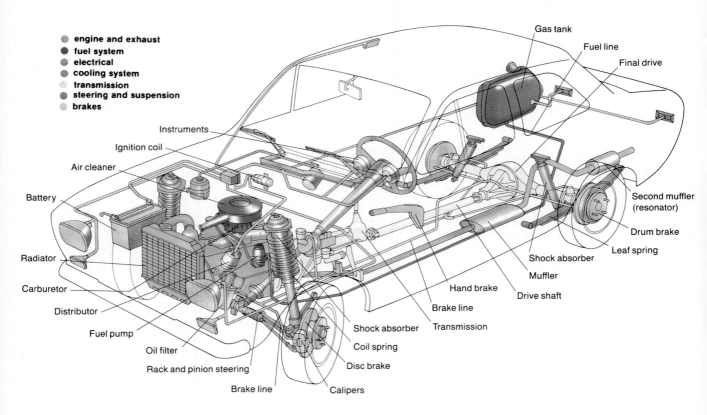

- ● engine and exhaust
- ● fuel system
- ● electrical
- ● cooling system
- ● transmission
- ● steering and suspension
- ● brakes

Instruments
Ignition coil
Air cleaner
Battery
Radiator
Carburetor
Distributor
Fuel pump
Oil filter
Rack and pinion steering
Brake line
Calipers
Disc brake
Coil spring
Shock absorber
Brake line
Transmission
Hand brake
Drive shaft
Muffler
Shock absorber
Second muffler (resonator)
Drum brake
Leaf spring
Gas tank
Fuel line
Final drive

line or in a V-shape with three cylinders in each arm of the V. These engines are called V-6's. The cylinders in an eight-cylinder engine are nearly always arranged in a V, and such engines are called V-8's. Generally, the more cylinders that an engine has, the more powerful that it is.

When an internal-combustion engine is running, the burning gas expands, pushing a piston inside the cylinder. This happens very rapidly, one piston after the other, in each of the engine's cylinders. A connecting rod connects each piston to a shaft, called the **crankshaft**. As each piston is pushed by the gas, it forces the crankshaft to turn. This turning motion is passed through the drive train to the drive wheels. For more information on how these engines work, consult the articles INTERNAL-COMBUSTION ENGINES and DIESEL ENGINES in this encyclopedia.

The Fuel System

Fuel stored in the automobile's fuel tank is drawn to the engine by a **fuel pump.** A **carburetor** then mixes the fuel with air and sends the gaseous mixture to the **intake manifold** and on into the cylinders of the engine. Instead of a carburetor, some cars have a **fuel-injection system** that sprays controlled amounts of gasoline into intake ports close to the cylinders. The fuel-air mixture goes into the cylinder when an **intake valve** opens.

Filters in the fuel line clean the fuel, but they can block the flow of fuel when they get clogged with dirt. They need to be changed regularly or the engine will not run properly.

Some modern, high-performance cars have **turbochargers** that suck in extra air and force it into the cylinders of the engine. This creates more pressure as the fuel is burned and enables the engine to produce greater power.

The Exhaust System

When the fuel burns inside an engine, gases are formed. These gases must be removed from the engine so that new fuel may be burned. This is a fast-moving, continual process. The operation of the piston in each cylinder forces the gases out an **exhaust valve** and then into an **exhaust manifold** that collects exhaust gases from all the cylinders. The gases then pass through **mufflers**, into **tail pipes**, and out the rear of the automobile. They must be forced away from the car because they are poisonous and can cause death when breathed by the driver or passengers.

Most automobiles have one or more mufflers in the exhaust system to muffle the loud noise of the burning fuel. Modern cars also have **emission-control devices** to reduce the amount of carbon monoxide, hydrocarbons, and nitrogen oxide, the harmful chemicals in the exhaust gases. Some cars pump some of the exhaust back through the engine to use every last bit of the fuel. Others have devices such as a **catalytic converter** to convert (change) the harmful gases to a less harmful form. Most states have laws to regulate the maximum amounts of harmful chemicals that may be present in automobile exhaust gases.

The Electrical System

Electrical energy is stored in a rechargeable battery that, on most modern cars, provides 12 volts of electricity. Whenever the engine is running, the battery is kept charged by an electrical generator called an **alternator.** The alternator is driven by a **belt,** a flexible loop attached to an engine-driven wheel. You will find more information on generators and alternators in the article ELECTRIC GENERATORS in Volume E. An article explaining how BATTERIES work is in Volume B.

When a driver turns the ignition key to the "start" position, power from the battery operates the electric starter motor. This motor turns the crankshaft, which pushes the pistons up and down, thus causing the gasoline engine to start. One part of the electrical system, called the **ignition system,** provides power to

The Ignition System

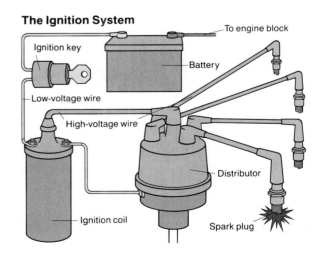

Ignition key
To engine block
Battery
Low-voltage wire
High-voltage wire
Distributor
Ignition coil
Spark plug

the spark plugs, which ignite the gas in the cylinders.

A spark strong enough to ignite the fuel requires far more than 12 volts of electricity. Thus the electricity from the battery is sent through an **ignition coil** that increases the voltage to about 20,000 volts. The current then passes through a **distributor** that sends it to the spark plug in each cylinder at the right time to ignite the gas in that cylinder.

The car's battery also provides electricity to operate the car's radio, horn, clock, instruments, lights, tape player, and other electric devices.

An automobile with a diesel engine has an electrical system to provide electrical energy for the starter motor, lights, and accessories. A diesel engine does not have spark plugs. Fuel is ignited when its temperature is raised to the burning point by very high compression of the fuel-air mixture in the cylinders.

The Lubrication System

Oil is essential to an internal-combustion engine. Oil coats the moving parts so that metal is not rubbing against metal inside the engine. Without lubrication, friction would cause the metal to become so hot that the engine would be destroyed. An **oil pump** in the engine forces the oil to every moving part.

Several quarts of oil are stored in the **crankcase** (the oil pan at the bottom of the engine). The oil pump draws oil from the crankcase and forces it around the engine. Eventually the oil drips back into the crankcase where it can be drawn up again. An oil filter in the system removes any dirt or tiny particles from the oil so they will not harm delicate engine parts. The oil and oil filter must be changed regularly to keep the engine running well.

The Cooling System

Modern internal-combustion automobile engines become very hot inside. They must be kept at an operating temperature that is cool enough to prevent damage from overheating yet warm enough for the most efficient operation. Some engines are **air-cooled.** As the car moves, air flows through the engine compartment to carry away excess heat. Other engines have **liquid cooling systems.** In these engines the cylinders have double walls. An engine-driven **water pump** forces **coolant** to flow between these walls. The coolant is usually a mixture of one-half water and one-half ethylene glycol, which acts as an antifreeze to keep the water from freezing. Usually anti-rust and anti-corrosion chemicals are added to the ethylene glycol. The coolant picks up heat from the cylinders and is then pumped through a **radiator** where airflow carries away the heat. A thermostat controls the flow of the coolant to keep the engine operating at the correct temperature.

Transmission and Final Drive

The engine is located at the beginning of the drive train of an automobile. The transmission receives the power from the engine and passes it on (transmits it) to the drive shaft, which in turn passes the power on to the drive wheels.

The transmission contains a series of gears that can be connected in different ways to produce different **gear ratios.** These permit the speed of the drive shaft to change in relation to the speed of the engine. The lowest gear ratio is called first gear and provides the greatest amount of torque, or twisting force, from the engine to the drive wheels. This gear is used for starting the car from a standstill. All cars have at least three gear ratios, and some

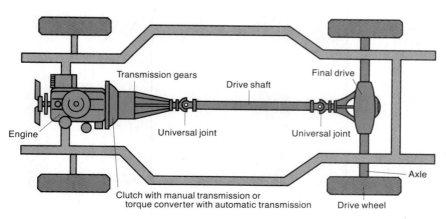

Transmission gears
Drive shaft
Final drive
Engine
Universal joint
Universal joint
Axle
Clutch with manual transmission or
torque converter with automatic transmission
Drive wheel

The Drive Train

The series of parts that carry power from the engine to the drive wheels is called the drive train. In the diagram the drive train is shown for a car with an engine located at the front of the car and with the drive wheels at the rear of the car. Front-wheel drive cars have the transmission and final drive located at the front. These cars do not have a drive shaft.

Manual Transmission

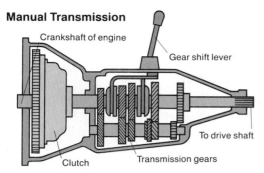

In a car equipped with a manual transmission, the driver selects the correct set of gears to match the engine speed to the road speed. In addition to a reverse gear, a manual transmission will have a neutral position and three, four, or five gears for forward movement.

Automatic Transmission

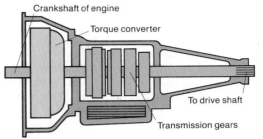

In a car equipped with an automatic transmission, the gears are shifted automatically from low to high as the car moves from a standing position to cruising speed. The transmission may shift into lower gears for climbing hills or for passing when more power is needed from the engine.

have four or even five. At the higher gear ratios, less torque is supplied to the drive wheels, but greater speed results at the drive shaft and at the drive wheels. The high gear ratios are used for highway travel. Transmissions also have a reverse gear that changes the direction in which the drive wheels turn, so that the car can back up. All transmissions also have a neutral position in which the engine is not connected to the drive shaft at all. This position permits the engine to run at any speed without the drive shaft or drive wheels turning.

Manual Transmissions. Some cars have a manual transmission that permits the driver to select the gear ratio best suited for the driving conditions. When changing from one gear to another, it is necessary to disconnect the transmission from the engine. This is accomplished by the **clutch,** which is located in the drive train between the engine and the transmission. When the clutch pedal is pushed down, the engine is disconnected from the transmission and the gears can be shifted. When the clutch pedal is allowed to come back up, the engine is again connected to the transmission and power flows to the drive wheels.

Automatic Transmission. An automatic transmission shifts the gears for the driver. All the driver must do is press down on the **accelerator** pedal (the ''gas'' pedal); the automatic transmission selects its lowest gear. Then, as speed increases, the transmission shifts itself into higher gears. No clutch is needed for a modern automatic transmission because it has a **fluid** (transmission oil) **coupling** between the gears and the engine.

If the car is going up a steep hill, the automatic transmission shifts itself down to a lower gear so that the engine can turn faster and provide more power. At the top of the hill, when the extra power is no longer needed, the transmission shifts back to a higher gear.

Many drivers prefer the direct control of a manual transmission. Others prefer the ease of an automatic.

For more detailed information on how a modern transmission works, consult the article Transmissions in Volume T.

Drive Shaft. In a front-engine car with rear-wheel drive, power from the transmission is carried to the final drive at the rear of the car by a drive shaft. The drive shaft is coupled to the transmission by means of a **universal joint.** This is a flexible joint that permits the rear axle of the car to move up and down without bend-

The Final Drive

The final drive carries power from the drive shaft to the drive wheels. It contains the differential gears that permit each of the drive wheels to turn at a different speed.

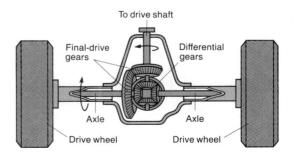

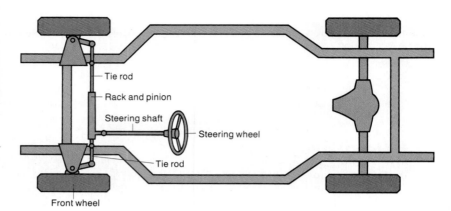

Rack and Pinion Steering

The steering system enables the driver to turn the front wheels and to control the direction of the car's movement. Some cars have power-assisted steering that uses power from the engine to make steering easier for the driver.

Tie rod

Rack and pinion

Steering shaft

Steering wheel

Tie rod

Front wheel

ing the drive shaft as the car goes over bumps. In a front-engine car with front-wheel drive, the transmission is connected directly to the final drive. A four-wheel drive car usually has two drive shafts and two final drives, one for each pair of drive wheels.

The final drive consists of a series of gears that carries the power from the drive shaft to the axles that turn the drive wheels. One set of gears causes the axle to turn at a slower speed than the drive shaft, and thus more torque is delivered to the drive wheels. A second set of gears, called the **differential,** permits each drive wheel to turn at a different speed when the car turns a corner. Because the inner wheel travels a smaller distance than the outer wheel, the inner wheel must turn at a slower speed to avoid skidding.

The Steering System

When the driver turns the steering wheel, gears are turned inside a **steering box** and this moves shafts attached to the front wheels. Some cars have a **rack-and-pinion** type of steering mechanism, in which gears act against a row of teeth.

If the car has power steering, a pump powered by the engine operates a hydraulic system that makes it easier for the driver to turn the wheels. The power assist works only when the engine is running.

Some automobiles have **four-wheel steering.** When the steering wheel is turned, both front and rear wheels turn. With four-wheel steering, a car can make U-turns in much less space. It is also easier to make the tight turns required to park in a small space.

The Brake System

The brake system enables the driver to slow down and to stop the car. The brake systems of modern cars operate on all four wheels and are either **drum brakes** or **disc brakes.** The basic principle of both types of brakes is the same: A friction pad is pressed against a rotating steel part that turns with the wheel, slowing or stopping the car. In drum brakes the metal part is cylinder-shaped, and the friction material is mounted on curved pieces called **brake shoes** that fit inside the drum. In disc brakes a steel disc turns with the wheel, and the friction material is in the form of **pads** that

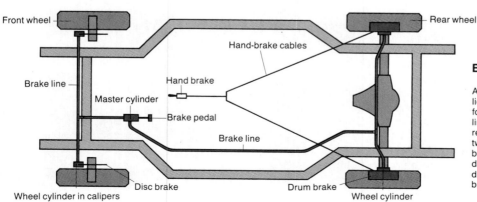

Front wheel

Rear wheel

Hand-brake cables

Brake line

Hand brake

Master cylinder

Brake pedal

Brake line

Disc brake

Wheel cylinder in calipers

Drum brake

Wheel cylinder

Brake System

All modern cars have hydraulic brakes that operate on all four wheels. Separate brake lines operate the front and rear brakes so that at least two wheels will have operating brakes if part of the system is damaged. The car shown has disc brakes in front and drum brakes in the rear.

are squeezed against both sides of the disc by a device called calipers.

Both types of brakes are operated by a hydraulic system. The main parts of the system are a **master cylinder** connected by steel tubes, called **brake lines,** to **wheel cylinders** at each wheel. When the driver steps on the brake pedal, a force is applied to a piston inside the master cylinder. The force is passed by the hydraulic fluid to a cylinder at each wheel where it moves another piston that pushes the friction material against the metal drum or disc. At the same time, an electric switch connected to the brake pedal turns on a red light at the rear of the car.

Many cars now have **power-assisted brakes** in which a vacuum system or a hydraulic pump operates on the master cylinder to increase the pressure applied by the driver. The power assist works only while the engine is running. All cars also have an emergency or hand brake that works independently of the hydraulic brake system.

A diagram of a hydraulic brake system appears in Volume H in the article HYDRAULIC AND PNEUMATIC SYSTEMS.

The Chassis and Body

The chassis includes the steel frame, the engine, drive train, and steering, brake, and suspension systems to which the body is fastened. The body includes the passenger compartments, the hood and trunk, and the fenders that cover the wheels. In earlier years the frame was manufactured first, and the body was then bolted to it. This method is still followed in the manufacture of cars that have fiberglass bodies and of trucks. Most modern automobiles are manufactured using **unitized body construction** in which the frame and body are made of a number of stamped steel panels that are welded together to make a one-piece combined chassis and body.

The Suspension. The suspension system supports the chassis and body and attaches them to the wheels. It absorbs the shock of hitting bumps in the road and improves safety by keeping good contact between the wheels and the road. The main parts of the suspension system are **springs** and **shock absorbers** located between the axles and the chassis at each wheel. The springs and shock absorbers resist pressure against the wheel caused by bumps in the road, smoothing out the movement of the chassis. Usually **coil springs** are used at the front wheels and **leaf springs** are used at the rear wheels. Some cars use coil springs at all four wheels or use **torsion bars** instead of springs. A torsion bar is a steel bar mounted so that a twisting force acts on it when the wheel moves up and down. The bar is elastic and resists the twisting force, acting much like a spring. Most cars have **independent suspension** at the front wheels that enables each wheel to move up and down separately. Shock absorbers are hydraulic devices that resist rapid changes of movement and smooth out the up and down movements of the wheels as they pass over bumps. There is usually one shock absorber at each wheel.

Wheels and Tires. Automobile wheels are made of pressed steel or an aluminum alloy. They are bolted to **hubs,** which are connected to the axles. The bolts are often covered by **hub caps** but must be easy to reach so that they can be removed when it is necessary to

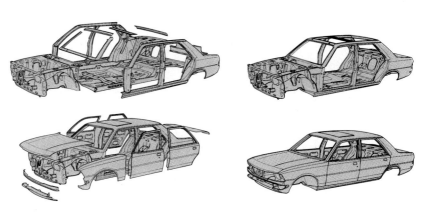

In unitized body construction, different parts of the body are stamped from sheet steel and welded together. The welding is often done by robots controlled by computers. The hood, trunk lid, front fenders, and doors are then added to complete the body.

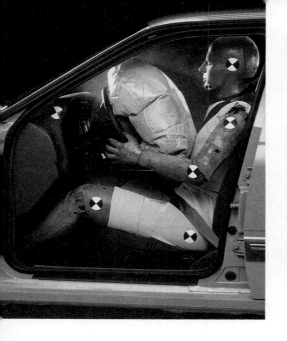

Left: In a test crash, an air bag inflates in a fraction of a second. The air bag prevents the dummy from smashing into the steering wheel or the windshield when the car stops abruptly. *Above:* Cars for sale in the United States are built so that the front end of the car will crumple and absorb some of the force that stops the car in a front-end accident.

remove a wheel, as in case of a flat tire. Modern tires are called **pneumatic tires** because they are filled with air that helps to cushion the ride. There are three kinds of tires used on automobiles: bias-ply, belted-bias, and radial. For more information about each type, see the article TIRES in Volume T.

Safety Features

All cars today have seat belts or some other restraint system to protect drivers and passengers in case of an accident. Many states now require drivers and passengers to fasten their belts every time they get into the car. In 1978 the state of Tennessee passed a law requiring that infants and children be placed in special restraints, and since then many states have also adopted this type of law. It has been proved that seat belts help prevent injury and even save lives.

Engineers are refining "air bag" systems that rapidly inflate from the steering wheel hub or the instrument panel if the car comes to a quick stop, such as in a collision. The resulting "balloon" would keep the driver from slamming into the wheel or dashboard or from flying out the front windshield. Many owners fear the system might activate at the wrong time and cause an accident, but this has never happened in cars that now use air bags. It is very likely that air bags will eventually be required equipment on all cars.

Other safety laws exist. Automobile bodies must be strong and often reinforced with steel bars in critical areas such as doors to protect the driver and passengers in case of accidents. Doors must have special locks that are crash resistant. Bumpers are now built to absorb some of the force of an accident. Brakes must meet certain performance standards, and fuel systems must be able to withstand crashes without spilling their flammable contents. Interiors of cars must be well padded, and outside mirrors must be available. Even the steering column on a modern car must be built to collapse, or otherwise absorb the impact of a crash. Tires, transmissions, and windshields must all be built with safety rules in mind.

How a New Model Is Created

A new model is made as a blend of what the public wants and needs and what the manufacturer thinks the public will buy. When the manufacturer decides to build a new model, the ideas of many people are considered. Engineers, stylists, designers, and economists decide how the car should look and perform and how much it should cost. Detailed drawings are then sent to hundreds of skilled specialists who plan the actual production of the car. Step-by-step they build the car from the ground up. They design and make working models of the various parts that will go into the car. Engineers may design and build a new engine for the new model. Other engineers may experiment with various types of axles, gears, brakes, and other components to see which will perform best for the new model.

Styling engineers select paint finishes, interior fabrics, and trim and also design the instrument panel and other accessories.

Finally a prototype, or sample version, of the car is built. It has probably taken months, even years, of careful research, design, and engineering to produce the final model. But questions still remain. Will the car perform correctly? Is it really the car the public wants?

Testing A New Model. The sample car is put through test after test to see if anything is wrong with it. It is placed in special "torture chambers" where it is frozen and thawed, drenched with water, heated and allowed to cool, and shaken and twisted until any flaws have been spotted and corrected. When the laboratory tests have been completed, the sample car is driven over a test track at the company proving ground. There it is subjected to far more severe punishment than the average automobile will have to face. Sample cars are also road tested to see how they perform on steep twisting mountain roads, on long flat straight roads, and in crowded city traffic. All this testing often leads to changes in design and then to more testing.

Mass Production of Automobiles

While the prototype model is going through its tests, engineers are planning how to manufacture the car in quantity. They design machines that will turn out the various parts of the car. Some of these machines, such as those that stamp out the roofs or fenders or doors, are the size of a small building. Other machines are designed so that parts, such as engine blocks, automatically move from one machine to another as different drilling, grinding, and other operations are performed.

Today's mass production of automobiles takes precise timing of every operation. Before mass production starts, engineers must determine the most efficient way to assemble the cars. Their plan must make sure that each machine manufacturing a part works in coordination with all the other machines so that the right parts meet at the right time and place on the final assembly line.

When everything is organized, full-scale production begins. Modern automobile production is like a great river. The main river is fed by side rivers, which are fed by streams. The "main river" of an automobile factory is

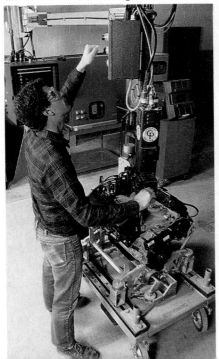

Right: Computers play a major part in the development of a new model. The shape of the car and the way people will fit in the car can be tried on a computer before even a model is made. *Below:* For some models, a new engine may be designed and tested to achieve the desired performance. *Below right:* A model of the new car is scanned by a device that records the car's shape. The data will be used in determining the final design.

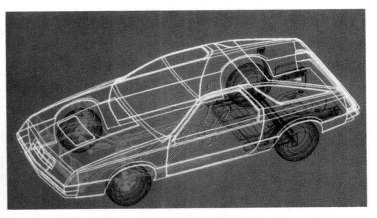

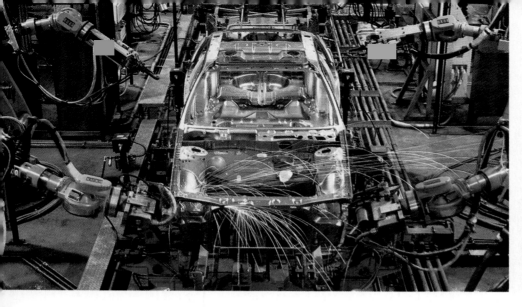

the final assembly line, an endless moving belt or chain that carries main components such as engine blocks.

The many sub-assembly lines are like the side rivers and streams, bringing parts and assembled sub-units—such as carburetors, fuel pumps, or alternators—into the main assembly line where they are attached by automatically controlled machines or by workers. A modern automobile has almost 20,000 separate parts, ranging in size from the roof and engine hood to tiny screws used inside the speedometer. Almost every part has been transported on an assembly line before it becomes a part of a finished automobile.

Once the engine and other sub-assemblies have been completed on their assembly lines, they are ready to be attached to the three major parts of the car—the chassis, the engine, and the body. With some models, the first two sub-assembly lines—carrying the chassis and the engine—meet and are fitted together. Then the chassis-engine assembly is joined to the body to produce a nearly completed car.

Other car models use an integrated, or single-unit, type of construction. Here, the body and chassis are welded together to make one instead of two major sub-assemblies.

Many additional operations are performed as the car moves down the assembly line. Parts are added at each station. Seats and floor carpets are installed, and the electrical systems are hooked up. Water hoses are attached, and various pieces of trim are added. Finally, at the very end of the line, gasoline is pumped into the tank and coolant into the radiator. Oil

has already been added to the engine on the engine's assembly line. A worker slides behind the wheel, starts the engine, and drives the car off the line.

But it is still not ready for its first owner. Quality-control inspectors examine the car for flaws. They adjust headlights and check details such as door, hood, and window fit.

Finally, at long last, the car is ready for the road.

The Automobile Industry

The automobile industry is one of the world's biggest producers and merchandisers of a product. It is also one of the biggest buyers. The industry consumes huge quantities of raw materials such as iron, copper, and rubber. In the United States it uses up one fourth of the country's steel production.

Excluding agricultural work, one out of every seven jobs in the United States is directly related to the manufacture and use of motor vehicles. These jobs support approximately 12,000,000 Americans. The center of automobile manufacturing in the United States is Detroit, Michigan, although in recent years major manufacturing plants have been built in several other states.

Beginning in the early years of the industry, manufacturers of automobiles have merged to form large corporations. In the United States, the three major manufacturers are General Motors, Ford, and Chrysler, each of which produces cars that still bear the names of the original independent companies. General Motors cars include Chevrolet, Pontiac, Oldsmo-

bile, and Cadillac. Cars manufactured by the Ford Motor Company include Ford, Mercury, and Lincoln. Chrysler Corporation cars include Chrysler, Plymouth, and Dodge. In Great Britain the major manufacturer of automobiles is the Rover Group, which produces the Land Rover and the Rover Stirling. The independent Rolls Royce Motor Cars Ltd. in England produces the famous Rolls Royce and Bentley cars. Also in England, the Jaguar-Daimler company produces the luxury Jaguar cars. In Germany the leading manufacturing companies are Volkswagen, Daimler-Benz (Mercedes), and BMW (Bayernische Motoren Werke). In France the leading manufacturing companies are Peugeot-Citroen and Renault. In Italy, the largest manufacturer of passenger cars is Fiat, but Fiat does not distribute cars in the United States. In Japan, the leading producers are Toyota, Nissan, and Honda.

In the early part of the 1990's more than 45,000,000 motor vehicles were manufactured worldwide each year. Of these, almost 35,000,000 were passenger cars and the remainder were trucks and buses. The five leading producers of passenger cars are Japan, United States, Germany, France, and Spain, in that order. Other countries that have a sizable automobile industry include Italy, the Russian Federation, the United Kingdom, Canada, and Korea. All of these countries, with the exception of Russia, export a large percentage of their output.

Throughout the world there are more than 386,000,000 cars on the road. If every person around the world climbed into an automobile at the same moment, there would be an average of twelve people in each car. But the number of people per automobile varies widely throughout the world. In the United States there are about two people per car, in Europe there are about five people per car, in Russia there are about 24 people per car, but in China there are more than 1,300 people per car.

In the early 1990's, there were more than 135,000,000 passenger cars on the road in the United States. More than two thirds of all the households in the United States have more than one motor vehicle. American motorists traveled just about 2,000,000,000,000 (trillion) miles in one year.

People in the United States own about 40 percent of the world's cars, trucks, and buses. Japan is in second place in the number owned. Other countries where ownership is high are Germany, France, Italy, the United Kingdom, and Canada.

When the automobile rolls off the assembly line, a number of businesses become involved. Trucking firms haul new cars from the factory to the dealers. The dealers employ staffs of salespeople and mechanics. Their advertisements bring business to newspapers and radio and television stations. Service stations supply gasoline and oil to keep the cars running. Service stations in turn purchase their supplies from oil companies. Cars need regular servicing, and this keeps many thousands of mechanics busy. In the United States, the automobile sales and service industry, including service station sales, accounts for more than $125,000,000,000 (billion) a year.

The car of the future may look like some cars of today, but it will be very different in the way that it operates. As new ideas and developments take place, they will be tried on a computer long before they are tested on the road.

Careers in the Automobile Industry

Manufacturing, selling, and servicing cars offer a wide range of career opportunities. Manufacturers employ many college graduates. Marketing experts determine what features the customers may want. Engineers, scientists, and artists design the cars. Production experts decide how to build them.

Manufacturing employees, such as machinists and tool and die workers, may have learned their skills in trade schools. They may serve several years as apprentices learning particular manufacturing skills. Others may be trained on the job to assemble cars.

Car dealers employ salespeople who are skillful in persuading customers to buy cars. Salespeople must be able to explain the cars' features and tell why these are desirable. This requires some mechanical knowledge.

Servicing cars offers a wide range of jobs— from pumping gas to making complicated repairs. Mechanics may be specialized in repairing certain areas such as transmissions, electrical systems, or car body repairs. Some of these skills may be learned in trade schools. Others may be taught by manufacturers' representatives or learned on the job. Large repair facilities have service managers and supervisors who make sure the work is done properly and efficiently.

The Car of the Future

The modern automobile is a marvelous machine. It is fast, sleek, comfortable, and beautiful to look at. But most automobile engineers know that the modern car will look like yesterday's noisy, smelly car when compared with the automobile of the future.

Experts predict that cars of the future will be made of plastics and carbon fibers that will be much stronger than steel and much lighter in weight. Even engines will be made of these materials.

Cars of the future will be smaller and lighter, but their design will probably be similar to the sleekest of the modern sports cars. There will probably not be any extreme design changes for a long time.

The real frontier for cars of the future lies not in body design but with computer activation. Cars may someday actually drive themselves. Highways would be wired so that cars could be programmed to travel a certain route and could make the trip with or without a driver. Everyone in the car would be able to relax, even take a nap, as the car speeds along at 200 miles (322 kilometers) per hour. The car would be radar- and computer-controlled to never touch other driverless cars or trucks and buses on the road. Changes of destination along the way could be made from the car, and a central computer could notify a computer at home.

Eventually the car would ease over to the right and pull off the high-speed roadway, navigate the city streets, and finally stop at the programmed destination.

Most automobile engineers believe that these cars are certain to be built, maybe even in the early 21st century—which would make it in your lifetime.

ROSS R. OLNEY
Author, *Car of the Future*

See also INTERNAL COMBUSTION ENGINES; DIESEL ENGINES; TRANSMISSIONS; BUSES AND BUS TRAVEL; TRUCKS AND TRUCKING; MASS PRODUCTION.

The ancient dream of flying has come true. These air show pilots are giving a thrilling demonstration of aerobatic flying, trailing white smoke to mark their paths in the sky.

AVIATION

People have always wanted to fly. The dream of flight appears in legends and myths of many cultures. It has been painted on cave walls, carved in stone, and inscribed on clay tablets. Through the centuries, stories have been told of magic flying carpets, winged horses, and chariots pulled by flying dragons.

The materials for simple aircraft have always been available. It would have been possible for ancient Chinese, Egyptians, or Incans to have made a hot-air balloon or a simple glider. Perhaps in a tiny village or on a remote mountainside someone did make a successful flight that was never recorded.

In the 20th century, the dream finally became a reality. Millions of people have flown in aircraft as varied as hot-air balloons, gliders, helicopters, 400-passenger airliners, and supersonic military fighters.

▶ EARLY ATTEMPTS TO FLY

One of the earliest concepts of flight came from watching the effortless soaring of birds. Many individuals tried to fly by strapping wood and fabric wings to their arms and jumping from a tower or a cliff—only to plunge straight to the ground.

A successful introduction to flight appeared in China several centuries before the birth of Christ. In a war a soldier could be sent up on a large kite to spy on the enemy army. But it was not the answer to the dream of flying, because the kite had to be attached to the ground by a long rope.

In the 16th century the great Italian artist, scientist, and inventor Leonardo da Vinci had many ideas for ways in which humans could fly. He drew designs for parachutes, helicopters, and human-powered ornithopters (aircraft with flapping wings) and may have experimented with kites and balloons. Da Vinci's sketches did not get people off the ground, but his work did prepare the way for the scientists of the 18th and 19th centuries who in turn set the stage for the explosion of flight that would take place after 1903.

This article is an overview of the subject of aviation. It covers major events in the history of flight. The development of commercial, military, and private aviation is discussed. Other subjects covered here are government regulations and safety standards, aircraft manufacture, and careers in aviation.

Descriptions of specific kinds of aircraft appear in the articles AIRPLANES; BALLOONS AND BALLOONING; GLIDERS; and HELICOPTERS. The physical laws of flight are found in AERODYNAMICS; the subject of flying faster than the speed of sound is covered under SUPERSONIC FLIGHT. The kinds of engines used on aircraft are described in detail in JET PROPULSION; INTERNAL-COMBUSTION ENGINES; and ROCKETS.

Other articles containing information related to aviation are AIRPORTS; NAVIGATION; PARACHUTES; RADAR, SONAR, LORAN, AND SHORAN; and UNITED STATES, ARMED FORCES OF.

Balloons

Over the centuries, people have observed that the smoke and sparks from a fire are carried upward in the currents of hot air. But no one thought to catch the hot air in a bag until the 18th century when the French brothers Joseph Michel and Jacques Étienne Montgolfier began experiments with balloons. They made a huge balloon, 100 feet (30.5 meters) around, which was a linen bag lined with paper. Lifted by hot air from a straw-fed fire, the balloon rose into the air on June 4, 1793. It was the first successful step on the road to flight.

About the same time, another French scientist, J. A. C. Charles, found that the newly discovered element hydrogen, which is lighter than air, could also lift a balloon. On August 24, 1783, he demonstrated his hydrogen balloon in Paris to a group that included an American inventor, Benjamin Franklin.

These two methods of balloon flight—gas-filled and hot-air balloons—are still in use today. Because hydrogen is flammable, helium now fills weather balloons, blimps, and even toy balloons. Hot-air ballooning has become a popular sport. Several people ride in a "basket" carried aloft by a large, brightly colored balloon that travels with the wind.

But balloons were not the solution for practical air transportation. Although they could lift heavy loads into the air, there was no way of controlling the direction of their flight.

Airships

In the late 18th century, efforts were being made to develop a balloon with power and a means to steer it. But it was not until 1852 that the first powered airship was flown. A French engineer, Henri Giffard, flew over Paris in a hydrogen-filled **dirigible.** Dirigible is the French word for "steerable" and is sometimes used as a name for powered, steerable lighter-than-air craft. Giffard's dirigible had a steam-powered propeller. Later dirigibles were powered by electric batteries or internal-combustion engines. Giffard's dirigibles were **nonrigid airships,** which means their shape was maintained by the pressure of the gas with which they were filled. They were shaped like huge, fat cigars. The British called them **blimps,** a term that is still used today.

In 1900 the first **rigid airship** flew. It was built by a German company owned by Ferdinand von Zeppelin. The shape of these **zeppelins,** as rigid airships are often called, was maintained by an internal metal framework which contained hydrogen-filled bags. Zeppelins had internal-combustion engines to power their propellers. More than 100 of these rigid airships were built, but they were not the ideal aircraft. The future of aviation was with the more slowly developing heavier-than-air craft.

Gliders

In the early 1800's, Sir George Cayley, an English inventor, believed it would be possible to build a heavier-than-air craft. Based on his observation of the flight of birds such as sea gulls, which soar for long distances without flapping their wings, he built model gliders with wings curved like a bird's wing. He added a combination rudder-elevator to make the glider turn and to climb or descend. These inventions are so important to all later

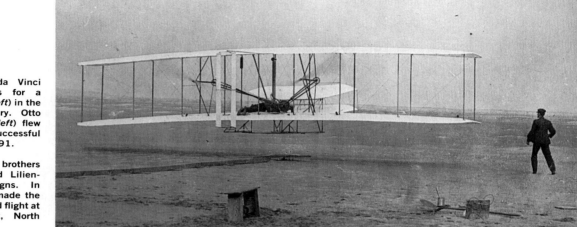

◀ Leonardo da Vinci drew plans for a glider (*far left*) in the 16th century. Otto Lilienthal (*left*) flew his first successful glider in 1891.

▶ The Wright brothers had studied Lilienthal's designs. In 1903 they made the first powered flight at Kitty Hawk, North Carolina.

aircraft designs that Cayley is often called the "father of aeronautics."

Power-driven model airplanes were being flown by the middle of the 19th century. The first was a steam-powered model designed and built by John Stringfellow, an English engineer. Steam remained the most popular source of power until the end of the 19th century. While tiny steam engines worked well enough in small model airplanes, steam engines large enough to power a full-size plane were too heavy to be practical. The development of the internal-combustion engine, light yet powerful, would one day be the solution. However, before powered flight was achieved, experiments with gliders large enough to carry a pilot solved the many problems of aircraft design and control.

Otto Lilienthal, a German, was one of the most successful designers of gliders. His first glider, built in 1891, was made of wood and cloth. The pilot hung from a frame in the center of the wing. Lilienthal took off in his glider by running down a hill with it until he was moving fast enough for the wind to lift the craft. He controlled the direction of flight by moving his body to one side or the other. Lilienthal made more than 2,000 flights. He was killed in 1896 while testing one of his new gliders.

▶POWERED FLIGHT

Lilienthal was the first engineer-pilot, designing, building, and flying his own aircraft. His work was an inspiration to two brothers from Ohio who made their living building bicycles. They were Wilbur and Orville Wright.

The Wright Brothers

In the amazingly short time of four years, the Wright brothers identified and solved the basic problems of flying a heavier-than-air craft. These were:

(1) Wings with enough surface area and the proper curve to provide lift.

(2) A means to control the direction of the aircraft's movement.

(3) Proper placement of weight to keep the aircraft balanced.

(4) A lightweight source of power.

(5) Efficient propellers.

(6) Piloting skills needed to fly the aircraft.

While the Wright brothers were solving these problems, others were also racing to be the first to fly in a powered aircraft. The Wrights' closest competitor may have been Samuel Pierpont Langley of the Smithsonian Institution.

After years of patient experiments and trials with models, Langley completed a full-size airplane called the *Aerodrome* in 1903. Langley's gasoline-powered machine was to be launched from the top of a houseboat in the Potomac River. On the first flight the *Aerodrome* crashed into the river. It was fished out and repaired and then launched again, only to crash a second time. Discouraged by the failures and by heavy criticism in the newspapers, Langley gave up his experiments.

The Wrights meanwhile had been creating a series of gliders. They had also built a wind tunnel, in which a fan forced air through a large tube. In this they could observe the effects of airflow on models of their aircraft designs. By 1903 they also had designed and built a lightweight internal-combustion engine and propellers to be connected to the engine by bicycle chains.

The First Flight

On December 17, 1903, a windy day at Kitty Hawk, North Carolina, Wilbur and Orville Wright made the first successful powered flight in a heavier-than-air craft. The first flight, made by Orville, was short—120 feet (36.6 meters) in 12 seconds—but it was followed by three more flights with the brothers taking turns. The last flight that day was made by Wilbur. It lasted for 59 seconds and covered 852 feet (254.8 meters). That distance would have been longer if there had not been a strong headwind.

Early Designers and Pilots

After the Wright brothers had solved the basic problems of powered flight, more people became excited about aviation and began to build and fly their own planes, often learning by trial and error. In Canada, Alexander Graham Bell, the inventor of the telephone, established the Aerial Experiment Association in 1907. One of the association's members was Glenn Hammond Curtiss, a designer of lightweight engines and a record-setting motorcycle racer. The association built several aircraft including the *June Bug,* in which Curtiss won a prize offered for flying more than one kilometer (.62 miles).

In France, interest in aviation was very high. Alberto Santos-Dumont, a Brazilian who lived there, made the first European flight in a powered biplane in 1906.

In 1909, Louis Bleriot, of France, became the first person to fly a plane across the English Channel. He made the flight in a monoplane that he had designed himself. Bleriot had added several new features to his airplane. The pilot sat in the cockpit of a covered fuselage (the body of the craft). He controlled the flight with a control stick and pedals, just as airplanes are flown today. The rudder and the elevators were at the rear of the plane. Bleriot's design became the standard for later airplane builders.

Soon the new designs created in Europe surpassed those in the United States. One reason for these rapid advances was that the military forces of the various European governments supported aviation development.

WORLD WAR I, 1914–1918

Although aircraft were only a small part of the total military effort in World War I, aviation was important right from the beginning of the conflict.

Airships were used by both sides for gathering information behind enemy lines. The British used blimps for spotting enemy submarines that could then be attacked by airplanes or ships. The Germans continued their pre-war development of zeppelins and used them in 53 bombing raids against England. Such raids were more notable for the fright they caused than for actual damage. By the end of the war, the disadvantage of airships was apparent. Zeppelins moved very slowly, making them easy targets. Gunfire from hostile airplanes or ground artillery could cause the hydrogen gas to burst into flames.

During the early years of the war, airplanes were also used for flying over enemy lines to gather information. But soon there were also squadrons of fighters and bombers with specialized airframes, engines, and weapons.

In 1914 a typical British aircraft was the B.E. 2a, a fragile biplane with a 35-foot (10.6-meter) wingspan and weighing only 1,274 pounds (573 kilograms). With its 70-horsepower Renault engine, it had a top speed of 70 miles (113 kilometers) per hour. It carried a pilot and an observer. Its weapons were pistols and hand-held bombs.

At the war's end, in November, 1918, the British Royal Air Force was flying the Handley-Page V/1500. The V/1500 had a wingspan of 126 feet (38.4 meters), weighed 24,000 pounds (19,800 kilograms), and was powered by four 375-horsepower Rolls-Royce engines. Its top speed was 97 miles (156 kilometers) per hour. The fighters were capable of speeds in excess of 140 miles (225 kilometers) per hour and strong enough to make the high speed turns, dives, and other maneuvers of air combat. There were aircraft carrying five machine guns and bombs weighing hundreds of pounds.

PEACETIME AVIATION, 1919–1938

After the war, former military pilots and many others used aircraft for peaceful purposes. They crossed the oceans, flew to unexplored areas of the world, and always tried to fly higher and faster.

Record Flights

In the ten years after World War I, the speed record went from 171 miles (275.2 kilometers) per hour to 370 miles (595 kilometers) per hour. The altitude record increased from 33,113 feet (10,093 meters) in 1920 to 43,166 feet (13,157 meters) in 1930.

The first aircraft to cross the Atlantic Ocean was the U.S. Navy's Curtiss NC-4. This four-engine **flying boat** (an aircraft that takes off and lands on the water) completed the trip in 19 days in May, 1919. The first nonstop flight across the Atlantic was made in the next month. British Lieutenants John Alcock and Arthur Whitten Brown flew a two-engine Vickers Vimy from Newfoundland to Ireland, a distance of 1,890 miles (3,043 kilometers), in 16 hours and 28 minutes.

In May, 1923, the first nonstop flight across the United States was made in a U.S. Army Air Service Fokker T-2, that was flown coast to coast in 26 hours and 50 minutes. In September, 1924, two U.S. Army Douglas World Cruisers completed a round-the-world flight that had taken 175 days.

The record-making flight that most excited the public was Charles A. Lindbergh's solo flight from New York to Paris. On the morning of May 20, 1927, he took off from Roosevelt Field on Long Island in a silver Ryan monoplane named the *Spirit of St. Louis*. Thirty-three hours and 30 minutes later, he landed in Paris where he was given a hero's welcome. His later flights and many public appearances created enthusiasm for aviation that speeded its progress for the next decade.

Early Commercial Aviation

For several years after World War I, the practical use of airplanes was limited because they were not large enough, reliable enough, or able to fly in bad weather. This meant that businesses could not make a profit by carrying passengers, nor could they compete economically with the railroads as freight carriers.

One thing airplanes could carry was the mail. In 1918 the United States Government established its own airmail service, with airfields and beacon lights across the country. In 1925, private companies were given the job of carrying the mail. They also began to carry other cargo and some passengers.

Aircraft design and construction improved, and the number of passengers began to grow. In 1926, Congress passed the Air Commerce Act, which set a system of licensing for airlines and pilots and established a federal airways system with light and radio beacons to mark the routes. Safety was improved with the addition of de-icers—devices on the wings that reduce the accumulation of ice in bad weather. Ice is dangerous because it destroys smooth airflow thus reducing lift. It also adds weight. Fire-extinguishing systems were installed, and new instruments and radio aids were developed to improve navigation and to allow safer flying. In 1927 more than 18,000 passengers traveled on commercial airlines.

Charles A. Lindbergh (*left*) stands beside the plane in which he made the first solo flight across the Atlantic Ocean (1927). Amelia Earhart (*right*) was the first woman to fly alone across the Atlantic (1932) and from Hawaii to California (1935).

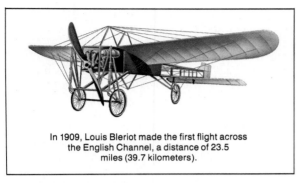

In 1909, Louis Bleriot made the first flight across the English Channel, a distance of 23.5 miles (39.7 kilometers).

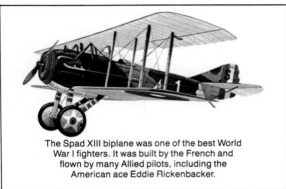

The Spad XIII biplane was one of the best World War I fighters. It was built by the French and flown by many Allied pilots, including the American ace Eddie Rickenbacker.

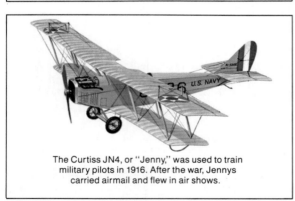

The Curtiss JN4, or "Jenny," was used to train military pilots in 1916. After the war, Jennys carried airmail and flew in air shows.

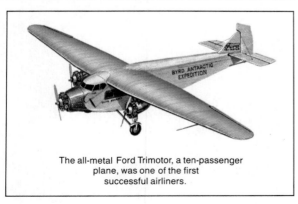

The all-metal Ford Trimotor, a ten-passenger plane, was one of the first successful airliners.

Zeppelins. At the same time that airplanes were being used for the first commercial flights, they had growing competition from rigid airships. The Germans built giant zeppelins. The first, in 1900, had been 419 feet (126 meters) long. By 1938 they had built the last and largest, which was 803 feet (41 meters) long, had four diesel engines, and could carry 30 tons of cargo across the ocean. Two American military airships actually carried five airplanes each and could launch them in the air.

But the possibility of damage by storms or from the use of highly flammable hydrogen gas made airship travel hazardous. When the zeppelin *Hindenburg* burst into flames while docking in Lakehurst, New Jersey, in May, 1937, the public finally rejected them as a passenger aircraft. By that time, airplanes had become safer and more convenient.

Successful Airliners. One of the first successful passenger planes was also used for explorations such as the pioneering flights made by American Rear Admiral Richard E. Byrd in Antarctica. The plane was the Ford Trimotor, one of the first all-metal aircraft. This ten-passenger plane was introduced in 1926, and many were still flying in the late 1930's.

In 1933, Boeing Aircraft Company introduced the 247, an all-metal plane with many new design features. Its cantilever wings were routed through the fuselage. The two engines had streamlined **cowling** (covers) into which the landing gear retracted. The new features were successful, but this plane also carried only ten passengers—too few for the growing airline businesses. However it paved the way for the first passenger plane capable of earning a profit. This was the legendary Douglas DC-3, introduced in 1936.

Douglas Aircraft Company engineers incorporated into the DC-3 all of the current technical developments of the time—all-metal structure, engine cowling, and retractable landing gear. It had **radial engines** (cylinders in a circle around the crankshaft) that were cooled by the air flowing over them, so they did not need heavy, complicated liquid cooling systems. The controllable pitch propellers could be changed to the most efficient angle for taking off or cruising. The landing flaps allowed the plane to land at lower speeds. In addition, the DC-3 carried 21 passengers. This plane made the United States a world leader in airline travel.

IN 2 DAYS TO NORTH AMERICA!
DEUTSCHE ZEPPELIN-REEDEREI

In the 1930's, intercontinental air travel increased. Giant zeppelins (*left*) carried passengers between Europe and North and South America. Flying boats, such as the Boeing 314 (*above*), were able to land on harbors and rivers next to many of the world's major cities.

The DC-3 was copied by many manufacturers in other countries and was the basis for airline growth all over the world. In World War II it was called the C-47 for use as a military transport. More than 13,000 civilian and military versions were built, many of which were still flying in the late 1980's.

Flying Boats. Another important passenger aircraft used in the 1930's was the flying boat. It was particularly useful for traveling long distances over oceans. It could land at many of the world's major cities that had no airports but were located on oceans, lakes, or rivers. Small flying boats were used for short trips in Europe, but only those built in the United States were capable of traveling long distances such as the 2,400 miles (38,640 kilometers) across the Pacific Ocean from California to Hawaii. Special piers were built for the flying boats to unload passengers and cargo. Sikorsky Aircraft Company's S.40 and S.42, the Martin M-130, and the Boeing 314 flew to the Far East, South America, and Europe. Flying boats were popular from the late 1930's until the end of World War II. By then, large airfields had been built all over the world, and there were land aircraft capable of carrying more passengers than the flying boats.

▶WORLD WAR II, 1939–1945

The technical advances used in the design of the DC-3 were also applied to the fighters and bombers of all the air forces that fought in World War II. The German Luftwaffe (air force) had already tested modern military aircraft such as the Messerschmitt Bf 109 fighter and Heinkel He 111 bomber in the Spanish Civil War. Civilians had learned the terrors of air warfare when German planes bombed and destroyed the Spanish city of Guernica. In 1939 and 1940 the Luftwaffe used tactics it had developed in Spain to support the German army in the conquest of Europe.

The English had matched the German aircraft development with its own fighters, the Spitfire and Hurricane. These were used to fight the Battle of Britain in August and September of 1940. By maintaining control of its own skies, the British Royal Air Force was able to prevent the Germans from invading or forcing a British surrender by heavy bombing. Although London and many British industrial cities were bombed, production of aircraft continued and the people's morale remained high.

The British had developed four-engine heavy bombers—the Short Stirling, Handley-

The British Spitfire was a World War II fighter. It could fly at more than 350 miles (560 kilometers) per hour.

The B-17 Flying Fortress, a World War II bomber, could carry 3 tons of bombs to targets 600 miles (966 kilometers) away.

The MiG 15, shown here with North Korean markings, was a Russian-built fighter used in the Korean War. Its top speed was 668 miles (1,075 kilometers) per hour.

The B-52 Strato Fortress was in service from the late 1950's through the 1980's. It can carry bombs to targets 12,500 miles (20,000 kilometers) away.

The F-15 Eagle is a U.S. jet fighter used in the 1980's. It can climb to 98,000 feet (30,000 meters) in 2.5 minutes.

Page Halifax, and Avro Lancaster. These, with the American Boeing B-17s and Consolidated B-24s, eventually carried large bomb loads deep into German territory, sometimes maintaining round-the-clock bombing of military, industrial, and railroad targets, as well as of major cities.

The Japanese and Allied forces used aircraft in combination with ships throughout the war in the Pacific. On December 7, 1941, the Japanese used carrier-based aircraft to attack Pearl Harbor, the U.S. Naval base in Hawaii. The first important aerial blow struck by the United States was a bombing raid in April, 1942. B-25s, normally land-based, were launched from aircraft carriers to attack Tokyo and other Japanese cities. Allied strength in the air grew, with carrier-based and land-based planes playing important parts in the war in the Pacific. The last blow of the war was struck in August, 1945, by two B-29s, each carrying a single atomic bomb.

The B-29 was one of two aircraft that demonstrate the effect the war had on aircraft design and technology. It could fly at 400 miles (644 kilometers) per hour, had a range of 5,333 miles (8,583 kilometers), and could carry up to 10,000 pounds (4,545 kilograms) of bombs. This was later increased to 20,000 pounds (9,000 kilograms).

The second plane was Germany's 550-mile (885-kilometer)-per-hour Messerschmitt Me 262 fighter, whose jet engines and swept wings clearly showed the way for future aircraft design.

Other important aviation developments came out of the war. One was the use of radar for aircraft identification, control, navigation, and bombardment. Another was the helicopter, which was used as a rescue aircraft.

Other developments included a worldwide network of landing fields, navigational aides, meteorological (weather forecasting) facilities, and repair sites. These helped the huge expansion of air travel in the next decade.

▶1945 TO THE PRESENT

Before World War II, new designs of aircraft had been limited by the power available from current engines. The jet engine changed this situation. It was so powerful that stronger, more steamlined airframes were required.

New Designs. One of the most visible design changes was the swept wing that had been used on the Me 262. These wings were used on the new fighters and bombers and, in 1954, on the prototype (original model) of the Boeing 707, which became the world's first successful jet airliner. New metals and new manufacturing techniques were also developed to meet the special needs of high speed and high altitude flight.

The jet engine was not the only new form of propulsion. In October, 1947, the Bell XS-1 research rocket plane flew faster than the speed of sound (760 miles, or 1,225 kilometers, per hour). Rockets were usually used in research aircraft and as auxiliary power to assist heavily loaded military planes to take off.

The North American F-100, the first supersonic fighter, was put into service in 1953. Three years later the first supersonic bomber, the delta-winged Convair B-58, followed. In 1969, co-operative effort by Britain and France made possible the flight of the Concorde, the first successful supersonic airliner.

New Records. The new technology meant that speed and altitude records would continue to be challenged and broken. An intense international rivalry developed. The first official postwar speed record of 602.87 miles (970.23 kilometers) per hour was set in 1945 by a British Gloster Meteor F4.

In 1956 a British Fairey Delta 2 exceeded the 1,000-miles-per-hour mark at a speed of 1,131.76 miles (1,821.39 kilometers) per hour. A Russian Mikoyan Type E166 raised this to 1,665.89 miles (2,681 kilometers) per hour in 1962. By 1976 a U.S. Lockheed SR-71A—nicknamed the "Blackbird"—flew at 2,193 miles (3,529.56 kilometers) per hour. After the war, speeds were referred to in **"Mach" numbers**—multiples of the speed of sound, which is called Mach 1.

Although the records are not official, the highest and fastest aircraft ever flown is the North American X-15 research plane. In 1963 the X-15 reached an altitude of 354,200 feet —over 67 miles (201.87 kilometers). Because this is considered to be a space flight, the pilots were awarded astronaut wings. In 1967 the X-15A-2 achieved a speed of Mach 6.72, or 4,534 miles (6,300 kilometers) per hour.

While speed and altitude records were made and broken, one major goal of flight in the atmosphere had not been achieved. This was a nonstop, nonrefueled flight around the world. In December, 1986, this goal was reached in *Voyager,* a fragile-appearing airplane built by Burt Rutan, an American aircraft designer. It had a wingspan of 111 feet (33.8 meters)— longer than a Boeing 727—weighed 2,680 pounds (1,206 kilograms), and carried almost 1,200 gallons (4,560 liters) of fuel, which weighed four times as much as the plane itself.

The flight of 26,718 miles (43,016 kilometers) was made in 9 days by pilots Dick Rutan and Jeana Yeager. It was a triumph of high-technology materials, computer-aided design, and the personal skill and bravery of its pilots.

Left: The DC-3, introduced in 1936, is one of the oldest airplanes in use today. This one is dropping fire fighters near a forest fire.

Right: Voyager is one of the latest airplane designs. In 1986 it made the first nonstop, nonrefueled flight around the world.

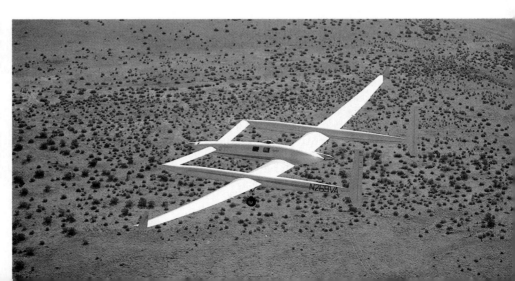

The 400-seat Boeing 747 (*above*) has its cockpit above the passenger area. The supersonic Concorde (*right*) has an adjustable nose section, shown here in the lowered position, allowing the pilot to see the runway better.

▶COMMERCIAL AVIATION TODAY

Air travel has changed our lives in many ways. Where once only the wealthy traveled from country to country, now the average citizen can do it, too. Two things that make this possible are larger airplanes and more fuel efficient engines. An airplane like the Boeing 747 can carry 400 people at a cost 25 percent lower per person than the 100-passenger 707.

Another factor in lowering the cost of flying is deregulation of the airlines. In 1984 the United States Government dissolved the Civil Aeronautics Board (CAB), the agency that had controlled the routes, fares, and some other airline activities. Now airlines compete for passengers by offering lower fares, better schedules, or different routes—things that once were set for them by the CAB.

Growth and Problems. After deregulation there was tremendous growth in the U.S. airline industry. But this growth has created problems, one of which is crowded airports. One of the busiest, O'Hare Field in Chicago, serves about 55,000,000 passengers a year. In such crowded, busy conditions, baggage sometimes gets lost, or more tickets are sold for a flight than there are seats on the airplane. Delays caused by weather or maintenance problems may result in lines of airplanes waiting for takeoff or circling overhead waiting for their turn to land. Air traffic controllers must direct rapidly growing numbers of flights of arriving and departing aircraft as well as those en route. Airport administrations, airline companies, and the federal government are all attempting to solve these problems.

The growth in passenger flying has created a need for new large and small airliners. The United States is the world leader in the manufacture of large planes such as the Boeing 767 and McDonnell Douglas MD11. But U.S. airlines also buy from foreign manufacturers. Regional airlines use smaller planes such as the German Fokker 100, the British de Havilland DHC-7, and the Italian Aerospace/Aeritalia ATR42.

Although many technical improvements have been made in passenger airplane construction, speeds have increased very little. The original Boeing 707s had a maximum cruising speed of about 600 miles (966 kilometers) per hour. A modern 747 can attain about 625 miles (1,006 kilometers) per hour. Except for the supersonic Concorde, most airliners fly at about 550 miles (885 kilometers) per hour. As a result, flight times have remained constant for the last 30 years.

▶FLYING SAFETY

The airlines have had a very good safety record, and statistics show it is safer to travel by airplane than by car. But many people remain concerned about the dangers of flying as the skies become more crowded. The government agency setting and maintaining standards of aviation safety is the Federal Aviation Administration (FAA). In addition to regulating air traffic, the FAA makes rules for aircraft construction and maintenance and pilot licensing and training. It also investigates accidents.

Because accident investigations often focus on pilot error, the FAA pays close attention to the training requirements of pilots. It gives pilot candidates written and flying tests for different levels of skill. A pilot is not allowed to fly for purposes beyond the level of the license earned. The airlines test their pilots further and periodically check their skills and send them to classes to refresh their knowledge.

▶GENERAL AVIATION

Aviation other than military or airline is called general aviation. For many years the United States has led the world in the number of private planes registered and in the total number of pilots licensed. In the late 1980's, there were 210,654 active general aviation aircraft, flown by 709,118 active pilots. A total of 34,063,000 hours were flown by general aviation pilots in 1985, out of 16,516 airports.

Flying corporate executives in swift jets and fighting forest fires in water bombers are general aviation activities. Others include delivering organs for transplants, controlling traffic and other police work, and simply sport flying.

The number and variety of airplanes using large airports have created problems: Each type of plane flies at a different airspeed when approaching to land, yet it is necessary to maintain a safe distance between them. The pilots may be students who have not yet earned their licenses, or they may have thousands of hours of flying experience.

In the late 1980's, owners and manufacturers of small planes, commercial and private pilots, and the FAA were seeking ways to protect flyers without overly restricting the use of the public airports. Controlled airspace around large airports is restricted to planes with two-way radios. In many such areas an aircraft must also have a **transponder**—a device on the plane that sends a signal identifying its position on the controller's radar screen.

▶AIRCRAFT MANUFACTURING

The cost of the new electronic equipment is high, as are the costs of buying, insuring, and maintaining aircraft. Flying lessons and renting airplanes are also expensive. This has reduced by about 85 percent the number of new general aviation aircraft sold between the late 1970's and the late 1980's. The greatest drop in production was in single-engine aircraft.

Total annual production of aircraft is about 10,000 per year (not including homebuilt planes). During World War II, U.S. manufacturers produced aircraft at a rate of 100,000 per year. But modern planes are far more com-

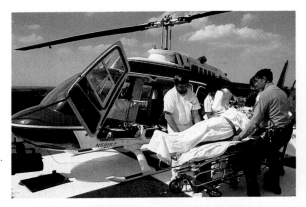

Aircraft serve many important purposes. Helicopters can be used to carry the ill or injured to hospitals (*top left*). Seaplanes carry people and supplies into remote areas where there are no airports (*bottom left*). Airplanes drop chemicals or water on forest fires (*below*).

plex. It may take seven years from the initial design to production of a warplane, and four years for a commercial airliner.

Every aspect of the design must be considered in order to achieve the combination of large size, high speed, and requirements for safety, reliability, and fuel economy. Engineers use many computer-aided design techniques. Before the first parts are built, there are computer tests of the design for strengths and weaknesses. New metals and composite materials such as plastic resins and graphite fibers are used because they combine strength and light weight. Sophisticated electronic equipment is also designed with the aid of computers.

The new materials and equipment and the time spent designing and building new planes are very costly. But planes are far more durable today than in the past. Whereas the early jet engines had to be overhauled every 25 hours of flying time, modern jet engines serve for tens of thousands of hours with much less maintenance. They last so long that weather-induced corrosion is more of a problem than are parts worn out by use. With careful maintenance and replacement of some parts with ones of newer design, an airliner can last 20 or 30 years, flying thousands of hours. This repays the owner's investment many times over.

▶CAREERS IN AVIATION

The growth of airline service since deregulation has increased the need for pilots. In the past, because there was always a large number of qualified pilots seeking positions with the airlines, the standards for hiring could be very high. However, as many as 50,000 additional pilots will be required before 1995. For this reason, airlines are looking for ways to have enough pilots with the necessary training and experience. Some are providing their own training programs in which the entire training of a pilot is done by the airline's methods, right from the start. These may be combined with college degree programs.

Another source of qualified pilots is former military flyers. Military flying training standards are very high, and the equipment used is up to date. However, pilots earning their wings in the military service have to serve a number of years before returning to civilian life. In addition, the military pay is now more competitive with that of civilian pilots.

There are also a number of independent civilian flight training schools. It may cost a student as much as $25,000 to earn ratings to qualify as a professional pilot. Such a course would include 260 hours of flying time. Graduates of these schools might work for small commuter airlines, air taxi services, businesses owning airplanes, or in other jobs in which they are paid to fly with passengers. For all of these positions, candidates must be 18 years old and have a commercial license, which requires 200 hours of flying time. They must also take a written test and pass a physical examination.

Airline pilots must meet stricter requirements. To obtain an Airline Transport Pilot license, extensive training and experience in airline equipment is required. In addition, written, physical, and flight examinations must be passed. Many airline pilots start out as flight engineers, for which they usually

In 1988, world records were set for distance and time aloft in a human-powered plane. Greek cycling champion Kanellos Kanellopoulos pedaled the American-built *Daedalus* for 3 hours and 54 minutes to complete the 74-mile (119-kilometer) flight between the Greek islands of Crete and Santorini.

The Beech Starship, a business plane, is built of light, strong composite materials. It has small forward wings, called canards, and winglets—sharply angled wingtips.

need both a commercial pilot's license and a flight engineer's license earned by passing written and practical tests.

Two licenses can be earned to become an airplane mechanic—either an airframe or engine mechanic's license; some positions require both. Aircraft mechanics maintain the complicated modern airliner. They often receive further training by the airline and by the manufacturer of the planes they maintain.

Each airline sets its own requirements and training for flight attendants. Their most important job is to see that the passengers are safe in normal operations and in emergencies. They also try to make the flight comfortable and enjoyable for the passengers.

Manufacturers employ engineers in many fields to design aircraft. Mechanics, electricians, and other expert workers are involved in the construction of the aircraft, and pilots are employed to test-fly them.

The FAA employs and trains air traffic controllers to work in airport control towers and other control centers. FAA pilots check the performance of commercial pilots, give flight exams to people seeking a pilot's license, and perform many safety-related tasks. Agency investigators try to discover the causes of all aviation accidents in order to prevent future ones.

▶ THE FUTURE IN AVIATION

Since the first brief powered flight in 1903, aviation has undergone huge changes and has brought equally great changes to the world.

Millions of people fly for business and pleasure. Two world wars and many other conflicts have shown the devastation of aerial conflict. And world leaders fly from one capital to another to attempt settlements of small wars before they become large ones.

The field of aviation will continue to change. New ideas in aircraft design will result in higher speeds and greater fuel economy. By the end of the 20th century, it may be possible to fly from New York City to Tokyo in less than two hours in a plane that flies at the edge of space.

Short flights from city center to city center will become more frequent with the further development of vertical-takeoff aircraft. The helicopter is a familiar version. Others will be similar to the tilt-rotor Bell XV-22, on which the angle of the engines can be changed for vertical or horizontal flight.

Cargo planes will be larger and able to carry heavier loads. The total weight of an aircraft, its fuel, and cargo might be as much as 1,000,000 pounds (450,000 kilograms). Cargo aircraft may be built in different shapes to carry certain large items. There are already specially modified planes that carry a single huge rocket engine. A modified 747 is used to carry the space shuttle on its back. More such uses will be devised.

Military aircraft will also have new shapes and be built of new materials. Some already have wings swept forward, and others have wings that can be moved from straight to swept positions. On-board computers assist in

MILESTONES OF AVIATION

1783	Jacques Étienne and Joseph Montgolfier of France launched first balloon (June).
1785	Jean Pierre Blanchard, French balloonist, made first successful voyage across English Channel.
1804	First winged glider made by Sir George Cayley, English aviation pioneer.
1848	John Stringfellow (English) constructed first successful power-driven model airplane.
1852	Henri Giffard flew steam-driven airship over Paris.
1891	Otto Lilienthal of Germany began his glider experiments.
1903	Wright brothers made first sustained, controlled flights in powered heavier-than-air craft at Kitty Hawk, North Carolina.
1909	Louis Blériot (French) made first crossing of English Channel in an airplane.
1911	Galbraith P. Rogers flew across United States, New York to California; flying time, 49 days.
	Eugene Ely accomplished first landing on deck of a ship.
1912	Harriet Quimby flew across English Channel, first woman to perform this feat.
1918	First airmail route established in United States.
1919	First crossing of Atlantic by air, accomplished by U.S. Navy seaplane; flying time, 54 hours.
	First nonstop air crossing of Atlantic made by two English airmen, Captain John Alcock and Lieutenant Arthur Whitten Brown.
1923	Two U.S. Army pilots made first nonstop transcontinental flight, New York to San Diego, California, in 26 hours, 50 minutes.
1924	U.S. Army pilots made first round-the-world flight, which was also first transpacific flight; flying time, 175 days.
1926	Lieutenant Commander Richard E. Byrd and Floyd Bennett flew across the North Pole, May 9.
1927	Charles A. Lindbergh made first solo nonstop transatlantic flight, New York to Paris; flying time, 33 hours, 30 minutes.
1929	Lieutenant James H. Doolittle, U.S. Army, made first flight using instruments only.
	Commander Richard E. Byrd and crew made first flight across South Pole, November 29.
	Fritz Opel of Germany flew first rocket plane.
1931	Wiley Post and Harold Gatty flew around the world in 8 days, 15 hours, 51 minutes.
1932	Amelia Earhart became first woman to fly Atlantic solo.
1939	First flight by jet aircraft made, in Germany.
1947	Captain Charles Yeager, USAF, made first supersonic flight.
1949	A USAF B-50, *Lucky Lady II,* completed first nonstop round-the-world flight.
1963	The X-15 flew to an altitude of 67 mi (202 km).
1965	Commander J. R. Williford, U.S. Navy, made longest direct helicopter flight—2,105.49 mi (3,388.46 km).
1967	First nonstop crossing of North Atlantic made by two USAF helicopters.
	The X-15A-2 achieved the speed of Mach 6.72 (4,534 mi, or 6,300 km, per hour).
1969	First flights of Supersonic Transports (SST's)—Soviet TU-144 and Anglo-French Concorde.
1970	Boeing 747's made first commercial flights.
1976	Concorde began first passenger-carrying supersonic service.
1977	The first human-powered aircraft, the *Gossamer Condor,* flew a course around pylons 0.31 mi (0.5 km) apart.
1979	The first human-powered aircraft, the *Gossamer Albatross,* was flown across the English Channel.
1981	Space shuttle orbiter Columbia, the first re-usable spacecraft, made an airplane-like landing after completing its first space mission.
1986	Richard Rutan and Jeana Yeager flew *Voyager* on the first nonstop, nonrefueled flight around the world.
1988	Record for distance (74 mi, or 118 km) and time aloft (3 hours, 54 minutes) set in a human-powered plane, the *Daedalus,* designed and built in the United States, flown by Kanellos Kanellopoulos (Greece).

the controlling of the aircraft and its weapons. New materials for the surface of the aircraft will make it less visible on radar.

New fuels such as hydrogen, methane, or nuclear fuels will be used. Solar energy has already been used to power a very lightweight experimental aircraft. Other experiments are being conducted in which ground antennas beam microwaves to an aircraft where they are converted to electric power.

New materials and designs will also be used in general aviation aircraft. Some of these ideas will come from those modern aviation pioneers, the designer-pilots. These pilots follow the path of the Wright brothers, sometimes setting world records and leading the way for aircraft manufacturers. Many of the pilots and companies exchange information and encouragement through such organiza- tions as the Experimental Aircraft Association of Oshkosh, Wisconsin.

Sport planes may soar with the birds at 20 miles per hour, fighters may roar 10 feet above the terrain in darkest weather, and airliners may whisk 1,000 passengers from New York City to Honolulu. All of these aircraft will be products of the human spirit that produced the original dream of flight. They are a tribute to the men and women who devote their lives to aviation.

WALTER J. BOYNE
Former Director
National Air and Space Museum
Smithsonian Institution

See also AERODYNAMICS; AIRPLANES; AIRPORTS; BALLOONS AND BALLOONING; GLIDERS; HELICOPTERS; INTERNAL-COMBUSTION ENGINES; JET PROPULSION; NAVIGATION; RADAR, SONAR, LORAN, AND SHORAN; ROCKETS; SUPERSONIC FLIGHT; TRANSPORTATION; UNITED STATES, ARMED FORCES OF THE.

AZERBAIJAN

Azerbaijan is a country situated in the eastern part of Transcaucasia—the region lying along the great Caucasus Mountain range, which traditionally forms part of the dividing line between Europe and Asia. The present-day borders of Azerbaijan date from the early 1800's, when it was divided between Russia and Persia (now Iran). Russian, or northern, Azerbaijan was briefly independent, from 1918 to 1920, before it was absorbed by the Soviet Union, which succeeded the Russian Empire. When the Soviet Union itself fell apart in late 1991, northern Azerbaijan declared its independence.

The People. The Azeri, or Azerbaijanis, are descended from Turkic-speaking peoples who migrated to the region from Central Asia in ancient times. Today, Azeri Turks make up about 85 percent of the country's population. The two largest ethnic minorities are Russians and Armenians. Azeri Turkish is the official language, although Russian continues in common usage. (In Iranian Azerbaijan, Persian is widely used.) The Azerbaijanis are Muslims, the Russians and Armenians Christians. There are also a small number of Jews, some of whom have preserved their faith since the days of the Khazar Kaganate, a once-powerful Turkic state in the region.

About half the people live in urban areas. The capital and largest city, Baku, is Azerbaijan's chief port on the Caspian Sea. With some 2 million people in its metropolitan area, Baku has more than one-quarter of the country's total population.

Azerbaijan's territory includes the Nagorno-Karabakh and Nakhichevan regions. Nagorno-Karabakh has been the scene of much bloody fighting between ethnic Armenians and Azeris. The Armenians, who make up a majority of its population, seek unification with Armenia.

The Land. Azerbaijan has a ruggedly beautiful landscape. Nearly half the land is covered by mountains. The Greater Caucasus forms Azerbaijan's natural boundary on the north; the Lesser Caucasus separates it from Armenia on the west; and the Talysh Mountains border

Looking as rugged as the mountains of her homeland, a woman of Azerbaijan contemplates her country's future. Azerbaijan was a constituent republic of the Soviet Union, before winning its independence as a result of the Soviet Union's collapse in 1991.

Iran to the south. Eastern Azerbaijan lies open to the Caspian Sea, which, despite its name, is the world's largest lake. Beyond the Caspian Sea are the deserts of Central Asia.

The Kura-Araks Lowland, which makes up the remaining land, takes its name from the country's two major rivers, the Kura and the Araks. The Araks marks the boundary with Iran. Fertile lowland plains, watered by the rivers and streams, stretch from the mountains to the Caspian Sea. The Apsheron Peninsula, jutting into the Caspian Sea, is the site of Baku.

Climate and Natural Resources. The climate varies widely, depending on elevation. The lowlands generally have mild winters and long, hot, and dry summers. Lowland temperatures in summer average 80°F (26°C). In the upper valleys and highlands, snow covers the ground in winter, while summers are comfortably cool.

The mountain forests are home to many kinds of wild animal life. The Caspian Sea teems with fish, including sturgeon, whose roe (eggs) are the source of the finest caviar. Azerbaijan is rich in mineral resources. In the early 1900's it produced half of the world's petroleum. Its mainland deposits are now exhausted, but crude oil is still extracted from offshore oil fields in the Caspian Sea.

The Economy. Economically, Azerbaijan has well-developed industry as well as a diversified agriculture that meets almost all of the food needs of its people. Heavy industry makes up about 80 percent of its gross national product (GNP), or the total value of its goods and services. It includes oil processing and the manufacture of petroleum products, chemical fertilizers, electrical equipment, machinery, metals, and related goods. The remaining 20 percent of the GNP is shared by agriculture and light industry, which includes processed agricultural products, textiles, footwear, and electrical household appliances and other consumer goods.

The varied climatic zones enable Azerbaijani farmers to grow a variety of crops. These include wheat and other grains, cotton, tea, tobacco, and almost all kinds of vegetables and fruits. Sheep are grazed on mountain pastures in summer and in the lowlands in winter.

History. As the only convenient land route through the Caucasus between Europe and Asia, Azerbaijan has been crossed by invading armies and migrating peoples since earliest times. The formation of Azerbaijan nationality dates from the A.D. 1000's, with the arrival of the last Turkic tribes, whose common language became Azeri Turkish. At only one period in its history, however, was all of Azerbaijan united under a single national ruler. In the 1500's, a native Azeri dynasty of the Safavids (or Safawids) created a great empire that eventually reached from Central Asia to the Persian Gulf. But in the 1600's the Safavid state fell under Persian rule.

The 1700's were marked by the struggle between Persia, Ottoman Turkey, and Russia for control of Azerbaijan and the rest of Transcaucasia. Under treaties signed in 1813 and 1828, Russia acquired the half of Azerbaijan north of the Araks River. After the Russian Revolution of 1917, Azeri leaders, on May 28, 1918, proclaimed an independent Azerbaijani republic. It lasted only until 1920, when Azerbaijan was invaded by forces of the Red (or Soviet) Army. It became a constituent republic of the Soviet Union in 1922. With the Soviet collapse in December 1991, Azerbaijan regained its independence.

Government. The country's legislative body is the National Assembly (Milli Mejlis). Executive authority is held by the president, who appoints the Council of Ministers, headed by a prime minister, to handle the day-to-day operations of the government. Geidar A. Aliyev was elected president in 1993. That same year the National Assembly approved Azerbaijan's entry into the Commonwealth of Independent States (CIS), an organization made up of most of the former Soviet republics.

ALEC RASIZADE
Visiting Research Fellow
The W. Averell Harriman Institute
Columbia University

FACTS and figures

AZERBAIJANI REPUBLIC is the official name of the country.

LOCATION: Eastern Transcaucasia.

AREA: 33,436 sq mi (86,600 km²).

POPULATION: 7,500,000 (estimate).

CAPITAL AND LARGEST CITY: Baku.

MAJOR LANGUAGE(S): Azeri Turkish (official), Russian.

MAJOR RELIGIOUS GROUP(S): Muslim.

GOVERNMENT: republic. **Head of state**—president. **Head of government**—prime minister. **Legislature**—National Assembly (Milli Mejlis).

CHIEF PRODUCTS: Agricultural—wheat and other grains, cotton, tea, tobacco, vegetables and fruits, livestock. **Manufactured**—petroleum products, chemical fertilizers, electrical machinery, metals, processed agricultural products, textiles, consumer goods. **Mineral**—petroleum and natural gas, aluminum, iron, copper, and zinc ores.

AZTECS

The Aztecs were an American Indian people of central Mexico, best known as the builders of an empire that swiftly fell under Spanish control during the years 1519 to 1521.

The defeat of the Aztecs was no ordinary conquest. The capital of their empire was a city larger than Rome. In its beauty it resembled Venice, set in the middle of a lake with canals for streets.

Although the city was demolished in the final battle of 1521, its fame has endured. Aztec civilization is remembered today for its elaborate religious life, complex social organization, elegant literature, and monumental works of sculpture.

▶ SOCIAL ORDER

What made Aztec society run smoothly? How was it organized?

Such questions cannot be answered fully. Yet there is a wealth of information in the writings of conquerors and missionaries. Aztecs themselves learned to use alphabetic script, and some of them wrote descriptions of life as it had been before the Spanish Conquest. These early accounts are our sources.

Family and Community

When a man tied the end of his cloak to the corner of a woman's blouse, she became his wife and he could marry no other. Though he might take one or more secondary "wives," only the children of his actual wife could inherit his property.

A man's duties included farming, soldiering, and the various trades, such as carpentry and metalwork. A woman took care of the home, wove cloth, or practiced medicine.

Children had responsibilities of their own. Girls helped with the weaving. Boys fetched firewood or went to the marketplace to pick up scraps of maize (corn) and beans left by the merchants.

Settlements. Families lived in villages, towns, or cities. Every town had neighborhoods, each with its chief. A city with many neighborhoods might be divided into four quarters, each quarter with its chief. These divisions made it easy to recruit people for military service or large work projects.

In the Valley of Mexico, the center of the Aztec world, there were dozens of cities. The largest was the capital, called Tenochtitlán, which may have had a population of 200,000. Tenochtitlán and its twin city, Tlatelolco, were located on islands in the middle of a shallow lake. The islands were connected to the mainland by earthen causeways.

Today the capital of the republic of Mexico is Mexico City. It is on the same site, but the lake, over the years, has been mostly drained.

Social Classes. Like cities today, the Aztec capital was a place of bustling activity, filled with people of all kinds. Everybody, however, fit into one of three categories: nobles, commoners, and *tlatlacotin*. The *tlatlacotin* were poor people who had sold themselves as permanent workers. Their children, however, were born free.

This drawing by Ignacio Marquina shows the Aztec capital Tenochtitlán as it appeared in 1519. It is based on the descriptions of Spanish conquerors and the remains of Aztec monuments.

High officials were usually chosen from the noble class. Commoners were also selected, if of proven ability.

Government

Each city was ruled by a king, who gave orders to neighborhood chiefs and to kings of cities under his control. There was no single chain of command but several, each ending with one of the important kings. These kings made alliances among themselves. Since Tenochtitlán was the strongest of the cities, its ruler can be called emperor or king of the empire.

Tribute. The reason for controlling other cities was to make them pay taxes, or tribute. Tribute goods included cloaks, hides, timber, stone, precious feathers, jewels, gold, and various foods.

Warfare. People did not like giving tribute to a king in a distant city. They were loyal to their own town. But if they refused to pay, they were threatened with armed attack.

Aztec armies were well equipped with bows and arrows, spears, and a kind of wooden sword, called *macana*, which was edged with sharp bits of stone.

If the governors or emperor heard of a far-away city rich in goods, they sent warriors to conquer it. Afterward they divided up the tribute and made sure that it kept coming regularly. This is how the empire grew.

▶ WAY OF LIFE

Traditional Aztec wisdom preached caution. The saying "The world is slick and slippery" meant it is easy to make mistakes in life. Aztecs also said, "Not twice on earth," meaning you only live once, so enjoy life while you can.

From Birth to Death

When a girl was born, she was presented with a tiny sewing basket. A boy was given a miniature shield and four little arrows. Before the age of 4, children had their ears pierced. At 5 or 6, children could go out to play, if they had finished their chores.

Education. At 10, children were legally responsible for their actions and could be sentenced to punishment. At this age all boys and girls were sent to neighborhood boarding schools. Some students learned trades. Others studied history, music, the art of speaking, and the interpretation of dreams.

At 15 a young woman was ready for marriage. The typical young man became a warrior and would marry later.

Dress. Men wore loincloths and simple cloaks knotted over one shoulder. Women wore sleeveless blouses and wrap-around skirts of cotton cloth.

Shelter and Food. Houses were of one story and might have several rooms, each facing a central courtyard. The kitchen with its fireplace was in the rear. A young family often lived in a single room in the house of the husband's father.

Maize, beans, squash, and turkey were important foods. Crops were grown on island gardens called *chinampas*, made of fertile soil scooped from the lake bottom.

Commerce. More unusual foods, such as cacao, pineapples, and vanilla, were brought by merchants from the lowlands. Cacao beans, the source of chocolate, were often used as money in the great marketplaces, where goods from all over the Aztec world were traded.

Goods came to market on the backs of porters. There were no beasts of burden and no wheeled vehicles. Water transport was by dugout canoe.

Old Age. Alcohol was restricted by law. But the elderly could drink as much as they wanted. This, along with retirement from work, was a privilege of old age.

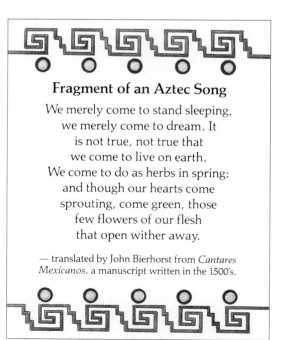

Fragment of an Aztec Song

We merely come to stand sleeping,
we merely come to dream. It
is not true, not true that
we come to live on earth.
We come to do as herbs in spring:
and though our hearts come
sprouting, come green, those
few flowers of our flesh
that open wither away.

— translated by John Bierhorst from *Cantares Mexicanos*, a manuscript written in the 1500's.

Aztec statues are noted for their massive size and mysterious details. *Left:* The great statue of the earth goddess Snake Skirt wearing a carved necklace of human hands and hearts. *Above:* The famous "calendar stone." In the center is the face of an Aztec earth god.

Funerals. Long prayers were said for a dead person. The corpse was either buried or cremated, together with a sewing basket and weaver's tools (for a woman) or weapons (for a man).

It was believed that most people went to the dead land beneath the earth. Those who had drowned went to the paradise of the rain god. The most honored dead were men killed in battle and women who had died in childbirth. They went to the sky to live with the sun.

Religion

Aztecs worshipped many gods in addition to the rain god and the sun. There was the fire god, called Old God. There was an earth goddess, called Snake Skirt, and a goddess of love, named Flower Plume.

Merchants and hunters had special gods who received their prayers. The city of Tenochtitlán had a tribal god, Huitzilopochtli (wee-tseel-oh-POACH-tlee), who protected the city's warriors.

Feasts and the Calendar. The year was divided into 18 "months," each with 20 days. In each of these months there was a feast in honor of one or more gods. The rain god and the maize god were remembered in the spring. One of the fall months was devoted to Cloud Snake, god of hunting. Religious feasts were marked by parades and music. At the end of the year were five unlucky days, when people stayed indoors.

At the close of every 52 years a special ceremony was held. All fires were put out. Then a priest kindled a new fire using a drilling stick. Runners with torches carried the new fire to each of the settlements in the Valley of Mexico.

The Payment. Aztecs believed that the gods demanded payment, perhaps an offering of food or a sacrifice of quail. For the new fire ceremony and other important feasts it was necessary to make the "human payment"— the sacrifice of a human being.

Arts

Architects, painters, and musicians were skilled professionals who enjoyed prestige in Aztec society.

The most impressive works of architecture were the pyramids, built in tiers like a wedding cake. At the top of a pyramid were one or more temples, housing statues of gods.

Gods were also depicted in books, made from long sheets of bark paper, rolled or folded. There were no words, only numbers and pictures that were outlined with black and filled in with brilliant colors. The books were used to record history, to explain the functions of gods, and to list the tribute each city had to pay.

Aztec literature as we know it today was not preserved in these old-style books. It was written after the Spanish Conquest, using the alphabetic script learned from missionaries.

It includes poetic speeches, myths, histories, and the texts of songs.

Songs, both before and after the Conquest, were accompanied by two kinds of drums: a skin drum, played with the hands, and a two-toned log drum, played with mallets. Songs, as well as speeches, often touch upon historical incidents that are explained more fully in other longer works of literature.

▶ HISTORY

Traditional Aztec histories begin with myths of world creation. They continue with legends about the Aztecs' predecessors, the Toltecs, who archaeologists have determined flourished between A.D. 900 and 1200. Their capital, Tula, now in ruins, is located 45 miles (75 kilometers) north of Mexico City. These legends are followed by historical accounts of the kings who built the Aztec empire.

Origin of the Aztecs

Aztecs claimed to have come from a region far to the north, migrating south toward Tula and into the Valley of Mexico. At about this time—according to legend—Tula's last ruler, the priest-king Quetzalcoatl (keh-tsahl-KOH-ahtl) broke his priestly vows and fled in disgrace to the eastern seashore. He disappeared over the water, promising one day to return. After he had gone, an Aztec tribe called Mexica founded Tenochtitlán, in 1325.

The Rise and Fall of the Aztec Empire

After years of warring with its neighbors, Tenochtitlán formed an alliance with two other cities, Texcoco and Tlacopán. This occurred about 1430. The new alliance, or empire, grew rapidly. By the time of the emperor Montezuma II, Aztecs controlled a territory stretching from the Pacific Ocean to the Gulf of Mexico and south to the present border of Guatemala.

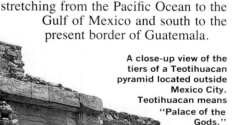

A close-up view of the tiers of a Teotihuacan pyramid located outside Mexico City. Teotihuacan means "Palace of the Gods."

Spanish Conquest. It was Montezuma II who greeted the conqueror Hernando Cortes in 1519 (or the year 1 Reed by the Aztec calendar). At first Montezuma believed Cortes was the legendary Quetzalcoatl, who was to return in the year 1 Reed. Hesitant to give offense, Montezuma was taken prisoner by the Spaniards and mysteriously killed. Unable then to restrain the populace by peaceful means, Cortes resorted to force. Firearms, horses, and steel armor gave the Spaniards an edge. But they could not have won without the help of Aztec cities that sided with them, eager to see Tenochtitlán humbled. The capital was reduced to rubble during the fierce battle of the summer of 1521. A new Spanish city began to rise in its place.

Aftermath. Smallpox and other diseases brought from Europe greatly diminished the Aztec population. The Aztecs, however, did not disappear. The succession of kings continued through the 1500's. Now known as *gobernadores* (governors), they served under Spanish authority. Although the *gobernadores* eventually lost what remained of their powers, people continued to read and write the Aztec language through the 1700's and to keep up many of the ancient customs.

Legacy of the Aztecs

The modern Aztec language, known as Nahuatl or *mexicano*, is still spoken by more than a million Nahua, who continue to plant maize, weave cotton cloth, and play instruments like the log drum. The Nahua live mostly in small towns and villages in central Mexico.

Nationally, Aztec art is recognized as an essential feature of Mexico's heritage. Aztec painting and sculpture have influenced Mexican artists such as Diego Rivera and Miguel Covarrubias. Modern poets such as Octavio Paz have been inspired by Aztec literature.

Perhaps the most widely known legacy of Aztec culture is in the realm of foods and recipes. *Avocado, chili, chocolate,* and *tomato* are all Aztec words. If you have been to a Mexican restaurant or have prepared Mexican food at home, you may have had *enchiladas, guacamole, tacos,* and *tamales.* These are dishes made with ingredients that go back to Aztec times.

JOHN BIERHORST
Author, *The Mythology of Mexico and Central America*

See also INDIANS, AMERICAN.

DICTIONARY ENTRIES

The following list contains brief biographies and short entries on many different subjects. It can be used for quick reference. To find references to all the information in the encyclopedia on a particular subject, consult the Index.

Abbott, Sir John Joseph Caldwell (1821–93), Canadian statesman, b. St. Andrews, Quebec. He was dean of the Faculty of Law at McGill University (1855–80). He served in the Legislative Assembly of Canada and the House of Commons (1859–74, 1881–87). He was appointed to the Senate (1887). He was the mayor of Montreal (1887–89), the Conservative Party leader, and prime minister (1891–92).

Abbott and Costello, American comedy team. Bud (William A.) Abbott (1895–1974), b. Asbury Park, N.J., and Lou Costello (Louis Francis Cristillo) (1908–59), b. Paterson, N.J., became one of the most popular comedy teams in the United States. Abbott portrayed a fast-talking con man who was always deceiving and upsetting the easily fooled Costello. Together they were famous for their routine ''Who's on First?'' Their many movies include *Hold That Ghost* (1941) and *Abbott and Costello Meet Frankenstein* (1948). They also hosted a television show that aired from 1952 to 1954.

Abelard (AB-el-ard), **Peter** (1079–1142), French philosopher and theologian, b. near Nantes. His fame as a teacher attracted students from many countries. But his philosophy offended the Church, and he was condemned for heresy (1140). His marriage to Héloïse displeased her uncle Fulbert, who was responsible for a physical attack upon Abelard. After the attack Abelard withdrew to a monastery, and Héloïse became a nun. Their letters and love story have become famous.

Abortion, the early ending of a pregnancy before the fetus (unborn child) has developed and grown enough to live outside the mother. If abortion happens naturally, before the 20th week of pregnancy, it is called a *spontaneous* abortion, or miscarriage. If abortion is caused by artificial means such as a medical procedure, it is called an *induced* abortion. In the United States, a debate rages over the ethical and legal aspects of induced abortion. Members of the right-to-life movement believe that abortion is morally wrong and should be restricted or prohibited. Other people, who refer to themselves as pro-choice, believe that women should have the right to choose for themselves whether or not to have an abortion. In 1973, in the *Roe* v. *Wade* case, the U.S. Supreme Court ruled that a woman could not be prevented from having an abortion during the first three months of pregnancy. Since then, the Court has allowed some restrictions on abortions; for example, states may require parental notification or a 24-hour waiting period.

Academy of Motion Picture Arts and Sciences

(AMPAS), an honorary organization composed of people in the motion picture industry. Each year it presents Academy Awards (''Oscars'') to those who have made outstanding contributions in such areas as acting, writing, and directing. The academy maintains a library covering all aspects of the motion picture industry. Founded in 1927, it has headquarters in Beverly Hills, California.

Acadia (a-CAY-dee-a), the French name for the area that is now Nova Scotia and New Brunswick, Canada. The French and English fought over the area from 1610 to 1713, when a treaty granted possession to England. In 1755, the English expelled all the French settlers (Acadians) who would not take an oath of allegiance to England. The deported Acadians, many of whom settled in Louisiana, are immortalized in Henry Wadsworth Longfellow's poem *Evangeline*.

Acanthus, a prickly plant found in the tropics and southern Europe. Some varieties have white or rose-colored flowers; others have no flowers. The plant grows to about 3 ft (1 m). Its graceful design was copied by the ancient Greeks in their architecture (Corinthian columns).

Achebe, Chinua (1930–   ), Nigerian writer, b. Ogidi. Achebe is considered one of the most accomplished African authors writing in English. His novels explore the effects of British colonialism on African society. After graduating from University College in Ibadan in 1953, Achebe worked for the Nigerian Broadcasting Company. Later, he was professor of English at the University of Nigeria and the editor of *Okike,* a literary journal. Achebe's novels include *Things Fall Apart* (1958), *Arrow of God* (1964), and *Anthills of the Savannah* (1987). He has also written short stories, poetry, essays, and books for children.

Acheson, Dean Gooderham (1893–1971), American lawyer and statesman, b. Middletown, Conn. He was undersecretary of the treasury (1933), assistant secretary of state (1941–45), and secretary of state (1949–53) under President Truman. He played an important role in founding NATO. His book, *Present at the Creation: My Years in the State Department,* won the 1970 Pulitzer prize for history.

Aclinic line (magnetic equator), an imaginary line on the earth's surface that lies close to the geographical equator. At any point along this line, the attraction between north and south magnetic poles is balanced, and a magnetic needle will show no dip.

Actaeon (ac-TE-on), in Greek mythology, a hunter who happened upon Artemis (goddess of the hunt) bathing naked in a river. Angered, Artemis changed him into a deer, and he was hunted down and eaten by his own hounds.

Act of God, a legal term for a natural event of overwhelming force, such as an earthquake or a disaster or accident that could not have been prevented by human action. Under the law of negligence, a person cannot be held responsible for damages or injuries caused by such an event.

Actors' Equity Association (AEA), a trade union of actors, dancers, singers, and other performers in the legitimate theater. It was the first union to include a clause in its contracts

Actors' Equity Association (continued)
providing for arbitration of all disputes. Founded in 1913, it has headquarters in New York, N.Y.

Adams, Ansel (1902–84), American photographer, b. San Francisco, Calif. He is best known for his realistic black-and-white photographs of American wilderness areas. Though trained to be a concert pianist, Adams decided on a career in photography in 1930. He helped to establish the department of photography at the Museum of Modern Art in New York City in 1940. Because of his interest in the environment, he was a strong conservationist.

Adams, Harriet Stratemeyer (1891–1982), American writer, b. Newark, N.J. In the early 1900's her father, Edward L. Stratemeyer, founded the Stratemeyer Syndicate, a group of writers who produced books for young readers, including the popular Nancy Drew, Hardy Boys, and Bobbsey Twins series. She joined the group soon after graduation from Wellesley College in 1914. After her father's death in 1930, she carried on his work. The series of books were published under pen names, such as Carolyn Keene, Franklin W. Dixon, and Laura Lee Hope. Like her father, Harriet Adams wrote some of the hundreds of books. But usually they were produced by other writers under her supervision. The stories were filled with adventure and always ended happily.

Adenauer (OD-en-our), **Konrad** (1876–1967), German statesman, b. Cologne. He held several political posts, including that of lord mayor of Cologne (1917–33), but was dismissed from office (1933) and imprisoned (1944) by the Nazis. Briefly reinstated as lord mayor (1945) by U.S. forces near the end of World War II, he was one of the founders and leaders of the Christian Democratic Union (CDU). Adenauer served as chancellor of the Federal Republic of Germany (West Germany) from 1949 to 1963, and was credited with much of West Germany's postwar economic and political development.

Adler (OD-ler), **Alfred** (1870–1937), Austrian psychiatrist, b. Penzing-Vienna. Originally a close associate of Sigmund Freud, he later disagreed with basic Freudian ideas. He developed the theory that the inferiority complex is the root of most psychological problems. He spent much time in the United States (after 1925) and finally settled in New York City in 1935. He lectured and taught at several medical schools and founded the School of Individual Psychology, Vienna. He started the *Journal of Individual Psychology* and was the author of numerous works, including *The Science of Living and The Pattern of Life*.

Adonis (a-DON-is), in Greek mythology, a handsome youth loved by Aphrodite and Persephone. He was ordered by Zeus to spend half the year with each goddess. Adonis was killed by a boar while hunting.

Adventist, a member of a religious group believing that the hope of the world lies in the second coming of Christ. The Adventist movement was founded by William Miller (1782–1849), a New England Baptist. He predicted that the world would come to an end in 1843, at which time Christ would appear. Many Adventist churches with differing views were organized in the 19th century. The largest, the Seventh-Day Adventist Church, does missionary work throughout the world.

Aeolus (EE-ol-us), in Greek mythology, the ruler of the winds. He lived in the Aeolian Islands, where the winds were kept. In the *Odyssey,* Aeolus gives a bag of wind to Odysseus (Ulysses) to help speed his ship home after the Trojan War.

Affirmative action, policies or programs designed to overcome the effects of past discrimination. U.S. President Lyndon B. Johnson first used the term in 1965 in ordering federal contractors to take "affirmative action" in hiring members of minority groups. The principle was later broadened to include educational institutions, some of which reserved a set number of places for minorities. These quota systems were challenged in a court case, *The Regents of the University of California v. Bakke.* Allan P. Bakke, a white man, charged that he was denied admission to a university medical college because of a rigid quota system. The U.S. Supreme Court ruled in 1978 that admissions plans favoring minorities are constitutional but that quota systems are not because they discriminate against whites.

Aga Khan (OG-a kahn), the spiritual leader of the Ismaili Muslim sect. He claims descent and spiritual authority from Mohammed through Mohammed's daughter Fatima. Shah Karim Khan (1936–   ) became Aga Khan IV upon the death of his grandfather Aga Khan III in 1957.

Agee (AY-gee), **James** (1909–55), American writer, b. Knoxville, Tenn. His novel *A Death in the Family* won a Pulitzer prize in 1958. With photographer Walker Evans, he produced *Let Us Now Praise Famous Men* (1941). This was a study of Depression tenant farmers, told in words and pictures. Agee was an influential film critic during the 1940's. Later, he turned to writing film scripts, including *The African Queen* (1951).

Agent Orange, a herbicide, or plant-killing chemical. It contains small amounts of dioxin, one of the world's most poisonous substances. During the Vietnam War, the U.S. Air Force sprayed Agent Orange on crops to reduce the enemy's food supplies and on jungles to expose enemy hiding places. U.S. soldiers who fought in the war later claimed that exposure to the herbicide caused a variety of health problems, ranging from cancer to birth defects in their children. In 1989, Congress approved legislation providing disability benefits for Vietnam War veterans who were exposed to Agent Orange.

Agnes, Saint, a Christian martyr and the patron saint of young girls, who lived during the 3rd century. She is thought to have been executed when only 12 or 13 years old. According to legend, a young girl could learn whom she would marry by following certain rituals on St. Agnes' Eve (January 20). The legend was used by Keats in his poem "The Eve of St. Agnes."

Agnosticism (ag-NAHS-tuh-siz-um), a philosophical belief that people cannot make judgments about things that can never be understood or proved, particularly the existence of God. The term dates from the 19th century, when T. H. Huxley stated that any knowledge of God was impossible because of the limited nature of the human mind. He coined the word *agnosticism* from two Greek words meaning "no knowledge."

Aguinaldo (og-e-NOLD-o), **Emilio** (1869–1964), Philippine leader and hero in the struggle for Philippine independence, b. Luzon. He led an unsuccessful revolt against Spain (1896). After the United States defeated Spain (1898), Aguinaldo pro-

Aguinaldo, Emilio (continued)

claimed Philippine independence and took office as first president (1899). When the colonial intentions of the United States became evident, he again headed a revolt (1899–1901) until captured. He pledged his loyalty to the United States, but he wore a black mourning bow tie until the Philippines finally achieved independence (1946). He ran for president (1935) but was defeated by Manuel Quezon. He later served on the Philippines Council of State.

Aikido

(i-kee-DOH), a Japanese self-defense method developed by Morihei Ueshiba (1883–1969) and based largely on jujitsu. When attacked, an aikido artist will control and direct the attacker's force so that the attacker is thrown off balance and down to the ground. The aikido artist may then hold the attacker with a lock that is not harmful but will prevent the attacker from resuming the fight.

Ailey (AY-lee), Alvin

(1931–89), American choreographer, b. Rogers, Texas. A leading figure in modern dance, Ailey was director of the Alvin Ailey American Dance Theater, which he founded in 1958. He worked with choreographer Lester Horton and appeared in Broadway shows before starting his own company. Many of Ailey's dances reflect his black Southern heritage and are set to jazz or gospel music. Among his best-known works are *Blues Suite* (1958), *Revelations* (1960), *Cry* (1971), *Memoria* (1979), and *Landscape* (1981).

Ajax

(A-jax), the name of two legendary Greek heroes of the Trojan War. Ajax the Greater was known for his strength and size. As a warrior, he was considered second only to Achilles. When Achilles died, Ajax and Odysseus (Ulysses) both claimed his armor, which had been given to him by the gods. The other warriors voted that Odysseus should receive the armor. Ajax planned revenge on them, but the goddess Athena made him temporarily insane so that he could not harm anybody. He killed a flock of sheep, thinking that they were soldiers, and then killed himself in shame. He is the subject of the play *Ajax* by Sophocles. Ajax the Lesser was punished by the sea god Poseidon (Neptune) for having violated the prophetess Cassandra after the fall of Troy. He was shipwrecked and drowned.

Akbar

(Jalal-ud-Din Muhammad) (1542–1605), the third emperor of the Mogul dynasty of India, b. Umarkot. Called Akbar the Great, he came to the throne in 1556 and extended his empire to include much of India, Kashmir, Afghanistan, and Baluchistan. He practiced religious and political tolerance and evolved a new religion, Din Ilahi.

Akiba ben Joseph

(50?–132), Jewish scholar, b. Lydda, Palestine (now Israel). He taught at a rabbinical school near Jaffa, Palestine. He developed a method of interpreting the Bible in which every word and sign has a particular significance. His collection of Jewish oral law was the basis of Mishnah (the first part of the Talmud, the book of Jewish civil and religious law). He supported Bar Kochba in a revolt against the Roman emperor Hadrian (132). He was executed for disobeying a Roman law that prohibited the teaching of Jewish law. He is one of the ten martyrs mentioned in the Jewish prayer of repentance.

Alaric

(AL-a-ric) (370?–410), king of the Visigoths; b. Peuce, an island at the mouth of the Danube River. For a time Alaric commanded Gothic troops serving in the Roman army. Elected king of the Visigoths (395), he led them in an invasion of Greece. The Romans made peace by appointing him military governor in the colony of Illyricum (now the western coast of the Balkan Peninsula). In 401 he invaded Italy. After several sieges he captured and devastated Rome in 410, signaling the final decline of the Roman Empire in the West. Alaric planned to establish a kingdom in northern Africa. But his fleet was wrecked by a storm, and he died soon after.

Albany Plan of Union,

the first formal plan for unification of the American colonies. It was proposed by Benjamin Franklin. The plan was adopted in 1754 by the Albany Congress, a convention of delegates from the colonies and representatives of Iroquois Indians. The plan called for a grand council, with representatives from each colony, which would deal with problems of taxation, defense, and trade. It was rejected by both Britain and the colonies, but it served as a basis for later plans of unification.

Albee (ALL-bee), Edward

(1928–), American playwright, b. Washington, D.C. He is best known for his drama *Who's Afraid of Virginia Woolf?* (1962). His plays deal with such themes as loneliness and human cruelty. They are written in a variety of styles and are often darkly humorous. Albee's first play was *The Zoo Story* (1959). Other works include *The Sand Box* (1960), *Tiny Alice* (1964), and three plays that won the Pulitzer Prize, *A Delicate Balance* (1966), *Seascape* (1975), and *Three Tall Women* (1994).

Albertus Magnus, Saint

(Albert, Count von Bollstadt) (1206?–80), German philosopher, theologian, scientist, and writer, b. Lauingen, Swabia. Called Albert the Great or Universal Doctor, he became a Dominican monk (1223). He was a teacher of Thomas Aquinas at Cologne (1248–54) and was Bishop of Ratisbon (1260–62). Recognized as one of the foremost scholars of his time, he was noted for his work on Aristotle and for his scientific investigations. He wrote *Summa de Creaturis*. He was beatified in 1622 and canonized in 1932.

Alexander, Harold Rupert Leofric George,

1st Earl Alexander of Tunis (1891–1969), British field marshal, b. County Tyrone, Ireland. As one of Britain's most successful generals of World War II, he commanded the withdrawal of British and Indian forces from Burma (1942) and successfully directed the Allied offensive to Tunis in North Africa (1943) and the invasion of Sicily and Italy (1943). After the war he served as governor-general of Canada (1946–52) and as minister of defense in Sir Winston Churchill's cabinet (1952–54). He was made a viscount in 1946 and an earl in 1952.

Alexander, Lloyd

(1924–), American writer of children's books, b. Philadelphia, Pa. Ancient Welsh legends inspired him to write the tales of Prydain, an imaginary land. He won the Newbery Medal in 1969 for the fifth book about Prydain, *The High King;* the National Book Award in 1971 for *The Marvelous Misadventures of Sebastian;* and the 1982 American Book Award for *Westmark.* Other works include *The Illyrian Adventure* (1986), *The El Dorado Adventure* (1987), and *The Drackenberg Adventure* (1988).

Alexander, Martha (1920–), American author and illustrator of children's books, b. Augusta, Ga. She develops her stories by sketching and writing almost at the same time. Her works include *Blackboard Bear* (1969), *Nobody Asked Me If I Wanted a Baby Sister* (1971), *I'll Protect You from the Jungle Beasts* (1973), and *Move Over, Twerp* (1981).

Alexander Nevski (1220?–63), Russian national hero and a saint of the Russian Orthodox Church, b. Vladimir. He defended Russia against invasions from the west. In 1240, he defeated the Swedes at the Neva River, earning the surname Nevski. He became grand duke of Kiev and Novgorod (1246) and of Vladimir (1252).

Alexius I Comnenus (com-NE-nus) (1048–1118), Byzantine emperor (1081–1118), b. Constantinople. Usurping the throne from Nicephorus III, he strengthened the military forces, reinforced the treasury, and through war and diplomacy resisted foreign enemies. He improved relations with the papacy, and the First Crusade (1196–99) took place during his reign. His life is recorded in the *Alexiad*, by his daughter Anna Comnena.

Aleykhem (or Aleichem) (a-LAI-kem), **Sholem** (Solomon J. Rabinovich) (1859–1916), Jewish writer and humorist, b. Kiev, Russia. He is considered one of the classic modern Yiddish writers. His witty and satiric stories about life in Russia and the United States are written in rich idiomatic style. Aleykhem inherited a large fortune, but he soon lost it in a publishing venture to encourage young Yiddish writers. He left Russia in 1905 and settled in New York. His books include *The Great Fair* and *The Writings of a Traveling Salesman*. Some of his stories were the basis for the musical *Fiddler on the Roof*.

Ali, Muhammad (Cassius Marcellus Clay, Jr.) (1942–), American boxer, b. Louisville, Ky. After winning an Olympic gold medal as a light-heavyweight in 1960, Ali became a professional boxer. He defeated Sonny Liston to win the world heavyweight title in 1964. A Muslim, Ali claimed that his religion exempted him from service in the armed forces. Convicted in court for refusing to serve, he lost his title. In 1971 the U.S. Supreme Court overturned the conviction. Ali regained the championship in a 1974 fight with George Foreman. He held the title until he was defeated in 1978 by Leon Spinks. Later that year, Ali regained the title in a rematch with Spinks. He thus became the first fighter to win the heavyweight title three times. Ali retired in 1981.

Allende (ah-YEN-day), **Salvador** (Salvador Allende Gossens) (1908–73), Chilean political leader, b. Valparaiso. A political activist at medical school, he was jailed for opposing the government. He was elected a national deputy in 1937. With Socialist and Communist support, he ran unsuccessfully for the presidency in 1952, 1958, and 1964. In 1970 he became the first Marxist-Socialist ever elected president of a Western democracy. Allende died in a violent seizure of power by Chile's armed forces in 1973.

Allied Powers, a term used to describe the nations that fought against Germany and its associates during the two world wars. During World War I the Allied Powers (also known as the Allies) fought the Central Powers. The original Allies included Great Britain, France, and Russia. They were joined by China, Italy, Japan, and 17 other nations. The United States joined forces with the Allies but was referred to as an "Associated Power." During World War II the Allied Powers fought the Axis Powers. The Allies included Great Britain, France, Poland, and later China, the United States, the Soviet Union, and 44 other nations around the world. The Allied Powers were victorious in both wars.

Alsace-Lorraine (al-SASS luh-RAIN), a historic region of eastern France. France and Germany fought for control of the area through the Thirty Years' War, the Franco-Prussian War, and World Wars I and II. The chief cities are Strasbourg, Metz, and Nancy. It is an agricultural area, noted for its wines. Lorraine has rich iron ore deposits.

Alum, a white solid chemical compound. The most common form contains potassium, aluminum, sulfur, and oxygen. It is widely used in purifying water, dyeing cloth, and making paper. It is used in styptic-pencil form to stop bleeding from small cuts.

Amado (a-MA-do), **Jorge** (1912–), Brazilian novelist, b. Ilhéus. His novels richly describe life in his native state of Bahia. Amado grew up on a cacao plantation similar to the one in his novel *The Violent Land* (1945). Later he became a Communist member of parliament and an outspoken reformer. *Gabriela, Clove and Cinnamon* (1958) reflects his concern about the social problems of Brazil. Many of Amado's novels, such as *Dona Flor and Her Two Husbands* (1966), are comic tales of the lives, loves, and troubles of everyday people who always win out. His books have been translated into more than thirty languages.

Amalekites (a-MAL-ek-ites), a fierce nomadic tribe of Biblical times. They were traditional enemies of the Israelites, who first encountered them during their exodus from Egypt. They fought each other many times.

Amateur Athletic Union of the United States (AAU), a federation of amateur athletic organizations that serves as the governing body of many competitive amateur sports. It sponsors National Championship competitions, represents the United States in international competition, provides uniform rules, and keeps records. The AAU was founded in 1888. It has headquarters in Indianapolis, Ind. It publishes rule books for various sports and a monthly magazine, *Info AAU*.

Amateur Softball Association of America (ASA), the governing body for amateur softball in the United States. It provides standardized rules of play. Founded in 1933, ASA has headquarters in Oklahoma City, Okla., and publishes *Balls and Strikes,* a monthly.

Amazons, in Greek mythology, a race of women warriors who lived around the Caucasus, allowing no men among them. Their children were fathered by men from neighboring nations, and the sons were either killed or sent back to their fathers. Their queen supposedly was killed by Achilles during the Trojan War.

Ambler, Eric (1909–), English author known for his spy thrillers, b. London. His heroes are often disenchanted secret agents, such as in his best-known novel, *A Coffin for Dimitrios*

Ambler, Eric (continued)

(1939). During World War II, Ambler served in the British Army in North Africa and Italy. He worked with a documentary film unit in the 1940's and later wrote the screenplays for many popular films.

Ambrosia,

in mythology, the food of the gods. Ambrosia supposedly gave immortality to those who ate it. In modern usage, it is anything extremely pleasing to the taste.

American Academy and Institute of Arts and Letters

(AAIAL), an honorary institution for the advancement of creative work in literature, music, and art. It was formed in 1976 by a merger of the American Academy of Arts and Letters (founded 1904) and the National Institute of Arts and Letters (founded 1898). Its 250 members are chosen on the basis of achievement. AAIAL presents annual awards for distinguished work. It has headquarters in New York, N.Y.

American Association for the Advancement of Science

(AAAS), the largest scientific organization in the United States. Its members represent all fields of science. AAAS was founded in 1848. It has headquarters in Washington, D.C., and publishes the weekly *Science*.

American Association of Retired Persons

(AARP), a national organization of 27 million members that works to improve the quality of life for older persons. Open to anyone age 50 and over, it offers retirement planning, group health insurance, and discounts on travel costs. Founded in 1958, AARP has its headquarters in Washington, D.C. It publishes the magazine *Modern Maturity* and a monthly news bulletin.

American Bar Association

(ABA), an organization of attorneys in good standing who are admitted to practice law before state bars. The ABA seeks high standards of legal education, sound federal and state legislation, uniform laws throughout the United States, and the improved administration of justice. Founded in 1878, it has headquarters in Chicago, Ill., and publishes the *American Bar Association Journal*.

American Bible Society

(ABS), a nonprofit organization devoted to the circulation of the Bible throughout the world. It translates and distributes copies of the Bible in more than 200 languages and in braille. Founded in 1816, it has international headquarters in New York, N.Y., and publishes the *American Bible Society Record*.

American Federation of Teachers

(AFT), a union of educational workers, mainly teachers, within the American Federation of Labor–Congress of Industrial Organizations (AFL-CIO). The AFT seeks to improve the salaries and working conditions of its members, as well as to provide a good education for all students. It also conducts research on educational issues. The AFT was founded in 1916. It has headquarters in Washington, D.C. The magazine *American Teacher* is among its publications. The Federation of Nurses and Health Professionals (FNHP), founded in 1978, is a division of the AFT. It represents the interests of nurses and other professional and technical workers in the health care field.

American Heart Association

(AHA), an organization devoted to the prevention and treatment of heart and circulatory diseases. With a membership of physicians, scientists, and lay persons, the organization promotes research, education, and community programs. Founded in 1924, it has headquarters in Dallas, Tex., and is financed by public contributions.

American Humane Association

(AHA), an organization of societies and individuals that acts to prevent cruelty to children and animals. It was founded in 1877 and has headquarters in Denver, Colo. Its publications include the *American Humane Shoptalk*.

American Jewish Committee,

a national organization of American Jews, founded in 1906. Its aims are to fight prejudice, to protect civil and religious liberties, and to promote understanding through education and human relations. Its publications include the bimonthly *Present Tense* and the monthly *Commentary*, an independent journal of opinion and criticism. Headquarters are in New York, N.Y.

American Jewish Congress

(AJC), an organization of American Jews dedicated to the unity and survival of Jews all over the world. It is active in helping the people of Israel. Founded in 1918 by Louis Brandeis and other prominent American Jewish leaders, it has headquarters in New York, N.Y., and publishes *Congress Monthly* and the quarterly *Judaism*.

American Legion

(AL), an organization of men and women veterans of World Wars I and II, the Korean War, and the Vietnam War. It supports patriotism and national defense and also works for veteran benefits. It was founded in 1919 by World War I veterans. It has headquarters in Indianapolis, Ind., and publishes the *American Legion Magazine*.

American Medical Association

(AMA), a national association of physicians. It provides professional information to its members and assists in setting and maintaining standards for medical schools. It also represents the medical profession in dealings with the federal government. Founded in 1847, it has headquarters in Chicago, Ill., and publishes the *Journal of the American Medical Association*.

Americans for Democratic Action

(ADA), an organization of politicians, people in business, labor leaders, and other citizens interested in liberal political ideas. It seeks to "formulate liberal domestic and foreign policies, based on the realities and changing needs of American democracy" and to obtain public support of such policies. The ADA tries to realize its ideas through the major American political parties. Founded in 1947, it has headquarters in Washington, D.C., and publishes *ADA World* monthly.

American Society of Composers, Authors and Publishers

(ASCAP), an association of music writers and publishers. It protects the copyrights of members by licensing commercial users of music, such as radio and TV stations and hotels. It also tabulates the number of public performances of a member's work and distributes royalties. ASCAP was founded in 1914 by Victor Herbert and others. Its headquarters are in New York, N.Y.

American Veterans Committee

(AVC), an organization of men and women who served in World Wars I and II, Korea, and Vietnam. Its purpose is "to achieve a more democratic and prosperous America and a more stable world." Founded in 1944, it has headquarters in Washington, D.C., and publishes the *AVC Bulletin*.

America's Cup, a yacht-racing trophy. It was won by the U.S. schooner *America* (1851) and was presented to the New York Yacht Club in 1857 to be used as an international challenge trophy. The first race was in 1870. American yachts won every cup until 1983, when it was won by *Australia II*. The American yacht *Stars and Stripes* won the cup back from Australia in 1987. A controversial 1988 race between the United States and New Zealand was decided in favor of the United States after a three-year legal battle. The United States won the cup again in 1992.

Amin (ah-MEEN), **Idi** (Field Marshall Idi Amin Dada) (1925–), Ugandan dictator, b. West Nile. As president, Amin was responsible for expelling Asians from his country and for killing thousands of Ugandan citizens who disagreed with him. Amin entered the army at age 21, gained control of the armed forces in 1966, and seized the presidency in 1971, ousting Milton Obote. In 1979 Amin was overthrown and driven out of the country by Tanzanian troops and Ugandan exiles.

Amnesty International, a human rights organization that won the Nobel Peace Prize in 1977. It was founded in 1961 to further human freedom by condemning torture and imprisonment because of religious and political beliefs. Its method is to adopt "prisoners of conscience" and plead their cases through mailings and other publicity. The organization has members in more than 150 countries. World headquarters are in London, England.

AMVETS (American Veterans of World War II and the Korean and Vietnam Wars), a veterans' organization that works to promote peace, encourage patriotism, and improve the welfare of veterans. Its goals include employment of the disabled. It was founded in 1944 and has headquarters in Lanham, MD.

Anarchism, a political theory that all law and government is evil. The word comes from the Greek *anarchia* ("without a ruler"). Anarchism has had followers since the days of ancient Greece. Modern anarchism is associated with Pierre Joseph Proudhon (1809–65), a Frenchman. He believed that people should work together freely in small groups, without laws, and that government should be abolished by whatever method was necessary. Some anarchists have favored the use of force to overthrow governments—President William McKinley was assassinated by an anarchist. Other anarchists have been opposed to violence. Anarchy is a condition of lawlessness or disorder resulting from a lack of governmental authority.

Andretti (an-DRET-tee), **Mario** (1940–), American race-car driver, b. Montona, Italy. Andretti won the Formula One Grand Prix world championship in 1978 and the Indianapolis 500 in 1969. His interest in racing began in Italy. He moved to the United States in 1955 and took up stock-car driving in 1958. During his career, Andretti has been U.S. Auto Club national driving champion three times (1965, 1966, and 1969).

Andropov (an-DRAW-pov), **Yuri Vladimirovich** (1914–84), Soviet political leader, b. southern Ukraine. He succeeded Leonid Brezhnev as general secretary (leader) of the Soviet Communist Party in 1982, and he was named chairman of the Presidium of the Supreme Soviet (head of state) the following year. Andropov rose through party ranks, holding several important posts, including head of the KGB (1967–82). He was a member of the Politburo from 1967 until his death. He was succeeded as head of the Soviet Communist Party by Konstantin Chernenko.

Anglund, Joan Walsh (1926–), American author and illustrator of children's books, b. Hinsdale, Ill. She is noted for her small, uniquely illustrated books, which often rhyme. Her works include *A Friend Is Someone Who Likes You* and *Love Is a Special Way of Feeling*.

Angström (ONG-strem), **Anders Jonas** (1814–74), Swedish physicist, b. Lödgö. He was a founder of spectroscopy—the science dealing with light separated into its various colors or wavelengths. His studies of wavelengths of light led to his discovery (1862) of hydrogen in the atmosphere. The angstrom unit (A), used in measuring wavelengths of light, is named in his honor.

Anguilla (an-GWIL-ah), one of the Leeward Islands in the Caribbean Sea. A British dependency, it has an area of about 35 sq mi (91 km²) and a population of about 7,000. The economy is based chiefly on fishing and farming. Anguilla was discovered by Christopher Columbus in 1493 and became a British colony in 1650. Formerly part of St. Kitts and Nevis, Anguilla broke away from the union in 1967.

Anne, Saint, mother of the Virgin Mary and wife of Joachim. She is often pictured wearing a veil. One of the many shrines dedicated to her is Ste. Anne de Beaupré near Quebec City, Canada. She is believed by many to have the power to effect miraculous cures. She is the patron saint of Quebec. Her feast day is July 26th.

Annunciation of the Virgin, in the New Testament (Luke), the announcement by the archangel Gabriel to the Virgin Mary that she would bear a son, to be called Jesus. The feast day is celebrated March 25.

Anthony of Padua, Saint (1195–1231), Franciscan monk and theologian, b. Lisbon, Portugal. He taught theology and preached in France and Italy. According to legend, once when he could not get people to listen to him, he turned and preached to a school of fish, which miraculously gave him their attention. He was canonized in 1232 and is the patron saint of Portugal. His feast day is June 13.

Antimatter, matter in which the electrical charges of the subatomic particles are the opposite of those in matter that makes up the world. An atom of matter has a nucleus of protons and neutrons surrounded by electrons. But an atom of antimatter would have a nucleus of antineutrons and antiprotons surrounded by positrons (positive electrons). When matter and antimatter are brought together, they destroy each other's mass, producing immense energy. Some antimatter has been produced in laboratories under special high-energy conditions.

Antivivisectionist (an-tee-VIV-ih-sec-shun-ist), a person opposed to vivisection, which is the use of live animals for scientific research. Antivivisectionists emphasize the rights of animals. They feel that many experiments are unnecessary and cruel. They believe that substitutes, such as one-celled organisms and human tissue grown in test tubes, can be used instead of animals. Organizations working to regulate experimentation on animals include the American Anti-Vivisection Society and the National Anti-Vivisection Society.

Appalachia (ap-a-LAY-chi-a), the name given to a region in the Appalachian Mountains in the eastern United States. The region consists of about 400 counties in 13 states from New York to Alabama.

Arab League, a league of Asian and African countries founded in 1945 to promote the political, cultural, and economic unity of the Arab community. The original members were Egypt, Iraq, Saudi Arabia, Syria, Lebanon, Jordan, and Yemen. Since then, many other Arab nations have joined. The league is made up of a council in which each country has one vote.

Arafat (AHR-a-fat), **Yasir** (1929–), Palestinian leader, b. Jerusalem. He graduated from Cairo University as an engineer. He also received commando and other military training in Egypt. He became head of al-Fatah, an anti-Israeli guerrilla group, and in 1969 was named chairman of the Palestine Liberation Organization (PLO). Long a foe of Israel, he nevertheless signed an accord with the Israelis in 1993 that provided for limited self-rule for Palestinians in the Gaza Strip and West Bank.

Arbus, Diane Nemerov (1923–71), American photographer, b. New York City. She is known for her stark photographs, in which her subjects—the odd, the unusual, and even the ugly—look directly at the camera. She and her husband, Allan Arbus, were fashion photographers, but she tired of that career in the late 1950's, studied documentary photography, and began to take pictures of people on the street.

Arcadia (ar-CAY-dia), a province of southern Greece. The mythical mountain home of the god Pan, it was almost inaccessible in ancient times. Poets have praised the peaceful life of Arcadian shepherds, and so "Arcadian" is often used to describe simple, pastoral living.

Arcaro, Eddie (Edward Arcaro) (1916–), American jockey, b. Cincinnati, Ohio. He rode over 4,000 winners, making him one of the leading jockeys in racing history. He was a five-time winner of the Kentucky Derby and the only jockey to ride two "triple crown" winners, Whirlaway in 1941 and Citation in 1948.

Archives (ARC-ives), a place in which public or private records and documents of historical value are preserved. The National Archives, established by the U.S. Congress in 1934, is located in Washington, D.C. It holds such notable documents as the Declaration of Independence, the Constitution, and the Bill of Rights. The Canada Archives, founded in 1872, is located in Ottawa.

Arias Sánchez, Oscar (1941–), Costa Rican political leader, b. Heredia. He served as president of Costa Rica from 1986 to 1990. A former professor in the school of political science at the University of Costa Rica (1969–72), Arias served as minister of national planning (1972–77). He was elected to the Costa Rican legislature, the Legislative Assembly (1978), and served (1979–84) as leader of the National Liberation Party (PLN). Arias was awarded the Nobel Peace Prize (1987) for his Central American peace plan.

Ark of the Covenant, a sacred chest containing the agreement between God and Israel made on Mt. Sinai. It was kept by the Israelites during their years of wandering in the desert. After they settled in the Promised Land, it was placed in King Solomon's temple in Jerusalem. Today the term refers to a holy chest holding the scroll of the Torah, or law of Moses. This is placed along the eastern wall of every synagogue as a symbol of the original.

Armageddon (ar-ma-GEDD-on), in the Bible, the place of the final battle between the powers of good and evil on judgment day (Revelation 16:16). Today people sometimes use the word to refer to a nuclear war or some other earth-shattering event.

Armstrong, Louis Daniel ("Satchmo") (1900?–71), American jazz trumpeter, singer, and bandleader, b. New Orleans, La. Armstrong was a street singer as a child. He later learned to play the cornet, performing in jazz bands in New Orleans, Chicago, and New York. By the end of the 1920's he had switched to the trumpet and had begun to lead his own bands. The swinging rhythms and clear tone of Armstrong's playing were widely admired and helped to popularize the type of jazz known as "swing." His mastery of the trumpet, as well as his distinctive, gravel-voiced singing style, made him one of the best-known personalities in jazz.

Armstrong, William H. (1914–), American author and educator, b. Lexington, Va. His book *Sounder* won the Newbery Medal in 1970. His other books for young readers include *Barefoot in the Grass: The Story of Grandma Moses* (1970), *The Education of Abraham Lincoln* (1974), and *Joanna's Miracle* (1977).

Arp, Jean (Hans) (1887–1966), French artist, b. Strasbourg, Alsace (then part of Germany but now part of France). He was a founder of the Dada movement in Zurich, Switzerland (1916). After 1925 he became a member of a group of surrealist painters in Paris. During the 1920's he did many abstract reliefs on wood, but after 1930 he devoted himself mainly to sculpture.

Árpád (AR-pod), (?–907), Hungarian national hero. Leader of the Magyar tribe, he was elected prince of all seven Hungarian tribes. He led nomadic tribes (896?) into the region of the Danube basin in what is now Hungary. He established the Árpád dynasty (890?–1301), of which Saint Stephen was the first crowned king and King Andrew was the last.

Arroyo, Martina (1936–), American singer, b. New York City to a Spanish father and an American mother. A leading soprano at the Metropolitan Opera House, she has sung in major concert halls and opera houses around the world and has produced records under several labels.

Aruba (a-RU-ba), island in the Caribbean Sea off the coast of Venezuela. A self-governing part of the Kingdom of the Netherlands, Aruba is scheduled to gain complete independence in 1996. The island's economy, once based on oil refining, is now largely dependent on tourism. Area: 75 sq mi (193 km²). Population: about 67,000. Capital and largest city: Oranjestad.

Aruego (ay-ar-u-A-go), **José** (1932–), author and illustrator of children's books, b. Manila, Philippines. He began his career in art as a cartoonist. Then he went on to do humorous drawings of animals in children's books. His illustrations may be seen in *Whose Mouse Are You?* (1970), *Leo the Late Bloomer* (1971), and *One Duck, Another Duck* (1984).

Ashbery, John (1927–), American poet, b. Rochester, N.Y. After studying at Harvard and Columbia universities, Ashbery worked as an art critic in New York and Paris. His first published books of poetry were *Turandot and Other Poems* (1953) and *Some Trees* (1956). He received widespread recognition in 1976, when he won the National Book Award, the National Book Critics Circle Award, and the Pulitzer Prize for *Self-Portrait in a Convex Mirror* (1975). His other collections of poems include *The Tennis Court Oath* (1962), *Houseboat Days* (1977), and *A Wave* (1984).

Ashe, Arthur Robert, Jr. (1943–93), American tennis player, b. Richmond, Va. Ashe played on the 1968, 1969, and 1970 winning Davis Cup teams. He became a professional in 1969. His major singles titles include the national intercollegiate in 1965, the U.S. amateur and U.S. championship in 1968, and Wimbledon in 1975. In 1979 he suffered serious illness, and he retired from competition the following year. Ashe was inducted into the International Tennis Hall of Fame in 1985. He died in 1993 of AIDS, having contracted the HIV virus through a blood transfusion. His autobiography, *Days of Grace: A Memoir,* was published the same year.

Ashkenazy (ahsh-ken-AH-zee), **Vladimir** (1937–), concert pianist and conductor, b. Gorki, Belarus. He is noted for his powerful, yet sensitive, interpretations of the music of Beethoven, Chopin, Rachmaninoff, and Mozart. In 1962 he shared first prize in the International Tchaikovsky Piano Competition held in Moscow. Ashkenazy became music director of the Royal Philharmonic Orchestra in 1987, but continued to tour as a pianist.

Asimov (AZ-i-mof), **Isaac** (1920–92), American writer and educator, b. Russia. He went to the United States in 1923. He attended Columbia University, where he took his Ph.D. in chemistry. He taught biochemistry at Boston University Medical School, but he left in 1958 to devote full time to writing. Asimov wrote more than three hundred books, including many works of science fiction. He is equally well known for his nonfiction books on science for the general reader.

Assad, Hafez al- (1928–), president of Syria, b. Qardaha. Assad, formerly commander of the Syrian Air Force and minister of defense, took power in a bloodless coup in 1970. He became president in 1971. He has ruled Syria longer than any other leader since its independence in 1944 and is a major representative of the Arab cause in the Middle East.

Assassins, a secret Muslim sect, founded in the 11th century, that believed in the murder of its enemies as a religious duty. Its name comes from the Arabic word *hashshashin,* meaning "hashish eaters," because the members were thought to be under the influence of that drug when they went on their murderous missions. The sect flourished in Syria and Persia, and it spread over much of the Middle East until it was subdued by Mongols and Mamelukes during the 13th century. Today the word "assassin" is applied to one who kills a political figure or other powerful leader.

Assemblies of God, Protestant denomination. This pentecostal sect, which does mainly evangelical and missionary work, was founded in 1914. Members believe in the second coming of Christ and in divine healing.

Astor, Lady (Nancy Witcher Langhorne Astor, Viscountess Astor) (1879–1964), first woman member of the British Parliament, b. Greenwood, Va., U.S.A. She succeeded her husband, Waldorf Astor, as Conservative member in the House of Commons (1919–45). She campaigned for women's rights, temperance, and child welfare.

Atheism (A-thee-iz-um), the denial of the existence of God. Atheism holds that everything in the world can be explained on a scientific or material basis rather than as the result of creation by a supreme being. Everything that exists now is said to have come from some form of matter that existed before. The term comes from the Greek word *atheos,* meaning "without God."

Athenaeum (ath-en-E-um), a literary or scientific association or club. The term is derived from the Greek "Athenaion" (Temple of Athena), where poets read their works. The name was also given to a school for the study of the arts built in Rome (2nd century A.D.) by the emperor Hadrian.

Atlantic Charter (August, 1941), declaration of common principles and war aims by President Franklin D. Roosevelt and Prime Minister Winston Churchill. The charter was signed aboard the battleship U.S.S. *Augusta* off the coast of Newfoundland. It expressed the hope that all people "may live out their lives in freedom from fear and want." It called for a general disarmament and the establishment of a permanent peacekeeping structure. Its provisions were endorsed by 15 anti-Axis nations and were later incorporated into the United Nations Declaration (1942).

Atlantis, a legendary island in the Atlantic Ocean, described by Plato as having an ideal state and a highly developed civilization. According to tradition, it was destroyed by an earthquake and sank beneath the sea.

Atwood, Margaret Eleanor (1939–), Canadian poet and novelist, b. Ottawa. She is best known for her portrayals of modern women in her novels. Her novels include *Surfacing* (1972), *Life Before Man* (1979), *Bodily Harm* (1982), and *The Handmaid's Tale* (1986). Atwood has written numerous volumes of poetry. One of these, *The Circle Game,* won the Canadian Governor-General's award in 1966. Her poems have a haunting quality, although they are written in simple language. Her book *Survival* (1972) is a study of modern Canadian literature.

Audubon Society, National (NAS), an organization devoted to the preservation of wildlife (birds, animals, plants) and the conservation of natural resources. The society is named

Audubon Society, National (continued)
after John J. Audubon, the famous painter of birds. It was founded in 1905 and has headquarters in New York, N.Y. It publishes *Audubon* magazine.

Aurora (uh-ROR-a), in Roman mythology, the goddess of the dawn. In Greek mythology she is known as Eos, the daughter of the Titan Hyperion and the sister of Helios (the sun god) and Selene (the moon goddess). She is said to have ushered in each new day by driving a chariot, drawn by two white horses, across the sky.

Autism (early childhood autism), a severe emotional and social disability in children. Autistic children, who withdraw from other people, often are unable to speak or relate to other people in a normal way. The cause of autism is unknown, but there are methods that can help autistic children, such as play therapy.

Avant-garde (ov-on-GARD), French term meaning "before the rest." It describes those people who lead their field in original designs, ideas, or techniques during any given period. It also means people who are ahead of their time and are therefore considered unconventional (out of the ordinary).

Avedon, Richard (1923–   ), American fashion and portrait photographer, b. New York City. He first became known for his photographs of fashion models in active, dramatic poses. His portraits emphasize the personalities of his subjects and often capture intense emotions. After serving two years (1942–44) in the photography branch of the U.S. Merchant Marine, Avedon worked as a staff photographer for *Harper's Bazaar* (1945–65) and later for *Vogue* magazine. His portraits have been exhibited in leading museums and published in books, including *Nothing Personal* (1964) and *Portraits* (1976).

Avogadro (ov-o-GA-dro), **Count Amedeo** (1776–1856), Italian scientist, b. Turin. He discovered a basic law of chemistry, Avogadro's law. This law states that equal amounts of different gases under equal conditions will have the same number of molecules.

AWACS, an airborne radar system capable of tracking aircraft over an area much wider than can be covered by ground-based radar. "AWACS" comes from the first letters of the words "*a*irborne *w*arning *a*nd *c*ontrol *s*ystem." An AWACS aircraft looks like a passenger airliner with a large radar dome on its back. It can detect and track up to 400 aircraft at a time. It can also give early warning about the approach of low-flying planes. Such planes often cannot be detected by ground-based radar.

AWOL, U.S. Army term meaning "absent without leave." It is a serious offense for those in the armed services to be absent from their duties or stations without official permission or authorization.

Axis Powers (Rome-Berlin-Tokyo Axis), the alliance of Italy, Germany, and Japan, which opposed the Allied Powers during World War II. The Axis was established in 1936 in a formal pact between Germany and Italy that pledged economic and military co-operation. The same year, in the Anti-Comintern Pact, Japan and Germany agreed to combine their efforts to combat Communism. They were joined by Italy in 1937. The Axis was solidified in 1939 in the Pact of Steel (Italy and Germany) and in 1940 in the Tripartite Pact (Germany, Italy, and Japan).

HOW TO USE THE INDEX

When travelers visit a large city, they use maps or guides to find their way about. When you want to find information in an encyclopedia, you need a guide, too. The Index is your guide to all the information in THE NEW BOOK OF KNOWLEDGE.

Each individual volume of THE NEW BOOK OF KNOWLEDGE contains the corresponding alphabetical division of the Index.

USING THE INDEX

When you look something up in this encyclopedia, you should always refer to the Index first. It will tell you where you can find what you want to know. Sometimes, if you need just one key fact, it will tell you all you want to know.

The Index brings together all the references to information about a particular subject. It tells you where that subject—and every subject related to it—is discussed. In most cases when you use the Index to look up a topic, you will find along with it a short definition or identifying phrase. This brief definition explains a term that may be unfamiliar to you and helps you make sure you have found the topic you are looking for.

HOW THE INDEX IS ARRANGED

The model entry and text in the next column and the diagram below explain what you will see if you look up a subject in the Index.

Anthropology (an-thro-POL-ogy) (study of human beings and human culture) **A:300–05** *see also* Human beings; Sociology
archaeology related to **A:**349, 362
blood groups studied **B:**258
Boas, Franz **B:**261
Leakey family **L:**96–97
Mead, Margaret **M:**195
Mexico City's National Museum of Anthropology **M:**252
prehistoric people **P:**438–42
races, human **R:**28–31

The subject you are looking up, **Anthropology**, is called the **heading** and is in boldface type. In parentheses next to the heading there is a **pronunciation guide** (an-thro-POL-ogy). This is provided for all heading words that may be difficult to pronounce.

Next to the pronunciation guide are a few words that identify the topic—"study of human beings and human culture." These words are called the **identification**. A volume letter and page numbers follow the identification—**A:304–09**. The volume letter is always in boldface type and tells you in which volume to look for the information about the subject. The page numbers tell you on which pages of the volume to look. If they are also in boldface type, they are directing you to an entire article about the subject; if they are in lightface type, the information is in another article. The heading, its identification, and its volume and page numbers together make up the **entry**.

Following the page number of the entry, you will find the words "*see also*," followed by two index headings. The "*see also*" listings are called **cross-**

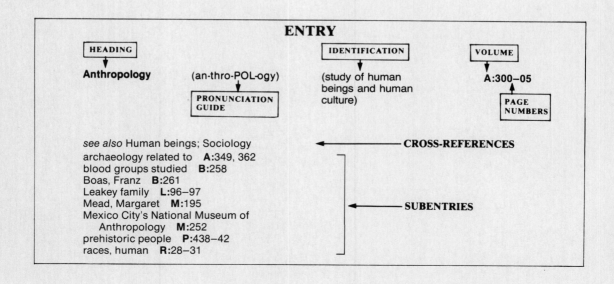

ENTRY

HEADING

Anthropology (an-thro-POL-ogy)

PRONUNCIATION GUIDE

IDENTIFICATION

(study of human beings and human culture)

VOLUME

A:300–05

PAGE NUMBERS

see also Human beings; Sociology
archaeology related to **A:**349, 362
blood groups studied **B:**258
Boas, Franz **B:**261
Leakey family **L:**96–97
Mead, Margaret **M:**195
Mexico City's National Museum of Anthropology **M:**252
prehistoric people **P:**438–42
races, human **R:**28–31

CROSS-REFERENCES

SUBENTRIES

references. They tell you where to look to find more information related to your subject. Cross-references are guides to Index entries, not to article titles.

Beneath the entry there is a list of additional references to your subject. These references are called **subentries**. They are indented and arranged in alphabetical order. The subentries refer to all the important information about your subject throughout the set. Unless you look in the Index, you may not think of all the points about your subject that have been covered in the encyclopedia. (Subentries, in turn, may appear as main entries in other parts of the Index under their own initial letters.)

In the case of **Anthropology** there are only a few subentries. But if you look up a broad topic, such as **Vocations**, you may find dozens of subentries. Subentries are helpful if you want to review the whole of a particular field.

Pictures are noted in the Index only if they fall on a page that is different from the main entry or if they are to be found in a different article.

Bohr, Niels (Danish atomic physicist)   **B:304**; **C:211**
   picture(s)   **P:232**
Bridges   **B:395–401**
   picture(s)
     swinging bridge   **J:157**

Maps are not noted in the Index. If you look up a country, state, or province article, you will find at least one map, often with its own index, included within the pages of the article.

Parentheses are used to enclose pronunciation guides and identifications. They are also used to enclose initials, alternative forms of names, and dates.

Initials: **Bay Area Rapid Transit System (BART)**
Alternative forms of names:
   Madison, Dolley (Dorothea Payne Todd Madison)

Dates: Dates are given for historical events that are summarized briefly in the Index.
   Mayflower Compact (1620)

What Shall I Look For?

Think of the specific word about which you need information and look for that. Go directly to the name you usually use for the thing you want. If you want to find out about baseball, turn directly to **Baseball** in the Index. You do not have to hunt first under **Sports**, although you would find baseball listed there, too.

How Do I Look Up a Person's Name?

Look for the last name, just as you do when you use the telephone book.

   Blake, William (English poet and artist)   **B:250b**

How Do I Look Up Names That Begin with "Mac" or "Mc"?

Names beginning with "Mac" and "Mc" are placed in alphabetical order, just as they are spelled.

   MacArthur, Douglas
   Macbeth
   Mac Cool
   Machine language
   Maze
   M' Bochi
   McAuliffe, Christa
   McKinley, William

What If the Person Is Known by More Than One Name?

Some persons are known by more than one name. Such entries are listed by their best-known names— **Buffalo Bill**; **Twain, Mark**; **Napoleon**. But if you should look under the person's official name, a cross-reference will tell you the right place to look.

   Bonaparte, Napoleon *see* Napoleon I
   Clemens, Samuel Langhorne *see* Twain, Mark
   Cody, William Frederick *see* Buffalo Bill

How Do I Look Up Names Beginning with "Saint" or "St."?

Saint is always spelled out. Place names beginning with Saint are listed under **Saint**.

   Saint Louis (Missouri)

But the names of saints are listed according to the name. "Saint" is placed after the name.

   Paul, Saint

What If There Is More Than One Spelling for My Topic?

If you use a different (but correct) spelling from the Index, you will also find a "*see*" reference.

   Aleichem, Sholem *see* Aleykhem, Sholem

How Are the Headings in the Index Arranged?

Because this is a Dictionary Index, it is arranged like a dictionary, letter by letter.

Mink
Minneapolis
Minnesingers
Minnesota

What If a Heading Is Made Up of More Than One Word?

Even when headings are made up of more than one word, they are still arranged alphabetically, letter by letter.

New Amsterdam
Newark
Newbery, John
New Castle

When there is a comma in the heading, the letter-by-letter arrangement goes through to the comma only—so that all the same names will be brought together

Black (color)
Black, Hugo La Fayette
Black, Joseph
Blackball
Black Hills
Black Market

What about Words in Parentheses, Titles, and Roman Numerals?

The alphabetical arrangement of headings is not affected by words in parentheses, titles, or Roman numerals. Just look up the heading as if it did not contain these added words or symbols.

Adler (OD-ler), **Alfred**
Adler (AD-ler), **Felix**

John I, II, and III (books of the Bible, New Testament)
John (king of England)
John II (king of France)
John XXIII (pope)
John, Saint (apostle of Jesus Christ)

How Do I Look Up a Heading That Begins with a Number?

If a number is the first word in a heading, the number is spelled out and put in its alphabetical place.

Seven Cities of Cíbola
Seven seas
Seven Sisters
Seventeenth Amendment (to the United States Constitution)
Seven wonders of the ancient world

When numbers appear in any other place in a heading, they come before letters.

Carbon
Carbon-14
Carbon black

Do I Look Up "A," "An," and "The"?

"A," "an," and "the" are not used in alphabetizing. If any one of these words is part of the title of a book or play, the word is put at the end of the title.

Cat in the Hat, The
Midsummer Night's Dream, A

How Are Initials Indexed?

You will find initials in their proper alphabetical order. A *"see"* reference along with them will lead you to the heading for which the initials stand.

CIA *see* Central Intelligence Agency

How Do I Look Up the Abbreviation "Mt."?

Mount is always spelled out and is placed after the name.

Everest, Mount

The word "lake," too, as a geographical term, is placed after the name.

Michigan, Lake

But you can look up the names of forts, towns, and rivers just as you would say them.

Fort Dearborn
Lake Placid
Mississippi River
Mount Vernon

How Do I Look Up a Poem?

Poems are listed individually by name and also by their authors.

"To Autumn" (poem by John Keats) **K:200**

Keats, John
   "To Autumn" **K:200**

How Do I Look Up a Story?

If the story you are looking for has been included in its complete form, you will find it listed under the heading **Stories** (told in full). If the story you want is part of a longer work, you will find it listed individually by its name.

Oliver Twist (book by Charles Dickens), *excerpt(s)*

Other listings similar to **Stories** are **Experiments and other science activities**; **Hobbies**; **How to.**

THE NEW BOOK OF KNOWLEDGE
PRONUNCIATION GUIDE

The pronunciation guide used in THE NEW BOOK OF KNOWLEDGE was designed to make the pronunciation of a word immediately recognizable, while making as few changes as possible in the original spelling. Known as the Minimal Change System, it was developed for this encyclopedia by Allana Cummings-Elovson of Columbia University and Jeanne Chall of Harvard University, after extensive research with children in elementary schools.

The system is based on the simplest and most direct way of presenting visually the pronunciation of a word. The words are broken down into letter groups that do not necessarily follow the rules of syllable division. Wherever possible, these letter groups are familiar short words or units. Consequently, the student is not required to learn something new or different from something previously learned. The system avoids the use of special marks, symbols, or extensive phonetic respellings.

It was conclusively demonstrated that elementary-school students using the Minimal Change System, in comparison with students using other pronunciation systems, (1) make fewer mistakes in their first attempts at figuring out the pronunciation of unfamiliar and difficult words, (2) make fewer mistakes in pronouncing the words when next seen without the benefit of pronunciation guides, and (3) make fewer spelling mistakes in the words after the pronunciation is learned.

Using the Pronunciation Guide

There are only a few basic rules with which anyone using this pronunciation guide needs to be acquainted. These rules will apply only when the familiar spelling of a letter group will not serve to properly identify a sound. In the majority of cases, natural responses to the letter groups will follow previously learned phonetic rules.

Stressed or Accented Syllables

The stressed or accented syllable is indicated by capital letters:

Achilles (ack-ILL-ese)
Adobe (ad-O-be)
Affenpinscher (AF-fen-pin-sher)
Airedale (AIR-dale)

Hard and Soft Consonant Sounds

The sound of *c* before *o, a,* and *u* is regularly hard, like the *c* in "collar," "card," and "cut." The sound of *c* before *e, i,* and *y* is always soft, like the *c* in *"cent," "city,"* and *"fancy."*

Canis (CAY-nis) hard *c*
Ceres (CE-rese) soft *c*

The sound of *g* is generally hard before *a, o,* and *u,* as in "game," "golf," and "gum." The sound *g* is generally soft before *i, e,* and *y,* as in "ginger," "gem," and "gymnasium."

Gabriel (GAY-bri-el) hard *g*
Genetics (gen-ET-ics) soft *g*

However, there are exceptions to this rule, as illustrated by comparing "ginger" and "girl," "gem" and "get." When the *g* is to retain the hard sound in spite of the vowel that follows it, the letter *h* will appear after the *g*.

Gezo (GHE-zo)
Gibbons (GHIB-ons)

Vowel Sounds

When the vowels *a, e, i, o,* and *u* are followed by a consonant (except for *r* and *l*) in a letter group, the vowel is usually pronounced with the short sound like the *a* in "bat," the *e* in "bet," the *i* in "bit," the *o* in "cot," the *u* in "but." The *r* and *l* sounds often modify the sound of the vowel, as in "tar," "err," "Irish," "cold," "pull."

A final *e* in a letter group gives the previous vowel its alphabetical, or long letter, sound, as illustrated by the vowel sound in "make," "cede," "like," "toe," "mute."

Galen (GALE-en)
Matisse (ma-TECE)

Index

A (first letter of the English alphabet) **A:**1 *see also* Alphabet
AA *see* Alcoholics Anonymous
Aa (AH-ah) (type of lava) **V:**382
AAA *see* Agricultural Adjustment Administration
Aachen (Germany)
    Charlemagne's palace chapel **F:**421–22
Aachen, Treaties of *see* Aix-la-Chapelle, Treaties of
Aalto (AHL-to), **Alvar Henrik** (Finnish architect and
    designer) **A:**385–86
    furniture **F:**517
    picture(s)
        molded plywood chair **F:**515
        stadium for the Polytechnical School (Otaniemi,
        Finland) **A:**385
AAM (air-to-air missiles) **M:**345, 349
Aardvark, African (animal) **M:**70
    picture(s) **M:**73
Aardwolf (animal) **H:**305
Aarhus (Denmark) **D:**112
Aaron (in the Old Testament) **B:**167
Aaron, Henry Louis (Hank) (American baseball player) **A:**142;
    B:88, 93
AAU *see* Amateur Athletic Union of the United States
Abaca (ab-a-KA) (plant fiber) **R:**333, 334
Abacha, Sani (Nigerian political leader) **N:**258
Abacus (AB-a-kus) (counting device) **A:**2–3; **N:**404–5
    early office machine **O:**53
    Japanese soroban **J:**30
Abalone (ab-al-O-ne) (mollusk) **O:**294
    picture(s) **S:**148
Abbai (ob-I) (name for the Blue Nile in Ethiopia) **E:**331
Abbasid (Muslim dynasty) **A:**345–46; **I:**349
Abbas the Great (Persian shah) **I:**309
Abbate, Niccolo dell' (Italian painter) **F:**424; **R:**171
Abbe, Ernst (German physicist) **E:**163
Abbey Theatre (Dublin, Ireland) **I:**326–27; **T:**161
    Yeats, William Butler **Y:**344
Abbot, Margaret (American golfer) **O:**108
Abbott, Sir John Joseph Caldwell (Canadian statesman) **A:**577
Abbott and Costello (American comedy team) **A:**577
Abbreviations **A:**4–5 *see also* individual letters of the alphabet
    amateur radio **R:**63
    library filing **L:**186
    Postal Service abbreviations **P:**401, 402
    shorthand systems based upon **S:**160
    states *see* individual state articles
    used as slang **S:**191
Abdomen (part of the body)
    bees **B:**116
    beetles **B:**124
    doctor's examination of **M:**208h
    insects **I:**230, 231
    shrimps **S:**167
    picture(s)
        CAT scan **X:**341
Abdul-Hamid II (AB-dul ha-MEED) (sultan of Turkey) **T:**349
Abdul-Jabbar, Kareem (Lew Alcindor) (American basketball
    player) **B:**95i
Abdullah ibn Hussein (king of Jordan) **J:**132
Abdul Rahman, Tunku *see* Rahman, Tunku Abdul
Abdul-Rauf, Mahmond (American basketball player)
    picture(s) **B:**95d
à Becket, Saint Thomas *see* Becket, Saint Thomas à
Abel *see* Cain and Abel
Abelard, Peter (French philosopher and theologian) **A:**577
Aberdeen (Scotland) **S:**87; **U:**58
Aberdeen (South Dakota) **S:**324–25

Abernathy, Ralph David (American minister and civil rights
    leader) **A:**142; **S:**115
    Poor People's March **P:**559
Aberrations (of lenses) **L:**148–49
Abhorrers (early English political party) **P:**369
Abidjan (ab-id-JON) (capital of the Ivory Coast) **I:**419–20
    picture(s) **I:**417
Abigail (in the Old Testament) **B:**167
Abilene (Kansas)
    Chisholm Trail **O:**282
    Eisenhower Center **K:**183
Ability
    individual differences in learning abilities **L:**106
    measurement by tests **T:**118
Ability grouping (of students) **E:**88–89
Abkhazians (a people of Europe) **G:**148
Able-bodied seamen (in the Merchant Marine) **U:**126
ABM systems *see* Antiballistic missile systems
Abnaki Confederacy (of American Indians) **I:**177; **M:**50
    Vermont **V:**318
Abolition movement (United States history) **A:**6–6b, 79f–79g;
    U:183
    Adams, John Quincy **A:**19
    Anthony, Susan B. **A:**299
    Brown, John **B:**411
    Civil War issue **C:**335, 336, 337, 342
    Douglass, Frederick **D:**289
    Dred Scott case **D:**321
    New York, history of **N:**224
    Pennsylvania **P:**139
    political parties, history of **P:**371
    Tubman, Harriet **T:**328
    Underground Railroad **U:**14–16
    What were the Gag Rules? **A:**6b
    Whittier, John Greenleaf **W:**169
    women's rights movement **W:**212–12a
Abomey (ah-BO-may) (capital of the kingdom of
    Dahomey) **B:**144
Abominable Snowman **H:**127
Aborigines (ab-or-IJ-in-ese), **Australian** (native people of
    Australia) **A:**7, 500, 517
    desert nomads **D:**127–28
    watercolor painting **A:**502
    picture(s) **A:**511
        schoolchildren **A:**499
Abortion (early ending of pregnancy) **A:**577
    ethics and society **E:**329
    Supreme Court of the United States **S:**509; **W:**213
Abraham (father of the Jews) **A:**8
    Dome of the Rock mosque in Jerusalem **J:**81
    Isaac was the son of **I:**345
    Islam **I:**346
    Jews, history of the **J:**102
    Muslim traditions **M:**199
    Old Testament **B:**158
Abraham, Plains of (site of the Battle of Quebec) **F:**466; **Q:**14,
    15
Abrahams, Harold (British runner) **O:**109
Abraham's Sacrifice (etching by Rembrandt)
    picture(s) **D:**360
Abramowitz, Shalom Jacob *see* Mendele Mocher Sefarim
Abrasives (a-BRAI-sives) (materials used for grinding and
    polishing) **G:**391–93
    ceramics **C:**178
    grinding machines **T:**236
    optical glass grinding **O:**185
Abruzzo, Ben (American balloonist) **B:**36
Absalom (in the Old Testament) **B:**167

Absalom and Achitophel (play by Dryden) **D:**340
Absalon (Danish bishop) **C:**544
Abscisic acid (plant hormone) **P:**312
Absentee ballots (for voting in elections) **E:**129
Absolute magnitude (of stars) **S:**429
Absolute zero **H:**88
Absolution (God's forgiveness delivered by a priest) **P:**431
Absorbent papers **P:**53
Absorption (process by which one substance takes in another substance or energy)
  color is determined by light wavelengths **C:**424; **L:**219
Absorption lines (on spectrum) **S:**489
Absorption refrigerating system **R:**135
Abstinence (from sexual intercourse) **B:**249
Abstinence syndrome see Withdrawal
Abstract algebra **M:**169
Abstract art (art movement) **M:**396b
  American art **U:**132
  Cézanne's influence **I:**106
  collage **C:**400–401
  concern with form **A:**438e
  Dutch painting **D:**364
  France **F:**432
  Germany's Blue Rider group **G:**172
  Kandinsky, Wassily **K:**173
  Latin America **L:**67
  Mondrian, Piet **M:**407
  Russia, art of **R:**375
Abstract expressionism (art movement) **E:**426; **M:**396b; **P:**31, 32; **U:**134
  Spain, art of **S:**387
  surrealism's influence on **S:**518
Abstract thought **C:**226
Abstract words **P:**94; **S:**116
Absurdist drama **D:**303
Abu Bakr (Islamic caliph) **I:**347
Abu Dhabi (United Arab Emirates) **U:**53
Abu-Gurab (site of ancient Egyptian temple) **E:**111–12
Abuja (Nigeria) **N:**256
Abuse of children see Child abuse
Abu Simbel (site of ancient Egyptian temples) **D:**21; **E:**114, 115
Abyssal (a-BISS-al) **plain** (of the ocean floor) **O:**21
  deep-sea vessels and underwater exploration **U:**21
Abyssal zone (of the ocean habitat) **O:**23
Abyssinia see Ethiopia
Abyssinian cats **C:**145
  picture(s) **C:**147
Abyssinian wild ass **H:**244
A.C. see Alternating current
Acacia (ak-A-sha) (tree)
  ants, relationship with **P:**317
Academic American Encyclopedia **E:**205
Academic dress **U:**223
Academy (school in Athens started by Plato) **P:**330
  picture(s) **A:**232
Academy of Arts (Russia) **R:**373
Academy of Model Aeronautics (Washington, D.C.) **A:**107
Academy of Motion Picture Arts and Sciences (AMPAS) **A:**577
Academy of Natural Sciences (Philadelphia) **P:**131
Academy of Painting and Sculpture (France) **F:**425, 430
Academy of Sciences (Russia) **R:**358
Acadia (French name for the area that is now Nova Scotia and New Brunswick) **A:**577; **C:**72; **N:**138, 138g, 350, 357
Acadia National Park (Maine) **M:**45
  picture(s) **U:**82
Acadians (original French habitants of New France) **C:**50; **N:**138g, 356, 357 see also Cajuns
  Maine settlers **M:**42
Acajutla (El Salvador) **E:**196
Acanthus (prickly plant) **A:**577
A cappella (ok-ap-PEL-la) (musical term) **M:**540
  choral music **C:**283

Acasta gneisses (rocks) **R:**266
Accelerando (musical term) **M:**540
Accelerated motion (in physics) **M:**474
Acceleration (change in speed of an object)
  gravity and gravitation **G:**320, 322
  human body, effects on **S:**340L–341
  law of falling bodies **F:**34
  measurement **W:**116–17
  motion **M:**475–76
  rockets and Newton's laws of motion **R:**256
Accelerators (ingredients in plastics) **P:**325
Accelerators, particle see Particle accelerators
Accelerometer (ak-sel-er-OM-et-er) (instrument to show changes in speed) **S:**340k
Accents (in music) **M:**540, 542
Accents (in poetry) **P:**353–54
Accents (marks of stress in pronunciation) **P:**486
Accessories (interior decorating) **I:**261, 263
Accidentals (in music) **M:**539, 540
Accident insurance see Insurance, accident
Accidents
  alcoholism is a leading cause of **A:**173
  avoiding health hazards **H:**76
  blindness, causes of **B:**252
  disabled people **D:**176–77
  driver education courses **D:**324–27
  first-aid treatment for **F:**157–63
  nuclear power plant leaks **P:**422
  occupational health and safety **O:**12–13
  poisoning **P:**355–56
  police investigate traffic accidents **P:**364
  safety **S:**3–7
  workers' compensation **W:**253
Accommodation, power of (of the eye) **E:**430; **L:**149–50
Accordion (folk music instrument) **F:**330; **K:**240
  picture(s) **K:**239
Accounting **B:**311, 312–14
Account manager (executive) (at advertising agencies) **A:**32
Accra (AK-kra) (capital of Ghana) **G:**196, 197
Accreditation (of hospitals) **H:**252
Accreditation (of universities and colleges) **U:**224
Accretion hypothesis (of origin of solar system) see Solar system—theories of formation
A.C.E. (abbreviation used with dates) **C:**16
Ace (hole in one) (in golf) **G:**254
Ace (in tennis) **T:**92
Acetate (AS-e-tate) **fibers** **N:**432, 436
Acetic (a-SE-tik) **acid** (in vinegar) **F:**345
Acetone (AS-e-tone) (chemical) **F:**91
Acetylcholine (transmitter agent in the nervous system) **B:**365; **N:**118
Acetylene (a-SET-il-ene) (gas) **G:**59, 60
  fuel **F:**490
Achaeans (a-KEE-ans) (a people of ancient Greece) **T:**316
Achaemenid dynasty (ancient Persia) **I:**308; **P:**154–55
Achard (OK-hart), **Franz Carl** (German chemist) **S:**485
Achebe, Chinua (Nigerian writer) **A:**76d, **577**
Acheson, Dean Gooderham (American statesman) **A:**577
Acheson, Edward (American inventor) **G:**392
Achievement tests **T:**118, 119–20
Achilles (ak-ILL-ese) (in Greek mythology) **G:**368–69
  Iliad **I:**61
  Trojan War **T:**316
  picture(s)
    Achilles playing dice, painting on a Greek vase of **A:**228
Achilles' heel **G:**366, 369
Achondroplasia see Dwarfism, human
Achromatic lenses **T:**59
Acid dyes **D:**373
Acid rain (precipitation that contains chemical pollutants) **A:**9–10, 124, 125; **W:**54, 67
  coal burning causes **C:**391
  conservation **C:**519

Advertising (cont.)
  photography **P:**218
  political campaigns **P:**373
  posters **P:**402
  radio programs **R:**59, 60, 61
  sales and marketing **S:**20, 21
  saving money by watching supermarket
    advertisements **F:**348
  silk-screen printing **S:**176
  smoking ads banned on radio and television **S:**207
  television **T:**68
  trade and commerce **T:**265
  trademarks **T:**266
  What is the difference between public relations and
    advertising? **P:**517
Advertising agency **A:**32–34, 35
Advocates *see* Lawyers
Adze (tool)
  picture(s) **T:**227
AEC *see* Atomic Energy Commission
A.E.F. *see* American Expeditionary Force
Aegean (e-JE-an) **civilization** **A:**438a; **P:**15–16; **S:**94–95
Aegean Sea **O:**43
  Greek islands **G:**333
Aegina (e-JY-na) (Greece)
  picture(s) **G:**336
Aeneas (an-E-as) (hero of Vergil's *Aeneid*) **A:**36; **G:**369
Aeneid (an-E-id) (epic poem by Vergil) **A:**36; **G:**369; **T:**316;
  V:304–5
Aeolus (in Greek mythology) **A:**578
Aerial acrobatics (aerials) (in free-style skiing) **S:**184d
Aerial acts (in a circus) **C:**312
  picture(s) **C:**309
Aerial Experiment Association **A:**560
Aerial perspective (in drawing) **D:**311–12
Aerial photography **P:**217
  archaeological sites, search for **A:**352
  ore, search for **M:**319
  petroleum, search for **P:**169
  photogrammetry **O:**183–84
Aeries (eagles' nests) **E:**2
Aerobatic flying
  picture(s) **A:**557
Aerobic exercises (for physical fitness) **P:**224–26
Aerobics (book by Cooper) **J:**113
Aerobraking (to slow a spacecraft) **S:**340d
Aerodrome (Samuel Langley's airplane) **A:**559
Aerodynamics (science of air in motion) **A:**37–41
  airplane design **A:**109, 565
  birds, flight of **B:**214–15
  glider flight **A:**558–59; **G:**239
  heavier-than-air craft **A:**559–60
  How does a helicopter fly? **H:**104–5
  hydrofoil boats **H:**301
  supersonic flight **S:**499–502
  picture(s)
    automobile design **A:**539
Aeroflot (Russian airline) **R:**363; **U:**42
Aeronautics *see* Aviation
Aerosol containers **G:**61
Aerospace engineers **E:**225
Aerospace industry **A:**567–68
Aeschylus (ESK-il-us) (Greek dramatist) **A:**229; **D:**296; **G:**355
Aesculapius (es-ku-LAPE-ee-us) (legendary Greek
  doctor) **M:**203
  picture(s)
    serpent wand of **M:**208c
Aesop (E-sop) (Greek author of fables) **F:**2–3; **H:**280
  "The Ant and the Grasshopper" **F:**5
  "The Four Oxen and the Lion" **F:**5
  "The Lion and the Mouse" **F:**4
  slavery **S:**196
  picture(s)
    "The Fox and the Crane" **C:**235

Aesthetics (es-THET-iks) (branch of philosophy) **P:**192
Aether (Aristotle's fifth element) **C:**207
Aetna, Mount *see* Etna, Mount
Afar (language) **E:**312
Afars (a people of northeastern Africa) **D:**232, 233
Afars and the Issas, French Territory of the *see* Djibouti
AFDC *see* Aid to Families with Dependent Children
Afewerki, Isaias (president of Eritrea) **E:**313
Affiliate stations (in television industry) **T:**68
Affinity (in the dyeing process) **D:**372
Affirmative action (to overcome discrimination) **A:**578; **L:**8
Afghanistan **A:**42–45
  Communism **C:**474
  USSR's invasion **U:**51–52
  picture(s)
    flag **F:**230
Aflatoxin (toxin made by molds) **F:**500
AFL-CIO *see* American Federation of Labor–Congress of
  Industrial Organizations
Africa **A:**46–69 *see also* the names of countries
  African American history **A:**79d
  agriculture **A:**92–93
  art and architecture *see* Africa, art and architecture of
  Congo River **C:**501
  conservation programs **C:**518, 521
  continents **C:**529, 530
  dance **D:**32
  doll making **D:**272
  drought **D:**328–29
  education **E:**86; **T:**43
  exploration and discovery **E:**414–15
  foods **F:**335
  France's former territories **F:**412, 420
  immigration **I:**94
  lakes of the world **L:**33–34
  languages **A:**305
  literature *see* Africa, literature of
  mountains **M:**505–6
  music *see* Africa, music of
  Nile River **N:**260–61
  Organization of African Unity **O:**220
  plant and animal community **A:**273
  population growth **P:**386, 388
  poverty **P:**418, 419, 420
  proverbs **P:**498
  refugees **R:**137
  Sahara **S:**8
  slavery, history of **A:**79d–79e
  Stanley and Livingstone explored **S:**424
  theater **T:**162
  universities **U:**226
  What and where are the Mountains of the Moon? **A:**61
  World Wars I and II **W:**275, 290
  picture(s)
    family **F:**45
    flags of African countries **F:**226–30
    traditional hairstyle **H:**6
  table(s)
    waterfalls **W:**63
Africa, art and architecture of **A:**70–76
  art of the artist **A:**438e
  Nigeria **N:**253–54
  use by Modigliani **M:**400
Africa, literature of **A:**76a–76d
  novels **N:**363
Africa, music of **A:**77–79; **M:**546–47
  picture(s) **M:**549
Africa Corps (German army in World War II) **R:**320
Africa Hall (Addis Ababa, Ethiopia) **E:**333
African American literature **A:**199–200, 202, 208, 211, 213,
  214, 214a
  Baldwin, James **B:**21
  children's literature **C:**238–39
  Du Bois, W. E. B. **D:**340

Dunbar, Paul Laurence **D:**349
folklore **F:**313
Harlem Renaissance **A:**79k
Hughes, Langston **H:**275
Johnson, James Weldon **J:**119
Morrison, Toni **M:**462
novels **N:**363
trickster stories carried from Africa **A:**76b
Washington, Booker T. **W:**27
Wright, Richard **W:**317
African American music
folk music **F:**327
hymns and spirituals **F:**324; **H:**310–11
jazz **J:**57–62; **U:**208
jazz-style big bands **R:**262a
rhythm and blues music **R:**262a, 262b
rock music **R:**262c
African Americans A:79a–80; **U:**157 *see also* the names of
African Americans
abolition movement **A:**6–6b
Alabama, history of **A:**142, 143
Arkansas's population **A:**420
baseball **B:**92
Boston's Black Heritage Trail **B:**342
civil rights **C:**328, 329
civil rights movement **C:**330–32
Civil War, United States **C:**334–38, 346
Confederate States **C:**496
Dred Scott decision **D:**321
education in the United States **E:**90
Emancipation Proclamation **E:**199–200
English language **E:**267
genealogical research **G:**76d
Liberia settled by freed American slaves **L:**165, 168
literature *see* African American literature
Maryland's population **M:**124
motion pictures, history of **M:**489–90
music *see* African American music
newspapers: Baltimore's *Afro-American* **M:**127
New York's population **N:**216
physicians trained at Meharry Medical College **N:**17
racism **R:**34a
Reconstruction Period **R:**117–20
segregation **S:**113–15
slavery **S:**194–97
Spingarn Medal **S:**409–10
thirteen American colonies **T:**166, 178
Uncle Tom's Cabin by Harriet Beecher Stowe **S:**465
Underground Railroad **U:**14–16
universities and colleges **U:**220
Washington, D.C., history of **W:**32, 34
What is Kwanzaa? **A:**80
picture(s)
Congress, first African American members of **U:**143
thirteen American colonies **T:**168
African elephants A:271; **E:**179–81
African gray parrot B:246
African hunting dog
picture(s) **D:**240
African kingdoms, early A:65–66, 79d
Dahomey **B:**144
Kimbundu in Angola **A:**261
Mali **M:**62
Nigeria, history of **N:**257
picture(s)
Zimbabwe, ruins of **Z:**376
African Methodist Episcopal Church P:140
African National Congress (ANC) S:273
African sleeping sickness (disease) *see* Sleeping sickness,
African
African violet (plant) **H:**267
picture(s) **H:**268
African warthogs (wild pigs) **H:**211; **P:**248

Afrikaans (af-rik-AHNS) (language spoken by South Africans of
Dutch descent) **A:**57; **N:**8; **S:**269
Afrikaners (South Africans of Dutch descent) **S:**269
Afro-American (newspaper) **M:**127
Afro-Americans *see* African Americans
Afro-Asian languages A:56
Afro-Brazilian dance L:69
Afrocentrism (African American educational approach) **A:**80
Afro-Cuban dance L:69
AFT *see* American Federation of Teachers
Afterimage (optical illusion) **O:**175–76
color illusions **C:**428
After the Bath (painting by Raphaelle Peale)
picture(s) **P:**110
A.G. Nova Scotia v. A.G. Canada (Canada, 1951) **S:**506
Agadez (Niger) **N:**252
picture(s)
mosque **I:**348
Aga Khan (spiritual leader of the Ismaili Muslim sect) **A:**578
Agam, Vaacov (Israeli painter)
Double Metamorphosis II (painting) **P:**32
picture(s)
Double Metamorphosis II (painting) **P:**31
Agamemnon (ag-a-MEM-non) (drama by Aeschylus) **D:**296
Agamemnon (in Greek mythology) **G:**368; **T:**316
Iliad **I:**61
Agapetus I, Saint (pope) **R:**290
Agapetus II (pope) **R:**290
Agar (gum obtained from algae) **A:**181; **R:**185
microbes, study of **M:**278
Agassiz (AG-as-se), **Elizabeth Cary** (wife of Jean Louis Rodolphe
Agassiz) **A:**81
Agassiz, Jean Louis Rodolphe (Swiss-born American geologist
and naturalist) **A:**81
glaciers **G:**221
ice age findings **I:**8–9
Agassiz, Lake (ancient glacial lake) **M:**80, 328; **N:**322
Agate (chalcedony quartz) **Q:**6
Agate Fossil Beds National Monument (Nebraska) **N:**90
Agatho, Saint (pope) **R:**290
Age *see* Aging
Aged, the *see* Old age
Agee, James (American writer) **A:**578
Agent Orange (herbicide) **A:**578
Agents (in publishing) *see* Literary agents
Agents provocateurs (oj-ONT prov-ok-a-TER) (spies) **S:**407
Age of Bronze, The (sculpture by Rodin) **R:**279
picture(s) **R:**279
Age of Exploration and Discovery E:405–8
geographical expeditions **G:**99
Age of Fish (Devonian period in geology) **F:**184
Age of Innocence, The (novel by Wharton) **W:**156
Age of Kings (17th and 18th centuries in
Europe) **A:**438d–438e
Age of Mammals (Tertiary Period) E:25; **F:**386–87
Age of Reason H:138
American literature **A:**203
Age of Reptiles F:383, 385–86
dinosaurs **D:**164
mammals, origin of **M:**67
Ageratums (aj-er-ATE-ums) (flowers) **G:**46
picture(s) **G:**50
Aggravated assault (crime) **J:**167
Agha Mohammed Khan (Persian ruler) **I:**309
Aghlabids (Tunisian dynasty) **T:**336
Agincourt (AJ-in-kourt), **Battle of** (1415) **H:**282
Aging A:82–87
Alzheimer's disease **D:**188
blindness **B:**251
cell aging and division **C:**159
deafness **D:**49
degenerative diseases **D:**185
horses' teeth **H:**236
How long do insects live? **I:**233–34

Aging (cont.)
old age **O:**96–101
percentages of older people in populations **P:**385–86
skeletal joints can stiffen **S:**184b
trees **T:**300
picture(s)
clam shell showing stages of growth **S:**149
Agitato (musical term) **M:**540
Agnes, Saint (Christian martyr) **A:578**
Agnew, Spiro T. (American public official) **N:**262f; **V:**330
picture(s) **N:**262d
Agnon, Shmuel Yosef (Samuel Joseph Czaczkes) (Hebrew novelist) **H:**101; **I:**371
Agnosticism (philosophical term) **A:578**
Agora (marketplace in Greek cities) **A:**374; **G:**341
Agoutis (a-GOO-tis) (rodents) **R:**276
Agra (India) **I:**132
Taj Mahal **T:**12
picture(s)
boatman on Jumna River **A:**445
Taj Mahal **I:**116
Agricola, Georgius (German mineralogist) **G:**109
Agricultural Adjustment Administration (AAA) **N:**138h; **R:**324
Agricultural engineers **E:**225
Agricultural fairs **F:**12
picture(s) **F:**13
Agricultural geography **G:**105
Agricultural Index **I:**115
Agricultural machinery *see* Farm machinery
Agricultural pests *see* Plant pests
Agricultural Revolution (early discoveries in agriculture) **A:**99
Agricultural Wheel (protest organization in Arkansas history) **A:**428
Agriculture **A:**88–100 *see also* Farms and farming (for specific information on how plants and animals are raised); the agriculture section of continent, country, province, and state articles; the names of domestic animals, livestock, and agricultural crops and products
agricultural engineering **E:**225
agricultural fairs **F:**12
Agriculture, United States Department of **A:**100a
antibiotics, uses for **A:**310–11
aquaculture **A:**336
atmosphere, effects on **A:**482
bacteria in agriculture **B:**12
Burbank's experimental work **B:**450
Carver's agricultural research **C:**130
collective and state farms of the USSR **U:**41
communes in China **C:**265
controlling plant pests **P:**289–91
desert farming **D:**127
farming the sea *see* Aquaculture
farms and farming **F:**48–62
feudal system **F:**99–103
food supply **F:**354–55
4-H clubs **F:**395–96
Future Farmers of America (FFA) **F:**525
gene splicing **G:**91
Indians, American **I:**165, 166, 170, 178, 200
irrigation **I:**339–41
kinds of industry **I:**225
migratory agriculture **J:**158
natural resources **N:**62
poverty caused by crop failure **P:**419
prehistoric people **F:**331; **P:**440–41
rain forest farmers **R:**100
trucks, uses of **T:**319
vegetable-growing on spacecraft **S:**344
world agriculture **W:**263–66
map(s)
world agriculture **W:**267
picture(s)
aerial spraying of crops **A:**108

Slovak farmer plowing with horses **S:**200
vegetable-growing on spacecraft **S:**342
Agriculture, United States Department of **A:**100a; **P:**450
food regulations and laws **F:**346
Forest Service **N:**29
4-H clubs **F:**395, 396
meat inspection **M:**198
National Agricultural Library **L:**178
Agrippina (ag-rip-PY-na) (Roman empress) **N:**114
Agronomy *see* Farms and farming
Aguinaldo, Emilio (Philippine hero) **A:578–79**; **P:**187
Ahab (A-hab) (king of Israel) **E:**189
Ahad Ha-am (AH-ad ha-OM) **(Asher Ginzberg)** (Hebrew writer) **H:**101
Ahasuerus (a-has-u-E-rus) (king of Persia)
Purim **P:**549
Xerxes **X:**339
Ahidjo, Ahmadou (Cameroon president) **C:**41
Ahimsa (a-HIM-sa) **(nonviolence)** (Hindu belief) **H:**129
also a teaching of Jainism **R:**147
Ahmadi (Kuwait) **K:**308
Ahmedabad (India) **I:**139
Ahmes papyrus (early mathematical handbook) **M:**162
Ahuizotl (Aztec ruler) **I:**172
Ahura Mazda (Zoroastrian god) **Z:**387
Ahvenanmaa *see* Aland Islands
AI *see* Artificial intelligence
Ai Ch'ing (Chinese poet) **C:**279
Aïda (ah-E-da) (opera by Verdi) **O:**149–50
Suez Canal opening commemorated **S:**481
picture(s) **O:**139
Aidid, Mohammed Farah (Somali leader) **S:**255
AIDS (Acquired Immune Deficiency Syndrome) **A:**100b
blood donations tested for AIDS antibodies **T:**273
condoms can protect against **B:**248
hypodermic needles of drug abusers can carry the AIDS virus **D:**330; **N:**15
immune system, disorders of **I:**98
pneumonia **D:**199
virus *see* HIV
picture(s)
halting the spread of AIDS **D:**212
Aid to Families with Dependent Children (AFDC) **W:**119
Aiken (South Carolina) **S:**308
Aiken, George L. (American dramatist) **D:**304
Aiken, Howard (American mathematician) **C:**487
Aikido (Japanese self-defense method) **A:579**
Ailerons (AIL-er-ons) (of airplanes) **A:**112
Ailey, Alvin (American choreographer) **A:579**; **D:**34
Ain Jalut, Battle of (1260) **B:**103f
Ainu (I-nu) (a people of Japan) **A:**455; **J:**26, 41; **R:**31
Air **A:**479–82
aerodynamics **A:**37–41
air conditioning **A:**101–3
ancient Greek theories of the elements **C:**206
balloons inflated with hot air **B:**34
Boyle's law **B:**354; **C:**207
burping and intestinal gases **B:**301
cloud formation **C:**382–83
gases **G:**57–58
jet streams **J:**91
light refraction **L:**215
liquefaction of gases **L:**254
matter, states of **M:**172
pollution *see* Air pollution
pressure *see* Air pressure
resistance to falling bodies **F:**33
weather **W:**77–95
Why does air move? **W:**184
winds **W:**184–87
Air, compressed *see* Compressed air
Air, liquid *see* Liquid air
Air bags (system to protect automobile passengers from injury) **A:**552; **C:**528

Airborne tanks **T:**15
Airborne warning and control system *see* AWACS
Air brakes **R:**88
    pneumatic systems **H:**300
    trucks **T:**319
    Westinghouse, George **W:**125
Air-breathing missiles **M:**344
Air carrier airports **A:**126
Air Commerce Act (United States, 1926) **A:**561
Air conditioning **A:**101–3
    air cycle system of refrigeration **R:**135
    heat pumps **H:**97
    refrigeration **R:**134, 135, 136
    spacecraft and space suits **S:**340h, 342–43
Air-cooled engines **A:**115, 548
Aircraft *see* Airplanes; Balloons and ballooning; Gliders;
    Helicopters
Aircraft carriers **S:**157; **U:**118
    picture(s)
        USS *Saratoga* **U:**116
Air deflectors (on trucks) **T:**319
Air division (Air Force unit) **U:**112
Airfields *see* Airports
Airfoil (surface that produces lift when air moves over
    it) **A:**109, 115
Air Force, Canada *see* Royal Canadian Air Force
Air Force, United States *see* United States Air Force
Air Force Communications Command **U:**112
Air Force Cross (American award)
    picture(s) **D:**66
Air Force Logistics Command **U:**112
Air Force Reserve **U:**114
Air Force Space Command **U:**112
Airframe (of an airplane) **A:**110
Air guns **G:**424
Air-launched cruise missiles (ALCM) *see* ALCM
Airlift, Berlin *see* Berlin Airlift
Airline flight attendants **A:**569
Airlines *see also* the transportation section of country, province,
    and state articles
    airports **A:**126–27, 129
    aviation **A:**561, 566
Airline stewardesses *see* Airline flight attendants
Airmail **A:**561; **P:**398
Air mass (in meteorology) **W:**82–83
Air National Guard (of the United States) **N:**41
Airplane models **A:**104–7
Airplanes **A:**108–21
    aerodynamics **A:**37–41
    airborne observatories **O:**8–9
    airports **A:**126–29
    aviation **A:**559–68
    battles **B:**103f
    Bermuda Triangle disappearances **B:**152
    fishing industry, use in **F:**218
    fuels **G:**63
    gliders compared to **G:**238
    gyroscopes **G:**437, 438
    hydraulic systems **H:**299
    inventions in air transportation **I:**284
    jet propulsion **J:**88–90
    models **A:**104–7
    rocket-powered **S:**502
    supersonic flight **S:**499–502
    transportation, history of **T:**287
    turboprop and turbojet engines **T:**343
    United States Air Force **U:**112
    United States Navy **U:**119
    used in farming **F:**56–57
    Wright brothers **W:**318
    picture(s)
        floatplane **C:**63
        jet liners **A:**566; **E:**212
        polluting the air **A:**125

    seaplane **A:**151
    servicing of **A:**128
Air pollution **A:**122–25 *see also* Dust; Fallout
    acid rain **A:**9–10
    automobiles are a cause of **A:**544
    coal **E:**220
    conservation **C:**519
    disease prevention **D:**212
    diseases, environmental **D:**186
    emphysema **D:**192
    environment, problems of **E:**299–301
    hazardous wastes **H:**72
    lead in gasoline **G:**63
    Los Angeles **L:**295
    pollution controls in automobiles **A:**547; **I:**269
    smog **F:**289
    Venice's stonework, destruction of **V:**301
Airports **A:**126–29; **H:**37 *see also* the transportation section of
    country, province, and state articles
    deregulation causes problems **A:**566
    world's first airport in Maryland **M:**120
    world's ten busiest airports, list of **A:**129
    picture(s)
        Riyadh (Saudi Arabia) **B:**437
Air (atmospheric) pressure **A:**480
    aerodynamics **A:**109
    air pollution affected by **A:**123
    barometer **B:**62
    barometer, how to make a **W:**93
    Boyle's law **B:**354; **C:**207
    climate **C:**361, 362
    how a tornado causes damage **H:**297–98
    how heat changes matter **H:**91–92
    hurricane, eye of **H:**293
    jet streams caused mainly by differences in **J:**91
    long-span roofs held up by air pressure **B:**437
    modern passenger jets are pressurized **A:**111
    pneumatic systems **H:**300
    pumps, action of **P:**539
    shown on weather maps **W:**88
    sonic booms **S:**501
    tornado damage **T:**243
    tunnel building **T:**338
    tunnels, underwater **T:**339
    vacuum formed by **V:**263, 265
    Venturi tube in aerodynamics **A:**38
    weather, creation of **W:**77, 79, 81, 82
    weather instruments to measure air pressure **W:**85
    What keeps a plane up in the air? **A:**38
    picture(s)
        supersonic flight **S:**499
Air resistance *see* Drag
Air sacs (alveoli) (of the lungs) **B:**279; **D:**199
    emphysema **D:**192
    picture(s) **B:**278
Airships **A:**558; **I:**284
    aerodynamics, principles of **A:**41
    World War I **A:**560
    picture(s)
        Goodyear blimp **H:**106
        weather balloon **W:**86
Airspeed (of an airplane) **A:**118
Airspeed indicator (in airplanes) **A:**118
Air terminals *see* Airports
Air-to-air missiles (AAM) *see* AAM
Air-to-surface missiles (ASM) *see* ASM
Air traffic control **A:**128–29
    picture(s) **A:**126; **N:**77; **R:**36
Air Training Command (of the United States Air Force) **U:**112
Air University (Alabama) **U:**112
Aitken, William Maxwell *see* Beaverbrook, Lord
Aix-la-Chapelle (EX-la-shap-ELL), Treaties of **F:**464
Ajanta (India) **I:**136, 139
Ajar, Emile *see* Gary, Romain

Ajax (name of two legendary Greek heroes) **A:579**
    picture(s)
        Ajax playing dice, painting on a Greek vase of **A:**228
Ajman (state, United Arab Emirates) **U:**53
Ajolotes (lizards) **L:**270
Akan (African language) **A:**78
Akan (African people) **A:**72, 74
Akbar (emperor of the Mogul dynasty of India) **A:579; I:**132, 137
Akers, Thomas D. (American astronaut) **S:**350
    picture(s) **S:**352, 371
Akhmatova, Anna (Russian poet) **R:**380
Akhnaton (Akhenaten; Amenhotep IV) (king of ancient Egypt) **A:**222; **E:**108, 115–16
Akiba ben Joseph (Jewish scholar) **A:579**
    Talmud **T:**13
Akihito (ah-ki-HE-to) (Crown Prince of Japan) **J:**47
Akii-Bua, John (Ugandan athlete) **O:**113
Akins, Zoë (American writer) **M:**380
Akosombo (Ghana)
    picture(s) **G:**197
Akron (Ohio) **O:**65, 72
    Soap Box Derby **S:**218a
Aksenfeld, Israel (Yiddish author) **Y:**350
Aksum (Ethiopia) **E:**333
    early African civilizations **A:**65
    Eritrea, history of **E:**313
Akureyri (ok-u-RAY-ri) (Iceland) **I:**35
Al- (in Arabic names) *see* the main part of name, as Azhar University, al-
ALA *see* American Library Association
Alabama **A:130–43**
    picture(s)
        Guntersville Lake **L:**27
Alabama (Indians of North America) **I:**178
Alabama, University of **A:**135
    football **A:**135
    picture(s)
        football **A:**134
Alabama Claims **G:**296
    Adams, Charles Francis **A:**11
Alabama River **A:**132
"Aladdin and the Wonderful Lamp" (story from *Arabian Nights*) **A:**341–42
Alajuela (Costa Rica) **C:**557
Alakaluf (Indians of South America) **I:**199
Alamein, El, Battle of (1942) **W:**295
Alamo, Battle of the (1836) **T:**124, 140
    Bowie, James, was a hero of **B:**347
    Crockett, Davy, was a hero of **C:**582
Alamo, The (San Antonio, Texas) **S:**26
    picture(s) **T:**136
Aland (OL-and) Islands (Finland) **I:**361
Al-Anon (program for the family and friends of alcoholics) **A:**173
Alarcón, Juan Ruiz de (Mexican-born Spanish playwright) **S:**390
Alarcón, Pedro Antonio de (Spanish writer) **S:**392
Alaric (king of the Visigoths) **A:579**
Alarm clock radio
    picture(s) **C:**370
Alas, Leopoldo *see* Clarín
Alaska **A:144–58; T:**111–12; **U:**82–83, 186
    Aleutian Islands **I:**361
    Alexander Archipelago **I:**362
    discovered by Vitus Bering **B:**145
    earthquake (1964) **E:**41
    Eskimos (Inuit) **E:**316–21; **I:**190–91
    glaciers **G:**223
    gold discoveries **G:**252
    pioneers **P:**262
    postal service **P:**397, 398
    Pribilof Islands **I:**367
    Yupik **I:**190–91

picture(s)
    Columbia Glacier **I:**5
    Denali National Park and Preserve **N:**44, 53
    Glacier Bay National Park **E:**13; **W:**51
    glaciers **G:**116
    Katmai National Park and Preserve **N:**53
    Mount McKinley **N:**44
Alaska, University of **A:**150–51
Alaska Air Command **U:**112
Alaska Federation of Natives (Inuit political group) **E:**321
Alaska Highway (North America) **A:**152, 158
    British Columbia **B:**405; **C:**63
    Yukon Territory **Y:**362
Alaska National Interest Lands Conservation Act (United States, 1980) **A:**158
Alaska Native Claims Settlement Act (United States, 1971) **A:**156, 158; **E:**321
Alaskan brown bears **B:**104, 107
    picture(s) **B:**106
Alaskan (Northern) fur seals **F:**518
    migration **H:**190
    picture(s) **H:**191
Alaskan malamute (working dog) **D:**247, 249
Alaska Peninsula (Alaska) **A:**146
Alaska Railroad **A:**153
Alaska Range (Alaska) **A:**146
Alaska State Museum (Juneau) **A:**151
Alateen (program for young people who live in an alcoholic family) **A:**173
Al-Azhar University *see* Azhar University, al-
Albacore (fish) **F:**217
Albania **A:159–62**
    Balkans **B:**22, 23
    picture(s)
        Albanian man from Kosovo **Y:**354
        flag **F:**235
Albanian (language) **A:**160
Albany (Australia) **A:**512, 515
Albany (capital of New York) **N:**220
    picture(s) **N:**221
Albany (Georgia) **G:**141
Albany Plan of Union (first formal plan for unification of the American colonies) **A:579**
    Franklin, Benjamin **F:**456
Albany Regency (New York political group) **V:**273
Albatrosses (birds) **B:**229
    incubation time **B:**227
    picture(s) **B:**231
        wandering albatross **B:**240
Albee, Edward (American playwright) **A:**214, **579**
Albéniz (al-BAY-neeth), Isaac (Spanish composer) **S:**392d
Albert (antipope) **R:**290
Albert (prince consort of Great Britain) **A:**163; **E:**250; **V:**332a
    first Christmas tree in England **C:**297
Albert, Carl B. (American legislator) **O:**94
Albert, Lake (Uganda–Zaïre) **U:**6
Albert I (king of Belgium) **A:**163; **B:**135; **W:**271–72
    picture(s) **W:**270
Albert II (king of Belgium) **A:**163; **B:**135
Albert I (prince of Monaco) **M:**406
Alberta (Canada) **A:164–72**
    Banff National Park **B:**46
    Edmonton **E:**73
    Jasper National Park **J:**54–55
    world's largest deposits of tar sands **E:**221
    picture(s)
        Banff National Park **C:**50
Alberti, Leon Battista (Italian architect) **A:**378; **I:**395; **R:**164–65
Albertus Magnus, Saint (German philosopher, theologian, scientist, and writer) **A:**340, **579**
Albertville (France)
    Olympic Games (1992) **O:**119–20
Albigensian (al-bi-JEN-sian) heresy **R:**286

Albrecht V (duke of Bavaria) **D:**261

Albright, Tenley (American figure skater) **O:**111

Album (for stamp collecting) **S:**421–22

Albumen (white of egg) **E:**99

Albumin glue **G:**243

Albuquerque (AL-bu-ker-ke) (New Mexico) **N:**180, 183, 185, 187, 189

Alcaeus (al-SE-us) (Greek lyric poet) **G:**354

Alcan Highway see Alaska Highway

Alcázar, The (castle, Segovia, Spain)
  picture(s) **C:**131; **S:**372

Alcázar, The (castle, Seville, Spain) **S:**383

Alcestis (al-SES-tis) (in Greek mythology) **G:**367

Alchemy (ancient practice of chemistry) **C:**207
  aging **A:**87
  distillation **D:**219
  extrasensory perception **E:**427
  picture(s) **C:**206

Alcibiades (Athenian statesman) **P:**120a

Alcindor, Lew see Abdul-Jabbar, Kareem

ALCM (air-launched cruise missiles) **M:**349

Alcmene (alk-ME-ne) (in Greek mythology) **G:**365–66

Alcohol **A:172**
  anesthesia **A:**256
  avoiding health hazards **H:**76
  beer and brewing **B:**114
  chemical term **C:**204
  common liquid **L:**256
  distillation process **D:**219
  driving under the influence of **D:**326–27; **P:**364
  fermentation **F:**90
  food taboos and customs **F:**334
  grain, uses of **G:**284–85
  juvenile crime **J:**169–70
  molecule model of its atoms **A:**483
  prohibition **P:**483–85
  specific weight **F:**251
  thermometers, use in **T:**163
  whiskey and other distilled beverages **W:**161

Alcohol, Drug Abuse, and Mental Health Administration **H:**78

Alcohol, Tobacco, and Firearms, Bureau of **T:**295

Alcoholics Anonymous (AA) **A:173**

Alcoholism **A:173**

Alcott, Amos Bronson (American educator) **A:**174

Alcott, Louisa May (American author) **A:174–75; C:**236
  Little Women, excerpt from **A:**174–75

Alcove Springs (Kansas) **K:**186

Aldebaran (al-DEB-ar-an) (star) **C:**525

Alden, John (Pilgrim settler) **P:**345

Alderney (one of the Channel Islands, Britain) **I:**363

Aldrin, Edwin E., Jr. (American astronaut) **A:**469; **E:**419; **S:**340f, 340h, 340j, 346
  picture(s) **M:**453; **S:**340i, 347

Aldus Manutius see Manutius, Aldus

Ale (type of beer) **B:**114, 115

Aleichem, Sholem see Aleykhem, Sholem

Aleijadinho (Brazilian sculptor) see Lisboa, Antonio Francisco

Aleixandre, Vicente (Spanish poet) **S:**392b

Alekseev, Konstantin see Stanislavski, Konstantin

Alemán (ol-ay-MON), Mateo (Spanish writer) **S:**390

Alemán, Miguel Valdés (Mexican president) **M:**251

Alençon (ol-on-SAWN) lace **L:**19

Aleppo (Syria) **S:**549

Alesia, Battle of (52 B.C.) **B:**103e

Alessandri Palma, Arturo (president of Chile) **C:**255

Alessandro Filipepi see Botticelli, Sandro

Aletsch (OL-ech) Glacier (Switzerland) **A:**194b

Aleut (language in the Eskimo-Aleut family) **E:**316

Aleut (Native Americans) **I:**191; **R:**29
  Alaska **A:**144, 150; **E:**316

Aleutian (a-LEU-tian) Islands **I:**361
  Alaska **A:**144, 146, 149, 158
  World War II **W:**295

Aleutian Range (Alaska) **A:**146

Alexander, Grover Cleveland (American baseball player) **B:**88

Alexander, Harold (1st Earl Alexander of Tunis, British field marshal) **A:**579; **W:**295

Alexander, Lloyd (American writer of children's books) **A:**579

Alexander, Martha (American author and illustrator of children's books) **A:580**

Alexander V (antipope) **R:**291

Alexander III (king of Macedonia) see Alexander the Great

Alexander I, Saint (pope) **R:**290

Alexander II (pope) **R:**290

Alexander III (pope) **R:**290

Alexander IV (pope) **R:**291

Alexander VI (pope) **E:**407; **R:**291

Alexander VII (pope) **R:**291

Alexander VIII (pope) **R:**291

Alexander I (emperor of Russia) **A:**176; **R:**365–66; **U:**46

Alexander II (emperor of Russia) **A:**176–77; **R:**366; **T:**116; **U:**47

Alexander III (emperor of Russia) **A:**177; **R:**366; **U:**47

Alexander and the Terrible, Horrible, No Good, Very Bad Day (book by Viorst)
  picture(s)
    Cruz illustration **C:**244

Alexander Archipelago (island group, Alaska) **I:**362
  Alaska's Panhandle **A:**146

Alexander Nevski (Russian national hero) **A:580**

Alexander the Great (king of Macedonia) **A:177–78**, 463; **G:**344
  Aristotle was teacher of **A:**397
  Greek civilization extended by **A:**230
  Middle East **M:**304
  Persia, ancient **P:**155
  submarine experiment **S:**473

Alexandra (Russian empress) **N:**249
  picture(s) **R:**367; **U:**47

Alexandria (Egypt) **E:**107; **M:**302
  Alexander the Great founds **A:**178
  library **E:**77; **L:**172
  mathematics, history of **M:**163
  Pharos lighthouse was a wonder of the ancient world **W:**219–20
  scientists of Alexandria **S:**63–64

Alexandria (Louisiana) **L:**310

Alexandria (Virginia) **V:**357

Alexandria, Museum of (ancient Egypt) **M:**521

Alexandrite (gemstone) **G:**75

Alexis (heir to Russian throne) **N:**249
  picture(s) **R:**367; **U:**47

Alexis (Russian Orthodox metropolitan) **I:**413

Alexius I Comnenus (Byzantine emperor) **A:580; C:**588

Aleykhem (Aleichem), Sholem (Jewish writer and humorist) **A:580; Y:**350–51

Alfaro (ol-FAR-o), Eloy (Ecuadorian political reformer) **E:**69

Alfheim (OLF-heim) (Norse fairyland) **N:**279

Alfieri (al-fi-AIR-i), Vittorio (Italian poet) **I:**408

Al fine (musical term) **M:**540

Alfonsín, Raúl (Argentinian political leader) **A:**396

Alfonso X, the Wise (king of Castile) **S:**389

Alfonso XII (Spanish king) **S:**380

Alfonso XIII (Spanish king) **S:**381

Alfred the Great (king of England) **A:179; E:**237–38
  English literature flourished under **E:**268–69
  spies **S:**408
  subject of legends **L:**130

Algae (AL-je) (simple organisms) **A:180–81; M:**275
  eutrophication of water sources **W:**65, 68
  fertilizers stimulate growth and cause pollution **E:**297
  food for the future **P:**221
  kingdoms of living things **K:**251
  ocean, uses of the **O:**28
  plankton **P:**283–84

Algebra (branch of mathematics) **A:182–84; M:**157 see also Arithmetic
  mathematics, history of **M:**163, 164, 165–66, 169

Alger, Horatio, Jr. (American author) **M:**148
Algeria **A:**185–88
  France, history of **F:**417, 420
  Organization of Petroleum Exporting Countries **O:**221
  picture(s)
      election **E:**127
      flag **F:**226
Algiers (capital of Algeria) **A:**185, 187
Algonkians (Indians of North America) **I:**177–78
  Massachusetts **M:**136, 146
  New England **N:**139
  New York, history of **N:**221
  Rhode Island, history of **R:**217
Alhambra palace (Spain) **I:**357
  fountains **F:**393
  Spain, art and architecture of **S:**383
  picture(s) **S:**383
      Court of the Lions **I:**356
Alhazen (ol-ha-ZEN) (Arab mathematician and optical
    scientist) **O:**178; **S:**65
Ali (cousin and son-in-law of the prophet Mohammed) **I:**306,
    348
Ali, Muhammad (Cassius Marcellus Clay, Jr.) (American
    boxer) **A:**580; **B:**353; **O:**111
Alia, Ramiz (Albanian political leader) **A:**162
Alianza Federal de Mercedes (Hispanic-American
    organization) **N:**194
Ali Baba (hero of story "The Forty Thieves" from *Arabian
    Nights*) **A:**342
Alibates Flint Quarries National Monument (Texas) **T:**134
Alice in Wonderland (book by Carroll) **C:**119, 120
  excerpt from **C:**120
  picture(s)
      Tenniel illustration **C:**234
Alice Springs (Australia) **A:**505, 513
Alice Tully Hall (Lincoln Center, New York City) **L:**248
Alien and Sedition Acts (United States, 1798) **A:**14, 189;
    U:178   ●
  freedom of speech and press curtailed **F:**462
Aliens **A:**189 *see also* Citizenship; Immigration;
    Naturalization
  compared to citizens **C:**324
  illegal Mexican immigrants, problem of **H:**133
  naturalization **N:**61
  passports and visas **P:**98
  refugees **R:**137–38
Ali Mahdi Mohammed (president of Somalia) **S:**255
Alimony (in divorce) **D:**230
Aliyev, Geidar A. (president of Azerbaijan) **A:**572
Alkali metals **C:**204; **E:**167
Alkaline batteries **B:**103b
Alkaline-earth metals **E:**167
Alkaline soils **S:**238
Alkalis (strong chemical bases) **C:**204
  soaps contain **D:**140
Alkyd (AL-kid) **resins** (types of liquid plastics) **P:**32
Allagash (AL-la-gash) **Wilderness Waterway** (Maine) **M:**45–46
Allah (Arabic name for God of Islam) **I:**346; **M:**401
Allahabad (al-la-ha-BAD) (India) **G:**25
All-America Football Conference **F:**366
All-American Canal (California) **C:**22
All-American Soap Box Derby *see* Soap Box Derby
"All Around the Kitchen" (folk song) **F:**324
Allegheny (AL-le-gainy) **Front** (escarpment) **O:**270
Allegheny Mountains (North America) **P:**128; **W:**128
Allegheny Plateau (eastern North America) **M:**122; **N:**213;
    O:62, 63; **P:**128; **W:**128
Allegheny River (United States) **P:**128, 266
Allegory (story to explain or teach something) **F:**111
  early English literature **E:**269
  early French literature **F:**436
  Everyman (greatest morality play) **E:**271
  Pilgrim's Progress **E:**276
Allegretto (musical term) **M:**540

Allegri, Antonio *see* Correggio, Antonio Allegri da
Allegro (musical term) **M:**540, 543
Allegro Brillante (ballet)
  picture(s) **B:**33
Allen, Ethan (American Revolutionary War hero) **A:**189; **R:**199;
    V:318
  sought Iroquois allies **I:**204
Allen, Gracie (American comedian) **B:**508
Allen, Horatio (American engineer) **R:**88–89
Allen, Joseph (American astronaut)
  picture(s) **S:**349
Allen, Richard (American religious leader) **A:**79e; **P:**140
Allen, Woody (American actor, writer, and filmmaker) **M:**493,
    497
Allenby, Sir Edmund H. H. (British general) **J:**79
Allende, Salvador (Chilean political leader) **A:**580; **C:**255
Allentown (Pennsylvania) **P:**135
Allergy (body's sensitivity to a normally harmless
    thing) **D:**184, 187–88
  hypoallergenic cosmetics **C:**552
  immune system, disorders of **I:**97
  insect stings **F:**162
All for Love (play by Dryden) **D:**340
All Hallows' Day **H:**13
Alliance for Progress (development program for Latin
    America) **K:**209
Alliances (of nations) **I:**274
All I Desire (motion picture) **M:**492
Allied Control Council (over Germany after World War II) **G:**164
Allied Powers (during the two world wars) **A:**580
  World War I **W:**272, 282
Allies (among nations) **I:**274
  allied army groups **U:**108
Allies Day, May 1917 (painting by Hassam)
  picture(s) **I:**106
Alligators **A:**284; **C:**582–84; **R:**179–80
  leather no longer available **L:**107
  picture(s) **U:**89
Alligator snapping turtle *see* Temminck's snapper
Alliteration (repetition of the same first sounds in a group of
    words) **P:**353
  Beowulf **B:**144b
Allosaurus (dinosaur) **D:**169
  picture(s)
      foot **D:**168
      skeleton reconstruction **D:**167
Allotropes (forms of a chemical element) **C:**204
Alloys **A:**190–91; **C:**204; **M:**236 *see also* Brass; Brazing;
    Bronze; Metals and metallurgy; Soldering; Welding
  aluminum **A:**194d
  bronze and brass **B:**409–10
  chemistry, history of **C:**206
  copper **C:**546
  gold alloyed with other metals **G:**248
  kinds of steel **I:**329
  magnesium alloys **M:**27
  magnets **M:**32, 33
  nickel **N:**249–50
  silver **S:**178
  standard jewelry alloys of gold **G:**248
  thermocouples, use in **T:**164
  tin, use of **T:**207
  tungsten and steel alloys **T:**332
Alloy steels **A:**190; **I:**329
All Quiet on the Western Front (novel by Remarque) **G:**182
All Saints Cathedral (England)
  picture(s)
      stained-glass window **S:**417
All Saints' Day **H:**13; **R:**154, 284
All Souls' Day (religious holiday) **R:**154, 284
  Latin America **L:**51
  Mexico **M:**242
Allspice **F:**334; **H:**114
All-star games (in baseball) **B:**84, 91

All's Well That Ends Well (play by Shakespeare) **S**:133
All-terrain bicycles (ATB's) **B**:175, 176, 177
"All the Friendly Beasts" (Christmas folk song) **F**:325
All the King's Men (novel by Warren) **A**:214; **W**:11
Alluvial (al-LU-vial) **deposits** **R**:237
   gold found in **G**:248–49
Alluvial Floodplain (area of Louisiana) **L**:300
Alluvial soils **S**:238
   North America **N**:291
Alluvium (river deposits) **R**:237
All-wheel drive (of a truck) **T**:319
Alma-Ata (capital of Kazakhstan) **K**:201; **U**:43
Almagest (book, Ptolemy) **A**:471
Almagro (ol-MA-gro), **Diego de** (Spanish soldier) **C**:253–54;
   E:411; **P**:268
Almanacs (type of reference book) **R**:129
   Poor Richard's Almanack **F**:454
Almandite (AL-mand-ite) (garnet gemstone) **G**:71
Almohads (Berber dynasty in Spain) **S**:379, 383
Almonds **N**:428
Almoravids (al-MO-ra-vids) (Berber dynasty) **M**:461; **S**:379
Almshouses (early hospitals for the poor) **H**:253
Alnico (alloy) **M**:32
Aloha State (nickname for Hawaii) **H**:48, 49
Alonso, Alicia (Cuban ballerina) **C**:597
"Alouette" (ol-oo-ETT) (folk song) **F**:322
Alpacas (al-PAK-as) (hoofed mammals) **H**:212
   picture(s) **H**:213
Alpha-amylase (al-fa-AM-il-ase) (digestive enzyme) **B**:296
Alphabet **A**:192–94a *see also* Writing systems; individual
      letters of the alphabet
   Arabic **A**:344
   Braille **B**:253
   Chinese alphabetic writing **C**:258–59
   communication advanced by **C**:463
   Danish has 29 letters **D**:108
   development of languages **L**:38
   encyclopedias in unit and split-lettered alphabetical
      systems **E**:204
   Hebrew **H**:98
   how to cut paper and fabric letters **B**:447
   indexes, learning to use **I**:115
   International Code of Signals for use at sea **F**:247
   Japanese language **J**:30
   Latin language **L**:76
   most used letter in English **E**:1
   phonics **P**:194
   pronunciation **P**:486
   Russian uses Cyrillic alphabet **R**:358, 376
   Should it be taught to a preschool child? **R**:108
   picture(s)
      cursive alphabet **H**:23
      manual alphabet of the deaf **D**:49
      manuscript alphabet **H**:22
Alpha brass (alloy) **B**:410
Alpha Centauri (star) **A**:474; **S**:355, 429, 488
Alpha particles (of radioactive atoms) **R**:67
Alpha rays (streams of alpha particles) **R**:67
   radioactive radiation **R**:47
Alpine Club of London (mountain climbing club) **M**:499
Alpine glaciers *see* Valley glaciers
Alpine horn (musical instrument)
   picture(s) **S**:540
Alpine skiing **S**:184c, 184e–184f, 185
Alpine tundra **T**:331
Alpine wildflowers **W**:171
Alps (mountains of Europe) **A**:194b
   Alpine regions of Austria **A**:520
   branches named and located **E**:344
   France **F**:407, 409
   Frejus tunnel **T**:339
   Italy **I**:384
   Liechtenstein **L**:191
   mountains of the world **M**:502, 504–5

   Switzerland **S**:540–41
   picture(s) **M**:503
      Alpine village **H**:169
      ibex **G**:244
      Matterhorn **E**:341
      Mont Blanc **G**:221
Al-Razi (Arab physician) *see* Rhazes
ALS *see* Amyotrophic lateral sclerosis
Alsace-Lorraine (historic region of eastern France) **A**:580;
   F:404, 417
   Franco-Prussian War **F**:452
Alsatian (dog) *see* German Shepherd
Al-Saud, Sultan Salman Abdelazize (Saudi Arabian astronaut)
   picture(s) **S**:351
Altaic languages **A**:455; **L**:40
Altair (al-TIRE) (star) **C**:525
Altamira cave paintings (Spain) **P**:15; **S**:382
   picture(s) **P**:14, 436
Alternate pattern (of leaf growth) **L**:115; **P**:306
Alternating current (A.C.) (in electricity) **E**:145
   electric clocks **C**:370
   electric generators **E**:133–34
   electric motors **E**:153–54
   transformers **T**:272
Alternation of generations (in biology)
   ferns **F**:94–95
   mosses **M**:473
   plants **P**:302
Alternators (of automobiles) **A**:547; **B**:103b, 103c
Altes ("Old") **Museum** (Berlin, Germany) **M**:522
Althing (Iceland's legislature) **I**:36; **L**:137; **V**:341
   oldest parliament in existence **P**:83
Altimeter (measures altitude) **A**:118; **B**:62
Altiplano regions (of South America) **S**:276
   Bolivia **B**:308
   Peru **P**:162
Altitude
   climatic control **C**:361, 364; **M**:507
   cloud formation **C**:382
   in geometry **G**:123
   temperature of environment affected by **L**:202
   vertical life zones **Z**:380–81
Alto (musical term) **C**:282
Altocumulus clouds **C**:385; **W**:84
   picture(s) **C**:384
Altostratus (AL-to-STRAIT-us) **clouds** **C**:385; **W**:84
   picture(s) **C**:384
Altricial (al-TRI-sial) **birds** **B**:229
"Alturas de Machu Picchu" (poem by Neruda)
   excerpt from **L**:71
Alum (chemical compound) **A**:580
   used as a mordant in dyeing **D**:371
   water purification **W**:57
Alumina *see* Aluminum oxide
Aluminum (aluminium) **A**:194c–194d; **E**:170
   acid rain's effect on soils **A**:10
   airplanes designed for subsonic flight **S**:501
   atomic structure **A**:486
   modern armor **A**:435
   non-ferrous alloys **A**:190, 191
   Washington, aluminum industry in **W**:19
   world distribution **W**:261
   map(s)
      world distribution **W**:260
   table(s) **M**:235
Aluminum bronze (alloy) **B**:410
Aluminum oxide (alumina) **A**:194c
   abrasive for grinding and polishing **G**:388
Alvarado (ol-va-RA-tho), **Pedro de** (Spanish soldier) **M**:187
Alvarez (AHL-vah-rez), **Luis Walter** (American
   physicist) **A**:194d; **D**:175
   geology **G**:111–12
Alvarez, Walter (American geologist) **A**:194d; **D**:175
Alveoli *see* Air sacs

ALVIN (deep submergence vehicle)
   picture(s) **O:**40; **S:**476
Always Prepared (motto of U.S. Coast Guard) *see* Semper
   Paratus
Alyssum, sweet (flower)
   picture(s) **G:**27, 28
Alzheimer's disease **D:**188
AM (radio) *see* Amplitude modulation
Amadeus (play by Shaffer)
   picture(s) **D:**295
Amado, Jorge (Brazilian novelist) **A:580; L:**72
Amager (island, Denmark) **C:**543
Amahl and the Night Visitors (opera by Menotti) **O:**150
   picture(s) **O:**151
Amalekites (tribe of Biblical times) **A:580**
Amalgam (a-MAL-gam) (alloy)
   gold and mercury **G:**247
   silver-mercury alloys **S:**178
Amalgamation (a-mal-ga-MAY-tion) (of ores) **M:**233
   gold-extracting process **G:**249
Amalienborg Palace (Copenhagen, Denmark) **C:**543
Amana (am-AN-a) **colonies** (Iowa) **I:**294, 298
Amanitas (am-a-NI-tas) (poisonous mushrooms) **F:**500;
   M:533
Amaral, Antonio H. (Brazilian artist) **L:**67
Amaranth (plant) **G:**286; **I:**165
Amarids (Muslim dynasty) **S:**379
Amarnath Cave (Hindu shrine, Kashmir)
   picture(s) **H:**126
Amateur Athletic Union of the United States (AAU) **A:580**
   gymnastic events **G:**433
   swimming **S:**536
Amateur Hockey Association of the United States *see* Hockey
   USA
Amateurism (in the Olympic Games) **O:**104, 106
Amateur radio *see* Radio, amateur
Amateur Radio Emergency Service **R:**63
Amateur Softball Association of America (ASA) **A:580**
Amateur telescope makers (ATM's) **T:**61
Amateur theatricals **T:**159
   putting on a play **P:**333–38
Amati (a-MA-ti) **family** (Italian violin makers) **B:**71; **V:**342
Amazing Stories (science-fiction magazine) **S:**84
Amazonite (AM-az-on-ite) (gemstone) **G:**76
Amazon Pact (to develop the resources of the Amazon rain
   forest) **A:194f; S:**291
Amazon parrot **B:**246
   picture(s) **P:**178
Amazon River (South America) **A:194e–194f; S:**277
   Brazil **B:**380
   How did the Amazon River get its name? **A:194f**
   tidal bore **T:**197
   picture(s)
     houseboat **R:**241
Amazons (in Greek mythology) **A:580**
   naming of the Amazon River **A:194f**
Ambartsumian, Victor (Armenian astrophysicist) **A:**431
Ambassadors (highest ranking officers in
   embassies) **F:**369–70; **I:**273
   forms of address **A:**22
Ambassadors, The (painting by Hans Holbein the Younger)
   picture(s) **N:**35
Amber (fossil resin) **R:**184
   discovery of static electricity **E:**136
   "display case" for insects **E:**374
   fossils preserved in **F:**379
   organic gems **G:**76
Ambergris (substance formed by whales) **W:**149, 154
   fixatives in perfumes **P:**151
Ambler, Eric (English author) **A:580–81; M:**564
Amboise Conspiracy (in French history) **F:**449
Ambon (Indonesia) **I:**211
Ambrogini, Angelo *see* Poliziano

Ambrose, Saint **C:**289; **R:**283
   converted Saint Augustine **A:**494
   hymn composer **H:**307
Ambrose Offshore Light Structure (off New York Harbor)
   picture(s) **L:**229
Ambrosia **A:581**
Ambulatory (in church architecture) **A:**376
Ambulatory surgery (surgery not requiring an overnight hospital
   stay) **H:**253
Amendments to the United States Constitution **U:**147, 155–60
   see also Bill of Rights, American
   civil rights amendments in the Bill of Rights **C:**328, 330
   Eleventh Amendment **J:**56
   first 10 are Bill of Rights **B:**182–83
   Fourteenth Amendment **J:**118
   freedom of religion, speech, and press in First
     Amendment **F:**462
Amenemhet I (om-en-EM-het) (king of ancient
   Egypt) **E:**112–13
Amenhotep III (om-en-HO-tep) (king of ancient Egypt) **E:**115
Amenhotep IV *see* Akhnaton
America *see also* Central America; Latin America; North
   America; South America; the names of countries
   Columbus discovered **C:**445–48
   exploration and discovery of **E:**406, 407, 409–11
   Vespucci, Amerigo, continents named for **V:**321
   Viking discovery of **V:**341
   Why was the New World named "America"? **E:**411
"America" (song by Smith) **N:**20, 22
American, The (book by Henry James) **J:**20
American Academy and Institute of Arts and Letters
   (AAIAL) **A:581**
American Antiquarian Society (Worcester,
   Massachusetts) **M:**145
American Anti-Slavery Society **A:**6, 6b
American architecture *see* United States, architecture of the
American art *see* United States, art of the
American Association for Affirmative Action **C:**328
American Association for the Advancement of Science
   (AAAS) **A:581**
American Association of Retired Persons (AARP) **A:581**
American Ballet Theatre **B:**33
American Bar Association (ABA) **A:581**
American Basketball Association (ABA) **B:**99
American beech (tree)
   picture(s) **T:**304
American Bible Society (ABS) **A:581**
American Bill of Rights *see* Bill of Rights, American
American bond (in masonry) *see* Common bond
American Book Awards *see* National Book Awards
American Bowling Congress (ABC) **B:**348, 350a
American Boy (magazine) **M:**17
American buffalo *see* Bison
American bullfrog **A:**214b
American Camping Association **C:**49
American Cancer Society **C:**93
American Canoe Association **C:**99
American Checker Federation **C:**192
American Civil Liberties Union (ACLU) **C:**328
American Civil War *see* Civil War, United States
American College Testing Program (ACTP) **T:**118
American colonies *see* Colonial life in America; Thirteen
   American colonies
American Colonization Society **L:**168; **S:**195
American crawl (swimming stroke) **S:**537
American Dictionary of the English Language, An (by
   Webster) **W:**99
American drama **D:**303–5
American eagles *see* Bald eagles
American elk (wapiti) **H:**214
   picture(s) **H:**215
American elm (tree)
   diagram(s)
     leaf **L:**113

picture(s) **T:**302
    state tree of Massachusetts **M:**137
    state tree of North Dakota **N:**323
American English **W:**240
    slang **S:**191
American Expeditionary Force (A.E.F.) **W:**279–80
    commanded by Pershing **P:**153
American Express credit card **C:**572
American Federation of Labor (AFL) **L:**14, 16
    Gompers, Samuel **G:**261
**American Federation of Labor–Congress of Industrial
    Organizations (AFL-CIO)** **L:**16–17
American Federation of Teachers (AFT) **A:**581
American flag *see* United States flags
American folklore *see* Folklore, American
American Folklore Society **F:**314
American Football Conference **F:**364
American Football League **F:**366
American Foundation for the Blind **B:**254
American Friends Service Committee (AFSC) **Q:**4a
American Friends Society *see* Quakers
American Fur Company (of John Jacob Astor) **F:**521, 523,
    524; **O:**216
American Gothic (painting by Wood) **W:**221
    picture(s) **W:**221
American Heart Association (AHA) **A:**581; **D:**212
American history *see* America; Thirteen American colonies;
    United States, history of the
American holly
    picture(s)
        state tree of Delaware **D:**89
American Home Economics Association **H:**165
American Humane Association (AHA) **A:**581
American Independent Party (in the United States) **P:**372
American Indian Movement (AIM) **C:**328
American Indians *see* Indians, American
Americanisms (in the English language) **W:**240
American Jewish Committee **A:**581
American Jewish Congress (AJC) **A:**581
American Kennel Club **D:**248, 249
American Labor Party **L:**18
American Lawn Bowling Association **B:**350b
American League (baseball) **B:**80, 84, 87, 93
    World Series records **B:**86
American Legion (AL) **A:**581
American Library Association **L:**180–81
    children's book awards **C:**228–29, 230–31
American lions *see* Mountain lions
American literature **A:**195–214a; **U:**98 *see also* African
    American literature; Canadian literature; Children's
    literature; Folklore, American; Humor; Latin America,
    literature of; Literary criticism; Magazines; Short
    stories; the names of writers
    African Americans *see* African American literature
    children's book awards **C:**228–29, 230–31
    drama *see* American drama
    essays **E:**322
    novels **N:**360, 361–62, 363
    Pulitzer Prizes **P:**533–37
    romanticism **R:**304
American Lung Association **D:**212
American Medical Association (AMA) **A:**581
American Museum of Immigration (Liberty Island, New
    York) **L:**169
American Museum of Natural History (New York City) **M:**523
American music *see* Folk music; Jazz; Spirituals; United States,
    music of the
American National Red Cross *see* Red Cross
American Nazi Party **N:**81
American Numismatic Association **C:**399, 400
American Nurses' Association **N:**421
American painting *see* United States, art of the
American Party *see* Know-Nothing Party
American Peace Society **P:**105

American Philosophical Society **F:**454; **P:**180, 181; **S:**70
American plan (of hotel rates) **H:**256
American Popular Revolutionary Alliance (APRA) (Peruvian
    political party) **P:**165
American Printing House for the Blind **B:**254
American Professional Football Association **F:**366
American Professional Soccer League (APSL) **S:**219
American Radio Relay League (ARRL) **R:**62, 63
American Red Cross *see* Red Cross
American regionalism (style of painting) **W:**221
American Revolution *see* Revolutionary War
American saddle horse **H:**244
American Samoa **P:**8, 10; **T:**114; **U:**93; **W:**124
American's Creed, The (by Page) **U:**161
Americans for Democratic Action (ADA) **A:**581
American Society for Information Science **L:**181
American Society for the Prevention of Cruelty to Animals *see*
    Society for the Prevention of Cruelty to Animals,
    American
**American Society of Composers, Authors and Publishers
    (ASCAP)** **A:**581
American Society of Free People of Color **A:**79f
American Society of Genealogists **G:**76a
American Society of Interior Designers (ASID) **I:**261
**American Sokol Educational and Physical Culture
    Organization** **G:**433
**American Standard Code for Information Interchange
    (ASCII)** **C:**494
American Standards Association (ASA) film speed index **P:**205
American Stock Exchange **S:**457
American Telephone and Telegraph Company **P:**523
    Johnson's "Chippendale Building" **J:**124
    picture(s)
        Bell Labs chemist **A:**79b
American Temperance Society **P:**484
American Tragedy, An (novel by Theodore Dreiser) **D:**322
American Upland cotton **C:**560
American Veterans Committee (AVC) **A:**581
American Veterans of World War II, Korean and Vietnam Wars *see*
    AMVETS
American War of Independence *see* Revolutionary War
American Water Ski Association **W:**73
American Woman Suffrage Association **W:**212a
American Youth Hostels, Inc. **H:**254
American Youth Soccer Organization **S:**222
America's Cup (yacht-racing trophy) **A:**582
America's Sweetheart (nickname for Mary Pickford) **M:**491
"America the Beautiful" (song by Bates) **N:**23
Americium (am-er-IS-ium) (element) **E:**170
Americo-Liberians (Liberian descendants of settlers from the
    United States) **L:**165, 168
Amerigo Vespucci *see* Vespucci, Amerigo
Amerindians *see* Indians, American
Amethyst (AM-eth-ist) (quartz gemstone) **G:**74, 75; **Q:**6
    picture(s) **G:**73
Amharas (a people of Ethiopia) **E:**330, 334
Amharic (am-HARR-ik) (language) **E:**330–31
Amherst, Lord Jeffrey (British soldier) **F:**465; **I:**203
Amiens, Treaty of (1802) **N:**11
Amiens Cathedral (France) **F:**423
Amin, Idi (Ugandan dictator) **A:**582; **U:**4, 7
Amine (chemical) **V:**370b
Amino (a-MI-no) **acids** (in body chemistry) **B:**188, 292–93,
    297–98
    digestion **D:**162–63
    enzymes **E:**303
    genetics **G:**84–85
    living things build proteins from **L:**199
    phenylketonuria **D:**198
    proteins in nutrition **N:**424
    structure of antibodies **I:**97
Aminopeptidase (digestive enzyme) **D:**162
Amis, Kingsley (English writer and teacher) **E:**290

Amish (OM-ish) (religious group)   F:295; P:134
    traditional agriculture   A:89
    picture(s)   P:127
Amistad National Recreation Area (Texas)   T:134
Amman (OM-mon) (capital of Jordan)   J:131
Ammonia (gas)   G:58, 60; N:262
    coal by-product   C:391
    nitrogen cycle   E:54
    refrigeration systems, use in   R:134–35
    Saturn's atmosphere   P:280; S:53
    structural formula   C:201
Ammonites (creatures with coiled shells)   P:433
Ammonium nitrate (chemical compound)   E:423
Ammunition   G:414–26
    explosives   E:421–25
    lead   L:92
Amnesty (freedom from prosecution)
    illegal aliens   I:93
Amnesty and Reconstruction, Proclamation of (1863)   R:117
Amnesty International (human rights organization)   A:582;
    C:329
Amniotic fluid (surrounding the fetus before birth)   B:2, 3
Amoebas (a-ME-bas) (one-celled animals)   M:276; P:496
    digestion   D:163
    reproduction   G:77
    picture(s)   P:495
Amon-Re (om-on-RAY) (Egyptian sun-god)   A:221
Amon-Re, Temple of (Karnak, Egypt)   A:221; E:114–15
    picture(s)   A:370
Amorphous materials   M:154
Amortization (of a debt)   R:112d
Amos (A-mos) (Hebrew prophet)   B:159; J:104
Amosite (mineral)   A:443
Amoskeag (AM-os-keg) Mills (Manchester, New
    Hampshire)   N:159, 162
Amperage (AM-per-age) (of electricity)   E:139–40
Ampere (ON-pare), André Marie   E:140
    electric motors, history of   E:154
    experiments in magnetism   M:31
Amperes (AM-peres) (measure of electric current)   B:103c;
    E:139–40; T:271, 272; W:117
Amphetamines (am-FET-a-means) (drugs)   D:331
Amphibians (am-FIB-ians) (aircraft)   A:115
Amphibians (land-water animals)   A:214b–216, 266–67
    acid rain's effects   A:10
    Earth, history of   E:27
    evolution from fish   F:185
    frogs and toads   F:476–78
    locomotion   A:278
    prehistoric animals   P:433
    three-chambered heart   M:76
Amphibious tanks   T:15
Amphibious vehicles
    picture(s)   U:122
Amphibious warfare
    United States Navy   U:118
    picture(s)
        United States Marine Corps   U:121
Amphibole (form of asbestos)   A:443
Amphoras (ancient Greek vases)
    picture(s)   A:363; D:73
Amplifiers (in electronics)
    amplified music is hazardous to hearing   S:258
    electronic music   E:155
    high-fidelity systems   H:121, 122–23
    modern stereo systems   S:267b
    radio   R:54
    transistors, uses for   T:276
    triodes   E:161
Amplitude (in physics)
    radio waves   R:52
    sound waves   S:258–59
Amplitude modulation (AM) (in radio)   R:53, 54, 56
Amputation (surgery)   S:513

Amritsar (India)   I:134
    picture(s)
        Golden Temple   I:118
Amsterdam (capital of the Netherlands)   N:120, 120c
    early stock exchange   S:455
    Olympic Games (1928)   O:109
    picture(s)   H:180; N:120a
        Rijksmuseum   M:526
Amsterdam Island (Indian Ocean)
    picture(s)   I:362
Amtrak (operator of U.S. passenger rail service)   R:80; T:290;
    U:103
    New Mexico   N:187
Amu Darya (om-U DAR-ya) (in ancient times called the Oxus
    River, in central Asia)   A:44; L:32; U:258
    Tajikistan   T:11
Amulets (AM-u-lets) (ornaments to ward off evil)   G:74
    picture(s)
        pre-Columbian amulet   D:73
Amundsen, Roald (Norwegian explorer)   N:339
    first Northwest Passage by sea   A:386d; E:416, 417
    first to reach South Pole   A:295
Amur (om-OOR) River (Asia)   R:240, 361; U:39
Amusement and theme parks   P:79–80
    Disneyland (California)   C:30; D:216
    Disneyland (Japan)   T:219
    Disney World (Florida)   D:216; F:269
    Holiday World (Indiana)   I:152
    Six Flags Great Adventure (New Jersey)   N:172
    picture(s)
        centrifugal effect of rides   G:323
        Disneyland (California)   D:215
        Disney World (Florida)   F:268; M:94
Amusements see Recreation
AMVETS (veterans' organization)   A:582
Amylase (digestive enzyme)   B:276; D:162
Amyotrophic lateral sclerosis
    Hawking, Stephen William   H:64
An see Anu
Anacletus, Saint (pope) see Cletus, Saint
Anacletus II (antipope)   R:290
Anaconda (an-a-KON-da) Company   M:442
Anacondas (snakes)   S:211
Anaerobic bacteria   B:11; L:203
    hyperbaric chambers used in treating infections   M:210
Anaerobic exercise   P:226
Anaerobic respiration (of plants)   P:315
Anagrams (word games)   G:17; W:236
Anal fins (of fish)   F:188
Analgesics (substances that relieve pain)   N:13
Analog devices   C:490
Analogies (test questions)   T:120
Analog sound storage   H:121
Analog synthesizer   E:156
Analog time display (in solid-state watches)   W:45
Anal sphincter (muscle at the end of the digestive
    tract)   B:301
Analysis (in chemistry)   C:204
Analytical chemistry   C:205
Analytical engine (early computer)   C:486
Analytical method (in philosophy)   P:189
Analytic geometry see Coordinate geometry
Anansi (hero of African folktales)   A:76b
Anapests (metrical feet in poetry)   P:354
Anaphylaxis (extreme allergic reaction)   D:188
Anarchism (political theory)   A:582
Anasazi see Cliff dwellers
Anastasius (antipope)   R:290
Anastasius I (pope)   R:290
Anastasius II (pope)   R:290
Anastasius III (pope)   R:290
Anastasius IV (pope)   R:290
Anatase (mineral)
    picture(s)   M:316

Anatidae (waterfowl family)   **D:**341
Anatolia (an-a-TO-lia) **(Asia Minor)** (region of Turkey)   **T:**345, 346 *see also* Asia Minor
   Ottoman Empire   **O:**261
Anatomy (a-NAT-omy), **comparative**   **A:**276–77
Anatomy, human (structure of human body)   **B:**268–88
   Vesalius, Andreas, was father of   **B:**195
Anatosaurus (dinosaur)
   picture(s)   **D:**172
Anawratha (Burman king)   **B:**457
Anaximander (Greek philosopher)   **S:**62
Anaya, Rudolfo (American writer)   **A:**214a
Ancestor worship   **R:**145
   Africa   **A:**60
   Africa, art of   **A:**70
   China   **C:**260
   ghosts   **G:**199
   Madagascar   **M:**8
   Rome, ancient   **R:**311
Anchises (an-KY-sese) (father of Aeneas)   **A:**36
Anchorage (ANK-or-age) (Alaska)   **A:**144, 150, 151, 152, 153, 158
   earthquake (1964)   **E:**41
"Anchors Aweigh" (song by A. H. Miles and R. Lovell)   **N:**23
Anchovies (fish)   **F:**200
Ancient civilizations   **A:**217–32 *see also* the names of ancient races and peoples; the names of countries of ancient times
   African kingdoms, early   **A:**65–66
   art *see* Ancient world, art of the
   Asia   **A:**463
   Aztecs   **A:**573–76
   bread and baking   **B:**388a–388b
   Celts   **C:**163–64
   eclipse studies   **E:**52
   education systems   **E:**74–77
   European civilization, development of   **E:**362–63
   exploration and discovery   **E:**400–402
   fairs and expositions   **F:**9
   food preparation in ancient times   **F:**333
   furniture   **F:**506–8
   historical writings   **H:**136
   homes   **H:**177–78
   Incas   **I:**107–10
   Indians, American   **I:**164–73
   libraries   **L:**171–72
   masonry of brick and stone   **B:**394
   Maya   **M:**184–87
   Mediterranean Sea regions   **M:**214
   Middle East called the cradle of civilization   **M:**304
   music *see* Ancient world, music of the
   mythology   **M:**565–68
   Persia, ancient   **P:**154–57
   Rome, ancient   **R:**309–17
   science, advances in   **S:**60
   slavery   **S:**192–93
   technology   **T:**40
   toys, history of   **T:**252–53
   wonders of the ancient world   **W:**216–20
   picture(s)
     Zimbabwe stone ruins   **Z:**376
Ancient history *see* Ancient civilizations
Ancient world, art of the   **A:**233–43
   art as a record   **A:**438a
   Persia   **P:**155, 157
Ancient world, music of the   **A:**243–47
Ancohuma (on-ko-OO-ma) (mountain in Bolivia)   **B:**307–8
Andalusia (an-da-lu-SI-a) (Spain)   **S:**373, 377
   folk music   **S:**392c
Andalusian cattle   **C:**153
Andaman (AN-da-man) **Islands** (India)   **I:**362
Andaman Sea   **O:**43
Andante (musical term)   **M:**540, 543
Anders, William A. (American astronaut)   **S:**346

Andersen, Hans Christian (Danish writer of fairy tales)   **A:**247–51; **C:**234; **F:**21
   Andersen Medal (book award)   **C:**230
   "The Emperor's New Clothes"   **A:**249–51
   Little Mermaid statue was inspired by his story   **C:**544
   "The Princess on the Pea"   **F:**26
   Scandinavian literature   **S:**58g
Anderson (South Carolina)   **S:**308
Anderson, Bill (American singer)   **C:**565
Anderson, Kenny (American basketball player)
   picture(s)   **B:**95d
Anderson, Marian (American singer)   **A:**79c, 79k, **251**; **N:**105
Anderson, Maxie (American balloonist)   **B:**36
Anderson, Maxwell (American playwright)   **D:**304; **N:**334
Anderson, Robert (American army officer)   **C:**334, 338–39
Anderson, Sherwood (American writer)   **A:**210; **O:**73; **S:**163
Andersonville National Historic Site (Georgia)   **G:**140
Andes (AN-dese) (mountains of South America)   **A:252–53**; **M:**504; **S:**276
   Argentina   **A:**388, 391–92
   Bolivia   **B:**307–8
   Colombia   **C:**404
   Ecuador   **E:**66
   Indians, American   **I:**168, 195–96
   Peru   **P:**161, 162
   Venezuela   **V:**296
Andes, Army of the   **S:**36
AND-gate (of a microprocessor)   **C:**493
Andorra   **A:**254–55
   picture(s)
     flag   **F:**235
Andorra la Vella (capital of Andorra)
   picture(s)   **A:**255
Andradite (an-DRA-dite) (gem mineral)   **G:**75
André (ON-dray), **John** (English spy)   **R:**206–7
   Arnold and André   **A:**436
   famous spies   **S:**408
   special medals awarded to his captors   **D:**65
Andrea Chénier (shain-YAY) (opera by Giordano)   **O:**150
Andrea del Sarto *see* Sarto, Andrea del
Andretti, Mario (American race-car driver)   **A:582**
Andrew, Saint (one of the 12 Apostles)   **A:**328–29
Andrew II (king of Hungary)   **H:**287
Andrews, Roy Chapman (American zoologist, explorer, and writer)   **W:**206
Andreyev (on-DRAY-ef), **Leonid** (Russian author)   **R:**379
Andromeda (an-DROM-e-da) (constellation)   **C:**525
   spiral galaxy in   **M:**309; **U:**214, 217
   picture(s)
     spiral galaxy in   **S:**340b
Andromeda (in Greek mythology)   **G:**365
Andronicus, Lucius Livius *see* Livius Andronicus, Lucius
Andropov, Yuri Vladimirovich (Soviet political leader)   **A:582**; **R:**369; **U:**51
Andros, Sir Edmund (English governor)   **C:**516
Androscoggin River (New Hampshire–Maine)   **M:**39–40; **N:**152
Anechoic chamber (room without echoes)   **S:**260–61
Anemia (deficiency of red cells or hemoglobin in the blood)   **D:**188
   deficiency disease   **B:**186–87; **V:**370c, 370d
   leukemia   **D:**196
   sickle-cell anemia   **D:**201
   transfusion used in treatment   **T:**273
Anemometers (an-em-OM-et-ers) (instruments that measure the strength of the wind)   **W:**84–85
   how to make   **W:**94
Anemones (a-NEM-o-nes), **sea** *see* Sea anemones
Aneroid (AN-er-oid) **barometer**   **B:**62
Anesthesia (an-es-THE-sia)   **A:**256–59 *see also* Drugs; Medicine, history of
   acupuncture   **M:**208b
   hospitals   **H:**248
   hypnosis   **H:**313, 314, 315
   progress in modern surgery   **M:**208a

Anesthesia (cont.)
    surgery S:513, 514, 515
    picture(s)
        first public demonstration S:512
Anesthesiologist (physician who specializes in
    anesthesia) A:257
Aneurysm (weak place in an artery) D:189
Angel (painting by Fra Angelico)
    picture(s) R:166
Angel Dust (drug) D:331
Angel Falls (Venezuela) S:277; V:296; W:62, 63
Angelfish
    picture(s) F:204
Angelico (on-JEL-ik-o), Fra (Italian painter) A:259; I:396;
    P:20
    Renaissance art R:166
    picture(s)
        Angel (painting) R:166
Angeli Laudantes (Praising Angels) (tapestry designed by
    Burne-Jones)
    picture(s) T:21
Angelou, Maya (American writer, stage performer, and
    composer) A:428
Anger, feeling of (in psychology) M:224
    death of loved one causes D:51
    divorce, attitudes toward D:231
Angerstein (ANG-er-stine), John Julius (English merchant and
    art patron) N:34
Angina (chest pains) D:193
Angiosperms (division of the plant kingdom) P:301, 302
Angkor (ancient city in Cambodia) C:35, 37
Angkor Thom (temple in Cambodia)
    picture(s) S:335
Angkor Wat (temple in Cambodia)
    picture(s) C:35
Angle, Edward (American orthodontist) O:237
Angle of incidence (in physics of light)
    diagram(s) L:212
Angle of reflection (in physics of light)
    diagram(s) L:212
Angler fish A:281; F:182
    picture(s) F:183
Anglers (persons who fish for sport) F:209
Angles (Germanic people, invaders of Britain) E:236
Angles (in geometry) G:122
    optical instruments that measure angles O:182–83
    diagram(s) G:123
Angleworms *see* Earthworms
Anglican Church (Protestant Episcopal Church) P:491–92 *see
    also* England, Church of
    Cranmer's prayer books E:243
    Reformation R:132–33
    United States C:294
Angling *see* Fishing
Anglo-Burmese wars B:457
Anglo-Egyptian Sudan *see* Sudan
Anglo-Norman French language F:434
Anglo-Saxon Chronicle E:268–69
Anglo-Saxon (Old English) language E:265
    compared with Anglo-Norman French F:434
    names N:4
Anglo-Saxon literature E:268–69
    Beowulf B:144a–144b
Anglo-Saxons (Teutonic peoples who settled in
    England) E:237
    Celtic and Anglo-Saxon art E:256–57
    conversion to Christianity C:290
    rulers of England, list of E:236
Anglund, Joan Walsh (American author and illustrator of
    children's books) A:582
Angola A:260–61; P:402
    Cuban military intervention C:600
    picture(s)
        flag F:226

Angora (now Ankara) (capital of Turkey) T:347
Angora goats C:152, 153
Angostura (Venezuela) *see* Ciudad Bolívar
Angry young men (in English literature) D:303
Angström, Anders Jonas (Swedish physicist) A:582
    units of measure W:117
Anguilla (one of the Leeward Islands in the Caribbean
    Sea) A:582; C:114; S:15
Angus (breed of beef cattle) C:148
Anhinga (bird)
    picture(s) A:277
Anicetus, Saint (pope) R:290
Animal behavior *see* Animal intelligence and behavior
Animal bites F:162
Animal breeding *see* Breeding, animal
Animal communication A:284; C:462
    ants A:318–19
    bee "dances" B:120
    birds B:223
    dogs D:247
    elephants E:180
    foxes F:396a
Animal defenses *see* Protective coloration; Protective devices
Animal diseases *see* Diseases, animal
Animal experimentation
    dogs D:243–44
Animal Farm (novel by Orwell) E:289; O:238
Animal feed *see* Feeding and feeds, animal
Animal gods M:568
Animal husbandry (art and science of livestock raising) C:154
    aquaculture A:336
    fish farming F:205–8
Animal intelligence and behavior
    beetles B:124–25
    birds B:220–23
    conditioning experiments in learning L:98–99
    dinosaurs tended their young D:171
    dolphins D:277–78
    experiments in learning P:504–8
    Lorenz, Konrad L:293
    parrots and other "talking" birds P:85–86
Animal kingdom A:265–67; K:249–50, 251, 252–56; L:209
    classes of animals A:264
    eggs and embryos E:99–102
Animal locomotion
    beetles B:124
    birds B:214–15
    dinosaurs D:168, 170–71, 172, 173
    dolphins D:275
    feet F:81–82
    fish F:198–99
    guidelines to animal life A:278–79
    hands F:83–84
    protozoans P:496–97
    snakes S:213–15
    spiders, ballooning of S:406
    starfishes S:427
    turtles T:356–57
    diagram(s)
        clams O:291
Animal rights F:504, 505
Animals A:262–87 *see also* Biology; Zoology; the animal life
        sections of continent, province, country, and state
        articles; the names of animal classes, as Birds, Insects;
        the names of animals as Elephants, etc.
    acid rain's effects A:10
    agents for dispersal of seeds F:284–85
    Arctic region A:386c
    biological clocks L:203–4
    bioluminescence B:203
    biomes B:204, 205, 206, 208, 210
    blood types B:258
    breeding *see* Breeding, animal
    cave dwellers C:157–58

Anne, Saint (mother of the Virgin Mary) **A:582**
Annealing (in metallurgy) **M:236**
    bronze and brass **B:410**
    glass **G:234**
    wire **W:190a**
Anne Boleyn see Boleyn, Anne
Annelids (AN-nel-ids) (worms) **E:42; W:309–10**
Anne of Cleves (4th wife of Henry VIII of England) **H:108**
    picture(s)
        portrait by Hans Holbein the Younger **G:167**
Anne of Green Gables (novel by Montgomery) **C:84–85**
Annie (musical)
    picture(s) **M:550**
Annobon see Pagalu
Annual (encyclopedia supplement) **E:205**
Annual layerings (in glaciers) **I:6**
Annuals (plants) **P:311**
    cultivated grasses **G:317**
    gardens and gardening **G:29–30, 46**
Annular eclipses **E:51**
Annulment of marriage **D:230**
Annunciation (painting by Martini)
    picture(s) **I:394**
Annunciation Day (religious holiday) **R:154**
Annunciation of the Virgin (in the New Testament) **A:582**
Anoles (a-NO-les) (lizards) **L:268**
Anonymity of sources (in journalism) **J:137**
Anopheles (a-NOF-el-ese) mosquito **H:260**
Anorexia nervosa (disease) **D:188**
Anorthosite (rock) **M:453**
Anouilh (on-NUI), Jean (French playwright) **F:442**
Anshar (Babylonian god) **M:565**
Ansky, S. (Yiddish author) **Y:351**
Answering machines **O:57; T:57**
Antagonists, narcotic see Narcotic antagonists
Antananarivo (capital of Madagascar) **M:8, 9**
"Ant and the Grasshopper, The" (fable by Aesop) **F:5**
Antarctic (south polar region)
    frigid (polar) zones **Z:380**
    icebergs **I:17, 18**
    ice sheet and ice shelves **I:5–6**
    map(s)
        penguins: where they live **P:121**
Antarctica (ant-ARK-tik-a) (continent) **A:292–95**
    Argentina's claims **A:391**
    Australian Antarctic Territory **A:495**
    Chile's claims **C:252**
    continental ice sheet **G:223, 224, 225**
    continents **C:529, 530**
    exploration and discovery **E:416–17**
    exploration by Byrd **B:485**
    marsupials once lived there **M:113**
    measuring the age of ice **I:7**
    mountains **M:506**
    ozone depletion over **A:480**
Antarctic Ocean **O:43**
Antarctic Treaty (1959) **A:295**
Ant cows see Aphids
Anteater civets (falanoucs) (mammals) **G:95**
Anteaters (mammals) **A:296; M:70**
    special diet in zoos **Z:385**
Anteaters, marsupial **M:116**
Anteaters, spiny see Spiny anteaters
Antelopes (hoofed mammals) **A:297–98; H:220**
    picture(s)
        antelope family **H:218**
        pronghorn **B:206; I:47**
        sable antelope **A:53**
        in zoo **Z:385**
Antennae (an-TENN-e) (of animals)
    ants **A:318**
    bees **B:116**
    butterflies and moths **B:475**
    crabs **C:571**

"feelers" (of insects) **I:230–31, 234–35**
    shrimps **S:167**
Antennas (in electronics)
    Apollo tracking antennas **S:340L**
    cable television **T:49**
    dish antennas **T:49, 67**
    microwave communications **T:50, 51**
    radar systems **R:37, 38**
    radar telescopes **R:73**
    radio **R:52, 53, 54, 57, 58**
    radio telescopes **R:70–71; T:60**
    television reception **T:64, 65**
    picture(s)
        dish antennas **T:50, 66**
        radio telescopes **R:69**
Anterus, Saint (pope) **R:290**
Anthem (musical form) **E:291; M:543**
Anthemius of Tralles (Byzantine architect) **B:489**
Anthems, national see National anthems and patriotic songs
Antheridia (of mosses) **M:473**
Anthers (of flowers) **F:279; P:307**
Anthocyanins (an-tho-SY-an-ins) (plant pigments) **T:308**
Anthony, Susan B. (American suffragist) **A:299; W:212, 212a**
    pictured on dollar coin **D:259**
    Stanton, Elizabeth Cady **S:424**
    picture(s) **W:214**
Anthony of Padua, Saint (Franciscan monk and
        theologian) **A:582**
Anthophyllite (mineral) **A:443**
Anthracite (hard coal) **C:388; F:487; P:126, 133, 135**
Anthrax (disease) **M:208**
    Koch discovers microbes causing **K:291**
    Pasteur, Louis **P:100**
Anthropology (an-thro-POL-o-jee) (study of human beings and
        human culture) **A:300–305** see also Human beings;
        Sociology
    archaeology related to **A:349, 362**
    blood groups studied **B:258**
    Boas, Franz **B:261**
    Leakey family **L:96–97**
    Mead, Margaret **M:195**
    Mexico City's National Museum of Anthropology **M:252**
    prehistoric people **P:438–42**
    races, human **R:28–31**
Anti-aircraft guns **G:426; T:14**
Anti-aircraft missiles **M:349**
Antibacterials (drugs) **D:333**
Antiballistic missile systems **N:379**
Antibiotics (drugs) **A:306–12; D:333, 334; M:208b**
    bacterial diseases are treated with **D:183**
    chemical control of pests **P:290**
    Fleming's work **F:249**
    made by fungi **F:500**
    surgery, history of **S:513**
    vitamin K deficiency may occur in users **V:370d**
Antibodies **A:313; V:260**
    acquired immunity **I:96–97; M:209, 210**
    autoimmune diseases **D:184**
    disease prevention and treatment **D:183, 208, 210, 211**
    monoclonal antibodies **C:93**
    rejection of organ transplants **M:211**
    structure and source **I:98**
    vaccination and inoculation **V:260, 261**
Anticline traps (rock formations that hold petroleum) **P:168**
Anti-Comintern Pact (1936) **W:286**
Anticorrosives see Corrosion
Anticosti Island (Quebec) **I:362**
Anticyclones (in meteorology) **W:79, 187**
Anti-Defamation League of B'nai B'rith **C:328**
Antidotes (remedies for effects of poisons) **P:355**
Antietam (an-TEE-tam), Battle of (Civil War battle near
        Sharpsburg, Virginia) **C:341**
Antietam National Battlefield Site (Maryland) **M:128**
Antifouling paints **P:33**

Antigens A:313; I:95, 96, 97
"Antigonish" (poem by Mearns) N:274
Antigua (an-TI-gwa) (Guatemala) G:396
  picture(s) G:397
Antigua (Caribbean island) *see* Antigua and Barbuda
Antigua (an-TI-ga) **and Barbuda** A:314; C:114, 115
  picture(s) N:283
    flag F:239
Antihistamines (drugs for allergic reactions) D:188, 191
Antihypertensives (drugs) D:333
Anti-inflammatories (drugs) D:209
Anti-Lebanon Mountains (Syria–Lebanon) L:120; S:548
Antilles (island group dividing Caribbean Sea from Atlantic
  Ocean) C:112–15
Antilles (an-TILL-es), **Greater** *see* Greater Antilles
Antilles, Lesser *see* Lesser Antilles
Antilles Current G:413
Antilocapridae (family of hoofed mammals) H:217
Antimasque (comic dance preceding masque) D:25
Antimatter A:582
Antimony (AN-tim-ony) (element) E:171
  producing regions of North America N:291
  table(s) M:235
Antinoüs (cult figure of ancient Rome)
  picture(s)
    statue R:319
Antioch (AN-ti-ok) (ancient city, now Antakya, Turkey)
  center of Apostles' missions to Gentiles R:282
  tarred torches lit L:231
Antiochus Epiphanes (an-TY-o-chus e-PIF-an-ese) (Syrian
  king) H:28
Antioxidants (an-ti-OX-id-ants) (in chemistry) V:319
  Vitamin E V:370d
Antipopes (pretenders to the papacy of the Roman Catholic
  Church) R:290–91
Antiques and antique collecting A:315–17
  dolls D:271
Antiquities (an-TI-quit-ies), **popular** F:302
Anti-Saloon League P:484
Anti-Semitism (hostility toward Jews and Judaism) J:108
Antiseptics (chemicals used to kill germs on the skin) D:214
  see also Disinfectants
  Lister, Joseph L:257
Antiserums (used to acquire passive immunity) A:313
Antitoxins (kind of antibody) D:203
  Behring, Emil von B:127a
Antitrust laws B:473
Antiviral drugs D:183
Antivivisectionist (person opposed to the use of live animals for
  scientific research) A:583
Antlers (of animals)
  deer D:81–82; H:214
  mammals' weapons M:67
Antlia (constellation) C:523
Antoinette Perry Memorial Award *see* Tony Award
Antonescu (on-to-NES-ku), **Ion** (Romanian political
  leader) R:300–301
Antoninus Pius (Roman emperor) R:316
Antony, Mark (Roman ruler) A:317; R:316
  Cicero's opposition to C:303
  Cleopatra C:355
Antony and Cleopatra (play by Shakespeare) S:133
Antonyms (words) S:546
Antrodemus (dinosaur) *see* Allosaurus
Antrum (part of the stomach) S:460
Ants A:318–24
  acacia plant, relationship with P:317
  household pests H:261–62
  strength of I:241
Antwerp (Belgium) B:134
  Olympic Games (1920) O:109
  trade, early development of S:455
Anu (Babylonian god) M:565, 566
Anubis (a-NU-bis) (in Egyptian legend) A:221; M:568

Anvil (bone in the ear) E:4, 6
  picture(s) E:5
Anxiety (emotion)
  mental illness D:186; M:227
  stuttering, causes of S:397–98
Anzio (Italy)
  beachhead battle (World War II) W:298
ANZUS Treaty (defense agreement) N:242
Aoki, Rocky (Japanese balloonist) B:36
Aorta (a-OR-ta) (artery carrying blood from heart) B:281;
  C:305; H:81
Aoudad (OWD-ad) (kind of wild sheep) S:145
Aouita, Saïd (Moroccan athlete) T:263
Aoun, Michel (Lebanese political leader) L:123
Apache (a-PACH-ee) (Indians of North America) I:184–85
  see also Cochise
  Arizona A:407, 414
  Geronimo G:190
  Indian Wars I:205
  New Mexico N:184, 190, 193
  picture(s)
    plant pollen used in ceremony P:295
Apalachee (Indians native to Florida) F:272; I:178
Apalachicola National Forest (Florida) F:267
Apartheid (a-PART-ite) (racial segregation in South
  Africa) S:269–70, 273
  abolition of C:329
  racism R:34a
Apartment houses H:182–83 *see also* Condominium
  ancient Rome H:178
  modern architecture A:384, 385
  New York City N:230
  picture(s)
    Brasília (Brazil) L:59
    Greenland G:372
    Habitat (Montreal) H:183
    Helsinki (Finland) F:131
    underground apartments on Florida coast H:184
Apatite (mineral)
  phosphate fertilizers F:97
  tooth enamel T:43
Apatosaurus (dinosaur) D:167, 170–71
Apelles (Greek painter) G:349
Apennines (AP-en-nines) (mountain range of Italy) I:384
  San Marino S:35
Apennines Mountains (on the moon)
  picture(s) M:450
Aperitif (a-per-i-TEEF) **(appetizer) wines** W:188
Aperture ring (of video cameras) V:332i
Apes A:325–27; M:418–19
  ancestors of apes E:379
  feet and hands F:83–84
  picture(s) M:417
Aphelion (a-FE-li-on) (point in comet's or planet's orbit farthest
  from the sun) S:242
  Mars M:105
  picture(s)
    Mercury's orbit R:144
Aphids (plant lice) P:289
  ants live with aphids A:324
  vectors of plant diseases V:284, 285, 367
Aphotic habitat (of the ocean) O:23
Aphrodite (af-rod-ITE-e) (Greek goddess) G:362, 364, 368
Aphrodite Terra (continent on Venus) V:303a
Apia (a-PI-a) (capital of Western Samoa) W:124
Apiary (APE-i-ary) (colony of bees) H:202
Apinaye (American Indian language) I:197
Aplodontia *see* Mountain beaver
Apocalypse (a-POK-a-lips) (type of writing that gives a
  revelation of the future) B:166
Apocrine sweat glands G:226
Apocrypha (a-POK-rif-a) B:156, 160–61, 163
Apogee (point of a satellite's orbit farthest from Earth) S:365
  moon's orbit M:446

Apollinaire, Guillaume (French poet) **F:**442
Apollo (Phoebus Apollo) (Greek and Roman god) **G:**362, 364
picture(s) **G:**361
Corinth temple ruins **G:**345
Apollo and Daphne (sculpture by Bernini)
picture(s) **I:**400
Apollodor of Damascus (Greek engineer) **E:**228
Apollodorus (Greek painter) **G:**349
Apollo program (to put astronauts on the moon) **M:**452, 453; **S:**340e
aerial photography **P:**217
Apollo 8 went through Van Allen belts **S:**345
Apollo 11 (first moon landing) **E:**419; **S:**340e, 340f–340j, 347
Apollo 17 **S:**342
Apollo-Soyuz mission **S:**348
integrated circuits' first large application **T:**278
lunar lander replica at National Air and Space Museum **P:**274
NASA programs **S:**338
portable life support system **S:**343
space flights and crews **S:**346, 348
space research and technology **S:**363
tracking network **S:**340k–340L
picture(s)
Apollo 11 (first moon landing) **M:**453
Aponeuroses (sheets of tissue joining muscles to bones) **M:**516
Apoplexy *see* Stroke
Apostle Islands National Lakeshore (Wisconsin) **W:**203
Apostles, The (12 disciples of Jesus Christ) **A:328–29; C:**286–87; **J:**83–87
New Testament of the Bible **B:**164
Peter, Saint **P:**166
Roman Catholic Church, history of **R:**281
Apostles' Creed **R:**293–94
Apostolic (ap-os-TOL-ik) **succession** **E:**45
Apostrophes (a-POS-tro-fese) (punctuation marks) **P:**542
Apotheosis of George Washington, The (painting by Brumidi) **C:**104
Appalachia (region in the eastern United States) **A:583**
poverty in the United States **P:**419–20
Appalachian Mountains (North America) **M:**502; **N:**285
Canada **C:**52; **N:**140; **Q:**8
overland trails **O:**270
Pennsylvania **P:**128
United States **U:**80
westward movement **W:**140–43
Appalachian National Scenic Trail (hiking trail from Maine to Georgia) **N:**52
Maryland **M:**122
Appalachian Plateau *see* Allegheny Plateau; Cumberland Plateau
Appaloosas (horses)
picture(s) **H:**238
Apparent magnitude (of stars) **S:**429
Appeals (in law) **C:**568
Supreme Court of the United States **S:**509
Appellate courts **C:**568
state courts (the judiciary) **S:**440
Supreme Court, jurisdiction of the **S:**507
United States, government of the **U:**171
Appendages (jointed limbs of crustaceans) **C:**592
Appendicitis (ap-pen-di-SY-tis) (infection in the appendix) **D:**188–89
Appendicular skeleton (of the body) **S:**183–84
Appendix (dead-end tube connected with the large intestine) **D:**188–89
appendectomy described **S:**514–15
Appert (ap-PARE), **Nicolas** (French chef) **F:**341; **I:**286
Appian Way (Roman road) **E:**227
Apple **A:329–33**
how to sprout apple seeds **A:**332
Johnny Appleseed, excerpt from **F:**315–16

Newton discovers law of gravitation **N:**206
storage **F:**52
picture(s) **F:**59
state flower of Arkansas **A:**417
state flower of Michigan **M:**259
trees and their leaves **T:**303
Applegate, Jesse (American political leader) **O:**277
Apples and Oranges (painting by Cézanne)
picture(s) **F:**430
Appleseed, Johnny (American folk hero) **F:**311–12
story about, excerpt from **F:**315–16
Appleton (Wisconsin) **W:**205
Appliances, electric *see* Electric appliances
Applied art *see* Commercial art; Industrial arts
Applied mathematics **M:**156
Applied research **R:**181
chemical industry **C:**197
Appliqué (needlecraft) **N:**101
Appomattox (app-o-MAT-tox) **Court House** (Virginia) **C:**346
Lee surrenders to Grant **L:**126
National Historical Park **V:**354
picture(s)
Lee surrenders to Grant **C:**347
Apportionment (of government representatives)
Supreme Court rulings **S:**509
Appreciation, notes of **L:**160–60a
Apprentices (persons learning a trade) **G:**405
automobile manufacturing **A:**556
colonial America **C:**415
plumbers **P:**340
Appropriations bills (suggested laws) **U:**168
Approximations, method of successive (in psychology) **P:**507–8
APRA *see* American Popular Revolutionary Alliance
Apricot **P:**107–8
April (4th month of the year) **A:334–35**
April (manuscript illustration by the Limburg brothers)
picture(s) **D:**351
April 19th Movement (in Colombia) **T:**117
April Fool's Day **H:**158
Apse (part of a church) **A:**374; **C:**134; **I:**392
Apsu (Babylonian god) **M:**565
Apt, Jerome (American astronaut) **S:**350
Aptitude tests **T:**118, 120–23
Apuleius (Roman writer) **L:**78
Apulia (Italy)
picture(s)
beehive houses **H:**175
Aqaba (Jordan) **J:**131
Aqaba (OK-a-ba), **Gulf of** (extension of the Red Sea)
Arab-Israeli wars **I:**376
Nasser closed gulf to Israeli ships **N:**17
Aquaculture (raising animals or plants in water environments) **A:336**
fish farming **F:**205–8
sea farming **O:**28, 29; **U:**26–27
shrimps **S:**168
Aqualung (for underwater swimming) **S:**187
oceanography, use in **O:**41
underwater exploration **U:**18
picture(s)
Cousteau and Aqualung **I:**281
Aquamarines (gemstones) **G:**71
picture(s) **G:**73
Aquanauts (underwater explorers) **U:**23–24
Aquaplaning *see* Waterskiing
Aqua regia (RE-jia) (hydrochloric and nitric acids) **G:**247
Aquariums **A:336–39; P:**179
fish as pets **F:**203–4
New Jersey State Aquarium **N:**172
picture(s)
National Aquarium (Baltimore) **M:**125
New Jersey State Aquarium **N:**168
Aquarius (constellation) **C:**522
picture(s) **C:**522

Aquatic animals
    animal plankton **P:**284–85
    beetles **B:**124
    dolphins **D:**273–78
    fish **F:**181–202
    fur seals **F:**518
    sea lions **S:**106
    seals **S:**107–8
    walruses **W:**6–7
    water pollution's effects **W:**65, 66, 69
    whales **W:**149–53
Aquatic plants
    aquarium plants **A:**337
    ferns **F:**94
    plant plankton **P:**283–84
    picture(s) **P:**320
        ferns **F:**93
Aquatic sports *see* Water sports
Aquatint (etching process) **E:**327; **G:**307
Aquavit (distilled beverage) **W:**161
Aqueducts **P:**339
    ancient Rome **A:**231; **M:**204; **R:**318; **U:**235
    picture(s) **R:**268
Aqueous humor (in the eye) **E:**431
Aquidneck Island (Rhode Island) **R:**223
Aquifers (water-bearing layers of permeable rocks) **G:**100; **W:**121–22
    Arizona **A:**406
    groundwater, pollution of **W:**65
Aquila (constellation) **C:**525
Aquinas (a-KWY-nas)**, Saint Thomas** (Italian monk and philosopher) **A:**340; **C:**291
    philosophy, history of **P:**190
    Roman Catholic Church, history of **R:**286
Aquino, Benigno S., Jr. (Philippine political leader) **A:**340; **P:**188
Aquino, Corazon C. (Philippine president) **A:**340; **P:**188
Arabesques (ar-a-BESKS) (pattern designs) **I:**351
    Islamic art **I:**355, 357, 358
    ornamentation of tapestry **T:**20
    Spain, art of **S:**384
    picture(s) **I:**349
        Islamic art **I:**354
Arabia (Arabian Peninsula) (southwestern Asia) **M:**300 *see also* Arabs
    Bahrain **B:**18–19
    Jewish communities of exile **J:**106
    Kuwait **K:**306–9
    Oman **O:**121
    Qatar **Q:**2–3
    Saudi Arabia **S:**57–58c
    United Arab Emirates **U:**53
    Yemen **Y:**347–49
    picture(s)
        desert **A:**346
Arabia Felix (Roman name for an area usually restricted to Yemen) **Y:**347
Arabian camels **C:**39; **H:**212
    picture(s) **H:**213
Arabian coffee plant **C:**396
Arabian Desert (Egypt) **E:**106
Arabian horses **H:**238, 244
    picture(s) **H:**237
Arabian Nights **A:**341–42
    early history of the short story **S:**161
Arabian Peninsula *see* Arabia
Arabian Sea **O:**43
Arabic-Hindu numerals *see* Hindu-Arabic numerals
Arabic language **A:**344; **L:**39; **M:**299
    anthropological studies **A:**305
    common language of early science **S:**64
    Islam, language of **I:**350, 351
    northern Africa **A:**56

    picture(s)
        alphabet **A:**194a
Arab-Israeli wars **A:**347; **I:**375–76; **J:**79–80, 111; **M:**305
    Egypt **E:**109
    Jordan **J:**132
    Kissinger, Henry **K:**266a
    Lebanon **L:**122
    Meir, Golda **M:**214
    Nasser, Gamal Abdel **N:**17
    Palestine **P:**40b
    refugees **R:**137
    Sadat, Anwar el- **S:**2
    Suez Canal **S:**481–82
    Syria **S:**550
    Thant, U **T:**156
Arab League **A:**583
Arable land **G:**100
Arabs **A:**55, 343–47
    alchemists **C:**207
    Iraq **I:**311
    Islam **I:**346–53
    mathematics, history of **M:**164
    Morocco **M:**458, 461
    Palestine **P:**40d
    preserved Greek knowledge in Middle Ages **A:**471
    Saudi Arabia **S:**57–58c
    Syria **S:**547
    picture(s)
        France **F:**405
Arachne (ar-AK-ne) (in Greek mythology) **S:**404; **W:**96
Arachnids (class of animals) **A:**348
    spiders **S:**402–6
    ticks **T:**192
Arafat, Yasir (Palestinian leader) **A:**583; **I:**376
    picture(s) **C:**368
Aragats, Mount (Armenia) **A:**431
Aragon (ancient kingdom in Spain) **F:**88; **S:**379
Aragon, Louis (French poet) **F:**442
Aral Sea (central Asia) **L:**32; **U:**39; **W:**54
Aramaic (ar-a-MAI-ik) **language** **H:**98
    alphabets derived from its syllabary **A:**194a
    in the Bible **B:**156, 157
    Dead Sea Scrolls **D:**47
    Persia, ancient **P:**155
Aramid (type of nylon) **N:**433
Aramis (a-ra-MEES) (one of *The Three Musketeers*) **D:**347–48
Aransas National Wildlife Refuge (Texas) **T:**131
Arantes do Nascimento, Edson *see* Pelé
Arapaho (Indians of North America) **I:**180
    Colorado **C:**443
Ararat, Mount (Asian Turkey) **T:**345
Araucanians (ar-auk-ON-ians) (Indians of South America) **C:**249, 251, 253, 254; **I:**199
Arawak (AR-a-wak) (Indians of South America) **I:**197
    Dominican Republic **D:**282
    Haiti **H:**11
    Jamaica **J:**15, 18
    Puerto Rico **P:**526
    Saint Vincent and the Grenadines **S:**20
    Suriname **S:**516
    Trinidad and Tobago **T:**315
Arawanas (fish) **F:**199–200
Arbeau (ar-BO)**, Thoinot** (French priest) **D:**27
Arbela, Battle of *see* Gaugamela, Battle of
Arbenz Guzmán, Jacobo (Guatemalan political leader) **G:**398
Arbitration
    international relations **I:**274
    labor-management relations **L:**8
    peace movements, goal of **P:**105
    provided for in treaties **T:**299
Arbor Day (holiday) **H:**150
    Jewish Arbor Day in Israel **R:**154
    origin in Nebraska **N:**82, 90
Arbuckle Mountains (Oklahoma) **O:**82, 84, 87

Arévalo, Juan José (Guatemalan political leader) **I:**194
Argali (AR-ga-li) (wild sheep) **S:**145
  picture(s) **H:**219
Argall, Samuel (English navigator and colonial official in America) **D:**89; **M:**50
Argand oil lamps **L:**233
Argentina **A:**388–96
  Buenos Aires **B:**426–28
  Chile, relations with **C:**252
  fascism in **F:**64
  Islas Malvinas (Falkland Islands) **I:**365; **S:**278
  life in Latin America **L:**47–61
  San Martín, José de **S:**36
  picture(s)
      cattle raising **S:**289
      flag **F:**238
      gaucho barbeque **L:**5
      Pampa, The **G:**314
      sheep ranch in Patagonia **P:**429
      Tierra del Fuego **S:**275
Argo (robot submarine) **O:**42
Argo Merchant (oil tanker)
  picture(s) **P:**176
Argon (element) **E:**171; **G:**58
  industrial uses **G:**61
  Langmuir's use in light bulbs **L:**35
  noble gases **N:**105, 106
  picture(s)
      use in welding **G:**59
Argonauts (in Greek mythology) **G:**367
Argumentation *see* Debates and debating
Aria (AR-ia) (accompanied song for the single voice) **B:**70; **M:**543; **O:**140, 141
Ariadne (arri-AD-ne) (in Greek mythology) **G:**368
  in story from *Tanglewood Tales* **H:**66
Arianism (AR-i-an-ism) (heresy of Arius) **C:**289
Arias Madrid, Arnulfo (Panamanian president) **P:**46
Arias Sánchez, Oscar (Costa Rican political leader) **A:**583; **C:**559
Arica (a-RI-ka) (Chile)
  rainfall least in world **R:**94
Ariel (moon of Uranus) **U:**233
Arienspace (space technology company) **S:**339
Aries (constellation) **C:**522
  picture(s) **C:**522
Arikara (a-RIK-a-ra) (Indians of North America) **I:**180; **S:**326
Ariosto (ar-i-OS-to), **Lodovico** (Italian poet) **I:**407
Aristarchus (ar-is-TARK-us) **of Samos** **A:**470; **S:**63–64
Aristide, Jean-Bertrand (Haitian president) **H:**12
Aristocracy (ar-i-STOK-ra-see) (type of government) **G:**273
Aristophanes (ar-is-TOF-an-ese) (Greek dramatist) **A:**229; **D:**297; **G:**357
Aristotle (Greek philosopher) **A:**396–97; **P:**189–90
  Alexander the Great, teacher of **A:**177
  ancient civilizations **A:**230
  astronomy, early history of **A:**471
  biologist of the ancient world **B:**193; **F:**184
  classification of living things **L:**207
  contributions to science, summary of **S:**63
  early encyclopedias **E:**205
  elements, theory of the **C:**206–7
  ethics **E:**328
  geology, history of **G:**107
  government systems **G:**273
  Greek literature **G:**359
  library of **L:**172
  medical advances **M:**203
  memory and the law of association **P:**503
  oratory and rhetoric **O:**190
Aristotle Contemplating the Bust of Homer (painting by Rembrandt)
  picture(s) **G:**358
Arithmetic **A:**398–401; **M:**157
  abacus **A:**2–3

binary number system **C:**494
decimal system **D:**56
fractions **F:**397–402
graphs **G:**309–13
interest **I:**255
numbers and number systems **N:**396–402
numerals and numeration systems **N:**403–9
percentage **P:**144–46
sets **S:**126–27
Arithmetic mean (kind of average of a set of numbers) **S:**441
Arithmetic sequences (of numbers) **N:**383
Arius (a-RY-us) (Greek theologian) **C:**289; **R:**283
Arizona **A:**402–15
  governor Mecham's impeachment **I:**99
  Grand Canyon National Park **G:**290–92
  Phoenix **P:**192–93
  Tucson **T:**329
  picture(s)
      flood damage **F:**252
      Grand Canyon National Park **W:**50, 216
      irrigated desert regions **D:**126
      Kitt Peak National Observatory **O:**8; **W:**77
      Meteor Crater **C:**449
      modern church architecture **C:**294
      Taliesin West **W:**316
Arizona, University of (Tucson) **T:**329
Arkansas **A:**416–29
  Clinton's governorship **C:**367
Arkansas, University of **A:**421
  traditional cheer **C:**194
Arkansas Post National Memorial (Arkansas) **A:**424
Arkansas River (United States) **A:**418, 423
  Colorado **C:**433
  Fryingpan-Arkansas Project **C:**435
  Oklahoma **O:**83
Arkansas-Verdigris River Navigation System **O:**88
Arkhangel'sk (Archangel) (Russia) **O:**47
Ark of the Covenant (sacred chest) **A:**583; **J:**148
  David brought to Jerusalem **J:**103
Arktika (nuclear-powered Soviet icebreaker) **A:**387
Arkwright, Richard (British inventor and early industrialist) **I:**219; **T:**143
Arlandes (ar-LOND), **Marquis d'** (French balloonist) **B:**34
Arlberg Pass (Austrian Alps) **A:**194b
Arles, Council of (314) **C:**290
Arlington House, The Robert E. Lee Memorial (formerly **Custis-Lee Mansion**, Virginia) **N:**25; **V:**354; **W:**30
  picture(s) **N:**24
Arlington National Cemetery (Virginia) **N:**24, 25–26; **V:**354
  Unknown Soldier **U:**227
  Washington, D.C. **W:**30
  picture(s)
      amphitheater **H:**224
Arm (part of the body) *see* Arms
Armada (ar-MA-da), **Spanish** (1588) **B:**103f; **E:**244; **S:**380
  Drake defeats King Philip's fleet **D:**293
  first naval battle fought entirely under sail **S:**155
  picture(s) **B:**103e
Armadillos (mammals) **M:**70–71
  offspring are identical quadruplets **E:**102
  picture(s) **A:**282; **M:**73
Armageddon (in the Bible) **A:**583
Armagh (Northern Ireland) **U:**60
Armature (framework used in clay modeling) **C:**354
Armatures (in electric motors) **E:**134, 152
Armed Forces, U.S. *see* United States, Armed Forces of the
Armed Forces Day **U:**106
Armed Forces of National Liberation **T:**117
Armenia (ar-ME-nia) **A:**430–32
  Kurds **K:**305
  languages of the USSR **U:**34
  popular foods **F:**335–36
  Yerevan **U:**43

Armenia (cont.)
picture(s)
    flag **F:**230
Armenian Apostolic Church **U:**35
Armenian language **A:**430, 432
Armenians (a people of western Asia) **A:**430
    Azerbaijan **A:**571
    Syria **S:**547
    picture(s)
        traditional costume **A:**431
Armies
    Alexander the Great **A:**177–78
    battles **B:**103d–103f
    Canadian armed forces **C:**80
    United States **U:**107–11
Armistice Day *see* Veterans' Day
Armonica (ar-MON-ik-a) (musical instrument) **F:**455
Armor **A:**433–35
    battles **B:**103d
    coats of arms **H:**110–12
    combat arms of United States Army **U:**107
    early decorations **D:**75
    knights, knighthood, and chivalry **K:**272–73
    Metropolitan Museum of Art collection **M:**239
    tanks **T:**14–15
Armored animals **A:**283
    dinosaurs **D:**173–74
Armory Show (New York art show, 1913) **P:**30; **U:**132
    modern art in the United States **M:**395
Arms (parts of the body)
    bones of the **F:**79; **S:**183
    siamang gibbon's long arms **A:**325
Arms control *see* Disarmament
Arms races (between nations)
    disarmament **D:**180
    between the World Wars **W:**282–85
Armstrong, Debbie (American skier) **O:**117
Armstrong, Edwin H. (American engineer) **R:**56
Armstrong, Henry (American boxer) **B:**354
Armstrong, Louis Daniel ("Satchmo") (American jazz trumpeter, singer, and bandleader) **A:**583
    jazz **J:**58–59; **L:**311
    picture(s)
        jazz **U:**208
Armstrong, Neil Alden (American astronaut) **A:**469; **E:**419; **O:**73; **S:**338, 340e, 340f, 340h, 340j, 346
    picture(s) **S:**340i, 347
Armstrong, William H. (American author) **A:**583; **C:**238
Army, Canadian *see* Canadian Armed Forces
Army, Roman **R:**310
Army, United States *see* United States Army
Army, United States Department of the
    national cemeteries **N:**24
Army ants **A:**324
    picture(s) **A:**318
Army National Guard (United States) **U:**111
Army of the Andes *see* Andes, Army of
Army of the Potomac *see* Potomac, Army of the
Army worms
    picture(s) **B:**483
Arnarson, Ingolfur (Norwegian Viking) **I:**36
    picture(s)
        statue in Reykjavik **I:**34
Arnaz, Desi (Cuban-American bandleader) **N:**224
Arnold, Benedict (American soldier and traitor) **A:**436
    Revolutionary War **R:**199, 201, 203, 204, 206–7
Arnold, Eddy (American singer) **C:**565
Arnold, Matthew (English author) **E:**284
Arno River (Italy) **I:**385
Aromatic plants *see* Herbs; Spices and condiments
Aroostook (a-ROOS-took) **County** (Maine) **M:**41, 42, 43
Aroostook War (Maine–New Brunswick boundary dispute) **M:**46, 51; **N:**138g
Arouet, François Marie *see* Voltaire

Arp, Jean (Hans) (French artist) **A:**583
    surrealism in modern art **M:**394; **S:**104
Arp220 (galaxy)
    picture(s) **U:**216
Árpád (Hungarian national hero) **A:**583
Arpeggio (in music) **M:**540
Arpino, Gerald (American choreographer) **B:**33
    picture(s)
        Clown (ballet) **D:**33
Arrack (alcoholic beverage from coconut palm) **C:**392
Arraignment (in law) **C:**567
Arrangement in Grey and Black, No. 1, Portrait of the Artist's Mother (painting by Whistler)
    picture(s) **W:**162
Array (radio telescope that has many reflectors) **R:**72
Arrays (flat rows of solar cells) **S:**240
Arrest (for breaking the law) **C:**566–67
    juvenile offenses **J:**167, 169
    steps in law enforcement **L:**87
"Arrow and the Song, The" (poem by Longfellow) **L:**293
Arrowhead Country (area of Minnesota) **M:**326
Arrowroot (edible starch)
    Saint Vincent and the Grenadines is the world's leading producer **S:**20
Arrows *see* Bows and arrows
Arrowworms (glassworms) (sea animals) **P:**285
Arroyo, Martina (American singer) **A:**583
Arroyos (dry river beds) **D:**124; **R:**237
Arsenal (building for storing weapons)
    Harper's Ferry National Historical Park (West Virginia) **W:**135
Arsenic (element) **E:**171
Ars nova (new art) (in French music) **F:**444
Arson **F:**153–54
    dogs trained to recognize fire-starting chemicals **D:**242
    juvenile crime **J:**167
Art **A:**437–38e *see also* the names of art forms, as Painting or Industrial design; the names of art periods, as Baroque art; the names of individual artists, such as Rembrandt; the names of specific countries, as Italy, art and architecture of
    Africa, art of **A:**70–76
    American *see* United States, art of the
    ancient **A:**233–43
    archaeology related to **A:**363
    computers, uses of **C:**492
    decorative arts **D:**68–80
    drawing **D:**306–12
    drawing, history of **D:**313–16
    engraving **E:**294
    etching **E:**326–27
    graphic arts **G:**302–8
    Latin America **L:**62–67
    mathematics in careers **M:**160
    Maya **M:**186
    modern **M:**386–96b
    museums *see* Art museums
    painting **P:**14–32
    prehistoric art **P:**435–37
    preschool children **T:**251
    religious *see* Religious art
    romanticism **R:**302–3
    sculpture **S:**90–105
    surrealism **S:**518
Art, commercial *see* Commercial art
Artabanus (Parthian king) **P:**156
Art cabinets (to hold curios and toys) **D:**261
Art deco (style of decorative arts) **C:**83; **D:**79
    furniture **F:**517
    picture(s)
        plastic radio **D:**78
Art directors
    books **B:**327
    commercial art **C:**457–58

Ashoka *see* Asoka
Ashton, Frederick (English choreographer) **B:**30–31
Ashton-Warner, Sylvia (New Zealand writer) **N:**236
Ashurbanipal (osh-ur-BA-ni-pol) (king of Assyria) **A:**225, 226;
  L:171
  picture(s)
    stone carving of him hunting **A:**240
Ashurnasirpal II (king of Assyria) **A:**240
  picture(s)
    statue **A:**241
Ash Wednesday (religious holiday) **R:**153, 284
  blessed ashes **R:**292
  Easter **E:**43
Asia **A:**444–67 *see also* the names of countries
  agriculture **A:**89, 90, 93
  Alexander the Great's conquests in **A:**177–78
  Arctic region **A:**386b–387
  boundary with Europe **C:**529
  conservation programs **C:**521
  continents **C:**529, 530
  emigration to the United States **I:**91, 92, 93
  Europe's geographic relation to Asia **E:**340
  exploration and discovery **E:**415
  immigration **I:**94
  lakes of the world **L:**30–33
  Middle East **M:**298–305
  mountains **M:**505
  music *see* Oriental music
  national dances **D:**31–32
  poverty **P:**418, 419, 420
  prairies **P:**426, 427–28
  refugees **R:**137
  rice diet **G:**282; **R:**228
  Siberia **S:**170
  Southeast Asia **S:**328–36
  terrorism **T:**117
  theater of the east **T:**162
  picture(s)
    flags of Asian countries **F:**230–34
  table(s)
    waterfalls **W:**63
Asia Minor (peninsula forming the western extremity of Asia)
  Asian Turkey **T:**345
  Hittite art and architecture **A:**238–39
  What and where is Asia Minor? **A:**451
Asian elephants *see* Indian elephants
Asian kraits (snakes) **S:**212
  picture(s) **S:**210
Asian music *see* Oriental music
Asimov, Isaac (American writer) **A:584**
ASM (air-to-surface missiles) **M:**345, 349
Asmara (capital of Eritrea) **E:**313
Asoka (king of Magadha, modern Bihar, India) **A:**463; **I:**130,
  135–36
Asparagus **P:**304; **V:**289
Asparagus fern (houseplant)
  picture(s) **H:**268
Aspartame (artificial sweetener) **S:**486
ASPCA *see* Society for the Prevention of Cruelty to Animals,
  American
Aspdin, Joseph (English bricklayer who invented Portland
  cement) **C:**165
Aspect ratio (in motion pictures) **M:**479
Aspen (Colorado)
  picture(s) **C:**438
Aspen (tree)
  picture(s) **T:**304
Aspen Festival (Aspen, Colorado) **M:**559
Aspergillus (fungus)
  picture(s) **M:**276
Asphalt (tarlike substance) **P:**172, 173
  La Brea Pits (Los Angeles, California) **L:**295–96
  road surfaces **R:**250
  Trinidad and Tobago has world's largest supply **T:**315

Aspirin (drug) **D:**329
  medicines from plants **P:**297
  poisonings in children **P:**355
  Reye's syndrome may be caused by **D:**200
  trademarks **T:**267
  treatment of rheumatoid arthritis **D:**189
Asquith, Herbert Henry (British statesman) **A:467**
Ass, wild *see* Wild ass
Assab (Eritrea) **E:**313
Assad, Hafez al- (president of Syria) **A:584; S:**550
Assam (state, India) **I:**129
Assassinations **P:**451; **V:**324
  Francis Ferdinand (archduke of Austria) **S:**125
  Gandhi, Indira **G:**23
  Gandhi, Mohandas Karamchand **G:**24
  Gandhi, Rajiv **G:**24
  Garfield, James A. **G:**52, 55
  George I (king of Greece) **G:**131
  Kennedy, John F. **K:**210
  Kennedy, John F.: Warren Report **W:**11
  Kennedy, Robert F. **K:**211
  King, Martin Luther, Jr. **K:**247
  Lincoln, Abraham **B:**335; **L:**247
  Malcolm X **M:**59
  McKinley, William **M:**194
  Sadat, Anwar el- **S:**2
  terrorism **T:**116
Assassin bug **V:**283
Assassins (secret Muslim sect) **A:584; T:**116
Assateague National Seashore (Virginia) **V:**350, 354
Assault (crime) **J:**167
Assemblages (works of art) **N:**137
Assemblage with Rainbow (collage by Schwitters) *see Merzbild
  mit Regenbogen*
Assemblies of God (Protestant denomination) **A:584**
Assembly, freedom of *see* Freedom of assembly
Assembly edit (in motion picture production) **M:**485
Assembly language (in computer programming) **C:**483
Assembly-line method (in manufacturing) **M:**88–89
  automobiles **A:**543, 553–54
  introduced by Henry Ford **F:**367; **T:**286
  technology, major developments in **T:**40, 41
  picture(s) **F:**342; **M:**265; **R:**253
Assessed value (of property) **R:**112d
Assets (shown in bookkeeping statements) **B:**311
Assimilation (of ethnic groups) **E:**335
  Jews in the Soviet Union **J:**109
Assiniboin (Indians of North America) **I:**180, 190
Assiniboine-Red River (Canada) **M:**80
Assist (in baseball) **B:**83
Assistant directors (for motion pictures) **M:**483
Associated Press (wire service) **J:**140
Associated states (of the United Kingdom) **U:**57
Associate's degree (in education) **U:**220
Association of ideas, law of (in psychology) **P:**503
Associative properties (of numbers) **N:**398–99
Assonance (kind of rhyme) **P:**353
Assumption of the Blessed Virgin Mary (holy day) **R:**284
Assumption of the Virgin (painting by Correggio) **I:**398
Assurbanipal *see* Ashurbanipal
Assyria (a-SIR-ia) (ancient empire of Asia) **A:**225–26
  art **A:**239–41
  libraries, history of **L:**171
  palaces **A:**371
  sculpture **S:**93–94
  picture(s)
    hairstyling **H:**6
Astaire, Fred (American dancer, singer, and actor) **D:**34;
  M:486
Astatine (AST-a-tene) (element) **E:**171
Aster (pattern of cell division) **C:**161, 162
Asterism (star effect in gemstones) **G:**70
Asterisms (groups of stars in constellations) **C:**523

Atkins, Chet (American singer, musician, and record producer) **C:**565

Atlanta (capital of Georgia) **A:**477; **G:**139, 141
  Civil War **C:**345
  Sherman captured the city **S:**150
  picture(s) **G:**142
    Civil War **C:**344

Atlanta Memorial Arts Center *see* Robert W. Woodruff Arts Center

Atlantic, Battle of the (1940–1941) **W:**291

Atlantic Basin (Canada) **C:**55, 57

Atlantic Charter **A:**584

Atlantic City (New Jersey) **N:**172
  picture(s) **N:**165

Atlantic Coastal Plain (United States) *see* Coastal Plain

Atlantic Fleet (of the United States Navy) **U:**116

Atlantic Intracoastal Waterway *see* Intracoastal Waterway

Atlantic Monthly (magazine) **H:**159b

Atlantic Ocean **A:**478–79
  Bermuda Triangle **B:**152
  cables, submarine **T:**54
  Gulf Stream **G:**413
  icebergs in the North Atlantic **I:**17, 18
  Mid-Atlantic Ridge **M:**504
  ocean liner crossings **O:**30–31, 32, 33

Atlantic Provinces (of Canada) *see* New Brunswick; Newfoundland; Nova Scotia; Prince Edward Island

Atlantis (legendary island) **A:**584
  Atlantic Ocean **A:**478

Atlantis (United States space shuttle) **S:**340j, 350, 351, 368
  picture(s) **S:**340b
    crew eating in microgravity **S:**341

Atlas (in Greek mythology) **A:**478; **G:**360, 366; **W:**243

Atlases (bound volumes of maps) **R:**129

Atlas Mountains (northern Africa) **A:**47–48, 185; **M:**460, 505
  picture(s) **A:**48; **M:**458

Atlatl (weapon) **I:**166

Atman (Hindu spiritual principle) *see* Brahman

Atmosphere (gases enveloping planets) **A:**479–82; **E:**20–21; **P:**277 *see also* Air; Meteorology
  acid rain **A:**9–10
  air pollution **A:**122–25; **E:**299–301
  chemical cycles in ecosystems **E:**54
  climatic changes, sources of **C:**363–64
  clouds **C:**382–85
  cosmic rays **C:**554–55
  Earth, history of **E:**23, 26
  Earth's atmosphere interferes with radiation from space **S:**370
  Earth's atmosphere supports life **L:**202
  ecosphere **N:**63
  Is the earth's atmosphere warming? **A:**482
  Jupiter **J:**159; **P:**279
  Mars **M:**105, 106, 108; **P:**278
  Mercury **M:**232; **P:**275–76
  meteorites **C:**450, 451
  moon lacks **M:**451, 453–54, 455
  Neptune **N:**111–12; **P:**282
  ozone layer **O:**287
  Pluto **P:**282, 343
  pressure centers are a climatic control **C:**362
  research with balloons **B:**36, 37
  Saturn **P:**280; **S:**53
  sun's atmosphere **E:**52; **S:**494–97
  Titan **P:**281; **S:**56
  Triton **N:**113; **P:**282
  twinkling layer of air **S:**434
  Uranus **P:**281; **U:**231–32
  Venus **V:**276; **V:**303a, 303b
  weather **W:**77–95
  picture(s)
    computer image **C:**487

Atmospheric pressure *see* Air pressure

ATM's *see* Amateur telescope makers; Automatic teller machines

Atolls (coral islands) **C:**548; **P:**3
  picture(s)
    Palau **P:**2

Atomic bomb *see* Atomic weapons

Atomic clocks (devices for measuring time with great accuracy) **C:**370, 371; **L:**46c; **T:**201

Atomic energy *see* Nuclear energy

Atomic Energy Commission **T:**326

Atomic numbers **A:**486; **C:**202, 204 *see also* Periodic table
  elements **E:**166–70

Atomic physics *see* Nuclear physics

Atomic power *see* Nuclear energy

Atomic second (basic unit of time measurement) **C:**370

Atomic weapons **N:**373, 374–75, 377–78
  aviation in World War II **A:**564
  battles **B:**103f
  Chicago, research in **I:**76
  Einstein's work on **E:**120
  fission **F:**223
  Hiroshima and Nagasaki (Japan) **J:**47
  New Mexico **N:**194
  Truman, Harry S., and bombing Japan **T:**325
  World War II **W:**308
  picture(s) **N:**194; **U:**196
    bombing of Hiroshima **A:**466

Atomic weight **A:**486; **C:**204
  Dalton's theory **D:**15
  elements **E:**166–67
  experimental measurements **C:**209
  isotopes **C:**205

Atomium (symbol of Brussels World's Fair) **F:**16

Atoms **A:**483–89
  alloy structures **A:**190, 191
  atomic theory **C:**198, 207, 209
  bonding **M:**151–52
  carbon chains and rings **C:**106
  chemical structure **C:**198, 201–3, 204
  chemistry, history of **C:**207, 209, 211
  chemistry of life **L:**198–99
  cosmic rays **C:**554–55
  crystals **C:**593–94; **M:**151
  Dalton's theory **D:**15
  electricity **E:**135–36
  electronics **E:**161
  elements, chemical **E:**166–70
  fission **F:**222–23
  ions and ionization **I:**287–89
  lightning, causes of **T:**185
  magnetism **M:**31–32
  materials science **M:**151–55
  matter and atoms **M:**176–78
  nuclear energy **N:**366–73
  radiation **R:**42
  radioactive dating **R:**64–66
  radioactive elements **R:**67
  Rutherford's theory **R:**383
  scanning electron microscope can examine **E:**164
  water molecule **W:**47
  Where does fission take place? **F:**223
  picture(s)
    water molecule **W:**48

Atoms for Peace Plan (1953) **D:**179

Atom smashing (process for studying atoms) **A:**488

Aton *see* Aten

Atonality (in music) **M:**397, 540
  Germany **G:**189

Atonement, Day of *see* Yom Kippur

ATP (adenosine triphosphate) **B:**298–99
  bioluminescence **B:**204
  muscle contraction **M:**519
  photosynthesis forms **P:**220, 315

Atrium (plural: **atria**) (chamber of the heart) **B:**280; **C:**305; **D:**193; **H:**80

Atrophy (wasting away of muscle fibers) **M:**519

Attachés (at-ta-SHAYS) (representatives of the armed forces in the Foreign Service) **F:**370

Attar of roses
Bulgaria is a major producer **B:**441

Atterbom, Per Daniel Amadeus (Swedish poet) **S:**58g

Attica (region around Athens)
Attic dialect became the language of Greece **G:**353
Attic vases **G:**348

Attic system (of numeration) *see* Herodianic system

Attila (king of the Huns) **A:**490; **B:**103d *see also* Huns
buried in Hungary according to legend **H:**287
subject of legends **L:**130

Attitude (of aircraft) **A:**117, 118
space terms **S:**340d

Attitude control system (of spacecraft) **S:**340k

Attitude scales (personality tests) **T:**119

Attlee, Clement (British prime minister) **A:**490
picture(s)
with Stalin at Potsdam Conference **S:**419

Attorney General (head of the United States Department of Justice) **C:**2; **J:**164; **P:**450
list of **J:**165

Attorneys *see* Lawyers

Attractants *see* Pheromones

Attucks, Crispus (American revolutionary patriot) **A:**79c; **R:**196

Attu Island (Alaska) **A:**144, 158

Atwood, Margaret (Canadian poet and novelist) **A:**584; **C:**85
picture(s) **C:**84

Aubrey, John (English scholar) **S:**462

Auburn (Maine) **M:**48

Auburn system (of punishment) **P:**482

Auburn University (Alabama) **A:**135

Auckland (New Zealand) **N:**240

Auctions
furs **F:**502–3
tobacco **T:**213

Audemars, Georges (Swiss scientist) **N:**435

Auden, W. H. (English-born American poet) **E:**288
odes **O:**50

Audible sounds **S:**258

Audio signal (television) **T:**64–65

Audiovisual materials and equipment
care of materials **L:**182
education **E:**89
special services of libraries **L:**177

Auditorium (part of a theater where the audience sits) **T:**158

Auditory memory (for things you hear) **S:**399

Audits (in bookkeeping) **B:**313

Audubon (AUD-u-bon), **John James** (American naturalist and painter) **A:**491; **U:**129
Audubon Memorial State Park (Louisiana) **L:**308
passenger pigeons of Kentucky **K:**216
watercolor painting **W:**60

Audubon Park Zoo (New Orleans, Louisiana) **Z:**383

Audubon Society, National (NAS) **A:**584–85; **C:**520

Aue, Hartmann von *see* Hartmann von Aue

Auerbach, "Red" (American basketball coach) **B:**95b

Augean (au-JE-an) **stables** (in Greek mythology) **G:**366

Auger (AUG-er) **bits** (tools) **T:**231; **W:**230

Augier, Emile (French dramatist) **D:**300

Augmented interval (in music) **M:**540

Augsburg, Peace of (1555) **G:**160

Augsburg Confession (1530) **P:**491

August (8th month of the year) **A:**492–93

Augusta (capital of Maine) **M:**47

Augusta (Georgia) **G:**141

Auguste clown **C:**387

Augustin I *see* Iturbide, Agustín de

Augustine, Saint (354–430, early Christian thinker and Bishop of Hippo) **A:**494; **C:**289–90
father of Latin theology **R:**283
philosophy, history of **P:**190
picture(s) **C:**288

Augustine, Saint (?–604, archbishop of Canterbury) **R:**284
Anglo-Saxons converted to Christianity **C:**290; **E:**237

Augustus (emperor of Rome) **R:**316
Aeneid written in honor of Augustus **A:**36
Antony, Mark **A:**317
Latin literature, golden age of **L:**77–78
picture(s)
statue **S:**96

"Auld Lang Syne" (song by Burns) **B:**459

Aulos (double oboe of ancient Greece) **A:**247

Aung San (Burmese political leader) **B:**458

Aung San Suu Kyi (Burmese political leader) **B:**458

Aurangzeb (AUR-ang-zeb) (emperor of Mogul dynasty of India) **I:**132

Aurelian (Roman emperor) **R:**317

Aureomycin (aur-e-o-MY-sin) (antibiotic) **A:**308

Auricle *see* Pinna

Aurochs (AUR-oks) (extinct wild cattle) **H:**220

Aurora (in Roman mythology) **A:**585

Aurora australis (aus-TRAY-lis) **(southern lights)** (in the Antarctic) **I:**289

Aurora borealis (bo-re-AL-is) **(northern lights)** (in the Arctic) **I:**289
picture(s) **I:**288; **S:**496

Auroras (polar lights) **I:**289
radiation belts **R:**49
solar flares **S:**497
solar wind **S:**475, 497

Auschwitz concentration camp (Poland) **H:**159c

Ausonius, Decimus Magnus (Roman writer) **L:**78

Austen, Jane (English novelist) **A:**494; **E:**283
style and themes of her novels **N:**359

Austerlitz, Battle of (1805) **N:**11

Austin (capital of Texas) **T:**136
"outlaw" country music **C:**565

Austin, Moses (American pioneer miner) **N:**366

Austin, Stephen F. (American pioneer) **T:**138

Australia **A:**495–517
aborigines **A:**7
Australia Day **H:**154
Canberra (capital of Australia) **C:**89
continents **C:**529, 530
dependencies **C:**461
exploration and discovery **E:**413
explored by Captain Cook **C:**531
favorite foods **F:**336
gold discoveries **G:**252; **M:**324
humans migrated by land during Ice Age **I:**13
immigration **I:**94
kangaroos **K:**174–75
koalas **K:**290
lakes **L:**34
Melbourne **M:**215
mountains **M:**506
New Guinea **N:**149; **P:**59
prairies **P:**426, 427, 428–29
rabbit plague **R:**24
snakes **S:**212
Sydney **S:**545–46
theater **T:**162
What is the Great Barrier Reef? **P:**5
Wollomombi waterfall **W:**63
picture(s)
flag **F:**241
western desert area **D:**125

Australia Day **H:**154

Australian Alps **A:**503, 507; **M:**506

Australian-American Memorial (Canberra, Australia) **C:**89

Australian Antarctic Territory **A:**495

Australian ballot **E:**131

Australian Capital Territory **A:**514; **C:**89

Australian cassowaries (flightless birds) **O:**247

Australian crawl (swimming stroke) **S:**536

Australian Elizabethan Theatre Trust **T:**162

Autonomy (stage of child development) C:226
Auto pilot *see* Automatic pilot
Autry, Gene (American actor and singer) C:564
Autumn (season) S:109–11 *see also* the names of months
  constellations C:525–26
  flowers for fall G:49
  Why do leaves change color in the autumn? P:306
  picture(s)
    constellations C:525
Autun (France)
  French Romanesque sculpture F:422
Auvergne (region of France) F:405
Auxiliaries (in grammar) G:289
Auxiliary personnel (in hospitals) H:249
Auxins (plant hormones) P:312
Avalanche (mass of snow or ice that slides rapidly down a
    mountain slope) A:521
  Austrian Alps A:521
  caused by sympathetic vibrations of sound S:261
  volcanoes: glowing avalanches V:383
Avalon Peninsula (Newfoundland)
  landforms of Canada C:52
Avant-garde A:585
Avedon, Richard (American photographer) A:585
Avenida 9 de Julio (Buenos Aires, Argentina)
  picture(s) B:427
Avenida de José Antonio (Gran Via) (Madrid, Spain)
  picture(s) M:15
Aventurine (av-ENT-ur-ene) (quartz) Q:6
Avenue, Middelharnis, Holland, The (painting by Hobbema)
  picture(s) D:363
Averages (values of sets of numbers) S:441
Averina, Tatiana (Soviet speed skater) O:115
Avery Fisher Hall (Lincoln Center for the Performing Arts, New
    York City) L:248
Aves (A-vese) (class name for birds) B:211
Avesta (av-ES-ta) (holy book of Zoroastrianism) Z:387
Aviaries (bird exhibits in zoos) Z:383
Aviation A:557–70
  aerodynamics A:37–41
  aerospace engineers E:225
  airplanes A:108–21
  airports A:126–29
  balloons and ballooning B:34–38
  Berlin airlift B:149; G:164
  Earhart, Amelia E:7
  Federal Aviation Administration T:293
  gliders G:238–40
  ground-controlled approach (GCA) radar R:39
  helicopters H:103–5
  inventions I:280, 284
  jet propulsion J:88–90
  Lindbergh's New York-Paris flight L:250
  mail service P:398
  mathematics in careers M:161
  Missouri's place in the history of M:375
  National Air and Space Museum P:273–74
  navigation N:72, 73, 77–78
  parachutes P:60
  record flights A:561, 565
  supersonic flight S:499–502
  transportation, history of T:287–88
  United States Air Force U:112–15
  United States air transportation U:103
  United States Army U:107
  United States Marine Corps U:122–23
  United States Navy U:119
  World War I W:277
  Wright, Wilbur and Orville W:318
  picture(s)
    Berlin airlift B:148
Aviation Challenge (science education program) S:340a
Avicenna (Persian philosopher) S:64
  geology, history of G:109

Avignon (ov-ene-YON) (France)
  seat of papacy for 70 years R:287
Ávila, Pedro Arias de *see* Pedrarias Dávila
Ávila Camacho (OB-i-la ka-MA-cho), Manuel (Mexican
    president) M:251
Avilés, Pedro Menéndez de *see* Menéndez de Avilés, Pedro
Avocado (fruit) M:78
Avocations *see* Hobbies
Avodire (tree)
  picture(s)
    uses of the wood and its grain W:223
Avogadro, Count Amedeo (Italian scientist) A:585
Avoirdupois (av-er-du-POIS) (weight) W:115
Avvakum, Archpriest (Russian religious leader) R:376
AWACS (airborne radar system) A:585
Awards, literary *see also* National Book Awards
  children's book awards C:228–31
  Nobel prizes N:265–66
  Pulitzer prizes P:533–37
Awls (tools for piercing holes) S:158
  needles probably developed from N:102
AWOL (U.S. Army term) A:585
A.W.S.A. *see* American Water Ski Association
Axial skeleton (of the body) S:183
Axioms (mathematical assumptions) M:157
  geometry G:121
Axis (in coordinate geometry) A:184
Axis (of a lens) L:144–45
Axis (of celestial bodies)
  Earth E:9; G:100
  Mars M:105
  moon M:446
  Uranus U:231
  picture(s)
    tilt of each planet on its axis P:278–79
Axis Powers (alliance of Italy, Germany, and Japan during World
    War II) A:585; W:282
Axles (of wheels) W:159, 160
Axminster carpets R:354–55
Axons (of neurons) B:364–65, 366; N:117, 118
Axum (Ethiopia) *see* Aksum
Ayatollahs (Muslim leaders) I:306, 308, 349
Aycock, Charles Brantley (American statesman) N:320
Aye-ayes (EYE-eyes) (lemurs) M:418
Ayer Directory of Publications M:19
Ayllón (ile-YONE), Lucas Vázquez de (Spanish explorer) S:309
Aylwin Azócar, Patricio (president of Chile) C:255
Aymará (eye-ma-RA) (Indian language of South
    America) P:159
Aymará (Indians of South America) I:173, 196; L:30
  Bolivia B:306
  Peru P:162
Ayres (songs) E:292; R:173
Ayrshire (breed of dairy cattle) C:149
  picture(s) D:5
Ayub Khan (a-YUBE KAHN), Field Marshal Mohammed
    (Pakistani political leader) P:40–40a
Ayutthaya (early kings of Thailand) T:153
Azad ("Free") Kashmir (Pakistani-controlled section of
    Kashmir) K:199
Azaleas (a-ZALE-yas) (shrubs)
  picture(s) G:28, 36
Azania (former name of East African coast and Zanzibar) T:19
Azcona Hoyo, José (president of Honduras) H:199
Azerbaijan A:571–72
  Baku U:43
  Commonwealth of Independent States C:460
  Kurds K:305
  picture(s)
    flag F:230
Azeri (Azerbaijani) (Turkic people) A:571; U:34
Azhar University, al- (Cairo, Egypt) C:8; E:104; U:219
Azimuthal (az-i-MUTH-al) equidistant projection (of
    maps) M:97

PHOTO CREDITS

The following list credits the sources of photos used in THE NEW BOOK OF KNOWLEDGE. Credits are listed, by page, photo by photo—left to right, top to bottom. Wherever appropriate, the name of the photographer has been listed with the source, the two being separated by a dash. When two or more photos by different photographers appear on one page, their credits are separated by semicolons.

A

2 © Terry Madison—The Image Bank
6 © The Granger Collection; © The Granger Collection.
6a © The Bettmann Archive; © The Granger Collection; © The Granger Collection; © The Granger Collection.
6b © The Bettmann Archive
7 © Jack S. Grove—Gamma Liaison
8 Giraudon
9 David Like, University of Vermont Biology Dept.
10 Ted Spiegel—Black Star
11 © The Granger Collection
12 © The White House Historical Association: Photographed by the National Geographic Society; The Granger Collection.
13 National Gallery of Art, Washington; Gift of Mrs. Robert Homans
14 Courtesy of Maryland Historical Society
15 Yale University Art Gallery
16 Corcoran Gallery of Art; The Granger Collection; The Bettmann Archive.
18 The Bettmann Archive; The Granger Collection.
19 The Bettmann Archive
20 © The Granger Collection
21 Historical Pictures Service
28 Courtesy of Binney & Smith Inc.
29 Courtesy of Young & Rubicam, New York
30 © Danilo Boschung—Leo de Wys Inc.; Courtesy of the American Cancer Society.
31 Courtesy of Grolier Enterprises Corp.
33 Courtesy of J. Walter Thompson
35 Warshaw Collection of Business Americana
37 © British Aerospace
39 Courtesy of Chrysler Corporation
41 © Steve Swope—Indy 500 Photos; © Yogi, Inc.
42 © Hernandez—Sipa Press
44 © Dr. Arthur C. Twomey—Photo Researchers; © Peter Knapp—The Image Bank.
45 © Sygma
46 © Sally Mayman—Tony Stone Images; © R.I.M. Campbell—Bruce Coleman Limited; © Gerald Cubitt; © Fridmar Damm—Leo de Wys Inc.; © Gerald Cubitt.
47 © Hiroyuki Matsumoto—Black Star; © Pedro Coll—The Stock Market; © Michael J. Howell—Leo de Wys Inc.
48 © Robert Everts—Tony Stone Images; © Hiroyuki Matsumoto—Black Star.
49 © Carl Frank—Photo Researchers
52 © James P. Rowan—Tony Stone Images
53 © MP Kahl—Black Star; © Alan Binks—Anthony Bannister Picture Library; © Mitch Kezar—Tony Stone Images.
54 © Gerald Cubitt; © Betty Press—Woodfin Camp & Assoc.; © Nicholas DeVore—Tony Stone Images; © Pedro Coll—The Stock Market.
55 © Kerstin Beier—Anthony Bannister Picture Library; © Tony Stone Images; © Martin Rogers—Tony Stone Images.
56 © Marc & Evelyne Bernheim—Woodfin Camp & Assoc.; © Paul Stepan—Photo Researchers.
57 © Michael Coyne—Black Star; © Gerald Cubitt; © Marc & Evelyne Bernheim—Woodfin Camp & Assoc.
58 © Robert Frerck—Tony Stone Images; © J. Bertrand—Leo de Wys Inc.
60 © Betty Press—Woodfin Camp & Assoc.; © Kerstin Beier—A.B.P.L.
61 © Betty Press—Woodfin Camp & Assoc.
62 © Hubertus Kanus—Photo Researchers; © Hubertus Kanus—Photo Researchers
63 © V. Englebert—Photo Researchers; © Rick Falco—Black Star.
64 © Pierre Boulat Cosmos—Woodfin Camp & Assoc.; © Jason Laure—Woodfin Camp & Assoc.
65 © The Granger Collection
66 © The Granger Collection; © The Granger Collection.
69 © Brooks Kraft—Sygma
70 © Richard Saunders—Leo de Wys Inc.
71 © George Holton—Photo Researchers; Photographed by Kathy Corday. National Museum of African Art, Eliot Elisofon Photographic Archives, Smithsonian Institution.
72 Photographed by Franko Khoury. National Museum of African Art, Eliot Elisofon Photographic Archives, Smithsonian Institution; Photographed by Franko Khoury. National Museum of African Art, Eliot Elisofon Photographic Archives, Smithsonian Institution; Photographed by Franko Khoury. National Museum of African Art, Eliot Elisofon Photographic Archives, Smithsonian Institution.
73 Photographed by Dick Beaulieux. Ethnographic Museum, Antwerp; © Lee Boltin; © Lee Boltin.
74 Photographed by Franko Khoury. National Museum of African Art, Eliot Elisofon Photographic Archives, Smithsonian Institution. Gift of Dr. Ernst Anspach and museum purchase; © Lee Boltin; © Lee Boltin.
75 Photographed by Franko Khoury. National Museum of African Art and National Museum of Natural History, Eliot Elisofon Photographic Archives, Smithsonian Institution; Photographed by Jim Young. National Museum of African Art, Eliot Elisofon Photographic Archives, Smithsonian Institution.
76 © Strauss—Curtis—The Stock Market
76a © Marc & Evelyne Bernheim—Woodfin Camp & Assoc.
77 © Paul Funston—Anthony Bannister Picture Library; © Bill Kaufman—Leo de Wys Inc.; © Marc & Evelyne Bernheim—Woodfin Camp & Assoc.
79a © Jeffrey Henson Scales; © George Olson—Woodfin Camp & Assoc.
79b © Nick Kelsh—Kelsh Wilson Design Inc.; © Momatiuk—Eastcott—Woodfin Camp & Assoc.
79c © Jeffrey Allan Salter
79d © The Granger Collection
79e © Peter Newark's American Pictures; © Schomburg Center for Research in Black Culture—The New York Public Library—Astor, Lenox and Tilden Foundations.
79f © The Granger Collection
79g © The Granger Collection; © Peter Newark's American Pictures.
79h © Schomburg Center for Research in Black Culture
79i © Peter Newark's American Pictures; © The Bettmann Archive.
79j © The Granger Collection; © Peter Newark's American Pictures.
79k © UPI/Bettmann Newsphotos; © The Bettmann Archive.
79l © Driggs Collection—Magnum Photos; © David Diaz, courtesy of HarperCollins Publisher; © The Bettmann Archive; © National Museum of American Art, Smithsonian Institution, Washington, DC. Gift of the Harmon Foundation—Art Resource, NY; © Schomburg Center for Research in Black Culture.
79m © Philadelphia Museum of Art: Gift of Dr. and Mrs. Mathew T. Moore; © Peter Newark's American Pictures.
79n © UPI/Bettmann Newsphotos; © Topham—The Image Works.
79o © Ted Russell—Sygma; © Charles Moore—Black Star.
79p © Kenneth Jarecke—Contact Press Images; © Peter Newark's American Pictures.
80 © E. Adams—Sygma; © Kathy Banks—Sygma; © Walter Iooss Jr.; © Anthony Barboza; © Micheline Pelletier—Sygma; © Albert Trotman—Allford Trotman Associates.
81 Archives, Museum of Comparative Zoology Library, Harvard University
82 © Dugald Stermer
84 © William Hubbell—Woodfin Camp & Assoc.
85 © Phil Huber—Black Star; © Ira Wyman—Sygma.
86 Gerald Davis—Contact
87 The Bettmann Archive
88 © Earl Roberge—Photo Researchers
89 © Jules Bucher—Photo Researchers
90 © Andrew Holbrooke—Wheeler Pictures; © Ronny Jacques—Photo Researchers.
91 © Andrew Holbrooke—Wheeler Pictures
92 © Bill Backman—Photo Researchers; © George Holton—Photo Researchers.
93 © Louis Goldman—Photo Researchers; © Ulrike Welsch—Stock Boston.
94 © Joe Munroe—Photo Researchers
95 © Photo Action Press—Photo Researchers
96 Grant Heilman
98 The Granger Collection
99 National Gallery of Art, Washington, DC, Garbisch Collection
100 © Liane Enkelis—Stock Boston
100a U.S. Department of Agriculture
101 The Bettmann Archive
104 *Model Airplane News*
106 Robert Schleicher
107 Courtesy of Byron Originals
108 © James A. Anderson—Unicorn Stock Photos; Photo Edit; Courtesy, Cessna; Brent Jones.
110 © R. Caton—H. Armstrong Roberts, Inc.
111 © Ingrid Johnsson—Journalism Services
112 Courtesy, British Aerospace
113 © Dennis Barnes; © David Brownell.
114 © Heinz Steenmans—Wheeler Pictures; Leonard Lee Rue III—Bruce Coleman Inc.
115 © Joseph Jacobson—Journalism Services
116 © Lepper—Miller—H. Armstrong Roberts; NASA.
117 © Randa Bishop
119 Boeing Aircraft Co.
120 Courtesy, McDonnell Douglas Corporation; © Photo Edit.